The World

SOCIAL STUDIES · SCOTT FORESMAN · THE WORLD · SCOTT FORESMAN

Grade 6
Teacher's Edition
VOLUME TWO

Editorial Offices: Glenview, Illinois • Parsippany, New Jersey • New York, New York
Sales Offices: Parsippany, New Jersey • Duluth, Georgia • Glenview, Illinois
Coppell, Texas • Ontario, California

ISBN: 0-328-01893-7

4 5 6 7 8 9 10 V063 11 10 09 08 07 06 05 04 03

What makes this program different and better?

People make the difference. The people behind Scott Foresman Social Studies share a personal commitment to this program. They believe it can change students' lives and help build a better future.

PROGRAM AUTHORS

Dr. Candy Dawson Boyd
Professor, School of Education
Director of Reading Programs
St. Mary's College
Moraga, California

Dr. C. Frederick Risinger
Director, Professional Development and Social Studies Education
Indiana University
Bloomington, Indiana

Dr. Allen D. Glenn
Professor and Dean Emeritus
College of Education
Curriculum and Instruc
University of Washingto
Seattle, Washington

Dr. Geneva Gay
Professor of Education
University of Washington
Seattle, Washington

Sara Miranda Sanchez
Elementary and Early Childhood Curriculum Coordinator
Albuquerque Public Schools
Albuquerque, New Mexico

Dr. Carole L. Hahn
Professor, Educational Studies
Emory University
Atlanta, Georgia

CONTRIBUTING AUTHORS

Rita Geiger
Director of Social Studies and Foreign Languages
Norman Public Schools
Norman, Oklahoma

Dr. Carol Berkin
Professor of History
Baruch College and the Graduate Center,
The City University of New York
New York, New York

Dr. M. Gail Hickey
Professor of Education
Indiana University-Purd
University
Ft. Wayne, Indiana

Dr. James B. Kracht
Associate Dean for Undergraduate Programs and Teacher Education
College of Education
Texas A & M University
College Station, Texas

Lee A. Chase
Staff Development Specialist
Chesterfield County Public Schools
Chesterfield County, Virginia

Dr. Bonnie Meszaro
Associate Director
Center for Economic Education and Entrepreneurship
University of Delaware
Newark, Delaware

Dr. Valerie Ooka Pang
Professor of Teacher Education
San Diego State University
San Diego, California

Dr. Jim Cummins
Professor of Curriculum
Ontario Institute for Studies in Education
University of Toronto
Toronto, Canada

How do I teach my students important conter

Children need to understand the key strands of social studies so they can fully participate in their world. Scott Foresman Social Studies helps every child become an active, involved, and informed citizen.

★ BIOGRAPHY ★

George Washington
1732–1799

George Washington was chosen to command the American Army during the Revolutionary War. As a young man, he learned the skills that later helped him to become a strong military leader. When he was 16 he began working as a surveyor, mapping the mountains of western Virginia. His first night in the woods was memorable. He wrote in his journal:

> "I...went into the bed, as they called it, when to my surprise I found it to be nothing but a little straw matted together...with double its weight of vermin such as lice, fleas, etc."

Surveying was difficult and tiring, but Washington seemed made for it. At 16 he was already an expert horseman. And he was very strong, standing well over six feet tall, with broad shoulders and powerful arms. According to friends he was nearly impossible to beat in wrestling.

BIOFACT
This set of Washington's false teeth was carved from walrus or hippopotamus teeth.

Washington worked as a surveyor for three years. The experience was valuable for the lessons it taught him about hard work, commitment, and leadership under challenging conditions. Thirty years later General George Washington would draw on these lessons while leading his fellow colonists to victory in the American Revolution.

Learn from Biographies
In 1789 George Washington became our nation's first President. How do you think his work as a surveyor helped prepare him for this job?

For more information, go online to Meet the ... at www.sfsocialstudies.com

283

HISTORY TO ENGAGE AND INSPIRE

★ Up-to-date, accurate, and comprehensive

★ Fully aligned to curriculum standards

★ Biographies that bring key figures to life

★ Primary sources with eyewitness accounts

★ Museum-quality artwork, photographs, and diagrams

★ Web-based updates and activities

★ Interactive multimedia

★ PRIMARY SOURCE ★

> "We hold these truths to be self-evident, that all men are created equal; that they are endowed [given] by their Creator with certain unalienable rights, that among these are life, liberty, and the pursuit of happiness."

MAP SKILL
Expansion of the United States, 1783–1898

ALASKA PURCHASE 1867
CANADA
OREGON TERRITORY TREATY 1846
TREATY WITH BRITAIN 1818
TREATY WITH BRITAIN 1842
PACIFIC OCEAN
MEXICAN WAR TREATY 1848
LOUISIANA PURCHASE 1803
UNITED STATES 1783
GADSDEN PURCHASE 1853
TEXAS 1845
ATLANTIC OCEAN
HAWAII 1898
PACIFIC OCEAN
FLORIDA 1819
Present-day boundaries are shown.
MEXICO
Gulf of Mexico

▶ As a result of the Mexican War, the territory of the United States extended to the Pacific Ocean.

MAP SKILL Place What was the last state to become part of the United States?

GEOGRAPHY TO LINK PEOPLE AND PLACES

★ Exclusive maps that are custom built for Scott Foresman by MapQuest™

★ Maps that show change and movement

★ Beautifully illustrated map adventures

★ Lessons that build map and globe skills

★ Online atlas with up-to-the-minute maps and current information

MAPQUEST.

CITIZEN HEROES

Racing to the Rescue

On a day of terrifying attacks, the heroic actions of New York City firefighters saved thousands of lives.

New York City's Ladder Company 21 has a long history of fighting fires and saving lives. When the company was first formed in 1890, firefighters rushed to fires on a truck pulled by three horses. Today Ladder Company 21 has computers and modern trucks. But some things have not changed. Firefighting is still a dangerous job that requires great courage. This is why New Yorkers have nicknamed the city's firefighters "New York's Bravest."

On the morning of September 11, 2001, terrorists crashed two planes into New York's World Trade Center. The call for help arrived in fire stations all over the city. At Ladder Company 21, Benjamin Suarez was one many firefighters who were just finishing a 24-hour shift. But Suarez did not even think about leaving the job. He called his wife and said,

1 *"I have to help the people."*

Then he and his fellow firefighters jumped on their trucks and raced to the scene of the attacks.

As firefighters arrived from around the city, they saw that the twin towers of the World Trade Center were on fire. They rushed into the buildings and up the stairs. "We saw them going up the stairs as we were going down," said a woman who escaped from one of the towers. The firefighters helped people who were injured or lost in the smoke. With **2** the firefighters' help, thousands of people escaped to safety.

Not everyone survived, however. About 4,000 people were trapped in the buildings when they collapsed. More than 300 firefighters, including Benjamin Suarez, died while trying to save the lives of others. Like so many heroes on that terrible day, Suarez put the desire to help other people ahead of his own safety. "That's what Benny was about," said Captain Michael Farrell of Ladder Company 21.

In the days following the terrorist attacks, neighbors visited Ladder Company 21 to show their sympathy for the firefighters who had lost their lives. Many people left flowers and made donations to the firefighters' families. Children wrote letters in which they thanked firefighters for saving lives. Some children drew pictures showing firefighters performing brave actions. The firefighters hung these letters and pictures on the wall of the fire station. **3** Similar scenes took place at fire stations all over the city.

Rudolph Giuliani, the mayor of New York City, thanked firefighters for their incredible courage:

4 *"Without courage, nothing else can really happen. And there is no better example, none, than the courage of the Fire Department of the City of New York."*

New York's firefighters not only saved thousands of lives. Their actions inspired the entire nation. In a time of fear and danger, firefighters helped Americans have the courage to face the difficult times ahead.

Courage in Action

Link to Current Events Every day, firefighters, police officers, and other rescue workers perform heroic acts in communities all over the nation. Read a newspaper from your community to find out about the recent actions of your local firefighters or other emergency workers. What actions did they take? How did these actions show courage?

BUILDING CITIZENSHIP
Caring
Respect
Responsibility
Fairness
Honesty
★ Courage

667

CITIZENSHIP LESSONS TO HELP STUDENTS MAKE A DIFFERENCE

★ Built-in lessons in the student book teach good citizenship skills: Caring, Respect, Responsibility, Fairness, Courage, and Honesty.

★ Historic figures and everyday citizen heroes inspire students.

★ Engaging, real-life applications

Content that covers the key social studies strands

SOCIAL STUDIES STRAND
Citizenship

SOCIAL STUDIES STRAND
Culture

SOCIAL STUDIES STRAND
Economics

SOCIAL STUDIES STRAND
Geography

SOCIAL STUDIES STRAND
Government

SOCIAL STUDIES STRAND
History

SOCIAL STUDIES STRAND
Science • Technology

Content organized for the way you teach

If time is short, use the Quick Teaching Plan to cover the core content and skills.

OR

To add depth and richer enjoyment, use the wealth of information in each lesson.

Quick Teaching Plan

If time is short, have students write on a chart: *Boston Massacre, Tea Act, Boston Tea Party, Intolerable Acts.*

• Have students write a summary of the roles that the colonists and British played in these events.

Then and Now
The Boston Massacre

In the center of Boston, you can find a patch of cobblestones near the Old State House. They have been preserved in memory of Crispus Attucks and the other protesters who were killed at this spot—the site of the Boston Massacre.

▶ An engraving *(left)* shows the Boston Massacre with the Old State House in the background. The building *(above)* still stands today.

277

What can I do to reach all my students?

If students are going to gain insight and perspective, they need to be able to read this richly detailed story. Scott Foresman Social Studies provides systematic instruction to improve comprehension and to reach out to all learners.

UNIT 4

Reading Social Studies

The American Revolution

 Cause and Effect

Learning to find causes and effects can help you understand what you read. Study the diagram below.

| **Cause** A **cause** is why something happens. | → | **Effect** An **effect** is what happens. |

- Sometimes writers use clue words such as *because, so,* or *since* to signal cause and effect.
- A cause may have more than one effect. An effect may have more than one cause.

Read the following paragraph. **Cause** and **effect** have been highlighted.

In Chapter 7, you read about the French and Indian War. What caused this war? Both Britain and France wanted to control land west of the Appalachian Mountains, and both sides were prepared to fight for it. The effect was the French and Indian War, which lasted nine long years. The French and Indian War was the first link in a chain of events that led to the American Revolution.

264

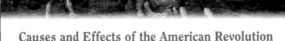

Causes and Effects of the American Revolution

After the French and Indian War, Britain needed money. As a result, the British government placed taxes on the American colonists. The British thought that the colonists should help pay for the war since it had been fought partly to defend the colonies

The first tax was the Stamp Act. It said that colonists had to buy tax stamps for printed materials. Many colonists refused to pay. They said they had not voted on the tax.

Since the Stamp Act did not work, Britain replaced it with a tax on imported goods. So colonists refused to buy imports. They made their own cloth and tea.

As a result of colonists' protests, Britain removed all taxes except the tax on tea. Angry Boston colonists led by

Samuel Adams threw a load of tea off a British ship. That action caused Britain to punish Boston further.

In response, Americans representing 12 colonies met in Philadelphia for the First Continental Congress. They voted to stop trading with Britain and to start training colonists to fight.

In April 1775, British soldiers marched from Boston to seize colonists' military supplies. American riders warned people along the way. Shooting started at Lexington and Concord.

The Second Continental Congress met later that year, and created a Continental Army. Congress also declared independence from Britain. That meant war.

 **Apply it!**

Use the reading strategy of cause and effect to answer these questions.

❶ What caused the British to tax the colonies?

❷ What effect did Americans' reaction to the Stamp Act have?

❸ What was the effect of dumping of tea in Boston Harbor?

265

DEVELOPING READING SKILLS WITH SOCIAL STUDIES

★ Built-in comprehension skill lessons in every unit

★ Preteach a target comprehension skill, then apply the same skill throughout the unit for sustained practice

★ Graphic organizers provide visual support, giving students access to content.

LOOK FOR THE TARGET SKILL ICON!

★ At the beginning of lessons

★ In Lesson Reviews

★ Throughout chapters

★ In Chapter Reviews

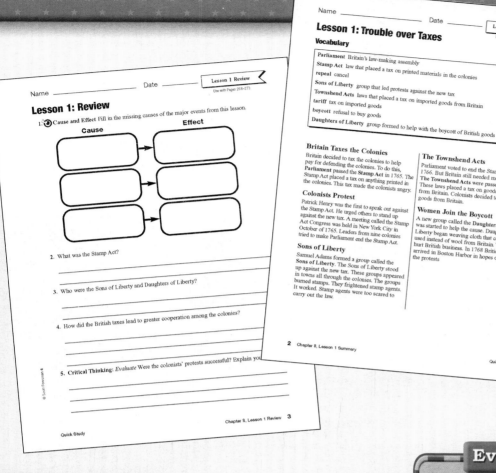

Lesson 1: Review

1. Cause and Effect Fill in the missing causes of the major events from this lesson.

Cause → Effect

2. What was the Stamp Act?

3. Who were the Sons of Liberty and Daughters of Liberty?

4. How did the British taxes lead to greater cooperation among the colonies?

5. Critical Thinking: *Evaluate* Were the colonists' protests successful? Explain yo...

Lesson 1: Trouble over Taxes

Vocabulary

Parliament Britain's law-making assembly
Stamp Act law that placed a tax on printed materials in the colonies
repeal cancel
Sons of Liberty group that led protests against the new law
Townshend Acts laws that placed a tax on imported goods from Britain
tariff tax on imported goods
boycott refusal to buy goods
Daughters of Liberty group formed to help with the boycott of British goods

Britain Taxes the Colonies
Britain decided to tax the colonies to help pay for defending the colonies. To do this, **Parliament** passed the **Stamp Act** in 1765. The Stamp Act placed a tax on anything printed in the colonies. This tax made the colonists angry.

Colonists Protest
Patrick Henry was the first to speak out against the Stamp Act. He urged others to stand up against the new tax. A meeting called the Stamp Act Congress was held in New York City in October of 1765. Leaders from nine colonies tried to make Parliament end the Stamp Act.

Sons of Liberty
Samuel Adams formed a group called the **Sons of Liberty**. The Sons of Liberty stood up against the new tax. These groups appeared in towns all through the colonies. The groups burned stamps. They frightened stamp agents. It worked. Stamp agents were too scared to carry out the law.

The Townshend Acts
Parliament voted to end the Stamp Act in 1766. But Britain still needed money. **The Townshend Acts** were passed in 1767. These laws placed a tax on goods brought from Britain. Colonists decided to **boycott** goods from Britain.

Women Join the Boycott
A new group called the **Daughters of Liberty** was started to help the cause. Daughters of Liberty began weaving cloth that could be used instead of wool from Britain. The boycott hurt British business. In 1768 British warships arrived in Boston Harbor in hopes of stopping the protests

Document declaring the 13 American colonies independent of Great Britain, written mainly by Thomas Jefferson and adopted on July 4, 1776 by the Second Continental Congress.

Declaration of Independence

AUDIO TEXT AND VOCABULARY CARDS TO HELP ALL STUDENTS ACCESS CONTENT

★ All lessons are recorded so students can listen and read along.

★ Vocabulary cards for key terms include the definition on one side.

QUICK STUDY GUIDE FOR LESSON SUPPORT

★ Easy-to-read summaries of each lesson

★ Scaffolding for the struggling reader

★ Lesson reviews with graphic organizers

MEETING INDIVIDUAL NEEDS
Leveled Practice

Write a Newspaper Article Have students write about the closing of Boston Harbor for a newspaper of that time.

Easy Ask students to write a two- or three-sentence "news brief" for a colonial newspaper telling what is happening in Boston since the harbor's closing. **Reteach**

On-Level Have students write a two-paragraph newspaper article for a colonial newspaper describing how the harbor's closing is affecting the city and changing people's attitudes. **Extend**

Challenge Have students write a three-paragraph newspaper article for a British newspaper about how the harbor's closing is affecting the Loyalists and is changing people's attitudes. Students should describe how the Loyalists are being treated by some Patriots. **Enrich**

For a Lesson Summary, use Quick Study, p. 62.

LEVELED PRACTICE TO MATCH STUDENTS' ABILITIES

★ The same activity at three instructional levels to reach all learners

★ Specific strategies for various learning styles

★ Promotes active participation and learning in every lesson

Every Student Learns

★ Access prior knowledge/build background: poster discussions, read alouds, word banks, word webs, and activity ideas

★ Access content: lesson summaries, graphic organizers, and blackline practice worksheets

★ Extend language: activities that use the language and content of the lesson

ESL EXTEND LANGUAGE
ESL Support

Examine Word Meanings Have students explore the meaning of *militia*.

Beginning Help students understand *militia* by using illustrations such as the one on p. 281. Invite them to share any cognates from their home languages.

Intermediate Ask students to demonstrate an understanding of *militia* by composing and sharing definitions.

Advanced Ask students to use dictionaries to find similar words and discuss how their meanings are related. For example, *militant* is related to *militia*. Militant means "aggressive; fighting; warlike." The Patriot *militia* was *militant*.

For additional ESL support, use Every Student Learns Guide, pp. 122–125.

LANGUAGE STRATEGIES AT POINT OF USE

★ Effective strategies for Beginning, Intermediate, and Advanced language learners in every lesson

★ Explore word meanings, usage, and form as well as cognates, etymologies, and more

How can I engage and motivate my students?

Scott Foresman Social Studies is brimming with compelling visuals, intriguing facts, and heart-pounding drama. It makes every student an interested social studies student who feels, knows, and thinks.

SMITHSONIAN VISUAL LESSONS

★ Developed exclusively for Scott Foresman in cooperation with the Smithsonian Institution

★ Brilliant visual lessons that bring students up close to national treasures and fascinating artifacts

★ A museum in every student book

DORLING KINDERSLEY VISUAL LESSONS

★ Recognized around the world for its visually stunning informational books and resources

★ Bold, large-as-life photographs with interesting, fact-filled expository captions

★ Helps students visualize their world and its past

DORLING KINDERSLEY

A NOTE FROM THE SMITHSONIAN
Viewing treasures of the past

What makes us want to see the flag that inspired the national anthem? Why do we stand in awe before George Washington's historic uniform?

These are treasured icons of our nation. They tell the story of America, our story. It is a story filled with great courage and sacrifice, with heartfelt convictions and a lasting belief in liberty and justice for all. These treasured icons, these priceless relics, bring us closer to who we are and what we believe as a nation.

The mission of the Smithsonian Institution is "the increase and diffusion of knowledge." Nowhere is the knowledge of our past more useful than in the minds and hearts of our children. Museum objects and their unique stories bring history alive and make it more exciting for children to learn. It is an honor to fulfill our mission this way by sharing these objects with a new generation of students.

Social Studies Plus!

A HANDS-ON APPROACH

★ Long-term and short-term projects and activities to extend lessons

★ Social Studies Fair ideas, Readers Theater, learning center ideas, holiday celebrations, writing and research activities, and more

★ Inspires hands-on, mind-on learning

UNIT
5 Project

Two Sides

Tune in to the past for a special town meeting.

1 **Prepare** to hold a town meeting to present arguments for and against the Virginia Plan and the New Jersey Plan.

2 **Assign** roles. Include roles for reporters, spokespersons for each plan, and audience members to ask questions.

3 **Research** the arguments for and against each plan. Write questions to ask each spokesperson. The spokespersons of each plan will respond to audience questions and comments.

4 **Stage** the town meeting. Take turns asking questions and giving responses.

Internet Activity
Learn more about the United States and its growth as a nation. Go to www.sfsocialstudies.com/activities and select your grade and unit.

392

You Are There

It is late at night, April 18, 1775. The streets of Boston are quiet.

Most people are at home. You are outside gathering wood for the fire. Suddenly you hear the pounding feet of a young man as he races past you. He looks upset and seems intent on getting somewhere quickly.

You wonder, "Where is he going?" You don't know it at the time, but he carries important information. He is bringing it to Paul Revere. The young man has learned the British soldiers are on the move. Where are they going? What do they plan to do? How will all of this affect the colonists?

▶ **Paul Revere warned colonists that the British were advancing.**

DISCOVERY CHANNEL SCHOOL PROJECTS

★ From one of the world's leading providers of educational multimedia

★ Exclusive, hands-on unit projects synthesize and enhance learning.

★ Exciting Web-based activities extend lessons.

DISCOVERY CHANNEL SCHOOL

YOU ARE THERE

★ Captivating, suspense-packed reading that builds excitement and sets the stage for each lesson

★ Lets students experience the event from a personal perspective

★ Spellbinding audio to help students visualize and feel the drama

WEB-BASED INFORMATION CENTER

★ Continually updated information, maps, and biographies

★ Exclusive, customized **Factmonster™** from **Infoplease®**

★ Motivating, interactive learning games

*H*ow will I know my students are successful?

**Students need to become critical thinkers who can solve problems, work together, and make decisions.
Scott Foresman Social Studies provides built-in skill lessons and multiple assessment tools to develop thinking citizens.**

Research and Writing Skills

Gather and Report Information

What? To write a report, you will often have to find information beyond what is available in your textbook. Where can you find facts on topics you want to learn more about? The library and the Internet hold a vast amount of resources that provide information on almost any topic. But gathering a lot of information does not guarantee a good report. You must also know how to organize your report, including the most important information, and how to write it clearly.

Why? In the previous lesson, you learned that the Federalists worked for the ratification of the Constitution and the Antifederalists worked against it. Suppose you want to gather more information on the Federalists to write a report. First, you have to collect facts a[bout]...

Thinking Skills

Evaluate Advertisements

What? An advertisement tries to sell people goods, or services, or ideas. An advertisement, often called ad for short, may be printed, spoken, sung, or found on the Internet. The purpose is always the same—to interest people in what the advertiser is selling.

The advertiser may be selling any kind of goods, from toothbrushes, to clothing, to cars. Or the advertiser may be selling services, such as haircuts, cooking lessons, or a trip. Or the advertiser may even be selling an idea, such as urging people to vote for a person running for office.

The advertisement shown here was published in a newspaper in New York City during the early years of the gold rush.

Map and Globe Skills

Compare Maps at Different Scales

What? You know that a map scale uses a unit of measurement, such as one inch, to represent an actual larger distance on Earth, such as one mile. On a **small-scale map** an inch on the map represents a very large distance on Earth. Therefore, a small-scale map shows a big area of Earth, such as a state or a country. Map A is a small-scale map.

On a **large-scale map** an inch represents a shorter distance on Earth. Therefore, this kind [of map shows more] details than a [small-scale map.]

Chart and Graph Skills

Read a Cross-Section Diagram

What? A cross-section diagram is a drawing that shows a view of something as if you could slice through it. Cross-section diagrams can be used to show you how something works.

Why? It is difficult to understand how a device works if you cannot see inside it. In a cross-section diagram, the artist "removes" part of the outside so that you can see how the inside

works. A cross-section diagram helps you see how canals like the Erie Canal work.

How? To use a cross-section diagram, you have to study the drawing carefully. Read the labels to identify each part of the diagram.

The diagram on this page shows how a boat moves from higher to lower water in the lock of a canal. A lock is a section of a canal that is closed off so that water can be removed or added. The water coming in or going out changes the level of the water in the lock so that a boat can be moved higher or lower.

Look at the cross-section diagram. Notice that the boat has to be moved to a lower water level. Locate the gates that will keep the boat in the lock while the water level is

being changed. Notice where the boat will go after the water level has been changed.

Think and Apply

1. What is the purpose of a canal lock?

2. What do the lock gates do?

3. This cross-section shows how a boat is moved from a higher water level to a lower water level. How do you think a lock could be used to move a boat from a lower water level to a higher water level?

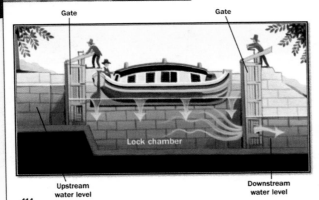

Gate   Gate

Lock chamber

Upstream water level   Downstream water level

414

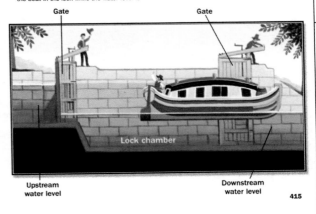

Gate   Gate

Lock chamber

Upstream water level   Downstream water level

415

BUILT-IN SKILL LESSONS IN EVERY UNIT

★ Teach and apply relevant skills within a social studies context

★ Graphics that support the content

INFORMAL ASSESSMENT OPPORTUNITIES

★ Monitor students' learning as you teach

★ If/then guidelines with specific reteaching strategies and effective practice

★ Assess instruction and make adjustments

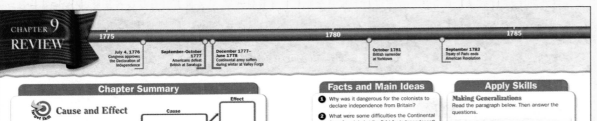

✓ Ongoing Assessment

If... students do not understand the British and colonists' views of the Intolerable Acts,

then... have students make a list of the punishments Britain placed on Boston and another list of the actions colonists planned as a result of these punishments.

FORMAL ASSESSMENT OPPORTUNITIES

★ Assess students' learning and provide practice for key test-taking skills

★ Built-in Lesson, Chapter, and Unit Reviews in the student book

★ Chapter Tests and Unit Tests in the Assessment Handbook

★ Standardized test format with multiple-choice, open-ended, and written responses

★ Performance-based assessments

CHAPTER 9
REVIEW

1775   1780   1785

July 4, 1776 Congress approves the Declaration of Independence

September–October 1777 Americans defeat British at Saratoga

December 1777– June 1778 Continental army suffers during winter at Valley Forge

October 1781 British surrender at Yorktown

September 1783 Treaty of Paris ends American Revolution

Chapter Summary

Cause and Effect

On a separate sheet of paper, fill in three effects that followed from the cause.

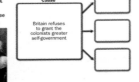

Cause

Britain refuses to grant the colonists greater self-government

Effect

Vocabulary

Match each word with the correct definition or description.

1. **Olive Branch Petition** (p. 297)
2. **traitor** (p. 300)
3. **mercenary** (p. 303)
4. **Battle of Saratoga** (p. 305)
5. **Treaty of Paris** (p. 319)

a. soldier who is paid to fight for another country

b. document that ended the American Revolution

c. person who acts against his or her country

d. letter Congress sent to Britain to try to avoid war

e. turning point of the American Revolution

People and Groups

Write a sentence explaining why each of the following people or groups was important in winning the American Revolution. You may use two or more in a single sentence.

1. Continental Army (p. 297)
2. Thomas Paine (p. 298)
3. Richard Henry Lee (p. 298)
4. Green Mountain Boys (p. 303)
5. Thaddeus Kosciusko (p. 305)
6. James Armistead (p. 306)
7. Mary Ludwig Hays (p. 307)
8. Marquis de Lafayette (p. 315)
9. Bernardo de Gálvez (p. 315)
10. John Paul Jones (p. 316)

Facts and Main Ideas

1. Why was it dangerous for the colonists to declare independence from Britain?

2. What were some difficulties the Continental Army faced during the fight for independence?

3. Why did George Washington attack Trenton, New Jersey, and what was the result of the attack?

4. **Time Line** How many years were there between the Declaration of Independence and the Treaty of Paris?

5. **Main Idea** What key events led the American colonists to declare their independence from Britain?

6. **Main Idea** How did women and African Americans contribute to the success of the United States in the war?

7. **Main Idea** How did other countries help the Americans in their victory over the British?

8. **Critical Thinking: Draw Conclusions** Why do you think people from other countries helped the Americans in their battle for independence?

Write About History

1. **Write a journal** that an American soldier might have written during the American Revolution. Describe what you see and the dangers you face.

2. **Write a story** about George Rogers Clark's army marching through icy swamplands to launch an attack at Fort Vincennes. Describe how the soldiers survived to go on to defeat the British.

3. **Write a letter** that Martha Washington might have written to American soldiers at Valley Forge to raise their spirits.

Apply Skills

Making Generalizations

Read the paragraph below. Then answer the questions.

During the American Revolution, Benjamin Franklin of Pennsylvania went to France to gain French support against Britain for the cause of American independence. John Jay of New York represented the colonies in Spain to try to gain support and recognition for the Americans in their fight against Britain. John Adams of Massachusetts went to Holland to gain Dutch support, and Francis Dana of Massachusetts served the United States in Russia.

1. What common theme can you find in the information in this paragraph?

2. Why did each of these men go to the various countries?

3. What generalization can you make about the paragraph?

Internet Activity

To get help with vocabulary, people, and terms, select dictionary or encyclopedia from Social Studies Library at www.sfsocialstudies.com.

322   323

Test Talk

TEST-TAKING STRATEGY LESSONS

★ Develop test-taking strategies right in the student book

★ Test preparation for national and state tests

★ Transparencies and worksheets to support instruction

UNIT 2

Review

Test Talk

Find key words in the text.

Main Ideas and Vocabulary

Read the passage below and use it to answer the questions that follow.

After Europeans arrived in the Americas, a great variety of plants and animals, foods and customs traveled in both directions across the Atlantic Ocean. This movement is known as the Columbian Exchange. It is a process that began with Columbus's first voyage and continues to this day.

Unfortunately, germs that cause diseases also made the ocean crossing in both directions. Many Indians and settlers died from diseases that were new to them.

Spain was the first European country to set up colonies in the Americas. Spanish explorers and soldiers claimed some islands in the Caribbean Sea for their country. Then they defeated the Aztecs in Mexico and established the colony of New Spain, with a capital at Mexico City. Later, they conquered the Inca Empire in what is now Peru.

Despite Spain's power at sea, England challenged Spain's powerful armada and defeated it in 1588. After that, England sent its explorers and settlers to form a colony in the Americas.

Roanoke, the first of the English colonies, disappeared mysteriously. The colony established at Jamestown in 1607 faced many difficulties but managed to survive. The Pilgrims and the Puritans came seeking freedom from religious persecution. They established colonies in New England.

Meanwhile, French and Dutch settlers were establishing colonies near the English. The French colonies were in what is now Canada. The English eventually captured the Dutch colonies.

By the early 1700s there were thirteen English colonies in North America.

1. According to this passage, what is the Columbian Exchange?
A the goods Columbus gave to Native Americans to buy land
B the Spanish conquest of Native American empires in the Americas
C the establishment of European colonies in the Americas
D the movement of plants, animals, and people between Europe and the Americas

2. In the passage, the word colony means—
A a settlement
B a company
C a fort
D a trade agreement

3. In the passage, the word persecution means—
A trial in court
B unjust treatment because of beliefs
C a fair process of investigation
D religious freedom

4. What is the main idea of this passage?
A European countries established colonies for various reasons.
B England established thirteen colonies in North America to challenge other European powers.
C The English colonies were generally better than colonies of other countries.
D Indians got sick and many died of European diseases.

190

The World

★ Teacher's Edition Table of Contents ★

Teacher Resources

The World

PROGRAM AUTHORS

Dr. Candy Dawson Boyd
Professor, School of Education
Director of Reading Programs
St. Mary's College
Moraga, California

Dr. Geneva Gay
Professor of Education
University of Washington
Seattle, Washington

Rita Geiger
**Director of Social Studies and
    Foreign Languages**
Norman Public Schools
Norman, Oklahoma

Dr. James B. Kracht
**Associate Dean for Undergraduate
    Programs and Teacher Education**
College of Education
Texas A&M University
College Station, Texas

Dr. Valerie Ooka Pang
Professor of Teacher Education
San Diego State University
San Diego, California

Dr. C. Frederick Risinger
**Director, Professional Development
    and Social Studies Education**
Indiana University
Bloomington, Indiana

Sara Miranda Sanchez
**Elementary and Early Childhood
    Curriculum Coordinator**
Albuquerque Public Schools
Albuquerque, New Mexico

CONTRIBUTING AUTHORS

Dr. Carol Berkin
Professor of History
Baruch College and the Graduate
    Center
The City University of New York
New York, New York

Lee A. Chase
Staff Development Specialist
Chesterfield County Public Schools
Chesterfield County, Virginia

Dr. Jim Cummins
Professor of Curriculum
Ontario Institute for Studies in
    Education
University of Toronto
Toronto, Canada

Dr. Allen D. Glenn
Professor and Dean Emeritus
Curriculum and Instruction
College of Education
University of Washington
Seattle, Washington

Dr. Carole L. Hahn
Professor, Educational Studies
Emory University
Atlanta, Georgia

Dr. M. Gail Hickey
Professor of Education
Indiana University-Purdue
    University
Fort Wayne, Indiana

Dr. Bonnie Meszaros
Associate Director
Center for Economic Education and
    Entrepreneurship
University of Delaware
Newark, Delaware

Editorial Offices: Glenview, Illinois • Parsippany, New Jersey • New York, New York
Sales Office: Parsippany, New Jersey • Duluth, Georgia • Glenview, Illinois •
    Coppell, Texas • Ontario, California

www.sfsocialstudies.com

Content Consultants

Catherine Deans-Barrett
World History Specialist
Northbrook, Illinois

Dr. Michael Frassetto
Studies in Religions
Independent Scholar
Chicago, Illinois

Dr. Gerald Greenfield
Hispanic-Latino Studies
History Department
University of Wisconsin, Parkside
Kenosha, Wisconsin

Dr. Frederick Hoxie
Native American Studies
University of Illinois
Champaign, Illinois

Dr. Cheryl Johnson-Odim
Dean of Liberal Arts and Sciences and
    Professor of History
African American
    History Specialist
Columbia College
Chicago, Illinois

Dr. Michael Khodarkovsky
Eastern European Studies
University of Chicago
Chicago, Illinois

Robert Moffet
U.S. History Specialist
Northbrook, Illinois

Dr. Ralph Nichols
East Asian History
University of Chicago
Chicago, Illinois

Classroom Reviewers

Diana Vicknair Ard
Woodlake Elementary School
St. Tammany Parish
Mandeville, Louisiana

Dr. Charlotte R. Bennett
St. John School
Newburgh, Indiana

Sharon Berenson
Freehold Learning Center
Freehold, New Jersey

Betsy Blandford
Pocahontas Elementary School
Powhatan, Virginia

Gloria Cantatore
Public School #5
West New York, New Jersey

LuAnn Curran
Westgate Elementary School
St. Petersburg, Florida

Louis De Angelo
Office of Catholic Education
Archdiocese of Philadelphia
Philadelphia, Pennsylvania

Dr. Trish Dolasinski
Paradise Valley School District
Arrowhead Elementary School
Glendale, Arizona

Dr. John R. Doyle
Director of Social Studies Curriculum
Miami-Dade County Schools
Miami, Florida

Dr. Roceal Duke
District of Columbia Public Schools
Washington, D.C.

Peggy Flanagan
Roosevelt Elementary School
Community Consolidated School
    District #64
Park Ridge, Illinois

Mary Flynn
Arrowhead Elementary School
Glendale, Arizona

Sue Gendron
Spring Branch ISD
Houston, Texas

Su Hickenbottom
Totem Falls Elementary School
Snohomish School District
Snohomish, Washington

Sally Hunter
Highland Park Elementary School
Austin ISD
Austin, Texas

Allan Jones
North Branch Public Schools
North Branch, Minnesota

Brandy Bowers Kerbow
Bettye Haun Elementary School
Plano ISD
Plano, Texas

Sandra López
PSJA Service Center
San Juan, Texas

Martha Sutton Maple
Shreve Island School
Shreveport, Louisiana

Lyn Metzger
Carpenter Elementary School
Community Consolidated School
    District #64
Park Ridge, Illinois

Marsha Munsey
Riverbend Elementary School
West Monroe, Louisiana

Christine Nixon
Warrington Elementary School
Escambia County School District
Pensacola, Florida

Liz Salinas
Supervisor
Edgewood ISD
San Antonio, Texas

Beverly Scaling
Desert Hills Elementary School
Las Cruces, New Mexico

Madeleine Schmitt
St. Louis Public Schools
St. Louis, Missouri

Barbara Schwartz
Central Square Intermediate School
Central Square, New York

Ronald Snapp
North Lawrence Community Schools
Bedford, Indiana

Lesley Ann Stahl
West Side Catholic Consolidated
    School
Evansville, Indiana

Carolyn Moss Woodall
Loudoun County of Virginia Public
    Schools
Leesburg, Virginia

Suzanne Zeremba
J. B. Fisher Model School
Richmond Public Schools
Richmond, Virginia

5 6 7 8 9 10 V057 11 10 09 08 07 06 05 04 03

Contents

Unit 1   Early Civilizations and Cultures

"With patience and a spirit of adventure, nothing is too far away."

—Said by Father Alberto de Agostini about the Cave of the Hands, 1941

Unit 2 Early Civilizations in Africa and Asia

"I will lead the army on water and on land, to bring marvels from God's-Land."

—Probably said by Queen Hatshepsut of Egypt

Unit 3 Early Civilizations in the Americas

"With such wonderful sights to gaze on we did not know what to say, or if this was real that we saw before our eyes."

—account given by Spaniard Bernal Diaz on seeing Tenochtitlan, c. 1560.

Unit 4 Mediterranean Empires

"Let them enjoy indeed the title of citizens."

—Emperor Claudius, as recorded by Tacitus, A.D. 48

Unit 5 The Medieval World

"I have not told half of what I saw."

—Said by Marco Polo on his deathbed about his travels across Asia, 1324

viii

Unit 6 Discovery, Expansion, and Revolutions

"Get gold, humanely if possible, but at all hazards— get gold."

—King Ferdinand of Spain, 1511

ix

Unit 7 A World in Opposition

"Never in the field of human conflict has so much been owed by so many to so few."

—said by Winston Churchill during the Battle of Britain, August 20, 1940

Unit 8 New Nations and a New Century

"We must learn to think globally. . . . No single region or nation can isolate itself from the rest of the world."

—Gro Harlem Brundtland in *Our Common Future*, a 1987 United Nations report

Reference Guide

★BIOGRAPHY★

Charts, Graphs, Tables & Diagrams

Time Lines

Notes

★ UNIT 5 ★
The Medieval World

The Medieval World

UNIT 5

Unit Planning Guide

Unit 5 • The Medieval World

Begin with a Primary Source pp. 314–315

Meet the People pp. 316–317

Reading Social Studies, Sequence pp. 318–319

Chapter Titles	Pacing	Main Ideas
Chapter 11 **Byzantine Empire and Ancient Arabia** pp. 320–341 ✓ **Chapter 11 Review** pp. 342–343	5 days	• Physical features, climate, and Roman and Greek culture influenced how people lived in the Byzantine Empire. • Under the rule of Justinian, the Byzantine Empire became great. • Islam brought changes to lands in Southwest Asia. • Trade and conquest helped spread religion and language throughout the Islamic world.
Chapter 12 **Asian Empires** pp. 344–365 ✓ **Chapter 12 Review** pp. 366–367	6 days	• Asia has a variety of climates and landforms that influenced several different cultures. • Medieval Chinese dynasties made several significant contributions to trade and technology. • For hundreds of years, the Khmer culture dominated the peninsula of Southeast Asia. • Japan became isolated, or separated, from most of the world but still carried on some trade.
Chapter 13 **African Empires** pp. 368–387 ✓ **Chapter 13 Review** pp. 388–389	5 days	• People throughout Africa have adapted to a variety of environments. • Many kingdoms developed in the savanna and forested areas of West Africa. • Trading empires developed in eastern, central, and southern Africa that interacted with Arabia, India, and China.
Chapter 14 **Medieval Europe** pp. 390–413 ✓ **Chapter 14 Review** pp. 414–415	6 days	• The landforms and climate of Europe affect the way Europeans live. • After a series of rulers and invaders, medieval government in Europe experienced a change. • The Church, feudalism, and manor life formed the foundation of European medieval life. • Routes promoted trade, travel, and communication, as well as the Plague, between Europe, Africa, and Asia.

✓ = Assessment Options

End with a Legend pp. 416–417   ✓ **Unit 5 Project** p. 420

✓ **Unit 5 Review** pp. 418–419

Saddle bags like this one were used to carry water and trade goods.

Resources	Meeting Individual Needs
• Workbook, pp. 77–82 • Every Student Learns Guide, pp. 146–161 • Transparencies 1, 9, 20, 39 • Quick Study, pp. 74–81 • Workbook, p. 83 ✓ Chapter 11 Content Test, Assessment Book, pp. 57–59 ✓ Chapter 11 Skills Test, Assessment Book, pp. 59–60	• ESL Support, TE pp. 318, 323, 328, 331, 335 • Leveled Practice, TE pp. 325, 327, 333, 337 • Learning Styles, TE p. 338 ✓ Chapter 11 Performance Assessment, TE p. 342
• Workbook, pp. 84–89 • Every Student Learns Guide, pp. 162–177 • Transparencies 1, 10, 20, 40, 41 • Quick Study, pp. 82–89 • Workbook, p. 90 ✓ Chapter 12 Content Test, Assessment Book, pp. 61–63 ✓ Chapter 12 Skills Test, Assessment Book, pp. 63–64	• ESL Support, TE pp. 347, 352, 358, 361 • Leveled Practice, TE pp. 349, 351, 357, 363, 364 • Learning Styles, TE p. 355 ✓ Chapter 12 Performance Assessment, TE p. 366
• Workbook, pp. 91–95 • Every Student Learns Guide, pp. 178–189 • Transparencies 6, 42 • Quick Study, pp. 90–95 • Workbook, p. 96 ✓ Chapter 13 Content Test, Assessment Book, pp. 65–67 ✓ Chapter 13 Skills Test, Assessment Book, pp. 67–68	• ESL Support, TE pp. 371, 375, 382 • Leveled Practice, TE pp. 372, 376, 383 • Learning Styles, TE pp. 377, 385 ✓ Chapter 13 Performance Assessment, TE p. 388
• Workbook, pp. 97–102 • Every Student Learns Guide, pp. 190–205 • Transparencies 1, 10, 20, 43, 44, 45 • Quick Study, pp. 96–103 • Workbook, p. 103 ✓ Chapter 14 Content Test, Assessment Book, pp. 69–70 ✓ Chapter 14 Skills Test, Assessment Book, pp. 71–72	• Leveled Practice, TE pp. 393, 397, 401, 408 • ESL Support, TE pp. 394, 398, 404, 407 • Learning Styles, TE pp. 409, 413 ✓ Chapter 14 Performance Assessment, TE p. 414

Providing More Depth

 Multimedia Library

- *Castle,* by Christopher Gravett
- *A Street Through Time,* by Anne Millard
- **Songs and Music**
- **Video Field Trips**
- **Software**

Additional Resources

- Family Activities
- Vocabulary Cards
- Daily Activity Bank
- Social Studies Plus!
- Big Book Atlas
- Student Atlas
- Outline Maps
- Desk Maps

 ADDITIONAL Technology

- AudioText
- The test maker
- Teacher Resources CD-ROM
- Map Resources CD-ROM
- **www.sfsocialstudies.com**

 To establish guidelines for your students' safe and responsible use of the Internet, use the Scott Foresman Internet Guide.

Additional Internet Links

To find out more about:

- Medieval art and architecture, visit **www.getty.edu**
- Life in the Middle Ages, click on *Social Studies and History* at **www.learner.org**

Key Internet Search Terms

- medieval or medieval world
- Middle Ages
- ancient Africa

Unit 5 Objectives

Assessment Options

✓ Formal Assessment

- **Lesson Reviews,** PE/TE pp. 325, 328, 333, 338, 349, 355, 359, 363, 373, 378, 385, 395, 398, 405, 411
- **Chapter Reviews,** PE/TE pp. 342–343, 366–367, 388–389, 414–415
- **Chapter Tests,** Assessment Book, pp. 57–72
- **Unit Review,** PE/TE pp. 418–419
- **Unit Tests,** Assessment Book, pp. 73–76
- **The test maker** (test-generator software)

✓ Informal Assessment

- **Teacher's Edition Questions,** throughout Lessons and Features
- **Section Reviews,** PE/TE pp. 323–325, 327–328, 331, 333, 335, 337–338, 347–349, 351, 353, 355, 357, 359, 361, 363, 371–373, 375, 377–378, 381–385, 393–395, 397–398, 401–405, 407–409, 411
- **Close and Assess,** PE/TE pp. 325, 328–329, 333, 338–339, 341, 349, 354–355, 359, 363, 365, 373, 378–379, 385, 387, 395, 398–399, 405, 411, 413

Ongoing Assessment

Ongoing Assessment is found throughout the Teacher's Edition lessons using an **If…Then** model.

If = students' observable behavior,	**Then =** reteaching and enrichment suggestions

✓ Portfolio Assessment

- **Portfolio Assessment,** TE pp. 313, 314, 419
- **Leveled Practice,** TE pp. 325, 327, 333, 337, 349, 351, 357, 363, 364, 372, 376, 383, 393, 397, 401, 408
- **Workbook Pages,** pp. 76–104
- **Chapter Review: Write About History,** PE/TE pp. 343, 367, 389, 415
- **Unit Review: Apply Skills,** PE/TE p. 419
- **Curriculum Connection: Writing** PE/TE pp. 325, 349, 355; TE pp. 315, 341, 365, 379

✓ Performance Assessment

- **Hands-on Unit Project** (Unit 5 Performance Assessment), PE/TE p. 313
- **Internet Activity,** PE p. 420
- **Chapter 11 Performance Assessment,** PE/TE p. 342
- **Chapter 12 Performance Assessment,** PE/TE p. 366
- **Chapter 13 Performance Assessment,** PE/TE p. 388
- **Chapter 14 Performance Assessment,** PE/TE p. 414
- **Unit Review: Write and Share,** PE/TE p. 419
- **Scoring Guides,** TE pp. 419–420

 Test Talk

Test-Taking Strategies

Understand the Question
- **Locate Key Words in the Question,** TE pp. 376, 409
- **Locate Key Words in the Text,** TE p. 382

Understand the Answer
- **Choose the Right Answer,** Test Talk Practice Book
- **Use Information from the Text,** TE p. 324
- **Use Information from Graphics,** PE/TE p. 419, TE p. 352
- **Write Your Answer to Score High,** TE p. 343

Featured Strategy

Use Information from Graphics

Students will:

- Understand the question and form a statement that begins "I need to find out …"

- Skim the graphics to find the right information to support their answer.

PE/TE p. 419, **TE** p. 352

Curriculum Connections

Integrating Your Day

The lessons, skills, and features of Unit 5 provide many opportunities to make connections between social studies and other areas of the elementary curriculum.

Social Studies

READING

Reading Skill—Sequence, PE/TE pp. 318–319, 322, 326, 346, 396

Lesson Review—Sequence, PE/TE pp. 325, 328, 349, 399

Link to Reading, PE/TE p. 363

WRITING

Write Journal Entries, TE p. 315

Link to Writing, PE/TE pp. 325, 349, 355, 398

Write About Line Graphs, TE p. 341

Create a How-to Guide, TE p. 365

Writing Metaphors, TE p. 379

MATH

Create Line Graphs, TE p. 340

West African Kingdoms, TE p. 378

Solving Problems with Time, TE p. 412

SCIENCE

Research Trade Routes, TE p. 324

Research Flood Control, TE p. 357

Link to Science, PE/TE pp. 373, 385, 411

Research and Report on Irrigation, TE p. 381

LITERATURE

Read Biographies, TE p. 316

Explore Travel Books, TE p. 339

Learn More About Cambodia, TE p. 359

African Tales, TE p. 373

Life in Medieval Times, TE p. 403

King Arthur, TE p. 417

ART

Create a Mural, TE p. 324

Illustrate Chinese Topics, TE p. 353

Link to Art, PE/TE pp. 359, 378, 395

Create Posters, TE p. 410

MUSIC / DRAMA

Role Play an Interview, TE p. 384

Perform a Skit, TE p. 404

Link to Drama, PE/TE p. 405

 Look for this symbol throughout the Teacher's Edition to find **Curriculum Connections.**

Professional Development

The Value of Literature

by Valerie Ooka Pang, Ph.D.
San Diego State University

Children's literature is one of the most important tools that teachers can use in social studies education. Literature brings the hope and joy of life into the classroom. It celebrates the human spirit. It describes the human condition. Well-written books can demonstrate how people from diverse communities work together to create a more compassionate and just society.

Literature can also show the struggle of individuals who have fought against oppressive practices and triumphed. Through literature, children are given the opportunity to look at life from many different people's perspectives.

Sometimes children's literature allows teachers to bring into the classroom controversial subjects to which children might not otherwise be exposed. Children's books can encourage young people to consider complex social issues and the dilemmas they pose.

In more specific terms, children's literature can be used to teach specific social science skills such as finding evidence, understanding chronology, reaching conclusions, posing questions, identifying social problems, investigating issues, examining solutions, making decisions, and acting to make social change.

Below are several ways in which Scott Foresman Social Studies *incorporates literature into its lessons.*

- *The Bibliography on p. 313h of the Teacher's Edition lists books to use as additional resources to enhance the lessons. Award-winning selections are suggested throughout the unit.*

- *The Literature Curriculum Connections invite students to use literature to expand their understanding of topics such as Cambodia, African culture, and feudalism.*

ESL Support

By Jim Cummins, Ph.D.
University of Toronto

In Unit 5, you can use the following fundamental strategies to activate students' prior knowledge and to build background:

Activate Prior Knowledge/ Build Background

Brainstorming and discussion as a whole class, in small groups, or in pairs can be a highly effective strategy. Students can interview each other in pairs to find out what each knows about a particular topic. Discussion can make abstract concepts more concrete and comprehensible.

Dramatization or role-playing can be used to express students' prior knowledge or intuitions about various concepts or events in social studies (e.g., they can dramatize the process of making and selling goods and the role of money in economic organization).

Having students write about what they know is also a worthwhile strategy. Students can do a "quick write" in which they write down words they associate with a particular concept or event, or they can write responses to written prompts.

The following examples in the Teacher's Edition will help you activate prior knowledge and build background for ESL students:

- *Share Knowledge About Asia on p. 347 asks advanced learners to list as many Asian countries and physical features as they can. Students then write sentences indicating what they already know about each item on the list.*

- *Share Knowledge About Climates on p. 371 invites intermediate ESL learners to brainstorm for a list of various climates in places they already know about. This will aid in their understanding of climate zones of Africa.*

Read Aloud

from the *Justinian Code*

Justice is the constant and perpetual wish to render everyone his due…. The maxims of law are these: to live honestly, to hurt no one, to give every one his due…. [T]he law which natural reason appoints for all mankind obtains equally among all nations, because all nations make use of it.

Build Background

- Share with students that these words come from the Justinian Code, named after the Byzantine emperor Justinian (527–565).
- Justinian wanted to create a large empire that he would rule with a uniform, or consistent, code of laws. He appointed a special commission that worked for years to collect and systemize existing Roman laws.
- The Justinian Code is still the basis of law for most countries in Europe.

Definitions

- *perpetual:* continuous or everlasting
- *maxims:* sayings or proverbs
- *obtains:* applies

Read Alouds and Primary Sources

- *Read Alouds and Primary Sources* contains additional selections to be used with Unit 5.

Bibliography

Cathedral: The Story of Its Construction, by David Macaulay (Houghton Mifflin Co., ISBN 0-395-17513-5, 1973) **Easy** *Caldecott Honor, New York Times Best Illustrator*

Maples in the Mist: Children's Poems from the Tang Dynasty, edited by Minfong Ho (Lothrop, Lee, & Shephard, ISBN 0-688-12044-X, 1996) **Easy** *ALA Notable Book*

The Silk Route: 7,000 Miles of History, by John S. Major (Harper Trophy, ISBN 0-064-43468-0, 1996) **Easy**

Muhammad of Mecca: Prophet of Islam, by Elsa Marston (Franklin Watts, Inc., ISBN 0-531-15554-4, 2001) **On-Level**

One World, Many Religions: The Ways We Worship, by Mary Pope Osborne (Knopf, ISBN 0-679-83930-5, 1996) **On-Level** *Orbis Pictus Honor*

Sons of Charlemagne, by Barbara Willard (Bethlehem Books, ISBN 1-883-93730-2, 1998) **On-Level**

Genghis Khan, by R. P. Lister (Cooper Square Press, ISBN 0-815-41052-2, 2000) **Challenge**

In the Land of the Taj Mahal: The World of the Fabulous Mughals, by Ed Rothfarb (Henry Holt and Co., Inc., ISBN 0-805-05299-2, 1998) **Challenge**

The Story of Mankind, by Hendrik Willem Van Loon (W. W. Norton and Company, ISBN 0-871-40175-4, 1999) **Challenge** *Newbery Medal*

A Companion to Justinian's Institutes, edited by Ernest Metzger (Cornell University Press, ISBN 0-801-48584-3, 1999) **Teacher reference**

Discovery Channel School Videos

Times Medieval This four-segment video features medieval feudal life, castles, knights' armor, and the Legend of King Arthur. (Item # 717470, 26 minutes)

- To order *Discovery Channel School* videos, please call the following toll-free number: 1-888-892-3484.
- Free online lesson plans are available at **DiscoverySchool.com.**

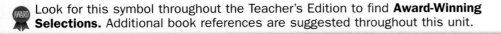

Look for this symbol throughout the Teacher's Edition to find **Award-Winning Selections.** Additional book references are suggested throughout this unit.

The Medieval World

How does trade connect peoples, cultures, and ideas?

313

The Medieval World

Unit Overview

The geography and climate of Europe, Africa, and Asia greatly affected how people lived and worked during the Medieval Age. People adapted to and modified their environments to meet their basic needs. Trade and other interactions between peoples led to the spread of cultures and beliefs.

Unit Outline

Unit Question

- Have students read the question under the painting.

- To activate prior knowledge, discuss the word *trade*, reminding students that people throughout history have traded goods and services with others to get what they need and want. Have students discuss questions such as *How does trade connect people? How would people exchange ideas as well as goods?* and *What ideas or items in our lives do you think may be the result of trade between nations?*

- Create a list of students' ideas about the ways in which trade connects people and cultures and influences the spread of ideas.

- ✓ **Portfolio Assessment** Keep this list to review with students at the end of the unit on p. 419.

Practice and Extend

Hands-on Unit Project

✓ **Unit 5 Performance Assessment**
- The Unit Project, *A Day in the Life*, found on p. 420, is an ongoing performance assessment project to enrich students' learning throughout the unit.
- This project, which has students do research and write about a day in a typical medieval village, and build a model of the village, may be started now or at any time during this unit of study.
- A performance assessment scoring guide is located on p. 420.

Begin with a Primary Source

Objective
- Use primary sources to acquire information.

Resource
- Poster 9

Interpret a Primary Source

- Tell students that the quotation that appears here is Marco Polo's deathbed statement. He had been asked to say that his stories were invented, not factual.

- Marco Polo was the son of a family of wealthy merchants who had long traded goods to the Middle East.

- ✓**Portfolio Assessment** Remind students of the list they began about how trade connects peoples and may spread culture and ideas (see p. 313). As students read the unit, they can keep a list of the interactions between cultures and the results of these interactions. Review students' lists at the end of the unit on p. 419.

Interpret Fine Art

- This picture shows a caravan traveling across the desert. A caravan is a group of people—usually merchants—who travel together for protection. People making long journeys usually traveled in caravans.

- Ask students what might make crossing the desert dangerous and how traveling in a caravan might benefit the people in this picture.

- Ask students to draw conclusions about how the people in this painting adapted to the desert environment. (Camels are well equipped to travel long distances without water, the clothing would protect the people from the sun and heat, and so on.)

500	600	700	800	900	1000

c. 527
The Byzantine Empire begins to expand.

c. 622
Islam begins to spread throughout Southwest Asia.

c. 800
Rise of feudalism in Europe

about 900
Height of early trading kingdoms and empires in East and West Africa

314

1

Practice and Extend

SOCIAL STUDIES
Background

About Marco Polo

- With his father and uncle, who were merchants in jewels and other precious goods, Marco Polo set out from Venice, Italy, in A.D. 1271.

- The Polos' route took them through present-day Israel, Turkey, Iran, and Afghanistan into China, then ruled by Kublai Khan. He made the Polos welcome and took a liking to young Marco and his stories of other lands.

- When Marco Polo returned to Europe, his book about his amazing journey, *Il Milione*, became a sensation. Christopher Columbus studied it closely before his voyage in search of the wealth of the Indies.

> *"I have not told half of what I saw."*
>
> —Said by Marco Polo on his deathbed about his travels across Asia, 1324

uana es partida del impi

anar raleatavo :

The Catalan Atlas of 1375 illustrates the caravan of Marco Polo crossing Asia.

| 1100 | 1200 | 1300 | 1400 | 1500 | 1600 |

1206 Genghis Khan unifies Mongolia.

1215 The Magna Carta is signed by King John.

1347 The Plague spreads across Europe.

3

1526 The Mogul Empire is established.

1095 The beginning of the Crusades

2

c. 1500 Portuguese invasions begin in Africa.

315

Meet the Artist

- This atlas was compiled and based on the writings of Marco Polo.

- Catalan is a language spoken in Spain and France. The earliest written materials in this romance language date to the twelfth century.

Use the Time Line

This time line at the bottom of the page covers a period of about one thousand years. People who lived in the fifteenth and sixteenth centuries named the period the Middle Ages. They believed that the heights of culture and civilization were reached before and after the period that lasted from about 350 to 1450. The word *medieval* comes from the Latin words *medium* (middle) and *aevum* (age).

1 **What does the letter c. in front of the entry for the year 527 tell you?** The exact year for beginning of the expansion of the Byzantine Empire is not known. The letter c stands for the Latin word *circa,* which means "about" or "approximately." Interpret Time Lines

2 **How many years passed between the beginning of the Crusades and King John's signing of the Magna Carta?** 120 years Analyze Information

3 **Which event on the time line shows that a serious illness affected a large population?** The Plague spreads across Europe. Draw Conclusions

---

CURRICULUM CONNECTION
Writing

Write Journal Entries

- Have students examine the painting and the quotation. Ask students to discuss what it might be like to travel in a caravan like the one depicted. What might the travelers have been thinking? What daily activities would they have needed to carry out to survive such a journey?

- Using ideas from the discussion, students can step into the shoes of one of the people in the painting and write a series of three or four journal entries. They might describe why they are taking the journey, the activities that fill their day, and how they feel as they travel through the desert.

- Remind students to use the first-person point of view, using words such as *I* and *we* to give the writing a feeling of immediacy.

Meet the People

Objective

- Identify the contributions of significant individuals during the Middle Ages.

Resource

- Poster 10

Research the People

Each of the people pictured on these pages played an important part in the medieval world. Have students conduct research to find out the answers to the following questions.

- **How did Sundiata Keita expand the Mali Empire? How did he strengthen its economy?** Sundiata Keita made the Sudanese Empire and the gold fields of West Africa part of the Mali Empire. He not only controlled the gold fields, but he also took care of the most important trade routes to keep the economy strong.

- **How was Mansa Musa related to Sundiata Keita?** Musa was most likely Sundiata Keita's grandson or grandnephew.

- **What modern-day countries had their beginnings in Charlemagne's empire?** France and Germany

- **What was Genghis Khan's name when he was a child?** Temujin (Temujen), in honor of an enemy his father defeated when Genghis Khan was an infant.

Students may wish to write their own questions about other people on these pages for the rest of the class to answer.

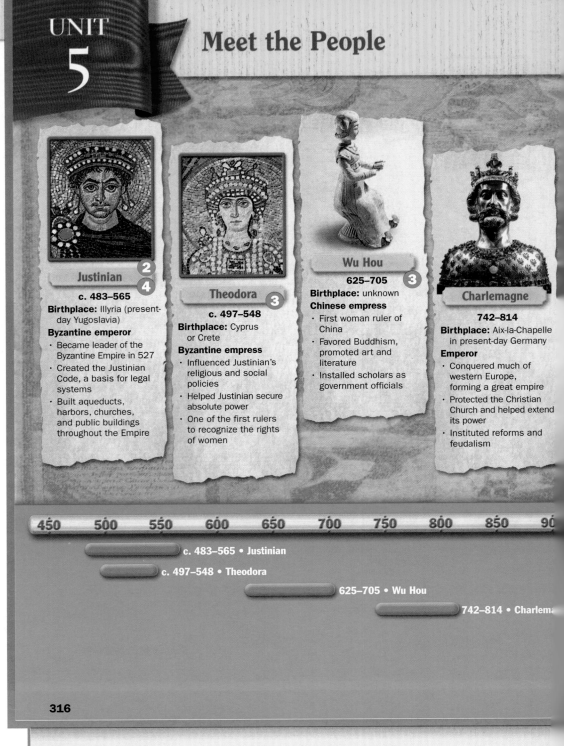

UNIT 5

Meet the People

Justinian ②④

c. 483–565

Birthplace: Illyria (present-day Yugoslavia)

Byzantine emperor

- Became leader of the Byzantine Empire in 527
- Created the Justinian Code, a basis for legal systems
- Built aqueducts, harbors, churches, and public buildings throughout the Empire

Theodora ③

c. 497–548

Birthplace: Cyprus or Crete

Byzantine empress

- Influenced Justinian's religious and social policies
- Helped Justinian secure absolute power
- One of the first rulers to recognize the rights of women

Wu Hou

625–705 ③

Birthplace: unknown

Chinese empress

- First woman ruler of China
- Favored Buddhism, promoted art and literature
- Installed scholars as government officials

Charlemagne

742–814

Birthplace: Aix-la-Chapelle in present-day Germany

Emperor

- Conquered much of western Europe, forming a great empire
- Protected the Christian Church and helped extend its power
- Instituted reforms and feudalism

| 450 | 500 | 550 | 600 | 650 | 700 | 750 | 800 | 850 | 90 |

c. 483–565 • Justinian

c. 497–548 • Theodora

625–705 • Wu Hou

742–814 • Charlema

316

Practice and Extend

CURRICULUM CONNECTION
Literature

Read Biographies

Use the following biography selections to extend the content.

Empress of China, Wu Ze Tian, by Cheng-An Chiang (Victory Press, ISBN 1-878-21732-1, 1998) **Easy**

Justinian (The Medieval World Series), by John Moorhead (Addison-Wesley Publishing, ISBN 0-582-06303-5, 1994) **On-Level**

Charlemagne, by Roger Collins (University of Toronto Press, ISBN 0-802-08218-1, 1998) **Challenge**

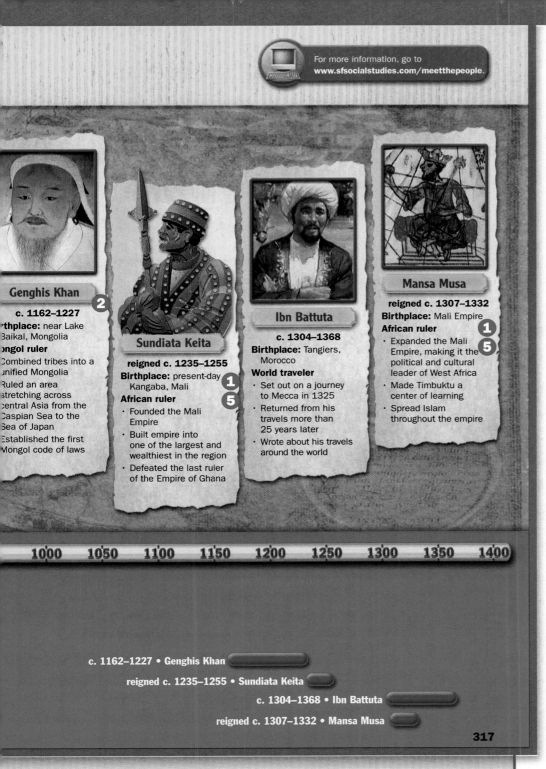

Genghis Khan

c. 1162–1227
Birthplace: near Lake
Baikal, Mongolia
Mongol ruler
· Combined tribes into a
unified Mongolia
· Ruled an area
stretching across
central Asia from the
Caspian Sea to the
Sea of Japan
· Established the first
Mongol code of laws

Sundiata Keita

reigned c. 1235–1255
Birthplace: present-day
Kangaba, Mali
African ruler
· Founded the Mali
Empire
· Built empire into
one of the largest and
wealthiest in the region
· Defeated the last ruler
of the Empire of Ghana

Ibn Battuta

c. 1304–1368
Birthplace: Tangiers,
Morocco
World traveler
· Set out on a journey
to Mecca in 1325
· Returned from his
travels more than
25 years later
· Wrote about his travels
around the world

Mansa Musa

reigned c. 1307–1332
Birthplace: Mali Empire
African ruler
· Expanded the Mali
Empire, making it the
political and cultural
leader of West Africa
· Made Timbuktu a
center of learning
· Spread Islam
throughout the empire

1000   1050   1100   1150   1200   1250   1300   1350   1400

c. 1162–1227 • Genghis Khan

reigned c. 1235–1255 • Sundiata Keita

c. 1304–1368 • Ibn Battuta

reigned c. 1307–1332 • Mansa Musa

317

For more information, go to
www.sfsocialstudies.com/meetthepeople.

WEB SITE
Technology

Students can research the
lives of people on this page by
clicking on *Meet the People* at
www.sfsocialstudies.com.

Use the Time Line

Have students use the time line and
biographies to answer the following
questions.

1 **Which people are not listed by their
dates of birth and death? What do the
dates by their names indicate? Why do
you think they are listed this way?**
Sundiata Keita and Mansa Musa are
listed according to the dates they
reigned. Their dates of birth and death
may not be known. **Draw Conclusions**

2 **What did Justinian and Genghis
Khan have in common?** Both developed
systems of laws to rule their empires.
Compare and Contrast

3 **What did Theodora and Wu Hou
have in common?** Both were empresses
in the Middle Ages. **Compare and Contrast**

4 **Which person listed with date of
birth had the longest life?** Justinian
Interpret Time Lines

5 **How many years after Sundiata
Keita's reign ended did Mansa Musa's
rule begin?** 52 years **Interpret Time Lines**

Biographies

Four of the people shown here are
discussed more extensively in the
Biography pages in Unit 5.

Read About the People

The people shown here are discussed in
the text on the following pages in Unit 5.

Reading Social Studies

Sequence

Objective

 Analyze information by determining the sequence of events.

Resource

• Workbook, p. 76

About the Unit Target Skill

• The target reading skill for this unit is Sequence.
• Students are introduced to the unit target skill here and are given an opportunity to practice it.
• Further opportunities to determine sequence are found throughout Unit 5.

1 Introduce and Motivate

Preview To activate prior knowledge, list some major events that were described in a previous chapter on the board. Write them out of order, and ask students to put them in the correct sequence. You might prompt students by asking leading questions such as *Which event happened first? What happened after that? What happened next?* and *What finally happened?*

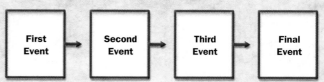
The Medieval World

Sequence

Events in sequence are listed in the order in which they happened.

| First Event | → | Second Event | → | Third Event | → | Final Event |

• Sometimes writers use words such as *before, initially, after, later,* and *finally* to signal sequence.
• Noting the dates of events will help you keep them in the correct sequence.
• Use a time line or a list to help you keep track of the sequence of events.

Read the following paragraph. The words that tell the sequence of events have been highlighted.

As you will read in this unit, the history of a place is often tied to the people living in that location. For example, the Hagia Sophia (ah YEE uh soh FEE uh) is one of the world's greatest buildings. Initially, the Hagia Sophia was a Christian church, built by a Roman emperor. Later, the Ottoman Turks conquered the region, converting the church into a mosque, a Muslim house of worship. Finally, in the twentieth century, it became a museum.

318

Practice and Extend

ESL ACCESS CONTENT
ESL Support

Practice Determining Sequence Guide students to understand the process of figuring out and retelling a sequence of events.

Beginning Display three or four pictures that clearly show steps in a simple sequence. Guide students as they help you put the pictures in sequential order.

Intermediate Display several pictures or drawings that show the steps in a process or convey the main events of a familiar story. Hold up one finger and say the word *first*. A volunteer can identify which happens first. Continue in the same way with the rest of the pictures.

Advanced Write simple sentences that tell a clear sequence of events on strips of paper, one event per strip. Guide students as they read the sentences, being sure they understand what each means. Then have students work in small groups to put the strips in order. Ask students to read the entire sequence aloud.

The Many Lives of the Hagia Sophia

In the fourth century, Emperor Constantine ordered that the first Hagia Sophia be built. On the same site where an earlier church that had been burned once stood, Emperor Justinian began the construction of a new church in 532. As the largest church in Constantinople, it was called "The Great Church."

The Hagia Sophia was constructed between the years 532 and 537. Even before the interior was completed, earthquakes rocked the building, cracking the great dome and the eastern half-dome. In 559 earthquakes made the main dome collapse. The church was reconstructed and later reopened by 563.

An earthquake in 869 toppled one of its half-domes. Another earthquake in 989 demolished the great dome. The building was reopened for religious services in 994. Today, periodic earthquakes continue to shake the Hagia Sophia.

Between 726 and 842, all of the church's religious pictures and figures were removed. In 1204 an army of crusaders looted, or robbed, the Hagia Sophia. Many of the holy relics, or remains, are now displayed in European museums.

After the Turkish army conquered the region in 1453, it took over the church. When Sultan Mehmed II entered the city, he was sad to see that the magnificent church was in need of repair.

The Turks converted the Hagia Sophia into a mosque and maintained the building for nearly 500 years. Finally, in 1935, the Hagia Sophia, located in Istanbul, Turkey, was converted into a museum.

Use the reading strategy of sequence to answer these questions.

1 What events took place within the first 300 years of the church's existence?

2 How did the Hagia Sophia change over time?

319

Workbook, p. 76

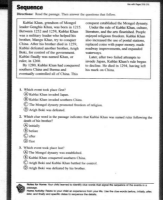

2 Teach and Discuss

- Explain that events that are in sequence are in the order in which they really happen or happened. Clue words, such as *before, initially, after, later,* and *finally* often help readers figure out the correct order of events. Dates can also help readers place the events in their proper sequence.

- Have students read the paragraph on p. 318. Make sure they realize that the highlighted words indicate sequence. Students may need help to understand how the word *initially* signals sequence.

- Then have students read the longer practice sample on p. 319 and answer the questions that follow.

- Ask students why, when studying history, it is important to understand sequence. (To understand history, we need to know which events happened before others. Often one event leads to or causes another. It is important to know how various events in history are connected to one another.)

3 Close and Assess

Apply it!

1. It was damaged by several earthquakes, including one in 559 that caused the dome to collapse. Removal of the church's religious pictures and figures began in 726.

2. Built as a Christian church, Hagia Sophia had been destroyed and rebuilt by 532; it was damaged and reconstructed by 559; religious pictures and figures were removed from it between 726 and 842; it became a mosque after 1453; it was finally converted into a museum in 1935.

Chapter Planning Guide

Chapter 11 • Byzantine Empire and Ancient Arabia

Locating Time and Place pp. 320–321

Lesson Titles	Pacing	Main Ideas
Lesson 1 **Geography of the Byzantine Empire** pp. 322–325	1 day	• Physical features, climate, and Roman and Greek culture influenced how people lived in the Byzantine Empire.
Lesson 2 **The Greatness of the Byzantine Empire** pp. 326–328	1 day	• Under the rule of Justinian, the Byzantine Empire became great.
Biography: **Justinian and Theodora** p. 329		• Justinian, a ruler of the Byzantine Empire, trusted his wife, Theodora, to give him advice about running the empire.
Lesson 3 **Development of Islam** pp. 330–333	1 day	• Islam brought changes to lands in Southwest Asia.
Lesson 4 **The Islamic World** pp. 334–338	2 days	• Trade and conquest helped spread religion and language throughout the Islamic world.
Citizen Heroes: Respect **Respecting Other Cultures** p. 339		• During his extensive travels, Ibn Battuta learned much about various cultures while showing respect for the people he met.
Chart and Graph Skills: **Interpret Line Graphs** pp. 340–341		• A line graph depicts how a variable or measured quantity changes over time.

✔ **Chapter 11 Review**
pp. 342–343

► **The Quran is the holy book of Islam.**

✔ = **Assessment Options**

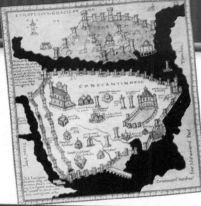

▶ The walls around Constantinople protected it from attack.

Vocabulary	Resources	Meeting Individual Needs
hippodrome	• Workbook, p. 78 • Transparency 9 • Every Student Learns Guide, pp. 146–149 • Quick Study, pp. 74–75	• ESL Support, TE p. 323 • Leveled Practice, TE p. 325
cathedral icon	• Workbook, p. 79 • Transparency 9 • Every Student Learns Guide, pp. 150–153 • Quick Study, pp. 76–77	• Leveled Practice, TE p. 327 • ESL Support, TE p. 328
pilgrimage caravan mosque	• Workbook, p. 80 • Transparencies 1, 39 • Every Student Learns Guide, pp. 154–157 • Quick Study, pp. 78–79	• ESL Support, TE p. 331 • Leveled Practice, TE p. 333
astrolabe	• Workbook, p. 81 • Transparency 20 • Every Student Learns Guide, pp. 158–161 • Quick Study, pp. 80–81 • Workbook, p. 82	• ESL Support, TE p. 335 • Leveled Practice, TE p. 337 • Learning Styles, TE p. 338
	✓ Chapter 11 Content Test, Assessment Book, pp. 57–59 ✓ Chapter 11 Skills Test, Assessment Book, pp. 59–60	✓ Chapter 11 Performance Assessment, TE p. 342

Providing More Depth

Additional Resources
- Vocabulary Cards
- Daily Activity Bank
- Social Studies Plus!
- Big Book Atlas
- Student Atlas
- Outline Maps
- Desk Maps

 Technology

- AudioText
- The test maker
- Teacher Resources CD-ROM
- Map Resources CD-ROM
- **www.sfsocialstudies.com**

 To establish guidelines for your students' safe and responsible use of the Internet, use the Scott Foresman Internet Guide.

Additional Internet Links
To find out more about:
- An illustrated time line of the Byzantine Empire, visit **www.metmuseum.org**
- The history and uses of the astrolabe, visit **www.astrolabes.org**

Key Internet Search Terms
- Byzantine Empire
- Islam
- Mecca

Workbook Support

Use the following Workbook pages to support content and skills development as you teach Chapter 11. You can also view and print Workbook pages from the Teacher Resources CD-ROM.

Workbook, p. 76

Sequence

Use with Pages 318–319.

Directions: Read the passage. Then answer the questions that follow.

Kublai Khan, grandson of Mongol leader Genghis Khan, was born in 1215. Between 1252 and 1259, Kublai Khan was a military leader who helped his brother, Mangu Khan, try to conquer China. After his brother died in 1259, Kublai defeated another brother, Arigh Boki, for control of the government. Kublai finally was named Khan, or ruler, in 1260.

By 1280, Kublai Khan had conquered southern China and Burma and eventually controlled all of China. This conquest established the Mongol dynasty.

Under the rule of Kublai Khan, culture, literature, and the arts flourished. People enjoyed religious freedom. Kublai Khan also increased the use of postal stations, replaced coins with paper money, made roadway improvements, and expanded waterways.

Later, after two failed attempts to invade Japan, Kublai Khan's rule began to decline. He died in 1294, having left his mark on China.

1. Which event took place first?
   - (A) Kublai Khan invaded Japan.
   - (B) Kublai Khan invaded southern China.
   - (C) The Mongol dynasty promoted freedom of religion.
   - ● Arigh Boki was defeated.

2. Which clue word in the passage indicates that Kublai Khan was named ruler following the death of his brother?
   - (A) initially
   - (B) before
   - ● after
   - (D) first

3. Which event took place last?
   - ● The Mongol dynasty was established.
   - (B) Kublai Khan conquered southern China.
   - (C) Arigh Boki and Kublai Khan battled for control.
   - (D) Arigh Boki was defeated by his brother.

 Notes for Home: Your child learned to identify clue words that signal the sequence of the events in a passage.
Home Activity: Relate to your child an experience from your life. Use the clue words *before, initially, after, later,* and *finally* and specific dates to sequence the details.

Use with Pupil Edition, p. 319

Workbook, p. 77

Vocabulary Preview

Use with Chapter 11.

Directions: Read each sentence. Then replace the words in italics with a vocabulary word from the box and write it on the line provided. You may use your glossary.

hippodrome	icon	caravan	astrolabe
cathedral	pilgrimage	mosque	

1. Many Muslims plan to make a *journey to a place of religious importance* to Mecca one time in their life.

   pilgrimage

2. A disagreement over the use of an *image of Jesus or a saint* as part of worship led to a split in the Christian church in 1054.

   icon

3. Muslim astronomers used an *instrument to map the stars in the sky* to determine directions.

   astrolabe

4. In medieval Arabia a *group of people and animals traveling together* was a common sight.

   caravan

5. The Hagia Sophia is an example of a *large, important Christian church.*

   cathedral

6. The *ancient Greek stadium used for horse and chariot racing* in Constantinople was the center of entertainment.

   hippodrome

7. Five daily prayers are offered in a *Muslim place of worship.*

   mosque

 Notes for Home: Your child learned the vocabulary terms for Chapter 11.
Home Activity: With your child, write a story about the Byzantine Empire using all of the vocabulary words correctly.

Use with Pupil Edition, p. 320

Workbook, p. 78

Lesson 1: Geography of the Byzantine Empire

Use with Pages 322–325.

Directions: Read the following statements. Then write *T* (True) or *F* (False) on the line before each statement. If the answer is false, correct the statement to make it true. You may use your textbook.

1. **F** In the southern and eastern European parts of the Byzantine Empire, people enjoyed mild, rainy summers and cool, wet winters.

   hot, dry summers

2. **T** Farmers raised such crops as grapes, olives, wheat, and barley.

3. **F** In the southern and eastern European parts of the Byzantine Empire, most people lived in large cities.

   villages

4. **F** The desert regions in the Byzantine Empire received heavy rainfall.

   very little rainfall

5. **F** People in northern Africa and across much of southwestern Asia lived their entire lives in the same town.

   moved from place to place

6. **F** Constantinople was renamed Byzantium.

   Byzantium, Constantinople

7. **T** Constantinople was protected on three sides by water.

8. **F** Constantinople was the entertainment center of the Byzantine Empire.

   educational

9. **F** The Byzantine Empire crumbled before the Roman Empire.

   Roman, Byzantine

 Notes for Home: Your child learned how the geography of the Byzantine Empire influenced the people who lived there.
Home Activity: With your child, discuss how physical features and climate affect people in your community.

Use with Pupil Edition, p. 325

Workbook, p. 79

Lesson 2: The Greatness of the Byzantine Empire

Use with Pages 326–328.

During the rule of Justinian, the Byzantine Empire reached its height.

Directions: Fill in the organizer below with facts about life during Justinian's rule. You may use your textbook.

Religion
1. emperors and church had strong ties
2. Byzantine Orthodox, official church
3. controlled cultural and political life

Law
1. Justinian Code organized laws
2. many legal systems today based on Justinian Code
3. empire operated efficiently

Rule of Justinian I

Art and Architecture
1. new harbors, aqueducts, and public buildings
2. cathedrals decorated in great detail
3. Hagia Sophia, greatest cathedral

Politics
1. wanted to restore Roman Empire
2. conquered North Africa, Italy, some of Spain, Mediterranean islands
3. wife, Theodora, trusted advisor

 Notes for Home: Your child learned about the rule of Justinian.
Home Activity: With your child, discuss why it is important to have an organized, written code of law.

Use with Pupil Edition, p. 328

Workbook Support

Workbook, p. 80

Lesson 3: Development of Islam

Use with Pages 330–333.

Directions: Match each person or term in the first column with the correct description in the second column.

<u>d</u> 1. Mecca   a. the holy book of Islam

<u>g</u> 2. Islam   b. founder of the religion Islam

<u>b</u> 3. Muhammad   c. religious duty in Islam

<u>a</u> 4. Quran   d. holy city of Islam

<u>f</u> 5. Muslim   e. five basic duties of Muslims

<u>e</u> 6. "Pillars of Islam"   f. believer in Islam

<u>c</u> 7. jihad   g. religion revealed to Muhammad

Directions: Reread the Five Pillars on pp. 332–333 of your textbook and summarize each duty in your own words in the chart below.

First pillar	Muslims believe in one god and several prophets, including Muhammad.
Second pillar	Muslims pray five times daily, following specific guidelines.
Third pillar	Muslims donate funds to help others.
Fourth pillar	Daily fasting is one way Muslims celebrate Ramadan.
Fifth pillar	Muslims make a pilgrimage to Mecca at least once in a lifetime.

 Notes for Home: Your child learned about the establishment of Islam and some of its basic principles.
Home Activity: Discuss with your child the role religious beliefs play in your family. In what religious customs and celebrations do you participate?

Use with Pupil Edition, p. 333

Workbook, p. 81

Lesson 4: The Islamic World

Use with Pages 334–338.

Muslim traders and travelers exchanged ideas and technology throughout the empire and with different parts of the world.

Directions: Look at each innovation listed in the first column of the chart. Complete the chart by identifying the advantages of these innovations to Muslims in the 1300s and to society today.

Innovations	Advantages to Muslims	Advantages Today
Branch banking	Made trading easier and safer	Makes banking convenient
Irrigation systems	Helped crops grow in areas lacking rainfall	Are used to water lawns and help crops grow
Algebra	Helped in determining distance between two points	Helps people perform calculations
Astronomy	Helped in mapmaking	Helps scientists find out about our universe
Mapmaking	Helped Muslims locate Mecca	Helps people find locations worldwide
Medical encyclopedia	Combined medical knowledge from various sources	Serves as a medical reference

 Notes for Home: Your child learned how trade helped spread ideas and technology throughout the Islamic world and the rest of the world.
Home Activity: With your child, discuss which of the innovations in the chart have had the greatest impact on the world. Support your choice with modern-day examples.

Use with Pupil Edition, p. 338

Workbook, p. 82

Interpret Line Graphs

Use with Pages 340–341.

Line graphs show how a measurement changes as time passes. **Directions:** Study the line graph about the number of people who have made a pilgrimage to Mecca since 1950. Then answer the questions that follow.

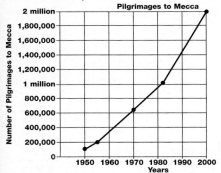

1. What time span does this graph cover?

   about 50 years, from 1950 to 2000

2. About how many pilgrimages were made to Mecca in 1983?

   about 1 million

3. What trend does this graph show, and what do you think is the reason?

   The number of pilgrimages to Mecca is increasing considerably, possibly because travel is becoming easier and more affordable, or because Mecca is offering more services to accommodate the Muslims.

 Notes for Home: Your child learned to use line graphs.
Home Activity: With your child, use the Internet or community resources to make a line graph plotting changes in population in your community between 1950 and 2000. What trend does your data show?

Use with Pupil Edition, p. 341

Workbook, p. 83

Vocabulary Review

Use with Chapter 11.

Directions: Use the vocabulary words from Chapter 11 to complete each item. Use the numbered letters to answer the clue that follows.

hippodrome	icon	caravan	astrolabe
cathedral	pilgrimage	mosque	

1. Ancient Greek stadium for horse and chariot racing   <u>h i p p o d r o m e</u>

2. Large or important Christian church   <u>c a t h e d r a l</u>

3. Image of Jesus or a saint   <u>i c o n</u>

4. Journey to a place of religious importance   <u>p i l g r i m a g e</u>

5. Group of people and animals traveling together   <u>c a r a v a n</u>

6. Muslim house of worship   <u>m o s q u e</u>

7. Instrument to map the stars in the sky   <u>a s t r o l a b e</u>

Clue: This prophet from Mecca founded the religion of Islam.

<u>M u h a m m a d</u>
1 2 3 4 5 6 7 8

 Notes for Home: Your child learned the vocabulary terms for Chapter 11.
Home Activity: Have your child write sentences using each vocabulary word or make vocabulary cards and practice saying the definitions together.

Use with Pupil Edition, p. 343

Assessment Support

Use these Assessment Book pages and the test maker to assess content and skills in Chapter 11. You can also view and print Assessment Book pages from the Teacher Resources CD-ROM.

Assessment Book, p. 57

Chapter 11 Test

Part 1: Content Test

Directions: Fill in the circle next to the correct answer.

Lesson Objective (1:3)

1. In what way was the Byzantine Empire related to the Roman Empire?
   - Ⓐ empire before the Roman Empire
   - Ⓑ middle part of the Roman Empire
   - ● continuation of the Roman Empire
   - Ⓓ another name for the Roman Empire

Lesson Objective (1:1)

2. Which describes the climate in the southern European part of the Empire?
   - ● hot, dry summers and cool, wet winters
   - Ⓑ desert conditions
   - Ⓒ dry summers and very cold winters
   - Ⓓ mild and humid all year

Lesson Objective (1:1)

3. How did the physical geography of the Byzantine Empire affect how people lived?
   - Ⓐ Wheat was grown throughout the Empire.
   - Ⓑ Desert conditions were good for growing crops.
   - Ⓒ Herders built villages and lived in one place.
   - ● It determined how the people earned a living.

Lesson Objective (1:2)

4. Where was Constantinople located?
   - Ⓐ on a strait linking the Mediterranean Sea with the Atlantic Ocean
   - Ⓑ on a river delta at the northern edge of Africa
   - ● on a peninsula at the southeastern end of Europe
   - Ⓓ on an island in the southern part of the Mediterranean Sea

Lesson Objective (1:2, 4)

5. Why was Constantinople an important center of trade?
   - Ⓐ It was guarded on three sides by water.
   - ● Ships traveling from the Black Sea to the Mediterranean Sea passed by there.
   - Ⓒ The ancient city of Byzantium was renamed Constantinople in 330.
   - Ⓓ Many wealthy people lived there.

Lesson Objective (2:2)

6. What was one goal of the emperor Justinian for the Byzantine Empire?
   - Ⓐ destroy the Hagia Sophia and build a palace in its place
   - Ⓑ reunite the Roman Catholic and Eastern Orthodox Churches
   - Ⓒ rewrite ancient Roman laws to suit modern needs
   - ● restore the Roman Empire and govern it as a whole

Lesson Objective (2:2)

7. Which was NOT a contribution made by Justinian to the Byzantine Empire?
   - Ⓐ Justinian rebuilt the famous cathedral Hagia Sophia.
   - Ⓑ Justinian conquered North Africa.
   - ● The Roman Catholic and Eastern Orthodox Churches were united.
   - Ⓓ Justinian organized the laws of the Romans into a code.

Use with Pupil Edition, p. 342

Assessment Book, p. 58

Lesson Objective (2:4)

8. Which is one reason why Justinian rebuild the Hagia Sophia?
   - Ⓐ to split the Christian church
   - Ⓑ to protect the Empire from invasions
   - Ⓒ to govern the Roman Empire as a whole
   - ● to show his strong ties to the church

Lesson Objective (2:3)

9. Which of the following played a role in the split of the Christian church?
   - Ⓐ the rebuilding of the Hagia Sophia
   - Ⓑ the collection and organization of the Justinian Code
   - Ⓒ Theodora's plans for defending Constantinople against attacks
   - ● the use of icons as part of worship

Lesson Objective (3:2)

10. Who founded the religion of Islam?
    - Ⓐ Ramadan
    - Ⓑ Justinian
    - Ⓒ Abraham
    - ● Muhammad

Lesson Objective (3:4)

11. How did Islam first begin to spread?
    - Ⓐ Muhammad's disciples began to preach the message of Islam.
    - Ⓑ Muhammad sent copies of the Quran to people throughout Arabia.
    - Ⓒ While in Africa Muhammad taught only traders about Islam.
    - ● In Medina Muhammad found many people eager to hear his teachings.

Lesson Objective (3:1)

12. Which is NOT a pillar of Islam?
    - Ⓐ a profession of faith in God
    - ● an annual pilgrimage to Rome
    - Ⓒ charity for the poor
    - Ⓓ five daily prayers

Lesson Objective (3:3, 5)

13. Why is the Quran important to Muslims?
    - Ⓐ It contains stories of Muhammad's journeys to Rome.
    - ● It covers many topics that Muslims face on a daily basis.
    - Ⓒ Muhammad wrote the Quran as a letter to his friends.
    - Ⓓ The sixth pillar, jihad, is described in detail.

Lesson Objective (4:1, 2, 4)

14. How were lands that were once part of the Byzantine Empire added to the Islamic world?
    - ● through Muslim wars and conquests
    - Ⓑ through the building of cathedrals
    - Ⓒ through the spread of the Arabic language
    - Ⓓ through the desire of their citizens to become Muslims

Lesson Objective (4:1, 2)

15. Which is NOT true about the spread of Islam?
    - ● Although Islam was known in many places, it never spread outside of the Arabian Peninsula.
    - Ⓑ The Arabic language spread along with Islam.
    - Ⓒ Through Muslim conquests, Islam spread to include much of what was once part of the Byzantine Empire.
    - Ⓓ Traders brought Islam to Southeast Asia, Central Asia and China, and other lands.

Lesson Objective (4:3)

16. Which was required of non-Muslims wherever Muslims ruled?
    - Ⓐ marry Muslim women
    - Ⓑ worship in the open
    - Ⓒ hold positions of power
    - ● pay a special tax

Use with Pupil Edition, p. 342

Assessment Support

Assessment Book, p. 59

Part 2: Skills Test

Directions: Use complete sentences to answer questions 1–6. Use a separate sheet of paper if you need more space.

1. What did people living in the different parts of the Byzantine Empire do to make a living? **Compare and Contrast**

   In southern and eastern Europe, people grew crops or raised sheep or goats. In northern Africa and southwestern Asia, some people were nomadic herders of sheep, goats, and camels. Others were merchants and artisans.

2. How did Constantinople become the capital of the Byzantine Empire? Write the events in the order in which they happened. **Sequence**

   The ancient city of Byzantium stood on a peninsula and served as a "bridge" between Europe and Asia. It was chosen as the Roman capital by Constantine I. Leaders of the city built walls on all sides. It was renamed Constantinople in A.D. 330.

3. In what five basic duties do followers of Islam believe? **Main Idea and Details**

   profession of faith in one god; five daily prayers; giving to the poor; fasting during Ramadan; and a pilgrimage to Mecca

4. How did Islamic culture spread throughout the Muslim Empire? **Cause and Effect**

   Wars added lands to the Islamic world, and the people there adopted Islam. Muslim traders took their religious beliefs to the lands with which they traded.

Use with Pupil Edition, p. 342

Assessment Book, p. 60

5. Which Muslim contributions to science and technology do you think have had the greatest impact on the world? Explain. **Draw Conclusions**

   Possible answer: Advances in irrigation systems allow people in dry areas to grow crops to eat and trade.

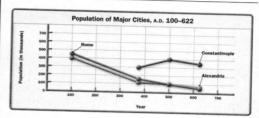

Population of Major Cities, A.D. 100–622

6. Use the graph to answer the questions. **Interpret Line Graphs**
   a. What does the graph show?

   how the population of three major cities changed from A.D. 100 to A.D. 622

   b. In A.D. 500 which city had the largest population?

   Constantinople

   c. How did the population of Rome change from A.D. 100 to A.D. 500?

   The population decreased from about 450,000 to about 100,000.

Use with Pupil Edition, p. 342

CHAPTER 11

Byzantine Empire and Ancient Arabia

Chapter 11 Outline

- **Lesson 1:** *Geography of the Byzantine Empire,* pp. 322–325
- **Lesson 2:** *The Greatness of the Byzantine Empire,* pp. 326–328
- **Biography:** *Justinian and Theodora,* p. 329
- **Lesson 3:** *Development of Islam,* pp. 330–333
- **Lesson 4:** *The Islamic World,* pp. 334–338
- **Citizen Heroes:** *Respecting Other Cultures,* p. 339
- **Chart and Graph Skills:** *Interpret Line Graphs,* pp. 340–341

Resources

- Workbook, p. 77: Vocabulary Preview
- Vocabulary Cards
- Social Studies Plus!

500, Constantinople (Byzantium): Lesson 1

Tell students this picture is a portolan chart or map, created by navigators to show the coastline. Have students describe the details (a city with a waterfront, a wall next to the coastline, large and small buildings).

527, Constantinople: Lesson 2

Ask students what this piece of art reveals about the people who lived in Constantinople. What may have been important to them? (art, architecture, their religion)

613, Mecca: Lesson 3

Tell students that this is a picture of a page from the Quran, the holy book of Islam. Ask students what they notice about it. (elaborate decorations)

700, Arabian Peninsula: Lesson 4

Tell students that the picture provides a glimpse into daily life. Ask students what it might be like to travel this way. (The time it would take to go from place to place would depend on wind and water conditions.)

320 Unit 5 • The Medieval World

CHAPTER 11

Byzantine Empire and Ancient Arabia

Lesson 1

500
Constantinople (Byzantium)
Constantinople becomes the center of the Byzantine Empire.

Lesson 2

527
Constantinople
Justinian becomes emperor of the Byzantine Empire.

Lesson 3

613
Mecca
Islam brings changes to lands in Southwest Asia.

Lesson 4

700
Arabian Peninsula
Islamic culture expands outside the Arabian Peninsula.

320

Practice and Extend

Vocabulary Preview

- Use Workbook p. 77 to help students preview the vocabulary words in this chapter.
- Use Vocabulary Cards to preview key concept words in this chapter.

 Also on Teacher Resources CD-ROM.

Workbook, p. 77

Vocabulary Preview

Directions: Read each sentence. Then replace the words in italics with a vocabulary word from the box and write it on the line provided. You may use your glossary.

| hippodrome | icon | caravan | astrolabe |
| cathedral | | pilgrimage | mosque |

1. Many Muslims plan to make a *journey to a place of religious importance* to Mecca one time in their life.

2. A *disagreement over the use of an image of Jesus or a saint* as part of worship led to a split in the Christian church in 1054.

3. Muslim astronomers used *an instrument to map the stars in the sky* to determine directions.

4. In medieval Arabia *a group of people and animals traveling together* was a common sight.

5. The Hagia Sophia is an example of a *large, important Christian church.*

6. The ancient Greek stadium used for horse and chariot racing in Constantinople was the *center of entertainment.*

7. Five daily prayers are offered in a *Muslim place of worship.*

Notes for Home: Your child learned the vocabulary terms for Chapter 11.
Home Activity: With your child, write a story about the Byzantine Empire using all of the vocabulary words correctly.

Locating Time and Place

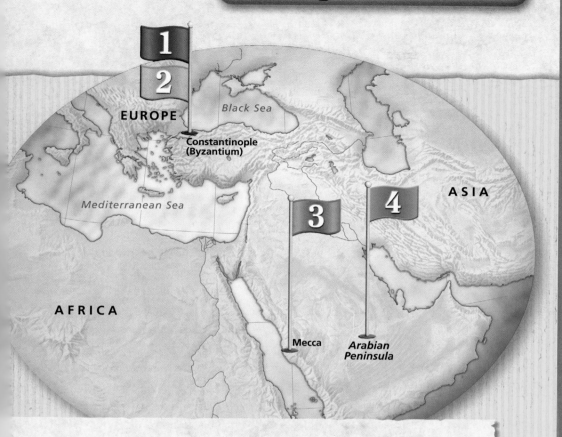

Black Sea

EUROPE

Constantinople
(Byzantium)

Mediterranean Sea

ASIA

AFRICA

Mecca

Arabian
Peninsula

Why We Remember

Some of today's practices and customs have their roots in the Byzantine Empire and in ancient Arabia. For example, parts of the legal codes, or laws, of many countries are similar to the code developed in the sixth century by Emperor Justinian. Islam, founded in the seventh century, is now a major world religion. It spread to other lands through a vast system of trade routes and conquests. Many of the trade routes developed in the seventh and eighth centuries are still used today.

321

- Have students examine the pictures shown on p. 320 for Lessons 1, 2, 3, and 4.

- Remind students that each picture is coded with a number and a color to link it to a place on the map on p. 321.

Why We Remember

Have students read the "Why We Remember" paragraph on p. 321, and ask them why events in this chapter might be important to them. Have students recall situations throughout history in which items or beliefs have been spread from one place to another through trade or other interactions. Have students discuss whether this type of interaction and sharing of ideas still takes place today.

WEB SITE
Technology

You can learn more about Byzantium, Constantinople, Mecca, and the Arabian Peninsula by clicking on *Atlas* at **www.sfsocialstudies.com.**

SOCIAL STUDIES STRAND
Geography

Mental Mapping On a outline map of the Eastern Hemisphere, have students use different colored pencils to shade in the areas of Europe, North Africa, and Southwest Asia where Islam and Christianity were widely practiced. Have them place dots and labels for Rome, Constantinople, Jerusalem, and Mecca. Discuss how the close proximity of different religions could be a source of conflict.

Geography of the Byzantine Empire

Objectives

- Describe how the physical geography and climate of the Byzantine Empire affected how people lived.

- Explain the significance of Constantinople to the Byzantine Empire.

- Explain how the Byzantine Empire was related to the Roman Empire.

- Explain how Constantinople became a center of trade.

Vocabulary

hippodrome, p. 324

Resources

- Workbook, p. 78
- Transparency 9
- Every Student Learns Guide, pp. 146–149
- Quick Study, pp. 74–75

Quick Teaching Plan

If time is short, have students write the words *Byzantine Empire* in the center of a word web.

- As students read independently, they can add details about the geography and climate.

1 Introduce and Motivate

Preview Ask students to recall what they have learned about the Byzantine Empire. Tell students that they will learn more about this empire as they read Lesson 1.

You Are There Ask students why they think that so many languages were spoken in Constantinople. (Many different cultures were brought together in the empire.)

LESSON 1

Geography of the Byzantine Empire

PREVIEW

Focus on the Main Idea
Physical features, climate, and Roman and Greek culture influenced how people lived in the Byzantine Empire.

PLACES
Constantinople
Bosporus
Black Sea
Sea of Marmara
Byzantium
Hippodrome

VOCABULARY
hippodrome

▶ Even today shoppers enjoy strolling through open-air markets and bazaars in what was once the Byzantine Empire.

 You Are There

About A.D. 500: You're strolling along Mese—the wide, straight main street of Constantinople (kahn stan tuh NOH pul). The clatter of the metal wheels moving along the paving blocks is loud. Merchants with carts are heading for the marketplace at the public square. The air is filled with many languages: Arabic, Greek, and Latin. The street is crowded. You step aside to let camels with spices and furs pass. It's noon. Jugglers, street musicians, magicians, and fortunetellers entertain the crowd. Customers buy silks, furs, fish, honey, and amber—a brownish, yellowish fossil used in making ornaments and jewelry. At the end of the street is the Imperial Palace. Constantinople (Byzantium) is the capital city of the Byzantine (BIH zan teen) Empire. It's truly the world's marketplace.

Sequence As you read, keep events in their correct time order.

Practice and Extend

 READING SKILL
Sequence

In the Lesson Review, students complete a graphic organizer like the one below. You may want to provide students with a copy of Transparency 9 to complete as they read the lesson.

Use Transparency 9

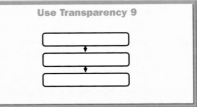

WEB SITE
Technology

- You can look up vocabulary words by clicking on *Social Studies Library* and selecting the dictionary at **www.sfsocialstudies.com.**

- Students can learn more about current news by clicking on *Current Events* at **www.sfsocialstudies.com.**

- Explore other events that occurred on this day by clicking on *This Day in History* at **www.sfsocialstudies.com.**

Roots of an Empire

The Byzantine Empire was considered a continuation of the Roman Empire. It stretched across lands that once formed the eastern part of the Roman Empire. At its height, the Byzantine Empire included parts of southern and eastern Europe and the Balkan Peninsula. It also included parts of northern Africa and southwestern Asia.

In the southern and eastern European parts of the empire, the people enjoyed hot, dry summers and cool, wet winters. They raised grapes, olives, and sometimes wheat and barley. The area often supported herds of sheep or goats. Most people lived in villages.

Life was different for people living in northern Africa and across much of southwestern Asia. There the summers were hotter and drier than in southern and eastern Europe. The winters were either mild or warm.

The desert regions received very little rainfall. In the country, people survived as herders, moving from place to place so that their sheep,

▶ The Byzantine Empire's location and barriers kept out invaders for nearly a thousand years. Today, Turkish women thresh wheat in what was once the Byzantine Empire.

goats, or camels could find food. In towns and large cities, merchants and artisans sold goods and practiced their trades.

REVIEW Did the Byzantine Empire rise before or after the Roman Empire? ⟳ Sequence

ASIA

Bosporus Strait

Byzantium

Black Sea

BALKAN PENINSULA

Sea of Marmara

EUROPE

ATLANTIC OCEAN

Mediterranean Sea

ASIA

Red Sea

AFRICA

323

Roots of an Empire

🕐 ***Quick Summary*** The Byzantine Empire stretched across lands that were in the eastern part of the Roman Empire. Its climate influenced the way in which the people lived.

① **How do you think the size of the empire may have affected how it was governed and how people communicated with each other?** Possible answers: It may have been difficult to govern, because many people lived far from its center. Communication would most likely be difficult and take a long time. **Make Inferences**

② **What effect did the dry, hot climate of northern Africa and southwestern Asia have on the jobs people did there?** People raised animals and moved from place to place to find food for their herds. **Cause and Effect**

③ **Choose two different parts of the Byzantine Empire and compare and contrast their climates.** Possible answer: In the southern and eastern European parts of the empire, summers were hot and dry, and winters were cool and wet. The summers in northern Africa were hotter and drier, and the winters were either mild or warm. **Compare and Contrast**

Ongoing Assessment

If... students are unable to compare and contrast the climates of two different parts of the empire,

then... lead them in creating a Venn diagram on the board. Draw two overlapping circles and label them with the names of different regions. Volunteers can supply details, indicating whether those details describe both of those locations or only one.

✓ **REVIEW ANSWER** After the Roman Empire ⟳ **Sequence**

Ultimate Location

🕐 *Quick Summary* Constantinople's location on a peninsula protected it from invaders while providing a safe and convenient route for trade.

Test Talk

Use Information from the Text

④ What evidence is given to support the opinion "Constantinople was a perfect location for the capital of the Byzantine Empire?" Tell students to look back in the text to find details about Constantinople's location. The city was located on a peninsula, offering it protection from three sides; the city controlled an important waterway for trade. **Fact and Opinion**

✓ **REVIEW ANSWER** In the year 330
🔄 Sequence

A Blend of Culture

🕐 *Quick Summary* Culture in the Byzantine Empire was a blend of Roman, Greek, and Asian cultures. Roman baths and horse races in the Hippodrome, a huge stadium modeled after buildings in ancient Greece, were popular forms of entertainment. Constantinople was a center of art, architecture, and learning.

⑤ How did the residents of Constantinople entertain themselves? They went to public baths, watched chariot races, and celebrated with ceremonies and military triumphs. **Main Idea and Details**

Ultimate Location

Constantinople was a perfect location for the capital of the Byzantine Empire. The city stands on a peninsula at the southeastern end of Europe. It serves as a "bridge" between Europe and Asia.

The peninsula itself extends into the **Bosporus,** a narrow strait linking the **Black Sea** and the **Sea of Marmara.** Ships traveling from the Black Sea to the Mediterranean Sea must pass through this 19-mile stretch of water. The waterway and city that controls it are both very important to trade.

People have lived at this location for thousands of years. The ancient city of **Byzantium** (bih ZAN tee um) was located on these shores. The Roman emperor Constantine I chose this location for his capital. As you read in Unit 4, the city was renamed Constantinople in 330 to honor him.

④ Because of its location on a triangular peninsula, the city was guarded on three sides by water. For additional protection, leaders built sea walls along the coast. At the western edge of the city stood elaborate walls that were rebuilt and expanded to protect Constantinople from land attacks. Some sections of these walls still stand today.

REVIEW When was Byzantium renamed Constantinople? 🔄 Sequence

A Blend of Culture

Isolated from Europe, the Byzantine Empire created an identity of its own. By blending Greek languages and Roman traditions, Byzantine culture flourished.

Based on Roman influence, most houses in Constantinople were made of wood. However, the rich lived in stone mansions. Many of these mansions had enclosed courtyards.

Aspects of Roman culture filled the Byzantine Empire. Based on Roman tradition, the city offered public baths that included steam rooms and swimming pools. Chariot races were a favorite form of entertainment in Byzantium, much as they were in the Roman Empire. They were held in a huge building called the **Hippodrome** (HIHP uh drohm).

A **hippodrome** is an ancient Greek stadium used for horse and chariot racing. The largest of the time, the Hippodrome in Constantinople was completed by Constantine in 330. With seating for more than 60,000 spectators, the Hippodrome was the center of entertainment. It also hosted other events such as ceremonies and celebrations of military triumphs.

▶ The word *Bosporus* comes from the Greek words meaning "ox" and "ford." Parts of the strait were once so narrow that cattle could cross, or ford, the water.

324

Practice and Extend

CURRICULUM CONNECTION
Science

Research Trade Routes

- Encourage students to research trade routes that have been used throughout time, particularly ones that are still in use today.
- Ask students to find out what goods are shipped along these routes and how long they have been used. They can make maps of their findings.
- Have students focus on the science involved in locks, canals, and other techniques that make trade routes easier to use.

CURRICULUM CONNECTION
Art

Create a Mural

- Review with students the forms of entertainment that were part of life in Constantinople.
- Invite students to illustrate a scene showing one of these forms of entertainment and write a short caption explaining it.
- Combine students' work in a wall display. Encourage students to suggest a descriptive title for the display.

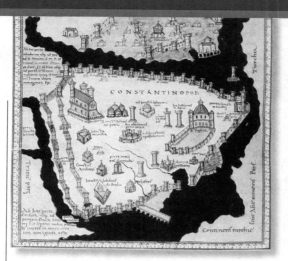

▶ Portolan charts, such as this one of Constantinople in the fifteenth century, helped navigators at sea. Notice the high sea walls, details of the coastline, and the city's major attractions.

Constantinople became the educational center of the Byzantine Empire. The Byzantines called themselves Romans even though they spoke Greek. The ancient Greek language was used for official purposes. However, it differed from the form of Greek spoken by most Byzantines. In the early history of the Empire, Byzantine emperors spoke Latin.

With hundreds of churches and plenty of palaces, mansions, schools, and hospitals, Constantinople thrived. The city's location brought forth a great blend of European and Asian culture. Art, architecture, and learning attracted many people to Constantinople. As the capital prospered, or flourished, so did the Byzantine Empire. All of this prosperity in the eastern part of the Roman Empire began after the western portion of the Roman Empire crumbled.

REVIEW Did Constantinople become a center of trade before or after the western part of the Roman Empire fell? 🔄 **Sequence**

Summarize the Lesson

- The Byzantine Empire was a continuation of the Roman Empire.
- Climate in parts of the Byzantine Empire was hot and dry.
- Constantinople, the capital of the Byzantine Empire, stood along the waterway connecting the Black Sea and the Sea of Marmara.

LESSON 1 REVIEW

Check Facts and Main Ideas

1. 🔄 **Sequence** The following events are not in chronological order. On a separate piece of paper, list them in their correct time order.

B
A
C

- A city is established at the strait of Bosporus.
- The Roman Empire weakens.
- Constantinople is fortified with sea and land walls.

2. Describe how the physical geography and climate of the Byzantine Empire affected the way people lived.

3. What city was the capital of the Byzantine Empire?

4. How was the Byzantine Empire related to the Roman Empire?

5. **Critical Thinking:** *Make Inferences* Why did Constantinople become a center of trade?

Link to ⟷ **Writing**

Write a Letter Suppose you are a member of Constantinople's merchant class. Write a letter to a merchant in another place explaining why Constantinople would be a good place to relocate his or her business.

325

✓ **REVIEW ANSWER** Before the fall of the Roman Empire 🔄 **Sequence**

3 Close and Assess

Summarize the Lesson

Tell students to read the summary and brainstorm key words related to each point. Students can use these words to create a crossword puzzle or clue-based word search to share with classmates.

✓ **LESSON 1   REVIEW**

1. 🔄 **Sequence** For possible answers, see the reduced pupil page.

2. The geography of the Empire, including its climate and land, was suitable for farming and herding, so many people were farmers or herders. The Empire's location along the Mediterranean Sea encouraged trading.

3. Constantinople

4. It was a continuation of the Roman Empire and included aspects of Roman and Greek cultures such as language, entertainment, and influences on art and architecture.

5. **Critical Thinking:** *Make Inferences* The city was located on a peninsula and a narrow strait linking the Black and Mediterranean Seas. Many trading ships and merchants passed through the Bosporus.

Link to ⟷ **Writing**

Students' letters should be persuasive, stating an opinion and including facts about the city.

MEETING INDIVIDUAL NEEDS
Leveled Practice

Create an Atlas Page Invite students to create an atlas focusing on the Byzantine Empire.

Easy Students can create a fact file for the atlas page by choosing one aspect of the empire and listing facts about it. **Reteach**

On-Level Students should create a map and a list of facts for their atlas page. Students' maps should show Constantinople and major waterways. **Extend**

Challenge Invite students to plan a web page for an online atlas, including interactive games, point-and-click maps that reveal facts about the area, and so on. **Enrich**

For a Lesson Summary, use Quick Study, p. 74.

Workbook, p. 78

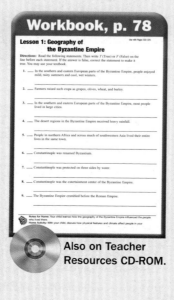

Lesson 1: Geography of the Byzantine Empire

Directions: Read the following statements. Then write *T* (True) or *F* (False) on the line before each statement. If the answer is false, correct the statement to make it true. You may use your textbook.

1. ____ In the southern and eastern European parts of the Byzantine Empire, people enjoyed mild, rainy summers and cool, wet winters.

2. ____ Farmers raised such crops as grapes, olives, wheat, and barley.

3. ____ In the southern and eastern European parts of the Byzantine Empire, most people lived in large cities.

4. ____ The desert regions in the Byzantine Empire received heavy rainfall.

5. ____ People in northern Africa and across much of southwestern Asia lived their entire lives in the same town.

6. ____ Constantinople was renamed Byzantium.

7. ____ Constantinople was protected on three sides by water.

8. ____ Constantinople was the entertainment center of the Byzantine Empire.

9. ____ The Byzantine Empire crumbled before the Roman Empire.

Also on Teacher Resources CD-ROM.

The Greatness of the Byzantine Empire

Objectives

- Explain the significance of the Hagia Sophia to the Byzantine Empire.
- Explain who Justinian and Theodora were, as well as their contributions to the Byzantine Empire.
- Explain what icons are and describe their role in the split of the Christian church.
- Explain why Justinian built Hagia Sophia in part to maintain close ties with the church.

Vocabulary

cathedral, p. 327; **icon,** p. 328

Resources

- Workbook, p. 79
- Transparency 9
- Every Student Learns Guide, pp. 150–153
- Quick Study, pp. 76–77

Quick *Teaching Plan*

If time is short, have students preview the lesson, make a list of questions, and take notes that answer their questions as they read independently.

1 Introduce and Motivate

Preview Ask students to summarize what they know about the Byzantine Empire. Tell students that in Lesson 2 they will learn more about the height of the Byzantine Empire.

 Ask students what the Hagia Sophia reveals about the culture and values of the Byzantine empire. (Religion was highly valued; architects and builders were very skilled.)

326 Unit 5 • The Medieval World

LESSON 2

500			1000
527 Justinian becomes emperor of the Byzantine Empire.	**537** The Hagia Sophia is completed.		**1000** The Byzantine Empire begins to weaken.

PREVIEW

Focus on the Main Idea
Under the rule of Justinian, the Byzantine Empire became great.

PLACES
Hagia Sophia
Constantinople

PEOPLE
Justinian
Theodora

VOCABULARY
cathedral
icon

TERMS
Justinian Code

▶ Outside, the Hagia Sophia is large and massive. Inside, well-placed arches and windows make the gigantic shapes appear to float in space.

326

The Greatness of the Byzantine Empire

You Are There A.D. 537: The city is buzzing with excitement. Today, after about five years of construction, the great Hagia Sophia [ah YEE uh soh FEE uh] will be opened. It will be the biggest church in the empire! You've sneaked into the church unnoticed as several of the emperor's guests arrive. The multicolored marble walls and columns seem to glow. A ring of 40 arched windows circles a great dome. Looking up at the dome makes you dizzy. How did the architects design such a magnificent building? The procession of animal sacrifices has begun. One hundred oxen, 6,000 sheep, 600 stags, 1,000 pigs, 10,000 hens, and 10,000 roosters are being offered as part of the celebration.

Sequence As you read, keep events in their correct time order.

Practice and Extend

READING SKILL Sequence

In the Lesson Review, students complete a graphic organizer like the one below. You may want to provide students with a copy of Transparency 9 to complete as they read the lesson.

Use Transparency 9

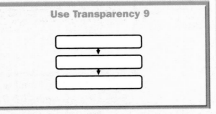

WEB SITE Technology

- You can look up vocabulary words by clicking on *Social Studies Library* and selecting the dictionary at **www.sfsocialstudies.com.**
- Students can learn more about current news by clicking on *Current Events* at **www.sfsocialstudies.com.**
- Explore other events that occurred on this day by clicking on *This Day in History* at **www.sfsocialstudies.com.**

Byzantine Glory

Emperor **Justinian** was responsible for rebuilding this magnificent **cathedral,** or large, important Christian church, the **Hagia Sophia,** in **Constantinople.** During his rule, the Byzantine Empire reached its height.

When Emperor Justinian came to the throne in 527, he wanted to restore the Roman Empire and govern it as a whole. To achieve his goal, he began by paying the Persian kings so that they would stop threatening the far western part of Asia. He later expanded the Empire by conquering North Africa, Italy, a small part of southern Spain, and islands in the western Mediterranean.

Justinian's wife, **Theodora** (THEE uh dor uh), became his most trusted advisor. He valued her intelligence and political wisdom. For example, she encouraged him to defend the city of Constantinople when it was attacked in 532. Read more about Theodora's wise advice to Justinian in the biography on page 329.

Justinian told Byzantine scholars to collect and organize the laws of the Romans into a code. This code, called the **Justinian Code,** made the laws clearer. Today, the code is the basis of many legal systems. The Justinian Code allowed the Empire to operate with an efficient and fair central government.

REVIEW What was the Justinian Code?
Main Idea and Details

The Byzantine Empire

MAP SKILL

Byzantine Empire, about 565
Byzantine Empire, about 1020
Eastern Orthodox, after 1054
Roman Catholic, after 1054

► The Byzantine Empire stretched across Southwest Asia, southern and eastern Europe, and northern Africa.

MAP SKILL Understand Borders and Capitals *Which present-day countries were part of the Byzantine Empire in 565?*

327

Write and Deliver a Speech Ask students to write and deliver short speeches about Justinian and his contributions to the Byzantine Empire.

Easy Ask students to "introduce" Justinian by giving basic details, such as where and when he lived and one thing he did to expand the Empire. **Reteach**

On-Level Students can write speeches to tell what they consider Justinian's most important accomplishment. As they give their speeches, they should tell what makes the accomplishment they chose so valuable. **Extend**

Challenge Speaking from Justinian's point of view, students can give speeches outlining plans for the Byzantine Empire. They can explain why their plans are important to all who are living in the Empire. **Enrich**

For a Lesson Summary, use Quick Study, p. 76.

---

2 Teach and Discuss

PAGE 327

Byzantine Glory

Quick Summary Emperor Justinian worked to expand the Byzantine Empire. He had scholars organize Roman laws into the Justinian Code.

1 **Why do you think it was important to Justinian to restore the Roman Empire?** Possible answer: Because the people of the Byzantine Empire thought of themselves as Romans, he wanted the Empire to regain its former size and strength. **Make Inferences**

SOCIAL STUDIES STRAND
Citizenship

A citizen of the Byzantine Empire followed the rules of the Justinian Code, which were contained in four books. Book I covered laws about people, including slaves, marriage, adoption, and the powers of parents.

2 **Why do you think it was important for the Empire to have such an extensive legal code?** Possible answer: Because the Empire was so large, laws needed to cover many situations in many places. Laws had to be clear so that everyone could understand them. **Draw Conclusions**

✔ **REVIEW ANSWER** The Justinian Code was the legal system developed during Justinian's rule. **Main Idea and Details**

The Byzantine Empire

3 **Where was the Eastern Orthodox religion concentrated after 1054?** In Russia, Greece, and the area near Constantinople **Interpret Maps**

MAP SKILL **Answer** Italy, Greece, Syria, Egypt

The Glorious Church

🕐 *Quick Summary* Under Justinian, art and architecture flourished. The Hagia Sophia symbolized his Empire's commitment to the church.

Primary Source

4 **What were Justinian's feelings about his relationship with the church and with God?** Possible answer: He was humble and thankful for God's help in building the church.
Analyze Primary Sources

✓ **REVIEW ANSWER** Justinian and the Church had close ties. The Church protected Justinian. **Summarize**

3 Close and Assess

Summarize the Lesson

Tell students to examine the vertical time line. Have students work in small groups to list three important details about each event on the time line.

✓ **LESSON 2 REVIEW**

1. 🔄 **Sequence** For possible answers, see the reduced pupil page.

2. It was the greatest cathedral in the Empire and showed the Church was an important part of the Empire.

3. Byzantine emperor Justinian expanded the empire and created a code of laws and many building projects. Theodora was his wife and trusted advisor.

4. Icons are images of Jesus and the saints. Disagreements about them led to the Byzantine Orthodox Church's split with the Roman Catholic Church.

5. **Critical Thinking:** *Fact or Opinion* Answers may vary. Though Justinian constructed many cathedrals at this time, rebuilding the greatest cathedral, the Hagia Sophia, probably strengthened his already close ties with the Christian church.

Link to 🔗 Speech
Students' speeches should give facts and specific reasons in support of opinions.

328 Unit 5 • The Medieval World

The Glorious Church

Art and architecture flourished during Justinian's rule. Justinian called for new harbors, aqueducts, and public buildings throughout the Empire. Many cathedrals were constructed. The interiors of these domed cathedrals were decorated with great detail. The greatest cathedral in the Empire was the Hagia Sophia. On its completion Justinian proclaimed:

> *"My thanks and gratitude to my Lord, for enabling me the means for creating such a glorious temple!"*

4

Byzantine emperors and the church had strong ties. The Byzantine, or Eastern, Orthodox Church was the official church. It also controlled cultural and political life. Justinian believed that God had chosen him to run the Empire. The church supported this belief and protected the emperor. The Empire that Justinian built lasted almost 500 years. In about 1000, the Empire began to weaken.

As you read in Unit 4, the Christian church divided in 1054. One major disagreement that

▶ **The use of religious icons, such as this one of the crucifixion of Christ, divided the Christian church.**

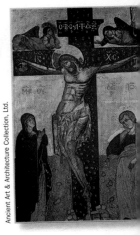

Ancient Art & Architecture Collection, Ltd.

led to the split was over the use of icons as part of worship. Religious **icons** are pictures or images of Jesus and saints. After 1054, the Roman Catholic Church and the Byzantine Orthodox Church existed separately.

REVIEW What was the relationship between Justinian and the church? **Summarize**

Summarize the Lesson

— **527** Justinian began to rule the Byzantine Empire.
— **537** The Hagia Sophia was completed.
— **1000** The Byzantine Empire began to decline.
— **1054** The Christian church split.

LESSON 2 REVIEW

Check Facts and Main Ideas

1. 🔄 **Sequence** The following events are not in the correct order. On a separate piece of paper, list them in chronological order.

   C A B
   • The Hagia Sophia was built in Constantinople.
   • Justinian added Italy to the Byzantine Empire.
   • Theodora encouraged Justinian to defend Constantinople.

2. What was the significance of the Hagia Sophia to the Byzantine Empire?

3. Who were Justinian and Theodora?

4. What are icons and explain their significance in the Byzantine Orthodox Church?

5. **Critical Thinking:** *Fact or Opinion* Justinian built the Hagia Sophia to keep close ties with the Christian church.

Link to 🔗 Speech

Write a Speech Suppose you are a member of Justinian's government. Write and present a speech supporting Justinian's proposal for a code of laws.

Practice and Extend

ESL **ACTIVATE PRIOR KNOWLEDGE**
ESL Support

Build Meaning Help students understand *disagreement, divided, split,* and *separately.*

Beginning Remind students of an activity in which the class split into teams. Write *divided* and *split* on the board and explain their similar meanings.

Intermediate Have students recall a time when they completed an independent assignment. Did they separate themselves from the group? Help students make a chart showing *divide* and its synonyms.

Advanced Have students write about a group that split into two or more smaller groups.

For additional ESL support, use Every Student Learns Guide, pp. 150–153.

Workbook, p. 79

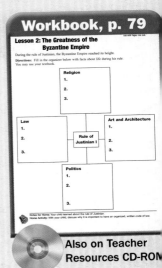

Lesson 2: The Greatness of the Byzantine Empire

🔘 **Also on Teacher Resources CD-ROM**

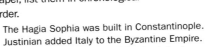

Justinian and Theodora

A.D. 500s

The year was 532. A revolt had broken out in Constantinople. The emperor, Justinian, and his advisors were trying to decide what to do. Many advisors urged Justinian to flee the city. However, Justinian's wife and most trusted advisor, Theodora, urged him to stay and fight. She encouraged him to rule with a firm hand. Standing in front of the emperor's most important advisors, she looked at them with disgust. She believed that they should fight until death: **1**

"If you resolve [decide], O Caesar, to fly, you have ships . . . . For my own part, I prefer the old saying that . . . . Imperial purple makes the best burial sheet!" **2**

Justinian relied heavily on the counsel of Theodora. As a result, he stayed and put down the revolt.

Theodora had an unusual background. She was an actress, a profession most people did not respect. After her death, Justinian's rule weakened significantly.

Justinian, who ruled from 527 to 565, was the greatest of Byzantine emperors. During his reign, Justinian came close to regaining all of the lands that the western Roman Empire had held at its height.

However, the extent of the empire did not last long. Within a few years of Justinian's death, German tribes drove the Byzantine armies out of Italy.

During the Byzantine Empire, mosaics, or pictures made of small pieces of stone, glass, or wood, were the leading art form.

Learn from Biographies

How did Theodora influence her husband's decisions as a ruler?

For more information, go online to *Meet the People* at **www.sfsocialstudies.com**.

329

Decision Making

Use a Decision-Making Process

- Make a list on the board of circumstances facing Justinian during the revolt in Constantinople as well as the resources available to him as emperor. Have students use these lists to brainstorm for an answer to the following question: **Imagine that you are an advisor to Justinian at the moment that he is making up his mind whether to stay in the city or flee. Empress Theodora has already urged the emperor to stay. Do you have the same advice?**

- Students should use the decision-making process to gather more information. They should then use the information to identify what other options Justinian has—where he might go and what he might do if he leaves the city. Students should predict the consequences of each option and then choose one.

1. **Identify a situation that requires a decision.**
2. **Gather information.**
3. **Identify options.**
4. **Predict consequences.**
5. **Take action to implement a decision.**

Justinian and Theodora

Objective

- Recognize the accomplishments of significant individuals such as Justinian and Theodora.

1 Introduce and Motivate

Preview Ask students what they learned about Justinian in Lesson 2. Tell students they will learn more about Justinian and his wife, Theodora.

2 Teach and Discuss

H SOCIAL STUDIES STRAND
History

Tell students that a rival emperor had already been chosen to replace Justinian.

1 Compare and contrast Theodora's advice during the revolt with the advice of Justinian's other advisors. Justinian's other advisors told him to leave the city. Theodora urged him to stay.
Compare and Contrast

C SOCIAL STUDIES STRAND
Culture

Let students know that only the Imperial family, the emperor and empress, were allowed to wear the color purple.

2 Explain the meaning of the proverb "Royal purple makes the best burial sheet." What did Theodora mean? Possible answer: It is better to die as royalty than leave the Empire and lose one's honor and status.
Analyze Primary Sources

3 Close and Assess

Learn from Biographies Answer

Possible answer: She was not afraid to speak her mind in front of the emperor and his most powerful advisors.

Development of Islam

Objectives

- List the major beliefs and roots of Islam.
- Explain the relationship between Islam and Muhammad.
- Explain what the Quran is and its significance in Islam.
- Explain how the spread of Islam affected Southwest Asia.
- Explain how the Quran affects the daily lives of Muslims.

Vocabulary

pilgrimage, p. 331; **caravan,** p. 331; **mosque,** p. 332

Resources

- Workbook, p. 80
- Transparency 1
- Every Student Learns Guide, pp. 154–157
- Quick Study, pp. 78–79

Quick Teaching Plan

If time is short, have students create outlines.

- Preview the chapter, noting the headings. Remind students that they could use the headings as section titles in their outlines.
- As students read the lesson, have them add important details.

1 Introduce and Motivate

Preview Have students read the list of places, vocabulary words, and terms. Ask them what they already know about these topics. Tell them that in Lesson 3, they will learn how Islam began and how it spread throughout Southwest Asia.

You Are There Ask students to recall what they have learned about cities in which people could find many different kinds of merchandise.

500	600

c. 570 Muhammad is born.

c. 613 Muhammad establishes Islam.

about 622 Islam begins to spread throughout Southwest Asi

Development of Islam

PREVIEW

Focus on the Main Idea
Islam brought changes to lands in Southwest Asia.

PLACES
Mecca
Medina

VOCABULARY
pilgrimage
caravan
mosque

TERMS
Islam
Quran
Muslim
caliph

You Are There

It's 1183, and you're watching a small group of men enter Mecca. You see pearls, perfumes, sapphires, and medicines—all for sale.

You've heard Mecca described as a place filled with all kinds of goods. Your mouth waters as you look over the figs and grapes. From Spain merchants have brought fresh foods to sell. Everything looks inviting, especially after traveling across the desert for days. Peaches, lemon, walnuts, watermelons, cucumbers, eggplants, and pumpkins shine in the sun.

A group from another land in the region has come to worship. They have brought wheat, almonds, grains, fruit, and kidney beans. Your eyes focus on th tempting honey and butter. You see tha traders make the journey to Mecca eve more worthwhile.

▶ **Muslim artists used elaborate artwork and calligraphy to illustrate pages, such as this one from the Quran.**

Main Idea and Details As you read, identify the main beliefs of Islam.

330

Practice and Extend

READING SKILL
Main Idea and Details

In the Lesson Review, students complete a graphic organizer like the one below. You may want to provide students with a copy of Transparency 1 to complete as they read the lesson.

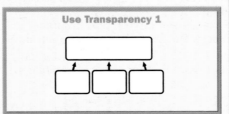

Use Transparency 1

WEB SITE
Technology

- You can look up vocabulary words by clicking on *Social Studies Library* and selecting the dictionary at **www.sfsocialstudies.com.**
- Students can learn more about current news by clicking on *Current Events* at **www.sfsocialstudies.com.**
- Explore other events that occurred on this day by clicking on *This Day in History* at **www.sfsocialstudies.com.**

Birth of Islam

A **pilgrimage** is a journey to a place of religious importance. The pilgrimage, or hajj (haj), to **Mecca** is an essential part of **Islam,** the religion revealed to Muhammad (moo HAM uhd). Muhammad, whose name means "Praised One," was born about 570 in Mecca. At an early age, he was orphaned and had to be raised by an uncle. For some time, Muhammad lived with a desert tribe, learning to tend sheep and camels. He eventually married and had a daughter. It is likely that he traveled on caravan journeys through Arabia at this time. **Caravans** are groups of people and animals traveling together.

In Muhammad's time, most people in this region were polytheistic, or worshiped many gods. People prayed to spirits and idols, or images or objects used in worship. This troubled Muhammad, and he went to the desert to pray and meditate alone. In 610, while Muhammad was meditating, according to Islamic beliefs, an angel visited him and said:

> *"Arise and warn, magnify thy Lord
> . . . wait patiently for Him."*

At first, Muhammad probably told only a few friends and family members about his vision. But according to the **Quran** (kuh RAN), the holy book

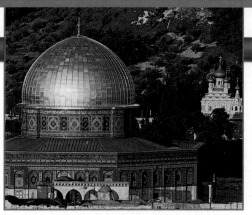

▶ The foundation of the Dome of the Rock, a Muslim mosque in Jerusalem, is holy to Muslims, Jews, and Christians.

of Islam, he had more visions. By about 613, he began to preach in public. Muhammad brought a new message to his people. He taught that there is only one God and that this God requires people to submit to, or obey, him. The Arabic word for submission, *Islam,* became the name of the religion. Believers in Islam are called **Muslims,** and they believe that the words Muhammad heard came directly from God.

In Mecca Muhammad found few people who supported his teachings. Muslims were being persecuted for their beliefs. In 622 Muhammad fled to the town of **Medina,** where he found many people eager to hear his teachings.

REVIEW What is the Quran?
Main Idea and Details

▶ If at all possible, every Muslim makes at least one pilgrimage, or hajj, to Mecca during his or her lifetime. Muslims consider the Ka'ba, a small shrine located near the center of the Great Mosque in Mecca, as the most sacred spot on Earth.

ESL ACCESS CONTENT
ESL Support

Sequence of Events Help students order and retell events.

Beginning Help students make a "Muhammad" time line showing the years and events described on the page. Students should include a small drawing for each event.

Intermediate Write each major event in Muhammad's life in a simple sentence on an index card. Read the sentences aloud, discussing ideas or words as needed. Mix up the cards and give one to each student. Students should place themselves in order and read their cards aloud.

Advanced Write sentence starters on the board that clearly show sequence, such as *Early in his life, Muhammad _____. Later, he _____.* Invite students to complete the sentences with the proper sequence of events. Students should include any other relevant sentences.

For additional ESL support, use Every Student Learns Guide, pp. 154–157.

🕐 *Quick Summary* Muhammad's visions led him to preach the message of a new religion, which came to be known as Islam.

H SOCIAL STUDIES STRAND
History

Although Mecca is a real city, the word *mecca* also means "a place that a person wants to visit" and "a goal of one's desires or ambitions."

1 **How do you think that the word *mecca* gained its other, more general meanings?** A trip to Mecca is a goal of Islam. Mecca is a place that Muslims want to visit. The more general meanings of *mecca* evolved from these definitions. **Hypothesize**

Primary Source
Cited in *The World Book* Encyclopedia

2 **What words in this message imply that Muhammad was intended to share his visions with others?** Possible answer: The words *warn* and *magnify* might show that Muhammad intended to share his vision. **Analyze Primary Sources**

C SOCIAL STUDIES STRAND
Culture

Tell students that 622 is the start of the Islamic calendar.

3 **Why is Medina an important place for Muslims?** When Muhammad went to the town, he found many people who were eager to hear his teachings. Tell students that Muhammad's journey is called the *hejira*. **Cause and Effect**

✓ **REVIEW ANSWER** The Quran is the holy book of Islam. It describes the founding of Islam by Muhammad. **Main Ideas and Details**

The Message of Islam

 Quick Summary Islam spread throughout parts of Asia and Africa. Muslims everywhere believe in five basic duties, known as the "Pillars of Islam."

4 **To which parts of the world did Islam spread after Muhammad's death?** Africa, Europe, India, the Malay Peninsula, and China. **Main Idea and Details**

Spread of Islam

5 **Where did Muhammad's hejira begin and end?** It began in Mecca and ended in Medina **Interpret Maps**

MAP SKILL **Answer** Islam spread first north from Mecca to Medina and then east and west.

H **SOCIAL STUDIES STRAND**
History

Let students know that in the past, Muhammad's name was often spelled *Mohammed,* and for this reason Muslims were often called Moslems, or even Mohammedans. The preferred usage today is *Muhammad* and *Muslims*.

6 **What do Muslims do before they offer their daily prayers?** They ritually cleanse themselves. **Sequence**

7 **Why does the third pillar require that Muslims give to the poor?** Because by giving to the poor, Muslims unite the community. **Main Idea and Details**

✓ Ongoing Assessment

| **If...** students are unable to tell why Muslims give to the poor, | **then...** ask students how they feel when a friend shares his or her food or possessions. Discuss how sharing can strengthen the bonds between people. |

✓ REVIEW ANSWER Profession of faith, five daily prayers, charity, fasting, and pilgrimage **Main Idea and Details**

The Message of Islam

After 622 Islam spread quickly throughout Southwest Asia. After Muhammad's death in 632, **caliphs** (KAY luhfs), or successors, carried on his mission. Islam spread to Africa, Europe, and places such as India, the Malay Peninsula, and China. Many different peoples became part of the Islamic world.

All Muslims acknowledge five basic duties. These duties are known as the "Pillars of Islam."

First pillar: The profession of faith: "There is no god but God and Muhammad is his prophet." Muslims believe that God has sent many prophets, or great spiritual teachers. These included Abraham, Moses, and Jesus. They believe that Muhammad was the last and most important prophet.

Second pillar: Five daily prayers are generally offered in a group in a **mosque,** a Muslim place of worship. After a ritual washing, Muslims face in the direction of the holy city of Mecca.

Third pillar: Muslims must give charity to the poor. By giving part of what they own to the poor, Muslims unite the community.

Fourth pillar: Muslims fast during the ninth month of the Muslim calendar, Ramadan. Daily fasting begins at daybreak and ends at sunset. During the day eating and drinking, among other things, are forbidden.

▶ **Five times a day Muslims are called to prayer by a muezzin, such as this one, who calls out from a minaret (a tower in a mosque).**

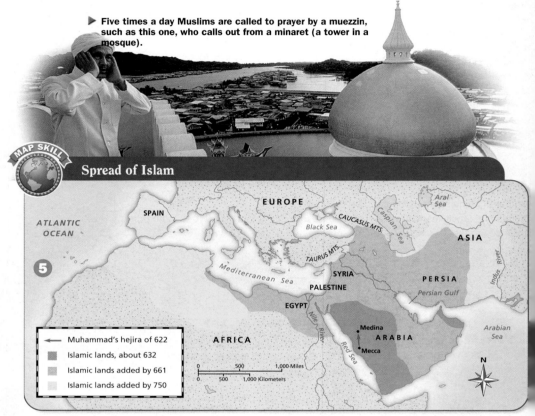

MAP SKILL
Spread of Islam

Muhammad's hejira of 622
Islamic lands, about 632
Islamic lands added by 661
Islamic lands added by 750

▶ **Muhammad fled from Mecca to Medina in what is called the *hejira*.**
MAP SKILL Trace Movement on Maps *In which directions did Islam spread?*

Practice and Extend

FYI **SOCIAL STUDIES**
Background

More About the Quran

- Muslims consider the Quran to be the words of Allah, spoken directly to Muhammad. Muhammad then recited the words. The word *Quran* means "recitation."
- Muslims value the art of reciting the Quran. A person who has memorized the entire Quran is called *hafiz,* "one who keeps the Quran in his or her heart."
- The Quran has 114 chapters. Its main topic is God's relationship with humanity.
- Many versions of the Quran have elaborate calligraphy and illustrations, showing the respect that Muslims have for the book. Verses from the Quran appear as decorations on mosques and other public buildings.
- In the past, the word *Quran* was sometimes spelled *Koran*.

Fifth pillar: A pilgrimage, a hajj, must be made to Mecca. This pilgrimage is required of every Muslim at least once in a lifetime—if at all possible.

REVIEW What are the Five Pillars of Islam? **Main Idea and Details**

Way of Life

Islam is a way of life for most Muslims. In addition to the Five Pillars, Muslims observe certain practices in their everyday lives.

▶ **After noon worship, Muslims leave a mosque in Manama, Bahrain.**

The **jihad** (jee HAD) is a religious duty in Islam. *Jihad* means "struggle." It can refer to a military struggle but can also mean a peaceful struggle—for the good of the Muslim community.

The Quran covers many topics that Muslims face on a daily basis. It tells them what not to eat or drink, such as pork or alcohol. The Quran has a moral code on marriage, divorce, business affairs, and other matters.

Muslims worship in mosques on Friday afternoons. Unlike some other religions, Islam does not have a central religious leader. However, Islam does have religious teachers who study the Quran and the acts of Muhammad and apply them to everyday life. **8**

REVIEW How do Muslims apply Islam to their everyday lives? **Main Idea and Details**

Summarize the Lesson

- **c. 570** Muhammad was born.
- **c. 613** According to Islamic beliefs, Islam was revealed to Muhammad.
- **c. 622** Islam began to spread throughout Southwest Asia.

LESSON 3   REVIEW

Check Facts and Main Ideas

1. **Main Idea and Details** On a separate piece of paper, copy the diagram below. Fill in the missing detail that describes Islam.

```
        Islam is a major world religion.
         /          |          \
Taught by      The Quran is      Teaches
prophet        the holy          Five Pillars
Muhammad       book of
               Islam.
```

2. What is the relationship between Muhammad and Islam?

3. What is the Quran?

4. What changes did Islam bring to Southwest Asia?

5. **Critical Thinking:** *Make Inferences* Why might a Muslim look at the Quran when faced with a business decision?

Link to ○─○ Geography

Use Maps Using maps from an atlas and the map on page 332, list the present-day countries to which Islam had spread by 750.

333

Way of Life

🕐 *Quick Summary* Muslims observe certain customs in their everyday lives, such as using the Quran for guidance and worshipping in mosques on Friday afternoons.

8 **How is Islam different from some other religions?** It does not have a central religious leader. **Compare and Contrast**

✓ REVIEW ANSWER The five pillars of Islam guide Muslims in the way they live and worship. The Quran provides a moral code and specific instructions on behavior. **Main Idea and Details**

3 Close and Assess

Summarize the Lesson

Tell students to examine the vertical time line. Copy it on the board and ask volunteers to place important events in the life of Muhammad and the development of Islam in the appropriate places on the time line.

✓

LESSON 3   REVIEW

1. **Main Idea and Details** For possible answers, see the reduced pupil page.

2. Muhammad was the prophet who founded Islam.

3. A record of the revelations Muhammad received from God

4. Possible answer: Islam replaced the worship of many gods with the worship of a single God.

5. **Critical Thinking:** *Make Inferences* Because the Quran can be applied to everyday life including business decisions, he or she could look to the Quran for guidance.

Link to ○─○ Geography

By the year 750, Islam had spread to all of the Arabian Peninsula, Egypt, North Africa, Spain, Palestine, Syria, and parts of Persia and Asia.

The Islamic World

Objectives

- Explain how the spread of Islam gave rise to the Islamic world.

- Explain how Islam spread outside of the Arabian Peninsula.

- Explain how and why non-Muslims were treated in the Islamic world.

- Explain how lands were united to create the Islamic world.

- Explain how the development of technology in navigation helped expand the Islamic world.

Vocabulary

astrolabe, p. 337

Resources

- Workbook, p. 81
- Transparency 20
- Every Student Learns Guide, pp. 158–161
- Quick Study, pp. 80–81

Quick Teaching Plan

If time is short, have students make a two-column chart labeled *Islamic Culture Spreads* and *Trading Ideas*.

- As students read, they should add details about conflict and trade as factors in the spread of Islam.

1 Introduce and Motivate

Preview To activate prior knowledge, have students recall what they learned about Islam and how it spread. Tell students that, in Lesson 4, they will find out more about how Islam united people to form an empire.

You Are There Tell students that the thick, wide pads on the soles of a camel's feet are also adaptations to the desert. Ask students to explain whether they would have liked to have worked at a caravansary.

| 1200 | 1300 | 1400 | 1500 |

1300s Muslims from Central Asia settle in Anatolia.

1325 Ibn Battuta sets out on his pilgrimage to Mecca.

1453 Constantinople falls to the Ottoman Empire

The Islamic World

PREVIEW

Focus on the Main Idea
Trade and conquest helped spread religion and language throughout the Islamic world.

PLACES
Arabian Peninsula
Anatolia

PEOPLE
Ibn Battuta

VOCABULARY
astrolabe

You Are There You work with your father and uncle at an inn where caravans stop. At night, you clean the rooms and stables surrounding the courtyard of the inn. Many caravans move during the cool of night, stopping at the caravansary, or caravan inn, in the morning. Once they arrive, you help care for the camels. Sometimes there are as many as 10,000 camels in a single caravan! It's hard work. But the animals work hard too. Each camel in a trade caravan may carry as many as 990 pounds. They go for days with little or no food and water, or they may eat only desert scrub—the plants that grow close to the ground. At the inn, you feed them dates, wheat, and oats. You're careful to stay away from the camel's sharp teeth. You recognize that the camel plays an important role in trade in the Islamic world.

▶ **Crossing the desert, travelers often used saddle bags on camels and horses to carry water and transport trade goods.**

Cause and Effect As you read, think about the effects and influence of Muslim trade.

334

Practice and Extend

READING SKILL
Cause and Effect

In the Lesson Review, students complete a graphic organizer like the one below. You may want to provide students with a copy of Transparency 20 to complete as they read the lesson.

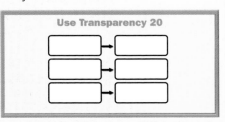

Use Transparency 20

WEB SITE
Technology

- You can look up vocabulary words by clicking on *Social Studies Library* and selecting the dictionary at **www.sfsocialstudies.com.**

- Students can learn more about current news by clicking on *Current Events* at **www.sfsocialstudies.com.**

- Explore other events that occurred on this day by clicking on *This Day in History* at **www.sfsocialstudies.com.**

Islamic Culture Spreads

According to the Quran, Muhammad wished to spread the word of God beyond the Arabian Peninsula and throughout the world. One way to do this was through trade on caravans. Another way that Islam spread was through war.

From the seventh to the tenth century, Muslim conquests added many lands to the Islamic world. Islam expanded outside of the Arabian Peninsula. In the 1300s, Muslims from Central Asia—called Turks—settled in Anatolia, (as Turkey was called in the Byzantine Empire). By 1453 they had conquered Constantinople, which became the capital of their empire, the Ottoman Empire. The Islamic world grew to include much of what was once part of the Byzantine Empire.

The first caliph, Abu Bakr (AH boo BAH kuhr), established a code, or law, for Muslim soldiers:

1 *"... Do not kill an old man, a woman or a child. Do not injure date palms and do not cut down fruit trees."*

Islam also expanded through trade. In addition to trade goods, Muslim traders brought Islam to Southeast Asia, Central Asia and China, North Africa, and sub-Saharan Africa, where they created an international slave trade.

Islam brought with it a system of government, laws, and society. Because the only acceptable version of the Quran was in Arabic, the Arabic language spread along with Islam. Wherever Muslims ruled, there was always a way to distinguish Muslims from non-Muslims. For example, non-Muslims had to pay a special tax. They could not marry Muslim women. Their houses and churches or synagogues could not be out in the open. They could not hold positions of power.

By the end of the tenth century, the Islamic culture, including its religion and language, was known throughout many lands. Muslim traders also brought knowledge about great advancements in mathematics and science in their contacts with Europe, Asia, and Africa.

REVIEW Why did the Arabic language spread with Islam? **Cause and Effect**

▶ This illustration from a tenth-century book shows Muslims capturing a city in Sicily in the 840s.

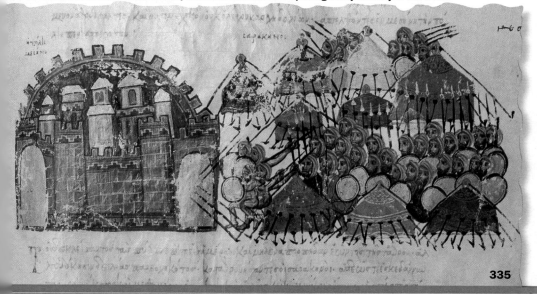

335

BUILD BACKGROUND
ESL Support

Introduce the Idea of Expansion Blow up a balloon, pausing to say "It's expanding." Then display a map and use your hands to frame where the Islamic world began. Say *expand* as you move your hands to show the expansion of the Islamic world. Have students make a two-column chart with the headings *Before Expansion* and *After Expansion.*

Beginning Have students complete the first column with *small* and a drawing of a small balloon and the second with *large* and a large balloon.

Intermediate Students can write short sentences about the balloon or map in the appropriate columns.

Advanced Students can write descriptive sentences about the map in the appropriate column.

For additional ESL support, use Every Student Learns Guide, pp. 158–161.

🕐 **Quick Summary** After the death of Muhammad, Islam continued to spread by means of both conquest and trade.

Primary Source

1 **What values of Islam are shown in this quotation from the caliph, Abu Bakr?** Possible answer: Respect for the elderly, for women, and for children, respect for the environment **Analyze Primary Sources**

✓ **Ongoing Assessment**

If... students are unable to identify respect for life as an Islamic value,	then... have students list who or what could not be killed or hurt. Ask students what these people and things have in common. (They are alive.)

H **SOCIAL STUDIES STRAND**
History

Let students know that the Ottoman Empire was named after Osman, the leader of the Turkish warriors. Osman led the Turks in their first major victory against the Byzantine Empire.

2 **In what ways did the religion and culture of Islam spread? Where did it extend?** Muslim conquests added land to the Islamic world. More peoples heard of Islam as they traded with Muslims. The Islamic world came to include much of what was once part of the Byzantine Empire. **Summarize**

✓ **REVIEW ANSWER** Possible answer: The only acceptable version of the Quran was in Arabic. If someone wished to become a Muslim, he or she would have to learn Arabic. **Cause and Effect**

Trading Ideas

 Quick Summary In addition to goods, Muslim trade and conquest spread ideas, arts, and technology throughout the Islamic world.

③ How did the spread of Islam eventually lead to the sharing of ideas and technology? Islamic traders took their religion and goods, as well as ideas and technology, and exchanged them with other traders across the Islamic world. **Cause and Effect**

⑤ SOCIAL STUDIES STRAND
Economics

Point out that branch-banking is used in the United States today and ask students what branch banks exist in your community.

④ How would branch-banking make trade safer? Traders no longer had to carry gold and silver on the trade routes where thieves were waiting. **Main Idea and Details**

Trading Ideas

Muslim traders carried goods throughout the Islamic world. Through trade and conquest, ideas, the arts, and technology traveled back and forth between cultures.

③ A great traveler and historian of the time was **Ibn Battuta** (IHB uhn ba TOO tah). He set out on a hajj, or pilgrimage, to Mecca in 1325. Through his many travels, he learned much about different peoples and lands. He traded goods and ideas throughout the Islamic world. He wrote about his adventures, which informed readers about other cultures. You will read more about Ibn Battuta later in this lesson.

The Muslims were the first people to use branch-banking. This means that several different banks functioned as one bank in different locations throughout the Islamic world. Checks, or letters of credit, could be cashed at any of the branch banks. This saved time and made **④** trade safer. Traders no longer had to carry gold and silver on the trade routes, where thieves were waiting.

Muslim engineers built water clocks and made complex irrigation systems. Muslim scientists made important breakthroughs in chemistry. For example, the Muslims were the first to make sulfuric (suhl FYOO rik) acid for use in manufacturing. In an effort to turn some metals into gold, they developed new chemical processes.

The Muslims expanded their knowledge of mathematics after building on ideas from the Hindus and the Greeks. Muslims were among the first people to work with the zero. As you read in Unit 3, the Maya in Central America made this same discovery much earlier. The word *algebra* comes from the Arabic word *al-jabr*, which means "restoring." Algebra was developed by a Muslim, al-Khwarizmi (al KWAR uhz mee).

▶ **Waterwheels, used for irrigation, were introduced and used throughout the Islamic world.**

336

Algebra had many uses in the Islamic world. With the help of algebra, surveyors could figure out the distance across a river. Algebra also helped determine the distance between objects in the sky. Muslim scientists even used the branch of mathematics called trigonometry to try to measure the distance around the Earth. By using information from the Greeks and trigonometry, Islamic scholars estimated that the distance around the world was about 20,400 miles. The ancient Greek mathematician Ptolemy believed that the distance was about 20,000 miles. (The actual distance is about 25,000 miles.)

Muslims found many other uses for mathematics. They used it to determine the times of day to call Muslims to prayer. They also needed mathematics to learn how to make maps. Accurate maps would help faithful believers of Islam find their way on their pilgrimage to Mecca.

Practice and Extend

ⓕⓨⓘ SOCIAL STUDIES
Background

Sulfuric Acid

- Let students know that sulfuric acid is a main component of batteries—for example, the average car battery contains about a gallon of acid.

- Sulfuric acid is also used to manufacture fertilizers and detergents, as well as many pigments and dyes.

FAST FACTS

Lesson 4 describes some accomplishments of the Islamic world by the fourteenth century, around the time of Ibn Battuta's travels. Share with students some of the various inventions that were created during Muhammad's lifetime:

- **580:** Women in China invent matches to use for heating and cooking.
- **590:** This year marks the first-known use of toilet paper, in China.
- **600:** In Persia windmills are invented to grind grain.
- **600:** In the Middle East, royal courts first use forks. They are used to hold food in place, not lift it.
- **610:** Japanese writings mention "burning water" that is used to light lamps. This water may have been petroleum.
- **650:** A Greek doctor first lists the symptoms of lead poisoning.

Muslim interest in astronomy, or study of the moon, planets, and stars, was also tied closely to Islam. By looking at the position of the stars with an **astrolabe** (AS truh layb), Muslim astronomers could determine directions and make accurate maps for navigators.

By looking at the position of the moon, Muslim astronomers produced a calendar. Maps were made for navigation and trade. But with calendars, maps could also help other Muslims in the Islamic world know when and in which direction to head toward Mecca. This was useful for pilgrimages and

▶ **Astrolabes were used by astronomers to determine latitude.**

knowing which direction to face when praying.

Muslims made advancements in medicine. One scholar put together an encyclopedia of medicine. He combined the studies and knowledge of Greek, Arabic, and Indian sources. Muslim doctors also discovered that blood circulates throughout the human body. **⑥**

REVIEW What are some ideas and technology the Muslims spread throughout the Islamic world? **Summarize**

⑤ How did Muslims use technology to help them practice Islam? Mathematics and astronomy helped Muslims know what times to pray and in which direction they needed to face to be looking toward Mecca. Mathematics helped them to make accurate maps for use on pilgrimages to Mecca. **Summarize**

⑥ Cite facts to support the following opinion: *The Muslim culture was amazing and ahead of its time.* Possible answer: Muslims were the first to use branch-banking and the first to use sulfuric acid in manufacturing. A Muslim mathematician developed algebra. A Muslim scholar compiled medical knowledge from Greek, Arabic, and Indian sources. **Fact and Opinion**

✓ **REVIEW ANSWER** Muslims spread the use of branch-banking; they built on the ideas of the Hindus and the Greeks in mathematics; they spread their knowledge of astronomy; they made advancements in medicine. **Summarize**

Map Adventure

You're a Navigator Ibn Battuta is relying on your knowledge of the monsoon season for his travels, which begin in 1325 and last more than 25 years. (Refer back to Unit 2 for information on the monsoon season.) Off the coast of China, the summer monsoons blow from southwest to northeast, and winter monsoons blow from northeast to southwest.

1. During which monsoon season will you and Ibn Battuta plan to leave Quanzhou, China, to go to Samudra? Explain why.

2. The trip from Calicut to Zafar will take about 28 days. Will the monsoon winds be blowing during the trip from Calicut to Zafar? How do you know?

3. During which season would it be easiest to make this trip? Why?

337

Map Adventure **Answers**

1. Winter; the wind blows from northeast to southwest

2. No; monsoons occur in summer and winter, and this trip occurs during spring.

3. Winter; because the monsoons blow from northeast to southwest, and the direction of travel is from east to west.

Experts at Sea

Quick Summary Proficiency at navigation helped Muslims expand their trade at sea, as well as on land.

7 **Why was it important to Muslims to develop trade routes at sea?** Sea routes helped Muslims reach parts of the Islamic world located near water and travel to lands that were farther away.
Make Inferences

✓ **REVIEW ANSWER** Their instruments, including astrolabes, their use of triangular sails, and their ability to sail into the wind **Main Idea and Details**

3 Close and Assess

Summarize the Lesson

Examine the vertical time line with students. Then give students three minutes to list as many new ideas and philosophies as they can that began in the Islamic world and were spread through trade or conflict.

✓ | LESSON 4 | REVIEW |

1. **Cause and Effect** For possible answers, see the reduced pupil page.

2. Through trade and conquest

3. They had to pay a special tax; they could not marry Muslim women; their houses and churches or synagogues could not be in the open; they could not hold positions of power.

4. Religion, language, trade

5. **Critical Thinking: *Make Generalizations*** Possible answer: Muslim sailors could use their knowledge to reach many parts of the world.

Link to —◯◯— Speech

Students' reports should be factual. They should include the idea that people who were not Muslims faced discrimination.

Experts at Sea

As you have read, trade expanded throughout the Islamic world. A good transportation network was needed to keep trade moving. While land routes grew, so did sea routes.

Muslim sailors were exceptional navigators. They used many different kinds of instruments to help guide them. By measuring the angle of the North Star above the horizon with astrolabes, navigators could find their position at sea.

The Muslim sailors could travel in all kinds of weather. They made sailing vessels that could sail into the wind as well as with the wind. Astrolabes and triangular sails also gave them **7** the ability to master sailing and expand the Islamic world.

REVIEW What made the Muslim sailors exceptional navigators? **Main Idea and Details**

▶ The triangular sail, called a lateen sail, was used by Arab merchants and the Ottoman fleet. These sails made it possible for ships to sail well against the wind.

Summarize the Lesson

— **1300s** Muslims from Central Asia settled in Anatolia.

— **1325** Ibn Battuta began his pilgrimage to Mecca.

| LESSON 4 | REVIEW |

Check Facts and Main Ideas

1. **Cause and Effect** On a separate piece of paper, copy the diagram below. Fill in an effect for each of the following causes.

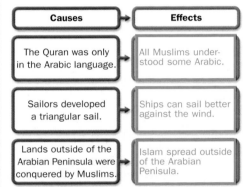

Causes	→	Effects
The Quran was only in the Arabic language.		All Muslims understood some Arabic.
Sailors developed a triangular sail.		Ships can sail better against the wind.
Lands outside of the Arabian Peninsula were conquered by Muslims.		Islam spread outside of the Arabian Penisula.

2. How did Islam spread beyond the Arabian Peninsula?

3. In the Islamic world, how were non-Muslims treated differently?

4. What united the lands in the Islamic world?

5. **Critical Thinking: *Make Generalizations*** How did knowledge of the oceans and the development of technology in navigation help expand the Islamic world?

Link to —◯◯— Speech

Write a News Report Suppose you are a television news anchor in one of the countries the Muslims conquered. Prepare a report on how the lives of Muslims and non-Muslims are different.

Practice and Extend

MEETING INDIVIDUAL NEEDS
Learning Styles

Report on the Islamic World Using their individual learning styles, students can report on what they learned in Lesson 4.

Verbal Learning Have students take the perspective of world travelers who have gone on an excursion with Ibn Battuta. Have them tell stories about what they have seen, heard, and learned during their travels.

Musical Learning Have students write and present songs or poems that celebrate an important aspect of life in the Islamic world, such as the use of navigation, the life of Muhammad, the importance of the camel, and so on.

Workbook, p. 81

Lesson 4: The Islamic World

Muslim traders and travelers exchanged ideas and technology throughout the empire and with different parts of the world.

Directions: Look at each innovation listed in the first column of the chart. Complete the chart by identifying the advantages of these innovations to Muslims in the 1300s and to society today.

Innovations	Advantages to Muslims	Advantages Today
Branch banking		
Irrigation systems		
Algebra		
Astronomy		
Mapmaking		
Medical encyclopedia		

Also on Teacher Resources CD-RO

CITIZEN HEROES

BUILDING CITIZENSHIP
Caring
★ Respect
Responsibility
Fairness
Honesty
Courage

Respecting Other Cultures

As he grew up, Ibn Battuta studied Arabic and Islamic law, hoping to become a lawyer or a judge. Instead, he became a world traveler and came into contact with many different peoples. He learned to respect other cultures.

In the 1320s, at the age of 21, Battuta set out on a pilgrimage to Mecca and Medina, some 3,000 miles away from his home. He had to cross deserts and mountains, while suffering sickness and risking attacks by thieves. Despite the dangers, Battuta discovered in himself a passion, or strong desire, for travel. He did not return home after his pilgrimage but continued his travels.

Determined to see as much of the world as possible, Battuta tried never to travel the same route twice. Battuta remained on the road for more than 25 years and covered some 75,000 miles. He visited nearly every Islamic kingdom in the world. Battuta was eager to learn about the way people of other lands lived. He was greatly impressed by the West African empire of Mali. Although he found the customs of Mali different from what he knew, he recorded them respectfully:

> "[The] women . . . are shown more respect than men . . . . No one claims descent from his father but from his mother's brother. A person's heirs are his sister's sons, not his own sons."

At the request of the leader of Morocco, Battuta told the story of his life travels to a scribe. The result was the *Rihla (Travels)*, one of the most famous travel books ever written.

National Geographic Image Collection

Respect in Action

Link to Current Events Research the story of a person today who has shown respect when coming into contact with different cultures.

339

Respecting Other Cultures

Objective

- Identify the contributions of significant individuals in the medieval world.

1 Introduce and Motivate

Preview Ask students to recall what they know about Ibn Battuta. What did Battuta learn on his travels? Ask students what they have learned on their travels.

2 Teach and Discuss

1 What motivated Battuta to travel? At first he wanted to make a pilgrimage to Mecca and Medina. Later he had a deep desire to see as much of the world as possible. **Cause and Effect**

Primary Source

Cited in *The Travels of Ibn Battuta,* by Ibn Battuta

2 What does Battuta's quotation reveal about his personality? Possible answer: He was respectful of other cultures. He tried to learn about the people he met on his travels. **Analyze Primary Sources**

3 Close and Assess

Respect in Action

Link to Current Events

Students should realize that cultural differences can sometimes cause misunderstandings, so it is important to show respect to prevent misunderstandings. Ask students to discuss the value of cultural interaction. You might have students share their own experiences or role-play situations in which people from different cultures come into contact. Can students model appropriate behavior? How do they think Battuta may have introduced himself and gained people's trust?

Interpret Line Graphs

Objective
- Interpret data in a line graph.

Resource
- Workbook, p. 82

1 Introduce and Motivate

What is a line graph? Lead a discussion about how a historian might use a line graph to study a general trend, such as a shift in population. Invite students to share their own experiences with line graphs. You might have them look at graphs in their math or science texts to refresh their memories. Then have students read the **What?** section of text on p. 340.

Why use a line graph? Have students read the **Why?** section of text on p. 340. Ask them why a line graph is easier to "read" than a paragraph about the same topic.

2 Teach and Discuss

How is this skill used? Examine with students the graphs on pp. 340–341.

- Point out that a line graph has a title. The title reveals what data are included in the graph. Both of the axes are labeled.

- Show students that each interval on the graph represents the same amount. For example, each interval on the vertical axis of the graph on p. 340 represents 100,000 people. The intervals on the horizontal axis represent 100 years. The intervals have to remain consistent for the graph to be useful.

- Have students read the **How?** section of text on p. 340.

Interpret Line Graphs

What? Line graphs show how a measurement changes as time passes. They help you understand how a variable, or measured quantity, changes over time.

Why? Line graphs can make it easier to interpret or understand data that changes over time. At a glance, you can see the highs and lows of the data. Line graphs also help you recognize trends. Trends can tell you whether a variable is increasing, decreasing, or staying about the same over time.

How? To use a line graph to answer specific questions, you need to compare the data plot to the horizontal and vertical axes. For example, the graph on page 340 can be used to answer the question, "Which city had the greatest population in A.D. 500?"
1. First find 500 on the horizontal axis.
2. Follow the grid line for 500 until it meets the blue data plot.
3. Next, read across to find out what the population was in 500 for Constantinople. The data plot meets the vertical axis at 400,000. Constantinople had the greatest population in 500.

▶ In a line graph, the quantity/amount variable is shown along the vertical axis. For this graph, the vertical axis shows the population (in thousands) in Alexandria, Rome, and Constantinople between A.D. 100 and 622.

▶ The title of a line graph tells you what variable is measured.

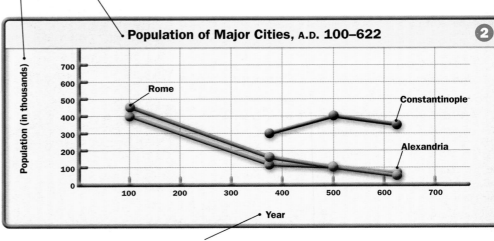

Population of Major Cities, A.D. 100–622 ②

▶ In a line graph, the time interval, or space between events, is shown along the horizontal axis. For this graph, time is measured in years.

340

Practice and Extend

CURRICULUM CONNECTION
Math

Create Line Graphs

Invite students to create line graphs of their own. Students can gather data from almanacs or other books of statistics, or they can write questions to ask classmates or family members. Students should graph the results. Possible questions include:
- How many barrels of oil has the United States imported in each of the last ten years?
- How many Muslims were recorded as U.S. residents in the last five censuses?
- How many Nobel Prizes have been awarded to women in each of the past ten years?
- How many CDs has (name of recording artist) sold in each of the last three years?

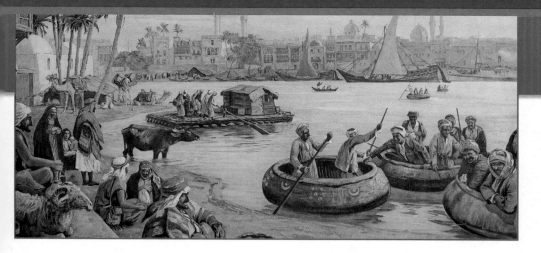

Note that sometimes the data plot will meet the vertical axis between two numbers. In these cases, you will need to estimate the vertical axis number. For example, on the line graph below, the population of Córdoba in A.D. 1150 was 60,000.

Look at the line graphs on pages 340–341, and then answer the questions.

Think and Apply

1 Which city had the greatest population growth?

2 Look at both line graphs on pages 340–341. Which cities had a decline in population between A.D. 500 and A.D. 1150?

3 From what you have learned in this chapter, why do you think Constantinople's population declined after A.D. 1000?

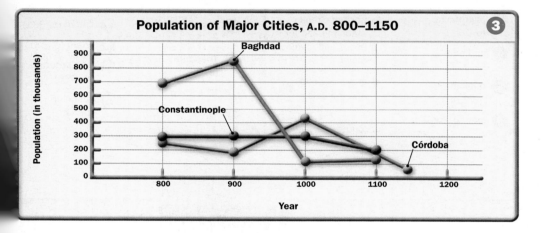

Population of Major Cities, A.D. 800–1150

1 **What is the first step in using a line graph to answer a question?** Find the appropriate value on the horizontal axis. **Sequence**

2 **In what year did Rome have its largest population? What was the population?** 100; about 450,000 people **Interpret Graphs**

3 **Which city's population changed the least over time—Córdoba or Baghdad?** Córdoba **Compare and Contrast**

Close and Assess

Think and Apply

1. Córdoba

2. All of them: Rome, Constantinople, Alexandria, Baghdad, and Córdoba

3. Constantinople's population began to decline after 1000 because the Byzantine Empire began to weaken at that time.

341

CURRICULUM CONNECTION
Writing

Write About Line Graphs

- Have students search through newspapers and magazines to find line graphs. (National newspapers and news magazines often contain line graphs.)

- Students should cut out the line graph, attach it to a sheet of paper, and write a question on the sheet of paper. Remind students to write questions that can be answered by reading the graph. They can write the answer on the back of the sheet.

Have small groups of students share their graphs and questions.

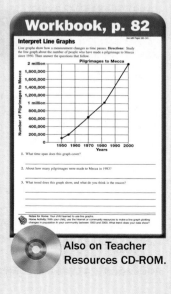

Workbook, p. 82

Also on Teacher Resources CD-ROM.

Resources

- Assessment Book, pp. 57–60
- Workbook, p. 83: Vocabulary Review

Chapter Summary

For possible answers, see the reduced pupil page.

Vocabulary

1. c, **2.** d, **3.** a, **4.** b, **5.** e

People and Terms

Possible answers:

1. The Justinian Code was a code of laws put together under Justinian's rule. The code organized a collection of Roman laws.

2. Theodora was the wife and most trusted advisor of Justinian, emperor of the Byzantine Empire. She greatly influenced his rule.

3. A Muslim is a follower of Islam.

4. A caliph is a successor to Muhammad.

5. The Quran is the holy book of Islam and contains a moral code for the daily lives of Muslims.

6. Islam is the religion revealed to Muhammad in 610.

7. Ibn Battuta was a traveler and historian who set out on a pilgrimage and continued to travel around the world.

8. Justinian, emperor of the Byzantine Empire from 527 to 565, established the Justinian Code, rebuilt the Hagia Sophia, and expanded the Byzantine Empire.

Facts and Main Ideas

1. Constantinople's location allowed it to control an important trade waterway and defend itself because it was surrounded on three sides by water.

2. Islam brought with it a system of government, laws, and society, the Arabic language, and preferential treatment for Muslims.

CHAPTER 11
REVIEW

A.D. 600

about 500
The Byzantine Empire began to expand.

about 622
Islam began to spread.

Chapter Summary

 Sequence

On a separate piece of paper, organize the following events in the correct order.

B
A
C
E
D

- Hagia Sophia is completed.
- Emperor Justinian comes to the throne.
- Muhammad is born.
- The Byzantine Empire begins to crumble.
- Islam spreads beyond the Arabian Peninsula.

Vocabulary

Match each word with the correct definition or description.

1 caravan (p. 331)

2 pilgrimage (p. 331)

3 cathedral (p. 327)

4 hippodrome (p. 324)

5 icon (p. 328)

a. an important Christian church

b. ancient Greek stadium used for horse and chariot racing

c. group of people and animals traveling together

d. journey for religious purpose

e. religious picture of Jesus and saints

People and Terms

Write a sentence explaining why each of the following people and terms is important in the study of the Byzantine Empire and ancient Arabia. You may use two or more in a single sentence.

1 Justinian Code (p. 327)

2 Theodora (p. 327)

3 Muslim (p. 331)

4 Caliph (p. 332)

5 Quran (p. 331)

6 Islam (p. 331)

7 Ibn Battuta (p. 336)

8 Justinian (p. 327)

342

Practice and Extend

Assessment Options

✓ Chapter 11 Assessment

- Chapter 11 Content Test: Use Assessment Book, pp. 57–59.
- Chapter 11 Skills Test: Use Assessment Book, pp. 59–60.

Standardized Test Prep

- Chapter 11 Tests contain standardized test format.

✓ Chapter 11 Performance Assessment

- Have students create a portfolio of the Byzantine Empire or the Islamic world.
- Portfolios may include a map, a time line, a list of key people and their contributions, and the student's opinion about the most impressive aspects of the topic they chose. Students may also include artwork.
- Assess students' understanding of daily life. Students' work should show that they understand how and why ideas spread throughout the Byzantine Empire or the Islamic world.

800   1000   1200   1400

1000
The Byzantine Empire began to weaken.

1054
The Christian church split.

1325
Ibn Battuta set out on his pilgrimage to Mecca.

Facts and Main Ideas

1 Why was Constantinople considered a great capital city?

2 What effects did Islam have on countries where it was introduced?

3 **Time Line** Did the Byzantine Empire decline before or after Islam spread?

4 **Main Idea** How are the Byzantine Empire and the Roman Empire related?

5 **Main Idea** How did Theodora influence Justinian's rule of the Byzantine Empire?

6 **Main Idea** What are the main beliefs of Islam?

7 **Main Idea** In what two ways did Islam spread?

8 **Critical Thinking:** *Make Inferences* What part did the dry, arid climate of Arabia play in the spread of Islam?

Write About History

1 **Write a travel brochure** describing travel adventures to such places as Constantinople or Mecca. Include reasons why a person in the Byzantine Empire or Islamic world might wish to travel to these locations.

2 **Write a point-of-view editorial** describing the benefits of trade with people outside of your town or village.

3 **Write a newspaper article** giving a short biography of Justinian and Theodora. Report on where they lived and how they ruled.

Apply Skills

Interpret Line Graphs
Use the line graph below that shows the growth of urban population to answer the questions.

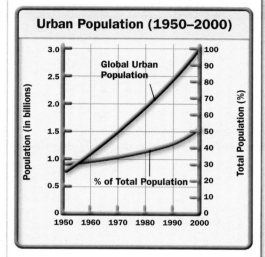

Urban Population (1950–2000)

Global Urban Population

% of Total Population

1 What generalization can you make about world population in urban areas over time?

2 What was the urban population in 1965?

Internet Activity

To get help with vocabulary, people, and terms, go online and select the dictionary, encyclopedia, or almanac from *Social Studies Library* at **www.sfsocialstudies.com**.

343

Hands-on Unit Project

✓ **Unit 5 Performance Assessment**
- See p. 420 for information about using the Unit Project as a means of performance assessment.
- A scoring guide is provided on p. 420.

WEB SITE Technology

For more information, students can select the almanac, dictionary, or encyclopedia from *Social Studies Library* at **www.sfsocialstudies.com**.

Workbook, p. 83

Vocabulary Review
Directions: Use the vocabulary words from Chapter 11 to complete each item. Use the numbered letters to answer the clue that follows.

| hippodrome | icon | caravan | astrolabe |
| cathedral | pilgrimage | mosque | |

1. Ancient Greek stadium for horse and chariot racing
2. Large or important Christian church
3. Image of Jesus or a saint
4. Journey to a place of religious importance
5. Group of people and animals traveling together
6. Muslim house of worship
7. Instrument to map the stars in the sky

Clue: This prophet from Mecca founded the religion of Islam.

Notes for Home: Your child learned the vocabulary terms for Chapter 11.
Home Activity: Have your child make sentences using each vocabulary word or make vocabulary cards and practice saying the definitions together.

Also on Teacher Resources CD-ROM.

---

3. After

4. The Byzantine Empire was a continuation of the Roman Empire.

5. Theodora was Justinian's most trusted adviser. She convinced him to stay in Constantinople when a revolt broke out.

6. The main beliefs are that there is a single God, Muslims must pray five times each day, they must give charity to the poor, they must fast during Ramadan, and they must try to make a pilgrimage to Mecca.

7. Through trade and conquest

8. Because of the climate, many people had to move often to find food, and they had to trade with each other and outsiders to get goods. This movement and interaction helped Islam spread.

Write About History

1. Brochures should include vivid descriptions, and the language should be persuasive and engaging.

Test Talk

Write Your Answer to Score High

2. Editorials should begin with statements that describe the point of view and contain persuasive facts to support that point of view. Ask students to reread their answer to make sure it is correct, complete, and focused.

3. Students' biographies should contain facts from the chapter. Students should use time-order words in their writing.

Apply Skills

1. It has increased.

2. Between 1.0 and 1.5 billion

Chapter Planning Guide

Chapter 12 • Asian Empires

Locating Time and Place pp. 344–345

Lesson Titles	Pacing	Main Ideas
Lesson 1 **Empire of Asia** pp. 346–349	1 day	• Asia has a variety of climates and landforms that influenced several different cultures.
Lesson 2 **Chinese Dynasties** pp. 350–355 📖 **Paper, Printing, and Books** p. 354	2 days	• Medieval Chinese dynasties made several significant contributions to trade and technology. • Paper and printing were very important Chinese inventions.
Lesson 3 **The Khmer** pp. 356–359	1 day	• For hundreds of years, the Khmer culture dominated the peninsula of Southeast Asia.
Lesson 4 **Japan in Isolation** pp. 360–363 **Research and Writing Skills: Gather and Report Information** pp. 364–365	2 days	• Japan became isolated, or separated, from most of the world but still carried on some trade. • When using reference sources, it is important to choose a source that is suited to the research question or task.

✓ **Chapter 12 Review** pp. 366–367

◀ This stone statue is of the Hindu god Vishnu, the protector of the world.

✓ = Assessment Options

◀ **This astronomical clock tower was built during the Song dynasty in 1088.**

Vocabulary	Resources	Meeting Individual Needs
	• Workbook, p. 85 • Transparency 10 • Every Student Learns Guide, pp. 162–165 • Quick Study, pp. 82–83	• ESL Support, TE p. 347 • Leveled Practice, TE p. 349
	• Workbook, p. 86 • Transparencies 1, 40 • Every Student Learns Guide, pp. 166–169 • Quick Study, pp. 84–85	• Leveled Practice, TE p. 351 • ESL Support, TE p. 352 • Learning Styles, TE p. 355
	• Workbook, p. 87 • Transparencies 20, 41 • Every Student Learns Guide, pp. 170–173 • Quick Study, pp. 86–87	• Leveled Practice, TE p. 357 • ESL Support, TE p. 358
aristocrat samurai typhoon daimyo shogun	• Workbook, p. 88 • Transparency 20 • Every Student Learns Guide, pp. 174–177 • Quick Study, pp. 88–89 • Workbook, p. 89	• ESL Support, TE p. 361 • Leveled Practice, TE p. 363 • Leveled Practice, TE p. 364
	✓ Chapter 12 Content Test, Assessment Book, pp. 61–63 ✓ Chapter 12 Skills Test, Assessment Book, pp. 63–64	✓ Chapter 12 Performance Assessment, TE p. 366

Providing More Depth

Additional Resources
• Vocabulary Cards
• Daily Activity Bank
• Social Studies Plus!
• Big Book Atlas
• Student Atlas
• Outline Maps
• Desk Maps

 Technology

• AudioText
• The test maker
• Teacher Resources CD-ROM
• Map Resources CD-ROM
• **www.sfsocialstudies.com**

 To establish guidelines for your students' safe and responsible use of the Internet, use the Scott Foresman Internet Guide.

Additional Internet Links
To find out more about:
• India in the past and present, search on India, then click on *India: Past and Present* at **library.thinkquest.org**
• A museum display focusing on Genghis Khan, click on *Virtual Exhibitions* at **www.pma.edmonton.ab.ca**
• A virtual tour of Edo, Japan, click on *Resources* and *Culture* at **www.us-japan.org**

Key Internet Search Terms
• India, Taj Mahal
• Mongolia, Ming dynasty
• Cambodia, Khmer
• Japan

Workbook Support

Use the following Workbook pages to support content and skills development as you teach Chapter 12. You can also view and print Workbook pages from the Teacher Resources CD-ROM.

Workbook, p. 84

Vocabulary Preview

Use with Chapter 12.

Directions: Circle the vocabulary term that best completes each sentence. Then write the definition of that word on the lines provided. You may use your glossary.

1. A (samurai, daimyo, shogun) was a ruler who governed large areas of farmland.

   the most powerful samurai; ruling leader who controlled other samurai and governed land

2. A (snow storm, typhoon, drought) is most likely to occur at sea.

   tropical storm with heavy winds and rough seas

3. A person who held a special, high-ranking military office in early Japan was a (samurai, daimyo, shogun).

   high-ranking military officer in early Japan

4. An (aristocrat, samurai, shogun) is a member of a high social class.

   noble of a high social class

5. A (samurai, daimyo, shogun) was a warrior who defended the land and kept order in society.

   member of the warrior class

Notes for Home: Your child learned the vocabulary terms for Chapter 12.
Home Activity: Have your child use these terms to tell you about society in early Japan.

Use with Pupil Edition, p. 344

Workbook, p. 85

Lesson 1: Empire of Asia

Use with Pages 346–349.

Directions: Circle the response that best completes each sentence. You may use your textbook.

1. Asia covers about (one-fourth, one-third, one-half) of Earth's land surface.

2. One ocean that does not border Asia is the (Indian Ocean, Pacific Ocean, Atlantic Ocean, Arctic Ocean).

3. The climate of Asia (varies greatly, varies somewhat, is the same) from region to region.

4. Most Asians live (in mountain ranges, in river or mountain valleys, in the desert).

5. The most important economic activity in Asia is (trade, manufacturing, agriculture).

Directions: Compare and contrast Mogul emperors Akbar and Aurangzeb by completing the following chart.

	Akbar	Aurangzeb
How did the emperor treat non-Muslims?	Tried to win their loyalty	Forced Hindus and other non-Muslims to pay a special tax
How well did the emperor control the government? How do you know?	Well; kept empire unified, reformed and strengthened central government	Not well; caused people of western and southern India to rebel
Brought or kept what area under Mogul control?	Most of the Indian subcontinent	Area around the city of Delhi in northern India

Notes for Home: Your child learned the role landforms and climate played in the growth of the Mogul Empire.
Home Activity: With your child, trace Asia's important rivers on the map on p. 347. Then look at the physical map of the United States in an atlas. How does the flow of major rivers affect how and where people live?

Use with Pupil Edition, p. 349

Workbook, p. 86

Lesson 2: Chinese Dynasties

Use with Pages 350–355.

Directions: Match each dynasty in the box below to its achievement, accomplishment, or description. Write the name of the dynasty on the line. You will use each dynasty more than once. You may use your textbook.

Sui	Tang	Song	Mongol	Ming

1. **Mongol** China ruled by non-Chinese ruler for first time
2. **Song** Military used gunpowder for first time
3. **Ming** Great advancements made in exploration
4. **Tang** Literature and fine arts flourished
5. **Sui** High taxes and forced labor caused collapse of dynasty
6. **Mongol** Improvements made in conquered lands
7. **Song** Improvements made in iron production, agriculture, and construction
8. **Ming** China isolated from the rest of the world
9. **Sui** System of connected waterways established
10. **Tang** Trade increased with Central and western Asia
11. **Mongol** Improved road and water travel for traders
12. **Song** First to use fractions
13. **Mongol** China led the world in sailing expertise
14. **Ming** Reinforced and extended Great Wall for protection
15. **Tang** China ruled by its first female ruler, Wu Hou

Notes for Home: Your child learned about the contributions of medieval Chinese dynasties to trade and technology.
Home Activity: With your child, review the Fact File on p. 351 of achievements and advancements during early Chinese dynasties. Discuss one achievement each of you considers to have had the greatest impact on the world.

Use with Pupil Edition, p. 355

Workbook, p. 87

Lesson 3: The Khmer

Use with Pages 356–359.

Directions: Use complete sentences to answer the following questions. You may use your textbook.

1. Where was the Khmer kingdom located?

   It was located in Southeast Asia, in the lands we know today as Cambodia and Laos on the Indochina Peninsula.

2. Which culture was a major influence on the Khmer civilization?

   Indian culture was a major influence on the Khmer civilization.

3. Why was it valuable for a Khmer ruler to be a deva-raja?

   Being a deva-raja allowed Khmer rulers to have absolute power.

4. Why was the irrigation system important to the Khmer economy?

   It stored water to irrigate crops in the dry season, prevented flooding during heavy rains, and improved agriculture to strengthen the economy.

5. What do you think is meant by a "golden age" of a civilization?

   Possible answer: The term refers to the wealthiest, or "golden," part of a civilization's culture, often shown by advances in literature and the arts, architecture, and thinking.

6. For what purpose was the Angkor Wat built? In what ways is it the same and different today?

   It was a temple to honor the Hindu god Vishnu. Possible answer: Although it still is a place of worship, Angkor Wat is recognized today as an architectural and cultural icon for the Khmer and the world.

Notes for Home: Your child learned about the Khmer kingdom in Southeast Asia.
Home Activity: With your child, discuss the importance of a national symbol to a people, such as the symbolism of the Angkor Wat to the Khmer.

Use with Pupil Edition, p. 359

Workbook Support

Workbook, p. 88

Lesson 4: Japan in Isolation

Use with Pages 360-363.

Directions: Sequence the following events in the order in which they took place by numbering them from *1* (earliest) to *10* (most recent). You may use your textbook.

__5__ Shogun Tokugawa Ieyasu rose to power.

__8__ The merchant class grew.

__2__ Nobles worked to weaken the emperor's power.

__10__ The class system began to crumble.

__3__ The Mongols in China made two attempts to invade and conquer Japan.

__1__ Japan's states were united under the country's first constitution.

__9__ Edo became a large city.

__7__ Foreigners were forced out of Japan.

__4__ Japan fell into a long civil war.

__6__ A four-class system was enforced under shogun rule.

Directions: Complete the cause-and-effect chart by identifying three effects of the shogun's control of trade in Japan in the 1600s.

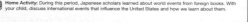

The shogun controlled trade in Japan in the 1600s.

→ 1. Possible answer: Trade increased.

→ 2. Possible answer: The merchant class grew.

→ 3. Possible answer: Edo became a large city.

Notes for Home: Your child learned about early Japan and its policy of isolation in the 1600s.
Home Activity: During this period, Japanese scholars learned about world events from foreign books. With your child, discuss international events that influence the United States and how we learn about them.

Use with Pupil Edition, p. 363

Workbook, p. 89

Gather and Report Information

Use with Pages 364-365.

Directions: Review the list of print and online sources in the box below and read each of the following topics about Japan. Identify in which sources you might look for information on each subject and write the sources on the lines provided. Not all sources will be used. Answers to each topic are located at the bottom of the page.

almanac	gazetteer	magazine or periodical
atlas	geographical dictionary	primary source
biographical dictionary	encyclopedia	thesaurus
dictionary	newspaper	yearbook

1. Number of years shoguns ruled in Japan
Possible Sources: __encyclopedia, almanac, primary source__

2. Distance between Tokyo and Kyoto
Possible Sources: __atlas, almanac, gazetteer__

3. Number of main islands in Japan
Possible Sources: __encyclopedia, geographical dictionary, atlas__

4. Meaning of *emperor*
Possible Sources: __dictionary, thesaurus__

5. When Edo was founded
Possible Sources: __geographical dictionary, encyclopedia, almanac__

6. Languages spoken by Crown Princess Masako
Possible Sources: __periodical, newspaper, primary source__

Answers: 1. About 700 years; 2. About 230 miles; 3. Four; 4. Ruler of an empire; 5. Around 1456; 6. Japanese, English, French, German.

Notes for Home: Your child learned to gather and report information.
Home Activity: With your child, create a short news program with your child as the news anchor. Gather and report information that has been in the news for the past few days.

Use with Pupil Edition, p. 365

Workbook, p. 90

Vocabulary Review

Use with Chapter 12.

Directions: Use each of the vocabulary terms from Chapter 12 in an original sentence. Write the sentences on the lines provided. You may use your glossary.

1. aristocrat

Possible answer: An aristocrat might not understand what it is like to be a poor farmer.

2. samurai

Possible answer: A samurai protected the people who lived on the land because he was a brave warrior.

3. typhoon

Possible answer: The boat was lost at sea because it sailed into a typhoon.

4. daimyo

Possible answer: Japan fell into a civil war because the daimyo fought for power and land.

5. shogun

Possible answer: Tokugawa Ieyasu became a powerful shogun in 1603.

Notes for Home: Your child learned the vocabulary terms for Chapter 12.
Home Activity: Have your child explain how these five terms are related to Japan and the role the shoguns played in the evolution of social classes in Japan.

Use with Pupil Edition, p. 367

Assessment Support

Use these Assessment Book pages and the test maker to assess content and skills in Chapter 12. You can also view and print Assessment Book pages from the Teacher Resources CD-ROM.

Assessment Book, p. 61

Chapter 12 Test

Part 1: Content Test

Directions: Fill in the circle next to the correct answer.

Lesson Objective (1:2)

1. Why is there a variety of cultures in Asia?
   - ● Asia has a variety of physical features and climates.
   - Ⓑ Asia covers about three-fourths of Earth's land.
   - Ⓒ Parts of the continent are covered by snow year-round.
   - Ⓓ Agriculture is the most important economic activity in Asia.

Lesson Objective (1:1, 3)

2. How was the Mogul Empire created?
   - Ⓐ The Gupta dynasty unified India.
   - Ⓑ Akbar built a capital at Agra.
   - ● Babur seized power in parts of northern India.
   - Ⓓ The central government was reformed and strengthened.

Lesson Objective (1:4)

3. What was unusual about Akbar's tax policy?
   - Ⓐ Taxes were paid only by farmers and their families.
   - Ⓑ Only non-Muslims were required to pay taxes.
   - Ⓒ Nobles were not required to pay taxes.
   - ● Taxes applied to every member of the Empire.

Lesson Objective (1:4, 5)

4. How did Akbar unify the Mogul Empire?
   - Ⓐ He built the Taj Majal to unify religion in the Empire.
   - ● He allowed many Hindus to hold important positions in the government.
   - Ⓒ He asked Hindus and other non-Muslims to pay a special tax.
   - Ⓓ He forced Hindus to adopt Islam, leading to rebellion.

Lesson Objective (2:5)

5. How did Empress Wu Hou change the civil service examination?
   - Ⓐ She added sections on science and reading.
   - Ⓑ She eliminated the exam requirement for high-ranking officials.
   - ● She strengthened it and made poetry writing part of the test.
   - Ⓓ She required candidates to take courses in literature and fine arts.

Lesson Objective (2:2)

6. Which of the following contributions was made during the Song dynasty?
   - Ⓐ playwriting
   - Ⓑ Great Wall
   - Ⓒ paper money
   - ● use of iron plow

Lesson Objective (2:1, 2)

7. Which was a contribution of the Mongol dynasty?
   - Ⓐ development of block printing
   - ● improvements in water travel
   - Ⓒ establishment of a canal system
   - Ⓓ improvements in ceramic glazes

Use with Pupil Edition, p. 366

Assessment Book, p. 62

Lesson Objective (2:3)

8. What was the Forbidden City?
   - ● emperor's palace during Ming dynasty
   - Ⓑ foreigners' nickname for Beijing
   - Ⓒ expensive voyages of Ibn Battuta
   - Ⓓ complex system of canals

Lesson Objective (2:4)

9. Why did the Ming emperor encourage Zheng He's expeditions?
   - Ⓐ He wanted people to fear traveling to and around China.
   - ● He hoped China would be seen as a wealthy power.
   - Ⓒ He wanted ships to return with gold, silver, and silk.
   - Ⓓ He hoped sailors would return with trade maps of the places they visited.

Lesson Objective (3:1, 4)

10. What allowed Khmer rulers to act with absolute power?
    - Ⓐ the constitution of the Khmer kingdom
    - Ⓑ religion of Buddhism
    - Ⓒ internal conflicts during the eighth century
    - ● their status as deva-rajas, or god-kings

Lesson Objective (3:3, 4)

11. Which had the greatest influence on the Khmer economy?
    - Ⓐ Hindu god Vishnu
    - Ⓑ monsoon rains
    - Ⓒ Angkor Wat
    - ● irrigation system

Lesson Objective (3:2)

12. Where was the location of the first Khmer royal city?
    - ● Angkor
    - Ⓑ Jayavarman
    - Ⓒ Laos
    - Ⓓ Wat

Lesson Objective (3:5)

13. Which is NOT a purpose for Angkor Wat?
    - Ⓐ reminder of the Khmer culture
    - ● model of the buildings of ancient Greece
    - Ⓒ tribute to the Hindu god Vishnu
    - Ⓓ tomb of the Khmer king

Lesson Objective (4:2)

14. What is one difference between samurai and shoguns?
    - ● Samurai provided protection; shoguns were military leaders.
    - Ⓑ Samurai were nobles; shoguns were not.
    - Ⓒ Shoguns were the most powerful samurai.
    - Ⓓ Samurai collected taxes that the shoguns paid.

Lesson Objective (4:1)

15. Which city was the capital of Japan during the rule of the Tokugawa shogun dynasty?
    - ● Edo
    - Ⓑ Kyoto
    - Ⓒ Osaka
    - Ⓓ Beijing

Lesson Objective (4:3)

16. When did Japan begin its policy of isolation?
    - Ⓐ when the first Japanese constitution was written
    - Ⓑ when the Mongols tried to invade Japan
    - Ⓒ when General Hideyoshi united warring groups
    - ● when shogun rulers took control of Japan's international trade

Use with Pupil Edition, p. 366

Assessment Support

Lesson Objective (4:4)

17. Why did Japan continue trade with a few countries during its isolationist period?
    - Ⓐ The shoguns wanted to travel abroad.
    - Ⓑ The shoguns felt the policy was unfair.
    - ● The shoguns wanted some contact with the outside world.
    - Ⓓ The shoguns hoped to conquer those countries.

Lesson Objective (4:3)

18. Which was NOT a result of Japan's policy of isolation?
    - Ⓐ Trade increased.
    - ● Trade with China stopped.
    - Ⓒ The merchant class grew.
    - Ⓓ Edo became a large city.

Part 2: Skills Test

Directions: Use complete sentences to answer questions 1–7. Use a separate sheet of paper if you need more space.

1. Which Mogul emperor do you think was the most successful? Why? **Point of View**

   Possible answer: Akbar was the most successful. He unified his people and created a strong government.

2. Which Chinese dynasty do you think made the greatest contributions to China? Explain. **Express Ideas**

   Possible answer: The Song dynasty made the greatest contribution. Methods of producing iron improved agriculture, defense, and construction projects.

3. What influence do you think the name of the Ming palace had on the way people viewed their emperor? **Make Inferences**

   Possible answer: The palace was called the Forbidden City because only the government's highest officials could enter it. The citizens of the Empire probably felt isolated from their emperor. The emperor was probably seen as unapproachable.

Use with Pupil Edition, p. 366

4. Describe the evolution of Khmer architecture. **Sequence**

   Khmer builders first constructed isolated towers of brick during the seventh century. Later they built small temples set on pyramids. Over time they added covered galleries and made the temples more elaborate. Instead of using brick, they began to use stone. Then the builders began to carve the stone.

5. What does having an image of Angkor Wat on Cambodia's flag indicate? **Draw Conclusions**

   Possible answer: The image of Angkor Wat on the flag of Cambodia reminds the people of their country's culture and achievements. Recognizing their history must be important to them since they include this architectural achievement on their national flag.

6. Write three details to support the following main idea: **The shoguns were a powerful group in Japan. Main Idea and Details**

   Possible answers: The shoguns operated gold and silver mines, controlled about 25 percent of the country's farmland, controlled trade, outlawed travel abroad, and banned nearly all foreign books.

7. What caused the shogun government to collapse? **Cause and Effect**

   The shogun government eventually fell into debt. As the merchant class became wealthier and more powerful, farmers rioted. As a result, the class system began to crumble.

Use with Pupil Edition, p. 366

Asian Empires

Chapter 12 Outline

- **Lesson 1:** *Empire of Asia,* pp. 346–349
- **Lesson 2:** *Chinese Dynasties,* pp. 350–355
- DK *Paper, Printing, and Books,* p. 354
- **Lesson 3:** *The Khmer,* pp. 356–359
- **Lesson 4:** *Japan in Isolation,* pp. 360–363
- **Research and Writing Skills:** *Gather and Report Information,* pp. 364–365

Resources

- Workbook, p. 84: Vocabulary Preview
- Vocabulary Cards
- Social Studies Plus!

1630, Agra: Lesson 1

Students may recognize the Taj Mahal. Ask them what they know about it. Then ask students whether the year 1630 comes before or after the beginning of the Mogul Empire. (After)

1368, Beijing: Lesson 2

This image shows a delicately painted porcelain vase. Ask students what they know or have heard about Ming dynasty pottery and what they think such works tell about the people who made them. (Ming ceramics are rare and valuable; the people of the Ming era valued artistry and beauty.)

c. 1120, Angkor: Lesson 3

This picture shows the towers of Angkor Wat, a royal city in Cambodia. Encourage students to compare and contrast the building shown here with India's Taj Mahal. Ask students what may account for the similarities and differences in these buildings.

1603, Edo (Tokyo): Lesson 4

Tell students that most of the castle seen here was built by a powerful samurai warlord. Ask students which elements of the castle's design seem well-suited to defending the castle against armed warriors. (The high walls would be hard to climb; no easy way to get in; it would be easy to watch enemy movements.)

CHAPTER 12

Asian Empires

Lesson 1

1630 Agra
Construction of the Taj Mahal begins.

1

Lesson 2

1368 Beijing
The Ming dynasty develops into one of China's greatest dynasties.

2

Lesson 3

c. 1120 Angkor
The Khmer build Angkor Wat.

3

Lesson 4

1603 Edo (Tokyo)
Tokugawa Japan emerges.

4

344

Practice and Extend

Vocabulary Preview

- Use Workbook p. 84 to help students preview the vocabulary words in this chapter.
- Use Vocabulary Cards to preview key concept words in this chapter.

 Also on Teacher Resources CD-ROM.

Workbook, p. 84

Vocabulary Preview

Directions: Circle the vocabulary term that best completes each sentence. Then write the definition of that word on the lines provided. You may use your glossary.

1. A (samurai, daimyo, shogun) was a ruler who governed large areas of farmland.

2. A (snow storm, typhoon, drought) is most likely to occur at sea.

3. A person who held a special, high-ranking military office in early Japan was a (samurai, daimyo, shogun).

4. An (aristocrat, samurai, shogun) is a member of a high social class.

5. A (samurai, daimyo, shogun) was a warrior who defended the land and kept order in society.

Locating Time and Place

A S I A

1 Agra
INDIA

2 Beijing
CHINA

3 Angkor
CAMBODIA

4 Edo (Tokyo)
JAPAN

PACIFIC
OCEAN

INDIAN OCEAN

Why We Remember

The great expanse of Asia has always been home to a large percentage of the world's population. For many years, the customs and activities of the people were shielded from outsiders. However, through trade, people outside of Asia were able to enjoy some of the goods—such as fine silk and porcelain—of the region. More importantly, ideas and technology that originated in Asia—such as paper money, civil service examinations, and gunpowder—also reached countries far away. Many things we have and use today came from Asia years ago.

345

WEB SITE
Technology

You can learn more about Agra, India; Beijing, China; Angkor, Cambodia; and Edo (Tokyo), Japan, by clicking on *Atlas* at **www.sfsocialstudies.com.**

SOCIAL STUDIES STRAND
Geography

Mental Mapping On a map of the Eastern Hemisphere, label the Arabian Peninsula, China, India, Japan, and Southeast Asia. Discuss which area might be in the best geographic location to influence or control other civilizations and why.

Locating Time and Place

- Have students examine the pictures shown on p. 344 for Lessons 1, 2, 3, and 4.

- Remind students that each picture is coded with both a number and a color to link it to a place on the map on p. 345.

Why We Remember

Have students read the "Why We Remember" paragraph on p. 345 and ask them why events in this chapter might be important to them. Have students consider how the goods and technology that are listed affect their daily lives. Ask them to think about how these items and ideas eventually spread throughout the world. What do they think makes some ideas last longer than others?

Empire of Asia

Objectives

- Explain the rise and fall of the Mogul Empire.

- Describe the variety of cultures in Asia.

- Identify who the first ruler of the Mogul Empire was and explain his contributions.

- Explain how Akbar's policies were different from those of past rulers.

- Explain how cooperation between Hindus and Muslims led to a unified Mogul Empire.

Resources

- Workbook, p. 85
- Transparency 10
- Every Student Learns Guide, pp. 162–165
- Quick Study, pp. 82–83

Quick Teaching Plan

If time is short, have students create "5 W's Charts" with the headings *Who? What? When? Where?* and *Why?*

- As students read independently, they can record answers to as many of the questions as they can.

1 Introduce and Motivate

Preview To activate prior knowledge, ask students what they learned about Islam and the Quran as they read Chapter 11. Tell students that, in Lesson 1, they will learn how Islam played an important role in the history of India.

You Are There Tell students that one of the buildings near the central structure is a mosque, a Muslim place of worship. There is also an enclosed garden, which is a Muslim symbol of paradise. Ask students to think about the importance of Islam in India at the time that the Taj Mahal was built.

LESSON 1

400	1000	1600

455
Huns and other groups begin to invade India.

1526
Babur establishes the Mogul Empire.

about 1630
Construction of the Taj Mahal begins.

Empires of Asia

PREVIEW

Focus on the Main Idea
Asia has a variety of climates and landforms that influenced several different cultures.

PLACES
Taj Mahal
Agra

PEOPLE
Babur
Akbar
Shah Jahan

You Are There It's a hot, sunny day in northern India. The sunlight reflecting from the building is so bright that you need to squint to protect your eyes. A few light clouds pass by. You rest your eyes on the white marble building that stands on a red sandstone platform. You're at the Taj Mahal (TAHZH muh HAHL). This magnificent tomb was built by the Indian ruler Shah Jahan (SHAH juh HAHN) in memory of his wife, Mumtaz. Shah Jahan tried to make the tomb as beautiful as the love he and Mumtaz had for each other.

As you step closer, you see that semiprecious stones such as jade and turquoise have been set in the white marble. You also see passages—from what you are told are from the Quran—that decorate the outside.

 Sequence As you read, keep the events in their correct time order.

▶ The Taj Mahal was constructed over a period of more than 20 years, from about 1630 to 1650. The project employed nearly 20,000 workers from Europe and parts of Asia.

346

Practice and Extend

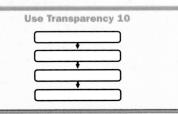 **READING SKILL**
Sequence

In the Lesson Review, students complete a graphic organizer like the one below. You may want to provide students with a copy of Transparency 10 to complete as they read the lesson.

> **Use Transparency 10**
>
> ▢
> ↓
> ▢
> ↓
> ▢
> ↓
> ▢

 WEB SITE
Technology

- You can look up vocabulary words by clicking on *Social Studies Library* and selecting the dictionary at **www.sfsocialstudies.com.**

- Students can learn more about current news by clicking on *Current Events* at **www.sfsocialstudies.com.**

- Explore other events that occurred on this day by clicking on *This Day in History* at **www.sfsocialstudies.com.**

Asia

The Taj Mahal is in Agra, India, which is located in Asia, the largest continent on Earth. Asia covers about one-third of the Earth's land surface. The Arctic Ocean forms Asia's northern boundary, while the Pacific Ocean forms its eastern boundary. To the south of Asia lies the Indian Ocean. On the map below, you can see that Asia's western boundary includes Europe, the Black Sea, the Greek Islands, the Mediterranean Sea, and the Red Sea.

Asia has a great variety of physical features and climates. In Asia there are vast flat lands, as well as the tallest mountains on Earth. Snow covers parts of northern Asia year-round, while tropical rain forests stand tall in southeastern Asia.

The mountain chains of Central Asia supply the continent's great rivers with water. Over time, people have migrated from the dry areas of Central Asia through the mountain passes into South Asia. They have moved from the dry areas of southwestern Asia to Southeast Asia and from the Arabian Peninsula to Indonesia and the Malay Peninsula. Mountain chains gave the Korean, Japanese, and Chinese peoples some protection from other peoples.

Today, most Asians live in river or mountain valleys. Other Asians live near seacoasts where they farm or fish. Agriculture is the most important economic activity in Asia.

REVIEW How did the mountains of Central Asia influence migration? *Cause and Effect*

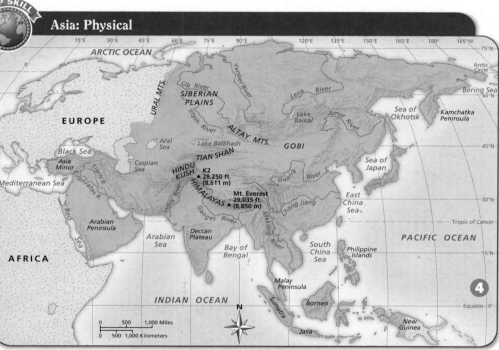

Asia: Physical

▶ The two highest points on Earth are located in Asia.

MAP SKILL Understand Map Symbols Where are the highest points in Asia located?

347

ESL Support

ACTIVATE PRIOR KNOWLEDGE

Share Knowledge About Asia Students may already know a few things about Asia.

Beginning Using the map of Asia, students can point to any features such as mountains, rivers, and oceans that they know. Help them pronounce the names and match photographs of Asia's physical features to the names.

Intermediate Have students say anything they know about Asian mountains, valleys, rain forests, and bodies of water. Then ask students what they want to learn. Record students' responses in a K-W-L chart.

Advanced Have students list as many Asian physical features as they can. Then have them write sentences indicating what they already know about each item on their list.

For additional ESL support, use Every Student Learns Guide, pp. 162–165.

---

2 Teach and Discuss

Asia

🕐 **Quick Summary** Asia, the largest continent on Earth, has a wide variety of physical features and climates.

1 **Support the following statement:** *Asia is a land of contrasts.* Asia has flat lands as well as the highest mountains on Earth. While some of Asia is covered with snow year-round, other parts have tropical rain forests.
Analyze Information

Ongoing Assessment

| **If...** students are unable to support the statement, | **then...** direct students' attention to the third paragraph. |

2 **To what part of Asia would you go if you wanted to experience warm, tropical weather?** Southeastern Asia, to the tropical rain forests
Main Idea and Details

3 **How do the climate and physical features of Asia affect the way people live?** Most Asians live in river or mountain valleys or near seacoasts. Many make a living by farming or fishing.
Cause and Effect

Asia: Physical

4 **What is the highest point in Asia?** Mt. Everest at 29,035 feet
Interpret Maps

MAP SKILL **Answer** In the Himalayas

✓ **REVIEW ANSWER** The mountains probably limited the migration of people from one place to another.
Cause and Effect

The Mogul Empire

 **PAGE 348**

> ⏱ *Quick Summary* Central Asian leader Babur began the Mogul Empire when he seized power in northern India in 1526. His grandson, Akbar, took measures to unify the empire.

5 **Did the Huns invade India before or after the Mogul Empire was established? Who rule the Empire first—Babur or Akbar?** Before; Babur. 🔄 Sequence

🌐 **Mogul Empire**

6 **What two cities were part of the Mogul Empire in 1539?** Delhi and Agra **Interpret Maps**

MAP SKILL **Answer** South, southeast, southwest

💲 **SOCIAL STUDIES STRAND**
Economics

Share with students that most property owners in the United States pay property taxes on buildings—homes, office buildings, and factories—and on land. These property taxes are collected by state and local governments, not by the U.S. government.

7 **Compare and contrast Akbar's tax policy with property taxes in the United States today.** Akbar taxed property, just as is done today. He was a national leader, however, and applied the tax to everyone in the empire. Today in the United States, state and local governments determine and collect property taxes. **Compare and Contrast**

8 **Do you think Akbar was a fair ruler? Explain.** Possible answer: Yes; he helped both Muslim and non-Muslim citizens of the empire. He collected taxes from both farmers and nobles. He allowed each province, district, and village to have its own leaders. **Evaluate**

✓ **REVIEW ANSWER** He tried to win the loyalty of his non-Muslim subjects. He reformed and strengthened the central government in ways that helped both nobles and farmers. **Summarize**

348 Unit 5 • The Medieval World

The Mogul Empire

As you read in Unit 2, the Gupta dynasty unified northern India in about A.D. 320. Then different groups of people began to invade India from 455 to the early 1500s. The Huns and Muslims from other parts of Asia were among the invaders who conquered parts of India.

5 In 1526 a Central Asian leader named **Babur** (BAH ber) seized power in parts of northern India. This marked the beginning of the Mogul (MOH gahl) Empire. During his four-year rule, Babur conquered much of northern India. Babur's son succeeded him, but it was Babur's grandson, **Akbar** (AK bahr), who became the greatest

🌐 **MAP SKILL**

Mogul Empire

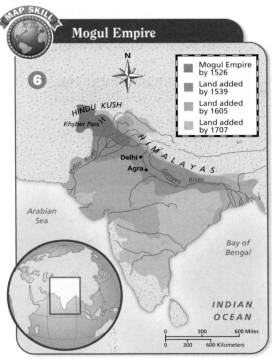

6

Legend:
- Mogul Empire by 1526
- Land added by 1539
- Land added by 1605
- Land added by 1707

HINDU KUSH
Khyber Pass
Indus River
HIMALAYAS
Delhi
Agra
Ganges River
Arabian Sea
Bay of Bengal
INDIAN OCEAN

0 300 600 Miles
0 300 600 Kilometers

▶ The Mogul Empire expanded until 1707. By 1739 the Persians had massacred much of the population of Delhi, and the Empire weakened.

MAP SKILL Use a Map Key *In what direction(s) did the Mogul Empire expand between 1605 and 1707?*

348

▶ The rise of the Mogul Empire brought Arab and Persian influences to India. In this illustration from 1528, Babur meets with two envoys, or diplomats, in a garden in Agra.

Victoria & Albert Museum, London

Mogul emperor. During his reign from 1556 to 1605, Akbar brought most of the Indian subcontinent under Mogul rule. He made his capital city at Agra.

In order to keep his empire unified, Akbar tried to win the loyalty of his non-Muslim subjects. He reformed and strengthened the central government. Akbar then organized the Empire into provinces, districts, and villages, each with its own administration, or government officials.

Akbar made changes that helped both the nobility and farmers. Nobles were allowed to keep their families' territories. In return, they had to recognize Akbar as emperor, pay taxes to the government, and supply troops on demand.

The most unusual part of Akbar's government was his method of tax collection. Akbar's land tax was equal to one-third of the value of the crops produced on the land each year. The tax was applied to every member of the Empire, including nobles and peasants. This was not a common practice by rulers at this time, as past rulers had only taxed the crops of farmers.

REVIEW How did Akbar govern his empire? Summarize

Practice and Extend

FAST FACTS

Share with students events that were happening around the world during the time of the Mogul Empire.

- Toward the end of the sixteenth century, five Native American nations formed the Iroquois Confederacy in what is now the northeastern United States. This league formed a constitution to make decisions as a group.
- Hernándo Cortés, a Spanish conquistador, conquered the Aztec Empire in 1521.
- Sir Walter Raleigh planted the first potato in Ireland in 1596.
- Pilgrims from England landed in Massachusetts in 1620, fifteen years after the end of Akbar's reign.
- In 1531 a large comet, later named Halley's Comet, worried some people who saw it streak across the sky.
- From 1551 through 1568, William Turner published *A New Herbal,* which marked the beginning of botany, or the study of plants, in England.

From Rise to Fall

The Mogul emperors were Muslims who ruled a largely Hindu nation. Under Akbar, some Hindus served as Mogul generals and governors. Other Hindus served as administrators and clerks. Hindus and Muslims were working, living, and interacting peacefully. Soon, the Mogul Empire came to be among the richest and most powerful in the world.

Akbar's grandson, **Shah Jahan** (SHAH juh HAHN), ruled from 1628 to 1658. He was responsible for the construction of the greatest building in India, the Taj Mahal. The Taj Mahal was built to honor the memory of Shah Jahan's wife, Mumtaz.

When Aurangzeb (or ANG seb), Shah Jahan's son, took his place, Indians found themselves under a harsh ruler. Aurangzeb forced Hindus, as well as other non-Muslims, to pay a special tax. Hindus held Aurangzeb responsible for destroying many Hindu temples and trying to force Hindus to convert to Islam. Aurangzeb's policies were very unpopular. As a result, the people of western

▶ Shah Jahan built the Taj Mahal as a large tomb for his wife, Mumtaz Mahal, pictured here.

India rebelled. Then many local leaders in the south rebelled. The Mogul Empire began to crumble. By the mid-1700s, Mogul control was limited to the area around the city of Delhi in northern India.

REVIEW How did Aurangzeb's policies affect the Hindus in India? Cause and Effect

Summarize the Lesson

- **c. 320** The Gupta dynasty unified northern India.
- **455** Huns and other groups invaded India.
- **1526** The Mogul Empire was established by Babur.

LESSON 1   REVIEW

Check Facts and Main Ideas

1. ⟳ Sequence On a separate piece of paper, list the following events in correct chronological order.

   B · Mogul forces control much of northern India.
   D · The Mogul Empire crumbles.
   A · Babur establishes Mogul Empire.
   C · Akbar rules much of India.

2. Why is there a variety of cultures in Asia?

3. Who was the first Mogul ruler of India?

4. What was unusual about Akbar's tax policy?

5. **Critical Thinking:** *Make Inferences* How would cooperation between the Hindus and Muslims help build a rich and powerful Empire?

Link to [⬡⬡] Writing

Write an Announcement You are a member of the nobility in India. Compose a flyer or announcement for a meeting to protest Akbar's tax system. Your announcement will be posted in the village square. Be sure to give reasons for your views.

349

From Rise to Fall

🕐 *Quick Summary* The powerful and wealthy Mogul Empire was peaceful and unified until Aurangzeb became emperor. By the mid-1700s, the Mogul influence was very limited in India.

9 Why was the Taj Mahal built? Shah Jahan had the Taj Mahal built to honor the memory of his wife.
Main Idea and Details

✓ **REVIEW ANSWER** Hindu temples were destroyed, Hindus were forced to pay a special tax, and they were pressured to convert. Rebellions followed, and the Mogul Empire began to crumble.
Cause and Effect

3 Close and Assess

Summarize the Lesson

Have students work in small groups to expand the time line by adding important events in the Mogul Empire. If time allows, students can use their time lines to write short summaries detailing the Empire.

✓ **LESSON 1   REVIEW**

1. ⟳ **Sequence** For possible answers, see the reduced pupil page.

2. Cultures developed in isolation from each other; Asia is enormous and has many physically distinct regions and climates.

3. Babur

4. He taxed everyone, including the nobles. This was not common in his time.

5. **Critical Thinking:** *Make Inferences* Their cooperation would preserve the nation's wealth and people would live, interact, and work together ensuring peace in the Empire.

Link to [⬡⬡] Writing

Students' flyers should be persuasive, providing specific reasons to support the opinion that the tax is not fair. Students should include the fact that leaders previous to Akbar had not taxed the nobility.

MEETING INDIVIDUAL NEEDS
Leveled Practice

Design a Graphic Source Ask students to represent the rise and fall of the Mogul Empire.

Easy Draw an upside down V and have students add events in the rise of the Empire on the left and in the fall on the right. **Reteach**

On-Level Have students create storyboards for a documentary about the Empire. Students should add descriptive paragraphs. **Extend**

Challenge Have students create political cartoons about the Mogul Empire. Provide samples for reference. **Enrich**

For a Lesson Summary, use Quick Study, p. 82.

Workbook, p. 85

Lesson 1: Empire of Asia

Directions: Circle the response that best completes each sentence. You may use your textbook.

1. Asia covers about (one-fourth, one-third, one-half) of Earth's land surface.
2. One ocean that does not border Asia is the (Indian Ocean, Pacific Ocean, Atlantic Ocean, Arctic Ocean).
3. The climate of Asia (varies greatly, varies somewhat, is the same) from region to region.
4. Most Asians live (in mountain ranges, in river or mountain valleys, in the desert).
5. The most important economic activity in Asia is (trade, manufacturing, agriculture).

Directions: Compare and contrast Mogul emperors Akbar and Aurangzeb by completing the following chart.

	Akbar	Aurangzeb
How did the emperor treat non-Muslims?		
How well did the emperor control the government? How do you know?		
Brought or kept what area under Mogul control?		

Notes for Home: Your child learned the role landforms and climate played in the growth of the Mogul Empire.
Home Activity: With your child, trace Asia's important rivers on the map on p. 347. Then look at the physical map of the United States in an atlas. How does the flow of major rivers affect how and where...

💿 **Also on Teacher Resources CD-ROM.**

Chinese Dynasties

Objectives

- List some of the major contributions of the Mongol dynasty in China.

- List and describe some of the major contributions made by the medieval Chinese dynasties.

- Explain what the Forbidden City was and where it was located.

- Explain the purpose behind Zheng He's expeditions.

- Explain how civil service exams changed the way government positions were filled in China.

Resources

- Workbook, p. 86
- Transparency 1
- Every Student Learns Guide, pp. 166–169
- Quick Study, pp. 84–85

Quick Teaching Plan

If time is short, have students create a time line of the dynasties as they read. Completed time lines should include the beginning and ending dates of each dynasty in the lesson.

1 Introduce and Motivate

Preview To activate prior knowledge, ask students if they know the meaning of the word *dynasty*. (a succession of rulers from the same family) Tell students that, in Lesson 2, they will find out about various dynasties that ruled China.

You Are There The Forbidden City was occupied by China's imperial families beginning in the year 1420, and it was the seat of power in China until 1911. Have students choose details from the text that show how the Forbidden City might have reflected the values of the people who built it and the dignity of the emperor.

LESSON 2

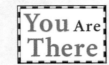

MONGOLIA
Beijing •
CHINA

500	1000	1500
589 The Sui dynasty unifies China.	**1206** Genghis Khan forms a unified Mongolia.	**1433** China c its port foreigne
	1406 Construction begins on the Forbidden City.	

PREVIEW

Focus on the Main Idea
Medieval Chinese dynasties made several significant contributions to trade and technology.

PLACES
Forbidden City
China
Mongolia
Beijing

PEOPLE
Wu Hou
Genghis Khan
Kublai Khan
Zheng He

TERMS
Sui dynasty
Tang dynasty
Song dynasty
Mongol (Yuan) dynasty
Ming dynasty

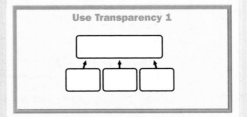

350

Chinese Dynasties

You Are There 1421: You're standing at the south gate of the Forbidden City. You're excited that your family has sent you here to be a servant to the royal family. You're one of the few people allowed inside the Forbidden City. You can't wait to explore the 9,999 rooms.

You first notice that the walled city is rectangular. After you cross a long, deep moat, you reach the brick walls surrounding the city. The red bricks glow with the color that symbolizes joy. Inside the gate, you see that the buildings—all made of wood—are coated in gold-colored paint, which is reserved for the royal family. Your attention is drawn to the yellow glazed tile roofs. The decorations in the palace are made of gold. Even the bricks on the ground shine! All of these details and ornaments have a special meaning to the history and traditions of China. You feel honored to be chosen to spend your life within the city, serving the royal family.

Main Idea and Details As you read, identify the major contributions of the Chinese dynasties.

Practice and Extend

READING SKILL
Main Idea and Details

In the Lesson Review, students complete a graphic organizer like the one below. You may want to provide students with a copy of Transparency 1 to complete as they read.

Use Transparency 1

WEB SITE
Technology

- You can look up vocabulary words by clicking on *Social Studies Library* and selecting the dictionary at **www.sfsocialstudies.com.**

- Students can learn more about current news by clicking on *Current Events* at **www.sfsocialstudies.com.**

- Explore other events that occurred on this day by clicking on *This Day in History* at **www.sfsocialstudies.com.**

Sui, Tang, and Song Dynasties

The **Forbidden City,** which still stands in **China** today, was built by one of the greatest Chinese dynasties. A summary of China's dynasties between the late sixth and mid-seventeenth centuries, along with some of their accomplishments, appears in the table to the right.

Before the **Sui** (SWAY) **dynasty,** China suffered through nearly four centuries of unrest. In 589 the Sui dynasty reunified the country. However, rulers made harsh demands on the people. High taxes and forced labor caused the collapse of the Sui dynasty.

The **Tang dynasty** is considered one of China's greatest dynasties. Empress **Wu Hou** (WOO JOW) came to power in the early years of the Tang dynasty. She was China's first female ruler. Her position was unusual. A Chinese philosopher claimed that having a woman rule would be as unnatural as having "a hen crow like a rooster at daybreak."

But Empress Wu Hou proved him wrong. She strengthened the civil service examinations. Wu Hou even included writing poetry as a requirement for high-ranking government jobs. As a result, literature and fine arts flourished under Tang rule.

Under Wu Hou, trade expanded, and China's contact and interaction with people and cultures of central and western Asia increased. Following the Tang dynasty were more than 50 years of warfare and corruption.

In 960 the **Song dynasty** united warring groups and established a strong central rule. Trade provided a large source of income for the government. The iron plow improved agricultural production. More efficient methods for producing iron were discovered. Iron could now be used as body armor for soldiers and as construction material for bridges.

REVIEW Which dynasty reunified China after 400 years of unrest? **Main Idea and Details**

FACT FILE

Dynasty	Achievements and Advancements
Sui, 581–618	• Canal system connecting waterways is established. Grand Canal eventually will carry water throughout China.
Tang, 618–907	• Civil service examinations bring talented people to government. • Block printing allows pages to be reprinted. • Paper money first printed
Five Dynasties and Ten Kingdoms, 907–960	• Widespread use of block printing helps spread ability to read.
Song, 960–1279	• First military use of gunpowder • First known use of fractions • Printers use movable type. • First chain-driven mechanism for celestial clock (tells time of day, day of month, and moon movements)
Mongol (Yuan), 1280–1368	• China leads world in sailing expertise. • Great age of Chinese playwriting ④ • Expert horsemanship skills
Ming, 1368–1644	• Improvements in ceramic glazes, the potter's wheel, and high-temperature kilns produce high-quality porcelain. • The Great Wall is reinforced and extended to protect against northern invaders.

351

MEETING INDIVIDUAL NEEDS
Leveled Practice

Write and Deliver a Speech Ask students to write and deliver a speech centered on a persuasive topic.

Easy Students can discuss the importance of making civil service examinations challenging in order to attract quality people to government positions. **Reteach**

On-Level According to the text, the Tang dynasty is "considered one of China's greatest dynasties." Ask students to craft arguments to prove that this statement is true. **Extend**

Challenge Students can use the chart on p. 351 to compare and contrast the various dynasties. They can choose the dynasty they think made the most valuable contribution to China. In their speeches, they can name the "winning" dynasty and tell what made it so noteworthy. **Enrich**

For a Lesson Summary, use Quick Study, p. 84.

---

2 Teach and Discuss

Sui, Tang, and Song Dynasties

Quick Summary The Sui dynasty reunified China, the Tang dynasty saw vast improvements to the country, and the Song dynasty established a strong central government.

SOCIAL STUDIES STRAND
Citizenship

Civil service workers work for the government of a state or country. They are usually not elected to their posts. Instead, they take examinations and are appointed based on merit.

① **Why is it important that civil service examinations be challenging?** Difficult examinations help ensure that the most qualified candidates obtain government jobs. **Draw Conclusions**

SOCIAL STUDIES STRAND
Economics

Tell students that the Tang dynasty encouraged trade with several nations and maintained peaceful relations with people who lived along important trade routes.

② **How might China's trade status during the Tang dynasty have benefited the people who lived in China?** Possible answer: Multiple trading partners and safe trade routes would have helped the Chinese buy and sell more goods. Welcoming foreign goods into China might have made other nations more likely to buy Chinese goods. **Evaluate**

③ **In what ways was iron important in the Song dynasty?** The iron plow improved agricultural production. Iron could be used for construction material and body armor. **Summarize**

✓ **REVIEW ANSWER** The Sui dynasty
Main Idea and Details

FACT FILE

④ **Which dynasty is known for its excellent horsemanship skills?** The Mongol dynasty **Interpret Charts**

Mongol and Ming Dynasties

Quick Summary Genghis Khan united the nomadic tribes of northern Asia to form Mongolia and then extended his empire into China. Several decades later the Ming dynasty came to power and led China into a period of isolation.

Primary Source

Cited in *The Travels of Ibn Battuta,* by Ibn Battuta

5 **What does this quotation reveal about Genghis Khan's personality?** Possible answer: He was ruthless and power-hungry. **Analyze Primary Sources**

6 **How did the Mongol dynasty differ from the previous dynasties?** The Mongol dynasty marked the first time that China was ruled by someone who was not Chinese. **Compare and Contrast**

 **Mongol Empire**

Point out to students that the Mongol Empire was so large that it included parts of present-day Europe, Russia, and Korea.

 **Test Talk**

Use Information from Graphics

7 **Over what two continents did the Mongol Empire spread?** Remind students to look at the legend to help them answer the question. Europe and Asia **Interpret Maps**

MAP SKILL **Answer** Southwest, west, northwest, southeast, and south

---

Mongol and Ming Dynasties

Near the end of the Song dynasty, a warrior leader came to power. His name was Temujin, and he united the nomadic, or wandering, groups of northern Asia to form a unified **Mongolia** in 1206. These groups named Temujin **Genghis Khan** (JEHNG gihs kahn), or universal ruler. Genghis Khan expanded his empire until his death in 1227.

Terror was Genghis Khan's greatest weapon. He ordered his army to give no mercy:

> *"The greatest happiness is to vanquish [conquer] your enemies, to chase them before you, to rob them of their wealth."*
>
> **5**

▶ In this thirteenth-century tapestry, Kublai Khan's army attacks the Chinese near the Chang Jiang River.

His army, some 110,000 men, was loyal and disciplined. Mongol warriors perfected their horsemanship skills and could shoot arrows even while riding at top speed. Most had as many as four horses so that a fresh and energetic horse was always available.

Genghis Khan defeated the peoples of northern China and Persia. But his sons expanded the empire even more after his death. His grandson, **Kublai Khan,** conquered both southern China and Burma by 1280. This conquest marked the beginning of the **Mongol, or Yuan, dynasty.** It was the first time China had a non-Chinese ruler. By 1294 Mongol power reached its height. **6**

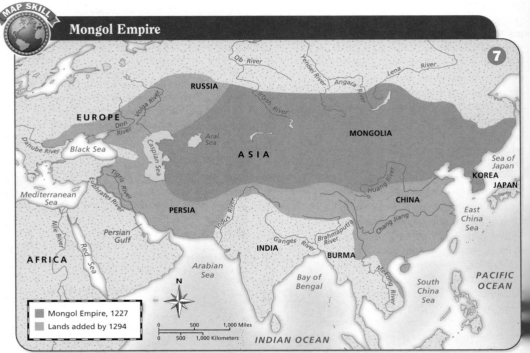

MAP SKILL **Mongol Empire**

Mongol Empire, 1227
Lands added by 1294

▶ The Mongol Empire at the time of the Yuan dynasty was extensive. After Genghis Khan's death, lands he had conquered were ruled by his sons.

MAP SKILL Use Intermediate Directions *After 1227 in which directions did the Mongol Empire expand?*

Practice and Extend

 **EXTEND LANGUAGE**
ESL Support

Examine Words with ex- Two words beginning with *ex-* appear on this page: *expand* and *extensive*. In words derived from Latin, *ex-* can mean "out."

Beginning Take a rubber band and stretch it out over the Mongolian Empire map as you say *expand*. Write *expand = stretch out; open out* on the board. Have students repeat the word *expand* and make a picture definition for it.

Intermediate Write the word *expand* on the board. Demonstrate its meaning as you make up a sentence using the word. Do the same for *extensive*. Then have students write simple sentences that include the words.

Advanced Write the words *expand* and *extensive* on the board and read the sentences in which the words appear on the page. Ask students how the words are alike. (They start with *ex-*.) Invite students to suggest other words that begin with *ex-*. (*extension, extent, express*)

For additional ESL support, use Every Student Learns Guide, pp. 166–169.

Despite the terror that the Mongols used in their conquests, they also made improvements in the lands they conquered. They improved roads and water travel. The Mongols recognized that trade brought wealth and made sure that travel was safe for traders throughout the empire. World traveler Ibn Battuta visited China during the Mongol dynasty. Battuta described the safety of travel in China:

> *"You can travel all alone across the land for nine months without fear, even if you are carrying much wealth."*

After several decades of conflict and natural disasters, the Mongols were overthrown, and the Ming dynasty came to power in 1368. At its height, the Ming dynasty ruled as many as 100 million people. There were great achievements made in the sciences and the arts.

For protection, the Ming dynasty emperors continued to strengthen and add onto the Great Wall. (Look on pages 110–111 to review the time line of the Great Wall.) Construction of the emperor's palace began in 1406. The palace was located in the heart of Beijing. Named the Forbidden City and occupied by the emperor in 1421, the palace was actually a collection of hundreds of buildings, surrounded by walls that were up to 35 feet tall. Only the government's highest officials could enter the Forbidden City.

During the Ming dynasty, people began to believe that China had the greatest civilization in the world. They believed that anything—and anyone—from outside of China should be avoided. As a result, China entered a long period of little contact with foreigners—but not before setting out on great voyages to other countries. ⑩

REVIEW How did the Mongol, or Yuan, dynasty show its concern for trade? *Cause and Effect*

(Look on pages 110–111 to review the time line of the Great Wall.)

▶ The Forbidden City was laid out in the form of a rectangle because the Chinese believed that Earth was square.

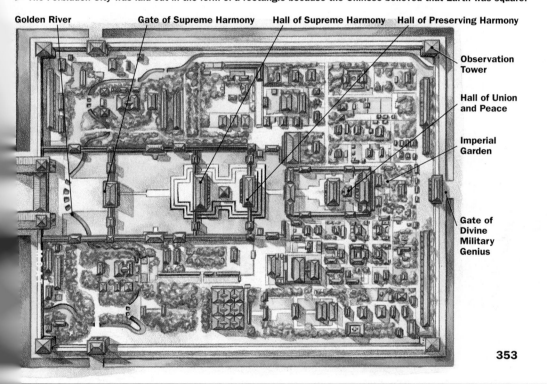

Golden River — Gate of Supreme Harmony — Hall of Supreme Harmony — Hall of Preserving Harmony

Observation Tower

Hall of Union and Peace

Imperial Garden

Gate of Divine Military Genius

353

Primary Source
Cited in *The Travels of Ibn Battuta*, by Ibn Battuta

❽ **Based on this quotation, how did Ibn Battuta feel about the country?** He felt that the country was friendly and safe. *Analyze Primary Sources*

❾ **What events led to the overthrow of the Mongol dynasty?** Decades of conflict and natural disasters *Cause and Effect*

⑩ **Explain the reason behind China's period of isolation during the Ming dynasty.** China made great achievements in science and the arts, which led people to believe that they had the greatest civilization in the world. They thought influences from outside of China should be avoided. *Cause and Effect*

✓ **Ongoing Assessment**

If... students are not able to pinpoint the cause and effect,

then... work with them to create a cause-and-effect graphic organizer. Draw two boxes on the board, label them *cause* and *effect*, and draw an arrow from the cause to the effect. Write the effect—China's isolation—in the appropriate box. Then have students reread the last paragraph on the page to find the cause.

✓ **REVIEW ANSWER** It improved roads and made sure that travel through the empire was safe for traders. *Cause and Effect*

CURRICULUM CONNECTION
Art

Illustrate Chinese Topics

Invite students to create artwork based on ideas in this lesson. Suggest topics such as the following:

- Make a poster that shows the most important contributions of the various dynasties.

- Create an illustrated time line showing the time periods of each of the dynasties. Include the years of the dynasties as well as important people, places, and events that occurred during each dynasty.

- Draw a building in the Forbidden City and write an explanatory caption or paragraph.

Dorling Kindersley

Paper, Printing, and Books

Objective

- Use primary and secondary sources such as visual materials to acquire information.

1 Introduce and Motivate

- Tell students that paper and printing were important Chinese inventions that had many practical and decorative uses.

- Before students read this page, ask them to make a list of the ways that they think paper and printing might have contributed to Chinese society.

2 Teach and Discuss

1 From what materials did Chinese people make paper? Silk rags, bamboo, and mulberry bark **Main Idea and Details**

2 What do the writing brush and decorated writing papers reveal about Chinese culture at the time those items were made? The people who lived in China at the time valued the arts. It was important to them to create things that were beautiful as well as useful. **Draw Conclusions**

3 Close and Assess

- Encourage students to find out more about various types of printing used in China and in other countries.

- Ask students to add to the lists they started before they read the page. They should consider how printing affected the spread of Chinese culture.

DORLING KINDERSLEY EYEWITNESS BOOK

Paper, Printing, and Books

Paper and printing were very important Chinese inventions. Credit for the successful manufacture of paper is given to Tsai Lun, an official of the imperial workshops, in A.D. 105. The first paper was made from silk rags. Later, other fibrous materials were used such as bamboo and mulberry bark. During the Han dynasty, there was a great demand for paper from the civil service. Paper was produced in large quantities in government factories. In the ninth century, large-scale woodblock printing was developed, making reading material available to more people.

Soft, springy brush tip probably made of wolf hair

Seal Prints
Seals were the first form of printing used in China. They were impressed on official documents, personal letters, and artwork.

Woodblock Printing
Since the ninth century, the Chinese printed books from large wooden blocks. The characters were carved in reverse. A print was taken by inking the surface of the block, laying a piece of paper over it, and then rubbing gently with a dry brush.

A Treasured Possession
This decorative writing brush from the Ming dynasty is made of lacquered, or varnished, wood.

A classical garden is illustrated in mother-of-pearl inlay.

Book cover with colorful flowers

Stylish Notepaper
This collection of illustrative papers is an example of colored woodblock printing. In sixteenth-century China, colored woodblock printing flourished. Scholars used beautifully designed papers for decorative letters. The illustrations were intended to be written over.

354

Practice and Extend

SOCIAL STUDIES
Background

More About Paper, Printing, and Books

- Making paper from bamboo was a multistep process. First, the bamboo was soaked to soften it. Then it was boiled and pounded to form a pulp. A fine screen was dipped into the pulp to gather a thin film of fibers. Next, the screen was pressed to remove the water and left to dry on a heated wall. When dry, the finished sheet of paper was peeled off the screen.

- Early books were made by rolling paper with handwritten text into scrolls.

- In the year 868, woodblock printing was used to create the earliest known printed book in China, a Buddhist text called the *Diamond Sutra.*

- In the tenth century, readily available books increased the spread of literacy. Buddhist texts and prayers were among the most popular printed materials.

China Explores

The Ming dynasty was a time of advancement in exploration. Even before the Europeans set sail to find sea routes to the East, Chinese explorer **Zheng He** (JUNG HUH) went westward. He led the first of seven voyages in 1405. His crews numbered more than 25,000 men. As many as 300 ships went on a single expedition.

Zheng He traveled to Southeast Asia and India. Later, he traveled to Africa and Southwest Asia. The Ming emperor encouraged Zheng He's expeditions. He spent a lot of money filling expedition ships with riches such as gold, silver, and silk. He asked that Zheng He give them as gifts to the people he encountered on his voyages.

The emperor hoped that China would be seen by others as a great and wealthy power. He also hoped that expensive gifts would encourage other countries to send envoys to China. At first,

▶ During the Ming dynasty, China became a major sea power led by Admiral Zheng He.

foreign countries began to send envoys. However, the Ming emperor died and the expensive voyages stopped by 1433. Under a new emperor, China soon cut itself off from the rest of the world, welcoming few foreigners. ⑪

REVIEW Did Zheng He explore west before or after the Europeans explored east?
 Sequence

Summarize the Lesson

- **589** The Sui dynasty unified China.
- **c. 1206** Genghis Khan formed a unified Mongolia.
- **1406** Construction of the Forbidden City began.
- **1433** China closed its ports to foreigners.

LESSON 2 REVIEW

Check Facts and Main Ideas

1. **Main Idea and Details** On a separate piece of paper, fill in the missing details below.

> The Mongol dynasty made several improvements in China.
>
> - China was safe for travelers.
> - Roads and water travel were improved.
> - Trade brought wealth to China.

2. Identify some of the contributions made by Chinese dynasties.

3. Where and what is the Forbidden City?

4. What was the purpose behind Zheng He's expeditions abroad?

5. **Critical Thinking:** *Make Inferences* What benefits might government officials have if positions in China were based on examination results, rather than family ties?

Link to ⬤─⬤ Writing

Write a Press Release You are the communications director for Empress Wu Hou. Your task is to write a press release, informing the public that civil service examinations must be taken in order to qualify for government jobs.

355

China Explores

🕐 *Quick Summary* During the Ming dynasty, Zheng He led seven voyages to explore west. Soon afterward China isolated itself.

🗺 Problem Solving

Ask students to think of another way that the Ming emperor might have encouraged envoys from foreign countries to visit China.

⑪ **How did China's policy toward foreign visitors change during the Ming dynasty?** At first the emperor hoped that other countries would send envoys to China. Later China allowed few foreigners into the country. **Summarize**

✓ **REVIEW ANSWER** Before 🔄 **Sequence**

③ Close and Assess

Summarize the Lesson

Play Match the Dynasty. Name a person, event, or accomplishment, and have students tell to which dynasty each one belongs.

✓ **LESSON 2 REVIEW**

1. **Main Idea and Details** For possible answers, see the reduced pupil page.

2. Block printing, paper money, gunpowder, sailing expertise, potter's wheel, and iron plow

3. The Forbidden City is a complex of government buildings in Beijing. Everyone but the highest government officials was forbidden to enter.

4. The emperor hoped China would be seen as a great and wealthy power and that other countries would send envoys to China.

5. **Critical Thinking:** *Make Inferences* The people hired might be more able to fulfill job requirements and do a better job at their work.

Link to ─⬤── Writing

Students' press releases should include subjects covered by the exams and the reasons exams are important.

The Khmer

Objectives

- Explain how the Khmer kingdom was ruled and thrived.

- Describe the location of the first Khmer royal city.

- Describe the role irrigation played in the Khmer economy.

- Explain why the Khmer were able to dominate Southeast Asia for centuries.

- Explain what Angkor Wat was and its significance to the Khmer kingdom.

Resources

- Workbook, p. 87
- Transparency 20
- Every Student Learns Guide, pp. 170–173
- Quick Study, pp. 86–87

Quick Teaching Plan

If time is short, have students write journal entries from the perspective of archaeologists.

- Provide several guiding questions, such as *What is most important about the Khmer culture?* Ask students to think of additional questions.

- As students read, they can write the answers and any other observations they may make.

1 Introduce and Motivate

Preview To activate prior knowledge, discuss with students religious buildings from previous lessons, such as the Hagia Sophia and Islamic mosques. Tell students that Angkor Wat is an important religious building in the Khmer Kingdom, located in what is now Cambodia.

You Are There As students read p. 356, have them look for clues about the climate and the Khmer culture. The details about irrigation, for example, reveal that the climate is sometimes too dry for growing.

LESSON 3

800	1000	1200	1400

802 Jayavarman II reunites the Khmer kingdom.

1113 Suryavarman II takes the throne.

about 1120 Construction begins on Angkor Wat.

1431 Invaders destroy the capital city of Angkor.

The Khmer

PREVIEW

Focus on the Main Idea
For hundreds of years, the Khmer culture dominated the peninsula of Southeast Asia.

PLACES
Cambodia
Laos
Indochina Peninsula
Angkor
Angkor Wat

PEOPLE
Jayavarman II
Suryavarman II

TERMS
deva-raja
absolute power

You Are There
On a mid-winter break, you and your family travel to Southeast Asia. It's the middle of the cool, dry season in Cambodia. What a great day to explore part of Angkor Wat (ANG kwar WAHT), one of the great temples built in the twelfth century! The temple is rectangular in shape. As you walk along the paved main entryway to the temple, you see that it is surrounded by artificial lakes, canals, and moats. These are used for water control and rice irrigation. The central pineapple-shaped tower in front of you stands more than 200 feet tall. Carvings on the walls to your left show scenes of war and legends. To your right are carvings describing everyday life. Everywhere you look, carvings of dancers greet you.

Cause and Effect As you read, identify the causes and effects of the rise and fall of the Khmer.

▶ The centuries-old Angkor Wat is the world's largest religious building. Construction of the temple began about 1120.

356

Practice and Extend

READING SKILL
Cause and Effect

In the Lesson Review, students complete a graphic organizer like the one below. You may want to provide students with a copy of Transparency 20 to complete as they read the lesson.

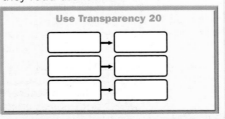

Use Transparency 20

WEB SITE
Technology

- You can look up vocabulary words by clicking on *Social Studies Library* and selecting the dictionary at **www.sfsocialstudies.com.**

- Students can learn more about current news by clicking on *Current Events* at **www.sfsocialstudies.com.**

- Explore other events that occurred on this day by clicking on *This Day in History* at **www.sfsocialstudies.com.**

The Khmer Kingdom

The Khmer (kuh MER) kingdom was one of the wealthiest kingdoms in Southeast Asia. *Khmer* is also the name of the people who lived in the kingdom.

In the sixth century, the Khmer ruled the lands we know today as **Cambodia** and **Laos** on the **Indochina Peninsula.** The Khmer civilization was influenced by Indian culture. Buddhism also flourished, along with the worship of Shiva and of other Hindu gods.

Internal conflicts divided the kingdom during the eighth century. But **Jayavarman II** (jah yah VAHR mahn) reunited the kingdom in 802. He was crowned king according to Hindu rites, which declared he was a **deva-raja** (DEE vah RA juh), or god-king. Being a deva-raja allowed Khmer rulers to act with **absolute power,** or the power to control every part of society. They used this power to form large armies that could defend the kingdom, as well as to invade its neighbors. In addition, the kings could force both the Khmer and slaves to work on the extensive irrigation system.

The irrigation system was key to the successful economy. During the monsoon season, the large reservoirs, levees, moats, and ponds helped prevent the farmland from being flooded. They also stored water to be used during the dry season. This irrigation system allowed

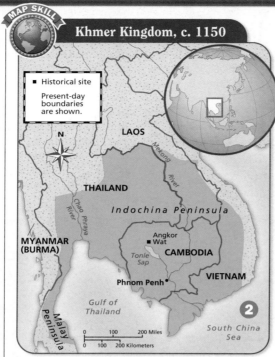

Khmer Kingdom, c. 1150

MAP SKILL

- Historical site

Present-day boundaries are shown.

LAOS

THAILAND

Chao Phraya River

Mekong River

Indochina Peninsula

MYANMAR (BURMA)

Angkor Wat

Tonle Sap

CAMBODIA

VIETNAM

Phnom Penh

Gulf of Thailand

Malay Peninsula

South China Sea

0   100   200 Miles
0   100   200 Kilometers

▶ By the twelfth century, the deva-rajas of the Khmer kingdom controlled a vast region of the Indochina Peninsula.

MAP SKILL Region *In what region of the world was the Khmer kingdom located?*

farmers to grow crops as many as two to three times a year.

Agricultural surpluses helped strengthen the kingdom's economy. For more than 500 years, the Khmer kingdom was an important influence in Southeast Asia.

The first royal city was built at **Angkor** in the tenth century. This marked the beginning of the empire's golden age. Under **Suryavarman II** (sur yuh VAHR mun) the empire reached its peak in the early twelfth century. During his rule from 1113 to 1150, he oversaw the construction of the magnificent towers of the temple **Angkor Wat.**

REVIEW How did the position of deva-raja affect expansion of Khmer rule? Cause and Effect

357

The Khmer Kingdom

⏱ **Quick Summary** The Khmer, a wealthy kingdom in Southeast Asia, was ruled by deva-rajas who had absolute power.

1 Do you think the Khmer were likely to have been tolerant toward different religions? Why do you think so? Possible answer: Yes; the Khmer were Buddhists as well as followers of Hindu gods. **Make Inferences**

MAP SKILL

Khmer Kingdom, c. 1150

2 How many present-day nations are shown on the map? Five: Vietnam, Cambodia, Laos, Thailand, and Myanmar (Burma) **Analyze Information**

MAP SKILL Answer In southeast Asia

3 How did the irrigation system help the Khmer economy? Irrigation gave farmers the right amount of water year-round and helped them grow crops two to three times a year. **Cause and Effect**

✓ **REVIEW ANSWER** Because the deva-raja had absolute power, he could force his people to form armies to invade neighboring nations. **Cause and Effect**

CURRICULUM CONNECTION Science

Research Flood Control

- Have students research answers to questions such as the following about methods the Khmer used to control floods.

- How can reforestation help control floods, and what role might erosion play in flooding?

- How do dams and levees keep flood waters in check?

- How do floodways divert floodwaters and help the soil?

MEETING INDIVIDUAL NEEDS Leveled Practice

Explore Khmer Accomplishments Have students describe the significant achievements of the Khmer kingdom.

Easy Have students list the accomplishments and write a sentence summarizing them. **Reteach**

On-Level Have students use the text on p. 357 to make a labeled drawing of the irrigation system during a monsoon and during a dry season. **Extend**

Challenge Have students compare and contrast the Khmer irrigation systems with those used in other parts of the ancient world, such as Peru or southwestern North America (See Unit 3.). **Enrich**

For a Lesson Summary, use Quick Study, p. 86.

A Stone Wonder

Quick Summary The Khmer demonstrated their skills in architecture and sculpture when they built magnificent stone temples.

The Khmer

Tell students that Jayavarman II renamed the Khmer kingdom Kambuja, an early version of Kampuchea, or Cambodia.

4 How has the leadership changed in the area that is now Cambodia? Since 1993, the government has been led by an elected prime minister. **Summarize**

5 How did the later temples differ from the ones that were first built? The building material evolved from brick to plain stone to carved stone. Later temples were larger and more elaborate than earlier ones. **Compare and Contrast**

✓ Ongoing Assessment

| **If...** students have difficulty understanding how later temples differed from earlier ones, | **then...** have them make a two-column chart and list details about the construction of earlier and later temples in the columns. |

Primary Source

6 What do you think may have been so impressive about the ruins at Angkor? Possible answer: The buildings were elaborate and extensive, and much work obviously went into creating them. **Analyze Primary Sources**

The Khmer

In 1431 the Thai people invaded and destroyed the capital city of Angkor. The Khmer kingdom never recovered. In addition, Angkor was ruled by one or another of its neighbors for hundreds of years. In the late 1800s, the French began to colonize the area. But by 1953, Cambodia won its independence. The Khmer, as a people, remained in Cambodia and today make up some 90 percent of the people who live there.

In 1993 a part of the former Khmer kingdom proclaimed itself the Kingdom of Cambodia, or Kampuchea (cam POOH chee uh). Currently, the head of state is King Norodom Sihanouk (SEE ha nook). The government is led by an elected prime minister. **4**

▶ Rice, rubber, cassava, sweet potatoes, corn, soy beans and tobacco are the main agricultural products of present-day Cambodia. This woman is transporting rice stalks.

A Stone Wonder

With some Indian influence on style, the Khmer became very skilled in art, architecture, and sculpture. The earliest known Khmer monuments are isolated towers of brick. They probably date from the seventh century. Later, the Khmer built small temples set on stepped pyramids. Over time, they added more and more covered galleries. The temples became more elaborate. **5** Soon stone replaced brick. Then, carved stone replaced plain stone.

By the end of Khmer dominance in the region, more than 70 huge temple and monument complexes stood at Angkor. Many of the temple walls have scenes of everyday life or battles. Some show men fishing, while others are of markets and entertainment. When French naturalist Henri Mouhot came upon Angkor in the mid-nineteenth century, he considered the ruins of the ancient Khmer capital to be:

> *"Grander than anything left by Greece or Rome."*

Of the dozens of temples, Angkor Wat stands as the finest example of Khmer architecture. It covers nearly one square mile.

358

Practice and Extend

EXTEND LANGUAGE
ESL Support

Endings Used to Compare Have students explore adjectives. Write the quote on p. 358 on the board. Write the word *grand* above *Grander*.

Beginning Explain that grand can mean "big." Point out the *-er* ending on *grander*. Display two books of different sizes, and describe them as *grand* and *grander*. Have students use these words or *big* and *bigger* to describe other pairs of objects.

Intermediate Have students explain how *grand* and *grander* differ. Then ask students to make similar word pairs from adjectives such as *tall, small, happy,* and *sad* and to use the words in sentences.

Advanced Write *grandest* on the board below *grand* and *grander*. Have students explain how the three words differ and use them in sentences.

For additional ESL support, use Every Student Learns Guide, pp. 170–173.

The builders of Angkor Wat wanted to honor the Hindu god Vishnu. Later, Angkor Wat became the tomb of the Khmer king who had ordered its construction. Nearly 50,000 artisans, workers, and slaves worked on the temple, which took nearly 40 years to complete. Today, Angkor Wat appears on Cambodia's flag. It is there to remind people of the Khmer culture and its achievements.

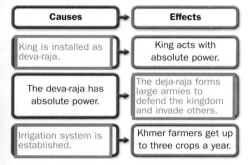

▶ Hinduism spread from South Asia to the Khmer kingdom in its early history. This stone statue is of the Hindu god Vishnu, the protector of the world.

Musee National de Phnom Penh, Cambodia/Bridgeman Art Library Int'l. Ltd. (U.S.)

▶ This Cambodian stamp featuring Angkor Wat was produced after Cambodia won its independence from France.

REVIEW What have we learned about the Khmer from the temples and monuments they left behind? **Draw Conclusions**

Summarize the Lesson

- **802** Jayavarman II reunited Khmer kingdom.
- **1113** Suryavarman II took the throne.
- **about 1120** Construction began on Angkor Wat.
- **1431** Invaders destroyed the capital city of Angkor.

LESSON 3   REVIEW

Check Facts and Main Ideas

1. **Cause and Effect** On a separate piece of paper, copy the diagram below and fill in one cause or effect for each blank.

Causes		Effects
King is installed as deva-raja.	→	King acts with absolute power.
The deva-raja has absolute power.	→	The deja-raja forms large armies to defend the kingdom and invade others.
Irrigation system is established.	→	Khmer farmers get up to three crops a year.

2. Where was the first royal city located?

3. What role did irrigation play in the Khmer economy?

4. Why were the Khmer able to dominate Southeast Asia for centuries?

5. **Critical Thinking:** *Make Generalizations* Why do you think the Khmer were willing to devote so much time and energy to constructing the temple complex?

Link to ∞ **Art**

Make a Poster Suppose you are a member of a team charged with carving a vast expanse of stone for the temple. Make a poster describing the type of artisan you would need. Be sure to describe the work, include job qualifications, and show pictures of designs you would like to see on the temple.

359

Workbook, p. 87

Lesson 3: The Khmer

Directions: Use complete sentences to answer the following questions. You may use your textbook.

1. Where was the Khmer kingdom located?

2. Which culture was a major influence on Khmer civilization?

3. Why was it valuable for a Khmer ruler to be a deva-raja?

4. Why was the irrigation system important to the Khmer economy?

5. What do you think is meant by a "golden age" of a civilization?

6. For what purpose was the Angkor Wat built? In what ways is it the same and different today?

Notes for Home: Your child learned about the Khmer kingdom in Southeast Asia. **Home Activity:** With your child, discuss the importance of a national symbol to a people, such as the symbolism of the Angkor Wat to the Khmer.

 Also on Teacher Resources CD-ROM.

---

⑦ **What importance does Angkor Wat hold in present-day Cambodia? How do the people show that it is important?** Angkor Wat reminds people of the accomplishments of the Khmer. It appears on Cambodia's flag, so it is a national symbol. **Main Idea and Details**

✓ **REVIEW ANSWER** They were highly skilled in art, architecture, and sculpture. **Draw Conclusions**

3 Close and Assess

Summarize the Lesson

Have students examine the vertical time line. Then allow time for students to work in pairs to devise quiz questions about the material. Use the questions to review the lesson with the class.

✓ **LESSON 3   REVIEW**

1. **Cause and Effect** For possible answers, see the reduced pupil page.

2. Angkor

3. Irrigation led to improved crop yield and a successful economy, which provided stability for the government.

4. The extensive irrigation system led to a successful economy. A large army could defend the nation. This helped the Khmer to dominate the region.

5. **Critical Thinking:** *Make Generalizations* They wanted to honor the Hindu god Vishnu and create a suitable burial place for their king.

Link to ∞ **Art**

Students' posters should be consistent with the details in the lesson. Students should include ideas such as the amount of hard work required by the job, the time the job may take, and what may be depicted in the carvings.

Japan in Isolation

Objectives

- Name and explain the location of the shogun's capital.
- Explain the difference between a shogun and a samurai.
- Explain how Japan's policy of isolation affected Japanese trade and culture.
- Explain why the shogun allowed some trade with foreigners during the period of isolation.

Vocabulary

aristocrat, p. 361; **samurai,** p. 361; **typhoon,** p. 361; **daimyo,** p. 361; **shogun,** p. 362

Resources

- Workbook, p. 88
- Transparency 20
- Every Student Learns Guide, pp. 174–177
- Quick Study, pp. 88–89

Quick Teaching Plan

If time is short, have students make K-W-L charts to guide their reading of the lesson.

- First, have students fill out a chart headed "Early Japan," and then have them read the lesson.
- Then, have students create a K-W-L chart titled "Tokugawa Rule." Make sure they note differences between the earlier and later eras as they fill out the chart.

1 Introduce and Motivate

Preview Have students recall the reasons that China isolated itself during the Ming dynasty. Tell students that they will find out why Japan adopted a similar policy as they read Lesson 4.

You Are There Ask students why they think there were checkpoints along the roads. Share with them that one of the concerns of the country's government at the time was the spread of Christianity. Ask students how the checkpoints might have contributed to Japan's isolation.

LESSON 4

500   **1000**   **1500**

1000s
Lady Murasaki Shikibu writes *The Tale of Genji.*

1200s
The Mongols make unsuccessful attempts to invade Japan.

1603
Beginning rule by the Tokugawa

PREVIEW

Focus on the Main Idea
Japan became isolated, or separated, from most of the world but still carried on some trade.

PLACES
Edo
Kyoto
Osaka
Nagasaki

PEOPLE
Murasaki Shikibu
Toyotomi Hideyoshi
Tokugawa Ieyasu

VOCABULARY
artistocrat
samurai
typhoon
daimyo
shogun

TERMS
Tokugawa dynasty
policy of isolation

▶ Farmers, merchants, warriors, and artisans were stopped at checkpoints along the main road of Japan, as this nineteenth-century woodcut shows.

360

Japan in Isolation

You Are There 1603: You're a messenger on the *Tokaido,* the main road from Kyoto (kee OH toh) to Edo (modern Tokyo). Although it's early morning, the road is busy. You're pushed and shoved as you move through a crowd of poor farmers and laborers. They're wearing cotton robes, called kimonos, and straw sandals. Ahead of you is a group of wealthy farmers. They're wearing kimonos with fancy designs and wooden sandals. You stop at one of 53 checkpoints along the road. At each, guards carefully check people for swords or other weapons. Most of the people at the checkpoint carry only turnips, cabbage, and other vegetables. A merchant takes out coins to pay a tax on the goods he plans to sell. The guards then place an official stamp on the goods. When they see that you have no weapons, they point you toward the gate that leads to Edo.

Cause and Effect As you read, identify the causes and effects of isolation on Japan.

Practice and Extend

READING SKILL
Cause and Effect

In the Lesson Review, students complete a graphic organizer like the one below. You may want to provide students with a copy of Transparency 20 to complete as they read the lesson.

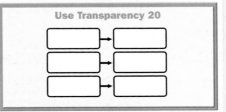

Use Transparency 20

WEB SITE
Technology

- You can look up vocabulary words by clicking on *Social Studies Library* and selecting the dictionary at **www.sfsocialstudies.com.**
- Students can learn more about current news by clicking on *Current Events* at **www.sfsocialstudies.com.**
- Explore other events that occurred on this day by clicking on *This Day in History* at **www.sfsocialstudies.com.**

Early Japan

Messengers traveled all over **Edo,** one of the major cities in unified Japan. Early in its history, Japan was made up of 100 states that were scattered over four islands. By the early 600s, these states were united under the country's first constitution.

Contact with China and Korea brought Buddhism and the Chinese system of writing to Japan. A unique blend of cultures began to develop toward the end of the eighth century. In the early 1000s, Lady **Murasaki Shikibu** (mer a SA kee shee KEE boo) wrote what is considered to be the world's first novel, *The Tale of Genji.*

Noble families soon occupied an important place in the government. They worked to weaken the emperor's power. For example, they created private estates, or plots of land that were free from the emperor's interference and taxes. The government, as well as the **aristocrats,** or nobles, began to rely on the warrior class for protection. These warriors, called **samurai** (SAM uh rye), defended their land and kept order in society. In 1192 the samurai took away all ruling powers from the emperor.

In the late 1200s, the Mongols in China made two attempts to invade and conquer Japan. During each attempt, the invaders were met by a **typhoon,** a tropical storm with heavy winds and rough seas. Typhoons helped Japan defeat any invaders.

▶ Some people name Lady Murasaki Shikibu as the world's first modern novelist.

These victories led to a feeling of national pride. The Japanese believed that the *kamikaze,* or "divine wind," destroyed the Mongols because the Japanese were a divinely protected people.

The years that followed the Mongol attacks were filled with a series of conflicts. The most powerful samurai became **daimyo** (DY mee oh), or ruling leaders, who controlled many other samurai and governed large areas of farmland. During the 1500s, the daimyo fought one another for power and land. As a result, Japan fell into a long civil war.

In 1590 General **Toyotomi Hideyoshi** (hee day HOH shee) united several warring groups, bringing most of Japan under his control. After his death, an ambitious daimyo, **Tokugawa Ieyasu** (toh kuh GAH wah ee YAY yah soo), rose to power, establishing the **Tokugawa dynasty.**

REVIEW What was the difference between a samurai and a daimyo? *Compare and Contrast*

▶ The Himeji Castle was built by the Akamatsu family in the 1300s. It was reconstructed by Toyotomi Hideyoshi in the late 1500s.

361

PAGE 361

2 Teach and Discuss

Early Japan

🕐 ***Quick Summary*** The 100 states of Japan were unified under one constitution. A series of internal and external conflicts allowed a powerful warrior to rise to power.

❶ Why were the Mongols unable to invade Japan? To what did the Japanese attribute their success at holding off Mongol invasion? Twice the Mongol forces were met by typhoons. The Japanese believed they were protected by the *kamikaze,* or divine wind. **Cause and Effect**

❷ Why do you think that military leaders rose to power in Japan? Possible answer: Noble families respected military leaders and depended on them to keep order and protect the land. **Draw Conclusions**

❸ Did civil war in Japan come before or after the attempted invasions by the Mongols? About how many years came between the two events? After; about 300 years ↩ **Sequence**

✓ **REVIEW ANSWER** A samurai was a professional warrior or soldier. The most powerful samurai became a daimyo who controlled many other samurai and governed large areas of farmland. **Compare and Contrast**

ACCESS CONTENT
ESL Support

Follow the Sequence of Events Help students follow the main events and learn the key concepts on p. 361.

Beginning Write key terms on the board, such as *aristocrats, samurai,* and *typhoon.* Say the words aloud and define them for students, using pictures if possible. Then have students match the words to the pictures or to simple definitions.

Intermediate Create a time line on the board and place blanks for key events using vocabulary such as *aristocrats, samurai,* and *typhoon.* As you read through the material with students, pause and ask students to fill in the blanks.

Advanced Discuss the rulers who rose to power. Have students write sentences about why those rulers wanted to control the country.

For additional ESL support, use Every Student Learns Guide, pp. 174–177.

SOCIAL STUDIES
Background

More About Lady Murasaki

- Lady Murasaki, the daughter of a provincial governor, was a respected scholar.
- The imperial family brought her to their court in 1001.
- For two years Murasaki kept a journal of her observations of the daily activities and attitudes of the upper class.
- While still at court, she used her observations to write much of her novel, *The Tale of Genji,* which is a story about a fictitious prince.

Tokugawa Rule

Quick Summary In 1603 the emperor gave Tokugawa Ieyasu the title of shogun, which led to 265 years of rule under the shogun of the Tokugawa dynasty. A policy of isolation and a four-class social system distinguished this period of Japanese history.

4 **What powers did the shogun have during the Tokugawa dynasty? What powers were reserved for the daimyo?** The shoguns controlled foreign trade, operated gold mines, ruled major cities, and controlled about twenty-five percent of the country's farmland. The daimyo issued laws and collected taxes on and governed the remaining farmland. *Main Idea and Details*

5 **Describe the social class system during the Tokugawa dynasty rule, and explain how that system gave power to the shoguns.** There were four classes— samurai, who were the ruling class, merchants, artisans, and farmers. The shoguns played one group of daimyos against another, thus ensuring their control. *Summarize*

6 **Why did the shoguns take control of foreign trade?** They wanted to prevent the daimyos from gaining too much wealth or power as a result of trade. *Cause and Effect*

Japan, 1603

7 **What bodies of water surround Japan?** Sea of Japan, Pacific Ocean, East China Sea *Interpret Maps*

MAP SKILL **Answer** Near the important cities of Edo, Kyoto, and Osaka; in east-central Japan

---

▶ Tokugawa Ieyasu was the first in a long line of Tokugawa dynasty shoguns who ruled Japan for more than 250 years.

Bridgeman Art Library Int'l. Ltd. (U.S.)

Tokugawa Rule

In 1603 the emperor gave Tokugawa Ieyasu the title of **shogun** (SHOH guhn), a special, high-ranking military office. This marked the start of 265 years of rule under the Tokugawa dynasty shoguns.

As a result, shoguns of the Tokugawa dynasty controlled foreign trade and operated gold and silver mines. They ruled major cities, including **Kyoto**, **Osaka** (oh SAH kuh), and Edo, the shogun's capital. In addition, shoguns controlled the emperor's land holdings, or about 25 percent of the country's farmland. (See the map to the right.)

4 The daimyo controlled the remaining 75 percent of Japan's farmland. There were about 270 daimyo, and each governed his own domain. The shogun had to share authority with the daimyo. This meant that the daimyo, not the shogun, issued laws and collected taxes.

During the rule of the Tokugawa dynasty shoguns, there was a strict four-class system. The samurai were at the top of the social system. They were originally warriors, but without wars they became members of the ruling class. Merchants, artisans, and farmers made up the remaining classes.

5 The divisions between the four social classes were essential to Tokugawa shogun power. Shoguns would make agreements with local daimyo, playing one group against another.

Because the shoguns took control of Japan's international trade, daimyos could not gain too

362

much wealth and power. Soon, most foreigners were forced out of the country. Only a few Dutch and Chinese traders were allowed to return to Japan to conduct business in one port, **Nagasaki.**

6 The shoguns outlawed traveling abroad and banned nearly all foreign books. The Dutch, who were from the Netherlands in Europe, brought books for Japanese scholars to read. These books helped scholars learn about studies in Europe and elsewhere. Shipbuilding, mapmaking, astronomy, and medicine were among the subjects of Japanese interest.

MAP SKILL

Japan, 1603

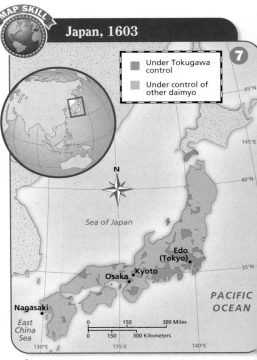

7

Under Tokugawa control

Under control of other daimyo

Sea of Japan

Edo (Tokyo)

Osaka • Kyoto

Nagasaki

East China Sea

PACIFIC OCEAN

0 150 300 Miles
0 150 300 Kilometers

▶ The emperor owned about 25 percent of Japan's farmland.

MAP SKILL Use a Map Key *Where was most of the emperor's land concentrated?*

Practice and Extend

SOCIAL STUDIES
Background

Time Line of the Shogun

- **Eighth century:** The term *shogun* describes a general sent to control local groups.
- **1192:** The overlord of Japan is called a shogun.
- **1333–1336:** Shoguns do not rule, as an emperor directly governs Japan.
- **1467–1568:** Civil war occurs as the shoguns and daimyos clash over control of the country.
- **1603:** Reign of Tokugawa dynasty shoguns begins.
- **1868:** Rebellion, brought on by the Tokugawa dynasty's inability to keep Japan isolated, brings direct imperial rule back to Japan.

The **policy of isolation** cut off Japan from the goods and culture of most countries. The only countries Japan still traded with were the Netherlands, China, and Korea, because shoguns wanted some contact with the outside world. In fact, shogun control caused trade to increase. The merchant class grew, and Edo became a large city. Dutchman Engelbert Kampfer commented during an official trade visit in 1691:

> *"The roads are always thronged [crowded] by ordinary citizens on business . . . . It is on most days more crowded than a public street in . . . Europe."*

The shogun government of the Tokugawa dynasty remained in place for about 250 years, but it eventually fell into debt. As the merchant class began to grow wealthier and more powerful, taxes were raised, causing farmers to riot. As a result, the class system began to crumble.

REVIEW How did the Tokugawa shoguns try to isolate Japan? **Cause and Effect**

Summarize the Lesson

- **600s** Japanese culture was influenced by China and Korea.

- **1603** Rule by shoguns of the Tokugawa dynasty began.

▶ A full suit of samurai armor could weigh up to 40 pounds.

LESSON 4 ⟩ REVIEW

Check Facts and Main Ideas

1. Cause and Effect On a separate piece of paper, copy the diagram below. Fill in the missing cause or effect.

Causes	→	Effects
The shogun controls all foreign trade.	→	Daimyos can no longer gain too much wealth and power.
Japan follows a policy of isolation.	→	Most foreigners are cut off from trading with Japan.
The merchant class grew wealthier and more powerful and the shogun government weakened.	→	Farmers riot.

2. Which Japanese city was the shogun's capital during the Tokugawa dynasty?

3. What is the difference between a samurai and a shogun?

4. How did Japan's policy of isolation affect Japanese trade and culture?

5. Critical Thinking: *Make Inferences* Why did shoguns allow some trade with other countries?

Link to ∞ Reading

Detect Bias Otsuki Gentaku wrote this passage in the 1700s after reading a book brought over by Dutch traders during Japan's policy of isolation. What biases has he learned from the Dutch book?

In terms of size, Egypt, a territory of Africa, should be termed the center of the world . . . . China and Japan are at the eastern end of the world, and Holland and the other European nations at the northwest.

363

Workbook, p. 88

Lesson 4: Japan in Isolation

Directions: Sequence the following events in the order in which they took place by numbering them from 1 (earliest) to 10 (most recent). You may use your textbook.

____ Shogun Tokugawa Ieyasu rose to power.

____ The merchant class grew.

____ Nobles worked to weaken the emperor's power.

____ The class system began to crumble.

____ The Mongols in China made two attempts to invade and conquer Japan.

____ Japan's states were united under the country's first constitution.

____ Edo became a large city.

____ Foreigners were forced out of Japan.

____ Japan fell into a long civil war.

____ A four-class system was enforced under shogun rule.

Directions: Complete the cause-and-effect chart by identifying three effects of the shogun's control of trade in Japan in the 1600s.

The shogun controlled trade in Japan in the 1600s.	→	1.
	→	2.
	→	3.

Also on Teacher Resources CD-ROM.

---

8 **What do Kampfer's observations reveal about Edo in 1691?** Possible answers: People led busy lives; business and economy were thriving.
Analyze Primary Sources

✓ **REVIEW ANSWER** They restricted trade, forced foreigners out of the country, forbade traveling abroad, and banned nearly all foreign books.
Cause and Effect

3 Close and Assess

Summarize the Lesson

Examine the vertical time line with students. Then ask students to work in small groups to list at least three important details about each point on the line. Allow time for students to share their ideas.

✓ **LESSON 4** **REVIEW**

1. Cause and Effect For possible answers, see the reduced pupil page.

2. Edo

3. A samurai is a member of the warrior class. Shogun is a title given by the emperor to a samurai, which marks a special, high-ranking military post.

4. It restricted trade to a few countries, but it actually increased the total amount of trade. It allowed only selected books into the country and prohibited foreign travel, so cultural exchange was severely limited.

5. Critical Thinking: *Make Inferences* Possible answer: They were controlling trade to limit the power and wealth of the daimyo, so they still allowed some trade to increase their own power and wealth.

Link to ∞ Reading

Students should point out that this Dutch book has helped Gentaku place his country in a position relative to other countries in the world. Thinking of Japan this way makes it seem less isolated and more a part of a greater world organization.

Gather and Report Information

Objective
- Identify reference sources and the kinds of information they provide.

Resource
- Workbook, p. 89

1 Introduce and Motivate

What sources can be used for gathering information? Encourage discussion of how historians use sources of information during the research process. Elicit students' experiences with reference sources, asking them to discuss various sources they have used. Then have students read the **What?** section of text on p. 364.

Why use particular reference sources? Have students read the **Why?** section of text on p. 365. Ask them where they might look for information that is often updated. Ask them where they might look to find general information about a person or topic.

2 Teach and Discuss

How is this skill used? Examine with students the graphics on pp. 364–365.

- Point out that matching the reference source to the type of information that is needed is the key to conducting research efficiently. For example, if you want to know the meaning of a word, you would not consult an encyclopedia.

- Ask students what type of information they would most likely find in a news periodical. For what types of research would they use this particular source?

- Have students read the **How?** section of text on p. 365.

Gather and Report Information

What? There is a wide variety of resources you can use to gather and report information on a particular subject. Your search for information will be easier if you are familiar with the resources available, as well as the kinds of information they contain. This is true whether you choose an online resource or a bound book.

Your choices for gathering information include primary sources and general resources such as an almanac, atlas, encyclopedia, dictionary,

yearbook, thesaurus, guidebook, and directory. In addition, there are specia resources such as a biographical dict graphical dictionary, and books of fam quotations.

Why? Every day more and more i is available about locations, people, a One way to organize the information i similar information in a single referer

An atlas or a gazetteer gives the exact location of Tokyo, Japan. Look up Tokyo in the alphabetical listing. The location of Tokyo, Japan, is about 35°N, 139°E.

An encyclopedia is a reference book that gives information on many subjects or concentrates on a single topic.

364

Practice and Extend

 **MEETING INDIVIDUAL NEEDS**
Leveled Practice

Give Directions Ask students to give directions for using a reference source.

Easy Refer students to the **How?** section of the text and help them restate in their own words how to use an almanac, atlas, or general encyclopedia. **Reteac**

On-Level Have students give oral step-by-step directions for using one of the reference sources. Remind them to use time-order words to make their directions clear. **Extend**

Challenge Have students write step-by-step instructions for finding appropriate resources. Remind them to use time order words such as *first, second, next,* and *finally* in their instructions. **Enrich**

How? To use the reference sources efficiently, you need to gain some familiarity with their contents. Suppose you wanted to learn more about Japan, the country you just studied.

A general encyclopedia will help you learn about the history of Japan. Look for the information under the guideword, or key word, *Japan*. A general encyclopedia will have information about the *samurai* and the *shoguns*.

An almanac might be best to gather current information on how many cell phones are in use in Japan today. Find *cellular telephones* in the almanac's general index. Turn to the page listed and you will find a table giving the number of cell phones in use in several different countries.

Most almanacs are published once a year. They often contain many kinds of information such as a calendar, important dates and events, and facts about governments, history, geography, and weather. An almanac may also give figures on population, industry, and sports.

▶ The key to gathering and reporting information is to know which type of resource to use.

Think and Apply

Gather the following information from at least two sources. Report both on the information you found and the resource you used.

1 How tall is Mount Fuji in Japan? How was it formed?

2 How was the *Tokaido* important to Japan?

3 What are the main exports and imports of Japan today?

365

1 **Why would an encyclopedia be a good source of information on the history of Japan?** The encyclopedia would give general information. The history of Japan has not drastically changed in recent years—a constantly updated source is not needed to find these historical facts. **Draw Conclusions**

2 **What is the first step in using an almanac to find a specific fact?** Use the index to find the correct page.
Sequence

3 **What is a gazetteer? What type of information would you find in it?** A gazetteer is a geographical index. It would give the exact locations of various places in the world, including their latitude and longitude.
Main Idea and Details

3 Close and Assess

Think and Apply

1. Possible answers: 12,388 feet or 3,776 meters; volcanic eruptions; atlas and encyclopedia

2. Possible answer: As a highway, it helped move people and goods around the country; Internet and encyclopedia

3. Possible answer: Machinery, electronic equipment, and automobiles; guidebook, almanac and Internet

CURRICULUM CONNECTION
Writing

Create a How-to Guide

Invite students to create research guides for their school or local library.

- Students could include a map of the library, showing where each type of reference source can be found and compose a guide to using various sources.

- The research guide could include a list of what types of resources are appropriate for finding different types of information, as well as how-tos for specific processes, such as using the card catalog/electronic database or the *Readers' Guide to Periodical Literature*.

Workbook, p. 89

Also on Teacher Resources CD-ROM.

Resources

- Assessment Book, pp. 61–64
- Workbook, p. 90: Vocabulary Review

Chapter Summary

For possible answers, see the reduced pupil page.

Vocabulary

1. b, **2.** a, **3.** c, **4.** d, **5.** e

People and Terms

Possible answers:

1. Tokugawa Ieyasu was the first of many Tokugawa shoguns, a group who ruled Japan for 265 years.

2. Zheng He was a Chinese explorer who was sent by the emperor to demonstrate the wealth of China to others around the world.

3. Khmer was one of the wealthiest kingdoms in the history of Southeast Asia.

4. The policy of isolation limited trade and contact between Japan and foreign nations.

5. Suryavarman II ruled the Khmer kingdom from 1113 to 1150.

6. Kublai Khan conquered southern China and Burma.

7. Akbar, the greatest Mogul ruler, was Babur's grandson.

8. Wu Hou, China's only female leader, ruled during the Tang dynasty.

9. Murasaki Shikibu wrote what is considered to be the world's first novel, *The Tale of Genji*.

10. Genghis Khan defeated the peoples of northern China and Persia.

11. Shah Jahan, a leader in India, had the Taj Mahal built in honor of his late wife.

12. Because Khmer deva-rajas were given absolute power according to Hindu rites, they controlled every aspect of society.

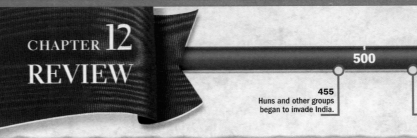

CHAPTER 12
REVIEW

	500	700
	455 Huns and other groups began to invade India.	**589** The Sui dynasty unified China.

Chapter Summary

 Target Skill

Sequence

On a separate piece of paper, put the following events on a time line in correct chronological order.

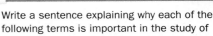
| 200 | 700 | 1200 | 1700 |

- Gupta dynasty rules northern India.
- Genghis Khan forms a unified Mongolia.
- Angkor Wat is constructed.
- Taj Mahal is constructed.
- Tokugawa shogun rule begins in Japan.

320
1206
1120
1630
1603

Vocabulary

Match each word with the correct definition or description.

1. **aristocrat** (p. 361)
2. **samurai** (p. 361)
3. **daimyo** (p. 361)
4. **shogun** (p. 362)
5. **typhoon** (p. 361)

a. warrior class
b. noble of a high social class
c. powerful samurai
d. high-ranking military post
e. tropical storm

People and Terms

Write a sentence explaining why each of the following terms is important in the study of Asia. You may use two or more in a single sentence.

1. Tokugawa Ieyasu (p. 361)
2. Zheng He (p. 355)
3. Khmer (p. 357)
4. policy of isolation (p. 363)
5. Suryavarman II (p. 357)
6. Kublai Khan (p. 352)
7. Akbar (p. 348)
8. Wu Hou (p. 351)
9. Murasaki Shikibu (p. 361)
10. Genghis Khan (p. 352)
11. Shah Jahan (p. 349)
12. absolute power (p. 357)

Practice and Extend

Assessment Options

✓ **Chapter 12 Assessment**

- Chapter 12 Content Test: Use Assessment Book, pp. 61–62.
- Chapter 12 Skills Test: Use Assessment Book, pp. 63–64.

Standardized Test Prep

- Chapter 12 Tests contain standardized test format.

✓ **Chapter 12 Performance Assessment**

- Have students make an illustrated map to summarize the information in Chapter 12.
- Give students large outline maps of the world and have them color-code the civilizations.
- Students can add sentences and paragraphs with details including dates, events, and people.
- Assess students' understanding of ancient Asia empires. Students' work should show that they understand the cultures of the various places in Chapter 12.

802
Khmer kingdom was reunited.

about 1206
Genghis Khan formed a unified Mongolia.

1433
China closed its ports to foreigners.

1526
The Mogul Empire was established.

1603
Japan began policy of isolation.

Facts and Main Ideas

1 Why did the Khmer, Chinese, and Japanese peoples tend to be isolated?

2 What was the result of early Japan's interaction with Korea and China?

3 **Time Line** Did China follow a policy of isolation before or after Japan?

4 **Main Idea** How was Akbar's tax policy like others of the time? How was it different?

5 **Main Idea** What major changes occurred in China during the Ming dynasty?

6 **Main Idea** How was irrigation linked to the Khmer economy?

7 **Main Idea** How did the Japanese policy of isolation affect Japanese trade?

8 **Critical Thinking:** *Detect Bias* How would the Japanese scholars determine whether the books they received from the Dutch showed biases?

Internet Activity

To get help with vocabulary, people, and terms, select dictionary, encyclopedia, or almanac from *Social Studies Library* at **www.sfsocialstudies.com.**

Apply Skills

Gather and Report Information

Make a chart with the following information on one of the countries you read about in this chapter: country map, population, major languages, exports and imports, and form of government. Document the information you gather by including a bibliography. You may use pictures or drawings from the sources you use. Present your chart to the class.

On a separate piece of paper, answer the following questions.

1 How many sources did you use to make your chart?

2 What kinds of sources did you use?

3 Why did you choose these sources for the information?

Write About History

1 Write a **biography** of a samurai who has become a daimyo. Be sure to research the characteristics of each class.

2 Write a **civil service test** that you would use to screen people who are applying for government jobs, such as postal workers.

3 Write a **magazine article** telling people about Angkor Wat. Describe the temple and explain who built it and when.

367

Hands-on Unit Project

✔ **Unit 5 Performance Assessment**

- See p. 420 for information about using the Unit Project as a means of performance assessment.
- A scoring guide is provided on p. 420.

WEB SITE
Technology

For more information, students can select the dictionary, encyclopedia, or almanac from *Social Studies Library* at **www.sfsocialstudies.com.**

Workbook, p. 90

Vocabulary Review

Directions: Use each of the vocabulary terms from Chapter 12 in an original sentence. Write the sentences on the lines provided. You may use your glossary.

1. aristocrat

2. samurai

3. typhoon

4. daimyo

5. shogun

Notes for Home: Your child learned the vocabulary terms for Chapter 12.
Home Activity: Have your child explain how these five terms are related to Japan and the role the shoguns played in the evolution of social classes in Japan.

Also on Teacher Resources CD-ROM.

Facts and Main Ideas

1. Physical geography: Khmer—peninsula, China—mountains, and Japan—islands. Attitudes: the Chinese built a Great Wall, and during the Ming dynasty, the Chinese began to avoid all foreign influence. A policy of isolation in Japan began during the Tokugawa dynasty.

2. The Japanese built upon the Chinese system of writing. They also accepted Buddhism.

3. Before

4. Similar: It taxed farmers. Different: It also taxed nobility.

5. During the Ming dynasty, people began to think that anything outside of China should be avoided. China began a period of isolation.

6. Large reservoirs, dikes, moats, and ponds helped prevent floods during monsoons. They also stored water for use during the dry season. This allowed farmers to grow two to three crops a year, which created a strong economy.

7. Japan's policy of isolation limited trade to only a few countries.

8. Because Japan was isolated, the Japanese scholars would have to compare the information from the Dutch books with the limited information they received from China and Korea.

Apply Skills

Students should use a variety of sources and explain why they chose each source.

Write About History

1. Biographies should be written from the third-person point of view and in chronological order. Facts should be consistent with ideas in the text on the rise of a daimyo. Conflicts between the shogun and daimyo should be noted.

2. Questions should test a candidate's knowledge of the job's subject area and a candidate's character and morals.

3. Students should include vivid and descriptive details to help readers picture the temple in their minds.

Chapter Planning Guide

Chapter 13 • African Empires

Locating Time and Place pp. 368–369

Lesson Titles	Pacing	Main Ideas
Lesson 1 **The Geography of Africa** pp. 370–373	1 day	• People throughout Africa have adapted to a variety of environments.
Lesson 2 **West African Kingdoms** pp. 374–378	2 days	• Many kingdoms developed in the savanna and forested areas of West Africa.
Biography: Sundiata p. 379		• Sundiata overcame disease and his adversaries to become the greatly respected king of Mali.
Lesson 3 **East, Central, and Southern Africa** pp. 380–385	2 days	• Trading empires developed in eastern, central, and southern Africa that interacted with Arabia, India, and China.
Research and Writing Skills: Use the Internet pp. 386–387		• The Internet provides an almost limitless source of information for research.
✓ **Chapter 13 Review** pp. 388–389		

◀ **Discovered at Great Zimbabwe, these bronze bangle bracelets were probably originally from India.**

✓ = Assessment Options

◀ **These bars of salt are ready to be traded at the market.**

Vocabulary	Resources	Meeting Individual Needs
savanna	• Workbook, p. 92 • Transparency 6 • Every Student Learns Guide, pp. 178–181 • Quick Study, pp. 90–91	• ESL Support, TE p. 371 • Leveled Practice, TE p. 372
griot	• Workbook, p. 93 • Transparencies 6, 42 • Every Student Learns Guide, pp. 182–185 • Quick Study, pp. 92–93	• ESL Support, TE p. 375 • Leveled Practice, TE p. 376 • Learning Styles, TE p. 377
Swahili oba	• Workbook, p. 94 • Transparency 6 • Every Student Learns Guide, pp. 186–189 • Quick Study, pp. 94–95 • Workbook, p. 95	• ESL Support, TE p. 382 • Leveled Practice, TE p. 383 • Learning Styles, TE p. 385
	✓ Chapter 13 Content Test, Assessment Book, pp. 65–67 ✓ Chapter 13 Skills Test, Assessment Book, pp. 67–68	✓ Chapter 13 Performance Assessment, TE p. 388

Providing More Depth

Additional Resources

- Vocabulary Cards
- Daily Activity Bank
- Social Studies Plus!
- Big Book Atlas
- Student Atlas
- Outline Maps
- Desk Maps

 Technology

- AudioText
- The test maker
- Teacher Resources CD-ROM
- Map Resources CD-ROM
- **www.sfsocialstudies.com**

 To establish guidelines for your students' safe and responsible use of the Internet, use the Scott Foresman Internet Guide.

Additional Internet Links

To find out more about:

- The Sahara Desert, visit **www.calacademy.org**
- Bantu, visit **www.thinkquest.org**
- Oral tradition in West Africa, visit **www.si.umich.edu**

Key Internet Search Terms

- Africa
- Sahara
- Bantu

Workbook Support

Use the following Workbook pages to support content and skills development as you teach Chapter 13. You can also view and print Workbook pages from the Teacher Resources CD-ROM.

Workbook, p. 91

Vocabulary Preview

Use with Chapter 13.

Directions: Choose the vocabulary word from the box and write it on the line beside its definition. You may use your textbook. Then use each word in an original sentence on the lines provided.

| savanna | griot | Swahili | oba |

1. __griot__ professional storyteller
   Possible answer: Griots have helped preserve Africa's history.

2. __oba__ king in Benin
   Possible answer: The oba's house was much sturdier than other people's houses.

3. __Swahili__ both a language and a culture; combination of Muslim and East African cultures
   Possible answer: My aunt learned Swahili while she was in college.

4. __savanna__ short, grassy plains
   Possible answer: I would like to see the animals that live on the African savanna.

 Notes for Home: Your child learned the vocabulary terms for Chapter 13.
Home Activity: Work together with your child to use these terms and details in the chapter to tell a story about African culture.

Use with Pupil Edition, p. 368

Workbook, p. 92

Lesson 1: The Geography of Africa

Use with Pages 370-373.

Directions: Decide whether each detail describes a desert, savanna, rain forest, or Mediterranean climate zone in Africa. For desert write a *D* in the blank, for savanna write an *S*, for rain forest write an *R*, and for Mediterranean write an *M*. Then answer the questions that follow. You may use your textbook.

__S__ 1. about half of Africa
__M__ 2. mostly hot summers
__R__ 3. thick vegetation
__D__ 4. hot and dry
__M__ 5. suitable for agriculture
__S__ 6. south of the Sahara
__D__ 7. little vegetation and few animals
__R__ 8. farming nearly impossible
__R__ 9. covers a very small area of the continent
__M__ 10. generally mild and rainy winters
__D__ 11. the Sahara

12. What made the journeys across Africa dangerous?
   In the desert, people faced sandstorms, high heat, and few water sources. Elsewhere, they also faced barriers such as mountains, plateaus, and cataracts.

13. Why did people migrate to other areas of Africa?
   Possible answers: Changes in climate; they had used up all the resources in a certain place.

 Notes for Home: Your child learned how the geography of Africa affects its people.
Home Activity: Select a climate zone discussed in this chapter. With your child, compare and contrast characteristics of its climate to the climate where you live.

Use with Pupil Edition, p. 373

Workbook, p. 93

Lesson 2: West African Kingdoms

Use with Pages 374-378.

Ghana, Mali, and Songhai were wealthy kingdoms in West Africa.
Directions: Complete the outline with information from this lesson about these empires. You may use your textbook.

I. Ghana
   A. People
      1. Religion of __Islam__
      2. Adopted Arabic system of __writing__
   B. Economy and Trade
      1. __Farmed, fished, and herded cattle__ for a living
      2. Capital city __Koumbi__, major center of trade
   C. Political Rule
      1. Founded by __Soninke__, who __lost control of__ empire by 1203

II. Mali
   A. People
      1. An Arab __architect__ built mosques, and __scholars__ brought Muslim learning
      2. __Jenne-jenno__, oldest known city in sub-Saharan Africa: 200 B.C. to A.D. 1400
   B. Economy and Trade
      1. Strong __agricultural__ economy, but relied on __trade__ for wealth
   C. Political Rule
      1. __Mansa Musa__ greatest king, took pilgrimage to __Mecca__

III. Songhai
   A. People
      1. __Fighting__ among different Muslim groups contributed to end of empire
   B. Economy and Trade
      1. Bigger center of __trade and learning__ than Mali
   C. Political Rule
      1. __Sonni Ali__, important king who divided land into __provinces__
      2. Professional __army and navy__ protected kingdom, defeated by __Moroccans__

Notes for Home: Your child learned about three empires of West Africa.
Home Activity: With your child, review the information in this outline. Together, create a Venn diagram to compare and contrast the empires of Ghana, Mali, and Songhai.

Use with Pupil Edition, p. 378

Workbook Support

Workbook, p. 94

Use with Pages 380–385.

Lesson 3: East, Central, and Southern Africa

Directions: Match the places in the box to the clues and write the terms on the lines provided. You will use each term more than once. You may use your textbook.

| Axum | Ethiopia | Kilwa | Great Zimbabwe | Benin |

1. exported ivory, frankincense, and myrrh __**Axum**__
2. destroyed by change in climate and trade routes __**Axum**__
3. known for its great art __**Benin**__
4. used Swahili to help traders communicate __**Kilwa**__
5. ruled by Solomonids after overthrow of Zagwe dynasty __**Ethiopia**__
6. ruled by kings called obas __**Benin**__
7. replaced Axum civilization __**Ethiopia**__
8. attacked by Portuguese for control of Indian Ocean trade __**Kilwa**__
9. ruled by Ezana __**Axum**__
10. abandoned when population exhausted resources __**Great Zimbabwe**__
11. built several churches out of solid rock __**Ethiopia**__
12. gained wealth by taxing trade goods __**Great Zimbabwe**__
13. located in a fertile forest region near Niger River __**Benin**__
14. built stone enclosures to show king's power __**Great Zimbabwe**__

 Notes for Home: Your child learned about trading empires in eastern, central, and southern Africa.
Home Activity: With your child, discuss the importance of trade to your community and state. What resources does your community sell to other places?

Use with Pupil Edition, p. 385

Workbook, p. 95

Use with Pages 386–387.

Use the Internet

The Internet contains millions of pages of information on all kinds of topics. You can access the Internet through your computer and use a search engine to help you find information on a particular topic. **Directions:** Answer the following questions about using the Internet on the lines provided.

1. Why do you think it can be helpful to use a search engine when looking for information on the Internet?

   Possible answer: Search engines can help locate or narrow information about a topic.

2. What is one advantage of researching a topic on the Internet?

   Possible answers: More current information, more choices, speed

3. What is one disadvantage of researching a topic on the Internet?

   Possible answer: The information may not be accurate.

4. What keywords might you type in to locate information about Mansa Musa's journey to the Middle East?

   Possible answers: Mansa Musa, empire of Mali, Mali civilization, Mali Africa

Directions: Complete the flowchart by using the terms in the box to sequence the steps for using a search engine.

| Select a search engine. | Narrow your topic, if necessary. | Choose a topic. |
| Type in the keywords. | Access the Internet. | |

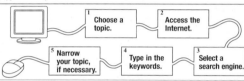

 Notes for Home: Your child learned how to use search engines on the Internet.
Home Activity: With your child, practice using various Internet search engines on a home or library computer to research a topic of interest.

Use with Pupil Edition, p. 386

Workbook, p. 96

Use with Chapter 13.

Vocabulary Review

Directions: Match each term or description in the box below to a vocabulary word from this chapter. Write the term or description on a line on the concept maps.

trading language	tells about life of Sundiata	ruled powerful empire
storyteller	about half of Africa	south of the Sahara
"people of the coast"	lived in a beautiful palace	kingdom of Benin
people herd cattle	empire of Mali	king
fertile soil	African and Muslim cultures	climate zone
culture and language		oral stories

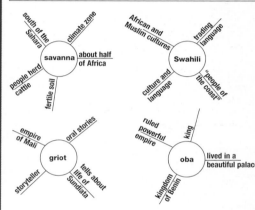

Notes for Home: Your child learned the vocabulary terms for Chapter 13.
Home Activity: After your child has categorized all the terms, verbally summarize for your child the information recorded in each concept map. Have your child listen carefully and correct any errors noticed in your summary.

Use with Pupil Edition, p. 389

Assessment Support

Use these Assessment Book pages and the test maker to assess content and skills in Chapter 13. You can also view and print Assessment Book pages from the Teacher Resources CD-ROM.

Assessment Book, p. 65

Chapter 13 Test

Part 1: Content Test

Directions: Fill in the circle next to the correct answer.

Lesson Objective (1:1)

1. Which describes the geography of Africa's savanna?
   - Ⓐ little vegetation
   - ● short grassy plains
   - Ⓒ thick vegetation
   - Ⓓ fertile land

Lesson Objective (1:2)

2. What are winters generally like in the Mediterranean climate zone of Africa?
   - Ⓐ hot and dry
   - Ⓑ hot and rainy
   - ● mild and rainy
   - Ⓓ mild and dry

Lesson Objective (1:1)

3. Which of the following landforms is NOT located in Africa?
   - Ⓐ Great Rift Valley
   - Ⓑ Mount Kilimanjaro
   - Ⓒ Sahara
   - ● Arabian Peninsula

Lesson Objective (1:3)

4. Which are the three major interior rivers in Africa?
   - ● Zambezi, Niger, and Congo
   - Ⓑ Tigris, Euphrates, and Ganges
   - Ⓒ Huang, Me-kong, and Yang-tze
   - Ⓓ Danube, Seine, and Thames

Lesson Objective (1:4)

5. Why did people migrate from one place to another in Africa?
   - ● The environment of their area changed and resources were used up.
   - Ⓑ They had too many resources.
   - Ⓒ The rivers of their area flooded, destroying their crops and homes.
   - Ⓓ They wanted to draw cave paintings in other areas.

Lesson Objective (1:5)

6. How do the Bantu languages help historians study migration in Africa?
   - Ⓐ Stories of migration are written in the Bantu languages.
   - Ⓑ Each language is unique and is spoken by very few people.
   - ● The languages are similar and have spread with people as they migrated.
   - Ⓓ Older Africans who speak these languages share their knowledge with historians.

Lesson Objective (2:1)

7. What influence did gold have on the empires of West Africa?
   - Ⓐ It allowed emperors to decorate their palaces.
   - Ⓑ It was used to make the coins of the empires.
   - Ⓒ It brought prospectors in hopes of finding gold.
   - ● It brought in trade goods from many other lands.

Use with Pupil Edition, p. 388

Assessment Book, p. 66

Lesson Objective (2:1, 2)

8. How did the location of Ghana help it become a wealthy empire?
   - Ⓐ It was on the coast, allowing traders to move goods to and from there by ship.
   - ● It was between the salt mines in the Sahara and the gold fields in Wangara.
   - Ⓒ It was in two climate zones, so farmers could raise either horses or camels.
   - Ⓓ It was located near the major trading centers of Koumbi and Baghdad.

Lesson Objective (2:3)

9. For what is Mansa Musa best known?
   - ● pilgrimage to Mecca
   - Ⓑ interest in Muslim learning and scholarship
   - Ⓒ interest in architecture
   - Ⓓ vast supply of gold and camels

Lesson Objective (2:5)

10. Why did European mapmakers begin to include Mali on their maps?
    - ● Mansa Musa's pilgrimage to Mecca caught their attention.
    - Ⓑ They wanted other Muslims to make a pilgrimage to Mecca.
    - Ⓒ They did not want sailors to get lost sailing around Africa.
    - Ⓓ They wanted architects to build mosques in Mali.

Lesson Objective (2:3)

11. What impact did Mansa Musa have on African history?
    - Ⓐ He forced people to convert to Islam.
    - ● Europeans became interested in the gold and resources in Mali.
    - Ⓒ He destroyed the empire of Mali.
    - Ⓓ He built new mosques in Europe.

Lesson Objective (2:4)

12. Which is true of most West African kingdoms?
    - ● They were crossroads for trade.
    - Ⓑ They were ruled by Sundiata.
    - Ⓒ They had agricultural economies.
    - Ⓓ They refused to pay tribute to Mali.

Lesson Objective (3:2)

13. Which was NOT a good exported by the kingdom of Axum?
    - Ⓐ ivory
    - ● gold
    - Ⓒ myrrh
    - Ⓓ frankincense

Lesson Objective (3:1)

14. Which country replaced the Axum civilization?
    - Ⓐ Zimbabwe
    - Ⓑ Mali
    - Ⓒ Ghana
    - ● Ethiopia

Lesson Objective (3:1)

15. Which of the following were the two major dynasties of Ethiopia?
    - ● Zagwe and Solomonid
    - Ⓑ Mogul and Mongol
    - Ⓒ Tang and Ming
    - Ⓓ Khmer and Tokugawa

Lesson Objective (3:4)

16. Why did the Portuguese attack many cities of East Africa in the 1500s?
    - Ⓐ to capture and enslave the residents
    - Ⓑ to rebuild European cities in their place
    - Ⓒ to steal gold and ivory reserves in the cities
    - ● to gain control of Indian Ocean trade

Use with Pupil Edition, p. 388

Assessment Support

Assessment Book, p. 67

Lesson Objective (3:3)

17. How were the stone enclosures of Great Zimbabwe different from the walls of Benin?
    - Ⓐ They were built to protect the city from high winds and violent storms.
    - Ⓑ They were built around the king's palace to protect his riches.
    - ⬤ They were built to show the power and importance of the king.
    - Ⓓ They were built to protect the city from invaders.

Lesson Objective (3:5)

18. What effect did international trade have on the kingdom of Benin?
    - ⬤ Benin grew to become a powerful empire.
    - Ⓑ Many people in Benin moved to Europe.
    - Ⓒ Merchants became more powerful than the king.
    - Ⓓ People in Benin learned several foreign languages.

Part 2: Skills Test

Directions: Use complete sentences to answer questions 1–7. Use a separate sheet of paper if you need more space.

1. Which of the main African climate zones is best suited for agriculture? In which part of Africa is this climate zone found? **Generalize**

   Mediterranean; Hot summers and mild, rainy winters, along with fertile soil, make the North African coast and southern tip of Africa ideal for agriculture.

2. How might people who study languages help historians learn more about an area's past? **Make Inferences**

   Possible answer: Linguists study similarities between languages and determine their origins. This could help historians understand how people have moved around. In addition, linguists might communicate with older members of a group and learn about their experiences.

3. What three factors made Ghana a wealthy kingdom? **Cause and Effect**

   Ghana became wealthy because of its safe trade routes, its location between gold fields and salt mines, and the income it earned from the taxes it placed on trade goods.

Use with Pupil Edition, p. 388

Assessment Book, p. 68

4. In what ways does the economy of Mali compare with the economy of Ghana? **Compare and Contrast**

   Same: both kingdoms relied on trade, particularly for gold, with other African nations for their wealth. Different: Mali also traded with Europeans and had a strong agricultural economy.

5. Identify and explain the role of storytellers in Mali. **Analyze Information**

   Over time, griots, or professional storytellers, have passed from one generation to the next stories about the history of the empire. Today griots still carry on the tradition of oral storytelling.

6. What three points would you include in a summary of Christianity in East Africa? **Summarize**

   Possible answer: Christian kingdoms were first established in northeastern Africa about 330 when the Axum king Ezana converted to Christianity. People in the kingdoms of Noba and Makurra converted between the years of 500 and 650. One Zagwe king, Lalibela, showed his faith by having 11 churches built out of solid rock during his reign.

7. By whom could the following statement have been made? **It is exciting to get to move with the king two or three times a year!** Support your answer. **Point of View**

   The statement could have been made by a member of the Solomonid king's royal court. They moved around the kingdom as often as two or three times a year. This allowed the king to stay in close contact with all the regions in the kingdom.

Use with Pupil Edition, p. 388

African Empires

Chapter 13 Outline

Resources

- Workbook, p. 91: Vocabulary Preview
- Vocabulary Cards
- Social Studies Plus!

c. 2500 B.C., The Sahara: Lesson 1

Ask students to describe the hardships of the Sahara. (Possible answers: Difficult to travel over, hot, dry, no food or water)

A.D. 1324, Mali: Lesson 2

Explain to students that this picture shows Mansa Musa during his pilgrimage to Mecca in 1324. Ask them to tell what they think travel was like at that time. (People traveled by camel; tents provided shelter.)

1450, Great Zimbabwe: Lesson 3

Ask students to share their impressions of the stone enclosures. (Possible answer: The enclosures seem like a good defense; they look a little like a maze.)

African Empires

Lesson 1

c. 2500 B.C.
The Sahara
The Sahara begins to dry up and people migrate to other parts of Africa.

Lesson 2

A.D. 1324
Mali
Mansa Musa, the king of Mali, goes on a pilgrimage to Mecca.

Lesson 3

1450
Great Zimbabwe
The Shona people complete the stone enclosures of Great Zimbabwe.

368

Practice and Extend

Vocabulary Preview

- Use Workbook p. 91 to help students preview the vocabulary words in this chapter.
- Use Vocabulary Cards to preview key concept words in this chapter.

 Also on Teacher Resources CD-ROM.

Workbook, p. 91

Vocabulary Preview

Directions: Choose the vocabulary word from the box and write it on the line beside its definition. You may use your textbook. Then use each word in an original sentence on the lines provided.

savanna	griot	Swahili	oba

1. _____ professional storyteller

2. _____ king in Benin

3. _____ both a language and a culture; combination of Muslim and East African cultures

4. _____ short, grassy plains

Locating Time and Place

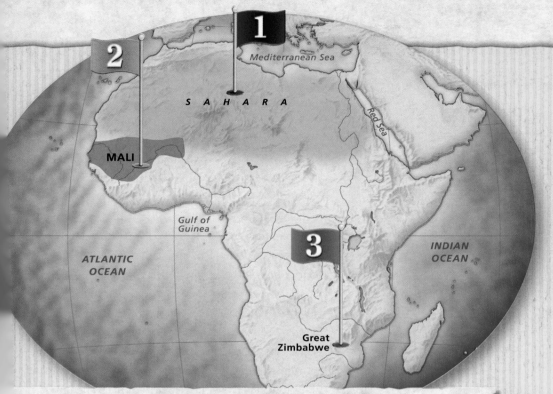

Why We Remember

Powerful African kingdoms were a major source of gold long before they caught the attention of Europeans in the late 1400s. West African states served as middlemen for the gold that came from the south. East African empires and city-states traded gold and iron with the peoples of Europe and Asia. These trade goods made the East and West African empires and city-states wealthy. Trade also helped Islam spread into East and West Africa and Christianity into East Africa. Europeans soon turned their attention to Africa's valuable resources. Today, many of these valuable resources are sold in the United States.

369

SOCIAL STUDIES STRAND
Geography

Mental Mapping On a piece of paper, have students make a compass rose at the bottom. Ask them to make a freehand outline of Africa. Next, have them label the Atlantic Ocean, Indian Ocean, Mediterranean Sea, and Red Sea. Finally, ask them to draw and label the Nile and Congo Rivers along with the Sahara and the Great Rift Valley. Discuss how the size of Africa and its geographic features may contribute to cultural isolation.

- Have students examine the pictures shown on p. 368 for Lessons 1, 2, and 3.

- Remind students that each picture is coded with both a number and a color to link it to a place on the map on p. 369.

Why We Remember

Have students read the "Why We Remember" paragraph on p. 369, and ask them why events in this chapter might be important to them. Have students discuss how the exchange of goods and ideas helps cultures develop.

The Geography of Africa

Objectives

- Describe how the physical geography of Africa is diverse with many physical features.

- List and describe the major climate zones of Africa.

- List and locate the major rivers of Africa.

- Explain how Africans have adapted to their environment.

- Explain why some linguists believe that Bantu speakers spread across Africa.

Vocabulary

savanna, p. 371

Resources

- Workbook, p. 92
- Transparency 6
- Every Student Learns Guide, pp. 178–181
- Quick Study, pp. 90–91

Quick Teaching Plan

If time is short, have students summarize the geography of Africa on a two-column chart with the headings *Climate Zones* and *Physical Features.*

- Have students fill in the chart as they read the lesson independently.

- Ask students to tell how they think these features might affect the way people live.

1 Introduce and Motivate

Preview Ask students to recall what they learned in Chapter 11 about how climate and geography affected the Byzantine Empire. Tell students that in Lesson 1 they will learn how climate and geography affected African life.

You Are There The desert climate can be dangerous. Have students identify precautions to take when living in or traveling through the harsh desert.

370 Unit 5 • The Medieval World

SAHARA

| 2500 B.C. | 1500 | 500 | A.D. 500 | 1500 |

c. 2500 B.C.
The Sahara begins to dry up and people migrate to other parts of Africa.

c. 100 B.C.–A.D. 1500
The Bantu people slowly spread across Africa.

PREVIEW

Focus on the Main Idea
People throughout Africa have adapted to a variety of environments.

PLACES
Sahara
Atlas Mountains
Great Rift Valley
Mount Kilimanjaro

VOCABULARY
savanna

TERMS
Bantu

The Geography of Africa

You Are There
You're walking through the desert. One foot sinks into the sand and then the other. A lizard pops its head out of one of the footprints you made in the sand. It dives back in to hide from the sun. You adjust your hat to make sure your head is covered from the scorching sun. Beads of sweat pour down your back. Your clothes are soaked. You look like you've been swimming in a river. How much longer will it be to the next oasis, where you can get a cool drink of water? You feel like you've been walking for days. A few people dressed in blue garments pass you. The men are wearing veils to protect their faces from the blowing sand. All of a sudden, the wind becomes stronger, and the sky turns gray. A sandstorm is coming.

Summarize As you read, summarize the different environments in Africa.

► Tuaregs are Berber-speaking peoples who have lived in North Africa since at least 1000 B.C.

370

Practice and Extend

READING SKILL
Summarize

In the Lesson Review, students complete a graphic organizer like the one below. You may want to provide students with a copy of Transparency 6 to complete as they read the lesson.

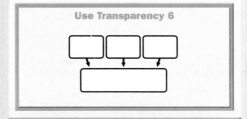
Use Transparency 6

WEB SITE
Technology

- You can look up vocabulary words by clicking on *Social Studies Library* and selecting the dictionary at **www.sfsocialstudies.com.**

- Students can learn more about current news by clicking on *Current Events* at **www.sfsocialstudies.com.**

- Explore other events that occurred on this day by clicking on *This Day in History* at **www.sfsocialstudies.com.**

Climate Zones

The desert that you just read about is in Africa, the second largest continent on Earth after Asia. There are eight climate zones in Africa. The main zones include desert, savanna, rain forest, and Mediterranean.

The desert climate zone is hot and dry. Little vegetation and few animals live in the desert. The Sahara is the largest desert in the world. It is located in northern Africa. Look at the map below to see the vast area it covers. Notice that the Atlas Mountains separate the Sahara from the Mediterranean Sea. Winds and sandstorms shape the sand dunes that cover about 25 percent of the Sahara.

South of the Sahara lies the savanna, or short, grassy plains. About half of Africa is savanna. The soil in the savanna is generally fertile.

▶ Burchell's zebras graze in the savanna grasslands of a South African nature reserve.

In areas of the savanna that are drier, people herd cattle.

Tropical rain forest biomes cover a very small area of the continent. Thick vegetation makes farming nearly impossible in this climate region.

The Mediterranean climate on the North African coast and southern tip of Africa is mild. Summers are mostly hot, while winters are generally mild and rainy. Land is fertile in some of these areas, making them suitable for agriculture.

REVIEW How are the climate zones of Africa alike and different? Compare and Contrast

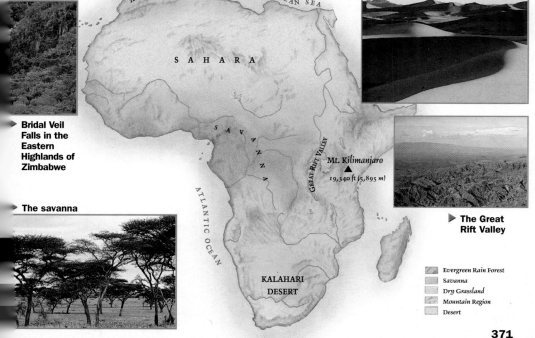

ATLAS MOUNTAINS
MEDITERRANEAN SEA
SAHARA
SAVANNA
GREAT RIFT VALLEY
Mt. Kilimanjaro
19,340 ft (5,895 m)
ATLANTIC OCEAN
KALAHARI DESERT

▶ Bridal Veil Falls in the Eastern Highlands of Zimbabwe

▶ The savanna

▶ The Sahara

▶ The Great Rift Valley

Evergreen Rain Forest
Savanna
Dry Grassland
Mountain Region
Desert

371

2 Teach and Discuss

PAGE 371

Climate Zones

Quick Summary Of the eight climate zones in Africa, the main ones include desert, savanna, rain forest, and Mediterranean.

1 Which climate zone covers about half of Africa? The savanna
Analyze Information

$ SOCIAL STUDIES STRAND Economics

2 In which two climate zones is agriculture not an important part of the economy? Why? The desert, because it is hot and dry; the rain forest, because thick vegetation makes farming nearly impossible. **Cause and Effect**

✓ **REVIEW ANSWER** Possible answer: Alike: Fertile soil in the savanna and in some areas with Mediterranean climate; desert and Mediterranean summers are hot; deserts and some savanna areas are dry; Different: Desert has little vegetation and few animals, rain forest has thick vegetation, and savanna is grassy plains; desert climate is dry and Mediterranean is warm. **Compare and Contrast**

ESL ACTIVATE PRIOR KNOWLEDGE ESL Support

Share Knowledge About Climates Find out what students already know about climates in places where they have lived or visited.

Beginning Show labeled pictures of different kinds of climates. Then have students answer *yes* or *no* to questions you ask about the climate in your region and other regions they know.

Intermediate Have students brainstorm a list of various climates in places familiar to them. Discuss conditions related to each type, helping students focus on words that help them to discuss: *humid, arid,* or *temperate.*

Advanced Have students describe a climate in another place they have lived or visited. Ask them to include information about vegetation, animals, and outdoor activities.

For additional ESL support, use Every Student Learns Guide, pp. 178–181.

FYI SOCIAL STUDIES Background

African Rain Forests
- Rain forests in Africa cover about 810,000 square miles. The largest area of rain forest stretches from the Democratic Republic of the Congo west to the Atlantic Ocean.
- Ebony and mahogany are valuable woods that grow in the rain forest.
- Animals of the African rain forests include squirrels, monkeys, wild hogs, gorillas, and chimpanzees.

Mountains and Rivers

🕐 *Quick Summary* Throughout history, people have made dangerous journeys across the mountains, deserts, plateaus, and cataracts of Africa.

③ **Why do you think people journeyed across the dangerous barriers of Africa?** Possible answer: They wanted to reach fertile land where they could grow food; traders may have wanted to exchange goods with people in other regions. **Make Inferences**

✓ **Ongoing Assessment**

| **If...** students have difficulty making inferences about why people journeyed across dangerous barriers, | **then...** point out on a map of Africa barriers such as deserts, mountains, and plateaus. Explain that people were willing to take risks to reach places where they could produce or obtain food and where they could trade for goods that they wanted. |

④ **Why are rivers and waterways important in Africa?** People use them to move trade goods from place to place. **Analyze Information**

✓ **REVIEW ANSWER** By camel caravans, rivers, seas, and oceans **Summarize**

Spread of Peoples

🕐 *Quick Summary* As the climate changed and resources were used up, people spread from West Africa to other parts of Africa.

⑤ **What tells us that the Sahara once had a different climate?** Prehistoric cave paintings and dried-up riverbeds **Main Idea and Details**

Mountains and Rivers

The climate in Africa affects the movement of people and goods. As you have read, camel caravans crossed the Sahara in northern Africa. These journeys were dangerous. Traders in the caravans faced sandstorms, high heat, and few water sources. In other parts of Africa, people faced barriers such as mountains, plateaus, and cataracts. Remember how people crossed the cataracts in ancient Egypt and Nubia?

③ In prehistoric times, a rift, or crack, may have formed in the earth, creating the 4,000-mile-long Great Rift Valley in East Africa. This fertile valley stretches across lakes, highlands, and other, smaller valleys. You can even see it from space! On one of these highlands is Mount Kilimanjaro. At 19,340 feet, it is the highest mountain in Africa.

Plateaus cover much of the interior of Africa. Many rivers flow from the plateaus to the coast. The Zambezi, Congo, and Niger are the major interior rivers in Africa. You have already read about the longest river in Africa and the world, the Nile. Many people used these rivers to move trade goods from place to place. The Red Sea and the Indian Ocean served as ways to transport goods and people to the Middle East.

④ **REVIEW** How did people and goods move throughout Africa? **Summarize**

Spread of Peoples

Over time, changes in climate caused people to migrate to other areas of Africa. For example, in ancient times, the Sahara was very different from the way it is today. It contained rivers, grassy plains, and forests. We know this because of prehistoric cave paintings and dried-up riverbeds. Many scientists believe that by about 2500 B.C., the climate began to change. Rain did not fall anymore, and the land dried out.

⑤ As the environment changed and resources were used up, people moved to the east and to the south.

▶ Mount Kilimanjaro, the highest mountain in Africa, as viewed from the Great Rift Valley. The Masai people and their herds of cattle live along the Great Rift Valley.

372

Practice and Extend

MEETING INDIVIDUAL NEEDS
Leveled Practice

Describe the Relationship Between Geography and Economics Have students describe how the geography of Africa influenced economic practices.

Easy Have students write a paragraph telling where they would prefer to live in Africa—in the Sahara or along one of the rivers. Have them explain their choice. **Reteach**

On-Level Tell students to suppose that they have just journeyed across the Sahara to the Great Rift Valley. Have them write a diary entry describing their journey and sharing their hopes of how they expect to live in their new environment. **Extend**

Challenge Have students research reference materials and online resources to learn more about the geography and economy of a specific location, such as Mozambique along the Great Rift Valley. Have them give oral presentations of their findings. **Enrich**

For a Lesson Summary, use Quick Study, p. 90.

Spread of Bantu Speakers

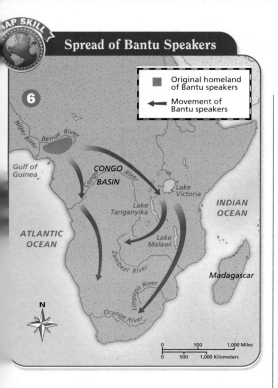

Original homeland of Bantu speakers

← Movement of Bantu speakers

⑥

Niger River
Benue River
Gulf of Guinea
CONGO BASIN
Congo River
Lake Victoria
Lake Tanganyika
INDIAN OCEAN
ATLANTIC OCEAN
Zambezi River
Lake Malawi
Madagascar
Limpopo River
Orange River

N

0   500   1,000 Miles
0   500   1,000 Kilometers

▶ About 100 B.C., Bantu speakers left the Niger-Benue area.

MAP SKILL Trace Movement on Maps *In which direction did the Bantu speakers move?*

One group of people is considered to be the ancestor of many different African groups today. It is estimated that between about 100 B.C. and A.D. 1500, people living in West Africa began to slowly spread to other parts of Africa. Linguists, or people who study languages, have traced this movement of West Africans by looking at the languages spoken in Africa. The Bantu languages are a group of languages spoken in large parts of Africa. Many of the words in these languages are similar. As the Bantu speakers traveled south, their languages spread with them. ⑦

REVIEW Why did people move to other parts of Africa? Main Idea and Details

Summarize the Lesson

- **c. 2500 B.C.** The Sahara began to dry up and people migrated to other parts of Africa.
- **c. 100 B.C.–A.D. 1500** The Bantu people slowly moved across Africa.

LESSON 1   REVIEW

Check Facts and Main Ideas

1. Summarize On a separate piece of paper, write three short sentences to form the summary below.

> The Sahara, the largest desert in the world, is located in Africa.

> Savanna covers about half of Africa.

> The Great Rift Valley is located in eastern Africa.

↓

> Africa is a diverse continent with many different physical features.

2. Describe the major climate zones of Africa.

3. What are the major rivers of Africa?

4. How did Africans adapt to their environment?

5. Critical Thinking: *Make Generalizations* Why do linguists believe that the Bantu speakers spread across Africa?

Link to ⌘ Science

Research Climate Zones Research the climate zone that you live in. Go to the library or look on the Internet to help gather information about the climate zone in which you live. Do you live in a type of climate zone that can also be found in Africa?

373

Workbook, p. 92

Lesson 1: The Geography of Africa

Directions: Decide whether each detail describes a desert, savanna, rain forest, or Mediterranean climate zone in Africa. For desert write a *D* in the blank, for savanna write an *S*, for rain forest write an *R*, and for Mediterranean write an *M*. Then answer the questions that follow. You may use your textbook.

___ 1. about half of Africa
___ 2. mostly hot summers
___ 3. thick vegetation
___ 4. hot and dry
___ 5. suitable for agriculture
___ 6. south of the Sahara
___ 7. little vegetation and few animals
___ 8. farming nearly impossible
___ 9. covers a very small area of the continent
___ 10. generally mild and rainy winters
___ 11. the Sahara

12. What made the journeys across Africa dangerous?

_____

13. Why did people migrate to other areas of Africa?

_____

Notes for Home: Your child learned how the geography of Africa affects its people.
Home Activity: Select a climate zone discussed in this chapter. With your child, compare and contrast characteristics of its climate to the climate where you live.

Also on Teacher Resources CD-ROM.

Help students locate the Bantu homelands near the confluence of the Niger and Benue Rivers.

⑥ **About how far did Bantu-speaking people migrate?** It is about 3,000 miles to the southern coast of Africa from the Niger-Benue area. Interpret Maps

MAP SKILL **Answer** South and southeast

⑦ **What was one effect of the movement of people out of West Africa?** The spread of the Bantu languages Cause and Effect

---

✓ **REVIEW ANSWER** The climate had changed and people had used up important food and fuel resources. Main Idea and Details

③ Close and Assess

Summarize the Lesson

Read the time line with students. Then discuss the geography and climate of the areas of Africa to which the Bantu people began to spread.

✓ **LESSON 1   REVIEW**

1. Summarize For possible answers, see the reduced pupil page.

2. Desert: hot, dry, little vegetation, few animals; Savanna: covers almost half of Africa, fertile soil, grassy plains for raising cattle; Rain forest: covers less of Africa than other zones, thick vegetation makes farming nearly impossible; Mediterranean: mild, rainy, fertile soil

3. Zambezi, Congo, Niger, and Nile

4. By migrating when climates changed or when resources were used up.

5. Critical Thinking: *Make Generalizations* Because many of the words in these languages are similar across Africa

Link to ⌘ Science

Students might make a climate zone map of the United States, highlighting the climate zone in which they live, and including keys that list statistics about the region's climate.

West African Kingdoms

Objectives

- Explain how gold and trade made the kingdoms and empires of West Africa wealthy.

- Explain the role of the empire of Ghana in promoting the movement of trade goods across the Sahara.

- Explain who Mansa Musa was and his significance in medieval African history.

- Explain how the West African kingdoms were crossroads for trade.

- Explain how and why European map makers included Mali on maps after the pilgrimage of Mansa Musa.

Vocabulary

griot, p. 376

Resources

- Workbook, p. 93
- Transparency 6
- Every Student Learns Guide, pp. 182–185
- Quick Study, pp. 92–93

Quick Teaching Plan

If time is short, have students create fact sheets for each West African empire described as they read Lesson 2.

1 Introduce and Motivate

Preview Ask students to tell about a leader they have learned about and admire. Have them give reasons for their choice.

You Are There Show students a map of Africa and Asia to help them understand how far Mansa Musa and his followers traveled from West Africa to Mecca. Ask students to tell what effect they think Mansa Musa's caravan might have had on people in the towns through which it passed.

LESSON 2

800	1000	1200	1400	1600

A.D. 900 Height of the empire of Ghana

1324 Mansa Musa sets out on a pilgrimage to Mecca.

1591 Empire of Songhai declines.

Koumbi •   Timbuktu • Gao
Jenne-jenno •

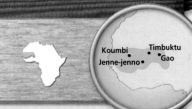

West African Kingdoms

PREVIEW

Focus on the Main Idea
Many kingdoms developed in the savanna and forested areas of West Africa.

PLACES
Ghana
Koumbi
Mali
Timbuktu
Jenne-jenno
Gao

PEOPLE
Sumanguru
Sundiata
Mansa Musa
Sonni Ali

VOCABULARY
griot

You Are There You're one of thousands of people traveling with your king, Mansa Musa. He has brought you along on his pilgrimage to Mecca. You travel for many days across the Sahara before reaching Egypt. Mansa Musa pulls out some of the hundreds of pounds of gold that he has brought on the journey. The people in Cairo shake their heads. All this gold means that gold prices will be lowered for years. The king buys the finest clothing for his top officials. Mansa Musa is a generous king. You have even heard that he gives handfuls of gold dust to beggars who come up to him.

As you leave the city, you hear praise singers honoring your king. They sing of his generosity and kindness.

Summarize As you read, summarize the details about the West African kingdoms.

▶ **This Spanish map from the fourteenth century shows Mansa Musa (seated, wearing a crown) during his pilgrimage to Mecca, which began in 1324.**

374

Practice and Extend

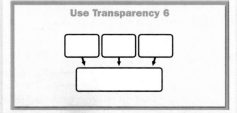

READING SKILL
Summarize

In the Lesson Review, students complete a graphic organizer like the one below. You may want to provide students with a copy of Transparency 6 to complete as they read the lesson.

Use Transparency 6

WEB SITE
Technology

- You can look up vocabulary words by clicking on *Social Studies Library* and selecting the dictionary at **www.sfsocialstudies.com.**

- Students can learn more about current news by clicking on *Current Events* at **www.sfsocialstudies.com.**

- Explore other events that occurred on this day by clicking on *This Day in History* at **www.sfsocialstudies.com.**

Ghana

Gold was a valuable resource to the empires of West Africa. It made them very wealthy and brought in trade goods from other lands. The ancient kingdom of **Ghana** was so well known that knowledge of its trade in gold had reached as far as Baghdad (modern Iraq) by the eighth century. (The kingdom of Ghana is not to be confused with the present-day country of Ghana in Africa.)

Most of what is known about Ghana comes from the Arabs, who wrote down what they heard about the kingdom from traders and travelers. Ghana had existed since about A.D. 300. It was founded by the Soninke (suhn IHN kay) people who began to act as middlemen for the gold that was mined to the south of Ghana.

People in Ghana probably farmed, fished, and herded cattle. They produced many goods to trade with others. Berber peoples in North Africa led traders across the Sahara. Thieves often attacked camel caravans. But the Berbers still tried to keep the thieves away so that the trade routes would be safe.

Safe trade routes meant that Ghana's capital, **Koumbi,** remained a major center of trade. By the late 900s, Ghana was thriving and had become a great trading empire.

▶ This person is filling shallow pits with salt water. Once the salt water has evaporated, a cake of dried salt will be retrieved from the pits.

▶ These bars of salt are tied together and ready to take to the market.

Its location between the salt mines in the Sahara and the gold fields in Wangara made the middlemen wealthy and turned Ghana into an empire. Traders in Ghana took gold, copper, and palm oil from the south. From the north, they took salt, glass, and ceramics. Taxes on these goods added more wealth to the empire.

Along with trade goods and wealth came ideas and religion that were brought by Muslim traders. Many of the Soninke people converted to Islam. They also adopted the Arabic system of writing. However, beginning in the 1000s, the Soninke people began to lose control of the empire. Different groups fought for political power. By 1203 King **Sumanguru** defeated the Soninke king and controlled Koumbi. To learn more about Sumanguru, see page 379.

REVIEW How long did the Soninke have control of the empire of Ghana? ⟳ Sequence

375

EXTEND LANGUAGE
ESL Support

Examine Word Meanings Help students understand the term *middleman*.

Beginning Draw three squares on the chalkboard and have students identify the middle one. Then have two students, each holding a different kind of object, stand about ten feet apart. Have another student stand between them to demonstrate the role of the *middleman* in trading the objects.

Intermediate Display a map showing the locations of the Sahara, Ghana, and Wangara. Discuss why being in the middle might be beneficial to Ghana. Ask what problems traders from the Sahara and Wangara might have had if they could not trade in Ghana.

Advanced Have students create a story in which a *middleman* is able to solve a problem or make a situation easier. Have students relate their stories to the text.

For additional ESL support, use Every Student Learns Guide, pp. 182–185.

2 Teach and Discuss

PAGE 375

Ghana

⏱ **Quick Summary** Ghana, a major center of the gold trade, was a wealthy and powerful empire.

🧩 **Problem Solving**

❶ **What problem would Ghana have had if the Berbers had not made the trade routes safe?** Thieves would have stolen gold and other trade goods. People would not have come to trade in Ghana, and it would not have become as wealthy or powerful as it did. **Solve Problems**

💲 **SOCIAL STUDIES STRAND**
Economics

Explain to students that some African traders could use salt as a medium of exchange, like money, because it was so scarce. It was also valuable because it could be used for so many purposes. Not only is salt needed by the human body, but it was also used as a cleanser, to set dyes in fabric, to soften leather, and as a bleaching agent.

❷ **How did Ghana's location help it become a center for trade?** Its location between the salt mines in the Sahara and the gold fields in Wangara made traders natural middlemen in the trading that occurred between these two regions. **Main Idea and Details**

✓ **Ongoing Assessment**

If... students have difficulty understanding why Ghana thrived as a center for trade, **then...** explain that Ghana did not produce all the goods it traded; traders in Ghana served as go-betweens to facilitate trade between regions to the north and south.

✓ **REVIEW ANSWER** For about 900 years ⟳ Sequence

Mali

 **Quick Summary** Sundiata helped Mali become one of the greatest trading kingdoms in Africa, and Mansa Musa's pilgrimage to Mecca drew European attention to Mali's resources.

Test Talk

Locate Key Words in the Question

3 **What was the main source of wealth in Mali?** Have students turn the question into a statement. Students should use the key words *main source* and *wealth* in a sentence that begins "I need to find out. . . ." Trade
Main Idea and Details

4 **About how long did it take Mali to become the most powerful empire in Africa?** About 65 years **Sequence**

Literature and Social Studies

Have students read the introduction and excerpt from *The Royal Kingdoms of Ghana, Mali, and Songhay.*

5 **What did Sundiata hope to accomplish by sending his sons and daughters to live with other rulers?** Possible answer: He hoped to prevent future wars. **Make Inferences**

Mali

West Africa remained under the control of various smaller states until A.D. 1235. In that year, **Sundiata** defeated King Sumanguru at the Battle of Kirina and established the empire of **Mali.** Read more about Sundiata in the biography on page 379. We know about Sundiata's life because of oral stories that are still told today by griots (GREE oats). **Griots** are professional storytellers.

The empire of Mali was expanded to include more land than had been controlled by the empire of Ghana. People in Mali grew crops such as rice, onions, grains, and yams. They also grew cotton. Although Mali had a strong agricultural economy, it relied on trade for wealth. New discoveries of gold along the Niger River made Mali wealthy. By 1300 Mali had become the most powerful empire in West Africa.

Perhaps the greatest king of Mali to follow Sundiata was his grandson, **Mansa Musa.** He was a strong Muslim ruler. Many people converted to Islam under his rule.

Mansa Musa is best known for his pilgrimage to Mecca. He took with him thousands of people, hundreds of pounds of gold, dozens of camels, and other supplies. Along the way he stopped in Egypt. His wealth, intelligence, and generosity made a lasting impression on Egyptian writers.

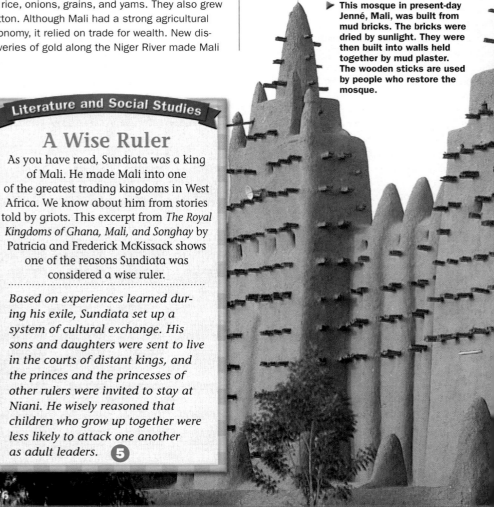

▶ This mosque in present-day Jenné, Mali, was built from mud bricks. The bricks were dried by sunlight. They were then built into walls held together by mud plaster. The wooden sticks are used by people who restore the mosque.

Literature and Social Studies

A Wise Ruler

As you have read, Sundiata was a king of Mali. He made Mali into one of the greatest trading kingdoms in West Africa. We know about him from stories told by griots. This excerpt from *The Royal Kingdoms of Ghana, Mali, and Songhay* by Patricia and Frederick McKissack shows one of the reasons Sundiata was considered a wise ruler.

Based on experiences learned during his exile, Sundiata set up a system of cultural exchange. His sons and daughters were sent to live in the courts of distant kings, and the princes and the princesses of other rulers were invited to stay at Niani. He wisely reasoned that children who grow up together were less likely to attack one another as adult leaders. **5**

376

Practice and Extend

 SOCIAL STUDIES STRAND
Culture

Griots

- Before West Africans had a written language, griots preserved West African culture by traveling from village to village telling stories. Their job was to keep an oral record of the traditions of their societies and to entertain people with songs and tales.

- Among the instruments griots used while telling their tales were *shekeres,* gourds that rattle when shaken, and *koras* and *halams,* which were various types of lutes or early guitars.

 MEETING INDIVIDUAL NEEDS
Leveled Practice

Act as a Griot Have groups of students assume the roles of griots and present an African tale orally to the class.

Easy Have students work in small groups to create short oral summaries of the story about Sundiata on p. 376. **Reteach**

On-Level Have students create detailed oral summaries of the story about Sundiata on p. 376. Students should describe Sundiata's feelings about sending his children away and an incident or two that might have happened to the children while they were living at distant courts. **Extend**

Challenge Have small groups of students use the library or online resources to find an African folktale of their choice, which they will then present orally to the class. Students should convey both the plot and specific details of the tale in their presentations. **Enrich**

For a Lesson Summary, use Quick Study, p. 92.

On his return from Mecca, Mansa Musa brought back an Arab architect who built new mosques in **Timbuktu,** one of the major trading cities in Mali. He also brought with him Arab scholars to teach Muslim beliefs and scholarship.

Mansa Musa's pilgrimage to Mecca caught the attention of European mapmakers. The Europeans began to take an interest in the gold and other resources Mali had to offer.

REVIEW What is most significant about the empire of Mali? **Summarize**

Jenne-jenno

Jenne-jenno was an ancient city located southwest of Timbuktu on the Niger River. It was the oldest known city in sub-Saharan Africa. People first settled there about 200 B.C.

The people of Jenne-jenno fished, kept live-stock, and grew crops such as rice and sorghum. Archaeologists believe that the people of Jenne-jenno traded with other peoples long before the empire of Mali did.

During the height of the empire of Mali, trade goods were brought by land to Jenne-jenno from the south and west. From Jenne-jenno the trade goods would be shipped up river to Timbuktu.

After A.D. 1200, the city of Jenne-jenno started to weaken. It was completely abandoned by about 1400. No one is certain why the people left. However, some believe that they wanted to live in the newer city of Jenné, which was just next door.

REVIEW Why is Jenne-jenno considered an important city in ancient West Africa? **Main Idea and Details**

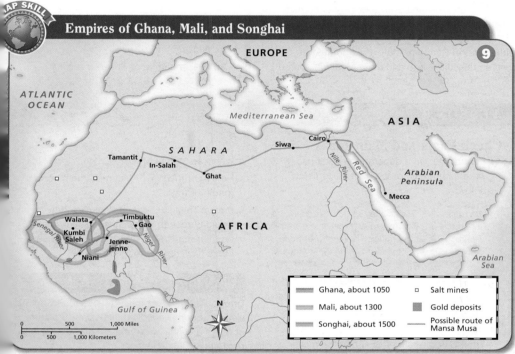

MAP SKILL Empires of Ghana, Mali, and Songhai

Legend:
- Ghana, about 1050
- Mali, about 1300
- Songhai, about 1500
- Salt mines
- Gold deposits
- Possible route of Mansa Musa

▶ In 1324 Mansa Musa set out on his pilgrimage to Mecca.

MAP SKILL Use Routes *Describe the route Mansa Musa took on his pilgrimage to Mecca.*

377

---

6 **What did Mansa Musa bring back from his pilgrimage to Mecca?** An Arab architect who built mosques in Timbuktu and Arab scholars to teach Muslim beliefs and scholarship **Main Idea and Details**

7 **What was likely to happen when Europeans took an interest in Mali's resources?** Possible answer: Europeans would send traders to buy gold and other resources from Mali. **Predict**

✓ **REVIEW ANSWER** Trade, which brought Islam, wealth, and attention to the empire **Summarize**

PAGE 377

Jenne-jenno

Quick Summary Jenne-jenno was an ancient city along Mali's trade route.

8 **What contribution did Jenne-jenno make to the Mali Empire?** It provided a place for traded goods to be brought and then shipped by river to Timbuktu in Mali. **Analyze Information**

✓ **REVIEW ANSWER** It is the oldest known city in sub-Saharan Africa. Its people traded with other peoples long before the rise of the empire of Mali. It became an important point along Mali's trade route. **Main Idea and Details**

MAP SKILL Empires of Ghana, Mali, and Songhai

Have students compare the Ghana, Mali, and Songhai Empires.

9 **In what direction would you travel to go from the region of salt mines to the region of gold deposits?** South, southeast, or southwest **Interpret Maps**

MAP SKILL **Answer** Mansa Musa traveled generally northeast, southeast, northeast again, and finally southeast to Mecca.

SOCIAL STUDIES
Background

The Djingareyber Mosque
- The Djingareyber Mosque in Timbuktu is one of many built by Mansa Musa and the architect he brought back from Mecca, Abu Ishap-Es-Saheli Altouwaidjin. This mosque is built mostly of earth mixed with materials such as straw and wood.

In 1853, the German explorer Heinrich Barth was still able to see the date 1327 and the name Kankan Moussa (meaning Mansa Musa) on the mosque.

MEETING INDIVIDUAL NEEDS
Learning Styles

Describe the Goods of Africa
Using their individual learning styles, students review pp. 375–377 to list and describe goods available in Africa.

Musical Learning Have students write and present short songs about goods available in Africa.

Visual Learning Have students draw and label pictures of goods available in Africa.

Songhai

⏱ *Quick Summary* The Songhai Empire was larger than Ghana or Mali, but it lasted only from about 1464 to 1591.

⑩ Where and how did the Songhai Empire begin? It began at the city of Gao, which was controlled by Mali in the early 1300s. About 1375, the Songhai people refused to pay tribute to Mali, and by 1464 they began taking over the territory around them.
Main Idea and Details

✓ **REVIEW ANSWER** Songhai became an even bigger center for learning than Ghana and Mali, but it did not last as long. Sonni Ali divided the land into provinces and had governors oversee them; he created a professional army to protect his trade. **Compare and Contrast**

③ Close and Assess

Summarize the Lesson

Tell students to examine the vertical time line. Ask them to describe the cause of each event listed.

✓ **LESSON 2   REVIEW**

1. **Summarize** For possible answers, see the reduced pupil page.

2. Its location between salt mines and gold fields made Ghana and its capital a major center of trade.

3. King of Mali; he made a famous pilgrimage to Mecca.

4. West African kingdoms helped traders by maintaining safe roads, providing shipping, and serving as receivers of trade goods.

5. **Critical Thinking:** *Make Inferences* Mali was a wealthy trading kingdom; Europeans began to take an interest in the gold and other resources that Mali had to offer.

Link to  **Art**

Have students reread *You Are There* on p. 374 to recall details about Musa's visit to Cairo.

Songhai

Along the Niger River lived a group of farmers, traders, and warriors called the Songhai. The Songhai people had fought to remain independent from the empire of Mali. The eastern border of the empire of Songhai began at the city of **Gao** (GOW), east of Timbuktu. Gao was under the control of Mali during the rule of Mansa Musa. At first the city was dominated by Mali. However, in about 1375, the Songhai refused to pay tribute to Mali. By about 1464, they began
⑩ taking over the territory around them.

Under King **Sonni Ali,** Songhai became an even bigger center of trade and learning than Mali had been. Sonni Ali made many changes to the territory he controlled. He divided the land into provinces and had governors oversee them. He created a professional army and navy to protect his kingdom and trade.

While the empire of Songhai was larger than either that of Ghana or Mali, it did not last as long as they did. More and more Muslims poured

▶ **This gold Moroccan coin dates from the empire of Songhai.**

into Gao, Songhai's capital. Fighting among different groups soon led to some states leaving the empire. However, a threat from the north ended the last great empire of West Africa. In 1591 Songhai was attacked by Moroccans from North Africa. The Moroccans were armed with guns. This new form of technology proved successful, and the empire of Songhai was defeated.

REVIEW How was the empire of Songhai different from the empires of Ghana and Mali? **Compare and Contrast**

Summarize the Lesson

● **A.D. 900** Height of the empire of Ghana.

┌ **1324** Mansa Musa made a pilgrimage to Mecca.

└ **1591** The empire of Songhai declined.

LESSON 2 ▶ REVIEW

Check Facts and Main Ideas

1. **Summarize** On a separate piece of paper, write a summary of the sentences listed below.

Trade made Ghana a wealthy empire.	Mali traded with its great quantities of gold.	Songhai became a great center of trade in West Africa.

↓

Trade made the empires of Ghana, Mali, and Songhai wealthy.

2. What was the role of Ghana in the movement of trade goods across the Sahara?

3. Who was Mansa Musa?

4. How were the West African kingdoms crossroads for trade?

5. **Critical Thinking:** *Make Inferences* Why would European mapmakers include Mali on their maps after hearing about Mansa Musa's pilgrimage to Mecca?

Link to **Art**

Draw a Picture What might Mansa Musa's visit to Cairo have looked like? Draw a picture or make a collage from the details you have read about in this lesson.

Practice and Extend

CURRICULUM CONNECTION Math

West African Kingdoms

● Have students identify the years of the beginning and the end of the empires of Ghana, Mali, and Songhai.

● Have them calculate how long each empire lasted. (Ghana: 300–1203, 903 years; Mali: 1235–1464, 229 years; Songhai: 1464–1591, 127 years)

Workbook, p. 93

Lesson 2: West African Kingdoms

Ghana, Mali, and Songhai were wealthy kingdoms in West Africa.
Directions: Complete the outline with information from this lesson about these empires. You may use your textbook.

I. Ghana
  A. People
    1. Religion of _____
    2. Adopted Arabic system of _____
  B. Economy and Trade
    1. _____ for a living
    2. Capital city _____ major center of trade
  C. Political Rule
    1. Founded by _____ who _____ empire by 1203
II. Mali
  A. People
    1. An Arab _____ built mosques, and _____ brought Muslim learning
    2. _____ oldest known city in sub-Saharan Africa; 200 B.C. to A.D. 1400
  B. Economy and Trade
    1. Strong _____ economy, but relied on _____ for wealth
  C. Political Rule
    1. _____ greatest king, took pilgrimage to _____
III. Songhai
  A. People
    1. _____ among different Muslim groups contributed to end of empire
  B. Economy and Trade
    1. Bigger center of _____ than Mali
  C. Political Rule
    1. _____ important king who divided land into _____
    2. Professional _____ protected kingdom, defeated by _____

Notes for Home: Your child learned about three empires of West Africa.
Home Activity: With your child, review the information in this outline. Together, create a Venn diagram to compare and contrast the empires of Ghana, Mali, and Songhai.

Also on Teacher Resources CD-ROM.

Sundiata

reigned about A.D. 1235–1255

Most information about Sundiata can be found in oral stories that are still told today by griots, or storytellers. They say that Sundiata was destined to be king. However, Sundiata was sick as a child. He could not speak or walk until he was at least seven years old.

Griots also tell us that the enemy of Sundiata's father was Sumanguru, who had conquered the Kingdom of Kangaba and killed all 11 of Sundiata's brothers. Sundiata outgrew his childhood illness and organized a group of men to rise up against Sumanguru.

According to the griots, at the Battle of Kirina, about 1235, Sundiata fought against Sumanguru. He wanted revenge. Sundiata declared:

> *"I am the rain that extinguishes the cinder;*
> *I am the boisterous [violent] torrent [outburst]*
> *that will carry you off."* ❶

Sundiata was successful and defeated Sumanguru.

Griots say that Sundiata worked to create a stable political structure. The political structure he created lasted hundreds of years after his reign.

After 1240 he moved the capital of his empire to Niani (later known as Mali), which was between the Sankarani and Niger rivers. This site attracted many merchants. It soon ❷ became a very important trading point for the entire Sudan region. Sundiata converted to Islam but continued ❸ to allow his people to practice their own religion.

According to legend, Sundiata had special powers. He used these powers to defeat Sumanguru at the Battle of Kirina.

BIOFACT

Learn from Biographies

Sundiata ruled over many different people when he created the empire of Mali. What advantage was there in allowing people to practice their own religion?

For more information, go online to *Meet the People* at **www.sfsocialstudies.com**.

379

Sundiata

Objective

- Identify the accomplishments of significant individuals, including Sundiata.

1 Introduce and Motivate

Preview Ask students to recall what they read about Sundiata on p. 376. Tell students they will learn how Sundiata created an empire that lasted hundreds of years.

Ask why it is important to know about the contributions of past leaders. (Possible answer: We can see how their ideas and contributions are still important in present-day government.)

2 Teach and Discuss

Primary Source

❶ **What message did Sundiata want to send in his declaration?** He wanted Sumanguru to know he would defeat him in battle. **Analyze Primary Sources**

❷ **Why did the capital of the empire attract many merchants?** Possible answer: Because it was located between two rivers, which were used to transport goods **Cause and Effect**

❸ **What qualities do you think Sundiata had as emperor? Explain.** Possible answer: Tolerant, wise, powerful; he allowed his people to practice their own religion and created an empire that lasted hundreds of years **Draw Conclusions**

3 Close and Assess

Learn from Biographies Answer

Possible answer: It promoted tolerance and unity among different peoples. People were less likely to revolt if they were allowed to practice their own religions.

WEB SITE
Technology

Students can find out more about Sundiata by clicking on *Meet the People* at **www.sfsocialstudies.com**.

CURRICULUM CONNECTION
Writing

Writing Metaphors

- Remind students that a metaphor is a comparison that does not use the words *like* or *as*.
- Review the metaphors used by Sundiata in his declaration.
- Have students write additional metaphors Sundiata might have used to represent other actions of his life.
- Have students read their metaphors aloud.

East, Central, and Southern Africa

Objectives

- Explain the history and origin of Ethiopia.

- List and describe the goods that were traded in and out of east, central, and southern Africa.

- Compare and contrast the civilizations that existed in east, central, and southern Africa.

- Explain how the civilizations of east, central, and southern Africa were influenced by other civilizations in the Indian Ocean trade network.

- Explain how international trade affected the east, central, and southern regions of Africa.

Vocabulary

Swahili, p. 383; **oba,** p. 384

Resources

- Workbook, p. 94
- Transparency 6
- Every Student Learns Guide, pp. 186–189
- Quick Study, pp. 94–95

Quick Teaching Plan

If time is short, have students create time lines showing the sequence of events in Lesson 3 as they read it independently.

1 Introduce and Motivate

Preview To activate prior knowledge, ask students to describe how the empires of west Africa thrived and grew. Tell them that in lesson 3 they will learn how empires developed in east, central, and southern Africa.

You Are There The stone enclosures described here are in Great Zimbabwe. Have students tell about a time when they visited an exciting new place. What did they notice about this place?

LESSON 3

300   600   900   1200   1500

A.D. 350
The kingdom of Axum invades the former Kush capital of Meroë.

1185–1225
Lalibela builds 11 rock churches in Ethiopia.

1450
Stone enclosures of Great Zimbabwe are completed.

AXUM (ETHIOPIA)
BENIN
Kilwa
Great Zimbabwe • Sofala

PREVIEW

Focus on the Main Idea
Trading empires developed in eastern, central, and southern Africa that interacted with Arabia, India, and China.

PLACES
Axum
Ethiopia
Adefa
Sofala
Kilwa
Great Zimbabwe
Benin

PEOPLE
Ezana
Lalibela

VOCABULARY
Swahili
oba

TERMS
Zagwe dynasty
Solomonid dynasty

▶ These bronze bangle bracelets, discovered at Great Zimbabwe, are probably from India.

380

East, Central, and Southern Africa

You Are There This is the first time your father has taken you on one of his many travels. Your father is a merchant trader. He travels between Sofala and the state of Great Zimbabwe to trade gold and ivory for trade goods such as ceramics from India and China. You want to see for yourself the amazing place he has been describing to you. When you arrive, you see the stone enclosures that rise more than 30 feet in the air. As you take a closer look, you realize that nothing is holding the stones together. They have been cut to fit tightly together, like a giant jigsaw puzzle.

You hear shouts. People are telling you and others in the crowd that you must leave the area because the king is coming. You have heard from your father that the king is a mysterious and powerful person. Most people never get to see him. Your father tells you that the gold and ivory have been loaded and it is time to go. Even after walking several miles, you are still able to see the stone enclosures.

Summarize As you read, summarize information about the civilizations that developed in eastern, central, and southern Africa.

Practice and Extend

READING SKILL
Summarize

In the Lesson Review, students complete a graphic organizer like the one below. You may want to provide students with a copy of Transparency 6 to complete as they read the lesson.

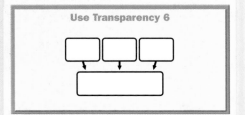

Use Transparency 6

WEB SITE
Technology

- You can look up vocabulary words by clicking on *Social Studies Library* and selecting the dictionary at **www.sfsocialstudies.com.**

- Students can learn more about current news by clicking on *Current Events* at **www.sfsocialstudies.com.**

- Explore other events that occurred on this day by clicking on *This Day in History* at **www.sfsocialstudies.com.**

East Africa

What were these great stone enclosures, or walls? They were constructed by people who began to live in eastern Africa about A.D. 300. These people interacted with people living in the trading city-states that arose along the eastern coast of Africa.

In about 350, the iron-rich trade center of Meroë, which you read about in Unit 2, was invaded by forces from the kingdom of **Axum** in the Ethiopian highlands. Axum had begun as a trading settlement in the sixth century B.C. Over time, it had grown into a powerful empire.

Axum exported ivory, frankincense, and myrrh to Greece and Rome. Both myrrh and frankincense were made from the resin of trees that grew in the mountainous areas of Axum. Craftworkers also created luxury goods from

brass, copper, and crystal. In exchange for these trade goods, Axum received cloth, jewelry, metals, and steel, which was used to make weapons. Axum traders bartered as a means for the exchange of trade goods.

Christian kingdoms existed in northeastern Africa since about 330, when the king of Axum, **Ezana,** converted to Christianity. To the northwest of Axum were the Christian kingdoms of Noba and Makurra, located between the first and fifth cataracts of the Nile River. The people in these kingdoms converted to Christianity between 500 and 650. After Arabs invaded Egypt in the seventh century, the kingdoms continued to exist.

Arab invasions did not destroy Axum. But changing climatic conditions and trade routes that moved away from the Red Sea forced people to abandon Axum. As a result, many people moved inland.

REVIEW Did Meroë fall before or after Axum became a trading settlement? ⟳ Sequence

▶ The kings of Axum commemorated their glories with stone stelae, or ceremonial stone slabs, sometimes up to 100 feet high, which were built above underground royal tombs. These stone towers could also have been built as symbols of power.

▶ The kings of Axum wore elaborate crowns such as this one.

381

East Africa

🕐 *Quick Summary* Located on the coast of the Red Sea, Axum became a powerful trading empire. Changes in climate and trade routes eventually forced people to leave Axum and move inland.

1 **What advantages did Axum have that enabled it to become a powerful empire?** Possible answer: Good location for trade; exported ivory, frankincense, and myrrh; made luxury goods from brass, copper, and glass crystal **Main Idea and Details**

2 **What effect do you think the loss of trade routes might eventually have on Axum? Why?** Possible answer: Since Axum depended on trade for its power and wealth, losing the trade routes might eventually mean the end of the empire. **Hypothesize**

✓ **Ongoing Assessment**

If... students do not recognize the importance of the trade routes,	**then...** have them locate Axum on a map and ask guiding questions, such as *Where is Axum in relation to the Red Sea? Why was trade so important to Axum? What might happen if the people of Axum can no longer trade?*

✓ **REVIEW ANSWER** After ⟳ Sequence

CURRICULUM CONNECTION
Science

Research and Report on Irrigation

Point out that the people of Axum used irrigation to water their crops. Have several partners or small groups research and report on different aspects of irrigation.

• List the following topics on the board: *History of Irrigation, Different Ways to Irrigate,* and *Advantages and Disadvantages of Irrigation.*

• Have each pair or small group of students choose one topic on which to do research and report.

• Have students present their reports to the class.

• Some students may be interested in building and displaying models to demonstrate the irrigation process.

Ethiopia

> *Quick Summary* In about 1150, Ethiopia replaced the Axum civilization, and Christianity was firmly established under the Zagwe dynasty.

3 **Compare and contrast the religion of the Zagwe dynasty to those of Sundiata, Mansa Musa, and Ezana.** Sundiata and Mansa Musa were followers of Islam. Ezana and the rulers of the Zagwe dynasty were Christians. **Compare and Contrast**

Test Talk

Locate Key Words in the Text

4 **Why did the Solomonid king move so frequently?** Have students skim the text to locate key words such as *king, move,* and *frequently;* remind them that they may find synonyms for some key words, such as *often* for *frequently.* Moving enabled the king to stay in contact with all the regions in the kingdom, so people would be more loyal to him. **Cause and Effect**

5 **Do you think constantly moving the capital is an idea that could be practiced in the United States today? Why or why not?** Possible answers: No, the government is too large; Yes, with the technological advances available today, government business can be done from anywhere. **Express Ideas**

✓ **REVIEW ANSWER** He was the king of Ethiopia during the Zagwe dynasty. He built 11 churches made of rock to show his faith and gain respect for his leadership. **Main Idea and Details**

Ethiopia

3 **Ethiopia** replaced the Axum civilization. About 1150 a new dynasty, the **Zagwe dynasty,** took the throne from the old line of Axumite kings. Christianity became firmly established in Ethiopia under the Zagwe. The capital was moved to **Adefa** on the central highlands.

A Zagwe king, **Lalibela,** ruled from about 1185 to 1225. During his rule, he had 11 churches built out of solid rock at the new capital. He built these churches to show his faith and to gain respect for his leadership. The largest church, called Savior of the World, is more than 100 feet long, 75 feet wide, and 35 feet high.

In 1270 the Zagwe dynasty was taken over by the **Solomonid dynasty** (SAW loh moh nihd).

▶ A modern painting of King Lalibela, who promoted Eastern Orthodox Christianity in his kingdom

Private Collection/Bridgeman Art Library Int'l. Ltd. (U.S.)

The Solomonid rulers claimed to be descendants of the original rulers of ancient Axum. Their rule of Ethiopia would last until 1974.

The Solomonids stopped building great stone churches and palaces in Ethiopia. The Solomonid kings and their royal courts, which included government and military officials, instead began to live in more modest structures. One result of this was that there was no longer a permanent capital.

The king and his court moved as often as two or three times a year. This was how the king could stay in close contact with all of the regions in the kingdom. As a result, people of the kingdom were more loyal to their king. However, the king's royal court included so many people that every time they moved into a region, they would use up all of its food and fuel supplies.

REVIEW Who was Lalibela and what did he do? **Main Idea and Details**

▶ The rooftop of the church of St. George, one of the churches carved out of solid rock during the rule of King Lalibela

382

Practice and Extend

ESL **BUILD BACKGROUND**
ESL Support

Use Visuals Help build background for learning about Ethiopia's history. Show students a map of Africa with Ethiopia and the capital, Adefa, labeled; a photo or drawing of a church in Adefa; and a drawing of a crown.

Beginning Have students use the visuals mentioned above as clues to answer simple questions, such as *In what part of Africa is Ethiopa? What was its capital city? What kinds of buildings were built there? What kinds of leaders did it have?*

Intermediate Based on the visual clues presented, have students say and write anything they can about Ethiopia.

Advanced Have students use the visual clues to write about Ethiopia. Then have them refer to another source, such as an encyclopedia, to find one or two facts about Ethiopia's history to share with the group.

For additional ESL support, use Every Student Learns Guide, pp. 186–189.

African Trade Routes

By land and sea, the Indian Ocean trade network exchanged goods, language, and culture.

MAP SKILL Use a Historical Map *Where were the trading cities located on sea routes?*

Kilwa

As Islam spread in the seventh and eighth centuries, cities along the eastern coast of Africa became more involved in Indian Ocean trade. At first this trade involved northern cities. By the ninth century, more southern cities such as **Sofala** and **Kilwa** were involved in the gold and ivory trade. In 1331 Ibn Battuta visited Kilwa and described its elegance. One Arab trader remarked of Kilwa that:

> *"Their mosques are very strongly constructed of wood. . . it is one of the most beautiful and well-constructed towns in the world."*

The Indian Ocean trade network extended from East Africa to India and China, as well as to Arabia. Arabs settled in East African coastal cities such as Mombasa. Muslim and East African culture mixed, creating a **Swahili** culture and language. *Swahili* is the Arabic word for "people of the coast." Both Arabic and Swahili were used as trading languages to help more traders communicate.

The Portuguese began to attack Kilwa and Mombasa in the early 1500s. They wanted control of Indian Ocean trade. The attacks were successful, but Swahili groups again gained control of many ports along the coast.

REVIEW How did Arab settlement in East African coastal cities affect language and culture? *Cause and Effect*

383

Kilwa

Quick Summary Southern cities such as Kilwa became involved in the Indian Ocean trade. Muslim and East African cultures blended, creating a Swahili culture and language.

African Trade Routes

Have students note the extent of the trade routes.

6 **Through which seas did African trade routes pass?** The Red, Arabian, and South China Seas **Interpret Maps**

MAP SKILL **Answer** Along the coasts of Africa, Arabia, and India.

Primary Source

Cited in *African Civilization Revisited*, by Basil Davidson

7 **What religion was practiced in Kilwa? How can you tell?** Islam; the quotation mentions mosques.
Analyze Primary Sources

8 **Why do you think the Portuguese lost control of the trade network?** Possible answer: The Swahili groups may have united and overpowered them.
Draw Conclusions

✓ **REVIEW ANSWER** The mix of Arab and East African languages and cultures eventually created the Swahili culture and language. **Cause and Effect**

MEETING INDIVIDUAL NEEDS
Leveled Practice

Identify Results of Trade Have students identify how trade affected East Africa.

Easy List the following possible effects on the chalkboard: *became powerful and rich, developed new language, created new cultures, climate changed,* and *became more isolated.* Have students tell whether or not each effect was the result of trade. **Reteach**

On-Level List the following headings on the board: *Religion, Culture, Language, Wealth.* Have students brainstorm and list the effects trade had on each of these in East Africa. **Extend**

Challenge Ask students to use books and online resources to find out more about Kilwa. Have students describe how it grew after the ninth century when it became involved in the gold and ivory trade. **Enrich**

For a Lesson Summary, use Quick Study, p. 94.

SOCIAL STUDIES
Background

Ethiopian Churches

- Some of the churches Lalibela built were below ground level.
- Tunnels and passageways were built that connected the churches to each other.
- It is said that the Church of St. George at Lalibela still has St. George's horse's hoof print in its courtyard.

Great Zimbabwe

⏱ *Quick Summary* Great Zimbabwe reached its height about 1400. It was abandoned about 1450 and eventually the area was taken over by the Portuguese.

⑨ Summarize how Great Zimbabwe amassed most of its wealth. It taxed trade goods such as gold and ivory. **Summarize**

⑩ Why did the people of Zimbabwe have trouble growing crops around 1450? Possible answer: They probably exhausted the nutrients in the soil so that it was no longer fertile. **Main idea and Details**

✓ **REVIEW ANSWER** Great Zimbabwe was a trading kingdom with stone enclosures built by the Shona people between 1200 and 1450. **Summarize**

Benin

⏱ *Quick Summary* Benin was a forest kingdom that by 1500 grew into a powerful empire through trade. Benin was known for its great art.

⑪ How did the physical features and climate of Benin affect people's activities? It was a forest region that had fertile soil and received lots of rain, so people could grow crops such as yams and cotton. **Apply Information**

Great Zimbabwe

The stone enclosures of **Great Zimbabwe** were built by the Shona people between 1200 and 1450. *Zimbabwe* means "houses of stone" in the Shona language. The enclosures were not built for defense but to show the power and importance of the king.

Like Kilwa, the city of Great Zimbabwe reached its height about 1400. Great Zimbabwe participated in the gold and ivory trade that eventually made its way to Kilwa. Gold was not actually mined in the region but taxing the trade goods provided a major source of wealth for Great Zimbabwe.

By the early fifteenth century, there were about 11,000 people living in and around Great Zimbabwe. Then, in about 1450, people abandoned Great Zimbabwe. The large population had exhausted resources such as trees for timber, soil for growing crops, and grasses for grazing farm animals. The Portuguese invaded the area about 100 years later and finally conquered the kingdom in the late 1600s.

REVIEW What was Great Zimbabwe? **Summarize**

Benin

Near the delta of the Niger River was the forest kingdom of **Benin** (buh NIN). The kings in Benin were called **obas** (OH buhz). They took power about 1300.

▶ Great Zimbabwe was one of the largest, wealthiest, and most sophisticated of the ancient sub-Saharan cultures.

A v-shaped pattern decorated part of the outside wall.

The ruler and his attendants lived in round thatched houses inside the enclosure.

The outside wall was 16 feet thick at the base and 32 feet tall.

The stone cone-shaped tower was solid all the way through.

▶ Archaeologists do not know what function the cone-shaped tower served. But they believe it could have been used for religious purposes.

Practice and Extend

🔷 **CURRICULUM CONNECTION**
Drama

Role-Play an Interview

Have partners role-play an interview with a subject of Great Zimbabwe.

- Have partners work together to create a list of questions an interviewer might ask a person who is leaving Great Zimbabwe in the mid-1400s.
- Allow students time to research more information about Great Zimbabwe.
- Partners can work together to answer the questions, then choose the role of the interviewer or the person being interviewed.
- Have partners conduct their interviews for the class.

In the late 1400s, the Portuguese began to trade coral beads and cloth for ivory, animal skins, and pepper with Benin. By 1500 Benin grew to become a powerful empire. By then Benin was trading its ivory, cloth, spices, and slaves.

This forest region had fertile soil and received lots of rain. People grew crops such as yams and cotton. They lived in Benin City, the capital city, as well as in the country. Houses were made of mud. However, the oba's palace had doors made of metal and had beautiful designs and pictures.

In addition to trade, Benin was known for its great art. Many artists used bronze, ivory, and wood to make sculptures and carvings. Craftspeople made beautiful bronze and brass sculptures to decorate the oba's palace. This was how the artists showed the greatness of the oba.

▶ Bronze sculptors in present-day Benin still practice the "lost wax" process of casting.

To protect these riches, high wooden walls were built around the oba's palace.

REVIEW How did contact with the Portuguese affect Benin's growth? *Cause and Effect*

Summarize the Lesson

- **A.D. 350** Axum invaded the former Kush capital of Meroë.

- **1185–1225** Lalibela built 11 rock churches in Ethiopia.

- **1450** The Shona people completed the stone enclosures of Great Zimbabwe.

LESSON 3 REVIEW

Check Facts and Main Ideas

1. **Summarize** On a separate piece of paper, fill the missing detail that completes the summary below.

> Axum was abandoned after Arab invasions.

> Meroë was replaced by Axum in A.D. 350.

> Ethiopia took over the position of the old kingdom of Axum.

↓

> Ethiopia began as a trade center at Meroë and was later replaced by the kingdom of Axum in A.D. 3500.

2. List goods that were traded in eastern, central, and southern Africa.

3. How were the civilizations that existed in eastern, central, and southern Africa alike and different?

4. How were these civilizations influenced by other civilizations in the Indian Ocean trade network?

5. **Critical Thinking:** *Make Inferences* What might life have been like in these regions if they had not participated in international trade? Explain your answer.

Link to ━━ Science

Build a Wall Research how the Shona people would have kept the stones together to build the enclosures at Great Zimbabwe. Use small blocks to build a wall like those in Great Zimbabwe and explain why the blocks stay together.

385

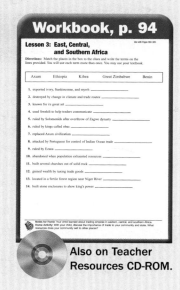

Workbook, p. 94

Lesson 3: East, Central, and Southern Africa

Directions: Match the places in the box to the clues and write the terms on the lines provided. You will use each term more than once. You may use your textbook.

| Axum | Ethiopia | Kilwa | Great Zimbabwe | Benin |

1. exported ivory, frankincense, and myrrh _____
2. destroyed by change in climate and trade route _____
3. known for its great art _____
4. used Swahili to help traders communicate _____
5. ruled by Solomonids after overthrow of Zagwe dynasty _____
6. ruled by kings called obas _____
7. replaced Axum civilization _____
8. attacked by Portuguese for control of Indian Ocean trade _____
9. ruled by Ezana _____
10. abandoned when population exhausted resources _____
11. built several churches out of solid rock _____
12. gained wealth by taxing trade goods _____
13. located in a fertile forest region near Niger River _____
14. built stone enclosures to show king's power _____

Also on Teacher Resources CD-ROM.

---

12. **How were the people of Benin and Great Zimbabwe alike in their actions toward their kings? How were they different?** They both considered their kings to be powerful and important. The people of Great Zimbabwe built stone enclosures to show this, while the craftspeople of Benin built beautiful bronze and brass sculptures to decorate their king's palace. **Compare and Contrast**

✓ **REVIEW ANSWER** Benin grew to be a powerful empire through trade with the Portuguese. **Cause and Effect**

③ Close and Assess

Summarize the Lesson

Tell students to examine the vertical time line. Ask them to copy the time line and insert dates and information about other African kingdoms they read about in this chapter.

✓ **LESSON 3 REVIEW**

1. **Summarize** For possible answers, see the reduced pupil page.

2. Gold, ivory, frankincense, myrrh, spices, cloth

3. The civilizations differed in religion, in culture, and in the trading partners they had. They were alike in that several of them, especially Great Zimbabwe and Benin, relied on trade to become great.

4. Muslim and East African culture combined to create Swahili culture and language. The Portuguese attacked several civilizations but helped Benin grow by trading with it.

5. **Critical Thinking:** *Make Inferences* Possible answer: People would have focused on producing necessities and local goods just for themselves; wealthy empires might not have developed without the exchange of goods and ideas that trade brought.

Link to ━━ Science

Students should realize that the stones are cut into shapes that fit together and support each other. If students need help, have them reread *You Are There* on p. 380.

Use the Internet

Objective

- Identify how to use the Internet to find information on a topic.

Resource

- Workbook, p. 95

1 Introduce and Motivate

What is the Internet? Ask students to share any prior knowledge or experience they have had using the Internet. Then have students read the **What?** section of text on p. 386.

Why use the Internet? Have students read the **Why?** section of text on p. 387. Ask them to give examples of situations in which the Internet would be the best resource to find information.

2 Teach and Discuss

How is this skill used? Examine with students the image and text on p. 386.

- Discuss the term *search engine* with students. Have them discuss the necessity for a search engine.

- Point out that the Internet is a vast source for information that would be impossible to locate without search engines. Explain that there are many search engines students can use, some of which are specifically designed for students.

- Have students read the **How?** section of text on p. 387.

Research and Writing Skills

Use the Internet

What? The Internet, which you can access through a computer, contains millions of pages on all kinds of topics. In order to find information on a particular topic, you use a search engine. A search engine is a Web site that has directories of information and offers key word searches.

Q? How do I begin my search?

A: Start with a search engine. Then type in a key word or key words for the information you want.

Search Engine

search key word East Africa

Q? How do I know if a site is dependable?

A: Government and educational sites that end in .gov or .edu, such as museums and colleges, usually have more dependable information than other sites. Also, use what you have learned about telling fact from opinion to judge how dependable a Web site is.

.gov

.org

.edu

386

Practice and Extend

SOCIAL STUDIES Background

How the Internet Works

- The Internet is a worldwide network of information that is made up of many smaller networks, each connected to one another.
- Most networks that make up the Internet can be shared by anyone connecting to the network.
- It is estimated that there were 61 million Internet users by the end of 1996, 148 million by the end of 1998, and 700 million in 2001.

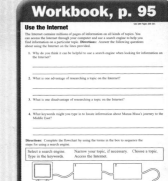

Workbook, p. 95

Use the Internet

The Internet contains millions of pages of information on all kinds of topics. You can access the Internet through your computer and use a search engine to help you find information on a particular topic. **Directions:** Answer the following questions about using the Internet on the lines provided.

1. Why do you think it can be helpful to use a search engine when looking for information on the Internet?

2. What is one advantage of researching a topic on the Internet?

3. What is one disadvantage of researching a topic on the Internet?

4. What keywords might you type in to locate information about Mansa Musa's journey to the Middle East?

Directions: Complete the flowchart by using the terms in the box to sequence the steps for using a search engine.

| Select a search engine. | Narrow your topic, if necessary. | Choose a topic. |
| Type in the keywords. | Access the Internet. |

Notes for Home: Your child learned how to use search engines on the Internet.
Home Activity: With your child, practice using various Internet search engines on a home or school computer to research a topic of interest.

Also on Teacher Resources CD-RO

Why? The Internet is a tool that students can use to find information on a topic. It was created during the 1960s to allow governments to share information. The Internet allowed researchers in different parts of the world to keep in touch with other researchers.

The World Wide Web was created in the 1990s so that more people could use the Internet. Now, anyone can put information on the Internet. But how can you find the information you are looking for and how do you know it is accurate? Search engines were created to help people find information about specific topics. When you enter keywords, or words related to the topic, you are telling the search engine to search the Internet for those keywords.

Using search engines to locate information on the Internet does not replace researching a topic by looking at books. However, the Internet may contain more current information than what is available in books.

How? The following steps will help you use a search engine.

- Access the Internet through your computer.
- A teacher or librarian can help you select a search engine that will help you conduct your research.
- Look for the word *search* with a long rectangular box on the first page of the search engine. Type in a topic that you are researching, such as East Africa. You could also type in the name of a more specific place such as Great Zimbabwe. **①**
- After you click on the *search* button, a search engine will return a list of items called "hits." Some of these hits might contain useful information on your topic. Remember, sometimes the information may not be useful. You may need to try narrowing your topic to bring up more specific information. **②**
- Some of the information you find on the Web may not be accurate. Make sure you compare the information from a Web site to at least one other appropriate source. **③**

Think and Apply

① Try researching the spread of the Bantu languages. What words or phrases would you type to begin the search?

② How would you choose which sites to visit from the list created by the search engine?

③ Which Web site gives you more useful information? Why?

387

---

① **How do you conduct a key word search?** Go to a search engine and type in a key word that describes the information you want. Next, click on the search or "go" button.  **Sequence**

② **How do you narrow your topic?** Identify a key word that is a more specific part of the larger topic. **Apply Information**

③ **What is an example of an assignment for which you would use a resource other than the Internet?** Possible answers: Write a book report; interview a famous person or someone you admire. **Apply Information**

3 Close and Assess

Think and Apply

1. Possible answer: *Spread of Bantu languages*

2. Choose a title and description that seem closely related to your topic.

3. A government or educational site is likely to be more useful because it probably has more extensive and reliable information than other kinds of sites.

Problem Solving

Use a Problem-Solving Process

- Have students consider the following problem-solving scenario: **You want to use the Internet to find information about the Ethiopian capital, Adefa. When you type Adefa into your search engine, no relevant Web sites are found. What can you do?**

- Students should use the following problem-solving process to decide on what they can do to improve their search. Ask students to work in small groups to discuss what other topics they can use as key words, or what other search engines or references they can use. Then have students use their ideas on the Internet to see if their solutions work. Write the steps above on the board or read them aloud.

1. Identify a problem.
2. Gather information.
3. List and consider options.
4. Consider advantages and disadvantages.
5. Choose and implement a solution.
6. Evaluate the effectiveness of a solution.

Resources

- Assessment Book, pp. 65–68
- Workbook, p. 96: Vocabulary Review

Chapter Summary

For possible answers, see the reduced pupil pages.

Vocabulary and Terms

1. b, **2.** a, **3.** c, **4.** d

People and Places

Possible answers:

1. In 1235, Sundiata defeated King Sumanguru and established the empire of Mali.

2. Mansa Musa was a strong Muslim king of Mali, best known for his pilgrimage to Mecca in 1324.

3. The Great Rift Valley is a fertile valley that stretches across lakes, highlands, and smaller valleys in East Africa.

4. Stone enclosures of Great Zimbabwe were built to show the power and importance of the king.

5. Songhai, the last great empire of West Africa, flourished between 1464 and 1591.

6. Its location between salt mines in the Sahara and gold fields in Wangara helped Ghana become a wealthy trading center.

7. Mali had a strong agricultural economy, but it relied on trade for wealth.

8. Axum, which began as a trading settlement in the sixth century B.C., grew into a powerful East African empire.

9. Christianity became firmly established in Ethiopia under the Zagwe dynasty.

10. Under King Sonni Ali, Songhai became an important center for trade and learning in West Africa.

CHAPTER **13**
REVIEW

300	500	7

about
A.D. 300–1200
Empire of Ghana

c. 350
Axum invaded Meroë.

Chapter Summary

Sequence

Target Skill

On a separate piece of paper, put the following events in their correct time order.

D · Songhai declines as a great trading empire in West Africa.

A · The Sahara begins to dry out.

B · Great Zimbabwe is completed.

C · The Portuguese invade Kilwa.

Vocabulary and Terms

Match each word with the correct definition or description.

1 savanna (p. 371)

2 griot (p. 376)

3 Swahili (p. 383)

4 Bantu (p. 373)

a. storyteller

b. short, grassy plain

c. language and culture mix of Muslims and East Africans

d. group of languages that was spread by farmers who left West Africa about 100 B.C.

People and Places

Write a sentence explaining why each of the following people and places is important in the study of medieval Africa. You may use two or more in a single sentence.

1 Sundiata (p. 376)

2 Mansa Musa (p. 376)

3 Great Rift Valley (p. 372)

4 Great Zimbabwe (p. 384)

5 Songhai (p. 378)

6 Ghana (p. 375)

7 Mali (p. 376)

8 Axum (p. 381)

9 Ethiopia (p. 382)

10 Sonni Ali (p. 378)

388

Practice and Extend

Assessment Options

✓ Chapter 13 Assessment

- Chapter 13 Content Test: Use Assessment Book, pp. 65–66.
- Chapter 13 Skills Test: Use Assessment Book, pp. 67–68.

⭐ Standardized Test Prep

- Chapter 13 Tests contain standardized test format.

✓ Chapter 13 Performance Assessment

- Assign each pair or small group of students the name of an African empire discussed in this chapter. Have students create riddles using facts and details related to their empire.

- Have groups take turns reading their riddles as other classmates try to solve them.

- Assess students' understanding of significant information about each empire, including geography, culture, and religion.

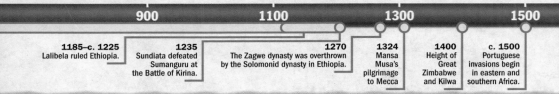

1185–c. 1225 Lalibela ruled Ethiopia.

1235 Sundiata defeated Sumanguru at the Battle of Kirina.

1270 The Zagwe dynasty was overthrown by the Solomonid dynasty in Ethiopia.

1324 Mansa Musa's pilgrimage to Mecca.

1400 Height of Great Zimbabwe and Kilwa.

c. 1500 Portuguese invasions begin in eastern and southern Africa.

Facts and Main Ideas

1. How was trade important culturally and economically?

2. With whom did states in East Africa trade?

3. With whom did kingdoms in West Africa trade?

4. **Time Line** What kingdoms in West Africa and East Africa thrived at the same time?

5. **Main Idea** Why did people leave the Sahara after 2500 B.C.?

6. **Main Idea** Why was gold so important to the African kingdoms and empires?

7. **Main Idea** Why were Arabic and Swahili used as trading languages?

8. **Critical Thinking:** *Make Generalizations* What was important about the locations of the trading kingdoms?

Apply Skills

Use the Internet

Use the Internet to find a translation of a primary source from a time period in this chapter. Think about some of the events you have read about in this chapter. Answer the following questions after you have found the appropriate Web site for the event.

1. How do you know that what you have found is a primary source?

2. Is the Web site an appropriate one that would provide accurate information? Explain your answer.

3. Does the Web site lead you to other Web sites with helpful resources and information?

Write About History

1. Write a **journal entry** from the point of view of someone accompanying Mansa Musa on his pilgrimage to Mecca.

2. Write a **news bulletin** describing some trade and travel problems for people traveling on the caravan routes in the Sahara or on the Red Sea.

3. Write a **magazine article** about how trade caused the mixing and blending of cultures in Africa.

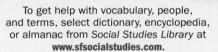

To get help with vocabulary, people, and terms, select dictionary, encyclopedia, or almanac from *Social Studies Library* at **www.sfsocialstudies.com.**

389

Hands-on Unit Project

✓ **Unit 5 Performance Assessment**

- See p. 420 for information about using the Unit Project as a means of performance assessment.
- A scoring guide is provided on p. 420.

WEB SITE
Technology

For more information, students can select the dictionary, encyclopedia, or almanac from *Social Studies Library* at **www.sfsocialstudies.com.**

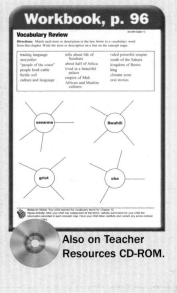

Workbook, p. 96

Vocabulary Review

Also on Teacher Resources CD-ROM.

1. Trade spread new ideas such as religion and language, and trade made states rich and powerful.

2. They traded with Arabia, India, and China.

3. They traded with people in North Africa. Some of their trade goods, such as gold, eventually ended up in Europe.

4. Ghana and Ethiopia

5. They left because the Sahara dried up, and they had used up important food and fuel resources.

6. Gold made empires wealthy and brought in trade goods from other lands.

7. Common languages made it easier for people to work together.

8. They were located near good farm land, near good land or sea trade routes, and near places that produced trade goods. They were a crossroads for trade.

Write About History

1. Encourage students to include supplies they would have on their journey as well as descriptions of the sights they would see.

2. Before writing their bulletins, have students brainstorm a list of the kinds of problems these travelers faced, such as difficult weather, rough terrain, and the threat of thieves.

3. Some students may wish to write their articles as opinions about the results of trade.

Apply Skills

1. Because it was created by someone who experienced the event(s) firsthand.

2. Students should demonstrate that they know that information from educational and government sites is usually more dependable.

3. Answers will vary. Most useful sites have links to other such sites.

Chapter Planning Guide

Chapter 14 • Medieval Europe

Locating Time and Place pp. 390–391

Lesson Titles	Pacing	Main Ideas
Lesson 1 **Geography of Europe** pp. 392–395	1 day	• The landforms and climate of Europe affect the way Europeans live.
Lesson 2 **Rulers and Invaders** pp. 396–398 **Biography: Charlemagne** p. 399	1 day	• After a series of rulers and invaders, medieval government in Europe experienced a change. • Charlemagne became emperor of the former Roman Empire in western Europe. He wrote a wide range of laws and promoted culture and learning in his empire.
Lesson 3 **Life in the Middle Ages** pp. 400–405	2 days	• The church, feudalism, and manor life formed the foundation of European medieval life.
Lesson 4 **Crusades, Trade, and the Plague** pp. 406–411 **Map and Globe Skills:** **Use a Time Zone Map** pp. 412–413	2 days	• Routes promoted trade, travel, and communication, as well as the Plague, between Europe, Africa, and Asia. • You can use time zone maps to compare the time of any location around the world to the time where you live.

✔ **Chapter 14 Review**
pp. 414–415

◄ **A manuscript by William of Tyre illustrates the First Crusade.**

✔ = Assessment Options

◄ **The Domesday Book**

Vocabulary	Resources	Meeting Individual Needs
	• Workbook, p. 98 • Transparency 20 • Every Student Learns Guide, pp. 190–193 • Quick Study, pp. 96–97	• Leveled Practice, TE p. 393 • ESL Support, TE p. 394
	• Workbook, p. 99 • Transparencies 10, 43 • Every Student Learns Guide, pp. 194–197 • Quick Study, pp. 98–99	• Leveled Practice, TE p. 397 • ESL Support, TE p. 398
monk nun monastery convent missionary monarch serf knight chivalry guild lady	• Workbook, p. 100 • Transparency 1 • Every Student Learns Guide, pp. 198–201 • Quick Study, pp. 100–101	• Leveled Practice, TE p. 401 • ESL Support, TE p. 404
epidemic	• Workbook, p. 101 • Transparencies 20, 44, 45 • Every Student Learns Guide, pp. 202–205 • Quick Study, pp. 102–103 • Workbook, p. 102	• ESL Support, TE p. 407 • Leveled Practice, TE p. 408 • Learning Styles, TE p. 409 • Learning Styles, TE p. 413
	✓ Chapter 14 Content Test, Assessment Book, pp. 69–70 ✓ Chapter 14 Skills Test, Assessment Book, pp. 71–72	✓ Chapter 14 Performance Assessment, TE p. 414

Providing More Depth

Additional Resources
- Vocabulary Cards
- Daily Activity Bank
- Social Studies Plus!
- Big Book Atlas
- Student Atlas
- Outline Maps
- Desk Maps

 Technology

- AudioText
- The test maker
- Teacher Resources CD-ROM
- Map Resources CD-ROM
- **www.sfsocialstudies.com**

 To establish guidelines for your students' safe and responsible use of the Internet, use the Scott Foresman Internet Guide.

Additional Internet Links

To find out more about:
- The Magna Carta, visit **www.nara.gov**
- Life during the Crusades, click on The New Jerusalem Mosaic at **jeru.huji.ac.il**

Key Internet Search Terms
- Magna Carta
- feudalism
- crusades

Workbook Support

Use the following Workbook pages to support content and skills development as you teach Chapter 14. You can also view and print Workbook pages from the Teacher Resources CD-ROM.

Workbook, p. 97

Vocabulary Preview

Use with Chapter 14.

Directions: Circle the word that best completes each sentence. You may use your textbook.

1. A baker, goldsmith, tailor, or weaver might have joined a craft (epidemic, **guild**, monarch) to unite common interests.

2. The (lady, **monarch**, serf) was the supreme ruler at the top of the feudalism social structure.

3. A (knight, **serf**, lady) was someone who farmed the land owned by the lords.

4. A man who devoted his life to religion was called a (**monk**, nun, monarch).

5. A (monastery, **convent**, missionary) served as a center of religion and education for the nuns who lived there.

6. A trained warrior in the third level in the feudalism pyramid was called a (**knight**, monarch, guild).

7. A (serf, **lady**, knight) was of noble birth but had little opportunity to make life decisions without direction from a spouse.

8. In addition to prayer and studies, a (lady, knight, **nun**, or woman devoted to religion, also cultivated crops and helped the poor.

9. The Plague was an aggressive (**epidemic**, monarch, guild) that killed about 25 percent of Europe's people in about five years.

10. According to a code of (guild, **chivalry**, missionary), a knight pledged to use his strength to stand against injustice.

11. A (**missionary**, knight, monastery) teaches a religion to people with different beliefs.

12. Monks studied, prayed, and lived in a community called a (convent, **monastery**, monarch).

Notes for Home: Your child learned the vocabulary terms for Chapter 14.
Home Activity: Have your child write each vocabulary word on a slip of paper and copy the definition on the back. Laying each paper with the term facing up, help your child define each word.

Use with Pupil Edition, p. 390

Workbook, p. 98

Lesson 1: Geography of Europe

Use with Pages 392-395.

The climate and landforms across Europe affect where and how people live.
Directions: Review each term in the box below. Copy the terms into the correct section of the organizer to describe the four major land regions of Europe. Some terms will be used more than once.

pastureland	mountains	vast area
rocky soil	steep slopes	fertile farming
forests	flat, rolling land	thin soil
		poor farming

Northwest Mountains
- mountains
- poor farming
- thin soil
- steep slopes

Central Uplands
- forests
- rocky soil
- mountains

Land Regions of Europe

North European Plain
- fertile farming
- vast area
- flat, rolling land

Alpine Mountain System
- mountains
- fertile farming
- forests
- pastureland

Notes for Home: Your child learned about the climate and landforms of Europe.
Home Activity: With your child, discuss how the climate and landforms where you live affect how people live and work. Then compare your region to the four land regions of Europe.

Use with Pupil Edition, p. 395

Workbook, p. 99

Lesson 2: Rulers and Invaders

Use with Pages 396-398.

Directions: Match each phrase in Column A to the phrase in Column B that best completes the sentence. Write the letter from Column B on the line in front of Column A. You may use your textbook.

	Column A		Column B
e	1. Before the Domesday Book was put together in 1086,	a.	it fell apart after his death.
b	2. Because Charlemagne gave large areas of land to the nobles,	b.	they were loyal to him and maintained roads, bridges, and defense walls on their estates.
a	3. Despite Charlemagne's efforts to strengthen his kingdom,	c.	civil war broke out in England.
d	4. After the Vikings looted the lands they conquered,	d.	they set up trading centers and trade routes.
i	5. After the Normans settled in northern France,	e.	no one really knew how many people lived in England.
h	6. Because King John governed with more force than earlier kings did,	f.	some of the articles eventually helped all people.
c	7. After King John lost an important battle against France,	g.	royal power was limited.
j	8. Rather than face defeat in England's civil war,	h.	English lords became angry with his rule.
f	9. Although most of the clauses of the Magna Carta helped the lords and other landholders,	i.	they adopted Frankish customs and became Christians and church leaders.
g	10. When King John agreed to the set of promises in the Magna Carta,	j.	King John agreed to the Magna Carta.

Notes for Home: Your child learned about medieval government in Europe under different rulers and invaders.
Home Activity: Review the articles of the Magna Carta discussed on p. 398. With your child, review the rules you have at home. Discuss why rules exist and why they are valuable.

Use with Pupil Edition, p. 398

Workbook, p. 100

Lesson 3: Life in the Middle Ages

Use with Pages 400-405.

Directions: Complete the concept map below. Classify each description in the box by listing it in one of the levels of feudalism. You may use your textbook.

received land from the lord	kings or queens	granted estates to lords
gave military support	protected serfs	no loyalty to monarchs or lords
trained to fight on horseback	supreme rulers	followed code of behavior
owned land and crops	peasants	
	lived on and farmed the land	

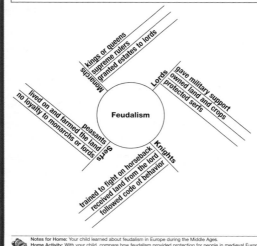

Notes for Home: Your child learned about feudalism in Europe during the Middle Ages.
Home Activity: With your child, compare how feudalism provided protection for people in medieval Europe and how people in democracies are protected today.

Use with Pupil Edition, p. 405

Workbook Support

Workbook, p. 101

Lesson 4: Crusades, Trade, and the Plague

Use with Pages 406–411.

Directions: Read the following statements. Then circle *T* (True) or *F* (False) for each statement. If the answer is false, correct the statement to make it true. You may use your textbook.

T **(F)** **1.** Christians in western Europe organized twelve Crusades to establish trade routes and defeat the Byzantine Empire.

> **organized eight Crusades to win back control of Palestine**
> **and protect the Byzantine Empire**

(T) F **2.** Because people began to want goods that were not available on a manor, they purchased the goods at fairs.

T **(F)** **3.** If traders wanted goods from Asia, they had to travel to Asia to buy them.

> **did not need to travel to Asia because the goods would**
> **reach the trader through a series of middlemen**

T **(F)** **4.** The Silk Road is a single route across Central Asia.

> **is several different routes and branches, each passing**
> **through different settlements**

(T) F **5.** Some historians believe that the Plague began in Central Asia and spread east to China and west along the Silk Road.

T **(F)** **6.** The Plague killed about three-fourths of Europe's people from 1347 to 1352.

> **killed about one-fourth to one-third of Europe's people from**
> **1347 to 1352**

 Notes for Home: Your child learned about the development of trade routes and their effect on communication between Europe, Africa, and Asia.
Home Activity: With your child, compare how epidemics from the Middle Ages and today are spread and are contained.

Use with Pupil Edition, p. 411

Workbook, p. 102

Use a Time Zone Map

Use with Pages 412–413.

A time zone map of the United States shows six of the world's time zones. The time in each zone is different by one hour from the time zone next to it. When it is 5 A.M. in Hawaii, it is 8 A.M. in Phoenix, 9 A.M. in Dallas, and 10 A.M. in Washington, D.C.

Directions: Use the time zone map of the United States to answer the questions that follow.

1. Suppose you are about to fly from Albuquerque, New Mexico, to Dallas, Texas. It is about a two-hour flight to Dallas and the plane is scheduled to depart at 10:00 A.M. About what time will you arrive in Dallas?

  (A) 12:00 P.M. (B) 12:00 A.M. ● 1:00 P.M. (D) 11:00 A.M.

2. Suppose it is 10:30 A.M. in Anchorage, Alaska. What time is it in Chicago, Illinois?

  (A) 11:30 A.M. (B) 12:30 A.M. ● 12:00 P.M. (D) 1:30 P.M.

3. Suppose you live in Chicago, Illinois, and you want to call a friend in California at 6:00 P.M. Pacific time. At what time in Chicago should you make the call?

  (A) 6:00 P.M. (B) 7:00 P.M. ● 8:00 P.M. (D) 9:00 P.M.

4. Suppose you are in New York City and want to call your uncle in San Francisco. At what time will you place the call from New York to reach him during his lunch hour?

  (A) 1:30 P.M. ● 3:30 P.M. (C) 10:30 A.M. (D) 12:30 P.M.

Notes for Home: Your child learned to use a time zone map.
Home Activity: With your child, use this map to practice converting time to other time zones of the United States.

Use with Pupil Edition, p. 413

Workbook, p. 103

Vocabulary Review

Use with Chapter 14.

Directions: Choose the vocabulary word from the box that best completes each sentence. Write the word on the line provided. Not all words will be used.

monk	convent	serf	guild
nun	missionary	knight	lady
monastery	monarch	chivalry	epidemic

1. A group of people united by a common interest is a _____**guild**_____.

2. A _____**monastery**_____ served as a center of religion and education, as well as a community in which monks lived.

3. _____**Epidemic**_____ is another word for a disease that spreads quickly over a wide area.

4. A woman who devoted her life to religion in the Christian church was called a _____**nun**_____.

5. Knights had a code of behavior called _____**chivalry**_____.

6. A monk sometimes became a _____**missionary**_____ to teach his religion to people with different beliefs.

Directions: On the lines provided, write a short paragraph using at least three of the six words not used above. Use information from the chapter in your paragraph.

Students' paragraphs should include three of the unused
vocabulary words (*monk, convent, monarch, serf, knight,* or
***lady*) to relate information from the text.**

 Notes for Home: Your child learned the vocabulary terms for Chapter 14.
Home Activity: Read aloud each word in the box. Ask your child to define each term.

Use with Pupil Edition, p. 415

Workbook, p. 104

Unit 5 Project   A Day in the Life

Directions: In a group, make a documentary about living in a medieval village.

1. The ✔ shows the topics included in our documentary:

  ____ location of village ____ village buildings ____ building materials

  ____ surrounding landscape ____ people in the village ____ farming

  ____ animals ____ technology ____ other activities

2. Facts to include in our script:

  _____

  _____

  _____

  _____

3. Parts of the village that we want to include in our model:

  _____ _____

  _____ _____

  _____ _____

Have students reread sections of the textbook about the
Middle Ages. Query students to ensure that they include and
correctly describe important parts of their village.

✔ **Checklist for Students**

____ We chose topics about life in a medieval village.
____ We researched the topics.
____ We wrote the script for our documentary.
____ We built a model of a medieval village.
____ We presented our documentary to the class.

Notes for Home: Your child learned about life in a medieval village.
Home Activity: With your child, make a Venn diagram to compare and contrast a medieval village to the city or town in which you live. Include information about location, buildings, people, and activities in your diagram.

Use with Pupil Edition, p. 420

Assessment Support

Use these Assessment Book pages and the test maker to assess content and skills in Chapter 14 and Unit 5. You can also view and print Assessment Book pages from the Teacher Resources CD-ROM.

Assessment Book, p. 69

Chapter 14 Test

Part 1: Content Test

Directions: Fill in the circle next to the correct answer.

Lesson Objective (1:2)

1. Which landform separates Europe from Asia?
   - Ⓐ Northwest Mountains
   - ● Ural Mountains
   - Ⓒ Carpathian Mountains
   - Ⓓ Black Forest

Lesson Objective (1:1)

2. In which two regions would you find most of Europe's farms?
   - Ⓐ Central Uplands and Alpine Mountain System
   - Ⓑ Northwest Mountains and North European Plain
   - Ⓒ Northwest Mountains and Central Uplands
   - ● North European Plain and Alpine Mountain System

Lesson Objective (1:3)

3. Which is Europe's longest river?
   - ● Volga River
   - Ⓑ Don River
   - Ⓒ Danube River
   - Ⓓ Rhine River

Lesson Objective (1:4)

4. How did Europe's landforms influence people's lives in the Middle Ages?
   - Ⓐ The Gulf Stream limited opportunities for the economy.
   - ● Deforestation led to planting crops on fertile farmlands.
   - Ⓒ People cut timber from the lower elevations of mountains such as the Alps.
   - Ⓓ Rivers were not navigable and prohibited trade.

Lesson Objective (1:5)

5. What is the climate like across most of Europe?
   - Ⓐ hot and dry
   - Ⓑ Mediterranean
   - Ⓒ snowy and cold
   - ● temperate

Lesson Objective (2:1)

6. Which of the following describes Charlemagne?
   - Ⓐ leader of the Normans in northern France
   - Ⓑ ruler who conquered and looted England and France
   - Ⓒ king who agreed to the articles of the Magna Carta
   - ● ruler who was crowned emperor by Pope Leo III

Lesson Objective (2:2)

7. What was the name for fierce pirates and warriors from Scandinavia?
   - Ⓐ Normans
   - ● Vikings
   - Ⓒ Christians
   - Ⓓ Franks

Lesson Objective (2:3)

8. Which of the following is true about the Magna Carta?
   - Ⓐ It gave the king more money and power.
   - ● It contained 63 clauses and limited the power of the king.
   - Ⓒ It was signed before the civil war in England.
   - Ⓓ It demanded that lords provide military service to the king.

Use with Pupil Edition, p. 414

Assessment Book, p. 70

Lesson Objective (2:1, 2)

9. Which of these events happened first?
   - Ⓐ The Magna Carta was signed by King John of England.
   - Ⓑ Vikings invaded Europe and set up trade routes.
   - ● Charlemagne was crowned emperor.
   - Ⓓ The Normans, led by William the Conqueror, invaded England.

Lesson Objective (3:1, 2)

10. In the system of feudalism, who farmed the land?
    - Ⓐ knights
    - Ⓑ lords
    - ● serfs
    - Ⓓ monarchs

Lesson Objective (3:4)

11. How did feudalism affect the lives of the nobility?
    - Ⓐ The system elevated the serfs to a level equal to lords and knights.
    - Ⓑ Monarchs were not allowed to build their own manor houses.
    - Ⓒ The monarchs established guilds to help serfs work the land.
    - ● Lords and knights were loyal to the monarch and provided protection.

Lesson Objective (3:5)

12. What effect did the manor system have on cities and towns?
    - ● Because there were crop surpluses in the towns, the towns grew.
    - Ⓑ Many lords moved from manor houses into the cities.
    - Ⓒ Manor houses were built close to towns, causing overcrowding.
    - Ⓓ People living in cities and towns received surplus crops for free.

Lesson Objective (3:3)

13. Which of the following was NOT a purpose of guilds?
    - Ⓐ guarantee a fair price for goods
    - Ⓑ buy large quantities of goods cheaply
    - Ⓒ control the marketplace of each town
    - ● identify new markets for surplus goods grown on manors

Lesson Objective (4:1)

14. Which event marked the decline of Byzantine control over Asia Minor?
    - Ⓐ William the Conqueror converted to Christianity.
    - Ⓑ The Jews were forced by the Romans to leave Judea.
    - Ⓒ Christians in western Europe organized the first of the Crusades.
    - ● A group of Muslim Seljuk Turks defeated a Byzantine army.

Lesson Objective (4:2)

15. Why did Emperor Alexius Comnenus ask Pope Urban II for help?
    - Ⓐ He wanted to change the name of Judea to Palestine.
    - ● He needed Christian knights to help fight against the Turks.
    - Ⓒ He hoped to invade England and defeat William the Conqueror.
    - Ⓓ He wanted to defeat the Byzantine Empire.

Lesson Objective (4:3)

16. Which of the following trade goods was NOT carried along the Silk Road?
    - Ⓐ ivory
    - Ⓑ gold
    - Ⓒ precious stones
    - ● cotton

Use with Pupil Edition, p. 414

Assessment Book, p. 71

Part 2: Skills Test

Directions: Use complete sentences to answer questions 1–7. Use a separate sheet of paper if you need more space.

1. How did the people of Europe use the continent's waterways? **Main Idea and Details**

   Europeans used the waterways to transport goods, to power waterwheels for grinding grain, and to provide fish to eat and sell.

2. What was the purpose of the Domesday Book? **Draw Conclusions**

   It was a census, or count, of all the people, animals, and businesses in medieval England. It also provided King William with information about his subjects and how they might be taxed.

3. How would you describe Charlemagne's relationship with the nobles? Explain. **Summarize**

   Possible answer: Charlemagne and the nobles had a good relationship. He gave large areas of land to the nobles. In return, the nobles pledged loyalty to him. They maintained the roads, bridges, and defense walls on their estates.

4. In what ways were the Vikings in Scandinavia and Normans, led by William the Conqueror, alike and different? **Compare and Contrast**

   Same: both were groups of Vikings during the Middle Ages and raided parts of Italy and England; Different: the Vikings were fierce warriors who raided many European countries and set up trading centers in some. The Normans adopted Frankish customs after settling in northern France. Many converted to Christianity and became church leaders.

Use with Pupil Edition, p. 414

Assessment Book, p. 72

5. How did the Magna Carta affect the rule of England? **Analyze Information**

   It contained 63 clauses that helped lords, land holders, and eventually all the people of England. The power of the king was limited by the law. The king could not make demands for money or imprison a free man without the consent of the lords or except by law. The king had to obey the law.

6. How did the bubonic plague affect the economy of Europe in the 1300s? **Cause and Effect**

   The decline in population led to a decrease in food production. Labor shortages took place in other industries as well. Because trade slowed down, some towns disappeared.

Time Zones of the World

7. Use the map to answer the questions. **Use a Time Zone Map**
   a. Into how many time zones is Earth divided? **24 time zones**

   b. What is the time difference between Lima and San Francisco? **3 hours**

   c. If the time in Beijing is 6 P.M., what is the time in Washington, D.C.? **5 A.M.**

Use with Pupil Edition, p. 414

Assessment Support

Assessment Book, p. 73

Unit 5 Test

Part 1: Content Test

Directions: Fill in the circle next to the correct answer.

Lesson Objective (11–1:3)

1. Which of the following describes the Byzantine Empire?
   - ● It was a continuation of the Roman Empire.
   - Ⓑ Its capital city was Byzantium.
   - Ⓒ Citizens shared one language and culture.
   - Ⓓ The entire Empire had a similar climate and geography.

Lesson Objective (11–1:2, 4)

2. How did the location of Constantinople help it become a center of trade?
   - Ⓐ It was located on a hill on the northwestern end of Europe.
   - Ⓑ Sea walls along the coast opened the city to trade.
   - ● Its location on a strait linking the Black and Marmara Seas made it important to trade.
   - Ⓓ It was located on the western bank of the Nile River.

Lesson Objective (11–2:1, 2, 3, 5)

3. Which of these events happened first?
   - Ⓐ The Hagia Sophia was built.
   - ● Justinian wanted to restore the Roman Empire and govern it as a whole.
   - Ⓒ Leaders of the Christian church disagreed over the use of icons.
   - Ⓓ Theodora encouraged her husband to defend Constantinople.

Lesson Objective (11–3:2, 3, 4, 5)

4. Which of the following statements is true about Islam?
   - Ⓐ The Torah is the holy book of Islam.
   - ● Islam began as a result of the visions and teachings of Muhammad.
   - Ⓒ The Quran does not cover topics of importance to Muslim followers.
   - Ⓓ Islam became important only in and around Mecca.

Lesson Objective (11–4:1, 2, 3, 4, 5)

5. Which of these was most important in establishing the Islamic world?
   - Ⓐ Muslim engineers built water clocks.
   - Ⓑ Non-Muslims had to pay a special tax.
   - ● Islam spread outside the Arabian Peninsula through conquests and trade.
   - Ⓓ Astronomers studied the position of the moon to locate Mecca.

Lesson Objective (12–1:2)

6. How has the geography of Asia influenced cultures located there?
   - Ⓐ The abundance of rivers has made travel very easy.
   - Ⓑ There is only one culture in Asia due to its small area.
   - ● A variety of landforms and climates gave rise to several different cultures.
   - Ⓓ Its rivers allowed the Indonesian people to remain isolated.

Use with Pupil Edition, p. 418

Assessment Book, p. 74

Lesson Objective (12–1:1, 3, 4, 5)

7. Which is NOT true about the Mogul Empire?
   - ● It began after Akbar became the greatest Mogul emperor.
   - Ⓑ Taxes under Akbar were imposed on every member of the Empire.
   - Ⓒ Its first ruler was a Central Asian leader named Babur.
   - Ⓓ Hindus and Muslims worked together to create a powerful Empire.

Lesson Objective (12–2:1, 2, 4, 5)

8. Which of these events happened in China during the Mongol dynasty?
   - Ⓐ Zheng He explored the West.
   - Ⓑ The Forbidden City was built.
   - Ⓒ Civil service examinations were strengthened.
   - ● China was ruled by a non-Chinese emperor.

Lesson Objective (12–3:1, 4)

9. Which of the following statements accurately describes the Khmer kingdom?
   - Ⓐ Angkor, the first Khmer ruler, reunited the kingdom in 802.
   - Ⓑ The first royal city of the kingdom was built in Beijing.
   - Ⓒ The kingdom's irrigation system had little influence on its economy.
   - ● The kingdom was ruled with absolute power.

Lesson Objective (12–4:1, 2, 3)

10. Which event happened before shoguns became rulers of Japan?
    - ● Japan suffered a long civil war.
    - Ⓑ Edo became the shogun capital.
    - Ⓒ Samurai became the ruling class.
    - Ⓓ Japan was cut off from the goods and culture of many other countries.

Lesson Objective (13–1:4)

11. How did the people of Africa adapt to their environment?
    - ● They migrated to the east and to the south.
    - Ⓑ They grew more rain forests.
    - Ⓒ They learned Bantu languages.
    - Ⓓ The Sahara dried up.

Lesson Objective (13–2:1, 2, 4)

12. Which of the following had the greatest influence on the economy of Ghana?
    - ● trade in gold
    - Ⓑ religion of Islam
    - Ⓒ camel caravans
    - Ⓓ safe trade routes

Lesson Objective (14–1:1, 2, 3, 4)

13. Which of these probably had the most influence on early European traders?
    - Ⓐ North European Plain
    - Ⓑ Volga River
    - Ⓒ Ural Mountains
    - Ⓓ Mediterranean climate

Lesson Objective (14–2:1, 2, 3)

14. Which of these events happened last?
    - Ⓐ Vikings invaded Europe.
    - Ⓑ Charlemagne was crowned emperor.
    - ● King John signed the Magna Carta.
    - Ⓓ The Normans invaded England.

Lesson Objective (14–4:1, 2, 3, 4)

15. Which of these events directly caused a decline in medieval culture?
    - ● A bubonic plague spread through Europe.
    - Ⓑ Alexius Comnenus asked for Christian knights to help fight against the Turks.
    - Ⓒ The trade of goods increased along the Silk Road.
    - Ⓓ Islam gradually replaced Christianity.

Use with Pupil Edition, p. 418

Assessment Book, p. 75

Part 2: Skills Test

Directions: Use complete sentences to answer questions 1–7. Use a separate sheet of paper if you need more space.

1. What ties did Justinian and Charlemagne have to religion? **Analyze Information**

   The Byzantine Orthodox Church was the official church of Justinian's Byzantine Empire, and it supported his belief that God had chosen him to run the Empire. The Roman Catholic Church was the official church of Charlemagne's kingdom. His close ties with the church in Rome allowed him to be crowned emperor.

2. What effect did the second and fifth "Pillars of Islam" have on early Muslim mathematicians, mapmakers, and astronomers? **Cause and Effect**

   Muslim mathematicians determined the times to call Muslims to prayer to fulfill part of the second pillar. To completely fulfill the second and fifth pillars, mapmakers and astronomers pinpointed the direction, distance, and location of Mecca for pilgrimages.

3. Identify the major achievements and advancements made in early China during the Tang dynasty. **Summarize**

   Wu Hou strengthened civil service examinations and caused literature and fine arts to flourish. Trade and contact with Central and western Asia increased. Advancements were made in block printing, and paper money was printed.

4. How did the geography of Japan support the shogun policy of isolation? **Draw Conclusions**

   Japan does not share a border with any other countries.

Use with Pupil Edition, p. 418

Assessment Book, p. 76

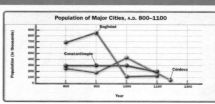

5. Use the graph to answer the questions. **Interpret Line Graphs**
   a. What do the labels along the left side of the graph show?

      the population in thousands

   b. Which city had the most growth over a 100-year period? When did the growth occur?

      Córdoba had the greatest growth from 900 A.D. to 1000 A.D.

   c. Estimate Baghdad's population in 950 A.D.

      about 450 thousand

Time Zones of the United States

6. Use the map to answer the questions. **Use a Time Zone Map**
   a. If you traveled from Philadelphia to Salt Lake City, how many time zones would you cross?

      3 time zones

   b. You live in Santa Fe. At 4:00 P.M. you phone a friend in Chicago. What time does the friend receive the call? **5:00 P.M.**

   c. When the time is 5 A.M. in Seattle, what is the time in Anchorage? **4 A.M.**

Use with Pupil Edition, p. 418

Medieval Europe

Chapter 14 Outline

Resources

- Workbook, p. 97: Vocabulary Preview
- Vocabulary Cards
- Social Studies Plus!

Europe: Lesson 1

Tell students the image shows a farmer in northern Europe. Ask students to describe the scene in the picture and to predict the climate in this area. (Possible answer: It had to have been mild enough for farming. The area shown is probably a temperate zone.)

1215, England: Lesson 2

Ask students to describe the document in the image. (Filled with writing, two big holes, probably an old document) Tell students that this is the Magna Carta, which was created in the 1200s.

c. 800, Europe: Lesson 3

Tell students the image here illustrates what a typical medieval community might have looked like. Ask students to identify the buildings in the picture and predict their functions. (Possible answer: Castle where kings, lords, and knights live; church for religion; farm house where serfs live)

1095, Rome: Lesson 4

Tell students the image shows some technology used in medieval warfare. Have students describe the picture. (People on horseback are attacking a building. People are armed with spears, axes, and swords.)

CHAPTER
14

Medieval Europe

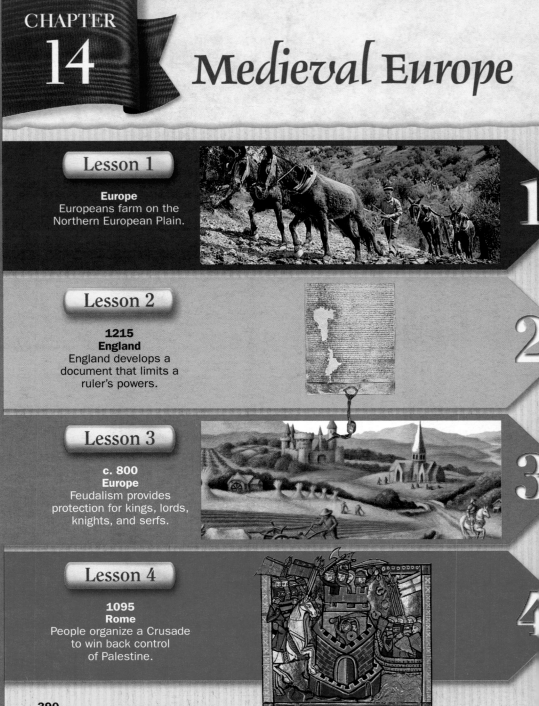

Lesson 1

Europe
Europeans farm on the Northern European Plain.

1

Lesson 2

1215
England
England develops a document that limits a ruler's powers.

2

Lesson 3

c. 800
Europe
Feudalism provides protection for kings, lords, knights, and serfs.

3

Lesson 4

1095
Rome
People organize a Crusade to win back control of Palestine.

4

390

Practice and Extend

Vocabulary Preview

- Use Workbook p. 97 to help students preview the vocabulary words in this chapter.
- Use Vocabulary Cards to preview key concept words in this chapter.

 Also on Teacher Resources CD-ROM.

Workbook, p. 97

Vocabulary Preview

Directions: Circle the word that best completes each sentence. You may use your textbook.

1. A baker, goldsmith, tailor, or weaver might have joined a craft (epidemic, **guild**, monarch) to unite common interests.
2. The (lady, **monarch**, serf) was the supreme ruler at the top of the feudalism social structure.
3. A (knight, **serf**, lady) was someone who farmed the land owned by the lords.
4. A man who devoted his life to religion was called a (**monk**, nun, monarch).
5. A (monastery, **convent**, missionary) served as a center of religion and education for the nuns who lived there.
6. A trained warrior in the third level in the feudalism pyramid was called a (**knight**, monarch, guild).
7. A (serf, **lady**, knight) was of noble birth but had little opportunity to make life decisions without direction from a spouse.
8. In addition to prayer and studies, a (lady, knight, **nun**), or woman devoted to religion, also cultivated crops and helped the poor.
9. The Plague was an aggressive (**epidemic**, monarch, guild) that killed about 25 percent of Europe's people in about five years.
10. According to a code of (guild, **chivalry**, missionary), a knight pledged to use his strength to stand against injustice.
11. A (missionary, knight, monastery) teaches a religion to people with different beliefs.
12. Monks studied, prayed, and lived in a community called a (convent, **monastery**, monarch).

Notes for Home: Your child learned the vocabulary terms for Chapter 14.
Home Activity: Have your child write each vocabulary word on a slip of paper and copy the definition on the back. Laying each paper with the term facing up, help your child define each word.

Locating Time and Place

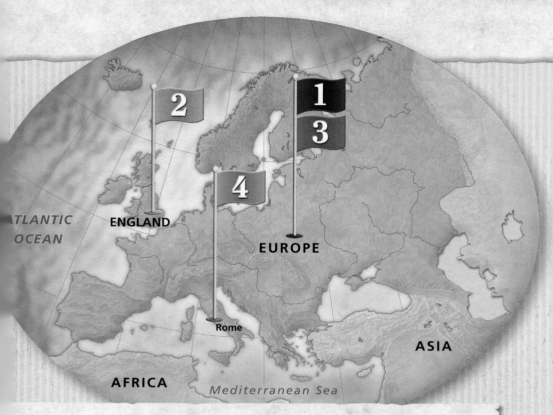

ATLANTIC OCEAN

ENGLAND

EUROPE

Rome

ASIA

AFRICA

Mediterranean Sea

Why We Remember

Medieval Europe provides a glimpse into one of the ways people organized themselves into a society. People worked together to be self-sufficient. Trade, then towns, began to prosper. Great strides were made in the movement of people and goods in the Middle Ages. During this time, military campaigns moved from Europe to the Holy Land in Southwest Asia. Trade routes began to branch out to even more locations. These routes, which had hugged the European coastline, moved inward. Goods and ideas were traded across different cultures. When Europeans came to America, they brought many goods and ideas that we use today.

391

- Have students examine the pictures shown on p. 390 for Lessons 1, 2, 3, and 4.

- Remind students that each picture is coded with both a number and a color to link it to a place on the map on p. 391.

Why We Remember

Have students read the "Why We Remember" paragraph on p. 391, and ask them why events in this chapter might be important to them. Have students name foods or traditions that may have originated in Europe.

WEB SITE
Technology

You can learn more about Europe, England, and Rome by clicking on *Atlas* at **www.sfsocialstudies.com**.

SOCIAL STUDIES STRAND
Geography

Mental Mapping On an outline map of Europe, ask students to label the Alps, Atlantic Ocean, Black Sea, Danube River, Mediterranean Sea, and Rhine River. Next, have them add England, France, Norway, and Spain. Discuss how Europe's smaller size and fewer geographic barriers may contribute to more cultural interaction and diffusion in Europe.

Geography of Europe

Objectives

- Explain how the different regions of Europe affect how people live and work.

- Locate and describe how the Ural Mountains served as a natural border between Europe and Asia.

- List and describe the major rivers of Europe.

- Explain how the landforms of Europe have influenced the way people live.

- List and describe the different climate regions of Europe.

Resources

- Workbook, p. 98
- Transparency 20
- Every Student Learns Guide, pp. 190–193
- Quick Study, pp. 96–97

Quick Teaching Plan

If time is short, have students create an almanac page about Europe.

- As they read each section independently, have students take notes about the landforms, waterways, and climate of Europe.

- Have students use their notes to write an almanac page titled *Fast Facts About Europe.*

1 Introduce and Motivate

Preview To activate prior knowledge, ask students to recall the kind of information they typically learn when studying the geography of an area. Tell students that, in Lesson 1, they will learn about European geography and its relationship to the history of Europe.

You Are There The geography and climate of an area affect the way its inhabitants live. Ask students to use clues from this passage to predict the climate and geography of Europe.

LESSON 1

Geography of Europe

PREVIEW

Focus on the Main Idea
The landforms and climate of Europe affect the way Europeans live.

PLACES
Europe
Ural Mountains
North European Plain
Volga River
Danube River
Rhine River

You Are There You're sitting in a room full of desks. Your fingers are cramped. It's winter, so the day is short and cold. Father Abbot fears a fire, so there is no source of heat or light in the room. You and each of the other scribes are copying a text. You write one letter, one word, one line at a time. "Two fingers hold the pen, but the whole body toils [labors]." You've been copying this same text onto paper for weeks. The last book you copied was an account of ancient Rome. When you finish a chapter, your copy is proofread. Corrections will be made. Titles will be added. Then, special pages are sent to an illustrator, who will supply any needed illustrations or art. Finally, the book will be bound. You look out the window for a moment to rest your eyes. The landscape of rolling hills and blowing grass is peaceful. This is Europe, your homeland.

Cause and Effect As you read, consider how the physical geography of Europe affects how people live.

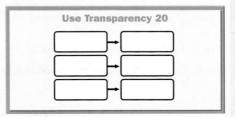

Practice and Extend

READING SKILL
Cause and Effect

In the Lesson Review, students complete a graphic organizer like the one below. You may want to provide students with a copy of Transparency 20 to complete as they read the lesson.

Use Transparency 20

WEB SITE
Technology

- You can look up vocabulary words by clicking on *Social Studies Library* and selecting the dictionary at **www.sfsocialstudies.com.**

- Students can learn more about current news by clicking on *Current Events* at **www.sfsocialstudies.com.**

- Explore other events that occurred on this day by clicking on *This Day in History* at **www.sfsocialstudies.com.**

Europe

Europe is the second smallest continent on Earth and extends from the Arctic Ocean in the north to the Mediterranean Sea in the south. Its western boundary is the Atlantic Ocean. In the east, the Ural (YOOR ul) Mountains separate Europe from Asia. The Urals are old, low mountains.

Europe has four major land regions: (1) the Northwest Mountains, (2) the North European Plain, (3) the Central Uplands, and (4) the Alpine Mountain System. The thin soil and steep slopes of the Northwest Mountain region make it poor for farming. The North European Plain is part of the Great European Plain, which covers a vast expanse of Europe, including part of southeast-ern England. The flat and rolling land includes some of the world's most fertile farmland.

The Central Uplands includes low mountains, high plateaus, and forests throughout the central region of Europe. Much of the land is rocky, but some is suitable for farming.

The Alpine Mountain System includes several mountain chains such as the Alps and the Carpathian Mountains. Lower mountain slopes and wide valleys provide good farmland. Heavy forests cover many of the higher slopes. Meadows above the timberline, or where the trees stop growing, are used as pastureland.

REVIEW How would you describe the major land regions of Europe? Summarize

MAP SKILL
Europe: Physical

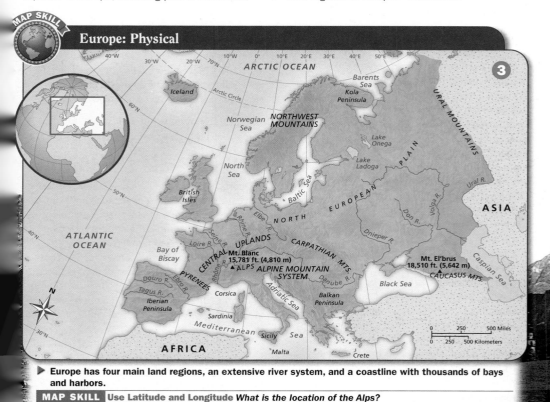

▶ Europe has four main land regions, an extensive river system, and a coastline with thousands of bays and harbors.

MAP SKILL Use Latitude and Longitude *What is the location of the Alps?*

393

MEETING INDIVIDUAL NEEDS
Leveled Practice

Identify Geographical Features Have students identify the major geographical features of Europe.

Easy List the following descriptive phrases on the board: *thin soil, steep slopes, flat and rolling land, fertile farmland, low mountains, high plateaus, forests, rocky land, meadows,* and *wide valleys.* Have volunteers read each phrase and identify the region that matches it. **Reteach**

On-Level Have students make a chart with one column for each region: the Northwest Mountains, the North European Plain, the Central Uplands, and the Alpine Mountain System. Have them list the features of each region. **Extend**

Challenge Have students use reference materials and online resources to find illustrative pictures of the different regions of Europe. Have them create and present their illustrated reports to the class. **Enrich**

For a Lesson Summary, use Quick Study, p. 96.

---

2 Teach and Discuss

PAGE 393
Europe

🕐 **Quick Summary** Europe has four major land regions, each with unique features.

1 Describe Europe's boundaries.
The northern, western and southern boundaries are all bodies of water; the eastern boundary is a mountain range. **Main Idea and Details**

2 Why is the North European Plain a better region for farming than the Northwest Mountains or the Central Uplands? The plains have flat rolling land with fertile soil, whereas the mountains have thin soil and steep slopes, and the uplands are mostly rocky. **Cause and Effect**

✓ **Ongoing Assessment**

If... students cannot explain why the North European Plain is better for farming, | **then...** work with students to complete a chart that lists the effects of living in a region with fertile soil and a region with poor, rocky soil. Then discuss which regions belong in each category and why.

✓ **REVIEW ANSWER** They include mountains, plains, and plateaus. Some land is rocky and not good for farming. The North European Plain has very fertile farmland. **Summarize**

MAP SKILL
Europe: Physical

Have students note the variety of landforms in Europe.

3 Which mountains separate the Iberian Peninsula from the rest of Europe? The Pyrenees **Interpret Maps**

MAP SKILL Answer 45°N, 5°E

Europe's River System

Quick Summary Europe's river system is one of its greatest natural resources. It has helped the European economy to thrive.

4 **Why do winds warmed by the Gulf Stream affect most of Europe?** There is no large mountain barrier to block them. **Cause and Effect**

Point out that cities often emerge along rivers and become centers for trade and shipping.

5 **What economic advantages did cities along rivers have?** Their proximity to rivers provided them with the means to transport goods to distant places and to grind grain to sell. **Main Idea and Details**

✓ **REVIEW ANSWER** It carries warm water from the Gulf of Mexico to the western coast of Europe. It gives Europe a milder climate. **Cause and Effect**

Climate and Landforms

Quick Summary Forests were cut down to clear land for farming. Much of Europe has a mild climate, which is good for farming.

6 **What main geographical features influence farming?** Climate and landforms **Main Idea and Details**

▶ The capital city of Budapest, Hungary, sits on both sides of the Danube River.

Europe's River System

The many rivers of Europe serve as major transportation routes. The **Volga** (VAHL guh) **River** is Europe's longest river. It flows through Russia to the Caspian (KAS pih un) Sea. Canals link the Volga with the Arctic Ocean, the Baltic Sea, and the Don River. The **Danube River** is Europe's second longest river. It is the main water route in the south-central part of the continent. The **Rhine River** is the backbone of the busiest inland system of waterways in the western part of Europe. The Rhine flows from the Alps through western Germany and the Netherlands to the North Sea.

Europe generally has milder weather than parts of Asia and North America at the same latitude. Europe's mild climate is caused by winds warmed by the Gulf Stream. The Gulf Stream is a powerful ocean current. It carries warm water from the Gulf of Mexico to the western coast of Europe. The winds affect most of the continent because no **4** mountain barrier is large enough to block them.

For more than 2,000 years, European traders have transported goods on the waterways of Europe. Farmers used the power of the flowing water to turn waterwheels to grind grain. Many cities emerged alongside rivers, where their economies thrived. Europeans began to fish in the North Atlantic. Fishing grew to become an important part of Europe's economy.

REVIEW How does the Gulf Stream affect Europe's climate? **Cause and Effect**

Climate and Landforms

During the early Middle Ages, Europeans began to clear the land to farm. This process of cutting down forests to clear the land is called deforestation. Climate and landforms affected how and where people chose to farm crops.

There are different climates across the continent of Europe. However, most of Europe has a temperate, or mild, climate. As you read earlier, the North European Plain is the most fertile farmland in Europe. Wheat and other grains are grown on this plain.

Along the Atlantic coast, winters are mild and summers are cool. This type of climate is good for farming. Crops that are grown in this area include potatoes, cabbage, and onions.

394

Practice and Extend

ESL ACTIVATE PRIOR KNOWLEDGE **ESL Support**

Use Knowledge Have students use what they already know about rivers to help them understand Europe's river system.

Beginning Help students brainstorm for the names of rivers they know. If necessary, show maps of the appropriate countries. List the rivers and any descriptive words students can say about each one. You may want to use pantomime or pictures to help with vocabulary.

Intermediate Have students complete a three-column chart with the headings *River, Location,* and *Description.*

Advanced Have students choose one or two rivers they know about to describe in webs. Have them write the name of the river in the center circle and descriptive words about the river and how it is used in the connecting circles. Students can use their webs to discuss the rivers.

For additional ESL support, use Every Student Learns Guide, pp. 190–193.

In southern Europe, the climate region is Mediterranean. As you remember from Unit 3, this climate region has hot, dry summers and mild, rainy winters. The ancient Greeks used irrigation to farm. Over time, these lands were overused, and farming declined in the region.

In the Northwest Mountain region, the climate varies. At higher elevations, the climate is cooler. At the lower elevations, people can cultivate

► **This farmer plows olive groves in Spain. Today, Spain and Greece are the world leaders in olive production.**

crops because the climate is more moderate. However, many people in these regions also herd animals and cut timber.

Just like Europe's climate, Europeans are diverse in their cultures and the languages they speak. In this chapter, you will learn about how these peoples interacted with each other and with people from other lands.

7

REVIEW How does location affect people who live and work in the major climate regions of Europe? *Cause and Effect*

Summarize the Lesson

- Europe has four major land regions: the Northwest Mountains, the North European Plain, the Central Uplands, and the Alpine Mountain System.
- Europe has an extensive river and waterway system for transportation.
- Europe's diverse climate affects how people live and work.

LESSON 1 REVIEW

Check Facts and Main Ideas

1. **Cause and Effect** On a separate piece of paper, fill in the missing cause and effects.

Causes		Effects
The North European Plain has fertile land.	→	People cultivate crops such as wheat and grains.
The Northwest Mountain Region has poor soil and dense forests.	→	People in the Northwest Mountain region herd animals and cut timber.
Europe has many rivers and waterways.	→	People use the rivers as transporation routes.

2. What major landform separates Europe from Asia?

3. What are the major rivers of Europe?

4. Identify some ways in which Europeans modified their landscape.

5. **Critical Thinking:** *Accuracy of Information* If you read in a book that Europe had climate regions that were mostly dry and hot, would that be correct? Explain.

Link to ⊂⊃ **Art**

Create an Advertisement Create a travel advertisement to attract visitors to Europe. Use photographs or drawings, as well as descriptions, of European geography. Think about what would appeal to people living in other countries.

395

SOCIAL STUDIES
FYI Background

The Alpine Mountain System

- Among the best known areas of the Alpine Mountain System are the Alps.
- The Alpine Mountain System extends about 750 miles from the Gulf of Genoa to Vienna and covers an area of about 80,000 square miles.
- Located on the border between France and Italy, Mt. Blanc is the highest peak in the Alps, with an elevation of 15,771 feet.
- The Alps support activities such as tourism, dairy farming, forestry, and mining of salt and iron ore.

Workbook, p. 98

Lesson 1: Geography of Europe

Also on Teacher Resources CD-ROM.

7 **What are some examples of Europe's diversity?** Possible answers: Different regions have different climates and landforms. Europeans have diverse cultures and speak many languages. **Main Idea and Details**

✓ **REVIEW ANSWER** Along the Atlantic coast, winters are warm and summers are cool, a climate that is good for farming. The Mediterranean region has hot, dry summers and mild, rainy winters, but farming here has declined because of overused land. At lower elevations in the Northwest Mountain region, the climate is moderate and people can cultivate crops. At higher elevations, where the climate is cooler, people herd animals and cut timber. **Cause and Effect**

3 Close and Assess

Summarize the Lesson

Tell students to read each main idea in the summary. Ask pairs of students to choose one main idea and write at least three details to support it. Have students share their work.

✓ **LESSON 1 REVIEW**

1. **Cause and Effect** For possible answers, see the reduced pupil page.

2. The Ural Mountains

3. Volga, Danube, and Rhine

4. They cut down forests, created irrigation systems, and overused farmland.

5. **Critical Thinking:** *Accuracy of Information* No, Europe has diverse climates that are more temperate than hot and dry.

Link to ⊂⊃ **Art**

Students may wish to look at travel brochures to give them ideas on how to design their ads. Tell students to be sure to include information about the climate and geography of Europe in their ads.

Rulers and Invaders

Objectives

- Explain what title Charlemagne was given by Pope Leo III and why.

- Explain who the Vikings were and what they did in Europe.

- Explain how the Magna Carta limited royal power.

Resources

- Workbook, p. 99
- Transparency 10
- Every Student Learns Guide, pp. 194–197
- Quick Study, pp. 98–99

Quick Teaching Plan

If time is short, have students write mini-biographies.

- Ask students to write the names of rulers and invaders on index cards as they read the lesson independently.

- Have students write facts about each person on the back of the card.

- Students can then compare their cards and add information they may have omitted.

1 Introduce and Motivate

Preview To activate prior knowledge, ask students to recall information they remember about rulers of the African empires. Tell students that, in Lesson 2, they will learn about rulers and invaders of Europe during the Middle Ages.

You Are There — Have students focus on how this passage demonstrates the great authority the king of England had. Ask students to compare the Domesday Book to a government census today.

LESSON 2

700	900	1100	1300

768–814
Much of Europe is united under the rule of Charlemagne.

c. 800–1100
Viking warriors and traders invade Charlemagne's empire.

1215
The Magna Ca is signed, limit royal power.

ENGLAND   SCANDINAVIA

Rulers and Invaders

PREVIEW

Focus on the Main Idea
After a series of rulers and invaders, medieval government in Europe experienced a change.

PLACES
England
Scandinavia
Runnymede

PEOPLE
Charlemagne
William the Conqueror
King John

TERMS
Domesday Book
Middle Ages
Magna Carta

▶ The Domesday Book contains specific information about life in England during the Middle Ages. For example, some 6,000 mills were used to grind grain.

396

You Are There

1086: You're tired. You've ridden on horseback for three hours to reach a small village in the south of England. Yesterday you were in a seaside town. Tomorrow you will be at a lord's castle. You must carry out King William's order that all of England be surveyed. You ask the same questions in every town and village: "Who is the lord of the manor? How much land is here? How many villagers live here? How many sheep? How many pigs? How many fisheries?" There are dozens of other similar questions to ask. Just yesterday some peasants asked what will be done with the Domesday (DOOMS day) Book—for that's what people have been calling it. You're not sure. But you and your fellow workers think that King William will use the information to see if he can get more tax money from the countryside. At the very least you guess that, when it's finished, the Domesday Book will give an accurate picture of life at this time.

Sequence As you read, keep in mind the order in which events happen.

Practice and Extend

READING SKILL
Sequence

In the Lesson Review, students complete a graphic organizer like the one below. You may want to provide students with a copy of Transparency 10 to complete as they read the lesson.

Use Transparency 10

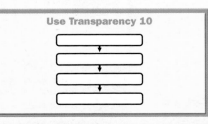

WEB SITE
Technology

- You can look up vocabulary words by clicking on *Social Studies Library* and selecting the dictionary at **www.sfsocialstudies.com.**

- Students can learn more about current news by clicking on *Current Events* at **www.sfsocialstudies.com.**

- Explore other events that occurred on this day by clicking on *This Day in History* at **www.sfsocialstudies.com.**

A European Empire

The Domesday Book helped keep track of people in England during the Middle Ages, or the period in Europe from about A.D. 500 to 1500. It also helped the ruler set up a tax system. Before the Domesday Book was put together in 1086, no one really knew how many people lived in England.

During the Middle Ages, rulers in Europe such as Charlemagne (SHAHR luh mayn) had to rely on records kept by nobles. In 771 Charlemagne became the sole ruler of his kingdom and by 800, he had been crowned emperor.

He gave large areas of land to loyal nobles. In return, the nobles gave an oath, or a pledge, of loyalty to him. The nobles were responsible for maintaining roads, bridges, and fortifications, or defense walls, on their estates. Read more about Charlemagne in the biography on page 399.

REVIEW How did Charlemagne strengthen his kingdom? Main Ideas and Details

Invaders

Despite Charlemagne's efforts to strengthen his kingdom, it fell apart after his death. First, Vikings, or fierce pirates and warriors from Scandinavia, invaded the empire. The Vikings came from the present-day countries of Denmark, Norway, and Sweden.

From about 800 to 1100, the Vikings launched several invasions. They conquered and looted, or robbed, parts of England and France. Then they raided Germany, Ireland, Italy, Russia, and Spain. At first, they raided these areas to steal goods. Later, they set up trading centers and trade routes.

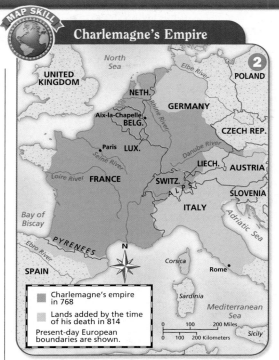

MAP SKILL Charlemagne's Empire

Charlemagne restored much of the old Roman Empire.

MAP SKILL Use Map Scale *How far west of the Rhine River did Charlemagne's empire stretch?*

In the early 900s, another group of Vikings, the Normans, settled in northern France. There they became Christians and church leaders. They also adopted Frankish customs. Under the leadership of William the Conqueror, they marched into England and later advanced into southern Italy.

REVIEW After the Vikings looted the lands they conquered, what did they do? Sequence

The Bayeux Tapestry shows William, Duke of Normandy, invading England with an army of well-trained cavalry troops.

Musée de la Tapisserie, Bayeux, France/Bridgeman Art Library Int'l. Ltd. (U.S.)

MEETING INDIVIDUAL NEEDS
Leveled Practice

Create a Domesday Book Tell students that the Domesday Book was first used by William the Conqueror and included a count of fields, ponds, animals, tools, and other items. Have students provide information for this book.

Easy Help students list people and items to be counted for one farm family. Have them present the information in a chart. **Reteach**

On-Level Have students suppose that they are doing an official count for a farming village. Tell them to design a system for recording their findings. Data should include a count of people, buildings, businesses, and tools. **Extend**

Challenge Have students work in small groups to present a count of people and property for a town or village. Then have them devise a system of taxation based on the information. Encourage groups to share their ideas and discuss the advantages of each. **Enrich**

For a Lesson Summary, use Quick Study, p. 98.

A European Empire

 Quick Summary The Domesday Book tracked people and helped set taxes. Nobles received land and were responsible for its defense and upkeep.

Problem Solving

1 What problems did the Domesday Book help solve? It helped solve the problem of keeping track of people in an empire and helped the ruler set up a tax system. **Solve Problems**

✓ **REVIEW ANSWER** Charlemagne gave land to loyal nobles. In return, nobles pledged their loyalty to him. They maintained roads, bridges, defense walls, and estates. **Main Idea and Details**

MAP SKILL **Charlemagne's Empire**

2 Which part of Europe did Charlemagne's empire include? Western Europe **Interpret Maps**

MAP SKILL Answer About 400 miles

Invaders

 Quick Summary The Vikings and Normans invaded and conquered many parts of Europe.

SOCIAL STUDIES STRAND
Geography

The Vikings came from a region of Europe that includes the present-day countries of Denmark, Norway, and Sweden.

3 What happened to Charlemagne's kingdom after his death? It fell apart when the Vikings invaded from Scandinavia. **Analyze Information**

✓ **REVIEW ANSWER** They established trading centers and trade routes.
 Sequence

A Change in Government

⏱ **Quick Summary** English lords became angry with King John's rule. The Magna Carta was written in 1215 to curb his power.

④ Order the major events that led to the signing of the Magna Carta. King John demanded more military service and money, and he sold royal positions to the highest bidders; he lost a battle against France; civil war broke out in England; he agreed to a set of promises rather than face defeat. 🔄 Sequence

Ongoing Assessment

If... students have difficulty ordering the events that led to the signing of the Magna Carta,

then... display a sequence graphic organizer and work together with students to order the events correctly.

✓ **REVIEW ANSWER** It limited royal power because even the king had to obey the law. **Main Idea and Details**

3 Close and Assess

Summarize the Lesson

Tell students to read the events shown on the time line and identify as many effects of each event as they can.

✓ **LESSON 2   REVIEW**

1. 🔄 **Sequence** For answers, see the reduced pupil page.

2. Emperor of the former Roman Empire in western Europe

3. It helped kings keep track of people and property.

4. The Magna Carta limited royal power by stating that the king could not make demands for money or imprison a free man without the consent of the lords or the sanction of law.

5. **Critical Thinking:** *Fact or Opinion* Fact

Students should realize that the law protected people's rights.

A Change in Government

From about 1066 through the 1100s, most of the kings who ruled England were strong and governed justly. They followed accepted customs that established both the lords' duties and what was expected of the king. However, there was no real limit on the king's power. **King John,** crowned in 1199, governed with more force than earlier kings did. He demanded more military service and greater amounts of money. He also sold royal positions to the highest bidders.

English lords were angry with John's rule. In 1214 John lost an important battle against France. Then civil war broke out in England. Rather than face defeat, John agreed to a set of promises on June 15, 1215, at **Runnymede.** The document was called the **Magna Carta,** or the "Great Charter."

The Magna Carta contained 63 clauses, or articles. Most of the clauses helped lords and other landholders. Some articles eventually helped all people. For example, the charter stated that the king could make no special demands for money

without the consent of the lords. The document stated that no free man could be imprisoned, exiled, or deprived of property, except by law. The greatest value of the Magna Carta was that it limited royal power. The king had to obey the law.

▶ **King John's Great Seal is attached by string to the Magna Carta.**

REVIEW What was the greatest value of the Magna Carta? **Main Idea and Details**

Summarize the Lesson

768–814 Much of Europe was united under the rule of Charlemagne.

c. 800–1100 Viking warriors and traders invaded Charlemagne's empire.

1215 The Magna Carta was signed.

LESSON 2   REVIEW

Check Facts and Main Ideas

1. 🔄 **Sequence** On a separate piece of paper, put these events in their correct chronological order.

   D
   A
   C
   B

   • King John signs the Magna Carta.
   • Charlemagne is crowned emperor.
   • William the Conqueror invades England.
   • The Vikings invade Europe.

2. What title did Pope Leo III give Charlemagne?

3. How did the Domesday Book help kings rule their kingdoms?

4. How did the Magna Carta limit royal power?

5. **Critical Thinking:** *Fact or Opinion* The Magna Carta indicated that there should be no taxation without the consent of the lords.

Link to 🔗 Writing

Interpret a Law Write a paragraph explaining the excerpt below from the Magna Carta.

No free man shall be taken, or imprisoned . . . except by the legal judgement of his peers, or by the law of the land.

Practice and Extend

ESL **EXTEND LANGUAGE ESL Support**

Explore Limits Help students understand the limits the Magna Carta placed on King John.

Beginning Discuss with students why a king might demand money from his subjects. Remind students that the Magna Carta limited King John's power.

Intermediate Help students chart the powers King John had before the Magna Carta and the limits that the document imposed.

Advanced Have students write a personal opinion paragraph about whether or not the Magna Carta was a fair and necessary document.

For additional ESL support, use Every Student Learns Guide, pp. 194–197.

Workbook, p. 99

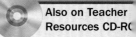

Lesson 2: Rulers and Invaders

Directions: Match each phrase in Column A to the phrase in Column B that completes the sentence. Write the letter from Column B on the line in front of Column A. You may use your textbook.

Column A	Column B
___ 1. Before the Domesday Book was put together in 1086,	a. it fell apart after his death.
___ 2. Because Charlemagne gave large areas of land to the nobles,	b. they were loyal to him and maintained roads, bridges, and defense walls on their estates.
___ 3. Despite Charlemagne's efforts to strengthen his kingdom,	c. civil war broke out in England.
___ 4. After the Vikings looted the lands they conquered,	d. they set up trading centers and trade routes.
___ 5. After the Normans settled in northern France,	e. no one really knew how many people lived in England.
___ 6. Because King John governed with more force than earlier kings did,	f. some of the articles eventually helped all people.
___ 7. After King John lost an important battle against France,	g. royal power was limited.
___ 8. Rather than face defeat in England's civil war,	h. English lords became angry with his rule.
___ 9. Although most of the clauses of the Magna Carta helped the lords and other landholders,	i. they adopted Frankish customs and became Christians and church leaders.
___ 10. When King John agreed to the set of promises in the Magna Carta,	j. King John agreed to the Magna Carta.

Notes for Home: Your child learned about medieval government in Europe under different rulers and invaders.
Home Activity: Review the articles of the Magna Carta discussed on p. 398. With your child, review the set of promises at home. Discuss why rules exist and why they are valuable.

💿 **Also on Teacher Resources CD-RO[M]**

Charlemagne
c. 742–814

Charlemagne was the son of Pepin III. Charlemagne ruled the kingdom of the Franks with his brother. The Franks had invaded the western Roman Empire in the 400s. Charlemagne was educated and raised as a Christian.

In 768 Pepin III died, and Charlemagne and his brother took over their father's kingdom. Charlemagne's brother died in 771, making Charlemagne the sole ruler of the Franks. He immediately set out to conquer neighboring lands and expand his power. Leading his army into battle, Charlemagne at nearly 6 feet 4 inches tall, towered over most men.

Once he conquered a region, Charlemagne forced the people to become Christians. He maintained close ties with the Roman church throughout his reign. At Christmas Mass in 800, Pope Leo III crowned Charlemagne emperor of the former Roman Empire in western Europe. People attending the Mass gave this salute:

1 *"To Charles Augustus, crowned by God, great and peace-giving Emperor . . . ."*

Charlemagne ruled much of western Europe, except England and Scandinavia. As ruler of such a large empire, Charlemagne issued a series of legal decrees, or commands, called capitularies. These written laws covered everything from church matters to punishment. Charlemagne also promoted culture and learning in his empire. He invited leading European scholars to his court and asked them to further educate clergy.

BIOFACT
Even after being crowned emperor, Charlemagne could not read or write. He kept writing tablets under his pillows to try to learn but never succeeded.

2 The scholars also supervised the copying by hand of classic Roman literature. Had these works not been copied, we would not know about many of them today. The originals have been lost.

Learn from Biographies
After Charlemagne conquered a region, what did he do?

For more information, go online to *Meet the People* at **www.sfsocialstudies.com.**

399

SOCIAL STUDIES STRAND
Economics

Economic Growth Under Charlemagne

- During Charlemagne's conquest, few town or cities existed. People farmed for a living, raising barely enough food to feed themselves.
- Under Charlemagne's rule, better farming methods increased the food supply. People could buy or trade food. As a result, towns arose.
- Charlemagne then introduced silver coins as money, which promoted trade.

Charlemagne

Objective
- Identify the contributions of significant individuals, such as Charlemagne, during the Middle Ages.

1 Introduce and Motivate

Preview To activate prior knowledge, ask students to share what they recall about Charlemagne. Tell students that they will read about how he ruled his empire and the contributions he made.

Ask why it might be useful to know about the contributions made by an emperor from the Middle Ages. (It can show which contributions have influenced present-day cultures throughout the world.)

2 Teach and Discuss

C **SOCIAL STUDIES STRAND**
Culture

Tell students that a mass is a celebrational ceremony of the Roman Catholic Church

1 How did people attending Christmas Mass in 800 feel about Charlemagne? They saluted him as a great and peace-giving emperor. **Analyze Primary Sources**

2 How did Charlemagne promote learning and culture in his empire? He invited European scholars to further educate the clergy and to supervise the copying of classic Roman literature. **Main Idea and Details**

3 Close and Assess

Learn from Biographies Answer

He forced conquered peoples to become Christians, issued legal decrees, and promoted culture and education.

Life in the Middle Ages

Objectives

- Explain the role of serfs in feudalism.
- List and describe the different levels of feudalism.
- Explain the purpose of craft guilds.
- Explain how feudalism and the manor system affected the lives of the nobility in medieval Europe.
- Explain how the manor system led to the growth of towns and cities.

Vocabulary

monk, p. 401; **nun,** p. 401; **monastery,** p. 401; **convent,** p. 401; **missionary,** p. 401; **monarch,** p. 401; **serf,** p. 401; **knight,** p. 401; **chivalry,** p. 401; **guild,** p. 404; **lady,** p. 405

Resources

- Workbook, p. 100
- Transparency 1
- Every Student Learns Guide, pp. 198–201
- Quick Study, pp. 100–101

Quick Teaching Plan

If time is short, have students create expanded glossaries, listing, defining, and providing an example for each of the vocabulary words.

1 Introduce and Motivate

Preview To activate prior knowledge, ask students what they know about kings and knights. Tell students that, in Lesson 3, they will learn what life was like for knights and kings in the Middle Ages.

You Are There Have students focus on the items offered for sale described in this passage. Ask them to draw conclusions about life in feudal times based on the kinds of items and activities included in the fair.

| 700 | 900 | 1100 | 1300 |

c. 700 Manor system begins.

c. 800 Feudalism begins to rise.

c. 1200 The Manor system starts to decline.

1400 Feudalism starts to decline.

PREVIEW

Focus on the Main Idea
The church, feudalism, and manor life formed the foundation of European medieval life.

PLACES
Europe

PEOPLE
Christine de Pisan

VOCABULARY
monk
nun
monastery
convent
missionary
monarch
serf
knight
chivalry
guild
lady

TERMS
feudalism
manor system
three-field rotation

▶ The goal of Nine Men's Morris is to get three markers in a row.

400

Life in the Middle Ages

You Are There It's September, and the cold night has lasted until morning. You pull the quilt up to your chin to stay warm—Wait! Today is Michaelmas—a holiday! Everyone will be at the fair. You rush to dress, eat, and leave for the commons. As you near the fair, you see stalls offering pottery, saddles, jewelry, fabric, glassware, bread, and even armor for sale. The merchants have come from miles away. You make your way through musicians, acrobats, and candy sellers. You can smell the Michaelmas goose cooking, and you want to make sure to get a taste of it for good luck. Beyond the food, you stop to watch a few wrestling matches, followed by archery contests. On your left are more food stalls. These are full of all things ginger—cake, beverages, cookies, and caramels. You meet a friend and together you play several games of Nine Men's Morris before you head home.

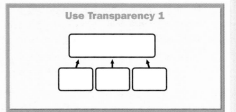

Main Idea and Details As you read, identify details of daily life in medieval Europe.

Practice and Extend

READING SKILL
Main Idea and Details

In the Lesson Review, students complete a graphic organizer like the one below. You may want to provide students with a copy of Transparency 1 to complete as they read the lesson.

Use Transparency 1

WEB SITE
Technology

- You can look up vocabulary words by clicking on *Social Studies Library* and selecting the dictionary at **www.sfsocialstudies.com.**
- Students can learn more about current news by clicking on *Current Events* at **www.sfsocialstudies.com.**
- Explore other events that occurred on this day by clicking on *This Day in History* at **www.sfsocialstudies.com.**

The Church

The Michaelmas holiday you just read about was one of the many Christian feast days celebrated in medieval **Europe.** During the Middle Ages, Christianity was an important part of daily life.

Not all Europeans were Christians; some were Jews and others were Muslims. But most were Christians. Like Muslims, Christians showed their devotion by going on a pilgrimage—to Rome or Jerusalem, not Mecca. To Jews, Christians, and Muslims, Jerusalem was a holy city. However, Rome was the holy center of Christendom, or "kingdom of the Christians." The Christian leader, or pope, lived in Rome. He was just as powerful as a king was.

Building cathedrals with magnificent stained-glass windows became a major focus of medieval life. Entire towns worked to build these large churches that took decades or even hundreds of years to finish. For example, the construction of the Chartres Cathedral in northwestern France began about 1145. After a fire, Chartres was reconstructed and completed by 1260.

The Christian faith centered around the Christian church. Some young people even devoted their lives to religion. Some men who did this were called **monks,** and women were called **nuns.** Monks studied, prayed, and lived in communities called **monasteries.** Nuns lived in similar communities called **convents.**

Both monasteries and convents served as centers of religion and education. In addition to praying and studying, monks and nuns cultivated crops and helped the poor. Some monks became **missionaries,** or people who teach a religion to people with different beliefs.

REVIEW What role did the Christian church have in medieval Europe? **Summarize**

▶ Chartres Cathedral has 176 stained-glass windows.

Feudalism

During the Middle Ages, Europe had few strong central governments. People formed their own system to meet their need for protection and justice. **Feudalism** was a political, social, and economic system that began in the 800s. It provided the needed protection for people.

Feudalism resembled a social structure. At the top was the **monarch,** a king or queen who was the supreme ruler. The next level included lords who pledged their loyalty to the monarch and military support in the event of a war or conflict. In return, the monarch granted the lord an estate.

The lord owned the land. He also received a large percentage of the crops produced on the land and received all the income from the crops. He collected taxes, maintained order, enforced laws, and protected the serfs. **Serfs** were the people who lived on the land and farmed it. A saying of the time was "No land without a lord, and no lord without land." ❷

Many lords had **knights,** or warriors trained and prepared to fight on horseback. Knights had a code of behavior called **chivalry.** According to the code, a true knight had deep faith, was ready to die for the church, gave generously to all, and used his strength to stand against injustice. Between 1100 and 1300, most knights received some land from their lords. ❸

REVIEW Why did a monarch give large estates to lords? Main Idea and Details

monarch

lords

knights

serfs or peasants

▶ During feudalism peasants made up 90 percent of the population. Monarchs, lords, and the church had all the power and wealth.

401

The Church

🕐 *Quick Summary* The church was the center of life in Medieval Europe. Major cathedrals were built, and some people became monks, nuns, or missionaries.

C SOCIAL STUDIES STRAND
Culture

Many of the stained-glass windows in Chartres Cathedral tell Bible stories.

❶ **What event slowed the construction of Chartres Cathedral?** A fire
Main Idea and Details

✓ **REVIEW ANSWER** Central. Many people devoted their lives to Christianity. **Summarize**

Feudalism

🕐 *Quick Summary* During the Middle Ages, most of Europe had a political, social, and economic system known as feudalism.

Primary Source

Cited in *The World Book Encyclopedia*

Tell students that "No land without a lord, and no lord without land" describes feudalism as a form of decentralized government. The lord's local administration had more effect on people's lives than the monarch's.

❷ **How did this saying show the importance of the lord of the land?** Possible answer: It states that every estate or piece of land must be overseen by a lord. **Analyze Primary Sources**

❸ **What personal qualities were knights expected to have in the feudal social structure?** Possible answers: Strong religious belief, bravery, loyalty, generosity, and strength
Draw Conclusions

✓ **REVIEW ANSWER** To get the lords' loyalty and military support, and so that the lords would maintain order for them
Main Idea and Details

Feudalism Declines

⏱ *Quick Summary* As lords grew more powerful, they became independent of the monarch. Military support was replaced by monetary payments, and by the 1400s the feudal system was in decline.

4 **What caused the decline of feudalism?** Some lords built up their own military power and became independent of the monarch. The lords substituted payment in money for military support. **Cause and Effect**

✓ **REVIEW ANSWER** Advantages: Serfs were not slaves. They could not be bought or sold. Disadvantages: Serfs were tied to the land and could not leave without the lord's permission, nor could they rise above serfdom to become knights. **Main Idea and Details**

The Manor System

⏱ *Quick Summary* The manor system was a way to manage feudal lands. Serfs used a three-field rotation system to avoid exhausting the soil.

5 **What did the typical manor have that kept it self-sufficient?** Farmland to grow food, a mill for grinding grain into flour, homes to shelter the serfs that worked the land, and a church **Analyze Information**

Feudalism Declines

Serfs, who are sometimes called peasants, formed the base of the society in the Middle Ages. Unlike kings, lords, and knights, who were bound to be faithful to one another, serfs had no such loyalty to anyone. Serfs were not slaves, yet could not become knights. They could not be bought or sold separate from the land. Even so, serfs were tied to the land they worked and could not leave it without the lord's permission.

As time passed, some lords had many faithful knights, therefore building up much military power. These lords became independent of the monarch, who originally granted the land to them. The lords substituted payment in money for actual military support. By the 1400s, feudalism had begun to decline.

4

REVIEW What advantages did feudalism provide serfs? Disadvantages? **Main Idea and Details**

The Manor System

Because feudalism was based on holding land, it is sometimes confused with the manor system, which was a way of organizing agricultural labor.

The **manor system,** common from the 700s to the 1200s, was a way to manage feudal lands. Manors usually had four parts: the manor house and village; farmland; meadowland; and wasteland. The manor house or castle was home to the lord of the estate. Gardens, orchards, and farm buildings often surrounded the manor house. Most manors included a church and a mill for grinding grain into flour.

Serfs' cottages were clustered together, forming a small village. The mud brick cottages had reinforced straw walls, dirt floors, and straw thatched roofs. A cottage usually consisted

5

▶ The manor system allowed the lord of the manor along with the knights and serfs to be self-sufficient, providing opportunities to grow or make everything they needed.

castle or manor house

church

knight

Practice and Extend

FYI **SOCIAL STUDIES**
Background

Serfdom

- Most of the European population of the Middle Ages were serfs.
- Serfs had to get their lord's permission if they wanted to marry someone from another manor, and sometimes pay a fine as well.
- A serf had to pay a fine if his or her son wanted to leave the manor to become a priest or a monk.
- Serfs had to pay their lords to use the mill, oven, and carts.
- A serf could gain freedom by escaping from the land, by paying for freedom, or by being formally freed.

of a single room with little floor space and a low ceiling. Many cottages had small vegetable and fruit gardens.

Many serfs shared their cottages with livestock and other animals on the manor. They heated their cottages with wood that they chopped from nearby forests. In addition to working in the fields all day, many serfs worshiped in church. Serfdom was a difficult life. The church offered hope and peace.

After about 1000, serfs worked the manor lands using the **three-field rotation** system.

▶ The serf's most important tool—the moldboard plow—required a team of four to eight oxen.

Ancient Art & Architecture Collection, Ltd.

In this system, every serf was assigned a strip of land in each of the manor's three fields. In the fall, one field was planted with wheat or rye. In the spring, the second field was planted with oats or barley. The third field was unplanted so that the soil would stay fertile. Each year the fields were rotated. **6**

Fields were divided into long strips about one acre in size. Some of the strips contained good soil, some poor. The best soil was set aside for the lord of the manor. In addition to their own strips, peasants had to work on the lord's land at least three days a week.

The manor's working animals grazed on the meadowland. Meadowlands and wastelands often included ponds and streams for fishing. They provided summer pasture for animals, as well as wood for fuel and building materials. They also provided foods such as nuts, berries, honey, rabbits, and wild fowl.

The manor system generally met all the needs of the lord, knights, and serfs living there. It even allowed for crop surpluses. Serfs could sell the surpluses from the strips to people living in towns and cities. With a surplus, towns and cities began to grow. **7**

REVIEW Name the advantages and disadvantages of the manor system.
Main Idea and Details

lord

serf

403

One-acre strips of land were all that could be plowed in one day's worth of work.

6 **How many strips of land would each serf have to farm in a year? How can you tell?** Two; each serf had one strip of land in each of the manor's three fields, and one field was always left unplanted. **Apply Information**

7 **How did selling crop surpluses help towns and cities grow?** Possible answer: More people could move into towns and cities knowing that food was available there. They could specialize in a trade or craft because they didn't have to grow their own food. **Draw Conclusions**

✓ **Ongoing Assessment**

If... students cannot explain how crop surpluses led to the growth of towns,

then... have them compare the roles of farmer and tradesman. Help them understand why having a source of food would be of concern to a craftsman living in a village.

✓ **REVIEW ANSWER** Disadvantages: Serfdom was a difficult life; peasants might not get good soil, and they had to work the lord's land as well as their own. Advantages: Generally all the needs of the lords, knights, and serfs were met; serfs were allowed to sell crop surpluses to people in cities and towns, which helped the cities and towns grow. **Main Idea and Details**

CURRICULUM CONNECTION
Literature

Life in Medieval Times

Use the following selections to extend content.

Marguerite Makes a Book, by Bruce Robertson (Getty Publications, ISBN 0-89236-372-X, 1999) **Easy**

If You Lived in the Days of the Knights, by Ann McGovern (Scholastic Trade, ISBN 0-439-10565-X, 2001) **On-Level**

The Midwife's Apprentice, by Karen Cushman (HarperTrophy, ISBN 0-06-440630-X, 1996) **Challenge** **Newbery Medal**

Guilds

Quick Summary Guilds were associations formed to protect town merchants and craftspeople from outside competition.

8 How did merchant guilds protect town merchants from competition? Merchants who were not members of the town's guild could not sell goods in the town. **Analyze Information**

C SOCIAL STUDIES STRAND
Culture

To earn guild membership, a young man or boy was bound to a master of a craft for several years. As an apprentice, he learned his craft's basics. Next, as a journeyman he earned wages for his work. Finally, after making a *masterpiece* (a particularly fine piece of work), he became a craft master.

✓ **REVIEW ANSWER** Membership would show that he made quality goods and would limit the competition he might face in a particular town. **Draw Conclusions**

The Beothuk

9 What effect did the Europeans have on the Beothuk's way of life? Possible answer: Europeans left behind objects such as nails, fishhooks, scraps of iron, and kettles. The Beothuk shaped these objects into arrowheads, spear points, and other tools. **Cause and Effect**

Guilds

By about 1000, once cities began to flourish, guilds formed. A **guild** was a group of people united by a common interest. A merchant guild included all of the traders in a town. The guild worked together to buy large quantities of goods cheaply and to control the market. A merchant who was not a member of the town's guild could **8** not sell goods in the town. Guilds also guaranteed a fair price for goods.

Workers such as bakers, goldsmiths, tailors, and weavers formed craft guilds. These guilds controlled the quality and quantity of production. Guilds protected the town's merchants and craftspeople from having to compete with those from outside the town.

REVIEW Why would a baker or weaver want to join a craft guild? **Draw Conclusions**

▶ Each guild had its own emblem, or symbol. Emblems were often based on the tools used by the craftspeople.

The Beothuk

At the same time that ancient Europeans were clearing lands for farms, a group of about 1,000 Beothuk (BE ah thuck) were hunter-gatherers living on the island of Newfoundland. The Beothuk ate a rich and varied diet including seals, polar bears, and beavers. They also ate caribou, fish, geese, and many other animals.

In the 1500s, some Europeans sailed to the Newfoundland region to fish. They built fishing structures to use during the summer months. The Europeans left behind a number of items when they moved on. The Beothuk found these objects—nails, fishhooks, and scraps of iron and kettles. They shaped them into arrowheads and spear points. They made harpoon points and animal hide scrapers.

The Beothuk had an unusual opportunity. They acquired these European goods without having to exchange Beothuk goods for them.

▶ The Beothuk often collected metal objects, such as these, by visiting abandoned European fishing locations.

▶ This Beothuk carved bone object was found on the island of Newfoundland. **9**

404

Practice and Extend

CURRICULUM CONNECTIONS
Drama

Perform a Skit Have students work in pairs to write and perform a skit about the Beothuk.

- Have students work in pairs to write a brief skit depicting two Beothuk fishers discussing life in Newfoundland during the 1500s.
- Have students include a scene in which the two fishers come across items left behind by the Europeans.
- Have partners present their skits to the class.

ESL EXTEND LANGUAGE
ESL Support

Economic Overview Have students explore the advantages of guilds.

Beginning Have students look through supermarket flyers or office supply brochures to compare prices of single items to those for the same items bought in bulk. Help students see that when you can buy more of an item the price is often less per item. Explain that this is one thing guilds did.

Intermediate Have students make a web with *guild* in the center circle. In each connecting circle, guide students to write a characteristic of a guild, such as *guaranteed fair prices.*

Advanced Have students create an advertisement attempting to bring members into a specific merchant or craft guild during the Middle Ages. Be sure students mention the benefits members of the guild will enjoy.

For additional ESL support, use Every Student Learns Guide, pp. 198–201.

Medieval Women

During the Middle Ages, most women had few rights. Unmarried women who owned some land did have rights. However, when they married they had to give up their rights. A **lady,** or a woman of noble birth, was given little opportunity to make decisions about her own life. Usually a lady's actions were directed by her father or husband. She often had little to do with the estate. Servants managed the lord's affairs, and nurses took care of the children. In contrast, a woman living in a village had more work to do. Wives often worked on the land with their husbands. Unmarried women worked as servant girls or as hired agricultural workers. Women living in towns worked in nearly all the trades. Even though they could participate in the craft, they were kept out of decision-making discussions.

Some women did break out of the common roles led by medieval women. One of these was **Christine de Pisan.** She was one of the few

▶ In this painting, Christine de Pisan is writing at her desk in France.

medieval women to earn a living by writing. She wrote poetry and books protesting the way women were both glorified and insulted by male authors.

REVIEW It has been said that "The greater a medieval woman's wealth and social standing, the lower her status." Do you agree with this statement? **Main Idea and Details**

Summarize the Lesson

- **c. 800s** Feudalism began.
- **c. 1200** The Manor system began to decline.
- **c. 1400** Feudalism began to decline.

LESSON 3 REVIEW

Check Facts and Main Ideas

1. **Main Idea and Details** On a separate piece of paper, fill in the missing main idea that is supported by the details.

```
┌─────────────────────────────────┐
│ Serfs had few rights in the     │
│ feudal system.                  │
└─────────────────────────────────┘
```

| Serfs were bound to the land. | Serfs were not slaves. | Serfs could not leave the land without permission from the lord. |

2. Name the four levels in feudalism.

3. What was the purpose of a craft guild?

4. Identify some ways in which feudalism and the manor system affected the lives of the nobility.

5. **Critical Thinking:** *Make Inferences* What feature of the manor system allowed the growth of towns and cities? Explain.

Link to ⚭ **Drama**

Prepare a Skit Choose the role of a guild member. Prepare a skit in which you explain why the guild is good for your town.

405

FAST FACTS

Christine de Pisan wrote poetry and prose and advocated women's active participation in society. Here are the first two stanzas of one of her poems.

Christine to Her Son
I have no great fortune, my son,
To make you rich. In place of one
Here are some lessons I have learned—
The finest things I've ever earned.

Before the world has borne you far,
Try to know people as they are.
Knowing that will help you take
The path that keeps you from mistake.

Workbook, p. 100

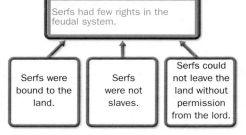

Lesson 3: Life in the Middle Ages

Directions: Complete the concept map below. Classify each description in the box by listing it in one of the levels of feudalism. You may use your textbook.

received land from the lord	kings or queens	granted estates to lords
gave military support	protected serfs	no loyalty to monarchs or lords
trained to fight on horseback	supreme rulers	followed code of behavior
owned land and crops	peasants	
	lived on and farmed the land	

Feudalism

Also on Teacher Resources CD-ROM.

Medieval Women

🕐 ***Quick Summary*** Medieval women had few rights and few opportunities to make decisions about their lives.

🔟 **In terms of rights, which village women most closely resembled women of noble birth?** Married women
Make Inferences

✓ **REVIEW ANSWER** Possible answers: Students may agree. Noblewomen were directed by husbands and fathers, whereas village women could be members of craft guilds.
Main Idea and Details

③ Close and Assess

Summarize the Lesson

Tell students to read the summary. Have them share in pairs what they know about feudalism, the manor system, and how the two are related.

✓ **LESSON 3 REVIEW**

1. **Main Idea and Details** For possible answer, see the reduced pupil page.

2. The monarch, the lords, the knights, and the serfs

3. To control the quality and quantity of goods produced and to protect members from outside competition.

4. In the feudal system, a monarch granted a lord land, and in return the lord pledged loyalty and military support to the monarch. The lord maintained order, received income from the crops produced on his estate, and collected taxes. The manor system guaranteed that there would be serfs to work the lord's land.

5. **Critical Thinking:** *Make Inferences* The three-field rotation system resulted in crop surpluses that serfs could sell to people who did not raise their own food.

Link to ⚭ **Drama**

Students should demonstrate the advantages the townspeople gained from the guilds.

Crusades, Trade, and the Plague

Objectives

- List and explain some of the major events that affected Europe in the late Middle Ages.

- Explain who issued the call for the Crusades and why.

- List and describe some of the major trade goods that traveled over trade routes, such as the Silk Road, in the Middle Ages.

- Explain what a bubonic plague is and how it affects humans.

- Explain what the different theories are regarding how the Plague reached Europe.

Vocabulary

epidemic, p. 410

Resources

- Workbook, p. 101
- Transparency 20
- Every Student Learns Guide, pp. 202–205
- Quick Study, pp. 102–103

Quick Teaching Plan

If time is short, have students complete a four-column chart with the headings *Event, What Happened, When,* and *Why.*

1 Introduce and Motivate

Preview Ask students to recall what they know about the effects of trade on a region. Explain that they will learn about European trade during the time of the Crusades.

You Are There Tell students the Crusades were religious wars fought during the early 1000s. Note that a *squire* is a knight's personal attendant, and that the word *mail* comes from the French word *maille,* meaning "mesh." Ask students to describe the problems they think knights might have had when preparing for battle in the Crusades.

LESSON 4

| 1000 | | 1500 |

1000
Trade begins to expand in Europe.

1095
Urban II calls for the First Crusade.

c. 1347
A Bubonic plague spreads throughout Europe.

Crusades, Trade, and the Plague

PREVIEW

Focus on the Main Idea
Routes promoted trade, travel, and communication, as well as the Plague, between Europe, Africa, and Asia.

PLACES
Palestine
Rome
Chang'an
Dunhuang
Genoa

PEOPLE
Alexius Comnenus
Urban II
Marco Polo

VOCABULARY
epidemic

TERMS
Crusades
Silk Road
Plague
bubonic plague

▶ This illustration from a twelfth-century tapestry shows a typical full suit of chain mail armor.

You Are There Hooray! It's your 14th birthday and your parents are sending you to work as a squire to Sir John. You will go on the Second Crusade with him. You will act as his servant much of the time. But, best of all, you will be in charge of Sir John's chain mail armor. It's a great responsibility. Sir John has the latest in armor technology. His chain mail has hundreds of iron rings linked together. It looks like mesh. Even his horse wears some chain mail armor. Sir John's armor weighs about 50 pounds. Sir John will need your help getting in and out of his armor. Once he is in it, you will hand him his weapons. These include a two-edged sword to hang from his waist and a dagger to tuck into his belt. After you help him onto his horse, you will hand him his lance and battle-ax. Then, because of your help, Sir John will be ready for battle.

Cause and Effect As you read, identify the causes and effects of the Crusades, expansion of trade, and the Plague.

406

Practice and Extend

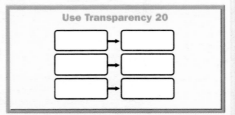

The Crusades

After Charlemagne, battles for religion meant that more and more Christian knights were needed to fight. Two hundred years earlier, Islam had spread through North Africa and Asia Minor. Lands to the north and west of the Mediterranean Sea were mainly Christian. Lands along the eastern shores of the Mediterranean were Muslim.

In the mid-1000s, a group of Muslim Seljuk Turks from Central Asia rose up and defeated a Byzantine army. This marked the decline of Byzantine control over Asia Minor. During this time, the Turks conquered many lands, including **Palestine.** In the first century, Judea had been renamed Palestine by the Romans, who then forced the Jews to leave the region.

Christians considered Palestine the Holy Land. According to the New Testament, this is where Jesus had lived and preached. In the Mediterranean and Black Sea regions, Islam had gradually replaced Christianity, and the Turkish language had replaced Greek. In 1095 Byzantine Emperor **Alexius Comnenus** asked Pope **Urban II** in **Rome** for help. He wanted Christian knights to fight against the Turks. Urban II responded by issuing a plea to free the Holy Land from the Muslims:

> *"I, Urban, by the permission of God . . . have come into these parts as an ambassador . . . to you, the servants of God."*

Between 1095 and 1214, Christians in western Europe responded by organizing eight major military expeditions called the **Crusades.** Kings, nobles, knights, peasants, and townspeople became crusaders and set out to win back control of Palestine.

REVIEW What were the Crusades?
Main Idea and Details

The First Crusade

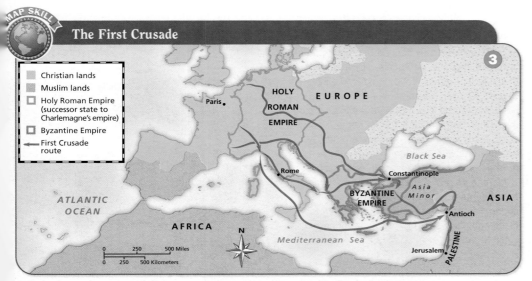

▶ While there were many Crusades, the first one produced the most significant results.

MAP SKILL Trace Movement on Maps *Describe the route of the First Crusade.*

407

Quick Summary The Crusades, which began in 1095, were eight major military expeditions fought to win back the Holy Land and protect the Byzantine Empire.

1 Why did Christians want to win back Palestine? They considered it to be their Holy Land because it was where Jesus had lived and preached.
Cause and Effect

✓ **Ongoing Assessment**

If... students do not understand why Christians wanted to take back Palestine,	then... explain that because the Christian religion had its beginnings in Palestine, Christians considered it to be their Holy Land.

Primary Source
Cited in *A Source Book for Medieval History,* edited by Oliver J. Thatcher and Edgar Holmes McNeal

2 What was the purpose of Pope Urban II's plea? To help free Palestine from Muslim control
Analyze Primary Sources

✓ **REVIEW ANSWER** Military expeditions to win back control of the Holy Land and to protect the Byzantine Empire
Main Idea and Details

The First Crusade

3 In which areas did Islam and Christianity flourish? Christianity flourished in Europe, while Islam flourished in Asia, Africa, and a small part of western Europe.
Interpret Maps

MAP SKILL Answer Crusaders from Europe marched south and east by various routes to Antioch, and then south to Jerusalem.

ESL EXTEND LANGUAGE
ESL Support

Examine Word Meanings Help students understand that while the word *crusades* in the text is a noun meaning "wars with religious purposes approved by the church," *crusade* can also mean "a campaign against something or for something," as well as a verb meaning "to fight for or to take up a cause."

Beginning Say the word *crusade* and have students repeat the pronunciation. List examples of nonviolent crusades, such as walks to help people with diabetes. Guide them in making simple posters about a cause.

Intermediate Have students use a thesaurus or dictionary to create word webs of synonyms for the word *crusade* used as a noun and as a verb. Then have them write sentences using *crusade* as a noun and as a verb.

Advanced Discuss the meaning of the word *crusade* as a verb. Have students write a paragraph telling how they would fight for a cause.

For additional ESL support, use Every Student Learns Guide, pp. 202–205.

East and West

🕐 *Quick Summary* The Crusades increased contact between the West and the East, which expanded opportunities for trade.

4 **What were the effects of the Crusades?** Although the Crusades did not have a permanent effect on rule in the region, they did increase trade and commerce between the West and the East. **Summarize**

✓ **REVIEW ANSWER** Each area had different goods and products, and the new contact stimulated interest in them. **Draw Conclusions**

Trade Grows

🕐 *Quick Summary* A network of European trade routes developed, linking Africa, Asia Minor, China, and the Far East. This allowed foreign goods to be sold at fairs throughout Europe.

5 **Why did the need for goods that were not available on the manor increase?** Serfs needed iron for better farming tools, and lords wanted new products, such as wool and furs, to show off their wealth. **Cause and Effect**

6 **What benefits did trade routes have for traders?** Traders were able to exchange local goods for foreign goods through middlemen without having to travel to the markets of Asia. **Main Idea and Details**

✓ **REVIEW ANSWER** Africa, Asia Minor, China, the Far East, and other Muslim lands **Main Idea and Details**

East and West

The crusaders marched to the East to win control of the Holy Land. Many of the crusaders also fought for themselves. They sought to increase their power, territory, and riches. The Crusades occurred at a time when western Europe's economy was expanding. Its military forces were increasing. The crusaders won some battles. They established crusader states along the eastern shore of the Mediterranean Sea. Although their victories had no permanent effect on the rule of the region, the Crusades increased the contacts between the West and the East. These contacts led to additional trade and commerce.

4 **REVIEW** Why would contact between the East and the West lead to increased trade? **Draw Conclusions**

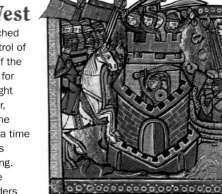

▶ A manuscript by William of Tyre illustrates the First Crusade, the Siege of Antioch.

Bibliotheque Nationale, Paris, France

A network of European trade routes developed to serve these fairs. Traders developed standard, or regular, trade routes. Along these routes, traders and merchants exchanged local goods for foreign goods. A trader did not need to travel to the markets of Asia. Instead, goods from Asia would reach the trader through a series of middlemen, rather like a relay race.

The European trade routes linked to Muslim trade routes, providing goods from Africa, Asia Minor, and other Muslim lands. For goods from China and the Far East, European trade routes linked to the primary trade route through Asia, the Silk Road, one of the oldest and most important land routes.

REVIEW What locations or regions were part of the European trade network? **Main Idea and Details**

Trade Grows

During the early Middle Ages, in about 1000, people had what they needed to produce their own food, clothing, and shelter. Occasionally they might barter for goods produced elsewhere. However, over time, people began to need and want goods that were not available on the manor. Serfs needed iron for better farming tools. Lords wanted ways to show off their wealth—fine wool and furs. These goods reached people on the manor by way of a fair.

Merchants and craftspeople in local guilds set up tents or stalls to display and sell their goods. Fairs occurred regularly and often took place on holidays, or holy days, or during celebrations.

▶ This image from the thirteenth century shows a typical medieval shop filled with goods.

408

Practice and Extend

🔆 **MEETING INDIVIDUAL NEEDS**
Leveled Practice

Describe a Process Have students show the steps involved in obtaining and selling foreign goods at fairs.

Easy Have students arrange the steps that merchants followed in correct order: (1) Obtain European goods to be traded. (2) Go to places along trade routes. (3) Trade European goods for foreign goods. (4) Display and sell foreign goods at fairs in Europe. **Reteach**

On-Level Have students complete a sequence chart to show the order of events that took place for European merchants to sell foreign goods at fairs. **Extend**

Challenge Have students write and perform a skit showing a European merchant preparing to travel to markets along the trade routes to obtain foreign goods. Have students include plans the merchant made for traveling and for the goods he hoped to bring back. **Enrich**

For a Lesson Summary, use Quick Study, p. 102.

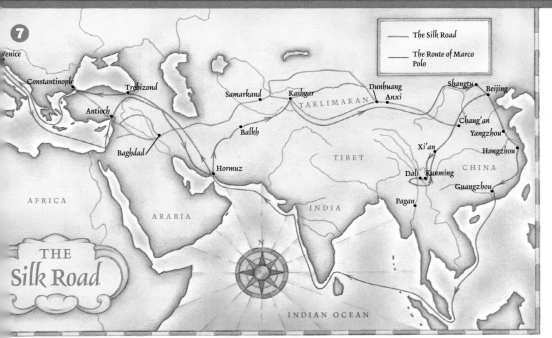

The name *Silk Road* is a nineteenth-century term coined by the German scholar Ferdinand von Richthofen. Marco Polo traveled the entire length of the Silk Road to cross Asia.

The Silk Road

We know much about the Silk Road from the travels of **Marco Polo.** His accounts of China's riches fascinated Europeans.

At about 4,000 miles in length, the Silk Road was not one single route across Central Asia. It was several different routes and branches, each passing through different settlements. However, all routes set out from the Chinese capital, **Chang'an** under the Han dynasty. They all reached **Dunhuang** on the edge of the Taklimakan Desert. At Dunhuang the road branched. The northern route, which led to Baghdad, is shown above on the map.

Caravans to China carried gold, ivory, and precious stones. Caravans from China brought silk, furs, ceramics, jade, bronze objects, lacquer, and iron. Ideas traveled both ways—Buddhism came to China via the Silk Road.

The Silk Road was physically difficult for travel. In addition, bandits made travel dangerous.

Caravans needed their own defense forces. In some places, forts and defensive walls were constructed along part of the route to protect the caravans.

In 1271 Marco Polo left Venice, Italy, for Shangtu. Under the Mongols, Polo remained in China as a guest for 17 years. In his writings, he describes how Genghis Khan unified the region:

> *"He then made himself master of cities and provinces . . . . and appointed governors to them."* 9

Once the numerous states in the region were united under the Mongol Empire, the Silk Road became important as a path for communication between different parts of the Empire. When the Silk Road came under the protection of the Mongols, it became safe for travel. 10

REVIEW What goods traveled along the Silk Road to and from China? Main Idea and Details

409

The Silk Road

Quick Summary The Silk Road was a series of trade routes beginning in China. Both the trading of goods and cultural exchanges took place along these trade routes.

7 **In what direction would a trader travel to get from Kashgar to Dunhuang? How many routes between these cities does the map show?** East; two Interpret Maps

C SOCIAL STUDIES STRAND
Culture

Tell students that lacquer is a highly polished varnish used to coat wood and other materials. The word *lacquer* can also refer to the coated items themselves, which are often decorated with ivory or metal.

8 **How did the Silk Road influence Chinese culture?** Caravans carried goods and ideas to China from the West. Buddhism also came to China via the Silk Road. Analyze Information

Primary Source
Cited in *Il Milione*, by Marco Polo

9 **According to Marco Polo, how did Genghis Khan unify the region?** He made himself head of cities and provinces over governors whom he appointed. Analyze Primary Sources

Test Talk

Locate Key Words in the Question

10 **What caused the Mongols to make the Silk Road safe for travel?** Have students identify the key words and phrases in the question. *(Mongols, Silk Road, safe)* Because they used the Silk Road to communicate with different parts of the empire, they wanted it to be safe. Cause and Effect

✓ **REVIEW ANSWER** Gold, ivory, and precious stones went to China. Furs, silks, ceramics, jade, bronze objects, lacquer, and iron came from China. Main Idea and Details

The Plague

Quick Summary The bubonic plague was an epidemic that spread throughout Europe, killing about one-fourth to one-third of Europe's population between 1347 and 1352.

MAP SKILL
The Spread of the Plague

Have students note the extent of the Plague throughout Europe.

11 **Why might areas surrounding the Mediterranean Sea be among the first to be affected by the Plague?** Possible answer: The Plague might have been spread on ships that carried goods from one port to another. **Analyze Information**

MAP SKILL **Answer** Areas unaffected by the Plague are located west and north of Barcelona, north of Genoa, southwest of Cologne, and west of Prague.

12 **Describe how the bubonic plague spread.** The bacteria that cause the disease are carried by rodents. Fleas infest the rodents. Then the fleas transfer the bacteria from a rodent to a human. Both the rodent and the human die, while the fleas live. **Sequence**

Primary Source

Cited in *The Black Death,* translated by William M. Bowsky

13 **What did the teachers and physicians in this account say caused the Plague?** God's will **Cause and Effect**

14 **What are some theories about how the Plague began?** Some historians believe it may have come from central Asia along the Silk Road; others believe it may have spread from country to country on ships. **Analyze Information**

Primary Source

Cited in *The Black Death*, translated by William M. Bowsky

15 **What conclusion about the Plague can you draw from this account?** Great numbers of people were dying at a fast rate from bubonic plague. **Analyze Primary Sources**

410 Unit 5 • The Medieval World

The Plague

When medieval culture was at its greatest strength, the **Plague** hit Europe.

The Plague was a **bubonic plague,** a very aggressive **epidemic,** or the rapid spread of a disease over a wide area. Bacteria, usually carried by rodents, caused the Plague.

A bubonic plague occurs when fleas infest rodents, usually rats, and then they move to humans. The fleas then transfer the

National Library of Australia

▶ Carved 75 years after the Plague, this woodcut illustrates the connection between trade and the spread of disease.

bacteria from the rat, through a bite, to the human. The rat and the human die, while the flea lives.

Today, we know how a bubonic plague spreads. However, in the fourteenth century, no one knew how and why the Plague spread. As one account says,

> *"And from what this epidemic came, all wise teachers and physicians could only say that it was God's will."*

Some historians suggest that the Plague began in Central Asia in the late 1320s and spread east to China. The Plague then spread west along the Silk Road, reaching the Black Sea by 1347.

The first European cases of the disease started in **Genoa,** Italy. An epidemic in a seaport town such as Genoa is especially dangerous. Ships from all directions came to and from Genoa. As a result, rats could spread the Plague from country to country in ships.

People were terrified that they would get the Plague. Some thought that they could get it by looking at someone who had the Plague. Here is an eyewitness account from Agnolo di Tura, of Siena:

> *". . . And they died by the hundreds, both day and night, and all were thrown in those ditches and covered with earth. And as soon as those ditches were filled, more were dug."*

MAP SKILL
The Spread of the Plague

Approximate extent of areas affected by:
- 1347
- 1348
- 1349
- 1350
- After 1350
- Largely unaffected
- Little or no information available

11 N

0   250   500 Miles
0   250   500 Kilometers

ATLANTIC OCEAN

North Sea
Baltic Sea

Stockholm
Moscow
London
Cologne
Warsaw
Paris
Prague
Vienna
Genoa
Venice
Kaffa
Black Sea
Marseille
Barcelona
Constantinople
Lisbon
Palermo
Marrakech
Mediterranean Sea
Tripoli
Alexandria

▶ Scholars do not know for certain why some small pockets in Europe were not affected by the Plague.

MAP SKILL **Use a Map Key** *What areas were largely unaffected by the Plague?*

410

Practice and Extend

SOCIAL STUDIES
Background

Symptoms of the Bubonic Plague

- The first symptoms are usually headache, nausea, and sore joints.
- Lymph nodes may swell to the size of an egg.
- Victims get a fever of between 101°F and 105°F.
- Victims' pulse and breathing accelerate.
- The disease can kill its victims in about four days.

CURRICULUM CONNECTIONS
Art

Create Posters

- Have students design posters that might have been posted along roads leading to towns that were infested with the Plague.
- Tell students their posters would be used to warn people of the dangers they will encounter ahead if they continue into the town infested with the Plague.

Effects of the Plague

- 25–33% Population loss in Europe
- Businesses go bankrupt
- Deaths cause labor shortages
- Trade declines and towns disappear
- Construction and building projects stop
- Food supply decreases and people starve

CHART SKILL Interpret a Chart *How did the Plague affect the growth of towns?*

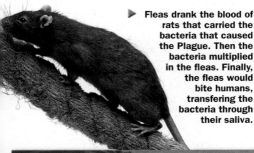

▶ Fleas drank the blood of rats that carried the bacteria that caused the Plague. Then the bacteria multiplied in the fleas. Finally, the fleas would bite humans, transfering the bacteria through their saliva.

An attack of bubonic plague does not last long, but the disease has a very high death rate. The Plague killed about one-fourth to one-third of Europe's population from 1347 to 1352. Despite the negative effects of the Plague (see chart at the left), fewer people meant that serfs became more valuable to lords. Serfs enjoyed a higher standard of living and more independence.

REVIEW What economic effects did the Plague have on Europe? **Cause and Effect**

Summarize the Lesson

- **1000** Trade began to grow in Europe.
- **1095** Pope Urban II called for the Crusades.
- **1271** Marco Polo traveled to China along the Silk Road.
- **about 1347** The Plague reached Europe.

LESSON 4 REVIEW

Check Facts and Main Ideas

1. **Cause and Effect** On a separate piece of paper, fill in the missing cause or effect in the blanks below.

Causes		Effects
The Seljuk Turks take over the Holy Land.	→	Pope Urban II calls for the Crusades.
Manors produce a food surplus.		Towns begin to flourish.
The Plague hits Europe.		European population declines by at least 25 percent.

2. Who issued the call for the Crusades, and why?

3. In addition to goods, what else traveled along trade routes such as the Silk Road.

4. What caused the Plague?

5. **Critical Thinking:** *Detect Bias* Why might some historians say that the Plague began in Central Asia?

Link to Science

Make a Hypothesis The bacteria that caused the Plague was *yersinia pestis*. Look in an encyclopedia, science book, or on the Internet to determine how bacteria form. Write a hypothesis, or educated guess, explaining how bacteria divide and spread.

411

The Plague

- Before the Plague, population growth had made it difficult to feed everyone. Afterward, food was more abundant.
- Workers were more valued after the Plague, because there were fewer people but the same amount of land and natural resources to be worked.
- Fewer people to feed meant less land had to be farmed. This made it profitable for landowners to run more sheep. This also shifted employment toward the manufacture of woolen goods. Fewer serfs were tied to farms and more were engaged in trade.

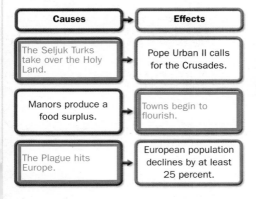

Workbook, p. 101

Lesson 4: Crusades, Trade, and the Plague

Directions: Read the following statements. Then circle *T* (True) or *F* (False) for each statement. If the answer is false, correct the statement to make it true. You may use your textbook.

T F 1. Christians in western Europe organized twelve Crusades to establish trade routes and defeat the Byzantine Empire.

T F 2. Because people began to want goods that were not available on a manor, they purchased the goods at fairs.

T F 3. If traders wanted goods from Asia, they had to travel to Asia to buy them.

T F 4. The Silk Road is a single route across Central Asia.

T F 5. Some historians believe that the Plague began in Central Asia and spread east to China and west along the Silk Road.

T F 6. The Plague killed about three-fourths of Europe's people from 1347 to 1352.

Notes for Home: Your child learned about the development of trade routes and their effect on communication between Europe, Africa, and Asia.
Home Activity: With your child, compare how epidemics from the Middle Ages and today are spread and controlled.

Also on Teacher Resources CD-ROM.

CHART SKILL Answer Towns stopped growing or disappeared because, as population died, businesses went bankrupt and construction projects stopped.

✓ **REVIEW ANSWER** The Plague killed about one-fourth to one-third of the population. Businesses went bankrupt, trade declined, and the food supply decreased. There was also a labor shortage, and construction projects stopped. Nevertheless, because labor was in short supply, serfs were more valuable to lords. Their standard of living and level of independence went up. **Cause and Effect**

Close and Assess

Summarize the Lesson

Tell students to read the events listed on the vertical time line. Have them list each event in the cause box of a cause-and-effect chart. Have them write at least two effects for each cause they list.

✓ **LESSON 1 REVIEW**

1. **Cause and Effect** For possible answers, see the reduced pupil page.

2. Pope Urban II called for the Crusades to regain the Holy Land and protect the Byzantine Empire.

3. Religions, ideas, and diseases

4. Bacteria that lived in rodents caused the Plague. The Plague was transferred to humans through saliva from flea bites.

5. **Critical Thinking:** *Detect Bias* Possible answer: Some European historians might want to blame Asia for the epidemic.

Link to Science

Before students write their hypotheses, discuss the habits of rats, such as where they live and what they eat.

Use a Time Zone Map

Objective
- Locate time zones on a map.

Resource
- Workbook, p. 102

1 Introduce and Motivate

What is a time zone map? Ask students to share any experiences they have had traveling from one time zone to another. Then have students read the **What?** section of text on p. 412.

Why have different time zones? Have students read the **Why?** section of text on p. 413. Ask them to give examples of when they might use a time zone map.

2 Teach and Discuss

How is this skill used? Examine with students the time zone map on p. 412.

- Point out that the time in all places within a single time zone is always the same.

- Point out that, as you move west from Greenwich, each time zone is one hour earlier. As you move east from Greenwich, each time zone is one hour later.

- Have students read the **How?** section of text on p. 413.

Use a Time Zone Map

What? A time zone map is a map that indicates the relative time for a location. Earth is divided into 24 standard time zones, 23 full zones and two half zones. Each of the full zones represents a time interval of one hour.

The International Date Line is an imaginary line halfway around the world from Greenwich, England. It roughly parallels the 180° longitude line. The world's nations have agreed that this line will be used to designate where new days begin on Earth.

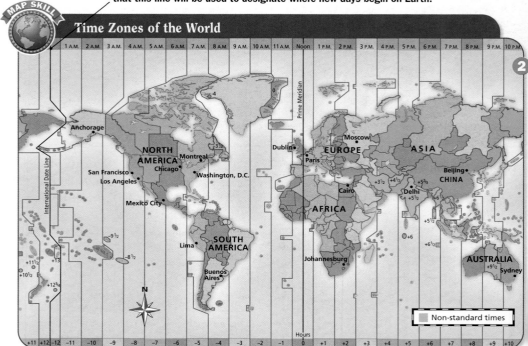

Time Zones of the World

Positive and negative numbers show the difference between local time and Greenwich Mean Time (GMT).

Anchorage   Los Angeles   Chicago   Montreal   Buenos Aires

412

Practice and Extend

CURRICULUM CONNECTION
Math

Solving Problems with Time

Have students use the time zone map to solve the following problem: It takes Jason five hours to fly from New York City, New York, to Los Angeles, California. What time will he arrive in Los Angeles if he departed New York at 9:00 A.M.? (11:00 A.M.)

SOCIAL STUDIES STRAND
Geography

The following map resources are available:
- Big Book Atlas
- Student Atlas
- Outline Maps
- Desk Maps
- Map Resources CD-ROM

Why? In the late 1880s, international scientists created 24 time zones to standardize time keeping. They divided Earth into 24 time zones because since Earth rotates 360° every day (or 24 hours), they could establish each time zone 15° apart. To simplify, 360 divided by 15 equals 24. Sometimes, boundaries of the time zones had to be changed to keep with political boundaries such as countries.

How? The following steps will help you use a time zone map to find the local time for a specific location—for example Moscow, Russia.

1. Find Moscow on the time zone map.

2. Match the color with positive and negative numbers at the top of the map to the color used for Moscow's time zone.

3. Read the time given, 3:00 P.M.

Think and Apply

1. How did scientists create the time zones?

2. According to the time zone map, what is the time difference between Los Angeles, California, and Washington, D.C.?

3. If it is 6 P.M. in Washington, D.C., what is the local time in Los Angeles?

4. What is the time difference between Mexico City, Mexico, and Chicago, Illinois? Explain.

Internet Activity

For more information, go online to the Atlas at www.sfsocialstudies.com.

Paris	Moscow	Delhi	Beijing	Sydney

413

Workbook, p. 102

Use a Time Zone Map

A time zone map of the United States shows six of the world's time zones. The time in each zone is different by one hour from the time zone next to it. When it is 5 A.M. in Hawaii, it is 8 A.M. in Phoenix, 9 A.M. in Dallas, and 10 A.M. in Washington, D.C.

Directions: Use the time zone map of the United States to answer the questions that follow.

1. Suppose you are about to fly from Albuquerque, New Mexico, to Dallas, Texas. It is about a two-hour flight to Dallas and the plane is scheduled to depart at 10:00 A.M. About what time will you arrive in Dallas?
   Ⓐ 12:00 P.M. Ⓑ 12:00 A.M. Ⓒ 1:00 P.M. Ⓓ 11:00 A.M.

2. Suppose it is 10:30 A.M. in Anchorage, Alaska. What time is it in Chicago, Illinois?
   Ⓐ 11:30 A.M. Ⓑ 12:30 A.M. Ⓒ 12:00 P.M. Ⓓ 1:30 P.M.

3. Suppose you live in Chicago, Illinois, and you want to call a friend in California at 6:00 P.M. Pacific time. At what time in Chicago should you make the call?
   Ⓐ 6:00 A.M. Ⓑ 7:00 A.M. Ⓒ 8:00 P.M. Ⓓ 9:00 A.M.

4. Suppose you are in New York City and want to call your uncle in San Francisco. At what time will you place the call from New York to reach him during his lunch hour?
   Ⓐ 1:30 P.M. Ⓑ 3:30 P.M. Ⓒ 10:30 A.M. Ⓓ 12:30 P.M.

Notes for Home: Your child learned to use a time zone map.
Home Activity: With your child, use this map to practice converting time to other time zones of the United States.

Also on Teacher Resources CD-ROM.

---

① **What is the purpose of the International Date Line?** This line is used to show where new days begin on Earth. **Analyze Information**

② **How do you determine the local time in a particular zone on a time zone map?** Match the color at the bottom of that zone of the map to the time written in the matching colored area at the top of the map. **Interpret Maps**

③ **What do positive and negative numbers indicate?** They show the difference between local time and Greenwich mean time. **Analyze Information**

3 Close and Assess

Think and Apply

1. They divided 360 by 24 because the earth rotates 360° each day. They set each time zone 15° apart.

2. Three hours

3. 3:00 P.M.

4. There is none. They share the same time zone, which is irregularly shaped to follow political boundaries.

Resources

- Assessment Book, pp. 69–72
- Workbook, p. 103: Vocabulary Review

Chapter Summary

For answers, see the reduced pupil page.

Vocabulary

1. e, **2.** c, **3.** b, **4.** a, **5.** d, **6.** f

People and Terms

Possible answers:

1. Charlemagne was a powerful European emperor who promoted learning and culture during the Middle Ages.

2. The Magna Carta was a document that placed limitations on royal power and included provisions that even the king had to obey the law.

3. The three-field rotation system was a system of planting crops to conserve the soil. In autumn one field is planted, in spring a second field is planted, and a third field is left unplanted each year.

4. The Crusades were major military expeditions designed to win back control of the Holy Land.

5. The Silk Road is the name for several trade routes across Central Asia, which allowed for the exchange of goods and ideas.

6. The North European Plain has some of the world's most fertile farmland.

7. The Rhine River is a major river in western Europe.

8. In 800 Pope Leo III crowned Charlemagne as emperor of the former Roman Empire in western Europe.

9. The Domesday Book contains information about the people and villages of England in 1086.

10. Christine de Pisan was one of the few medieval women who earned a living by writing books and poetry.

CHAPTER 14
REVIEW

600	800

800
Charlemagne was crowned emperor by Pope Leo III.
c. 800
Vikings began to invade Charlemagne's empire.
Feudalism began to rise.

Chapter Summary

Sequence

On a separate piece of paper, put these events in their correct order.

D A B C

- The Magna Carta is signed.
- Vikings launch invasions on Europe.
- Charlemagne becomes ruler.
- The First Crusade takes place.

```
[ ] → [ ] → [ ] → [ ]
```

Vocabulary

Match each word with the correct definition or description.

1. **monarch** (p. 401)
2. **feudalism** (p. 401)
3. **serf** (p. 401)
4. **knight** (p. 401)
5. **guild** (p. 404)
6. **chivalry** (p. 401)

a. warrior trained to fight on horseback

b. person who lived and farmed on land owned by a lord

c. social, political, and economic system of the Middle Ages

d. group of people united by a common trade

e. supreme ruler

f. knight's code

People and Terms

Write a sentence explaining why each of the following people and terms is important in the study of the Middle Ages. You may use two or more in a single sentence.

1. Charlemagne (p. 397)
2. Magna Carta (p. 398)
3. three-field rotation (p. 403)
4. Crusades (p. 407)
5. Silk Road (p. 409)
6. North European Plain (p. 393)
7. Rhine River (p. 394)
8. Leo III (p. 399)
9. Domesday Book (p. 397)
10. Christine de Pisan (p. 405)

414

Practice and Extend

Assessment Options

✓ Chapter 14 Assessment

- Chapter 14 Content Test: Use Assessment Book, pp. 69–70.
- Chapter 14 Skills Test: Use Assessment Book, pp. 71–72.

Standardized Test Prep

- Chapter 14 Tests contain standardized test format.

✓ Chapter 14 Performance Assessment

- Assign small groups a specific ruler or person belonging to a group discussed in the chapter, such as Charlemagne, King John, a serf on a manor, a merchant in a guild, or a knight in the Crusades. Have groups work together to write an autobiography their assigned person might write.

- Have one member of each group read aloud the group's autobiography without naming its subject, as classmates try to identify the person.

- Assess students' understanding of significant people and events of Europe in the Middle Ages.

1000   1200   1400

1086
The Domesday Book
was created.

1215
The Magna Carta
was signed.

1400
Feudalism began to decline.

1347
The Plague reached Europe.

Facts and Main Ideas

1. Who called for the First Crusade?

2. How were serfs and slaves alike and different?

3. **Time Line** About how long did the feudal system last?

4. **Main Idea** What are the four major land regions of Europe?

5. **Main Idea** How did the Magna Carta change the way England was ruled?

6. **Main Idea** How did people's lives change during feudalism?

7. **Main Idea** How were the Crusades, trade, and the Plague related?

8. **Critical Thinking:** *Evaluate Information* What do you think was the greatest advancement in culture people made during the Middle Ages? Why?

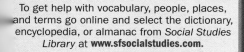
Write About History

1. **Write a journal entry** as a crusader who has reached Palestine (the Holy Land) during the First Crusade. What do you see? What do you hope to accomplish?

2. **Write a news bulletin** announcing the signing of the Magna Carta. Describe its contents and why it is newsworthy.

3. **Write a "help wanted" ad** inviting people to become merchants and traders along the Silk Road. Describe what qualifications are needed. Tell what kinds of people and things the merchant can expect to meet and see along the way.

Apply Skills

Use a Time Zone Map
Using the time zone map on page 412, answer the following questions.

1. What is the time difference, if any, between your state and Washington, D.C.?

2. How many time zones are in China?

3. If it is 9 A.M. in San Francisco, California, what time is it in Delhi, India?

Hands-on Unit Project

✓ **Unit 5 Performance Assessment**
- See p. 420 for information about using the Unit Project as a means of performance assessment.
- A scoring guide is provided on p. 420.

WEB SITE Technology

For more information, students can select the dictionary, encyclopedia or almanac from *Social Studies Library* at **www.sfsocialstudies.com**.

Workbook, p. 103

Vocabulary Review

Directions: Choose the vocabulary word from the box that best completes each sentence. Write the word on the line provided. Not all words will be used.

monk	convent	serf	guild
nun	missionary	knight	lady
monastery	monarch	chivalry	epidemic

1. A group of people united by a common interest is a _____

2. A _____ served as a center of religion and education, as well as a community in which monks lived.

3. _____ is another word for a disease that spreads quickly over a wide area.

4. A woman who devoted her life to religion in the Christian church was called a _____

5. Knights had a code of behavior called _____

6. A monk sometimes became a _____ to teach his religion to people with different beliefs.

Directions: On the lines provided, write a short paragraph using at least three of the six words not used above. Use information from the chapter in your paragraph.

_____
_____
_____
_____
_____

Also on Teacher Resources CD-ROM.

Facts and Main Ideas

1. Pope Urban II

2. Both serfs and slaves had to work the land. Neither had a say on where they would place their loyalty. Neither could leave the land without permission. However, serfs could not be sold apart from the land, but slaves could be sold.

3. About 600 years

4. The Northwest Mountains, the North European Plain, the Central Uplands, and the Alpine Mountain System.

5. It limited royal power by requiring the monarch to obey the law. The king needed the consent of the lords to demand money.

6. A social structure developed in which lords received land and the right to collect crops and taxes in exchange for loyalty and providing military support to the monarch. Serfs received protection in exchange for working the land; as they began to raise surplus crops, towns and cities grew.

7. They each followed trade routes between Europe, Central Asia, and the Far East.

8. Possible answer: Trade routes; they promoted the exchange of goods and ideas between the East and the West.

Write About History

1. Students' entries should clearly identify the purpose of the Crusades.

2. News bulletins should explain who signed the document and why it was significant.

3. Students' ads should include both advantages and disadvantages of trading along the Silk Road.

Apply Skills

1. Students should locate Washington, D.C., and their town or city on the map and use the time zones to calculate the time difference.

2. Five

3. 10:30 P.M.

The Round Table

Objectives

- Identify significant examples of literature from the medieval world.

- Explain how literature may reflect the times during which it was written.

1 Introduce and Motivate

Preview To activate prior knowledge, ask students what they know about King Arthur or Merlin the Magician. Tell students that they will read about the son of Sir Lancelot, one of the most famous knights of the Round Table. Ask students how legends might be useful. (They can provide an interesting and entertaining way to learn about a time period.)

2 Teach and Discuss

1 What significant prediction was made about a knight's sitting on the seat of danger? The days of the Round Table would be coming to an end. **Main Idea and Details**

C SOCIAL STUDIES STRAND
Culture

The world *Celtic* describes the people, languages, and cultures from the European areas of Brittany, Cornwall, Wales, Scotland, Ireland, and the Isle of Man.

2 Why were the knights so surprised when Sir Galahad sat on the seat of danger? No one before him had ever been able to sit on the seat of danger and live. **Cause and Effect**

The Round Table

Tales and legends are stories that are usually made up. Sometimes they try to explain something such as an historical event. This excerpt is from a medieval legend about King Arthur's Round Table. King Arthur appears in legends as early as A.D. 600 and as late as the 1300s. According to legend, Arthur was a Celtic ruler who fought against invaders from England. From this passage, what can you learn about the Middle Ages?

King Arthur filled his Round Table with the best knights in all the world. But for many years, one seat remained empty. No one could sit on it and live, which is why it was called the Siege Perilous, or seat of danger. Merlin prophesied that when a knight came to claim the Siege Perilous, the days of the Round Table would be drawing to a close.

One day a young knight clad in red armor appeared at court, without weapons. He bowed to King Arthur, walked straight to the Siege Perilous, and sat down. The knights gasped. But behind the young knight appeared in letters of gold, "Galahad, the High Prince."

"Welcome," said King Arthur. "Please tell us who you are."

"I am Sir Galahad, and my mother, Elaine, is the daughter of King Pelles, the Maimed King."

"I have heard of King Pelles, who lies crippled at the castle of Carbonek. But I did not know he had a grandson. And yet, Sir Galahad, I feel I know you. You look like Sir Lancelot as a young man."

"This is not surprising," said Lancelot, "for he is my son."

[from DK The Illustrated Book of Myths: Tales and Legends of the World, retold by Neil Philip]

416

Practice and Extend

FYI SOCIAL STUDIES
Background

King Arthur

- King Arthur of Celtic legend was a great hero given credit for such accomplishments as slaying giants, monsters, and witches.
- Legend also has it that Arthur took possession of the magic cauldron of Annwn and thus became immortal.
- Some of Arthur's knights were Sir Kay, Sir Gareth, and Sir Lancelot. King Arthur's wife was Queen Guinevere.

417

3 **Who was Sir Lancelot?** One of the knights of the Round Table and the father of Sir Galahad. **Analyze Information**

4 **Based on what you know about the Middle Ages, how did the knights of the Round Table help King Arthur?** Possible answer: They fought battles for him and helped to protect his kingdom. **Draw Conclusions**

3 Close and Assess

- Have students orally retell the story in the excerpt in their own words.

- Ask students to make a list of people and items in this excerpt that shows it takes place during the Middle Ages. (Possible answers: Knights, armor)

CURRICULUM CONNECTION
Literature

King Arthur

Students may enjoy reading other books about King Arthur:

The Kitchen Knight: A Tale of King Arthur, by Margaret Hodges (Holiday House, ISBN 0-8234-0787-X, 1990) **Easy**

Eyewitness Classics: King Arthur, by Rosalind Kerven (DK Publishing, ISBN 0-7894-2887-3, 1998) **On-Level**

The Story of King Arthur and His Knights, by Howard Pyle (Dover Publications, ISBN 0-486-21445-1, 1996) **Challenge**

Resource
- Assessment Book, pp. 73–76

Main Ideas and Vocabulary TEST PREP

1. c, **2.** b, **3.** d, **4.** c

People and Terms

1. b, **2.** d, **3.** f, **4.** e, **5.** c, **6.** a

Apply Skills

- Some students may draw and label time zones on a pre-printed map and then attach the map to poster board.

- Others may draw an outline map of the world and then draw and label the time zones.

- Suggest that students compare their maps to the one shown on p. 412.

Test Talk

Use Information from Graphics
Use Apply Skills to model the Test Talk strategy.

Understand the question.
Have students identify places in the question. Students should finish the statement "I need to find out . . . ."

Use information from graphics.
Ask students to skim the map to find the right information to support their answer.

Main Ideas and Vocabulary TEST PREP

Read the passage below and use it to answer the questions that follow.

The years from about 500 to 1500 are often called the Middle Ages. During that period, people from different parts of the world came into contact with one another, often for the first time. This contact and interaction included armed conflicts and the bartering of goods.

The Byzantine Empire maintained a capital at Constantinople, a city at the center of several trade routes. Christianity flourished in the Byzantine Empire until the 1000s, when the empire began to decline as it fought losing battles against the Muslims.

In the 600s, Islam, based on the teachings of Muhammad, rose in Arabia. Under Muhammad's successors, Muslim Arabs conquered northern Africa, bringing Islam with them. Muslim traders and sailors also spread Islam. African empires in eastern, western, and southern Africa developed along major trade routes.

Isolation helped Chinese society to be both stable and self-sufficient. In the 1200s, Mongol warriors, led by Kublai Khan, swept into China. The Khan established the Mongol Empire, marking the first time that China came under foreign rule.

Japanese culture was influenced by contact with China. For example, the Japanese borrowed the Chinese system of writing. Japan began to cast off Chinese influences during the late 700s and early 800s. The 1100s marked civil wars resulting in a form of military government led by a shogun.

In Europe feudalism and the manor system rose and declined. Royal power was limited under the Magna Carta. To take back the Holy Land, the Crusades were launched in 1095. Towns grew and trade thrived. But much of that changed when the plague hit Europe.

1 According to the passage, what two items helped influence the future of world regions?
- **A** feudalism and serfs
- **B** Islam and empires
- **C** conflicts and trade
- **D** language and time

2 In the passage, the word *bartering* means—
- **A** growing
- **C** throwing away
- **B** trading
- **D** making

3 According to the passage, what religion was carried by traders?
- **A** Christianity
- **C** feudalism
- **B** Buddhism
- **D** Islam

4 What is the main idea of the passage?
- **A** There were many wars between 500 and 1500.
- **B** Muslim traders conquered lands.
- **C** Trade and religion helped shape the future of many regions.
- **D** Japan borrowed ideas from China.

418

Practice and Extend

Assessment Options

✓ Unit 5 Assessment
- Use Unit 5 Content Test: Use Assessment Book, pp. 73–74.
- Use Unit 5 Skills Test: Use Assessment Book, pp. 75–76.

Standardized Test Prep
- Unit 5 Tests contain standardized test format.

✓ Unit 5 Performance Assessment
- See p. 420 for information about using the Unit Project as a means of Performance Assessment.
- A scoring guide for the Unit 5 Project is provided in the teacher's notes on p. 420.

Test Talk
- Test Talk Practice Book

WEB SITE Technology

For more information, you can select the dictionary, encyclopedia, or almanac from *Social Studies Library* at **www.sfsocialstudies.com.**

Test Talk

Use the map to help you find the answer.

People and Terms

Match each person or term to its definition.

1. Sumanguru (p. 375)
2. Genghis Khan (p. 352)
3. Shah Jahan (p. 349)
4. Ming dynasty (p. 353)
5. Solomonid dynasty (p. 382)
6. bubonic plague (p. 410)

a. an epidemic
b. defeated by Sundiata at Battle of Kirina
c. ruled Ethiopia for more than 700 years
d. ruthless Mongol warrior
e. overthrew the Mongols
f. built Taj Mahal for his wife

Apply Skills

Prepare a Time Zone Map
Make a time zone map. Show the time zones on a globe or map for several different cities around the world.

Write and Share

Present a Television News Magazine Segment
Prepare a 10-minute segment about the impact of trade in the Middle Ages. Work with your classmates to choose a news anchor, a reporter, and people to interview. Be sure to include the viewpoints of people such as rulers, traders, merchants, serfs, and religious leaders. Have the remaining classmates write questions for the reporter to ask. Present your news segment to another class in your school.

Read on Your Own

Look for books like these in the library.

419

Revisit the Unit Question

✓ Portfolio Assessment

- Have students look at the list of ways trade connects people that they made at the beginning of the unit.
- Have students look at the list of interactions between cultures and the results of these interactions.
- Ask students to compare and contrast their lists.

- Have students write a summary expressing how their understanding of how trade and other factors influence interaction between peoples and cultures.
- Have students add these lists and summaries to their Social Studies Portfolio.

Write and Share

- Before students begin working on the segment, discuss the different people and jobs involved in a television magazine news segment. If possible, show students an example of a television news magazine program.

- Some students may wish to design and make simple costumes for the people being interviewed. Others can work on set design.

- If possible, videotape the segment and present the video to other classes.

- Use the following scoring guide.

✓ Assessment Scoring Guide

Television News Magazine Segment	
4	Creates a well-organized presentation that provides detailed information about life in medieval Europe, including the living conditions, dangers, and goals unique to each of at least five different people interviewed.
3	Provides an organized presentation in which at least three people from different backgrounds are interviewed and gives relevant information about their living conditions during the Middle Ages.
2	Provides a presentation in which three or fewer people are interviewed and gives general information about life in the Middle Ages.
1	Is unable to provide an organized presentation.

Read on Your Own

Fa Mulan: The Story of a Woman Warrior, by Robert D. San Souci (Hyperion Press, ISBN 0-786-82287-2, 1998) **Easy**

Sundiata: Lion King of Mali, by David Wisniewski (Clarion Books, ISBN 0-395-76481-5, 1999) **On-Level**

 Catherine, Called Birdy, by Karen Cushman (Houghton Mifflin, ISBN 0-395-68186-3, 1994) **Challenge** *Newbery Honor Book*

A Day in the Life

Objective
- Describe life in a medieval manor village.

Resource
- Workbook, p. 104

Materials
milk cartons, egg cartons, foam containers, cardboard, shoeboxes, pipe cleaners, twigs, poster board, markers, pencils, paper, reference materials from the library or Internet

Follow This Procedure
- Tell students that they will write a script and build a model for a documentary about life in a medieval manor village. Explain that a documentary is a film that presents material in a factual and informative manner.

- Divide students into groups of three or four. Have a discussion about village life, farming, and technology available during the Middle Ages.

- Encourage students to write a list of facts before writing their script and to sketch their village before creating their model.

- Allow class time for students to build their models. Students may choose to bring in additional materials from home.

- Invite students to present their documentaries to the class.

✓ Assessment Scoring Guide

A Day in the Life	
4	Provides detailed descriptions of life in a medieval village using accurate information and precise word choices.
3	Provides some detailed descriptions of life in a medieval village using mostly accurate information and clear word choices.
2	Provides few details to describe life in a medieval village and uses some inaccurate information and vague word choices.
1	Provides few or no details to describe life in a medieval village and uses inaccurate information and incorrect word choices.

Discovery Channel School UNIT 5 Project

A Day in the Life

Make a documentary about living in a medieval village.

1 **Form** groups to choose topics to research about life in a medieval village. Find information about the village's buildings and the activities of people living in the village.

2 **Write** a script about people living in a medieval village.

3 **Build** a model of your village. Include buildings and the surrounding landscape.

4 **Present** your documentary to the class.

Internet Activity
Explore the Middle Ages on the Internet. Go to **www.sfsocialstudies.com/activities** and select your grade and unit.

420

Practice and Extend

Hands-on Unit Project

✓ Performance Assessment
- The Unit Project can also be used as a performance assessment activity.
- Use the scoring guide to assess each group's work.

WEB SITE Technology

Students can launch the Internet Activity by clicking on *Grade 6, Unit 5* at **www.sfsocialstudies.com/activities**.

Workbook, p. 104

5 Project A Day in the Life

Directions: In a group, make a documentary about living in a medieval village.

1. The ✓ shows the topics included in our documentary.
____ location of village ____ village buildings ____ building materials
____ surrounding landscape ____ people in the village ____ farming
____ animals ____ technology ____ other activities

2. Facts to include in our script: _____

3. Parts of the village that we want to include in our model: _____

✓ Checklist for Students
____ We chose topics about life in a medieval village.
____ We researched the topics.
____ We wrote the script for our documentary.
____ We built a model of a medieval village.
____ We presented our documentary to the class.

Notes for Home: Your child learned about life in a medieval village.
Home Activity: With your child, make a Venn diagram to compare and contrast a medieval village to the city or town in which you live. Include information about location, buildings, people, and activities in your diagram.

Also on Teacher Resources CD-ROM

★ UNIT 6 ★

Discovery, Expansion, and Revolutions

Discovery, Expansion, and Revolutions

UNIT 6

Unit Planning Guide

Unit 6 • Discovery, Expansion, and Revolutions

Begin with a Primary Source pp. 422–423

Meet the People pp. 424–425

 Reading Social Studies, Summarize pp. 426–427

Chapter Titles	Pacing	Main Ideas
Chapter 15 **New Beginnings** pp. 428–451 ✓ **Chapter 15 Review** pp. 452–453	6 days	• From the mid-1400s to the 1600s, Europeans had a renewed interest in art, literature, education, and the cultures of ancient Greece and Rome. • European traders and rulers wanted additional trade routes and to increase their empires. • As Europeans reached new lands, they spread their culture through settlement and colonization.
Chapter 16 **Ideas and Movements** pp. 454–481 ✓ **Chapter 16 Review** pp. 482–483	7 days	• New nations in the Americas break free of European rule. • The path of revolution turned violent in France. • The Industrial Revolution began in Great Britain and soon spread to other nations. • While business owners gained more freedom from government controls, workers struggled to improve their working conditions.
Chapter 17 **Imperialism, Nationalism, and Unification** pp. 484–503 ✓ **Chapter 17 Review** pp. 504–505	6 days	• By the 1800s, many European nations were building empires by conquering and colonizing other countries and territories. • China and Japan experienced Western imperialism in different ways. • Nationalism led to new nations in Europe and the British colonies.

End with a Song pp. 506–507

✓ **Unit 6 Review** pp. 508–509

✓ = Assessment Options   ✓ **Unit 6 Project** p. 510

◀ **Watches were first made in the early 1500s.**

Resources	Meeting Individual Needs
• Workbook, pp. 106–110 • Every Student Learns Guide, pp. 206–217 • Transparencies 6, 46, 47, 48, 49 • Quick Study, pp. 104–109 • Workbook, p. 111 ✓ Chapter 15 Content Test, Assessment Book, pp. 77–78 ✓ Chapter 15 Skills Test, Assessment Book, pp. 79–80	• ESL Support, TE pp. 431, 441, 449 • Learning Styles, TE p. 434 • Leveled Practice, TE pp. 435, 439, 446 ✓ Chapter 15 Performance Assessment, TE p. 452
• Workbook, pp. 112–118 • Every Student Learns Guide, pp. 218–233 • Transparencies 1, 6, 13 • Quick Study, pp. 110–117 • Workbook, p. 119 ✓ Chapter 16 Content Test, Assessment Book, pp. 81–82 ✓ Chapter 16 Skills Test, Assessment Book, pp. 83–84	• ESL Support, TE pp. 459, 470, 472, 476, 479 • Leveled Practice, TE pp. 461, 468, 477, 480 • Learning Styles, TE pp. 462, 473, 481 ✓ Chapter 16 Performance Assessment, TE p. 482
• Workbook, pp. 120–124 • Every Student Learns Guide, pp. 234–245 • Transparencies 6, 11, 20, 50, 51, 52 • Quick Study, pp. 118–123 • Workbook, p. 125 ✓ Chapter 17 Content Test, Assessment Book, pp. 85–86 ✓ Chapter 17 Skills Test, Assessment Book, pp. 87–88	• Leveled Practice, TE pp. 487, 495, 503 • ESL Support, TE pp. 488, 494, 500 • Learning Styles, TE pp. 496, 501 ✓ Chapter 17 Performance Assessment, TE p. 504

Providing More Depth

 Multimedia Library

• *Invention,* by Lionel Bender
• *To Be a Slave,* by Julius Lester
• **Songs and Music**
• **Video Field Trips**
• **Software**

Additional Resources

• Family Activities
• Vocabulary Cards
• Daily Activity Bank
• Social Studies Plus!
• Big Book Atlas
• Student Atlas
• Outline Maps
• Desk Maps

 ADDITIONAL Technology

• AudioText
• The test maker
• Teacher Resources CD-ROM
• Map Resources CD-ROM
• **www.sfsocialstudies.com**

 To establish guidelines for your students' safe and responsible use of the Internet, use the Scott Foresman Internet Guide.

Additional Internet Links
To find out more about:
• The Renaissance, visit **www.learner.org**
• Tenements, visit **www.thirteen.org**
• The British Empire, search for *Queen Victoria's Empire* at **www.pbs.org**

Key Internet Search Terms
• European exploration
• French Revolution
• Italy, Germany, or China

Unit 6 Objectives

Beginning of Unit 6
- Acquire information from primary sources. (p. 422)
- Identify the contributions of significant individuals between the fifteenth and twentieth centuries in Europe, South America, and Asia. (p. 424)
- Summarize information by writing the main points and important details. (p. 426)

Chapter 15

Lesson 1 The Renaissance
pp. 430–437
- Describe three of the great changes that occurred in Europe during the Renaissance.
- Explain the influence Petrarch had on the Renaissance in Europe.
- Identify the practices within the Roman Catholic Church that led to the Reformation.
- Explain how people's thinking changed during the Renaissance.
- Explain the effects that the Renaissance continues to have on us today.

Lesson 2 Trade Routes and Conquests
pp. 438–442
- Explain why Europeans began to make voyages of exploration.
- Explain the reasons why Europeans were so interested in exploring Africa.
- Identify the location of the Cape of Good Hope.
- Describe how the European exploration of the Americas would have been different if the Spanish had been convinced that there was little or no gold to be found in the Americas.
- Identify the accomplishments of significant individuals such as Queen Elizabeth I during the period of European exploration. (p. 443)

Lesson 3 European Colonization
pp. 444–449
- Explain how the economic system of mercantilism works.
- Describe what a colony is and explain why colonies enabled European countries to grow more wealthy and powerful.
- Explain how the system of encomienda worked.
- Identify some of the reasons that Europe started founding colonies.
- Describe ways that Europe could have created colonies without forcing the native peoples who lived there to work for them.
- Interpret the message of a political cartoon. (p. 450)

Chapter 16

Lesson 1 Revolutions in the Americas
pp. 456–462

- Describe the similarities and differences between the revolutions in North America and those in South America.
- Explain why the North American colonists wanted independence from British rule.
- Explain the significance of Father Miguel Hidalgo to the revolution in Mexico.
- Identify the restrictions that the Spanish government put on the people of Latin America.
- Explain the reasons why the fight for independence in South America took so many years.
- Identify the contributions of significant individuals, including Simón Bolívar, who helped South American countries gain independence. (p. 463)
- Analyze images and artifacts to better understand early American history. (p. 464)

Lesson 2 The French Revolution
pp. 466–470
- Identify the main causes of the French Revolution.
- Explain what the three estates were and who belonged to each of them.
- Explain who Robespierre was and his role in the French Revolution.
- Identify the accomplishments of the French Republic.
- Explain why other European countries banded together to defeat Napoleon.
- Identify individuals, such as Marie-Olympe de Gouges, who made significant contributions in the area of women's rights. (p. 471)
- Analyze how one primary source may have influenced another primary source. (p. 472)

Lesson 3 The Industrial Revolution
pp. 474–477
- Describe how goods were produced differently as a result of the Industrial Revolution.
- Describe the contributions of James Watt.
- Identify the factors that allowed Great Britain to get a head start in the Industrial Revolution.
- Explain why so many people moved from the country to the city between 1800 and 1850 in Great Britain.
- Explain what made conditions so bad in London factories and London slums.

Lesson 4 The Second Industrial Revolution pp. 478–481
- List some of the machines we use today that were invented during the Second Industrial Revolution.
- Explain what a corporation is and how it differs from other types of companies.
- Explain why reformers wanted to improve working conditions.

- Explain who Karl Marx was and describe his ideas about socialism and capitalism.
- Explain why Thomas Edison's inventions did or did not improve people's lives.

Chapter 17

Lesson 1 Expanding Empires
pp. 486–489
- List ways in which nationalism and imperialism led European nations to form empires in the 1800s.
- Explain why some Europeans believed that imperialism would benefit people in their colonies.
- Identify ways in which King Leopold's rule in the Congo was harsh.
- Locate the parts of the world where European countries built empires in the 1800s.
- Explain why Cecil Rhodes's ideas did or did not have solid evidence to support them.
- Interpret data from circle graphs that describe parts of a whole. (p. 490)

Lesson 2 Imperialism in East Asia
pp. 492–496
- Describe how the Western nations affected China and Japan in the 1800s.
- Describe the belief behind China's reference to itself as the "Middle Kingdom."
- Describe the ways in which Japan changed after Meiji came to power in 1868.
- Describe the relationships that China and Japan had with Western countries before the 1800s.
- Explain why the Qing Dynasty did or did not provide leadership necessary to modernize China.
- Identify the contributions of significant individuals, including Meiji, who helped modernize Asian nations. (p. 497)

Lesson 3 New Nations pp. 498–503
- List these important events in chronological order: Australia and Canada become dominions, Garibaldi liberates southern Italy, Germany becomes an empire, and Greece becomes independent.
- Describe the influence Greece had on Germany and Italy.
- Identify Prussia's most important contribution to the German Empire.
- Explain the importance of nationalism in the formation of a unified Italy and a unified Germany.
- Explain whether or not the British dominions were truly independent.

End of Unit 6
- Interpret how feelings and attitudes such as nationalism can be expressed through music. (p. 506)
- Describe how an invention has benefited society. (p. 510)

Assessment Options

✓ Formal Assessment

- **Lesson Reviews,** PE/TE pp. 437, 442, 449, 462, 470, 477, 481, 489, 496, 503
- **Chapter Reviews,** PE/TE pp. 452–453, 482–483, 504–505
- **Chapter Tests,** Assessment Book, pp. 77–88
- **Unit Review,** PE/TE pp. 508–509
- **Unit Tests,** Assessment Book, pp. 89–92
- **The test maker** (test-generator software)

✓ Informal Assessment

- **Teacher's Edition Questions,** throughout Lessons and Features
- **Section Reviews,** PE/TE pp. 431–437, 439–442, 445–448, 457–462, 467–470, 475–477, 479–481, 487–489, 493–496, 499–503
- **Close and Assess,** PE/TE pp. 427, 437, 442, 443, 449, 451, 462, 463, 465, 470, 471, 473, 477, 481, 489, 491, 496, 497, 503, 507

Ongoing Assessment

Ongoing Assessment is found throughout the Teacher's Edition lessons using an **If...then** model.

If = students' observable behavior,	**then** = reteaching and enrichment suggestions

✓ Portfolio Assessment

- **Portfolio Assessment,** TE pp. 421, 422, 509
- **Leveled Practice,** TE pp. 435, 439, 446, 461, 468, 477, 480, 487, 495, 503
- **Workbook,** pp. 105–126
- **Chapter Review: Write About History,** PE/TE pp. 453, 483, 505
- **Unit Review: Apply Skills,** PE/TE p. 509
- **Curriculum Connection: Writing** PE/TE pp. 437, 442, 449, 470, 489, 503; TE pp. 437, 491, 497, 499, 503, 506

✓ Performance Assessment

- **Hands-on Unit Project** (Unit 6 Performance Assessment), TE pp. 421, 453, 483, 505, 510
- **Internet Activity,** PE p. 510
- **Chapter 15 Performance Assessment,** PE/TE p. 452
- **Chapter 16 Performance Assessment,** PE/TE p. 482
- **Chapter 17 Performance Assessment,** PE/TE p. 504
- **Unit Review: Write and Share,** PE/TE p. 509
- **Scoring Guides,** TE pp. 509, 510

Test Talk

Test-Taking Strategies

Understand the Question
- **Locate Key Words in the Question,** TE p. 493
- **Locate Key Words in the Text,** TE p. 495

Understand the Answer
- **Choose the Right Answer,** Test Talk Practice Book
- **Use Information from the Text,** TE p. 500
- **Use Information from Graphics,** TE pp. 446, 460
- **Write Your Answer to Score High,** PE/TE p. 509

For additional practice, use the Test Talk Practice Book.

Featured Strategy

Write Your Answer to Score High
Students will:
- Make sure their answer is correct.
- Make sure their answer is complete.
- Make sure their answer is focused.

PE/TE p. 509

Curriculum Connections

Integrating Your Day

The lessons, skills, and features of Unit 6 provide many opportunities to make connections between social studies and other areas of the elementary curriculum.

Social Studies

READING

Reading Skill—Summarize, PE/TE pp. 426–427, 430, 438, 444, 466, 486

Lesson Review— Summarize, PE/TE pp. 437, 442, 449, 470, 489

WRITING

Write an Opinion Paragraph, TE p. 437

Link to Writing, PE/TE pp. 437, 442, 449, 470, 489, 503

Write About Circle Graphs, TE p. 491

Write About Influential Leaders, TE p. 497

What Is a Nation?, TE p. 499

Write an Editorial, TE p. 503

Write a Poem, TE p. 506

MATH

Write Math Questions, TE p. 423

Three-dimensional Shapes in Art, TE p. 433

Calculate Continental Army Supplies, TE p. 464

Create Circle Graphs, TE p. 490

LITERATURE

Read Biographies, TE pp. 424, 443, 463

Read More About Slavery, TE p. 448

Read About Women's Rights, TE p. 471

SCIENCE

Research Diseases, TE p. 442

Inventions and How They Work, TE p. 475

Link to Science, PE/TE pp. 477, 481

MUSIC / DRAMA

Compose a Song, TE p. 451

ART

Make a Poster, TE p. 445

Create a Political Cartoon, TE pp. 450, 467

Expressions of Freedom, TE p. 458

Create a Mural, TE p. 489

Link to Art, PE/TE p. 496

Create a CD Cover, TE p. 507

 Look for this symbol throughout the Teacher's Edition to find **Curriculum Connections.**

Professional Development

Social Studies and History

by Rita Geiger
Norman Public Schools

History is a story, and who doesn't like an interesting story? It is the challenge of every social studies teacher to pique students' imaginations and help them understand their part in keeping our heritage alive and well. To do this successfully, history instruction must be woven into the social studies curriculum. Below are several ways *Scott Foresman Social Studies* incorporates history into its program.

Studying the Past

Two important goals of history instruction are to make the past seem real and to help students gain insight into how their own lives and current events have been shaped by the events and people of the past. Studying the past can help explain the present. When students make these connections between the past and the present, they are better equipped to carry on important traditions of civic pride and responsibility.

- *Lesson 1 in Chapter 15 examines the impact that art, literature, science, and technology of the Renaissance period have had on life today. Copernicus and Galileo, as well as the invention of the printing press, are discussed.*

Examining Art

The use of music, art, and literature related to certain historical time periods immerses students in the culture of that era.

- *The Art Curriculum Connection on p. 458 of the Teacher's Edition asks students to reflect on a painting of the signing of the Declaration of Independence. Students use the painting as a springboard for additional activities.*

ESL Support

by Jim Cummins, Ph.D.
University of Toronto

In Unit 6, you can use the following fundamental strategy to help English Language Learners expand their language abilities:

Extend Language

Word formation follows some very predictable patterns. When students know some of the rules or conventions of how academic words are formed, they have an edge in extending their vocabulary. Such knowledge helps them figure out not only the meanings of individual words, but also how to form different parts of speech from these words.

For example, students might brainstorm words that are directly related to the word *revolution*. They would then explore the meanings of different word forms. Thus, they would discover that the verb related to *revolution* is *revolve;* the adjective is *revolutionary*. They would also discover semantically related words, such as *revolt* and *revolting*. Dictionaries and thesauruses, as well as electronic resources, can be used in this language detective work.

The following examples in the Teacher's Edition will help you extend the language abilities of ESL students:

- *Identify Related Words on p. 441 invites English Language Learners to identify words associated with ships. Advanced students create a web with the word* ships *and related words.*

- *Examine Word Meanings on p. 470 helps ESL students learn the meanings of past-tense verbs and related nouns. Advanced learners name nouns that are related to the verbs* conquered, invaded, defeated, ruled, *and* escaped.

Read Aloud

Thoughts of a Renaissance Man
by Leonardo da Vinci

Iron rusts from disuse; stagnant water loses its purity and in cold weather becomes frozen; even so does inaction sap the vigour of the mind.

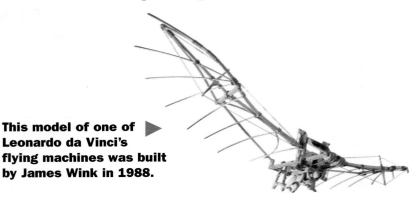

This model of one of Leonardo da Vinci's flying machines was built by James Wink in 1988.

Build Background

- Leonardo da Vinci (1452–1519) was the ideal Renaissance man. He was an exceptionally talented painter, sculptor, architect, scientist, and inventor.

- This quotation shows the importance he placed on thinking and learning.

Definitions

- *stagnant:* standing still
- *sap:* drain
- *vigour:* strength

Read Alouds and Primary Sources

- *Read Alouds and Primary Sources* contains additional selections to be used with Unit 6.

Bibliography

Good Queen Bess: The Story Of Elizabeth I of England, by Diane Stanley (HarperCollins, ISBN 0-688-17961-4, 2001) **Easy**
ALA Notable Book, Boston Globe Horn Book Honors

Jamestown Colony (Cornerstones of Freedom), by Gail Sakurai (Children's Press, ISBN 0-516-26138-X, 1997) **Easy**

Leonardo da Vinci, by Diane Stanley (Harper Trophy, ISBN 0-688-16155-3, 2000) **Easy**
ALA Notable Book, Boston Globe Horn Book Honors, Orbis Pictus Award

Morning Girl, by Michael Dorris (Hyperion Books, ISBN 0-786-81358-X, 1999) **On-Level** *Scott O'Dell Award*

Renaissance, by Andrew Langley (Knopf, ISBN 0-375-80136-7, 1999) **On-Level**

The Spanish Armada, by John Tincey, Richard Hook (Illustrator) (Osprey Publishing, ISBN 1-841-76028-5, 2000) **On-Level**

Elizabeth I, Red Rose of the House of Tudor, by Kathryn Lasky (Scholastic, ISBN 0-590-68484-1, 1999) **Challenge**

The Voyage of the Armada: The Spanish Story, by David Howarth (Lyons Press, ISBN 1-585-74424-7, 2001) **Challenge**

What Life Was Like Among Samurai and Shoguns: Japan, A.D. 1000–1700, by Time Life Books, ed. (Time-Life Inc., ISBN 0-783-55462-1, 2001) **Challenge**

Famous Men of the Renaissance and Reformation, by Robert G. Shearer (Greenleaf Press, ISBN 1-882-51410-6, 1996) **Teacher reference**

A Short History of the French Revolution, by Jeremy D. Popkin (Prentice Hall, ISBN 0-130-60032-6, 2001) **Teacher reference**

Discovery Channel School Videos

Conquerors: Napoleon This video explores the accomplishments of a man who seized control by virtue of his brilliant military strategy and excellent timing. (Item # 722769, 27 minutes)

Conquerors: Peter the Great Discover how this Russian monarch's passion and perseverance spawned military victories, modern cities, and a renewed national pride. (Item # 715912E, 26 minutes)

Conquerors: Suleyman the Magnificent Explore how this sultan transformed Constantinople into Istanbul, allowed conquered subjects to have autonomy, and defended his Ottoman Empire. (Item # 722744E, 27 minutes)

The Revolutionary War This video provides a concise and compelling look at America's birth. (Item # 716746, 53 minutes)

- To order *Discovery Channel School* videos, please call the following toll-free number: 1-888-892-3484.

- Free online lesson plans are available at **DiscoverySchool.com.**

 Look for this symbol throughout the Teacher's Edition to find **Award-Winning Selections.** Additional book references are found throughout this unit.

Discovery, Expansion, and Revolutions

How do ideas make a nation?

421

Discovery, Expansion, and Revolutions

Unit Overview

The 1400s began an awakening of the Western world that would change life around the globe, influencing civilization to the present day. Every aspect of life was affected, including the arts, culture, exploration, trade, and colonization.

Unit Outline

Unit Question

- Have students read the question under the picture.

- To activate prior knowledge, discuss the kinds of ideas that make a nation, including economic, cultural, social, and political ideas. Ask students which kinds of ideas they think are most important to the building of a nation and why.

- Create a list of students' opinions of the most important kinds of ideas in the development of a nation.

✓ **Portfolio Assessment** Keep this list to review with students at the end of the unit on p. 509.

Practice and Extend

Hands-on Unit Project

✓ **Unit 6 Performance Assessment**

- The Unit Project, *Arts and Letters,* found on p. 510, is an ongoing performance assessment project to enrich students' learning throughout the unit.

- This project, which has students create an infomercial about an important invention, may be started now or at any time during this unit of study.

- A performance assessment scoring guide is located on p. 510.

Begin with a Primary Source

Objective
- Acquire information from primary sources.

Resource
- Poster 11

Interpret a Primary Source

- Tell students that this primary source is a quotation from King Ferdinand of Spain, who ruled Spain along with his wife, Queen Isabella.

- These words show that King Ferdinand wanted explorers to get gold at all costs to enrich Spain.

- ✓ **Portfolio Assessment** Remind students of the lists that they created of the most important kinds of ideas in the development of a nation (see p. 421). Have students add specific ideas that influenced various nations as they continue reading the unit. Review students' lists at the end of the unit on p. 509.

Interpret Fine Art

- Have students read the caption and describe what they see in the picture.

- Ask students why they think this picture was chosen for the opening of a unit about discovery, expansion, and revolutions.

- Discuss with students why owning ships like those in the picture was probably important to European countries.

- Ask students to consider how their lives might be different if ships like these had not been built.

1450	1500	1550	1600	1650

1455 Gutenberg Bible is printed.

1492 Columbus begins first voyage to the Americas.

1519 Magellan begins first voyage around the world.

1588 Spanish Armada is defeated by England.

1607 Jamestown is founded.

422

Practice and Extend

 **SOCIAL STUDIES Background**

About the Primary Source

- Spain began its expansion to the west with the explorations of Columbus in 1492.
- In 1519 Spain's Hernando Cortés conquered the Aztec Empire in Mexico.
- It was during the 1530s that Spain gained tremendous wealth with the discovery of gold and silver in its colonies in the Americas.
- By the mid-1500s, Spain ruled almost all of South America, Central America, Florida, Cuba, and the Philippine Islands.

> "*Get gold, humanely if possible, but at all hazards—get gold.*"
>
> —King Ferdinand of Spain, 1511

The power that European nations gained after 1500 was fueled by great advances in shipbuilding and navigation. This battle in the Gulf of Naples was painted by Pieter Brueghel.

Meet the Artist

- Pieter Brueghel the Younger (1564–1638) was the son of the well-known Flemish landscape painter Pieter Brueghel the Elder.

- Brueghel the Younger is best known for his skillful copies of his father's paintings.

Use the Time Line

The time line at the bottom of pp. 422–423 covers the 450 years from the printing of the Gutenberg Bible through the age of European exploration to the end of the nineteenth century.

1 **About how many years were there between the printing of the Gutenberg Bible and the improvement of the steam engine?** About 300 years
Interpret Time Lines

2 **How many years after the Declaration of Independence was written did the Reign of Terror begin?** 17 years Interpret Time Lines

3 **Was the German Empire created before or after Mexico became independent?** After Interpret Time Lines

1700   1750   1800   1850   1900

1760s
James Watt improves the steam engine. **1**

1776 U.S. Declaration of Independence

1793
Reign of Terror begins in France.

1821
Mexico wins independence.

1871
German Empire is created.

2   **3**   **423**

CURRICULUM CONNECTION
Math

Write Math Questions

- Have students study the time line and the events listed.
- Have students create questions about the time lapses between specific events.
- Students can then exchange and answer each other's questions.

Meet the People

Objective

- Identify the contributions of significant individuals between the fifteenth and twentieth centuries in Europe, South America, and Asia.

Resource

- Poster 12

Research the People

The people pictured on these pages played an important role in the development of their respective nations. Have students conduct research to find out the answers to the following questions.

- **What are some areas of science that Leonardo da Vinci studied and researched?** Anatomy, optics, hydraulics

- **What did Martin Luther join in 1505?** The Augustinian monastery in Erfurt

- **Who were the parents of Elizabeth I?** Henry VIII and his second wife, Anne Boleyn

- **On which continents did Simón Bolívar live?** South America and Europe

Students may wish to write their own questions about other people on these pages for the rest of the class to answer.

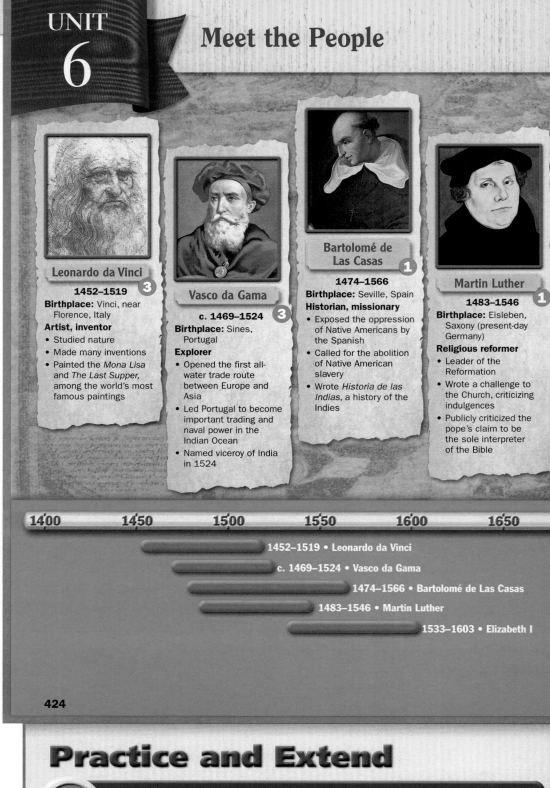

UNIT
6

Meet the People

Leonardo da Vinci
1452–1519
Birthplace: Vinci, near Florence, Italy
Artist, inventor
- Studied nature
- Made many inventions
- Painted the *Mona Lisa* and *The Last Supper*, among the world's most famous paintings

Vasco da Gama
c. 1469–1524
Birthplace: Sines, Portugal
Explorer
- Opened the first all-water trade route between Europe and Asia
- Led Portugal to become important trading and naval power in the Indian Ocean
- Named viceroy of India in 1524

Bartolomé de Las Casas
1474–1566
Birthplace: Seville, Spain
Historian, missionary
- Exposed the oppression of Native Americans by the Spanish
- Called for the abolition of Native American slavery
- Wrote *Historia de las Indias,* a history of the Indies

Martin Luther
1483–1546
Birthplace: Eisleben, Saxony (present-day Germany)
Religious reformer
- Leader of the Reformation
- Wrote a challenge to the Church, criticizing indulgences
- Publicly criticized the pope's claim to be the sole interpreter of the Bible

| 1400 | 1450 | 1500 | 1550 | 1600 | 1650 |

1452–1519 • Leonardo da Vinci
c. 1469–1524 • Vasco da Gama
1474–1566 • Bartolomé de Las Casas
1483–1546 • Martin Luther
1533–1603 • Elizabeth I

Practice and Extend

CURRICULUM CONNECTION
Literature

Read Biographies

Use the following biography selections to extend the content.

A Long and Uncertain Journey: The 27,000 Mile Voyage of Vasco da Gama, by Joan Elizabeth Goodman (Mikaya Press, ISBN 0-965-04937-X, 2001) **Easy**

Elizabeth I, by Catherine Bush (Chelsea House, ISBN 0-877-54579-0, 1987) **On-Level**

Leonardo Da Vinci for Kids: His Life and Ideas, by Janis Herbert (Chicago Review Press, ISBN 1-556-52298-3, 1998) **Challenge**

For more information, go to
www.sfsocialstudies.com/meetthepeople.

Elizabeth I
1533–1603
Birthplace: Greenwich, near London, England
English queen
· Reigned from 1558 until her death in 1603
· Under her reign, made Protestantism important in England
· Made England a great sea power and defeated the Spanish Armada

Marie-Olympe de Gouges
1748–1793
Birthplace: Montauban, France
Political activist, feminist
· Wrote *Declaration of the Rights of Woman and the Female Citizen,* calling for the equality of women
· Opposed the execution of Louis XVI
· Influenced feminists in other countries

Simón Bolívar
1783–1830
Birthplace: Caracas in present-day Venezuela
South American general, dictator, president
· Won independence for Bolivia, Colombia, Ecuador, Peru, and Venezuela from Spain
· President of Ecuador and Colombia
· Dictator of Peru
· Drew up constitution for Bolivia

Meiji
1852–1912
Birthplace: Kyoto, Japan
Japanese emperor
· Presided over the end of shogun rule of Japan
· Oversaw Japan's development into an industrial and military power
· Namesake of Meiji Era in Japan

1700   1750   1800   1850   1900   1950

· Marie-Olympe de Gouges
1783–1830 · Simón Bolívar
1852–1912 · Meiji

425

Use the Time Line

Have students use the time line and biographies to answer the following questions.

1 **What common methods did Martin Luther, Marie-Olympe de Gouges, and Bartolomé de Las Casas use to express their viewpoints?** They all wrote and spoke about their viewpoints.
Compare and Contrast

2 **What did Elizabeth I and Simón Bolívar have in common?** Both were rulers of their countries.
Compare and Contrast

3 **About how many years after Leonardo da Vinci's birth was Vasco da Gama born?** About 17 years
Interpret Time Lines

4 **About how old was Meiji when he died?** About 60 years old
Interpret Time Lines

Biographies

Three of the people shown here are discussed more extensively in the Biography pages in Unit 6.

Read About the People

The people shown here are discussed in the text on the following pages in Unit 6.

WEB SITE
Technology

Students can research the lives of people on this page by clicking on *Meet the People* at **www.sfsocialstudies.com**.

Reading Social Studies

Summarize

Objective

Summarize information by writing the main points and important details.

Resource

- Workbook, p. 105

About the Unit Target Skill

- The target reading skill for this unit is Summarize.
- Students are introduced to the unit target skill here and are given an opportunity to practice it.
- Further opportunities to summarize are found throughout Unit 6.

1 Introduce and Motivate

Preview To activate prior knowledge, ask students to summarize information from a previous chapter or lesson of this textbook. (In Unit 5, Chapter 14, Lesson 3, students read about feudalism. Have students summarize what feudalism is.)

Discovery, Expansion, and Revolutions

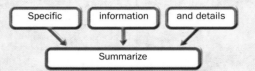

Summarize

Summarizing information will help you pick out the main points of what you read. It will also help you make sense of the ideas you read or hear about.

You can use these four steps to write a summary.

- Read from start to finish.
- List the main points.
- Add important details to the list.
- Turn your list into a paragraph.

Specific	information	and details

↓ ↓

Summarize

Read the paragraph. Then read the **summary** that follows.

> The Renaissance (rehn uh SAHNS) lasted from the 1400s to the 1600s. It began in Italy and spread to England, France, and other countries. During the Renaissance, scholars and artists studied the cultures of ancient Greece and Rome.
>
> In summary, the Renaissance began in the 1400s. It spread from Italy to other European countries. During this time, people studied ancient Greek and Roman culture.

Practice and Extend

 ACCESS CONTENT
ESL Support

Summarize an Experience Have students summarize an enjoyable experience they had.

Beginning Have students draw a picture of an enjoyable experience they had, such as a trip or a visit. Help them write one sentence to tell what the picture shows.

Intermediate Have students orally describe a recent enjoyable activity. Help students summarize their experience by asking questions such as *Who were you with? Where were you?* and *What happened?*

Advanced Have students write a paragraph about a recent experience. Remind them to begin their summaries with a main idea sentence and then add several supporting details.

The Work of Bartolomé de Las Casas

Bartolomé de Las Casas (bahr toh loh MAY day lahs KAH sahs) lived from 1474 until 1566. He was one of the first Spanish missionaries to reach the island of Hispaniola, in the West Indies.

Las Casas was among the first Europeans to defend the rights of the native peoples. He worked hard to improve conditions for them. He wrote many essays and pamphlets, each detailing the thought processes that led him to oppose the Spanish treatment of these peoples.

One of his works was *In Defense of the Indians* (1552). In it Las Casas argues that every human being is free and rational by nature, and capable of unlimited growth.

Las Casas's views were contrary to those of philosophers such as Aristotle, who held that some people were slaves by nature and made to serve others.

Las Casas defended Native American resistance to Spanish conquest. He explained that the Spanish were coming to the Americas and acting as if they were kings in these new lands.

> *"Every king . . . can prohibit any person from entering his land, whether to engage in trade or to reside therein or for any other cause."*

Las Casas pointed out that Spanish explorers and generals acted as if they had a right to the gold. In support of his argument, he asked what the Spanish king would do if the French marched into Spain and took possession of the Spanish silver mines or the king's store of gold.

Las Casas continued to argue for the rights of the Native Americans until his death.

Use the reading strategy of summarize to answer these questions. Then write a summary of the selection.

1 What is the main idea of the selection?

2 What details will you place in your summary?

427

Workbook, p. 105

Summarize

Directions: Read the following passage. Then fill in the circle next to the correct answers.

Leonardo da Vinci is considered one of the greatest painters, sculptors, architects, engineers, and scientists of the Renaissance period. He could paint, sculpt, sketch, and even design and build weapons, buildings, and machinery.

Da Vinci was interested in many things, but he rarely finished what he started. In fact, in a 17-year period, many art historians believe Da Vinci completed only six paintings, including *The Last Supper*, his masterpiece. He also painted the *Mona Lisa*, one of the world's most celebrated portraits. Da Vinci produced theater designs, architectural designs, models, and statues. However, many were never finished or were lost or destroyed. He also made several scientific discoveries and even invented a large number of machines. Among them was an underwater diving suit and several flying devices.

1. Which of the following best summarizes the passage?
   Ⓐ Da Vinci mainly was a painter.
   Ⓑ Da Vinci's interests were so broad, he rarely finished a painting.
   Ⓒ Da Vinci introduced approaches and styles to his art in an entirely new way.
   Ⓓ Da Vinci was one of the greatest artists of the Renaissance period.

2. What is the main idea of the second paragraph?
   Ⓐ Da Vinci completed only six paintings during his lifetime.
   Ⓑ Because his interests were so broad, Da Vinci rarely finished works that he started.
   Ⓒ *The Last Supper* is Da Vinci's masterpiece.
   Ⓓ Da Vinci produced architectural designs and made scientific discoveries.

3. Which detail does NOT contribute to a summary of this passage?
   Ⓐ Many of Da Vinci's works were lost or destroyed.
   Ⓑ Da Vinci is recognized as one of the world's great Renaissance painters.
   Ⓒ Da Vinci made several contributions to the arts and sciences.
   Ⓓ Da Vinci's interests extended far beyond painting and sculpting.

Notes for Home: Your child learned how to summarize within passages.
Home Activity: Read a newspaper article, magazine article, or story with your child. Then ask your child to verbally summarize the passage.

Teach and Discuss

- Explain that as they read, students should focus on the main points of the passage or selection.

- Have students read the sample paragraph on p. 426. Make sure they realize that the main point of the paragraph is to tell what the Renaissance was. Ask what details were included in the summary. (1400s to 1600s; spread to other European countries from Italy; scholars and artists studied the cultures of Ancient Greece and Rome.)

- Then have students read the longer practice sample on p. 427 and answer the questions that follow.

- Ask students why, when they are studying history, it is important to be able to summarize what they read. (By summarizing they can focus on the most important ideas and therefore make the information easier to understand and remember.)

Close and Assess

Apply it!

1. Las Casas was among the first Europeans to defend the rights of the native peoples and worked hard to improve conditions for them.

2. Wrote essays and pamphlets; wrote *In Defense of the Indians;* argued that every human being is free by nature; had a different view from Aristotle; felt Native Americans had a right to resist Spanish conquest

Chapter Planning Guide

Chapter 15 • New Beginnings

Locating Time and Place pp. 428–429

Lesson Titles	Pacing	Main Ideas
Lesson 1 **The Renaissance** pp. 430–437	2 days	• From the mid-1400s to the 1600s, Europeans had a renewed interest in art, literature, education, and the cultures of ancient Greece and Rome.
Lesson 2 **Trade Routes and Conquests** pp. 438–442	2 days	• European traders wanted additional trade routes and rulers wanted to establish empires.
Biography: Elizabeth I p. 443		• The early life of Elizabeth influenced her rule as Queen of England.
Lesson 3 **European Colonization** pp. 444–449	2 days	• As Europeans reached new lands, they spread their culture through settlement and colonization.
Research and Writing Skills: **Interpret Political Cartoons** pp. 450–451		• Political cartoons express opinions, often using humor to soften a difficult or painful issue.

✓ **Chapter 15 Review**
pp. 452–453

✓ = Assessment Options

◀ **Modern reproduction of the Gutenberg printing press**

Vocabulary	Resources	Meeting Individual Needs
commerce indulgence excommunicate	• Workbook, p. 107 • Transparencies 6, 46 • Every Student Learns Guide, pp. 206–209 • Quick Study, pp. 104–105	• ESL Support, TE p. 431 • Learning Styles, TE p. 434 • Leveled Practice, TE p. 435
circumnavigate conquistador	• Workbook, p. 108 • Transparencies 6, 47 • Every Student Learns Guide, pp. 210–213 • Quick Study, pp. 106–107	• Leveled Practice, TE p. 439 • ESL Support, TE p. 441
colony mercantilism	• Workbook, p. 109 • Transparencies 6, 48, 49 • Every Student Learns Guide, pp. 214–217 • Quick Study, pp. 108–109 • Workbook, p. 110	• Leveled Practice, TE p. 446 • ESL Support, TE p. 449
	✓ Chapter 15 Content Test, Assessment Book, pp. 77–78 ✓ Chapter 15 Skills Test, Assessment Book, pp. 79–80	✓ Chapter 15 Performance Assessment, TE p. 452

◀ **This diagram shows how slaves were packed into slave ships without regard for safety or comfort.**

Providing More Depth

Additional Resources
• Vocabulary Cards
• Daily Activity Bank
• Social Studies Plus!
• Big Book Atlas
• Student Atlas
• Outline Maps
• Desk Maps

 Technology

• AudioText
• The test maker
• Teacher Resources CD-ROM
• Map Resources CD-ROM
• **www.sfsocialstudies.com**

 To establish guidelines for your students' safe and responsible use of the Internet, use the Scott Foresman Internet Guide.

Additional Internet Links
To find out more about:
• The Renaissance, visit an online exhibit at **www.learner.org**
• European exploration, visit **www.thinkquest.org**
• Kings and queens of England, visit **www.royal.gov.uk**

Key Internet Search Terms
• Renaissance
• European explorations
• Spanish Armada

Workbook Support

Use the following Workbook pages to support content and skills development as you teach Chapter 15. You can also view and print Workbook pages from the Teacher Resources CD-ROM.

Workbook, p. 105

Summarize

Use with Pages 426–427.

Directions: Read the following passage. Then fill in the circle next to the correct answer.

> Leonardo da Vinci is considered one of the greatest painters, sculptors, architects, engineers, and scientists of the Renaissance period. He could paint, sculpt, sketch, and even design and build weapons, buildings, and machinery.
>
> Da Vinci was interested in many things, but he rarely finished what he started. In fact, in a 17-year period, many art historians believe Da Vinci completed only six paintings, including
>
> *The Last Supper,* his masterpiece. He also painted the *Mona Lisa,* one of the world's most celebrated portraits.
>
> Da Vinci produced theater designs, architectural designs, models, and statues. However, many were never finished or were lost or destroyed. He also made several scientific discoveries and even invented a large number of machines. Among them was an underwater diving suit and several flying devices.

1. Which of the following best summarizes the passage?
   - (A) Da Vinci mainly was a painter.
   - (B) Da Vinci's interests were so broad, he rarely finished a painting.
   - (C) Da Vinci introduced approaches and styles to his art in an entirely new way.
   - ● Da Vinci was one of the greatest artists of the Renaissance period.

2. What is the main idea of the second paragraph?
   - (A) Da Vinci completed only six paintings during his lifetime.
   - ● Because his interests were so broad, Da Vinci rarely finished works that he started.
   - (C) *The Last Supper* is Da Vinci's masterpiece.
   - (D) Da Vinci produced architectural designs and made scientific discoveries.

3. Which detail does NOT contribute to a summary of this passage?
   - ● Many of Da Vinci's works were lost or destroyed.
   - (B) Da Vinci is recognized as one of the world's great Renaissance painters.
   - (C) Da Vinci made several contributions to the arts and sciences.
   - (D) Da Vinci's interests extended far beyond painting and sculpting.

Notes for Home: Your child learned how to summarize written passages.
Home Activity: Read a newspaper article, magazine article, or story with your child. Then ask your child to verbally summarize the passage.

Use with Pupil Edition, p. 427

Workbook, p. 106

Vocabulary Preview

Use with Chapter 15.

Directions: Use the vocabulary terms in the box to complete each sentence. Write the term on the lines. Then unscramble the letters marked with a star to answer the clue that follows.

commerce	excommunicate	conquistador	mercantilism
indulgence	circumnavigate	colony	

1. One of Magellan's ships was the first to <u>c i r c u m n a v i g a t e</u>, or sail completely around, the world.

2. An economic system by which a country uses colonies to obtain raw materials is called <u>m e r c a n t i l i s m</u>.

3. An <u>i n d u l g e n c e</u> is a church's pardon from punishment for a sin.

4. Hernando Cortés was a Spanish conqueror, or <u>c o n q u i s t a d o r</u>, who acquired wealth by conquering a wealthy civilization.

5. The buying and selling of a large quantity of goods is called <u>c o m m e r c e</u>.

6. A settlement physically separate from—but under the control of—the ruling country is a <u>c o l o n y</u>.

7. Church officials could <u>e x c o m m u n i c a t e</u>, or expel, someone who challenged the church.

Clue: What is the name of the intellectual and economic movement that saw a revived interest in art and the social, scientific, and political thoughts of ancient Greece and Rome?

<u>R e n a i s s a n c e</u>

Notes for Home: Your child learned the vocabulary terms for Chapter 15.
Home Activity: With your child, review the above sentences. Then have your child give the definition for each vocabulary term.

Use with Pupil Edition, p. 428

Workbook, p. 107

Lesson 1: The Renaissance

Use with Pages 430–437.

Directions: Use complete sentences to answer the following questions on the lines provided. You may use your textbook.

1. Why did the Renaissance begin?

   Trade and commerce had made the city-states wealthy, and they flourished economically and intellectually. People wanted to understand ancient cultures and find ways to display their wealth.

2. How was Renaissance art different from medieval European art?

   Renaissance painters and sculptors portrayed people and nature realistically. They mastered perspective and proportion to make figures appear full and real to the viewer.

Directions: Complete the chart with information about the Reformation and the Catholic Counter-Reformation. You may use your textbook.

	Reformation	Catholic Counter-Reformation
Why did the movement occur?	Church's practices challenged; some Christians rejected church.	Church was against the Reformation.
What were followers' beliefs?	People should read and interpret the Bible themselves.	Only the Church could explain the Bible; Pope was highest Church authority.
What actions did followers take?	Challenged Catholic Church; Martin Luther asked for debate.	Called Council of Trent; banned sale of indulgences.

Notes for Home: Your child learned about the changes in Europe brought on by the Renaissance.
Home Activity: With your child, discuss how events that occurred during the Renaissance affect us today.

Use with Pupil Edition, p. 437

Workbook Support

Workbook, p. 108

Use with Pages 438–442.

Lesson 2: Trade Routes and Conquests

Directions: Match each name or term in the box to its description. Write the letter of the term on the line provided. You may use your textbook.

a. Portugal	f. Spain	k. Columbian Exchange
b. Ptolemy's map	g. Queen Isabella	l. Elizabeth I
c. Vasco da Gama	h. Pope Nicholas V	m. Armada
d. Ferdinand Magellan	i. Treaty of Tordesillas	
e. Christopher Columbus	j. Hernando Cortés	

j 1. conquistador who acquired wealth by conquering a wealthy civilization

l 2. queen of England; funded many expeditions and supported Dutch Protestants who were fighting against Catholic Spain

h 3. allowed explorers to make slaves of native peoples in newly explored lands

c 4. sailed around the Cape of Good Hope, which marked the first all-water trade route between Europe and Asia

i 5. agreement dividing the Americas between Spain and Portugal

d 6. sea captain whose ship was the first to sail completely around the world

b 7. world map used widely by navigators and sailors

m 8. fleet of Spanish warships defeated by English ships

g 9. funded Columbus's expedition to Asia; wanted to spread Christianity and compete with Portugal for wealth

a 10. important trading and naval power; took the lead in expeditions to find new sea routes

k 11. process of exchanging goods and diseases between the Americas and Europe

e 12. Italian sailor who sailed for Spain in search of a western route to Asia

f 13. Portugal's rival for wealth from voyages of exploration

Notes for Home: Your child learned about European expeditions, trade routes, and conquests.
Home Activity: With your child, imagine you are about to go on a voyage that will last several months. Make a list of the items and supplies you need to take with you. Discuss why each item is important.

Use with Pupil Edition, p. 442

Workbook, p. 109

Use with Pages 444–449.

Lesson 3: European Colonization

Directions: Identify the European country associated with each of the following events. For Portugal write *P* in the blank, for Spain write *S*, for England write *E*, and for France write *F*. You may use your textbook.

S 1. a colony was formed in the region where Aztecs had been defeated

E 2. thirteen colonies had been established in North America by 1732

P 3. began exploring Africa in the early 1400s to spread Christianity

S 4. encomienda system of forced labor was established by government

E 5. colonization caught the interest of merchants and other people who sought wealth and religious and political freedom

F 6. clashes over land rights with Native Americans and British resulted in war in North America

P 7. first colony was settled by citizens who did not own land in home country

E 8. convicts were sent to settle New South Wales, Australia

P 9. landed in South America as early as 1500

F 10. control of Canada was lost after defeat by Great Britain

S 11. Mexico, Central America, part of South America, islands in the Caribbean, and the southwestern United States were controlled by 1550

F 12. Canada was claimed after explorations by Jacques Cartier

F 13. first colony was founded at Quebec

P 14. Brazil was first colony

E 15. first successful North American colony, Jamestown, was established

P 16. set up sugar cane plantations and forced Native Americans to work in Brazil

Notes for Home: Your child learned about early colonization by the Portuguese, Spanish, English, and French.
Home Activity: With your child, discuss how Europeans changed the ways of life of the native peoples in the lands they conquered and settled.

Use with Pupil Edition, p. 449

Workbook, p. 110

Use with Pages 450–451.

Interpret Political Cartoons

Political cartoons use humor and pictures to express the opinion or point of view of the cartoonist. This type of editorial usually focuses on public figures, political events, or economic conditions of a particular time and place. The cartoons often exaggerate events or personal qualities of the subject to make the cartoonist's point of view or message more obvious to the reader.

Directions: Read the questions about political cartoons. Fill in the circle next to the correct answer.

1. What is a political cartoon?
   - Ⓐ advertisement for a political figure
   - Ⓑ newspaper article written by a reporter
   - Ⓒ small caption that explains a photograph in a newspaper
   - ● interpretation of a current event through pictures and some words

2. Which of the following is NOT used in political cartoons to make a point?
   - Ⓐ drawings
   - Ⓑ captions
   - ● explanations
   - Ⓓ symbols

3. Which is NOT a reason why cartoonists use political cartoons to make a point?
   - ● Readers prefer straight text with no bias.
   - Ⓑ Cartoons are able to communicate meaning on several levels.
   - Ⓒ Their use of humor may soften a difficult or painful situation.
   - Ⓓ Readers often are more open to a visual message.

4. Which of the following activities may NOT help readers interpret political cartoons?
   - Ⓐ Study the relationships between the characters and symbols.
   - Ⓑ Identify any bias.
   - Ⓒ Determine the cartoonist's point of view on the topic.
   - ● Look for context clues in the articles surrounding the cartoon.

Directions: On a separate sheet of paper, draw a political cartoon about a newsworthy event.

Notes for Home: Your child learned to interpret political cartoons.
Home Activity: Using recent newspapers and magazines, help your child select a political cartoon to study. Discuss the cartoon's message and the cartoonist's point of view.

Use with Pupil Edition, p. 451

Workbook, p. 111

Use with Chapter 15.

Vocabulary Review

Directions: Circle the vocabulary term that best completes each sentence. Then write the definition of that term on the line. You may use your textbook.

1. A practice of churches in western Europe that was most objected to was a willingness to accept money for a pardon, or (excommunicate, mercantilism, (indulgence)).

   a church's pardon from punishment for a sin

2. The Treaty of Tordesillas divided the Americas between Spain and Portugal and allowed a (colony, (conquistador), commerce) to claim a portion of the Americas for either Spain or Portugal.

   Spanish conqueror

3. A ((colony), circumnavigate, conquistador) helped make a ruling country wealthy and powerful by serving as a new market that could trade only with the ruling country.

   settlement physically separate from—but under the control of—the ruling country

4. The city-states of Florence, Milan, and Venice grew through trade and ((commerce), mercantilism, indulgence).

   buying and selling of a large quantity of goods

5. Following Ferdinand Magellan's death, the last remaining ship in his voyage was the first to (conquistador, excommunicate, (circumnavigate)) the world.

   sail completely around

6. The Europeans used an economic policy called ((mercantilism), indulgence, colony) in their colonies to gain wealth and power.

   system in which a country uses colonies to obtain raw materials, and colonies can trade only with the ruling country

7. When Martin Luther wrote a challenge to the Roman Catholic Church, church officials decided to (circumnavigate, indulgence, (excommunicate)) him from the church.

   to expel

Notes for Home: Your child learned the vocabulary terms for Chapter 15.
Home Activity: With your child, make a set of vocabulary cards. Write the vocabulary words on one side. On the other side, write the definitions. Shuffle the cards and hold up each card, allowing your child to give you the matching word or definition.

Use with Pupil Edition, p. 453

Assessment Support

Use these Assessment Book pages and the test maker to assess content and skills in Chapter 15. You can also view and print Assessment Book pages from the Teacher Resources CD-ROM.

Assessment Book, p. 77

Chapter 15 Test
Part 1: Content Test
Directions: Fill in the circle next to the correct answer.

Lesson Objective (1:4)

1. How did Europeans' way of thinking change during the Renaissance?
   - ● renewed interest in the art, science, and social and political thought of ancient Greece and Rome
   - Ⓑ decline in interest in the arts, politics, and religion
   - Ⓒ renewed interest in conquering the peoples of Greece and Rome
   - Ⓓ new belief that all areas of life should be governed by religion

Lesson Objective (1:2)

2. How did the poet Petrarch influence people during the Renaissance in Europe?
   - Ⓐ He helped others display their art.
   - Ⓑ He mastered the art of perspective.
   - Ⓒ He was the finest sculptor of the Renaissance.
   - ● He encouraged people to study philosophy and literature.

Lesson Objective (1:2)

3. Which was the first country to experience a cultural and economic rebirth in Europe?
   - Ⓐ France
   - ● Italy
   - Ⓒ Spain
   - Ⓒ Germany

Lesson Objective (1:1)

4. Which of the following is NOT a change that took place during the Renaissance?
   - Ⓐ Art became more realistic.
   - Ⓑ Scientists made new discoveries about the solar system.
   - ● Religion became more unified.
   - Ⓓ Technology became more advanced.

Lesson Objective (1:5)

5. What was one effect of the Renaissance invention of the printing press?
   - Ⓐ Books became more expensive.
   - Ⓑ The demand for books declined.
   - ● More people learned to read.
   - Ⓓ Fewer books were produced.

Lesson Objective (1:5)

6. Which of the following effects of the Renaissance continues to affect people today?
   - ● invention of the watch
   - Ⓑ sale of indulgences in the Catholic Church
   - Ⓒ use of the Gutenberg press to print religious books
   - Ⓓ emphasis on studying only ancient cultures

Lesson Objective (1:3)

7. Which practice of the Roman Catholic Church led to the Reformation?
   - Ⓐ allowing people to interpret the Bible
   - ● selling indulgences
   - Ⓒ excommunicating members
   - Ⓓ fasting

Lesson Objective (2:2)

8. What did Europeans hope to find by exploring Africa?
   - Ⓐ cinnamon and other spices
   - Ⓑ new ocean routes
   - Ⓒ silk and other cloths
   - ● gold and other riches

Use with Pupil Edition, p. 452

Assessment Book, p. 78

Lesson Objective (2:1)

9. Why did many European countries search for ocean routes to Africa?
   - ● Land routes were dangerous and costly.
   - Ⓑ Traveling by land was convenient.
   - Ⓒ Traveling by sea was the only way to reach Africa.
   - Ⓓ Land routes were controlled by Asian traders.

Lesson Objective (2:3)

10. Where is the Cape of Good Hope?
    - Ⓐ along the western edge of Europe
    - Ⓑ between Spain and Portugal
    - Ⓒ on the east coast of Asia
    - ● on the southern tip of Africa

Lesson Objective (2:5)

11. Why did European explorers conquer regions of the Americas?
    - ● They were searching for wealth.
    - Ⓑ They were in a war with South American countries.
    - Ⓒ They wanted to bring South Americans back to Spain.
    - Ⓓ They wanted to stop the spread of Christianity.

Lesson Objective (2:4)

12. Which describes the Columbian Exchange?
    - Ⓐ official letter allowing explorers to make slaves of native peoples
    - ● exchange of goods between the Americas and Europe
    - Ⓒ the spread of Native American diseases such as smallpox, measles, and influenza
    - Ⓓ attempt to convert the native peoples to Christianity

Lesson Objective (3:2, 4)

13. How could a colony increase the wealth of the ruling country?
    - Ⓐ by preventing new trade routes
    - Ⓑ by bringing more people into the country
    - ● by providing new markets that could trade only with the ruling country
    - Ⓓ by encouraging more exploration

Lesson Objective (3:5)

14. Under mercantilism, what did a colony supply to the ruling country?
    - Ⓐ new European citizens
    - Ⓑ finished products
    - Ⓒ religious converts
    - ● raw materials

Lesson Objective (3:5)

15. Why did European colonists force Native Americans to work for them?
    - Ⓐ They hoped to learn from the Native Americans.
    - Ⓑ They did not know how to farm.
    - ● They needed people to provide labor.
    - Ⓓ They wanted to anger the Native Americans.

Lesson Objective (3:3)

16. What system allowed Spanish colonists to demand labor from Native Americans?
    - Ⓐ mercantilism
    - ● encomienda
    - Ⓒ colonization
    - Ⓓ exploration

Use with Pupil Edition, p. 452

Assessment Support

Lesson Objective (3:3)

17. How did the encomienda system work?
    A. Some colonists went to North America after Protestantism was outlawed in France.
    B. Native Americans worked the land in exchange for their freedom.
    ● Some Europeans were granted the right to force Native Americans to work for them.
    D. Some convicts worked in exchange for shorter prison sentences.

Lesson Objective (3:4)

18. Which of the following was NOT a reason for European colonization?
    A. expansion of power
    B. religious freedom
    C. increased wealth
    ● to establish friendships with natives

Part 2: Skills Test

Directions: Use complete sentences to answer questions 1–7. Use a separate sheet of paper if you need more space.

1. What sequence of events led to the Renaissance? **Sequence**

   As Italy's city-states grew through trade and commerce, they flourished economically and intellectually. This led to a revived interest in the art, social, scientific, and political ideas of ancient Greece and Rome.

2. What techniques were introduced in painting and sculpture during the Renaissance? **Main Idea and Details**

   Artists began using perspective, depth, and proportion to make their art appear more realistic.

3. What differences in religious beliefs brought about the Reformation? **Point of View**

   Some people believed that the church had become corrupt and should not be allowed to sell indulgences. They also believed that individuals should interpret the Bible themselves. Others believed that only the Pope or other church officials could interpret the Bible. This led some people to leave the Roman Catholic Church.

4. Why did European countries sponsor explorations to other lands? **Summarize**

   Possible answers: Many European countries hoped to open new trade routes, find gold and other riches, establish colonies, spread Christianity, and increase their power.

5. What was the result of the Columbian Exchange? **Make Inferences**

   Possible answer: Through the Columbian Exchange, new diseases, animals, and foods were introduced to the Americas and to European countries.

6. What did European countries gain from establishing colonies in different parts of the world? **Cause and Effect**

   Possible answer: They were able to become wealthy and powerful by colonizing other lands, acquiring new materials, creating markets for European goods, and spreading Christianity to their colonies.

7. How did European colonization expand the slave trade? **Analyze Information**

   Many times there were not enough colonists to perform all the work in the colony. As a result, Europeans in the Americas often forced native peoples to work for them or brought in slaves from Africa to provide labor.

New Beginnings

Resources

- Workbook, p. 106: Vocabulary Preview
- Vocabulary Cards
- Social Studies Plus!

1400s, Florence: Lesson 1

The painting shows a mother and child. The image was painted during the Renaissance. Have students describe the people in the picture. Ask students whom they think this painting portrays. (The Mother of Jesus)

1492, West Indies: Lesson 2

This image shows a map of the known world in the early fifteenth century. Its portrayal of the world is based on the work of a second-century geographer, astronomer, and mathematician, Claudius Ptolemaeus, known as Ptolemy. Ask students to tell what continents they see on this map. Have volunteers trace a possible trade route from one continent to another.

1607, Jamestown: Lesson 3

The image shown is a modern interpretation of the building of Jamestown. Have students tell about what might be happening in this picture. Then ask them where this action is taking place. (Settlers seem to be building a place to live; in some sort of harbor)

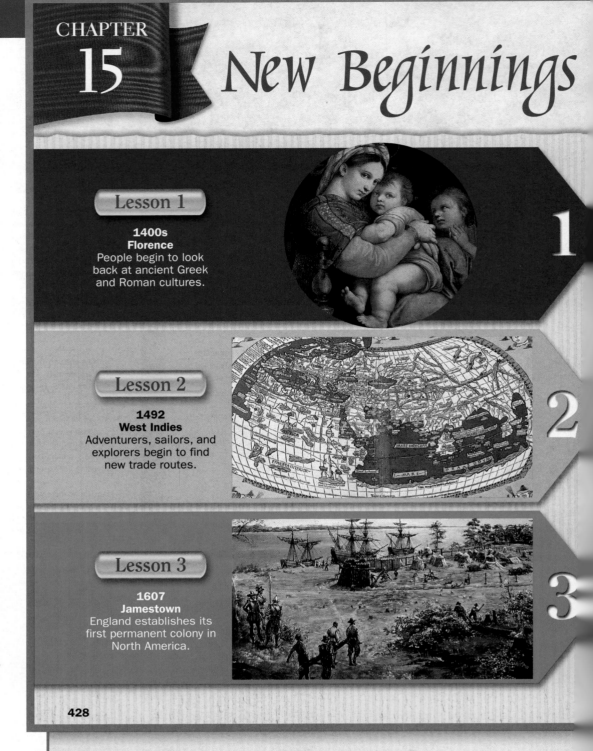

CHAPTER
15 New Beginnings

Lesson 1

1400s
Florence
People begin to look back at ancient Greek and Roman cultures.

1

Lesson 2

1492
West Indies
Adventurers, sailors, and explorers begin to find new trade routes.

2

Lesson 3

1607
Jamestown
England establishes its first permanent colony in North America.

3

428

Practice and Extend

Vocabulary Preview

- Use Workbook p. 106 to help students preview the vocabulary words in this chapter.
- Use Vocabulary Cards to preview key concept words in this chapter.

 Also on Teacher Resources CD-ROM.

Workbook, p. 106

Vocabulary Preview

Vocabulary Preview
Directions: Use the vocabulary terms in the box to complete each sentence. Write the term on the lines. Then unscramble the letters marked with a star to answer the clue that follows.

| commerce | excommunicate | conquistador | mercantilism |
| indulgence | circumnavigate | colony | |

1. One of Magellan's ships was the first to _____, or sail completely around, the world.
2. An economic system by which a country uses colonies to obtain raw materials is called _____.
3. An _____ is a church's pardon from punishment for a sin.
4. Hernando Cortes was a Spanish conqueror, or _____, who acquired wealth by conquering a wealthy civilization.
5. The buying and selling of a large quantity of goods is called _____.
6. A settlement physically separate from—but under the control of—the ruling country is a _____.
7. Church officials could _____, or expel, someone who challenged the church.

Clue: What is the name of the intellectual and economic movement that saw a revived interest in art and the social, scientific, and political thoughts of ancient Greece and Rome?

_____

Notes for Home: Your child learned the vocabulary terms for Chapter 15.
Home Activity: With your child, review the above sentences. Then have your child give the definition for each vocabulary term.

Locating Time and Place

Locating Time and Place

- Have students examine the pictures shown on p. 428 for Lessons 1, 2, and 3.

- Remind students that each picture is coded with a number and a color to link it to a place on the map on p. 429.

Why We Remember

Have students read the "Why We Remember" paragraph on p. 429, and ask them why events in this chapter might be important to them. Have students discuss how knowledge of the European explorations can help them understand their own country's beginnings.

Why We Remember

In the 1400s, the effects of the Plague began to decrease. This is also when the Western world became interested in building a culture as grand as the cultures of ancient Rome and Greece. People took an interest in art, poetry, history, and moral philosophy. Adventurers sought new trade routes. Instead they found lands they did not know about. In their quest for riches, some people took advantage of native populations. All of these factors were a powerful influence on the world as we know it today.

429

WEB SITE
Technology

You can learn more about Florence, Italy; Hispanola, West Indies; and Jamestown, Virginia, by clicking on *Atlas* at **www.sfsocialstudies.com.**

SOCIAL STUDIES STRAND
Geography

Mental Mapping On an outline map showing the continents of the world, have students retrace the route of the Silk Road from Constantinople to China. Next, ask students to trace a sea route to the East that might be safer and faster. Then, have students discuss their choice, including supporting reasons.

The Renaissance

Objectives

- Describe three of the great changes that occurred in Europe during the Renaissance.
- Explain the influence Petrarch had on the Renaissance in Europe.
- Identify the practices within the Roman Catholic Church that led to the Reformation.
- Explain how people's thinking changed during the Renaissance.
- Explain the effects that the Renaissance continues to have on us today.

Vocabulary

commerce, p. 431; **indulgence,** p. 436; **excommunicate,** p. 437

Resources

- Workbook, p. 107
- Transparency 6
- Every Student Learns Guide, pp. 206–209
- Quick Study, pp. 104–105

Quick Teaching Plan

If time is short, have students create a separate note card for each of these topics: art, science, technology, religion.

- As students read independently, have them note contributions or changes that occurred during the Renaissance.

1 Introduce and Motivate

Preview To activate prior knowledge, ask students to recall the effects of the Plague on Europe. Tell students that in Lesson 1 they will learn more about developments in Europe after the Plague faded and finally ended.

 The word *renaissance* means "rebirth." Europe experienced a rebirth in many areas, such as art, science, technology, and religion. Have students identify and discuss examples described on this page and ask them what conclusions they can draw about their importance.

LESSON 1

Milan • Venice • Florence
ITALY

1400			1500

mid-1400s
Renaissance begins.

1455
Gutenberg introduces a Bible printed on a printing press.

1517
The Reformation begins.

PREVIEW

Focus on the Main Idea
From the mid-1400s to the 1600s, Europeans had a renewed interest in art, literature, education, and the cultures of ancient Greece and Rome.

PLACES
Florence
Milan
Venice

PEOPLE
Petrarch
Raphael
Michelangelo
Leonardo da Vinci
Copernicus
Galileo
Johannes Gutenberg
Martin Luther

VOCABULARY
commerce
indulgence
excommunicate

TERMS
Renaissance
moveable type
Protestantism

EVENTS
Reformation
Council of Trent
Counter-Reformation

430

The Renaissance

You Are There
It's a warm, sunny day in Florence, Italy, in the late 1500s. Yesterday, you watched the city celebrate the feast of Saint John, Florence's patron saint. The main event was a horse race through the city. Today, you're enjoying a stroll through the Boboli Gardens, behind the Pitti Palace. The palace belongs to the Medici, the most powerful family in Florence. At the far end of the gardens, on top of a hill, stands the newly built Forte Belvedere. You climb up to the battlements, and look out the openings to get a complete view of the city. You cannot miss the Duomo of Florence, a splendid cathedral. Next to it stands the Baptistery with its famous bronze doors. The cathedral's dome and the Baptistery's doors are just two examples of the stunning art of the time. From your perch on the Forte, you see that the city-state of Florence is a truly beautiful place.

 Summarize As you read, summarize the events of the Renaissance to help you organize your learning.

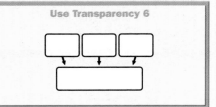

Practice and Extend

READING SKILL
Summarize

In the Lesson Review, students complete a graphic organizer like the one below. You may want to provide students with a copy of Transparency 6 to complete as they read the lesson.

Use Transparency 6

WEB SITE
Technology

- You can look up vocabulary words by clicking on *Social Studies Library* and selecting the dictionary at **www.sfsocialstudies.com.**
- Students can learn more about current news by clicking on *Current Events* at **www.sfsocialstudies.com.**
- Explore other events that occurred on this day by clicking on *This Day in History* at **www.sfsocialstudies.com.**

The Awakening

In 1350 Italy consisted of many separate city-states. Three of the most important of these were **Florence**, **Milan**, and **Venice**. All of these city-states grew to importance through trade and commerce. **Commerce** is the buying and selling of a large quantity of goods. With great wealth, these city-states flourished economically, as well as intellectually.

Florence was the birthplace of the **Renaissance** (rehn uh SAHNS), the intellectual and economic movement that saw a revived interest in the art, social, scientific, and political ideas of ancient Greece and Rome. Some people believed that an understanding and appreciation of the cultures of ancient times could help people conduct their own lives. **Petrarch** (PEH trahrk), a poet and scholar, was a powerful influence on the early Renaissance. Petrarch encouraged people to seek out and study the philosophy and literature of the past. He also encouraged people to speak and write thoughtfully:

> *"The style is the man."*

▶ Florence is known as the birthplace of the Renaissance. The large cathedral shown here is the Duomo of Florence.

Petrarch meant that careless expression was a sign of careless thought.

As markets grew, merchants, bankers, and tradespeople became more prosperous. Prosperous people searched for ways to display their wealth. They wanted fine clothing and larger, more luxurious homes to display works of art. This cultural and economic rebirth began in Italy in the 1400s. By the 1600s it had spread to England, France, Germany, the Netherlands, and Spain.

REVIEW What did the Renaissance represent?
🔁 Summarize

MAP SKILL — Italian City-States, c. 1500 ③

Other Italian states

SWISS CONFEDERATION

FRANCE · DUCHY OF SAVOY · DUCHY OF MILAN · REPUBLIC OF VENICE · HUNGARY

REPUBLIC OF GENOA · REPUBLIC OF FLORENCE · PAPAL STATES · *Adriatic Sea* · OTTOMAN EMPIRE

REPUBLIC OF GENOA

N

KINGDOM OF SARDINIA · KINGDOM OF NAPLES · *Tyrrhenian Sea*

KINGDOM OF SICILY · *Mediterranean Sea*

0   100   200 Miles
0   100   200 Kilometers

▶ Several regions of fifteenth-century Italy were city-states.

MAP SKILL Understand Borders *Which city-states bordered both the Adriatic Sea and the Tyrrhenian Sea?*

431

2 Teach and Discuss

The Awakening

⏱ **Quick Summary** The Renaissance, characterized by a renewal of interest in art, science, education, and the cultures of ancient Greece and Rome, began in Italy during the 1400s.

① **What helped Florence, Milan, and Venice flourish economically?** Trade and commerce **Cause and Effect**

✓ **Ongoing Assessment**

If... students have difficulty understanding how commerce and trade create wealth,	**then...** remind students that commerce is buying and selling. Then tell students trading and selling are economic activities that make money, or wealth, for traders and sellers.

Primary Source

Cited in *World Book Encyclopedia*

② **What does this quote suggest about those who speak and write correctly?** Possible answer: That they have style; they are careful and knowledgeable people.
Analyze Primary Sources

MAP SKILL — Italian City-States, c. 1500

③ **Which city-states were islands?** Part of the Republic of Genoa, the Kingdom of Sardinia, and the Kingdom of Sicily **Apply Information**

MAP SKILL **Answer** Papal states, Kingdom of Naples

✓ **REVIEW ANSWER** It represented a rebirth of the cultures of ancient Greece and Rome. 🔁 Summarize

Art in the Renaissance

Quick Summary During the Renaissance, artists—including Raphael, Michelangelo, and Leonardo da Vinci—created beautiful works of art.

4 **What conclusion can you draw about art before the Renaissance?**
Possible answer: People and nature were not portrayed realistically.
Draw Conclusions

5 **What is the art of perspective?** It is the illusion of depth an artist puts into a picture; the people, buildings, and other things are in proportion to one another.
Summarize

6 **Why might Michelangelo have created a sculpture of David that was so tall?** Possible answers: He thought David was an important biblical figure; the large scale helped Michelangelo show details of the human body.
Make Inferences

Art in the Renaissance

There were several reasons why the Renaissance began in Italy. Ancient ruins could be seen all over the Italian Peninsula. Trade made the Italian city-states wealthy. This wealth encouraged political leaders, businessmen, and the Catholic Church to hire artists to create beautiful works of art. There was a new respect for what humans were able to achieve.

4 Unlike medieval European artists, Renaissance painters and sculptors portrayed people and nature realistically. They were inspired by ancient Greek and Roman artists. They mastered the art of perspective, which creates the illusion that objects in paintings are closer or farther from the viewer. They learned to give depth to pictures as well as proportion to people,
5 things, and buildings.

▶ This painting of the Mother of Jesus was painted by Raphael.

Among the most well-known Italian Renaissance artists were **Raphael, Michelangelo,** and **Leonardo da Vinci.** They were famous in their own time. Many people today still consider them to be geniuses. Raphael was noted for his lovely portraits of the Mother of Jesus. He was also noted for his mastery of perspective and architecture.

Michelangelo was not only a painter but also the finest sculptor of the Renaissance. He painted the Sistine Chapel in fresco and sculpted a series of works known as the *Pietà*. These statues portrayed the Mother of Jesus holding her son after he had been taken down from the cross. Michelangelo carefully chose his marble blocks by visiting the quarry where they were mined. There, he would wait until the sun rose, so that he could watch the sun shine through the marble. If there was a flaw in the marble, he could see it.

The greatest of the Renaissance artists may have been Leonardo da Vinci. He was a painter, sculptor, engineer, and scientist. His most famous paintings were the *Mona Lisa* and *The Last Supper*. He created statues of men and horses. As a scientist he investigated optics, or the study of light and vision, and dissected human bodies to study anatomy.

6 ▶ Michelangelo's statue of David was sculpted in marble and stands more than 13 feet tall.

The Granger Collection

432

Practice and Extend

FAST FACTS

Here are some interesting facts about Leonardo da Vinci.

- Da Vinci's theories and ideas were not made known to the world during his lifetime.
- Several of his theories, while unheard of in his time, were investigated many years after his death and discovered to be at least partially accurate, including those relating to blood circulation, eye action, and the effect of the moon on tides and continent formation.
- He invented an underwater diving suit.
- His design for a flying machine had wings that flapped.

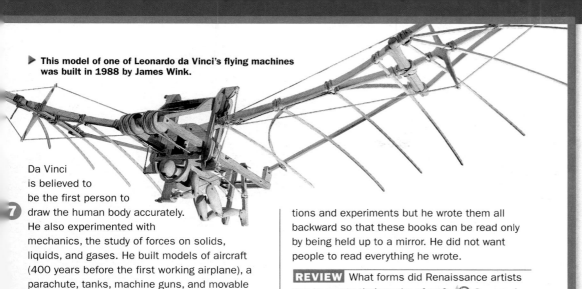

▶ This model of one of Leonardo da Vinci's flying machines was built in 1988 by James Wink.

Da Vinci is believed to be the first person to draw the human body accurately. He also experimented with mechanics, the study of forces on solids, liquids, and gases. He built models of aircraft (400 years before the first working airplane), a parachute, tanks, machine guns, and movable bridges. He kept notebooks on all his observations and experiments but he wrote them all backward so that these books can be read only by being held up to a mirror. He did not want people to read everything he wrote.

REVIEW What forms did Renaissance artists use to create their works of art? ◈ Summarize

 **An Asian Renaissance**

At the same time the Renaissance was spreading throughout Europe, China and Japan were experiencing a cultural renaissance of their own. In China during the Ming dynasty there was a renewal of literature and the arts. Novels and dramas flourished. The Forbidden City, a beautiful palace, was built in Beijing. Theater thrived in Japan. Kabuki theater combined music, dancing, and elaborate costumes in performances that often lasted from morning to evening. Sometimes actors would stop the play so that they could talk to the audience. Sometimes the audience talked back. Other art forms grew prominent in Japan. Haiku poems, which have three lines and 17 syllables, became popular. The art of wood-block prints flourished. Multicolored wood-block art soon followed. This period made important contributions to urban Japanese culture.

▶ Kabuki theater began in Japan in the 1500s. This actor is part of a present-day Kabuki performance.

8

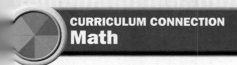

MING DYNASTY

JAPAN

N

▶ Matsuo Basho perfected Haiku poetry.

433

⑦ **How important do you think art was to Michelangelo and Leonardo da Vinci? Explain.** Very important. Michelangelo carefully examined his marble for flaws. Da Vinci dissected human bodies, and this study of anatomy helped him draw the human body accurately. **Draw Conclusions**

✓ **REVIEW ANSWER** Paintings and sculpture ◈ Summarize

An Asian Renaissance

⑧ **What art forms characterized the Asian Renaissance?** Novels, theater, architecture, poetry (haiku), wood-block prints, and multicolored wood-block art ◈ Summarize

Revolution in Science

🕐 **Quick Summary** Two significant Renaissance scientists, Copernicus and Galileo, taught that Earth moved around the sun. The Catholic Church criticized Galileo for this theory.

ST SOCIAL STUDIES STRAND
Science • Technology

9 **How did Renaissance scientists contribute to present-day scientific understanding?** Possible answer: They realized that Earth moves around the sun, which we know today is correct.
Analyze Information

10 **Summarize the impact of Renaissance scientists.** They helped spread ideas, and other scientists went on to perform experiments and to make their ideas known. 🔄 Summarize

✓ **REVIEW ANSWER** Copernicus taught that Earth was not the center of the universe. Galileo studied the motion of pendulums and the physics of motion.
🔄 Summarize

Revolution in Science

Renaissance thinkers believed that people should use reasoned thought and the scientific method to understand how the world works. Two of the most significant Renaissance scientists were **Copernicus** and **Galileo.** Both were astronomers and both taught that Earth moves around the sun.

Copernicus taught at the University of Cracow in Poland. His astronomical observations convinced Copernicus that Earth was not the center of the universe. He wrote out his ideas by 1510, but chose not to allow them to be published until 1540.

Galileo lived in Italy and taught at the University of Pisa. When he spoke out in favor of Copernicus's ideas, he was criticized by the Catholic Church. In 1609, only a year after the telescope was invented, Galileo built an improved telescope. He then did something revolutionary—he became the first person to point his telescope toward the sky. He used it to study the sky. However, Galileo's studies challenged the authority of the Catholic Church. He was put on trial and under house arrest for the

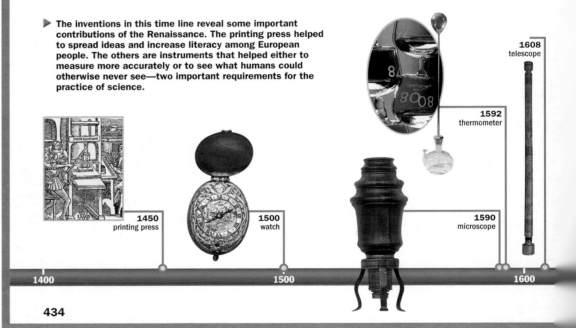

▶ Copernicus (left) and Galileo (below) helped to revolutionize our understanding of the universe.

rest of his life. Even so, Galileo went on to describe the motion of pendulums and the physics of motion. Other scientists invented new instruments, performed experiments, and made their ideas known. **10**

REVIEW How did Copernicus and Galileo change people's ideas about the world?
🔄 Summarize

▶ The inventions in this time line reveal some important contributions of the Renaissance. The printing press helped to spread ideas and increase literacy among European people. The others are instruments that helped either to measure more accurately or to see what humans could otherwise never see—two important requirements for the practice of science.

1450 printing press

1500 watch

1590 microscope

1592 thermometer

1608 telescope

1400   1500   1600

434

Practice and Extend

❄ MEETING INDIVIDUAL NEEDS
Learning Styles

Summarize Theories Have students use their individual learning styles, to summarize the scientific theories that emerged during the Renaissance.

Verbal Learning Have students give an oral presentation that summarizes the scientific theories of the Renaissance.

Linguistic Learning Have students pretend they are newspaper reporters during the time of the Renaissance. Have them write an article summarizing the latest scientific theories.

Visual Learning Have students make a diagram showing one scientific theory, such as how Earth revolves around the sun.

Renaissance Inventions

Probably the greatest advance in technology was **Johannes Gutenberg's** invention of a printing press that used **movable type,** or small reusable metal pieces for each letter and number. Gutenberg worked on his invention throughout the 1440s. In 1455 he introduced a Bible printed on his printing press.

Up until this time, books had to be copied by hand. Gutenberg's press produced books far more quickly than they could be produced by hand. As a result, books became affordable for the educated middle class. Readers wanted a variety of books, such as almanacs, travel books, romances, and poetry. As the demand for books grew, the book trade flourished throughout Europe. Other related industries, such as paper making and printing press building, also thrived. As a result, more people became literate and the economy strengthened.

In addition to the printing press, a variety of inventions was introduced during the Renaissance. Some have proven to be quite useful to society both then and now.

The Granger Collection

▶ Johannes Gutenberg (on the far right) spent years perfecting his movable-type printing press. Here, he examines a page fresh off the press.

▶ **This is a modern reproduction of the Gutenberg printing press.**

As you already have read, Leonardo da Vinci experimented with mechanics, which is the study of forces on solids, liquids, and gases. Unfortunately, many of his inventions were too advanced for the existing technology of his time.

Other practical inventions included the watch, which was created in the early 1500s. A Dutchman invented a mainspring to power clocks. Until then, clocks had been driven by falling weights and had to remain stationary and upright for the weights to accurately operate. The mainspring allowed clocks to be portable and movable. In the late 1500s, a Dutch maker of eyeglasses discovered the principle of the compound microscope. In the 1670s, a single lens microscope was invented that could magnify an object up to 270 times its real size.

Another Dutch optician used the same principle to create an optical telescope in 1608. As you have read, Galileo soon improved on the original design of the telescope.

The air thermometer was invented in 1592. It worked by measuring a column of air in a glass tube. A person could use it to estimate temperature.

REVIEW How did Gutenberg's printing press change conditions in Europe? ⟳ **Summarize**

435

Renaissance Inventions

🕐 *Quick Summary* A variety of inventions were introduced during the Renaissance, including the printing press, which Johannes Gutenberg worked on during the 1440s.

⓫ **How did the printing press work?** It used movable type—small reusable letters and numbers. ⟳ **Summarize**

Ⓢ|Ⓣ SOCIAL STUDIES STRAND
Science • Technology

⓬ **Which industries directly benefited from the invention of the printing press?** The paper and book industries, and the manufacturing industry (making printing presses) **Cause and Effect**

⓭ **What other inventions were introduced during the Renaissance?** The watch, a single-lens microscope, an optical telescope, and the air thermometer **Main Idea and Details**

✓ **REVIEW ANSWER** As a result of the printing press, people read more and the book trade flourished throughout Europe. ⟳ **Summarize**

The Need for Church Reform

Quick Summary One of the most vocal critics of the Roman Catholic Church, Martin Luther, was eventually excommunicated from the Church, initiating the Reformation and the Counter-Reformation.

14 **What were the two main objections Luther had to the Roman Catholic Church?** He criticized the Church for selling indulgences for money and for its dictate that only the pope or other church officials could interpret the Bible.
↻ Summarize

Problem Solving

Point out that Martin Luther attempted to solve the problems he found within his church.

15 **How did Martin Luther suggest the church might respond to his objections?** He asked for a debate.
Solve Problems

Spread of Protestantism

16 **Which religions were practiced in Ireland at this time?** Protestant and Roman Catholic religions **Interpret Maps**

MAP SKILL **Answer** Parts of Prussia, Poland and Lithuania, and France

---

The Need for Church Reform

Many Renaissance scholars in northern and western Europe turned their attention to the study of the Roman Catholic Church and its practices. The Church had become wealthy during the Middle Ages. With that wealth came corruption.

Among the practices these scholars objected to was the Church's willingness to accept money for **indulgences,** or pardons from punishment for sins. Originally, an indulgence could be gained only by performing works of charity. For example, a person could fast, give money to the poor, or make pilgrimages to holy places. However, by the beginning of the Renaissance, the Church allowed people to buy indulgences as a way to buy pardons for their sins. Indulgences were also granted to the crusaders before they set off for war.

One of the most vocal critics of this practice was **Martin Luther.** He believed that Christians should not be judged by the good works they

▶ **This wood engraving from the early 1500s depicts a church official selling indulgences.**

performed, but by their belief in God. In 1517 Luther wrote a challenge to the Church. He attacked the sale of indulgences. He stated that people should read and interpret the Bible themselves. The church dictated that only the pope, the leader of the Roman Catholic Church, or other church officials such as bishops and monks, could interpret the Bible on their own. Luther asked for a debate, or a public discussion.

14

15

MAP SKILL

Spread of Protestantism

16

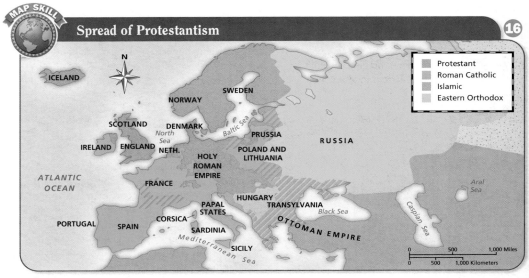

	Protestant
	Roman Catholic
	Islamic
	Eastern Orthodox

ICELAND · N · NORWAY · SWEDEN · SCOTLAND · DENMARK · North Sea · Baltic Sea · PRUSSIA · RUSSIA · IRELAND · ENGLAND · NETH. · POLAND AND LITHUANIA · HOLY ROMAN EMPIRE · ATLANTIC OCEAN · FRANCE · HUNGARY · TRANSYLVANIA · Aral Sea · PORTUGAL · SPAIN · CORSICA · PAPAL STATES · Black Sea · Caspian Sea · SARDINIA · OTTOMAN EMPIRE · Mediterranean Sea · SICILY

0 500 1,000 Miles
0 500 1,000 Kilometers

▶ **By 1590 Protestantism had spread to many parts of Europe.**
MAP SKILL **Use a Map Key** *In which countries did Roman Catholic areas overlap with Protestant areas?*

Practice and Extend

SOCIAL STUDIES
Background

Martin Luther

- A descendant of peasants, Luther's father, Hans, was a copper miner in Mansfeld, Germany.
- Luther became a monk in 1506 and a priest in 1507.
- He obtained a bachelor's degree in theology in 1509.
- He received his doctorate in theology in 1512.

Church officials reacted by **excommunicating,** or expelling, Luther from the Church. When he was asked if he would reconsider and take back his objections, Luther said,

> **⑰** *". . . my conscience is captive to the Word of God. I cannot and I will not recant [take back] anything . . ."*

People who agreed with Luther and followed his teachings became known as Lutherans. Soon there were other groups of Christians, such as the followers of John Calvin, who no longer wished to be a part of the Roman Catholic Church.

These events were called the **Reformation** because these people wanted to reform, or change, Church beliefs and practices. This began a movement called **Protestantism,** since its supporters had protested against the Church.

The Catholic Church responded by calling the **Council of Trent** in 1545. These efforts were called the **Counter-Reformation** because they were against the Reformation. Roman Catholics

▶ **Martin Luther was the leader of the Protestant Reformation.**

still accepted that only the Church could explain the Bible. They also insisted that the pope was the highest authority in the Church. However, the council did begin some reforms, including a ban on the sale of indulgences.

As you read in Unit 4, Christianity split into an eastern church and a western church in 1054. Now the Reformation and the Counter-Reformation split western Christianity once again: into Catholics and Protestants.

REVIEW What were the Reformation and the Counter-Reformation? 🔄 Summarize

Summarize the Lesson

— **mid-1400s** The Renaissance began.

└ **1455** Gutenberg published a printed version of the Bible.

└ **1517** The Reformation began.

LESSON 1 REVIEW

Check Facts and Main Ideas

1. 🔄 **Summarize** On a separate piece of paper, write three short sentences that lead to the summary.

The printing press helped make more Europeans literate.	Artists portrayed people and nature realistically.	Scientists discovered that Earth orbits around the sun.

↓

Events during the Renaissance brought great changes in the arts, science, literature, and ideas to Europe.

2. How did Petrarch influence the Renaissance?

3. What practices of the Roman Catholic Church led to the Reformation?

4. How does the Renaissance affect us today?

5. **Critical Thinking:** *Make Inferences* How did the Renaissance change people's thinking?

Link to ∞ Writing

Write an Essay Suppose you are Petrarch's assistant. Write an essay that describes and illustrates his quote: "The style is the man." Exchange your essay with a partner and ask him or her to evaluate it.

437

Workbook, p. 107

Lesson 1: The Renaissance

Directions: Use complete sentences to answer the following questions on the lines provided. You may use your textbook.

1. Why did the Renaissance begin?

2. How was Renaissance art different from medieval European art?

Directions: Complete the chart with information about the Reformation and the Catholic Counter-Reformation. You may use your textbook.

	Reformation	Catholic Counter-Reformation
Why did the movement occur?		
What were followers' beliefs?		
What actions did followers take?		

Notes for Home: Your child learned about the changes in Europe brought on by the Renaissance.
Home Activity: With your child, discuss how events that occurred during the Renaissance affect us today.

Also on Teacher Resources CD-ROM.

Spoken by Martin Luther at the Imperial Diet of Worms

⑰ What was the main point Luther was trying to make in this quotation? He believed his objections were based on the Word of God and taking them back would be going against God.
Analyze Primary Sources

✓ **REVIEW ANSWER** Movement to bring reform to the Roman Catholic Church, leading to Protestantism; movement to reform the Roman Catholic Church to keep Christians from becoming Protestants 🔄 Summarize

Close and Assess

Summarize the Lesson

Tell students to read the events in the time line. Have them add other important events from the lesson.

✓ **LESSON 1 REVIEW**

1. 🔄 **Summarize** For possible answers, see the reduced pupil page.

2. He encouraged people to study the philosophy and literature of the past and to speak and write thoughtfully.

3. Sale of indulgences and interpretation of the Bible by only the Pope and church officials

4. People are richer for the art, literature, science, and technology that came from the Renaissance. The variety of Protestant religions came from the Reformation, a result of the Renaissance.

5. **Critical Thinking:** *Make Inferences* It encouraged people to use reasoned thought and the scientific method as they thought about their world. It also encouraged them to value art, literature, technology, and science.

Link to ∞ Writing

Before students begin their essays, have them brainstorm a list of character traits a person's style might reflect, such as being careful, neat, neglectful, disorderly, or thorough.

Trade Routes and Conquests

Objectives

- Explain why Europeans began to make voyages of exploration.
- Explain the reasons why Europeans were so interested in exploring Africa.
- Identify the location of the Cape of Good Hope.
- Describe how the European exploration of the Americas would have been different if the Spanish had been convinced that there was little or no gold to be found in the Americas.

Vocabulary

circumnavigate, p. 439;
conquistador, p. 441

Resources

- Workbook, p. 108
- Transparency 6
- Every Student Learns Guide, pp. 210–213
- Quick Study, pp. 106–107

Quick Teaching Plan

If time is short, have students read independently and take notes in a chart or other graphic organizer for each country.

- Have them include information stating *Who, What, Where, When,* and *Why* each exploration took place.

1 Introduce and Motivate

Preview To activate prior knowledge, ask students what they know about Christopher Columbus or any other explorers. Tell students that in Lesson 2 they will learn about the explorations from the point of view of the Europeans.

You Are There Point out that Prince Henry was ruler of Portugal in the 1400s. Have students discuss why Portugal may have felt it was so important to trade with Africa.

LESSON 2

1450		1500	
	1492 Columbus's first expedition to the Americas		**1519** Magellan begins his journey around the world.
		1497 Vasco da Gama begins expedition to India.	

PREVIEW

Focus on the Main Idea
European traders wanted additional trade routes, and rulers wanted to establish empires.

PLACES
Cape of Good Hope
West Indies

PEOPLE
Henry the Navigator
Bartolomeu Dias
Vasco da Gama
Ferdinand Magellan
Christopher Columbus
Isabella
Elizabeth I

VOCABULARY
circumnavigate
conquistador

TERMS
Treaty of Tordesillas
Columbian Exchange
Armada

Trade Routes and Conquests

You Are There — As Prince Henry's economic advisor, you've been asked to compare the cost of bringing gold to Portugal from Africa by sea to the cost of transporting it by land. Travel logs show that a single camel can travel about 3.5 miles per hour for about 10 hours a day—34 miles in one day. One camel can carry about 990 pounds of cargo. Most camel caravans have 1,000 camels.

Next, you discover that a ship travels about 2 miles per hour. However, the ship can move 24 hours a day. Most important is how much cargo a ship can carry—between 50 and 160 tons of cargo.

After you have made your calculations, you approach Prince Henry. You recommend that he spend whatever is necessary to establish and protect sea routes for trade with Africa.

 Summarize As you read, summarize the information to help you better understand how Europeans started exploring and conquering other lands.

438

Practice and Extend

READING SKILL
Summarize

In the Lesson Review, students complete a graphic organizer like the one below. You may want to provide students with a copy of Transparency 6 to complete as they read the lesson.

Use Transparency 6

WEB SITE
Technology

- You can look up vocabulary words by clicking on *Social Studies Library* and selecting the dictionary at **www.sfsocialstudies.com.**
- Students can learn more about current news by clicking on *Current Events* at **www.sfsocialstudies.com.**
- Explore other events that occurred on this day by clicking on *This Day in History* at **www.sfsocialstudies.com.**

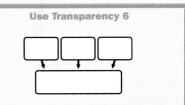

Portuguese Explorers

During the 1400s, Europeans developed an interest in gold and other riches from Africa. For years, travelers brought gold, silver, and ivory across land routes that connected Africa to the Mediterranean region. As you read in Unit 5, the land routes were costly, dangerous, and controlled by Muslim traders. As a Christian country, Portugal wanted to avoid land routes controlled by Muslims. Portugal took the lead in the expeditions to find new sea routes.

From 1419 until his death in 1460, Prince **Henry** of Portugal sent several expeditions to explore the west coast of Africa. He hoped to establish colonies there and break the Muslim control on trade routes. Henry's influence on voyages of exploration was so important that he came to be called Henry the Navigator.

In 1488 **Bartolomeu Dias** of Portugal sailed around the **Cape of Good Hope** at the southern tip of Africa. He would have continued on to India, but the ship's supplies were low. After consulting with his officers, Dias decided to turn back.

In 1497 **Vasco da Gama** sailed around the Cape of Good Hope to India. His voyage marked the first all-water

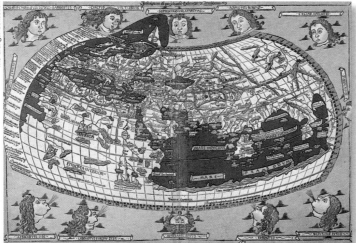

The Granger Collection

▶ Thanks to the printing press, this world map, originally drawn by Ptolemy about A.D. 150, was widely available to navigators and sailors.

trade route between Europe and Asia. Da Gama's second voyage to India, in 1502, established a Portuguese presence in India. Portugal soon became an important trading and naval power in the Indian Ocean.

Other nations soon took Portugal's lead. However, it was a Portuguese sea captain named **Ferdinand Magellan** who made one of the most important sea voyages of the age. Magellan thought it possible to reach the east by sailing around the southern tip of South America. In 1519 Magellan set out with five ships. Magellan did not live long enough to complete the voyage himself. He was killed while he and his crew visited an island in the Pacific Ocean.

In 1522, three years after Magellan had begun his voyage, a single ship—all that was left of the original five—arrived in Spain. It was the first ship to **circumnavigate,** or sail completely around, the world. ❶

REVIEW Why did Catholic countries such as Portugal wish to find an ocean route to the African coasts? **Cause and Effect**

▶ Galleons were sailing ships used mainly by the Spanish and Portuguese during the fifteenth and sixteenth centuries.

439

2 Teach and Discuss

PAGE 439

Portuguese Explorers

🕐 *Quick Summary* Portugal initiated the search for new sea routes to Africa, Asia, and eventually around the world.

❶ **Summarize the important Portuguese sea voyages made during the 1400s and 1500s.** Dias sailed around the Cape of Good Hope at the southern tip of Africa in 1488; da Gama sailed to India in 1497 and in 1502; Ferdinand Magellan's ships circumnavigated the world from 1519 to 1522. 🔄 Summarize

✓ **Ongoing Assessment**

If... students have difficulty summarizing Portuguese explorations,

then... list the following names on the chalkboard and have students write a sentence about each explorer's voyage: Dias, Vasco da Gama, Magellan.

✓ **REVIEW ANSWER** To avoid the land routes that were controlled by Muslims and to acquire goods at a lower cost **Cause and Effect**

❄ **MEETING INDIVIDUAL NEEDS**
Leveled Practice

Sequence Explorations Have students sequence the important Portuguese explorations during the 1400s and 1500s.

Easy Have students put the following in order: da Gama sails around the Cape of Good Hope (2); Dias sails around the Cape of Good Hope (1); Magellan's ships circumnavigate the world (4); da Gama establishes a Portuguese presence in India (3). **Reteach**

On-Level Have students complete a sequence chart listing the major Portuguese voyages of the 1400s and 1500s. **Extend**

Challenge Have students research additional Portuguese voyages of this time. Have students sequence these voyages and the voyages from the text in a time line. **Enrich**

For a Lesson Summary, use Quick Study, p. 106.

East to West

🕐 **Quick Summary** Some European rulers and explorers thought they could reach Asia by sailing west. This was Columbus's goal as he set sail from Spain in 1492.

2 **Explain the reactions Portugal and Spain each had to Columbus's request for funding.** Portugal turned him down; it wanted to continue to explore the African coast. Spain agreed to fund his voyage; it wanted to spread Christianity and compete with Portugal for wealth. **Compare and Contrast**

Primary Source

Cited in *Early European Adventurers and the Opening of Japan*, by Richard Pflederer

3 **What does Columbus's statement indicate about the world maps of the fifteenth century?** Possible answers: They were not accurate; they probably showed inaccurate distances; they didn't include the Americas. **Analyze Primary Sources**

✓ **REVIEW ANSWER** She hoped to be able to convert other people to Christianity and to compete with Portugal for wealth. **Cause and Effect**

Map Adventure Answers

1. Southwest, then southeast; **2.** About 4 months; **3.** Because the only other sailors who had come to the area were Muslims; **4.** Indian Ocean

East to West

As the economy improved in parts of Europe, the demand for goods from Asia—such as peppercorns, cloves, nutmeg, cinnamon, precious gems, and fine silk—increased. While the Portuguese worked to reach Asia by sailing around Africa, others thought sailing west would be easier. Among these was **Christopher Columbus,** an Italian sailor living in Portugal. In 1484 Columbus asked King John II of Portugal to sponsor a voyage to reach Asia by a western route. Because Portugal was committed to exploring the gold-producing coast of Africa, King John turned him down.

Columbus turned to Spain for funding. His first few requests were refused. Eventually, however, Queen **Isabella** agreed to fund Columbus's expedition. She wanted to spread Christianity and to **2** compete with Portugal for wealth.

Columbus sailed from Spain on August 3, 1492. On October 12 he sighted land, an island in what is now called the **West Indies.** About two weeks later he sighted what he thought was Japan, also called Zipangu at that time.

> *"All my globes and world maps seem to indicate that the island of Japan is in this vicinity and I am sure that Cuba and Zipangu are one."* **3**

By 1504 Columbus had completed three more expeditions.

REVIEW What benefits did Queen Isabella expect to get from Columbus's expedition? **Cause and Effect**

Map Adventure

You're an Explorer

It is 1497. Vasco da Gama has asked you to join his crew. You will be working on one of his four ships, sailing around the Cape of Good Hope. This voyage could open up trade routes to both India and China.

1. In July, you depart from Lisbon, Portugal. What direction do you sail to head toward the Cape of Good Hope?

2. You round the tip of Africa in November. How many months have you traveled?

3. You drop anchor off the coast of Mozambique. The people living there think that you are all Muslims. Why?

4. Your next major stop before India is Malindi. An Arab navigator joins your crew to show da Gama how to use the monsoon winds to reach Calicut. What ocean must you cross?

440

Practice and Extend

Decision Making

Use a Decision-Making Process

● Have students consider the following decision-making scenario: **Suppose you are the advisor to King John II of Portugal. The king asks your advice about funding Columbus's voyage to the west to reach Asia.**

● Students should use the following decision-making process to decide what advice they will give. For each step in the process, have groups of students discuss and write about what must be considered as they make their decision. Write the steps listed above on the board or read them aloud.

1. Identify a situation that requires a decision.
2. Gather information.
3. Identify options.
4. Predict consequences.
5. Take action to implement a decision.

Conquering the Americas

As the Portuguese began exploring Africa, the Church expressed an interest in new territories. In 1452 Pope Nicholas V wrote an official letter that allowed explorers to make slaves of the native peoples of newly explored lands. Expeditions began to include missionaries, who tried to convert the native peoples to Christianity.

In 1494 the Church helped to draw up the **Treaty of Tordesillas.** This treaty divided the Americas between Spain and Portugal. This allowed the conquerors to claim great portions of the Americas for either Spain or Portugal.

The Spanish and Portuguese explorers believed that there was great wealth in the Americas. As you read in Unit 3, Hernando Cortes and Francisco Pizarro were **conquistadors,** or Spanish conquerors, who acquired wealth by conquering wealthy civilizations.

However, the conquerors soon discovered other riches: the foods grown by the Native Americans. These included maize (corn), tomatoes, potatoes, chocolate, and squash. Europeans introduced plants and animals to the Americas: wheat, sugar cane, cattle, pigs, and horses, among others. This exchange of goods between the Americas and Europe is known as the **Columbian Exchange.**

Diseases were also exchanged. Europeans brought over diseases such as smallpox, measles, and influenza. The Native Americans had never encountered these diseases before. Many died.

REVIEW What was the Treaty of Tordesillas?
⟳ **Summarize**

4

MAP SKILL
European Voyages of Exploration

5

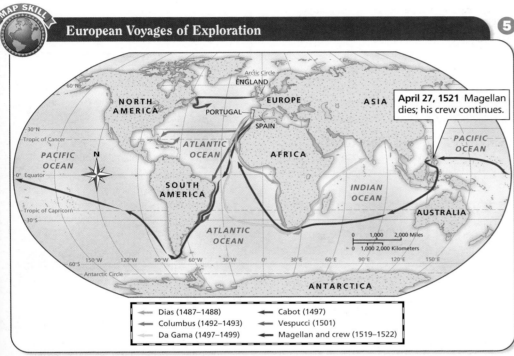

April 27, 1521 Magellan dies; his crew continues.

Key:
← Dias (1487–1488)   ← Cabot (1497)
← Columbus (1492–1493)   ← Vespucci (1501)
← Da Gama (1497–1499)   ← Magellan and crew (1519–1522)

▶ From 1487 to 1522, a number of explorers completed voyages with different rates of success.

MAP SKILL Use Latitude *Which explorer traveled to the farthest northern latitude? Which explorer traveled to the farthest southern latitude?*

441

Conquering the Americas

Quick Summary Motivated by the Church's interest in exploring new territories and converting their people to Christianity, Spain and Portugal conquered regions of the Americas during the late fifteenth and early sixteenth centuries.

4 **Did the Church and the explorers have the same reasons for exploring and conquering new lands? Explain.** No; the Church wanted to convert people to Christianity, while the explorers wanted to gain wealth by conquering wealthy civilizations. **Compare and Contrast**

MAP SKILL
European Voyages of Exploration

5 **Which two explorers were traveling during the same year? Which year was it?** Da Gama and Cabot both traveled during 1497. **Interpret Maps**

MAP SKILL **Answer** Northern: Cabot; southern: Magellan and crew

✓ **REVIEW ANSWER** This treaty was drawn up in 1494 by the Church. It divided the Americas between Spain and Portugal, allowing them to claim great portions of the Americas. ⟳ **Summarize**

ESL Support
EXTEND LANGUAGE

Identify Related Words Guide students in identifying words associated with ships.

Beginning Show students labeled pictures of people associated with ships, such as an explorer, pirate, navigator, captain, and sailor. Remove the labels and have students identify the people.

Intermediate Have students create sentences that tell what each kind of person on a ship does; for example, *Explorers explore new places.*

Advanced Have students create a web with *ships* in the center circle and related words, such as *fleet, warships,* and *pirates,* in the connecting circles.

For additional ESL support, use Every Student Learns Guide, pp. 210–213.

The Spanish Armada

🕐 **Quick Summary** England's powerful ships defeated the Spanish Armada, which the king of Spain sent as a response to English pirate attacks.

6 **How were sixteenth-century England and Spain alike? How were they different?** Possible answers: Both wanted to explore and conquer new lands; England was Protestant, Spain was Catholic. **Compare and Contrast**

✓ **REVIEW ANSWER** Queen Elizabeth funded many sea expeditions. **Main Idea and Details**

3 Close and Assess

Summarize the Lesson

Have students read the three events listed in the time line and write an effect of each.

✓ **LESSON 2   REVIEW**

1. 🔄 **Summarize** For possible answers, see the reduced pupil page.

2. They believed the continent was a source of great amounts of gold and other riches.

3. At the southern tip of Africa

4. The exchange of plants, animals, and other goods between Europe and the Americas

5. **Critical Thinking: *Make Inferences*** Possible answer: Expeditions to the Americas might have been fewer or stopped altogether for a time.

Link to ⚭ **Writing**

Have students include the scope of the expedition, their direction, and final destination. Remind students to write persuasively and to include facts to convince the investors.

The Spanish Armada

In 1496 King Henry VII of England funded the expedition of Italian explorer John Cabot to find a western route to Asia. When the expedition sailed the following year, Cabot explored the coast of North America. After Henry VII died, his son Henry VIII focused his attention on the religious changes taking place in Europe, not exploration. England became a Protestant nation under his rule. Under his daughter, **Elizabeth I,** England became a world sea power. Read more about Elizabeth I in the biography on page 443.

As queen of England, Elizabeth funded many expeditions after she came to power in 1558. Some of the English navigators, such as Sir Francis Drake, were pirates as well as explorers. These pirates attacked Spanish ships filled with gold and riches from their expeditions.

Elizabeth also supported Dutch Protestants **6** who were fighting against Catholic Spain. In response in 1588, King Philip II of Spain sent the **Armada** (ar MAH dah), a fleet of about 130 warships, to attack England. The gold and intricate

▶ The Spanish Armada clashes with English ships in this painting by Hendrik Cornelisz Vroom.

designs on the Spanish ships were beautiful, but they made the ships heavy and slow. The plainer but swifter English ships had bigger and more powerful guns. Within a few days, the Armada was defeated.

REVIEW How did Queen Elizabeth make England a major sea power? **Main Idea and Details**

Summarize the Lesson

- **1488** Bartolomeu Dias reached the Cape of Good Hope.

- **1492** Christopher Columbus began his first expedition.

- **1519** Magellan began a journey around the world.

LESSON 2   REVIEW

Check Facts and Main Ideas

1. 🔄 **Summarize** On a separate piece of paper, fill in the summary from the details given below.

| The Portuguese explored sea routes to India. | Columbus sailed west to reach Asia. | Magellan's crew sailed around the world. |

↓

While trying to increase their wealth and empire, Europeans explored many new sea routes.

2. Why were Europeans interested in exploring Africa?

3. Where is the Cape of Good Hope?

4. What was the Columbian Exchange?

5. **Critical Thinking: *Make Inferences*** What do you think would have happened if the first Spanish explorers had been convinced there was little or no gold to be found in the Americas?

Link to ⚭ **Writing**

Write a Grant Request Suppose you are working with Christopher Columbus or Ferdinand Magellan. Your assignment is to prepare a grant request, asking investors for money to fund your expedition. Be sure you explain what the money will be used for and what the investor can expect in return.

Practice and Extend

CURRICULUM CONNECTION
Science

Research Diseases

- Have students work in small groups or pairs to research one of the diseases that was brought from Europe to the Americas: smallpox, measles, or influenza.

- Students should find out the history of the disease in the Americas and how the medical community has coped with it.

- Have students illustrate their findings with pictures, diagrams, or time lines.

Workbook, p. 108

Lesson 2: Trade Routes and Conquests

Directions: Match each name or term in the box to its description. Write the letter of the term on the line provided. You may use your textbook.

a. Portugal	f. Spain	k. Columbian Exchange
b. Ptolemy's map	g. Queen Isabella	l. Elizabeth I
c. Vasco da Gama	h. Pope Nicholas V	
d. Ferdinand Magellan	i. Treaty of Tordesillas	
e. Christopher Columbus	j. Hernando Cortés	

_____ 1. conqueror who acquired wealth by conquering a wealthy civilization
_____ 2. queen of England; funded many expeditions and supported Dutch Protestants who were fighting against Catholic Spain
_____ 3. allowed explorers to make slaves of native peoples in newly explored lands
_____ 4. sailed around the Cape of Good Hope, which marked the first all-water trade route between Europe and Asia
_____ 5. agreement dividing the Americas between Spain and Portugal
_____ 6. sea captain whose ship was the first to sail completely around the world
_____ 7. world map used widely by navigators and sailors
_____ 8. fleet of Spanish warships defeated by English ships
_____ 9. funded Columbus's expedition to Asia; wanted to spread Christianity and compete with Portugal for wealth
_____ 10. important trading and naval power; took the lead in expeditions to find new sea routes
_____ 11. process of exchanging goods and diseases between the Americas and Europe
_____ 12. Italian sailor who sailed for Spain in search of a western route to Asia
_____ 13. Portugal's rival for wealth from voyages of exploration

Notes for Home: Your child learned about European expeditions, trade routes, and conquests. *Home Activity:* With your child, imagine you are about to go on a voyage that will last several months. Make a list of the items and supplies you need to take with you. Discuss why each item is important.

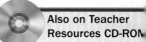

Also on Teacher Resources CD-ROM

Elizabeth I

1533–1603

Elizabeth I was the daughter of King Henry VIII of England. She received an excellent education. She studied French, Greek, Latin, and Italian. She wrote poetry.

When she was young, Elizabeth was caught in the religious power struggles between Catholics and Protestants. When her father died, Elizabeth's Protestant half-brother Edward VI became king. When a plot against Edward's life was discovered, Elizabeth was a suspect. Although she was only 15, she was brave and answered her accusers. Elizabeth was soon cleared of the charges.

After Edward died, Elizabeth's Catholic half-sister Mary became queen of England. When plans to overthrow Mary were discovered, Elizabeth, who was Protestant, was again accused. She was imprisoned in the Tower of London.

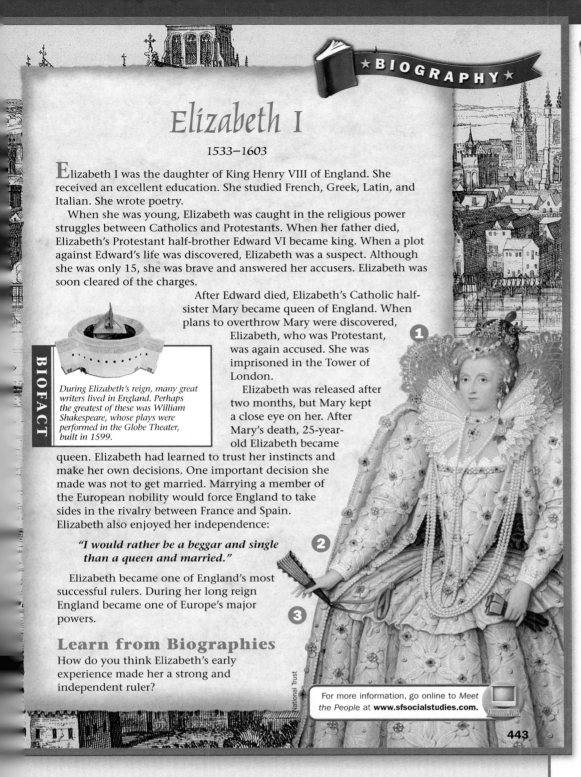

Elizabeth was released after two months, but Mary kept a close eye on her. After Mary's death, 25-year-old Elizabeth became queen. Elizabeth had learned to trust her instincts and make her own decisions. One important decision she made was not to get married. Marrying a member of the European nobility would force England to take sides in the rivalry between France and Spain. Elizabeth also enjoyed her independence:

"I would rather be a beggar and single than a queen and married."

Elizabeth became one of England's most successful rulers. During her long reign England became one of Europe's major powers.

Learn from Biographies

How do you think Elizabeth's early experience made her a strong and independent ruler?

BIOFACT

During Elizabeth's reign, many great writers lived in England. Perhaps the greatest of these was William Shakespeare, whose plays were performed in the Globe Theater, built in 1599.

For more information, go online to *Meet the People* at **www.sfsocialstudies.com.**

443

CURRICULUM CONNECTION
Literature

Read Biographies

Use the following selections to extend the content.

Good Queen Bess: The Story of Elizabeth I of England, by Diane Stanley (HarperCollins, ISBN 0-688-17961-4, 2001) **Easy** *ALA Notable Book, Boston Globe Horn Book Honors*

The Lyons Throne (Lyon Saga Series), by M. L. Stainer (Chicken Soup Press, ISBN 1-893-33702-2, 1999) **On-Level**

Beware, Princess Elizabeth (Young Royals), by Carolyn Meyer (Harcourt, ISBN 0-152-02659-2, 2001) **Challenge**

Elizabeth I

Objective

• Identify the accomplishments of significant individuals, such as Queen Elizabeth I, during the period of European exploration.

1 Introduce and Motivate

Preview To activate prior knowledge, ask students to recall what they learned about Elizabeth I in this chapter. Tell students that they will learn about the decisions Elizabeth made that influenced her reign.

2 Teach and Discuss

1 Why was Elizabeth a suspect in a plot to overthrow her sister when Mary was queen of England? Mary was Catholic and Elizabeth was Protestant.
Cause and Effect

Primary Source

Cited in *The Dictionary of Biographical Quotation*, Richard Kenin and Justin Wintle, eds.

2 Why was it important to Elizabeth to remain unmarried? Because she did not want to take sides in the rivalry between France and Spain and because she enjoyed her independence
Analyze Primary Sources

3 What qualities did Elizabeth possess? Possible answer: She was strong, independent, and decisive.
Draw Conclusions

3 Close and Assess

Learn from Biographies Answer

Possible answer: Being under suspicion for the plots to kill her brother and overthrow her sister made Elizabeth rely on her own instincts. She learned to make her own decisions.

European Colonization

Objectives

- Explain how the economic system of mercantilism works.
- Describe what a colony is and explain why colonies enabled European countries to grow more wealthy and powerful.
- Explain how the system of encomienda worked.
- Identify some of the reasons that Europe started founding colonies.
- Describe ways that Europe could have created colonies without forcing the native peoples who lived there to work for them.

Vocabulary

colony, p. 445; **mercantilism,** p. 445

Resources

- Workbook, p. 109
- Transparency 5
- Every Student Learns Guide, pp. 214–217
- Quick Study, pp. 108–109

Quick Teaching Plan

If time is short, have students create a chart with three headings: *Portugal and Spain, England, France.*

- As students read the lesson independently, have them take notes about each country's involvement in American colonization.

1 Introduce and Motivate

Preview To activate prior knowledge, ask students to share what they recall about the reasons for European colonization. Tell students that in Lesson 3 they will learn the effects European colonization had on the Americas.

You Are There Reasons for taking part in expeditions were varied. Have students predict some of the goals English explorers may have had in traveling to the new world.

1500	1600
1500s The Spanish and Portuguese establish colonies in the Americas.	**1607** Jamestown becomes the first permanent English settlement in North America.
	1608 The French establish their first settlement in North America at Quebec.

THE 13 COLONIES Quebec
Jamestown
Sandwich Islands   BRAZIL   NEW SOUTH WALES

PREVIEW

Focus on the Main Idea
As Europeans reached new lands, they spread their culture through settlement and colonization.

PLACES
Sandwich Islands
Brazil
Jamestown
New South Wales
Quebec

PEOPLE
James Cook
Jacques Cartier

VOCABULARY
colony
mercantilism

TERMS
encomienda
triangular trade

European Colonization

You Are There
You're one of the crew members on Captain James Cook's ship, the *Resolution.* Leaving your family in England in 1776 was hard. But being part of this expedition has been a life-changing experience. You've met many interesting people. However, you're all anxious to find what you're looking for—a northern passage that connects the Pacific Ocean to the Atlantic Ocean. After searching for months, you and your sister ship, the *Discovery,* head south.

You finally reach some islands. Captain Cook names them after a friend of his, the Earl of Sandwich. You search for weeks for a good harbor among these islands. When you finally set anchor, many people come to greet you.

▶ **This chief's ceremonial headdress is from the Cook Islands in the South Pacific Ocean.**

 Summarize As you read, try to write a brief summary for each section to keep track of how Europeans colonized other lands.

444

Practice and Extend

 **READING SKILL Summarize**

In the Lesson Review, students complete a graphic organizer like the one below. You may want to provide students with a copy of Transparency 5 to complete as they read the lesson.

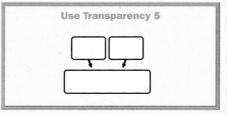
Use Transparency 5

 **WEB SITE Technology**

- You can look up vocabulary words by clicking on *Social Studies Library* and selecting the dictionary at **www.sfsocialstudies.com.**
- Students can learn more about current news by clicking on *Current Events* at **www.sfsocialstudies.com.**
- Explore other events that occurred on this day by clicking on *This Day in History* at **www.sfsocialstudies.com.**

Early Colonization

Where did **James Cook** land? The lands that Cook named the **Sandwich Islands** are in the Pacific Ocean. Today, we know them as the Hawaiian Islands.

Europeans began to look for faster passages to the east. On their expeditions and search for riches, they made contact with new peoples.

At first, Europeans were interested in finding new trade routes or new sources of trade goods. When Europeans arrived in a new land, they often wanted to use the resources there. Resources included more than just gold, silver, and ivory. Europeans also wanted to cultivate crops that they could export. They needed human labor to grow and harvest these crops.

The Europeans encouraged their fellow citizens to settle in the newly conquered lands. There the Europeans could manage the land. They could oversee the labor. These European settlements

► This portrait of James Cook was painted by Nathaniel Dance.

National Maritime Museum

were called **colonies** because they were physically separate from—but under the control of— another country.

The Europeans used an economic policy called **mercantilism** in their colonies. In this system, a country uses colonies to obtain raw materials to make into products. The colonies would also serve as new markets that could trade only with the ruling country. Under mercantilism, the function of a colony is to make the ruling country more wealthy and powerful. **1**

REVIEW What advantages did ruling countries get from establishing colonies? *Draw Conclusions*

► This cave painting of a European ship was created by Native Australians. It provides a glimpse of the impressions the people of Australia had during their early encounters with Europeans.

445

CURRICULUM CONNECTION
Art

Make a Poster

- Tell students to think about how explorers might persuade European citizens to settle in the colonies in the Americas.
- Have students create a poster encouraging European citizens to participate in the next expedition to the Americas.
- Students should include pictures and text showing the benefits and opportunities European citizens will find in the colonies.

Early Colonization

🕐 **Quick Summary** Europeans used the people and resources of the colonies in which they settled. Europeans were the colonies' exclusive trading partners.

1 Summarize the process Europeans followed as they colonized new lands. Europeans set off on expeditions. When they arrived in new lands, they used the resources there and cultivated crops for export. Other European citizens came to manage the land. The European countries then traded with their colonies to increase their own wealth.
↪ **Summarize**

Ongoing Assessment

If... students cannot summarize the process,

then... have them order the following steps in a sequence chart: *Bring other European citizens to new land* (2); *Set off on expeditions* (1); *Use resources and cultivate crops in new lands* (3); *Trade with colonies* (4).

✓ **REVIEW ANSWER** Colonies provided raw materials and other resources to trade and produce goods. They also provided populations of people to work the land and buy goods.
Draw Conclusions

Portugal and Spain

🕐 **Quick Summary** By 1550 Portugal and Spain had explored and controlled lands in South America, Mexico, Central America, the Caribbean, and what is now the southwestern United States.

2 What was Portugal's and Spain's aim in exploring the Americas? Colonization **Main Idea and Details**

3 What point of view do you think that the Native Americans had about the Portuguese colonists? Possible answer: They probably resented the Portuguese because Portuguese colonists took their land and forced them to work on sugar cane plantations. **Point of View**

European Colonization of the Americas by 1620

Test Talk

Use Information from Graphics

4 Which country had the most colonies in South America? Tell students to go back and look at the map to find the right answers. Spain **Interpret Maps**

MAP SKILL **Answer** Portugal and Spain

Portugal and Spain

Portugal had begun exploring Africa in the early 1400s. The Portuguese had several motives. They wanted better access to the spice trade and they wanted to spread Christianity. However, when Portugal, along with Spain, looked to the **2** Americas, they had an additional aim: colonization.

The Portuguese had landed in South America as early as 1500. However, they settled their first colony, **Brazil,** only when other European countries threatened to take it from them. Many Portuguese who did not own land in Portugal moved to Brazil to take a piece of land for themselves. There they set up sugar cane plantations and forced the Native Americans to work for them. **3**

MAP SKILL
European Colonization of the Americas by 1620 **4**

Territory held by:
- Great Britain
- France
- Spain
- Portugal
- Netherlands
- Russia

Present-day country names and borders are used.

▶ By 1620 many European nations had claimed territory in the Americas.

MAP SKILL Understand the Equator *Which European nations held territories on the equator in the Americas?*

446

Practice and Extend

MEETING INDIVIDUAL NEEDS
Leveled Practice

Interpret Maps Have students further explore the map on this page.

Easy Have students identify the color that represents each country's colonies. Then have students make statements about the map, such as "Most of Spain's colonies were in South America." **Reteach**

On-Level Have students compare and contrast the location and size of Portuguese and Spanish colonies in the Americas. **Extend**

Challenge Have pairs of students research two present-day countries, one that was a Portuguese colony and one that was a Spanish colony. If possible, students should describe how the country's history as a colony influences its customs, language, music, and architecture. **Enrich**

For a Lesson Summary, use Quick Study, p. 108.

▶ This sixteenth-century picture shows a Portuguese soldier in the West African kingdom of Benin.

The Spanish formed a colony in the region where they had defeated the Aztecs. The Spanish colonists introduced the teachings of Christianity. They also forced the Native Americans to work. This system was known as the **encomienda.** The Spanish government allowed certain colonists the right to demand labor from the Native Americans of a particular area.

As you read in Lesson 2, Spanish conquests of lands in the Americas continued. By 1550 Spain controlled Mexico, Central America, part of South America, islands in the Caribbean, and part of the present-day southwestern United States.

REVIEW What was the cause of colonization? **Cause and Effect**

English Colonies

Other European countries became interested in acquiring colonies. In England, there were several reasons why people began to think seriously about colonization. English merchants and other wealthy people saw colonies as a great source for new wealth. At the same time, some people in England were seeking religious and political freedom.

▶ These colonists are shown building Jamestown, England's first permanent colony in North America.

The first successful English colony in North America was established in Jamestown in 1607. It was planned by a group of investors who hoped it would bring them wealth. It paved the way for other settlements. England had established thirteen colonies in North America by 1732. By that time England had become part of Great Britain.

The British also set up the colony of New South Wales in Australia in 1788. Many of these colonists were convicts. At the time, Great Britain shipped criminals out of the country to relieve crowding in British prisons.   **6**

REVIEW Name two of the reasons the English wanted colonies in North America.
◀ Summarize

French Colonies

Explorations by Jacques Cartier in the 1530s led to France's claim to Canada. The French were disappointed when explorers were unable to find the kind of mineral riches the Spanish had found in Mexico and Peru. But Canada offered other kinds of riches to the French, especially furs such as beaver pelts. In 1608 France founded its first settlement in North America, Quebec. During the 1700s, the French settled in southern Canada and in what is today the U.S. state of Louisiana.

▶ Jacques Cartier explored Canada for France.

The Granger Collection

Clashes over land rights among the Native Americans, French, and British led to war in 1763 in North America. Great Britain defeated the French and the Native Americans seven years later, gaining all of Canada.   **7**

REVIEW Why did the French settle in North America? ◀ Summarize

447

---

5 **What is the difference between mercantilism and the encomienda system?** Mercantilism uses a colony's natural resources and markets; the encomienda system uses a colony's people by forcing them to work. **Compare and Contrast**

✓ **REVIEW ANSWER** A desire for better access to the spice trade and to spread Christianity **Cause and Effect**

PAGE 447

English Colonies

🕐 *Quick Summary* For a variety of reasons, English citizens began to take an interest in colonization in North America and in Australia.

6 **Why did England set up the colony of New South Wales in Australia?** They shipped criminals there to relieve overcrowding in British prisons. **Cause and Effect**

✓ **REVIEW ANSWER** To find wealth and to seek religious or political freedom
◀ Summarize

French Colonies

🕐 *Quick Summary* The French began their settlements in present-day Canada, and also in the present-day state of Louisiana in the United States.

7 **What caused the war in 1763?** Disagreements among the British, French, and Native Americans over land rights **Cause and Effect**

✓ **REVIEW ANSWER** Because Canada and the United States offered riches in the form of furs such as beaver pelts
◀ Summarize

The Slave Trade

 Quick Summary As the need for additional workers increased, Europeans brought people from Africa to work as slaves in their colonies in the Americas.

8 Why were more workers needed in the Portuguese and Spanish colonies? Because many of the enslaved Native American workers died, rebelled, or escaped Main Idea and Details

9 How did the Europeans acquire slaves for their colonies in the Americas? They went to Africa and purchased people whom the Africans had captured in battle, and then they shipped the people to the Americas. Summarize

Slavery and the Triangular Trade

10 After slave ships left Africa, where did they travel next? The West Indies Interpret Maps

MAP SKILL **Answer** Southeast

11 What was the Middle Passage? How did it affect the enslaved people? The part of the journey from Africa to America across the Atlantic Ocean; the enslaved people had to endure tight quarters, extreme heat, painful illnesses, and poor living conditions— many enslaved people died during the trip. Main Idea and Details

✓ REVIEW ANSWER Triangular trade describes the exchange of manufactured goods from New England for West African slaves. The enslaved people were sent to the West Indies and sold for sugar cane, and the sugar cane was sent to New England to be made into rum. Summarize

The Slave Trade

Earlier in this lesson, you learned that the Portuguese and the Spanish had enslaved many Native Americans in their colonies. As time went by, the demand for additional workers increased. Many Native Americans were dying from over-work, cruel treatment, and exposure to European **8** diseases. They often rebelled or escaped. Faced with this problem, European merchants began to transport slaves from Africa to work in America.

Europeans were familiar with the African custom of making prisoners of people they captured in battle. These captives usually were treated fairly and might one day expect to gain their free-dom. Europeans began to purchase captives from **9** the African leaders.

The English had also begun plantation agriculture in their colonies in the West Indies and on the North American mainland. Africans were first brought to Virginia in 1619. At first, many of these Africans were regarded as servants. They were bound for a period of years to the master who paid the ship captain for transporting them

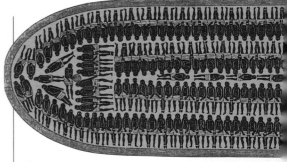

▶ This diagram shows how slaves were transported on the slave ships. This arrangement was meant to fit as many slaves as possible, with no concern for the comfort or safety of the slaves.

to America. However, by the 1640s, most Africans brought to the colonies were slaves, with no hope of freedom.

In 1672, England set up the Royal African Company. Colonial merchants also entered the business of transporting slaves to the colonies. These traders sold manufactured goods to leaders in West Africa in exchange for slaves.

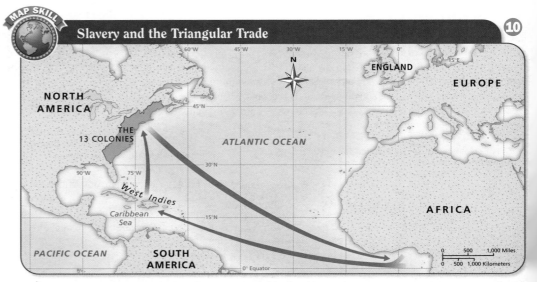

Slavery and the Triangular Trade **10**

▶ Slaves were shipped to the Americas as part of the triangular trade.

MAP SKILL Trace Movement on Maps *In which direction did ships leaving the 13 colonies travel on the triangular trade?*

448

Practice and Extend

 CURRICULUM CONNECTION
Literature

Read More About Slavery

You may use the following selections to extend the content:

Bound for America: The Forced Migration of Africans to the New World, by James Haskins, et al. (Lothrop Lee & Shepard, ISBN 0-688-10258-1, 1999) **Easy**

They Came in Chains: The Story of the Slave Ships (Great Journeys), by Milton Meltzer (Benchmark Books, ISBN 0-761-40967-X, 2000) **On-Level**

Escape from the Slave Traders, by Dave Jackson, et al. (Bethany House, ISBN 1-556-61263-X, 1992) **Challenge**

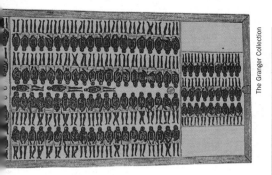

The Granger Collection

The slaves were transported to the West Indies. There, they were sold for sugar cane. The sugar cane was shipped to New England to be made into rum and other manufactured products. This trade arrangement came to be known as the **triangular trade.**

The most dehumanizing part of this trade may have been the Middle Passage. This was the journey of the slave ships across the Atlantic from Africa to America. The slaves were packed tightly into the holds of ships and chained together. They suffered through intense heat, painful illnesses, poor living conditions, and

rough seas. Many of the slaves would die during this grueling voyage, which lasted from four to six weeks.

To the European colonists, slaves were nothing but property. For the slaves, there was almost no hope of ever gaining freedom. Torn from their homelands and loved ones, most slaves ended up on plantations. There they worked very long hours in the fields six days a week. They lived in shacks under very harsh conditions. Each colony passed severe law codes that totally deprived African American slaves of any legal rights.

⑪

REVIEW What was the triangular trade and how did it work? ⓢ **Summarize**

Summarize the Lesson

- **1500s** The Portuguese and Spanish established colonies in the Americas.
- **1607** Jamestown became the first permanent English settlement in North America.
- **1608** The French established their first North American settlement at Quebec.

LESSON 3   REVIEW

Check Facts and Main Ideas

1. ⓢ **Summarize** On a separate piece of paper, fill in the missing details that lead to the summary.

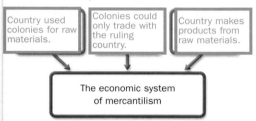

| Country used colonies for raw materials. | Colonies could only trade with the ruling country. | Country makes products from raw materials. |

→ The economic system of mercantilism

2. What are colonies and how did they make European countries wealthy and powerful?

3. What was the encomienda?

4. What were some of the reasons for European colonization?

5. **Critical Thinking:** *Solve Complex Problems* How could Europeans have colonized other lands without forcing the native peoples to work for them?

Link to   **Writing**

Write a Dialogue Write a dialogue between Native Americans and colonists who have just arrived from Europe. Write equal numbers of lines from the perspective of European colonists and of Native Americans.

449

---

3 Close and Assess

Summarize the Lesson

Tell students to read the events listed in the time line. Have them discuss what they know about each colony on the time line.

✓ **LESSON 3**   **REVIEW**

1. ⓢ **Summarize** For possible answers, see the reduced pupil page.

2. Settlements of land ruled by countries that might be far away; by sending raw materials to the ruling European countries and by trading only with those countries.

3. A system that gave Spanish colonists the right to demand that Native Americans in a certain area work for the colonists

4. To find new trade routes; to get raw materials; to find new markets for their products; to acquire more land; to build wealth and power; to find religious or political freedom; to relieve overcrowding in prisons

5. **Critical Thinking:** *Solve Complex Problems* Possible answer: They could have brought more settlers from Europe.

Link to   **Writing**

Have students work in pairs as they write the dialogues. Ask volunteers to perform their dialogues aloud for the class.

Workbook, p. 109

Lesson 3: European Colonization

Directions: Identify the European country associated with each of the following events. For Portugal write *P* in the blank, for Spain write *S*, for England write *E*, and for France write *F*. You may use your textbook.

___ 1. a colony was formed in the region where Aztecs had been defeated

___ 2. thirteen colonies had been established in North America by 1752

___ 3. began exploring Africa in the early 1400s to spread Christianity

___ 4. encomienda system of forced labor was established by government

___ 5. colonization caught the interest of merchants and other people who sought wealth and religious and political freedom

___ 6. clashes over land rights with Native Americans and British resulted in war in North America

___ 7. first colony was settled by citizens who did not own land in home country

___ 8. convicts were sent to settle New South Wales, Australia

___ 9. landed in South America as early as 1500

___ 10. control of Canada was lost after defeat by Great Britain

___ 11. Mexico, Central America, part of South America, islands in the Caribbean, and the southwestern United States were controlled by 1550

___ 12. Canada was claimed after explorations by Jacques Cartier

___ 13. first colony was founded at Quebec

___ 14. Brazil was first colony

___ 15. first successful North American colony, Jamestown, was established

___ 16. set up sugar cane plantations and forced Native Americans to work in Brazil

Notes for Home: Your child learned about early colonization by the Portuguese, Spanish, English, and French.
Home Activity: With your child, discuss how Europeans changed the ways of life of the native peoples they conquered and settled.

Also on Teacher Resources CD-ROM.

Interpret Political Cartoons

Objective
- Interpret the message of a political cartoon.

Resource
- Workbook, p. 110

1 Introduce and Motivate

What is a political cartoon?
Ask students to define the words *political* and *cartoon*. Use students' understanding of these words to predict the purpose of a political cartoon. Then have students read the **What?** section of text on p. 450.

Why use political cartoons? Have students read the **Why?** section of text on p. 450. Ask them why political cartoons may have wider appeal than an opinion paragraph or essay. (Readers are often more open to a visual message than to straight text.)

2 Teach and Discuss

How is this skill used? Examine with students the political cartoon on p. 450.

- Point out that, as in most works of art, political cartoons are open to individual interpretation.

- In this cartoon, King Henry VIII is using Pope Clement VII as a footstool, so the viewer knows that Henry VIII is more powerful than the pope, at least according to the cartoonist.

- Have students read the **How?** section of text on p. 451.

Interpret Political Cartoons

What? You have probably turned to the editorial page in a newspaper. In editorials, news writers express opinions about current events. A political cartoon is a kind of editorial. It uses an image, often humorous, to make a point. Some political cartoons include some text. Others rely on pictures alone. ❶

The cartoon on the left is an example of an early political cartoon. It shows Henry VIII, the king of England, seated upon his throne. The room is full of people. Some, but not all of them, appear to be upset. The cartoon is telling a story about an important moment in English history.

Why? According to a familiar saying, "a picture is worth a thousand words." This statement certainly rings true for political cartoons. As an image, a cartoon is able to communicate meaning on several levels. Its use of humor may soften a difficult or painful issue. Readers are often more open to a visual message than to straight text. ❷

▶ This cartoon deals with an important event during the rule of Henry VIII of England.

450

Practice and Extend

CURRICULUM CONNECTION
Art

Create a Political Cartoon

- Have students choose an event they read about in this chapter, such as the Renaissance, Spanish explorations, or European colonialism.

- Students can work in pairs to design a political cartoon showing their opinion about what happened.

- Have partners display their cartoons and discuss the viewpoint they wanted to convey.

Mike Keefe 97 The Denver Post

► This modern political cartoon was created in 1997, at a time when many people were starting to use the Internet.

How? To understand a political cartoon, you must be able to identify the visual details. You must also interpret them correctly. What details do you notice in the cartoon of Henry VIII?

Notice that several of the people in this cartoon have their names written across their clothing. They were real people who were involved in this important event. This tradition—writing labels on people and objects to let readers know who they are or what they symbolize—is still used by many political cartoonists today. Henry VIII's name does not appear in the cartoon. The artist may have assumed (or hoped) that people would recognize the king. In political cartoons it is important to draw important people in a way that everyone can recognize them immediately.

Did you notice the figure lying down in front of the king? Notice that Henry is resting his feet on the man's back, hiding part of the man's name. This is Pope Clement VII of the Roman Catholic Church. Next to him is an English priest, who is trying to comfort the Pope. Alongside the king are two of his most important advisors.

In 1533 Henry VIII declared that he, not the Pope, was the head of the Church of England. This led England to break with Catholicism and become a Protestant nation.

Think and Apply

1. Look at the modern political cartoon at the top of this page. There are no famous people shown in this cartoon. It does not refer to a single event. However, it still deals with an important change in the world. In this cartoon, the changes are related to the growth of the computer industry and the Internet. What do you think the cartoonist is trying to tell us? Write your interpretation of this cartoon.

2. What are some other ways a cartoonist might show the same message in a political cartoon? You can sketch your cartoon idea or write a paragraph explaining what you would show.

3. Search for a political cartoon in a recent newspaper or magazine. Do you understand the point the cartoonist is trying to make? Write your interpretation of the cartoon. You may need to do some additional research to understand the cartoon's message.

451

Resources

- Assessment Book, pp. 77–80
- Workbook, p. 111: Vocabulary Review

Chapter Summary

For possible answers, see the reduced pupil page.

Vocabulary and Terms

1. b, **2.** e, **3.** d, **4.** a, **5.** c

People and Events

1. The Reformation, a movement to challenge some church practices, resulted in Protestant religions.

2. The Council of Trent was called by church officials in response to the Reformation.

3. Isabella was the Spanish queen who funded Columbus's 1492 voyage.

4. Elizabeth I supported many expeditions after she came to power in 1558.

5. Galileo was criticized by the Roman Catholic Church when he supported Copernicus's theory that Earth moves around the sun.

6. The Spanish Armada was a fleet of about 130 ships that unsuccessfully attacked England in 1588.

7. James Cook was an English adventurer who sought a northern passage to the Pacific Ocean.

8. Johannes Gutenberg's invention of the printing press was probably the greatest advance in technology.

9. The greatest of the Renaissance artists may have been Leonardo da Vinci.

10. The Counter-Reformation was an effort to stop the movement called the Reformation.

CHAPTER 15
REVIEW

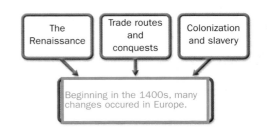

1450

1455
Gutenberg Bible was printed.

1492
Columbus began his westward voyages.

Chapter Summary

 Summarize

On a separate piece of paper, write a summary that combines the ideas in this chapter.

| The Renaissance | Trade routes and conquests | Colonization and slavery |

Beginning in the 1400s, many changes occured in Europe.

Vocabulary and Terms

Match each word with the correct definition or description.

1 commerce (p. 431)

2 encomienda (p. 447)

3 conquistador (p. 441)

4 circumnavigate (p. 439)

5 mercantilism (p. 445)

a. sail completely around the world

b. the buying and selling of goods

c. a system in which colonies are a source of raw materials

d. Spanish conquerors

e. a system that forced Native Americans to work for the Spanish

People and Events

Write a sentence explaining why each of the following people, terms, events is important. You may use two or more in a single sentence.

1 Reformation (p. 437)

2 Council of Trent (p. 437)

3 Isabella (p. 440)

4 Elizabeth I (p. 442)

5 Galileo (p. 434)

6 Armada (p. 442)

7 James Cook (p. 445)

8 Johannes Gutenberg (p. 435)

9 Leonardo da Vinci (p. 432)

10 Counter-Reformation (p. 437)

452

Practice and Extend

Assessment Options

✓ **Chapter 15 Assessment**

- Chapter 15 Content Test: Use Assessment Book, pp. 77–78.
- Chapter 15 Skills Test: Use Assessment Book, pp. 79–80.

Standardized Test Prep

- Chapter 15 Tests contain standardized test format.

✓ **Chapter 15 Performance Assessment**

- Display the following newspaper headlines: *Renaissance Comes to Europe, Portugal Explores New Lands, Spain Conquers Land in the Americas,* and *England Settles New Colonies.*
- Have students work in small groups to write the article that belongs to each headline.
- Assess students' understanding of Renaissance, explorations, and colonization as they read their newspaper articles.

1500s Portuguese began to colonize in South America.

1517 Reformation began.

1588 Spanish Armada was defeated by England.

1607 Jamestown colony was settled.

Facts and Main Ideas

1 Why was Prince Henry the Navigator looking for a new trade route?

2 What was the first permanent British colony in North America? When was it established?

3 What is slavery and how did the Europeans use it to create prosperous colonies?

4 **Time Line** Which three events occurred while the Portuguese were colonizing South America?

5 **Main Idea** What effect did Gutenberg's printing press have on European people?

6 **Main Idea** Name one reason why the English colonized North America.

7 **Main Idea** Explain how the triangular trade worked.

8 **Critical Thinking:** *Make Inferences* How were the searches for new trade routes related to colonization and slavery?

Write About History

1 **Write a journal entry** as a sailor on Magellan's ship. What do you see? What is the purpose of your journey?

2 **Write a grant request** asking Queen Isabella to pay for a voyage to determine how to reach Asia by sailing west. Indicate what you think you will be able to bring the queen in return for her grant.

3 **Write a broadside poster** encouraging people to rethink their attitudes about slavery. Include reasons why slavery should be abolished, even if it is economically profitable.

Apply Skills

Interpret Political Cartoons

Study the political cartoon below and then answer the questions.

1 Who is the person pictured in this cartoon?

2 Describe what the person in this cartoon is doing.

3 What is the cartoonist trying to say in this cartoon? Explain your answer.

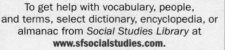

Internet Activity

To get help with vocabulary, people, and terms, select dictionary, encyclopedia, or almanac from *Social Studies Library* at **www.sfsocialstudies.com.**

453

Hands-on Unit Project

✓ Unit 6 Performance Assessment

- See p. 510 for information about using the Unit Project as a means of performance assessment.
- A scoring guide is provided on p. 510.

WEB SITE
Technology

Students can select the dictionary, encyclopedia, or almanac from *Social Studies Library* at **www.sfsocialstudies.com.**

Workbook, p. 111

Vocabulary Review

Directions: Circle the vocabulary term that best completes each sentence. Then write the definition of that term on the line. You may use your textbook.

1. A practice of churches in western Europe that was most objected to was a willingness to accept money for a pardon, or (excommunicate, mercantilism, indulgence).

2. The Treaty of Tordesillas divided the Americas between Spain and Portugal and allowed a (colony, conquistador, commerce) to claim a portion of the Americas for either Spain or Portugal.

3. A (colony, circumnavigate, conquistador) helped make a ruling country wealthy and powerful by serving as a new market that could trade only with the ruling country.

4. The city-states of Florence, Milan, and Venice grew through trade and (commerce, mercantilism, indulgence).

5. Following Ferdinand Magellan's death, the last remaining ship in his voyage was the first to (conquistador, excommunicate, circumnavigate) the world.

6. The Europeans used an economic policy called (mercantilism, indulgence, colony) in their colonies to gain wealth and power.

7. When Martin Luther wrote a challenge to the Roman Catholic Church, church officials decided to (circumnavigate, indulgence, excommunicate) him from the church.

Notes for Home: Your child learned the vocabulary terms for Chapter 15.
Home Activity: With your child, make a set of vocabulary cards. Write the vocabulary words on one side. On the other side, write the definitions. Shuffle the cards and hold up each card, allowing your child to give the matching word or definition.

Also on Teacher Resources CD-ROM.

Facts and Main Ideas

1. To reach Africa's gold, bypassing the routes controlled by Muslims

2. Jamestown; 1607

3. Forcing people to work, often in harsh conditions, and not paying them; they did not have to pay workers and they could make them work long hours.

4. The Reformation, the defeat of the Spanish Armada

5. People read more and became more educated.

6. Possible answers: Political or religious freedom; wealth

7. The enslaved people were sent to the West Indies from Africa and sold for sugar cane, and the sugar cane was sent to New England to be made into rum. Rum and other manufactured goods were sent to Africa.

8. They led European explorers to unfamiliar lands, which were colonized in order to make wealth for European nations. Native Americans were first enslaved to do the work in the colonies, and later enslaved Africans provided the labor.

Write About History

1. To help students take the perspective of a sailor, have them think about taking a journey in a small ship to an unknown part of the world.

2. Students' writing should be respectful but persuasive.

3. Students may want to begin by listing phrases that describe slavery.

Apply Skills

1. Galileo.

2. Using a telescope to look into space

3. Galileo helped look at and shape the future by being the first to turn his telescope toward the night sky.

Chapter Planning Guide

Chapter 16 • Ideas and Movements

Locating Time and Place pp. 454–455

Lesson Titles	Pacing	Main Ideas
Lesson 1 **Revolutions in the Americas** pp. 456–462		• New nations in the Americas broke free of European rule.
Biography: Simón Bolívar p. 463	3 days	• Inspired by the ideas of liberty proclaimed during the French Revolution, Simón Bolívar devoted his life to winning freedom for South America.
Smithsonian Institution: **American Revolution** pp. 464–465		• Art and artifacts from this historical period help make this time come alive.
Lesson 2 **The French Revolution** pp. 466–470		• The path of revolution turned violent in France.
⭐ **Citizen Heroes:** Fairness **A Pioneer for Women's Rights** p. 471	2 days	• During the French Revolution, Marie-Olympe de Gouges asked for equal rights for women in her *Declaration of the Rights of Women and the Female Citizen.*
Research and Writing Skills: Compare Primary Sources pp. 472–473		• Comparing primary sources helps readers understand how one document might have influenced the writing of another.
Lesson 3 **The Industrial Revolution** pp. 474–477	1 day	• The Industrial Revolution began in Great Britain and soon spread to other nations.
Lesson 4 **The Second Industrial Revolution** pp. 478–481	1 day	• While business owners gained more freedom from government controls, workers struggled to improve their working conditions.

✔ **Chapter 16 Review**
pp. 482–483

◀ **The telephone was invented in 1876.**

✔ = **Assessment Options**

This edition of the Napoleonic Code was published in 1804.

Vocabulary	Resources	Meeting Individual Needs
legislature massacre	• Workbook, p. 113 • Transparency 13 • Every Student Learns Guide, pp. 218–221 • Quick Study, pp. 110–111 • Workbook, p. 114	• ESL Support, TE p. 459 • Leveled Practice, TE p. 461 • Learning Styles, TE p. 462
monarchy	• Workbook, p. 115 • Transparency 6 • Every Student Learns Guide, pp. 222–225 • Quick Study, pp. 112–113 • Workbook, p. 116	• Leveled Practice, TE p. 468 • ESL Support, TE p. 470 • ESL Support, TE p. 472 • Learning Styles, TE p. 473
textile factory tenement	• Workbook, p. 117 • Transparency 13 • Every Student Learns Guide, pp. 226–229 • Quick Study, pp. 114–115	• ESL Support, TE p. 476 • Leveled Practice, TE p. 477
corporation reformer strike	• Workbook, p. 118 • Transparency 1 • Every Student Learns Guide, pp. 230–233 • Quick Study, pp. 116–117	• ESL Support, TE p. 479 • Leveled Practice, TE p. 480 • Learning Styles, TE p. 481
	✓ Chapter 16 Content Test, Assessment Book, pp. 81–82 ✓ Chapter 16 Skills Test, Assessment Book, pp. 83–84	✓ Chapter 16 Performance Assessment, TE p. 482

Providing More Depth

Additional Resources

- Vocabulary Cards
- Daily Activity Bank
- Social Studies Plus!
- Big Book Atlas
- Student Atlas
- Outline Maps
- Desk Maps

 Technology

- AudioText
- The test maker
- Teacher Resources CD-ROM
- Map Resources CD-ROM
- **www.sfsocialstudies.com**

 To establish guidelines for your students' safe and responsible use of the Internet, use the Scott Foresman Internet Guide.

Additional Internet Links

To find out more about:

- Loyalty and liberty, based on the American Revolution, visit **www.history.org**
- Napoleon Bonaparte, visit **www.pbs.org**
- Technology in 1900, visit **www.pbs.org**

Key Internet Search Terms

- American Revolution
- French Revolution
- Industrial Revolution

Workbook Support

Use the following Workbook pages to support content and skills development as you teach Chapter 16. You can also view and print Workbook pages from the Teacher Resources CD-ROM.

Workbook, p. 112

Vocabulary Preview

Use with Chapter 16.

Directions: Match each vocabulary word in the box below with its meaning. Write the vocabulary word on the line next to its meaning.

legislature	textile	corporation
massacre	factory	reformer
monarchy	tenement	strike

1. **tenement** — overcrowded slum apartment
2. **reformer** — person who wanted to keep capitalism but improve it
3. **monarchy** — government in which a king, queen, or emperor has supreme power
4. **legislature** — lawmaking body
5. **textile** — cloth that is either woven or knitted
6. **massacre** — event that causes the death of unresisting or helpless people
7. **strike** — refusal to work until certain demands are granted
8. **factory** — large place where machines are grouped together
9. **corporation** — business organization that raises money by selling stock shares to the public

 Notes for Home: Your child learned the vocabulary terms for Chapter 16.
Home Activity: Call out each term and have your child use it in an original sentence.

Use with Pupil Edition, p. 454

Workbook, p. 113

Lesson 1: Revolutions in the Americas

Use with Pages 456–462.

Directions: Complete the cause-and-effect chart with information from Lesson 1. You may use your textbook.

Cause		Effect
1. Cause Great Britain was deeply in debt.	→	**Effect** It decided to tax the colonies.
2. Cause Colonists in Boston Harbor threw cases of tea overboard. They called this the Boston Tea Party.	→	**Effect** British government closed the port and sent troops to Boston.
3. Cause Great Britain sent over more troops to force the colonists to obey Parliament's laws.	→	**Effect** Colonists declared their independence.
4. Cause George Washington forced a British force at Yorktown to surrender.	→	**Effect** In 1783 the British accepted the United States as an independent nation.
5. Cause In 1791 Toussaint L'Ouverture led enslaved Africans in a revolt against French rule.	→	**Effect** The French were driven from Haiti.
6. Cause Father Miguel Hidalgo called for Mexicans to revolt against the Spanish.	→	**Effect** His words set off a struggle for freedom in Mexico and Latin America.

 Notes for Home: Your child learned how nations in the Americas were able to break free of European rule.
Home Activity: With your child, make a chart comparing and contrasting the ways citizens of these countries gained their independence.

Use with Pupil Edition, p. 462

Workbook, p. 114

American Revolution

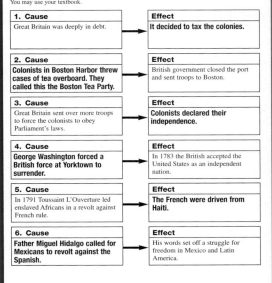

The American struggle for independence from Great Britain lasted five long years before the former colonies emerged as a new nation.

Directions: Imagine you are a soldier serving under General George Washington in the Continental Army during the American Revolution. Use the items and descriptions shown on pp. 464–465 to help you write a diary entry in which you describe the hardships encountered by Americans on the road to becoming a new nation. Write your diary entry on the lines provided. Use a separate sheet of paper if you need more space.

Students' diary entries should reflect information from the
lesson and an understanding of the hardships faced by
Americans during the American Revolution.

 Notes for Home: Your child learned about the American struggle for independence.
Home Activity: With your child, discuss why it was important for the colonies to gain independence from Great Britain. Discuss how life today might be different if the United States had remained separate colonies under the rule of Great Britain.

Use with Pupil Edition, p. 465

Workbook, p. 115

Lesson 2: The French Revolution

Use with Pages 466–470.

Directions: Sequence the events in the order in which they occurred. Number the events from 1 (earliest) to 12 (most recent). You may use your textbook.

6 Radicals take control of the revolution and make France a republic.

2 Members of the Third Estate form the National Assembly and write a constitution for France.

7 King Louis XVI is put on trial as a traitor, convicted, and put to death.

3 The French Revolution begins.

11 Napoleon's armies conquer Spain, much of what is now Germany, and Austria.

5 Fearing that the French Revolution might spread, other European rulers send armies into France, causing panic.

8 During the Reign of Terror, thousands of citizens suspected of being against the revolution are put to death.

4 The National Assembly adopts a *Declaration of the Rights of Man and of Citizen.*

10 The Napoleonic Code preserves important reforms made by the republic during the French Revolution, but women lose some of the rights of citizenship they had gained.

1 King Louis XVI calls a meeting of the Estates-General. The Third Estate demands that each person at the meeting have one vote, but the king refuses.

9 Napoleon Bonaparte overthrows the French republic. He becomes emperor of France.

12 Napoleon is defeated by Britain and European allies at the Battle of Waterloo.

 Notes for Home: Your child learned about events occurring during the French Revolution.
Home Activity: With your child, discuss several events that have led to revolutions. Identify nonviolent means of bringing about change.

Use with Pupil Edition, p. 470

Workbook Support

Workbook, p. 116

Compare Primary Sources

Use with Pages 472–473.

One way people learn about the past is by comparing primary sources, or the records of events made by people who witnessed them. In addition to written sources such as speeches, articles, and letters, primary sources include paintings, photographs, and artifacts.

Directions: In your textbook, locate and analyze the primary sources listed in the following chart. Then complete the chart to compare and contrast the sources.

Textbook Page	Primary Source	Information Provided in Primary Source	Draw Conclusions by Comparing Sources
p. 423	Quotation from King Ferdinand of Spain (1511)	**King Ferdinand wanted gold at any cost.**	How do the points of view in these quotations compare? **Possible answer: The speakers have opposite points of view. The king thinks that he has the right to any resources.**
p. 427	Quotation from *In Defense of the Indians* by Bartolomé de Las Casas (1552)	**Some Europeans thought that Native Americans had every right to protect their resources from Europeans.**	**Las Casas thinks that the king did not have the right to take resources or property from any land.**
p. 111	Quotation from Ban Zhao, a female Chinese historian (some time around 100 B.C.)	**Women in China were not educated; men were.**	How are these quotations alike and different? **Possible answer: Alike: Both quotations show that women were not treated equally to men.**
p. 471	Quotation from *Declaration of the Rights of Woman and the Female Citizen* by Marie-Olympe De Gouges (1791)	**Women in France at that time did not have equal rights with men.**	**Different: The women were from different periods in history and from different cultures.**

 Notes for Home: Your child learned to compare primary sources.
Home Activity: Have your child think of a time when he or she had a disagreement or argument with someone. Together, compare your child's account of the argument to what might have been the other person's account. Discuss the similarities and differences in the two primary sources.

Use with Pupil Edition, p. 473

Workbook, p. 117

Lesson 3: The Industrial Revolution

Use with Pages 474–477.

In Europe after 1750, new ideas arose about how to make and use machines to produce goods faster and on a larger scale. This period is known as the Industrial Revolution.

Directions: Complete the chart with information about inventions or improvements made during the Industrial Revolution. You may use your textbook.

Invention	Inventor	Date	Purpose
Improvement of the Steam Engine	James Watt	1760s	To use steam to power large machines
Steamboat	Robert Fulton	1807	To use the power of steam to increase the speed of ships
Train Engine	George Stephenson	1825	To speed up transportation by attaching a steam engine to wheels and putting it on rails

Directions: Answer the following questions on the lines provided.

1. How and why did cities in Europe change during the Industrial Revolution?

   Cities grew rapidly as people from farms and villages moved there to take jobs in new factories. An increased use of machinery on farms had eliminated the need for many of these workers.

2. What kinds of problems did Europe's growing cities experience?

   Possible answers: Few public services, overcrowded housing, poor safety conditions at home and at work

 Notes for Home: Your child learned about the beginning of the Industrial Revolution in Great Britain.
Home Activity: With your child, compare and contrast a typical day for a young British factory worker in the mid-1800s with a typical day in the life of your child.

Use with Pupil Edition, p. 477

Workbook, p. 118

Lesson 4: The Second Industrial Revolution

Use with Pages 478–481.

Directions: Write each term in the box beside its example or description.

Second Industrial Revolution	capitalism	labor union
internal combustion engine	market economy	socialism
electricity	*laissez faire*	Karl Marx
assembly line	reformer	

Karl Marx 1. popularized socialist ideas and supported a classless society

labor union 2. organization formed to represent the workers in a factory or industry and demand higher wages and better working conditions

capitalism 3. economic system in which private individuals own and run businesses for profit

internal combustion engine 4. run by oil made into gasoline

Second Industrial Revolution 5. inventions that used electricity, oil, and steel for power and changed the way people lived and worked

assembly line 6. manufacturing process in which individual workers add one part or perform one task to complete a product, such as an automobile

laissez faire 7. French expression meaning "leave it alone"; belief that government should not control business

electricity 8. supplied light and power to machines; led to new forms of communication

socialism 9. economic system in which the government owns most industries, businesses, land, and natural resources

reformer 10. person who wanted to keep capitalism but correct abuses in the system

market economy 11. economy in which people make their own decisions about how to spend their money

 Notes for Home: Your child learned about the Second Industrial Revolution and the struggle to improve conditions for workers.
Home Activity: With your child, create a Venn diagram to compare and contrast capitalism and socialism. Discuss which form of government the United States has today.

Use with Pupil Edition, p. 481

Workbook, p. 119

Vocabulary Review

Use with Chapter 16.

Directions: Read the following statements. Then write T (True) or F (False) on the line before each statement. If the answer is false, correct the statement to make it true. Not all words will be used. You may use your textbook.

T 1. A legislature is a lawmaking body that sets taxes and makes laws.

F 2. A reformer is a government in which a king, queen, or emperor has supreme power.

   A monarchy is a government in which a king, queen, or emperor has supreme power.

F 3. Workers bought raw materials such as cotton and produced thread to make tenements, or cloth that is either woven or knitted.

   Workers bought raw materials such as cotton and produced thread to make textiles, or cloth that is either woven or knitted.

T 4. Businesspeople lowered costs by grouping machines together in one large factory.

F 5. In the cities, many workers lived in overcrowded slum apartments, called monarchies.

   In the cities, many workers lived in overcrowded slum apartments, called tenements.

T 6. A strike is a refusal to work until certain demands are granted.

 Notes for Home: Your child learned the vocabulary terms for Chapter 16.
Home Activity: With your child, scan the articles in a local newspaper. Locate as many of the vocabulary terms as you can and discuss how each term is used in the article.

Use with Pupil Edition, p. 483

Assessment Support

Use these Assessment Book pages and the test maker to assess content and skills in Chapter 16. You can also view and print Assessment Book pages from the Teacher Resources CD-ROM.

Assessment Book, p. 81

Chapter 16 Test

Part 1: Content Test

Directions: Fill in the circle next to the correct answer.

Lesson Objective (1:2)

1. Why did North American colonists want to be independent from Great Britain?
   - Ⓐ to insult King George
   - ● to end unfair taxation
   - Ⓒ to name their own king
   - Ⓓ to keep Great Britain from becoming too powerful

Lesson Objective (1:3)

2. Who inspired people in Mexico to fight for their independence from Spain?
   - Ⓐ George Washington
   - Ⓑ Toussaint L'Ouverture
   - ● Father Miguel Hidalgo
   - Ⓓ Simón Bolívar

Lesson Objective (1:4)

3. Which economic restriction did the Spanish government place on Latin Americans?
   - Ⓐ They were not paid for working.
   - Ⓑ They could not travel overseas.
   - Ⓒ They could not transport any goods.
   - ● They were not allowed to trade with any country except Spain.

Lesson Objective (1:5)

4. Why did the struggle for independence in South America take so long?
   - ● Many countries had to gain their independence.
   - Ⓑ The Spanish army was stronger than expected.
   - Ⓒ South American armies were unorganized and unprepared.
   - Ⓓ People in South America did not feel strongly about independence.

Lesson Objective (2:1)

5. Which of the following is NOT a cause of the French Revolution?
   - Ⓐ separation of citizens into distinct classes
   - Ⓑ unfair taxation
   - Ⓒ unequal representation
   - ● Reign of Terror

Lesson Objective (2:2)

6. Who belonged to the Third Estate in the French society?
   - Ⓐ priests
   - Ⓑ the king
   - Ⓒ nobles
   - ● peasants and the middle class

Lesson Objective (2:3)

7. Who led the government of the new Republic of France?
   - Ⓐ King Louis XVI
   - Ⓑ Marie Antoinette
   - ● Maximilien de Robespierre
   - Ⓓ Napoleon Bonaparte

Lesson Objective (2:4)

8. What was one accomplishment of the Republic of France?
   - Ⓐ establishing a separate estate for peasants
   - ● ending slavery in all French colonies
   - Ⓒ strengthening the country's military forces
   - Ⓓ creating a fair system of justice

Use with Pupil Edition, p. 482

Assessment Book, p. 82

Lesson Objective (2:5)

9. Why did several European countries band together to defeat Napoleon?
   - Ⓐ He overthrew the government of France.
   - Ⓑ They supported equal rights for all French citizens.
   - ● They wanted to prevent him from conquering all of Europe.
   - Ⓓ They wanted to reestablish the Republic of France.

Lesson Objective (3:1)

10. Before the Industrial Revolution, where were most goods made?
    - Ⓐ markets
    - Ⓑ factories
    - Ⓒ cities
    - ● homes

Lesson Objective (3:2)

11. Who made a steam engine that could power other large machines?
    - ● James Watt
    - Ⓑ George Stephenson
    - Ⓒ Robert Fulton
    - Ⓓ Charles Dickens

Lesson Objective (3:3)

12. What gave Great Britain a head start in the Industrial Revolution?
    - Ⓐ many unskilled workers
    - ● a good transportation network
    - Ⓒ available land
    - Ⓓ schools and universities

Lesson Objective (3:5)

13. Which of the following did NOT contribute to poor working conditions in early factories?
    - ● faulty air conditioning systems
    - Ⓑ low wages
    - Ⓒ long hours
    - Ⓓ dangerous machines

Lesson Objective (3:4)

14. Why did many people in Great Britain move to cities between 1800 and 1850?
    - Ⓐ They did not like living in the country.
    - Ⓑ Living conditions were better in the city.
    - ● They were looking for jobs because fewer farm workers were needed.
    - Ⓓ Cities could not support the growing population.

Lesson Objective (4:1)

15. Which of the following inventions that we use today was created during the Second Industrial Revolution?
    - ● light bulb
    - Ⓑ television
    - Ⓒ washing machine
    - Ⓓ computer

Lesson Objective (4:2)

16. How does a corporation differ from other types of businesses?
    - Ⓐ It uses only factories to produce its goods.
    - Ⓑ It is smaller and less expensive than other types of businesses.
    - Ⓒ It is made up of one business owner and a few employees.
    - ● It sells shares of stock to raise money.

Use with Pupil Edition, p. 482

Assessment Support

Assessment Book, p. 83

Lesson Objective (4:3)

17. Why did some people work to reform capitalism?
    Ⓐ They believed that the government had too much control of business.
    Ⓑ They wanted to increase competition among businesses.
    ● They wanted to improve poor working conditions.
    Ⓓ They felt that some corporations were becoming too large.

Lesson Objective (4:4)

18. What type of economic system did Karl Marx support?
    Ⓐ democracy
    Ⓑ capitalism
    Ⓒ communism
    ● socialism

Part 2: Skills Test

Directions: Use complete sentences to answer questions 1–7. Use a separate sheet of paper if you need more space.

1. What events led up to the American Revolution? Sequence the events in the order in which they occurred. **Sequence**

   Great Britain taxed the colonies, the colonists protested, fighting broke out between the colonists and British soldiers, the colonists declared independence, and war broke out.

2. How were the revolutions in North America and South America similar and different? **Compare and Contrast**

   Possible answers: Similar: people in both North and South America fought for independence from a strong European power because they believed that they were being treated unfairly; Different: revolutions in South America lasted much longer than the ones in North America.

Use with Pupil Edition, p. 482

Assessment Book, p. 84

3. What changes did the National Assembly make in France during the French Revolution? **Summarize**

   It took privileges away from the Church and nobles, gave peasants new rights, taxed nobles and church officials, and established basic rights for all French citizens.

4. What might have happened to Europe had Napoleon not been defeated at the Battle of Waterloo? **Hypothesize**

   Possible answer: Napoleon might have continued conquering countries in Europe until most of Europe was under his rule.

5. How did the Industrial Revolution change how many goods were produced? **Cause and Effect**

   The Industrial Revolution made it possible for many goods to be made by machines rather than by hand. As a result, many goods began to be produced in large factories in cities, rather than in homes.

6. In what ways have Thomas Edison's inventions improved people's lives? **Evaluate**

   Possible answer: His inventions have led people to use machines powered by electricity, operate electric lights in houses and businesses, develop machines to communicate over long distances, and watch motion pictures.

7. Why was the invention of the assembly line a significant event? **Draw Conclusions**

   Assembly lines greatly sped up the manufacturing process. They allowed parts to travel on a moving belt where they could be assembled by a line of people who each performed one specific task to manufacture the item.

Use with Pupil Edition, p. 482

Ideas and Movements

Chapter 16 Outline

Resources

- Workbook, p. 112: Vocabulary Preview
- Vocabulary Cards
- Social Studies Plus!

1773, Boston: Lesson 1

Tell students that the people in the picture are European colonists dressed as Native Americans. Have students describe what the people are doing. (Some people are carrying boxes. Other people are swinging axes or hatchets.)

1789, Paris: Lesson 2

Tell students that the people in the picture are outside a French prison. Have students compare this picture to the picture for Lesson 1. (Both pictures show a group of people who seem determined, and who are taking action.)

After 1750, Great Britain: Lesson 3

Ask students to describe the scene in the painting. (Several children are working with a large machine.)

1876, Menlo Park: Lesson 4

Tell students that the picture shows two important inventions. Have students describe them. Then tell students that the picture shows an early phonograph and a movie camera.

Ideas and Movements

Lesson 1

1773
Boston
New nations emerge in the Americas.

1

Lesson 2

1789
Paris
An angry mob storms the Bastille.

2

Lesson 3

After 1750
Great Britain
The Industrial Revolution begins in Great Britain.

3

Lesson 4

1876
Menlo Park
Thomas Edison's laboratory becomes a center of invention.

4

454

Practice and Extend

Vocabulary Preview

- Use Workbook p. 112 to help students preview the vocabulary words in this chapter.
- Use Vocabulary Cards to preview key concept words in this chapter.

 Also on Teacher Resources CD-ROM.

Workbook, p. 112

Vocabulary Preview

Directions: Match each vocabulary word in the box below with its meaning. Write the vocabulary word on the line next to its meaning.

legislature	textile	corporation
massacre	factory	reformer
monarchy	tenement	strike

1. _____ overcrowded slum apartment
2. _____ person who wanted to keep capitalism, but improve it
3. _____ government in which a king, queen, or emperor has supreme power
4. _____ lawmaking body
5. _____ cloth that is either woven or knitted
6. _____ event that causes the death of unresisting or helpless people
7. _____ refusal to work until certain demands are granted
8. _____ large place where machines are grouped together
9. _____ business organization that raises money by selling stock shares to the public

Notes for Home: Your child learned the vocabulary terms for Chapter 16.
Home Activity: Call out each term and have your child use it in an original sentence.

Locating Time and Place

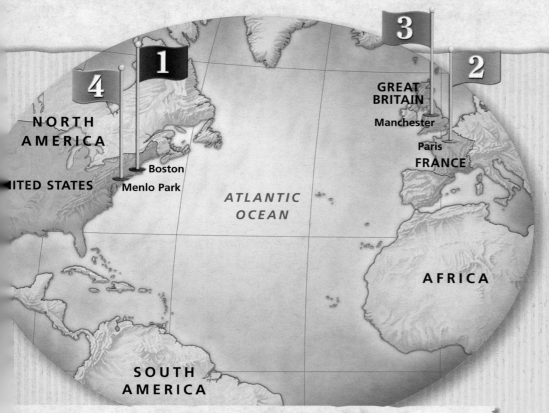

Why We Remember

The way our government works, the kind of work we do, and the machines we use every day—all of these things have changed greatly in the last 200 years. Colonies in the Western Hemisphere became independent of their European masters. A revolution in France showed the world that kings could not be protected from new ideas about government. The Industrial Revolution and factory system transformed the way people make things. The Second Industrial Revolution brought us wave after wave of inventions that changed people's lives even further. Our way of life today is the result of a series of revolutions.

455

- Have students examine the pictures shown on p. 454 for Lessons 1, 2, 3, and 4.

- Remind students that each picture is coded with a number and a color to link it to a place on the map on p. 455.

Why We Remember

Have students read the "Why We Remember" paragraph on p. 455, and ask them why events in this chapter might be important to them. Ask students how their lives would be different if they made instead of bought most of the items they use. What do students think it would be like to live in a country in which their basic freedoms and rights were not guaranteed? Touch on the idea of revolution. Point out that the word can mean "rebellion" but it can also mean "change." Students can list various revolutions that they know of and the changes those revolutions caused.

WEB SITE
Technology

You can learn more about Boston, Massachusetts; Paris, France; Manchester, Great Britain; and Menlo Park, New Jersey, by clicking on *Atlas* at **www.sfsocialstudies.com.**

SOCIAL STUDIES STRAND
Geography

Mental Mapping On a piece of paper, ask students to draw an outline map of the eastern coast of the United States from the border with Canada to Florida. Next, ask them to label the Atlantic Ocean and then to shade in and label the Appalachian Mountains. Finally, have students label the 13 colonies in order from north to south in their approximate locations. Discuss why the colonies all bordered the ocean.

Revolutions in the Americas

Objectives

- Describe the similarities and differences between the revolutions in North America and those in South America.

- Explain why the North American colonists wanted independence from British rule.

- Explain the significance of Father Miguel Hidalgo to the revolution in Mexico.

- Identify the restrictions that the Spanish government put on the people of Latin America.

- Explain the reasons why the fight for independence in South America took so many years.

Vocabulary

legislature, p. 457; **massacre,** p. 457

Resources

- Workbook, p. 113
- Transparency 13
- Every Student Learns Guide, pp. 218–221
- Quick Study, pp. 110–111

Quick Teaching Plan

If time is short, have students record details about the lesson on a web centered around the word *revolution*.

1 Introduce and Motivate

Preview Discuss with students previous struggles for freedom that they have read about in this book. Tell students they will learn more about struggles for freedom in Lesson 1.

You Are There Lexington, Massachusetts, was the site of the first clash of the American Revolution on April 19, 1775. About 700 British soldiers were met by about 70 colonial minutemen. Eight men were killed in the skirmish. Ask students to discuss whether freedom is worth fighting for.

LESSON 1

1750   1800   1850

1776
The 13 British colonies declare independence.

1821
Mexico wins independence.

1824
Simón Bolívar frees Peru from Spanish rule.

PREVIEW

Focus on the Main Idea
New nations in the Americas broke free from European rule.

PLACES
Boston
Haiti
Dolores

PEOPLE
George Washington
Toussaint L'Ouverture
Miguel Hidalgo
José María Morelos
Agustín de Iturbide
Simón Bolívar
José de San Martín
Bernardo O'Higgins

VOCABULARY
legislature
massacre

TERMS
Declaration of Independence
United Provinces of Central America

EVENTS
Boston Massacre
Boston Tea Party
American Revolution
Battle of Saratoga

456

Revolutions in the Americas

You Are There
Your brother is out of breath. He just ran across town with the news. Your parents can barely believe it.

All last night, British troops were marching toward the town of Lexington. They were sure they would surprise the colonists.

The British arrived in Lexington just after daybreak. To their surprise, they found about 70 colonists waiting at the village green. Captain John Parker, the colonial leader, gave last-minute orders:

"Stand your ground. Don't fire unless fired upon. But if they want a war, let it begin here!"

A shot rang out and both sides began firing. As you listen to your brother's news, your family is a little afraid—but very excited. If we go to war now, you wonder, will we really be able to break free of British rule?

▶ **This soldier from the American Revolution wears the uniform of an infantryman in the Continental Army.**

Compare and Contrast As you read, look for the similarities and differences among the revolutions in the Americas.

Practice and Extend

READING SKILL
Compare and Contrast

In the Lesson Review, students complete a graphic organizer like the one below. You may want to provide students with a copy of Transparency 13 to complete as they read the lesson.

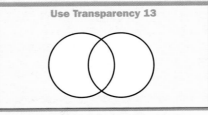

Use Transparency 13

WEB SITE
Technology

- You can look up vocabulary words by clicking on *Social Studies Library* and selecting the dictionary at **www.sfsocialstudies.com.**

- Students can learn more about current news by clicking on *Current Events* at **www.sfsocialstudies.com.**

- Explore other events that occurred on this day by clicking on *This Day in History* at **www.sfsocialstudies.com.**

The Roots of Conflict

For many years, the 13 British colonies in North America had largely governed themselves. Every colony had its own **legislature**, or lawmaking body. These legislatures made laws and set taxes.

This was about to change. Great Britain was deeply in debt. The British decided to tax the colonies. The colonists were furious. They believed that they should not be taxed without their approval. This was reflected in their rallying cry:

> *"No taxation without representation!"*

In 1770 an event occurred that weakened relations between the colonies and Great Britain. One winter night in **Boston**, Massachusetts, colonists began heckling British soldiers and throwing stones at them. Some soldiers fired into the crowd, killing several colonists. The incident became known as the **Boston Massacre.** A **massacre** is an event that causes the death of unresisting or helpless people.

New laws made the colonists angrier. In Boston colonists protested British rules that said that all tea had to be bought from only one company. On the night of December 16, 1773, about 60 colonists disguised as Native Americans boarded a tea ship in Boston Harbor. They threw the tea overboard, case by case. Colonists called this the **Boston Tea Party.** The act led the British government to close the port and to send troops to patrol the streets of Boston.

REVIEW What led the colonists to stage the Boston Tea Party? Cause and Effect

MAP SKILL The 13 Colonies ③

▶ After 1770, the 13 British colonies in North America came into increasing conflict with Great Britain.

MAP SKILL Understanding Continents and Oceans *Which North American colony did not have a coastline on the Atlantic Ocean?*

The Granger Collection

▶ On the night of December 16, 1773, protesting colonists destroyed a shipload of tea from Great Britain.

457

The Boston Massacre and the Boston Tea Party

- The British soldiers involved in the Boston Massacre were stationed in Boston to discourage angry colonists from protesting duties on imports into the colonies.

- Nine British soldiers were arrested and tried for murder. Two of them were found guilty of manslaughter, and the others were acquitted.

- Samuel Adams was able to use the Boston Massacre to stir patriotism and intense feelings against the British.

- The Boston Tea Party was initiated when the citizens of Boston refused to unload the British ships that arrived in Boston with 342 chests of tea. The royal governor of Massachusetts, however, refused to let the ship return to England unless the tea was paid for. The British closed the port because Boston's government refused to pay for the tea that had been destroyed.

The Roots of Conflict

🕐 ***Quick Summary*** Self-government of the thirteen North American colonies ended when Great Britain made the decision to levy taxes. The Boston Massacre and Boston Tea Party were watershed events in the conflict.

Primary Source

Popular colonial slogan, widely cited

① **How do you think this quotation rallied the colonists?** Possible answer: It sums up the unfairness of the situation in a way that would make people want to fight for their rights. **Analyze Primary Sources**

② **Which happened first, the Boston Massacre or Boston Tea Party? How many years passed between these events?** The Boston Massacre; three years **Sequence**

✓ **REVIEW ANSWER** The British had ruled that all tea had to be bought from one company. **Cause and Effect**

MAP SKILL **The 13 Colonies**

Show students a present-day map of the United States.

③ **Which present-day state was part of the colony of Massachusetts?** Maine **Apply Information**

MAP SKILL **Answer** Pennsylvania

The American Revolution

Quick Summary After a five-year war against British forces, the United States was finally accepted as an independent nation in 1783.

Primary Source

Cited in the Declaration of Independence

4 **In what ways had the British government denied the colonists "life, liberty, and the pursuit of happiness"?** The British government had denied colonists the right to represent themselves and had imposed rules that limited their freedom. The colonists were no doubt fearful after the Boston Massacre that disagreeing with their government could lead to death. **Analyze Primary Sources**

5 **Why do you think the colonists wrote the Declaration of Independence as they began to fight the British?** Possible answers: The colonists wanted the British and the world to know why they were fighting. The Declaration would serve as a unifying force during the battles to come. **Draw Conclusions**

SOCIAL STUDIES STRAND
History

Share with students the fact that France and Great Britain had fought with each other many times. The French and Indian War, in which France and Great Britain were on opposite sides, had been fought about twelve years before the American Revolution.

6 **What do you think may have motivated France to ally with the Americans?** France and Great Britain had been on opposite sides in previous wars. If the Americans won, Great Britain would be weakened because of the loss of the prosperous colonies. **Draw Conclusions**

✓ **REVIEW ANSWER** The American victory at the Battle of Saratoga convinced the French that the Americans could win the war. **Summarize**

The American Revolution

When Great Britain sent over more troops to force the colonists to obey Parliament's laws, the colonists decided to declare their independence. The result was the **Declaration of Independence.** The Americans clearly stated why they were splitting from Great Britain:

4 *"We hold these truths to be self-evident [clear], that all men are created equal, that they are endowed [given] by their Creator with certain unalienable [absolute] rights; that among these, are life, liberty, and the pursuit of happiness."*

On July 4, 1776, the Declaration was approved. Now the Americans had to win their independence on the battlefield. The **5** **American Revolution** would last five long years.

There was bitter fighting in every colony. One key victory came in 1777, when the Americans won the **Battle of Saratoga** in New York. Until that point, the Americans had been fighting alone. The victory at Saratoga convinced France that the Americans could win the war. As a result of the victory, France joined in an alliance with the **6** Americans.

The war then shifted to the southern colonies, where the Americans won some important victories. Then, with the support of the French, General **George Washington** trapped a British force at Yorktown and forced it to surrender. In 1783 the British accepted the United States as an independent nation.

REVIEW Why did France decide to form an alliance with the Americans? **Summarize**

▶ The Declaration of Independence was written mostly by Thomas Jefferson.

▶ The Declaration of Independence, which announced the colonists' determination to split away from Great Britain, was approved on July 4, 1776, at Independence Hall in Philadelphia.

The Granger Collection

458

Practice and Extend

CURRICULUM CONNECTION
Art

Expressions of Freedom Examine the picture of the signing of the Declaration of Independence with students. Ask them to reflect on it.

- Students can write captions for the picture. In their captions, they can describe what is happening as well as what the figures in the picture may be thinking.
- Students can draw another scene that reflects a "moment of freedom" in the history of the United States. They should include descriptive captions.
- Students can design an assignment based on this piece of art. They could, for example, find another piece of art and compare and contrast it with this one or write a critique of the art focusing on artistic elements such as color and composition.

Revolution in Haiti

In 1790 all of the lands south of the new United States were colonies of Europe. Spain ruled most of this territory. However, the first spark of revolt did not appear in a Spanish colony. It appeared in **Haiti,** then a colony of France. A few French planters controlled the island's great wealth. Most Haitians worked long hours on plantations as slaves.

In 1791 enslaved Africans revolted against French rule. **Toussaint L'Ouverture** (too SAINT loo ver TOOR) became the leader of the rebellion. L'Ouverture had escaped slavery and educated himself. Under his leadership, the slaves were able to drive French forces from the island. When French forces attempted to retake Haiti in 1802, L'Ouverture was captured and thrown into prison. Still, he did not give up the struggle. Before he died in prison he wrote:

> *"In overthrowing me, the French have only felled the tree of black liberty in [Haiti]. It will shoot up again for it is deeply rooted and its roots are many."*

The French failed to retake the island. In 1804 the Haitians declared their independence. Haiti became the first independent country in Latin America and the first republic led by a person of African descent.

REVIEW How was the revolution in Haiti different from the American Revolution? **Compare and Contrast**

► **Toussaint L'Ouverture (seated) became the leader of the Haitian Revolution.**

The Revolution Spreads

Meanwhile, much of Latin America remained under Spanish rule. On September 16, 1810, the struggle began to end colonial rule. A local priest in the village of **Dolores,** Mexico, called together villagers by ringing the church bell. Father **Miguel Hidalgo** (ee DAHL goh) asked them to revolt against the Spanish:

> *"My children, will you be free? Will you make the effort to recover from the hated Spaniards the lands stolen from your forefathers 300 years ago?"* **9**

His words set off a struggle for freedom in Mexico. But the struggle did not end there. Father Hidalgo's words echoed throughout Latin America. They would become the rallying cry for Latin Americans who wanted independence. Many people under Spanish colonial rule longed for political and economic freedom.

Latin Americans were not allowed self-government. Officials appointed by the Spanish king made all of the important decisions. Latin American merchants could trade only with Spain. They could transport their goods only on Spanish ships. These strict rules held back Latin America's economic growth.

► **Father Miguel Hidalgo set off Mexico's struggle for freedom from Spain.**

National History Museum Mexico City/Dagli Orti/Art Archive

REVIEW Why did the people of Latin America struggle against Spanish rule? **Summarize**

459

Revolution in Haiti

🕐 ***Quick Summary*** Led by Toussaint L'Ouverture, Haitians fought for independence. Haiti became the first independent country in Latin America in 1804.

7 **What role did L'Ouverture play in the quest for independence for Haiti?** He escaped from slavery and educated himself, showing that it was possible for slaves to join in an uprising. He was an inspiration to the slaves in the revolt even after he was imprisoned. **Summarize**

Primary Source

Cited in *The History of the Haitian Revolution and the Economic Adjustment to Emancipation*, by Sapna Mehta

8 **Why do you think L'Ouverture compared himself to a tree?** Possible answer: A tree is strong, but it has roots and branches, not just a trunk. L'Ouverture saw himself as the strong trunk and thought the roots could sprout other "trees" to work for freedom for Haitians. **Analyze Primary Sources**

✓ **REVIEW ANSWER** The Americans were colonists trying to break free of British rule. The Haitians were mostly slaves trying to win their freedom from France. **Compare and Contrast**

The Revolution Spreads

🕐 ***Quick Summary*** Latin Americans, inspired by Father Miguel Hidalgo, struggled for freedom from Spanish rule.

Primary Source

Cited in *Diez y Seis Fiesta* from Pecos Enterprise

9 **What strong, persuasive words did Father Hidalgo use to stir people's desire for freedom?** He used words such as *hated Spaniards* and *stolen* to stir people's feelings. **Analyze Primary Sources**

✓ **REVIEW ANSWER** The people of Latin America wanted to rule themselves and to trade with countries other than Spain. **Summarize**

ESL **ACTIVATE PRIOR KNOWLEDGE**
ESL Support

Use Visuals Students can use visuals to share what they know about Haiti, Latin America, or revolutions.

Beginning Have students find Haiti and France on a world map. Ask what language many Haitians speak (French). Name several Latin American countries for students to point to on the map. Then have them find Spain. Ask what language most Latin Americans speak (Spanish).

Intermediate Write *revolt* and *revolution* on the board and ask students to define the words. Have students list countries that have had revolutions and identify against whom they revolted. Begin with Mexico and Spain.

Advanced Have students make a poster of a country they know about. They should add details about any revolutions in which it was involved.

For additional ESL support, use Every Student Learns Guide, pp. 218–221.

Mexico, Central America, and South America

10 Which island country in the Caribbean Sea became independent between 1900 and 1950? Cuba, in 1902 Interpret Maps

SOCIAL STUDIES STRAND
Geography

If necessary, remind students that Central America is the strip of land between Mexico and South America that connects North and South America.

11 Which Central American countries became independent in 1838?
Honduras, Nicaragua, and Costa Rica
Interpret Maps

Use Information from Graphics

12 What generalization can you make about the years that most of the countries in South America became independent? Tell students that the dates next to the country names can help them answer the question. Have students list these dates and then ask themselves how these dates are similar. Most countries in South America became independent in the 1800s.
Generalize

MAP SKILL Answer Puerto Rico, French Guiana, the Galapagos Islands, and the Falkland Islands

Mexico, Central America, and South America

▶ Beginning in the early 1800s, independence movements swept through Mexico, Central America, South America, and the Caribbean.

MAP SKILL Use a Historical Map Which parts of Central America, South America, and the Caribbean still are not independent?

460

Practice and Extend

FAST FACTS

The events in this lesson took place in the late 1700s and 1800s. Share with students some other events that took place during this period of time:

- **1773** James Cook crosses the Antarctic Circle and goes around Antarctica.
- **1774** British scientist Joseph Priestley identifies a gas he calls "dephlogisticated air." This gas is later known as *oxygen*.
- **1780** Pennsylvania was the first state to abolish slavery.
- **1783** The first successful flight is made in a hot-air balloon.
- **1787** The first professionally performed American comedy is *The Contrast*.

Mexico's struggle for independence from Spain is captured in this painting by Diego Rivera.

Independence for Mexico and Central America

Father Hidalgo's army began marching toward Mexico City. Father Hidalgo was captured by the Spanish and executed in 1811. But other leaders kept up the fight.

José María Morelos (moh RAY lohs) was a farm worker who had studied to become a priest. By 1813 his army controlled a large part of southern Mexico. However, Morelos frightened many Mexicans by announcing that he would seize land and give it to the peasants. Without support, Morelos was captured by the Spanish and executed in 1815.

A new revolution broke out in 1820. It was led by an army officer, **Agustín de Iturbide** (ah gus TEEN day ee toor BEE day), who had once supported the Spanish. In 1821 Iturbide fought off the Spanish and proclaimed independence for Mexico. Then he made himself emperor of Mexico. Opponents threw him out of office in 1823.

The people of Central America were inspired by Mexico's struggle for freedom. In 1821 they threw out the Spanish and joined Iturbide's short-lived empire of

Mexico. But Central Americans did not want to be ruled by another country. So, in 1823, after Iturbide was removed from power, they joined together and formed the **United Provinces of Central America.** Later, the United Provinces split into the nations of Costa Rica, El Salvador, Guatemala, Honduras, and Nicaragua.

REVIEW What inspired the people of Central America to revolt against the Spanish? **Cause and Effect**

Literature and Social Studies

Latin American Liberator

Simón Bolívar is often called "the liberator" because he freed his people from Spanish rule. He did not seek power and greatness just for himself. In this passage from the biography *Simón Bolívar: Latin American Liberator* by Frank de Varona, do you think that Bolívar showed good judgment?

....

Simón Bolívar thought about the glory that would one day belong to the person who freed South America. But he also understood the danger of using this fame to seek personal power rather than freedom for all people. From then on, his ambition in life would be to achieve both liberty and glory.

461

Independence for Mexico and Central America

⏱ *Quick Summary* Following Mexico's lead, other countries in Central America fought for freedom from the Spanish.

13 **Why do you think that José María Morelos did not have widespread support throughout Mexico?** Morelos had pledged to seize land and give it to peasants. Not all Mexicans were peasants, and some stood to lose a great deal if Morelos's ideas were implemented. **Evaluate**

14 **Why was the United Provinces of Central America formed? What are the modern nations that made up the group?** The group was formed to promote self-rule rather than rule by another country. The provinces comprised the modern nations of Costa Rica, El Salvador, Guatemala, Honduras, and Nicaragua. **Main Idea and Details**

✓ **REVIEW ANSWER** They were inspired by Mexico's struggle for freedom. **Cause and Effect**

Literature and Social Studies

Latin American Liberator

Be sure that students understand the meaning of the word *liberator* as "one who liberates, or frees, people."

15 **How do you think Simón Bolívar wanted to use his glory?** He wanted to draw attention to the struggle of South American peoples for freedom rather than draw attention to his own personal accomplishments. **Draw Conclusions**

MEETING INDIVIDUAL NEEDS
Leveled Practice

Contribute to a Freedom Hall of Fame Invite students to contribute to a Hall of Fame based on the "liberators" in this lesson.

Easy Students can choose one of the historical figures in this lesson, such as Toussaint L'Ouverture, Father Hidalgo, Simón Bolívar, or José María Morelos, and list that person's accomplishments in the quest for freedom. **Reteach**

On-Level Students can choose one of the historical figures and write a speech persuading Hall of Fame organizers to include this person in the Freedom Hall. Speeches should include facts to support opinions. **Extend**

Challenge Encourage students to create multimedia presentations about one of the people in the lesson. The presentations could include biographies, artwork that is copied or downloaded from the Internet, excerpts from speeches and writings, and maps of important places. **Enrich**

For a Lesson Summary, use Quick Study, p. 110.

Independence for South America

🕐 *Quick Summary* The struggle for independence in South America took many years and cost many lives.

16 Describe the events leading to South American independence. Simón Bolívar led forces in the northern part of the continent, while José de San Martín forced out Spanish rulers in southern South America. Eventually, Chile and Peru were both freed from Spanish rule.
Main Idea and Details

✓ **REVIEW ANSWER** Simón Bolívar liberated northwestern South America. José de San Martín and Bernardo O'Higgins drove the Spanish out of Chile. ⟳ Summarize

3 Close and Assess

Summarize the Lesson

Have students provide supporting details about the main events in the time line.

✓ **LESSON 1**   **REVIEW**

1. **Compare and Contrast** For possible answers, see the reduced pupil page.

2. Colonists believed that the British government was denying them certain rights. They also wanted to govern themselves.

3. He was a priest from Dolores, Mexico, whose words set off a revolt against the Spanish in Mexico.

4. Latin American merchants could trade only with Spain and transport their goods only on Spanish ships.

5. **Critical Thinking:** *Evaluate Information* Possible answer: The rugged mountain terrain and the steamy rain forests may have made it difficult for troops to move from place to place quickly.

 **Link to**   **Geography**

Students should identify the towering Andes and the harsh desert as difficult areas to cross.

Independence for South America

The struggle for South American independence took many years. In the northwestern part of South America, a brilliant young leader emerged. **Simón Bolívar** (see MOHN boh LEE vahr) dreamed of freeing South America from Spanish rule. Read more about Bolívar in the Biography on page 463. For 15 years, he led his troops through steamy rain forests and frigid mountains.

In the south, **José de San Martín** (hoh SAY day sahn mahr TEEN) forced out the Spanish. In Chile **Bernardo O'Higgins** organized an army. San Martín led his army through the rugged mountain passes of the Andes to join O'Higgins' army. Together, the two leaders defeated the Spanish. Chile became independent in 1818.

Peru had declared independence in 1821, but it lacked the strength to drive out all the Spanish forces. In 1824, high in the Andes, Bolívar's

► This painting shows José de San Martín and Bernardo O'Higgins crossing the Andes Mountains into Chile.

The Granger Collection

troops crushed a Spanish-led army. The struggle that had started with Father Hidalgo in Dolores was now complete. Almost all of Latin America was politically independent.

REVIEW Who were the leading figures of the South American revolutions and what did they accomplish? ⟳ Summarize

Summarize the Lesson

1776 The 13 British colonies declared independence.

1821 Mexico won independence.

1824 Simón Bolívar freed Peru from Spanish rule.

LESSON 1   **REVIEW**

Check Facts and Main Ideas

1. **Compare and Contrast** On a separate piece of paper, fill in the diagram to compare and contrast the revolutions in the Americas.

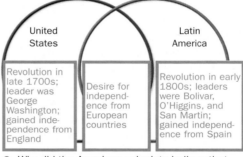

United States — Revolution in late 1700s; leader was George Washington; gained independence from England

Desire for independence from European countries

Latin America — Revolution in early 1800s; leaders were Bolívar, O'Higgins, and San Martin; gained independence from Spain

2. Why did the American colonists believe that they needed to break free of British rule?

3. Who was Father Miguel Hidalgo?

4. Name two restrictions that the Spanish government put on the people of Latin America.

5. **Critical Thinking:** *Evaluate Information* Why do you think the fight for South American independence took so many years?

Link to   **Geography**

Write a Description Study a relief map of South America. Write a report about the kind of landforms José de San Martín and his army should expect to find in Chile.

Practice and Extend

❄ **MEETING INDIVIDUAL NEEDS**
Learning Styles

Revolutions in the Americas Using their individual learning styles, students explore revolutions in the Americas.

Visual Learners Ask students to compare and contrast two of the revolutions, using Venn diagrams.

Logical Learners Ask students to create detailed, illustrated time lines that show revolutions and when they took place. Encourage students to add many supporting details for each revolution.

Kinesthetic Learners Invite students to create a short play, or skit, that depicts an important turning point in a revolution.

Workbook, p. 113

Lesson 1: Revolutions in the Americas
Directions: Complete the cause-and-effect chart with information from Lesson 1. You may use your textbook.

1. Cause	Effect
Great Britain was deeply in debt.	
2. Cause	Effect
	British government closed the port and sent troops to Boston.
3. Cause	Effect
Great Britain sent over more troops to force the colonists to obey Parliament's laws.	
4. Cause	Effect
	In 1783 the British accepted the United States as an independent nation.
5. Cause	Effect
In 1791 Toussaint L'Ouverture led enslaved Africans in a revolt against French rule.	
6. Cause	Effect
	His words set off a struggle for freedom in Mexico and Latin America.

Also on Teacher Resources CD-ROM

Simón Bolívar
1783–1830

Simón Bolívar was the son of wealthy Venezuelan landowners. Both his parents died when he was still a child. He was raised by an uncle and sent to study in Europe. Bolívar soon became interested in the ideas of liberty that had inspired the French Revolution of 1789. He was also greatly influenced by his teacher Simón Rodríguez. Bolívar credited Rodriguez with the revolutionary spirit that guided his life:

"You molded my heart for liberty, justice, greatness, and beauty." ❶

As a young adult, Bolívar pledged to devote his life to freeing South America from Spanish rule. He began by freeing the black slaves who worked on his land. He then turned toward freeing entire nations. In 1813 he led an army from Colombia (then known as New Granada) into Venezuela and defeated the Spanish. However, forces loyal to Spain soon regained control of Venezuela. Bolívar regrouped his army. In 1819 he led them across the Andes Mountains and into Colombia. His troops took the Spanish by surprise and defeated them. ❷

BIOFACT

In 1828 Bolívar narrowly escaped assassination by diving out of a window minutes before his would-be murderers burst into his bedroom.

Bolívar played a key role in gaining independence for Colombia, Venezuela, Ecuador, Peru, and Upper Peru (present-day Bolivia). Bolívar wanted the newly independent nations to become a Federation of the Andes with himself as leader. However, his plan did not succeed. Revolts and disagreements brought an end to the federation. Even though Bolívar became very unpopular, today he is honored as the founding father of South American independence.

Learn from Biographies
Who and what influenced Simón Bolívar to fight for South American independence from Spain?

For more information, go online to *Meet the People* at **www.sfsocialstudies.com.**

463

WEB SITE
Technology

Students can find out more about Simón Bolívar by clicking on *Meet the People* at **www.sfsocialstudies.com.**

CURRICULUM CONNECTION
Literature

Read Biographies
Students may want to read more about Simón Bolívar.
Simón Bolívar: Latin American Liberator, by Frank De Varona (Millbrook Press, ISBN 1-562-94278-6, 1993) **Easy**
Simón Bolívar: South American Liberator, by David Goodnough (Enslow Publishers, ISBN 0-766-01044-9, 1998) **On-Level**
Bolívar: Liberator of a Continent, by Bill Boyd (Capital Books, ISBN 1-892-12316-9, 2000) **Challenge**

Simón Bolívar

Objective
• Identify the contributions of significant individuals, including Simón Bolívar, who helped South American countries gain independence.

1 Introduce and Motivate

Preview To activate prior knowledge, ask students to recall what they learned about Simón Bolívar in Lesson 1. How did he help gain independence for South America? Tell students that they will learn more about Bolívar's role.

2 Teach and Discuss

Primary Source
Cited in *Historic World Leaders*, by Anne Commire, ed.

❶ **What did Bolívar mean by the words "molded my heart"?** He believed that Simón Rodríguez influenced his values. Rodríguez inspired Bolívar to seek liberty, justice, greatness, and beauty. **Analyze Primary Sources**

SOCIAL STUDIES STRAND
Geography

More than 50 of the mountains in the Andes chain are more than 20,000 feet high.

❷ **Why do you think Spanish troops were surprised by Bolívar's invasion of Colombia?** The Andes Mountains would be difficult to cross. The troops were probably not expecting an assault from that direction. **Draw Conclusions**

3 Close and Assess

Learn from Biographies Answer
Ideas from the French Revolution and his teacher Simón Rodríguez

American Revolution

Objective

- Analyze images and artifacts to better understand American history.

1 Introduce and Motivate

- Tell students that examining objects and images associated with an event can provide more information about the event.

- Before students read these pages, have them draw detailed sketches of people and/or events connected to the American Revolution. Tell students that they will learn more details as they read these pages.

- Students will add to their sketches or draw new ones as part of the assessment for these pages.

2 Teach and Discuss

(H) SOCIAL STUDIES STRAND
History

The engraved version of the Boston Massacre at the bottom of p. 464 was drawn by a Boston patriot named Paul Revere. Revere wanted his picture to stir up anti-British sentiment and convince people that the British were tyrants who had attacked innocent and peaceful Bostonians. In fact, before the massacre began, the colonial protesters had been throwing ice and wood at the British soldiers and daring them to shoot.

1 What details in the engraving at the bottom of p. 464 might be biased to support the view that the British troops "massacred" Boston protesters? Explain. Possible answer: The British troops are organized in a straight line and firing directly into the crowd of seemingly unarmed colonists. The colonists are gathered in a confused mass, not fighting back, and many of them are bleeding and collapsed on the ground. Recognize Bias

---

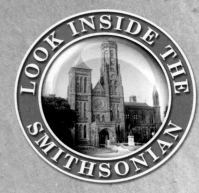

American Revolution

The American struggle for independence from Great Britain lasted five long years. The Americans had to endure many hardships—harsh winters and a lack of supplies—on the road to victory. Thanks to the leadership of George Washington and an alliance with France, the former colonies emerged from the war as a new nation: the United States.

The Boston Massacre
1 This engraving by Paul Revere depicts the moment that British troops opened fire on a crowd of protesting colonists on March 5, 1770.

464

Washington's Field Tent
This field tent was used by George Washington during the American Revolution.

Washington Reviewing His Ragged Army at Valley Forge
William T. Trego's painting captures the hardship the Continental Army suffered during the winter 1777. The image was used on a series of posta, stamps issued as part of the United States Bicentennial in 1976.

Washington's Field Glass
George Washington used this field glass during American Revolution. He may have used it to sp on enemy activity.

Practice and Extend

CURRICULUM CONNECTION
Math

Calculate Continental Army Supplies

- Tell students that in 1777, Congress voted to give each man in the Continental Army half a gill of rice and a tablespoonful of vinegar for Thanksgiving dinner.

- Write on the board that two gills equals one cup. One cup equals 16 tablespoons. One gallon equals 16 cups.

- Ask students to use this information to calculate the following: If the Continental Army consisted of 12,000 men in November of 1777, how many gallons of rice and how many gallons of vinegar would be needed for their Thanksgiving dinner? Answers: 12,000 half gills of rice equals 6,000 gills. 6,000 gills equals 3,000 cups. 3,000 cups equals 187.5 gallons of rice. 12,000 tablespoons of vinegar equals 750 cups or 46.9 gallons of vinegar.

Washington Crossing the Delaware
From a Painting by Emanuel Leutze / Eastman Johnson

Washington Crossing the Delaware
This painting by Emanuel Leutze shows General George Washington and his troops as they crossed the Delaware River in December 1776, on their way to the Battle of Trenton. In 1976, as part of the United States Bicentennial, this image was released as a series of postage stamps.

American Grenadier Cap
Caps such as this one were worn by grenadiers, who were among the bravest and best-trained soldiers of the 1700s. This cap may have been worn by a grenadier fighting in the Battle of Trenton.

Officer's Regimental Coat
This coat was worn by Peter Gansevoort, a colonel with the Third New York Continental Regiment. Gansevoort would eventually become a general.

Artifacts are from the ✳ Smithsonian Institution.

465

Workbook, p. 114

American Revolution

The American struggle for independence from Great Britain lasted five long years before the former colonies emerged as a new nation.

Directions: Imagine you are a soldier serving under General George Washington in the Continental Army during the American Revolution. Use the items and descriptions shown on pp. 464–465 to help you write a diary entry in which you describe the hardships encountered by Americans on the road to becoming a new nation. Write your diary entry on the lines provided. Use a separate sheet of paper if you need more space.

Notes for Home: Your child learned about the American struggle for independence.
Home Activity: With your child, discuss why it was important for the colonies to gain independence from Great Britain. Discuss how life today might be different if the United States had remained separate colonies under the rule of Great Britain.

Also on Teacher Resources CD-ROM.

Bicentennial means a celebration of the two-hundredth anniversary of an event. The United States Bicentennial celebrated the two-hundredth anniversary of the signing of the Declaration of Independence in 1776. Other events of the American Revolution were also honored at this time. Some people celebrated with museum exhibits, historical reenactments, and festivals, while the United States Mint marked the occasion by releasing special bicentennial versions of the quarter, half dollar, and dollar coins.

2 **How does the picture at the top of p. 465, which was used for a postage stamp during the U.S. Bicentennial celebration, present George Washington as a heroic figure?** Possible answers: In the picture Washington takes a commanding and inspiring pose at the front of the boat, clearly leading his troops across the icy waters. The picture shows the men in the boat symbolically moving from the stormy darkness behind them toward a lighter sky, which promises hope and victory.
Analyze Pictures

3 **How do the American regimental coat and grenadier cap shown here compare with the British uniforms shown in the engraving of the Boston Massacre on page 464?** The British uniforms are bright red, while the American coat is dark blue. The British soldiers wear black caps, while the grenadier cap is pointed and colorful.
Compare and Contrast

3 Close and Assess

- Encourage students to learn more about the American Revolution. They may look in encyclopedias or history books.

- Ask students to add details to their earlier sketches or draw new sketches of people and events of the American Revolution. Have students discuss what they learned from the pictures on these pages about the people and events of the American Revolution.

The French Revolution

Objectives

- Identify the main causes of the French Revolution.

- Explain what the three estates were and who belonged to each of them.

- Explain who Robespierre was and his role in the French Revolution.

- Identify the accomplishments of the French Republic.

- Explain why other European countries banded together to defeat Napoleon.

Vocabulary

monarchy, p. 467

Resources

- Workbook, p. 115
- Transparency 6
- Every Student Learns Guide, pp. 222–225
- Quick Study, pp. 112–113

 Quick *Teaching Plan*

If time is short, have students create a time line of important events in the lesson. As students read independently, they can note events on their time lines.

1 Introduce and Motivate

Preview To activate prior knowledge, ask students what they know about the American Revolution. Tell them that in Lesson 2 they will learn about a revolution in France.

You Are There Many historians consider the French Revolution one of the most important events in Europe's history because it provided a model for popular rebellion elsewhere. Have students discuss the two different points of view presented in the dialogue.

1774 Louis XVI comes to the throne.

1789 The Bastille falls; the *Declaration of the Rights of Man and of Citizen* is issued.

1793 Reign of Terror beg

The French Revolution

PREVIEW

Focus on the Main Idea
The path of revolution turned violent in France.

PLACES
Paris

PEOPLE
Louis XVI
Marie Antoinette
Maximilien de Robespierre
Napoleon Bonaparte

VOCABULARY
monarchy

TERMS
Estates-General
estate
National Assembly
Bastille
Declaration of the Rights of Man and of Citizen
Reign of Terror
Napoleonic Code

EVENTS
French Revolution
Battle of Waterloo

You Are There *1793:* As you sit in a courtroom in Paris, you listen to the following dialogue:

JUDGE: Citizen, do you have anything to say before we pass sentence?

PRISONER: This trial is illegal. I am the king of France, and you are my subjects. You have no right to charge me with anything.

JUDGE: You have committed terrible crimes against the people of France. You have tried to destroy the Revolution. You have committed treason by conspiring with the enemies of France.

PRISONER: Rubbish! How can I commit treason against myself? I rule by the divine right of God and it is only to him that I have to answer.

JUDGE: Citizen, you have committed treason against the Revolution. You are sentenced to death.

▶ **This painting captures the determination of the Third Estate as they gathered to create a constitution for France.**

Summarize As you read, summarize the most important events of the French Revolution.

466

Practice and Extend

 READING SKILL Summarize

In the Lesson Review, students complete a graphic organizer like the one below. You may want to provide students with a copy of Transparency 6 to complete as they read the lesson.

Use Transparency 6

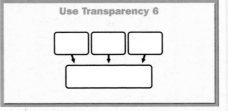

 WEB SITE Technology

- You can look up vocabulary words by clicking on *Social Studies Library* and selecting the dictionary at **www.sfsocialstudies.com.**

- Students can learn more about current news by clicking on *Current Events* at **www.sfsocialstudies.com.**

- Explore other events that occurred on this day by clicking on *This Day in History* at **www.sfsocialstudies.com.**

France in Trouble

France was one of the most powerful countries in Europe. Yet, by the middle of the 1700s, France's **monarchy,** or government in which a king, queen, or emperor has supreme power, was on the edge of collapse.

France's tax system was unfair. Peasants and the middle class paid heavy taxes while nobles paid almost nothing. The nobles, who made up about one percent of the population, owned nearly one-third of the land in France.

Louis XVI (LOO ee), who became king in 1774, was a weak ruler. Finding himself short of money, Louis decided to call a meeting of the Estates-General. The **Estates-General** was a group of advisers to the king.

The Estates-General represented the three **estates,** or classes, into which French society was officially divided. The First Estate was made up of church officials. The Second Estate was made up of nobles. The other 98 percent of the French people belonged to the Third Estate.

Each estate was represented in the Estates-General. Because the Third Estate represented most of the population, it demanded that each person at the meeting have one vote. When the king refused to grant this demand, members of the Third Estate formed into a group called the **National Assembly.** They then began to write a constitution for France. The **French Revolution** had begun.

REVIEW What were the three estates into which France was divided? Who belonged to each? **Main Idea and Details**

The Art Archive/Musée Carnavalet Paris/Jean-Loup Charmet

▶ In this political cartoon, the Third Estate is shown carrying the nobles and priests on its back.

▶ Louis XVI was the king of France at the beginning of the French Revolution.

Lauros-Giraudon/Bridgeman Art Library Int'l. Ltd. (U.S.)

467

France in Trouble

⏱ *Quick Summary* The powers of the monarchy and the unfair system of taxation led to the stirrings of the French Revolution in the late 1700s.

1 Describe France's system of taxation in the 1700s, and tell what made it unfair. The nobles paid almost no taxes, while the peasants and middle class paid heavy taxes. Those who were least able to pay had to pay the most. **Summarize**

2 What were estates? Explain how they led to the revolution in France. Estates were social classes. Two of the three estates made up a very small portion of the population, yet those estates had a larger say in the governing of the country. The third estate, or lowest class, wanted more rights. **Main Idea and Details**

3 Explain the title of this section. Why was France in trouble? France was in financial trouble, and its citizens were unhappy because of the tax system and the lack of representation in the government. **Summarize**

✓ **REVIEW ANSWER** The First Estate was made up of church leaders. The Second Estate was made up of nobles. The rest of the French people belonged to the Third Estate. **Main Idea and Details**

CURRICULUM CONNECTION
Art

Create a Political Cartoon

Using the political cartoon on p. 467 as a model, students can create political cartoons of their own.

- Ask students to describe the cartoon and to tell what point the cartoon is trying to make. Help students understand that a political cartoon makes a statement by using pictures rather than words.

- Ask students to choose a topic for their political cartoons. They could use the same topic depicted on this page, or they could choose a topic concerning one of the three estates described in this section.

- When students have completed their cartoons, invite them to share their work with others. Have other students summarize the points that various cartoons are trying to make.

New and Old Privileges

Quick Summary The attack on the Bastille and the adoption of the Declaration of the Rights of Man were important events in the French Revolution.

4 **Summarize the changes made by the National Assembly.** The National Assembly took away the privileges of the church and nobles. Peasants were paid, and nobles and church leaders had to pay taxes. The Assembly adopted a Declaration of the Rights of Man.
Summarize

✓ **REVIEW ANSWER** They were afraid that the French Revolution would encourage the people in their countries to start their own revolutions.
Draw Conclusions

The Reign of Terror

Quick Summary During the Reign of Terror, 40,000 people who were thought to be against the revolution were executed.

5 **How did the government of France change when the radicals took over the country?** Power was taken away from the king, and the country became a republic. Louis was put on trial as a traitor and executed. Marie Antoinette, and anyone else who was thought to be against the revolution, was executed as well.
Cause and Effect

6 **Why do you think Maximilien de Robespierre executed political enemies instead of trying to control them in other ways?** By executing them, he was sure not to have any opposition. He could rule the country as he pleased.
Draw Conclusions

New and Old Privileges

King Louis began gathering troops near the meeting. The people of **Paris** were outraged. On July 14, 1789, an angry mob attacked the **Bastille** (bah STEEL), a prison in Paris. The mob captured the prison and took the weapons stored there.

In its first days, the National Assembly took away all the privileges of the Church and nobles. Peasants no longer had to work without pay for nobles. Nobles and church leaders had to pay taxes. Many nobles had to sell their land at cheap prices to peasants.

In August 1789, the National Assembly adopted a *Declaration of the Rights of Man and of Citizen.*
4 This document was inspired by the U.S. Declaration of Independence. The French declaration stated that all men are equal and have certain rights. These include freedom of speech, assembly, and religion, and the right to a fair trial.

Other rulers in Europe were frightened by the

▶ **Marie Antoinette**

French Revolution. Fearing that the revolution might spread, they sent armies into France. At first, the French armies were badly beaten. Panic swept the country. Mobs in Paris blamed Louis and the queen, **Marie Antoinette** (muh REE an twa NET), for the defeats.

REVIEW Why would other European rulers be frightened by the French Revolution?
Draw Conclusions

The Reign of Terror

Radical, or extreme, leaders soon took control of the revolution. In 1792 they took away all of the king's power and made France a republic.

The following year, the radicals put Louis on trial as a traitor. He was convicted by a single vote and put to death. Ten months later, Marie Antoinette was also executed.

A period of violence followed. It was known as the **Reign of Terror.** Thousands of citizens who were suspected of being against the revolution were put to death.

▶ **A mob stormed the Bastille in Paris on July 14, 1789.**

Practice and Extend

MEETING INDIVIDUAL NEEDS
Leveled Practice

The Declaration of the Rights of Man Invite students to explore the declaration adopted by the Assembly in 1789.

Easy Ask students to revisit the lesson and make a list of the basic rights granted by the *Declaration of the Rights of Man*. Have students look up unfamiliar terms so that they understand these rights. **Reteach**

On-Level Ask students to compare and contrast the *Declaration of the Rights of Man* with the U.S. Declaration of Independence. **Extend**

Challenge Encourage students to think of rights that should be included in a declaration of rights. Have them make a list of the rights, and then write the list in the form of a declaration. Alternatively, students could research governing documents for various nations, compare and contrast them, and then evaluate their fairness and effectiveness. **Enrich**

For a Lesson Summary, use Quick Study, p. 112.

▶ **Maximilien de Robespierre**

A committee led by **Maximilien de Robespierre** (rohbz pee AIR) took over the government. Before long, the committee began executing anyone it suspected of being against the revolution.

Between 1793 and 1794, about 40,000 French people were executed. About half were beheaded by a new machine known as the guillotine (gee oh TEEN). Many leaders began to fear that they would be next to climb the steps to the guillotine. The final victims of the Reign of Terror were its leaders, including Robespierre.

Despite the violence of the Reign of Terror, the republic made many accomplishments. For example, slavery was ended in all of the French colonies. The republic also stripped away the privileges of the wealthy classes.

REVIEW Describe the Reign of Terror.
⟳ Summarize

Napoleon

When the French Revolution began, **Napoleon Bonaparte** was a young officer in the army. Napoleon's rise to power was swift. He led the French army in victories against Great Britain and Austria and became a general at the age of 24. In 1799 Napoleon overthrew the republic. In 1804 he became emperor of France.

Napoleon strengthened the French government and restored order. He established a new system of laws for France called the **Napoleonic Code.** The Code is still the basis of French law today. The Code was based on the principles of Roman law. It preserved some of the important reforms made by the republic during the French Revolution. However, women lost some of the rights of citizenship that they had gained during the revolution.

8

▶ **This edition of the Napoleonic Code was published in 1804.**

REVIEW What was the Napoleonic Code and how did it affect the lives of women?
⟳ Summarize

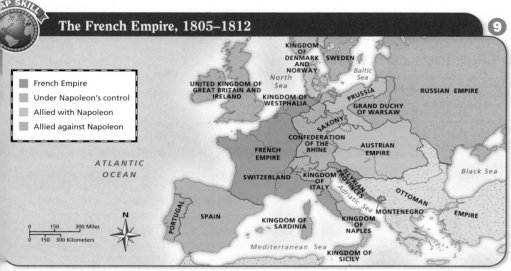

The French Empire, 1805–1812 **9**

Legend:
- French Empire
- Under Napoleon's control
- Allied with Napoleon
- Allied against Napoleon

KINGDOM OF DENMARK AND NORWAY, SWEDEN, UNITED KINGDOM OF GREAT BRITAIN AND IRELAND, North Sea, Baltic Sea, KINGDOM OF WESTPHALIA, PRUSSIA, RUSSIAN EMPIRE, GRAND DUCHY OF WARSAW, SAXONY, CONFEDERATION OF THE RHINE, AUSTRIAN EMPIRE, FRENCH EMPIRE, ATLANTIC OCEAN, SWITZERLAND, KINGDOM OF ITALY, ILLYRIAN PROVINCES, Adriatic Sea, Black Sea, OTTOMAN EMPIRE, PORTUGAL, SPAIN, KINGDOM OF SARDINIA, KINGDOM OF NAPLES, MONTENEGRO, Mediterranean Sea, KINGDOM OF SICILY

0 150 300 Miles
0 150 300 Kilometers
N

▶ **Napoleon made many conquests in Europe.**

MAP SKILL Use a Map Key *Which nations were allied with France? Which nations were allied against France?*

469

SOCIAL STUDIES
Background

More About the Napoleonic Code

- The Code of laws was not Napoleon's sole accomplishment in establishing order in the nation. He also negotiated an agreement with the pope, which ended many of the problems between France and the Roman Catholic Church.

- Napoleon's laws included simplifying the court system and reorganizing the educational system.

- The Napoleonic Code addresses civil laws, including rights of people and rights related to property. Later additions to the Napoleonic Code addressed commercial and criminal law.

- The Code has been praised for its simplicity and clarity and served as a model for laws in many modern nations, such as Belgium, the Netherlands, Italy, Spain, some Latin American republics, and the state of Louisiana.

---

7 **How did the invention of the guillotine affect executions during the Reign of Terror?** The guillotine made it easier to execute people.
Cause and Effect

✓ Ongoing Assessment

| **If...** students are unable to connect a cause and effect in relation to the guillotine, | **then...** help them create a graphic organizer, using *invention of the guillotine* as the cause. |

✓ REVIEW ANSWER The Reign of Terror was a violent period during which people who were suspected of being against the revolution were executed.
⟳ Summarize

PAGE 469

Napoleon

🕐 *Quick Summary* Napoleon Bonaparte strengthened the French government and restored order by establishing a system of laws for France.

8 **How did Napoleon establish himself as a leader?** As a young officer, he led the French army to important victories.
Main Idea and Details

✓ REVIEW ANSWER The Napoleonic Code was a new system of laws for France. Women lost some of the rights of citizenship under these laws.
⟳ Summarize

The French Empire, 1805–1812

9 **Which countries were under Napoleon's control?** Spain, Kingdom of Italy, Saxony, Kingdom of Westphalia, Kingdom of Naples, Confederation of the Rhine, the Grand Duchy of Warsaw
Interpret Maps

MAP SKILL Answer Allied with France: Kingdom of Norway and Denmark, Prussia, Austrian Empire; allied against France: United Kingdom of Great Britain and Ireland, Portugal, Sweden, Russian Empire, Kingdom of Sardinia, Montenegro, Kingdom of Sicily

Napoleon's Conquests

🕐 **Quick Summary** Napoleon's goal to establish his own empire resulted in Napoleon's defeat and eventual exile.

10 **What was Napoleon's goal? Why did he fail to accomplish it?** Napoleon wanted to reestablish the Holy Roman Empire. The monarchs of Europe banded together against Napoleon.  **Summarize**

✓ **REVIEW ANSWER** He conquered Spain, much of present-day Germany, and Austria. 🔄 **Summarize**

3 Close and Assess

Summarize the Lesson

Ask students to provide positive and negative effects of the French Revolution for a two-column chart with the heads *Plus* and *Minus*.

✓ **LESSON 2**   **REVIEW**

1. For possible answers, see the reduced pupil page. 🔄 **Summarize**

2. He strengthened the French government and restored order.

3. He was the leader of a committee that took over the French government. This committee executed people it suspected of opposing the revolution.

4. The republic ended slavery in the French colonies and took away the privileges of the wealthy classes.

5. **Critical Thinking:** *Recognize Point of View* They banded together because they feared that he would attack them and take away their power.

Link to ⚭ **Writing**

Remind students to use a respectful tone that is appropriate for writing to a publication. Students should state their opinions first and then support them with facts.

470 Unit 6 • Discovery, Expansion, and Revolutions

Napoleon's Conquests

Napoleon's goal was to establish his own empire. Napoleon made major conquests in Europe. His armies conquered Spain, much of present-day Germany, and Austria. However, the French Empire began to collapse in 1812, when Napoleon invaded Russia. Many French soldiers died in the invasion because they did not have the clothing or equipment needed during Russia's harsh winter.

Once again, the monarchs of Europe banded together. This time, they were successful. In 1813 the European allies defeated Napoleon. They exiled him, or forced him to leave. He was sent to an island in the Mediterranean Sea. However, he escaped to France in 1815.

Réunion des Musées Nationaux

▶ **Napoleon Bonaparte strikes a heroic pose in this painting by Jacques Louis David.**

Napoleon ruled France for 100 days. He was finally defeated by Britain and the European allies at the **Battle of Waterloo.** Napoleon was sent to the far-off island of St. Helena in the Atlantic Ocean, where he died in 1821.

REVIEW What were Napoleon's major conquests in Europe? 🔄 **Summarize**

Summarize the Lesson

- **1774** Louis XVI came to the throne.
- **1789** Bastille fell; *Declaration of Rights of Man and of Citizenship* was issued.
- **1793** Reign of Terror

LESSON 2 ▷ REVIEW

Check Facts and Main Ideas

1. 🔄 **Summarize** On a separate piece of paper, write a brief summary of the main points below.

```
The French              The Estates-
monarchy                General did            France's tax
had too much            not give equal         system was
power.                  representation         unfair.
                        to the estates.
```

By the mid-1700s, France's monarchy was on the edge of collapse.

2. How did Napoleon improve conditions in France?

3. Who was Robespierre?

4. What accomplishments did the republic bring to France?

5. **Critical Thinking:** *Recognize Point of View* Why would other European leaders band together to defeat Napoleon?

Link to ⚭ **Writing**

Write a Letter Write a letter to a newspaper editor explaining why you believe that the republic is important to France. Be sure to include comparisons of the republic with the French monarchy that came before it.

470

Practice and Extend

ESL **EXTEND LANGUAGE**
ESL Support

Examine Word Meanings Students use past-tense verbs and related nouns to explore word meanings.

Beginning Have students scan the first paragraph for two words beginning with *con-*. Help students understand the words. Repeat with the two words beginning with *in-*.

Intermediate Have students list five past-tense verbs from the text and use them in sentences.

Advanced Write on the board *conquered, invaded, defeated, ruled,* and *escaped.* Have students identify a related noun for each word and use the noun in a sentence.

For additional ESL support, use Every Student Learns Guide, pp. 222–225.

Workbook, p. 115

Lesson 2: The French Revolution

Directions: Sequence the events in the order in which they occurred. Number the events from 1 (earliest) to 12 (most recent). You may use your textbook.

_____ Radicals take control of the revolution and make France a republic.

_____ Members of the Third Estate form the National Assembly and write a constitution for France.

_____ King Louis XVI is put on trial as a traitor, convicted, and put to death.

_____ The French Revolution begins.

_____ Napoleon's armies conquer Spain, much of what is now Germany, and Austria.

_____ Fearing that the French Revolution might spread, other European rulers send troops into France, causing panic.

_____ During the Reign of Terror, thousands of citizens suspected of being against the revolution are put to death.

_____ The National Assembly adopts a *Declaration of the Rights of Man and of Citizen.*

_____ The Napoleonic Code preserves important reforms made by the republic during the French Revolution, but women lose some of the rights of citizenship they had gained.

_____ King Louis XVI calls a meeting of the Estates-General. The Third Estate demands that each person at the meeting have one vote, but the king refuses.

_____ Napoleon Bonaparte overthrows the French republic. He becomes emperor of France.

_____ Napoleon is defeated by Britain and European allies at the Battle of Waterloo.

Notes for Home: Your child learned about events occurring during the French Revolution.
Home Activity: With your child, discuss several events that have led to revolutions. Identify motivated means of bringing about change.

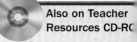

Also on Teacher Resources CD-RO

A Pioneer for Women's Rights

During the years of the French Revolution, Marie-Olympe de Gouges (oh LAMP duh GOOZH) asked that women be granted the same rights as men. Her demand was met with rejection and laughter from both men and women, but she continued to fight for what she believed in.

BUILDING CITIZENSHIP
- Caring
- Respect
- Responsibility
- ★ Fairness
- Honesty
- Courage

Musee de la Ville de Paris, Musee Carnavalet, Paris France

De Gouges was born in southwestern France in 1748. She began her career as a playwright. De Gouges's plays were considered extreme and often were not performed. The plays that were produced received harsh criticism.

De Gouges found other ways to spread her ideas about equality. She published pamphlets and articles. De Gouges's most famous work is the *Declaration of the Rights of Woman and the Female Citizen* (1791). This document was the first feminist manifesto, or public declaration. She began the *Declaration* with this challenge:

> "Man are you capable of being just? It is a woman who asks you this question. Who has given you the authority to oppress my sex?" ❶

Bibliothèque Nationale de France

In the *Declaration,* de Gouges stated that women should have the same legal rights as men. She said that women should also receive an equal education. De Gouges was ahead of her time and was viewed as a threat. She was arrested, found guilty of treason, and sent to the guillotine. ❷

De Gouges's work influenced women in other countries. A year after the *Declaration* was published, British writer Mary Wollstonecraft wrote a book about equal rights and education for women. These works helped to encourage the movement for women's rights.

Fairness in Action

Link to Current Events Research strategies the women's rights movement used to fight for equal rights. How do their experiences compare with de Gouges's experiences?

471

CITIZEN HEROES

A Pioneer for Women's Rights

Objective
- Identify individuals, such as Marie-Olympe de Gouges, who made significant contributions in the area of women's rights.

1 Introduce and Motivate

Preview Ask students what they remember about the Napoleonic Code. Remind students that the Code took away some of women's civil rights. Tell students that they will learn about Marie-Olympe de Gouges, a pioneer for women's rights.

2 Teach and Discuss

Primary Source
Cited in *Historic World Leaders 2,* by Anne Commire, ed.

❶ **What challenge does de Gouges make to men in this declaration?** She challenges men by asking them who gave them the authority to oppress, or dominate, women.
Analyze Primary Sources

❷ **Why do you think de Gouges was eventually executed?** Possible answer: Her ideas were considered too revolutionary, and she was a threat to the way of life at the time.
Cause and Effect

3 Close and Assess

Fairness in Action

Students should identify women's rights activists such as Susan B. Anthony, Lucretia Mott, Elizabeth Cady Stanton, Lucy Stone, or Elizabeth Blackwell. Encourage them to use simple reference sources to find out more about the methods these women used and how they compared to those used by de Gouges.

WEB SITE Technology

Students can find out more about Marie-Olympe de Gouges by clicking on *Meet the People* at **www.sfsocialstudies.com.**

CURRICULUM CONNECTION Literature

Read About Women's Rights
Share the following title to help students explore the issue of equal rights for women.

Let It Shine: The Stories of Black Women Freedom Fighters, by Andrea Davis Pinckney (Harcourt, ISBN 0-152-01005-X, 2000)
On-Level

- Encourage students to research more titles about women's rights on line or at a library.

Compare Primary Sources

Objective

- Analyze how one primary source may have influenced another primary source.

Resource

- Workbook, p. 116

1 Introduce and Motivate

What is a primary source? Remind students that primary sources are eyewitness accounts or observations of history, made by people who participated in the events being described. Ask students how studying primary sources from different periods of time might provide them with broader "snapshots" of history. Then have students read the **What?** section of text on p. 472.

Why compare primary sources? Have students read the **Why?** section of text on p. 473. Ask them to think about the ways in which primary source documents have influenced other documents. The Declaration of the Rights of Man during the French Revolution, for example, was based largely on the ideas of the Declaration of Independence adopted by the U.S. colonies.

2 Teach and Discuss

How is this skill used? Examine with students the primary sources on p. 472.

- Encourage students to be careful about language and vocabulary as they read primary sources. Some words change their meaning over time. Students should consider the intent of the original documents, not only the words.

Compare Primary Sources

What? You have already learned that primary sources are snapshots of history. They come in many forms and translations.

You can use two primary sources from different time periods to compare and contrast how ideas were alike and different. Below are excerpts from the English Bill of Rights (1689) and the U.S. Constitution (1787).

XXVIII. WILLIAM the THIRD and MARY the SECOND, from 1688 to 1702.

BILL OF RIGHTS

The Granger Collection

"And for preventing all questions and divisions in this realm . . . in and upon which the unity, peace, tranquility and safety of this nation doth under God wholly consist and depend . . . the safety and welfare of this Protestant kingdom . . ."

tranquility: calmness, quiet
doth: does
posterity: later generations
ordain: pass into law

We the People

Article 1

The Granger Collection

We the People of the United States, in Order to form a more perfect Union, establish Justice, insure domestic Tranquility, provide for the common defence, promote the general Welfare, and secure the Blessings of Liberty to ourselves and our Posterity, do ordain and establish this Constitution for the United States of America.

472

Practice and Extend

Paraphrasing Help students paraphrase the excerpts and focus on the similarity of the main ideas of the sources.

Beginning Write simple sentences with some of the same ideas as the excerpt from the U.S. Constitution; for example, *The people of the United States wanted fairness and peace.* Have students read the sentences aloud. Ask questions to ensure that students understand the sentences. Then do the same with the excerpt from the English Bill of Rights. Help students see the similarities.

Intermediate Help students use reference sources such as dictionaries to find unfamiliar words. Then help them paraphrase a few lines in each excerpt and look at how similar their two paraphrasings are.

Advanced Help students paraphrase the two excerpts and discuss which ideas in them are similar (e.g., peace and safety in a country).

▶ This scene depicts the signing of the U.S. Constitution.

The Granger Collection

Why? By comparing primary sources, we can try to understand how one document might have influenced the writing of another.

The English wanted to limit the power of the monarchy. They used the main points of the Magna Carta (1215), which limited the king's power, to draw up the English Bill of Rights in 1689. This piece of legislation made England a **constitutional monarchy**, one in which the monarch's power is limited.

Beginning in the late 1600s, a philosophical movement called the **Enlightenment** began in Europe. This movement applied reason, or logical thinking, to understanding the laws of human nature. These ideas could then be used to improve society. Enlightenment writers such as John Locke inspired the American colonists to form ideas about self-government. The colonists then borrowed ideas from the Enlightenment, as well as the English Bill of Rights, to help in the writing of the Constitution.

How? In comparing primary sources, first you must use a dictionary to look up any words you do not know. You may be using a primary source that is in English but uses different words from those you are used to. For example, in the excerpt from the English Bill of Rights, you will see the word *doth*. We would say *does* instead of *doth*.

Then you must look for key words. In the selections that you read from both primary sources, make a list of key words, ideas, and subjects. Consider the writer or writers of the primary sources, as well as the audience.

③

Think and Apply

① What are some common key words and ideas in both excerpts?

② To whom are these documents addressed?

③ Summarize what you have learned by comparing these two primary sources.

473

- Lead students in comparing the two documents on p. 472. What parallels between the two can students find?

- Have students read the **How?** section of text on p. 473.

① **On what primary source was the English Bill of Rights based?** The Magna Carta Main Idea and Details

② **How did the Enlightenment affect the writing of the U.S. Constitution?** During the Enlightenment people applied reason to understanding human nature. Writers from the Enlightenment inspired American colonists to form their own ideas about self-government. They incorporated these ideas into the U.S. Constitution. Cause and Effect

③ **Why is it important to consider the writer of the primary source as well as the intended audience?** A writer who lived long ago may have used different words or language. If the writing were intended for a specific audience, the writer may have introduced bias into the piece. Draw Conclusions

3 Close and Assess

Think and Apply

1. *Unity/union, tranquility, safety and welfare/common defense, general welfare*

2. To ordinary people

3. That the English BIll of Rights probably influenced the U.S. Constitution

---

MEETING INDIVIDUAL NEEDS
Learning Styles

Comparing Primary Sources Students can use their own learning styles as they compare primary sources.

Logical Learning Encourage students to create flow charts or other graphic organizers to show the steps in comparing primary sources. The first step, for example, might be to paraphrase the sources.

Verbal Learning Have students work in small groups to paraphrase primary sources. Working with partners may help students understand the content of the sources.

Workbook, p. 116

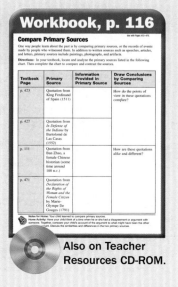

Compare Primary Sources

One way people learn about the past is by comparing primary sources, or the records of events made by people who witnessed them. In addition to written sources such as speeches, articles, and letters, primary sources include paintings, photographs, and artifacts.

Directions: In your textbook, locate and analyze the primary sources listed in the following chart. Then complete the chart to compare and contrast the sources.

Textbook Page	Primary Source	Information Provided in Primary Source	Draw Conclusions by Comparing Sources
p. 423	Quotation from King Ferdinand of Spain (1511)		How do the points of view in these quotations compare?
p. 427	Quotation from *In Defense of the Indians* by Bartolomé de Las Casas (1552)		
p. 111	Quotation from Ban Zhao, a female Chinese historian (some time around 100 B.C.)		How are these quotations alike and different?
p. 471	Quotation from *Declaration of the Rights of Woman and the Female Citizen* by Marie-Olympe De Gouges (1791)		

Notes for Home: Your child learned to compare primary sources.
Home Activity: Have your child think of a time when he or she had a disagreement or argument with someone. Together, compare your child's account of the argument to what might have been the other person's account. Discuss the similarities and differences in the two primary sources.

Also on Teacher Resources CD-ROM.

The Industrial Revolution

Objectives

- Describe how goods were produced differently as a result of the Industrial Revolution.
- Describe the contributions of James Watt.
- Identify the factors that allowed Great Britain to get a head start in the Industrial Revolution.
- Explain why so many people moved from the country to the city between 1800 and 1850 in Great Britain.
- Explain what made conditions so bad in London factories and London slums.

Vocabulary

textile, p. 475; **factory,** p. 475; **tenement,** p. 477

Resources

- Workbook, p. 117
- Transparency 13
- Every Student Learns Guide, pp. 226–229
- Quick Study, pp. 114–115

Quick Teaching Plan

If time is short, have students use K-W-L charts as they read the lesson independently.

1 Introduce and Motivate

Preview Ask students what they know about the how goods are created in factories. Tell students that in Lesson 3 they will learn more about factories and how they have changed.

You Are There In the late 1700s, some British children worked in cotton mills in exchange for their food and housing. Ask students how they might persuade factory owners to improve working conditions in factories.

LESSON 3

1750	1800	1850	1900

1760s James Watt improves the steam engine.

1807 Robert Fulton builds the first successful steamboat.

1829 The "Railroad Age" begins.

GREAT BRITAIN

UNITED STATES — New York City

PREVIEW

Focus on the Main Idea
The Industrial Revolution began in Great Britain and soon spread to other nations.

PLACES
Great Britain
Hudson River
New York City
Albany

PEOPLE
James Watt
George Stephenson
Robert Fulton
Charles Dickens

VOCABULARY
textile
factory
tenement

TERMS
domestic system
Industrial Revolution
steam engine
factory system

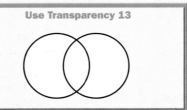
North Wind Picture Archives

474

The Industrial Revolution

You Are There

Letter to the Editor
Manchester, England
February 15, 1831

Dear Editor:

I'm 15 years old and I work in a mill here in Manchester. I start work at five o'clock in the morning, six days a week. Many days I don't stop working until eight at night. I work the spinning machines, and I'm on my feet all day. My boss likes to hire children because he can pay us less than adults. Children also have smaller hands that can fit better inside the machines. A week ago, a girl lost her right hand in a machine, which started turning while her hand was in it.

I've worked here for seven years. My knees always hurt. Sometimes it hurts to breathe, too, because the factory is filled with cotton dust. I cough all of the time.

I expect I will work here all my life. That's if I don't get hurt. If I get hurt and can't work, I will starve because there's no one here to look out for me.

—Sophia

Compare and Contrast As you read, think about the changes the Industrial Revolution made in the way goods were produced.

Practice and Extend

A New Way of Making Things

Between 1000 and 1750, humans or animals did nearly all of the work. There were some machines, but they were powered by hand, foot, or animal. Most goods were made at home. For example, workers would buy a raw material such as cotton from merchants, take it back to their cottages, and produce thread to make **textiles,** or cloth that is either woven or knitted. Making goods in the home is called the **domestic system.**

In Europe after 1750, new ideas arose about how to make and use machines to produce goods faster and on a larger scale. The change from human and animal power to machine power is known as the **Industrial Revolution.**

The invention of the **steam engine,** a machine that used the power of steam, kicked off the Industrial Revolution in **Great Britain.** The first useful steam engine was built early in the 1700s. During the 1760s, **James Watt** of Scotland improved the steam engine so that it could power large machines.

The next step was to lower costs by grouping machines together into one large place: a **factory.** Grouping machines in one place was known as the **factory system.**

REVIEW Summarize how the factory system was different from the domestic system.
🔁 Summarize

Great Britain and the Steam Engine

There were a number of reasons why Great Britain launched the Industrial Revolution. Great Britain had important natural resources, such as iron and coal. It also had many skilled workers, as well as people with money to invest in factories. It had a good transportation network, a system of roads and rivers to move goods to markets. Finally, it had colonies to supply raw materials and to buy goods.

By 1800 many new roads and canals had been built in Great Britain. Ten miles an hour was about as fast as anybody was able to travel in a horse-drawn coach or canal boat.

In 1825, **George Stephenson** attached a steam engine to wheels and put it on rails. The train engine could do the work of 40 teams of horses. In 1829 Stephenson's engine stunned people by reaching a top speed of 36 miles per hour. The "Railroad Age" had begun. **3**

Steam power was also used to increase the speed of ships. The first successful steamboat was built by American **Robert Fulton.** In 1807 Fulton sailed a steamboat up the **Hudson River** from **New York City** to **Albany,** New York, at a speed of five miles an hour. By the 1840s, steamships were crossing the Atlantic Ocean.

REVIEW Why was Great Britain able to get an early lead in the Industrial Revolution? **Main Idea and Details**

▶ The moving parts of a steam engine are set in motion by introducing steam through the steam inlet.

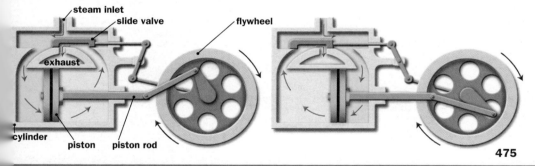

steam inlet
slide valve
flywheel
exhaust
cylinder
piston
piston rod

475

CURRICULUM CONNECTION
Science

Inventions and How They Work

Ask students to use one or more of the following ideas to explore inventions.

- Students can choose an inventor or invention and use simple reference sources to find out more. They might draw scale drawings or diagrams to show how the inventions work. Encourage them to find out about the lives of the inventors. What methods did they use? What other important discoveries did they make?

- Invite students to think of other inventions that caused major changes in the world. Ask them to add their ideas to a display of inventions that caused changes in the way people worked and lived. They can explain each invention and how it works and tell how the invention changed people's lives.

- Ask students to think of a need in their own lives that could be met with a new invention. They can draw it, describe how it works, and tell what it does.

A New Way of Making Things

🕐 **Quick Summary** The invention of the steam engine began the Industrial Revolution in Great Britain.

1 How did James Watt affect the way that goods were produced in England? Watt improved the steam engine so that it could power large machines to produce goods faster. **Cause and Effect**

2 How did the factory system affect the costs of production? Business people could lower costs by grouping larger machines together into one large place. The factory system made it cheaper to produce goods. **Draw Conclusions**

✓ **REVIEW ANSWER** Instead of goods being made on a small scale in a home, they were made by machines grouped together in a large place. 🔁 **Summarize**

Great Britain and the Steam Engine

🕐 **Quick Summary** Great Britain launched the Industrial Revolution for many reasons, including its good transportation network.

3 Why was George Stephenson's steam engine on wheels significant? The train engine was able to do the work of 40 teams of horses; it marked the beginning of the "Railroad Age." **Main Idea and Details**

✓ **REVIEW ANSWER** Because it had important natural resources, many skilled workers, money to invest, good transportation, and colonists to supply raw materials and buy goods **Main Idea and Details**

Terrible Conditions

🕐 *Quick Summary* In the early years of the Industrial Revolution, women and children worked long hours in dangerous conditions for little pay.

4 **Why do you think factory workers were treated so poorly?** Possible answer: There were many workers, so when one was injured, he or she was easy to replace. **Hypothesize**

✓ **Ongoing Assessment**

| **If...** students do not understand why workers were not treated well, | **then...** point out that many factory owners knew that people needed their jobs and that there were many people willing to work. |

Primary Source

Cited in *Connecting Spheres*, by Marilyn J. Boxer and Jean H. Guataert

5 **What details in the description of the mine support the main idea that the "road is very steep"?** *Go on my hands and feet, hold by a rope, [hold] by anything we can catch hold of* **Main Idea and Details**

✓ **REVIEW ANSWER** The factories were dark, dirty, and poorly ventilated. Workers (many of them women and children) worked 12 to 15 hours each day, 6 days a week. There were no safety devices on the machines. 🔄 **Summarize**

PAGES 476–477

Growing Cities Have Many Problems

🕐 *Quick Summary* The Industrial Revolution led to overcrowded cities and inadequate public services.

GRAPH SKILL **Answer** Between 1800 and 1850

Terrible Conditions

Early factories were dark, dirty, and had poor air quality. Workers labored 12 to 15 hours a day, six days a week.

In the early days of the Industrial Revolution, most of the workers were women and children. They were paid much less than men. Children as young as five could be sent to work in textile mills. Even after the British government halted the use of children under nine in the textile industry in 1833, young children were still used in other industries.

4 Safety conditions were often poor. The machines had few, if any safety devices. Workers were often badly hurt. A worker who lost an arm or leg usually was fired without any payment.

One of the most dangerous jobs was that of the "scavenger." The youngest workers in the textile factories were usually employed as scavengers. They had to pick up the loose cotton from under the machinery by crawling under the running machines.

Coal was the cheap fuel that helped to drive the Industrial Revolution. Working conditions in the coal mines also were hard and dangerous. This is how one woman described her job in the mine:

5 *"I have a belt round my waist and a chain passing between my legs, and I go on my hands and feet. The road is very steep, and we have to hold by a rope, and when there is no rope, by anything we can catch hold of."*

REVIEW Describe the working conditions in factories during the early Industrial Revolution. 🔄 **Summarize**

▶ The Industrial Revolution lured many people to cities such as London. Many lived in overcrowded slum apartments.

476

Population of Great Britain

Population (in millions) / Year

▶ The Industrial Revolution helped the population of Great Britain to increase dramatically between 1750 to 1850.

GRAPH SKILL Use a Bar Graph *Did the population of Great Britain increase more between 1750 and 1800, or between 1800 and 1850?*

Growing Cities Have Many Problems

During the 1800s, Europe saw huge population growth. For example, in Great Britain the population went from a little more than 10 million in 1800 to more than 20 million in 1850.

As a result, Europe's cities grew rapidly. Before the Industrial Revolution, most people in Europe lived on farms or in small villages. After the Industrial Revolution began, more people started to move into towns and cities.

Practice and Extend

ESL **ACCESS CONTENT** **ESL Support**

Taking Notes Help students take notes to access the content on the page.

Beginning Have students write *Terrible Conditions* on a sheet of paper. Explain the title's meaning. Read aloud the page, pausing to paraphrase, summarize, and make connections to the title. Have students add notes to their papers.

Intermediate Provide skeletal notes, such as sentences with blanks, for students to use. Use an overhead transparency to model how to take notes as you read the section aloud. Pause for students to take notes.

Advanced Provide skeletal notes for students to use as they read the section independently.

For additional ESL support, use Every Student Learns Guide, pp. 226–229.

People moved into the cities because they were no longer able to earn their living on farms. As the use of machinery on farms increased, fewer farm workers were needed. At the same time, the growing number of factories in the cities provided many new jobs for workers.

In the cities, many workers lived in overcrowded slum apartments, called **tenements.** There were few public services for people in the tenements. For example, in the 1830s, the city of Birmingham, England, still used pigs to eat the garbage residents produced.

Writer **Charles Dickens** described a London slum:

> *"It was a town of machinery and tall chimneys, out of which serpents of smoke trailed. It had a black canal in it, and a river that ran purple with ill-smelling dye."*

Museum of London, UK

▶ **Smoke filled the skies of industrial cities such as London.**

REVIEW Why did so many people in Europe move to cities in the first half of the nineteenth century? **Cause and Effect**

Summarize the Lesson

- **1760s** James Watt improved the steam engine.
- **1807** Robert Fulton built the first successful steamboat.
- **1829** The "Railroad Age" began.

LESSON 3 REVIEW

Check Facts and Main Ideas

1. **Compare and Contrast** On a separate piece of paper, complete the diagram below.

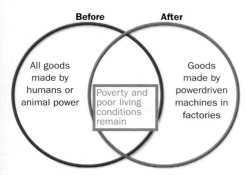

Before — All goods made by humans or animal power

Poverty and poor living conditions remain

After — Goods made by powerdriven machines in factories

2. What did James Watt's improvements to the steam engine accomplish?

3. What factors allowed Great Britain to get a head start in the Industrial Revolution?

4. Why did so many people move to cities between 1800 and 1850?

5. **Critical Thinking:** *Make Inferences* Why do you think the conditions were so bad in London factories and London slums?

Link to ⌒⌒ **Speech**

Write a Speech Write a speech in which you try to draw attention to the terrible health problems caused by overcrowded slums and poor factory conditions in London.

477

Workbook, p. 117

Lesson 3: The Industrial Revolution

In Europe after 1750, new ideas arose about how to make and use machines to produce goods faster and on a larger scale. This period is known as the Industrial Revolution.

Directions: Complete the chart with information about inventions or improvements made during the Industrial Revolution. You may use your textbook.

Invention	Inventor	Date	Purpose
Improvement of the Steam Engine			
Steamboat			
Train Engine			

Directions: Answer the following questions on the lines provided.

1. How and why did cities in Europe change during the Industrial Revolution?

2. What kinds of problems did Europe's growing cities experience?

Also on Teacher Resources CD-ROM.

Chapter 16 • Lesson 3 **477**

The Second Industrial Revolution

Objectives

- List some of the machines we use today that were invented during the Second Industrial Revolution.

- Explain what a corporation is and how it differs from other types of companies.

- Explain why reformers wanted to improve working conditions.

- Explain who Karl Marx was and describe his ideas about socialism and capitalism.

- Explain why Thomas Edison's inventions did or did not improve people's lives.

Vocabulary

corporation, p. 479; **reformer,** p. 480; **strike,** p. 480

Resources

- Workbook, p. 118
- Transparency 1
- Every Student Learns Guide, pp. 230–233
- Quick Study, pp. 116–117

Quick Teaching Plan

If time is short, have students record main ideas and details in outlines as they read independently.

1 Introduce and Motivate

Preview Have students recall what they know about the Industrial Revolution. Tell them they will learn about a Second Industrial Revolution in Lesson 4.

You Are There Edison originally invented the phonograph to be used as a dictating machine in offices. Ask students to predict how the first Industrial Revolution may have influenced the second.

1850	1900	1950

about 1850
U.S. industries start using crude oil.

1877
Edison invents the phonograph.

1913
Ford Motor Co. begins building automobiles on an assembly line.

Menlo Park
NEW JERSEY

PREVIEW

Focus on the Main Idea
While business owners gained more freedom from government controls, workers struggled to improve their working conditions.

PLACES
Menlo Park

PEOPLE
Thomas Edison
Karl Marx

VOCABULARY
corporation
reformer
strike

TERMS
Second Industrial Revolution
assembly line
capitalism
capitalist
market economy
traditional economy
laissez faire
labor union
socialism
command economy

The Second Industrial Revolution

You Are There

What will Thomas Edison dream up next? All your life you've been hearing about his wonderful inventions and how some day they will improve people's lives. You haven't actually met anyone who's used an electric light bulb in their home. You've only heard stories about the kineto-scope, an invention that seems to make photographs move. However, you've just seen another of Edison's inventions up close. It's a machine that holds a tube wrapped in tin foil. When the machine is turned on, the tube spins while a needle touches its surface.

All you can hear at first is a loud hissing and crackling. As you listen closer, you hear something else. It's a softer, more familiar sound. Somehow, that tube wrapped in tin foil can store and then replay a human voice.

Main Idea and Details
As you read, keep track of the machines you use today that were first introduced during the Second Industrial Revolution.

1877
phonograph

1879
light bulb

1876
telephone

1875

478

Practice and Extend

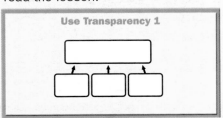

New Sources of Power

The first Industrial Revolution had been based on the steam engine and coal. After the 1850s, the Second Industrial Revolution was powered by electricity, oil, and steel. New inventions began to change the way people lived and worked.

Thomas Edison and his assistants were responsible for many of the inventions that we are familiar with today: the electric light bulb, the phonograph (the ancestor of today's CD player), motion pictures, or movies, and others. Edison and others made important discoveries. Many of these inventions came out of Edison's laboratory in Menlo Park, New Jersey.

Steel bridges could cross wide rivers. Buildings with steel skeletons could rise higher and higher. Steel plows could break the heavy soil of the American Great Plains for planting.

In the 1850s industries in the United States started using crude oil. At first, crude oil was used for lighting and heating. Then came the development of the internal combustion engine. Oil could be made into gasoline to run these engines. This engine is used today in most cars, trucks, and buses.

Just as important was the power of electricity. Electricity supplied light and power to machines. It led to the development of new forms of communication, such as the telephone and telegraph. Later, inventors discovered how to use radio waves to send voices and music over long distances in virtually no time.

REVIEW How was the Second Industrial Revolution different from the first? **Compare and Contrast**

Corporations and Assembly Lines

At the beginning of the Industrial Revolution, a handful of people could build a factory and keep it going. However, by the early 1800s, large amounts of money were needed to open a factory. Railroad and steel-making companies had grown so large that it became very expensive to buy machines and pay workers.

A new type of business organization developed. It was called a corporation. Corporations provided a way to raise millions of dollars. They raised money by selling stock shares, or parts of the company, to the public. If the corporation made profits, those profits would be divided among the shareholders.

In time, business leaders tried to develop new ways to manufacture items. One such way was the assembly line. The assembly line was developed in the early 1900s by the U.S. automobile manufacturer Henry Ford. On the assembly line, the automobile traveled along a moving belt past a number of workers. Each worker added one part to the car, such as a door, until the car was complete. The assembly line made it possible to manufacture more items in a shorter period of time.

REVIEW What effect did the assembly line have on the manufacturing process? **Cause and Effect**

1885 automobile

1890 movie camera

1885 ——————————— 1895

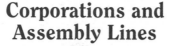

Teach and Discuss

PAGE 479

New Sources of Power

🕐 *Quick Summary* The Second Industrial Revolution was powered by electricity, oil, and steel rather than steam engines.

1 **How did crude oil and steel affect industry in the United States?** Steel was used in bridges, buildings, and plows. Crude oil was used as power for internal combustion engines used in transportation. **Cause and Effect**

✓ **REVIEW ANSWER** The first Industrial Revolution had been based on iron and the steam engine. The Second Industrial Revolution was powered by electricity, oil, and steel. **Compare and Contrast**

Corporations and Assembly Lines

🕐 *Quick Summary* As industry grew, assembly lines and corporations replaced small factories.

2 **Why were factories becoming too expensive to open and maintain?** The companies were becoming very large, and it became more expensive to buy new machinery. It was hard to pay all the workers. **Cause and Effect**

3 **Explain how a corporation works.** Corporations raise money by selling stock to the public. If the corporation profits, then it shares its profits with shareholders. **Summarize**

✓ **Ongoing Assessment**

If... students cannot explain how a corporation works, | **then...** guide them through the steps a corporation takes as it sells its stock and divides any profit among its stockholders.

✓ **REVIEW ANSWER** It made it possible to build more items in a shorter period of time. **Cause and Effect**

Capitalism and Reformers

🕐 **Quick Summary** As capitalists ran their businesses to make profits, reformers pushed for government controls on businesses.

④ How did capitalists feel about the government controls on their businesses? Why did they feel that way? The capitalists did not want government regulations. They wanted control over their own businesses.

🔁 **Summarize**

✓ **REVIEW ANSWER** The reformers did not believe that business owners would improve harsh factory conditions without some kind of government control.
Draw Conclusions

Working Conditions

🕐 **Quick Summary** Governments regulated businesses to improve living and working conditions. Many workers formed labor unions in order to improve their working conditions.

🗺️ Decision Making

⑤ Unions sometimes use strikes in order to have their demands met in the workplace. Do you think that the decision to strike is effective? Why or why not? Possible answer: If the business is vital, then going on strike would be effective because consumers miss the goods or services provided by that business. **Make Decisions**

✓ **REVIEW ANSWER** Reformers persuaded governments to create laws to protect workers. Workers formed labor unions to demand better conditions in the factory. 🔁 **Summarize**

Capitalism and Reformers

The economic system that arose during the Industrial Revolution was called capitalism. Under **capitalism,** private individuals own most factories and industries. These people run the businesses in order to make a profit. People who invested money were known as **capitalists.**

The capitalism that took hold in the industrialized nations was a market economy. In a **market economy,** the people make their own decisions about how to spend their money. To succeed in a market economy, capitalists have to know what people want. This influences the decisions that capitalists make about their businesses.

The market economy brought on by capitalism replaced a traditional economy. In a **traditional economy,** people work and spend their money in ways that do not change much from generation to generation.

One result of this change from a traditional to a market economy was that change occurred at a much quicker pace. Many questioned if all of these changes were better for people. Some people wanted the government to have some control over business.

Most capitalists believed that government controls were harmful to the growth of their businesses. The capitalists wanted to run their factories and businesses freely, without any government controls. These ideas about business were called *laissez faire* (LAY zay FAIR). *Laissez* *faire* is a French expression that means "leave it alone." Business owners believed that the system worked best when the government did not try to control it.

Many people were disturbed by the harsh conditions in the factory system. They rejected *laissez faire* ideas and wanted the government to correct many of the abuses. These people were known as **reformers,** because they wanted to keep capitalism but improve, or reform, it.

REVIEW Why did reformers reject *laissez faire* ideas? **Draw Conclusions**

480

Working Conditions

Pressure from reformers led governments in Europe and North America to pass laws that improved living and working conditions. For example, a British law limited the work day for children and women to ten hours. Other laws restricted the use of children and stopped the use of women, girls, and young boys in mines.

The workers themselves played a key role in improving conditions. They began to form labor unions to push their demands for better conditions. **Labor unions** represent all of the workers in a factory or an industry. They try to make the factory owner raise wages and improve working conditions. Unions use **strikes,** or the refusal to work, until their demands are granted.

In the 1700s, British workers had begun the first associations to help improve their working conditions. These were the first labor unions in Great Britain. As the unions grew more politically active, employers and the government grew hostile. In the early 1800s, many laws were passed to forbid labor unions. However, unions eventually became legal. By the late 1800s, workers' unions had become strong.

REVIEW How did people try to improve conditions for workers? 🔁 **Summarize**

▶ Union workers used strikes as a way of demanding better working conditions.

North Wind Picture Archives

Practice and Extend

❄️ MEETING INDIVIDUALS NEEDS
Leveled Practice

Build Meaning Help students understand the terms *capitalism, market economy, traditional economy, laissez faire,* and *reformer.*

Easy Have students work in a group and choose one or two terms for which to write definitions. Ask students to read aloud their definition so that one or two other group members can use the term in a sentence. **Reteach**

On-Level Have students write sentences comparing or contrasting two of the terms. Students will need to use at least one term twice. Pairs can exchange papers and discuss their sentences. **Extend**

Challenge Have students use the terms in a paragraph that explains how the terms are related. Alternatively, students may write an expository paragraph about each term. **Enrich**

For a Lesson Summary, use Quick Study, p. 116.

The Socialists

Reformers did not reject capitalism. They wanted to improve it. However, there were some people who blamed capitalism for many of society's problems. Some wanted to replace capitalism with an economic system called socialism. Under **socialism,** most industries, businesses, land, and natural resources are owned by the government, instead of individuals. Socialism was a form of **command economy,** in which the government or other central authority controls the flow of money.

Most socialists used peaceful means to promote their ideas. They formed political parties and struggled to win control of their nation's government in elections. However, some called for a revolution. One person who popularized socialist ideas and a revolt against the government was the German **Karl Marx.** He predicted a worldwide revolution that would bring about a society that had no separate economic classes.

During the 1800s and 1900s, many nations improved wages and working conditions. Workers in these nations gained many freedoms. They saw no need to overthrow the system.

► **Karl Marx was an early leader of the International Working Men's Association. Membership in this group was a mixture of reformers and socialists.**

REVIEW How were Karl Marx's ideas different from those of many other socialists? **Main Idea and Details**

Summarize the Lesson

- **c. 1850** Industries in the United States started using crude oil.
- **1877** Edison invented the phonograph.
- **1913** Ford Motor Co. began building automobiles on an assembly line.

LESSON 4 REVIEW

Check Facts and Main Ideas

1. **Main Idea and Details** On a separate piece of paper, fill in the diagram to give examples of familiar machines that were invented during the Second Industrial Revolution.

   > Many machines we use today were invented during the Second Industrial Revolution.

   | telephone | electric light bulbs | movie camera |

2. What is a corporation?

3. Why did reformers want to improve working conditions?

4. Who was Karl Marx?

5. **Critical Thinking: *Make Generalizations*** Do you believe that Thomas Edison's inventions improved people's lives? Explain your answer.

   Link to — Science

   Research on Your Own Thomas Edison spent years trying to develop electric lighting. Do some research to learn about the details of his experiments to design the light bulb.

481

The Socialists

Quick Summary Socialists were alarmed at the problems caused by capitalism and envisioned a society in which everyone could benefit from industry.

6 **How does capitalism differ from socialism?** In capitalism businesses are owned by individuals or corporations. In socialism most businesses, land, and natural resources are owned by the government. **Compare and Contrast**

✓ **REVIEW ANSWER** Karl Marx promoted a revolution and a society with no economic classes. **Main Idea and Details**

3 Close and Assess

Summarize the Lesson

Give students three minutes to list new ideas, inventions, and philosophies that came about during the Second Industrial Revolution. Lead students to compare and contrast the two Industrial Revolutions.

✓ **LESSON 4   REVIEW**

1. **Main Idea and Details** For possible answers, see the reduced pupil page.

2. It is a type of business organization that raises money by selling parts, or shares, of the company to the public, and then divides profits among its shareholders.

3. They were disturbed by the harsh conditions in the factory system.

4. He was a German who made socialist ideas popular. He favored a worldwide revolution to create a society with no economic classes.

5. **Critical Thinking: *Make Generalizations*** Students should mention a specific invention and give reasons to support their opinion.

Link to — Science

Encourage students to draw diagrams showing the parts of the light bulb and how they work.

❄ MEETING INDIVIDUAL NEEDS
Learning Styles

Report on the Second Industrial Revolution
Using their individual learning styles, students can report on the Second Industrial Revolution.

Visual Learning Students can create illustrated time lines of the Second Industrial Revolution. Encourage them to conduct research to find other inventions that were created during this time period and then add them to the time line, along with their dates of invention.

Linguistic Learning Students can write "a day in the life of…" journal entries. They can write from the point of view of a laborer, a capitalist, or a reformer.

Workbook, p. 118

Lesson 4: The Second Industrial Revolution
Directions: Write each term in the box beside its example or description.

Second Industrial Revolution	capitalism	labor union
internal combustion engine	market economy	socialism
electricity	laissez faire	Karl Marx
assembly line	reformer	

1. popularized socialist ideas and supported a classless society
2. organization formed to represent factory workers and demand higher wages and better working conditions
3. economic system in which private individuals own and run businesses for profit
4. run by oil made into gasoline
5. inventions that used electricity, oil, and steel for power and changed the way people lived and worked
6. manufacturing process in which individual workers add one part or perform one task to complete a product, such as an automobile
7. French expression meaning "leave alone;" beliefs that government should not control the business system
8. supplied light and power to machines, led to new forms of communication
9. economic system in which the government owns most industries, businesses, land, and natural resources
10. person who wanted to keep capitalism but correct abuses in the system
11. economy in which people make their own decisions about how to spend their money

Notes for Home: Your child learned about the Second Industrial Revolution and the struggle to improve conditions for workers.
Home Activity: With your child, create a Venn diagram to compare and contrast capitalism and socialism, and discuss the role of government in the United States today.

Also on Teacher Resources CD-ROM.

Resources

- Assessment Book, pp. 81–84
- Workbook, p. 119: Vocabulary Review

Chapter Summary

For possible answers, see the reduced pupil page.

Vocabulary

1. e, **2.** d, **3.** a, **4.** c, **5.** b

People and Terms

1. With the help of the French, General George Washington and the American army trapped the British force at Yorktown, forcing its surrender.

2. Simón Bolívar was the leader whose victories liberated northern South America from Spain.

3. Bernardo O'Higgins organized an army that joined forces with José de San Martín's army to force the Spanish out of Chile.

4. The Declaration of Independence was written to clearly state why the colonists were splitting from Great Britain.

5. During the Industrial Revolution, machines were developed that produced goods more quickly and cheaply.

6. Thomas Edison and his assistants were responsible for many inventions, including the electric light bulb, phonograph, and motion pictures.

7. Louis XVI was a weak king of France who was killed during the French Revolution.

8. Capitalism is the economic system in which private individuals own most businesses.

9. Socialism is an economic system where land, resources, and businesses are owned by the government and not by private citizens.

10. The Napoleonic Code was a system of laws developed by Napoleon to strengthen the government and to restore order following the French Revolution.

1750	1775	
1760s James Watt improved the steam engine.	**1789** Bastille fell; *Declaration of Rights of Man and of Citizen* issued.	**1793** Reign of Terror beg
1776 13 British colonies declared independence.		

Chapter Summary

Summarize

On a separate piece of paper, fill in the missing summary from the details.

Many skilled workers	Large quantities of natural resources	A market for goods to be purchased

Great Britain was well-suited to launch the Industrial Revolution

Vocabulary

Match each word with the correct definition or description.

1. **legislature** (p. 457)
2. **monarchy** (p. 467)
3. **textile** (p. 475)
4. **factory** (p. 475)
5. **strike** (p. 480)

a. cloth that is either woven or knitted

b. the refusal to work

c. a place where machines are grouped together

d. a government in which a king, queen, or emperor has supreme power

e. lawmaking body

People and Terms

Write a sentence identifying each of the following people and terms and explain their significance.

1. George Washington (p. 458)
2. Simón Bolívar (p. 462)
3. Bernardo O'Higgins (p. 462)
4. Declaration of Independence (p. 458)
5. Industrial Revolution (p. 475)
6. Thomas Edison (p. 479)
7. Louis XVI (p. 467)
8. capitalism (p. 480)
9. socialism (p. 481)
10. Napoleonic Code (p. 469)

Practice and Extend

Assessment Options

✓ Chapter 16 Assessment

- Chapter 16 Content Test: Use Assessment Book, pp. 81–82.
- Chapter 16 Skills Test: Use Assessment Book, pp. 83–84.

Standardized Test Prep

- Chapter 16 Tests contain standardized test format.

✓ Chapter 16 Performance Assessment

- Ask students to create Revolution Portfolios, focusing on the two different types of revolutions studied in this chapter.

- Students should define the two types of revolutions and create annotated collages for each type. Students can also add a time line to each collage with details about the revolutions in this chapter.

- Assess students' understanding of the ideas in this chapter as you read through their portfolios. Use students' work to ask probing questions about the material.

1800   1825   1850   1875   1900   1925

1821
Mexico won independence.

1876
Alexander Graham Bell invented the telephone.

1890
Edison invented a motion picture camera.

1913
Ford Motor Co. began building automobiles on an assembly line.

Facts and Main Ideas

1 Why did the British government tax the American colonists?

2 **Time Line** Which occurred first: the invention of the motion picture camera or the independence of Mexico?

3 **Main Idea** How did the policies of European nations lead to revolutions in the Americas?

4 **Main Idea** How did the French Revolution affect France and the rest of Europe?

5 **Main Idea** How did the Industrial Revolution affect people and economies?

6 **Main Idea** What was one important advantage to forming a corporation during the Second Industrial Revolution?

7 **Critical Thinking:** *Recognize Point of View* Do you think that the colonists in the Americas had the right to rebel against their government? Why or why not?

Write About History

1 Write a **journal entry** from the viewpoint of a French woman during the French Revolution. Should men and women get the same rights of citizenship?

2 Write a **"What If" story** describing what life might be like today if the Industrial Revolution had not occurred.

3 Write an **advertisement** urging colonists to join the movement to liberate Mexico. Make a poster using slogans, drawings, or other attention-grabbing techniques.

Apply Skills

Compare Primary Sources
Read the primary source below. Then answer the questions.

In 1819 the South American revolutionary leader Simón Bolívar spoke to other political leaders about the people and lands just liberated from the Spanish:

"We find that our quest for liberty is now even more difficult . . . for we, having been placed in a state lower than slavery, had been robbed not only of our freedom but also of the right to exercise an active domestic tyranny."

1 What important key word in this primary source is also used in one of the primary sources on page 472?

2 How is the meaning of that key word different in this primary source?

3 What was Simón Bolívar trying to tell his listeners?

Internet Activity

To get help with vocabulary, people, and terms, select dictionary, encyclopedia, or almanac from Social Studies Library at **www.sfsocialstudies.com**.

483

Hands-on Unit Project

✓ Unit 6 Performance Assessment

- See p. 510 for information about using the Unit Project as a means of performance assessment.
- A scoring guide is provided on p. 510.

WEB SITE
Technology

Students can select the dictionary, encyclopedia, or almanac from *Social Studies Library* at **www.sfsocialstudies.com**.

Workbook, p. 119

Vocabulary Review

Directions: Read the following statements. Then write T (True) or F (False) on the line before each statement. If the answer is false, correct the statement to make it true. Not all words will be used. You may use your textbook.

___ 1. A legislature is a lawmaking body that sets taxes and makes laws.

___ 2. A reformer is a government in which a king, queen, or emperor has supreme power.

___ 3. Workers bought raw materials such as cotton and produced thread to make textiles, or cloth that is either woven or knitted.

___ 4. Businesspeople lowered costs by grouping machines together in one large factory.

___ 5. In the cities, many workers lived in overcrowded slum apartments, called monarchies.

___ 6. A strike is a refusal to work until certain demands are granted.

Also on Teacher Resources CD-ROM.

Facts and Main Ideas

1. Because Great Britain was deeply in debt.

2. The independence of Mexico

3. European policies limiting or prohibiting self-government and controlling colonial wealth led to revolutions.

4. It ended the French monarchy and gained more rights for ordinary people, but it also resulted in great violence and many executions. The rest of Europe feared that the revolution would spread beyond France.

5. It created the factory system and better transportation but also led to poor working and living conditions in crowded city slums.

6. By selling stock shares to the public, corporations could afford to pay workers and buy machines.

7. Possible answers: Yes; because of unfair treatment (high taxes), lack of individual freedoms, desire to make decisions for themselves (self-government), limited economic opportunities under colonial rule. No; they were breaking the law, which would lead to conflict and bloodshed, and European nations provided safety and security for their colonies.

Write About History

1. Journal entries should be written from the first-person point of view and refer to the limits on women's rights.

2. Students' "what-ifs" will most likely include the idea of the domestic system. Accept reasonable ideas that are supported with details.

3. Students' advertisements should be persuasive and attention-grabbing. Consider teaching students about the use of such advertising techniques as loaded language, bandwagon approaches, and so on.

Apply Skills

1. *liberty*

2. Bolívar states that the people's lack of liberty denied them the right even to exercise control over their own domain.

3. The Spanish have not allowed South Americans the freedom to govern themselves.

CHAPTER 17

Chapter Planning Guide

Chapter 17 • Imperialism, Nationalism, and Unification

Locating Time and Place pp. 484–485

Lesson Titles	Pacing	Main Ideas
Lesson 1 **Expanding Empires** pp. 486–489	2 days	• By the 1800s, many European nations were building empires by conquering and colonizing other countries and territories.
Chart and Graph Skills: Interpret Circle Graphs pp. 490–491		• A circle graph shows the relationship between parts and the whole.
Lesson 2 **Imperialism in East Asia** pp. 492–496	2 days	• China and Japan experienced Western imperialism in different ways.
Biography: Meiji p. 497		• Emperor Meiji of Japan took an active role in government, leading the Japanese system toward democracy.
Lesson 3 **New Nations** pp. 498–503	2 days	• Nationalism led to new nations in Europe and the British colonies.
✓ **Chapter 17 Review** pp. 504–505		

This vase, created during the Qing dynasty, features the crucifixion of Jesus.

✓ = Assessment Options

Japanese Emperor Meiji was influenced by Western ideas and customs. ▶

Vocabulary	Resources	Meeting Individual Needs
nationalism imperialism imperialist	• Workbook, p. 121 • Transparencies 6, 50 • Every Student Learns Guide, pp. 234–237 • Quick Study, pp. 118–119 • Workbook, p. 122	• Leveled Practice, TE p. 487 • ESL Support, TE p. 488
treaty port compound modernization	• Workbook, p. 123 • Transparency 20 • Every Student Learns Guide, pp. 238–241 • Quick Study, pp. 120–121	• ESL Support, TE p. 494 • Leveled Practice, TE p. 495 • Learning Styles, TE p. 496
dominion parliament	• Workbook, p. 124 • Transparencies 11, 51, 52 • Every Student Learns Guide, pp. 242–245 • Quick Study, pp. 122–123	• ESL Support, TE p. 500 • Learning Styles, TE p. 501 • Leveled Practice, TE p. 503
	✓Chapter 17 Content Test, Assessment Book, pp. 85–86 ✓Chapter 17 Skills Test, Assessment Book, pp. 87–88	✓Chapter 17 Performance Assessment, TE p. 504

Providing More Depth

Additional Resources
- Vocabulary Cards
- Daily Activity Bank
- Social Studies Plus!
- Big Book Atlas
- Student Atlas
- Outline Maps
- Desk Maps

 Technology

- AudioText
- The test maker
- Teacher Resources CD-ROM
- Map Resources CD-ROM
- **www.sfsocialstudies.com**

 To establish guidelines for your students' safe and responsible use of the Internet, use the Scott Foresman Internet Guide.

Additional Internet Links
To find out more about:
- Queen Victoria, go to *History* and click on *Empires* at **www.pbs.org**
- Formosa, click on *Academics,* then *Departments, History, Research Aids* at **web.reed.edu**
- A detailed time line of Canadian history, click on *Time, Best Links, Canadian History* at **www.cbc4kids.ca**

Key Internet Search Terms
- Indian Mutiny
- Qing Dynasty
- Sardinia
- Australia

Workbook Support

Use the following Workbook pages to support content and skills development as you teach Chapter 17. You can also view and print Workbook pages from the Teacher Resources CD-ROM.

Workbook, p. 120

Use with Chapter 17.

Vocabulary Preview

Directions: Find the meaning of each vocabulary term from Chapter 17. Write the meaning on the lines provided. You may use your textbook.

1. nationalism

   strong devotion to one's own country

2. imperialism

   building up an empire by controlling or conquering lands in Africa, Asia, and elsewhere

3. imperialist

   European who promoted imperialism

4. treaty port

   port city where Europeans had special trading rights

5. compound

   enclosed area with buildings in it run by Europeans

6. modernization

   process of bringing ways and standards into the present day

7. dominion

   self-governing nation that still has ties with the ruling empire

8. parliament

   elected legislature that enacts laws and selects national leaders from its own members

 Notes for Home: Your child learned the vocabulary terms for Chapter 17.
Home Activity: Use each term in an original sentence. Have your child restate the meaning of each vocabulary term in his or her own words.

Use with Pupil Edition, p. 484

Workbook, p. 121

Use with Pages 486–489.

Lesson 1: Expanding Empires

Directions: Circle the term that best completes each sentence.

1. (Nationalism) Imperialism, Colonization), or a strong devotion to one's own country, was a powerful force that swept over Europe in the 1800s.

2. Europeans made huge profits by selling factory-made goods created from raw materials obtained from their (enemies, allies, (colonies)).

3. In the age of imperialism, (Spain, (Great Britain,) China) had the largest empire in the world.

4. During the 1800s (India,) Indochina, Egypt), was one of Great Britain's most valuable colonies.

5. Because many Indians were unhappy with British rule, called the (imperialism, reign, (Raj)), they rebelled.

6. The Indian National Congress, formed in 1885, began a movement toward (war, (independence) destruction) for India.

7. Because the ((Suez Canal,) Raj, Indians) shortened the sea route from England to India, the British wanted to control it.

8. Imperialism was at its height in (China, (Africa,) Asia), where lands were claimed by the European powers.

9. After the Berlin Conference, the only two African countries remaining independent were (Egypt and Libya, Ethiopia and Angola, (Ethiopia and Liberia)).

10. King Leopold II of Belgium controlled the Congo and forced Africans living there to (leave the region, (work for him,) go to war).

Directions: Sequence the events below on the time line.

British buy Egypt's ownership of Suez Canal	Indian troops rebel against British
European powers partition Africa	French begin Suez Canal

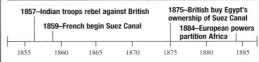

1857–Indian troops rebel against British **1875–British buy Egypt's ownership of Suez Canal**
1859–French begin Suez Canal **1884–European powers partition Africa**

1855 1860 1865 1870 1875 1880 1885

 Notes for Home: Your child learned about European expansion in Africa in the 1800s.
Home Activity: With your child, review this lesson and make a list of the effects of imperialism on Africa.

Use with Pupil Edition, p. 489

Workbook, p. 122

Use with Pages 490–491.

Interpret Circle Graphs

Directions: Answer the following questions about circle graphs on the lines provided. You may use your textbook.

1. What information does a circle graph show?

   the relationship between the parts of an item to the whole item

2. How is information on a circle graph represented?

   Possible answers: As portions or slices of a circle, with labels, color, or shading used to show what percentage each slice represents

3. What percentage of a whole does an entire circle represent? Half a circle? A quarter of a circle?

   100 percent; 50 percent; 25 percent

4. How do you read a circle graph to analyze the information on it?

   compare the sizes of the graph portions and draw conclusions from the information

5. When might someone choose to show information on a circle graph rather than as a paragraph of text?

   Possible answer: When the information gives parts of a whole and can be more easily understood in a graph than as text in a paragraph

 Notes for Home: Your child learned to interpret circle graphs.
Home Activity: With your child, identify how much time your child spends sleeping, at school, and on other activities in a typical day. Use this information to make a circle graph.

Use with Pupil Edition, p. 491

Workbook, p. 123

Use with Pages 492–496.

Lesson 2: Imperialism in East Asia

The actions of the European imperialists affected China and Japan differently.

Directions: Complete the chart by placing a (✔) in the correct column to identify where each event occurred. If the event occurred both in China and Japan, check the column labeled *Both*.

	China	Japan	Both
1. Qing dynasty powerless to keep out foreigners	✔		
2. Lost much of its land to other countries	✔		
3. Forced to open treaty ports			✔
4. Built up their armed forces and became more powerful		✔	
5. Could not arrest Europeans	✔		
6. Competed with Russia for control of Manchuria		✔	
7. Fought in the first and second Opium Wars	✔		
8. Began to be treated equally with Europeans		✔	
9. Started on a path of modernization under new ruler		✔	
10. Forced to open up country to trade			✔
11. "Boxers" wanted to destroy all foreign influences	✔		
12. Attracted European imperialists			✔
13. Gained island of Formosa and won influence in Korea		✔	
14. Went to war with Japan and was defeated	✔		
15. Considered a great world power after defeating Russia		✔	
16. Learned much about Western science and industry		✔	

 Notes for Home: Your child learned how imperialism affected China and Japan differently.
Home Activity: With your child, review information from the chapter and discuss what caused China to lose power while Japan became a world power. What might China have done differently to remain in control?

Use with Pupil Edition, p. 496

Workbook Support

Workbook, p. 124

Lesson 3: New Nations

Use with Pages 498-503.

Directions: Sequence the events leading to a united Italy in the order in which they took place. Number them from 1 (earliest) to 8 (most recent). You may use your textbook.

5 1. Southern Italy unites with the rest of the country; the kingdom of Italy is formally announced.

1 2. A movement for Italian unification builds.

7 3. Italy takes over Rome and makes it the Italian capital.

4 4. Giuseppe Garibaldi's army frees Sicily, Naples, and other parts of southern Italy.

2 5. Camillo di Cavour of the Kingdom of Sardinia forms an alliance with France; the allies attack Austria and drive the Austrians out of most of northern Italy.

8 6. Italy becomes a united nation.

3 7. Most states in northern and central Italy join with Sardinia under Victor Emmanuel II.

6 8. Italy takes over Venice and other nearby lands.

Directions: Match each dominion of the British Empire in the box to its description. Write the name of the dominion on the line. The terms will be used more than once.

Canada	Australia	New Zealand

Australia 9. began when colonists and convicts settled in New South Wales

Canada 10. included four provinces: Quebec, Ontario, New Brunswick, and Nova Scotia

New Zealand 11. originally settled by Polynesian people called the Maori

New Zealand 12. became a British dominion in 1907

New Zealand 13. William Hobson signed treaty making this a British colony

Australia 14. Sir Edmund Barton drew up constitution making this a British dominion in 1901

Canada 15. became first British dominion in 1867

 Notes for Home: Your child learned about new nations in Europe and the British colonies.
Home Activity: With your child, compare and contrast the German, Italian, and British nations. Why did they want to unify and build new nations? What changes did the governments make during the spread of nationalism?

Use with Pupil Edition, p. 503

Workbook, p. 125

Vocabulary Review

Use with Chapter 17.

Directions: Circle the vocabulary term that best completes each sentence. You may use your textbook.

1. Because the British were pressured by some of their colonies for self-rule, they prepared each colony to become a (parliament, (dominion,) treaty port).

2. A European treaty port ran its own (dominion, parliament, (compound,) or enclosed area.

3. A powerful feeling called (parliament, (nationalism,) modernization) led some people to believe that their country was better than all others.

4. Meiji and his advisors started Japan on a path of rapid (parliament, nationalism, (modernization,) because Japan wanted to catch up with the West.

5. An elected legislature, or ((parliament,) compound, imperialist), enacts laws and selects national leaders from its own members.

6. A European who promoted building up an empire by controlling or conquering lands was called an (imperialism, dominion, (imperialist).)

7. A city such as Shanghai, where Europeans had special trading rights, was called a ((treaty port,) dominion, compound).

8. An idea often linked to the nationalism of the 1800s was (modernization, parliament, (imperialism,) which meant building up an empire by controlling or conquering lands in Africa, Asia, and elsewhere.

Directions: Answer the following question on the lines provided.

9. How did Japan use modernization to become a great world power?

Japan studied Western science and industry and built up their armed forces to become more powerful. After Japan defeated both China and Russia, it was seen as a great world power.

 Notes for Home: Your child learned the vocabulary terms for Chapter 17.
Home Activity: Write each vocabulary word on a small slip of paper. Then make a second set of papers on which you write the definitions. Have your child practice matching each term with its definition.

Use with Pupil Edition, p. 505

Workbook, p. 126

6 Project **Arts and Letters**

Discovery SCHOOL

Directions: In a group, advertise an important invention in an infomercial.

1. Our invention: _____

2. The ✔ shows the information included in our infomercial:

___ invention name   ___ value (how it is helpful)

___ inventor's name   ___ price

___ description   ___ importance of invention

___ how to use it   ___ other: _____

3. Brief infomercial script (including facts about information above):

_____

_____

_____

_____

_____

_____

You may wish to gather relevant resources from your school or local library. Assist students, as needed, in selecting an invention and locating relevant information.

✔ Checklist for Students

___ We chose an invention.

___ We researched facts about the invention.

___ We wrote a script for our infomercial.

___ We made a poster to advertise the invention.

___ We presented our infomercial to the class.

Notes for Home: Your child learned about important inventions.
Home Activity: With your child, look for items in your home that are important to people's daily lives. Discuss how life might be different if these items had never been invented or produced.

Use with Pupil Edition, p. 510

Assessment Support

Use these Assessment Book pages and the test maker to assess content and skills in Chapter 17 and Unit 6. You can also view and print Assessment Book pages from the Teacher Resources CD-ROM.

Assessment Book, p. 85

Chapter 17 Test
Part 1: Content Test
Directions: Fill in the circle next to the correct answer.

Lesson Objective (1:1)
1. What effect did nationalism and imperialism have on some European countries in the 1800s?
● led them to expand their empires
Ⓑ reduced profits on factory-made goods
Ⓒ decreased feelings of patriotism
Ⓓ led to political unrest among citizens

Lesson Objective (1:2)
2. How did many Europeans feel about the effects of imperialism in their colonies?
Ⓐ They felt that people in the colonies wanted to become English citizens.
● They felt that people in the colonies were better off due to European influence.
Ⓒ They felt that people in the colonies were worse off than before colonization.
Ⓓ They felt that there were no benefits to the colonies.

Lesson Objective (1:5)
3. Why are Cecil Rhodes's ideas about English superiority considered to be opinions rather than facts?
Ⓐ They can be proven true.
● They cannot be proven true.
Ⓒ Rhodes never really claimed English superiority.
Ⓓ They are facts, not opinions.

Lesson Objective (1:4)
4. Which of the following areas was most affected by imperialism in the 1800s?
Ⓐ North America
Ⓑ South America
Ⓒ Eastern Europe
● Africa

Lesson Objective (1:3)
5. How might King Leopold's rule of the Congo be described?
Ⓐ fair
● cruel
Ⓒ peaceful
Ⓓ friendly

Lesson Objective (2:4)
6. What relationship did China have with Europe before the 1800s?
Ⓐ violent opposition
Ⓑ free access
● limited trade
Ⓓ forced cooperation

Lesson Objective (2:2)
7. What did the Chinese mean when they said that China was the "Middle Kingdom"?
● It was the center of civilization.
Ⓑ It was located in the middle of Asia.
Ⓒ It was neither the largest nor the smallest country.
Ⓓ It was at the midpoint of all ocean trade routes.

Lesson Objective (2:5)
8. How did the Qing dynasty prevent China from becoming modernized?
Ⓐ It limited opportunities for learning.
Ⓑ It stopped all trade with all other countries.
● It isolated China from European influences.
Ⓓ It insisted that the Chinese return to ancient traditions.

Use with Pupil Edition, p. 504

Assessment Book, p. 86

Lesson Objective (2:1)
9. What was the result of the first Opium War between Britain and China?
● Britain took Hong Kong and forced China to open five treaty ports.
Ⓑ China forced Britain out of Asia.
Ⓒ Britain occupied Beijing.
Ⓓ Millions of Chinese people died.

Lesson Objective (2:3)
10. What changes occurred in Japan after the Meiji emperor came to power?
● The country focused on technology and modernization.
Ⓑ Japanese shoguns took control of the government.
Ⓒ China and Japan worked together to keep out Western ideas.
Ⓓ The government became a victim of Western imperialism.

Lesson Objective (2:1)
11. Which of the following countries was most influenced by Western ideas?
Ⓐ China
● Japan
Ⓒ Hong Kong
Ⓓ Korea

Lesson Objective (3:4)
12. Why did Germans and Italians want to create their own nations?
Ⓐ They wanted to have their own colonies in the Americas.
Ⓑ They were unhappy with the Catholic Church.
Ⓒ They had no common languages or customs.
● They felt a strong sense of nationalism.

Lesson Objective (3:2)
13. What country served as a role model for Germans and Italians?
● Greece
Ⓑ France
Ⓒ Austria
Ⓓ Turkey

Lesson Objective (3:3)
14. How did Prussia help create a unified German empire?
Ⓐ set up a democratic system of government
Ⓑ negotiated deals with several other countries
● defeated neighboring countries in wars
Ⓓ inspired Germans to rise up and overthrow their rulers

Lesson Objective (3:4)
15. Which of the following was NOT a leader in the nationalist effort to unify Italy?
Ⓐ Giuseppe Mazzini
● Wilhelm II
Ⓒ Camillo di Cavour
Ⓓ Giuseppe Garibaldi

Lesson Objective (3:5)
16. How are British dominions different from other independent nations?
Ⓐ Dominions are self-governing nations.
Ⓑ They overthrew their rulers to form new nations.
● Dominions still have ties with the ruling nation.
Ⓓ They won their independence through war.

Use with Pupil Edition, p. 504

Assessment Book, p. 87

Part 2: Skills Test
Directions: Use complete sentences to answer questions 1–7. Use a separate sheet of paper if you need more space.

1. How did Europeans connect nationalism to imperialism? **Summarize**

   Nationalism is a strong feeling of devotion to one's country. For some people, nationalism meant believing their country was better than all others. This led to imperialism, or building an empire by conquering other lands.

2. How do you think Cecil Rhodes felt about citizens of Great Britain? Support your response. **Point of View**

   He believed the British were better than other people. He called them the "first race" and said that the world was better off because of British imperialism.

3. How did China and Japan respond to Western influences? **Generalize**

   China tried to isolate itself from Western influences; therefore, it could not keep up with advances in technology. Japan wanted to modernize, so it studied Western science and industry.

4. How did Japan establish itself as a world power in the late 1800s? **Summarize**

   Japan learned all it could about Western ideas and built on them to become competitive with the West. The Japanese then used these ideas to develop new technology, modernize their armed forces, and take over other lands.

Use with Pupil Edition, p. 504

Assessment Book, p. 88

5. How were the roads to independence similar for Germany and Italy? How were they different? **Compare and Contrast**

   Similar: both countries were formed by people who spoke the same language, shared customs, and wanted to create their own nation. Different: Germans fought three wars to conquer neighboring countries, then they declared their independence. Italians overthrew local rulers to unite as an independent nation.

6. Do you think the British dominions were truly independent? Explain. **Evaluate**

   Possible answer: No; The dominions were self-governing, but they were closely tied to Great Britain in language, culture, and system of government.

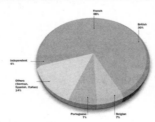

7. Use the circle graph to answer the questions. **Interpret Circle Graphs**
   a. What kind of information does a circle graph show?

   the relationship among the parts of a whole

   b. What does the whole circle represent? Africa's entire land area

   c. Who colonized the largest area of African land? How do you know?

   the French; the French portion of the graph is the largest.

Use with Pupil Edition, p. 504

Assessment Support

Unit 6 Test

Part 1: Content Test

Directions: Fill in the circle next to the correct answer.

Lesson Objective (15–1:1)

1. Which of the following is NOT a change that occurred in Europe during the Renaissance?
   - ● stronger ties to the Catholic Church
   - Ⓑ a renewed interest in art and science
   - Ⓒ more realistic art and sculpture
   - Ⓓ advances in technology

Lesson Objective (15–1:3)

2. What caused the Reformation?
   - Ⓐ the emergence of Protestantism
   - Ⓑ growing support of the Pope
   - ● disputes over indulgences and the interpretation of the Bible
   - Ⓓ belief that the Church had complete authority over people's lives

Lesson Objective (15–2:2)

3. What prompted European countries to explore Africa?
   - Ⓐ a desire to establish cities there
   - ● the hope of finding gold and other riches
   - Ⓒ a growing demand for silk and spices
   - Ⓓ the desire for independence

Lesson Objective (15–2:1)

4. Why did many European countries search for ocean routes to Africa?
   - Ⓐ Land routes were controlled by Asian traders.
   - Ⓑ Traveling by land was convenient.
   - Ⓒ Traveling by sea was the only way to reach Africa.
   - ● Land routes were dangerous and costly.

Lesson Objective (15–3:4)

5. Which is NOT a reason why European countries founded colonies?
   - ● decrease the country's population
   - Ⓑ establish new markets
   - Ⓒ obtain new resources
   - Ⓓ increase their wealth

Lesson Objective (15–3:3)

6. What did the encomienda system allow some colonists to do?
   - Ⓐ keep any gold or silver that they found
   - ● force Native Americans to work for them
   - Ⓒ set up new governments
   - Ⓓ force Native Americans to form new colonies

Lesson Objective (16–1:2)

7. Why did colonists in North America want independence from British rule?
   - Ⓐ They could not afford to pay more for tea.
   - Ⓑ The British government had promised not to raise taxes again.
   - ● They felt that they were being taxed without fair representation.
   - Ⓓ They thought Great Britain exaggerated the cost of government.

Lesson Objective (16–1:3)

8. Who was Miguel Hidalgo?
   - Ⓐ an army officer who defeated the Spanish army in Peru
   - Ⓑ a ruler who overthrew the Mexican government
   - Ⓒ a military leader who fought for the independence of Haiti
   - ● a Mexican priest who urged all Mexicans to fight for independence

Lesson Objective (16–2:1)

9. What led to the French Revolution?
   - Ⓐ the struggle of French colonies to become independent
   - ● an unfair system of taxation
   - Ⓒ religious differences among French citizens
   - Ⓓ a standoff between the king and the French army

Lesson Objective (16–3:1, 4, 5)

10. Which of the following was NOT an effect of the Industrial Revolution?
    - Ⓐ Many people in Great Britain moved from the country to the city.
    - Ⓑ Many goods began to be produced in large factories.
    - ● Several countries experienced hard economic times.
    - Ⓓ Living and working conditions grew worse in large cities.

Lesson Objective (16–4:1)

11. Which of the following machines that we use today was invented during the Second Industrial Revolution?
    - Ⓐ television
    - ● telephone
    - Ⓒ washing machine
    - Ⓓ microwave oven

Lesson Objective (17–1:1)

12. Why did some European countries begin to build large empires in the 1800s?
    - Ⓐ They wanted to build large factories there.
    - Ⓑ They needed to spread Christianity.
    - Ⓒ They wanted to buy raw materials for their factories.
    - ● They were swept up by a sense of nationalism.

Lesson Objective (17–2:1)

13. Which country isolated itself in the 1800s to avoid Western influences?
    - ● China
    - Ⓑ Japan
    - Ⓒ Taiwan
    - Ⓓ Korean

Lesson Objective (17–2:3)

14. What was the effect of the Meiji emperor's efforts to modernize Japan?
    - Ⓐ Other countries broke off trade relations with Japan.
    - ● Japan became a world power.
    - Ⓒ Cooperation between Japan and China increased.
    - Ⓓ Japan fell further behind Western countries.

Lesson Objective (17–3:4)

15. What led to independence for Italy and Germany?
    - ● a strong sense of nationalism among Germans and Italians
    - Ⓑ Prussia's friendship with Denmark
    - Ⓒ rising tensions between Austria and France over Italy and Germany
    - Ⓓ the decline of many large European empires

Lesson Objective (17–3:5)

16. In what way were British dominions not independent?
    - Ⓐ The legislatures selected their own leaders.
    - Ⓑ They were settled by the British and other Europeans.
    - Ⓒ Each made laws for its country.
    - ● Each government included a governor-general, who represented the British monarchy.

Part 2: Skills Test

Directions: Use complete sentences to answer questions 1–6. Use a separate sheet of paper if you need more space.

1. What effects of the Renaissance can still be seen today? **Apply Information**

   Many of the techniques in art and new technologies developed during the Renaissance are still used today. Many of our ideas about science are based on discoveries made during the Renaissance.

2. Why do you think so many revolutions took place around the world between 1700 and 1800? **Draw Conclusions**

   Possible answer: Each revolution influenced the next one. The ideas of freedom and independence quickly spread to different areas and encouraged others toward self-rule.

3. How did the First and Second Industrial Revolutions change the world? **Summarize**

   Possible answer: The Industrial Revolution used machine power, such as the steam engine, rather than human and animal power to make goods more quickly and on a larger scale. Inventions of the Second Industrial Revolution, such as the electric light bulb and electric power, changed how everyday people lived and worked.

4. How did the responses of China and Japan to Western imperialism in the 1800s differ? **Compare and Contrast**

   Both countries had been forced to open treaty ports to European trade. In China this led to resentment, then to revolts within the country, and to war with Japan. Japan used Western influences to achieve modernization and become a world power, rather than a victim of imperialism.

5. How did nationalism affect Europe during the 1800s? **Cause and Effect**

   Nationalism contributed to imperialism by encouraging some European countries to expand their empires and establish colonies around the world. It also encouraged some Europeans to unite and form their own nations.

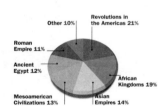

Other 10%
Revolutions in the Americas 21%
Roman Empire 11%
Ancient Egypt 12%
African Kingdoms 19%
Mesoamerican Civilizations 13%
Asian Empires 14%

6. The graph shows the results of a student questionnaire about the world history topics they enjoyed the most. Use the graph to answer the questions. **Interpret Circle Graphs**
   a. What do the percentages represent on the graph?

   the percent of students who prefer each topic

   b. Which topic is the most popular?

   Revolutions in the Americas

   c. How does the circle graph help you quickly interpret the results of the questionnaire?

   Possible answer: Comparing the size of the circle pieces is quicker and easier than comparing the actual percentages.

Imperialism, Nationalism, and Unification

Chapter 17 Outline

- **Lesson 1,** *Expanding Empires,* pp. 486–489
- **Chart and Graph Skills:** *Interpret Circle Graphs,* pp. 490–491
- **Lesson 2,** *Imperialism in East Asia,* pp. 492–496
- **Biography:** *Meiji,* p. 497
- **Lesson 3,** *New Nations,* pp. 498–503

Resources

- Workbook, p. 120: Vocabulary Preview
- Vocabulary Cards
- Social Studies Plus!

late 1800s, South Africa: Lesson 1

This picture shows a diamond mine in South Africa. Ask students why a mine like this might be important to a country's economy.

1900, China: Lesson 2

This image shows a harbor in a busy Chinese trading port around the turn of the 19th century. Ask students what evidence they can see in the picture that China has opened its doors to other nations. (A European ship appears in among the Chinese boats.)

1867, Canada: Lesson 3

Tell students that these three stamps are from countries that Great Britain once controlled. Have students name these places (Canada, New Zealand, Australia) and locate them on a world map.

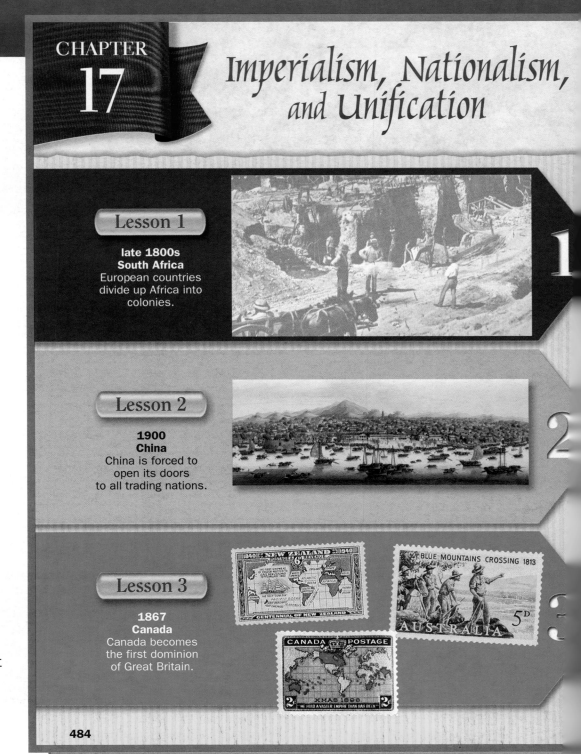

CHAPTER
17

Imperialism, Nationalism, and Unification

Lesson 1

late 1800s
South Africa
European countries divide up Africa into colonies.

Lesson 2

1900
China
China is forced to open its doors to all trading nations.

Lesson 3

1867
Canada
Canada becomes the first dominion of Great Britain.

484

Practice and Extend

Vocabulary Preview

- Use Workbook p. 120 to help students preview the vocabulary words in this chapter.
- Use Vocabulary Cards to preview key concept words in this chapter.

Also on Teacher Resources CD-ROM.

Workbook, p. 120

Vocabulary Preview

Directions: Find the meaning of each vocabulary term from Chapter 17. Write the meaning on the lines provided. You may use your textbook.

1. nationalism

2. imperialism

3. imperialist

4. treaty port

5. compound

6. modernization

7. dominion

8. parliament

Locating Time and Place

Locating Time and Place

- Have students examine the pictures shown on p. 484 for Lessons 1, 2, and 3.

- Remind students that each picture is coded with both a number and a color to link it to a place on the map on p. 485.

Why We Remember

Have students read the "Why We Remember" paragraph on p. 485, and ask them why events in this chapter might be important to them. Explain that colonization was one way a nation could grow in wealth and power. Ask students what they think it would be like to live in a colony that belongs to another country and what effects they think colonization has had on the modern world.

Why We Remember

Today we live in a global culture. Most of us come into contact with people of many ethnic groups, nationalities, and religions. However, in the 1800s, interaction was more limited. For many people, such contact was only through the creation of colonies. The European powers wanted more resources. They were anxious to create empires. European powers began to search for lands they could colonize. The experiences of colonization brought diverse cultures face to face on a large scale. Colonization has had lasting effects on the world we live in today.

485

WEB SITE
Technology

You can learn more about South Africa, China, and Canada by clicking on *Atlas* at www.sfsocialstudies.com.

SOCIAL STUDIES STRAND
Geography

Mental Mapping On an outline map of the countries of the world, have students label the following: Australia, Canada, China, Egypt, England, France, Germany, India, Indochina, Italy, Japan, and South Africa. Then, using colored pencils, ask them to circle the names of those nations who were imperialist powers in 1900. Finally, have students underline in the same colors the names of those areas under each one's colonial control.

Expanding Empires

Objectives

- List ways in which nationalism and imperialism led European nations to form empires in the 1800s.

- Explain why some Europeans believed that imperialism would benefit people in their colonies.

- Identify ways in which King Leopold's rule in the Congo was harsh.

- Locate the parts of the world where European countries built empires in the 1800s.

- Explain why Cecil Rhodes's ideas did or did not have solid evidence to support them.

Vocabulary

nationalism, p. 487; **imperialism,** p. 487; **imperialist,** p. 487

Resources

- Workbook, p. 121
- Transparency 6
- Every Student Learns Guide, pp. 234–237
- Quick Study, pp. 118–119

Quick Teaching Plan

If time is short, have students create webs with *empire* as the central concept and record details about empires on the "spokes" of the web as they read the lesson independently.

1 Introduce and Motivate

Preview Have students recall empires they have already studied. Tell students they will learn more about empires created by Europeans in the 1800s as they read Lesson 1.

You Are There Some Europeans hoped to strengthen their countries and increase their wealth by creating colonies in Africa. Ask students how they might have felt if they had been forced to change their way of life.

486 Unit 6 • Discovery, Expansion, and Revolutions

LESSON 1

1850

1857
Indian Mutiny

1869
Suez Canal opens.

1885
Congo Free State is set up.

1900

GERMANY — Berlin
Suez Canal
EGYPT
CONGO FREE STATE
INDIA — FRENCH INDOCHINA
SOUTH AFRICA

PREVIEW

Focus on the Main Idea
By the 1800s, many European nations were building empires by conquering and colonizing other countries and territories.

PLACES
South Africa
India
Suez Canal
Indochina
Berlin
Congo Free State

PEOPLE
Cecil Rhodes
Victoria
Tilak
Leopold II

VOCABULARY
nationalism
imperialism
imperialist

EVENTS
Indian Mutiny
Berlin Conference

Expanding Empires

You Are There

Another work day begins. You watch as the people before you prepare for 12 hours of hot, hard, dirty work. At noon they receive a cold baked yam, some dry corn, and a little water to drink. The work master allows exactly 20 minutes for this snack he calls a meal.

You barely remember the days before the European masters came to this part of the Congo. At one time your family raised corn, yams, and beans in their own fields. With older brothers and sisters you fished in the big river. Life was lively in your village. In the evenings, elders shared stories about village ancestors. You shared songs and jokes. Now it's sad to think these memories are growing dimmer and dimmer.

▶ **Africans labored under harsh, often cruel conditions for the European conquerors.**

Summarize As you read, try to summarize how European nations built world empires.

486

Practice and Extend

READING SKILL
Summarize

In the Lesson Review, students complete a graphic organizer like the one below. You may want to provide students with a copy of Transparency 6 to complete as they read the lesson.

Use Transparency 6

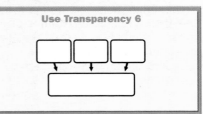

WEB SITE
Technology

- You can look up vocabulary words by clicking on *Social Studies Library* and selecting the dictionary at **www.sfsocialstudies.com.**

- Students can learn more about current news by clicking on *Current Events* at **www.sfsocialstudies.com.**

- Explore other events that occurred on this day by clicking on *This Day in History* at **www.sfsocialstudies.com.**

Nationalism and Imperialism

Why did the Europeans go into the Congo in Africa, conquer African peoples, and force them to work for their European masters? A powerful force called nationalism swept over Europe in the 1800s. **Nationalism** is a strong devotion to one's own country. For some people, nationalism meant wanting to unify or strengthen their country. For others, it meant believing that their country was better than all others.

Another idea that was often linked to nationalism was imperialism. In the 1800s, **imperialism** meant building up an empire by controlling or conquering lands in Africa, Asia, and elsewhere. The Europeans who promoted imperialism were called **imperialists.**

Imperialism made huge profits for the Europeans. European countries got raw materials such as cotton, rubber, oil, minerals, sugar, tea, and coffee from their colonies. In return, Europeans sold their own factory-made goods to the colonies—always at a nice profit.

▶ **Cecil Rhodes made a fortune in the diamond mines of South Africa.**

They believed that the conquered peoples were better off because of European influence. They believed they were spreading Christianity and European civilization to people they considered less advanced.

Many Europeans believed that they were better than the non-Europeans in their colonies. **Cecil Rhodes** was one such person. This British empire-builder developed diamond mines in **South Africa.** He became very rich. Rhodes said:

> *"I say that we are the first race in the world, and that the more of the world we inhabit [live in] the better it is for the human race."*

❸

REVIEW Summarize the two powerful forces that swept over Europe in the 1800s.
⤶ Summarize

▶ **The Kimberley Mine in South Africa was founded after farmers started discovering diamonds on their land. This photo is from 1872, shortly after mining operations began.**

487

Teach and Discuss

Nationalism and Imperialism

🕐 ***Quick Summary*** As nationalism and imperialism swept over Europe, Europeans established colonies to extend their power and wealth.

❶ **Give at least two effects of nationalism.** Strong devotion to one's own country, which could mean a desire to unify or strengthen that country or a belief that one's country is better than others **Cause and Effect**

Ⓗ **SOCIAL STUDIES STRAND**
History

❷ **How did imperialism benefit the Europeans who established the colonies? How did it affect the non-Europeans?** The Europeans made large profits because the colonies were a source of raw materials and a market for European factory-made goods. Those who were conquered often lost their traditional way of life and much of their freedom. ⤶ **Summarize**

Primary Source

Cited in *A Global History* by L. S. Stavrianos

❸ **What do you think may have contributed to Rhodes's feelings of superiority?** Possible answer: Rhodes was probably influenced by nationalism. He may not have had an understanding of South African culture and therefore judged it as inferior. **Analyze Primary Sources**

✓ Ongoing Assessment

If... students are unable to suggest reasons for Rhodes's attitude,	**then...** remind students that the world was not as "connected" in the nineteenth century as it is today. Many people did not have the opportunity to learn about other cultures and thought their way of life was best.

✓ REVIEW ANSWER Nationalism and imperialism ⤶ Summarize

Empires in Asia and Africa

 Quick Summary Several European countries established colonies in Asia and Africa.

4 **Why did the British call India the "jewel in the crown"?** India held great riches and was very valuable to Great Britain. **Main Idea and Details**

Primary Source

Cited in *A Global History* by L. S. Stavrianos

5 **What caused Indians like Tilak to revolt? What was the result of their rebellion?** Tilak felt that he had a right to be free; like Tilak, many Indians were unhappy under British rule. The Indian Mutiny was put down, but in 1885 a group of Indians formed the Indian National Congress, which would lead the way to India's independence movement. **Cause and Effect**

6 **Why was the Suez Canal so important to Great Britain?** The canal provided a shorter route from Great Britain to India. This would allow the British to strengthen their empire and continue to build their wealth. **Draw Conclusions**

MAP SKILL **Impact of the Suez Canal on European–Indian Trade**

7 **Describe the shorter route from London to Bombay.** A ship would travel south from London on the Atlantic Ocean, east across the Mediterranean Sea, south through the Suez Canal and Red Sea, and east across the Arabian Sea to India. **Interpret Maps**

MAP SKILL **Answer** About 5,000 miles

8 **What was the purpose of the Berlin Conference?** Several European powers wanted to claim African lands; they met in Berlin to divide up Africa. **Main Idea and Details**

Empires in Asia and Africa

In the age of imperialism, Great Britain had the world's largest empire. British colonies were scattered all over the globe. During the reign of Queen **Victoria,** Great Britain's monarch, it was claimed that "the sun never sets on the British Empire." This meant that the British Empire had colonies all over the world. So even when the sun was setting in Great Britain, it was rising somewhere else in the empire.

India was a valuable colony to Great Britain. The British called India the "jewel in the crown." **4** India held great riches. Great Britain had controlled parts of India since the 1600s. British rule there became known as the *Raj.* This word means "rule" or "reign" in Hindi, a language of India.

Many Indians were unhappy under the Raj. In 1857 Indian troops rebelled. The revolt, called the **Indian Mutiny,** was soon put down. In 1885 a group of Indians formed the Indian National Congress. In time, this organization would lead the way to that country's independence movement. A rebel Indian leader named **Tilak** expressed:

5 *"Freedom is my birthright and I will have it!"*

▶ This illustration shows ships passing through the Suez Canal shortly after it was completed in 1869.

488

Great Britain extended its imperial activities into Egypt. The French had dug the **Suez Canal** across Egypt, beginning in 1859 and finishing ten years later. This waterway linked the Mediterranean Sea to the Indian Ocean. Because the canal shortened the sea route from England to India, the British wanted to control it. In an effort to fight French control of the canal, the British bought all of Egypt's ownership (44 percent) of the canal in 1875.

Other European nations also colonized in South and Southeast Asia. France took control of **Indochina.** This region includes present-day Vietnam, Cambodia, and Laos. The Netherlands controlled the islands that became Indonesia.

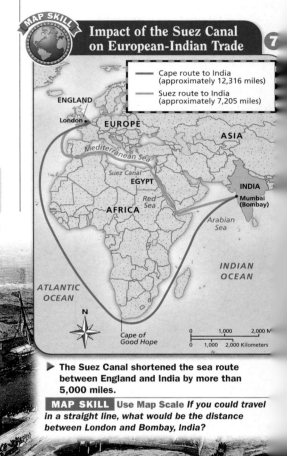

MAP SKILL **Impact of the Suez Canal on European-Indian Trade** **7**

Cape route to India (approximately 12,316 miles)
Suez route to India (approximately 7,205 miles)

ENGLAND
London
EUROPE
Mediterranean Sea
ASIA
Suez Canal
EGYPT
INDIA
Mumbai (Bombay)
Red Sea
AFRICA
Arabian Sea
ATLANTIC OCEAN
INDIAN OCEAN
N
Cape of Good Hope
0 1,000 2,000 M
0 1,000 2,000 Kilometers

▶ The Suez Canal shortened the sea route between England and India by more than 5,000 miles.

MAP SKILL Use Map Scale *If you could travel in a straight line, what would be the distance between London and Bombay, India?*

Practice and Extend

ESL **EXTEND LANGUAGE** **ESL Support**

Examine Context Clues Help students use context clues and visuals, if necessary, to determine the meanings of unfamiliar words and figures of speech.

Beginning Model using simple words, pantomime, or pictures to present the meanings of these words according to their context in the first paragraph on p. 489: *scramble, meet, invite,* and *remained.* Then have students take turns giving clues for and identifying the words.

Intermediate Have students identify the context clue for *partition* in the first paragraph on p. 489 ("divide up"). Then have students reread the entire second paragraph to figure out the meaning of *harshest.*

Advanced Tell students that words are sometimes used in ways that differ from their usual meanings. Help students use context clues to explain the phrases *cast a long shadow* and *reached its height* on p. 489.

For additional ESL support, use Every Student Learns Guide, pp. 234–237.

However, European imperialism reached its height in Africa. Spain and Portugal had long held lands there. Other European powers began to "scramble" for African lands. In 1884 the European powers decided to meet in **Berlin,** Germany, to partition, or divide up, Africa. They never invited any Africans to attend. At the **Berlin Conference,** France, Great Britain, Germany, Belgium, and Italy all claimed parts of African territory. Finally, only two African countries remained independent: Ethiopia and Liberia.

In Africa, European imperialism was at its harshest. Belgium's King **Leopold II** controlled the Congo region of Central Africa. In 1885 he

▶ **This woodcut offers a glimpse of life in an African village before contact with European conquerors.**

managed to have the **Congo Free State** set up with himself as ruler. Africans living in this area were forced to work for Leopold. Leopold was widely criticized for cruel treatment of the Africans. After 20 years of this cruelty, the Congo's population had fallen by about one-half.

European imperialism cast a long shadow over Africa's future. In Unit 8 you will read how, after years of struggle, the African nations gained their independence.

REVIEW Why did Great Britain want control of the Suez Canal? *Draw Conclusions*

Summarize the Lesson

— **1857** Indian troops, unhappy with British rule, revolted in the Indian Mutiny.

— **1869** Egypt's Suez Canal opened, making travel between Europe and India much faster.

— **1885** Belgium's King Leopold II set up the Congo Free State, which treated Africans brutally.

LESSON 1   REVIEW

Check Facts and Main Ideas

1. 🔄 **Summarize** On a separate piece of paper, fill in the details of the summary.

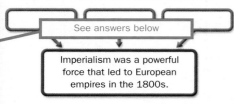

See answers below

Imperialism was a powerful force that led to European empires in the 1800s.

2. Why did some Europeans believe that imperialism would benefit people in colonies?

3. What evidence could you offer to show that King Leopold's rule in the Congo was harsh?

ef in superiority white race | Countries competing for colonies | Industrialization created a need for raw materials and new markets.

4. In what parts of the world did Europeans build their empires in the 1800s?

5. **Critical Thinking:** *Detect Bias* Do you think that Cecil Rhodes could back up his opinions with solid evidence? Why or why not?

Link to ⦿⦿ **Writing**

Write a Paragraph Explain whether or not you think that it was fair that no Africans were invited to the Berlin Conference. Explain how the outcome of the conference might have been different if they had attended.

489

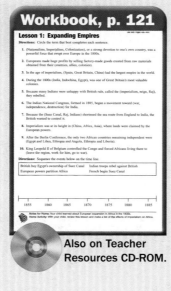

Workbook, p. 121

Lesson 1: Expanding Empires

Directions: Circle the term that best completes each sentence.

1. (Nationalism, Imperialism, Colonization), or a strong devotion to one's own country, was a powerful force that swept over Europe in the 1800s.

2. Europeans made huge profits by selling factory-made goods created from raw materials obtained from their (enemies, allies, colonies).

3. In the age of imperialism, (Spain, Great Britain, China) had the largest empire in the world.

4. During the 1800s (India, Indochina, Egypt), was one of Great Britain's most valuable colonies.

5. Because many Indians were unhappy with British rule, called the (imperialism, reign, Raj), they rebelled.

6. The Indian National Congress, formed in 1885, began a movement toward (war, independence, destruction) for India.

7. Because the (Suez Canal, Raj, Indian) shortened the sea route from England to India, the British wanted to control it.

8. Imperialism was at its height in (China, Africa, Asia), where lands were claimed by the European powers.

9. After the Berlin Conference, the only two African countries remaining independent were (Egypt and Libya, Ethiopia and Angola, Ethiopia and Liberia).

10. King Leopold II of Belgium controlled the Congo and forced Africans living there to (leave the region, work for him, go to war).

Directions: Sequence the events below on the time line.

British buy Egypt's ownership of Suez Canal | Indian troops rebel against British
European powers partition Africa | French begin Suez Canal

1855 1860 1865 1870 1875 1880 1885

Also on Teacher Resources CD-ROM.

✓ **REVIEW ANSWER** If the British controlled the Suez Canal, they could command the shortest route to India. **Draw Conclusions**

③ Close and Assess

Summarize the Lesson

Ask students to explain the motivation for and effects of each event on the time line.

✓ **LESSON 1   REVIEW**

1. 🔄 **Summarize** For possible answers, see the reduced pupil page.

2. They believed that imperialism would bring Christianity and the benefits of civilization to people in their colonies.

3. The population of the Congo dropped by about one-half in the first 20 years of the Congo Free State.

4. In the 1800s Europeans built their empires mostly in Asia and Africa.

5. **Critical Thinking:** *Detect Bias* Rhodes said that the English and the white race were above other nationalities and races. But he could not have had much information about other nations, cultures, and races, so his opinions were biased in favor of what he did know about.

Link to ⦿⦿ **Writing**

Encourage students to state their opinions at the beginning of their paragraphs and to include as many facts as possible to support these opinions. Accept reasonable explanations for differing outcomes.

Interpret Circle Graphs

Objective

- Interpret data from circle graphs that describe parts of a whole.

Resource

- Workbook, p. 122

1 Introduce and Motivate

What is a circle graph? Spark discussion on how historians might use a circle graph, or a graph that shows parts of a whole. You might have students find circle graphs in math or other texts to discover what types of data are represented with circle graphs. Then have students read the **What?** section of text on p. 490.

Why use a circle graph? Have students read the **Why?** section of text on p. 491. Ask them what the "slices" on a circle graph represent.

2 Teach and Discuss

How is this skill used? Examine with students the graph and the map on pp. 490–491.

- Point out that the graph has a title that tells what information is being shown. In any circle graph, the entire circle represents 100 percent of something. Students should note that the individual numbers, when added, will equal 100.

- Have students compare the graph to the map on p. 491. Explain that circle graphs convey data at a glance to make it easier to understand. Ask students why a circle graph is easier to use than a simple list of percentages. (A circle graph gives a picture of how parts of something are related to the whole.)

- Have students read the **How?** section of text on p. 491.

Interpret Circle Graphs

What? A circle graph shows the relationship between the parts and a whole. It can help you understand the relative proportions of the parts that make a whole. In a circle graph, an entire circle represents all, or 100 percent, of something. Half the circle represents 50 percent. A quarter circle represents 25 percent.

African Colonies and Protectorates (Area), 1914

The title of a circle graph tells you what quantity is illustrated. This graph illustrates the extent of colonization in Africa in 1914.

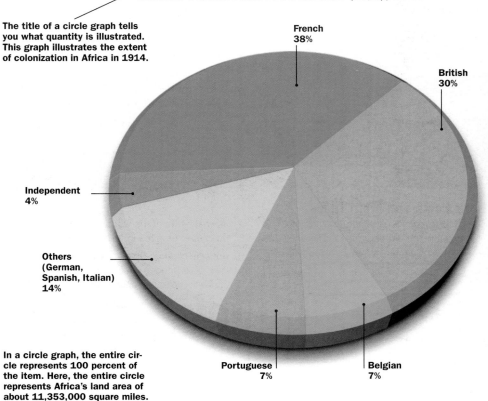

- French 38%
- British 30%
- Belgian 7%
- Portuguese 7%
- Others (German, Spanish, Italian) 14%
- Independent 4%

In a circle graph, the entire circle represents 100 percent of the item. Here, the entire circle represents Africa's land area of about 11,353,000 square miles.

In a circle graph, percents of the whole are shown by portions of the entire circle. Here, 38 percent is represented by a little more than one third of the circle. From the graph you can read that 38 percent of Africa's land area was colonized by the French.

490

Practice and Extend

 CURRICULUM CONNECTION
Math

Create Circle Graphs

Have students create circle graphs.

- Students can survey classmates on a particular topic and then display the results in a circle graph.
- Students might also make circle graphs to represent data from reference sources such as almanacs.
- You may want to provide compasses and protractors to help students draw their graphs.

Why? A circle graph can make it easier to interpret data that describes parts of a whole. Smaller slices stand for smaller amounts. Larger slices stand for larger amounts.

Imperialism in Africa, 1914

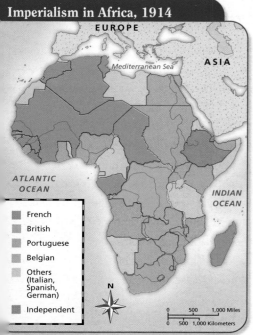

EUROPE

ASIA

Mediterranean Sea

ATLANTIC OCEAN

INDIAN OCEAN

- ◼ French
- ◼ British
- ◼ Portuguese
- ◼ Belgian
- ◼ Others (Italian, Spanish, German)
- ◻ Independent

N

0   500   1,000 Miles
0   500   1,000 Kilometers

► **Use the colors indicated on the map and map key to match the countries with the circle graph on page 490.**

How? To use a circle graph to answer specific questions, compare the sizes of the graph portions. Often these portions are labeled with the percent of the whole they represent. For example, the graph on the previous page can be used to answer the questions "Which European country colonized the greatest portion of Africa?" and "Over how much land did it rule?"

First find the greatest portion on the graph. You can see that 38 percent is the greatest area represented.

Check the label to find out which country's holdings are represented. You can see that the French colonies covered about 38 percent of Africa in 1914.

❸
❹

Think and Apply

❶ About what percent of Africa's land was ruled by the British?

❷ Whose land holdings in Africa were greater, those of Great Britain or France? How do you know?

❸ Explain how to use the graph to tell whether the following statement is true. "Together France and Great Britain controlled two-thirds of Africa's lands."

491

❶ What do you think makes a circle graph easy to use? A circle graph shows the relationship between the parts and a whole. When you look at a circle graph, it is easy to identify the largest segment as the largest percentage of the whole. **Generalize**

❷ Compare and contrast the circle graph and the map in terms of the information they give. Both give information about African colonies. The map shows the exact location of the colonies, while the circle graph tells the relative amount of land held by each country. **Compare and Contrast**

❸ What percentage of Africa was independent in 1914? 4% **Interpret Graphs**

❹ Who held more land in Africa—the Portuguese or British? British **Compare and Contrast**

❸ Close and Assess

Think and Apply

1. About 30%

2. The graph shows that France held a greater portion of land in Africa, 38% compared with Great Britain's 30%.

3. Two-thirds of a whole is about 67%. Adding together the percentage of land area controlled by the French (38%) and the area controlled by the British (30%) shows it is true that these two countries controlled more than two-thirds of Africa's land (68%).

CURRICULUM CONNECTION
Writing

Write About Circle Graphs

- Ask students to write detailed explanations of their answers to Think and Apply. Encourage them to use sequence words to show the steps in the process.

  Have students write directions for creating circle graphs. Encourage them to illustrate each step in the process.

  Help students locate a circle graph in another class text. Have them write three questions about the graph for classmates to answer.

Workbook, p. 122

Interpret Circle Graphs

Directions: Answer the following questions about circle graphs on the lines provided. You may use your textbook.

1. What information does a circle graph show?

2. How is information on a circle graph represented?

3. What percentage of a whole does an entire circle represent? Half a circle? A quarter of a circle?

4. How do you read a circle graph to analyze the information on it?

5. When might someone choose to show information on a circle graph rather than a paragraph of text?

Notes for Home: Your child learned to interpret circle graphs.
Home Activity: With your child, identify how much time your child spends sleeping, at school, and on other activities in a typical day. Use this information to make a circle graph.

Also on Teacher Resources CD-ROM.

Imperialism in East Asia

Objectives

- Describe how the Western nations affected China and Japan in the 1800s.

- Describe the belief behind China's reference to itself as the "Middle Kingdom."

- Describe the ways in which Japan changed after Meiji came to power in 1868.

- Describe the relationships that China and Japan had with Western countries before the 1800s.

- Explain why the Qing Dynasty did or did not provide leadership necessary to modernize China.

Vocabulary

treaty port, p. 494; **compound,** p. 494; **modernization,** p. 495

Resources

- Workbook, p. 123
- Transparency 20
- Every Student Learns Guide, pp. 238–241
- Quick Study, pp. 120–121

Quick *Teaching Plan*

If time is short, provide outline maps showing the locations listed under *Places* on p. 492. Students can take notes about these places as they read the lesson independently.

1 Introduce and Motivate

Preview Have students recall what motivated imperialism in Africa and the problems that resulted. Tell students they will learn about imperialism in East Asia as they read Lesson 2.

You Are There In the 1800s, many Europeans established colonies in Asia. Have students predict what life may have been like for Europeans living in East Asia during this period.

| 1800 | 1850 | 1900 | 1950 |

1839
First Opium War

1900
The Open Door Policy opens China's ports to all trading nations.

1904
Russia and Japan go to war over Manchuria.

Imperialism in East Asia

PREVIEW

Focus on the Main Idea
China and Japan experienced Western imperialism in different ways.

PLACES
Hong Kong
Canton
Shanghai
Beijing
Macao
Formosa (Taiwan)
Manchuria

PEOPLE
Ci Xi
Matthew Perry
Meiji
Theodore Roosevelt

VOCABULARY
treaty port
compound
modernization

TERMS
Qing dynasty
Open Door Policy

EVENTS
Opium War

492

 You Are There

May 30, 1888

Dear Diary,

The weather in Shanghai was beautiful again today. We had a picnic in Victoria Park. (It has a Chinese name, but I can't spell it.) The food was tasty. I had fun talking to Yvette in French. She says my accent is quite good! Yvette's father works in the treaty port, just like my poppa. But he works for France instead of England.

Sometimes I wonder what Chinese children are like. We never see them. Only workers and traders come into the European compound. I'd love to know what kinds of games the Chinese children play and which subjects they study in school. I bet Chinese children are not much different from Yvette and me.

Yours truly,
Claire

Cause and Effect As you read, keep in mind how actions of the European imperialists affected China and Japan.

Practice and Extend

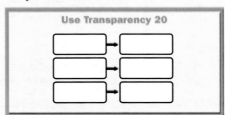

READING SKILL
Cause and Effect

In the Lesson Review, students complete a graphic organizer like the one below. You may want to provide students with a copy of Transparency 20 to complete as they read the lesson.

Use Transparency 20

WEB SITE
Technology

- You can look up vocabulary words by clicking on *Social Studies Library* and selecting the dictionary at **www.sfsocialstudies.com.**

- Students can learn more about current news by clicking on *Current Events* at **www.sfsocialstudies.com.**

- Explore other events that occurred on this day by clicking on *This Day in History* at **www.sfsocialstudies.com.**

The Middle Kingdom

Europeans colonized other parts of the world besides Africa. They were attracted to the riches of China. During the 1700s Britain had traded in China for tea, silk, and porcelain. However, Chinese officials strictly controlled this trade. They wanted as little contact with Europeans as possible.

Chinese culture was often isolated, or set apart, from other cultures. Their own word for China means "Middle Kingdom." The Chinese traditionally believed that their country was surrounded on all sides by inferior, "barbarian" peoples. The Chinese considered all foreigners who did not share Chinese customs, culture, and language to be barbarians.

As you read in Chapter 12, the Ming dynasty came to power in 1368. When that dynasty weakened, the **Qing** (CHIHNG) **dynasty** took power in 1644. Arts, learning, and trade flourished under

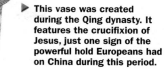

▶ This vase was created during the Qing dynasty. It features the crucifixion of Jesus, just one sign of the powerful hold Europeans had on China during this period.

the Qing. However, the Chinese would soon pay a price for trying to avoid contact with Europeans and European ideas.

In spite of its proud past, Chinese technology was not able to match the progress made by the Europeans. By the 1800s, China had fallen far behind Western nations. Chinese boats and weapons were inferior to modern European ships and guns. As time went on, the Qing dynasty became powerless to keep out the foreigners.

REVIEW Why were the Chinese opposed to foreigners? Main Idea and Details

▶ This view of Canton in about 1800 shows the increasing European presence in China. Note the European-style buildings.

493

SOCIAL STUDIES
Background

China in the 1800s

- At the end of the eighteenth century, the population of China was about 300 million. The Qing dynasty had established order, and the nation was peaceful and prosperous.
- By 1850 the population had jumped to more than 400 million. All the land in China that could be cultivated was already in use, so there was no land available to grow additional food.
- In the mid-1800s many Chinese lived in poverty. They were unable to cope with natural disasters such as floods and droughts.
- While the country expanded, the government remained the same size. It was unprepared to provide services for a rapidly growing population.

Teach and Discuss
PAGE 493

The Middle Kingdom

🕐 *Quick Summary* Despite a long self-imposed isolation, China was unable to keep out foreigners who wanted to control trade and share in the country's riches.

Test Talk

Locate Key Words in the Question

❶ **Why did China put tight controls on trade with other countries?** Make sure students understand the question. Then have them find the key words *China, controlled,* and *trade.* Chinese officials wanted as little contact with Europeans as possible. **Main Idea and Details**

❷ **What characteristic of nationalism was part of the Chinese tradition?** The Chinese considered themselves superior to foreigners who did not share Chinese customs, culture, and language. **Apply Information**

❸ **What do you think the Chinese people valued? Why do you think so?** Chinese people valued their heritage and tried to preserve it. They wanted as little contact with Europeans as possible. **Evaluate**

❹ **Why did Chinese technology lag behind technology in other parts of the world?** Because of its policy of isolation, China did not share ideas with Europeans who were developing new technology. Arts and a traditional way of life were more valued than technological progress. **Draw Conclusions**

✓ **REVIEW ANSWER** They believed that Chinese customs, culture, and language were better than anyone else's. Anyone who was not Chinese was considered a barbarian. **Main Idea and Details**

Western Imperialists in China

Quick Summary European imperialists gained control by forcing China to open its port cities and grant the Europeans trading rights.

$ SOCIAL STUDIES STRAND
Economics

Establishing trade relations with foreign countries provided Great Britain with additional markets for its goods and strengthened the British economy.

5 Why was it important for the British to have treaty ports in China? The British had special trading rights in these cities, so they were guaranteed markets for their goods and the profits that this trade would bring.
Analyze Information

---

6 Why do you think the Chinese government was powerless to stop the spread of imperialism in its country? Possible answer: Several European countries wanted to take land in China, and the Chinese lacked the technology to fight all the imperialists. **Draw Conclusions**

✓ Ongoing Assessment

| **If...** students are unable to draw a conclusion as to why the Chinese were powerless to stop the spread of imperialism, | **then...** have students reread the last paragraph on p. 493 and share with them the background information on that page. Ask students what advantages Europe had over China. |

China: Territory Gained by European Imperialists and Japan

7 Which parts of China remained free of foreign influence? The central part and a strip of land in the southeast
Interpret Maps

MAP SKILL Answer Japan

Western Imperialists in China

In the late 1700s, the British started bringing opium into China to trade for Chinese goods. Opium is a powerful and addictive drug. The Chinese government repeatedly told Great Britain to stop exporting opium. Great Britain refused. In 1839 China and Great Britain went to war over this issue. This war is known as the first **Opium War.** By 1842 Great Britain had defeated China. The British received **Hong Kong** in return. They then forced China to open five treaty ports. **5 Treaty ports** were port cities such as **Canton** and **Shanghai,** where Europeans had special trading rights. Europeans ran their own **compounds,** or enclosed areas with buildings in them. The Chinese police were not even allowed to arrest Europeans.

Soon, Great Britain wanted more treaty ports. In the late 1850s, the British, now joined by the French, fought against China in the second Opium War. They occupied China's capital, **Beijing** (bay JEENG), and forced China to open more treaty ports. By this time, Russia, Germany, and other countries wanted a piece of China. Even Portugal took the port of **Macao** (muh KOW).

Meanwhile, resentment had been growing in China. The Chinese government appeared unable to stop the European imperialists. A huge rebellion broke out in 1850. The Qing dynasty finally put down the revolt in 1864, but only after millions of Chinese had died.

A final blow for China came in 1894 when it went to war with Japan. Japanese forces easily defeated Chinese troops by 1895.

MAP SKILL China: Territory Gained by European Imperialists and Japan

▶ Japan became an imperialist nation and gained territories from several countries.

 MAP SKILL **Use Latitude and Longitude** Which imperialist nation gained the territory located at 40° north, 120° east?

494

Practice and Extend

ESL ACCESS CONTENT
ESL Support

Use Graphic Organizers Use various types of graphic organizers to understand the page.

Beginning Have students write the heading *Countries That Occupied China in the 1800s* on a sheet of paper. Below it have students draw a large circle with *China* written on it and below it six connecting circles with a country name in each one. (Great Britain, France, Russia, Germany, Portugal, Japan).

Intermediate Have students make a time line indicating what happened in China on these dates: 1842, late 1850s, 1864, 1894.

Advanced Have students make a cause-and-effect chart that allows for multiple effects. Under *Cause* have students write *Great Britain defeated China in the Opium Wars.* Then have students list effects (e.g., *Great Britain got treaty ports.*) and possible effects of those effects (e.g., *British ran compounds.*).
For additional ESL support, use Every Student Learns Guide, pp. 238–241.

► Empress Ci Xi was one of the most powerful women in China's history.

The Qing empress **Ci Xi** (tsee SHYEE), who kept out foreigners and prevented progress in China, expressed China's anger:

"The foreigners are the curse of China . . . . For forty years I have lain on brushwood and eaten bitterness because of them." ⑧

In 1898 another revolt broke out in China. A powerful group known as "the Boxers" wanted to destroy all foreign influences. But again, the Europeans gained the upper hand. In 1900 they sent another army into Beijing and defeated the Boxers. The United States, which also was interested in China, set up an **Open Door Policy** in 1900. According to this policy, every country had equal opportunity to trade with China. With this policy, foreigners remained in control of China.

The days of European control of China were numbered. In Unit 7 you will read how the twentieth century brought dramatic changes to China.

REVIEW What were the effects of European imperialism on China? *Cause and Effect*

► The Chinese were powerless to prevent the British from bringing opium into China.

Japan and the West

In 1853 U.S. naval official **Matthew Perry** sailed warships into a Japanese harbor. He demanded that the Japanese authorities accept a letter from the U.S. president, demanding that Japan open treaty ports. In 1854 Japan opened its ports to trade.

As you read in Unit 5, Japan's shoguns had kept their country closed off from the outside world for two centuries. But some Japanese had begun to worry. They wondered if Japan would end up like China, a victim of Western imperialism.

In 1868, the last shogun handed over his power to a forward-looking emperor. This new leader, **Meiji** (MAY jee), and his advisors started Japan on a path of rapid modernization. **Modernization** is the process of bringing ways and standards into the present day. In this case, Japan wanted to improve technology to catch up with the West.

The Japanese now began to study Western science and industry. They built up and modernized their armed forces.

As Japan became more powerful, Western imperialists began to treat it differently from China. They ended their treaty port policies in Japan. Some governments even began to treat Japanese diplomats equally with Europeans.

As you have read, Japan defeated China in a war in 1895. As a result, Japan gained the island of **Formosa** (Taiwan). Japan also won influence in Korea, which it took over in 1910.

REVIEW Put the following events in correct order and give a date for each: Japan went to war with China; Japan took over Korea; The last shogun handed power over to Meiji; Matthew Perry arrived in Japan. *Sequence*

► The first railway line in Japan began service in 1872. This painting details one of the train stations along the route. ⑩

495

Primary Source
Cited in *The Dragon Empress*, by Marina Warner

⑧ **What did the empress mean when she said that she had "eaten bitterness"?** Possible answer: She had tasted, or experienced, suffering and sadness because people from foreign lands had invaded China and taken control of many territories.
Analyze Primary Sources

Test Talk

Locate Key Words in the Text

⑨ **Summarize the provisions of the Open Door Policy.** Have students find key words from the text such as *policy, China, equal,* and *trade* to support their answer. Every country had equal opportunity to trade with China, so foreigners remained in control of China. **Summarize**

✓ **REVIEW ANSWER** China went to war with the Europeans and Japan. China was forced to open treaty ports for all of those countries interested. The Chinese people rebelled against the government. **Cause and Effect**

PAGE 495

Japan and the West

🕐 *Quick Summary* As Japan adopted a policy of modernization and became more powerful, the country gained the respect of Western imperialists.

⑩ **Why was there a difference between the way Western imperialists treated Japan and the way they treated China?** Japan started on a path of rapid modernization. The Japanese improved technology and modernized their armed forces. Some governments began to regard Japan as an equal. **Cause and Effect**

✓ **REVIEW ANSWER** Matthew Perry arrived in Japan—1853; the last shogun handed power over to Meiji—1868; Japan went to war with China—1894; Japan took over Korea—1910. **Sequence**

A New World Power

🕐 **Quick Summary** Japan's victory over Russia in the battle for control of Manchuria established Japan as a world power.

⑪ **Why do you think Western imperialists were shocked when Japan defeated Russia?** Possible answer: Japan had been considered technologically inferior to European countries, and therefore less powerful. **Draw Conclusions**

✓ **REVIEW ANSWER** Victory in the war against Russia in 1904
Main Idea and Details

3 Close and Assess

Summarize the Lesson

Ask students to write quiz questions about content in this lesson. Use the questions to conduct a class review session.

✓ **LESSON 2** **REVIEW**

1. **Cause and Effect** For possible answers, see the reduced pupil page.

2. The Chinese traditionally believed that their country was surrounded on all sides by inferior "barbarian" peoples who did not share their customs, culture, and language.

3. Japan borrowed ideas from the West and modernized rapidly.

4. China wanted as little contact with Europeans as possible so trade was strictly controlled. Japan had been closed off from the outside world for two centuries.

5. **Critical Thinking: Make Inferences** Possible answer: No; the Qing policy of avoiding contact with Europeans prevented them from sharing ideas that would have fostered technological growth.

Link to 🔗 Art

Students should include details that indicate advanced technology, such as a modern transportation system.

A New World Power

Meanwhile, Japan and Russia competed for control of **Manchuria**, the northeastern region of China. In 1904 they went to war. To the shock of the Western imperialists, Japan defeated Russia quickly. Japan was ⑪ then considered a great world power, much like those in Europe. In 1905 Japan and Russia agreed to a peace treaty offered by U.S. President **Theodore Roosevelt.** Roosevelt later won a Nobel Peace Prize for helping to end this war.

Japan had proven that Asians could hold their own against the Western powers. In Unit 7 you will read how Japan and the United States clashed in a war.

REVIEW What event caused Japan to be considered a world power? **Main Idea and Details**

▶ Japanese troops await an attack from the Russians in Manchuria in 1905.

Summarize the Lesson

- **1839** The first Opium War began after Chinese officials demanded that Great Britain stop bringing opium into China.

- **1900** The Open Door Policy opened China's ports to all trading nations.

- **1904** Russia and Japan went to war over control of Manchuria.

LESSON 2 **REVIEW**

Check Facts and Main Ideas

1. **Cause and Effect** On a separate piece of paper, fill in the missing cause or effect.

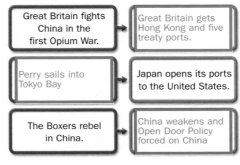

Great Britain fights China in the first Opium War.	→	Great Britain gets Hong Kong and five treaty ports.
Perry sails into Tokyo Bay	→	Japan opens its ports to the United States.
The Boxers rebel in China.	→	China weakens and Open Door Policy forced on China

2. What traditional Chinese belief explains the name "Middle Kingdom" for China?

3. How did Japan change after Meiji came to power in 1868?

4. Before the 1800s, what contact did China and Japan have with Western countries?

5. **Critical Thinking: Make Inferences** Do you think the Qing dynasty provided the leadership needed to modernize China in the 1800s? Explain your answer.

Link to 🔗 Art

Analyze Visual Art Look at the Japanese painting in the right-hand column on page 495. What can you learn from this painting about Western influence in Japan?

Practice and Extend

MEETING INDIVIDUAL NEEDS
Learning Styles

Imperialism in Eastern Asia Students can use their individual learning styles to explore the ideas about imperialism.

Visual Learning Ask students to create a piece of art or a political cartoon that emphasizes the differences between China and Japan and the way in which the two countries were viewed by imperialists.

Verbal Learning Students can work in pairs to play a game. One student gives a clue about China, Japan, or both; the other identifies which country is being described.

Workbook, p. 123

Lesson 2: Imperialism in East Asia
The actions of the European imperialists affected China and Japan differently.
Directions: Complete the chart by placing a (✓) in the correct column to identify where each event occurred. If the event occurred in both in China and Japan, check the column labeled *Both.*

	China	Japan	Both
1. Qing dynasty powerless to keep out foreigners			
2. Lost touch of its land to other countries			
3. Forced to open treaty ports			
4. Built up their armed forces and became more powerful			
5. Could not arrest Europeans			
6. Competed with Russia for control of Manchuria			
7. Fought in the first and second Opium Wars			
8. Began to be treated equally with Europeans			
9. Started on a path of modernization under new ruler			
10. Forced to open up country to trade			
11. "Boxers" wanted to destroy all foreign influences			
12. Attracted European imperialism			
13. Gained island of Formosa and won influence in Korea			
14. Went to war with Japan and was defeated			
15. Considered a great world power after defeating Russia			
16. Learned much about Western science and industry			

Notes for Home: Your child learned how imperialism affected China and Japan differently.
Home Activity: With your child, review information from the chapter and discuss what caused China to change and Japan to become a world power. What might China have done differently to avoid...

Also on Teacher Resources CD-ROM

Meiji

1852–1912

Emperor Meiji was the first Japanese ruler in more than two centuries who did not view Western nations and ideas with suspicion. The young emperor studied traditional Japanese subjects. However, he also studied German and European politics. These all greatly influenced his thought and rule.

In 1868 he was crowned emperor and changed his name from Mutsuhito to Meiji, which means "enlightened rule." He then took the "Charter Oath of Five Principles." The Charter Oath said that the Japanese would no longer live in the past:

"Evil customs of the past shall be discontinued, and new customs shall be based on the just laws of nature."

The government, economy, and military were modeled after those in the West. Meiji wore Western-style clothes and ate Western food. When Japan's first railway opened, Meiji appeared before the public to mark the occasion. Meiji also took an active role in the government.

BIOFACT

Emperor Meiji wrote more than 100,000 traditional Japanese poems during his lifetime.

Although government officials were responsible for writing laws, Meiji had to approve all legislation.

In 1889 Japan passed its first constitution. The new constitution reduced the emperor's role significantly. However, Meiji remained involved in the government, especially in military matters. When war broke out against China in 1894, he left Tokyo for eight months to supervise the military. During Meiji's rule, Japan became a major world power.

Learn from Biographies

How did Meiji's new government lean toward democratic principles?

Réunion des Musées Nationaux

For more information, go online to *Meet the People* at **www.sfsocialstudies.com.**

CURRICULUM CONNECTION
Writing

Write About Influential Leaders

- Students can write an original poem about Meiji and his influence on modern Japan. Encourage them to use colorful, descriptive words.

- Students can write about other influential leaders who caused great change in their nations. Remind students to include background information and a list of accomplishments.

Meiji

Objective

- Identify the contributions of significant individuals, including Meiji, who helped modernize Asian nations.

1 Introduce and Motivate

Preview To activate prior knowledge, ask students what they know about Meiji and his role in modernizing Japan. Tell them they will learn more about Meiji and how his ideas impacted Japan's rise to the status of a world power.

Ask what Meiji's actions show about accepting new ideas. (New philosophies can be blended with traditions to strengthen a country.)

2 Teach and Discuss

- Ask students what influenced Meiji's thoughts and actions. (He studied German, European politics, and traditional Japanese subjects.)

- Ask students what influences their thoughts and actions. (Ideas of parents and teachers, things they read)

① Compare and contrast Meiji with the emperors who had preceded him. Like emperors who had come before him, Meiji wanted what was best for Japan. Unlike previous rulers, he adopted Western ideas, modeling the government, economy, and military after those in the West. **Compare and Contrast**

3 Close and Assess

Learn from Biographies Answer

It passed its first constitution, which significantly reduced the emperor's role in the government.

New Nations

Objectives

- List these important events in chronological order: Australia and Canada become dominions, Garibaldi liberates southern Italy, Germany becomes an empire, and Greece becomes independent.

- Describe the influence Greece had on Germany and Italy.

- Identify Prussia's most important contribution to the German Empire.

- Explain the importance of nationalism in the formation of a unified Italy and a unified Germany.

- Explain whether or not the British dominions were truly independent.

Vocabulary

dominion, p. 502; **parliament,** p. 502

Resources

- Workbook, p. 124
- Transparency 11
- Every Student Learns Guide, pp. 242–245
- Quick Study, pp. 122–123

Quick Teaching Plan

If time is short, have students list each new nation, explain how it was formed, and tell who was involved in its formation as they read the lesson independently.

1 Introduce and Motivate

Preview Ask students to think about the challenges of living in an empire where people have different languages, customs, and traditions. Tell students that they will learn about the unification of regions that had been controlled by various nations as they read Lesson 3.

You Are There Italian patriots favored the formation of an Italian nation. Have students tell whether or not they agree and give reasons for their opinion.

LESSON 3

1850   1900

1861
Italy becomes a unified nation.

1871
German Empire is created.

1867
Canada becomes a dominion.

PREVIEW

Focus on the Main Idea
Nationalism led to new nations in Europe and the British colonies.

PLACES
Germany
Italy
Prussia
Venice
Rome
Canada
Australia
New Zealand

PEOPLE
Giuseppe Mazzini
Otto von Bismarck
Wilhelm II
Camillo di Cavour
Victor Emmanuel II
Giuseppe Garibaldi
Sir John MacDonald
Sir Edmund Barton
William Hobson

VOCABULARY
dominion
parliament

New Nations

You Are There Over dessert and coffee your father and Uncle Karl have a loud and bitter argument. Your father says that Italy has been divided up like a pie for too long. Italians should have their own nation. Uncle Karl protests that Italy is better off under the strong, protective arm of Austria. They go back and forth arguing until their faces turn bright red. Everyone at the table shifts and squirms. Mother and Aunt Cecilia try to change the subject. Later you begin to think about what has been said. Doesn't it make sense for Italians to have their own country? Why should Austria—or any other country—rule Italy? You wonder if someone will come forward to lead Italy in becoming a unified nation.

▶ Parts of present-day Germany and present-day Italy were controlled by Austria-Hungary, whose flag is pictured here.

Sequence As you read, keep the events that led to new nations in their correct chronological order.

498

Practice and Extend

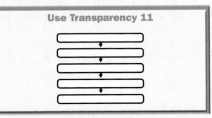

READING SKILL
Sequence

In the Lesson Review, students complete a graphic organizer like the one below. You may want to provide students with a copy of Transparency 11 to complete as they read the lesson.

Use Transparency 11

WEB SITE
Technology

- You can look up vocabulary words by clicking on *Social Studies Library* and selecting the dictionary at **www.sfsocialstudies.com.**

- Students can learn more about current news by clicking on *Current Events* at **www.sfsocialstudies.com.**

- Explore other events that occurred on this day by clicking on *This Day in History* at **www.sfsocialstudies.com.**

Nationalism and Unification

In Lesson 1, you read how European nationalism contributed to imperialism. Nationalism also encouraged some countries to unify and build new nations. Two such nations were **Germany** and **Italy**.

Giuseppe Mazzini was an influential Italian patriot.

For hundreds of years, there had been no German or Italian nation. France and Austria controlled parts of Germany. Austria also controlled northern Italy. A king ruled over the "Kingdom of the Two Sicilies" in southern Italy. The pope, or head of the Roman Catholic Church, ruled territories in central Italy.

In the 1800s, an Italian patriot named **Giuseppe Mazzini** (joo SEH peh mat ZEE nee) said:

> **1** *"A nation is the universality [sum total] of citizens speaking the same language."*

The people of Italy wanted their own nation. Likewise, the people of Germany wanted a nation of their own.

Germans and Italians looked to Greece as an example. For nearly 500 years, the Ottoman Empire had ruled Greece. The Ottomans had a different language, customs, history, and religion than Greece had. In the 1820s, the people of Greece had fought a war of independence. Finally, in 1830, Greece became an independent nation. By the mid-1800s, the Germans and Italians were ready to fight for their own nations too.

REVIEW Describe the states of Germany and Italy before the 1850s. ⟳ Summarize

MAP SKILL Italy and Germany, 1850 **4**

▶ In 1850, Italy and Germany were made up of many states and territories, some of which were under the control of Austria-Hungary.

MAP SKILL Use an Inset Map *What continent lies just to the south of the island of Sicily?*

499

Nationalism and Unification

🕐 ***Quick Summary*** The spirit of nationalism prompted Germany and Italy to form independent nations.

Primary Source

Cited in *Europe: A History*, by Norman Davies

1 **Do you agree with Mazzini's definition of *nation*? Explain.** Possible answer: Speaking the same language may unify a group of people, but sharing the same customs, history, and values may be even more important in forming a nation. **Analyze Primary Sources**

2 **Describe what Germany and Italy were like prior to the early 1800s. How did nationalism affect the people who lived there?** Italy and Germany were made up of smaller states. The people wanted to create unified nations. **Main Idea and Details**

3 **How did events in Greece affect Italians and Germans?** Greece had gained independence from the Ottoman Empire. Events in Greece inspired Italians and Germans to seek their own independence. **Cause and Effect**

✓ **REVIEW ANSWER** Germany and Italy were not nations; instead, each was made up of states and territories. Foreign powers ruled in both countries—Austria, a king, and the pope ruled in Italy; Austria and France controlled parts of Germany. ⟳ Summarize

Italy and Germany, 1850

4 **Of which country was Hanover a part? Which country included the Papal States?** Hanover was part of Germany; the Papal States were part of Italy. **Interpret Maps**

MAP SKILL Answer Africa

CURRICULUM CONNECTION
Writing

What Is a Nation?

- Giuseppe Mazzini defined *nation* as the "universality of citizens speaking the same language." Encourage students to write in response to the question: What is a nation?

- Students could write poems or essays. They might interview classmates and family members to gather various ideas about the definition of *nation*.

- Allow time for students to share their work with the class, and discuss the various interpretations of *nation*.

A German Nation

 **Quick Summary** After winning several key victories, Prussians declared Germany a united empire. Germany became a powerful country.

Test Talk

Use Information from the Text

5 What was Otto von Bismarck's goal? How did he obtain it? Tell students to skim the text to find the names and places that will support their answer. His goal was to unify the German Empire and make it a major power in Europe. He obtained his goal by leading Prussia to victory in wars against Denmark, Austria, and France. **Summarize**

Primary Source

Cited in *Oxford Dictionary of Quotations*, by Elizabeth Knowles

6 What attitudes did Kaiser Wilhelm convey in this quotation? Explain your answer. Possible answer: Wilhelm conveyed confidence, ambition, and a sense of superiority. He says that Germany has a place in the sun, or a favored position, and it will not give up its power. **Analyze Primary Sources**

✓ **REVIEW ANSWER** The new kaiser, Wilhelm II, was ambitious and determined that Germany should remain a great world power. This made other European powers fearful. **Cause and Effect**

German Reunification

Have students look at the large photograph of the Berlin Wall.

7 Which images in the photograph indicate the separate "Germanys"? Possible answers: Soldiers, weapons, barbed wire **Analyze Pictures**

A German Nation

Prussia was the largest and most powerful German state. **Otto von Bismarck** was its clever prime minister, or head of government. He led Prussia in three wars to unify Germany. Bismarck said he wanted to "put Germany in the saddle" in Europe.

Prussia first defeated its neighbor Denmark in 1864. Then it turned on Austria in 1866 and won a quick victory. Finally, Prussia fought France in 1870–1871. Again, Prussia won a quick victory. With all of these interfering neighbors out of the way, the Prussians declared Germany a united empire. Prussia's king became the kaiser (KEYE zuhr), or emperor, of unified Germany.

Germany grew rapidly into a powerful country. But its government, located in Prussia, was not democratic. Prussia was also the center of support for the military and warfare. A new kaiser, **Wilhelm II,** later explained:

> *"We have . . . fought for our place in the sun and have won it. It will be my business to see that we retain this place in the sun unchallenged."* **6**

Wilhelm II meant that Germany had fought to become a great world power. France, Great Britain, and other European countries began to fear Germany's power and ambition. In Chapter 18, you will read how these fears helped draw Europe into war in 1914.

REVIEW Why were France and the other European powers fearful of a united Germany? **Cause and Effect**

German Reunification

In this lesson you have learned how German states united into one Germany in 1871. In 1990 Germany was reunited once again. How did this happen? After World War II, the United States and the Soviet Union set up separate "Germanys"—a democratic one in the west and a communist one in the east. Germany remained divided until the late 1980s. Changes in the Soviet Union allowed Germans to reach out across their borders. Today, Germany is again one country.

7

▶ The Brandenburg Gate (below) was completed in the 1790s to represent peace but became part of the Berlin Wall which separated East and West Germany from 1961 to 1989.

▶ The Berlin Wall was a grim reminder of a Germany divided in half. Finally, it was broken through in November 1989.

500

Practice and Extend

 BUILD BACKGROUND
ESL Support

Use Maps and Discussions Help students build background for learning about how the first united Germany began.

Beginning Give students a labeled outline map showing the divided German states and their neighboring countries. Have students point to or color Prussia, Denmark, Austria, and France.

Intermediate Have students decide which would be more powerful—one German state by itself or the group of states unified—and why.

Advanced Have students make a web with the words *No Democracy* in the center. In connecting circles they can write characteristics of a nondemocratic country.

For additional ESL support, use Every Student Learns Guide, pp. 242–245.

A United Italy

Meanwhile, a movement for unification was building in Italy. One leader of this movement, Giuseppe Mazzini, wanted Italians to overthrow their rulers and form a united, democratic Italy.

Another supporter of a united Italy was **Camillo di Cavour** (kuh VOOR), prime minister of the Kingdom of Sardinia. Cavour wanted to unify Italy under Sardinia's king, **Victor Emmanuel II.**

In 1859 Cavour formed an alliance with France to attack Austria, which controlled northern Italy. These allies soon drove the Austrians out of most

> Garibaldi (seated beneath the tree) is surrounded by his patriotic troops, the Redshirts.

Italy and Germany, 1871 ⑧

> By 1871 Italy and Germany were unified nations.

MAP SKILL Observe Change Through Maps
Using this map and the map on page 499, explain what changes occurred in Italy and Germany between 1850 and 1871.

of northern Italy. Most states in northern and central Italy then agreed to join with Sardinia under Victor Emmanuel II.

Another leader in the fight to unify Italy was **Giuseppe Garibaldi** (GAIR uh BALL dee). He gathered a small army known as the "Redshirts." To these brave patriots, Garibaldi said: ⑨

> *"I can offer you neither honors nor wages; I offer you hunger, thirst, forced marches, battles and death. Anyone who loves his country, follow me."* ⑩

Garibaldi's Redshirts freed Sicily, Naples, and other parts of southern Italy. In 1860 southern Italy united with most of the rest of the country under Victor Emmanuel II. In early 1861 the kingdom of Italy was formally announced. It would continue to grow for another nine years.

In 1866 Austria was involved in the war against Prussia that you read about. That gave Italy the opportunity to take over **Venice** and other nearby lands ruled by Austria. Finally, Italy took over **Rome** in 1870 and made that city the Italian capital.

REVIEW Summarize the main events leading to a united Italy in 1861. ⚙ Summarize

501

A United Italy

🕐 *Quick Summary* Surging nationalism led to the events that resulted in a united Italy in 1870.

Italy and Germany, 1871

⑧ **Which empires bordered the German Empire?** The Russian Empire and the Austro-Hungarian Empire
Interpret Maps

MAP SKILL Answer The states and territories were unified in each nation.

⑨ **Name important leaders in the movement for a united Italy and describe their roles.** Giuseppe Mazzini encouraged people to overthrow their rulers and create a democratic country. Camillo di Cavour formed an alliance with France to drive Austria out of northern Italy. Giuseppe Garibaldi and his Redshirts freed Sicily, Naples, and other parts of southern Italy.
⚙ Summarize

Ongoing Assessment ✓

| **If...** students have difficulty identifying these leaders and describing their roles, | **then...** have students skim the text to find people's names, and encourage them to read about the accomplishments of each person. |

Primary Source
Cited in *Oxford Dictionary of Quotations*, by Elizabeth Knowles, ed.

⑩ **Why do you think Garibaldi painted a bleak picture of life in the army?** Possible answer: He wanted to be honest about the obstacles patriots would face, and he wanted to appeal to their bravery and patriotism.
Analyze Primary Sources

✓ **REVIEW ANSWER** Cavour drove Austria out of most of northern Italy; states in northern and central Italy joined together under Sardinia's King Victor Emmanuel II; Garibaldi's Redshirts freed southern Italy, which then joined united Italy; Italy took Venice from Austria and, in 1870, took over Rome, making that city its capital.
⚙ Summarize

British Dominions

🕐 **Quick Summary** Many colonies belonging to the British pressured Great Britain for self-rule. These colonies became dominions.

⓫ **Describe how the government of a dominion is set up.** Each dominion sets up a government like that of Great Britain. An elected legislature enacts the laws and selects national leaders from its own members. A governor-general represents the British king or queen but has little real power. **Main Idea and Details**

⓬ **What do you think might be an advantage of living in a dominion?** Possible answer: A dominion is able to govern itself but still has the protection and shared resources of the rest of the empire. **Evaluate**

Ⓖ **SOCIAL STUDIES STRAND**
Government

Explain to students that a province is a division of a country. A territory is an area of a country that is not a state or a province. It has a separate organized government.

⓭ **Compare and contrast dominions with states in the United States.** States have their own governments just as dominions do. Dominions, however, are more like countries that have ties to their empires. The states in the United States are also governed closely by the federal government. **Compare and Contrast**

Canada, New Zealand, and Australia

⓮ **Which of the three dominions is the largest?** Canada **Interpret Maps**

MAP SKILL Answer Australia and New Zealand

British Dominions

By the mid-1800s, the British were being pressured by some of their colonies for self-rule. **Canada**, **Australia**, and **New Zealand** had been settled by the British and other Europeans. Great Britain began preparing these colonies to become dominions. A **dominion** is a self-governing nation that still has ties with the ruling empire, in this case, the British Empire.

Each dominion set up a form of government like that of Great Britain. In this system, an elected legislature, or **parliament**, enacts laws and selects national leaders from its own members. Each dominion also had a governor-general, who represented the British king or queen but had little real power.

In 1867 the British Parliament made Canada the first dominion. Canada included four provinces: Quebec, Ontario, New Brunswick, and Nova Scotia. Canada set up its capital at Ottawa. **Sir John MacDonald** became Canada's first prime minister. In time, other provinces joined. Today, Canada has ten provinces and three territories.

British colonization of Australia began when colonists and convicts started to settle in New South Wales in 1788. This was the part of Australia that Captain James Cook had claimed for Great Britain. Soon many other people came to Australia and started other British colonies.

▶ Canada, Australia, and New Zealand all made the transition from British colonies to dominions.

MAP SKILL
Canada, New Zealand, and Australia

▶ Between 1867 and 1907, the British colonies of Canada, Australia, and New Zealand became dominions.

MAP SKILL Understand the Equator *Which British dominions lie south of the equator?*

502

Practice and Extend

Ⓕ**Ⓨ**Ⓘ **SOCIAL STUDIES**
Background

More About Australia

- British interest in Australia began when William Dampier landed on the continent in 1688. He urged the English government to continue to explore this continent to gain its riches.

- During the eighteenth century, Europeans became more interested in global exploration. This ushered in new interest in Australia.

- In 1768 James Cook took a three-year trip to the Pacific. He landed in Australia, chartered the region near Botany Bay, and named the place New South Wales.

- Europeans did not want to settle in this harsh land. At the time, however, people believed that the best way to combat crime was to remove criminals from society, so Great Britain established a prison settlement in Australia.

Many of the Aborigines, the original people to inhabit Australia, were pushed off their land by colonists. The lands the Aborigines were forced onto were often harsh and dry. It has been estimated that in the first half-century of colonial rule, the Aboriginal population of Australia dropped by one-half.

By the late 1800s, many Australians believed that their colonies should be united into a single nation. **Sir Edmund Barton** led the efforts to draw up a constitution for Australia. With British approval, Australia became a British dominion in 1901. Barton served as Australia's first prime minister.

New Zealand had originally been settled by Polynesian people called the Maori. British missionaries started to arrive in New Zealand in 1814, soon followed by other British colonists.

The alarmed Maori rebelled but were put down by British colonial forces. In 1840 British naval officer **William Hobson** signed a treaty with Maori chiefs. The treaty made New Zealand a British colony.

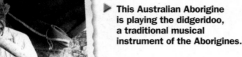

▶ **This Australian Aborigine is playing the didgeridoo, a traditional musical instrument of the Aborigines.**

In 1907 New Zealand became another British dominion. The new nation grew prosperous and attracted immigrants. However, strained relations continued between the Europeans and the Maori.

REVIEW Why do you think Canada, Australia, and New Zealand adopted a parliamentary form of government like Great Britain's? **Draw Conclusions**

Summarize the Lesson

- **1861** Italy became a united nation under King Victor Emmanuel II of Sardinia.
- **1867** Canada became the first British dominion.
- **1871** Germany became a united nation and declared itself an empire.

LESSON 3 REVIEW

Check Facts and Main Ideas

1. **Sequence** On a separate piece of paper, put the events in their correct time order.

   E C B D A

   - Australia became a dominion.
   - Canada became a dominion.
   - Garibaldi freed southern Italy.
   - Germany became an empire.
   - Greece became independent.

2. How did the example of Greece give hope to nationalistic Germans and Italians?

3. What did the German Empire inherit from the powerful German state of Prussia?

4. How did nationalism lead to the formation of a unified Germany and Italy?

5. **Critical Thinking:** *Evaluate Information* Do you think that the British dominions were truly independent? Explain your answer.

Link to ⎯⎯ **Writing**

Write a letter from Giuseppe Mazzini to Camillo di Cavour explaining why a united Italy should be democratic.

503

MEETING INDIVIDUAL NEEDS
Leveled Practice

Write an Editorial Have students write editorials on issues of nationalism and unification.

Easy Have students state their position on unification and write three sentences supporting that position. **Reteach**

On-Level Have students describe Bismarck's actions from the point of view of an Austrian. **Extend**

Challenge Have pairs of students express opposing viewpoints on unification. **Enrich**

For a Lesson Summary, use Quick Study, p. 122.

Workbook, p. 124

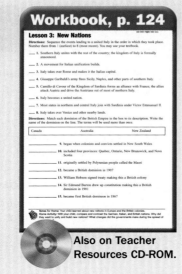

Lesson 3: New Nations

Directions: Sequence the events leading to a united Italy in the order in which they took place. Number them from 1 (earliest) to 8 (most recent). You may use your textbook.

____ 1. Southern Italy unites with the rest of the country; the kingdom of Italy is formally announced.

____ 2. A movement for Italian unification builds.

____ 3. Italy takes over Rome and makes it the Italian capital.

____ 4. Giuseppe Garibaldi's army frees Sicily, Naples, and other parts of southern Italy.

____ 5. Camillo di Cavour of the Kingdom of Sardinia forms an alliance with France; the allies attack Austria and drive the Austrians out of most of northern Italy.

____ 6. Italy becomes a united nation.

____ 7. Most states in northern and central Italy join with Sardinia under Victor Emmanuel II.

____ 8. Italy takes over Venice and other nearby lands.

Directions: Match each dominion of the British Empire in the box to its description. Write the name of the dominion on the line. The terms will be used more than once.

Canada	Australia	New Zealand

____ 9. began where colonists and convicts settled in New South Wales

____ 10. included four provinces: Quebec, Ontario, New Brunswick, and Nova Scotia

____ 11. originally settled by Polynesian people called the Maori

____ 12. became a British dominion in 1907

____ 13. William Hobson signed treaty making this a British colony

____ 14. Sir Edmund Barton drew up constitution making this a British dominion in 1901

____ 15. became first British dominion in 1867

Notes for Home: Your child learned about new nations in Europe and the British colonies.
Home Activity: With your child, compare and contrast the German, Italian, and British nations. Why did they want to unify and build new nations? What changes did the governments make during the spread of...

Also on Teacher Resources CD-ROM.

---

15 **Describe the effects of the arrival of British colonists in the area that is now New Zealand.** The original settlers, the Maori, rebelled but were put down by the British. Eventually, a treaty was signed making New Zealand a British colony. **Cause and Effect**

✓ **REVIEW ANSWER** Each of these dominions was settled mostly by British people who naturally modeled their government on that of the home country; colonists knew they would have to establish a government the British Parliament would approve. **Draw Conclusions**

3 Close and Assess

Summarize the Lesson

Tell students to use the three events as main topics in an outline and have them list details that tell about each one.

✓ **LESSON 3 REVIEW**

1. **Sequence** For possible answers, see the reduced pupil page.

2. Greece had gained its independence from the Ottoman Empire.

3. Nondemocratic government, support of the army

4. Nationalism inspired people to establish strong, independent nations whose people shared the same language, customs, and history.

5. **Critical Thinking:** *Evaluate Information* The dominions were not completely independent. A colony had to have approval from the British Parliament to become a dominion, and a dominion still had ties to the British Empire.

Link to ⎯⎯ **Writing**

Students' letters should give clear reasons. Encourage students to use logical arguments and to put their most persuasive reasons at the end.

Resources

- Assessment Book, pp. 85–88
- Workbook, p. 125: Vocabulary Review

Chapter Summary

For possible answers, see the reduced pupil page.

Vocabulary and Terms

1. d, **2.** c, **3.** e, **4.** a, **5.** b

People and Events

Possible answers:

1. Otto von Bismarck was the Prussian prime minister who guided Germany to unification.

2. In 1857 Indian troops rebelled against British rule in a revolt called the Indian Mutiny.

3. Queen Victoria reigned over Great Britain during the period when "the sun never set" on its empire.

4. Camillo di Cavour unified most states in northern and central Italy with Sardinia under King Victor Emmanuel II.

5. As a result of the Opium Wars, Great Britain gained land in China and forced the Chinese to open treaty ports.

6. Ci Xi ruled China around the time of the Boxer rebellion.

7. William Hobson negotiated a treaty with Maori chiefs, making New Zealand a British colony.

8. Several European powers met at the Berlin Conference in 1884 to divide up Africa among themselves.

9. Theodore Roosevelt was the U.S. president who persuaded Russia and Japan to accept a peace treaty ending the war between them.

10. Sir John MacDonald was the first prime minister of the Dominion of Canada.

1840	1850

1839 First Opium War began.

1854 Japan opened to trade.

1857 Indian Mutiny

Chapter Summary

Summarize

On a separate piece of paper, break down the summary into three short sentences.

Greece became independent after centuries of Ottoman rule	Italy had a great history and now desired unification	Newly unified Germany warred against other nations to prove its strength

Nationalism led to new nations.

Vocabulary and Terms

Match the correct definition to the words below.

1. **treaty port** (p. 494)
2. **dominion** (p. 502)
3. **nationalism** (p. 487)
4. **parliament** (p. 502)
5. **imperialism** (p. 487)

a. an elected legislature

b. to build an empire by controlling or conquering lands

c. a self-governing nation that still has ties with a ruling empire

d. port city where Europeans had special rights

e. a devotion to one's own country

People and Events

Write a sentence explaining why each of the following people or events was important in the age of imperialism, nationalism, and unification. You may use two or more in a single sentence.

1. Otto von Bismarck (p. 500)
2. Indian Mutiny (p. 488)
3. Victoria (p. 488)
4. Camillo di Cavour (p. 501)
5. Opium War (p. 494)
6. Ci Xi (p. 495)
7. William Hobson (p. 503)
8. Berlin Conference (p. 489)
9. Theodore Roosevelt (p. 496)
10. Sir John MacDonald (p. 502)

504

Practice and Extend

Assessment Options

✓ Chapter 17 Assessment

- Chapter 17 Content Test: Use Assessment Book, pp. 85–86.
- Chapter 17 Skills Test: Use Assessment Book, pp. 87–88.

Standardized Test Prep

- Chapter 17 Tests contain standardized test format.

✓ Chapter 17 Performance Assessment

- Ask students to create large three-column charts with the words from the title of this chapter—*imperialism, nationalism,* and *unification.*

- In their charts, students can write definitions of each of the terms. Then they can list important people, places, and events that convey the ideas behind these three words.

- Assess students' understanding of the ideas in this chapter as you examine their portfolios. Ask probing follow-up questions based on the ideas students wrote.

1870	1880	1890	1890

1861 aly became unified ation.

1871 German Empire was created.

1869 Suez Canal opened.

1867 Canada became a dominion.

1885 Congo Free State was set up.

1898 Boxer Rebellion began.

1904 War between Japan and Russia began.

acts and Main Ideas

hat did the British call "the jewel in the own"? Why?

hich African countries remained dependent after the Berlin Conference?

plain why Great Britain and China fought e first Opium War.

me Line How many years separated Italy's ification and the Boxer Rebellion?

in Idea Why did the European imperialists nt colonies?

in Idea According to Giuseppe Mazzini, at defined a nation?

in Idea How did Japan avoid becoming a get of Western imperialists?

tical Thinking: *Detect Bias* Do you think t King Leopold II shared Cecil Rhodes's nion that the white race was better than er races? Explain your answer.

rite About History

te a **meeting notice** for an upcoming ting of the Indian National Congress. persuasive writing to encourage fellow ans to attend.

e a **letter** from Beijing, China, to the ed States about your feelings as a gner during the Boxer Rebellion.

e a **diplomatic note** to the British ament asking that the Maori be given ight to their land in New Zealand.

Apply Skills

Interpret Circle Graphs

Students voted for the world history topics they enjoyed the most so far this school year. They then put the results into a circle graph.

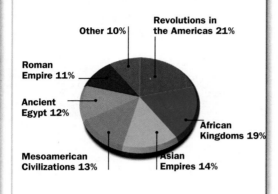

- Other 10%
- Revolutions in the Americas 21%
- Roman Empire 11%
- Ancient Egypt 12%
- African Kingdoms 19%
- Mesoamerican Civilizations 13%
- Asian Empires 14%

1 Which topic was the students' favorite?

2 Which three topics took place on the continent of Africa?

3 Which topic was more popular, the Roman Empire or African kingdoms?

Internet Activity

To get help with vocabulary, people, and terms, select dictionary, encyclopedia, or almanac from *Social Studies Library* at **www.sfsocialstudies.com**.

505

Hands-on Unit Project

Unit 6 Performance Assessment

See p. 510 for information about using the Unit Project as a means of performance assessment.

A scoring guide is provided on p. 510.

WEB SITE Technology

or more information, students can select the ictionary, encyclopedia, or almanac from *Social tudies Library* at **www.sfsocialstudies.com**.

Workbook, p. 125

Vocabulary Review

Directions: Circle the vocabulary term that best completes each sentence. You may use your textbook.

1. Because the British were pressured by some of their colonies for self-rule, they prepared each colony to become a (parliament, dominion, treaty port).

2. A European treaty port ran its own (dominion, parliament, compound, or enclosed area.

3. A powerful feeling called (parliament, nationalism, modernization) led some people to believe that their country was better than all others.

4. Meiji and his advisors started Japan on a path of rapid (parliament, nationalism, modernization), because Japan wanted to catch up with the West.

5. An elected legislature, or (parliament, compound, imperialist), enacts laws and selects national leaders from its own members.

6. A European who promoted building up an empire by controlling or conquering lands was called an (imperialism, dominion, imperialist).

7. A city such as Shanghai, where Europeans had special trading rights, was called a (treaty port, dominion, compound).

8. An idea often linked to the nationalism of the 1800s was (modernization, parliament, imperialism), which meant building up an empire by controlling or conquering lands in Africa, Asia, and elsewhere.

Directions: Answer the following question on the lines provided.

9. How did Japan use modernization to become a great world power?

Also on Teacher Resources CD-ROM.

Facts and Main Ideas

1. India; the British viewed it as a valuable colonial possession.

2. Ethiopia and Liberia

3. Chinese officials wanted to shut down the opium trade, but Britain wanted to continue bringing opium into China.

4. 37 years

5. As sources for raw materials and markets where they could sell their own factory-made goods for big profits

6. A group of people who all speak the same language

7. Japan improved its technology, modernized its armed forces, and gained the respect of Western imperialists.

8. It is reasonable to assume that King Leopold II shared Rhodes's opinion because he allowed cruel treatment of black Africans in the Congo, showing that he had no respect for their basic human rights.

Write About History

1. Students' notices should give facts telling why Indians may want to work for independence from Great Britain.

2. Remind students to consider the Boxers' viewpoint on foreigners as they compose their letters.

3. Students' notes should be persuasive and include specific reasons that the Maori should be allowed to keep their own land.

Apply Skills

1. Revolutions in the Americas

2. Roman Empire, Ancient Egypt, and African Kingdoms

3. African Kingdoms

Así es mi tierra

Objectives

- Interpret how feelings and attitudes, such as nationalism, can be expressed through music.

1 Introduce and Motivate

Preview To activate prior knowledge, ask students to recall the definition of *nationalism.* Point out that nationalism can be pride in one's country. How might a song express pride in a nation?

Ask students how studying a song from a particular country or culture can be useful. (It can provide a way to understand the people's culture and what they value most. It can help us understand what the people think about their nation.)

2 Teach and Discuss

1 **What does this song honor?** An important battle in Mexican history
Main Idea and Details

UNIT
6
End with a Song

Así es mi tierra

This song was written by Ignacío Fernández Esperón describing the beauty of Mexico. In English the title of this song means, "this is my land." Mexicans sometimes sing this song, which

1 honors an important battle in Mexican history. After reading the translation, do you think that Esperón had a strong sense

2 of nationalism when he wrote these words?

Words and Music by Ignacío Fernandez Esperón

A-sí es mi tie - rra, more - ni - ta y lu - mi - no - sa; A-sí es mi
This is my coun-try, It's a land that's bright with beau-ty; This is my

tie - rra, tie-ne el al - ma he-cha de a - mor. A - sí es mi
coun - try, It's a land that's made to love. This is my

tie - rra, a - bun - dan - te y ge - ne - ro - sa; ¡Ay, tie - rra
coun - try, It has giv - en so much to me; Oh, my dear

mí - a co - mo es gra - to tu ca - lor!
coun - try, Wel-come are your gifts of love.

2nd time to next stanza

506

Practice and Extend

CURRICULUM CONNECTION
Writing

Write a Poem

- Discuss with students the special features that characterize a region or country in which they have lived. Encourage them to express their feelings about this place.
- Help students brainstorm a list of words and phrases that describe the place and convey their feelings.
- Have students use words from their lists to compose a poem. Some may want to write in the form of an acrostic, using the letters in the place name to begin each line of the poem.

AUDIO CD
Technology

Play the CD, *Songs and Music,* to listen to the song.

This is my land, both sun-bronzed and bright,
This is my land, with a soul made for love.
This is my land, abundant and generous,
Oh, my land, how pleasant is your warmth!
Your dawnings are so full of joy,
And your serenades are well-suited for love.
This is my land, flower of sadness,
Oh, my land, how pleasant is your warmth!

❸
❹

G₇   C

Sus   al-bo-ra-das   tan lle-ni-tas, de a-le-grí-a.   Sus se-re-
When morn-ing   light comes, Peo-ple greet the day with   glad-ness.   In hap-py

G₇   C

na-tas   tan pro-pi-cias al   a-mor.   A-sí es   mi
sing-ing   we hear mel-o-dies of   love.   This   is   my

C   F   G₇

tie-rra,   flor de   la   me-lan-co-lí-a.   ¡Ay, tie-rra
coun-try,   Leav-ing fills me with such   sad-ness;   Oh, my dear

C   G₇   C

mí-a   co-mo es   gra-to   tu   ca-lor!
coun-try,   Wel-come   are   your   gifts   of   love.

507

❷ This song is a translation from Spanish. Why might you need to know that this a translation rather than the original song? A translation usually conveys approximately the same meaning as the original, but the translation may not be word for word. Also, the rhythm of the words may be different in the translation.
Draw Conclusions

❸ What positive qualities of Mexico are described in this song? Its warmth, its beauty, its generosity and giving spirit
Main Idea and Details

❹ What kinds of sensory images does Esperón use in the song? Give examples. The sense of sight: sun-bronzed; the sense of hearing: serenades; the sense of touch: warmth
Generalize

3 Close and Assess

- Have students practice singing the song. Be sure that they know how to pronounce words that may be unfamiliar to them. If anyone in the class speaks Spanish, ask him or her to sing the song in Spanish.

- Ask students to write a few sentences that tell what the song reveals about Mexico. What do people in Mexico seem to value about their country?

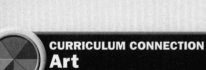

CURRICULUM CONNECTION
Art

Create a CD Cover
- Have students use watercolors, chalk, or another medium to create a cover for a CD of this song.
- Students may want to look at photographs depicting various parts of Mexico to decide what images might be appropriate. Have them list key words from the song that might influence the choice of art for the cover of the CD.

Resource

• Assessment Book, pp. 89–92

Main Ideas and Vocabulary

1. c, **2.** a, **3.** d, **4.** a

People and Terms

1. The encomienda was a Spanish colonial system that taught Christianity and enslaved Native Americans.

2. The Reign of Terror was a violent period after radical leaders took control of the French Revolution.

3. Capitalism is an economic system in which private individuals own and run businesses to make a profit.

4. The Open Door Policy allowed all countries to trade with China.

5. Karl Marx predicted a worldwide revolution that would bring about a society without economic classes.

6. The Suez Canal shortened the sea route from England to India.

7. Marie-Olympe de Gouges believed that women should have the same legal rights as men and that women should receive an equal education.

8. Mercantilism is an economic system in which a country uses colonies as sources of raw materials and as markets for its goods.

9. During the reign of Elizabeth I, England became a world sea power.

Main Ideas and Vocabulary

TEST PREP

Read the passage below and use it to answer the questions that follow.

During the Renaissance, Europeans developed a renewed interest in classical Greek and Roman culture. This inspired great changes in art, science, thought, and religion. Countries sought more profitable ways to bring goods to Europe. Adventurers explored the Americas, lands previously unknown to Europeans. The quest for wealth and power led Spain and Portugal to conquer the new lands. They mistreated the Native Americans. With Great Britain, they engaged in trading goods for slaves brought from Africa.

In the late 1700s people began to revolt against European rule in parts of the Americas. At about the same time, people in France rose up against their leaders, igniting the French Revolution.

Political revolutions were soon followed by the Industrial Revolution. Technological advances such as the steam engine and machines for producing textiles powered the Industrial Revolution. Economies changed from mostly rural and agricultural to mostly urban and industrial. New economic systems came into being, including capitalism and socialism.

European powers sought to <u>colonize</u> more lands, especially in Africa. But the European desires were the same as with the Americas—gain riches and work to rule and convert the people.

In the 1800s, some conflicts even led to the formation of new unified countries, such as Germany and Italy.

1 According to the passage, how did the industrial revolution affect European economies?

A They changed from wealthy to poor.

B They changed from agricultural and urban to industrial and rural.

C They changed from agricultural and rural to industrial and urban.

D They changed to colonial.

2 In the passage, the word *colonize* means—

A take over a territory far from the country that governs it

B bring Christianity to natives

C start a revolution

D begin a war

3 According to the passage, what items contributed to the Industrial Revolution?

A trade

B colonization of Africa

C capitalism

D steam engine and machines for making textiles

4 What is the main idea of the passage?

A There have been a variety of changes since the 1700s.

B Political revolutions produce industrial revolutions.

C Ancient Greek and Roman culture inspired changes in religion and art.

D African colonies prospered under European rule.

508

Practice and Extend

Assessment Options

✓ **Unit 6 Assessment**

• Use Unit 6 Content Test: Use Assessment Book, pp. 89–90.

• Use Unit 6 Skills Test: Use Assessment Book, pp. 91–92.

Standardized Test Prep

• Unit 6 Tests contain standardized test format.

✓ **Unit 6 Performance Assessment**

• See p. 510 for information about using the Unit Project as a means of Performance Assessment.

• A scoring guide for the Unit 6 Project is provided in the teacher's notes on p. 510.

 Test Talk

• Test Talk Practice Book

 WEB SITE Technology

For more information you can select the dictionary, encyclopedia, or almanac from *Social Studies Library* at **www.sfsocialstudies.com**.

People and Terms

Write a complete sentence defining each term or explaining the importance of each person listed.

1 encomienda (p. 447)

2 Reign of Terror (p. 468)

3 capitalism (p. 480)

4 Open Door Policy (p. 495)

5 Karl Marx (p. 481)

6 Suez Canal (p. 488)

7 Marie-Olympe de Gouges (p. 471)

8 mercantilism (p. 445)

9 Elizabeth I (p. 442)

10 Armada (p. 442)

Apply Skills

Create a Political Cartoon Draw a cartoon that shows your point of view about an important event. The cartoon can be about an event at your school, in the news, or in your own life. You can label different parts of your drawing to help people understand its meaning.

Write and Share

Present a Round Table Discussion Choose classmates to represent the points of view of the British government, British traders, and African natives. Form a round table discussion with a host. Write questions to ask the guests appearing on the show. Allow time for the guests to write the answers to the questions before the discussion starts. Invite another class to sit in on your discussion.

Read on Your Own

Look for books like these in the library.

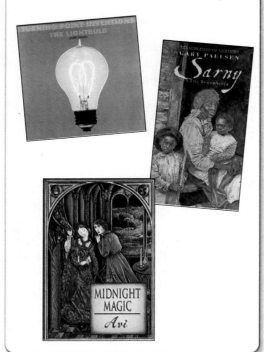

509

Revisit the Unit Question

✓**Portfolio Assessment**

Have students look at their Unit 6 lists of ideas that they think are most important to the building of a nation.

Have students look at their Unit 6 lists of specific ideas that influenced the development of various nations.

- Ask students to compare and contrast their lists.
- Have students write a summary expressing how their own opinions of what ideas are most important to the building of a nation may have changed.
- Have students add these lists and summaries to their Social Studies Portfolio.

---

10. The British defeated the Armada, a fleet of Spanish warships.

Apply Skills

Have students choose an important event about which to express an opinion.

Write and Share

- Students may want to use additional reference materials as they form their points of view for discussion.
- Spend time working on strategies for effective speaking.
- Use the following scoring guide.

✓**Assessment Scoring Guide**

Present a Round Table Discussion	
4	Answers clearly and thoughtfully, using facts and relevant ideas.
3	Correctly answers questions, using relevant ideas and not minor details.
2	Some answers are incorrect or unsupported.
1	Is unable to write questions or answer them correctly.

Test Talk

Write Your Answer to Score High
Use Write and Share to model the Test Talk strategy.

Make sure the answer is correct.
Students should make sure their written answer has only correct details.

Make sure the answer is complete.
Have students include numerous details in their written answer.

Make sure the answer is focused.
Students should make sure their written answer has only details that answer the question/complete the assignment.

Read on Your Own

Have students prepare oral reports, using the following books.

The Lightbulb (Turning Point Inventions), by Joseph Wallace (Atheneum, ISBN 0-689-82816-0, 1999) **Easy**

Sarny: A Life Remembered, by Gary Paulsen (Random House Inc., ISBN 0-440-21973-6, 1999) **On-Level**

Midnight Magic, by Avi (Scholastic, Inc., ISBN 0-590-36035-3, 1999) **Challenge**

Unit Project

Arts and Letters

Objective
- Describe how an invention has benefited society.

Resource
- Workbook, p. 126

Materials
large sheets of paper, pencils, paints, markers, reference materials from the library or Internet

Follow This Procedure
- Tell students that they will write a script and make a poster for an infomercial about an invention in this unit. Explain that an infomercial is a television program that advertises a product with demonstrations and discussions.

- Divide students into groups of three or four. Encourage each group to choose a different invention. Have students research the benefits that their inventions have contributed to society. Challenge them to create presentations that convey the importance of their inventions to the people who used them.

- Have students make a poster advertising the invention.

- Invite each group to present their infomercials to the class.

✓ Assessment Scoring Guide

	Arts and Letters
4	Provides detailed descriptions of how an invention benefited society using accurate content and a variety of supporting facts.
3	Provides some detailed descriptions of how an invention benefited society using mostly accurate content and some variety of supporting facts.
2	Provides few accurate descriptions of how an invention benefited society and very little variety of supporting facts.
1	Provides no accurate descriptions of how an invention benefited society and little or no variety of supporting facts.

510 Unit 6 • Discovery, Expansion, and Revolutions

UNIT 6 Project

Arts and Letters

Create an infomercial about an important invention.

1 Form a group and choose an invention studied in this unit.

2 Research the invention. Write about the inventor and tell why he or she made the invention and when it was invented. Describe how the invention has helped people.

3 Make a poster or backdrop to advertise your invention.

4 Present your infomercial to your class. You may want to dress in the clothing of the time and add sound effects.

Internet Activity
Explore inventions on the Internet. Go to www.sfsocialstudies.com/activities and select your grade and unit.

510

Practice and Extend

 Hands-on Unit Project

✓ Performance Assessment
- The Unit Project can also be used as a performance assessment activity.
- Use the scoring guide to assess each group's work.

 WEB SITE Technology

Students can launch the Internet Activity by clicking on *Grade 6, Unit 6* at www.sfsocialstudies.com/activities.

Workbook, p. 126

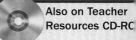 **Also on Teacher Resources CD-RC**

★ UNIT 7 ★
A World in Opposition

A World in Opposition

Unit Planning Guide

Unit 7 • A World in Opposition

Begin with a Primary Source pp. 512–513

Meet the People pp. 514–515

Target Skill **Reading Social Studies, Cause and Effect** pp. 516–517

Chapter Titles	Pacing	Main Ideas
Chapter 18 **The World at War** pp. 518–537 ✓ **Chapter 18 Review** pp. 538–539	5 days	• Competition between nations pushed Europe toward war. • The Great War caused much destruction. • The Allies tried to make a peace treaty that would solve all of Europe's problems.
Chapter 19 **From Peace to War** pp. 540–563 ✓ **Chapter 19 Review** pp. 564–565	7 days	• Hard times set the stage for another world war. • World War II caused millions of deaths and great destruction. • The Allies formed the United Nations and helped shattered nations rebuild.
Chapter 20 **The Cold War** pp. 566–589 ✓ **Chapter 20 Review** pp. 590–591	6 days	• After 1945 the Soviet Union and the Allies broke off relations. • In a century of revolution, communists took control of China. • The Cold War became a "hot" war in Korea and Vietnam.

End with a Song pp. 592–593

✓ **Unit 7 Review** pp. 594–595

✓ **Unit 7 Project** p. 596

✓ = Assessment Options

The British *Dreadnought* was completed in 1905.

Providing More Depth

  Multimedia Library

- *World War II,* by Simon Adams
- *Eleanor Everywhere: The Life of Eleanor Roosevelt,* by Monica Kulling
- **Songs and Music**
- **Video Field Trips**
- **Software**

Additional Resources

- Family Activities
- Vocabulary Cards
- Daily Activity Bank
- Social Studies Plus!
- Big Book Atlas
- Student Atlas
- Outline Maps
- Desk Maps

 ADDITIONAL Technology

- AudioText
- The test maker
- Teacher Resources CD-ROM
- Map Resources CD-ROM
- **www.sfsocialstudies.com**

 To establish guidelines for your students' safe and responsible use of the Internet, use the Scott Foresman Internet Guide.

Additional Internet Links

To find out more about:

- The *Lusitania,* visit **www.pbs.org**
- The Great Depression, visit **www.newdeal.feri.org**
- Churchill's speeches, click on *Spoken Word* at **www.winstonchurchill.org**

Key Internet Search Terms

- The Great Depression
- World War I
- World War II
- Cold War
- Korean War

Resources	Meeting Individual Needs
• Workbook, pp. 128–132 • Every Student Learns Guide, pp. 246–257 • Transparencies 16, 20, 21, 53, 54 • Quick Study, pp. 124–129 • Workbook, p. 133 ✓ Chapter 18 Content Test, Assessment Book, pp. 93–94 ✓ Chapter 18 Skills Test, Assessment Book, pp. 95–96	• Leveled Practice, TE pp. 521, 524, 527, 536 • ESL Support, TE pp. 522, 530, 535 • Learning Styles, TE p. 529 ✓ Chapter 18 Performance Assessment, TE p. 538
• Workbook, pp. 134–139 • Every Student Learns Guide, pp. 258–269 • Transparencies 18, 20, 21, 55, 56 • Quick Study, pp. 130–135 • Workbook, p. 140 ✓ Chapter 19 Content Test, Assessment Book, pp. 97–98 ✓ Chapter 19 Skills Test, Assessment Book, pp. 99–100	• ESL Support, TE pp. 543, 550, 559 • Leveled Practice, TE pp. 544, 552, 560 • Learning Styles, TE pp. 545, 562 ✓ Chapter 19 Performance Assessment, TE p. 564
• Workbook, pp. 141–145 • Every Student Learns Guide, pp. 270–281 • Transparencies 19, 20, 57, 58, 59 • Quick Study, pp. 136–141 • Workbook, p. 146 ✓ Chapter 20 Content Test, Assessment Book, pp. 101–102 ✓ Chapter 20 Skills Test, Assessment Book, pp. 103–104	• Leveled Practice, TE pp. 569, 575, 579, 585, 586 • ESL Support, TE pp. 570, 578, 587 • Learning Styles, TE pp. 574, 584 ✓ Chapter 20 Performance Assessment, TE p. 590

Nikita Khrushchev was the Soviet leader during the Cuban Missile Crisis.

Unit 7 Objectives

Beginning of Unit 7
- Acquire information from primary sources. (p. 512)
- Identify the contributions of significant individuals during the twentieth century. (p. 514)
- Analyze information by identifying cause-and-effect relationships. (p. 516)

Chapter 18

Lesson 1 Headed Toward War
pp. 520–523
- List some of the causes of the Great War.
- List the strong forces that caused friction between the countries of Europe in the years leading up to 1914.
- Explain how the taking of the French provinces by Germany caused friction.
- Explain how imperialism increased competition between France and Germany.
- Describe and explain the impact of alliances on the start of the Great War.
- Compare parallel time lines to show a time relationship between events happening in different places. (p. 524)

Lesson 2 The Great War pp. 526–532
- List the events that caused the United States to enter the Great War.
- List and describe weapons first used in the Great War. Explain how they differed from earlier weapons.
- Describe how Lenin and the Communists persuaded the Russian people to support the Russian Revolution.
- Explain the significance of the Battles of Verdun and the Somme.
- Describe how peoples' attitudes toward the Great War may have been affected by the high number of casualties.
- Learn how war affected an average young person growing up in Great Britain during the Great War. (p. 533)

Lesson 3 After the War pp. 534–537
- List the two provisions of the Treaty of Versailles that were included to show that Germany was being blamed for starting the Great War.
- Explain how the map of Europe changed according to the Treaty of Versailles.
- Explain the opposition President Wilson faced in trying to get his plan for a fair peace with Germany approved.
- Explain how paying reparations affected the German economy.

Chapter 19

Lesson 1 Good to Bad Times
pp. 542–547
- List and describe the significant events that happened during Stalin's reign and their impact on the Soviet Union.
- Define inflation. Explain how inflation and the Great Depression impacted the world economy.
- Explain fascism and list two examples of fascist countries.
- Describe how conditions in Italy and Germany led to the rise of dictators.
- Explain Hitler's motivation for breaking the Treaty of Versailles in the 1930s.

Lesson 2 World War II pp. 548–554
- List and describe the effects of Germany's attacks on countries in Europe.
- Explain why Hitler gave up on invading Great Britain.
- Explain the significance of D-Day.
- Explain the significance and effects of the bombings on Hiroshima and Nagasaki.
- Explain the effect of the U.S. entry into World War II.
- Identify the contributions of significant individuals, such as Winston Churchill, during World War II. (p. 555)
- Acquire information from primary and secondary sources, such as visual materials. (p. 556)

Lesson 3 The Aftermath pp. 558–561
- List and explain some of the outcomes of World War II.
- Describe how the dropping of atomic bombs on Hiroshima and Nagasaki affected the Japanese people.
- Explain how we know about Anne Frank.
- Explain and describe the significance of the United Nations.
- Describe the Marshall Plan and explain why the Eastern European countries did not benefit from it.
- Read and interpret a bar graph. (p. 562)

Chapter 20

Lesson 1 The Soviets Advance
pp. 568–572
- List the causes of the Cold War.
- Explain the significance of the Berlin airlift.
- Identify the central issue behind the Cuban missile crisis.

- Explain how iron curtain described the map of Europe after 1945.
- Explain the significance of NATO and describe its effect on Stalin's blockade of Berlin.
- Identify the accomplishments of Tenzing Norgay. (p. 573)
- Evaluate Tenzing Norgay's decision to reveal that he was the second to reach the summit of Mt. Everest. (p. 573)
- Solve complex problems by identifying options, considering them carefully, and choosing a plan of action. (p. 574)

Lesson 2 Communism in China
pp. 576–580
- List the causes and effects of the Long March.
- Name the political parties that fought for control of China in the 1940s.
- Identify Jiang Qing and explain her role in communist China.
- List and describe the revolutions that occurred in China in the twentieth century.
- Explain why the leaders of the two Chinese governments could not be relied on to make accurate statements about each other.
- Identify the early life experiences of Mao Zedong that may have contributed to his later ideas and his decision to lead the Cultural Revolution. (p. 581)

Lesson 3 The Cold War Heats Up
pp. 582–587
- List some of the causes and effects of the Korean War and Vietnam War.
- Describe U.S. involvement in the Vietnam War under President Eisenhower.
- Explain the change in U.S. involvement in the Vietnam War in the 1960s.
- Compare and contrast the wars in Korea and Vietnam and other events of the Cold War.
- Explain how events in other parts of the world would have convinced people that the domino effect would occur if Vietnam became a communist country.
- Examine U.S. public attitudes toward involvement in the Vietnam War. (p. 588)

End of Unit 7
- Identify significant examples of music from various periods in U.S. history. (p. 592)
- Describe a significant historic event. (p. 596)

Assessment Options

✓ Formal Assessment

- **Lesson Reviews,** PE/TE pp. 523, 532, 537, 547, 554, 561, 572, 580, 587
- **Chapter Reviews,** PE/TE pp. 538–539, 564–565, 590–591
- **Chapter Tests,** Assessment Book, pp. 93–104
- **Unit Review,** PE/TE pp. 594–595
- **Unit Tests,** Assessment Book, pp. 105–108
- **TestWorks** (test-generator software)

✓ Informal Assessment

- **Teacher's Edition Questions,** throughout Lessons and Features
- **Section Reviews,** PE/TE pp. 521, 523, 527, 529–532, 535–536, 537, 543, 545–547, 549–554, 559, 561, 569–572, 577–580, 583, 585, 587
- **Close and Assess,** TE pp. 517, 523, 525, 532, 533, 537, 547, 554, 555, 557, 561, 563, 572, 573, 575, 580, 581, 587, 589, 593

Ongoing Assessment

Ongoing Assessment is found throughout the Teacher's Edition lessons using an **If...then** model.

If = students' observable behavior,	**then** = reteaching and enrichment suggestions

✓ Portfolio Assessment

- **Portfolio Assessment,** TE pp. 511, 512, 595
- **Leveled Practice,** TE pp. 521, 524, 527, 536, 544, 552, 560, 569, 575, 579, 585, 586
- **Workbook Pages,** pp. 127–147
- **Chapter Review: Write About History,** PE/TE pp. 539, 565, 591
- **Unit Review: Apply Skills,** PE/TE p. 594
- **Curriculum Connection: Writing** PE/TE pp. 561, 572, 587; TE pp. 531, 536, 552, 580

✓ Performance Assessment

- **Hands-on Unit Project** (Unit 7 Performance Assessment), PE/TE pp. 511, 539, 565, 591, 594, 596
- **Internet Activity,** PE p. 596
- **Chapter 18 Performance Assessment,** PE/TE p. 538
- **Chapter 19 Performance Assessment,** PE/TE p. 564
- **Chapter 20 Performance Assessment,** PE/TE p. 590
- **Unit Review: Write and Share,** PE/TE p. 595
- **Scoring Guide,** TE p. 595

Test Talk

Test-Taking Strategies

Understand the Question
- **Locate Key Words in the Question,** TE p. 521
- **Locate Key Words in the Text,** TE p. 527

Understand the Answer
- **Choose the Right Answer,** PE/TE p. 594
- **Use Information from the Text,** TE p. 584
- **Use Information from Graphics,** TE p. 552
- **Write Your Answer to Score High,** TE p. 565

For additional practice, use the Test Talk Practice Book.

Featured Strategy

Choose the Right Answer
Students will:
- Narrow the answer choices and rule out choices they know are wrong.
- Choose the best answer.

PE/TE p. 594

Curriculum Connections

Integrating Your Day

The lessons, skills, and features of Unit 7 provide many opportunities to make connections between social studies and other areas of the elementary curriculum.

READING

Reading Skill—Cause and Effect, PE/TE pp. 516–517, 520, 526, 534, 542, 548, 558, 568, 576, 582

Lesson Review—Cause and Effect, PE/TE pp. 523, 532, 537, 547, 554, 561, 572, 580, 587

Link to Reading, PE/TE pp. 523, 537, 547

MATH

Deciphering Codes, TE p. 551

Writing Word Problems, TE p. 563

Link to Mathematics, PE/TE p. 580

WRITING

Write a Letter, TE p. 531

Write Peace Points, TE p. 536

Write a Wartime Communication, TE p. 552

Link to Writing, PE/TE pp. 561, 572, 587

Research Revolutions, TE p. 580

Social Studies

LITERATURE

Read Biographies, TE pp. 514, 555

Read Other Works, TE p. 533

Read About Mt. Everest, TE p. 573

Both Sides of the Vietnam War, TE p. 588

SCIENCE

Link to Science, PE/TE pp. 532

Need for Steel, TE p. 546

Research Nuclear Weapons, TE p. 571

ART

Interpret the Photograph, TE p. 512

Analyze a Photo, TE p. 527

Link to Art, PE/TE p. 554

Make Origami Cranes, TE p. 561

Create a Political Cartoon, TE p. 569

Design a Book Jacket, TE p. 581

Create Posters, TE p. 589

MUSIC / DRAMA

Present a Play, TE p. 524

Give a Speech, TE pp. 560, 586

Present a News Show, TE p. 575

Patriotic Songs, TE p. 593

 Look for this symbol throughout the Teacher's Edition to find **Curriculum Connections.**

Professional Development

Economics in the Classroom

by Bonnie Meszaros, Ph.D.
University of Delaware

Today's children will face many economic issues as adults. They will be required to make decisions that will impact their lives and the lives of others. They will decide what to buy, what careers to pursue, when and if they should change jobs, and how much of their income they should spend and how much they should save.

They will need to understand the fallacy in politicians' promises to cut taxes and expand government services. They will need to know how the closing of a plant by an auto manufacturer or the cutting of oil production by OPEC will impact their lives.

Adults without some understanding of economics and a grasp of economic reasoning will find many of these complex issues confusing. Their decisions will be based on faulty assumptions, incorrect information, and misconceptions that were not addressed during their school experience.

Children live in an economic world and bring economic knowledge and experience into the classroom. At an early age they make consumer choices involving spending, saving, and even borrowing. Young children learn early that they cannot have everything they want. Unfortunately, they do not always understand why this is the case or why each choice involves a cost. Students think that when they become adults, choices will no longer be a problem. Below are several ways that *Scott Foresman Social Studies* incorporates the study and history of economics into its program.

- *Chapter 19, Lesson 1, explains how overproduction and too much debt led to the Great Depression. Students are introduced to the concepts of borrowing and lending and inflation.*

- *In the Economics Social Studies Strand on p. 543 of the Teacher's Edition, students explore the concept of supply and demand.*

ESL Support

by Jim Cummins, Ph.D.
University of Toronto

In Unit 7, you can use the following fundamental strategies to help ESL students access social studies content:

Access Content

An important strategy in making the language of Social Studies comprehensible to ESL students involves activating and building students' background knowledge. The more background knowledge they have, the more they will understand the text. An additional way to support or scaffold students' learning is to modify the input itself. In doing so, we enable students to access meaning more easily.

The use of visuals is an effective way to help ESL students grasp new words and concepts. Pictures, photographs, objects, vocabulary cards, maps, globes, and graphic organizers are among the visuals we can use in presenting academic content. Dramatization and acting out also can be highly effective.

The following examples in the Teacher's Edition will help your ESL students better understand the content of the unit.

- *Understand Concepts on p. 543 invites ESL students to use play money and to role-play borrowing and lending in order to apply and understand these concepts.*

- *Names of Countries on p. 550 has ESL students use a globe to point out and name various countries and their locations. Advanced learners create sentences about countries in the lesson and use a globe to point them out.*

Read Aloud

from "Keep the Home-Fires Burning"
a song by Lena Ford
music by Ivor Novello

Keep the home-fires burning,
While your hearts are yearning,
Though your lads are far away
They dream of home;
There's a silver lining
Through the dark cloud shining,
Turn the dark cloud inside out
Till the boys come home.

Families at home sent photos like this to soldiers at war. ▶

Build Background

- Ford and Novello wrote this song in 1914.
- The song is sentimental, and it quickly became popular, particularly with English citizens who had family members fighting in the Great War (World War I).

Definitions

- *yearning:* wishing
- *lads:* young men

Read Alouds and Primary Sources

- *Read Alouds and Primary Sources* contains additional selections to be used with Unit 7.

Bibliography

(AWARD) *The Glorious Flight: Across the Channel with Louis Blériot,* by Alice Provensen and Martin Provensen (Viking Press, ISBN 0-14-050729-9, 1987) **Easy** **Caldecott Medal Winner**

(AWARD) *Passage to Freedom: The Sugihara Story,* by Ken Mochizuki (Lee & Low Books, ISBN 1-880000-49-0, 1999) **Easy** **American Bookseller Pick of the Lists**

Vietnam Veterans Memorial, by Jason Cooper (Rourke Book Company, ISBN 0-86593-549-1, 1999) **Easy**

Air Raid— Pearl Harbor!, by Theodore Taylor (Harcourt, ISBN 0-15-216421-9, 2001) **On-Level**

(AWARD) *Bud, Not Buddy,* by Christopher Paul Curtis (Delacorte Press, ISBN 0-385-32306-9, 1999) **On-Level** **Newbery Award Winner**

(AWARD) *Out of the Dust,* by Karen Hesse (Scholastic Paperbacks, 0-590-37125-8, 1999) **On-Level** *Newbery Award Winner*

Flags of Our Fathers, by James Bradley (adapted for young readers) (Delacorte Press, ISBN 0-385-72932-4, 2001) **Challenge**

The Good Fight: How WW II Was Won, by Stephen E. Ambrose (Atheneum, ISBN 0-689-84361-5, 2001) **Challenge**

The Nazi Olympics, by Susan D. Bachrach (Little, Brown, ISBN 0-316-07087-4, 2000) **Challenge**

Atlas of World History, by John Haywood (Metro Books, ISBN 1-58663-099-7, 2000) **Teacher reference**

The Timetables of History: A Horizontal Linkage of People and Events, by Bernard Grun (Simon & Schuster, ISBN 0-671-74271-X, 1991) **Teacher reference**

Discovery Channel School Videos

Jerusalem: City of Heaven Visit this city, which is holy to Jews, Christians, and Muslims and which continues to attract conflict and controversy. (Item # 716266D, 51 minutes)

Normandy: The Great Crusade Watch footage of the actual landing at Omaha Beach on D-Day, hear personal accounts of soldiers, and learn about the evolution of D-Day. (Item # 718361D, 53 minutes)

- To order *Discovery Channel School* videos, please call the following toll-free number: 1-888-892-3484.
- Free online lesson plans are available at **DiscoverySchool.com**.

(AWARD) Look for this symbol throughout the Teacher's Edition to find **Award-Winning Selections.** Additional book references are suggested throughout this unit.

A World in Opposition

Why was much of the twentieth century a time of war and change?

511

A World in Opposition

Unit Overview

Competition between European nations led to the Great War, which eventually drew in the United States. Economic depression and the rise of dictators in Germany and Italy brought on World War II, which again involved not only Europe, but also Asia and the United States. During the rest of the century, there were various smaller conflicts, especially in the Eastern Hemisphere.

Unit Outline

Chapter 18 *The World at War*
pp. 518–539

Chapter 19 *From Peace to War*
pp. 540–565

Chapter 20 *The Cold War*
pp. 566–591

Unit Question

- Have students read the question under the painting.

- To activate prior knowledge, ask students what kinds of things might cause wars to begin.

- Create a list of students' ideas about causes of war.

✓ **Portfolio Assessment** Keep this list to review with students at the end of the unit on p. 595.

Practice and Extend

Hands-on Unit Project

✓ **Unit Performance Assessment**

- The Unit Project, *We Interrupt This Program,* found on p. 596, is an ongoing performance assessment project to enrich students' learning throughout the unit.

- This project, which has students collecting information and old photos for a scrapbook, may be started now or at any time during this unit of study.

- A performance assessment scoring guide is located on p. 596.

Begin with a Primary Source

Objective
- Acquire information from primary sources.

Resource
- Poster 13

Interpret a Primary Source

- Tell students that this primary source is a quotation from a speech by Winston Churchill, who was Prime Minister of Great Britain during World War II.

- Winston Churchill was expressing gratitude to the Royal Air Force.

- ✓**Portfolio Assessment** Remind students of the list that they created of possible causes of war (see p. 511). Have students add to their list as they read the unit. Review students' lists at the end of the unit on p. 595.

Interpret the Photograph

- Point out that this photograph shows D-Day in 1944.

- *D-day* is the term for a secret day on which a military operation will begin. Here the Allies attacked the Germans in Normandy, France, on June 6, 1944, the most famous D-day in history.

- Have students discuss what they can learn about this battle from viewing the photograph.

1910	1920	1930	1940
1914–1918 The Great War (World War I)		**1929** Stock Market Crash	**1939–1945** World War II

512   1

Practice and Extend

FYI **SOCIAL STUDIES**
Background

About the Primary Source

- The primary source on p. 513 is quoted from Winston Churchill. He used it to express gratitude to Britain's Royal Air Force, which defeated the *Luftwaffe*, the German Air Force, during the Battle of Britain.

- German leaders wanted to invade Britain across the English Channel. In July 1940 the *Luftwaffe* began bombing along the British coast. After a while, the *Luftwaffe* bombed London nightly. Germany gave up its attempts to defeat Britain from the air in May 1941.

- Churchill symbolized the fierce British resistance to conquest by Germany. Churchill was an excellent orator and often encouraged the British people through his dynamic speeches.

> *"Never in the field of human conflict has so much been owed by so many to so few."*
>
> —said by Winston Churchill during the Battle of Britain, August 20, 1940

This photo of D-Day in 1944 shows all the forces of modern warfare—land, sea, and air—coming together for one big battle.

Use the Time Line

The time line at the bottom of pages 512–513 covers the 70 years from 1910 to 1980, when much of the world was in upheaval.

1 **How many years passed between the end of the Great War and the beginning of World War II?** 21 years
Analyze Information

2 **The United Nations was founded in 1945, but more wars followed. Discuss whether those wars were as large as those before its founding and why you think as you do.** Possible answer: Wars were as large. Wars were named after the countries where the wars were fought. These were not world wars.
Make Inferences

3 **Which war in this period lasted the longest? How long?** Vietnam War; 21 years Analyze Information

1950   1960   1970   1980

1945
United Nations
is founded.

Atomic
Age begins.

1950–1953
Korean War
2

1954–1975
Vietnam War
2 3

513

FYI SOCIAL STUDIES
Background

More About D-Day

- Thousands of American, British, Canadian, and French soldiers stormed a 50-mile stretch of French beach called Normandy.
- This Normandy invasion was also called Operation Overlord.

Meet the People

Objective

- Identify the contributions of significant individuals during the twentieth century.

Resource

- Poster 14

Research the People

Each of the people pictured on these pages played an important part in events of the twentieth century. Have students do research to find out the answers to the following questions.

- **What was the focus of President Wilson's campaign slogans for reelection in 1916? Give an example.** Peace; "He kept us out of war."

- **For what disaster in the Great War was Winston Churchill blamed?** The failed attack against the Turks in the Dardanelles and the Gallipoli Peninsula

- **What medal was Hitler awarded for his fighting in the Great War?** The Iron Cross

- **How long was Mao's Long March?** 6,000 miles, from Jiangxi province to Shaanxi

Students may wish to write their own questions about other people on these pages for the rest of the class to answer.

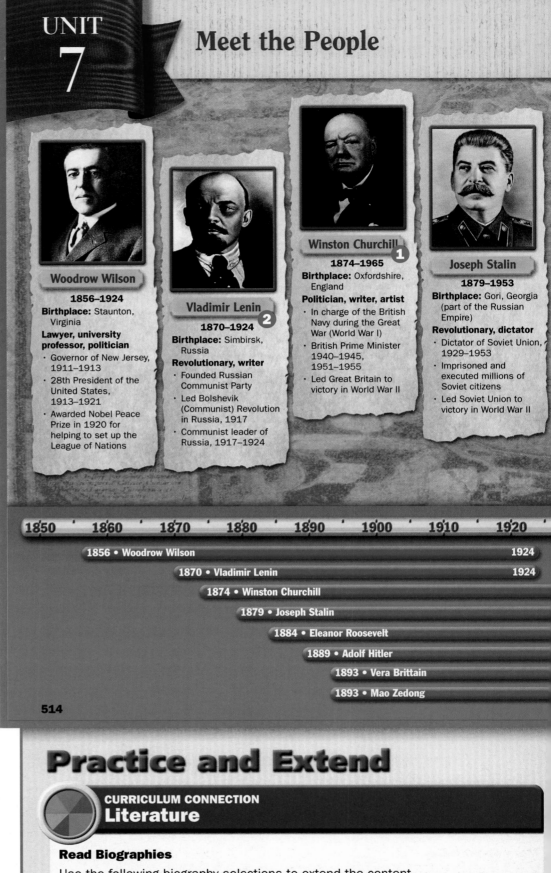

Woodrow Wilson

1856–1924

Birthplace: Staunton, Virginia

Lawyer, university professor, politician

- Governor of New Jersey, 1911–1913
- 28th President of the United States, 1913–1921
- Awarded Nobel Peace Prize in 1920 for helping to set up the League of Nations

Vladimir Lenin

1870–1924

Birthplace: Simbirsk, Russia

Revolutionary, writer

- Founded Russian Communist Party
- Led Bolshevik (Communist) Revolution in Russia, 1917
- Communist leader of Russia, 1917–1924

Winston Churchill

1874–1965

Birthplace: Oxfordshire, England

Politician, writer, artist

- In charge of the British Navy during the Great War (World War I)
- British Prime Minister 1940–1945, 1951–1955
- Led Great Britain to victory in World War II

Joseph Stalin

1879–1953

Birthplace: Gori, Georgia (part of the Russian Empire)

Revolutionary, dictator

- Dictator of Soviet Union, 1929–1953
- Imprisoned and executed millions of Soviet citizens
- Led Soviet Union to victory in World War II

1850	1860	1870	1880	1890	1900	1910	1920

1856 • Woodrow Wilson   1924

1870 • Vladimir Lenin   1924

1874 • Winston Churchill

1879 • Joseph Stalin

1884 • Eleanor Roosevelt

1889 • Adolf Hitler

1893 • Vera Brittain

1893 • Mao Zedong

514

Practice and Extend

CURRICULUM CONNECTION
Literature

Read Biographies

Use the following biography selections to extend the content.

Churchill and the British, by John Bradley (Gloucester Press, ISBN 0-531-17227-9, 1990) **Easy**

Woodrow Wilson, President, by Sallie Randolph (Walker & Co., ISBN 0-802-78143-8, 1992) **On-Level**

Eleanor Roosevelt: A Life of Discovery, by Russell Freedman (Houghton Mifflin Corp., ISBN 0-395-84520-3, 1997) **Challenge**

For more information, go to
www.sfsocialstudies.com/meetthepeople.

Eleanor Roosevelt

1884–1962 ④

Birthplace: New York, NY

Activist, writer, humanitarian

- First Lady of United States, 1933–1945
- United States delegate to United Nations, 1945, 1949–1951, 1961
- Helped draft the *United Nations Universal Declaration of Human Rights,* 1948

Adolf Hitler

1889–1945 ③

Birthplace: Braunau, Austria

Dictator

- Dictator of Germany, 1933–1945
- Rearmed Germany in the 1930s and started World War II in 1939
- Killed millions of Jews and others in the Holocaust

Vera Brittain

1893–1970 ⑤

Birthplace: Newcastle-under-Lyme, England

Writer, activist

- Volunteered as a nurse in the Great War
- Wrote *Testament of Youth* about her experiences in the war
- Supported women's rights, opposed war

Mao Zedong

1893–1976 ②

Birthplace: Shao-shan, Hunan province, China

Soldier, revolutionary, writer

- Led Communist Party during the Long March and afterward
- Established People's Republic of China in 1949 and was its leader until his death
- Started the Cultural Revolution in 1966

1930	1940	1950	1960	1970	1980	1990	2000

1965

1953

1962

1945

1970

1976

515

Use the Time Line

Have students use the time line and biographies to answer the following questions.

❶ Which historic figure led his country at two different times? Winston Churchill
Analyze Information

❷ Describe one similarity between the lives of Vladimir Lenin and Mao Zedong. Both led the Communist Party in their own country; both were revolutionaries and writers.
Analyze Information

❸ Which historic figure was born in one country and became the leader of another? Hitler was born in Austria and led Germany. Analyze Information

❹ Which historic figure served in an international capacity without being a leader of a nation? Eleanor Roosevelt, delegate to the UN Analyze Information

❺ Which historic figure never held a government office? Vera Brittain
Analyze Information

Biographies

Three of the people shown here are discussed more extensively in the Biography pages in Unit 7.

- Vera Brittain, p. 533
- Winston Churchill, p. 555
- Mao Zedong, p. 581

Read About the People

The people shown here are discussed in the text on the following pages in Unit 7.

- Woodrow Wilson, pp. 536–537
- Vladimir Lenin, pp. 531, 546
- Winston Churchill, pp. 549, 551, 555, 568–569
- Joseph Stalin, pp. 541, 546–547, 549, 551, 560, 569–571
- Eleanor Roosevelt, p. 560
- Adolf Hitler, pp. 541, 544–545, 549, 551, 560
- Vera Brittain, p. 533
- Mao Zedong, pp. 577–580, 581

WEB SITE
Technology

Students can research the lives of people on this page by clicking on *Meet the People* at **www.sfsocialstudies.com.**

Reading Social Studies

Cause and Effect

Objective

Analyze information by identifying cause-and-effect relationships.

Resource

- Workbook, p. 127

About the Unit Target Skill

- The target reading skill for this unit is Cause and Effect.
- Students are introduced to the unit target skill here and are given an opportunity to practice it.
- Further opportunities to use cause and effect are found throughout Unit 7.

1 Introduce and Motivate

Preview To activate prior knowledge, ask students for examples of cause-and-effect relationships from previous units of this textbook. [Example: In Unit 6, students read about expanding empires and the rise of imperialism (the cause), which caused competition among European nations (the effect).]

A World in Opposition

Cause and Effect

Cause	Effect
A **cause** is why something happens.	An **effect** is what happens.

- Sometimes writers use clue words and phrases such as *because*, *so*, *since*, *thus*, and *as a result* to signal cause and effect.

- A cause may have more than one effect. An effect may have more than one cause.

Read the following paragraph. **Cause** and **effect** have been highlighted.

In Chapter 17, you read about expanding empires and imperialism in the late 1800s. Nations wanted land, raw materials, and large numbers of people to buy their products. The effect was that these nations decided that they needed empires. Huge areas of Africa and Asia became colonies of Western countries. As a result, the people of those areas lost their independence.

516

Practice and Extend

 ACCESS CONTENT
ESL Support

Cause and Effect Have students identify possible causes or effects.

Beginning Say or show an effect (a full trash can), and have students tell the cause. Help students tell or act out possible causes, such as "No one emptied it." Help students identify the cause and the effect. Continue with other causes and effects.

Intermediate Mention a cause and have students supply the effect. For example, "Bob walks with his shoes untied. What might happen?" (Bob might trip and fall down.) Have students work in groups to create cause-and-effect pairs.

Advanced Have students suggest cause-and-effect pairs. Point out that an effect can be a cause in a new cause-and-effect pair. For example, Bob walks with his shoes untied, which *causes* him to fall (an *effect*). The fall *causes* him to break his leg (*effect*). Have students make cause-and-effect chains.

Imperialism and War

As European countries grew strong and wealthy in the 1800s, they began to look for lands to colonize. This desire to have overseas colonies led to tension among the European powers.

For example, war almost broke out in 1911 over Morocco, a country in North Africa. When Germany tried to seize a port city there, Great Britain and France joined forces to stop it.

Italy and Germany were both new countries that had formed from smaller territories in the 1860s and 1870s. These nations tried to catch up with countries such as Great Britain and France in the race for colonies. Imperialism in Europe was at its height. German leaders believed that they needed a powerful navy to take and keep colonies. They then challenged Great Britain as a naval power. The British ship *Dreadnought,* shown above, was built as a warning to the German Navy.

Russia, France, and Great Britain all wanted land that was controlled by the Ottoman Empire (present-day Turkey). When European imperialism erupted into war in 1914, the Ottoman Empire opposed these countries.

Use the reading strategy of cause and effect to answer these questions.

1. What major cause of tension among European countries does this passage identify?

2. What caused Great Britain to consider Germany a threat to peace?

3. What caused the Ottoman Empire (Turkey) to decide to fight against Russia, France, and Great Britain when war broke out?

517

Standardized Test Prep

- Use Workbook p. 127 to give students practice with standardized test format.
- Chapter and Unit Tests in the Assessment Book use standardized test format.
- Test-taking tips are contained in the front portion of the Assessment Book Teacher's Edition.

Also on Teacher Resources CD-ROM.

Workbook, p. 127

Cause and Effect

The European powers had several reasons for trying to expand their empires in the late 1800s.

Directions: Read p. 521 in your textbook. Then, for each of the following, fill in the circle next to the correct answer.

1. What caused intense competition among the nations of Europe during the late 1800s?
   Ⓐ communism
   Ⓑ nationalism
   Ⓒ imperialism
   Ⓓ nationalism and imperialism

2. What led some European nations to begin colonizing?
   Ⓐ They had too many people and needed a place where peasants could live.
   Ⓑ They did not like where they currently lived.
   Ⓒ They wanted to claim new resources for their growing industries.
   Ⓓ They were poor and needed money.

3. What did Germany do to make it easier to take and keep colonies?
   Ⓐ became allies with Great Britain
   Ⓑ became allies with France
   Ⓒ paid foreign peoples to become German citizens
   Ⓓ built a powerful navy

4. What caused many Africans and Asians to lose their independence during the nineteenth century?
   Ⓐ famine
   Ⓑ civil wars
   Ⓒ colonization by Western European countries
   Ⓓ disease

5. What led Great Britain and France to join forces against Germany in 1911?
   Ⓐ Germany tried to seize a Moroccan port.
   Ⓑ The Ottoman Empire was a target for colonization.
   Ⓒ Germany added to its naval power.
   Ⓓ They believed Germany already had too many colonies.

Notes for Home: Your child learned how the countries of Western Europe expanded their influence to other lands.
Home Activity: Discuss with your child how imperial expansion spreads the culture and influence of the colonizing nation to the nation being colonized. Brainstorm a list of ways your family's life might change if the United States were colonized by Great Britain, France, or Germany.

Teach and Discuss

- Explain that an effect (what happens) has a cause (a reason). As they read, ask students to look for clue words, such as *because, so, since, thus,* and *as a result,* to find causes and effects. Point out that sometimes there are no clue words.

- Have students read the sample paragraph on p. 516. Make sure they can state why the sentences highlighted in blue are the causes of the sentences highlighted in yellow, the effects.

- Then have students read the longer practice sample on p. 517 and answer the questions that follow.

- Ask students why, when studying history, it is important to understand causes and effects. (To understand history, we need to know why something happened and how one action led to another.)

Close and Assess

Apply it!

1. Imperialism, or the desire to have colonies

2. Germany built a large navy, challenging Great Britain as a naval power.

3. Because Russia, France, and Britain wanted land controlled by the Ottoman Empire

Chapter Planning Guide

Chapter 18 • The World at War

Locating Time and Place pp. 518–519

Lesson Titles	Pacing	Main Ideas
Lesson 1 **Headed Toward War** pp. 520–523	2 days	• Competition between nations pushes Europe toward a major war.
Chart and Graph Skills: **Compare Parallel Time Lines** pp. 524–525		• Parallel time lines can compare events happening in different places at the same time.
Lesson 2 **The Great War** pp. 526–532	2 days	• The Great War caused much destruction.
Biography: Vera Brittain p. 533		• The Great War changed a British woman's life.
Lesson 3 **After the War** pp. 534–537	1 day	• The Allies tried to make a peace treaty that would solve all of Europe's problems.

✓ **Chapter 18 Review**
pp. 538–539

► **Women from the Women's Royal Air Force celebrate the end of the Great War in 1918.**

✓ = Assessment Options

◀ **Gas masks like this one were used during the Great War.**

Vocabulary	Resources	Meeting Individual Needs
mobilization neutral	• Workbook, p. 129 • Transparency 20 • Every Student Learns Guide, p. 246–249 • Quick Study, pp. 124–125 • Workbook, p. 130	• Leveled Practice, TE p. 521 • ESL Support, TE p. 522 • Leveled Practice, TE p. 524
casualty trench warfare armistice	• Workbook, p. 131 • Transparencies 22, 53 • Every Student Learns Guide, p. 250–253 • Quick Study, pp. 126–127	• Leveled Practice, TE p. 527 • Learning Styles, TE p. 529 • ESL Support, TE p. 530
Holocaust reparation inflation	• Workbook, p. 132 • Transparencies 16, 54 • Every Student Learns Guide, p. 254–257 • Quick Study, pp. 128–129	• ESL Support, TE p. 535 • Leveled Practice, TE p. 536
	✓ Chapter 18 Content Test, Assessment Book, pp. 93–94 ✓ Chapter 18 Skills Test, Assessment Book, pp. 95–96	✓ Chapter 18 Performance Assessment, TE p. 538

Workbook Support

Use the following Workbook pages to support content and skills development as you teach Chapter 18. You can also view and print Workbook pages from the Teacher Resources CD-ROM.

Workbook, p. 127

Cause and Effect

The European powers had several reasons for trying to expand their empires in the late 1800s.

Directions: Read p. 521 in your textbook. Then, for each of the following, fill in the circle next to the correct answer.

1. What caused intense competition among the nations of Europe during the late 1800s?
   - (A) communism
   - (B) nationalism
   - (C) imperialism
   - ● nationalism and imperialism

2. What led some European nations to begin colonizing?
   - (A) They had too many people and needed a place where peasants could live.
   - (B) They did not like where they currently lived.
   - ● They wanted to claim new resources for their growing industries.
   - (D) They were poor and needed money.

3. What did Germany do to make it easier to take and keep colonies?
   - (A) became allies with Great Britain
   - (B) became allies with France
   - (C) paid foreign peoples to become German citizens
   - ● built a powerful navy

4. What caused many Africans and Asians to lose their independence during the nineteenth century?
   - (A) famine
   - (B) civil wars
   - ● colonization by Western European countries
   - (D) disease

5. What led Great Britain and France to join forces against Germany in 1911?
   - ● Germany tried to seize a Moroccan port.
   - (B) The Ottoman Empire was a target for colonization.
   - (C) Germany added to its naval power.
   - (D) They believed Germany already had too many colonies.

Notes for Home: Your child learned how the countries of Western Europe expanded their influence to other lands.
Home Activity: Discuss with your child how imperial expansion spreads the culture and influence of the colonizing nation to the nation being colonized. Brainstorm a list of ways your family's life might change if the United States were colonized by Great Britain, France, or Germany.

Use with Pupil Edition, p. 517

Workbook, p. 128

Vocabulary Preview

These are the vocabulary words for Chapter 18. How much do you know about these words?

Directions: Match each word with its meaning. Write the letter of the word on the line next to its meaning. You may use your glossary.

- a. mobilization
- b. neutral
- c. casualty
- d. trench warfare
- e. armistice
- f. holocaust
- g. reparation
- h. inflation

- **a** preparations nations make before sending their armies into battle
- **g** payment for war losses
- **b** not taking sides
- **h** rapid increase in prices
- **f** mass killing
- **e** a cease-fire agreement
- **c** wounded or killed soldier
- **d** armies dig deep ditches to shelter their troops

Directions: Write the vocabulary word that best completes each sentence.

1. When war broke out in 1914, the United States remained ___**neutral**___ by not entering the war immediately.

2. The Armenian ___**Holocaust**___ was the first of several mass killings in the twentieth century.

3. Germany's war-torn economy was largely the result of huge ___**reparation**___ payments to the Allies.

4. During periods of ___**inflation**___, money loses value.

Notes for Home: Your child learned the vocabulary terms for Chapter 18.
Home Activity: Help your child use each of the vocabulary words in an original sentence.

Use with Pupil Edition, p. 518

Workbook, p. 129

Lesson 1: Headed Toward War

Directions: The following is a list of the European Powers. Separate them into the alliances they formed. Write *TA* if the country was a member of the Triple Alliance. Write *TE* if it was a member of the Triple Entente. Then answer the questions that follow. You may use your textbook.

- **TE** 1. Great Britain
- **TA** 2. Italy
- **TE** 3. France
- **TA** 4. Germany
- **TA** 5. Austria-Hungary
- **TE** 6. Russia

7. What effect did these alliances have on the possibility of war?

   They helped push Europe toward war.

8. Name one advantage and one disadvantage of a country being part of a large alliance.

   Possible answers: Advantage: the country has the protection of the other countries in the alliance. Disadvantage: if one of the other countries is attacked, all the countries may have to go to war.

Notes for Home: Your child learned about the alliances formed by the European Powers before the Great War.
Home Activity: With your child, discuss the similarities and differences between a friendship and a formal alliance.

Use with Pupil Edition, p. 523

Workbook, p. 130

Compare Parallel Time Lines

Directions: Use the information in the parallel time lines to answer the following questions.

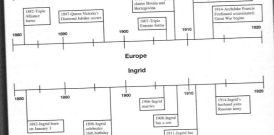

1. How old was Ingrid at the time of Queen Victoria's Diamond Jubilee?

   15

2. What important world event occurred the year after Ingrid married?

   Triple Entente formed

3. What world event may have contributed to Ingrid's husband's decision to join the Russian army?

   Archduke Ferdinand was assassinated.

4. What event happened in Ingrid's family the year Austria-Hungary claimed Bosnia and Herzegovina?

   Ingrid's son was born.

Notes for Home: Your child learned how to analyze relationships between parallel time lines.
Home Activity: With your child, create a time line of activities and events from your child's life over the past week or month. Then create a parallel time line of U.S. or world events.

Use with Pupil Edition, p. 525

Workbook Support

Use with Pages 526–532.

son 2: The Great War

ons: The Great War in Europe was fought along two fronts. Each of the
g phrases deals with either the Eastern Front, the Western Front, or both.
e number of each phrase under the appropriate heading in the Venn diagram
You may use your textbook.

erman, French, and British soldiers come to a standstill.

ussia battles Germany and Austria-Hungary.

oldiers use new weapons such as poisonous gas, machine guns, and tanks.

r the first time, airplanes are used to drop bombs on the enemy.

ermans attack Verdun.

housands of soldiers die.

llies storm German trenches.

ussian army suffers terrible casualties.

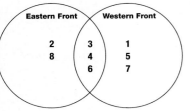

Eastern Front — 2, 8
(overlap) — 3, 4, 6
Western Front — 1, 5, 7

Notes for Home: Your child learned about the fighting in Europe during the Great War.
Home Activity: With your child, examine the map on p. 531. Discuss how people probably were affected
when the war front moved into their home area.

Use with Pupil Edition, p. 532

Use with Pages 534–537.

Lesson 3: After the War

The Great War caused events to follow in its aftermath.

Directions: Draw a line from each country in the first column to the corresponding
phrase in the second column. Then answer the questions that follow.

1. Ottoman Empire   **a.** its President created Fourteen Points

2. United States   **b.** site of Armenian Holocaust

3. Russia (Soviet Union)   **c.** its money became virtually worthless

4. Germany   **d.** suffered the greatest number of casualties

5. What organization was formed from President Wilson's plan for a "general association of nations"?

League of Nations

6. What three things did the Treaty of Versailles require from Germany?

**Accept blame for starting the war, remove forts and other
defenses from the Rhineland, pay huge reparations to the
Allies**

7. Look at the maps on p. 535. Name three new countries that appeared in Eastern Europe
after the war.

**Possible answers: Poland, Czechoslovakia, Austria,
Hungary, Yugoslavia, Estonia, Latvia, Lithuania, Finland**

Notes for Home: Your child learned about the results of the Great War.
Home Activity: Discuss with your child the provisions of the Treaty of Versailles. Ask him or her why the
Allies might want to punish Germany in this way.

Use with Pupil Edition, p. 536

Use with Chapter 18.

Vocabulary Review

Directions: Complete each sentence with the correct word or phrase.

mobilization	casualty	armistice	reparation
neutral	trench warfare	holocaust	inflation

1. In 1918 the Great War ended with an **armistice** .

2. Many families suffered at least one **casualty** due to the fighting in the
Great War.

3. The Germans were bound by the Treaty of Versailles to make **reparation**
payments to the Allies.

4. In Germany, **inflation** made money so worthless that many people burned it
for heat.

5. Some countries did not take sides in the war. They chose to remain **neutral** .

6. Europeans started the process of **mobilization** to prepare their armies for war.

7. Ottoman officials massacred between one-half million and one million Armenians in the first
holocaust of the twentieth century.

8. When engaging in **trench warfare** , soldiers had to crawl out to fight the enemy.

Directions: On the lines below, use as many words as possible from the box above
to write an imaginary news bulletin about the end of the Great War.

Notes for Home: Your child learned the vocabulary terms for Chapter 18.
Home Activity: Provide your child with one-word clues for each vocabulary term. Have him or her try to
answer with the correct term while using as few clues as possible.

Use with Pupil Edition, p. 539

Assessment Support

Use these Assessment Book pages and the test maker to assess content and skills in Chapter 18. You can also view and print Assessment Book pages from the Teacher Resources CD-ROM.

Assessment Book, p. 93

Chapter 18

Part 1: Content Test

Directions: Fill in the circle next to the correct answer.

Lesson Objective (1:1)

1. Which was a leading cause of the Great War?
   - Ⓐ invasion of France
   - ● competition among nations
   - Ⓒ assassination of Wilhelm II
   - Ⓓ invention of airplanes

Lesson Objective (1:3)

2. In the late 1800s, which two countries were in conflict over problems caused by imperialism?
   - ● Germany and France
   - Ⓑ Spain and Russia
   - Ⓒ Austria and Hungary
   - Ⓓ Serbia and Great Britain

Lesson Objective (1:3, 4)

3. When did Germany take over two provinces from France?
   - Ⓐ at the outbreak of the Great War
   - Ⓑ in 1945
   - ● after a war in 1870–1871
   - Ⓓ in the mid-1700s

Lesson Objective (1:2)

4. Which of the following events occurred first?
   - Ⓐ Austria-Hungary claimed two Serbian provinces.
   - Ⓑ The Triple Entente was formed.
   - Ⓒ Archduke Francis Ferdinand was assassinated.
   - ● The Triple Alliance was formed.

Lesson Objective (1:5)

5. How did alliances among European countries push them toward the Great War?
   - ● Allied countries began to mobilize for war.
   - Ⓑ The countries were too far from each other.
   - Ⓒ Different languages caused misunderstandings.
   - Ⓓ Alliances were declared for a limited time only.

Lesson Objective (2:2)

6. How did new weapons used in the Great War differ from those used in previous wars?
   - Ⓐ They were manufactured in Germany.
   - Ⓑ All weapons could be used in air attacks.
   - ● They were more destructive.
   - Ⓓ Untrained soldiers could use them.

Lesson Objective (2:2)

7. Which weapon was a silent killer?
   - Ⓐ tanks
   - ● poison gas
   - Ⓒ airplanes
   - Ⓓ machines guns

Lesson Objective (2:4)

8. What distinguished the Battles of the Somme and Verdun from other battles in the Great War?
   - Ⓐ Both were fought in the countryside.
   - Ⓑ Soldiers fought with rifles.
   - ● Both had an extremely high number of casualties.
   - Ⓓ The British led powerful attacks.

Use with Pupil Edition, p. 538

Assessment Book, p. 94

Lesson Objective (2:1)

9. What prompted the United States to join the Great War?
   - Ⓐ a peace treaty signed between Russia and Germany
   - Ⓑ the introduction of tanks and machine guns
   - Ⓒ the sinking of the *Lusitania* and the number of casualties at the Battle of Verdun
   - ● the sinking of the *Lusitania* and Germany's attempts to bribe Mexico with the promise of U.S. lands

Lesson Objective (2:4, 5)

10. What direct effect did American soldiers have on the war?
    - ● They became additional Allied casualties.
    - Ⓑ Fresh troops overpowered the Central Powers' soldiers.
    - Ⓒ They negotiated cease-fires with Germany.
    - Ⓓ More people at home became nurses and doctors.

Lesson Objective (2:3)

11. Which is NOT a reason why the Russian people were ready to support a revolution?
    - Ⓐ They had suffered terrible casualties on the Eastern Front.
    - Ⓑ The economy had collapsed.
    - Ⓒ Little food and fuel were available.
    - ● Russia was close to winning the war.

Lesson Objective (2:3)

12. Which communist leader took over the government in Russia in 1917?
    - Ⓐ Nicholas II
    - ● Vladimir Lenin
    - Ⓒ Joseph Stalin
    - Ⓓ Wilhelm II

Lesson Objective (3:1)

13. Which was NOT an outcome of the Great War?
    - Ⓐ More than 8 million soldiers were killed.
    - Ⓑ Nations incurred large debts to fight the war.
    - ● Russia and France signed a pact.
    - Ⓓ The map of Europe had to be redrawn because national borders changed.

Lesson Objective (3:1, 3)

14. What happened to the German Empire, the Russian Empire, the Ottoman Empire, and the empire of Austria-Hungary after the Great War?
    - ● They disappeared.
    - Ⓑ They grew more powerful.
    - Ⓒ They became U.S. territories.
    - Ⓓ They were unchanged by the war.

Lesson Objective (3:4)

15. Which nation opposed President Wilson's ideas for peace with Germany?
    - Ⓐ Great Britain
    - Ⓑ Italy
    - Ⓒ Russia
    - ● France

Lesson Objective (3:5)

16. How did the reparations ordered by the Treaty of Versailles affect the German economy?
    - ● The economy experienced high inflation.
    - Ⓑ German soldiers quit the military and moved home.
    - Ⓒ Germans rebelled against their leaders.
    - Ⓓ The German Empire had to be dissolved.

Use with Pupil Edition, p. 538

Assessment Support

Part 2: Skills Test

Directions: Use complete sentences to answer questions 1–6. Use a separate sheet of paper if you need more space.

1. What issues arose between Germany and the countries of France and Great Britain that ultimately helped lead to war? **Summarize**

   Germany had taken over two French provinces in a previous war, and France wanted them back. Germany's attempt to compete with Britain's navy caused tension between those two countries.

2. How might the outcome of the Great War have been different had new weapons not been widely used? **Make Inferences**

   Possible answer: There might have been fewer casualties. Airplanes, bombs, tanks, and poison gas allowed for greater destruction in wider areas than face-to-face combat.

3. How might the Great War have ended had the United States not joined the war effort? **Apply Information**

   Possible answers: The Allies might have lost to the Central Powers. The Central Powers, already exhausted, might have surrendered. The war might have continued for a longer period of time.

4. What effect did the Treaty of Versailles have on Germany? **Cause and Effect**

   Germany had to accept blame for the war and remove defenses from its border with France. It also had to pay for war losses incurred by the Allies. This caused skyrocketing inflation in Germany.

Use with Pupil Edition, p. 538

5. The Great War caused more suffering than any war up to that point. Which event do you think was most devastating: the loss of human life, destruction of property, or war debt? Explain. **Point of View**

   Possible answers: Human life is irreplaceable. Physical destruction took many years and a great deal of money to repair. Debts caused financial hardships for many Europeans for years after the war.

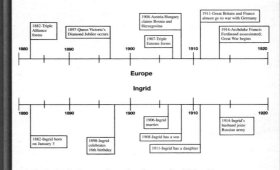

Europe

Ingrid

6. Use the time line to answer the questions. **Compare Parallel Time Lines**
   a. What do the longer vertical lines on the time lines stand for?

   the beginning of a 10-year period

   b. What war was in progress when Ingrid's husband joined the Russian Army?

   the Great War

   c. What event happened in Europe the year Ingrid was born?

   The Triple Alliance formed.

Use with Pupil Edition, p. 538

The World at War

Chapter 18 Outline

Resources

- Workbook, p. 128: Vocabulary Preview
- Vocabulary Cards
- Social Studies Plus!

1914, Sarajevo: Lesson 1

Ask students to describe the scene in the picture and to suggest what the people are doing. (It shows Sophia and Ferdinand shaking hands and greeting people.)

1916, Verdun: Lesson 2

The picture shows the battlefield at Verdun. Ask students to study the picture and describe what the soldiers are doing. (The soldiers are waiting in trenches.)

1919, Paris: Lesson 3

The picture shows the peace conference at Versailles that ended the Great War. Ask students how this picture differs from the picture just above. (In this picture, men are dressed formally, are seated calmly. In the picture above, the soldiers are dirty and are prepared to fight.)

Lesson 1

1914
Sarajevo
An assassination helps push nations into war.

Lesson 2

1916
Verdun
War rages in Europe.

Lesson 3

1919
Paris
A peace conference ends the Great War.

518

Practice and Extend

Vocabulary Preview

- Use Workbook p. 128 to help students preview the vocabulary words in this chapter.
- Use Vocabulary Cards to preview key concept words in this chapter.

 Also on Teacher Resources CD-ROM.

Workbook, p. 128

Vocabulary Preview
Use with Chapter 18.

These are the vocabulary words for Chapter 18. How much do you know about these words?

Directions: Match each word with its meaning. Write the letter of the word on the line next to its meaning. You may use your glossary.

a. mobilization ___ preparations nations make before sending their armies into battle
b. neutral ___ payment for war losses
c. casualty ___ not taking sides
d. trench warfare ___ rapid increase in prices
e. armistice ___ mass killing
f. holocaust ___ a cease-fire agreement
g. reparation ___ wounded or killed soldier
h. inflation ___ armies dig trenches to shelter their troops

Directions: Write the vocabulary word that best completes each sentence.

1. When war broke out in 1914, the United States remained _____ by not entering the war immediately.
2. The Armenian _____ was the first of several mass killings in the twentieth century.
3. Germany's war-torn economy was largely the result of huge _____ payments to the Allies.
4. During periods of _____ money loses value.

Notes for Home: Your child learned the vocabulary terms for Chapter 18.
Home Activity: Help your child use each of the vocabulary words in an original sentence.

Locating Time and Place

Why We Remember

Europeans are a variety of peoples living in countries on the same continent. They have their own cultures, languages, and customs. This has led to conflicts and civil wars. However, until 1914, most of these involved only a few countries. Some groups of people felt they were superior to others. Many had strong nationalist feelings about their country. This strained political relations between nations. These tensions eventually led to a world war. The effects of that war would continue to shape world events for the rest of the twentieth century.

519

- Have students examine the pictures shown on p. 518 for Lessons 1, 2, and 3.

- Remind students that each picture is coded with both a number and a color to link it to a place on the map on p. 519.

Why We Remember

Have students read the "Why We Remember" paragraph on p. 519, and ask them why events in this chapter might be important to them. Ask students if they think groups of people still feel superior to others.

WEB SITE
Technology

ou can learn more about
arajevo, Bosnia and Herzegovina;
erdun, France; and Paris, France
y clicking on *Atlas* at
ww.sfsocialstudies.com.

SOCIAL STUDIES STRAND
Geography

Mental Mapping On an outline map of Europe, ask students to label these countries or empires as of 1914: Austria-Hungary, France, Germany, Great Britain, Italy, Ottoman Empire, and Russia. Next, have them mark with an *X* the area in Europe where the major military campaigns took place. Finally, ask students to circle the names of the nations that were victorious in the Great War.

Headed Toward War

Objectives

- List some of the causes of the Great War.
- List the strong forces that caused friction between the countries of Europe in the years leading up to 1914.
- Explain how the taking of the French provinces by Germany caused friction.
- Explain how imperialism increased competition between France and Germany.
- Describe and explain the impact of alliances on the start of the Great War.

Vocabulary

mobilization, p. 522; **neutral,** p. 523

Resources

- Workbook, p. 129
- Transparency 20
- Every Student Learns Guide, pp. 246–249
- Quick Study, pp. 124–125

Quick Teaching Plan

If time is short, have students make a chart of conflicts.

- Have them label three columns: *Conflicting Nations, Cause,* and *Effect.*
- Students should write pairs, such as Germany/France, under *Conflicting Nations,* and then fill in the rest of the chart as they read.

1 Introduce and Motivate

Preview To activate prior knowledge, ask students to describe a time when they argued with someone about something they both wanted. Tell them that they will learn more about the effects of conflicts between nations as they read Lesson 1.

 You Are There The British enjoyed the Diamond Jubilee with its military display. But no one thought about why the British Empire had so many soldiers. Have students reflect on why this was so.

1880   **1900**   **192**

1882 Triple Alliance formed.

1907 Triple Entente formed.

1914 Great War begins.

AUSTRIA-HUNGARY
Sarajevo • SERBIA
BOSNIA AND HERZEGOVINA

Headed Toward War

PREVIEW

Focus on the Main Idea
Competition among nations pushed Europe toward war.

PLACES
Serbia
Bosnia and Herzegovina
Sarajevo

PEOPLE
Wilhelm II
Francis Ferdinand
Nicholas II

VOCABULARY
mobilization
neutral

TERMS
Triple Alliance
Triple Entente

You Are There For weeks you have been looking forward to the national celebration of Queen Victoria's Diamond Jubilee. It's the sixtieth anniversary of her reign in Great Britain. The special day in June 1897 arrives. You and many thousands of others line the streets for this grand parade. Colorfully dressed soldiers from all parts of the British Empire—East Indians, Africans, Australians, New Zealanders, Canadians, and others—march in step. At the high point of the parade, the queen herself passes in a magnificent coach. Everyone smiles and enjoys the celebration. How could anyone guess that war was to come within the next two decades?

▶ **Queen Victoria's Jubilees were often commemorated on stamps, plates, and mugs.**

Cause and Effect As you read, look for causes of tension among European nations and its effect on Europe and the world.

520

Practice and Extend

READING SKILL
Cause and Effect

In the Lesson Review, students complete a graphic organizer like the one below. You may want to provide students with a copy of Transparency 20 to complete as they read the lesson.

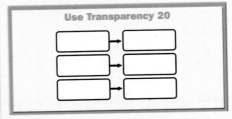
Use Transparency 20

WEB SITE
Technology

- You can look up vocabulary words by clicking on *Social Studies Library* and selecting the dictionary at **www.sfsocialstudies.com.**
- Students can learn more about current news by clicking on *Current Events* at **www.sfsocialstudies.com.**
- Explore other events that occurred on this day by clicking on *This Day in History* at **www.sfsocialstudies.com.**

Competition Among Nations

Queen Victoria's Diamond Jubilee was, in part, a celebration of the size and strength of Great Britain's empire. In Chapter 17, you read that nationalism and imperialism became strong forces in Europe in the late 1800s. They caused intense competition among the nations of Europe and produced dangerous disagreements.

A group of European nations challenged each other in a number of ways. These nations competed for colonies that were rich in natural resources. They used these resources to expand their growing industries. They tried to build up bigger navies and armies than their neighbors. In the early 1900s, the European Powers included Great Britain, France, Germany, Austria-Hungary, and Russia. Some thought that Italy belonged to this group too. As these nations competed, serious trouble developed.

France and Germany had problems left over from a war they fought in 1870–1871. After the war, Germany had taken over two French provinces. France wanted them back.

Since the early 1800s, the British Navy had ruled the seas. But by the 1890s, Germany's ruler, **Wilhelm II,** insisted on building a big, modern navy to compete with Great Britain. This caused tensions between Great Britain and Germany.

▶ **Kaiser Wilhelm II of Germany**

The British *Dreadnought* was completed in 1905.

Austria-Hungary contained many different ethnic groups, such as Poles, Czechs, and Slovaks. These ethnic groups wanted to have countries of their own. Their nationalism made the rulers of Austria-Hungary afraid. In 1908 Austria-Hungary claimed two provinces in **Serbia,** its neighbor to the south: **Bosnia** (BAHZ nee uh) and **Herzegovina** (hairt suh goh VEE nuh). This made the Serbians angry and caused friction between the two countries.

By the early 1900s, imperialism was causing tension among the Great Powers. Europeans wanted more resources and felt they had a right to take over lands in Africa, Asia, and other places. However, little land was left to colonize. Nations scrambled for what was left. In 1911 Great Britain and France almost went to war with Germany over a port in Morocco. Europe was near a boiling point.

REVIEW What was the cause of friction between Great Britain and Germany?
 Cause and Effect

521

Quick Summary European nations competed for colonies, built bigger navies and armies, and claimed provinces belonging to other nations. This led to friction between the nations.

❶ How did European nations challenge each other? They competed for colonies. They tried to build up bigger navies and armies than their neighbors.
Main Idea and Details

❷ What did Wilhelm II do to compete with Britain to obtain colonies? He built a big, modern navy. **Cause and Effect**

Test Talk

Locate Key Words in the Question

❸ Why were the rulers of Austria-Hungary worried? Repeat the question and have students ask themselves, "Who or what is this question about?" Nationalism was increasing among its many ethnic groups. **Analyze Information**

❹ How did imperialism cause problems in Europe? Nations competed to take control of parts of Africa and Asia, but little land was available.
Cause and Effect

✓ **REVIEW ANSWER** Wilhelm II began building a big, modern navy to compete with Great Britain. **Cause and Effect**

MEETING INDIVIDUAL NEEDS
Leveled Practice

Examine a Map Ask students to examine a map of Europe and North Africa.

Easy Locate all seven European countries mentioned in this section on a map. Also find Morocco. **Reteach**

On-Level Find one port in each nation of France, Germany, and Great Britain. Trace routes ships could take from each European port to a port in Morocco. **Extend**

Challenge Have students trace possible shipping routes from Morocco to France, Germany, and Great Britain. Then have students explain why Germany was at a disadvantage geographically in competing against Britain and France for Moroccan trade. **Enrich**

For a Lesson Summary, use Quick Study, p. 124.

Alliances Lead to War

Quick Summary Competing European nations formed two major alliances to protect themselves. The assassination of Archduke Ferdinand of Austria-Hungary started a chain reaction of events that led to war.

5 **What was good about alliances? What was dangerous about them?** They gave nations a feeling of security. One event could force nations to go to war to protect each other. **Compare and Contrast**

✓ Ongoing Assessment

If... students do not understand alliances,	**then...** have students think of an alliance as a group of nations working together as a single team.

Problem Solving

6 **Solve this problem: How do nations choose which alliances to join? Why did Britain and France join together? Why did Austria-Hungary join Germany?** Possible answer: If nations share the same enemy, they might join together because they can find strength in numbers. Both Britain and France feared Germany. The ruling class of both Germany and Austria-Hungary spoke the same language, and the countries shared a border. **Solve Problems**

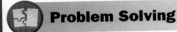

Europe in 1914

Point out that Europe was divided in two, with the Triple Entente against the Triple Alliance.

7 **Which three neutral countries bordered the Triple Alliance along its southeast border?** Montenegro, Serbia, and Romania **Interpret Maps**

MAP SKILL **Answer** Triple Alliance: Germany, Austria-Hungary, Italy; Triple Entente: Russia, France, Great Britain

---

Alliances Lead to War

In the years leading up to what became known as the Great War, the European Powers joined together in two opposing alliances. The countries agreed to protect each other in case of attack.

In 1882 Germany, Austria-Hungary, and Italy formed an alliance known as the **Triple Alliance.** Ties between Germany and Austria-Hungary were especially strong. The ruling class of Austria spoke German, and the two countries shared a long border.

In 1907, Russia, France, and Great Britain formed the **Triple Entente** (ahn TAHNT). In French, *entente* means "understanding." Each country understood that an attack on one meant an attack on all. On the map below, identify the countries in both alliances.

Though alliances made countries feel safe, they actually helped push Europe toward war. Countries promised to help their allies if trouble arose. Many began to mobilize for war.

Mobilization is the preparations nations make before sending their armies into battle. These preparations include getting troops, supplies, and weapons ready. Once mobilization started, it was almost impossible to stop it.

In the summer of 1914, members of the Triple Alliance and the Triple Entente became locked in a quarrel that soon led to an all-out war. On June 28, 1914, Archduke **Francis Ferdinand** of Austria-Hungary, next in line for his nation's throne, was assassinated in **Sarajevo** (sair uh YAY voh), the capital of Bosnia. Because a Serbian nationalist was responsible for the crime, the leaders of Austria-Hungary wanted to punish Serbia. Czar (zar) **Nicholas II,** the ruler of Russia, believed that his country should protect Serbia. Many people in Serbia and Russia belonged to the same religion: Orthodox Christianity. Nicholas II responded to Austria-Hungary's threats by mobilizing his army.

MAP SKILL Europe in 1914

▶ In 1914 Europe was divided into two main alliances. Notice that the Triple Entente surrounded the Triple Alliance.

MAP SKILL Use a Historical Map *What countries belonged to the Triple Alliance? What countries belonged to the Triple Entente?*

522

Practice and Extend

EXTEND LANGUAGE
ESL Support

Use Cause-and-Effect Words Point out that several causes and effects are described on pp. 522–523, but few clue words are used.

Beginning Help students use clue words from p. 516 to state events from their own lives Then help students use clue words to describe events that led to war.

Intermediate Choose one or two paragraphs from pp. 522–523. Read the paragraphs aloud. Then have students rephrase the paragraphs, adding clue words to show the causes and effects.

Advanced Have groups of students make a chart of the chain of events that led to war. Then have them use the chart to summarize the causes and effects, using clue words to make the connections clear.

For additional ESL support, use Every Student Learns Guide, pp. 246–249.

These events started a chain reaction that was soon felt throughout Europe. Germany declared war on Russia and Russia's ally, France. Then Germany invaded Belgium, Great Britain's ally and a **neutral** country, or one that does not take sides. Because Great Britain had a defensive treaty with Belgium, it declared war on Germany.

In August 1914, on the eve of the Great War, British foreign secretary Sir Edward Grey said,

> *"The lamps are going out all over Europe; we shall not see them lit again in our lifetime."*

The Great War—a war that affected many nations and peoples—had begun.

REVIEW What caused Great Britain to declare war on Germany in 1914? *Cause and Effect*

▶ This photo of Archduke Francis Ferdinand and his wife, Sophie, was taken just minutes before their death.

Summarize the Lesson

- **1882** Germany, Austria-Hungary, and Italy formed the Triple Alliance.
- **1907** Great Britain, France, and Russia formed the Triple Entente.
- **1914** Archduke Francis Ferdinand was assassinated, triggering the Great War in Europe.

LESSON 1 REVIEW

Check Facts and Main Ideas

1. *Cause and Effect* On a separate piece of paper, fill in the chart below by listing one cause or effect.

Causes	→	Effects
Germany took over two French provinces and France wanted them back.	→	Friction between France and Germany
Germany built a large, modern navy.	→	It caused relations to cool between Great Britain and Germany.
Members of the Triple Alliance and the Triple Entente became locked in a battle that led to war.	→	The Archduke of Austria-Hungary was assassinated.

2. What strong forces caused friction between the countries of Europe in the years leading up to 1914?

3. What was a cause of friction between France and Germany?

4. How did imperialism increase competition among nations in Europe?

5. **Critical Thinking:** *Make Inferences* Suppose the nations of Europe had not formed alliances in the years before 1914. Do you think a world war would have broken out? Explain.

Link to 🔗 Reading

Make Connections Czar Nicholas II was the last ruler of the old Russian Empire. *Czar* means *caesar.* Go back and read through your textbook. Where have you seen the word "caesar" before? What does this tell us about past civilizations?

523

Workbook, p. 129

Lesson 1: Headed Toward War

Directions: The following is a list of the European Powers. Separate them into the alliances they formed. Write *TA* if the country was a member of the Triple Alliance. Write *TE* if it was a member of the Triple Entente. Then answer the questions that follow. You may use your textbook.

___ 1. Great Britain
___ 2. Italy
___ 3. France
___ 4. Germany
___ 5. Austria-Hungary
___ 6. Russia

7. What effect did their alliances have on the possibility of war?

8. Name one advantage and one disadvantage of a country being part of a large alliance.

Also on Teacher Resources CD-ROM.

SOCIAL STUDIES STRAND
Geography

8 **Look at the map on p. 522 and determine which alliance had an easier time joining forces for protection and attack.** Possible answer: The Triple Alliance did because Germany and Austria-Hungary shared a border, as did Austria-Hungary and Italy. **Apply Information**

Primary Source
Cited in *Oxford Dictionary of Quotations*

9 **What do you think Sir Edward Grey meant by his statement?** Possible answer: The lamps were nations that were falling under German armies. **Analyze Primary Sources**

✓ **REVIEW ANSWER** Germany invaded Belgium. *Cause and Effect*

3 Close and Assess

Summarize the Lesson

Tell students to examine the vertical time line. Ask them to summarize the lesson by reviewing the events and explaining how they are related.

✓ **LESSON 1 REVIEW**

1. *Cause and Effect* For possible answers, see the reduced pupil page.

2. Nationalism and imperialism

3. Germany had taken two provinces from France.

4. Land for colonization was limited.

5. **Critical Thinking:** *Make Inferences* Possible answer: No, nations might have found ways to work out problems without resorting to war.

Link to 🔗 Reading

Caesar was used in ancient Rome. Cultural aspects are sometimes adapted from past great civilizations; the role of the Czar was probably similar to that of Caesar.

Compare Parallel Time Lines

Objective

- Compare parallel time lines to show a time relationship between events happening in different places.

Resource

- Workbook, p. 130

1 Introduce and Motivate

What are parallel time lines? Ask students what they might learn by comparing time lines that show the same time period from different perspectives. Then have students read the **What?** section of text on p. 524 to help set the purpose of the lesson.

Why use parallel time lines? Have students read the **Why?** section of text on p. 525. Ask them what kind of parallel time lines they could create to compare their lives with events in national headlines.

2 Teach and Discuss

How is this skill used? Examine with students the parallel time lines on p. 524.

- Point out that the parallel time lines shown compare events happening in an individual's life with world events. Parallel time lines can also be used to compare events happening in different nations at the same time.

- Explain that parallel time lines can be used to compare historical/political events with events occurring at the same time in the art world, in science and medicine, in music and literature, and in daily life.

- Have students read the **How?** section of text on p. 525.

Chart and Graph Skills

Compare Parallel Time Lines

What? A time line is a type of chart that allows you to show events in a period of time. Events are shown in the order in which they occurred.

Parallel describes lines that are the same distance apart at every point. You can compare parallel time lines to show interesting time relationships. Look at the following parallel time lines. The first time line shows important events in the Great War. The second shows events that Adele, a student in Milwaukee, Wisconsin, recorded in her diary during the war years.

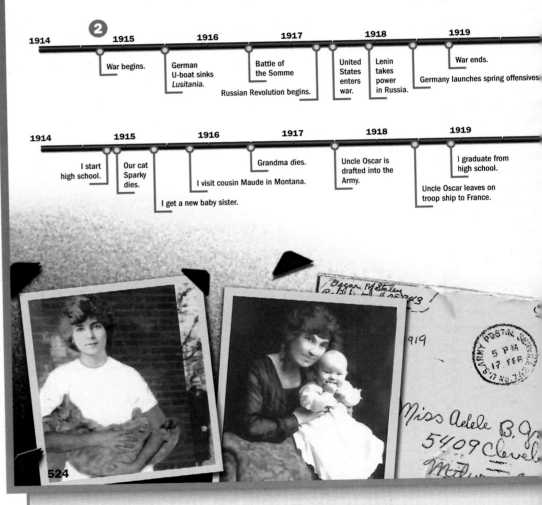

| 1914 | 1915 | 1916 | 1917 | 1918 | 1919 |

- War begins.
- German U-boat sinks *Lusitania*.
- Battle of the Somme
- Russian Revolution begins.
- United States enters war.
- Lenin takes power in Russia.
- War ends.
- Germany launches spring offensives

| 1914 | 1915 | 1916 | 1917 | 1918 | 1919 |

- I start high school.
- Our cat Sparky dies.
- I get a new baby sister.
- I visit cousin Maude in Montana.
- Grandma dies.
- Uncle Oscar is drafted into the Army.
- Uncle Oscar leaves on troop ship to France.
- I graduate from high school.

Practice and Extend

MEETING INDIVIDUAL NEEDS
Leveled Practice

Present a Play Have groups of students present short skits based on Adele's life and world events. Students will have to find a way to introduce the world events into Adele's life.

Easy Help students review the parallel time lines and discuss events of the time. Ask students to choose a world event and describe what Adele was doing when she heard the news. **Reteach**

On-Level Have students choose events in Adele's life and write a short skit about how she heard the world news and how she reacted to it. **Extend**

Challenge Have students write a skit in which a soldier in the Great War later reads Adele's diary. Tell students to discuss what he might say about Adele's life and about events that affected him. **Enrich**

Why? Parallel time lines help you compare events in different places or compare public events with personal events. In fact, as long as the time periods covered are the same, you can compare events from almost any place.

How? The parallel time lines on the previous page help you compare the public events of the Great War with the personal events in Adele's life.

One thing to be careful about when using a time line is reading dates correctly. Each blue tick mark on the time line stands for the beginning of a year (January 1). Everything to the *right*—until the next date's blue mark—is for that year. Look at the time line for Adele's diary. Find the *1915* label and blue mark. You can see on the time line that Adele's cat Sparky died toward the end of 1914. Adele's new baby sister was born sometime in early 1915.

Now look at the year 1914 on both time lines. You can see that the Great War began in Europe that year. During that same year, Adele started high school.

Think and Apply

1. What events happened in 1916? Which event do you think was most important to Adele? Why?

2. Which events in 1917 probably brought the war home to Adele?

3. Uncle Oscar fought for less than a year in the Great War. How do the parallel time lines give you this information?

525

---

1 What do the parallel time lines show? The first time line shows events in the Great War. The second shows events a student recorded in her diary during the war years.
Main Idea and Details

2 What important event happened in 1914? The Great War began.
Analyze Time Lines

3 Close and Assess

Think and Apply

1. The Battle of the Somme in the war and the death of Adele's grandma; her grandma's death was probably more important to Adele because it was a very personal event.

2. The United States entered the war, and Adele's Uncle Oscar was drafted into the army.

3. Adele's time line shows that Uncle Oscar left for France around early March 1918. Since the war ended in early November, he could not have fought for as long as one year.

FYI SOCIAL STUDIES Background

Events in 1914

Although the big event in 1914 was the beginning of the Great War in Europe, other important events also occurred at that time.

- The Panama Canal opened, connecting the Atlantic and Pacific Oceans.
- In Cleveland, Ohio, the first red and green electric traffic lights were installed.
- Construction of the Lincoln Memorial in Washington, D.C., began.

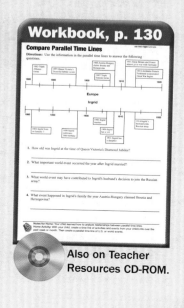

Workbook, p. 130

Also on Teacher Resources CD-ROM.

The Great War

Objectives

⟳ List the events that caused the United States to enter the Great War.

• List and describe weapons first used in the Great War. Explain how they differed from earlier weapons.

• Describe how Lenin and the Communists persuaded the Russian people to support the Russian Revolution.

• Explain the significance of the battles of Verdun and the Somme.

• Describe how peoples' attitudes toward the Great War may have been affected by the high number of casualties.

Vocabulary

casualty, p. 528;
trench warfare, p. 528;
armistice, p. 530

Resources

• Workbook, p. 131
• Transparency 22
• Every Student Learns Guide, p. 250–253
• Quick Study, pp. 126–127

Quick Teaching Plan

If time is short, have students make a table telling about the Great War.

• Column labels should read *nation, leader, alliance, battles won, battles lost, date entered war,* and *date exited war.*

1 Introduce and Motivate

Preview To activate prior knowledge, ask students what they know about the Great War, who fought it, and where it was fought. Tell students they will learn more about the Great War in Lesson 2.

You Are There This letter describes conditions representative of those on the front lines during the Great War. Mud and freezing temperatures plagued the soldiers. Ask students what they think happened in the Great War.

1915

1915
Italy joins the Allies.

1916
Battles of Verdun and the Somme

1917
Russian Revolution

1918
The Great War ends.

19

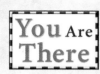

GERMANY RUSSIA
Paris • Verdun
FRANCE

The Great War

PREVIEW

Focus on the Main Idea
The Great War caused much destruction.

PLACES
Paris
Ottoman Empire
Verdun
Somme
Soviet Union

PEOPLE
Woodrow Wilson
Vladimir Lenin

VOCABULARY
casualty
trench warfare
armistice

TERMS
Allied Powers
Central Powers
communism
Soviets

EVENTS
Russian Revolution

You Are There

May 15, 1915
a battlefield in France

Dear Anne,

I surely miss being home with you, Mother, and Father in Great Britain. You can't imagine what it's like to live in a trench. It's really just a deep ditch. Dirt and mud are all around—not to mention mice, rats, and bugs! But worst of all is the sound of German shells screaming overhead day and night. It's usually safe down here, six or eight feet below the ground. But many times we have to climb out of the trench and march into enemy lines. It's scary, but I know that fighting in this war is my duty to our country.

Your loving brother,
Ralph

▶ **A British soldier eats his dinner in a trench during the Great War.**

Cause and Effect As you read, think about the effects of some of the most important battles of the Great War.

526

Practice and Extend

READING SKILL
Cause and Effect

In the Lesson Review, students complete a graphic organizer like the one below. You may want to provide students with a copy of Transparency 22 to complete as they read the lesson.

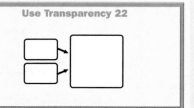

Use Transparency 22

WEB SITE
Technology

• You can look up vocabulary words by clicking on *Social Studies Library* and selecting the dictionary at **www.sfsocialstudies.com.**

• Students can learn more about current news by clicking on *Current Events* at **www.sfsocialstudies.com.**

• Explore other events that occurred on this day by clicking on *This Day in History* at **www.sfsocialstudies.com.**

The War Begins

At the beginning of the war in August 1914, Germany had a plan to defeat France in six weeks. It sent an army through Belgium and into France. This army was supposed to encircle **Paris,** the French capital, and then attack the British and French armies.

The generals soon discovered that planning a war on maps is not the same as soldiers trudging through enemy territory. As one British soldier wrote home:

> *"People out here seem to think that the war is going to be quite short, why, I don't know; personally I see nothing to prevent it [from] going on forever."*

In fact, the war continued for four long years. The German army came to a standstill opposite the French and British armies in France. This front, or line of battle, became known as the Western Front. Though huge battles raged, the armies hardly moved at all.

Meanwhile, Russia tried to push into Germany from the east. Russia also was fighting against Austria-Hungary, Germany's ally. The line of battle between Russia and Austria-Hungary became known as the Eastern Front. In August 1914, Germany won a great victory over Russia on Germany's eastern edge.

In November 1914 the **Ottoman Empire** entered the war on the side of Germany and Austria-Hungary. In 1915 Italy joined on the side of Great Britain, France, and Russia. The old Triple Entente, which you read about in Lesson 1, added Italy and became known as the **Allied Powers.** The old Triple Alliance—Germany and Austria-Hungary but minus Italy—was now known as the **Central Powers.** The Ottoman Empire and the border between Italy and Austria-Hungary soon became the sites of many battles.

REVIEW By 1915, what were the two main fronts in the Great War? Summarize

▶ **Many soldiers, such as these British soldiers, were forced to live in protective trenches during the Great War.**

The Granger Collection

527

2 Teach and Discuss

PAGE 527

The War Begins

Quick Summary In July 1914, Germany's fight against France and Britain bogged down on the Western Front. On the Eastern Front, Germany overwhelmed Russia. The Ottoman Empire entered the war and sided with Germany, while Italy switched alliances and joined France.

1 Compare Germany's plan to capture France with what actually happened. Germany planned to defeat France in six weeks by plunging through Belgium, circling Paris, and then taking the British and French armies. But fighting came to a standstill, and the war lasted four years instead of six weeks. **Compare and Contrast**

2 Which nation had to fight a war on both its eastern and western borders? Germany **Analyze Information**

Test Talk

Locate Key Words in the Text

3 By 1915, which nations were fighting in which alliances? Names, such as *Allied Powers* and *Central Powers,* are often key information in a text. Have students find these names and then look for answers to the question. Central Powers: Germany, Austria-Hungary, Ottoman Empire; Allied Powers: Great Britain, France, Russia, Italy **Main Idea and Details**

Decision Making

4 Suppose you were the leader of a neutral European country that was being greatly affected by the Great War. How would you decide which alliance to join? Possible answer: I would choose the side that held the same values and goals that my country did. **Make Decisions**

✓ **REVIEW ANSWER** Western and Eastern fronts **Summarize**

MEETING INDIVIDUAL NEEDS
Leveled Practice

Analyze a Photo Ask students to study the photo on p. 527 and another photo in the lesson.

Easy Have students read the captions about the photos and restate the information in their own words. **Reteach**

On-Level Have students look closely at the photos and notice details. Have groups of students list what they learned from studying the photos. **Extend**

Challenge Have groups of students study all the photos in the lesson to compare the material goods and technology of war with those of today. Students should speculate and decide whether it would have been harder to fight and survive back then or today. **Enrich**

For a Lesson Summary, use Quick Study, p. 126.

A New Kind of War

🕐 *Quick Summary* In the Great War, new technology such as tanks, machine guns, and poison gas increased the number of people who were killed. Trench warfare also caused many casualties.

5 **How were airplanes used in the Great War?** For dropping bombs, firing guns, and spying Analyze Information

6 **Give two reasons why the Great War was deadlier than earlier wars.** Deadly new weapons, such as machine guns, tanks, and poison gas; trench warfare ↺ Cause and Effect

Primary Source

Cited in *The First World War: A Complete History*, by Martin Gilbert

7 **Compare and contrast the quote on p. 528 to the You Are There letter. What is similar? Different?** Possible answer: Both the letter and the quote discuss the idea of trench warfare and what it feels like. The letter mentions inconveniences and being scared, but it is fairly upbeat. The quote is sad and perhaps shows that the speaker is frightened. **Compare and Contrast**

8 **Examine the illustration and the text, and then describe trenches and trench warfare. Note what was good and bad about each.** Trenches were deep ditches dug to shelter troops; barbed wire provided a barrier in front of them. They gave some protection to soldiers but were unsanitary. They were open to rain and cold weather. Shells could explode in them. Leaving a trench meant crawling through a no-man's land where machine guns were firing. **Compare and Contrast**

✓ Ongoing Assessment

If...	then...
If... students do not understand how trenches became part of the Western Front,	**then...** tell them that soldiers dug narrow holes about ten feet deep and often packed them with sandbags to keep the walls from caving in.

A New Kind of War

The Great War proved deadlier than any earlier war. Thousands of soldiers were killed daily in battle. One reason for these terrible casualties, or wounded and killed soldiers, was a group of deadly new weapons.

For the first time, the machine gun was widely used in a major war. It allowed soldiers to shoot many times without reloading.

Still another new weapon was the tank, an armored vehicle mounted with guns. Tanks moved on tracks instead of wheels. This helped them to roll over land that soldiers could not travel easily on by foot.

One of the most horrifying new weapons was poison gas, which injured or killed many soldiers. Soldiers started wearing gas masks so that they would not breathe the deadly poison gas.

The Great War was the first war in which airplanes were used. In airplanes army pilots could see what was going on in enemy territory.

▶ This gas mask was used during the Great War.

They could also drop bombs and fire guns from the airplanes.

Another reason for the war's high number of casualties was trench warfare. In trench warfare, armies dug deep trenches, or ditches, to shelter their troops. They strung barbed wire in front of the trenches to keep out the enemy.

When attacking, soldiers had to crawl out of the trench and move toward enemy soldiers, who were waiting in their own trenches. Machine-gun fire sprayed the advancing troops. Shells from the enemy's big guns exploded all around them. The strip of land between the trenches of opposing armies became known as "No-Man's Land" for a good reason. It was no place for anybody!

One British soldier described watching fellow soldiers leading the way into battle:

> *"We were able to see our comrades [friends] move forward in an attempt to cross No-Man's Land, only to be mown down like meadow grass. I felt sick at the sight . . . and remember weeping."*

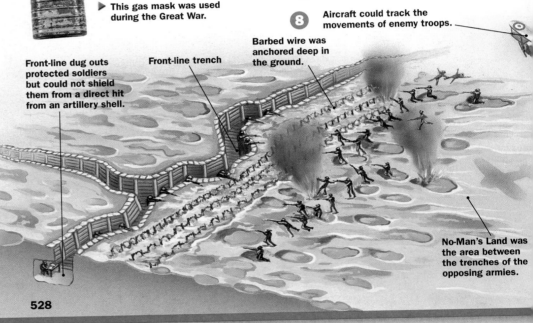

8 Aircraft could track the movements of enemy troops.

Barbed wire was anchored deep in the ground.

Front-line dug outs protected soldiers but could not shield them from a direct hit from an artillery shell.

Front-line trench

No-Man's Land was the area between the trenches of the opposing armies.

528

Practice and Extend

(FYI) SOCIAL STUDIES Background

Use of Poison Gas German troops were the first to use poison gas.

- On April 22, 1915, at Ypres, France, German troops released a cloud of chlorine gas. The gas, heavier than air, dropped into the trenches. Allied Troops fled.

- Both sides used poison gas in the war, although it was ineffective in extreme cold. To continue fighting, troops had to use gas masks. Soldiers put gas masks on the dogs and horses that were used in the war.

FAST FACTS

Lesson 2 describes the Great War. Other facts about this time include:

- The Red Baron was a real German. Baron Manfred von Richthofen was called the Red Baron. He shot down 80 planes in the war.

- After the United States joined the Great War, hamburgers, named after the German town of Hamburg, were called "liberty sandwiches."

The Battles of Verdun and the Somme

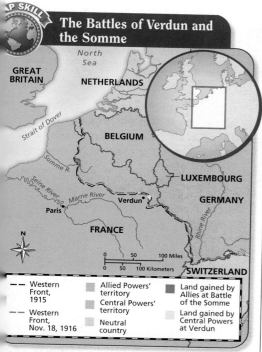

▶ Neither side was able to make much progress at the Battles of Verdun and the Somme.

MAP SKILL Use a Map Key **How did the Western Front change from 1915 to November 1916?**

Some of the war's fiercest battles were fought in these terrible conditions on the Western Front. Two of the worst took place in 1916. One was at **Verdun** (vair DUHN) in eastern France, and the other was at the **Somme** (SUHM) River.

Germany launched an attack on Verdun in February 1916. The French fought back, and the battle went on for the rest of the year. In the end, there were more than 500,000 French and German casualties. However, for all those months of death and suffering, Germany gained very little.

Meanwhile, the British Army led a powerful attack on the Germans at the Somme River. On July 1, 1916, the Allies stormed the German trenches. More British soldiers were killed that one day than on any other day in British history—

▶ British nurses help a wounded soldier onto a stretcher.

20,000. It was also the bloodiest day of the Great War. When the battle finally ended, the Allies had gained very little. ⑫

REVIEW Name at least one cause of the high number of casualties in the Great War. ↻ Cause and Effect

Women's War Work

Although the soldiers fighting in the war were all men, women served in military roles too. Some 57,000 served in the British Women's Auxiliary Army Corps.

British women performed supportive tasks, including teaching soldiers how to use gas masks, driving ambulances, working in factories, and growing crops to feed everyone. Women also served as nurses. Sometimes this brought them close to the front lines. Like the men, these women often put their own lives in danger.

Germany had a special women's service in major cities. These women sewed uniforms for soldiers and sheets for hospital beds. German women also cooked and performed nursing duties. ⑬

REVIEW Name three of the tasks performed by British women during the Great War. **Main Idea and Details**

529

---

⑨ **Compare and contrast the land gained by the Allies at the Somme with that gained by the Central Powers at Verdun.** Neither side gained much land at either battle. Compare and Contrast

MAP SKILL **Answer** The Western Front changed a little at Verdun but very little anywhere else.

⑩ **Why was Verdun a frustrating battle?** Neither side progressed, but there were 500,000 casualties. Draw Conclusions

⑪ **Did the Allied Powers fight as one army? Explain.** No. While the French army fought Germany at Verdun, the British fought a separate battle at the Somme River. Draw Conclusions

⑫ **What probably caused the record number of deaths of British soldiers on July 1, 1916?** Machine gun fire when British troops left the shelter of their trenches to attack German trenches Hypothesize

✓ **REVIEW ANSWER** Poison gas, machine guns, trench warfare ↻ Cause and Effect

PAGE 529

Women's War Work

Quick Summary Women on both sides of the Great War performed a variety of supportive tasks.

⑬ **Compare and contrast how British and German women participated in the war.** Possible answer: Similar: Both were involved in feeding soldiers and being nurses. Different: German women sewed uniforms and sheets; British women taught soldiers, drove ambulances, and worked in factories. Compare and Contrast

✓ **REVIEW ANSWER** (Any three of the following) teaching soldiers how to use gas masks, driving ambulances, working in factories, growing crops, and serving as nurses Main Idea and Details

---

❄ **MEETING INDIVIDUAL NEEDS**
Learning Styles

Describe the Western Front Using their individual learning styles, students can point out and tell about the Western Front.

Visual Learning Have students use the map on p. 529 to trace the Western Front of the Great War and explain to a partner the groups who were fighting along this front.

Kinesthetic Learning Have student groups draw a large map of the Western Front and transport toy armaments marked with the correct alliance to their proper positions along the front. The British need ships; everyone needs railroads.

Musical Learning Have students make up a song or rhythmic poem about the conditions at the Western Front during the Great War.

America Enters

⏱ **Quick Summary** Although America tried to stay neutral, the sinking of the *Lusitania* and Germany's attempts to ally itself with Mexico pushed the United States toward war.

14 **When the Great War started in 1914, what was the U.S. stance?** The United States remained neutral. **Evaluate**

15 **How did Germany intend to defeat Great Britain?** By destroying British shipping **Analyze Information**

16 **Why wasn't France as susceptible to submarine attacks as Great Britain?** Great Britain needed ships to bring it supplies. France could get supplies over land. **Make Inferences**

17 **Why did German submarines sink the *Lusitania*?** The British passenger ship supposedly carried weapons bound for Great Britain. **Main Idea and Details**

18 **What part did Mexico play in the Great War?** Germany offered to return to Mexico territory that the United States had taken in 1846 if Mexico would join the Central Powers. **Main Idea and Details**

Primary Source
Quoted in *Side-By-Side, A Photographic History of American Women in War,* by Vickie Lewis

19 **Using Cunningham's quote, describe what it might have been like for soldiers on the Western Front during the Great War.** Possible answer: Soldiers were often injured by guns and gas, and sometimes lost limbs. The noise of guns and shells exploding must have frightened them. **Analyze Primary Sources**

✓ **REVIEW ANSWER** The deaths of American citizens when Germany sank the *Lusitania* and other American ships, and the discovery of Germany's attempt to persuade Mexico to join the Central Powers; the effect was the entrance of two million American soldiers who helped turn the tide of the war for the Allies. ↩ **Cause and Effect**

America Enters

14 When war broke out in 1914, the United States adopted a policy of neutrality. Many people did not want to get involved in the war. Some were even against sending food and supplies to help Great Britain. If the United States was going to enter the war, there needed to be a good reason for it.

Germany's leaders decided to take a big gamble. They would try to drive Great Britain out of the war **15** by destroying British shipping. The British depended on trade for food and supplies. The Germans gambled that the British could be forced into defeat if German submarines sank **16** their ships, cutting off Great Britain's food supply.

Germany's submarines were powerful weapons. But in the end, they brought a dangerous new enemy into the war on the side of the Allies—the United States.

In May 1915 a German submarine sank the *Lusitania*, a British ship. The *Lusitania* was carry-**17** ing passengers, supplies, and probably weapons from the United States to Great Britain. Nearly 1,200 people died, including 128 Americans. The sinking of the *Lusitania* and several American commercial, or trade, ships by Germany pushed U.S. public opinion toward war.

In early 1917 many Americans also wanted to join the war after the British found a secret German telegram to the government of Mexico. In it Germany promised that it would restore to **18** Mexico land that the United States had taken from it in 1846, if Mexico joined the war on the side of the Central Powers. When Great Britain

The Granger Collection

CUNARD

EUROPE VIA LIVERPOOL
LUSITANIA
Fastest and Largest Steamer now in Atlantic Service Sails
SATURDAY, MAY 1, 10 A.M.
Transylvania, Fri., May 7, 5 P.M.
Orduna, - - Tues, May 18, 10 A.M.
Tuscania, - - Fri., May 21, 5 P.M.
LUSITANIA, Sat., May 29, 10 A.M.
Transylvania, Fri., June 4, 5 P.M.
Gibraltar—Genoa—Naples—Piraeus
S.S. Carpathia, Thur., May 13, Noon

NOTICE!
TRAVELLERS intending to embark on the Atlantic voyage are reminded that a state of war exists between Germany and her allies and Great Britain and her allies; that the zone of war includes the waters adjacent to the British Isles; that, in accordance with formal notice given by the Imperial German Government, vessels flying the flag of Great Britain, or of any of her allies, are liable to destruction in those waters and that travellers sailing in the war zone on ships of Great Britain or her allies do so at their own risk.

IMPERIAL GERMAN EMBASSY
WASHINGTON, D. C. APRIL 22, 1915.

▶ This advertisement from the *New York Herald* announces the sailing of the *Lusitania*. The "notice" in the advertisement is a warning to travelers about the dangers posed by German submarines.

showed this telegram to the United States, feelings against Germany became stronger. On April 6, 1917, the U.S. Congress declared war on Germany at the request of President **Woodrow Wilson.**

As 1918 began, American troops began pouring into battlefields in France. German attacks crushed the Allies on the Western Front throughout the spring of 1918. However, by summer, two million fresh American soldiers were turning the tide of the war for the Allies. Still, many soldiers were being killed or wounded. Fanny Louise Cunningham, an American nurse on the Western Front, wrote:

"It broke your heart to see these fine young men carried off on stretchers with missing limbs, blinded, burned with gas and, in some cases shell-shocked. Many were only boys."

By the fall of 1918, the Central Powers were exhausted. They gave up, one by one. First the Ottoman Empire surrendered, then Austria-Hungary. Germany held on until early November. Germany agreed to an **armistice,** or cease-fire, on November 11, 1918. After four long years, the fighting was finally over.

REVIEW What caused the United States to enter the war? What was the effect of this entry? ↩ **Cause and Effect**

The Russian Revolution
By 1917 people everywhere had grown tired of the war. In no other country were feelings running as strongly against the war as in Russia.

Practice and Extend

ESL **ACTIVATE PRIOR KNOWLEDGE**
ESL Support

Build Word Webs Discuss the word *island*. What do students think that word means? Have students write the word on a card and write below it the word for *island* in their home language.

Beginning Have students brainstorm things that might be important to people on an island and create a word web. For example, from the word *water*, the word *ship* might web out. From *ship*, students might web to *sail*, *sailor*, or *navy*.

Intermediate Have students create a word web with the word *island* in the center circle. After students create the webs, have them translate the words into their home language. Then choose important words for students to write on cards in English with the word in the home language below.

Advanced Ask students to create a word web using the word *island*. Then have groups of students write a paragraph using the words from that web.

For additional ESL support, use Every Student Learns Guide, pp. 250–253.

On the Eastern Front, the Russian Army had suffered terrible casualties, just as the French and British had on the Western Front. However, conditions in Russia were much worse. The Russian economy had collapsed. Military supplies were low. Food and fuel were limited.

The **Russian Revolution** broke out in March 1917. People demanded relief from their suffering. Russian soldiers joined the protesters. Russia's ruler, Czar Nicholas II, was forced to give up his throne. Russia's new rulers kept Russia in the war, but conditions did not improve. Russia was in a state of chaos, or disorder.

The Bolsheviks (BOHL shuh viks), or communists, led by **Vladimir Lenin** (LEH nuhn), promised peace, bread, and land to all Russians. They followed a form of socialism called **communism,** an economic and social system in which all resources are owned by a government led by a dictator. Aided by workers' and soldiers' councils called **Soviets,** the communists took over the government on November 7, 1917.

The Germans forced Russia to sign a treaty, giving up much land in the west. Lenin got peace,

▶ **Soldiers celebrate the Bolshevik Revolution.**

but at a high price.

Meanwhile, a bloody civil war broke out between the communists and the non-communists in Russia. The United States, Great Britain, Japan, and other nations sent troops and supplies to help the non-communists. The civil war in Russia raged on until 1920, when the communists triumphed. In 1922 Russia's communist leaders formed the **Soviet Union.**

REVIEW In Russia's civil war, which side had greater support among other nations? Explain your answer. Draw Conclusions

The Soviet Union in 1922

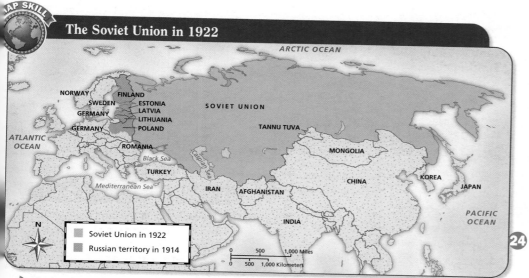

▶ **The borders of the Soviet Union were different from those of Russia.**

MAP SKILL Measure Distance *What was the distance between the eastern and western edges of the Soviet Union in 1922?*

531

The Russian Revolution

Quick Summary The Russian Revolution forced the czar from the throne and brought the Bolsheviks to power. Under Vladimir Lenin, Russia signed a peace treaty with Germany, yet civil war soon broke out.

20 **Why did Russian soldiers join the protest against the government in 1917?** Food, fuel, and military supplies were low. The Russian army had suffered terrible casualties.
Cause and Effect

21 **Who were the Soviets, and how were they involved in the government of Russia?** Workers' councils; they helped the Bolsheviks led by Lenin.
Analyze Information

22 **Who was leading the Russians at the start of the war? At the end?** Czar Nicholas II; Vladimir Lenin **Sequence**

23 **How did Russia get out of the Great War?** By signing a peace treaty with, and giving up land to, Germany
Analyze Information

The Soviet Union in 1922

Point out that the map shows changes in the land area of Russia that became the Soviet Union in 1922.

24 **Which countries in 1922 were located on land that had once been part of Russia?** Finland, Estonia, Latvia, Lithuania, and Poland **Interpret Maps**

MAP SKILL **Answer** About 6,000 miles

✓ **REVIEW ANSWER** Non-communists; The United States, Great Britain, Japan, and other nations sent troops and supplies to help the non-communists.
Draw Conclusions

CURRICULUM CONNECTION
Writing

Write a Letter

• Have students write a letter to Vladimir Lenin telling whether they agree or disagree with how Lenin got peace for Russia.

• Ask students to support their opinions.

WEB SITE
Technology

You can learn more about the area of one of the most significant sea battles in history, the Battle of Jutland, by clicking on *Atlas* at **www.sfsocialstudies.com.**

Another Victory

🕐 **Quick Summary** After the Great War, men and women returned to their pre-war responsibilities. In addition women gained the right to vote in many countries, including the United States.

㉕ **What right did many women win after the war?** The right to vote
Main Idea and Details

✓ **REVIEW ANSWER** Most women returned to taking care of their husbands and children. Women also won the right to vote in national elections. **Main Idea and Details**

③ Close and Assess

Summarize the Lesson

Tell students to examine the vertical time line. Ask them to summarize the lesson by describing how each of these events affected the outcome of the Great War.

| ✓ | LESSON 2 | REVIEW |

1. 🔄 **Cause and Effect** For sample answers, see the reduced pupil page.

2. Machine guns, tanks, poison gas, airplanes

3. Peace, bread, and land

4. They show how destructive—both in terms of land and human lives—the Great War was.

5. **Critical Thinking: *Make Inferences*** Possible answer: People must have raised this question because soldiers died by the thousands in battles that gained little or nothing for either side.

Link to 🔗 Science

Students should explain that fronts separate air masses of different temperature and moisture. Along weather fronts, these different air masses can clash and sometimes result in extremely turbulent weather, such as thunderstorms and tornadoes. War fronts also result in turbulent actions.

Another Victory

The end of the Great War was a cause for celebration for the victorious nations. Soldiers went back to their families. Most women went back to taking care of their husbands and children. Returning soldiers wanted their jobs back from women who had filled in during the war.

However, between 1917 and 1920, women did gain an important victory of their own—the right to vote in national elections. After years ㉕ of struggle by women, the Soviet Union, Canada, Germany, Great Britain, the United States, and others granted women the right to vote.

REVIEW How did women's lives change after the end of the Great War?
Main Idea and Details

▶ **Members of the Women's Royal Air Force celebrate the armistice signing in 1918.**

Hutton-Deutsch Collection/Corbis

Summarize the Lesson

- **1916** The Battle of Verdun and the Battle of the Somme raged on the Western Front.
- **1917** Lenin and the communists came to power in the Russian Revolution.
- **1918** The fighting ended when Germany signed an armistice on November 11.

| LESSON 2 | REVIEW |

Check Facts and Main Ideas

1. 🔄 **Cause and Effect** On a separate piece of paper, fill in the chart below by listing two causes that convinced the United States to enter the Great War.

```
┌──────────────────────┐
│ German submarine     │──┐
│ sank the Lusitania.  │  │      ┌──────────────┐
└──────────────────────┘  │      │    Effect    │
                          ├─────▶│ The United   │
┌──────────────────────┐  │      │ States       │
│ United States learned│  │      │ entered the  │
│ that Germany had     │──┘      │ Great War.   │
│ offered land to Mexico│        └──────────────┘
│ if Mexico joined the │
│ Central Powers.      │
└──────────────────────┘
```

2. What new weapons made the Great War deadlier than earlier wars?

3. What did Lenin and the communists promise the Russian people to gain their support in the Russian Revolution?

4. How do the battles of Verdun and the Somme summarize the experience of the Great War?

5. **Critical Thinking: *Make Inferences*** Given the terrible casualties in the Great War battles, do you think that some people questioned whether winning was worth the cost? Why or why not?

Link to 🔗 Science

Study Weather Fronts The term *front* is used for a line that separates enemy armies. It comes from meteorology, or weather science. Find a front on a weather map. Explain why it is like a front in war.

Practice and Extend

FAST FACTS

While war raged in Europe, scientists still worked and researched. During the Great War from 1914–1918,

- The Dodge brothers set up their Dodge car business in Detroit. It was the first successful attempt to manufacture an all-steel car.
- Alexander Graham Bell in New York and Dr. Thomas A. Watson in San Francisco completed the first transcontinental phone call.

Workbook, p. 131

Lesson 2: The Great War

Directions: The Great War in Europe was fought along two fronts. Each of the following phrases deals with either the Eastern Front, the Western Front, or both. Place the number of each phrase under the appropriate heading in the Venn diagram below. You may use your textbook.

1. German, French, and British soldiers come to a standstill.
2. Russia battles Germany and Austria-Hungary.
3. Soldiers use new weapons such as poisonous gas, machine guns, and tanks.
4. For the first time, airplanes are used to drop bombs on the enemy.
5. Germans attack Verdun.
6. Thousands of soldiers die.
7. Allies storm German trenches.
8. Russian army suffers terrible casualties.

Eastern Front   Western Front

Notes for Home: Your child learned about the fighting in Europe during the Great War.
Home Activity: With your child, examine the map on p. 531. Discuss how people probably were affected as the war moved into their home area.

💿 **Also on Teacher Resources CD-RO**

Vera Brittain

1893–1970

As a young girl growing up in Great Britain, Vera Brittain knew she wanted to be a writer. By the time she was 11, she had written and illustrated five "novels." Brittain loved to learn. She was determined to go to college, although it was uncommon for young women to attend college in the early 1900s. In 1914 she won a scholarship to a women's college at Oxford University in England. She started classes a few weeks after the Great War began. In 1915 Brittain left college to serve as a volunteer nurse in the war.

As a nurse, Brittain faced difficult experiences. She cared for wounded soldiers in freezing cold weather and poorly supplied field hospitals. Both her brother and one of her friends were killed in the war. The Great War turned Vera Brittain into a lifelong pacifist, or someone who opposes war. She once said:

1 *"I hold war to be a crime against humanity, whoever fights it and against whomever it is fought."*

After the war, she graduated from Oxford and began a career as a writer. Brittain hoped to use "the power of ideas to change the shape of the world and even help to eliminate its evils." Brittain wrote more than 25 books and many essays. A number of her writings speak out against war. She also spent much of her time promoting rights and freedoms for women. Her best-known book is her autobiography, *Testament of Youth* (1933), which describes the horrors of war. The book quickly became a best seller.

BIOFACT — *Brittain's* Testament of Youth *was made into a movie in 1979.*

Learn from Biographies

Do you think Brittain's attitude toward war was different before the war? Explain your answer.

For more information, go online to *Meet the People* at **www.sfsocialstudies.com.**

533

Vera Brittain

Objective

- Learn how war affected an average young person growing up in Great Britain during the Great War.

1 Introduce and Motivate

Preview To activate prior knowledge, ask students to consider how the Great War might have affected young people not only in the United States, but also in the rest of the world. Tell students they will learn about how the Great War affected a young British woman.

Ask why it is important to know how civilians lived during wars. (It gives a truer picture of the war's effects.)

2 Teach and Discuss

- Ask students why they think Vera Brittain left Oxford University to serve as a volunteer nurse in the war. (She wanted to help the war effort.)

- Ask students how they think Brittain's experiences in war affected her later life. (She wrote about the horrors of war, and perhaps her work as a nurse encouraged her to speak out about women's rights.)

1 **How does the quote from Brittain show she is a pacifist?** She says war is a crime no matter who fights.
Analyze Primary Sources

3 Close and Assess

Learn from Biographies Answer

Possible answer: Brittain probably developed her strong ideas about war once she saw its effects firsthand.

CURRICULUM CONNECTION
Literature

Read Other Works

Students may enjoy reading about other English authors from this period.

Meet A.A. Milne, by S. Ward (PowerKids Press, ISBN 0-823-95708-X, 2001) **Easy**

Frances Hodgson Burnett: Beyond the Secret Garden, by Angelica Shirley Carpenter (First Avenue Editions, ISBN 0-822-59610-5, 1992) **On-Level**

At Home with Beatrix Potter: The Creator of Peter Rabbit, by Susan Denver (Harry N. Abrams, ISBN 0-810-94112-0, 2000) **Challenge**

After the War

Objectives

- List the two provisions of the Treaty of Versailles that were included to show that Germany was being blamed for starting the Great War.

- Explain how the map of Europe changed according to the Treaty of Versailles.

- Explain the opposition President Wilson faced in trying to get his plan for a fair peace with Germany approved.

- Explain how paying reparations affected the German economy.

Vocabulary

holocaust, p. 535; **reparation,** p. 536; **inflation,** p. 537

Resources

- Workbook, p. 132
- Transparency 16
- Every Student Learns Guide, pp. 254–257
- Quick Study, pp. 128–129

Quick Teaching Plan

If time is short, have students expand the time line on p. 534. Next to each of the three points on the time line, add a column labeled *What Happened Next.* For each point, have students list what happened next.

1 Introduce and Motivate

Preview To activate prior knowledge ask students what makes them proud to be an American. Tell students they will learn more about the aftermath of the Great War as they read Lesson 3.

You Are There War usually makes everyone feel that they are a part of the effort. Many towns in Europe and the United States have monuments honoring those who died while fighting in the Great War. Have students find out if their community has a monument to the people who died as a result of the Great War.

LESSON 3

*Paris
FRANCE*

1918   1919

1918
Germany signs armistice, ending the Great War.

1918
President Woodrow Wilson arrives in France.

191
The
Germ
the
Vers

After the War

PREVIEW

Focus on the Main Idea
The Allies tried to make a peace treaty that would solve all of Europe's problems.

PLACES
Paris
Rhineland

PEOPLE
Georges Clemenceau

VOCABULARY
holocaust
reparations
inflation

TERMS
Fourteen Points
Treaty of Versailles
League of Nations

You Are There Your teacher calls your attention to current events, though it's hard for you to concentrate. Spring has come to your hometown. Soon, school will be out.

The delegates at the Paris peace conference are trying to make a fair peace after the Great War, which just ended last fall. A newspaper article says that President Wilson has become an important leader at the peace conference. People in Europe seem to look up to Wilson as an example of democratic leadership.

As an American, you feel proud . . . but you wonder if someday you'll be helping in the war effort, like your older brother and sister have just done.

▶ This painting by Sir William Orpen shows the delegates signing the peace treaty to end the Great War.

Art Archive/Imperi

Cause and Effect As you read, take note of the changes the Great War caused in the map of Europe and in people's lives.

534

Practice and Extend

READING SKILL
Cause and Effect

In the Lesson Review, students complete a graphic organizer like the one below. You may want to provide students with a copy of Transparency 16 to complete as they read the lesson.

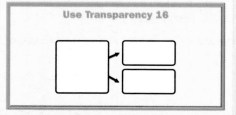

Use Transparency 16

WEB SITE
Technology

- You can look up vocabulary words by clicking on *Social Studies Library* and selecting the dictionary at **www.sfsocialstudies.com.**

- Students can learn more about current news by clicking on *Current Events* at **www.sfsocialstudies.com.**

- Explore other events that occurred on this day by clicking on *This Day in History* at **www.sfsocialstudies.com.**

Results of the War

The Great War caused more suffering than any previous war in history. No one knows exactly how many people died. Government statistics indicate that more than eight million soldiers were killed. This number is about the same as the population of a large city. Millions of civilians, or non-soldiers, died too.

During the war, Ottoman officials forced Armenians, a minority group, from their homes. This terrible event became known as the Armenian Holocaust. Though no one knew it at the time, this **holocaust,** or mass killing, would be only the first of several in the twentieth century.

The Great War caused great property destruction as well. Areas near the Western Front, in France and Belgium, were especially hard-hit. People were homeless, and businesses were destroyed. Nations had run up huge debts to fight

▶ Between one-half million and one million Armenians were killed in the Armenian Holocaust in 1915–1916. These children are boarding a train to an orphanage.

the war. It has been estimated that the war cost more than $300 billion.

The Great War changed the map of Europe. Compare the two maps below. Empires disappeared, including the German Empire ruled by Kaiser Wilhelm II, the Russian Empire ruled by Czar Nicholas II, the Ottoman Empire, and the Empire of Austria-Hungary.

REVIEW Give three details to support the main idea that the Great War changed conditions in Europe. **Main Idea and Details**

MAP SKILL

Europe in 1914

Europe in 1919

▶ The map of Europe changed significantly at the end of the Great War.

MAP SKILL Observe Change Through Maps *From which three old countries did the new nation of Poland receive land?*

535

2 Teach and Discuss

PAGE 535

Results of the War

🕐 **Quick Summary** The Great War caused more suffering than any previous war in history. The war also changed the map of Europe.

1 Compare the Armenian Holocaust to the deaths of civilians in France and Germany during the Great War. France and Germany were fighting a declared war. Civilians were not the target. Armenians were not at war with the Ottoman Empire nor were they an army. They were civilians targeted to be driven out of their homes and killed. **Evaluate**

2 Why did areas along the Western Front suffer the most damage during the Great War? The armies fought along this line for most of the war. **Analyze Information**

MAP SKILL Europe in 1914; Europe in 1919

Compare these maps to the other maps in Chapter 18.

3 How did the 1914 country of Austria-Hungary change at the end of the Great War? Possible answer: Its land was divided among several countries, including Austria, Hungary, Yugoslavia, Czechoslovakia, Poland, and Romania. It became two separate countries. **Sequence**

Ongoing Assessment

| **If...** students cannot see how Austria-Hungary changed, | **then...** have them compare the two maps and the names of the countries on each one. |

MAP SKILL **Answer** Germany, Russia, and Austria-Hungary

✓ **REVIEW ANSWER** The German Empire became Germany, and it lost territory in both the east and west; the Ottoman Empire disappeared and was replaced by the smaller Turkey; and new countries emerged in Eastern Europe. **Main Idea and Details**

Making Peace

🕐 **Quick Summary** Although President Wilson wanted a fair peace, the Treaty of Versailles was severe. Germany was forced to accept blame for the war, give up territory, remove its defenses from the Rhineland, and pay huge reparations.

FACT FILE

Casualties and Debt of the Great War

Point out that the file has not only the number of wounded but also the total number of casualties, which includes those wounded and those who died. It also shows the cost of fighting the Great War.

4 **Which nation suffered the most casualties during the Great War? Which nation spent the most money?** Russia; the British Empire **Interpreting Charts**

Primary Source

President Wilson quoted in *The Penguin Book of Twentieth Century Speeches,* by Brian MacArthur, ed.

5 **Explain what President Wilson meant by his words.** Possible answer: Wilson felt democracy was very important and that its ideas would help keep peace and freedom for citizens of other countries. **Analyze Primary Sources**

6 **What was the League of Nations?** An association of nations established to prevent future wars **Main Idea and Details**

✓ **REVIEW ANSWER** Huge reparations it had to pay to the Allies
🔄 **Cause and Effect**

FACT FILE

Casualties and Debt of the Great War

Country	Total Mobilized Forces	Wounded	Total Casualties	Cost in Dollars (rounded)
Russia (Soviet Union)	12,000,000	4,950,000	9,150,000	$22.3 billion
British Empire	8,904,467	2,090,212	3,190,235	$39.1 billion
France	8,410,000	4,266,000	6,160,800	$24.3 billion
Italy	5,615,000	947,000	2,197,000	$12.4 billion
United States	4,355,000	204,002	323,018	$22.6 billion
Japan	800,000	907	1,210	$40 million
Serbia	707,343	133,148	331,106	$400 million
Germany	11,000,000	4,216,058	7,142,558	$37.8 billion
Austria-Hungary	7,800,000	3,620,000	7,020,000	$20.6 billion
Ottoman Empire	2,850,000	400,000	975,000	$1.4 billion

▶ **Red Cross workers, pictured here, cared for the wounded on both sides during the Great War.**

Making Peace

On December 13, 1918, U.S. President Woodrow Wilson arrived in France. He came early to prepare for the peace conference that was to meet in **Paris** in January 1919. Many felt that Wilson's blueprint for peace, the **Fourteen Points,** would bring about a more democratic Europe and help prevent future wars.

When the peace conference opened, the leaders of Great Britain, France, and Italy joined the United States. From the start, Wilson and the French leader, **Georges Clemenceau** (KLEHM uhn soh), disagreed on almost every point. Clemenceau wanted to weaken Germany so that it could never again threaten France. This point of view collided with Wilson's ideas for a fair peace and cooperation between nations.

Earlier, President Wilson had said:

"The world must be made safe for democracy. Its peace must be planted upon the tested foundations of political liberty."

The final document, the **Treaty of Versailles** (vair SIGH), was a compromise containing ideas of both the French leader and Wilson. Wilson's fourteenth point, to create a "general association of nations" to help prevent future wars, became the **League of Nations.**

Under the Treaty of Versailles, Germany would have to accept blame for starting the war. It would have to remove forts and other defenses from the **Rhineland,** its western region bordering France. Finally, Germany would have to pay huge **reparations,** or payment for war losses, to the Allies.

536

Practice and Extend

MEETING INDIVIDUAL NEEDS
Leveled Practice

Write Peace Points Ask groups of students to take different points of view and write points for the basis of peace after the Great War.

Easy As Clemenceau of France, students can write three points that they think will keep Germany from attacking their country again. **Reteach**

On-Level As President Wilson, students can write three points that they think will end wars forever in Europe. **Extend**

Challenge As delegates to the Versailles Conference, students can discuss and negotiate to reach common ground. Then have students write their own treaty proposal. **Enrich**

For a Lesson Summary, use Quick Study, pp. 128–129.

On June 28, 1919, the Allies signed the Treaty of Versailles with Germany. Germany's war-torn economy could not stand up to the strain of huge reparation payments. By the early 1920s, Germany was experiencing skyrocketing **inflation,** or the rapid increase in prices. Money became almost worthless. People had to bring along piles of it just to buy groceries. They also burned money because it was cheaper than buying coal to burn for heat.

▶ **(seated left to right) Vittorio Orlando (Italy), David Lloyd George (Great Britain), Georges Clemenceau (France), and Woodrow Wilson (United States) at the peace conference in Paris**

By 1927 the German economy had recovered slightly. However, the German people never forgot their suffering.

REVIEW What was the cause of Germany's inflation in the early 1920s? ↻ **Cause and Effect**

Summarize the Lesson

- **December 1918** President Wilson arrived in France with ideas for establishing a fair peace.
- **January 1919** The peace conference began in Paris.
- **June 1919** Germany and the Allies signed the Treaty of Versailles.

LESSON 3 REVIEW

Check Facts and Main Ideas

1. ↻ **Cause and Effect** On a separate piece of paper, fill in the chart below by listing two effects in the blank boxes.

Cause → **Effects**

| Under the Treaty of Versailles, Germany is blamed for starting the war. | → | Removed defenses from Rhineland |
| | → | Paid reparations to Allies |

2. What part of Europe was most affected by boundary changes after the Great War?

3. In what ways did the Treaty of Versailles punish Germany?

4. What was the major stumbling block in establishing the kind of fair and just peace that President Wilson wanted?

5. **Critical Thinking:** *Solve Complex Problems* What impact did paying reparations to the Allies have on Germany's economy?

Link to  Reading

Interpret a Poem Flanders is located in Belgium. Canadian John M. McCrae wrote "In Flanders Fields." The poem's first two lines read:
*In Flanders fields the poppies blow
Between the crosses, row on row.*
What tells you that this poem deals with the high number of casualties in the Great War?

③ Close and Assess

Summarize the Lesson

Have students examine the vertical time line and discuss with a partner what happened before and immediately after each event on the time line.

✓ **LESSON 3** **REVIEW**

1. ↻ **Cause and Effect** For possible answers, see the reduced pupil page.

2. Eastern Europe

3. Germany had to accept blame for the war, leave the Rhineland undefended, and pay huge reparations to the Allies.

4. Georges Clemenceau wanted to weaken and punish Germany. President Wilson was more concerned about peace for all nations.

5. **Critical Thinking:** *Solve Complex Problems* Possible answer: Germany suffered from severe problems with inflation. Their money was worth almost nothing, and people could barely buy food and coal to heat their homes.

Link to  Reading

"Between the crosses, row on row" suggests a huge graveyard.

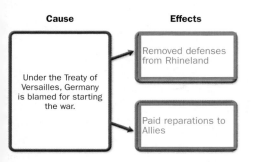
 Also on Teacher Resources CD-ROM.

⊞ Problem Solving

Use a Problem-Solving Process

- Have students consider the following problem: **Suppose you are in the German government after the Great War. How can you work to reduce your reparations?**

- Students should use the problem-solving process to decide how to ask former enemies for help. Have students discuss the exact economic issue that their group will work on and then come up with information and a marketing strategy to persuade other countries to help.

1. **Identify a problem.**
2. **Gather information.**
3. **List and consider options.**
4. **Consider advantages and disadvantages.**
5. **Choose and implement a solution.**
6. **Evaluate the effectiveness of the solution.**

Resources
- Assessment Book, pp. 93–96
- Workbook, p. 133: Vocabulary Review

Chapter Summary
For possible answers, see the reduced pupil page.

Vocabulary
1. e, **2.** c, **3.** a, **4.** b, **5.** d, **6.** g, **7.** f

People and Terms
Possible answers:

1. Wilhelm II was emperor of Germany before and during the Great War.

2. The assassination in 1914 of Archduke Francis Ferdinand, heir to the throne of Austria-Hungary, set off the Great War.

3. The Triple Alliance was an alliance among Germany, Austria-Hungary, and Italy formed in 1882.

4. The Central Powers were Germany and its allies, known before the war as the Triple Alliance.

5. Woodrow Wilson was President of the United States during the Great War and a leader of the Paris Peace Conference.

6. Vladimir Lenin was the leader of the Russian Revolution.

7. The Allied Powers was the old Triple Entente among Great Britain, France, Russia, and later the United States.

8. Vera Brittain was a nurse on the Western Front in the Great War who later wrote about her experiences.

9. The Fourteen Points were Woodrow Wilson's blueprint for peace after the Great War.

10. The League of Nations was the international peacekeeping body set up in the Treaty of Versailles after the Great War.

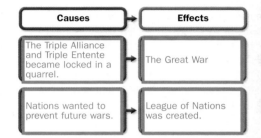

1880		1890

1882
Triple Alliance formed.

Chapter Summary

 Cause and Effect

On a separate piece of paper, fill in the chart by listing two causes and their effects of the Great War.

Causes	→	Effects
The Triple Alliance and Triple Entente became locked in a quarrel.	→	The Great War
Nations wanted to prevent future wars.	→	League of Nations was created.

Vocabulary

Match each word with the correct definition or description.

1. neutral (p. 523)
2. mobilization (p. 522)
3. armistice (p. 530)
4. holocaust (p. 535)
5. reparations (p. 536)
6. inflation (p. 537)
7. casualties (p. 528)

a. cease-fire
b. mass killing
c. preparations for war
d. sums of money paid for war losses
e. not taking sides
f. wounded and killed soldiers
g. rapid increase in prices

People and Terms

Write a sentence explaining why each of the following people or terms was important in the events of the Great War. You may use two or more in a single sentence.

1. Wilhelm II (p. 521)
2. Francis Ferdinand (p. 522)
3. Triple Alliance (p. 522)
4. Central Powers (p. 527)
5. Woodrow Wilson (p. 530)
6. Vladimir Lenin (p. 531)
7. Allied Powers (p. 527)
8. Vera Brittain (p. 533)
9. Fourteen Point (p. 536)
10. League of Nations (p. 53

538

Practice and Extend

Assessment Options

✓ Chapter 18 Assessment
- Chapter 18 Content Test: Use Assessment Book, pp. 93–94
- Chapter 18 Skills Test: Use Assessment Book, pp. 95–96

Standardized Test Prep
- Chapter 18 Tests contain standardized test format.

✓ Chapter 18 Performance Assessment
- Have students recreate the events of the Great War by studying the photos in Chapter 18 and writing a story about the war from the point of view of someone in one of the photos.
- The story should include factual information from the chapter and details brought out by the photos and maps.
- Assess students' understanding of the events in the story they choose to create.

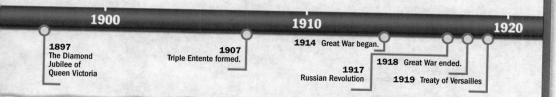

1897 The Diamond Jubilee of Queen Victoria

1907 Triple Entente formed.

1914 Great War began.

1917 Russian Revolution

1918 Great War ended.

1919 Treaty of Versailles

Facts and Main Ideas

- How did alliances help start the Great War?

- What type of warfare became common in battles during the Great War? Describe.

- How were Woodrow Wilson's goals for peace different from those of the other Allied leaders?

- **Time Line** About how many years after the start of the Great War did the Russian Revolution occur?

- **Main Idea** How did some European nations challenge each other in the years before the Great War?

- **Main Idea** Why did the United States enter the war in 1917?

- **Main Idea** What did Allied leaders hope to do when they wrote the Treaty of Versailles?

- **Critical Thinking:** *Recognize Point of View* From what you have read, do you think that Germany and Great Britain wanted to go to war? Explain.

Write About History

Write a want ad looking for someone to serve as note-taker at the meetings of the Paris peace conference.

Write a letter to a soldier fighting on the Western Front.

Write a short poem to honor soldiers who fought bravely in the Great War.

Apply Skills

Compare Parallel Time Lines

Study the parallel time lines. Then answer the questions.

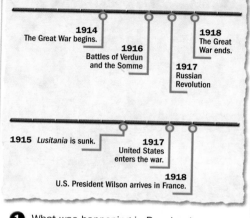

1914 The Great War begins.

1916 Battles of Verdun and the Somme

1918 The Great War ends.

1917 Russian Revolution

1915 *Lusitania* is sunk.

1917 United States enters the war.

1918 U.S. President Wilson arrives in France.

1. What was happening in Russia when the United States entered the war?

2. Was the Battle of Verdun before or after the sinking of the Lusitania?

3. How many years passed between the beginning of the Great War and the beginning of the U.S. involvement in the war?

Internet Activity

To get help with vocabulary, people, and terms, select dictionary, encyclopedia, or almanac from *Social Studies Library* at **www.sfsocialstudies.com**.

539

Hands-on Unit Project

Unit 7 Performance Assessment

See p. 596 for information about using the Unit Project as a means of performance assessment.

A scoring guide is provided on p. 596.

WEB SITE
Technology

or more information, students can select the ictionary, encyclopedia, or almanac from *Social tudies Library* at **www.sfsocialstudies.com**.

Workbook, p. 133

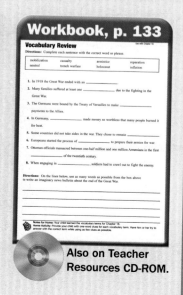

Vocabulary Review

Directions: Complete each sentence with the correct word or phrase.

| mobilization | casualty | armistice | reparation |
| neutral | trench warfare | holocaust | inflation |

1. In 1918 the Great War ended with an _____.
2. Many families suffered at least one _____ due to the fighting in the Great War.
3. The Germans were bound by the Treaty of Versailles to make _____ payments to the Allies.
4. In Germany, _____ made money so worthless that many people burned it for heat.
5. Some countries did not take sides in the war. They chose to remain _____.
6. Europeans started the process of _____ to prepare their armies for war.
7. Ottoman officials massacred between one-half million and one million Armenians in the first _____ of the twentieth century.
8. When engaging in _____, soldiers had to crawl out to fight the enemy.

Directions: On the lines below, use as many words as possible from the box above to write an imaginary news bulletin about the end of the Great War.

Notes for Home: Your child learned the vocabulary terms for Chapter 18.
Home Activity: Provide your child with one-word clues for each vocabulary term. Have him or her try to answer with the correct term while using as few clues as possible.

Also on Teacher Resources CD-ROM.

Facts and Main Ideas

1. When one nation of an alliance was attacked or threatened, other alliance members had to come to its defense. During the Great War, Russia mobilized its armies to protect Serbia, which was threatened by Austria-Hungary. Great Britain had to fight Germany because Germany attacked Belgium, an ally of Britain.

2. Trench warfare. Soldiers crouched in deep trenches to protect themselves. When ordered to attack, they rushed out into "no-man's land," where they were exposed to machine gun fire and shells.

3. Wilson's main concern was to prevent future wars. The other Allied leaders, particularly the leader of France, mostly wanted to punish Germany.

4. Three years

5. Imperialism brought these nations into conflict with one another.

6. Because of the sinking of the *Lusitania* and other American ships. Germany also sent a note promising Mexico territory lost to the United States if Mexico would join the Central Powers.

7. They hoped to prevent Germany or any other country from starting a war in the future.

8. Possible answer: Yes, they had built up navies to challenge each other. Both had also bickered over colonies.

Write About History

1. Students should choose a nation to write the ad for. It should state the purpose of the note-taking activities.

2. Have students note details from the chapter and from maps and photos.

3. Encourage students to use figurative language in their poems.

Apply Skills

1. Russian Revolution

2. After

3. Three years

Chapter Planning Guide

Chapter 19 • From Peace to War

Locating Time and Place pp. 540–541

Lesson Titles	Pacing	Main Ideas
Lesson 1 **Good to Bad Times** pp. 542–547	2 days	• Hard times set the stage for another world war.
Lesson 2 **World War II** pp. 548–554 **Biography: Winston Churchill** p. 555 **Smithsonian Institution:** **A World at War** pp. 556–557	3 days	• World War II caused millions of deaths and great destruction. • WInston Churchill rallied the British people to defeat fascism. • Life changed for most people in the United States an around the world during World War II.
Lesson 3 **The Aftermath** pp. 558–561 **Chart and Graph Skills:** **Interpret Bar Graphs** pp. 562–563	2 days	• The Allies formed the United Nations and helped shattered nations rebuild. • Bar graphs are often used to compare numbers and amounts.

✓ **Chapter 19 Review**
pp. 564–565

◄ **One of Winston Churchill's most effective tools was his powerful public-speaking ability.**

✓ = Assessment Options

◀ Many women contributed to the war effort. Women's Air Force Service Pilots towed targets for training and moved aircraft from factories to bases near enemy territory.

Vocabulary	Resources	Meeting Individual Needs
epression ascism azis ropaganda ggression nnex ppeasement ollective	• Workbook, p. 135 • Transparency 20 • Every Student Learns Guide, pp. 258–261 • Quick Study, pp. 130–131	• ESL Support, TE p. 543 • Leveled Practice, TE p. 544 • Learning Styles, TE p. 545
	• Workbook, p. 136 • Transparencies 18, 55, 56 • Every Student Learns Guide, pp. 262–265 • Quick Study, pp. 132–133 • Workbook, p. 137	• ESL Support, TE p. 550 • Leveled Practice, TE p. 552
ugee ncentration camp arter	• Workbook, p. 138 • Transparency 21 • Every Student Learns Guide, pp. 266–269 • Quick Study, pp. 134–135 • Workbook, p. 139	• ESL Support, TE p. 559 • Leveled Practice, TE p. 560 • Learning Styles, TE p. 562
	✓ Chapter 19 Content Test, Assessment Book, pp. 97–98 ✓ Chapter 19 Skills Test, Assessment Book, pp. 99–100	✓ Chapter 19 Performance Assessment, TE p. 564

Providing More Depth

Additional Resources

- Vocabulary Cards
- Daily Activity Bank
- Social Studies Plus!
- Big Book Atlas
- Student Atlas
- Outline Maps
- Desk Maps

 Technology

- AudioText
- The test maker
- Teacher Resources CD-ROM
- Map Resources CD-ROM
- **www.sfsocialstudies.com**

 To establish guidelines for your students' safe and responsible use of the Internet, use the Scott Foresman Internet Guide.

Additional Internet Links

To find out more about:

- World War II, search for *An American Scrapbook* at **www.thinkquest.org**
- Three teenagers who resisted the Holocaust, search for *Daring to Resist* at **www.pbs.org**
- Everyday life through the war, visit **www.si.edu**

Key Internet Search Terms

- Great Depression
- World War II
- United Nations

Workbook Support

Use the following Workbook pages to support content and skills development as you teach Chapter 19. You can also view and print Workbook pages from the Teacher Resources CD-ROM.

Workbook, p. 134

Name _____ Date _____

Vocabulary Preview

Use with Chapter 19.

These are the vocabulary words for Chapter 19. How much do you know about these words?

Directions: Match each vocabulary word to its meaning. Write the number of the word on the line next to its meaning. You may use your glossary.

1. depression
2. fascism
3. Nazi
4. propaganda
5. aggression
6. annex
7. appeasement
8. collective
9. Axis Powers
10. Allies
11. Big Three
12. Women's Army Corps
13. D-Day
14. kamikaze
15. refugee
16. concentration camp
17. charter

17 constitution

10 Great Britain, Soviet Union, China, and the United States

3 Germany's fascist party, the National Socialists

1 a period of economic decline

7 preserving peace by meeting the demands of an aggressor

9 Germany, Italy, and Japan

5 launching attacks on other countries

12 armed forces organization for women

6 to attack

15 a person who left his or her homeland for safety

13 June 6, 1944: history's largest invasion by sea

4 the planned spread of certain beliefs using posters, pamphlets, and speeches

16 a place that imprisoned people of a particular ethnic group or for their political or religious beliefs

11 Franklin Roosevelt, Joseph Stalin, and Winston Churchill

2 form of government that stresses the nation above individuals

8 farms grouped together and run by the government

14 Japanese pilots who flew their airplanes directly into enemy warships

Notes for Home: Your child learned the vocabulary terms for Chapter 19.

Use with Pupil Edition, p. 540

Workbook, p. 135

Lesson 1: Good to Bad Times

Use with Pages 542–547.

Directions: Think about what the following terms and names mean and how they relate to World War II. Then write them in the correct column in the chart. You may use your textbook.

Leaders	Events
Joseph Stalin	responsible for Kristallnacht
Emperor Hirohito	launched the Five-Year Plans
Adolf Hitler	became dictator of Italy
Benito Mussolini	took Manchuria

Country	Leader	Event
Italy	Benito Mussolini	became dictator of Italy
Germany	Adolf Hitler	responsible for Kristallnacht
Japan	Emperor Hirohito	took Manchuria
Soviet Union	Joseph Stalin	launched the Five-Year Plans

 Notes for Home: Your child learned about events leading to World War II.
Home Activity: With your child, review the chart. Discuss how all of these events were related during World War II.

Use with Pupil Edition, p. 547

Workbook, p. 136

Lesson 2: World War II

Use with Pages 54...

Directions: Read the following events from World War II. Put them in the order that they occurred by numbering them from 1 (earliest) to 10 (latest). You may use your textbook.

6 1. The United States and France drive Germany out of Paris.

10 2. Japan surrenders.

8 3. Nazi Germany surrenders.

1 4. Germany attacks Poland.

4 5. German troops surrender to the Soviet Army at Stalingrad.

7 6. President Roosevelt dies.

5 7. D-Day occurs at Normandy.

3 8. Great Britain wins the battle at El Alamein.

9 9. The United States drops an atomic bomb on Hiroshima.

2 10. Japan attacks Pearl Harbor.

Directions: Answer the questions below. Write your answers on the lines provided.

1. What were some important contributions women in the United States made during War II?

Possible answers: Formed Women's Airforce Service ▶ moved aircraft around the country and abroad; worke defense plants and factories

2. What might have happened if Japan had not ignored the United States warning ab atomic bomb?

Possible answer: The United States might not have dr the bombs on the cities of Hiroshima and Nagasaki.

Notes for Home: Your child learned about the sequence of events during World War II.
Home Activity: With your child, analyze the events in this worksheet to find cause-and-effect re...

Use with Pupil Edition, p. 554

Workbook Support

Workbook, p. 137

World at War

...ople learn about the world wars by studying artifacts such as objects people used
...uniforms soldiers wore. Artifacts help people to better understand what life was
...e during World War I and World War II.

...rections: Complete the chart below by describing some of the artifacts shown on
556–557.

Artifact	Description
...Military ...Decorations	Silver Star, Italian Cross, Purple Heart; awarded by the U.S. to American soldiers in World War II
...War Ration ...Book	Issued by the U.S. during World War II; reduced the usage of goods such as meat, butter, and petroleum
...Hand-Me- ...Downs	Uniforms left over from World War I worn by soldiers in World War II; army was short on uniforms
...Japanese ...Fighter	Mitsubishi Zero; introduced in 1940; Japan's best airplane in World War II
...Rosie the ...Riveter	Symbol of working American women in World War II

...ctions: Draw a picture of an artifact, different from those shown on pp. 556–
... to represent the life of a soldier or civilian during the world wars. Your artifact
...t be an object that civilians used during the world wars, a weapon used by
...rs, or a part of a soldier's uniform. Draw your picture in the box below.

...tudents' drawings should include an artifact to represent the
...fe of a soldier or civilian in one or both of the world wars.

Notes for Home: Your child learned about some of the artifacts that represent life during the world wars.
Home Activity: With your child, discuss some other artifacts that were used during World War I and World
War II. How does each artifact represent the daily life of civilians or soldiers during the world wars?

Use with Pupil Edition, p. 557

Workbook, p. 138

Use with Pages 558–561.

Lesson 3: The Aftermath

Directions: Complete each sentence with the correct term from the box. You may
use your textbook.

Joseph Stalin	Eleanor Roosevelt	Anne Frank
United Nations	Meyer Levin	Marshall Plan
6 million	13 billion	100,000

1. The atomic bomb left more than **100,000** dead and thousands more
   severely burned or sick with illnesses such as cancer.

2. Nazi Germany's "Final Solution" left at least **6 million** Jewish people
   dead.

3. American reporter **Meyer Levin** described the horrors of the Nazi
   concentration camps.

4. The **United Nations** was formed as an international peacekeeping organization.

5. The first U.S. delegate to the United Nations was **Eleanor Roosevelt**

6. After the war, aid was sent to Europe under the provisions of the
   Marshall Plan

7. The United States sent **13 billion** dollars in aid to help rebuild European
   economies.

8. **Joseph Stalin** forced Eastern European countries to refuse money from the
   United States after the war.

9. **Anne Frank** expressed personal feelings about the war in a diary.

Notes for Home: Your child learned about events that occurred immediately after World War II.
Home Activity: With your child, discuss the actions of the Axis Powers and the consequences they
suffered after the war. Then ask whether he or she thinks the Allies should have helped the Axis countries
rebuild. Discuss the reasons behind Allied aid.

Use with Pupil Edition, p. 561

Workbook, p. 139

Use with Pages 562–563.

Interpret Bar Graphs

Bar graphs help us understand relationships among amounts or numbers.

Directions: Look at the bar graphs and text on pages 562–563 of your textbook. Then read each
statement below. On the line beside each statement, write a *T* if it is true. If it is false, write an *F*
and then rewrite the false portion of the statement on the line provided to make it true.

F 1. Bar graphs have one axis.
___ **two axes** ___

T 2. The vertical axis on a graph is the y-axis.

F 3. On the graphs on pages 562–563, country names label the y-axis.
___ **x-axis** ___

F 4. The heights of the bars indicate exact figures.
___ **Possible answers: Approximate, rounded, estimated** ___

T 5. The title and axes labels on a graph help you read the information on the graph.

T 6. Italy had the fewest military casualties of all the countries represented on the graph.

F 7. On the graph, Japan spent the lowest percentage of its national income on defense.
___ **the United States** ___

Notes for Home: Your child learned to interpret a bar graph.
Home Activity: Using temperature data from a newspaper or weather broadcast, have your child create
bar graphs to represent the high and low temperatures for five U.S. cities on today's date. Then quiz your
child on the information recorded on the graphs.

Use with Pupil Edition, p. 563

Workbook, p. 140

Use with Chapter 19.

...cabulary Review

...are the vocabulary words for Chapter 19. How much do you know about these words?

...ions: Circle the word that best completes each sentence.

...ession	annex	Big Three	concentration camp
...sm	appeasement	Women's Army Corps	charter
	collective	D-Day	
...aganda	Axis Powers	kamikaze	
...ession	Allies	refugee	

...he (Nazis, charter) took away many democratic freedoms in Germany.

...ecause of the (depression, aggression), people around the world lacked hope.

... the political system called (appeasement, fascism) the leader has total control over the
...overnment and industry.

...he Nazis spread new ideas rapidly through the use of (aggression, propaganda).

...tler's and Mussolini's policies of (depression, aggression) helped lead to the outbreak of war.

...nder Stalin's rule, Russian farmers worked on the land of a (collective, fascist) every day.

... 1942, the United States had joined the war on the side of the (Axis Powers, Allies).

...tler decided to (annex, charter) Austria to gain more land.

...e World War II Allies created a (charter, propaganda) to guide the actions of the United
...tions.

...(appeasement, charter) means that peace can be preserved by meeting the demands of
...aggressor.

...rope, China, and other areas were overflowing with (Nazis, refugees) as a result of the
...mic bomb.

...e Nazis forced many Jewish people into (charters, concentration camps).

...rmany, Italy, and Japan made up the group known as the (Axis Powers, Allies).

...otes for Home: Your child learned the vocabulary terms for Chapter 19.
...ome Activity: Write each of the vocabulary words on an index card and then shuffle the cards. Have
...ur child draw a card from the stack and tell you one name, place, or event associated with that term in
...orld War II. Continue until all the cards have been chosen.

Use with Pupil Edition, p. 565

Assessment Support

Use these Assessment Book pages and the test maker to assess content and skills in Chapter 19. You can also view and print Assessment Book pages from the Teacher Resources CD-ROM.

Assessment Book, p. 97

Chapter 19

Part 1: Content Test

Directions: Fill in the circle next to the correct answer.

Lesson Objective (1:2)

1. During the 1930s, what affected the economies of most countries around the world?
   - ● the Great Depression
   - Ⓑ long-term stability
   - Ⓒ rising stock prices
   - Ⓓ wealth and prosperity

Lesson Objective (1:3)

2. What is the most important concern of a fascist government?
   - Ⓐ individual citizens
   - Ⓑ the rights of criminals
   - ● the nation
   - Ⓓ the church

Lesson Objective (1:3)

3. Which two European countries were led by fascist governments during the 1930s?
   - Ⓐ Germany and France
   - ● Germany and Italy
   - Ⓒ France and Italy
   - Ⓓ France and the Soviet Union

Lesson Objective (1:4)

4. Why did fascist dictators rise to power in some European countries in the 1930s?
   - ● They promised to end hard times.
   - Ⓑ They had friendly, likable personalities.
   - Ⓒ They promised another war.
   - Ⓓ They offered to personally pay off the country's debts.

Lesson Objective (1:5)

5. Why did France and Great Britain make little effort to stop Hitler's actions during the 1930s?
   - Ⓐ They supported his actions.
   - Ⓑ They did not know what he was doing.
   - Ⓒ They felt the countries he invaded deserved to be annexed.
   - ● They feared another war.

Lesson Objective (1:1)

6. Which is a reason why Stalin launched his Five-Year Plan?
   - Ⓐ to decrease the importance of farmers
   - Ⓑ to decrease industrial production
   - ● to increase crop production
   - Ⓓ to prepare the military for war

Lesson Objective (2:1)

7. What was the leading cause of World War II?
   - ● Hitler's effort to conquer Europe for Germany
   - Ⓑ the resignation of British Prime Minister Neville Chamberlain
   - Ⓒ the United States' attempt to remain neutral
   - Ⓓ Italy's alliance with Germany

Lesson Objective (2:1)

8. Which was NOT a country Hitler invaded prior to World War II?
   - Ⓐ Austria
   - ● Japan
   - Ⓒ Poland
   - Ⓓ Czechoslovakia

Use with Pupil Edition, p. 564

Assessment Book, p. 98

Lesson Objective (2:2)

9. Why did Hitler abandon the idea of capturing Great Britain?
   - Ⓐ His army revolted.
   - Ⓑ He decided Britain would be a better ally than enemy.
   - Ⓒ He chose to invade Japan instead.
   - ● He realized his forces could not defeat the Royal Air Force.

Lesson Objective (2:4)

10. Which event in June 1944 is remembered as history's largest invasion by sea?
    - Ⓐ V-J Day
    - Ⓑ Memorial Day
    - ● D-Day
    - Ⓓ V-E Day

Lesson Objective (2:3)

11. Which was NOT an effect of the United States' entry into World War II?
    - Ⓐ The Allies received thousands more weapons and vehicles.
    - Ⓑ The Germans were driven out of France.
    - ● The Soviets gave up Eastern Europe.
    - Ⓓ Allied forces won the Battle of Midway.

Lesson Objective (2:5)

12. Why did the Japanese emperor tell his government to surrender in 1945?
    - ● Atomic bombs had devastated the cities of Hiroshima and Nagasaki.
    - Ⓑ The Allies had won the Battle of the Coral Sea.
    - Ⓒ Kamikaze pilots were destroying Japanese warships.
    - Ⓓ U.S. forces had won a victory on Midway Island.

Lesson Objective (3:2)

13. What happened as a result of dropping atomic bombs on Hiroshima and Nagasaki?
    - Ⓐ From 40 to 50 million people were killed worldwide.
    - Ⓑ Tokyo was bombed to ruins.
    - Ⓒ Refugees fled to Japan.
    - ● More than 100,000 people died, and thousands more were injured or sick.

Lesson Objective (3:1)

14. The Allied victory in World War II put an end to which terrible practice?
    - Ⓐ the bombing of cities during wartime
    - ● placing Jews in concentration camps
    - Ⓒ the forming of alliances
    - Ⓓ the killing of people other than soldiers during wartime

Lesson Objective (3:4)

15. How did U.S. President Franklin D. Roosevelt hope to create a new and better world after World War II?
    - Ⓐ by promising the United States would never go to war again
    - Ⓑ by producing more atomic bombs
    - ● by forming an international peacekeeping organization
    - Ⓓ by arresting German war criminals

Lesson Objective (3:5)

16. Why did the Marshall Plan provide no help to the countries of Eastern Europe?
    - ● Stalin would not allow Eastern Europe to accept help from America.
    - Ⓑ The Americans did not want Eastern Europe to benefit from the plan.
    - Ⓒ Eastern Europe did not need to rebuild after the war.
    - Ⓓ The Marshall Plan was created only for Western European countries.

Use with Pupil Edition, p. 564

Assessment Support

Assessment Book, p. 99

Part 2: Skills Test

Directions: Use complete sentences to answer questions 1–8. Use a separate sheet of paper if you need more space.

1. When Europeans started to grow their own crops again after the Great War, how did it affect U.S. farmers? **Cause and Effect**

   The Europeans no longer needed to buy U.S. crops. This meant U.S. farmers made less money and could not repay their loans.

2. How did Hitler rise to power in Germany after the Great War? **Main Idea**

   Hitler convinced the Germans he would end hard times by restoring Germany's military power.

3. What might have happened if France and Great Britain had reacted differently when Hitler began to invade European countries during the 1930s? **Hypothesize**

   Possible answer: If they had taken action against Hitler sooner, they might have avoided a world war and prevented much of the death and destruction that occurred.

4. What was one advantage and one disadvantage of Stalin's plan to collectivize Soviet farms? **Analyze the Facts**

   Possible answers: Advantage: The government could control farming and increase production. Disadvantage: The farmers rebelled; production fell sharply; millions of Soviet people starved.

5. What were the human and economic results of Stalin's efforts to increase industrial production in the Soviet Union? **Cause and Effect**

   By the mid-1930s, the Soviet Union was second only to the United States in industrial production. However, the people began to rebel. In response, Stalin had millions of people either shot or sent to labor camps.

Use with Pupil Edition, p. 564

Assessment Book, p. 100

6. Why do you think Prime Minister Winston Churchill of Great Britain is considered one of the great leaders of World War II? **Draw Conclusions**

   Possible answer: He was a strong leader who was able to inspire his people to turn back the Germans when they attacked. He also was an important factor in the Allied victory.

7. Why do you think the Americans launched the Marshall Plan? **Draw Conclusions**

   Possible answers: They needed other countries to have healthy economies so they could buy U.S. products; They did not want the European people to continue suffering.

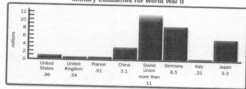

Military Casualties for World War II

	millions
United States .96	
United Kingdom .54	
France .61	
China 3.1	
Soviet Union more than 11	
Germany 8.5	
Italy .31	
Japan 5.3	

8. Use the graph to answer the questions. **Interpret Bar Graphs**
   a. What do the bars on the graph represent?

   the military casualties per country in World War II

   b. What information does the y-axis give?

   the number of military casualties in millions

   c. How many military casualties did Japan have?   about 6 million

Use with Pupil Edition, p. 564

From Peace to War

Resources

- Workbook, p. 134: Vocabulary Preview
- Vocabulary Cards
- Social Studies Plus!

The 1930s, Germany: Lesson 1

Tell students that the man in the middle of the picture is Prime Minister Neville Chamberlain of Great Britain. Ask students to describe what is happening in the picture. (Chamberlain is speaking to a crowd. The paper in his hand is probably something important. It looks like good news because the people are smiling.)

1939–1945, London: Lesson 2

Tell students that this is a picture of Londoners sleeping in the subway. Ask students to predict why they might be seeking shelter in the subway. (To avoid falling bombs)

1945–1948, New York City: Lesson 3

Ask students to tell what object is pictured. (A radio) Ask students to tell why a radio might be important. (Radios provided people with news and entertainment.)

CHAPTER

19 From Peace to War

Lesson 1

The 1930s Germany
The stage is set for another world war.

Lesson 2

1939–1945 London
World War II rages.

Lesson 3

1945 New York City
The world makes a new beginning.

540

Practice and Extend

Vocabulary Preview

- Use Workbook p. 134 to help students preview the vocabulary words in this chapter.
- Use Vocabulary Cards to preview key concept words in this chapter.

 Also on Teacher Resources CD-ROM.

Workbook, p. 134

Vocabulary Preview

Locating Time and Place

GREAT BRITAIN

London

GERMANY

Berlin

EUROPE

ATLANTIC OCEAN

New York City

UNITED STATES

AFRICA

Why We Remember

Today many people of the world either enjoy or desire the benefits of freedom. However, in the 1920s and 1930s, many countries made the decision to abandon democracy. Hard times from economic depression convinced many people that a strong ruler—a dictator—was needed. Adolf Hitler, Benito Mussolini, Joseph Stalin, and military dictators in Japan rose to power. Their plans for national glory brought on the most destructive war the world has ever seen: World War II. Millions fought and died. We are all the children of their sacrifice.

541

- Have students examine the pictures shown on p. 540 for Lessons 1, 2, and 3.

- Remind students that each picture is coded with both a number and a color to link it to a place on the map on p. 541.

Why We Remember

Have students read the "Why We Remember" paragraph on p. 541, and ask them why events in this chapter might be important to them. Have them consider how our lives would be different if soldiers had not fought to save us from dictators.

WEB SITE
Technology

...u can learn more about Berlin, ...rmany; London, England; ...d New York City, New York, ...clicking on *Atlas* at ...w.sfsocialstudies.com.

SOCIAL STUDIES STRAND
Geography

Mental Mapping On an outline map of the Eastern Hemisphere, have students label: Australia, China, Hawaii, India, Japan, Korea, Philippines, Southeast Asia, Soviet Union, and Taiwan. Next, ask students to color in the places under Japanese control at the height of Japan's power in the early 1940s. Discuss what advantages this empire might provide for Japan.

Good to Bad Times

Objectives

- List and describe the significant events that happened during Stalin's reign and their impact on the Soviet Union.

- Define *inflation.* Explain how inflation and the Great Depression impacted the world economy.

- Explain fascism and list two examples of fascist countries.

- Describe how conditions in Italy and Germany led to the rise of dictators.

- Explain Hitler's motivation for breaking the Treaty of Versailles in the 1930s.

Vocabulary

depression, p. 543; **fascism,** p. 544; **Nazis,** p. 544; **propaganda,** p. 545; **aggression,** p. 545; **annex,** p. 545; **appeasement,** p. 545; **collective,** p. 546

Resources

- Workbook, p. 135
- Transparency 20
- Every Student Learns Guide, pp. 258–261
- Quick Study, pp. 130–131

 Quick *Teaching Plan*

If time is short, have students draw five circles to represent the United States, Germany, Italy, Japan, and the Soviet Union.

- Have students read independently, noting what happened in each country in the appropriate circle.

1 Introduce and Motivate

Preview Ask students if they ever had a day where everything was so good they did not want it to end. Tell students that as they read Lesson 1, they will learn more about a decade when many people of the United States felt that way.

You Are There Good times don't last forever. Have students predict what might happen to this family if times get hard.

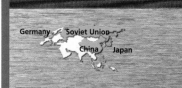

LESSON 1

1920   1930

1922
Fascists take
control of Italy.

1929
Stock market crash/Great
Depression begins.

1933
Hitler becomes
dictator of Germany.

1931
Japan takes Manchuria.

Germany   Soviet Union
China   Japan

PREVIEW

Focus on the Main Idea
Hard times set the stage for another world war.

PLACES
Germany
Japan
China
Soviet Union

PEOPLE
Benito Mussolini
Adolf Hitler
Neville Chamberlain
Hirohito
Joseph Stalin

VOCABULARY
depression
fascism
Nazis
propaganda
aggression
annex
appeasement
collective

TERMS
Five-Year Plan

EVENTS
Great Depression
Spanish Civil War

542

Good to Bad Times

You Are There On your walk home from school, yo
think about how nice it is that the w
is over. The weekend is finally here.
Father is taking you and your sister to a baseball game.
You've never seen Babe Ruth play. In fact, you've never
seen any of the New York Yankees play. You count the
hours until Saturday's game. When you reach your
driveway, Mother and Father greet
you with smiling faces. Before you
sits a beautiful, shiny black automobile with a red ribbon around it.

"Look what Father bought us!"
Mother cries.

WOW! A brand new car. You
can't believe how great things are.
You don't want these good times
to end.

FAVORITE—IN SMART CIRC

LA SALLE

▶ This advertisement for a luxury car
dates from about 1927.

 Cause and Effect As you read, think about
conditions that may have caused the rise of
dictators in Europe.

Practice and Extend

 READING SKILL
Cause and Effect

In the Lesson Review, students complete a graphic organizer like the one below. You may want to provide students with a copy of Transparency 20 to complete as they read the lesson.

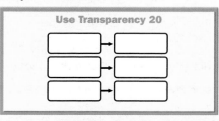
Use Transparency 20

 WEB SITE
Technology

- You can look up vocabulary wor
by clicking on *Social Studies Libr*
and selecting the dictionary at
www.sfsocialstudies.com.

- Students can learn more about current news by clicking on *Current Events* at **www.sfsocialstudies.com.**

- Explore other events that occurred on this day by clicking on *This Day in History* at **www.sfsocialstudies.com.**

The 1920s

After the war, the economies of many European countries were weak. **Germany** was paying reparations. Europe had to be rebuilt. However, the United States became the strongest economic power in the world. Most Americans were living the good life. Some writers called this time the "Roaring Twenties."

Good times in the United States lasted less than a decade. During the Great War, the U.S. government had encouraged farmers to buy more land to increase production. Farmers took out loans to buy land. They promised to pay back the loans after the war. But after the war, Europeans went back to growing their own crops. When they stopped buying U.S. agricultural products, prices went down. Farmers did not make enough money to pay back their loans.

After the Great War, Americans also wanted to buy goods that were not available during the war. Factories switched from making weapons to making automobiles and radios. Like farmers, other Americans bought these goods on credit. Consumers soon ran out of credit and could not buy any more goods. When factories produced

▶ *Life* magazine captures the good times of the 1920s.

more goods than Americans were able to buy, prices fell and people lost their jobs.

In the late 1920s, people also borrowed money to buy stocks, or shares of companies, on credit. People investing their money in the stock market began to lose confidence in the economy. In October 1929, large numbers of investors began to sell their stock. Prices fell rapidly. When brokers demanded that investors pay back their loans, most could not repay them. Both the brokers and investors lost money. Hundreds of banks and businesses closed.

The prosperity that had begun in the early 1920s was swept away by the **Great Depression,** a worldwide business slump. A **depression** is a period of economic decline. During depressions, businesses close, people lose their jobs, and prices fall. Every country was hit hard, not just the United States. People around the world were out of work, food, and hope.

REVIEW How was borrowing money on credit one cause of the Great Depression? ↻ **Cause and Effect**

▶ This investor was among thousands who lost all of their money after the stock market crash in 1929.

$100 WILL BUY THIS CAR. MUST HAVE CASH. LOST ALL ON THE STOCK MARKET

543

Teach and Discuss

PAGE 543

The 1920s

⏱ **Quick Summary** The United States became the strongest economic power in the world, but overproduction and too much debt brought on the Great Depression.

1 In the early 1920s, why was the United States stronger economically than the countries of Europe? The United States had no reparations to pay and did not have the physical damage from the war that Europe did. **Summarize**

2 Why were the 1920s called the Roaring Twenties? Possible answer: The U.S. economy was strong (roaring) during most of the decade. **Draw Conclusions**

$ **SOCIAL STUDIES STRAND**
Economics

Review the terms *supply* and *demand*.

3 What might happen when the supply of goods is greater than the demand? A factory cannot sell many of the goods it produces, prices may fall, and workers may lose their jobs. ↻ **Cause and Effect**

✓ **REVIEW ANSWER** Credit made it possible for people to buy more goods than they would have otherwise. However, when times got hard, people could not pay back the money they had borrowed on credit, causing problems for other people and businesses. ↻ **Cause and Effect**

New Dictators in Europe

Quick Summary Fascism, a new political movement that stressed the nation above individuals, became popular under the leadership of Adolf Hitler of Germany.

4 **Why might Italians and Germans have wanted fascist dictators?**
Possible answer: They believed that dictators could make quick and firm decisions and make their countries strong again. **Point of View**

5 **What was the name of Hitler's political party?** The National Socialists, or Nazis **Main Idea and Details**

Prices of Goods in the United States

6 **What does inflation cause?** An increase in prices **Cause and Effect**

7 **The actual cost of a table lamp increased $18 from 1932 to 2001. What was the increase in the actual cost of a sled that steers during that time?** $35.05 **Interpret Charts**

8 **The price of a table lamp in 2001 was 19 times more than the cost of a table lamp in 1932. How many times more did an adult sweater cost in 2001?** 30 **Apply Information**

9 **Why did the Nazis use propaganda?**
To spread their belief that the Jews were responsible for all of Germany's problems **Summarize**

✓ **REVIEW ANSWER** There were strikes, inflation, and unemployment in Italy and Germany after World War I. The dictators promised to put people back to work.
Cause and Effect

New Dictators in Europe

Italian soldiers returned from the Great War to a country in poor condition. Workers went on strike. Factories stopped producing goods. Thousands of returning soldiers faced unemployment.

A new political movement called **fascism** (FASH ism) grew out of this troubled situation. Fascism is a form of government that stresses the nation above individuals. In a fascist country, the leader is usually a dictator who has total control over the government and industry.

4 The head of the Italian fascists, **Benito Mussolini** (MOO soh LEE nee), promised to make things better. When the fascists marched on Rome in

► Benito Mussolini and Adolf Hitler became dictators in the 1920s and 1930s.

October 1922, Mussolini took over the government as dictator.

Germany was still paying reparations when the Great Depression hit. As a result, by 1932, six million Germans were unemployed. Thousands joined Germany's fascist party, the National Socialists, or **Nazis.** Their leader, **Adolf Hitler,** promised to end hard times by restoring German military power. Hitler's ideas and plans were well known in Germany in part because of his book, *Mein Kampf* ("My Struggle").

Prices of Goods in the United States

How much money would you have needed to buy a sled or a doll in the 1930s? Why are prices today higher than they were back then? When governments print more money, that makes more money available. However, printing more money can actually decrease the value of the money. This causes inflation. Inflation causes an increase in prices. Look at the chart below to compare prices of goods taken from 1932 and 2001 advertisements.

	1932	2001
adult winter coat	$28.00	$99
table tennis	$23.50	$150
doll	$1.95	$19
table lamp	$1.00	$19

sled that steers	
1932	$3.95
2001	$39.00

adult sweater	
1932	$1.00
2001	$30.00

544

Practice and Extend

MEETING INDIVIDUAL NEEDS
Leveled Practice

Interpret a Chart Have students make statements about the data in a chart.

Easy Have students compare the prices of two or three items and make a general statement about how prices have changed. **Reteach**

On-Level Have students choose two or three items in the chart and find the percentage change in the price. Students should find the difference and then divide the difference by the 1932 price. **Extend**

Challenge Students should hypothesize why some prices (adult sweater, for example) increase more rapidly than others (adult winter coat, for example). If necessary, prompt students to think about supply and demand. **Enrich**

For a Lesson Summary, use Quick Study, p. 130.

In January 1933 Hitler gained the top position in Germany's democratic government. Within two months, the Nazis took away most democratic freedoms. Hitler then became dictator of Germany.

Nazis were masters of **propaganda,** or the planned spread of certain beliefs. Propaganda was in the form of posters, pamphlets, or speeches. Nazis used propaganda to preach that the Jews were responsible for all of Germany's problems. They also said that the Germans were superior to all other ethnic groups.

Such Nazi ideas became widely known outside of Germany by 1938. Kristallnacht (krihs TAHL nahkt), a night of nationwide violence against Jews, showed the world how the Nazis treated Jews.

REVIEW What conditions in Germany and Italy led to the rise of dictators? Cause and Effect

Steps Toward War

Europe's new dictators quickly adopted a policy of **aggression,** which meant launching attacks on other countries. Both Hitler and Mussolini wanted to create empires. Beginning in the mid-1930s, they invaded lands that their armies could conquer easily. The leaders of Europe's strongest democracies, Great Britain and France, feared another war, so they did little to stop the aggressive acts.

Soon after taking power, Hitler began rebuilding Germany's armed forces, an action that violated the Treaty of Versailles. He had two goals: to regain territory in the east to bring together all German-speaking people and to take revenge for Germany's humiliating defeat in the Great War. The Treaty of Versailles had made the Rhineland, Germany's western region, off-limits to German troops. In 1936 Hitler ignored the treaty and sent troops into the Rhineland. Neither France nor Great Britain responded. Hitler's next move was to add Austria,

his homeland, to Germany. In March 1938, German troops marched into Austria and **annexed,** or attached, it to Germany. Both of these actions broke the Treaty of Versailles, but neither France nor Great Britain responded.

In September 1938 Hitler demanded that Czechoslovakia give up its German-speaking territories. He wanted to make them part of a greater Germany. To avoid war, British Prime Minister **Neville Chamberlain** suggested a conference. The result of the conference was an agreement: Germany was allowed to occupy the territory if Hitler promised to make no more claims in Europe. The agreement grew out of a policy called **appeasement,** or meeting the demands of an aggressor in order to preserve peace. In March 1939, however, Hitler broke the agreement. He seized the rest of Czechoslovakia.

Like Hitler, Mussolini had a plan of his own to take land for Italy. In 1935 he invaded Ethiopia in northeastern Africa. The League of Nations failed to stop this act of aggression. Then Italian and German troops went to Spain to join with fascist rebels against the government in the **Spanish Civil War.** This war ended with a fascist victory in 1939. Some historians later described this war as a "dress rehearsal" for what became World War II.

REVIEW Why did France and Great Britain ignore Hitler's breaking of the Treaty of Versailles? Cause and Effect

▶ In 1938 Prime Minister Neville Chamberlain waves an agreement reached with Hitler, declaring "peace with honor."

545

PAGE 545

Steps Toward War

🕐 **Quick Summary** Hitler and Mussolini began to build empires by attacking and controlling land belonging to other countries. France, Great Britain, and the League of Nations did little to stop them.

⑩ **What are some examples of Hitler's and Mussolini's policies of aggression?** Rebuilding armies, annexing Austria, occupying Czechoslovakia, invading Ethiopia **Summarize**

Decision Making

⑪ **If you were a leader of a country and saw other countries behaving aggressively, would you appease them or try to stop them? Give reasons for your answer.** Possible answers: Stop them because it would be my responsibility to try to keep peace. It would also be a way for me to try to keep my own country safe. Appease them because people are tired of war and are still trying to recover from the Great War. **Decision Making**

Ongoing Assessment

| **If...** students do not understand the meaning of *appeasement,* | **then...** help them imagine that a bully is demanding someone's lunch. If the policy is appeasement, would they tell the student to give the lunch to the bully and make the bully promise not to take anyone else's lunch or would they try to keep the lunch and fight? |

✓ **REVIEW ANSWER** France and Great Britain feared that if they stood up to Hitler, that would mean war. These countries did not want to go to war again. Cause and Effect

Japan Seizes an Empire

🕐 *Quick Summary* To gain more resources, Japan seized Manchuria, a region in northeastern China, and then declared war against China.

12 Compare and contrast Japan's nationalism and the nationalism of Italy and Germany. All three countries wanted more resources and land for expansion. All three countries wanted to gain glory through war and heroism. Italy and Germany were run by strong leaders. Japan was run by the military.
Compare and Contrast

13 What happened in Nanjing, the capital of China? The Japanese military showed its power by killing hundreds of thousands of people. **Make Inferences**

Japanese Aggression in China

14 What areas did Japan control in 1930? Korea, Taiwan, and small areas in southeastern China, including the area around Guangzhou. **Interpret Maps**

15 After the Japanese conquered Manchuria, in which directions did they extend their control into China? South and east **Interpret Maps**

MAP SKILL Answer The northeastern part, including the area around Nanjing

✓ **REVIEW ANSWER** Manchuria had coal and iron, which Japan needed.
🔄 Cause and Effect

A Soviet Dictator

🕐 *Quick Summary* The communists formed the Union of Soviet Socialist Republics, led first by Lenin and then by the dictator Stalin, who forced his country to try to catch up economically with the United States.

16 How did Russia's civil war affect the people? More than 10 million people died, and many millions more had no food. 🔄 Cause and Effect

Japan Seizes an Empire

By 1930 military leaders began influencing **Japan.** As in Europe, nationalism began to rise. Japan's government encouraged nationalism through the worship of Emperor **Hirohito** (hir oh HEE toh). War and heroism were glorified.

As an island nation with few natural resources, Japan was dependent on the United States and other countries for raw materials. Japan's military leaders believed they could get the raw materials they needed by seizing Manchuria, a region in northeastern **China** with rich coal and iron deposits. The Chinese government was not strong enough to fight back. In 1931 Japan easily overran Manchuria.

▶ **Hirohito became emper**‌ of Japan in 1926.

Japan launched a f‌ scale war against Ch‌ in 1937. The map below shows areas o‌ China that Japan invaded. Millions died ‌ the fighting. In Nanjing, then China's capital, the Japanese killed hundreds of thousands of the city's residents.

By late 1938, Japan's military leaders held m‌ of eastern China and were planning to bring all ‌ eastern and southeastern Asia under their contr‌

REVIEW What was the cause of Japan's invasion of Manchuria? 🔄 Cause and Effect

MAP SKILL

Japanese Aggression in China

Japanese territory, 1930

Territory seized by 1932

Territory seized by 1939

▶ **Japan took control of much of China in the 1930s.**

MAP SKILL Use a Map Key *What parts of China did Japan invade?*

546

A Soviet Dictator

In 1922 the communists in Russia formed the Union of Soviet Socialist Republics, or the **Soviet Union.** The birth of this first communist nation had been long and violent. More than te‌ million Russians died during the civil war, which‌ lasted from 1918 to 1920. Millions of Russian‌ were left without food.

The Soviet leader, Lenin, tried to improve the‌ failing economy. He allowed small peasant farr‌ ers and business people to operate without government control. This plan, called the New Economic Policy, helped the economy of the Soviet Union recover.

Lenin died in 1924, leaving the nation witho‌ a leader. Top Soviet officials became rivals in a‌ struggle for power. By the late 1920s, the secretary general of the Communist Party, **Joseph Stalin,** had defeated all his opponents. He was now a dictator.

In 1928 Stalin rejected Lenin's New Econom‌ Policy. That same year he launched the first of ‌ **Five-Year Plans.** His plan had two goals. One ‌ to turn farms into government collectives to increase crop production. **Collectives** are farm‌ that are grouped together and run as a unit.

Practice and Extend

CURRICULUM CONNECTION
Science

Need for Steel

- Tell students that iron and coal are important in making steel. Have students research the steel-making process to find out why Japan seized Manchuria. (Steel contains iron, and coal is needed as fuel to melt the iron.)

- Students should also find out how steel would have helped Japan reach its goals. (Steel is used in buildings, cars, and railroad rails.)

FAST FACTS

- During the 1920s and 1930s, radio delivered news, propaganda, and entertainment.
- President Roosevelt explained issues in "Fireside Chats."
- In 1938 Orson Welles' radio adaptation of *War of the Worlds* was so convincing that people thought an alien invasion was actually happening.
- Hitler's speeches also were broadcast.

The second goal was to make the Soviet Union into an industrial giant. Stalin gave his reasons:

> "We are 50 or 100 years behind the advanced countries. We must make good this lag in 10 years . . . or we will be crushed."

The peasants rebelled when Stalin tried to collectivize their land. Many of the wealthier peasants were sent to prison camps or killed. Farm production fell sharply, causing people to starve. Some historians believe five to seven million Soviet people died during this period.

Stalin's industrial drive was more successful. By the mid-1930s, the Soviet Union was second to the United States in industrial production. Still, many Soviet people did not like Stalin. In response, Stalin launched a program called the Great Terror. Millions of people were shot or sent to labor camps.

REVIEW How did Stalin plan to catch up to the economies of advanced countries? **Main Idea and Details**

▶ These Russian refugees were taken away by train during a famine in 1922.

Summarize the Lesson

- **1922** Fascists, led by Benito Mussolini, took control of Italy.
- **1931** Japan seized Manchuria from China.
- **1933** Adolf Hitler came to power in Germany.

LESSON 1 REVIEW

Check Facts and Main Ideas

1. 🔄 **Cause and Effect** On a separate piece of paper, fill in the chart below by listing one important effect or cause.

Causes		Effects
Stalin's Great Terror	→	Millions of people were shot or sent to labor camps.
Stalin wanted to increase crop production on Soviet farms.	→	Collectives
New Economic Policy	→	Soviet economy recovered.

2. Explain how inflation and the Great Depression affected world economies.

3. Define fascism and name two fascist countries from this lesson.

4. How did hard times lead to the rise of dictators in Italy and Germany?

5. **Critical Thinking:** *Make Inferences* Why do you think that Hitler repeatedly violated the Treaty of Versailles? Explain your answer.

Link to 🔗 Reading

Research Current Events Using newspapers, news magazines, and the Internet, research conflicts in the world today. Choose one conflict and prepare a report about it for your class.

547

Workbook, p. 135

Lesson 1: Good to Bad Times

Directions: Think about what the following terms and names mean and how they relate to World War II. Then write them in the correct column in the chart below. You may use your textbook.

Leaders	Events
Joseph Stalin	responsible for Kristallnacht
Emperor Hirohito	launched the Five-Year Plans
Adolf Hitler	became dictator of Italy
Benito Mussolini	took Manchuria

Country	Leader	Event
Italy		
Germany		
Japan		
Soviet Union		

Notes for Home: Your child learned about events leading to World War II.
Home Activity: With your child, review the chart. Discuss how all of these events were related during World War II.

Also on Teacher Resources CD-ROM.

Primary Source
Cited in *Why Lenin? Why Stalin?* by Von Laue

17 **What did Stalin mean by *advanced countries*?** Industrialized countries that produced more goods and food because of their technology **Analyze Primary Source**

18 **Why did farmers rebel against collectivization?** Possible answers: They did not want to give up their land; they did not like change. **Draw Conclusions**

✓ **REVIEW ANSWER** By turning farms into collectives and by making the Soviet Union an industrial giant **Main Idea and Details**

3 Close and Assess

Summarize the Lesson

Have students work with partners to come up with true-or-false questions about the major events of the 1920s and 1930s as discussed in the lesson. Then have pairs pose their questions to other pairs.

✓ **LESSON 1 REVIEW**

1. 🔄 **Cause and Effect** For possible answers see the reduced pupil page.

2. Possible answer: Inflation made goods cost more. People had less money, and many lost their jobs. Worldwide economies declined during the Great Depression.

3. Fascism is a type of government that stresses the nation over the individual. The leader, usually a dictator, controls the government and industry; Italy and Germany

4. People were desperate for jobs and willing to accept a strong leader who could change the situation.

5. **Critical Thinking:** *Make Inferences* Possible answer: Hitler wanted to see how much he could get away with because Great Britain and France were not enforcing the Treaty of Versailles.

Link to 🔗 Reading

Students should use more than one source for their research and then present their findings in an oral report.

World War II

Objectives

- List and describe the effects of Germany's attacks on countries in Europe.

- Explain why Hitler gave up on invading Great Britain.

- Explain the significance of D-Day.

- Explain the significance and effects of the bombings on Hiroshima and Nagasaki.

- Explain the effect of the U.S. entry into World War II.

Resources

- Workbook, p. 136
- Transparency 18
- Every Student Learns Guide, pp. 262–265
- Quick Study, pp. 132–133

Quick Teaching Plan

If time is short, have students draw a blank time line starting at the year 1939 and ending at the year 1945.

- Have students read the lesson independently.

- Tell students that any time they see a date, they should put the date and event on their time line.

1 Introduce and Motivate

Preview To activate prior knowledge, ask students what they know about World War II. Tell students that they will learn more about this historic event in Lesson 2.

You Are There Ask students how they might make the best of a bad situation today. Give the example of sitting in the school basement during a tornado alert.

LESSON 2

London Berlin
Stalingrad
Tokyo

PREVIEW

Focus on the Main Idea
World War II caused millions of deaths and great destruction.

PLACES
Poland
London
Pearl Harbor
Stalingrad
Normandy
Berlin
Midway Island
Tokyo
Hiroshima
Nagasaki

PEOPLE
Winston Churchill
Franklin Roosevelt
Oveta Culp Hobby
Dwight Eisenhower
Douglas MacArthur
Harry Truman

TERMS
Axis Powers
Allies
Big Three
Women's Army Corps
D-Day
kamikaze

EVENTS
Battle of Britain

548

1935	1940	1945

1939
World War II begins in Europe.

1941
Japan attacks U.S. ships at Pearl Harbor.

1945
Nazi Germany surrenders.

1945
Japan surrenders.

World War II

You Are There At first, it seems like a holiday. You're going down into the "tube"—the London subway—at night with Mum and Dad and the neighbors. Mrs. Fenway, that nice older lady from downstairs, compares the bombing of London to a big slumber party. You bring your pajamas, pillows, and blankets and stay up very late. Mum says that Londoners always make the best of a bad situation.

In November 1940 London is in pretty bad shape. The Battle of Britain is in full swing, and every night German bombs are falling. Oh! There's one now. First you hear the rumble of planes overhead, then the scream of falling bombs, then the crash and roar of the explosions. You know that your family and friends will be safe here below tonight . . . but will you find your home still standing tomorrow morning?

Londoners seeking shelter and safety sleep in the subway at night during air raids.

Cause and Effect As you read, look for the effects the actions of the Axis Powers had on the rest of the world.

Practice and Extend

READING SKILL
Cause and Effect

In the Lesson Review, students complete a graphic organizer like the one below. You may want to provide students with a copy of Transparency 18 to complete as they read the lesson.

Use Transparency 18

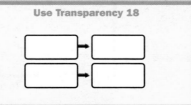

WEB SITE
Technology

- You can look up vocabulary words by clicking on *Social Studies Library* and selecting the dictionary at **www.sfsocialstudies.com.**

- Students can learn more about current news by clicking on *Current Events* at **www.sfsocialstudies.com.**

- Explore other events that occurred on this day by clicking on *This Day in History* at **www.sfsocialstudies.com.**

Hitler's Aggression to 1939

Legend:
- Germany in 1935
- German territory occupied by troops against treaty, 1936
- Foreign territory under German control, March 1939

ESTONIA, LATVIA, LITHUANIA, EAST PRUSSIA, DENMARK, SWEDEN, North Sea, Baltic Sea, Elbe River, Oder River, Vistula River, POLAND, NETHERLANDS, GERMANY, RHINELAND, CZECHOSLOVAKIA, Rhine River, Danube River, AUSTRIA, SWITZERLAND, YUGO., ITALY, Adriatic Sea

100   200 Miles
100 200 Kilometers

Germany violated the Treaty of Versailles when it occupied the Rhineland in 1936.

MAP SKILL Use a Locator Map *Germany is part of what continent?*

World War II Begins

In August 1939, Stalin and Hitler signed an agreement. The two dictators promised not to attack each other. They also secretly agreed to attack and divide up **Poland.**

Hitler then set out on his plan to conquer Europe. On September 1 waves of German bombers, tanks, and troops crossed over into neighboring Poland. Within a few days, Great Britain and France declared war on Germany. Soon after, the Soviet Army invaded Poland from the east. World War II had begun.

Poland's collapse was followed by a period of calm. Then, in April 1940, Germany was on the move again, conquering the northern European countries of Denmark and Norway.

Meanwhile, **Winston Churchill** became prime minister of Great Britain in May. Churchill was the strong leader Great Britain needed. He knew that Hitler could not be trusted.

The Germans then marched into the Netherlands and Belgium. Next, Germany invaded France. Italy joined Germany by declaring war on France and Great Britain in June. Within a couple of weeks, France surrendered to Germany, leaving Great Britain to fight on alone.

The German Air Force soon launched an attack on Great Britain. In the **Battle of Britain,** day after day, British pilots defended England against German bombers. The Germans staged air raids on **London** and other cities. However, they could not destroy Britain's Royal Air Force or the will of the British people. Churchill was determined that Great Britain would fight on:

> *"We shall defend our island, whatever the cost may be. We shall fight on the beaches, we shall fight on the landing grounds, we shall fight in the fields and in the streets . . . we shall never surrender."*

Churchill's words of encouragement worked. The British fought on, and Hitler gave up on Great Britain.

Hitler's next move broke his agreement with Stalin. On June 22, 1941, the Germans attacked their ally, the Soviet Union. Expecting a quick victory, the Germans marched into Russia. The Soviet Union joined the side of Great Britain. The Germans held on until 1943. Then they retreated, or went back, to Germany.

REVIEW Why do you think Hitler gave up on his attacks against Great Britain? Draw Conclusions

549

SOCIAL STUDIES
Background

About World War II

- What had once been called the Great War would now be known as World War I.
- *Blitzkrieg* is a German word that means "lightning war." With fast-moving modern equipment, such as tanks and airplanes, the German military attacked Poland so thoroughly and quickly that within days it was clear the Poles were defeated. However, Great Britain did not surrender despite repeated blitzes.

The United States Enters the War

Quick Summary President Roosevelt wanted to help democracies fight Hitler, but it wasn't until Japan bombed U.S. ships at Pearl Harbor that the United States officially joined the conflict.

5 **Which three countries made up the Axis Powers?** Germany, Italy, Japan
Main Idea and Details

6 **What event immediately preceded the Japanese decision to attack Pearl Harbor?** The United States stopped exporting goods to Japan.
Cause and Effect

Primary Source

Address to Congress, December 8, 1941, in *Public Papers*

7 **What words make this quote sound strong and outraged?** Possible answers: *Infamy, suddenly, deliberately, attacked*
Analyze Primary Sources

8 **Which came first, the relocation of Japanese Americans to camps or the bombing of Pearl Harbor?** The bombing of Pearl Harbor **Sequence**

✓ **REVIEW ANSWER** The United States went to war because Japan attacked Pearl Harbor in Hawaii on December 7, 1941. **Cause and Effect**

The United States Enters the War

5 At the beginning of the war, the United States was at peace. However, U.S. President **Franklin Roosevelt** argued that all free countries would be endangered if the **Axis Powers**—Germany, Italy, and Japan—won the war. In order to aid the **Allies** —Great Britain, the Soviet Union, and China— Roosevelt asked for changes in laws that kept the United States neutral. Congress agreed. They then let the Allies buy war supplies.

With Great Britain fighting for its survival, the United States was the only country that could stop Japan from conquering Asia. The United States stopped exporting goods to Japan. As a result, the Japanese government decided to **6** attack the United States.

On December 7, 1941, Japanese planes attacked the U.S. ships and airplanes anchored at **Pearl Harbor** in Hawaii. The surprise attack killed more than 2,300 people and destroyed or damaged 21 ships and 300 airplanes. President Roosevelt described the attack to Congress as follows:

7 "*Yesterday, December 7, 1941— a date which will live in infamy [public disgrace]—the United States of America was suddenly and deliberately attacked by naval and air forces of the Empire of Japan.*"

The United States immediately declared war on Japan. Germany and Italy then declared war on the United States.

▶ **Three damaged battleships during the Japanese attack on Pearl Harbor.**

The Granger Collection

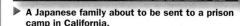
▶ A Japanese family about to be sent to a prison camp in California.

The attack on Pearl Harbor made many Americans angry toward all of the Japanese, including Japanese Americans. In 1942 Roosevelt responded to this growing pressure and ordered all people of Japanese descent, or relation, to leave their homes on the West Coast. They were then sent to prison camps in various U.S. states. Nearly 50 years later, in 1988, Congress voted to grant $20,000 to each of the surviving Japanese Americans who had been sent to these camps.

REVIEW Why did the United States go to war in 1941?
Cause and Effect

Practice and Extend

Dunkirk Evacuation

- Early in the war British forces were in France in anticipation of a German invasion.
- Germany invaded through Belgium, bypassing France's reinforced border, the Maginot Line.
- As German forces marched west, they stranded Allied forces at Dunkirk.
- Every available boat in Great Britain was pressed into service to ferry 338,000 stranded Allied troops to safety.

ESL **ACCESS CONTENT**
ESL Support

Names of Countries Have students find countries and continents on a globe.

Beginning Using a globe, point out and name the United States, Japan, Germany, Italy, Great Britain, and the former Soviet Union. Have students respond to questions such as "Where is _____?"or "What is the name of this country?"

Intermediate Using a globe, point out and name all the countries mentioned in the lesson. Have students ask each other questions about the countries' locations, such as "Where is _____?" or "What is the name of this country?"

Advanced Make sure students are familiar with the locations of the countries in the lesson and that they know the meaning of *attacked* and *conquered*. Have students point out countries as they create sentences about the lesson.

For additional ESL support, use Every Student Learns Guide, pp. 262–265.

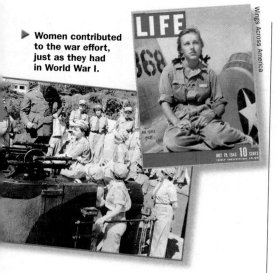

▶ Women contributed to the war effort, just as they had in World War I.

Wings Across America

Women in the War

During World War II women again helped in the war effort. As in World War I, women were not allowed to fight in combat. However, they had many more opportunities in war work that brought them closer to the front lines. Great Britain, the Soviet Union, and the United States all set up military organizations for women. Millions of women also went to work in defense plants, or factories that produced war weapons.

One U.S. organization that contributed to the war effort was the Women's Air Force Service Pilots (WASPs). Women pilots towed targets for training. They also moved aircraft around the country and abroad from factories to bases near enemy territory.

By the end of the war, the Soviet Union let women fight because of shortages in manpower. Great Britain also faced huge losses. For the first time in history, some British women were drafted, or called up for military service. However, British women were still not allowed to fight in combat. Germany did not allow women to help out much in the war. Many served as nurses or in the army in non-combat roles.

REVIEW How did women's roles in the war effort change over time? Compare and Contrast

The Tide Turns

By 1942 the United States and the Soviet Union had joined the Allies. The major Allied leaders—Franklin Roosevelt, Joseph Stalin, and Winston Churchill—were known as the **Big Three.** Roosevelt and Churchill agreed to concentrate on defeating Germany before Japan.

Stalin wanted a second fighting front, in Western Europe. Roosevelt and Churchill decided that the new front would be in Italy. However, the Allies first needed to drive the Axis Powers out of northern Africa. There the British were already fighting to hold on to Egypt and the Suez Canal.

In November 1942 the British stopped the Axis advance into Egypt at El Alamein. The battle was a turning point in the war. By May 1943 northern Africa was a clear base from which the Allies could invade Italy.

The Allies landed on the island of Sicily off the tip of Italy. In September 1943 they crossed over to the mainland and began a long, hard struggle up the Italian Peninsula. Though Italy had surrendered, Hitler and Mussolini still had control of central and northern Italy.

On the Eastern Front, intense Soviet fighting and the harsh winter of 1942 kept the Germans out of Moscow and Leningrad. In the spring, German forces moved south in an attempt to take Soviet oil fields. They met the Soviet Army at **Stalingrad** in late August. The battle raged for five months before the last German troops finally surrendered in February 1943. This battle was another key turning point in the war.

REVIEW What was the effect of the Battle of Stalingrad on Germany's invasion of the Soviet Union? Cause and Effect

▶ British officers lead troops of the British Empire from their desert camp in Egypt in 1940.

Hulton-Deutsch Collection/Corbis

551

PAGE 551

Women in the War

⏱ *Quick Summary* Women contributed to the war effort in many ways, especially in industry and the military.

9 **How did WASPs help in the United States' war effort?** They towed targets and flew planes from factories to bases. **Main Idea and Details**

✓ **REVIEW ANSWER** At first women were kept well away from the front lines, but as the war dragged on, women got closer and closer to combat lines. British women were drafted. Soviet women fought in combat. **Compare and Contrast**

The Tide Turns

⏱ *Quick Summary* The Allies fought Hitler in northern Africa, Italy, and the Soviet Union before the battle of Stalingrad finally stopped Hitler's eastward progress.

10 **In what order did the Big Three decide to fight their enemies?** Defeat Germany, then Japan **Sequence**

11 **How were challenges the Allies faced in Italy different from the ones they faced in the Soviet Union?** Possible answers: In Italy the soldiers were on enemy turf. In the Soviet Union the Allies were on their own turf. In Italy they were fighting to defeat Mussolini. In the Soviet Union they were fighting to keep the Germans from getting oil. **Compare and Contrast**

✓ **REVIEW ANSWER** Germany's advance to the east was finally stopped. Cause and Effect

---

CURRICULUM CONNECTION
Mathematics

Deciphering Codes

- Between the Great War and World War II, the German military acquired a code that seemed indecipherable. The Poles, however, recruited cryptographers who were mathematicians and fluent in German. These cryptographers looked for patterns that signaled the beginning of a message, and from that point the rest of the code could be deciphered.

In 1942 the U.S. military began using Navajo speakers to develop a new code. This code was based on the Navajo language, which is not written. Navajo code talkers provided the United States with a fast, secure code that was never broken.

Have students develop a code and use it to write a short message. They can exchange messages and try to crack each other's code.

Victory in Europe

Quick Summary With the help of the United States and its wartime production, the Allies were able to drive the Germans out of Paris while the Soviets drove the Germans from the Soviet Union and Eastern Europe.

Primary Source

Cited in *Side by Side: A Photographic History of American Women in War,* by Vickie Lewis

12 **Based on this quote, how do you think women felt about serving in the war and working in defense plants?** Possible answer: They felt they were helping and defending their country. **Analyze Primary Sources**

13 **How did the Allies show their strength in France during the summer of 1944?** U.S. General Dwight Eisenhower led the Allied forces in history's largest invasion by sea, and U.S. and French forces drove the Germans out of Paris. **Main Idea and Details**

World War II in Europe and Asia

Test Talk

Use Information from Graphics

14 **In which two regions of the world was World War II mainly fought?** Tell students to use the legend to find symbols for victories and atomic bomb targets. Then they should look for these symbols on the map. Europe and the Pacific **Interpret Maps**

MAP SKILL Answer 180°

✓ **REVIEW ANSWER** It gave the Allies the weapons they needed to launch the D-Day attack. 🌀 **Cause and Effect**

Victory in Europe

After being attacked by Japan in late 1941, the United States began preparing for war. Millions of men entered the armed forces. Women served too. The commander of the **Women's Army Corps, Oveta Culp Hobby,** declared that every woman who served released a man for combat. Beatrice Hood Stroup, who served under Hobby, described her feelings about the war:

12

"It wasn't just my brother's country, or my husband's country, it was my country as well. And so this war wasn't just their war, it was my war, and I needed to serve in it."

▶ Posters recruited women to work in factories to produce airplanes

France. However, the Germans lacked the strength to keep it going.

While the Western Allies were freeing France from the Nazis, the Soviets were advancing from the east. By the spring of 1944, the Soviet troops had driven the Germans from the Soviet Union and then crossed into Eastern Europe. By April 1945, the Soviets held nearly all of Eastern Europe.

The United States astonished the world with its wartime production, including 86,000 tanks and 297,000 airplanes.

U.S. military production was put to the test on June 6, 1944. On this day, also known as **D-Day,** U.S. General **Dwight Eisenhower** led the Allied forces in history's largest invasion by sea. More than 4,700 ships carried over 150,000 soldiers from southern Great Britain to **Normandy** on the northern coast of France. By late June, one million Allied troops had landed.

On August 25, U.S. and French forces drove the last Germans out of Paris. In December the German Army launched a final attack on the border between Belgium and

World War II in Europe and Asia

▶ The Allies defeated Germany and Italy in Europe and Japan in Asia.

Practice and Extend

MEETING INDIVIDUAL NEEDS
Leveled Practice

Write a Wartime Communication Have students research one of the events of the war and write as if they are involved in that event.

Easy Write a telegram telling someone about the event. Remember that every word in a telegram costs money! Also write who you are and to whom you are writing. **Reteach**

On-Level Write a letter telling someone about the event. Letters from the front lines were censored to make sure they did not give away any secret information. If you mention dates or places, mark them out with a black marker. **Extend**

Challenge Write a newspaper article fully informing the public about the event. Reporters usually put the most vital information at the beginning of an article and then write more detail in later paragraphs. That way, if there is not room to print the whole article, the last few paragraphs can be cut. **Enrich**

For a Lesson Summary, use Quick Study, p. 132.

The Soviets then surrounded Germany's capital, **Berlin.** The Allies had marched from the west, and stood just outside of Berlin. Nazi Germany was finished. It surrendered to the Allies on May 7, 1945.

REVIEW How did U.S. war production help the Allies? 🔄 Cause and Effect

Toward Victory Over Japan

The attack on Pearl Harbor gave Japan an important opportunity. While the United States was mobilizing for war, Japan expanded its empire in Asia. Within six months, Japan had conquered 100 million people. Japan easily took Hong Kong, Singapore, Thailand, and islands south of China. Japan already held large areas of China and Indochina, as well as all of Korea.

Only the islands of the Philippines, under U.S. General **Douglas MacArthur,** put up much resistance. MacArthur had to retreat from the Philippines in March 1942. By early May, the Philippines had surrendered. MacArthur promised, "I shall return."

Two sea battles cut off the Japanese advance in the Pacific. In May 1942, the Battle of the Coral Sea was fought entirely in the air between airplanes launched from aircraft carriers. Neither side won. However, it stopped the Japanese advance. In June the U.S. surprised and defeated the Japanese at **Midway Island,** west of Hawaii. The Battle of Midway was the first Allied victory in the Pacific.

REVIEW Why was the attack on Pearl Harbor an opportunity for the Japanese? Main Idea and Details

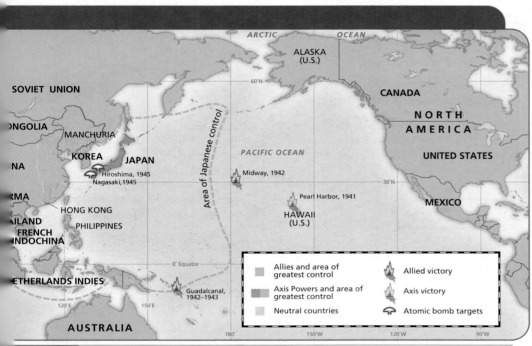

MAP SKILL Use Latitude and Longitude *What was the farthest eastern point of Japanese control?*

553

Toward Victory Over Japan

🕐 *Quick Summary* Japan expanded its empire quickly and with little resistance until the United States won the Battle of Midway.

15 **Why did Japan fight some battles completely on the sea or in the air?** Many of the areas Japan was conquering were islands or regions located near the sea. **Draw Conclusions**

16 **What were some difficulties Japan had in trying to defend a group of islands?** The enemy didn't have to get around their troops to move forward, their territory was spread out, and it was difficult to keep all their territories supplied. **Make Inferences**

✓ **REVIEW ANSWER** While the United States was recovering and mobilizing for war after the attack on Pearl Harbor, Japan expanded its empire in Asia. **Main Idea and Details**

SOCIAL STUDIES
Background

The Home Front

- In every country involved in the war, those at home had to make sacrifices to provide more for the war effort.
- In Germany and Japan food was rationed. In Great Britain meat and clothing were rationed. At different times during the war, the following items were rationed in the United States: gasoline, coffee, butter, tires, and sugar.
- Many Americans also participated in "drives" to collect materials, such as rubber and scrap metal, that could be used in the war.

Dropping the Atomic Bomb

⏱ **Quick Summary** After MacArthur captured the Philippines, the Japanese began kamikaze attacks. The war ended when President Truman ordered atomic bombs to be dropped on two Japanese cities.

17 **Even after the United States warned Japan to surrender or be destroyed, the Japanese did not surrender. How would you describe the Japanese military?** The military was extremely determined and loyal, willing to sacrifice anything in order to win. **Draw Conclusions**

✓ **REVIEW ANSWER** The use of atomic weapons on the cities of Hiroshima and Nagasaki 🔄 **Cause and Effect**

③ Close and Assess

Summarize the Lesson

Make a list of all the battles mentioned in the lesson. Locate them on the map on pp. 552–553.

✓ **LESSON 2   REVIEW**

1. 🔄 **Cause and Effect** For possible answers see the reduced pupil page.

2. Hitler could not defeat Great Britain's air force.

3. It was the largest invasion by sea in history. It stopped the German advance on the Western Front.

4. Possible answer: Japan finally decided to surrender.

5. **Critical Thinking: *Evaluate Information*** Possible answer: Either Germany would have won the war, or Germany and Great Britain would have continued to fight until both countries were exhausted.

Link to 🔗 Art
Students' posters should be positive and inspiring.

554 Unit 7 • A World in Opposition

Dropping the Atomic Bomb

In August 1942 the United States began a military campaign in the Pacific. The U.S. defeat of Japan at Guadalcanal in February 1943 was a major victory.

General MacArthur returned to the Philippines in October 1944. Nearly 300 ships were involved in a battle that crushed the Japanese. However, Japan fought back with a dreadful new weapon—the **kamikaze** (kah mih KAH zee). These were pilots who flew airplanes directly into enemy warships. They faced certain death. In 1945 kamikazes sank at least 30 ships.

In March 1945, U.S. planes dropped firebombs on the Japanese city of **Tokyo.** One-fourth of the city's buildings were destroyed in this attack.

Meanwhile, President Roosevelt died in April 1945. The new U.S. President, **Harry Truman,** learned of a top-secret government program called the Manhattan Project. The scientists working on the project were developing an atomic bomb. After testing a bomb in July, the United States warned Japan to surrender or be destroyed. Japan ignored the warning.

On August 6, 1945, the United States dropped an atomic bomb on the city of **Hiroshima** (hir uh SHEE muh). The bomb caused massive destruction and thousands of deaths. Still, Japan did not surrender. On August 9, the United States dropped a second atomic bomb, on the city of **Nagasaki** (nah guh SAH kee). Finally, the Japanese emperor urged his government to end the war. Japan surrendered on September 2, 1945. At last World War II was over.

REVIEW What finally caused Japan to surrender? 🔄 **Cause and Effect**

Summarize the Lesson

- **1941** The United States entered World War II after Japan attacked Pearl Harbor.
- **1945** Germany surrendered to the Allies.
- **1945** Japan surrendered to the Allies.

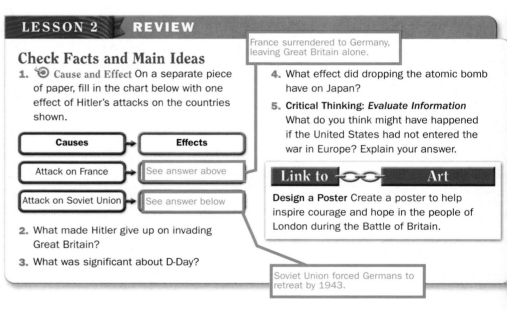

LESSON 2   REVIEW

Check Facts and Main Ideas

1. 🔄 **Cause and Effect** On a separate piece of paper, fill in the chart below with one effect of Hitler's attacks on the countries shown.

France surrendered to Germany, leaving Great Britain alone.

Causes	→	Effects
Attack on France	→	See answer above
Attack on Soviet Union	→	See answer below

Soviet Union forced Germans to retreat by 1943.

2. What made Hitler give up on invading Great Britain?

3. What was significant about D-Day?

4. What effect did dropping the atomic bomb have on Japan?

5. **Critical Thinking:** *Evaluate Information* What do you think might have happened if the United States had not entered the war in Europe? Explain your answer.

Link to 🔗 Art
Design a Poster Create a poster to help inspire courage and hope in the people of London during the Battle of Britain.

554

Practice and Extend

SOCIAL STUDIES Background

Development of the Atomic Bomb

- Albert Einstein, one of the many scientists who immigrated to Allied countries before the war, wrote to President Roosevelt in 1939 warning that Germany might be developing an atomic bomb.

- After the bombing of Pearl Harbor, the United States built research facilities in isolated areas, such as Los Alamos, New Mexico. The plutonium bomb was successfully tested at Alamogordo, New Mexico, on July 16, 1945.

Workbook, p. 136

Lesson 2: World War II

Directions: Read the following events from World War II. Put them in the order that they occurred by numbering them from 1 (earliest) to 10 (latest). You may use your textbook.

_____ 1. The United States and France drive Germany out of Paris.

_____ 2. Japan surrenders.

_____ 3. Nazi Germany surrenders.

_____ 4. Germany attacks Poland.

_____ 5. German troops surrender to The Soviet Army at Stalingrad.

_____ 6. President Roosevelt dies.

_____ 7. D-Day occurs at Normandy.

_____ 8. Great Britain wins the battle at El Alamein.

_____ 9. The United States drops atomic bomb on Hiroshima.

_____ 10. Japan attacks Pearl Harbor.

Directions: Answer the questions below. Write your answers on the lines provided.

1. What were some important contributions women in the United States made during World War II?

2. What might have happened if Japan had not ignored the United States warning of the atomic bomb?

Notes for Home: Your child learned about the sequence of events during World War II.
Home Activity: With your child, analyze the events in this worksheet to find cause-and-effect relationships.

💿 **Also on Teacher Resources CD-R**

Winston Churchill
1874–1965

Winston Churchill was born to an American mother and British father. He struggled in school as a child but later became one of the great leaders during World War II.

Throughout the 1920s, Winston Churchill was a member of Parliament in the British government. In the 1930s, he warned Great Britain of the growing threat of Nazism. When appeasement failed and Neville Chamberlain resigned as prime minister, Churchill accepted the position. He made it clear that Great Britain's goal was to defeat fascism. One of his most effective tools in rallying the British people was his gift of language. His first speech as prime minister was powerful and inspiring:

① *"You ask, what is our aim? I can answer in one word: victory, victory at all costs, victory in spite of all terror, victory however long and hard the road may be; for without victory there is no survival."*

During the war, Churchill woke at 8:00 A.M. every day. He spent hours reviewing the progress of the war. He then sent memos to military and government officials. After a one-hour nap, Churchill would work through the afternoon. He often spent the evening meeting with advisers until long after midnight.

During his long career, Churchill made mistakes and enemies. Few, however, would question his ability to use words to inspire others. As U.S. President John F. Kennedy once noted, Churchill "mobilized the English language and sent it into battle."

BIOFACT

Churchill was an amateur painter. He painted many landscapes using watercolors.

Learn from Biographies
From what you have read about Winston Churchill, how would you describe his personality?

For more information, go online to *Meet the People* at **www.sfsocialstudies.com.**

555

Winston Churchill

Objective
- Identify the contributions of significant individuals, such as Winston Churchill, during World War II.

1 Introduce and Motivate

Preview To activate prior knowledge, ask students what they know about Winston Churchill. Tell students that they will learn more about Churchill's leadership and work habits during the war as they read this page.

2 Teach and Discuss

- Ask students what Churchill believed to be Great Britain's goal.

- Ask students how he worked to meet this goal.

① **How did Churchill's words help the British people fight the war?** His words were inspiring, and they challenged people to make sacrifices and work hard. **Make Inferences**

3 Close and Assess

Learn from Biographies Answer

Possible response: Churchill was very determined, and he worked hard. He also had the ability to inspire others.

A World at War

Objective
- Acquire information from primary and secondary sources, such as visual materials.

Resource
- Workbook, p. 137

1 Introduce and Motivate

- Tell students that examining objects from a time period can tell you about the way people lived during that time period.

- Before students read these pages, have them write *Life in the Military* and *Life at Home* at the top of separate sheets of paper. Tell students to write or sketch details they know about the way people in each situation lived during World War II. Tell students that they will learn more details as they read these pages.

- Students will add to their lists of details as part of the assessment for these pages.

2 Teach and Discuss

1 Why might food and goods have needed to be rationed during World War II? The war might have reduced the supply of food and goods. Rationing would help make sure that everyone got a share and that supplies were not completely used up. **Make Inferences**

A World at War

We can learn about World War I and World War II through artifacts such as objects people used or uniforms soldiers wore. By studying these artifacts, we gain a better understanding of what a soldier's or civilian's life was like during the world wars.

Hand-Me-Downs
Because the army was short on uniforms in World War II, some soldiers had to wear uniforms like one that were left over from World War I.

Victory Gardens
During World War II, people were encouraged to grow their own gardens.

Kind of a Mess
American soldiers used this type of mess kit in World War II. Most of the food that soldiers ate came in cans.

Military Decorations
Some American soldiers were awarded medals such as the Silver Star, Italian Cross, and Purple Heart in World War II.

Limited Supplies
The United States issued the War Ration Book during World War II to reduce the usage of goods such as meat, butter, and petroleum.

556

Practice and Extend

SOCIAL STUDIES Background

The U.S. Marine Corps and the Battle of Iwo Jima

- Iwo Jima is a small island 660 miles south of Tokyo, Japan. The first American invasion of Japanese soil took place in Iwo Jima on February 19, 1945. The ensuing battle lasted for over a month.

- On the fifth day of the battle, five marines and a navy hospital corpsman raised an American flag on Mt. Suribachi, an extinct volcano the marines had captured. Photographer Joe Rosenthal won a Pulitzer Prize for his picture of the event. Sculptor Felix W. de Weldon built a model based on this picture that later became the basis for the sculpture on the U.S. Marine Corps Memorial. Three of the soldiers in the picture posed for de Weldon's sculpture.

- The U.S. Marine Corps Memorial was dedicated on November 10, 1954, the 179th anniversary of the U.S. Marine Corps.

nese Fighter
...Mitsubishi Zero was Japan's
...airplane in World War II. It
...first introduced in 1940.

❷

... the Riveter
...mage was the symbol of
...ng American women during
...War II. A song about Rosie
...bes her work making airplanes.

❸

Raising the Flag
The U.S. Marine Corps
Memorial honors all
marines who fought and
died in battle since 1775.
The flag being raised was
modeled after a famous
photograph taken at a
World War II battle site.

Artifacts are from the ✸ Smithsonian Institution.

557

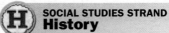
The Zero was a single-seat aircraft.
It had a 1,130-horsepower engine
and a 156-gallon fuel tank, was loaded
with two 7.7-mm machine guns and
two 2-mm cannons, and could carry
two 132-pound bombs under its wings.

**❷ Why do you think the Zero carried
only one fighter pilot?** Possible answer:
The engine, fuel tank, and weapons were
extremely heavy, so the less weight
added by humans, the more effective the
plane. **Make Inferences**

SOCIAL STUDIES STRAND
Culture

The last three lines of the song "Rosie
the Riveter" are "There's something true
about,/Red, white, and blue about,/
Rosie the Riveter."

**❸ Why would the song "Rosie the
Riveter" say there is something "red,
white, and blue about" her?** Red, white,
and blue are the colors of the American
flag. Rosie is these colors because she
is a patriotic American whose work helps
her country. **Draw Conclusions**

3 Close and Assess

- Encourage students to learn more
  about life in the military and life at
  home during World War II. They may
  look in encyclopedias or history books.

- Ask students to add to their lists of
  details about each living situation that
  they began earlier. Have students
  discuss what they learned from the
  pictures on these pages about life in
  the military and life at home during
  World War II.

WEB SITE
Technology

...u can visit the Smithsonian
...stitution online. Click on
...mithsonian at
...w.sfsocialstudies.com
...go to **www.si.edu.**

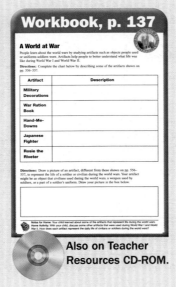

Workbook, p. 137

A World at War

People learn about the world wars by studying artifacts such as objects people used
or uniforms soldiers wore. Artifacts help people to better understand what life was
like during World War I and World War II.

Directions: Complete the chart below by describing some of the artifacts shown on
pp. 556–557.

Artifact	Description
Military Decorations	
War Ration Book	
Hand-Me-Downs	
Japanese Fighter	
Rosie the Riveter	

Directions: Draw a picture of an artifact, different from those shown on pp. 556–
557, to represent the life of a soldier or civilian during the world wars. Your artifact
might be an object that civilians used during the world wars, a weapon used by
soldiers, or a part of a soldier's uniform. Draw your picture in the box below.

Notes for Home: Your child learned about some of the artifacts that represent life during the world wars.
Home Activity: With your child, discuss some other artifacts that were used during World War I and World
War II. How does each artifact represent the daily life of civilians or soldiers during the world wars?

**Also on Teacher
Resources CD-ROM.**

The Aftermath

Objectives

- List and explain some of the outcomes of World War II.

- Describe how the dropping of atomic bombs on Hiroshima and Nagasaki affected the Japanese people.

- Explain how we know about Anne Frank.

- Explain and describe the significance of the United Nations.

- Describe the Marshall Plan and explain why the Eastern European countries did not benefit from it.

Vocabulary

refugee, p. 559;
concentration camp, p. 559;
charter, p. 560

Resources

- Workbook, p. 138
- Transparency 21
- Every Student Learns Guide, pp. 266–269
- Quick Study, pp. 134–135

Quick Teaching Plan

If time is short, have students read the lesson independently.

- Write *1946* on the board and have students list events from the lesson that happened before the date. Then have students list events that happened after 1946.

1 Introduce and Motivate

Preview To activate prior knowledge, ask students what they learned in Lesson 2 about the end of the war. Tell them they will find out more about events at the end of the war in this lesson.

 Ask students what the end of World War II might have been like. What other things might a young person be looking forward to or be concerned about?

LESSON 3

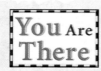
UN Headquarters
New York City

1945

1945
Founding of the United Nations

1948
Marshall Plan

PREVIEW

Focus on the Main Idea
The Allies formed the United Nations and helped shattered nations rebuild.

PLACES
New York City

PEOPLE
Eleanor Roosevelt
George Marshall
Anne Frank

VOCABULARY
refugee
concentration camp
charter

TERMS
United Nations
Marshall Plan

The Aftermath

You Are There
You're sitting at the kitchen table, helping Mom shell beans from the garden. It's so hot that you shift your chair to get directly in front of the electric fan for some relief. It's August, and a heat wave has hit your town.

You are enjoying a radio show when a voice interrupts with a news bulletin: "President Truman has just announced that the United States has exploded a bomb of tremendous destructive power over Hiroshima, Japan. The bomb is a new type of weapon called an atomic bomb."

Mom tells you that the war will probably be over soon. You're glad to hear this because that means that your brother will be coming home. At the same time, you feel frightened that something terrifying has entered the world.

The Granger Collection

▶ Radios such as this one provided people with news and entertainment.

Cause and Effect As you read, identify effects of the Allied victory in World War II on the postwar world.

558

Practice and Extend

 READING SKILL Cause and Effect

In the Lesson Review, students complete a graphic organizer like the one below. You may want to provide students with a copy of Transparency 21 to complete as they read the lesson.

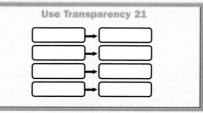
Use Transparency 21

 WEB SITE Technology

- You can look up vocabulary words by clicking on *Social Studies Library* and selecting the dictionary at **www.sfsocialstudies.com.**

- Students can learn more about current news by clicking on *Current Events* at **www.sfsocialstudies.com.**

- Explore other events that occurred on this day by clicking on *This Day in History* at **www.sfsocialstudies.com.**

The Most Terrible War

World War II was the first war in which an atomic bomb was used. It also brought more death and destruction than any other war. Cities such as Berlin and Tokyo had been bombed to ruins. About 40 to 50 million people were killed worldwide. Millions had been forced to flee their homes. Now Europe, China, and other areas were overflowing with **refugees,** or people who left their homeland for a safer place.

The Japanese cities of Hiroshima and Nagasaki had been hit by the first atomic bomb attacks in history. More than 100,000 were killed immediately. Thousands of survivors suffered burns and thousands more soon developed illnesses such as cancer.

However, nothing so horrified the world as the discovery of Nazi **concentration camps,** or places that held imprisoned people of a particular ethnic group or with particular political or religious beliefs. Nazi Germany put millions of people—mostly Jews—to death in such camps. The Nazi leaders had carried out their plan, which they called the "Final Solution," to get rid of Europe's Jews. They imprisoned millions in concentration camps, where people were forced to work.

No one will ever know exactly how many Jews were murdered in what came to be known as the Holocaust. Most historians believe that at least 6 million Jews died. As Allied troops entered Nazi territory, they saw unbelievable suffering in the

► **World War II produced millions of refugees.**

Nazi camps. American reporter Meyer Levin described the survivors he saw:

> *"They were like none we have ever seen. Skeletal with feverish, sunken eyes, shaven skulls."* ③

REVIEW What were three terrible effects of World War II? 🔄 **Cause and Effect**

These young people in a concentration camp await liberation by Russian soldiers in September 1945.

⏱ **Quick Summary** The war left cities in ruins, survivors who suffered from the atomic blasts, concentration camp victims who were barely alive, and refugees who were looking for a safe place to live.

❶ **Why were refugees unable to return to their homes?** Possible answers: Their homes had been destroyed; their lands were now occupied by someone else; they had no money to travel. **Make Inferences**

❷ **How did the atomic bomb affect the people of Hiroshima and Nagasaki?** More than one hundred thousand people were killed. Survivors suffered burns and developed illnesses such as cancer. 🔄 **Cause and Effect**

Primary Source
Cited in *A History of the Twentieth Century,* by Martin Gilbert

❸ **What words help us know what concentration camp victims looked like?** *Skeletal; feverish, sunken eyes; shaven skulls* **Analyze Primary Sources**

✓ **REVIEW ANSWER** A death toll of 40 to 50 million; the suffering of victims of atomic bomb attacks at Hiroshima and Nagasaki; Nazi Germany's "Final Solution," the killing of millions of Jews and others whom the Nazis wanted to eliminate 🔄 **Cause and Effect**

EXTEND LANGUAGE
ESL Support

Examine Word Meanings Explain and practice the concepts of the words *today, tomorrow,* and *yesterday.*

Beginning Point out days on a calender as you teach the words *today, tomorrow,* and *yesterday.* Use these words in short sentences emphasizing the appropriate verb tense. (e.g. "Yesterday we *went* on a field trip.")

Intermediate Review the concepts of *yesterday, today,* and *tomorrow.* Then practice past, present, and future tenses with a variety of verbs. Give students a list of irregular verbs to practice.

Advanced Give students a verb and hold up a card that says "Past," "Present," or "Future." Students should give the correct tense of the verb. After some oral practice ask students to read a selection from the textbook, choose ten verbs, and write their past, present, and future tenses.

For additional ESL support, use Every Student Learns Guide, pp. 266–269.

New Beginnings

⏱ **Quick Summary** The Allies hoped to make a better world by creating an international peacekeeping organization and by helping European countries to rebuild.

4 How did the experience with the League of Nations affect the Allies' development of the United Nations charter? The Allies learned from the failures of the League and tried to make the UN stronger. **Main Idea and Details**

5 How has the Universal Declaration of Human Rights influenced the world? Possible answers: By setting standards for how people should be treated and giving hope to people who are not treated fairly **Make Inferences**

✓ Ongoing Assessment

If... students do not understand what human rights are,

then... read the first part of the Declaration of Independence where it mentions life, liberty, and the pursuit of happiness. Those are general human rights. Talk about specific human rights that people should have, such as the right to vote.

6 Compare the way Western Europe recovered economically after World War II to the way it did after the Great War. What problems might a plan like the Marshall Plan have prevented? Possible answer: The economic recovery after the Great War was very slow, but because of the Marshall Plan, recovery after World War II was much faster. A plan to provide economic aid after the Great War might have prevented World War II. **Compare and Contrast**

New Beginnings

Out of the war's destruction the Allies hoped to fashion a new and better world. U.S. President Franklin D. Roosevelt, among others, believed that an international peacekeeping organization was needed. Roosevelt died on April 12, 1945, just before the **United Nations,** or UN, formed.

Others carried on the work. On April 25, 1945, the first United Nations conference met and drew up a **charter,** or constitution. The United Nations became effective on October 24, 1945. In 1951 the UN moved to permanent headquarters in **New York City.**

In Chapter 18 you read that the Allies, after the Great War, had set up the League of Nations. Learning from the League's failures, the World War II Allies tried to make the UN stronger.

U.S. President Harry Truman named **Eleanor Roosevelt** to serve as a delegate to the UN when it met in early 1946. Mrs. Roosevelt was the wife of the late President Roosevelt. She also was a writer and experienced public speaker.

▶ Eleanor Roosevelt fought for human rights.

At the UN, Eleanor Roosevelt's most important work was as chairperson of the committee that wrote the *Universal Declaration of Human Rights.* This document set standards for human rights. The declaration has been a guideline for nations and rulers since the UN adopted it in 1948.

In Germany and Japan, the Allies brought war criminals to justice. They arrested the most important leaders and put them on trial. However the chief war criminal, Adolf Hitler, escaped Allied justice. He had killed himself on April 30, 1945.

The economies of European countries failed to recover after the war. Europe needed to rebuild. It needed financial help. President Truman and his secretary of state, **George Marshall,** believed that the United States should help these countries. They persuaded Congress to pass the **Marshall Plan,** which went into effect in April 1948.

The United States sent $13 billion in aid Europe. The Marshall Plan was a tremendous success. Within a few years, the economies Western Europe were prospering. However, the countries of Eastern Europe were now under Soviet control. Soviet leader Joseph Stalin forced Eastern Europe countries to turn down America's offer of help. He did not want them rely on the United States.

▶ Ben Shahn's 1945 painting *Liberation* shows children playing in the rubble left by World War II.

Estate of Ben Shahn/Licensed by VAGA, New York, NY/Museum of Modern Art

560

Practice and Extend

MEETING INDIVIDUAL NEEDS
Leveled Practice

Give a Speech Have students prepare a speech to give in front of the UN.

Easy Prepare a speech about something that happened in World War II. List your concerns about it and what you feel should be done differently in the future. **Reteach**

On-Level Prepare a speech about something that you feel is a basic human right and how you feel it should be protected. **Extend**

Challenge Research what is contained in the actual Universal Declaration of Human Rights. Choose one right and give a speech explaining its importance and persuading the members to adopt it as part of the Declaration. **Enrich**

For a Lesson Summary, use Quick Study, p. 134.

As the world made a new beginning, no one had expressed hope for humanity as much as **Anne Frank.** Anne was a Jewish girl who had lived in the Netherlands, a country in Europe. She went into hiding with her family. Anne kept a diary and wrote about her life in hiding. In 1944 she and her family were discovered and sent to concentration camps. In her diary she wrote:

"In spite of everything I still believe that people are really good at heart."

REVIEW Why do you think the United States wanted to help nations rebuild after World War II? Draw Conclusions

Summarize the Lesson

- **1945** The United Nations charter was approved in April, and the United Nations opened in October.
- **1948** The United States began its aid program for Europe, the Marshall Plan.
- **1948** The United Nations adopted the Universal Declaration of Human Rights.

▶ Anne Frank's diary has been translated into more than 60 languages.

The Granger Collection

LESSON 3 ▶ REVIEW

Check Facts and Main Ideas

1. 🔄 **Cause and Effect** On a separate piece of paper, fill in the chart below by listing the cause of each of the effects listed.

Causes		Effects
International peace keeping organization needed.	→	The UN was founded.
Nazi leaders carried out their plan called "The Final Solution."	→	Survivors in Nazi camps were freed.
Economies of Europe needed to rebuild.	→	The U.S. helped Europe through the Marshall Plan.
Universal Declaration of Human Rights written.	→	Nazi and Japanese war criminals were tried.

2. What ill effects did survivors of the atomic bombings in Nagasaki and Hiroshima suffer?

3. Who was Anne Frank?

4. How did the United Nations give hope to the world?

5. **Critical Thinking:** *Evaluate Information* Why do you think Stalin did not want the Eastern European countries to take advantage of the Marshall Plan?

Link to 🔗 Writing

Write a Proposal You have been asked to write a proposal to give to your country's delegate to the United Nations. Use a topic from this lesson as the subject of your proposal. Suggest a solution to a problem or a way of preventing future problems.

561

Make Origami Cranes

Look at the novel ***Sadako and the Thousand Paper Cranes,*** by Eleanor Coerr (Puffin, ISBN 0-698-11802-2, 1999) **Easy**, and the nonfiction book about the real Sadako, a girl who survived the atom bomb but died later of cancer, ***One Thousand Paper Cranes: The Story of Sadako and the Children's Peace Statue,*** by Takayuki Ishii (Laurel Leaf, ISBN 0-440-22843-3, 2001) **On-Level**.

Find an origami book that shows how to make paper cranes and have students follow the directions.

Workbook, p. 138

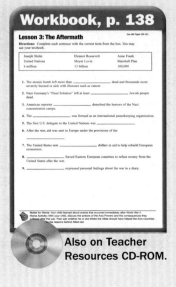

Lesson 3: The Aftermath

Directions: Complete each sentence with the correct term from the box. You may use your textbook.

Joseph Stalin	Eleanor Roosevelt	Anne Frank
United Nations	Meyer Levin	Marshall Plan
6 million	13 billion	100,000

1. The atomic bomb left more than _____ dead and thousands more severely burned or sick with illnesses such as cancer.

2. Nazi Germany's "Final Solution" left at least _____ Jewish people dead.

3. American reporter _____ described the horrors of the Nazi concentration camps.

4. The _____ was formed as an international peacekeeping organization.

5. The first U.S. delegate to the United Nations was _____.

6. After the war, aid was sent to Europe under the provisions of the _____.

7. The United States sent _____ dollars in aid to help rebuild European economies.

8. _____ forced Eastern European countries to refuse money from the United States after the war.

9. _____ expressed personal feelings about the war in a diary.

Notes for Home: Your child learned about events that occurred immediately after World War II.
Home Activity: With your child, discuss the actions of the Axis Powers and the consequences they suffered after the war. Then ask whether he or she thinks the Allies should have helped the Axis countries after the war. Have them give reasons behind Allied aid.

Also on Teacher Resources CD-ROM.

---

7 **What reasons might Anne Frank have had for thinking people are good at heart?** Possible answer: She saw examples of people who were good, such as those who hid her family. **Analyze Primary Sources**

✓ **REVIEW ANSWER** The economic hardships countries suffered after the Great War contributed to the beginning of World War II. **Draw Conclusions**

3 Close and Assess

Summarize the Lesson

Make a list of things from the lesson that Allied leaders hoped to prevent from ever happening again. Identify steps they took to prevent these things.

✓ **LESSON 3 REVIEW**

1. 🔄 **Cause and Effect** For possible answers see the reduced pupil page.

2. They suffered from burns, radiation sickness, and, years later, diseases such as cancer.

3. Anne Frank was a Jewish girl from the Netherlands who was sent to a Nazi camp and left behind a diary of her thoughts and experiences.

4. It passed the Declaration of Human Rights that became a guideline for countries and rulers.

5. **Critical Thinking:** *Evaluate Information* Possible answer: Stalin did not want those countries to be allied with the United States.

Link to 🔗 Writing

Proposals should include details from the lesson and a solution or way of preventing future problems.

Interpret Bar Graphs

Objective

* Read and interpret a bar graph.

Resource

* Workbook, p. 139

1 Introduce and Motivate

What is a bar graph? Ask students to share any prior experience they have had reading bar graphs. Where have they seen these types of graphs? (Possible answers: In science and math textbooks, newspaper articles, or magazines) Then have students read the **What?** section of text on p. 562.

Why read bar graphs? Have students read the **Why?** section of text on p. 563. Ask them to give examples of the kind of data best displayed on bar graphs. Point out that bar graphs often are used to compare numbers and amounts, as opposed to line graphs, which are usually used to show change over time.

2 Teach and Discuss

How is this skill used? Examine with students the graphs on pp. 562 and 563.

* Read the title of each graph. Have students discuss the kind of information each graph provides.

* Discuss the advantages of showing data on bar graphs. Ask students how this information might look if they had to show it in paragraph form. Students should realize that bar graphs allow them to compare a great deal of data visually and simultaneously.

* Have students read the **How?** section of text on p. 563.

562 Unit 7 • A World in Opposition

Chart and Graph Skills

Interpret Bar Graphs

What? A bar graph is a graph that shows different amounts by rectangles of different lengths. The three bar graphs shown here give information about World War II. The bars on each graph represent countries that were involved in the war. The numbers have been rounded off. For many of these countries, such as the Soviet Union, more exact numbers are not available for the first graph, *Military Casualties for World War II.*

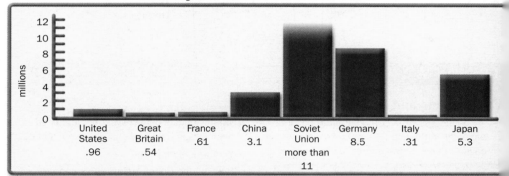

Military Casualties for World War II

Country	millions
United States	.96
Great Britain	.54
France	.61
China	3.1
Soviet Union	more than 11
Germany	8.5
Italy	.31
Japan	5.3

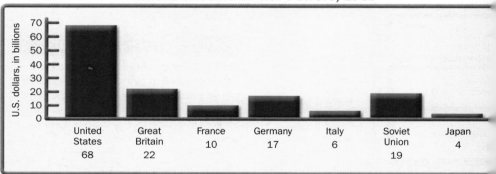

National Income of War Powers, 1937

Country	U.S. dollars, in billions
United States	68
Great Britain	22
France	10
Germany	17
Italy	6
Soviet Union	19
Japan	4

562

Practice and Extend

MEETING INDIVIDUAL NEEDS
Learning Styles

Summarize Data Using their individual learning styles, have students summarize the following data about the number of aircraft produced by the Allies and Axis Powers from 1939 through 1945:

	Total Aircraft Production Allies	Total Aircraft Production Axis Powers
1939	24,178	14,562
1940	39,518	16,815
1941	64,706	19,264
1942	101,519	26,670
1943	151,761	43,100
1944	167,654	67,987
1945	84,806	18,606

Verbal Learning Have students give a speech to the class, summarizing the data.

Logical Learning Have students make two bar graphs showing the data.

Linguistic Learning Have students write a paragraph summarizing the data.

Percentage of National Income Spent on Defense, 1937

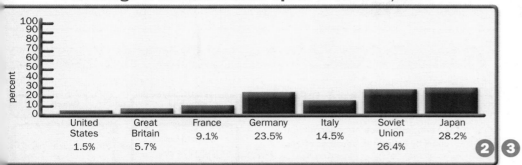

Percentage of National Income Spent on Defense, 1937

	percent
United States 1.5%	
Great Britain 5.7%	
France 9.1%	
Germany 23.5%	
Italy 14.5%	
Soviet Union 26.4%	
Japan 28.2%	

Why? Graphing helps us understand relationships between amounts or numbers easily. Bars are simple visual objects. They are very easy for our eyes to scan to gather information.

How? Every bar graph has two axes, or labeled sides. (The word *axes* is the plural form of *axis*.) Usually, one axis only has labels. The base of the bars sits on this axis. The other axis usually has both a scale and a label. In mathematics the horizontal (side-to-side) axis is called the x-axis. The vertical (up-and-down) axis is called the y-axis.

Look at the graph *Military Casualties for World War II*. What do you see along the x-axis? Along the y-axis? In this graph, the bottoms of the bars sit on the x-axis. Names of countries label this axis. One name goes with each bar. The y-axis is a scale with numbers. Its label tells us the number of military casualties—soldiers killed or wounded in the war.

Now read the number of casualties for a particular country. Look at the x-axis. Find the bar for the United States. Scan upward to find the top of the bar. Then scan left to the y-axis. Note where on the axis your eye falls. You can see that the United States bar stops a little lower than one notch on the scale. So its value must be a little

more than 900,000. Without a table of figures, you would not know the exact figure. But you could make a good guess based on the height of the bar.

Now study the other two graphs. One shows the national income of the World War II powers in 1937 (just before the war). The other shows the percentage of the national income being spent on defense during that same year.

Think and Apply

1. Which group of countries had more military casualties in World War II, the Allies or the Axis Powers?

2. Which group of countries had a higher total national income in 1937, the Allies or the Axis Powers?

3. Compare the bar graphs for *National Income of War Powers, 1937* and *Percentage of National Income Spent on Defense, 1937*. According to your comparison, which countries were mobilizing for war?

563

1 **Which countries suffered fewer than two million casualties?** United States, Great Britain, France, and Italy **Interpret Graphs**

2 **Which graphs would you use to determine the amount of money the United States spent on defense during 1937? How would you use them?** *National Income of War Powers, 1937* and *Percentage of National Income Spent on Defense 1937;* multiply the percentage of income spent by the United States in 1937 by the income for that year. 1.5% x $68,000,000,000 = $1,020,000,000 **Apply Information**

3 **Compare and contrast defense spending by the Soviet Union and Japan.** Possible answer: Both spent about the same percentage of their national income on defense, but the Soviet Union spent almost five times as much money as Japan; the Soviet Union spent 26.4% x $19,000,000,000 = $5,016,000,000; Japan spent 28.2% x $4,000,000,000 = $1,128,000,000. **Compare and Contrast**

3 Close and Assess

Think and Apply

1. The Allies

2. The Allies

3. Japan, the Soviet Union, and Germany

Workbook, p. 139

Interpret Bar Graphs

Bar graphs help us understand relationships among amounts or numbers.

Directions: Look at the bar graphs and text on pages 562–563 of your textbook. Then read each statement below. On the line beside each statement, write a *T* if it is true. If it is false, write an *F* and then rewrite the false portion of the statement on the line provided to make it true.

____ 1. Bar graphs have one axis.

____ 2. The vertical axis on a graph is the y-axis.

____ 3. On the graphs on pages 562–563, country names label the y-axis.

____ 4. The heights of the bars indicate exact figures.

____ 5. The title and axes labels on a graph help you read the information on the graph.

____ 6. Italy had the fewest military casualties of all the countries represented on the graph.

____ 7. On the graph, Japan spent the lowest percentage of its national income on defense.

Also on Teacher Resources CD-ROM.

Resources
- Assessment Book, pp. 97–100
- Workbook, p. 140: Vocabulary Review

Chapter Summary
For possible answers, see the reduced pupil page.

Vocabulary
1. d, **2.** b, **3.** e, **4.** c, **5.** a

People and Terms
Possible answers:

1. Benito Mussolini was the fascist dictator of Italy before and during World War II.

2. Adolf Hitler was the dictator of Germany and the person responsible for the murder of millions of Jews and others.

3. The Japanese government encouraged worship of Hirohito, the Emperor of Japan, as a way of promoting nationalism.

4. Germany, Italy, and Japan were the Axis Powers.

5. Winston Churchill was the British Prime Minister who led his nation to victory in World War II.

6. The Great Depression was the worldwide economic decline of the 1930s.

7. The Allies were Great Britain, the United States, the Soviet Union, and other countries that fought against the Axis Powers.

8. Dwight Eisenhower was commander of Allied troops during D-Day.

9. D-Day was the Allied invasion by sea of Normandy, France, in June 1944.

10. Eleanor Roosevelt helped draft the Universal Declaration of Human Rights, which was adopted by the United Nations in 1948.

CHAPTER 19
REVIEW

1920

1922
Fascists took control of Italy.

Chapter Summary

 Cause and Effect

On a separate piece of paper, fill in the chart by listing the cause or effect.

Causes	→	Effects
German-Soviet agreement	→	Start of World War II
The Japanese bombed Pearl Harbor.	→	United States entered World War II.
The dropping of the atomic bomb on Hiroshima	→	Japan surrendered.

Vocabulary

Match each word with the correct definition or description.

1. fascism (p. 544)
2. propaganda (p. 545)
3. Nazi (p. 544)
4. annex (p. 545)
5. charter (p. 560)

a. a constitution
b. planned spread of beliefs
c. attach or take a territory
d. form of government that stresses nation above individuals
e. Germany's fascist party

People and Terms

Write a sentence explaining why each of the lowing people or terms was important in the events of the 1930s and World War II. You m use two or more in a single sentence.

1. Benito Mussolini (p. 544)
2. Adolf Hitler (p. 544)
3. Hirohito (p. 546)
4. Axis Powers (p. 550)
5. Winston Churchill (p. 549)
6. Great Depres (p. 543)
7. Allies (p. 550
8. Dwight Eisenhower (p. 552)
9. D-Day (p. 55
10. Eleanor Roosevelt (p. 560)

564

Practice and Extend

Assessment Options

✓ Chapter 19 Assessment
- Chapter 19 Content Test: Use Assessment Book, pp. 97–98.
- Chapter 19 Skills Test: Use Assessment Book, pp. 99–100.

⭐ Standardized Test Prep
- Chapter 19 Tests contain standardized test format.

✓ Chapter 19 Performance Assessment
- Have students prepare a time line of at least 25 critically important events from the lesson.
- Have students prepare a radio documentary-style script (complete with sound effects, if desired) covering the sweep of events in the lesson with at least 25 critically important events mentioned.
- Assess students' understanding of the major events as you read or listen to their time lines or radio scripts.

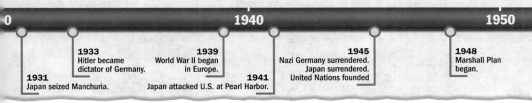
1931
Japan seized Manchuria.

1933
Hitler became dictator of Germany.

1939
World War II began in Europe.

1941
Japan attacked U.S. at Pearl Harbor.

1945
Nazi Germany surrendered.
Japan surrendered.
United Nations founded

1948
Marshall Plan began.

Facts and Main Ideas

What conditions helped dictators come to power in Italy and Germany after World War I?

What were the two goals of Stalin's first Five-Year Plan?

Why did the military leaders of Japan decide to bomb Pearl Harbor?

Time Line How long did World War II last in Europe?

Main Idea How did the rise of dictators help cause World War II?

Main Idea What event caused the United States to enter World War II?

Main Idea What did the Allies do to help the world recover after World War II?

Critical Thinking: *Evaluate Information* How accurate do you think the information about the Jews was in German propaganda?

Apply Skills

Interpret Bar Graphs

Use the skills you learned on pages 562–563 to answer the following questions. You will need to refer to the three bar graphs on those pages.

1 Based on the information shown, what country in 1937 may not have been worried about going to war?

2 What countries in 1937 may have been preparing to go to war?

3 What country shown on the bar graph had the lowest national income in 1937?

4 What country shown on the bar graph spent the highest percentage of its national income on defense in 1937?

Write About History

Write a paragraph from someone in the United States in 1940. Explain why you do—or do not—think the United States should get involved in the war in Europe between Nazi Germany and Great Britain.

Write a radio script for a radio broadcast at the time of the surrender of France in June 1940. Consider what the mood might have been at that time.

Write a verdict as a judge at a trial of a Nazi war criminal after World War II. Write a judgment at the end of the trial. Explain why you think the war criminal should be punished.

Internet Activity

To get help with vocabulary, people, and terms, select dictionary, encyclopedia, or almanac from *Social Studies Library* at **www.sfsocial studies.com**.

Facts and Main Ideas

1. Economic hard times

2. To collectivize private property and to make the Soviet Union an industrial giant

3. They knew that only the United States could stop Japan from building an Asian empire, so they decided to weaken the United States by attacking first.

4. Six years (1945 – 1939 = 6)

5. The dictators did not have to answer to democratic public opinion, so they felt bold enough to grab lands from other countries.

6. The bombing of Pearl Harbor in Hawaii

7. They formed the United Nations; they tried war criminals; the United States aided European countries through the Marshall Plan.

8. Possible answer: Not very accurate; it was full of bias against Jews.

Write About History

1. Students' work should show that it is 1940. Their reasons should be clear and unbiased.

2. Students' work should have a definite mood but put the best spin on things.

Test Talk

Write Your Answer to Score High

3. The writing should be logical and objective, with support for any sentence given. Remind students that their written answers should be correct, complete, and focused.

Apply Skills

1. The United States

2. Japan, the Soviet Union, and Germany

3. Japan

4. Japan

Hands-on Unit Project

Unit 7 Performance Assessment

See p. 596 for information about using the Unit Project as a means of performance assessment. A scoring guide is provided on p. 596.

WEB SITE Technology

For more information, students can select the dictionary, encyclopedia, or almanac from *Social Studies Library* at **www.sfsocialstudies.com**.

Workbook, p. 140

Vocabulary Review

These are the vocabulary words for Chapter 19. How much do you know about these words?

Directions: Circle the word that best completes each sentence.

depression	annex	Big Three	concentration camp
fascism	appeasement	Women's Army Corps	charter
Nazi	collective	D-Day	
propaganda	Axis Powers	kamikaze	
aggression	Allies	refugee	

1. The (Nazis, charter) took away many democratic freedoms in Germany.
2. Because of the (depression, aggression), people around the world lacked hope.
3. In the political system called (appeasement, fascism) the leader has total control over the government and industry.
4. The Nazis spread new ideas rapidly through the use of (aggression, propaganda).
5. Hitler's and Mussolini's policies of (depression, aggression) helped lead to the outbreak of war.
6. Under Stalin's rule, Russian farmers worked on the land of a (collective, fascist) every day.
7. By 1942, the United States had joined the war on the side of the (Axis Powers, Allies).
8. Hitler decided to (annex, charter) Austria to gain more land.
9. The World War II Allies created a (charter, propaganda) to guide the actions of the United Nations.
10. An (appeasement, charter) means that peace can be preserved by meeting the demands of an aggressor.
11. Europe, China, and other areas were overflowing with (Nazis, refugees) as a result of the atomic bomb.
12. The Nazis forced many Jewish people into (charters, concentration camps).
13. Germany, Italy, and Japan made up the group known as the (Axis Powers, Allies).

Notes for Home: Your child just learned the vocabulary terms for Chapter 19.
Home Activity: Write each of the vocabulary words on an index card and then shuffle the cards. Have your child draw a card from the stack and tell you one name, place, or event associated with that term in _. Continue until all the cards have been chosen.

Also on Teacher Resources CD-ROM.

Chapter Planning Guide

Chapter 20 • The Cold War

Locating Time and Place pp. 566–567

Lesson Titles	Pacing	Main Ideas
Lesson 1 **The Soviets Advance** pp. 568–572		• After 1945 the Soviet Union and the Allies broke off relations.
⭐ **Citizen Heroes:** Honesty **Reaching the Roof of the World** p. 573	2 days	• Tenzing Norgay reached his goal of climbing to the to of Mt. Everest, but he never realized his feat would become a political issue.
Thinking Skills: **Solve Complex Problems** pp. 574–575		• President Kennedy used a problem-solving strategy deal with the Cuban missile crisis in 1962.
Lesson 2 **Communism in China** pp. 576–580		• In a century of revolution, communists took control China.
Biography: Mao Zedong p. 581	2 days	• Born a peasant, as a child Mao Zedong developed t skills that would enable him one day to lead the Cultural Revolution in China.
Lesson 3 **The Cold War Heats Up** pp. 582–587		• The Cold War became a "hot" war in Korea and Vietnam.
Issues and Viewpoints: **The Public Speaks Out** pp. 588–589	2 days	• U.S. involvement in the Vietnam War divided the na as no other issue had since the Civil War.

✔ **Chapter 20 Review**
pp. 590–591

▲ **Many Americans protested U.S. involvement in the Vietnam War.**

✔ = Assessment Options

Mao Zedong led the Cultural Revolution in China. ▶

Vocabulary	Resources	Meeting Individual Needs
uclear ontainment	• Workbook, p. 142 • Transparencies 19, 57 • Every Student Learns Guide, pp. 270–273 • Quick Study, pp. 136–137 • Workbook, p. 143	• Leveled Practice, TE p. 569 • ESL Support, TE p. 570 • Learning Styles, TE p. 574 • Leveled Practice, TE p. 575
oletarian	• Workbook, p. 144 • Transparency 20 • Every Student Learns Guide, pp. 274–277 • Quick Study, pp. 138–139	• ESL Support, TE p. 578 • Leveled Practice, TE p. 579
errilla tente	• Workbook, p. 145 • Transparencies 20, 58, 59 • Every Student Learns Guide, pp. 278–281 • Quick Study, pp. 140–141	• Learning Styles, TE p. 584 • Leveled Practice, TE pp. 585, 586 • ESL Support, TE p. 587
	✓ Chapter 20 Content Test, Assessment Book, pp. 101–102 ✓ Chapter 20 Skills Test, Assessment Book, pp. 103–104	✓ Chapter 20 Performance Assessment, TE p. 590

Providing More Depth

Additional Resources

- Vocabulary Cards
- Daily Activity Bank
- Social Studies Plus!
- Big Book Atlas
- Student Atlas
- Outline Maps
- Desk Maps

Technology

- AudioText
- The test maker
- Teacher Resources CD-ROM
- Map Resources CD-ROM
- **www.sfsocialstudies.com**

 To establish guidelines for your students' safe and responsible use of the Internet, use the Scott Foresman Internet Guide.

Additional Internet Links

To find out more about:
- The Vietnam War, visit **www.pbs.org**
- The Korean War, visit **korea50.army.mil**

Key Internet Search Terms
- Cold War
- Korean War
- Vietnam War
- communism

Workbook Support

Use the following Workbook pages to support content and skills development as you teach Chapter 20. You can also view and print Workbook pages from the Teacher Resources CD-ROM.

Workbook, p. 141

Vocabulary Preview

Use with Chapter 20.

These are the vocabulary words from Chapter 20. How much do you know about these words?

Directions: Draw a line from the word to the correct definition.

1. nuclear
2. containment
3. proletarian
4. guerilla
5. détente

a. relaxation of tensions
b. a hit-and-run-fighter
c. atomic
d. preventing the spread of communism
e. "of the working class"

Directions: Suppose you are a newspaper reporter covering an international political crisis. Use the vocabulary words above to write a front-page story for your paper.

Students should use all five words correctly in their articles.

Notes for Home: Your child learned the vocabulary terms for Chapter 20.
Home Activity: These terms are all related to past political conflicts. With your child, read a newspaper article on current international disputes. Discuss how the conflict involves, or might lead to, the use of the terms shown above.

Use with Pupil Edition, p. 566

Workbook, p. 142

Lesson 1: The Soviets Advance

Use with Pages 568–572.

Directions: During the Cold War, tensions escalated between the United States and the Soviet Union. For every action one superpower took, the other nation responded. Read each action. Complete the table by identifying who took action, who reacted, and what the response was. You may use your textbook.

Action	By	Reaction	By
1. Stopped traffic into Berlin	Soviet Union	Ordered Berlin airlift	United States
2. Set up NATO	United States and its Western Allies	Formed Warsaw Pact	Soviet Union
3. Tested first H-bomb	United States	Created own H-bomb	Soviet Union
4. Began building missile bases in Cuba	Soviet Union	Set up naval blockade	United States

Notes for Home: Your child learned that actions by one superpower caused a reaction by another.
Home Activity: Discuss major events at home or at work that caused reactions by other parties to those events. Review the cause-and-effect sequence of the actions.

Use with Pupil Edition, p. 572

Workbook, p. 143

Solve Complex Problems

Use with Pages 574–575.

The race to develop and stockpile nuclear arms is one in which superpowers and smaller countries alike participate. Some people view this arms race as an advantage for their country. Others consider any race that could threaten entire nations with complete destruction to be a disadvantage.

Directions: Complete the following problem-solving chart with details to support your views on the nuclear arms race.

Problem-Solving Process	
1. Identify a problem.	Should countries develop and stockpile nuclear arms?
2. Gather information.	Possible answer: Small countries and superpowers alike are stockpiling weapons of mass destruction.
3. List and consider options.	Participate or not participate in arms race
4. Consider advantages and disadvantages.	Possible answers: Advantages: be able to defend oneself against attack; Disadvantages: economic cost, investment in weapons of mass destruction
5. Choose and implement a decision.	Answers should reflect independent thinking but be supported by logical conclusions.
6. Evaluate the effectiveness of a solution.	Answers should reflect independent thinking but be supported by logical conclusions.

Notes for Home: Your child learned to use a problem-solving process to solve complex problems.
Home Activity: Identify a complex issue with your child. Together, apply the steps in the problem-solving process to find a solution.

Use with Pupil Edition, p. 575

Workbook Support

Workbook, p. 144

Use with Pages 576–580.

Lesson 2: Communism in China

After the removal of China's emperor in 1911, China went through changes in its government.

Directions: Use the phrases in the box to compare the Nationalist and Communist parties. Then complete the Venn diagram with these phrases. You may use your textbook.

Tried to turn farms into collectives	Leader was Mao Zedong
Fought in a civil war	Started the Cultural Revolution
Kept seat in United Nations until 1971	Capital was Taipei
Invited to take UN seat in 1971	Fought Japan during World War II
Capital was Beijing	Leader was Chiang Kai-shek

Communist Party

Leader was Mao Zedong
Capital was Beijing
Invited to take UN seat in 1971
Tried to turn farms into collectives
Started the Cultural Revolution

Fought Japan during World War II
Fought in a civil war

Kept seat in United Nations until 1971
Leader was Chiang Kai-shek
Capital was Taipei

Nationalist Party

Notes for Home: Your child learned how leaders influenced the social and political direction of a country.
Home Activity: Discuss with your child the qualities effective leaders possess.

Use with Pupil Edition, p. 580

Workbook, p. 145

Use with Pages 582–587.

Lesson 3: The Cold War Heats Up

After World War II, the United States was involved in two wars in Asia. One war was fought in Korea, the other in Vietnam.

Directions: Read the following statements and decide which country is described. On the line beside each number, write a *K* for Korea or a *V* for Vietnam. Then answer the questions below. You may use your textbook.

- **K** 1. An invasion was launched on June 25, 1950.
- **V** 2. President Eisenhower promised help.
- **V** 3. A demonstration against the war brought protesters to Washington, D.C.
- **V** 4. The Tet offensive proved devastating to U.S. troops.
- **K** 5. General MacArthur was put in charge of American troops.
- **V** 6. Television brought the war to American homes.
- **K** 7. China came to the aid of communist forces.
- **V** 8. The war continued until April 1975.
- **K** 9. President Truman requested action from the United Nations.
- **K** 10. An armistice in 1953 ended the fighting.

1. Why did General MacArthur and President Truman disagree about how to fight in the Korean War?

   Truman and his advisors wanted to fight a limited war; MacArthur wanted to extend the war into China to win a complete victory.

2. Why did President Johnson think the United States had to fight in the war in Vietnam?

   Possible answer: Johnson concluded that communism would spread throughout Asia if Americans did not fight to control it.

Notes for Home: Your child learned about the United States' participation in wars in Korea and Vietnam.
Home Activity: Share with your child any recollections you or other family members may have of either conflict. Discuss reasons for your support for or protest of American involvement in these wars.

Use with Pupil Edition, p. 587

Workbook, p. 146

Use with Chapter 20.

Vocabulary Review

Directions: Complete each sentence with the correct vocabulary word from the box below.

nuclear	containment	proletarian	guerilla	détente

1. Unlike Korea, North Vietnam used **guerilla** fighters to attack its enemies.

2. President Truman used a policy of **containment** against communism.

3. Tensions between the Soviet Union and the United States during the Cold War escalated after the invention of **nuclear** weapons.

4. As the war in Vietnam came to an end, President Nixon enacted a plan of **détente**.

5. Mao Zedong started a new phase of revolution in China called the "Great **Proletarian** Cultural Revolution."

Directions: Use the vocabulary words from this chapter to create a fictional journal entry for Henry Kissinger. Explain the armistice between the United States and North Vietnam.

Journal entries should apply the vocabulary terms correctly.

Notes for Home: Your child learned the vocabulary terms for Chapter 20.
Home Activity: Discuss the importance of maintaining peace among world powers that are involved in ongoing political conflicts.

Use with Pupil Edition, p. 591

Workbook, p. 147

Project We Interrupt This Program

Directions: In a group, present a news conference about a historic event in Unit 7.

The historic event chosen: _____

Roles assigned for the news conference:

_____ news anchor(s) _____ reporter(s)

_____ government official(s) _____ citizen(s)

Press release (summary of the event):

Who: _____

What: _____

Where: _____

When: _____

Why: _____

How: _____

On a separate sheet of paper, write a summary of the event's importance in history.

You may wish to gather relevant resources from your school library. Assist students, as needed, in further researching events from the unit.

Checklist for Students

☐ We chose a historic event.
☐ We assigned roles for the news conference.
☐ We wrote a press release.
☐ We made a banner or brought materials to help describe the event.
☐ We presented our news conference to the class.

Notes for Home: Your child learned how to write a press release about an important event.
Home Activity: With your child, watch a local or national news program or news conference. Discuss how important events are summarized. Share details about the events and their importance to the world.

Use with Pupil Edition, p. 596

Assessment Support

Use these Assessment Book pages and the test maker to assess content and skills in Chapter 20 and Unit 7. You can also view and print Assessment Book pages from the Teacher Resources CD-ROM.

Assessment Book, p. 101

Chapter 20
Part 1: Content Test
Directions: Fill in the circle next to the correct answer.

Lesson Objective (1:4)

1. Which two areas were separated by the Iron Curtain?
   - (A) Eastern Europe and China
   - (B) Eastern Europe and the Soviet Union
   - (C) Western Europe and the United States
   - ● Eastern Europe and Western Europe

Lesson Objective (1:1)

2. Which was a leading cause of the Cold War?
   - ● Stalin forced countries in Eastern Europe to have communist governments.
   - (B) The Allied powers wanted the countries of Eastern Europe to have communist governments.
   - (C) The Truman Doctrine pledged support to all European countries.
   - (D) Germany was divided into four zones of occupation.

Lesson Objective (1:2)

3. How did the Berlin airlift in 1948 help the French, British, and Americans in Berlin?
   - (A) Troops were flown in to help defend the Allies.
   - (B) U.S. forces rescued people from the British and French zones.
   - ● Food and supplies were flown in to save the people from starvation.
   - (D) The airlift contained a naval blockade.

Lesson Objective (1:5)

4. How did the Soviet Union respond to the formation of NATO?
   - (A) The Soviet Union applied to join it.
   - ● The Soviet Union formed a similar alliance called the Warsaw Pact.
   - (C) The Soviet Union stopped its attempt to spread communism.
   - (D) The Soviet Union built the Berlin Wall.

Lesson Objective (1:3)

5. Who were the leaders of the world's superpowers at the time of the Cuban missile crisis?
   - ● John F. Kennedy and Nikita Khrushchev
   - (B) John F. Kennedy and Joseph Stalin
   - (C) Harry S. Truman and Joseph Stalin
   - (D) Franklin D. Roosevelt and Nikita Khrushchev

Lesson Objective (1:3)

6. In the early 1960s, where did the Soviet Union begin building missile bases?
   - (A) about 25 miles from U.S. soil
   - ● about 90 miles from U.S. soil
   - (C) about 250 miles from U.S. soil
   - (D) about 900 miles from U.S. soil

Lesson Objective (2:1)

7. What political event led to "the Long March"?
   - (A) Chiang Kai-shek died, and communists took control.
   - (B) China became a republic.
   - ● The Nationalist party tried to rid China of communists.
   - (D) A revolution left the Chinese without enough food.

Use with Pupil Edition, p. 590

Assessment Book, p. 102

Lesson Objective (2:2)

8. Who led the People's Republic of China when it was formed in 1949?
   - (A) Sun Yat-sen
   - ● Mao Zedong
   - (C) Jiang Qing
   - (D) Chiang Kai-shek

Lesson Objective (2:5)

9. What is one change that occurred when the Communist Party took over China from the Nationalist Party?
   - ● The Communists took away freedom of speech and religion.
   - (B) The Nationalists formed an alliance with the Soviets.
   - (C) Communist China immediately joined the United Nations.
   - (D) Taipei became the capital of Communist China.

Lesson Objective (2:3)

10. What role did Jiang Qing play in launching a classless society in China?
    - (A) She opposed Mao Zedong's Cultural Revolution.
    - (B) She led the marches of the Red Guards.
    - (C) She was leader of the Long March.
    - ● She was Mao's closest ally and a powerful revolutionary.

Lesson Objective (2:4)

11. What effect did the Cultural Revolution have on education in China?
    - (A) More universities were built.
    - (B) Older citizens became teachers.
    - (C) Education became a priority.
    - ● Many schools were closed.

Lesson Objective (2:4)

12. What brought China's Cultural Revolution to an end?
    - (A) death of Jiang Qing
    - (B) imprisonment of Nien Cheng
    - ● death of Mao Zedong
    - (D) Red Guard

Lesson Objective (3:1)

13. What was a leading cause of the Korean War?
    - (A) political pressure from China
    - (B) U.S. imperialism
    - ● communist expansion
    - (D) the death of Mao Zedong

Lesson Objective (3:5)

14. How did the Korean War affect U.S. involvement in the Vietnam War?
    - ● It caused U.S. leaders to focus on the spread of communism in Asia.
    - (B) It made the United States realize it could not defeat the communists.
    - (C) It made U.S. leaders eager to fight another war.
    - (D) It made all communists afraid to fight the United States.

Lesson Objective (3:2)

15. To what extent was the United States involved in the Vietnam War during President Eisenhower's administration?
    - (A) The United States remained neutral.
    - ● U.S. military advisors were sent to support South Vietnam.
    - (C) U.S. troops were sent to build up South Vietnam's army.
    - (D) The U.S. Air Force was sent to defend South Vietnam.

Use with Pupil Edition, p. 590

Assessment Book, p. 103

Lesson Objective (3:3)

16. How did President Johnson alter U.S. involvement in Vietnam?
    - ● He sent U.S. ground and air support to Vietnam.
    - (B) He signed a treaty with North Vietnam.
    - (C) He brought South Vietnamese troops to the United States for training.
    - (D) He withdrew all U.S. advisors and troops from Vietnam.

Lesson Objective (3:4)

17. How did the wars in Korea and Vietnam differ from the Cold War?
    - (A) They were based on the spread of communism.
    - (B) The United States was not involved in the Korean and Vietnam Wars.
    - (C) The Russians were communists; the Koreans and Vietnamese were not.
    - ● There was no physical fighting in the Cold War.

Part 2: Skills Test
Directions: Use complete sentences to answer questions 1–8. Write on a separate sheet of paper if you need more space.

1. How are NATO and the Warsaw Pact alike, and how are they different? **Compare and Contrast**

   Alike: Both were formed to support and defend member countries. Different: NATO was organized by the United States and its Western allies. The Warsaw Pact formed an alliance of communist countries in Eastern Europe.

2. How did the nuclear arms race between the United States and the Soviet Union escalate after 1945? Identify specific events in the order they occurred. **Sequence**

   The United States dropped the atomic bomb in 1945. The Soviet Union tested an atomic bomb in 1949. In the early 1950s, the United States built the H-bomb; the Soviet Union followed.

Use with Pupil Edition, p. 590

Assessment Book, p. 104

3. What two political parties struggled for control of China? Who were the parties' leaders? What beliefs did the parties support? **Summarize**

   Nationalist Party, first led by Sun Yat-sen and then Chiang Kai-shek, supported a republican form of government; Communist Party, headed by Mao Zedong and then Jiang Qing, supported a classless society.

4. Suppose you were a young person in China in the late 1960s. Would you have supported Mao's Cultural Revolution? Why or why not? **Point of View**

   Possible answer: Yes; I might have believed the ideals of the Cultural Revolution.

5. Why did President Truman replace General MacArthur with another general during the Korean War? **Draw Conclusions**

   President Truman wanted to fight a limited war, but MacArthur wanted an all-out war.

6. What misconception did President Johnson have that influenced his decision about the United States' involvement in Vietnam? **Fact and Opinion**

   He believed that if one Asian country fell to communism, others would follow. Events during the Vietnam War did not support this opinion.

7. Do you think you would have supported or protested U.S. involvement in the Vietnam War? Why? **Express Ideas**

   Possible answers: Supported; I would have wanted to stop the spread of communism; Protested; Too many people were dying.

8. Why do you think President Nixon entered a period of détente with the Soviet Union and China? **Draw Conclusions**

   Possible answer: After the domino theory was disproved and Americans protested the Vietnam War, he may have decided to try to forge a peaceful coexistence between the United States and communist countries.

Use with Pupil Edition, p. 590

Assessment Support

Assessment Book, p. 105

Use with Pupil Edition, p. 594

Unit 7 Test

Part 1: Content Test

Directions: Fill in the circle next to the correct answer.

Lesson Objective (18–1:5)

1. Which countries formed the Triple Alliance before the Great War?
   - Ⓐ Great Britain and Germany
   - Ⓑ Great Britain, France, and Russia
   - ● Germany, Austria-Hungary, and Italy
   - Ⓓ Italy and the United States

Lesson Objective (18–1:1)

2. What was sparked by the killing of Archduke Francis Ferdinand?
   - Ⓐ Triple Alliance
   - Ⓑ Great Depression
   - Ⓒ Triple Entente
   - ● Great War

Lesson Objective (18–2:2)

3. How did new weapons help create areas known as "no-man's land"?
   - ● Machine guns and tanks made land between battle trenches especially deadly.
   - Ⓑ Nuclear weapons were dropped on the border between Austria-Hungary and Germany.
   - Ⓒ Land mines filled the area between the Western Front and the Eastern Front.
   - Ⓓ Lasers were used to guard the Berlin Wall.

Lesson Objective (18–2:3)

4. Who became the leader of the Russian people after the Russian Revolution?
   - Ⓐ Czar Nicholas II
   - ● Vladimir Lenin
   - Ⓒ Karl Marx
   - Ⓓ Archduke Francis Ferdinand

Lesson Objective (18–3:2)

5. Which empire did NOT disappear after World War I?
   - Ⓐ Ottoman
   - Ⓑ Russian
   - ● British
   - Ⓓ German

Lesson Objective (18–3:3)

6. Which point of the Treaty of Versailles did Germany find hardest to support?
   - Ⓐ taking blame for the war
   - Ⓑ inflation
   - ● paying reparations
   - Ⓓ losing the Rhineland

Lesson Objective (19–1:2)

7. Which key problem led to the Great Depression?
   - Ⓐ a series of poor harvests
   - ● investors selling their stocks, causing prices to fall
   - Ⓒ European products flooding American markets
   - Ⓓ Americans buying goods that were unavailable during the 1920s

Lesson Objective (19–1:4)

8. What action did many Germans take as a result of the Great Depression?
   - Ⓐ They joined the military.
   - Ⓑ They refused to pay reparations to the Allies.
   - Ⓒ They joined the Communist party.
   - ● They joined the Nazi party.

Assessment Book, p. 106

Use with Pupil Edition, p. 594

Lesson Objective (19–2:1)

9. What event caused Great Britain and France to declare war on Germany?
   - ● Poland was invaded.
   - Ⓑ Czechoslovakia was invaded.
   - Ⓒ Italy was invaded.
   - Ⓓ Denmark was invaded.

Lesson Objective (19–2:2)

10. Why did Hitler give up on invading Great Britain?
    - ● The Royal Air Force and the British people's spirits were strong.
    - Ⓑ France declared its surrender.
    - Ⓒ He was afraid of Winston Churchill.
    - Ⓓ Italy mounted an attack on Germany.

Lesson Objective (19–3:2)

11. Which event brought World War II to an end?
    - Ⓐ return of General MacArthur
    - Ⓑ Battle of Midway
    - ● dropping the atomic bomb on Nagasaki
    - Ⓓ death of President Roosevelt

Lesson Objective (19–3:4)

12. What is the role of the United Nations?
    - Ⓐ an organization to remember war veterans
    - ● an organization for peacekeeping
    - Ⓒ an organization to promote international travel
    - Ⓓ an organization to monitor international finance

Lesson Objective (20–1:2)

13. Why did President Truman order an airlift into Berlin?
    - ● to deliver supplies to people in French, British, and American zones
    - Ⓑ to drop off troops to defend Americans in Berlin
    - Ⓒ to tear down the Berlin Wall
    - Ⓓ to pick up Americans and fly them home

Lesson Objective (19–3:5)

14. Why didn't the countries of Eastern Europe benefit from the Marshall Plan?
    - Ⓐ The financial aid was only offered to Western Europe.
    - Ⓑ Eastern Europe did not need any financial assistance.
    - ● Stalin forced Eastern Europe to turn down help.
    - Ⓓ Japan provided financial help to all of Eastern Europe.

Lesson Objective (20–1:4)

15. What was the Iron Curtain?
    - Ⓐ a wall that divided East Germany from West Germany
    - Ⓑ a nickname for an important German mining region
    - Ⓒ an expression to describe the Cold War
    - ● a term for the political separation of Eastern Europe and Western Europe

Lesson Objective (20–2:3)

16. What was Jiang Qing's role in communist China?
    - Ⓐ She opposed the Cultural Revolution.
    - ● She helped Mao Zedong launch the Cultural Revolution.
    - Ⓒ She was a target of the Red Guard.
    - Ⓓ She made the Cultural Revolution come to an end.

Lesson Objective (20–3:3)

17. To what extent was the United States involved in Vietnam under President Johnson?
    - Ⓐ No U.S. troops were in Vietnam at that time.
    - Ⓑ The United States sent peacekeeping troops only.
    - Ⓒ The number of U.S. troops dropped.
    - ● Half a million U.S. troops were sent to Vietnam.

Assessment Book, p. 107

Use with Pupil Edition, p. 594

Part 2: Skills Test

Directions: Use complete sentences to answer questions 1–6. Use a separate sheet of paper if you need more space.

1. Which events in Europe led to the Great War? **Cause and Effect**

   Alliances between European countries and competition for colonies led to disagreements and increased military buildup. The assassination of Archduke Francis Ferdinand set off the war.

2. How did Hitler change Germany once he took power? What methods did he use to accomplish his goals? **Main Idea and Details**

   Hitler's Nazi party took away most democratic freedoms; He used propaganda to unite the country against the Jewish population.

3. What role did American women play in World War II? **Main Idea and Details**

   Women took jobs in defense plants and factories to produce goods for the war effort. Many served as nurses, did volunteer work, or replaced men at their jobs.

4. World War II brought Americans face-to-face with terrible acts of violence against other human beings. What can you do to make sure such acts are not repeated in your lifetime? **Express Ideas**

   Possible answers: Learn from the tragedies of the Holocaust and the dropping of atomic bombs on the Asian people; become politically involved in finding peaceful solutions; support negotiations and peace processes

5. Which American President—Wilson, Roosevelt, Truman, Kennedy, Johnson, or Nixon—do you think dealt most effectively with communist threats? **Point of View**

   Answers should reflect independent thinking, be supported by information from the unit, and reflect a consistent attitude toward a limited or all-out response.

Assessment Book, p. 108

Use with Pupil Edition, p. 594

6. Use the time lines to answer the questions. **Compare Parallel Time Lines**
   a. Where on the time line would you place an event that occurred in June of 1916?

   to the right of 1916, halfway between 1916 and 1917

   b. Which occurred first: the beginning of the Great War or the sinking of the Lusitania?

   the beginning of the war

   c. How many years did the Great War last? **4 years**

The Cold War

Chapter 20 Outline

- **Lesson 1, *The Soviets Advance,*** pp. 568–572
- **Citizen Heroes: *Reaching the Roof of the World,*** p. 573
- **Thinking Skills: *Solve Complex Problems,*** pp. 574–575
- **Lesson 2, *Communism in China,*** pp. 576–580
- **Biography: *Mao Zedong,*** p. 581
- **Lesson 3, *The Cold War Heats Up,*** pp. 582–587
- **Issues and Viewpoints: *The Public Speaks Out,*** pp. 588–589

Resources

- Workbook, p. 141: Vocabulary Preview
- Vocabulary Cards
- Social Studies Plus!

1948, Berlin: Lesson 1

Tell students that the three men seated in this picture are the leaders of three important countries. Ask students to identify the men. (Joseph Stalin, Franklin Roosevelt, and Winston Churchill).

1949, Beijing: Lesson 2

This picture shows a rally held in Beijing in 1971, twenty-two years after China had become a Communist nation. Ask students what holiday celebrates the birth of our American nation. (Independence Day)

1960s–1970s, Hanoi: Lesson 3

Tell students that this picture shows Korean refugees leaving their village with their belongings. Ask students why they might be doing this. (Their village is in a war zone.)

CHAPTER
20 The Cold War

Lesson 1

1948
Berlin
Tensions increase between the United States and the Soviet Union.

Lesson 2

1949
Beijing
China becomes a communist nation.

Lesson 3

1960s–1970s
Hanoi
The Cold War leads to fighting in Korea and Vietnam.

566

Practice and Extend

Vocabulary Preview

- Use Workbook p. 141 to help students preview the vocabulary words in this chapter.
- Use Vocabulary Cards to preview key concept words in this chapter.

 Also on Teacher Resources CD-ROM.

Workbook, p. 141

Vocabulary Preview

These are the vocabulary words from Chapter 20. How much do you know about these words?

Directions: Draw a line from the word to the correct definition.

1. nuclear   a. relaxation of tensions
2. containment   b. a hit-and-run fighter
3. proletarian   c. atomic
4. guerrilla   d. preventing the spread of communism
5. détente   e. "of the working class"

Directions: Suppose you are a newspaper reporter covering an international political crisis. Use the vocabulary words above to write a front-page story for your paper.

Locating Time and Place

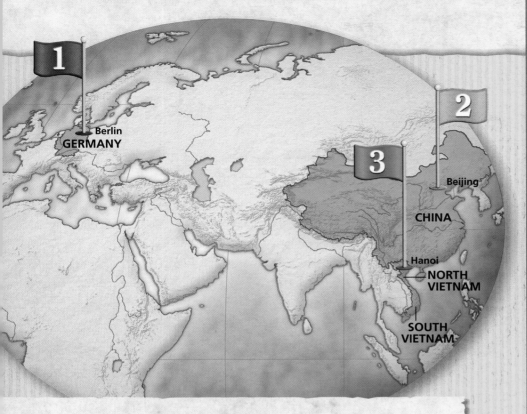

1 — Berlin, GERMANY

2 — Beijing

3 — CHINA

Hanoi — NORTH VIETNAM

SOUTH VIETNAM

Why We Remember

After World War II, people longed for peace. In the past, countries went to war because of imperialism or nationalism. Now competition between communism and democracy took center stage. Communist countries believed that their system of state ownership of properties and businesses was fairer than one of private ownership. However, to enforce their ideas, communists had to destroy democratic freedoms. In this atmosphere, tensions between the Soviet Union and the United States led to a new kind of war—a "cold war."

567

- Have students examine the pictures shown on p. 566 for Lessons 1, 2, and 3.

- Remind students that each picture is coded with both a number and a color to link it to a place on the map on p. 567.

Why We Remember

Have students read the "Why We Remember" paragraph on p. 567, and ask them why events in this chapter might be important to them. If necessary, clarify the difference between the terms *state ownership* and *private ownership.* Have students consider how their lives would be different if they lived in a communist country. Ask students if they can think of reasons Americans would want to halt the spread of communism.

WEB SITE Technology

u can learn more about Berlin, jing, and Hanoi by clicking on es at **www.sfsocialstudies.com.**

SOCIAL STUDIES STRAND Geography

Mental Mapping On an outline map of the countries of the world, have students lightly shade with a red pencil those countries or areas under communist control at the height of the Cold War. Then, with a pen or pencil, label on the map as many of the countries or areas as they can. Discuss what a major threat communist countries might pose to non-communist countries.

The Soviets Advance

Objectives

- List the causes of the Cold War.
- Explain the significance of the Berlin airlift.
- Identify the central issue behind the Cuban missile crisis.
- Explain how *iron curtain* described the map of Europe after 1945.
- Explain the significance of NATO and describe its effect on Stalin's blockade of Berlin.

Vocabulary

nuclear, p. 569; **containment,** p. 570

Resources

- Workbook, p. 142
- Transparency 19
- Every Student Learns Guide, pp. 270–273
- Quick Study, pp. 136–137

Quick Teaching Plan

If time is short, have students create a time line of major events.

- Model a time line and place the first event, World War II, on the time line.
- Remind students to add events and descriptions to the time line as they read independently.

1 Introduce and Motivate

Preview To activate prior knowledge, ask students what they know about the relationship between the United States and the former Soviet Union. Tell students they will learn more about the root of the tension between the two countries as they read Lesson 1.

You Are There Churchill delivered his speech in Fulton, Missouri. Ask students to speculate whether Churchill's phrase *iron curtain* is literal or figurative and what the phrase might mean for the countries involved.

568 Unit 7 • A World in Opposition

LESSON 1

1945		1955

1948–1949
Berlin airlift

1949
North Atlantic Treaty Organization (NATO) forms.

Soviet Union makes an atomic bomb.

1962
Cuban crisis

The Soviets Advance

PREVIEW

Focus on the Main Idea
After 1945 the Soviet Union and the Allies broke off relations.

PLACES
Berlin
West Germany
East Germany
Cuba

PEOPLE
Nikita Khrushchev
John F. Kennedy

VOCABULARY
nuclear
containment

TERMS
Cold War
Truman Doctrine
North Atlantic Treaty Organization (NATO)
Warsaw Pact

EVENTS
Berlin airlift

568

 You Are There

While you listen to the radio, your parents and some of your neighbors are at the dining room table. They are debating about the speech that Winston Churchill gave at nearby Westminster College the other night. They keep using a phrase you have never heard before: "the Iron Curtain." Finally, you turn down the radio so you can listen more closely.

You're a little confused. Wasn't the Soviet Union one of our allies in the war? In his speech, Churchill warned that the Soviet Union is going to cut Eastern Europe off from the rest of the world. It will be behind an iron curtain. The adults are debating whether the Soviets would actually do something like that.

You begin to wonder: Does this mean we will be going back to war?

▶ U.S. President Harr Truman introduces Churchill at Westmi College in 1946.

 Cause and Effect As you read, consider the effects of the actions by the Soviet Union and Western countries after World War II.

Practice and Extend

 READING SKILL
Cause and Effect

In the Lesson Review, students complete a graphic organizer like the one below. You may want to provide students with a copy of Transparency 19 to complete as they read the lesson.

Use Transparency 19

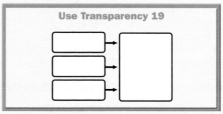

 WEB SITE
Technology

- You can look up vocabulary words by clicking on *Social Studies Library* and selecting the dictionary at **www.sfsocialstudies.com.**
- Students can learn more about current news by clicking on *Current Events* at **www.sfsocialstudies.com.**
- Explore other events that occurred on this day by clicking on *This Day in History* at **www.sfsocialstudies.com.**

New Superpowers

In the final weeks of World War II, Soviet troops met the Allied troops at Berlin, Germany. They had fought as Allies in a long war against Nazi Germany. Now their relationship was about to change.

With the Axis powers in ruins, the Soviet Union and the United States were now much stronger than any other countries. They had become "superpowers." However, the new superpowers soon found it hard to agree on anything.

During World War II, the "Big Three"—Great Britain's Churchill, U.S. President Roosevelt, and Soviet leader Stalin—had made plans for postwar Europe. They agreed to allow the nations of Eastern Europe to establish their own governments.

However, as the war drew to a close, Soviet troops marched into Eastern Europe. Stalin and the Soviet army forced communist governments in Poland, Czechoslovakia, Hungary, and other nations in the region. In this way, the Soviet Union gained political control of these countries. By 1948 all of Eastern Europe was communist.

Churchill said that the new communist rulers were putting up a wall between their countries and the West. This "wall" stopped trade and travel. In a speech Churchill made at Westminster College in Fulton, Missouri, he said:

Courtesy of FDR Library, Hyde Park, NY

▶ In 1945 the "Big Three" met to discuss plans for postwar Europe. Seated from left to right: Joseph Stalin, Franklin Roosevelt, and Winston Churchill.

"From Stettin in the Baltic to Trieste in the Adriatic an iron curtain has descended across the Continent."

②

Churchill's "iron curtain" became almost as familiar a term as "cold war." **Cold War** was the term used to describe the tension between the Soviet Union and the United States after World War II. The destructive power of **nuclear,** or atomic, weapons backed this "cold" war of words and threats.

REVIEW Why do you think the United States mistrusted the Soviet Union? Explain your answer. **Draw Conclusions**

The Iron Curtain was an imaginary wall that stretched from the Baltic Sea to the Adriatic Sea.

IRELAND · North Sea · DENMARK · Baltic Sea · UNITED KINGDOM · NETHERLANDS · EAST GERMANY · BELGIUM · POLAND · LUXEMBOURG · USSR · WEST GERMANY · ATLANTIC OCEAN · SWITZERLAND · CZECHOSLOVAKIA · FRANCE · HUNGARY · ITALY · AUSTRIA · ROMANIA · PORTUGAL · SPAIN · YUGOSLAVIA · Adriatic Sea · Black Sea · BULGARIA

569

New Superpowers

🕐 **Quick Summary** After World War II Soviet troops invaded Eastern Europe, setting up an "iron curtain" that halted trade and travel. This began the Cold War between the United States and the Soviet Union.

① Why did the United States and the Soviet Union become superpowers? Their relative strength was much greater than that of other countries. **Make Inferences**

✓ **Ongoing Assessment**

If... students are unable to figure out why the United States and the Soviet Union became superpowers, **then...** remind students that the Allies had won the war and that many other countries had been devastated.

Primary Source

Cited in *Oxford Dictionary of Quotations*, by Angela Partington, ed.

② How does the term "iron curtain" reveal what was happening in Europe? Possible answers: *Curtain* indicates that something is hidden or blocked from view. *Iron* shows that the curtain was difficult to cross. Trade and travel to Eastern Europe were virtually shut off. **Analyze Primary Sources**

③ Using the map, name the countries on either side of the iron curtain. Countries of the West: Portugal, Spain, France, Italy, Switzerland, Austria, Luxembourg, Belgium, West Germany, the Netherlands, Denmark, Ireland, Great Britain; communist countries of the East: East Germany, Poland, Czechoslovakia, Hungary, Romania, Yugoslavia, Albania, Bulgaria, USSR **Interpret Maps**

✓ **REVIEW ANSWER** Possible answer: Because the Soviet Union forced other nations in Eastern Europe to become communist and because the United States feared the spread of communism **Draw Conclusions**

A Divided Europe

🕐 **Quick Summary** The liberation of the U.S., British, and French zones of Berlin was one of many events that were part of President Harry S. Truman's policy of containment, the effort to halt the spread of communism.

Primary Source

Cited in *The Truman Doctrine*, March 12, 1947

4 **Why do you think President Truman pledged to involve the United States in maintaining freedom throughout the world?** Possible answers: Americans understood the value of freedom; countries that are free are more likely to be at peace with each other.
Analyze Primary Sources

Ⓗ SOCIAL STUDIES STRAND
History

Remind students that two groups of nations formed alliances. NATO still exists and works to keep peace in the world. During the mid-1990s NATO forces participated in peacekeeping operations in Bosnia and Herzegovina. The Warsaw Pact was dissolved on July 1, 1991, after democratic revolutions in Eastern Europe.

5 **Compare and contrast the goals of NATO and the Warsaw Pact.** Both were treaties designed to protect member nations from aggression. NATO's nations pledged to protect each other from Soviet aggression; the Warsaw Pact was similar, but involved Soviet-controlled countries in Eastern Europe.
Compare and Contrast

✓ **REVIEW ANSWER** Stalin tried to push the Western Allies out of Berlin by blockading supplies to their zones. The effect was a victory for the Western Allies over Stalin. 🕐 **Cause and Effect**

A Divided Europe

At the close of World War II, the Allies agreed to divide Germany into zones of occupation. The Soviet Union, France, Great Britain, and the United States would each control a zone. Germany's capital, **Berlin,** would then be divided up in the same way.

As relations between the Soviet Union and the other Allies turned sour, these arrangements began to cause problems. Berlin was located inside the Soviet zone of occupation.

In June 1948 Stalin decided to push the French, British, and Americans out of Berlin. He stopped traffic coming into their sections of the city. People living in those zones now faced the threat of starvation.

U.S. President Harry S. Truman responded quickly with the **Berlin airlift.** An airlift is the transport of supplies by airplanes. For nearly a year, the people in the U.S., British, and French zones of Berlin survived on these supplies. In the end, Stalin had to give up. Only three years after the defeat of the Nazis, Berlin became a symbol of freedom to the world.

Truman worked to prevent Soviet communism from spreading into any other countries. This became known as a policy of **containment.** When Greece and Turkey faced Soviet pressure in 1947, Truman committed the United States to help these nations. This promise became known

▶ **Berliners cheer as an American plane with supplies flies above them during the Berlin airlift.**

as the **Truman Doctrine.** In his address to Congress, Truman declared:

> *"The free peoples of the world look to us for support in maintaining their freedoms."*

The next year, Truman offered economic a[id] any country, both in the East and the West, t[o] encourage countries to resist communism.

In April 1949 the United States and its Western Allies set up the **North Atlantic Treaty Organization (NATO).** Members of thi[s] organization made a promise to each other. [They] promised that if one member were threatened by Soviet aggression, the others would come to its aid. In response, the Soviets set up the **Warsaw Pact.** This alliance was similar to NATO, but it was designed for the communist countries of Eastern Europe.

▶ **The offici[al] flag was a[dopted] in Octobe[r]**

In May 1949, the Western Allies combined their zones of occupation to form the countr[y] of **West Germany.** The Soviets created **East Germany** from their zone. Now more th[an] ever, an iron curtain divided Europe.

REVIEW What was the cause of the Berli[n air-]lift? What was its effect? 🕐 **Cause and Effe[ct]**

570

Practice and Extend

ⒺⓈⓁ EXTEND LANGUAGE
ESL Support

Examine Word Meanings Help students understand *aggression.*

Beginning Pronounce the word *aggression* and write it on the board. Add related words that students will understand, such as *fight* or *attack*. Say the words aloud, reinforcing the meaning with facial expressions or gestures.

Intermediate Pronounce and define *aggression* and then have students write i[t] in the middle of a word web. Students may list related words (*anger, attack*), antonyms (*cooperation, friendship*), and/or situations in which aggression might occur (an argument, an invasion of a country).

Advanced Introduce and define the noun *aggressor* and the adjective *aggressive*, relating them to the word *aggression*. Lead students to use the word[s] in sentences.

For additional ESL support, use Every Student Learns Guide, pp. 270–273.

The Nuclear Arms Race

In Chapter 19 you read how the United States dropped atomic bombs on two Japanese cities in 1945. Joseph Stalin realized that the Soviet Union would have to develop such weapons if it expected to keep up with the United States.

In 1949 the Soviet Union tested its first atomic bomb. This proved to the world that it was now a nuclear power too.

In the early 1950s, the United States tested a far more powerful weapon, the hydrogen bomb, or "H-bomb." Within a few years, the Soviet Union also had its own H-bombs. The Soviets and Americans, locked in their Cold War, now could threaten each other with complete destruction. Each side was determined to use the threat of nuclear war to make the other side back down. People in both countries were afraid. Children grew up practicing drills in school for what to do

in the event of a nuclear attack. Called "duck and cover," this drill resembled the procedure for a tornado drill. One student, looking back on this period, later reported:

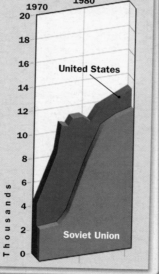

> "I was afraid because my parents and other adults seemed very worried. I remember our neighbors wondering if they should build a bomb shelter." **7**

REVIEW Why did Stalin think the Soviet Union needed to develop its own nuclear weapons?
Draw Conclusions

FACT FILE

The Nuclear Arms Race, 1945–1990

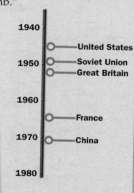

After the United States used atomic bombs in World War II, it was only a matter of time until other countries developed nuclear weapons. The time line shows when other nations had "the bomb."

- 1940
- 1950 — United States
- 1950 — Soviet Union
- 1950 — Great Britain
- 1960
- 1960 — France
- 1970 — China
- 1980

The nuclear race was mostly between the Soviet Union and the United States. By the 1980s, these two countries each had more than 10,000 nuclear weapons, as the graph at right shows.

United States

Soviet Union

Thousands: 0, 2, 4, 6, 8, 10, 12, 14, 16, 18, 20
1970   1980   1990

8 9

571

The Nuclear Arms Race

Quick Summary The escalating arms race between the United States and the Soviet Union caused fear in both countries.

6 Why do you think developing nuclear weapons was important to the Soviet Union? The Soviet Union believed it needed to keep up with the United States to maintain its superpower status. Developing weapons gave the country increased power.
Draw Conclusions

Primary Source

Quotation from Catherine Van Patten, Evanston, Illinois

7 What caused the student to be afraid? His parents' worry about the possibility of nuclear war.
Cause and Effect

✓ **REVIEW ANSWER** To keep up with the United Sates **Draw Conclusions**

FACT FILE

The Nuclear Arms Race, 1945–1990

Assist students in reading the time line. Lead them to draw conclusions about the number of nuclear weapons and when they were developed.

8 By 1960 which nations had developed nuclear arms? The United States, the Soviet Union, and Great Britain **Interpret Time Lines**

9 Compare and contrast the U.S. and Soviet Union's buildup of nuclear weapons from 1970 to 1990. Possible answer: Both nations increased the number of weapons they had. The United States always had more nuclear weapons than the Soviet Union, but the Soviet Union increased its number more consistently than the United States.
Interpret Graphs

CURRICULUM CONNECTION
Science

Research Nuclear Weapons

Encourage students to find out more about nuclear weapons. They might focus on the science involved in creating these weapons, the experiments that allowed these weapons to be developed, key players in the development of nuclear weapons, and so on.

Students could also create glossaries of terms such as *fission, fusion, chain reaction,* and *half-life.*

SOCIAL STUDIES STRAND
History

The Space Race

The United States and the Soviet Union were also involved in a "space race." Have students research answers to the following questions:

- What started the "space race"?
- What was the goal of NASA?
- What new technologies were developed and enhanced during the space race?

The Cuban Missile Crisis

⏱ *Quick Summary* When the Soviet Union began building missile bases in Cuba, President John F. Kennedy responded with a naval blockade.

🔟 How did the naval blockade end the crisis in Cuba? Soviet ships were unable to deliver materials needed to finish building missile bases.
↻ Cause and Effect

✓ **REVIEW ANSWER** People left East Germany before the Berlin Wall was built. **Sequence**

③ Close and Assess

Summarize the Lesson

Groups of students can make illustrated posters to show the most important details about a topic from the time line.

✓ **LESSON 1   REVIEW**

1. ↻ **Cause and Effect** For possible answers, see the reduced pupil page.

2. To ship supplies to the French, British, and American zones of Berlin

3. Soviet nuclear missile bases in Cuba

4. Possible answer: As communist countries in Eastern Europe closed off trade and travel to other countries, it seemed as if an iron curtain had fallen.

5. **Critical Thinking: *Make Inferences*** Possible answer: NATO members worried about Soviet aggression. NATO guaranteed that if one member was threatened, the other member nations would come to its aid.

Link to ∞ Writing

Students' notes should be respectful but firm, and they may describe possible consequences.

The Cuban Missile Crisis

Sharp disagreements between the superpowers continued. The fear of nuclear attack was behind every action made by either side. When the new Soviet leader, **Nikita Khrushchev,** declared in 1956, "We will bury you," people in the United States felt more uneasy than ever.

In 1961 people were leaving East Germany in huge numbers to reach West Germany. Khrushchev responded. He had a wall built through the middle of Berlin. It became known as the Berlin Wall and stood for more than 25 years.

In October 1962, the world came dangerously close to nuclear war. U.S. spy planes took photos

▶ Soviet leader Nikita Khrushchev speaks at a United Nations conference.

that showed that the Soviet Union was buildi missile bases in **Cuba,** a communist country. the bases were completed, Soviet nuclear mis siles would be only 90 miles from the souther tip of Florida. To keep missiles out of Cuba, President **John F. Kennedy** responded with a naval blockade, the use of force to prevent sl from reaching ports. For several days, the wo trembled with fear. Finally, Khrushchev backee down.

REVIEW Did people leave East Germany before or after the Berlin Wall was built? **Sequ**

Summarize the Lesso

1948–1949 The United States and its / launched the Berlin airlift.

1949 The Soviet Union successfully tes its first atomic bomb.

1962 The United States and the Soviet Union came close to starting a nuclear over Soviet missiles in Cuba.

LESSON 1   REVIEW

Check Facts and Main Ideas

1. ↻ **Cause and Effect** On a separate piece of paper, fill in the chart below by listing three causes of the Cold War.

See answer above →

See answer below → [The Cold War]

See answer below →

Soviet Union trade and travel was stopped.

Soviet Union developed nuclear weapons.

Eastern Europe became communist.

2. What was the purpose of the Berlin airlift?

3. What was the central issue of the Cuban missile crisis?

4. Why did Churchill's term, "the iron curtai seem to sum up the situation in Europe during the Cold War so well?

5. **Critical Thinking: *Make Inferences*** How w the founding of NATO an effect of Stalin' attempt to take over Berlin? Explain.

Link to ∞ Writing

Write a Message You are a U.S. diplomat 1948. The Soviets have just cut off all traf to the French, British, and American zones Berlin. Write a message to Joseph Stalin explaining why he should reconsider this action.

572

Practice and Extend

FYI **SOCIAL STUDIES Background**

More About the Berlin Wall

- After the final stages of construction, the Berlin Wall was 96 miles long. It was 12 feet high, with a concrete tube at the top.

- On November 9, 1989, travel restrictions were lifted, and more than 10,000 East Germans crossed the border to West Berlin. People later broke pieces off the wall to save as souvenirs.

- In October 1990 East and West Germany reunited into one country with Berlin as its capital.

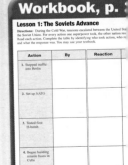

Workbook, p.

Lesson 1: The Soviets Advance

Action	By	Reaction
1. Stopped traffic into Berlin		
2. Set up NATO		
3. Tested first H-bomb		
4. Began building missile bases in Cuba		

Also on Tea Resources

Reaching the Roof of the World

CITIZEN HEROES

Reaching the Roof of the World

BUILDING CITIZENSHIP

Caring
Respect
Responsibility
Fairness
Honesty
Courage

enzing Norgay's dream came true one cold day in
953. He and Edmund Hillary became the first people
 reach the top of Mt. Everest, the world's tallest
ountain. However, Tenzing never thought that some
eople would turn his feat into a political issue.

Norgay was born in 1914 in Nepal, a country in southern Asia. His
age was in the shadow of the Himalayas. As a boy he dreamed of
mbing Mt. Everest. His people, the Sherpas, called it the "goddess
ther of the world." He recalled:

> *"The pull of Everest was stronger for me
> than any force on Earth."*

Early on May 29, 1953, Norgay and his partner, New Zealander
mund Hillary, set out from their camp. They were about 1,000 feet
n the top of the mountain. They took turns leading the way. Both of
m carefully planted their ice axes into the brittle ice as they inched
ward. At 11:30 A.M. they reached the top—the roof of the world!
Norgay and Hillary were hailed as heroes. However, because Norgay
 Asian and Hillary was of European descent, some people wanted
 laim the achievement for the East or the West. They demanded
 now who had reached the summit first.

Norgay gave the situation careful thought. Even though Norgay
w some people would be disappointed, he told the truth.
is autobiography *Tiger of the Snows* (1955), Norgay revealed
 Hillary reached the top first. Norgay reached the summit
ents later.

Honesty in Action

Link to Current Events Research the story of a
person today who has demonstrated honesty.
What risks did this person take in being honest in
that particular situation?

Edmund Hillary/Royal Geographical Society Picture Library

573

CURRICULUM CONNECTION
Literature

ead About Mt. Everest Use the following selections to extend the content.

e *Top of the World: Climbing Mount Everest,* by Steve Jenkins (Houghton
Mifflin, ISBN 0-395-94218-7, 1996) **Easy**

umph on Everest: A Photobiography of Sir Edmund Hillary,* by Broughton
Coburn and Mingma Norbu Sherpa (National Geographic Society, ISBN 0-792-
27114-9, 2000) **On-Level**

ching My Father's Soul: A Sherpa's Journey to the Top of Mt. Everest,* by
amling Tenzing Norgay and Jon Krakauer (Harper, ISBN 0-062-51687-6, 2001)
Challenge

Reaching the Roof of the World

Objectives
- Identify the accomplishments of Tenzing Norgay.
- Evaluate Tenzing Norgay's decision to reveal that he was the second to reach the summit of Mt. Everest.

1 Introduce and Motivate

Preview To activate prior knowledge, have students describe a time when they faced a difficult decision—whether or not to tell the truth. What would a lie have accomplished in the situation? What made telling the truth the "right thing" to do, even though it was difficult?

2 Teach and Discuss

Primary Source
Cited in *National Geographic World*, January, 1999; "Battling Everest" by Michael Burgan

1 What motivated Tenzing to make the dangerous trip to the top of Everest? He had always dreamed of climbing the mountain.
Cause and Effect

SOCIAL STUDIES STRAND
Citizenship

2 How were Tenzing's actions an example of honesty? He told the truth even though the truth could have disappointed many people. **Evaluate**

3 Close and Assess

Honesty in Action
- Encourage students to identify some of the risks that being honest may involve.
- You might have students create character trait webs to record their ideas about Tenzing.

Solve Complex Problems

Objective

- Solve complex problems by identifying options, considering them carefully, and choosing a plan of action.

Resources

- Workbook, p. 143
- Transparency 57

1 Introduce and Motivate

What is the problem to be solved? Ask students to recall the information they learned about the Cuban missile crisis in Lesson 1. Then have students read the **What?** section of text on p. 574 to help them understand the problem.

Why was it crucial to solve this problem effectively? Have students read the **Why?** section of text on p. 575. Ask them what made solving this problem so important. What could have happened if President Kennedy had not used good problem-solving skills?

2 Teach and Discuss

How is this skill used? Examine the crisis faced by President Kennedy.

- Help students define the problem concisely.

- Encourage them to think of possible solutions to the problem. Lead them in weighing the pros and cons of each of the proposed solutions.

- Have students read the **How?** section of text on p. 575.

1 Why do you think President Kennedy consulted others rather than solving the problem himself? Possible answers: He wanted to gather expert opinions; he wanted to consider many opinions before making a decision.
Draw Conclusions

Solve Complex Problems

▶ U.S. President Kennedy (right) and Soviet Leader Khrushchev (above) had to deal with the threat of a nuclear war.

What? A complex problem is one that needs to be considered car◀ If you make a bad decision in trying to solve a complex problem, the problem may only get worse. In October 1962, U.S. spy planes provide◀ President John F. Kennedy with evidence that the Soviet Union was bui◀ missile bases in Cuba. From only 90 miles south of Florida, the Soviets the Cubans would be able to launch nuclear missiles at any U.S. c◀ President Kennedy had to make difficult d◀ sions about how to get rid of the missiles— without setting off a nuclear war. Members o◀ Cabinet, military leaders, and others were ca◀ upon to advise him. Once decisions were ma◀ Kennedy had to communicate them to the So◀ leader, Nikita Khrushchev, in Moscow.

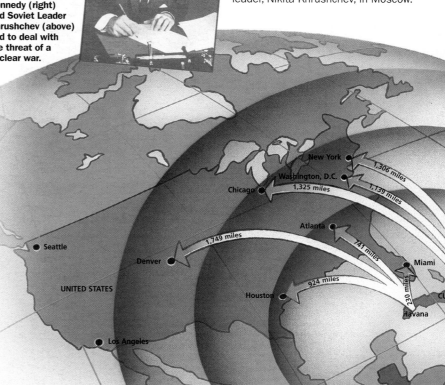

574

Practice and Extend

MEETING INDIVIDUAL NEEDS
Learning Styles

Use the Problem-Solving Process Using their individual learning styles, students review and use the problem-solving process.

Visual Learning Invite students to create flow charts to show the steps of the problem-solving process. Students can use the flow charts to work on problem◀ of their own.

Verbal Learning Small groups can discuss how they would have solved the problems that President Kennedy faced and what the outcomes of those solutions may have been. Alternatively, students could take the role of Presiden◀ Kennedy and explain their actions and what prompted them to act as they did.

Linguistic Learning Students can act as advisors to President Kennedy and write letters or position papers detailing the best solution to the problem and explaining why that solution would work.

U.S. spy planes took aerial photos such as this one of the missile bases being built by the Soviets in Cuba. Labels (added later) indicate the different parts of the missile base.

Why? It is always important to make decisions carefully. But when the stakes are high, finding effective ways to solve difficult problems is especially critical. President Kennedy had to deal with the Cuban missile crisis. He knew that the world's fate might rest in his hands. A poor decision might have led to nuclear war.

How? President Kennedy made a good decision right at the start. He carefully discussed his options, or possible actions, with a group of trusted advisers. By drawing on the experience of experts, he could feel confident of being well informed.

Next, President Kennedy refused to be rushed into making a decision. Some of his advisers wanted the United States to bomb the missile sites at once. However, the president realized that he had time to think. He knew the Soviets could not get the missile sites ready right away. He did not want to rush into any action.

Finally, Kennedy chose a plan of action. The plan satisfied the need to stop work on the missile sites without risking war with the Soviet Union. He placed a blockade on all Soviet ships going to Cuba. This means that the U.S. Navy would prevent Soviet ships from reaching Cuba. The blockade would keep more Soviet missiles out of Cuba. It should also buy time for the two sides to work out a settlement.

Like President Kennedy, you might use the following strategy to solve complex problems:

· Carefully consider all your options. Seek advice from experts, or people whose judgment you respect.
· Do not allow yourself to be rushed into a decision. Give yourself time to think things through.
· Consider the consequence of each option. Try to find a solution that satisfies all requirements or most of them.

Think and Apply

① What do you think might have happened in 1962 if President Kennedy had rushed into bombing the Cuban missile sites?

② Why do you think that it is important for a leader to be willing to ask people for advice and to listen? Explain your answer.

③ Think of a situation in which you had to make a difficult decision. Did you use any parts of the strategy discussed here? Explain.

575

---

② **Why could President Kennedy take time making his decision?** The Soviet Union was thousands of miles away and was not able to prepare the missile sites quickly enough for an immediate attack. ⟳ **Cause and Effect**

③ **Do you think that bombing the missile sites right away would have been a good strategy? Why or why not?** Possible answers: No, bombing might have started a war, putting people in immediate danger. Yes, the attack would have destroyed the sites and sent a clear message to the Soviet Union. **Evaluate**

3 Close and Assess

Think and Apply

1. Possible answer: An all-out nuclear war might have taken place. It might have destroyed both the United States and the Soviet Union and damaged Earth's atmosphere enough to make life on Earth difficult or impossible.

2. Possible answer: This quality enables a leader in times of crisis to get the best possible information.

3. Possible answer: Yes, I tried to think about different things I could do. Then I talked it over with two friends and made a decision. Then I discussed my decision with my parents before I took action.

Workbook, p. 143

Complex Problems

Also on Teacher Resources CD-ROM.

MEETING INDIVIDUAL NEEDS
Leveled Practice

Present a News Show Ask groups of students to create news shows depicting the events surrounding the Cuban missile crisis.

Easy Have students read aloud the **How?** section of the text. Help them retell the information in their own words. **Reteach**

On-Level Have students create original "on-the-spot" reports by reviewing the information in the **What?, Why?,** and **How?** sections. They can orally report the news to their classmates. **Extend**

Challenge Have students do additional research as they create their news stories. They can "interview" President Kennedy, his advisors, and so on as they report about the crisis and its solution. **Enrich**

Communism in China

Objectives

- List the causes and effects of the Long March.
- Name the political parties that fought for control of China in the 1940s.
- Identify Jiang Qing and explain her role in communist China.
- List and describe the revolutions that occurred in China in the twentieth century.
- Explain why the leaders of the two Chinese governments could not be relied on to make accurate statements about each other.

Vocabulary

proletarian, p. 579

Resources

- Workbook, p. 144
- Transparency 20
- Every Student Learns Guide, pp. 274–277
- Quick Study, pp. 138–139

Quick Teaching Plan

If time is short, have students create a "biography chart" as they read independently by listing the names of individuals included in Lesson 2 and explaining the role of each in twentieth-century China.

1 Introduce and Motivate

Preview Ask students to recall from Lesson 1 how communism spread throughout Europe. Tell students that they will learn in Lesson 2 how communism was introduced in China.

You Are There The Cultural Revolution was officially "launched" in August 1966. Mao Zedong shut down China's schools and encouraged the Red Guards to attack traditional values. Ask students what might happen in a country with so much unrest.

576 Unit 7 • A World in Opposition

Beijing
CHINA

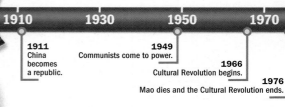

1910	1930	1950	1970

1911 China becomes a republic.

1949 Communists come to power.

1966 Cultural Revolution begins.

1976 Mao dies and the Cultural Revolution ends.

Communism in China

PREVIEW

Focus on the Main Idea
In a century of revolution, communists took control of China.

PLACES
Taiwan
People's Republic of China
Beijing
Taipei

PEOPLE
Sun Yat-sen
Chiang Kai-shek
Mao Zedong
Richard Nixon
Jiang Qing
Nien Cheng

VOCABULARY
proletarian

TERMS
Nationalist Party

EVENTS
Cultural Revolution

576

You Are There Today, coming home from school, y• notice that the street near your apar• ment building in Shanghai (shang H• China, is blocked. You hear what sounds like a noisy parade. You try to remember what day it is. Oh, yes, it's August 23, 1966. You're sure it's not a special holiday.

By looking more closely at the paraders, you notice something. They all seem young—about the age of you teenage sister. They're all wearing red armbands. Many shouting and waving a little red book. Some are carrying big poles that hold up huge banners. You try to make out some of the writing.

You turn to a girl next to you and ask, "What's going on?" "Don't you know?" she responds. "These are the Red Guards, marching in the Cultural Revolution."

▶ Copies of the "little red book": *Quotations from Chairman Mao Zedong*

 Cause and Effect As you read, try to identify causes and effects of the communist takeover of China in 1949.

Practice and Extend

 **READING SKILL Cause and Effect**

In the Lesson Review, students complete a graphic organizer like the one below. You may want to provide students with a copy of Transparency 20 to complete as they read the lesson.

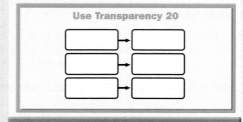
Use Transparency 20

 **WEB SITE Technology**

- You can look up vocabulary words by clicking on *Social Studies Library* and selecting the dictionary at **www.sfsocialstudies.com.**
- Students can learn more about current news by clicking on *Current Events* at **www.sfsocialstudies.com.**
- Explore other events that occurred on this day by clicking on *This Day in History* at **www.sfsocialstudies.com.**

A Struggle for Control of China

As you have just read, a revolution began in China in 1966. It was not the first revolution China went through in the twentieth century. In 1911 a revolution removed China's emperor and China became a country without a king or emperor—a republic. One of the leaders of that revolution was **Sun Yat-sen** (SUN YAHT SEN). Sun Yat-sen started the Guomindang (GWOAH en dang), or the **Nationalist Party.** When he died in 1925, **Chiang Kai-shek** (jee AHNG ky EK), became the Guomindang leader. Meanwhile, the Communist Party of China was formed in 1921. In a few years, **Mao Zedong** (OW ZUH DUNG) became the leader of the communists.

In the 1930s, the Nationalist Party ruled most of China. It wanted to get rid of the communists and nearly succeeded. However, a group of communists escaped to far northwest China. Their long, difficult journey during 1934 and 1935 became known as "The Long March." A man who later became an important government official described the Long March:

> *"For us, the darkest time . . . was . . . when we crossed the great grasslands near Tibet. . . . We not only had nothing to eat, we had nothing to drink."*

2

During World War II, the Nationalist Party and the communists had to put aside their differences to fight Japan. But afterward they fought in a civil war. In 1949 the communists won and took over China. The nationalists then fled to **Taiwan** (ty WAHN), an island off China's coast.

3

REVIEW What were the effects of the civil war in China? Cause and Effect

Yan'an · Huang Ho River · Chang Jiang River · Zunyi · Ruijin · CHINA · N · TAIWAN

— Main Route of Red Army
⌐⌐ Great Wall

Map Adventure

You're an American Journalist

The Chinese communists are making a 6,000-mile journey to escape from the nationalists. You're assigned to cover their story. The march begins in southeastern China in October 1934. About a year later, they set up a new base at Yan'an.

1. In January 1935, the communists hold a meeting at Zunyi. Locate Zunyi on the map.

2. What major river do the communists need to cross after turning their direction northward?

3. Along what human-made structure do the communists travel for many miles?

577

The Long March

Approximately 100,000 people began the Long March. Thirty-five of the marchers were women.

During their march, the communists were pursued by Kuomintang troops. Some of the marchers died from battle wounds, and many died from disease.

When the Long March ended in Shaanxi Province in October 1935, only 8,000 of the original 100,000 members still remained with the group.

Although the communists had been forced to retreat, the group turned the end of the march into a moral victory. They made the Red Army a fighting force that would be able to take over all of China by 1949.

A Struggle for Control of China

Quick Summary A revolution in 1911 resulted in China's becoming a republic, but after World War II, the communists took over China.

1 When was the Communist Party formed? Where does this date fall in relation to important dates in Nationalist leadership? 1921; Chiang Kai-shek became the leader of the Nationalist party in 1925. **Sequence**

Primary Source
Cited in Quotations from Premier Chou En-Lai

2 What do the conditions described in the primary source reveal about the communists who escaped in 1935? Possible answer: They were determined to escape. They withstood harsh circumstances to stand up for their beliefs. **Analyze Primary Sources**

3 Why do you think the clashing political parties in China united during World War II? The entire country was threatened during the war. If the country had been divided, then they would not have been able to fight successfully against Japan. **Express Ideas**

✓ **REVIEW ANSWER** The communists won control of the country; the Nationalist followers of Chiang Kai-Shek fled to Taiwan. Cause and Effect

Map Adventure Answers

1. Students should point to the south central part of the map. **2.** Chang Jiang River **3.** The Great Wall of China

The People's Republic of China

Quick Summary Mao led the communist takeover of China. The standard of living improved for some Chinese, but the government was faced with serious problems.

4 **What made Taiwan a problem for the People's Republic of China?**
Nationalists had formed a government on Taiwan and governed Taiwan as a separate nation. The country prospered while China had economic problems. The People's Republic believed that Taiwan belonged to China.
Cause and Effect

Ongoing Assessment

| **If...** students are unable to determine this cause-and-effect relationship, | **then...** point out Taiwan's close proximity to China on a map. Discuss how their relationship became strained. |

5 **Why do you think the United Nations removed Taiwan and invited the People's Republic of China to take its place?** The People's Republic was a large, powerful country, and Taiwan was not formally recognized as a nation.
Draw Conclusions

6 **Explain the state of Chinese-Soviet relations between 1949 and 1960.** In 1949 the communists formed an alliance with the Soviet Union. Later the two countries disagreed on the goals of communism and became involved in a border skirmish. They broke off relations by 1960. **Sequence**

7 **Do you consider Mao's transformation of China a success? Why or why not?** Possible answers: Yes, China became more modern and eventually the government was recognized by other nations. No, the famine and failing economy were proof that the changes were unsuccessful.
Analyze Information

REVIEW ANSWER Achievements: improved standard of living for most people, unification of China; Failures: loss of democratic freedoms, "The Great Leap Forward" **Summarize**

The People's Republic of China

When the communists took over China in 1949, they set up the **People's Republic of China** and made **Beijing** (bay JEENG) their capital. The Nationalist Party, led by Chiang, set up a government on Taiwan with its capital at **Taipei** (tie PAY).

The Communists began transforming China into a communist country. They also formed an alliance with the Soviet Union. In the next lesson, you will read how China supported its communist neighbor, North Korea, in the Korean War.

Mao and the Communists unified the country and improved the standard of living, especially for the poor. However, these improvements came at a cost. Mao's government took away democratic freedoms, including freedom of speech and religion. It invaded China's neighbor to the southwest, Tibet, forcing its leader to flee.

Mao's attempt to modernize China, "The Great Leap Forward," turned out to be a costly step backwards for China's economy. Like the Soviet Union in the 1930s, China tried to turn its farms into collectives. But the collectives were badly planned and badly run. The result was famine. A more serious attempt to change China was the **Cultural Revolution,** which you will read about in the next section.

▶ On his visit to China in 1972, U.S. President Richard Nixo_ shakes hands with China's leader, Mao Zedong.

Taiwan remained a problem for the People Republic. After the communist takeover of m_ land China, Taiwan took China's place in the United Nations, an organization that promot_ peace. As it prospered, Taiwan maintained i_ independence. But the People's Republic cla_ that Taiwan belonged to China.

In 1971 the United Nations dismissed Ta_ and invited the People's Republic of China t_ its seat. In 1972, U.S. President **Richard N** went to China and met with Mao. He hoped_ improve relations between the United State_ China. During this period, China had little t_ with the Soviet Union. The two countries ha_ broken off their friendship by 1960. _ had been fighting over the border be_ the two countries and disagreed on _ the aims of communism.

REVIEW What were two achieveme_ Mao's communist government in Chi_ What were two failures? **Summarize**

▶ The People's Republic of China adopt_ this as their national flag in 1949.

Practice and Extend

ESL **ACCESS CONTENT**
ESL Support

Examine Word Meanings *Unify* means "to make or form into one." Mao wanted to unify people to make the People's Republic of China a strong natio_

Beginning Ask several students to stand in the corners of the room. Say th_ word *unify* and have students come together in the center of the room. Expla_ that the separate students have unified, or become one.

Intermediate Relate the word *unify* to a team playing a game, pointing out_ all members of a team must work as one, or unify, to accomplish a goal. Ask_ students to describe other situations in which people need to unify.

Advanced List the words *unicycle*, *unity*, *uniform*, and *unify* on the board. A_ students how these words are the same. (All of them begin with *uni-*.) Ask _ students if they can figure out what the letters *uni-* mean when they appear_ word. ("one" or "single") Have students explain the meaning of each word.
For additional ESL support, use Every Student Learns Guide, pp. 274–277.

The Cultural Revolution

In 1966 Mao Zedong decided to start a new phase of revolution. He called this phase the "Great Proletarian Cultural Revolution." The word **proletarian** means "of the working class." The movement soon became known simply as the Cultural Revolution.

Mao's stated aim was to clear China of all "counter-revolutionary" elements. By this he meant all remaining privileges that interfered with his vision of an equal society without classes. Mao's closest ally in launching the Cultural Revolution was his wife, **Jiang Qing** (JANG CHEENG). For more than a decade, Jiang was to be one of the most powerful people in China.

Mao encouraged young people to take up his revolutionary cause. Millions of students joined the "Red Guards." They left their studies and marched in the streets. They teased and attacked many older people, as well as people in authority. Teachers and party officials came under attack, as did anyone who seemed to have a high standard of living. However, anyone opposed to the actions of the Red Guard could be seen as a counter-revolutionary element.

Soon, millions of people found their lives turned upside down. Attacks on older people and the well-educated became violent. Many people died.

Nien Cheng was a fairly wealthy resident of Shanghai in 1966. Because of her wealth, Nien Cheng was seen by the Red Guard as a privileged, counter-revolutionary element. She became a target of the Cultural Revolution. She later wrote about her experiences, describing the Red Guards in 1966:

> "Red Guards were stopping buses, distributing leaflets, lecturing the passengers, and punishing those whose clothes they disapproved of. . . . On the sidewalks, the Red Guards led the people to shout slogans. Each group of Red Guards was accompanied by drums and gongs and . . . Mao's portrait." ⑩

Nien Cheng was put in prison without any formal charge. She remained there for more than six years.

REVIEW What was the Cultural Revolution?
Main Idea and Details

▶ In 1971, during the Cultural Revolution, China marked the 22-year anniversary of the Communist Revolution. This rally was held at the Gate of Heavenly Peace in Beijing.

PAGE 579

The Cultural Revolution

🕐 **Quick Summary** In 1966 Mao launched the Cultural Revolution in order to create a classless, equal society.

⑧ What does it mean to have a high standard of living? Why were people with a high standard of living targeted during the Cultural Revolution? Individuals with a high standard of living usually have more money or privileges than other people. The Cultural Revolution was meant to create an equal, classless society in which everyone had the same standard of living. 🔄 **Cause and Effect**

C SOCIAL STUDIES STRAND
Culture

Point out that a class system is a social organization in which the rights and duties of individuals may be determined at birth. In some ancient cultures, people were born into certain classes, and people in lower classes had no hope of becoming a member of another class.

⑨ Why do you think Mao wanted to create a classless society? Possible answers: It was a goal of communism that in a classless society, no one would have more privileges than others; the wealth of a nation would be shared among all who lived there. **Evaluate**

Primary Source

Cited in *Life and Death in Shanghai*, by Nein Cheng

⑩ What methods did the Red Guards use to assert their ideals? What do you think the Chinese thought of the Red Guards' methods? Explain. The Red Guards distributed literature, shouted slogans, lectured people, and punished those of whom they disapproved. Possible answer: Many people probably disliked or resented these methods because they were disrespectful of older people and authorities. **Express Ideas**

✓ **REVIEW ANSWER** A movement to clear China of "counter-revolutionary" elements and create a classless society, in which everyone was equal
Main Idea and Details

Discuss and Research Social Classes Ask students to consider the idea of social classes.

Easy Ask students to define the phrase *social class*. Have them retell the goals of the Cultural Revolution in their own words. **Reteach**

On-Level Ask students to refer to the first paragraph on p. 579 to find the meaning of *proletarian*. Ask students to discuss why that class of people may have felt "left out" of Chinese society. As members of the proletarian class, students can make a case for the Cultural Revolution. **Extend**

Challenge Have students research the caste system in India and the election of President K. R. Narayanan. Ask students to compare and contrast the Cultural Revolution with Narayanan's election. **Enrich**

For a Lesson Summary, use Quick Study, p. 138.

The Last Years

Quick Summary The Cultural Revolution lasted ten years, ending in 1976 with the death of Mao.

11 **What happened in China after Mao died?** The Cultural Revolution ended. Mao's wife, Jiang Qing, held power until 1978, but she was imprisoned. New leadership took over the country. **Sequence**

✓ **REVIEW ANSWER** Students left their studies to join the Red Guards and march in the street; teachers and party officials came under attack; older people were harassed; and anybody who opposed the actions of the Red Guards was considered a counter-revolutionary element. ↻ **Cause and Effect**

3 Close and Assess

Summarize the Lesson

Have each student write a multiple-choice question based on information in the lesson. Collect the questions and use them for a class "quiz show."

✓ **LESSON 2** **REVIEW**

1. ↻ **Cause and Effect** For possible answers, see the reduced pupil page.

2. The Communist party and the Nationalist party

3. She was the wife of Mao Zedong and one of the most powerful people in China during the Cultural Revolution.

4. Possible answer: The 1911 revolution overthrew the emperor; in 1949 the communists took control of mainland China; in 1966 Mao launched the Cultural Revolution.

5. **Critical Thinking:** *Detect Bias* Possible answer: No, these governments have been enemies for more than fifty years. Each has reasons for criticizing the other.

Link to ⚭ Mathematics

Students should report the numbers they find correctly rounded to the nearest hundred million. Their answers should be fractions.

580 Unit 7 • A World in Opposition

The Last Years

The Cultural Revolution continued for a decade. Schools were closed and students were sent to the countryside to do farm work. The army, backed by Mao, took control of China.

When Mao died in 1976, the Cultural Revolution came to an end. Jiang Qing held on to power until 1978, but she was

► Jiang Qing was a cultural leader and spokeswoman.

then put on trial and imprisoned. Leaders with different ideas for China then took power. Some of these leaders had been targets of the Cultural Revolution themselves.

REVIEW What was the effect of the Cultural Revolution on China? ↻ Cause and Effect

Summarize the Lesson

- **1911** China became a republic when the emperor was overthrown.
- **1949** Mao Zedong and the communists came to power after winning the civil war.
- **1966** The Cultural Revolution began.
- **1976** Mao Zedong died, and the Cultural Revolution came to an end.

LESSON 2 **REVIEW**

Check Facts and Main Ideas

1. ↻ **Cause and Effect** On a separate piece of paper, fill in the chart below by listing causes and effects.

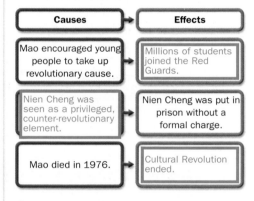

Causes	Effects
Mao encouraged young people to take up revolutionary cause.	Millions of students joined the Red Guards.
Nien Cheng was seen as a privileged, counter-revolutionary element.	Nien Cheng was put in prison without a formal charge.
Mao died in 1976.	Cultural Revolution ended.

2. What political parties fought for control of China during the civil war of the late 1940s?

3. Who was Jiang Qing and what was her role in China's history?

4. What details can you provide to support the statement "The twentieth century was an era of revolution in China"?

5. **Critical Thinking:** *Detect Bias* Do you think you could believe everything the communist leaders in Beijing said about the government of Taiwan? Could you believe everything Taiwan's leaders said about the People's Republic of China? Explain your answer.

Link to ⚭ Mathematics

Learn with Fractions Find the population of the United States and that of the People's Republic of China in a current almanac. To make the numbers easier to work with, round each figure to the nearest hundred million. Make a fraction like the model below:

$$\frac{\text{population of the United States}}{\text{population of China}}$$

Reduce the fraction to its lowest terms.

580

Practice and Extend

CURRICULUM CONNECTION **Writing**

Research Revolutions

Encourage students to find out more about revolutions in various countries throughout history. They might focus on one revolution and answer questions such as the following:

- When and where did the revolution take place?
- What circumstances prompted the revolution?
- What were the goals of the revolutionaries?
- What was the outcome of the revolution or uprising?

Students can write a few paragraphs comparing and contrasting the revolutions they studied with the Cultural Revolution in China.

Workbook, p. 14

Lesson 2: Communism in China

After the removal of China's emperor in 1911, China went through changes in its government.

Directions: Use the phrases in the box to compare the Nationalist and Communist Parties. Then complete the Venn diagram with these phrases. You may use your textbook.

Tried to turn farms into collectives	Leader was Mao Zedong
Fought in a civil war	Started the Cultural Revolution
Kept seat in United Nations until 1971	Capital was Taipei
Invited to take UN seat in 1971	Fought Japan during World War
Capital was Beijing	Leader was Chiang Kai-shek

Communist Party

Nationalist Party

Also on Teacher Resources CD

Mao Zedong
1893–1976

Mao was born a peasant. At the age of five, he was sent to work in rice fields. Two years later, he was allowed to go to school. Mao loved to read. He especially liked traditional Chinese novels about heroes who rebelled against their unfair rulers. Mao was a good student. However, his strict father made him quit school when he was 13 to return to farming.

In 1913 Mao attended a teacher's training school. There he became politically active. He joined in protests against the government.

When the Russian Revolution broke out, Mao adopted Marxism. In 1921 he became the founder of the Chinese Communist Party. Mao believed that communism would take power away from landowners and other privileged people. He claimed that communism would help poor rural peasants. In 1927 Mao showed his confidence in the peasants in China:

> *"[S]everal hundred million peasants will rise like a mighty storm, like a hurricane, a force so swift and violent that no power, however great, will be able to hold it back."*

All the peasants needed was a leader. Mao became that leader. After the 1949 revolution, he also became the leader of China.

BIOFACT

During the Cultural Revolution, people wore badges showing a picture of Mao. Some badges even glowed in the dark!

Learn from Biographies

What events in Mao's life first reveal his political beliefs as an adult?

For more information, go online to *Meet the People* at **www.sfsocialstudies.com**.

581

★ BIOGRAPHY ★

Mao Zedong

Objective
- Identify the early life experiences of Mao Zedong that may have contributed to his later ideas and his decision to lead the Cultural Revolution.

1 Introduce and Motivate

Preview To activate prior knowledge, ask students to recall information they learned about Mao Zedong in Lesson 2. Tell students that they will read about Mao's childhood and young adulthood.

Ask why it is helpful to know about a person's early life. (A person's early life often influences what he or she becomes.)

2 Teach and Discuss

- Ask students how Mao's early experiences may have contributed to his ideas about social classes.

- Discuss with students the beliefs that Mao expressed in the quotation on this page.

1 Why do you think that Mao felt qualified to lead the peasants to a new standing in China? Possible answer: Mao was born a peasant, so he could understand their difficulties. He attended school and was politically active. Mao believed that with a good leader, the peasants would be a powerful force in China. **Hypothesize**

3 Close and Assess

Learn from Biographies Answer

As a young student, Mao liked reading novels about heroes who rebelled against their unfair rulers. As a student in teacher's training school, he joined in protests against the government. Mao adopted Marxism when the Russian Revolution broke out.

CURRICULUM CONNECTION
Art

[De]sign a Book Jacket

[A]sk students to design book [ja]ckets for a biography of Mao [Z]edong. Remind them that a [b]iography is the story of [s]omeone's life.

[T]hey should include artwork on [the] cover and write copy for the [in]side flap of the book jacket.

[S]tudents can use facts from [th]is biography as well as from [L]esson 2 as they create their [b]ook jacket.

WEB SITE
Technology

Students can find out more about Mao Zedong by clicking on *Meet the People* at **www.sfsocialstudies.com**.

The Cold War Heats Up

Objectives

- List some of the causes and effects of the Korean War and Vietnam War.

- Describe U.S. involvement in the Vietnam War under President Eisenhower.

- Explain the change in U.S. involvement in the Vietnam War in the 1960s.

- Compare and contrast the wars in Korea and Vietnam and other events of the Cold War.

- Explain how events in other parts of the world would have convinced people that the domino effect would occur if Vietnam became a communist country.

Vocabulary

guerrilla, p. 584; **détente,** p. 587

Resources

- Workbook, p. 145
- Transparency 20
- Every Student Learns Guide, pp. 278–281
- Quick Study, pp. 140–141

Quick Teaching Plan

If time is short, ask students to make outlines as they read independently.

- Suggest that each section title can be a main idea.
- Have students note details to support each main idea.

1 Introduce and Motivate

Preview Review with students the issues involved in the Cold War. Tell students that they will learn in Lesson 3 how the same issues emerged in Asia.

You Are There Let students know that the letter on this page is fictitious, but based on a possible experience of a soldier. Point out North Korea and South Korea on a map. Ask students why they think the United States may have been involved in a war in this area.

582 Unit 7 • A World in Opposition

LESSON 3

1950	1960	1970

1950
The Korean War begins.

1953
The Korean War ends.

1965
The United States sends troops to Vietnam.

North takes ov...

The Cold War Heats Up

PREVIEW

Focus on the Main Idea
The Cold War became a "hot" war in Korea and Vietnam.

PLACES
North Korea
South Korea
Indochina
North Vietnam
South Vietnam
Cambodia
Laos
Hanoi

PEOPLE
Ho Chi Minh
John F. Kennedy
Lyndon Johnson
Robert MacNamara

VOCABULARY
guerrilla
détente

TERMS
Viet Cong
domino effect
Vietnamization

EVENTS
Tet Offensive

▶ These "dog tags" belonged to a U.S. soldier during the Vietnam War.

582

You Are There

December 3,

Dear Aunt Rosa,

   I'm sorry I missed this year's Thanksgiving dinner. I hope the feast was delicious.

   We got here just in time for the hottest summer K has had in years. The rains are supposed to help cool things off, but it was also a very dry summer.

   We were supposed to get six weeks of training whe got here. But instead, they sent us into the field almo immediately.

   Over Thanksgiving we were involved in some heav fighting. We had a lot of casualties. Even worse was t rumor I heard that we were not just fighting the Nor Koreans, but the Chinese too.

   They used to tell us we'd be out of here by Christm I'm starting to doubt it.

   Say hi to Uncle Julio and the kids.

Your nephew,

Juan

 Cause and Effect As you read, look for effects of the wars in Korea and Vietnam on the United States.

Practice and Extend

 READING SKILL Cause and Effect

In the Lesson Review, students complete a graphic organizer like the one below. You may want to provide students with a copy of Transparency 20 to complete as they read the lesson.

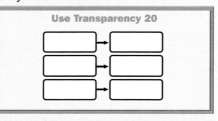

Use Transparency 20

 WEB SITE Technology

- You can look up vocabulary words by clicking on *Social Studies Library* and selecting the dictionary at **www.sfsocialstudies.com.**

- Students can learn more about current news by clicking on *Current Events* at **www.sfsocialstudies.com.**

- Explore other events that occurred on this day by clicking on *This Day in History* at **www.sfsocialstudies.com.**

The Korean War

In the previous lesson, you read that China became a communist nation under the leadership [of] Mao Zedong in 1949. Soon Asia, like Europe, became a battleground in the Cold War.

Since the end of World War II, Korea, a country [to] the southeast of China, had been a divided [na]tion. The communists had taken control of [the] north. They were allied with the Soviet Union. [No]n-communists ruled in the south.

[O]n June 25, 1950, **North Korea** launched [an] invasion of **South Korea.** President Harry S. [Tru]man immediately requested action from the [Un]ited Nations. In response, the United Nations agreed to support a military operation to help stop the invasion. However, the United States provided most of the equipment and troops.

President Truman appointed World War II hero Douglas MacArthur as the UN commander in Korea. MacArthur's troops made a brilliant landing on the west coast of South Korea. MacArthur's troops drove the North Korean army almost to the Chinese border.

China feared attack. They sent an army into North Korea against the UN troops. Soon the UN troops were forced to retreat.

General MacArthur and President Truman disagreed about how to fight the war. Truman and his advisers wanted to fight a limited war, not a total, all-out war. But MacArthur wanted to extend the war into China to win complete victory. In April 1951, Truman replaced MacArthur with another general.

In 1953 North Korea agreed to an armistice. The fighting stopped, but North and South Korea never officially signed a treaty to end the war.

REVIEW What event prompted U.S. and UN troops to fight a war in Korea?
Cause and Effect

Korea, 1953

CHINA

SOVIET UNION

NORTH KOREA

Sea of Japan

Armistice Border Line, 1953

Yellow Sea

SOUTH KOREA

Point of Farthest North Korean Advance, 1950

JAPAN

75   150 Miles

150 Kilometers

[Ko]rea remained divided after the Korean War.

[MA]P SKILL Use Latitude and Longitude
[What] was the latitude line that divided Korea?

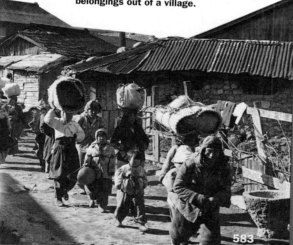

▶ Korean refugees transport their belongings out of a village.

583

SOCIAL STUDIES
Background

[Mo]re About Douglas MacArthur

[A]t age 50 Douglas MacArthur was [t]he youngest chief of staff.

[J]apanese forces surrendered to [M]acArthur to end World War II.

[A]fter MacArthur was fired by [P]resident Truman, ending his long [m]ilitary career, he delivered a [s]peech to Congress in which he [u]ttered the famous line, "Old [s]oldiers never die, they just [fa]de away."

FAST FACTS

Lesson 3 describes some world events during the 1950s. Other facts that reflect the time include:

- "I Love Lucy" and "The $64,000 Question" were two of the most popular TV shows.

- Important "firsts" include: business computers, a polio vaccine, open-heart surgery, and atomic-powered submarines.

2 Teach and Discuss

PAGE 583

The Korean War

Quick Summary When communist North Korea invaded noncommunist South Korea, the United States provided troops for a UN operation to stop the invasion.

1 How was Korea similar to postwar Germany? Just as Germany had been divided into East Germany and West Germany, Korea had been divided into North Korea and South Korea. In both cases, one nation was ruled by communists and the other was ruled by noncommunists. **Compare and Contrast**

2 Why do you think the United States joined the war in Korea? Possible answers: Because of the Cold War, the United States was determined to help those who were fighting against communism and against forces aligned with the Soviet Union. President Truman was enacting his policy of containment.
Cause and Effect

3 Compare and contrast President Truman's and Douglas MacArthur's ideas about fighting the war. President Truman wanted to fight a limited war; MacArthur wanted to extend the war into China to complete the victory.
Compare and Contrast

MAP SKILL
Korea, 1953

If necessary, review the concepts of latitude and longitude.

4 Describe the area of South Korea that had not been invaded by North Korea in 1950. Possible answer: Only a small area in the southeastern part of the country had not been invaded.
Interpret Maps

MAP SKILL Answer 38° N

✓ **REVIEW ANSWER** North Korea invaded South Korea on June 25, 1950.
Cause and Effect

The Vietnam War

Quick Summary When Ho Chi Minh and the Viet Cong decided to bring communist rule to South Vietnam, the United States entered into the conflict.

Test Talk

Use Information from the Text

5 **What happened just before Vietnam was split into two separate countries?** Students should look back at the text to make sure they have the right answer. Vietnam had been part of Indochina, a French colony. In 1954 the French lost the colony in a war against the Vietnamese. A peace conference divided the nation in two parts. **Sequence**

6 **Why do you think many Americans opposed the war in Vietnam?** Possible answers: Americans did not think that communism posed an immediate threat; Americans feared the death and injury of their troops; Americans opposed intervention in an internal, civil war. **Express Ideas**

Literature and Social Studies

Tell students that *The Clay Marble* (Sunburst, 1993) is the story of a Cambodian family forced by war to leave their home. After her father is executed, 12-year-old Dara and her family arrive at a refugee camp. Dara is later separated from her mother.

7 **What does this passage reveal about the reality of war for children?** Possible answer: Wars may be fought over large issues, but innocent people may get caught in the middle. **Make Inferences**

The Vietnam War

The Korean War forced U.S. leaders to focus on the spread of communism in Asia. The war also showed that China was willing to fight for its communist neighbors.

A country just south of China—Vietnam—seemed to have much in common with Korea. Before 1954 Vietnam had been part of **Indochina,** a French colony. In 1954 the French lost this colony in a war against the Vietnamese people. A peace conference split Vietnam into two countries: a communist **North Vietnam** and **5** a non-communist **South Vietnam.**

Unlike Korea, North Vietnam had a group of communist **guerrillas,** or hit-and-run fighters. The guerrillas were called the **Viet Cong** and they lived and fought mostly in South Vietnam. The Viet Cong and the North Vietnamese leader, **Ho Chi Minh** (HOH CHEE MIN), were determined to bring communist rule to the south.

▶ An American soldier helps an elderly Vietna[m] woman during the Vietnam War.

U.S. President Dwight D. Eisenhower pro[mised] to help South Vietnam fight against commu[nism]. The president sent military advisers to buil[d] South Vietnam's army and air force. In the e[arly] 1960s, President **John F. Kennedy** continue[d] policy and increased the number of advisers.

Meanwhile, South Vietnam's government w[as] losing control of the country to the Viet Cong.

1964 President **Lyndon Johr** decided to commit the Unite[d] States on a larger scale. He [acted] to prevent a communist take[over] of South Vietnam.

In early 1965 the U.S. Ai[r] Force began bombing North Vietnam. At the same time, United States sent thousan[ds of] ground troops to help the S[outh] Vietnamese army.

Still, the war with the com[mu]nists continued. The United [States] sent more and more troops. [By] 1966 there were 270,000 U[.S.] troops and by 1967, half a m[illion]. The Viet Cong and the North Vietnamese fought on.

As U.S. involvement dee[pened,] more and more Americans [fought] and died in Vietnam. Oppos[ition] to the war began to surface [in] the United States.

Literature and Social Studies

7 **The Clay Marble**

Minfong Ho wrote about the terrible suffering of Cambodian children in the 1970s in *The Clay Marble*. Cambodia is a country in Southeast Asia. It is next to Vietnam. Fighting in the Vietnam War stretched into Cambodia. In this passage, a little girl wonders where her mother is after they have been forced to separate.

If only I could climb up this tree to the moon, I thought, drowsily, and curl up against its smooth curve, how comfortable I'd be tonight. Or I could hang on to it as it swept across the night sky, and search down far below for my mother.

Practice and Extend

MEETING INDIVIDUAL NEEDS
Learning Styles

Report on Events Using their individual learning styles, students report on events that led up to and took place during the Vietnam War.

Visual/Logical Learning Have students make illustrated time lines to show the major events of the Vietnam War. They can use the dates listed on this pa[ge].

Verbal Learning Students may wish to report orally on the events leading up [to] the Vietnam War. Encourage them to use sequence words (e.g., *first, then, nex[t,] finally*) in their oral presentations to keep the facts organized.

Individual Learning Allow students to work on their own to devise ways to report on what they have learned. Encourage them to develop plans for your approval before they begin working.

President Johnson explained that the United
[St]ates had to fight in Vietnam because of the
[do]mino effect. When dominoes are lined up and
[on]e domino falls, it knocks over the next domino,
[wh]ich knocks over the domino next to it. This
[co]ntinues until all the dominoes have fallen.
[Pre]sident Johnson believed that if one country
[in] Southeast Asia fell to communism, soon all
[t]he countries in that region would fall.

[B]y 1967 protests against U.S. involvement in
[the] Vietnam War heated up all over the United
[Sta]tes. In October a demonstration against the
[war] brought 50,000 protesters to Washington,
[D.C]. Antiwar protest activity became widespread
[on] college campuses.

[T]elevision brought the Vietnam War into
[peo]ple's living rooms. Many Americans opposed
[the] U.S. bombing of North Vietnam. President

▶ This early protest against
the Vietnam War took
place in November 1965.

Johnson hoped the bombing would convince
North Vietnam to talk about peace.

REVIEW What was the domino effect, and why
was it used to explain U.S. involvement in
Vietnam? **Main Idea and Details**

Point out that the Vietnam War was
the first war to be widely covered by
television. Previous wars had been
covered only by newspapers, radio,
newsreels, and so on.

8 **How do you think that television
was able to shape people's opinions of
the Vietnam War?** Possible answer:
People could see the effects of war
on the civilian population and on the
troops. People felt better able to form
opinions because they were getting so
much news about the war.
Cause and Effect

War in Algeria

At the same time that the United States
was getting involved with Vietnam,
[Fran]ce was losing its hold on Algeria. Like Vietnam,
[Alg]eria had been a French colony since the 1880s.
[Alge]rians formed an armed group to resist the French
[in 19]54. This group carried out attacks on French
[colo]nists. The French responded by sending more
[troo]ps. By 1959 the French president stated that
[Alge]rians should be given the right to decide their
[own] future. Peace talks began in 1961. Algeria won
[its in]dependence in 1962.

[The]se Algerian troops fought for independence
[fr]om the French.

REFÉRENDUM D'AUTODÉTERMINATION
DU 1ᵉ JUILLET 1962

▶ This ballot was used
by Algerians to vote
whether or not Algeria
should become an
independent nation.

REFÉRENDUM D'AUTODÉTERMINATION
DU 1ᵉ JUILLET 1962

NON ✓

585

War in Algeria

Before students read, set a purpose for
them. Ask them to think about the
similarities and differences between
Algeria and Vietnam.

9 **Compare and contrast the situations
of Algeria and Vietnam.** Both countries
were French colonies that resisted French
forces to gain independence. Both were
given their independence, but Algeria
was not divided into two sections as
Vietnam was. **Compare and Contrast**

✓ **REVIEW ANSWER** It was the idea
that if one country in a region became
communist, the other countries in that
region would soon become communist.
It was used to explain U.S. involvement
in Vietnam as opposition to the war
began to increase. **Main Idea and Details**

MEETING INDIVIDUAL NEEDS
Leveled Practice

[Co]mpare and Contrast the Korean and Vietnam Wars Students can work
[inde]pendently or in small groups to compare and contrast the two wars.

[Easy] Write facts about the two wars on index cards. Give the cards to students,
[and] have them tack the cards on a bulletin board under the titles *Korean War,*
[Viet]nam War, or *Both Wars.* **Reteach**

[On-L]evel Students can create Venn diagrams to compare and contrast the two
[war]s. They should focus on the ideals and goals involved, the amount of U.S.
[invol]vement, and so on. **Extend**

[Cha]llenge Have students list facts about the Korean War and the Vietnam War.
[Stud]ents can then draw storyboards for a documentary video about one or both
[wars]. **Enrich**

▶ *Lesson Summary, use Quick Study, p. 140.*

The War's Final Chapter

Quick Summary President Nixon enacted his plan of Vietnamization and eventually worked out a peace plan with North Vietnam. Two years later communist troops took over South Vietnam.

10 **Explain Richard Nixon's policy of Vietnamization.** South Vietnamese troops would take over the majority of the ground fighting. As a result, the number of American troops in the war decreased after 1969.
Main Idea and Details

The Tet Offensive, 1968

Call students' attention to the inset map of Southeast Asia.

11 **During the Tet Offensive, the Viet Cong traveled through two countries other than South Vietnam. What were they?** Laos and Cambodia **Interpret Maps**

12 **Why do you think the major part of the Tet Offensive was outside Vietnam?** Possible answer: Because the Viet Cong would run into fewer South Vietnamese soldiers or American troops **Hypothesize**

MAP SKILL **Answer** South and east

13 **Why did many Americans feel that involvement in the war had been pointless?** Many Americans had died, the communists had achieved their aims despite the war, and the domino effect did not happen. **Summarize**

Primary Source

Cited in the *Oxford Dictionary of Quotations,* edited by Angela Partington

14 **How do Robert MacNamara's words reflect the feelings of many Americans?** Many Americans had been protesting U.S. involvement in the war for many years before it finally ended. Communist forces had achieved their aims, making the war seem futile. **Analyze Primary Sources**

586 Unit 7 • A World in Opposition

The War's Final Chapter

In 1968 the Viet Cong and North Vietnamese launched the **Tet Offensive.** This series of battles across South Vietnam showed that the North Vietnamese were a stronger opponent than the Americans had realized. His popularity damaged, President Johnson decided not to run for reelection. Richard Nixon became president in 1969. He had a plan to reduce the U.S. role in the Vietnam War. His plan was called
10 **Vietnamization,** which turned over most of the ground fighting to the South Vietnamese Army. The number of American troops in the war dropped after 1969. The United States and North Vietnam were now conducting peace talks.

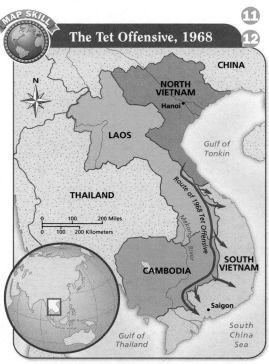

The Tet Offensive, 1968 **11** **12**

CHINA

NORTH VIETNAM
Hanoi

LAOS

Gulf of Tonkin

THAILAND

Route of 1968 Tet Offensive

0   100   200 Miles
0   100   200 Kilometers

Mekong River

SOUTH VIETNAM

CAMBODIA

Saigon

Gulf of Thailand

South China Sea

▶ The Tet Offensive was a turning point in the Vietnam War.

MAP SKILL Trace Movement on Maps
In which direction did the North Vietnamese move during the Tet Offensive?

586

However, the United States continued to bo North Vietnam heavily. The United States a extended the fighting into **Cambodia,** Sout Vietnam's neighbor.

The protests in the United States continu In May 1970, a demonstration at Kent Stat University in Ohio turned tragic. National Gu troops sent there to stop the protests fired students and killed four of them. That May, lege campuses exploded in protest.

By 1972 the number of American ground troops fell to about 70,000. However, the U States continued to bomb North Vietnam, Cambodia, and **Laos** from the air. In Decen 1972 the United States launched the Chris bombing of **Hanoi** and other cities in Vietn Many parts of Hanoi, including the airport, destroyed.

The bombings in December would be the major U.S. military action in Vietnam. One later, in January 1973, President Nixon and chief adviser, Henry Kissinger, worked out a armistice with North Vietnam. For the Unite States, the war was over, although the last troops did not leave until 1975. In Vietnam however, it continued until April 1975. In th month, communist troops took over South Vi

Some Americans felt that sacrifices in th Vietnam War had been pointless. Even with involvement, the communists had achieved aims in Vietnam. In addition, the domino ef proved false because most of the countries Southeast Asia remained non-communist. More than 58,000 Americans lost their live the war. Nearly 3.5 million Vietnamese had in 20 years of war.

Robert MacNamara, President Johnson' secretary of defense, later expressed his re about the Vietnam War:

> *"We . . . acted according to wh we thought were the principle . . . of this nation. We were wrong. We were terribly wron*

Practice and Extend

MEETING INDIVIDUAL NEEDS
Leveled Practice

Give a Speech Have students create persuasive speeches based on what th learned in Lesson 3.

Easy Ask students to decide whether they would have supported U.S. involvement in Vietnam. They can list three reasons that support their viewpoi and read their lists aloud to classmates. **Reteach**

On-Level Invite students to role-play one of the people in this lesson, such as President Truman, President Nixon, or a protesting student, and deliver a spee explaining his or her viewpoint on the Vietnam War. **Extend**

Challenge Challenge students to create a debate or panel discussion to pres several viewpoints about the issue of U.S. involvement in the Vietnam War. As them to use factual sources as the basis for their arguments. **Enrich**
For a Lesson Summary, use Quick Study, p. 140.

As U.S. involvement in the Vietnam War wound down, foreign relations were changing with other communist nations. Nixon and Kissinger started a period of **détente,** (day TAHNT) or the relaxation of tensions, with the Soviet Union and China. However, while relations improved, the nuclear arms race—and the Cold War—continued.

LESSON 3 REVIEW

Check Facts and Main Ideas

1. 🔄 **Cause and Effect** On a separate piece of paper, fill in the chart below by listing a cause or effect.

Causes		Effects
The Communists took control of North Korea.	→	UN troops were sent to Korea.
UN troops on the Chinese border		China sent an army into North Korea.
South Vietnam's government was losing control of the country to the Viet Cong.		President Johnson's decision not to run in 1968

2. How did President Eisenhower help the government of South Vietnam fight against the Communists?

3. How did U.S. involvement in the war change under President Nixon?

4. How were the wars in Korea and Vietnam different from other disagreements with communist countries during the Cold War?

5. **Critical Thinking: Make Inferences** What events in other parts of the world would have convinced people that the domino effect would occur if Vietnam became a communist country?

Link to ◦—◦ **Writing**

Write a Letter to the Editor Suppose the year is 1967. Your city's newspaper has just printed an editorial supporting President Johnson's policy in the Vietnam War. Decide whether you support or oppose the war. Write a letter to the editor explaining your opinion for or against the war.

REVIEW Do you think that the United States should or should not have become involved in the Vietnam War? Explain your answer. **Draw Conclusions**

Summarize the Lesson

- **1950** The Korean War began when North Korea invaded South Korea.
- **1953** An armistice ended the fighting in Korea.
- **1965** The United States sent troops to help South Vietnam fight against the communists.
- **1975** North Vietnam took over South Vietnam.

▶ **A U.S. government official greets former prisoners-of-war shortly after their release in February 1973.**

587

---

15 Why do you think the Cold War continued even during détente?
Possible answer: Building trust between countries would take time. **Evaluate**

✓ **REVIEW ANSWER** Possible answers: Yes, the United States was acting on its promises to contain communism. No, the United States should not have become involved in an internal civil war. **Draw Conclusions**

3 Close and Assess

Summarize the Lesson

Write on index cards important terms, people, and places from Lesson 3, one per card. Have pairs of students write a definition or example for one card and then share it with the class.

✓ **LESSON 3 REVIEW**

1. 🔄 **Cause and Effect** For possible answers, see the reduced pupil page.

2. He sent military advisors to build up the South Vietnamese military.

3. Eliminated the ground war but continued the air war

4. In Korea and Vietnam, outside countries became involved and were major players in the wars.

5. **Critical Thinking: Make Inferences** Russia became the communist Soviet Union; China, which shares a border with the Soviet Union, then became communist. Korea, which shares a border with China, then split in two, with the northern half becoming communist. Then Vietnam, which also shares a border with China, became partly communist.

Link to ◦—◦ **Writing**

Students' letters should clearly state a viewpoint and support their viewpoint with persuasive facts.

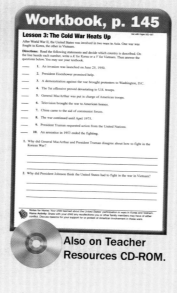

Workbook, p. 145

Lesson 3: The Cold War Heats Up

After World War II, the United States was involved in two wars in Asia. One war was fought in Korea, the other in Vietnam.

Directions: Read the following statements and decide which country is described. On the line beside each number, write a *K* for Korea or a *V* for Vietnam. Then answer the questions below. You may use your textbook.

_____ 1. An invasion was launched on June 25, 1950.
_____ 2. President Eisenhower promised help.
_____ 3. A demonstration against the war brought protesters to Washington, D.C.
_____ 4. The Tet offensive proved devastating to U.S. troops.
_____ 5. General MacArthur was put in charge of American troops.
_____ 6. Television brought the war to American homes.
_____ 7. China came to the aid of communist forces.
_____ 8. The war continued until April 1975.
_____ 9. President Truman requested action from the United Nations.
_____ 10. An armistice in 1953 ended the fighting.

1. Why did General MacArthur and President Truman disagree about how to fight in the Korean War?

2. Why did President Johnson think the United States had to fight in the war in Vietnam?

Also on Teacher Resources CD-ROM.

The Public Speaks Out

Objective
- Examine U.S. public attitudes toward involvement in the Vietnam War.

1 Introduce and Motivate

Preview To activate prior knowledge, ask students what they already know about protests against the Vietnam War. Ask them to describe other situations in which the public has protested an action of the U.S. government.

To introduce the issue of differing viewpoints on the Vietnam War, remind students that Americans were able to receive news and pictures by watching television, so viewers may have felt well-informed about the war in Vietnam.

2 Teach and Discuss

1 What were the reasons behind the moratorium held on October 15, 1969? To send a strong message; to show that many people did not support U.S. involvement in the Vietnam War; to demonstrate "strength in numbers"
Main Idea and Details

2 Why do you think some people supported U.S. involvement in Vietnam? Some people believed strongly in the threat of communism and the domino effect. Others believed that the United States was right to assist people whose freedom was at stake.
Point of View

3 Why might Martin Luther King, Jr., have believed that involvement in Vietnam was an enemy of the poor? The financial resources of the United States could have been spent on helping poor people. Instead much money was spent on arming and training troops and sending them to South Vietnam.
Evaluate

Issues and Viewpoints

The Public Speaks Out

U.S. involvement in the Vietnam War divided the nation. It split the nation like no other issue since the Civil War, some 100 years earlier.

By 1967 public opinion was split over the war in Vietnam. Though many Americans still supported the war, protests against the war were increasing. Some demonstrations were peaceful. However, clashes between people of opposing views could be intense. As a result, the demonstrations sometimes grew violent. Many supporters of the war believed that some demonstrators were provoking the police and pro-war demonstrators on purpose.

On October 15, 1969, the largest antiwar protest in U.S. history took place. Millions of Americans skipped work or school to attend marches, demonstrations, religious services, and rallies. In Boston more than 100,000 people listened to speeches against the war. This protest was called the "Moratorium [strike] to End the War in Vietnam." Its goal was to send a strong message to President Richard Nixon. The protest suggested that a large number of ordinary American citizens wanted U.S. troops out of Vietnam.

However, for many Americans, supporting the war was a way of showing support for their country and for the American soldiers already in Vietnam.

"Then came the buildup in Vietnam and I watched the [poverty] program broken . . . and I knew that America would never invest the necessary funds or energies in . . . its poor . . . So I was increasingly compelled to see the war as an enemy of the poor and to attack it as such."
Martin Luther King, Jr., *civil rights activist, 1967*

588

Practice and Extend

 CURRICULUM CONNECTION
Literature

Both Sides of the Vietnam War Use the following selections to extend students' understanding of the Vietnam War from the perspectives of Americans and Vietnamese.

Sweet Dried Apples: A Vietnamese Wartime Childhood, by Rosemary Breckler and Deborah Kogan Ray (Houghton Mifflin, ISBN 0-395-73570-X, 1996) **Easy**

Sing for Your Father, Su Phan, by Stella Pevsner and Fay Tang (Clarion Books, ISBN 0-395-82267-X, 1997) **On-Level**

The Valiant Women of the Vietnam War, by Karen Zeinert (Millbrook Press, ISBN 0-761-31268-4, 2000) **On-Level**

The Vietnam War: What Are We Fighting For? by Deborah Kent (Enslow Publishers, ISBN 0-766-601731-1, 2000) **Challenge**

> "China looms [appears] so high just beyond the frontiers that if South Vietnam went, it would . . . give the impression that the wave of the future in Southeast Asia was China and the Communists."

John F. Kennedy, *U.S. President, 1963*

> "This war has already stretched the generation gap so wide that it threatens to pull the country apart."

Frank Church, *U.S. senator, 1970*

> ". . . North Vietnam is carrying out . . . aggression against the South . . . The people of South Vietnam have chosen to resist this threat. At their request, the United States has taken its place beside them in their defensive struggle."

Aggression from the North,
State Department White Paper on Vietnam, 1965

Issues and You

Some Americans were against the idea of U.S. involvement in the Persian Gulf War of 1990–1991. Do some research to find out about the issues at stake and the reasons some Americans were against the use of force against Iraq. Write an essay to compare and contrast protests against the Gulf War with those against the Vietnam War.

589

4 **What does President John F. Kennedy's quotation say about the relationship between the United States and China?** President Kennedy saw China as a threat. A battle against North Vietnam was also a fight against Chinese aggression.
Analyze Primary Sources

5 **What is the "generation gap"? Why do you think the Vietnam War could have widened the generation gap?** Possible answer: The generation gap is the difference in outlook between people of different ages. The gap may have been increased by perceptions of U.S. involvement in the Vietnam War. People of different age groups may have had different feelings about the war.
Cause and Effect

6 **Compare and contrast the viewpoints expressed in two of the quotations on these pages.** Possible answer: Both President Kennedy and Dr. Martin Luther King, Jr., were worried. Kennedy saw communism in South Vietnam as a threat to all of Asia, and King saw the Vietnam War as a threat to the poor because it required federal money needed for the poverty program.
Point of View

3 Close and Assess

Issues and You

- Encourage students to write questions to guide their research. They might record their ideas in K-W-L charts before they begin working.

- Students should use at least three reference sources as they work. You might provide sources in various media, such as books, videotapes, CD-ROMs, and appropriate Internet sites.

- If students want to share their work in alternate forms, they might create Venn diagrams, draw posters that describe the various protests, assemble and display copies of news articles about protests on a bulletin board, and so on.

CURRICULUM CONNECTION
Art

eate Posters

Have students create posters advertising the "Moratorium Strike to End the War." They should include facts about why the protesters are gathering and use persuasive words that would entice people to attend.

Students could create posters supporting the war. These posters could state reasons people should support U.S. involvement n Vietnam. Invite students to display their work.

WEB SITE
Technology

You can learn more about the people discussed on these pages by clicking on *Meet the People* at **www.sfsocialstudies.com.**

CHAPTER 20 REVIEW

Resources

- Assessment Book, pp. 101–104
- Workbook, p. 146: Vocabulary Review

Chapter Summary

For possible answers, see the reduced pupil page.

Vocabulary

1. c, **2.** d, **3.** b, **4.** e, **5.** a

People and Terms

Possible answers:

1. John F. Kennedy was the U.S. President who successfully responded to the Cuban missile crisis.

2. The Cold War was the post-World War II period of tension between the United States and the Soviet Union that affected the entire world.

3. NATO, North Atlantic Treaty Organization, was a group of nations defending one another against Soviet aggression.

4. Nikita Khrushchev was the Soviet leader who in 1962 instigated the Cuban missile crisis.

5. Chiang Kai-shek was the leader of the Nationalist Party in China. The nationalists fled to Taiwan when the communists took over in 1949.

6. Mao Zedong became the leader of the Communist party in China and led the Cultural Revolution.

7. The People's Republic of China was the nation set up after the communist takeover of China in 1949.

8. Ho Chi Minh was the leader of North Vietnam and the Viet Cong.

9. The Viet Cong was a group of guerrillas who were determined to bring communist rule to South Vietnam.

10. President Nixon enacted the policy of Vietnamization to withdraw U.S. ground troops from Vietnam.

590 Unit 7 • A World in Opposition

CHAPTER 20 REVIEW

1950 — 1955

1949 NATO formed.

1950–1953 Korean War

1948–1949 Berlin airlift

Chapter Summary

Cause and Effect

On a separate piece of paper, fill in three effects of communist aggression during the Cold War.

Cause

Communist aggression during the Cold War

Trade and trave stopped in the Soviet Union.

China became divided countr

War broke out Korea and Vie

Vocabulary

Match each word with the correct definition or description.

1. containment (p. 570)
2. nuclear (p. 569)
3. détente (p. 587)
4. proletarian (p. 579)
5. guerrillas (p. 584)

a. loosely organized fighters
b. relaxation of tensions
c. preventing the spread of communism
d. atomic
e. of the working class

People and Terms

Write a sentence explaining why each of following people or terms was important events of the Cold War. You may use two more in a single sentence.

1. John F. Kennedy (p. 572)
2. Cold War (p. 569)
3. NATO (p. 570)
4. Nikita Khrushchev (p. 572)
5. Chiang Kai-shek (p. 577)
6. Mao Zedo (p. 577)
7. People's of China
8. Ho Chi M (p. 584)
9. Viet Cong (p. 584)
10. Vietnami (p. 586)

590

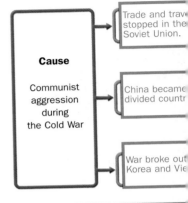

Practice and Extend

Assessment Options

✓ **Chapter 20 Assessment**
- Chapter 20 Content Test: Use Assessment Book, pp. 101–102.
- Chapter 20 Skills Test: Use Assessment Book, pp. 103–104.

TEST PREP Standardized Test Prep
- Chapter 20 Tests contain standardized test format.

✓ **Chapter 20 Performance Assessmer**
- Challenge students to assume the identit one of the U.S. presidents discussed in Chapter 20.
- Students can explain a major policy or decision. For example, students may cho to explain the Cuban Doctrine, Vietnamization, or the steps taken to res the Cuban missile crisis.
- Assess students' understanding of the events surrounding the policy or decisior

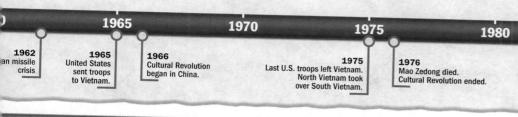

| 1962 an missile crisis | 1965 United States sent troops to Vietnam. | 1966 Cultural Revolution began in China. | 1975 Last U.S. troops left Vietnam. North Vietnam took over South Vietnam. | 1976 Mao Zedong died. Cultural Revolution ended. |

Facts and Main Ideas

What happened to the World War II alliance of the Soviet Union, Great Britain, and the United States?

Name two political changes in the world between 1945 and 1950.

What U.S. president expanded military support for South Vietnam?

Time Line How long were U.S. troops in Vietnam?

Main Idea What were the two main sides in the Cold War?

Main Idea What were the two groups that fought for power during the civil war in China in the late 1940s?

Main Idea What were two "hot wars" during the Cold War?

Critical Thinking: *Make Inferences* Why do you think the Soviets were so eager to drive the Allies out of Berlin?

Apply Skills

Solve Complex Problems

Consider the following situation. Think how you might use the strategies presented on pages 574–575 of this chapter to find a solution. Then answer the questions.

You have just lost your backpack at school. You notice that one of your classmates has a backpack identical to the one you lost. When you ask him about the backpack, he says it was a gift from a relative.

1 Should you tell your teacher about the backpack? Why or why not?

2 What might be some consequences of confronting your classmate?

3 Can you think of some creative solutions other than (1) telling your teacher, or (2) confronting your classmate?

Write About History

Write a **journal entry** as someone who lives in the American zone of Berlin during the Berlin airlift. Write an entry describing the frequent arrival of airplanes bringing in supplies. Describe your feelings.

Write a **television news report** informing U.S. citizens about the Cuban missile crisis right after the crisis has ended.

Write a **paragraph** describing relations between South Korea and North Korea in the years since the end of the Korean War. You will need to research this topic before you write your paragraph.

Internet Activity

To get help with vocabulary, people, and terms, select dictionary, encyclopedia, or almanac from *Social Studies Library* at **www.sfsocialstudies.com.**

591

Hands-on Unit Project

Unit 7 Performance Assessment

See p. 596 for information about using the Unit Project as a means of performance assessment. A scoring guide is provided on p. 596.

WEB SITE Technology

more information, students can select the onary, encyclopedia, or almanac from *Social ies Library* at **www.sfsocialstudies.com.**

Workbook, p. 146

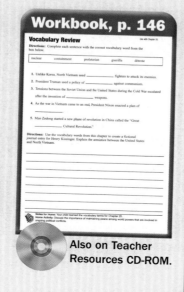

Vocabulary Review

Also on Teacher Resources CD-ROM.

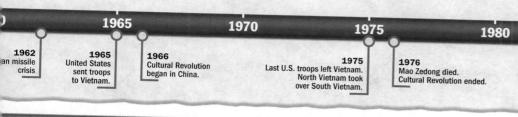

Facts and Main Ideas

1. Great Britain and the United States remained allies, but their relationship with the Soviet Union turned sour when the Soviet Union invaded several Eastern European countries and blockaded Western zones of occupation in Berlin.

2. Possible answer: Many Eastern European countries were taken over by communism. The Communists took over China.

3. President John F. Kennedy

4. Ten years

5. The United States and the Soviet Union

6. The Communist Party and the Nationalist Party

7. Korean War; Vietnam War

8. Possible answer: They wanted to take control of the entire city and that zone of Germany. They wanted to prevent Allied forces from entering their zone of occupation.

Write About History

1. Students should include facts surrounding the Berlin airlift and describe their feelings, which may include anger, relief, or happiness.

2. Students' reports should include facts about the events of the crisis. Reports might also feature background information about the Cold War and analysis of the way the situation was handled.

3. Help students find books and Internet sites that provide information about the relations between these two countries since 1953.

Apply Skills

1. Students will most likely say no, that they should take time to consider their options and "cool off."

2. Students may say that they could lose a good friend; they might examine the backpack and find that it is not theirs; or the classmate may admit that the backpack was stolen.

3. Accept reasonable answers. Help students explore the strengths and weaknesses of suggested solutions.

Over There

Objective

- Identify significant examples of music from various periods in U.S. history.

1 Introduce and Motivate

Preview To activate prior knowledge, ask students if they have heard the song "Over There" and if they know any of the history behind the song.

Ask students if they know what is meant by the word *Yank* in the third line of the song. (*Yank* is short for *Yankee*, a word that means "native or inhabitant of the United States.")

2 Teach and Discuss

1 What mood is expressed by this song? This song is optimistic. It shows patriotism and expresses confidence that the Americans can get the job done in the war. **Point of View**

UNIT
7
End with a Song

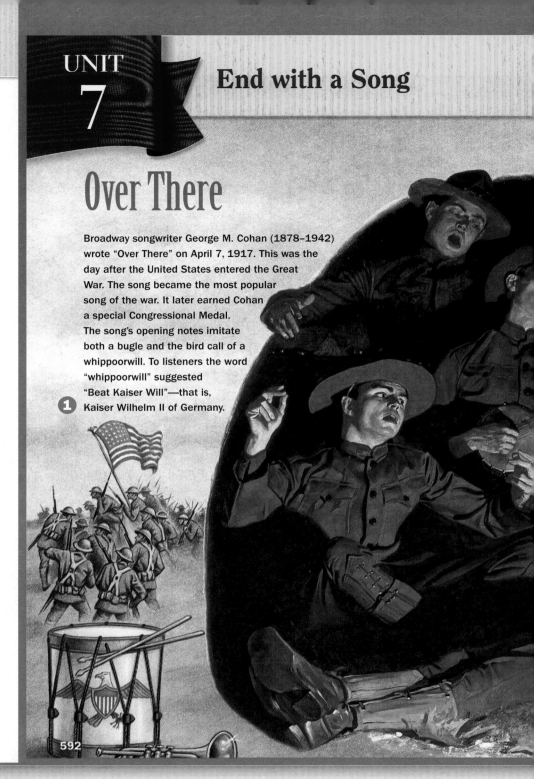

Over There

Broadway songwriter George M. Cohan (1878–1942) wrote "Over There" on April 7, 1917. This was the day after the United States entered the Great War. The song became the most popular song of the war. It later earned Cohan a special Congressional Medal. The song's opening notes imitate both a bugle and the bird call of a whippoorwill. To listeners the word "whippoorwill" suggested "Beat Kaiser Will"—that is, **1** Kaiser Wilhelm II of Germany.

592

Practice and Extend

 **SOCIAL STUDIES Background**

More About Yankee

- The term *Yankee* did not always have a positive connotation. By 1775 the British called the colonists "Yankees" to make fun of them. During the U.S. Civil War, southerners used the term *Yankee* in a harsh way to describe northerners. When U.S. troops landed in Europe during World War I, newspapers saluted them as *Yankees*.

- George M. Cohan (1878–1942) was a playwright, composer, producer, and actor. In his first successful musical, *Little Johnny Jones*, he played Yankee Doodle Boy. The role was associated with him for the rest of his career.

- Besides "Over There," Cohan wrote other popular songs, including "I'm a Yankee Doodle Boy," "You're a Grand Old Flag," and "Give My Regards to Broadway."

 **AUDIO CD Technology**

Play the *Songs and Music* CD to listen to "Over There."

Words and Music by George M. Cohan

O - ver there, o - ver there,

Send the word, send the word o - ver there

That the Yanks are com-ing, the Yanks are com-ing, The

drums rum tum - ming ev - 'ry - where.

So pre - pare, say a pray'r,

Send the word, send the word to be - ware

We'll be o - ver, we're com-ing o - ver, And we

won't come back 'till it's o - ver o - ver there.

593

---

2 **How do you think American soldiers felt when they heard this song? How do you think people who were counting on help from the United States might have felt?** Possible answers: American soldiers may have gained confidence and felt a sense of pride in the United States and what it was trying to do. Others may have felt that same optimism and been thankful for the involvement of forces that wanted to help.

Cause and Effect

3 Close and Assess

- Encourage students to sing this song. Students may want to play instruments to accompany the class.

- Ask students why they think this song became so popular during World War I. Point out that George M. Cohan won a medal of honor for writing the song. Why would a song such as this earn an award? What can students conclude about the importance of the song in the war effort?

Resource

- Assessment Book, pp. 105–108

Main Ideas and Vocabulary TEST PREP

1. c, **2.** d, **3.** a, **4.** c

Test Talk

Choose the Right Answer
Use Main Ideas and Vocabulary, question 3, to model the Test Talk strategy.

Narrow the answer choices.
Tell students to read each answer choice carefully. Students should rule out any choice that they know is wrong.

Choose the best answer.
After students make their answer choice, tell them to check their answer by comparing it with the text.

People and Terms

1. f, **2.** c, **3.** a, **4.** e, **5.** d, **6.** b

Apply Skills

- Have students use reference sources to find dates of important events.

- Be sure that events on the time lines are placed in chronological order.

UNIT 7 Review

Test Talk
Narrow the answer choices. Rule out answers you know are wrong.

Main Ideas and Vocabulary TEST P

Read the passage below and use it to answer the questions that follow.

The twentieth century was a time of warfare. Imperialism, nationalism, and other forms of competition pushed European nations toward war. When the archduke of Austria-Hungary was assassinated in 1914, countries started mobilizing for war.

People expected the war to end quickly, but it did not. People called it the "Great War." <u>Casualties</u> were enormous. After the war, the Allies tried to make a peace that would prevent future wars. But they treated Germany harshly. Germany was told it would have to pay for the Allied war losses.

A new form of government appeared in Russia during the Great War. It was a communist government. In a communist system, everything is owned by the state. Under Lenin and Stalin, Russia became the Soviet Union.

Hard times from the Great Depression led to the rise of dictators in Germany and Italy. Military leaders took control of Japan. These three Axis Powers committed acts of <u>aggression</u>. These acts set the stage for World War II.

The Allies, led by the United States, Great Britain, and the Soviet Union, defeated the Axis Powers. After the war, they set up the United Nations to deal with future disagreements between countries.

The Soviet dictator, Stalin, wanted to spread communism worldwide. Mao Zedong led another communist country, China, after 1949.

Now the world experienced another kind of war. It was a cold war between communist and non-communist countries. This was mostly words and threats. However, "hot" wars flared in Korea and Vietnam during the Cold War.

1 According to the passage, what new kind of government played a major part in the politics of the twentieth century?
- **A** republic
- **B** royal
- **C** communist
- **D** council

2 In the passage the word *casualties* means—
- **A** easygoing manners
- **B** kindnesses
- **C** false remarks
- **D** killed or wounded soldiers

3 In the passage the word *aggression* means—
- **A** forceful taking
- **B** concealment
- **C** generosity
- **D** going backwa

4 What is the main idea of this passa
- **A** The Great War was brutal.
- **B** The United States has become ve powerful.
- **C** The twentieth century was a time warfare.
- **D** Russia had a revolution.

594

Practice and Extend

Assessment Options

✔ **Unit 7 Assessment**
- Unit 7 Content Test: Use Assessment Book, pp. 105–106.
- Unit 7 Skills Test: Use Assessment Book, pp. 107–108.

 Standardized Test Prep
- Unit 7 Tests contain standardized test format.

✔ **Unit 7 Performance Assessment**
- See p. 596 for information about using the Unit Project as a means of Performance Assessment.
- A scoring guide for the Unit Project is provided in the teacher's notes on p. 596.

Test Talk
- Test Talk Practice Book

WEB SITE Technology
For more information, you can select the dictionary, encyclopedia, or almanac from *Social Studies Library* at **www.sfsocialstudies.com**.

People and Terms

[Matc]h each person or term to its definition.

[Triple] Entente
(p. 522)

[N]icholas II
[(]p. 522)

[G]eorges
[C]lemenceau
[(]p. 536)

[C]entral Powers
[(]p. 527)

[O]veta Culp Hobby
[(]p. 552)

[N]ationalist Party
[(]p. 577)

a. French leader during the Great War

b. group that removed the emperor and founded republic in China

c. ruler of Russia until 1917

d. head of the Women's Army Corps

e. alliance of Germany and Austria

f. alliance of Great Britain, France, and Russia

Apply Skills

[P]arallel Time Lines Create a poster dis-
[playing] parallel time lines. Use events from your
[lif]e on one time line. Use public events on
[the oth]er time line. Public events might include
[nation]al events such as elections, weather
[event]s, or sports events.

[You ca]n use the
[ma]rks on the
[lin]e to repre-
[sent ye]ars, months,
[or week]s.

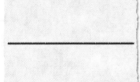

Write and Share

Honor Wartime Sacrifices The United States
honors the people who make sacrifices during
wartime. Many communities also have monuments and ceremonies to honor soldiers and
civilian workers who contributed in times of war.
Research ways in which your own community or
state honors veterans. Write a paper on the subject and present it to your class. After
presenting your paper, your class can break into
small groups. Each group can then propose its
own idea for a memorial or celebration in honor
of veterans.

Read on Your Own

Look for books like these in your library.

595

- Provide encyclopedias, nonfiction books, and access to the Internet for students to use in conducting their research.

- Encourage students to use an outline to organize the information for their papers.

- Encourage groups to write down their ideas and to create illustrations showing their memorial.

- Use the following scoring guide.

✓ **Assessment Scoring Guide**

Honor Wartime Sacrifices	
4	Writes a well-organized paper on a specific topic and includes several credible sources.
3	Writes a paper with relevant information and uses at least one credible source.
2	Writes a paper with general information and no credible sources.
1	Is unable to write an adequate paper.

Read on Your Own

Have students prepare oral reports using the following books.

Lost in the War, by Nancy Antle (Puffin, ISBN 0-141-30836-2, 2000) **Easy**

When the Soldiers Were Gone, by Vera W. Propp (Puffin, ISBN 0-698-11881-2, 2001) **On-Level**

Good Night, Maman, by Norma Fox Mazer and Jeannette Larson (Harcourt, Brace, ISBN 0-152-01468-3, 1999) **Challenge**

[R]evisit the Unit Question

[P]ortfolio Assessment

- [H]ave students look at the lists of [p]ossible causes for wars that they [c]reated at the beginning of the unit.

- [H]ave students look at the possible [c]auses for wars that they added to [t]heir lists as they read the unit.

- [A]sk students to compare and [c]ontrast their lists.

- Have students write a summary expressing how their own ideas about causes of wars may have changed.

- Have students add these lists and summaries to their Social Studies Portfolio.

We Interrupt This Program

Objective
- Describe a significant historic event.

Resource
- Workbook, p. 147

Materials
paper, pens, markers, poster board or large sheets of paper, poster paints

Follow This Procedure
- Tell students they will present a news conference about an important historic event in this unit.
- Discuss significant events in the unit to help groups choose topics. Encourage them to focus on particular aspects, such as a speech or battle within a war. Allow time for students to conduct research.
- Have students assign jobs such as news anchors and local citizens, government officials, and reporters.
- Have students create a banner for their news event. Encourage them to bring in props appropriate to the time period and event.
- Invite each group to present its news program to the class.

✓ Assessment Scoring Guide

We Interrupt This Program	
4	Describes a significant historic event using accurate content, elaborate details, and precise word choices in a creative presentation.
3	Describes a significant historic event using some accurate content, several details, and clear word choices in a somewhat creative presentation.
2	Describes an historic event using some inaccurate content, few details, and vague word choices in an ordinary presentation.
1	Describes an historic event using inaccurate content, no details, and incorrect word choices in an uncreative presentation.

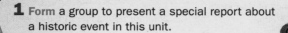
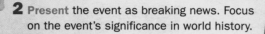

7 Projec

We Interrupt This Program

Participate in a "live" news conference from the past.

1 **Form** a group to present a special report about a historic event in this unit.

2 **Present** the event as breaking news. Focus on the event's significance in world history.

3 **Assign** jobs, including news anchors, government officials, reporters, and citizens.

4 **Write** a press release or a brief summary of the event and its significance.

5 **Create** a banner and bring in materials that help describe the event. You may choose to create a scenic background.

Internet Activity
Discover historic world events. Go to **www.sfsocialstudies.com/activities** and select your grade and unit.

596

Practice and Extend

Hands-on Unit Project

✓ Performance Assessment
- The Unit Project can also be used as a performance assessment activity.
- Use the scoring guide to assess each group's work.

WEB SITE Technology

Students can launch the Internet Activity by clicking on *Grade 6, Unit 7* at **www.sfsocialstudies.com/activities.**

Workbook, p. 1

7 Project We Interrupt This Program

Directions: In a group, present a news conference about a historic event in Unit

1. The historic event chosen: _____

2. Roles assigned for the news conference:
   _____ news anchor(s)
   _____ government official(s)

3. Press release (summary of the event):
   Who: _____
   What: _____
   Where: _____
   When: _____
   Why: _____
   How: _____

On a separate sheet of paper, write a summary of the event's importance in histo

✓ Checklist for Students
_____ We chose a historic event.
_____ We assigned roles for the news conference.
_____ We wrote a press release.
_____ We made a banner or brought materials to help describe the ev
_____ We presented our news conference to the class.

Also on Teach Resources CD

★ UNIT 8 ★

New Nations and a New Century

New Nations and a New Century

UNIT 8

Unit Planning Guide

Unit 8 • New Nations and a New Century

Begin with a Primary Source pp. 598–599

Meet the People pp. 600–601

 Reading Social Studies, Draw Conclusions pp. 602–603

Chapter Titles	Pacing	Main Ideas
Chapter 21 **New Nations** pp. 604–625 ✓ **Chapter 21 Review** pp. 626–627	6 days	• The end of colonialism brought an end to imperialism and European rule in Africa and Asia. • The end of European control and the creation of Israel change the Middle East. • Calls for greater freedom brought an end of communism in Eastern Europe.
Chapter 22 **Cooperation, Conflict, and Challenges** pp. 628–649 ✓ **Chapter 22 Review** pp. 650–651	6 days	• World and regional economies have become closely bound together. • Ethnic, political, and religious differences have led to violent conflicts around the world. • People around the world continue to stand up against terrorism and work toward peace.
Chapter 23 **Living in the 21st Century** pp. 652–671 ✓ **Chapter 23 Review** pp. 672–673	5 days	• Population growth and movement present challenges in today's world. • People are working together to repair damage to Earth's environment. • As energy sources become less plentiful, we look for new ways produce and conserve energy. • Technology gives us many benefits, but it cannot solve every human problem.

✓ **= Assessment Options**

End with a Poem pp. 674–675   ✓**Unit 8 Project** p. 678

✓**Unit 8 Review** pp. 676–677

Year after the gates
The Berlin Wall were
ed, East and West
any reunited.

Resources	Meeting Individual Needs

Workbook, pp. 149–153
Every Student Learns Guide, p. 282–293
Transparencies 23, 60, 61, 62, 63
Quick Study, pp. 142–147

- ESL Support, TE pp. 607, 618, 621
- Leveled Practice, TE pp. 609, 616, 622
- Learning Styles, TE p. 611

Workbook, p. 154
Chapter 21 Content Test, Assessment Book, pp. 109–110
Chapter 21 Skills Test, Assessment Book, pp. 111–112

✓ Chapter 21 Performance Assessment, TE p. 626

Workbook, pp. 155–159
Every Student Learns Guide, p. 294–305
Transparencies 20, 23, 64
Quick Study, pp. 148–153

- ESL Support, TE pp. 631, 637, 646
- Leveled Practice, TE pp. 633, 639, 647
- Learning Styles, TE pp. 635, 649

Workbook, p. 160
Chapter 22 Content Test, Assessment Book, pp. 113–114
Chapter 22 Skills Test, Assessment Book, pp. 115–116

✓ Chapter 22 Performance Assessment, TE p. 650

Workbook, pp. 161–166
Every Student Learns Guide, p. 306–321
Transparencies 21, 23
Quick Study, pp. 154–161

- ESL Support, TE pp. 655, 661, 665, 669
- Leveled Practice, TE pp. 656, 663, 667, 671
- Learning Styles, TE p. 670

Workbook, pp. 167
Chapter 23 Content Test, Assessment Book, pp. 117–118
Chapter 23 Skills Test, Assessment Book, pp. 119–120

✓ Chapter 23 Performance Assessment, TE p. 672

Providing More Depth

  Multimedia Library

- *Arctic and Antarctic*, by Barbara Taylor
- *Technology*, by Roger Bridgman
- **Songs and Music**
- **Video Field Trips**
- **Software**

Additional Resources

- Family Activities
- Vocabulary Cards
- Daily Activity Bank
- Social Studies Plus!
- Big Book Atlas
- Student Atlas
- Outline Maps
- Desk Maps

 ADDITIONAL **Technology**

- AudioText
- The test maker
- Teacher Resources CD-ROM
- Map Resources CD-ROM
- **www.sfsocialstudies.com**

 To establish guidelines for your students' safe and responsible use of the Internet, use the Scott Foresman Internet Guide.

Additional Internet Links
To find out more about:

- Nelson Mandela's life, visit **www.anc.org.za**
- Mairead Corrigan Maguire or Aung San Suu Kyi, visit the members area and click on *Peace,* then *Peace Heroes* at **www.wagingpeace.org**
- NAFTA, click on *Trade Policy,* then *NAFTA* at **www.fas.usda.gov**

Key Internet Search Terms

- Nelson Mandela
- African National Congress
- Tiananmen Square

Unit 8 Objectives

Beginning of Unit 8
- Acquire information from primary sources. (p. 598)
- Identify contributions of significant individuals in the twentieth century. (p. 600)
- Analyze information by drawing conclusions. (p. 602)

Chapter 21

Lesson 1 Independence pp. 606–612
- Explain when and how sub-Saharan African and Asian nations gained independence from European powers.
- Explain how black South Africans and the Western powers reacted to apartheid.
- Describe and explain how and why Gandhi used nonviolent civil disobedience to gain independence for India.
- List four new nations in Asia and sub-Saharan Africa since World War II.
- Identify the contributions of significant individuals such as Julius Nyerere during the decolonization of sub-Saharan Africa. (p. 613)

Lesson 2 The Middle East pp. 614–618
- Explain how Zionism, the Holocaust, and the Balfour Declaration led to the division of Palestine and the creation of the state of Israel.
- Explain how Arab nationalism affected the Middle East.
- Explain the outcome of the UN plan to divide Palestine into Jewish and Arab states.
- Describe and explain how Arab hopes for independence and Jewish hopes for a homeland in Palestine caused tension in the Middle East.
- Describe what the Oslo Accords were and explain how they affected the Arab-Israeli relationship.
- Identify the contributions of significant individuals such as Menachem Begin and Anwar el-Sadat during the twentieth century. (p. 619)

Lesson 3 Eastern Europe pp. 620–623
- List and explain the major events that led to the fall of communism in Eastern Europe.
- List and describe the events of the Revolution of 1989.
- Define *perestroika* and *glasnost* and explain why Gorbachev used them in his policy.
- Describe the changes in Eastern Europe that resulted from the end of communism in Eastern Europe and the Soviet Union.
- Explain how the Soviet Union's response to protests against the Soviet government changed under Gorbachev.

- Evaluate the credibility of a print resource. (p. 624)

Chapter 22

Lesson 1 Economic Cooperation pp. 630–633
- Explain the causes and effects of trading blocs, trade agreements, and trade disputes.
- Define *gross domestic product*.
- List four trading blocs and their members.
- Explain the role of the World Trade Organization.
- Explain what the benefits are of belonging to a trading bloc.
- Interpret cartograms to find particular information. (p. 634)

Lesson 2 Conflicts of Identity pp. 636–641
- List and describe three major conflicts over identity or ethnicity.
- Explain why thousands of refugees fled Bosnia and Herzegovina in the 1990s.
- Compare and contrast the conflicts in central Africa and Northern Ireland.
- List three places in the world where people have been struggling for freedoms or human rights.
- Explain why some countries do not give equal status to men and women.
- Identify the contributions of significant individuals such as Aung San Suu Kyi. (p. 642)
- Identify a significant individual, Rigoberta Menchú, who worked for human rights. (p. 643)

Lesson 3 Political Conflicts and Challenges pp. 644–649
- Provide examples of how, throughout history, people have stood up against terrorism.
- Define *terrorism* and explain how it is used.
- Explain how the United States has responded to acts of terrorism.
- Explain how people around the world have responded to acts of terrorism.
- Explain how governments around the world have stood up against terrorism.

Chapter 23

Lesson 1 Population Growth and Change pp. 654–657
- Explain why people migrate to urban areas in developed countries.
- Explain why more people migrate to urban than to rural areas.
- Identify the parts of the world where the population is growing the fastest.
- List and describe one challenge that population movement presents.

- Explain how immigration affects populations in developed and developing countries.
- Describe and identify the purpose of a distribution map. (p. 658)
- Analyze information from a population density map. (p. 658)

Lesson 2 Earth's Environment pp. 660–663
- List and describe how people harm the environment but also provide solutions to help the environment.
- Define *environmentalist*.
- Describe what carbon dioxide is and explain how it has increased in Earth's atmosphere.
- Explain how people have found solutions to help the environment in the last 50 years.
- Express an opinion about whether humans have done more good or harm to Earth.

Lesson 3 Energy pp. 664–667
- Explain why fossil fuels are nonrenewable resources that will eventually run out.
- List three fossil fuels and explain which one will run out first.
- Explain why nuclear energy has advantages and disadvantages as an alternative to energy from fossil fuels.
- List and explain four renewable alternative energy sources.
- Describe the characteristics of a perfect energy source.

Lesson 4 Technology pp. 668–671
- Explain how we have used technology.
- Explain why and how we have used technology in space.
- Explain what the Human Genome Project is.
- Give an example of a problem that technology can solve and give an example of a problem that technology cannot solve.
- Explain why some forms of technology are more important than others.

End of Unit 8
- Identify figurative language. (p. 674)
- Explain how literature may reflect the times during which it was written. (p. 674)
- Describe the history of a communications method and create an accompanying Web page. (p. 678)

Assessment Options

✓ Formal Assessment

- **Lesson Reviews,** PE/TE pp. 612, 618, 623, 633, 641, 649, 657, 663, 667, 671
- **Chapter Reviews,** PE/TE pp. 626–627, 650–651, 672–673
- **Chapter Tests,** Assessment Book, pp. 109–120
- **Unit Review,** PE/TE pp. 676–677
- **Unit Tests,** Assessment Book, pp. 121–124
- **The test maker** (test-generator software)

✓ Informal Assessment

- **Teacher's Edition Questions,** throughout Lessons and Features
- **Section Reviews,** PE/TE pp. 607, 609–612, 615–618, 621, 623, 631–633, 637–641, 645, 647–648, 655–657, 661–662, 665–667, 669–671
- **Close and Assess,** PE/TE pp. 603, 612–613, 618–619, 623, 625, 633, 635, 641–643, 649, 657, 659, 663, 667, 671, 675

Ongoing Assessment

Ongoing Assessment is found throughout the Teacher's Edition lessons using an **If...then** model.

If = students' observable behavior,	**then =** reteaching and enrichment suggestions

✓ Portfolio Assessment

- **Portfolio Assessment,** TE pp. 597, 598, 677
- **Leveled Practice,** TE pp. 609, 616, 622, 633, 639, 647, 656, 663, 667, 671
- **Workbook Pages,** pp. 148–168
- **Chapter Review: Write About History,** PE/TE pp. 627, 651, 673
- **Unit Review: Apply Skills,** PE p. 677, TE p. 676
- **Curriculum Connection: Writing,** PE/TE pp. 623, 649, TE pp. 598, 608, 622, 625, 638, 645, 658

✓ Performance Assessment

- **Hands-on Unit Project** (Unit 8 Performance Assessment), TE pp. 597, 627, 651, 673, 676, 678
- **Internet Activity,** PE p. 678
- **Chapter 21 Performance Assessment,** PE/TE p. 626
- **Chapter 22 Performance Assessment,** PE/TE p. 650
- **Chapter 23 Performance Assessment,** PE/TE p. 672
- **Unit Review: Write and Share,** PE/TE p. 677
- **Scoring Guides,** TE pp. 677, 678

Test Talk

Test-Taking Strategies

Understand the Question
- **Locate Key Words in the Question,** TE p. 616
- **Locate Key Words in the Text,** TE p. 646

Understand the Answer
- **Choose the Right Answer,** Test Talk Practice Book
- **Use Information from the Text,** TE p. 662
- **Use Information from Graphics,** PE/TE pp. 676–677
- **Write Your Answer to Score High,** TE p. 649

For additional practice, use the Test Talk Practice Book.

Featured Strategy

Use Information from Graphics

Students will:

- Understand the question and form a statement that begins "I need to find out ...."
- Skim the graphics to find the right information to support their answer.

PE/TE pp. 676–677

Curriculum Connections

Integrating Your Day

The lessons, skills, and features of Unit 8 provide many opportunities to make connections between social studies and other areas of the elementary curriculum.

READING

Reading Skill—Draw Conclusions, PE/TE pp. 602–603, 606, 614, 620, 636, 644, 654, 664, 668

Lesson Review—Draw Conclusions, PE/TE pp. 612, 618, 623, 641, 649, 657, 667, 671

Link to Reading, PE/TE p. 641

WRITING

Create a Global Citizens Web Guide, TE p. 598

Write About Colonies that Gained Freedom, TE p. 608

Write a Series of Journal Entries, TE p. 622

Link to Writing, PE/TE pp. 623, 649

Rate Information Sources, TE p. 625

Write Poems About Peace, TE p. 638

Write Historical Fiction, TE p. 645

Write a Summary, TE p. 658

MATH

Link to Mathematics, PE/TE pp. 618, 657

Create Line Graphs, TE p. 624

Create Cartograms, TE p. 634

Rate of Growth, TE p. 657

Social Studies

LITERATURE

Read Biographies, TE p. 600

Read About the Middle East, TE p. 619

More About Peace and Peacemakers, TE p. 643

Books About Energy, TE p. 666

SCIENCE

Make a School Population Distribution Map, TE p. 659

Link to Science, PE/TE pp. 663, 667

MUSIC / DRAMA

Celebrate Independence, TE p. 610

Give a Speech, TE p. 639

ART

Interpret Fine Art, TE pp. 598–599

Create a Mural, TE p. 599

Create a Display, TE p. 640

Create a Peace Display, TE p. 648

Create a Symbolic Garden, TE p. 675

 Look for this symbol throughout the Teacher's Edition to find **Curriculum Connections.**

Preparing Citizens of the 21st Century

by Carole L. Hahn, Ed.D.
Emory University

In the past, the old "expanding environments" view of social studies was that students first became aware of their local, then national, and finally, international communities. Very little, if anything, was said about their growing identity with an ethnic community. We now realize that a child simultaneously comes to identify with his or her ethnic community, a national community, and the global human community.

It is only by teaching social studies and language arts with a multicultural and global perspective that we will prepare students to be effective citizens in our culturally pluralistic democracy in an interdependent world.

Students need to see how decisions made in one part of the world affect citizens in other parts of the world and how decisions made by one generation have consequences for future generations. Students need to study issues that transcend national borders.

If we give students practice in analyzing issues and ask them to take the perspectives of others across time and space, we will help them appreciate their role as global citizens, as well as citizens in the national, local, and ethnic communities of which they are a part. Below are several ways *Scott Foresman Social Studies* helps students understand how they are connected to people around the world.

- *To answer the unit question on p. 597 of the Pupil's Edition, students are asked to name ways in which they can be global citizens as well as citizens of their own nations. Students then review this list when they reach the end of the unit.*

- *The Writing Curriculum Connection on p. 598 of the Teacher's Edition asks students to evaluate various Web sites that could be linked to a Web site for global citizens. Students then create a corresponding Web guide.*

ESL Support

by Jim Cummins, Ph.D.
University of Toronto

In Unit 8, you can use the following fundamental strategies to help activate prior knowledge and build background for ESL students.

Activate Prior Knowledge/ Build Background

Teachers can use a variety of strategies to activate prior knowledge and build background. Communicating to students that their identities are important will motivate them to invest their identities in their learning, and students will learn with increased confidence in their personal worth and their ability to succeed academically.

Using direct experiences, such as taking a walk or going on a field trip, is also an effective strategy. Afterwards, students dictate what they saw or learned as the teacher writes on chart paper. The teacher can then relate these observations to the content of the social studies lesson.

The following examples in the Teacher's Edition will help you activate prior knowledge and build background for ESL students:

- *Explore National Identity on p. 637 helps students understand the concept of identity by relating it to their personal identity. This leads to a discussion about national identity.*

- *Explore a Concept on p. 669 suggests that English Language Learners at the beginning level take a walk around the school to identify technological tools.*

Read Aloud

from The Works of Mohandas Gandhi

"Non-cooperation . . . is not directed against the Governors, but against the system they administer. The roots of non-cooperation lie not in hatred but in justice . . . ."

Gandhi wove his own clothes rather than buy British cloth. ▶

Build Background

- Mohandas Gandhi (1869–1948) led a nonviolent revolution to secure the freedom of his country, India, from Great Britain.
- Born in India and educated in law in London, Gandhi was sent to South Africa as a legal advisor. He found himself discriminated against and treated as a member of an "inferior race." After many imprisonments and severe beatings, Gandhi began to resist authorities in a nonviolent way.
- Even after his assassination following the granting of independence to India, Gandhi's influence and teachings were felt around the world. He was a role model for Martin Luther King, Jr.

Read Alouds and Primary Sources

- *Read Alouds and Primary Sources* contains additional selections to be used with Unit 8.

Bibliography

Gandhi, by Demi (Margaret McElderry, ISBN 0-689-84149-3, 2001) **Easy**

Sitti's Secrets, by Naomi Shahib Nye (Aladdin Paperbacks, ISBN 0-689-81706-1, 1997) **Easy** *Jane Addams Book Award*

World Population, by Nance Fyson (Franklin Watts, Inc., ISBN 0-531-14479-8, 1998) **Easy**

Biodiversity, by Dorothy Hinshaw Patent (Clarion Books, ISBN 0-395-68704-7, 1996) **On-Level**

The Environmental Movement: From Its Roots to the Challenges of a New Century, by Laurence Pringle (Morrow/Avon, ISBN 0-688-15626-6, 2000) **On-Level**

No More Strangers Now: Young Voices from a New South Africa, by Tim McKee, Anne Blackshaw (Photographer) (DK Publishing, ISBN 0-789-42663-3, 2000) **On-Level** *ALA Notable Books for Children*

The Chain Reaction: Pioneers of Nuclear Science, by Karen Fox (Franklin Watts, ISBN 0-531-11425-2, 1998) **Challenge**

Habibi, by Naomi Shihab Nye (Aladdin Paperbacks, ISBN 0-689-82523-4, 1999) **Challenge** *ALA Notable Book for Children*

Samir and Yonatan, by Daniella Carmi (Arthur A. Levine, ISBN 0-439-13504-4, 2000) **Challenge** *Mildred L. Batcheldor Award*

Mandela's Children: Growing Up in Post-Apartheid South Africa, by Oscar A. Barbarin and Linda M. Richter (Routledge, ISBN 0-415-92469-3, 2001) **Teacher reference**

Silent Spring, by Rachel Carson (Houghton Mifflin, ISBN 0-395-68329-7, 1994) **Teacher reference**

Discovery Channel School Videos

Technology at Work 2-Pack One of the seven segments in this video follows an electronic signal from the Daytona 500 to a television in a viewer's living room. (Item # 765628, 60 minutes)

Understanding: Television This video explores the impact of television on life in America beginning with the introduction of television at the 1939 World's Fair. (Item # 717686A, 51 minutes)

- To order Discovery Channel School videos, please call the following toll-free number: 1-888-892-3484.
- Free online lesson plans are available at **DiscoverySchool.com.**

Overflow ▸ Look for this symbol throughout the Teacher's Edition to find **Award-Winning Selections.** Additional book references are suggested throughout this unit.

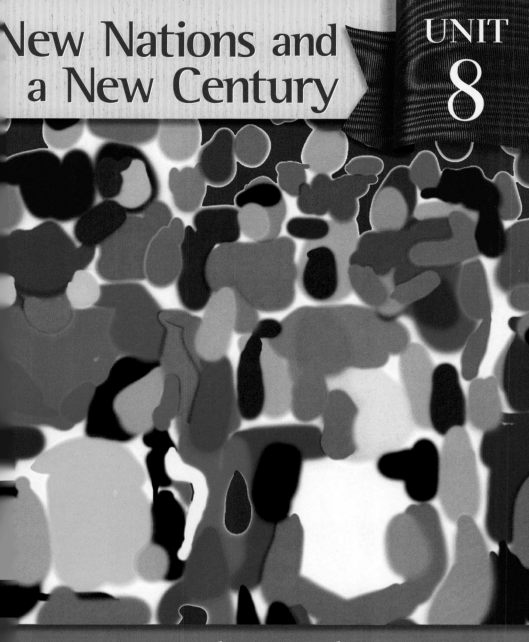

New Nations and a New Century

UNIT 8

How can you be a national citizen and a global citizen?

New Nations and a New Century

Unit Overview

During the twentieth century, many nations in sub-Saharan Africa and Asia gained their independence. Other nations have changed forms of government, aligned and realigned with other nations, and faced major identity clashes. Increasing concern over the environment and other global issues has caused people to think of themselves as citizens of the world.

Unit Outline

Unit Question

- Have students read the question under the picture.

- To activate prior knowledge, discuss the phrase *global citizen,* helping students to develop a definition of the term. Have students think of ways that they are connected with people around the world.

- Create a list of students' ideas about the ways in which they can be global citizens as well as citizens of their own nations. Suggest phrases such as *use resources wisely, vote for responsible leaders,* and *respect cultural diversity* to begin the discussion.

- ✓**Portfolio Assessment** Keep this list to review with students at the end of the unit on p. 677.

ractice and Extend

Hands-on Unit Project

Unit 8 Performance Assessment

The Unit Project, *Making Contact,* found on p. 678, is an ongoing performance assessment project to enrich students' learning throughout the unit.

This project, which has students design a Web page about the history of communication, may be started now or at any time during this unit of study.

A performance assessment scoring guide is located on p. 678.

Begin with a Primary Source

Objective

- Acquire information from primary sources.

Resource

- Poster 15

Interpret a Primary Source

- Tell students that this primary source is a quotation from Gro Harlem Brundtland, a Norwegian political leader.

- Brundtland served as the prime minister of Norway, was the chair of the World Commission on Environment and Development, and became director-general of the World Health Organization.

- ✓ **Portfolio Assessment** Remind students of the lists that they began of ways in which they can be global citizens (see p. 597). As students read through the unit, they can keep a list of various ways in which citizens around the world show their concern for the global community and how they might struggle to be an active voice in that community. Review students' lists at the end of the unit on p. 677.

Interpret Fine Art

- Point out that this picture shows a diverse group of people. Do students think that this picture accurately reflects the world around them? In what ways?

- Relate the picture to the quotation. Ask students how the painting reflects (or does not reflect) the idea of a global community.

- Invite students to think about why the artist may have chosen the particular colors she used and why she composed the picture as she did. What would students have done differently to express the same idea?

1950		1960		1970
1				
2	1957 The European Economic Community is created.	about 1960 Many sub-Saharan African countries begin to gain independence.	1967 The Six-Day War occurs in the Middle East.	
3 598				

Practice and Extend

CURRICULUM CONNECTION
Writing

Create a Global Citizens Web Guide

- Ask students to imagine that they are editors for a Web site for global citizen Their job is to locate and then evaluate various Web sites that could be linke to the network.

- Brainstorm for topics that could be entered in a student-appropriate search engine. Students may focus on such topics as the environment, human right activism, or volunteerism.

- As students find Web sites, they can document their findings. They should include the Web site address and title, a short description of the site conten and a rating to let users know the strengths and weaknesses of the site.

> *"We must learn to think globally . . . . No single region or nation can isolate itself from the rest of the world."*
> —Gro Harlem Brundtland in *Our Common Future,* a 1987 United Nations report

Diana Ong's 2000 piece, *The Beat Goes On,* suggests the world's human diversity.

Meet the Artist

- Diana Ong (1940–) was trained in art at the National Academy of Arts and the School of Visual Arts in New York. Her art has been featured on posters, book covers, greeting cards, and magazines in over 35 countries.

- Ong has created art in many different media, from woodcuts to paintings. She uses computers to create digital paintings.

Use the Time Line

The time line at the bottom of the page covers a time period from the mid- to the late-twentieth century.

1 **How many years passed between the appearance of the first personal computer and the fall of the Soviet Union?** About 16 years
Analyze Information

2 **Which event on the time line describes a demonstration or dispute?** Protest at Tiananmen Square
Draw Conclusions

3 **How many years passed between the beginning of the European Economic Community and the issuance of the euro?** About 42 years
Analyze Information

1980   **1990**   **2000**

975
rst personal computer

1989
Protest at Tiananmen Square

1991
Fall of the Soviet Union

1999 The euro is issued.

September 11, 2001
Terrorists attack the United States.

CURRICULUM CONNECTION
Art

reate a Mural

Discuss with students the events on the time line. Ask how the events show the emergence of global citizenship. What do the events reveal about the ways in which the world has changed during the twentieth century?

Encourage students to brainstorm for other events that have happened in the last 50 years that also demonstrate how people think globally. Invite students to choose one of the events from the list and create an illustration or painting of the event. As an alternative, students might choose an event from the time line. Additional research may be necessary.

Work with students to arrange their art into a classroom mural. Ask students to suggest appropriate titles for the finished work.

SOCIAL STUDIES
Background

More About the Euro

- The euro was issued in 1999.
- The euro was not put into general circulation until January 2002.

Meet the People

Objective
- Identify contributions of significant individuals in the twentieth century.

Resource
- Poster 16

Research the People

Each of the people pictured on these pages played an important part in world events during the twentieth century. Have students conduct research to find the answers to the following questions.

- **Name a book other than *Silent Spring* that Rachel Carson wrote.** Possible answers: *Under the Sea Wind, The Sea Around Us, The Edge of the Sea.*

- **Describe the relationship between the United States and Israel during the time that Menachem Begin served as prime minister.** The United States disagreed with Israel on some major policy issues, but the United States gave large amounts of economic and political assistance to the country.

- **Describe some of the cultural contributions made by Julius Nyerere.** Possible answers: Nyerere encouraged people to use the Swahili language rather than English, the language of Tanganyika's British colonial governors. His country was the only one on the continent whose official language was African, and he also translated Shakespeare's works into Swahili.

- **What are some ways Aung San Suu Kyi has tried to restore democracy in her country?** Possible answers: By going on a hunger strike; by giving speeches; by urging foreign businesses not to invest in her country until democracy is restored

Students may wish to write their own questions about other people on these pages for the rest of the class to answer.

Meet the People

Mohandas Gandhi

1869–1948
Birthplace: Porbandar, India
Lawyer, writer, political and spiritual leader
- Leader of independence movement in India
- Promoted nonviolent resistance
- Assassinated in 1948 by religious extremist
- Influenced other world leaders, including Martin Luther King, Jr.

Rachel Carson

1907–1964
Birthplace: Springdale, Pennsylvania
Biologist, writer
- Worked for U.S. Fish and Wildlife Service
- Wrote *Silent Spring* (1962), which led to restrictions on pesticides
- Writings inspired creation of modern environmental movement

Mother Teresa of Calcutta

1910–1997
Birthplace: Skopje, Macedonia
Nun, missionary
- Roman Catholic nun, nurse, and teacher
- Founded the Missionaries of Charity in Calcutta, India, where she worked with the poor for more than 40 years
- Awarded the Nobel Peace Prize in 1979

Menachem Begi[n]

1913–1992
Birthplace: Brest-Lito[vsk] Russia (present-day Belarus)
Military officer, politi[cal] leader
- Served in Israeli parliament, 1949–1[ ]
- Prime minister of Is[rael] 1977–1983
- Negotiated peace tre[aty] between Israel and E[gypt]
- Shared 1978 Nobel Peace Price with An[war] el-Sadat

| 1860 | 1870 | 1880 | 1890 | 1900 | 1910 | 1920 | 1930 |

1869 • Mohandas Gandhi

1907 • Rachel Carson

1910 • Mother Teresa of Calcut[ta]

1913 • Menachem Begin

1918 • Anwar el-Sa[dat]

1922 • Julius [ ]

600

Practice and Extend

CURRICULUM CONNECTION
Literature

Read Biographies
Use the following selections to extend the content.

Rachel Carson: Pioneer of Ecology (Women of Our Time), by Kathleen V. Kudlinski (Penguin Putnam, ISBN 0-140-32242-6, 1989) **Easy**

Aung San Suu Kyi: Fearless Voice of Burma, by Whitney Stewart (Lerner Publications, ISBN 0-822-54931-X, 1997) **On-Level**

Gandhi: Great Soul, by John B. Severance (Houghton Mifflin Co., ISBN 0-395-77179-X, 1997) **Challenge**

For more information, go to
www.sfsocialstudies.com/meetthepeople.

Anwar el-Sadat

1918–1981 ②

⑤

Birthplace: Mit Abu
l-Kum, Egypt

**Military officer, political
leader**

- President of Egypt,
1970–1981
- Negotiated peace treaty
between Egypt and
Israel
- Shared 1978 Nobel
Peace Price with
Menachem Begin
- Assassinated in 1981
by religious extremists

Julius Nyerere

1922–1999

Birthplace: Butiama,
Tanganyika (present-day
Tanzania)

**Teacher, writer, political
leader**

- Led independence
movement in Tanganyika
- Helped unite Tanganyika
and Zanzibar to form
Tanzania in 1964
- President of Tanzania,
1964–1984

Aung San Suu Kyi

1945– ②

Birthplace: Yangon
(Rangoon), Myanmar
(Burma)

**Writer, human rights
activist**

- Leader of opposition to
military dictatorship in
Myanmar (Burma)
- Won 1991 Nobel Peace
Prize for efforts to
restore democracy in her
country
- Awarded Presidential
Medal of Freedom

Rigoberta Menchu

1959– ②

Birthplace: Chimel,
Guatemala

**Agricultural laborer,
human rights activist**

- Continued her father's
fight for peace
- Activist for Indian rights
in Guatemala
- Won 1992 Nobel Peace
Prize for her efforts to
achieve social justice
for Guatemalan Indians

1940   1950   1960   1970   1980   1990   2000

1948

1964

1997

1992

1981

1999

1945 • Aung San Suu Kyi

1959 • Rigoberta Menchu

601

Use the Time Line

Have students use the time line and biographies to answer the following questions.

① Why do some of the lines on the time line extend to the edge of the page, where there is no date noted? These people were still alive when this book was published. **Analyze Information**

② What do four of the people on the time line, including Anwar el-Sadat, have in common? Who are the four people? Anwar el-Sadat, Menachem Begin, Aung San Suu Kyi, and Rigoberta Menchú all won the Nobel Peace Prize. **Compare and Contrast**

③ Which people lived to be the same age? Menachem Begin and Mohandas Gandhi **Analyze Information**

④ Which person was born before the turn of the twentieth century? Mohandas Gandhi **Interpret Time Lines**

⑤ Explain the connection between Menachem Begin and Anwar el-Sadat. The two worked together to negotiate a peace treaty between Egypt and Israel. They shared the Nobel Prize for Peace for this achievement. **Analyze Information**

Biographies

Four of the people shown here are discussed more extensively in the Biography pages in Unit 8.

- Menachem Begin, p. 619
- Anwar el-Sadat, p. 619
- Julius Nyerere, p. 613
- Aung San Suu Kyi, p. 642

Read About the People

The people shown here are discussed in the text on the following pages in Unit 8.

- Mohandas Gandhi, pp. 611–612
- Rachel Carson, p. 661
- Mother Teresa, p. 655
- Menachem Begin, pp. 618, 619
- Anwar el-Sadat, pp. 618, 619
- Julius Nyerere, pp. 607, 613
- Aung San Suu Kyi, pp. 640, 642
- Rigoberta Menchú, pp. 640, 643

WEB SITE
Technology

Students can research the lives
of people on this page by clicking
on *Meet the People* at
www.sfsocialstudies.com.

Reading Social Studies

Draw Conclusions

Objective
- Analyze information by drawing conclusions.

Resource
- Workbook, p. 148

About the Unit Target Skill
- The target reading skill for this unit is Draw Conclusions.
- Students are introduced to the unit target skill here and are given an opportunity to practice it.
- Further opportunities to draw conclusions are found throughout Unit 8.

1 Introduce and Motivate

Preview To activate prior knowledge, pose a scenario that invites students to draw conclusions. You might, for example, describe a familiar classroom situation without identifying it. (For example, you might describe lunch, recess, or a special assembly.) As you give clues, students can draw conclusions to determine the situation you are describing. Then allow students to give clues so that classmates can draw conclusions.

New Nations

Draw Conclusions

A good reader puts together facts he or she reads and then creates a new idea, or a conclusion. Sometimes you may have more than one conclusion.

Fact	
Fact	→ Conclusion
Fact	

- Try to make a logical conclusion from the clues you have read.
- Use your own knowledge and experience to help you draw conclusions.
- Check to make sure that your conclusions make sense and are supported by the facts.

In this paragraph, the facts are highlighted in blue. The conclusion is in boldface type.

Jomo Kenyatta (JOH moh ken YAHT uh), the first leader of independent Kenya, studied in Great Britain. India's independence leader, Mohandas Gandhi (moh HAHN dahs GAHN dee), also studied law in Great Britain. Kwame Nkrumah (KWAH mee en KROO muh), the independence leader of Ghana, studied at American and British universities. **Many African and Asian independence leaders studied at universities in Western countries.**

602

Practice and Extend

ACCESS CONTENT
ESL Support

Practice Drawing Conclusions Help students to draw conclusions.

Beginning Tell students you will describe a popular celebrity or other person in the news without naming him or her, and they will draw conclusions about who is. Give clues such as *He has brown hair and plays a detective.*

Intermediate Display several pictures with clear subjects. Ask a student to choose a picture without indicating which he or she chooses. The student should describe the picture without naming its subject. Tell students to draw conclusions about which picture is being described. Explain that to *draw conclusions* means "to use clues to figure out something."

Advanced Point out the Draw Conclusions graphic on p. 602. Then write facts on the board about a familiar place. Students can draw conclusions to identify the place. Then write a conclusion and have students write facts to support it.

Effects of Imperialism

European imperialism ended in most African and Asian nations more than 40 years ago. But people there are still experiencing the effects of imperialism. Sometimes these effects can be seen in the countries themselves.

You have read about some of the harsh rule of Europeans in Africa. Many colonial powers set up new economic and political systems. Some European countries did less to help their colonies prepare for independence than European countries did. Imperialist countries, such as Great Britain, took much of the wealth out of their colonies.

Nations in Africa and Asia have struggled to overcome the effects of these actions by European countries. Today, poverty and unstable governments in Africa can be partially traced back to imperialism.

On the other hand, Africans and Asians have gained some benefits from their former colonizers. Europeans helped many of their colonies set up universities. Two of these universities are located in Lagos, Nigeria, and Nairobi, Kenya. India has more than 8,000 universities and colleges.

Europeans also shared technology with Africans and Asians. You can see evidence of this in the skyscrapers of many African and Asian cities.

In India and other places, knowing the English language has been helpful. India is a huge land with many languages. The government encourages people to speak English as a second language. Knowledge of English has helped many Indians become successful in "hi-tech" industries such as computer software.

Use the reading strategy of drawing conclusions to respond to these items.

1. Explain why the following statement is or is *not* a good conclusion: "Imperialism affected the colonizing countries as much as their colonies."

2. Explain why the following statement is or is *not* a good conclusion: "The effects of European imperialism on Africa and Asia have been both harmful and beneficial."

3. List four facts that support the conclusion of this passage.

603

Workbook, p. 148

Draw Conclusions
Directions: Read the passage. Then answer the questions that follow.

From 1898 to 1997 Hong Kong, on the southeastern coast of China, was a British colony. For more than 150 years Hong Kong had been the financial center of Asia and the busiest shipping port in the world. Many people predicted this would change once Great Britain turned over Hong Kong to China.

Under British control, Hong Kong handled its own international trade. As part of the handover negotiations, China agreed not to interfere with Hong Kong's economy or democratic form of government for at least 50 years.

Although their economic and government systems are different, China and Hong Kong are in many ways interdependent. When Great Britain took control of Hong Kong, the population was mostly Chinese. Because the British did not force their

own culture upon the colony, Chinese culture remained an important influence on the people of Hong Kong. Their shared customs and heritage have created a strong cultural bond between them, and the people of Hong Kong feel a certain loyalty to China.

Hong Kong serves as a major port for the Pacific region, including China. Its absence of import tariffs also makes it an important export market for goods from China. Hong Kong's free market system serves as a model for China, which is trying to modernize its economy and government.

Interaction with China is also important for Hong Kong to meet the basic needs of its people. Hong Kong depends on China for nearly 50 percent of its food and almost half of its water.

1. Which of the following statements is a logical conclusion for this passage?
Ⓐ Hong Kong's economy would benefit from a communist government.
Ⓑ The relationship between Hong Kong and China benefits both of them.
Ⓒ British colonization had no effect on the economy of Hong Kong.
Ⓓ Hong Kong would benefit from cutting its ties to China.

2. What conclusion can you draw from the passage about the future relationship between Hong Kong and China?
Ⓐ Citizens of Hong Kong will petition for a return to British rule.
Ⓑ China will no longer depend on Hong Kong ports for exporting its goods to overseas markets.
Ⓒ Hong Kong will agree to abide by a communist government.
Ⓓ As China and Hong Kong become more interdependent, they will continue to influence each other economically.

Notes for Home: Your child learned how to draw conclusions from printed text.
Home Activity: State four related details or facts about a topic of your choice. Have your child practice drawing a conclusion from the clues in your facts.

2 Teach and Discuss

- Explain that a conclusion is an idea that is based on evidence. Conclusions are not mere guesses; they are based on facts. You can check a conclusion by asking whether the facts in a text support the conclusion.

- Have students read the paragraph on p. 602. Make sure they realize that the blue highlighting signals facts, or clues, while the part that is in boldface type is a conclusion. Encourage students to explain how each fact supports the conclusion.

- Then have students read the longer passage on p. 603 and answer the questions that follow.

- Ask students why, when studying history, it is important to know how to draw conclusions. (To understand history, we need to analyze the facts that we are given and reach new understandings based on those facts. We can draw conclusions about people and events.)

3 Close and Assess

Apply it!

1. It is not a good conclusion. The passage says nothing at all about the effects of imperialism on the colonizing countries.

2. It is a good conclusion. Paragraphs 2 and 3 describe harmful effects of imperialism. Paragraphs 4, 5, and 6 describe beneficial effects.

3. Possible answers: Facts supporting harmful effects: harshness of European rule in Africa, drain of wealth from colonies by imperial rule. Facts supporting beneficial effects: universities modeled on those in Europe, technology

Chapter Planning Guide

Chapter 21 • New Nations

Locating Time and Place pp. 604–605

Lesson Titles	Pacing	Main Ideas
Lesson 1 **Independence** pp. 606–612	2 days	• The end of colonialism brought an end to imperialism and European rule in Africa and Asia.
Biography: Julius Nyerere p. 613		• Nyerere led the movement to make Tanzania an independent nation in Africa.
Lesson 2 **The Middle East** pp. 614–618	2 days	• The end of European control and the creation of Israel changed the Middle East.
Biography: Menachem Begin and Anwar el-Sadat p. 619		• Begin and el-Sadat negotiated a treaty for peace between Israel and Egypt.
Lesson 3 **Eastern Europe** pp. 620–623	2 days	• Calls for greater freedom brought an end of communism in Eastern Europe.
Thinking Skills: Determine Accuracy of Information pp. 624–625		• Readers need to check the accuracy of sources to ensure that they are reading and using correct information.

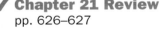 **Chapter 21 Review**
pp. 626–627

◀ **Menachem Begin and Anwar el-Sadat shared the Nobel Prize for Peace in 1978.**

✓ **= Assessment Options**

◀ **Tanzanian leader Julius Nyerere translated this play into Swahili.**

Vocabulary	Resources	Meeting Individual Needs
ecolonization oup d'état egregate partheid unction vil disobedience	• Workbook, p. 150 • Transparencies 23, 60, 61 • Every Student Learns Guide, pp. 282–285 • Quick Study, pp. 142–143	• ESL Support, TE p. 607 • Leveled Practice, TE p. 609 • Learning Styles, TE p. 611
onism	• Workbook, p. 151 • Transparencies 23, 62 • Every Student Learns Guide, pp. 286–289 • Quick Study, pp. 144–145	• Leveled Practice, TE p. 616 • ESL Support, TE p. 618
sident estroika snost	• Workbook, p. 152 • Transparencies 23, 63 • Every Student Learns Guide, pp. 290–293 • Quick Study, pp. 146–147 • Workbook, p. 153	• ESL Support, TE p. 621 • Leveled Practice, TE p. 622
	✓ Chapter 21 Content Test, Assessment Book, pp. 109–110 ✓ Chapter 21 Skills Test, Assessment Book, pp. 111–112	✓ Chapter 21 Performance Assessment, TE p. 626

Providing More Depth

Additional Resources

- Vocabulary Cards
- Daily Activity Bank
- Social Studies Plus!
- Big Book Atlas
- Student Atlas
- Outline Maps
- Desk Maps

 Technology

- AudioText
- The test maker
- Teacher Resources CD-ROM
- Map Resources CD-ROM
- **www.sfsocialstudies.com**

 To establish guidelines for your students' safe and responsible use of the Internet, use the Scott Foresman Internet Guide.

Additional Internet Links

To find out more about:

- Mohandas Gandhi, visit **web.mahatma.org**
- The rise and fall of the Berlin Wall, visit **www.wall-berlin.org**
- The rise of democracy in South Africa in the 1990s, visit **www.pbs.org**

Key Internet Search Terms

- African nations: Kenya, Ghana, Nigeria, Tanzania, Zimbabwe, South Africa
- Mohandas Gandhi
- Lech Walesa, Mikhail Gorbachev, Boris Yeltsin

Workbook Support

Use the following Workbook pages to support content and skills development as you teach Chapter 21. You can also view and print Workbook pages from the Teacher Resources CD-ROM.

Workbook, p. 148

Use with Pages 602–603.

Draw Conclusions

Directions: Read the passage. Then answer the questions that follow.

From 1898 to 1997 Hong Kong, on the southeastern coast of China, was a British colony. For more than 150 years Hong Kong had been the financial center of Asia and the busiest shipping port in the world. Many people predicted this would change once Great Britain turned over Hong Kong to China.

Under British control, Hong Kong handled its own international trade. As part of the handover negotiations, China agreed not to interfere with Hong Kong's economy or democratic form of government for at least 50 years.

Although their economic and government systems are different, China and Hong Kong are in many ways interdependent. When Great Britain took control of Hong Kong, the population was mostly Chinese. Because the British did not force their

own culture upon the colony, Chinese culture remained an important influence on the people of Hong Kong. Their shared customs and heritage have created a strong cultural bond between them, and the people of Hong Kong feel a certain loyalty to China.

Hong Kong serves as a major port for the Pacific region, including China. Its absence of import tariffs also makes it an important export market for goods from China. Hong Kong's free market system serves as a model for China, which is trying to modernize its economy and government.

Interaction with China is also important for Hong Kong to meet the basic needs of its people. Hong Kong depends on China for nearly 50 percent of its food and almost half of its water.

1. Which of the following statements is a logical conclusion for this passage?
   Ⓐ Hong Kong's economy would benefit from a communist government.
   ● The relationship between Hong Kong and China benefits both of them.
   Ⓒ British colonization had no effect on the economy of Hong Kong.
   Ⓓ Hong Kong would benefit from cutting its ties to China.

2. What conclusion can you draw from the passage about the future relationship between Hong Kong and China?
   Ⓐ Citizens of Hong Kong will petition for a return to British rule.
   Ⓑ China will no longer depend on Hong Kong ports for exporting its goods to overseas markets.
   Ⓒ Hong Kong will agree to abide by a communist government.
   ● As China and Hong Kong become more interdependent, they will continue to influence each other economically.

 Notes for Home: Your child learned how to draw conclusions from printed text.
Home Activity: State four related details or facts about a topic of your choice. Have your child practice drawing a conclusion from the clues in your facts.

Use with Pupil Edition, p. 603

Workbook, p. 149

Use with Chapter 21.

Vocabulary Preview

Directions: Read each sentence in the box. Match the underlined word in each sentence with its synonym or definition below. Write the underlined term on the line next to its definition. You may use your glossary.

- The decolonization of Kenya was complete on December 12, 1963.
- In 1965 Mobutu took control of the Congo in a coup d'état.
- The Afrikaner party passed laws to segregate whites from blacks in South Africa.
- Nelson Mandela was imprisoned for protesting against South Africa's laws of apartheid.
- In the 1980s, many countries placed a sanction on South Africa to force the government to do away with apartheid.
- Gandhi's method of civil disobedience attracted many followers in India.
- The movement to build a Jewish state in Palestine became known as Zionism.
- Vaclav Havel, a former dissident, became president of Czechoslovakia.
- When Mikhail Gorbachev became the Communist Party leader, he introduced perestroika to reform the Soviet economy.
- Glasnost was a policy that gave Soviet people some freedom of speech.

dissident	1.	protester against the government
apartheid	2.	system of laws enforcing segregation
coup d'état	3.	overthrow of the government
civil disobedience	4.	refusal to obey or cooperate with unjust laws
decolonization	5.	process of removing control by another country
segregate	6.	separate
sanction	7.	penalty
glasnost	8.	policy that allowed Soviet people some freedom of speech
perestroika	9.	policy introduced to reform the Soviet economy
Zionism	10.	establishment of a Jewish state in Palestine

 Notes for Home: Your child learned the vocabulary terms for Chapter 21.
Home Activity: Ask your child to use the terms from this chapter to explain to you the effects of decolonization in Africa, Asia, the Middle East, and Eastern Europe.

Use with Pupil Edition, p. 604

Workbook, p. 150

Use with Pages 606–612.

Lesson 1: Independence

Directions: Answer the following questions about the decolonization of Africa and Asia on the lines provided. You may use your textbook.

1. Why was decolonization important to the people of Africa and Asia?

   It led to independence, so the people could now govern themselves.

2. What challenges did some new sub-Saharan African nations face after decolonization?

   Possible answers: Setting up a strong government and army, finding strong leaders, and keeping peace

3. How did Western nations react to apartheid as a result of the protest in the town of Soweto?

   Many nations stopped trade relations with South Africa, and they used sanctions to make the government do away with apartheid.

4. What happened in South Africa as a result of Nelson Mandela's election as president?

   South Africa ended apartheid, adopted a new constitution, and was reshaped into a democracy.

5. What did Mohandas Gandhi urge people to do when he became the leader of India's independence movement?

   He urged people to stop buying and paying taxes on British goods and to use civil disobedience in their quest for freedom.

6. How did religion influence the formation of Pakistan?

   India was divided so that Pakistan could be a Muslim nation and Hindus could live in India.

 Notes for Home: Your child learned how nations in Africa and Asia gained independence from European rule.
Home Activity: With your child, discuss the advantages and disadvantages of independence for any

Use with Pupil Edition, p. 612

Workbook Support

Workbook, p. 151

Lesson 2: The Middle East
Use with Pages 614–618.

Directions: Match each cause with its effect. Write the letter of the effect on the line provided after each cause. You may use your textbook.

Cause	Effect
1. Jews face anti-Semitism in Europe. **d**	**a.** Israel gains a large portion of the land that was to become an Arab state.
2. Jews are persecuted in Nazi Germany. **i**	**b.** Leaders in the Middle East attempt to make peace.
3. A conflict grows between Arabs and Jews. **f**	**c.** Arab nationalism becomes a powerful force in the Middle East.
4. Arab states refuse to recognize the state of Israel. **h**	**d.** Many Jews leave Europe for Palestine and the United States.
5. Israel reaches an armistice with its Arab neighbors. **a**	**e.** Israel controls Palestine, the Gaza Strip, the West Bank, the Golan Heights, and the Sinai Peninsula.
6. A coup d'état ends the monarchy in Egypt. **g**	**f.** The United Nations proposes dividing Palestine into an Arab state and a Jewish state.
7. Nasser goes to war against France, Great Britain, and Israel. **c**	**g.** Gamal Abdel Nasser becomes the prime minister of Egypt.
8. Israel and its Arab neighbors fight the Six-Day War. **e**	**h.** War breaks out between Arabs and Jews.
9. Arab states attack Israel and place an embargo on oil exports to Western countries supporting Israel. **j**	**i.** The largest migration of Jews to Palestine takes place.
10. Anwar el-Sadat becomes president of Egypt. **b**	**j.** An international oil crisis occurs.

Notes for Home: Your child learned about conflicts in the Middle East between Arabs and Jews.
Home Activity: With your child, discuss the importance of finding nonviolent ways to solve disagreements. Have your child give examples of efforts to create peace in the Middle East.

Use with Pupil Edition, p. 618

Workbook, p. 152

Lesson 3: Eastern Europe
Use with Pages 620–623.

Directions: Sequence the events in the order in which they took place by numbering them from 1 (earliest) to 13 (most recent). You may use your textbook.

7 Mikhail Gorbachev calls for more freedoms for Soviet people.

4 The people of Hungary rebel against their communist government.

11 Boris Yeltsin and other leaders of the republics declare the end of the Soviet Union in December 1991.

10 The destruction of the Berlin Wall is complete.

12 Yeltsin begins to change the Russian economy and 15 new nations are created.

3 People in East Germany protest against their communist government.

9 East Germany and West Germany are reunited into one country.

6 Workers in Poland led by Lech Walesa force their government to accept Solidarity.

5 The people of Czechoslovakia want freedom, but their demands are rejected by the Soviet Union.

2 After World War II, the Soviet Union forces communist governments on countries in Eastern Europe.

8 Poland holds free elections in 1989.

1 Russia becomes a communist country.

13 Mikhail Gorbachev resigns as president of the Soviet Union.

Notes for Home: Your child learned about the end of communism in Eastern Europe and the Soviet Union.
Home Activity: With your child, discuss the freedoms citizens might lose in a communist country. Discuss why citizens of the former Soviet Union might want more personal freedoms.

Use with Pupil Edition, p. 623

Workbook, p. 153

Determine Accuracy of Information
Use with Pages 624–625.

When gathering information, it is important to use source material that is accurate and credible. Outdated information can provide old statistics and lead to false conclusions. An author who projects bias or is not a credible source for a topic can state opinions as facts, which can mislead the reader.

Directions: Fill in the circle next to the correct answer.

1. Which of the following online sources would be most likely to post unbiased information about a recent world crisis?
● government Web site
Ⓑ online chat room
Ⓒ family home page
Ⓓ e-mail from an eyewitness

2. Which of the following print sources would be most likely to provide a firsthand account of the fall of the Berlin Wall?
Ⓐ novel about the reunification of Germany
Ⓑ article from a recent monthly German teen magazine
● diary entry from an eyewitness to the event
Ⓓ entry in a world almanac

3. Which of the following print sources would be most likely to provide reliable statistics on the population of your state?
● publication of the U.S. Census Bureau
Ⓑ 1990 almanac
Ⓒ encyclopedia
Ⓓ geographic dictionary

4. Which of the following would be most likely an objective source for a report on the decolonization of India?
Ⓐ speech by Mohandas Gandhi
Ⓑ declaration by the British government
Ⓒ biography of Jawaharlal Nehru
● encyclopedia entry on the history of India in the twentieth century

Notes for Home: Your child learned how to analyze sources for accuracy of information.
Home Activity: With your child, read two accounts of the same event from different sources. Then compare the sources for accuracy, currentness, and objectivity.

Use with Pupil Edition, p. 625

Workbook, p. 154

Vocabulary Review
Use with Chapter 21.

Directions: Imagine you were present for one of the events in the chapter. Use the terms in the box to write a firsthand account about the event. Use the diary page below to write your paragraphs.

decolonization	apartheid	dissident
coup d'état	sanction	perestroika
segregate	civil disobedience	glasnost
	Zionism	

Review students' diary entries to confirm appropriate use of each vocabulary term.

Notes for Home: Your child learned the vocabulary words for Chapter 21.
Home Activity: Have your child use each word in context. Together, use the words to discuss more recent world events.

Use with Pupil Edition, p. 627

Assessment Support

Use these Assessment Book pages and the test maker to assess content and skills in Chapter 21. You can also view and print Assessment Book pages from the Teacher Resources CD-ROM.

Assessment Book, p. 109

Chapter 21 Test

Part 1: Content Test

Directions: Fill in the circle next to the correct answer.

Lesson Objective (1:4)

1. Which of the following countries did NOT gain its independence as a result of decolonization?
   - Ⓐ Kenya
   - Ⓑ the Congo
   - Ⓒ Tanzania
   - ● Great Britain

Lesson Objective (1:1)

2. When did many African nations gain their independence from European powers?
   - Ⓐ in the 1920s
   - ● after 1960
   - Ⓒ before World War II
   - Ⓓ within the last 5 years

Lesson Objective (1:2)

3. What does the word *apartheid* mean?
   - Ⓐ always
   - ● apartness
   - Ⓒ unity
   - Ⓓ strength

Lesson Objective (1:2)

4. Which African leader was imprisoned for his protests against apartheid?
   - ● Nelson Mandela
   - Ⓑ F. W. de Klerk
   - Ⓒ Robert Mugabe
   - Ⓓ Ian Smith

Lesson Objective (1:3)

5. What method did Mohandas Gandhi use to bring about India's independence from Great Britain?
   - Ⓐ declaration of war
   - Ⓑ violent conflict
   - ● nonviolent civil disobedience
   - Ⓓ compromise and negotiation

Lesson Objective (2:1)

6. Which of the following events did NOT lead to the creation of Israel?
   - ● Japan's defeat in World War II
   - Ⓑ the growth of Zionism in Palestine
   - Ⓒ the Holocaust and migration of Jews into Palestine
   - Ⓓ growing tensions between Arabs and Jews

Lesson Objective (2:3)

7. How did the United Nations hope to resolve the conflict between Arabs and Jews in Palestine?
   - ● by dividing Palestine into two separate states
   - Ⓑ by encouraging the two groups to resolve their problems peacefully
   - Ⓒ by requiring all Jewish refugees to return to their homeland
   - Ⓓ by giving control of the country to the strongest group

Use with Pupil Edition, p. 626

Assessment Book, p. 110

Lesson Objective (2:4)

8. How did the Arabs' and the Jews' quest for a homeland in Palestine affect the Middle East?
   - Ⓐ It helped to unify the people in the Middle East.
   - ● It resulted in wars and armed conflicts for many years.
   - Ⓒ It made Palestine the strongest nation in the Middle East.
   - Ⓓ It brought peace between Palestine and Israel.

Lesson Objective (2:2)

9. Which of the following ideas resulted in the building of strong Arab states?
   - Ⓐ decolonization
   - Ⓑ civil disobedience
   - Ⓒ Zionism
   - ● Arab nationalism

Lesson Objective (2:4)

10. What role did Yasir Arafat play in the conflicts in the Middle East?
    - Ⓐ He gave up Jordan's claims to the West Bank.
    - ● He led the PLO movement to create an independent Palestinian state.
    - Ⓒ He founded the nation of Israel.
    - Ⓓ He went to war against the British over the Suez Canal.

Lesson Objective (2:5)

11. What did the Oslo Accords do?
    - Ⓐ They officially established the nation of Israel.
    - Ⓑ They ended the Arab-Israeli conflict.
    - ● They tried to end the Arab-Israeli conflict, but their efforts failed.
    - Ⓓ They reunited Palestine and Israel into a single nation.

Lesson Objective (3:2)

12. What did the "Revolution of 1989" represent?
    - ● the end of communist rule in Eastern Europe
    - Ⓑ the spread of communism to countries in Eastern Europe
    - Ⓒ the beginning of the Cold War
    - Ⓓ increased tensions between the Soviet Union and United States

Lesson Objective (3:1, 2)

13. Which of the following events was NOT part of the "Revolution of 1989"?
    - Ⓐ tearing down of the Berlin Wall
    - Ⓑ collapse of East Germany's communist government
    - ● election of Mikhail Gorbachev
    - Ⓓ reunion of East and West Germany

Lesson Objective (3:4)

14. Which of the following events occurred in Eastern Europe after Poland held free elections in 1989?
    - Ⓐ The Cold War began.
    - Ⓑ The Soviet Union gained power.
    - Ⓒ Germany became a world superpower.
    - ● Many new nations were formed.

Lesson Objective (3:3)

15. What did Gorbachev hope to accomplish with *perestroika*?
    - Ⓐ less Soviet involvement in world affairs
    - Ⓑ stronger limits on people's freedoms
    - ● a restructuring of the Soviet economy
    - Ⓓ a return to stricter communist policies

Use with Pupil Edition, p. 626

Assessment Support

Assessment Book, p. 111

Lesson Objective (3:5)

16. What changes did Mikhail Gorbachev make in the Soviet Union?
    Ⓐ He strengthened communist rule.
    ● He allowed greater freedom in the country.
    Ⓒ He used force to extend the power of the Soviet Union.
    Ⓓ He overthrew the existing communist government.

Lesson Objective (3:3)

17. What was the purpose of *glasnost*?
    ● provide some freedom of speech to the Soviet people
    Ⓑ unify communist countries in Eastern Europe
    Ⓒ overthrow Gorbachev's government
    Ⓓ break up the Soviet Union

Part 2: Skills Test

Directions: Use complete sentences to answer questions 1–8. Use a separate sheet of paper if you need more space.

1. What effect did decolonization have on many African and Asian countries? **Cause and Effect**

   Many gained independence from European powers and set up new governments of their own.

2. How did many Western nations react to apartheid in South Africa? **Summarize**

   Many countries stopped trade relations with South Africa and enforced sanctions against the country.

3. What methods did Mohandas Gandhi use to protest British control of India? **Analyze Information**

   Gandhi used nonviolent civil disobedience to try to force Great Britain to give up control of India. Goods were boycotted, taxes were not paid, and peaceful protests were held.

Use with Pupil Edition, p. 626

Assessment Book, p. 112

4. Write at least three details to support the following main idea: **After World War II, many countries in Asia and Africa became independent. Main Idea and Details**

   Possible answers: Tanzania gained its independence from Great Britain in 1961. In 1965 Southern Rhodesia declared its independence. Myanmar, Malaya, and Singapore all became independent following World War II.

5. What caused the conflict between Arabs and Jews in Palestine in 1948? **Cause and Effect**

   Arab states opposed the division of Palestine to form the Jewish nation of Israel.

6. Why do you think the conflict in the Middle East has continued for so long? **Hypothesize**

   Possible answer: The opposing views of the Palestinians and the Israelis and increasing tensions have prevented a peaceful solution to their conflict. Each group feels very strongly about its cause and is unwilling to compromise with the other.

7. Why was the tearing down of the Berlin Wall a significant event? **Evaluate**

   The Berlin Wall had been a symbol of the Cold War and of communist rule in Eastern Europe. Tearing down the wall marked the end of the Cold War and communist rule. It signaled the introduction of democracy into the area.

8. What factors led to the end of the Soviet Union? **Draw Conclusions**

   Greater freedoms, an unhappiness with the Soviet economy, a loss of faith in the Soviet system, and a desire for greater self-rule led smaller countries to declare independence from the Soviet Union and set up their own governments.

Use with Pupil Edition, p. 626

New Nations

Chapter 21 Outline

Resources

- Workbook, p. 149: Vocabulary Preview
- Vocabulary Cards
- Social Studies Plus!

c. 1960, Africa: Lesson 1

The picture shows the national flags of South Africa, Zimbabwe, Kenya, Ghana, and Tanzania—all former colonies that achieved independence. Discuss with students the effect of independence on the people who live in a newly-independent nation. How might the people feel? What challenges would they face as a new nation?

1967, West Bank: Lesson 2

Tell students that this picture shows the Western Wall, a place that is sacred to Jews. Explain that this wall is part of a larger wall surrounding the Dome of the Rock, a place that is sacred to Muslims. Ask students to predict what might happen when one place is sacred to people of two different religions.

1989, Berlin: Lesson 3

This picture shows Berlin citizens dancing on top of the Berlin Wall. Ask students to comment on what the wall symbolized and why it was important for the wall to be torn down.

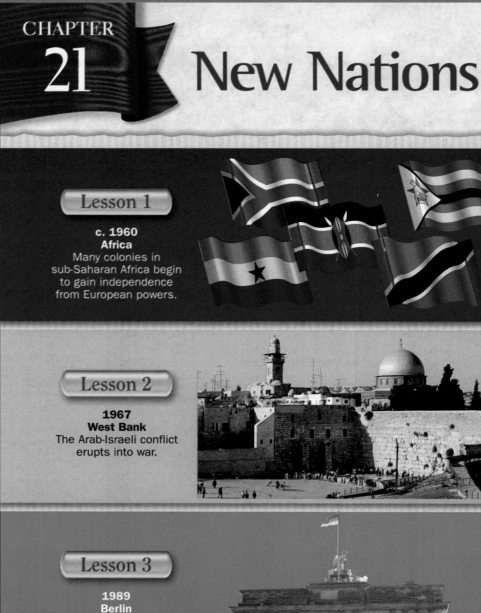

Lesson 1

c. 1960
Africa
Many colonies in sub-Saharan Africa begin to gain independence from European powers.

Lesson 2

1967
West Bank
The Arab-Israeli conflict erupts into war.

Lesson 3

1989
Berlin
The gates to the Berlin Wall open, and communism crumbles.

604

Practice and Extend

Vocabulary Preview

- Use Workbook p. 149 to help students preview the vocabulary words in this chapter.
- Use Vocabulary Cards to preview key concept words in this chapter.

 Also on Teacher Resources CD-ROM.

Workbook, p. 149

Vocabulary Preview

Directions: Read each sentence in the box. Match the underlined word in each sentence with a synonym or definition below. Write the underlined term on the line next to its definition. You may use your glossary.

- The decolonization of Kenya was complete on December 12, 1963.
- In 1965 Mobutu took control of the Congo in a coup d'état.
- The Afrikaner party passed laws to segregate whites from blacks in South Africa.
- Nelson Mandela was imprisoned for protesting against South Africa's laws of apartheid.
- In the 1980s, many countries placed a sanction on South Africa to force the government to do away with apartheid.
- Gandhi's method of civil disobedience attracted many followers in India.
- The movement to build a Jewish state in Palestine became known as Zionism.
- Vaclav Havel, a former dissident, became president of Czechoslovakia.
- When Mikhail Gorbachev became the Communist Party leader, he introduced perestroika to reform the Soviet economy.
- Glasnost was a policy that gave Soviet people some freedom of speech.

_____ 1. protester against the government

_____ 2. system of laws enforcing segregation

_____ 3. overthrow of the government

_____ 4. refusal to obey or cooperate with unjust laws

_____ 5. process of removing control by another country

_____ 6. separate

_____ 7. penalty

_____ 8. policy that allowed Soviet people some freedom of speech

_____ 9. policy introduced to reform the Soviet economy

_____ 10. establishment of a Jewish state in Palestine

Notes for Home: Your child learned the vocabulary terms for Chapter 21.
Home Activity: Ask your child to use the terms from this chapter to explain to you the effects of decolonization in Africa, Asia, the Middle East, and Eastern Europe.

Locating Time and Place

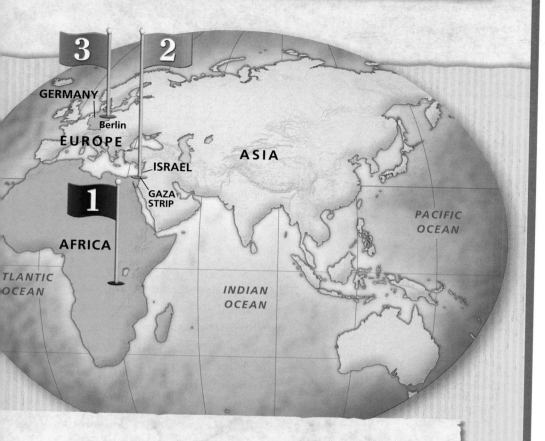

- Have students examine the pictures shown on p. 604 for Lessons 1, 2, and 3.

- Remind students that each picture is coded with both a number and a color to link it to a place on the map on p. 605.

Why We Remember

Have students read the "Why We Remember" paragraph on p. 605, and ask them why events in this chapter might be important to them. Have students think about changes in this country. The United States was once a colony. What beliefs did the patriots in the United States fight for? Why do struggles for independence continue to take place, and how do those struggles change the face of the globe?

Why We Remember

You may have seen an old globe that your parents or grandparents used when they were in school. You would probably see names and borders that looked strange. In fact, since you were born, some nations have formed and others have vanished. From the world wars to the present, nations and governments changed from time to time. To understand where these nations came from, how they disappeared, or how they affect our lives today, we study history and other branches of social studies.

605

WEB SITE
Technology

u can learn more about Africa; West Bank; and Berlin, rmany, by clicking on *Atlas* at w.sfsocialstudies.com.

SOCIAL STUDIES STRAND
Geography

Mental Mapping On a world map of the continents, have students mark with an X those regions where new nations might have gained their freedom during the second half of the twentieth century. Discuss what relationship there might be between these new nations and the imperialist movements discussed in previous chapters.

Independence

Objectives

- Explain when and how sub-Saharan African and Asian nations gained independence from European powers.

- Explain how black South Africans and the Western powers reacted to apartheid.

- Describe and explain how and why Gandhi used nonviolent civil disobedience to gain independence for India.

- List four new nations in Asia and sub-Saharan Africa since World War II.

Vocabulary

decolonization, p. 607;
coup d'état, p. 607; **segregate,** p. 609;
apartheid, p. 609; **sanction,** p. 609;
civil disobedience, p. 611

Resources

- Workbook, p. 150
- Transparency 23
- Every Student Learns Guide, pp. 282–285
- Quick Study, pp. 142–143

Quick Teaching Plan

If time is short, have students annotate a world outline map with notes about the lesson. They can jot down old and new names of nations, important dates and events, and so on.

1 Introduce and Motivate

Preview To activate prior knowledge, ask students to give examples of what *independence* means. Ask students what it means for a nation to gain independence. Tell students they will learn more about nations gaining independence in Lesson 1.

You Are There Kenya had undergone many tumultuous years before gaining its independence. What do students think may have caused new attitudes toward colonialism to emerge?

1940   **20**

1947
India and Pakistan gain independence.

about 1960
Many sub-Saharan African nations begin to gain independence from European countries.

1997
China takes control of Hong Kong.

Independence

PREVIEW

Focus on the Main Idea
The end of colonialism brought an end to imperialism and European rule in Africa and Asia.

PLACES
Kenya
Ghana
Tanzania
Zimbabwe
South Africa
Hong Kong
Pakistan

PEOPLE
Kwame Nkrumah
Jomo Kenyatta
Julius Nyerere
Mobutu Sese Seko
Robert Mugabe
Nelson Mandela
Mohandas Gandhi
Muhammed Ali Jinnah

VOCABULARY
decolonization
coup d'état
segregate
apartheid
sanction
civil disobedience

You Are There Never has there been such an exciting night. The skies above Nairobi explode with fireworks. Crowds clap and roar with each burst of color.

It's Kenya's independence day—December 12, 1963. A gentle breeze brushes across your face. Near the Equator in the highlands, Nairobi's weather is rather mild.

For longer than almost anyone can remember, the British have been ruling the country. Your father and mother worked for the Europeans, as did your grandparents and great-grandparents. Now Kenya will be truly free. Tomorrow morning your schoolmaster will raise a new flag. You will no longer sing "God Save the Queen."

Oh! Here comes the finale. The fireworks spell out *uhuru*. In Swahili, this means "freedom!"

Draw Conclusions As you read, try to put facts together to understand how former colonies became independent nations.

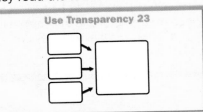

▶ **Hong Kong**   ▶ **India**

▶ **Ghana**   ▶ **Kenya**

606

Practice and Extend

READING SKILL
Draw Conclusions

In the Lesson Review, students complete a graphic organizer like the one below. You may want to provide students with a copy of Transparency 23 to complete as they read the lesson.

Use Transparency 23

WEB SITE
Technology

- You can look up vocabulary words by clicking on *Social Studies Library* and selecting the dictionary at **www.sfsocialstudies.com.**

- Students can learn more about current news by clicking on *Current Events* at **www.sfsocialstudies.com.**

- Explore other events that occurred on this day by clicking on *This Day in History* at **www.sfsocialstudies.com.**

Decolonization

How did countries in sub-Saharan Africa such as **Kenya** gain independence? In Chapter 17, you read how European imperialists set up colonies in Africa, Asia, and elsewhere. After World War II, Africans began organizing into political groups to demand independence and fight for decolonization. **Decolonization** is the process of removing colonial rule, or control by another country.

Kwame Nkrumah (KWAH may neh KROO muh) was an independence leader in **Ghana** in western Africa. He and other Africans believed that freedom belonged to all people:

> *"Freedom is not something that one people can bestow on [give to] another as a gift. They claim it as their own and none can keep it from them."*

The path to freedom was different from country to country. As you read in Unit 7, colonies such as Algeria fought bitter wars of independence. By the 1950s, attitudes in Europe were changing. Great Britain had the most colonies in Africa. Now it was time to let them go.

Guinea and Ghana launched independence movements in 1950. But after 1960, decolonization and independence swept through sub-Saharan Africa. Kenya won its independence under the leadership of **Jomo Kenyatta** (JOH moh ken YAHT uh) in 1963. See the map on page 608 for independence dates of other African countries. By the mid-1970s, most of Africa was free of European imperialism.

REVIEW Why was it important when Guinea and Ghana launched independence movements in 1950? ↻ Draw Conclusions

▶ **Zimbabwe**

nia

Challenges

In the early 1960s, many nations in sub-Saharan Africa were winning their independence from European countries. Some experienced decolonization very quickly. However, setting up strong governments proved difficult and challenging.

New African countries looked to their leaders for help. **Julius Nyerere** (nyuh RAIR ay) guided present-day **Tanzania** (tan zuh NEE uh) to independence from Great Britain beginning in 1961. Read more about Nyerere in the biography on page 613.

As you read in Unit 6, people living in the Belgian Congo had struggled under harsh colonial rule. Belgium gave little aid and training to the Congo army and government.

After the Congo won independence, the wealthy province of Katanga broke away from the Congo. The Congo then asked the United Nations (UN) for help. As a result, a UN army later forced Katanga to return to the Congo.

In 1965 **Mobutu Sese Seko** took control of the Congo in a **coup d'état** (KOO day TAH), or overthrow of the government. But the people of the Congo still were not free, as Mobutu ruled as a dictator for more than 30 years.

Some African nations had strong, capable leaders after decolonization, but others did not. Conflicts continued among some groups in sub-Saharan African nations. You will read more about some of these conflicts in Chapter 22.

REVIEW How did Mobutu disappoint hopes for a free Congo?

↻ Draw Conclusions

▶ **Jomo Kenyatta became Kenya's first president after independence was achieved.**

607

Southern Africa

Quick Summary Conflicts arose between the black majority and the white settlers in Southern Rhodesia. The apartheid system in South Africa segregated blacks and whites.

4 **Why did Great Britain at first refuse to grant independence to Rhodesia?** Because the country did not have a black majority in the government
Main Idea and Details

African Independence in the Twentieth Century

5 **Name the last African nation to gain its independence. In what year did this occur? Hint: It is on the shore of the Red Sea.** Eritrea; 1993
Interpret Maps

MAP SKILL **Answer** More countries are shown on the map on p. 608 than on p. 491. The map on p. 491 shows mostly African colonies, while the map on p. 608 shows mostly independent African nations.

6 **What happened after Ian Smith's declaration of Rhodesian independence?** After 14 years—and help from the British—blacks and whites reached a settlement. Elections were held, a black majority came to power, Robert Mugabe became prime minister, and the country's name was changed to Zimbabwe. **Sequence**

Southern Africa

In the 1700s, many Europeans had started to settle in southern Africa. The British colony of Southern Rhodesia attracted many settlers.

In the 1960s, white Southern Rhodesians asked Great Britain for independence. Whites made up only 5 percent of the population but held the most farmland and controlled the government. Great Britain refused to recognize independence until Southern Rhodesia had a black majority in the government. In 1962 a constitution denied civil rights to blacks. By this time, many blacks had already joined groups to fight against the white government. In 1965 Southern Rhodesia's new white prime minister, Ian Smith declared independence

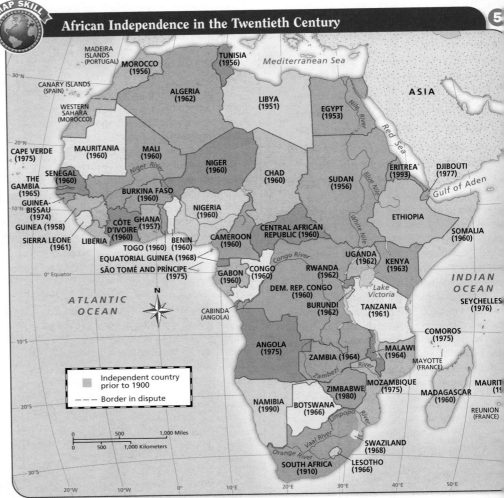

MAP SKILL **African Independence in the Twentieth Century**

▶ Many sub-Saharan African nations gained independence in the twentieth century.

MAP SKILL Observe Change Through Maps *Compare the 1914 colonization map on page 491 with this map. What differences do you observe?*

608

Practice and Extend

CURRICULUM CONNECTION
Writing

Write About Colonies That Gained Freedom

- Encourage students to conduct research to find out more about a colony that gained its freedom. Students could focus on one of the sub-Saharan African o Asian nations in this chapter or a different colony, perhaps even the United States of America.

- Students can use reference sources to find out more details about the circumstances surrounding the decolonization of the nation.

- Encourage students to report on their findings in a format other than as a report. They could write newspaper articles from the time period, create time lines of important events, write profiles of people who were instrumental in the gaining of independence, and so on.

Whites and blacks reached a settlement with the
[hel]p of the British in 1979. National elections
[bro]ught a black majority to power and a new prime
[mi]nister, **Robert Mugabe** (moo GAH bay), to lead
[th]e country in 1980. Southern Rhodesia's name
[wa]s then changed to **Zimbabwe** (zihm BAH bway).

South Africa has also had a long history of
[con]flict between whites and blacks. Dutch set-
[tle]rs called Boers (later called Afrikaners) first
[ca]me to the region in the 1600s. British settlers
[foll]owed. These whites settled among the black
[Afri]cans who were already living there, and they
[ga]ve few rights to blacks. Blacks could not vote
[an]d only some owned land.

[S]outh Africa became independent in 1910. In
[19]48 an Afrikaner political party came to power.
[Th]e government passed laws to **segregate,** or
[sep]arate, whites from blacks and Asians. Blacks
[wer]e forced to live apart from whites and go to
[sep]arate schools. This system of laws was called
[ap]**artheid** (uh PART hayt), which means "apart-
[nes]s" in the language of the Afrikaners.

[P]olitical groups that had formed years before
[incr]eased their protests against apartheid. One
[gro]up, the African National Congress (ANC), was
[led] by **Nelson Mandela.** In 1960 the South
[Afri]can government banned these groups and
[late]r imprisoned Mandela. Many young people
[bec]ame active in the protest against apartheid.
[In 1]976 government forces killed 25 black
[chil]dren at a protest in the town of Soweto.

[A]fter the incident in Soweto, few nations wanted
[to c]ontinue trade relations with South Africa
[bec]ause of apartheid. In the 1980s, many coun-
[tries] placed **sanctions,** or penalties, on South
[Afric]a. For example, the United States and many
[Euro]pean countries refused to buy South African

goods. They hoped that sanctions would make the
South African government do away with apartheid.

REVIEW Why did many countries place
sanctions on South Africa? Draw Conclusions

A New Era

In 1990 South Africa's president, F.W. de Klerk,
realized that the international boycott caused by
sanctions was hurting South Africa. He also
feared that apartheid would lead to civil war. As a
result, he released Nelson Mandela from prison
after 27 years. The two men held talks and made
plans to end apartheid.

In 1994 all South Africans gained full voting
rights, and Nelson Mandela was elected president. South Africa adopted a constitution that
reflected many of Mandela's own ideas:

> *"I have fought against white
> domination and . . . against
> black domination. I have cher-
> ished the ideal of a democratic
> and free society in which
> all persons live together in
> harmony and with equal
> opportunities."*

Mandela helped reshape South Africa into a
democracy. He served as president until 1999.

REVIEW Why was Mandela's election
as president of South Africa important?
Draw Conclusions

[In] this 1994 aerial photograph, South Africans in Soweto, a suburb of
[Jo]hannesburg, wait in line to vote. (right) Nelson Mandela and F.W. de
[Kl]erk join hands after a ceremony celebrating the end of apartheid.

609

---

7 **What do you think was the intended
effect of U.S. and European sanctions
in South Africa?** Sanctions limited South
African companies' ability to sell goods
abroad. They hoped that sanctions
would make the South African
government do away with apartheid.
Draw Conclusions

⭐ **SOCIAL STUDIES STRAND**
Citizenship

Point out that young black people in
South Africa boycotted going to school
when the government forced the high
schools to use the Afrikaans language
as the language for instruction.

8 **Do you think that boycotting is an
effective form of citizen protest?
Explain why this tactic would or would
not be effective.** Possible answer:
Boycotting shows people's feelings
without causing violence. White South
Africans, however, may not have cared
whether black students attended school.
Evaluate

✓ **REVIEW ANSWER** These countries
were responding to the killing of black
children in Soweto. They hoped that
sanctions would help end apartheid in
South Africa. Draw Conclusions

A New Era

🕐 **Quick Summary** In 1990 South
Africa's president began to make
plans with Nelson Mandela to end
apartheid.

Primary Source

Cited in Pretoria, South Africa, Supreme Court trial
records, April 20, 1964

9 **How were Nelson Mandela's ideas
different from those of many of his
fellow South Africans?** Mandela believed
in neither black nor white control of
South Africa. He wanted a democratic
society. Analyze Primary Sources

✓ **REVIEW ANSWER** He was a black
African who had been imprisoned for his
protests against apartheid. He believed
in democracy with full participation of
both blacks and whites.
Draw Conclusions

East and Southeast Asia

Quick Summary Beginning in the 1930s traces of European imperialism disappeared from Asia.

10 **Why would it be beneficial for a newly independent nation to join a federation, or group of nations?** Possible answer: Nations could pool resources and trade with each other, ensuring economic stability. Working as a group could make the new nations stronger. **Draw Conclusions**

11 **Name three European countries from which Asian countries gained independence.** France, Great Britain, the Netherlands Main Idea and Details

✓ **REVIEW ANSWER** Many countries became independent and some came together to form new nations.
Draw Conclusions

Independence in South and Southeast Asia

Point out that the year in which each country became independent appears on the map.

12 **Name three countries that became independent in 1949.** Bhutan, Laos, and Indonesia Interpret Maps

MAP SKILL **Answer** East Timor

East and Southeast Asia

Nations in East and Southeast Asia and the Pacific gained independence from European countries too. As in Africa, these nations gained independence in different ways.

In the 1930s, Japan took control of former European colonies. However, when the Allies defeated Japan in 1945, European countries tried to take back their former colonies in Asia.

In Chapter 20, you read about the long and bitter war in Vietnam. This war started as a struggle between the communists and France after World War II. France was forced to give up its control of Indochina (Vietnam) in 1954.

The British controlled Myanmar (Burma), Malaya, Singapore, and other lands in Southeast Asia. These countries became independent in the two decades following World War II. However, Malaya and some other states later joined to **10** form the new nation of Malaysia.

The Netherlands had long controlled the rich island country of Indonesia. Indonesia fought for **11** and won its independence in 1945. For independence dates of other countries in South and Southeast Asia, see the map below.

In Chapter 17, you read how Western imperialists took control of parts of China during the nineteenth century. In the twentieth century, the People's Republic of China was determined to end all foreign control of Chinese territory. **Hong Kong** had been held by the British for more than 150 years. In 1997 Great Britain turned over Hong Kong to China. Portugal gave its of Macao back to China in 1999. Both Hong and Macao became special administrative regions of China. European imperialism dis peared from this region.

REVIEW How did the end of European imperialism change South and Southeast Asia? **Draw Conclusions**

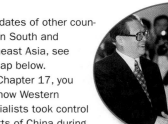
► At a cere before the of Hong K China, Ch President Zemin we Prince Ch of Great

MAP SKILL **Independence in South and Southeast Asia**

12

AFGHANISTAN (1919)
BHUTAN (1949)
PAKISTAN (1947)
NEPAL
PAKISTAN (1947) becomes BANGLADESH (1971)
MYANMAR (BURMA) (1947)
Arabian Sea
INDIA (1947)
LAOS (1949)
VIETNAM (1954)
Bay of Bengal
THAILAND
CAMBODIA (1954)
South China Sea
PHILIPPINES (1946)
SRI LANKA (1948)
MALDIVES (1965)
BRUNEI (1984)
MALAYSIA (1963)
SINGAPORE (1965)
INDIAN OCEAN
INDONESIA (1949)
EAST TIMOR (2002)
PACIFIC OC

Independent country prior to 1900

0   500   1,00
0   500   1,000 Kilomete

N

► **Which South and Southeast Asian nations were independent before 1900?**
MAP SKILL Use a Map Key **Which country became independent in the twenty-first century?**

Practice and Extend

CURRICULUM CONNECTION
Music

Celebrate Independence

- Ask students to suppose that they are residents of one of the nations in this lesson that has gained independence. Encourage students to visualize the celebration of the event.
- Students can create a song to commemorate the event.
- Allow time for students to share their song in a class "Independence Day Celebration."

New States in the Middle East

At about the same time that foreign domination was coming to an end in Africa [and] Asia, independence movements were spreading [throu]ghout the Middle East. The Ottoman Turks had [contr]olled much of this region since the sixteenth [centu]ry. During World War I, the British and French [fough]t against and defeated the Ottoman Empire. They [grante]d limited independence to many Arab countries. [But th]e British and French still controlled or managed [these] countries until full independence was gained. [Look] at the map at the right for the dates of independence [in the] Middle East.

13

[Th]e Indian Subcontinent

[In U]nit 6, you read that India was a colony of [Great] Britain. The Indian National Congress, or ["the C]ongress," opposed British rule. At first, the [Congr]ess attracted people of all religions. [Howe]ver, some Muslim members believed that [Hindu]s were dominating the Congress. In 1906 [these] Muslims broke away and formed the All-[India] Muslim League.

[Abo]ut 1920 **Mohandas Gandhi** became the [leade]r of India's independence movement. [Gandh]i knew that Great Britain could rule only as [long as] long as Indians cooperated. He urged [Indian] people to stop buying British [goods] goods such as cloth [and] and paying taxes on

goods such as salt. Gandhi, whom the people called "Mahatma," or "great soul," wrote:

14

> *"In my humble opinion, noncooperation with evil is as much a duty as coopera-tion with good."*

15

Gandhi's methods of peaceful protest for free-dom and democracy became known as nonviolent civil disobedience. **Civil disobedience** is the refusal to obey or cooperate with unjust laws. Gandhi's movement attracted millions of follow-ers in India. In the 1960s, Martin Luther King, Jr., used similar methods to help gain equality for black Americans in the Civil Rights Movement in the United States.

REVIEW Why is nonviolent civil disobedience used to take action? Draw Conclusions

▶ Here, Gandhi is making cotton thread to weave his own clothes.

611

The Indian Subcontinent

🕐 ***Quick Summary*** Mohandas Gandhi led the movement for the nation of India to become independent from Great Britain.

 ## New States in the Middle East

13 **Which Arab nation was the first one to gain its independence? In what year did this occur?** North Yemen; 1918
Interpret Maps

$ **SOCIAL STUDIES STRAND**
Economy

Point out that, just as the United States and Europe had boycotted goods from South Africa, people in India began to boycott British goods.

14 **How would refusal to buy British goods and pay taxes lead to independence for India?** Possible answer: Both of these actions would slow down the economy and would remove one of Great Britain's primary reasons for controlling India. **Evaluate**

Primary Source
Cited in *The Oxford Dictionary of Quotations*

15 **How did Ghandi view noncooperation with Great Britain?** He viewed it as a duty.
Interpret Primary Sources

H **SOCIAL STUDIES STRAND**
History

Remind students that nonviolent civil disobedience was also used by black South Africans fighting against apartheid.

✓ **REVIEW ANSWER** Nonviolent civil disobedience is an effective way to take action peacefully. Draw Conclusions

---

MEETING INDIVIDUAL NEEDS
Learning Styles

[Exp]lore the Use of Civil Disobedience Using their individual learning styles, [stu]dents can explore and report on the use of civil disobedience.

[Vis]ual Learning Have students create illustrated time lines that depict various [ins]tances in which civil disobedience has been used as a method of protest.

[So]cial Learning Encourage students to discuss in groups the pros and cons of [civi]l disobedience. What effects can taking these actions have? What downside [mig]ht exist to using such tactics to create change? Students can choose a [rep]orter to relate the main discussion points to the class.

[Lin]guistic Learning Have students write a speech that could be given by a [lea]der who advocated (or advocates) civil disobedience, such as Gandhi or [Ma]rtin Luther King, Jr. Speakers should explain the benefits of civil disobedience [as] well as what types of action would be most appropriate and effective.

India Divides

⏰ **Quick Summary** Religious differences in India resulted in the formation of Pakistan.

16 **Explain why Pakistan was created from land that had been part of India.**
Some members of the Congress believed that the group did not adequately address Muslim concerns. Pakistan became a Muslim nation, while most Hindus chose to live in India. **Main Idea and Details**

✓ **REVIEW ANSWER** Muslims felt that their concerns could best be addressed in a country of their own.
↺ **Draw Conclusions**

3 Close and Assess

Summarize the Lesson

Examine the time line with students. Encourage them to work in groups to list three important details about each of the events.

✓ **LESSON 1** **REVIEW**

1. ↺ **Draw Conclusions** For possible answers, see the reduced pupil page.

2. Black South Africans used nonviolent civil disobedience and protest. Western countries placed sanctions on South Africa.

3. Gandhi realized that if the Indian people refused to cooperate, Great Britain would no longer be able to rule.

4. Students should name any four of the countries from the maps on pp. 608 and 610 for which the year of independence is given.

5. **Critical Thinking: *Fact or Opinion***
Opinion: Nkrumah's belief that freedom belongs to all people; Fact: Most of the other sentences on the page express facts.

Link to ∞ Geography

Bodies of water such as the Arabian Sea and the Bay of Bengal surround much of the Indian subcontinent.

India Divides

Another Congress leader was **Muhammed Ali Jinnah.** He argued that the Congress did not pay enough attention to Muslim concerns. Jinnah left the Congress in the early 1930s and became head of the All-India Muslim League. He later demanded that Muslims have their own country.

Before World War II ended, British leaders had agreed to grant independence to India, but only if India's leaders could agree on a form of government. Indian and British leaders then divided India.

Pakistan —the Muslim nation that Jinnah
16 had wanted—was created in August 1947. India became independent on the same day. However, dividing the country caused chaos and violence to break out. As a result, millions of Hindus left Pakistan for India, and millions of Muslims left India for Pakistan.

In 1948 Gandhi was shot and killed by a Hindu extremist. Jawaharlal Nehru (juh wah hur LAHL NAY roo), who had worked closely with Gandhi, then led India to become the democratic country Gandhi had dreamed of.

Jinnah led Pakistan, which was created from parts of northwestern and northeastern India. As a result, East and West Pakistan were separated by more than 1,000 miles. In 1971 East Pakistan broke away to form the nation of Bangladesh.

▶ **Pakistan's national flag**

REVIEW Why did Muslims in India want their own country? ↺ **Draw Conclusions**

Summarize the Lesson

- **1947** India and Pakistan became independent when India was divided.
- **about 1960** Many sub-Saharan African colonies began to gain their independence from the European powers.
- **1997** Hong Kong became a special administrative region of China.

LESSON 1 **REVIEW**

Check Facts and Main Ideas

1. ↺ **Draw Conclusions** On a separate piece of paper, fill in the missing facts.

> Southern Rhodesia declared independence from Great Britain in 1965.

> Hong Kong and Macao became special administrative regions of China in the 1990s.

> India gained independence through nonviolent civil disobedience in 1947.

→ Independence from European Powers was achieved in different ways and at different times in sub-Saharan Africa and Asia.

2. How did black South Africans and Western countries react to apartheid?

3. Why did Gandhi believe that nonviolent civil disobedience was the way to gain independence for India?

4. Name four new nations that have formed in Asia and sub-Saharan Africa since World War II.

5. **Critical Thinking: *Fact or Opinion*** Find one fact and one opinion on page 607.

Link to ∞ Geography

Use a Map Look at the map on page 610. How is the Indian subcontinent separated from the rest of Asia?

Practice and Extend

FYI **SOCIAL STUDIES Background**

More About Jawaharlal Nehru

- Jawaharlal Nehru (1889–1964) joined the Indian National Congress in 1919 and soon became devoted to Gandhi.

- Nehru was a talented writer whose books detailed the struggles for Indian independence.

- Nehru was against the plan to divide India into two countries based on religion.

- Nehru played a major role in world politics, keeping India neutral during the Cold War, supervising a prisoner exchange at the end of the Korean War, and monitoring a truce after the First Indochina War.

Workbook, p. 15

Lesson 1: Independence

Directions: Answer the following questions about the decolonization of Africa and Asia on the lines provided. You may use your textbook.

1. Why was decolonization important to the people of Africa and Asia?

2. What challenges did some new sub-Saharan African nations face after decolonization?

3. How did Western nations react to apartheid as a result of the protest in the town of ____?

4. What happened in South Africa as a result of Nelson Mandela's election as president?

5. What did Mohandas Gandhi urge people to do when he became the leader of Indian independence movement?

6. How did religion influence the formation of Pakistan?

Notes for Home: Your child learned how nations in Africa and Asia gained independence from European rule.
Home Activity: With your child, discuss the advantages and disadvantages of independence.

Also on Teacher Resources CD-

Julius Nyerere
1922–1999

Julius Nyerere was born in Tanganyika (present-day Tanzania), which at the time was ruled by the British. Nyerere attended Tanganyika's only high school, where he soon became a top student.

Nyerere eventually won an academic scholarship to study history and economics at the University of Edinburgh in Scotland. He became the first Tanganyikan ever to study in Great Britain. While in Scotland, he began to plan his future:

"Tanganyika's politics must be the politics of independence."

Nyerere became one of the leaders of the independence movement in sub-Saharan Africa. In 1955 he gave a powerful speech before the United Nations on the subject of independence. In 1961 Tanganyika achieved independence, and Nyerere became prime minister. When Tanganyika and Zanzibar formed the country of Tanzania in 1964, Nyerere was elected president. **1**

Nyerere's vision for Tanzania was based on ideas of equality. Some of these ideas were rooted in socialism. Under his principle of *ujamaa,* or "familyhood," the government took control of industries and tried to improve harvests by forcing small farms to combine together. However, Nyerere's economic plans failed.

Nyerere translated two Shakespeare plays, Julius Caesar *and* The Merchant of Venice, *into Swahili.*

When Nyerere came to power, most Tanzanians could not read or write, and no national language existed. Tanzania was one of the world's poorest countries. Poverty and violence constantly threatened civil war. In 1985, after serving as president for four five-year terms, Nyerere resigned. By the end of his presidency, about 90 percent of Tanzanians could read and write. Nyerere's promotion of the Swahili language resulted in it becoming the country's national language. His free education policy has enabled more Tanzanians to read and write than the people of most other African nations. **2**

Learn from Biographies

What contributions did Nyerere make to help his country?

For more information, go online to *Meet the People* at **www.sfsocialstudies.com.**

613

SOCIAL STUDIES STRAND
History

More About Nyerere

- Nyerere preferred to be called Mwalimu, which means "teacher" in Swahili.

- He came out of retirement in the 1990s to act as mediator between warring groups in Burundi and Rwanda.

Julius Nyerere

Objective

- Identify the contributions of significant individuals, such as Julius Nyerere, during the decolonization of sub-Saharan Africa.

1 Introduce and Motivate

Preview To activate prior knowledge, ask students to recall what they learned about Julius Nyerere and the role he played in his African country, Tanzania. Tell students that they will learn more about the contributions that Nyerere made and the goals that he struggled to achieve.

2 Teach and Discuss

1 **After studying in Scotland, what three positions did Nyerere hold?** He was a leader of the independence movement in sub-Saharan Africa, then prime minister of Tanganyika, and finally president of Tanzania. Sequence

2 **Name one of Nyerere's greatest contributions as president.** His free education policy made it possible for many Tanzanians to learn to read and write. Main Idea and Details

3 Close and Assess

Learn from Biographies Answer

He provided stability and avoided civil war; he also set up a free education system.

The Middle East

Objectives

- Explain how Zionism, the Holocaust, and the Balfour Declaration led to the division of Palestine and the creation of the state of Israel.

- Explain how Arab nationalism affected the Middle East.

- Explain the outcome of the UN plan to divide Palestine into Jewish and Arab States.

- Describe and explain how Arab hopes for independence and Jewish hopes for a homeland in Palestine caused tension in the Middle East.

- Describe what the Oslo Accords were and explain how they affected the Arab-Israeli relationship.

Vocabulary

Zionism, p. 615

Resources

- Workbook, p. 151
- Transparency 23
- Every Student Learns Guide, pp. 286–289
- Quick Study, pp. 144–145

Quick Teaching Plan

If time is short, have students create K-W-L charts to guide their reading.

- Students should write names of places, people, terms, and events in the *K* column. Students should pause as they read to add questions to the *W* column and facts to the *L* column.

1 Introduce and Motivate

Preview Ask students what might make people want independence. Tell students that they will learn more about the conflict over creating an independent state in the Middle East in Lesson 2.

You Are There Ask students for other details that might have been in the film. Help students identify different points of view about an independent Jewish state in the Middle East.

1940

1948
The state of Israel is created.

1967
Six-Day War between Israel and Arab

1978
The Camp David Acc signed by Israel and

The Middle Eas

PREVIEW

Focus on the Main Idea
The end of European control and the creation of Israel changed the Middle East.

PLACES
Palestine
Jerusalem
Israel
Egypt
West Bank
Golan Heights
Sinai Peninsula
Gaza Strip

PEOPLE
David Ben-Gurion
Gamal Abdel Nasser
Anwar el-Sadat
Menachem Begin

VOCABULARY
Zionism

TERMS
Arab nationalism
Palestinian Liberation Organization
Camp David Accords
Oslo Accords

EVENTS
Six-Day War

▶ The Western Wall, sacred to Jews, forms part of a larger wall surrounding the Dome of the Rock, which is sacred to Muslims.

614

You Are There

You turn on the television in your ily room and find a documentary f on conflicts in the Middle East. Yo learn that this region stretches from the Mediterranea Sea to the western borders of Afghanistan and Pakista The program explains that this region was once part c Ottoman Empire from the 1500s until the end of Wor War I. At that time, Great Britain and France took cor of most of the Middle East.

You learn that the Babylonians forced many Jews of Judah in about 600 B.C. in to what is called the Diaspora. Over time, some Jews returned to Judah.

In the first century A.D., the Romans forced all of t Jews out of Judah, a land they called Palestine. Centu later many Jews began to call for a Jewish state in Palestine. During World War I, they persuaded the Bri government to support a Jewish state there.

Much of this is beginning to sound familiar to you, as you've heard it on the news.

Draw Conclusions As you read, identify the main facts of the Arab-Israeli conflict so that you can make logical conclusions.

Practice and Extend

READING SKILL
Draw Conclusions

In the Lesson Review, students complete a graphic organizer like the one below. You may want to provide students with a copy of Transparency 23 to complete as they read the lesson.

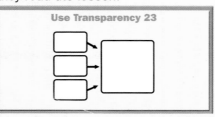

Use Transparency 23

WEB SITE
Technology

- You can look up vocabulary word by clicking on *Social Studies Libr* and selecting the dictionary at **www.sfsocialstudies.com.**

- Students can learn more about current news by clicking on *Current Events* at **www.sfsocialstudies.com.**

- Explore other events that occurred on this day by clicking on *This Day in History* at **www.sfsocialstudies.com.**

A Growing Palestine

...movement to build a Jewish state in
...ne became known as **Zionism** (zɪ uh nɪz
...onism comes from the word *Zion*, which
...e a synonym for **Jerusalem.** Zionism
...sed hopes of the Jewish people for a
...and. Since the late 1800s, Zionism has
...o mean the establishment of a Jewish
...Palestine. The British supported the
...shment of a "national home for Jewish
..." in Palestine.

...ough there had been growing tensions
...n the Arabs and the small community of
...ving in Palestine before World War I, they
...nerally lived in peace. In the 1930s, anti-
...sm, or discrimination against Jews, in
...caused more Jews to leave for Palestine
...e United States.

...ever, persecution by Nazi Germany and the
...ust led to the largest migration of Jews to
...ne. This large migration of Jews to
...ne soon led to growing tensions between
...and Jews.

...World War I, Great Britain and France took
...of a large part of the Middle East. Great
...had been governing Palestine. However,
...orld War II, Great Britain asked the United
...s (UN) to help with the growing conflict
...n Arabs and Jews. As a result, the UN
...ed dividing Palestine into two states,
...g one Arab state and one Jewish state.

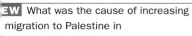 What was the cause of increasing
...migration to Palestine in
...30s? **Cause and Effect**

▶ **David Ben-Gurion became the first
prime minister of Israel in 1948.**

State of Israel

On May 14, 1948, the last British troops left
Palestine. Jewish leader **David Ben-Gurion**
declared the Jewish part of Palestine as the
state of **Israel.**

Jews in Palestine celebrated, but Arab states
opposed the division of Palestine and refused to
recognize Israel. War then broke out between
Arabs and Jews. The neighboring Arab countries
of Syria, **Egypt,** and Jordan joined the Palestinian
Arabs—now called Palestinians—in the fight
against Israel.

Israel reached an armistice with its Arab
neighbors by 1949. As a result, Israel gained
a large portion of the land the UN had put aside
for an Arab state. During the war, hundreds of
thousands of Palestinians had fled Palestine and
settled in refugee camps in Israel. Most settled
in neighboring Arab states. More battles were to
come between Israel and the Palestinians, as
well as Arab states, in what became known as
the Arab-Israeli conflict.

REVIEW How was the reaction different among
Arabs and Jews to the declaration of the state of
Israel? **Compare and Contrast**

615

---

2 Teach and Discuss

PAGE 615

A Growing Palestine

🕐 *Quick Summary* Large numbers
of new Jewish settlers moving to
Palestine caused tensions between
Arabs and Jews to increase.

**1 How did the United Nations propose
to solve the growing conflict between
Arabs and Jews in Palestine?** The UN
suggested splitting Palestine into one
Arab state and one Jewish state.
Main Idea and Details

✓ **REVIEW ANSWER** Anti-Semitism
in Europe led to increased Jewish
migration to Palestine. **Cause and Effect**

State of Israel

🕐 *Quick Summary* The declaration
of the nation of Israel led to the war
between Israelis and Palestinians.

**2 How long did the war between
Israel and its Arab neighbors last?**
About one year **Apply Information**

✓ **REVIEW ANSWER** Jews in Palestine
celebrated. The Arabs refused to
recognize Israel, and war broke out
between Arabs and Jews.
Compare and Contrast

🔵 SOCIAL STUDIES STRAND
History

...four Declaration

...document in which Great Britain declared its
...port for the establishment of a Jewish state
...called the Balfour Declaration. Arthur James
...our wrote this letter of declaration to Lord
...nschild on November 2, 1917.

**...His Majesty's Government view with favour the
...blishment in Palestine of a national home for the
...ish people, and will use their best endeavours to
...itate the achievement of this object, it being clearly
...erstood that nothing shall be done which may
...udice the civil and religious rights of existing non-
...ish communities in Palestine, or the rights and
...tical status enjoyed by Jews in any other country...."**

FYI SOCIAL STUDIES
Background

David Ben-Gurion

- Born October 16, 1886, David Gruen later changed his surname to Ben-
Gurion, an ancient Hebrew name.
- Turkish governors in Palestine were suspicious of Ben-Gurion's Zionist activity
at the onset of World War I. They arrested Ben-Gurion and forced him to leave
Palestine.
- Following the publication of the Balfour Declaration, Ben-Gurion returned to the
Middle East. He later became the first prime minister and defense minister of
Israel. He served from 1948 to 1953, then retired from his posts, only to
return again and serve from 1955 to 1963.

Arab States

⏱ **Quick Summary** Gamel Abdel Nasser's actions, taken against British influence in Egypt, stirred strong support from other Arab nations and helped lead to Arab nationalism.

Test Talk

Locate Key Words in the Question

3 **In what year did Nasser become the prime minister of Egypt? What was his goal?** Have students repeat the question. Students should ask themselves "Who or what is this question about?" 1954; he wanted to force the British to leave Egypt.
Analyze Information

✓ **REVIEW ANSWER** He stood up to Western nations by sending troops to block the Suez Canal in an effort to drive the British from Egypt, and he went to war with France, Great Britain, and Israel when they invaded Egypt.
Main Idea and Details

Continuing Conflict

⏱ **Quick Summary** Despite some moves toward peace in the Middle East, the conflict has continued between Arabs and Israelis, resulting in more violence.

4 **What did the Palestinian Liberation Organization hope to achieve? What was one method it used to try to achieve this goal?** The PLO wanted a Palestinian state; some leaders of the PLO supported Palestinian raids on Israel. **Main Idea and Details**

Arab States

In the 1930s and 1940s, many Arab states gained their independence—Iraq and Jordan from Great Britain, and Syria and Lebanon from France. By the 1950s, most states in the Middle East had decolonized.

In Unit 6, you read that Great Britain had some control in keeping the Suez Canal open for British ships. In 1952 a coup d'etat ended the monarchy in Egypt. Two years later, **Gamal Abdel Nasser** became the prime minister and was determined to drive the British completely out of his country. He sent his forces to block the canal. In 1956 France, Great Britain, and Israel invaded Egypt, starting a war over the Suez Canal.

▶ **Gamal Abdel Nasser became president of Egypt in 1956.**

Nasser's actions gained wide support in the Arab world. No Arab leader in the Middle East had ever before stood up to Western nations. His goal of greater Arab unity, or **Arab nationalism,** became a powerful force throughout the Middle East.

REVIEW How did Nasser gain support from other Arab leaders in the Middle East? **Main Idea and Details**

Continuing Conflict

Israel and its Arab neighbors continued to fight wars in 1967 and 1973. The 1967 war, or the **Six-Day War,** ended with Israel in control of Palestine. Israel seized the **West Bank,** a large piece of land between Israel and Jordan, from Jordan. From Syria, Israel took the **Golan Heights** and from Egypt the **Sinai Peninsula** and the **Gaza Strip.**

The Gaza Strip and West Bank were home to more than 1 million Palestinians. Many Palestinians

---

recognized the **Palestinian Liberation Organization** (PLO) as representative of all Palestinians. Led by Yasir Arafat the PLO worked to create a Palestinian state. Some Arab leaders supported Palestinian attacks on Israel, but over time came to think that the best strategy was to make peace with Israel.

In the 1973 war, Arab states attacked Israel to try to regain land they had lost in 1967. This war caused an international oil crisis because Arab states placed an embargo on oil exports to Western countries, such as the United States, that supported Israel.

Old City of Jerusalem

Practice and Extend

MEETING INDIVIDUAL NEEDS
Leveled Practice

Identify Main Ideas Ask students to write about the main ideas on p. 616.

Easy Provide sentence starter outlines, giving students skeletal outlines for them to complete with main points and/or details from the reading. **Reteach**

On-Level Ask students to create quiz questions about the lesson material. They should also write the answers. Use students' questions to create a tool for review or as the basis for a quiz show or game. **Extend**

Challenge Ask students to imagine that they have been asked to teach the material on this page. They need to create a lesson outline for one of the sections and develop a visual aid to accompany it, such as a map or a time line. Students may need to do additional research to add background information to their presentations. If time allows, invite students to present their lessons to the class. **Enrich**

For a Lesson Summary, use Quick Study, p. 144.

982 Israel invaded Lebanon following a
 of Palestinian raids. Arafat and some of
lowers fled to Tunisia in North Africa. In
Palestinians in the Occupied Territories car-
ut an uprising—riots, demonstrations, and
ce. Many Arab leaders wanted to stop the
g. King Hussein of Jordan gave up his
y's claims to the West Bank and East
alem.

EW How did the 1973 war between Israel
rab states affect Western countries? **Cause**
ffect

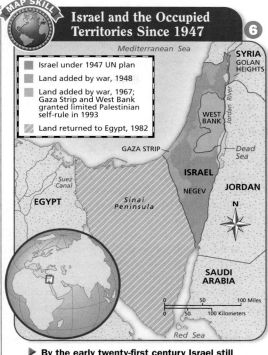

Israel and the Occupied Territories Since 1947 ⑥

MAP SKILL

- Israel under 1947 UN plan
- Land added by war, 1948
- Land added by war, 1967; Gaza Strip and West Bank granted limited Palestinian self-rule in 1993
- Land returned to Egypt, 1982

Mediterranean Sea

SYRIA
GOLAN HEIGHTS

WEST BANK

GAZA STRIP

Dead Sea

ISRAEL

Suez Canal

NEGEV

JORDAN

EGYPT

Sinai Peninsula

N

SAUDI ARABIA

0 50 100 Miles
0 50 100 Kilometers

Red Sea

▶ By the early twenty-first century Israel still occupied land taken in the Six-Day War.

MAP SKILL Human-Environment Interaction
What political boundary is formed by the Jordan River?

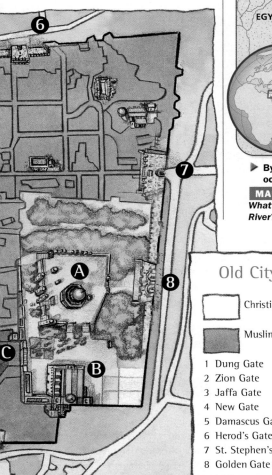

⑥

⑦

Ⓐ

C

Ⓑ

⑧

Old City of Jerusalem Map Key

- ☐ Christian
- ■ Muslim
- ■ Jewish
- ☐ Armenian (Eastern Orthodox)

1 Dung Gate
2 Zion Gate
3 Jaffa Gate
4 New Gate
5 Damascus Gate
6 Herod's Gate
7 St. Stephen's Gate
8 Golden Gate

A Dome of the Rock/Haram esh-Sharif
B El-Aqsa Mosque
C Western Wall of the Second Temple
D Church of the Holy Sepulchre
E The Citadel or Tower of David

617

⑤ **What can you tell about King Hussein from his actions after the 1987 Palestinian uprising in the Occupied Territories?** Possible answer: He wanted peace and was willing to make sacrifices to get it. ↻ **Draw Conclusions**

✓ **REVIEW ANSWER** It caused an international oil crisis because Arab states placed an embargo on oil exports to Western countries that supported Israel. **Cause and Effect**

MAP SKILL **Israel and the Occupied Territories Since 1947**

⑥ **Which part of Israel's Occupied Territories was returned to Egypt? When was it returned?** The Sinai Peninsula; 1982 **Interpret Maps**

MAP SKILL Answer The border between Jordan and Israel

FAST FACTS

at Happened in the World in 1947?

ackie Robinson became the first African American to play on a major league aseball team—the Brooklyn Dodgers.

enry Ford died, passing on a fortune worth over 600 million dollars.

More than one million veterans enrolled in college through the financial aid of he G.I. Bill.

he Diary of Anne Frank was published.

Drive-in movie theaters became a booming business.

Toward Peace

⏱ *Quick Summary* Despite many efforts towards peace, violence continues in the Middle East.

7 **Leaders from what three countries came together to create the Camp David Accords?** Egypt, Israel, and the United States **Main Idea and Details**

✓ **REVIEW ANSWER** Despite efforts toward peace, violence and the Arab-Israeli conflict have continued. **Summarize**

3 Close and Assess

Summarize the Lesson

Tell students to examine the time line. Then write on the board some of the people, places, and terms from p. 614. Ask volunteers to define these terms. Students can then use the terms to create crosswords, word searches, or other puzzles using the words.

✓ **LESSON 2** **REVIEW**

1. 🔄 **Draw Conclusions** For possible answers, see the reduced pupil page.

2. Arab nationalism encouraged other Arab states to stand up to the British and other Western nations. It also brought a sense of Arab unity.

3. Ben-Gurion declared the Jewish part of Palestine as Israel. The Arabs lost some of their land in war and were unable to establish their own state.

4. Arabs and Jews have fought over the same land to create their independent states.

5. **Critical Thinking:** *Evaluate Information* Possible answer: It is a fair trade because the Accords could lead to an Arab state and Jewish state existing together in Palestine, much as the UN proposed in the 1940s.

Link to 🔗 Mathematics
About 33

Toward Peace

In 1978 Egypt's president **Anwar el-Sadat** (AHN wahr el-suh DAHT) and Israeli Prime Minister **Menachem Begin** (muh NAH chuhm BAY gihn) began to work toward a peace agreement. With the help of U.S. President Jimmy Carter, they signed **7** the **Camp David Accords.** Read more about this agreement in the biography on page 619.

Some leaders in the Middle East have made moves toward peace. For example, in 1994 King Hussein of Jordan signed a peace treaty with Israel. In 1993 and 1995, Israeli Prime Minister Yitzhak Rabin (YIHT zak rah BEEN) and PLO leader Yasir Arafat signed the **Oslo Accords.** These agreements aimed at ending the Arab-Israeli conflict but resulted in failure and another Palestinian uprising in 2000.

Despite efforts to make peace, violence continues in the Middle East. Thousands of Arabs and

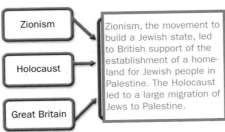

▶ U.S. President Jimmy Carter joins hands with Anwar Sadat and Menachem Begin after the signing of the Camp David Accords.

Israelis, as well as many of their leaders, have lost their lives in the Arab-Israeli conflict.

REVIEW How have efforts for peace on both sides affected the Arab-Israeli situation?

Summarize the Lesson

— **1948** The state of Israel, a homeland for Jews, was created.

— **1967** Israel and its Arab neighbors fought the Six-Day War.

—┘ **1978** Israel and the Egyptians signed the Camp David Accords.

LESSON 2 REVIEW

Check Facts and Main Ideas

1. 🔄 **Draw Conclusions** Copy the diagram below on a separate piece of paper. Then write a conclusion about how the state of Israel was created using the given clues.

```
┌──────────┐
│ Zionism  │───┐
└──────────┘   │     ┌──────────────────────────┐
               ├────▶│ Zionism, the movement to │
┌──────────┐   │     │ build a Jewish state, led │
│ Holocaust│───┤     │ to British support of the │
└──────────┘   │     │ establishment of a home-  │
               │     │ land for Jewish people in │
┌──────────┐   │     │ Palestine. The Holocaust  │
│Great     │───┘     │ led to a large migration  │
│Britain   │         │ of Jews to Palestine.     │
└──────────┘         └──────────────────────────┘
```

2. How did Arab nationalism affect the Middle East?

3. What was the result of the UN plan to divide Palestine into Jewish and Arab states?

4. How did Arab hopes for independence and Jewish hopes for a homeland in Palestine cause tension?

5. **Critical Thinking:** *Evaluate Information* In the Oslo Accords, Israel agreed to give land back to the Palestinians. The Palestinians then agreed to recognize Israel. Do you think this is a fair trade? Explain.

Link to 🔗 Mathematics

Compare Areas The area of the state of Israel is 8,130 square miles. The area of the state of Texas is 266,874 square miles. About how many states of Israel would fit inside Texas?

Practice and Extend

ESL **EXTEND LANGUAGE** **ESL Support**

Use Cognates Find Spanish cognates for lesson words.

Beginning Write *conflict* and *document* on the board. Next to each word write the Spanish: *conflicto, documento.*

Intermediate Have students make a 2-column chart. They should list Spanish words in the first column (*conflicto, documento, discriminación, tensión, control*) and English in the second.

Advanced Invite Spanish-speaking students to scan the lesson for words that have cognates in Spanish and to list the words in both languages.

For additional ESL support, use Every Student Learns Guide, pp. 286–289.

Workbook, p. 15

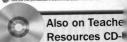

Lesson 2: The Middle East

Directions: Match each cause with its effect. Write the letter of the effect on the line provided after each cause. You may use your textbook.

Cause	Effect
1. Jews face anti-Semitism in Europe. ___	a. Israel gains a large portion of the land that was to become an Arab state.
2. Jews are persecuted in Nazi Germany. ___	b. Leaders in the Middle East attempt to make peace.
3. A conflict grows between Arabs and Jews. ___	c. Arab nationalism becomes a powerful force in the Middle East.
4. Arab states refuse to recognize the state of Israel. ___	d. Many Jews leave Europe for Palestine and the United States.
5. Israel reaches an armistice with its Arab neighbors. ___	e. Israel controls Palestine, the Gaza Strip, the West Bank, the Golan Heights, and the Sinai Peninsula.
6. A coup d'état ends the monarchy in Egypt. ___	f. The United Nations proposes dividing Palestine into an Arab state and a Jewish state.
7. Nasser goes to war against France, Great Britain, and Israel. ___	g. Gamal Abdel Nasser becomes prime minister of Egypt.
8. Israel and its Arab neighbors fight the Six-Day War. ___	h. War breaks out between Arabs and Jews.
9. Arab states attack Israel and place an embargo on all exports to Western countries supporting Israel. ___	i. The largest migration of Jews to Palestine takes place.
10. Anwar al-Sadat becomes president of Egypt. ___	j. An international oil crisis occurs.

Notes for Home: Your child learned about conflicts in the Middle East between Arabs and Jews.
Home Activity: With your child, discuss the importance of finding nonviolent ways to solve disputes. Have your child give examples of efforts to create peace in the Middle East.

Also on Teacher Resources CD-R

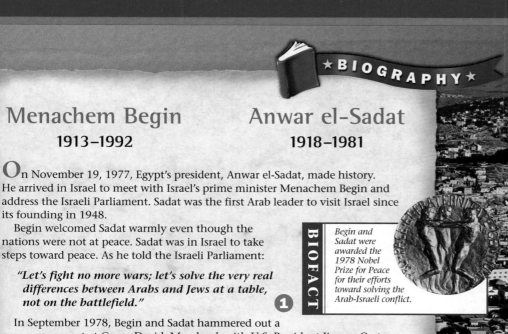

Menachem Begin
1913–1992

Anwar el-Sadat
1918–1981

On November 19, 1977, Egypt's president, Anwar el-Sadat, made history. He arrived in Israel to meet with Israel's prime minister Menachem Begin and address the Israeli Parliament. Sadat was the first Arab leader to visit Israel since its founding in 1948.

Begin welcomed Sadat warmly even though the nations were not at peace. Sadat was in Israel to take steps toward peace. As he told the Israeli Parliament:

> *"Let's fight no more wars; let's solve the very real differences between Arabs and Jews at a table, not on the battlefield."* ❶

In September 1978, Begin and Sadat hammered out a peace agreement at Camp David, Maryland, with U.S. President Jimmy Carter. Sadat and Begin soon signed two agreements, known as the Camp David Accords. Israel agreed to withdraw its troops that had occupied Egypt's Sinai Peninsula since 1967. In return, Egypt agreed to establish peace with Israel. The two leaders also set up a process for a transition to self-rule for the Palestinian Arabs living in the Israeli-occupied West Bank and Gaza Strip. As Begin explained, ❷

> *"We believe that if we achieve peace . . . we shall be able to assist one another . . . and a new era will be opened in the Middle East."*

The accords were hailed as a great achievement by most non-Arab states. However, many Arab states felt that Sadat was not backing the Arab cause. They did not want peace with Israel. In 1981 Sadat was assassinated by Muslim extremists.

Begin was also criticized for his role in the accords. A number of his supporters abandoned his political party after the accords were signed. In 1983 Begin resigned as prime minister following Israel's invasion of Lebanon.

BIOFACT

Begin and Sadat were awarded the 1978 Nobel Prize for Peace for their efforts toward solving the Arab-Israeli conflict.

Learn from Biographies

Why do you think Begin welcomed Sadat in 1977 even though Israel and Egypt were at war?

For more information, go online to *Meet the People* at **www.sfsocialstudies.com.**

619

CURRICULUM CONNECTION
Literature

[R]ead About the Middle East

[Th]e following selections may deepen students' [un]derstanding of issues in the Middle East.

[Th]e Arab-Israeli Conflict, by Tony McAleavy (Cambridge University Press, ISBN 0-521-62953-5, 1998) **On-Level**

[Ca]uses and Consequences of the Arab-Israeli Conflict, by Stewart Ross (Raintree/Steck-Vaughn, ISBN 0-817-24051-9, 1995) **On-Level**

[Isr]ael: An Illustrated History, by Daniel J. Schroeter [(]Oxford University Press, ISBN 0-195-10885-X, 1999) **Challenge**

Menachem Begin
Anwar el-Sadat

Objective

- Identify the contributions of significant individuals, such as Menachem Begin and Anwar el-Sadat, during the twentieth century.

1 Introduce and Motivate

Preview Ask students to recall what they learned about these men in Lesson 2. Tell students that they will learn more about the reasons that Begin and el-Sadat worked on a peace agreement and about the effects of that agreement in the Middle East.

Ask students what they can learn from reading about leaders such as Begin and el-Sadat. (They are good examples of people who strive for peace even though others may not agree with them.)

2 Teach and Discuss

Primary Source

Anwar el-Sadat, cited in *Great Lives of the Twentieth Century*; Menachem Begin, cited in *Les Prix Nobel 1978*

❶ **What point of view did el-Sadat express to Begin and to the Israeli people?** Possible answer: That Arabs and Jews could solve their problems peacefully by talking **Point of View**

❷ **Describe the compromises made by each side in the Camp David Accords.** Israel agreed to withdraw troops from the Sinai Peninsula. Egypt agreed to establish peace with Israel. **Main Idea and Details**

3 Close and Assess

Learn from Biographies Answer

Begin, too, was interested in trying to solve Israel and Egypt's differences without further bloodshed.

Eastern Europe

Objectives

- List and explain the major events that led to the fall of communism in Eastern Europe.

- List and describe the events of the Revolution of 1989.

- Define *perestroika* and *glasnost* and explain why Gorbachev used them in his policy.

- Describe the changes in Eastern Europe that resulted from the end of communism in Eastern Europe and the Soviet Union.

- Explain how the Soviet Union's response to protests against the Soviet government changed under Gorbachev.

Vocabulary

dissident, p. 621; *perestroika,* p. 622; **glasnost,** p. 622

Resources

- Workbook, p. 152
- Transparency 23
- Every Student Learns Guide, pp. 290–293
- Quick Study, pp. 146–147

Quick Teaching Plan

If time is short, have students create outlines as they read independently.

- Preview the lesson and write the headings on the board.
- As students read, they can jot down details from each section.

1 Introduce and Motivate

Preview Ask students what they already know about the Berlin Wall. Tell students that they will learn more about the Berlin Wall and the division between communist and noncommunist nations that it represented in Lesson 3.

You Are There Remind students that the wall was built by East German troops in August 1961. Ask students to explain why it was built.

LESSON 3

1980　　　　　1990　　　　20

1985
Mikhail Gorbachev becomes the Communist Party leader of the Soviet Union.

1991
The Soviet Union falls.

1989
The gates of the Berlin Wall open.

Eastern Europe

PREVIEW

Focus on the Main Idea
Calls for greater freedom brought an end to communism in Eastern Europe.

PLACES
Berlin Wall
Czech Republic
Slovak Republic
Slovenia
Croatia
Bosnia and Herzegovina
Macedonia

PEOPLE
Lech Walesa
Mikhail Gorbachev
Boris Yeltsin

VOCABULARY
dissident
perestroika
glasnost

TERMS
Solidarity
Kremlin
Commonwealth of Independent States

You Are There It's a crisp autumn night in November 1989. A huge party is taking place right here in the heart of Berlin, Germany. The gates of the Berlin Wall are open!

East German guards let cars, bicycles, and people through as fast as they can cross the checkpoints. These same soldiers used to forbid anyone from crossing the border. But everyone seems happy tonight. Some are singing, others are laughing. A few even chip away at the tall concrete wall with hammers or drills. Fireworks go off; the crowd applauds.

You hold your grandmother's hand tightly. Tears well in her eyes. "I remember when this wall went up," she says. "I never thought I'd see it come down." Even though it's well past your bedtime, you have been allowed to stay up late. You are excited to be part of history being made.

 Draw Conclusions As you read, identify facts about how communism ended in Eastern Europe.

▶ On November 10, 1989, on top of the Berlin Wall, Berliners celebrate the opening of the border between East and West Germany.

620

Practice and Extend

READING SKILL
Draw Conclusions

In the Lesson Review, students complete a graphic organizer like the one below. You may want to provide students with a copy of Transparency 23 to complete as they read the lesson.

Use Transparency 23

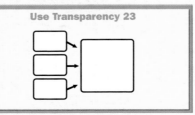

WEB SITE
Technology

- You can look up vocabulary words by clicking on *Social Studies Library* and selecting the dictionary at **www.sfsocialstudies.com.**

- Students can learn more about current news by clicking on *Current Events* at **www.sfsocialstudies.com.**

- Explore other events that occurred on this day by clicking on *This Day in History* at **www.sfsocialstudies.com.**

Changes in Eastern Europe

November 1989, the gates of the [Berlin] Wall were opened, allowing people [to mo]ve freely into West Germany. East [Germ]any's communist government soon [fell. I]n 1990 East and West Germany were [unit]ed into one country. By 1991 the [destr]uction of the Berlin Wall was complete.

[All] these events that ended communist rule [in Ea]stern Europe became known as the ["Rev]olution of 1989."

[In C]hapter 18, you read how Russia became [a com]munist country in 1917. After World War II, [the S]oviet Union forced communist governments [on co]untries in Eastern Europe. Soviet leaders [used] force to keep these countries united under [comm]unism.

[Beg]inning in the 1950s, some of these coun[tries] began to rebel against their communist [gover]nments. In 1953 people in East Germany [prote]sted against their communist government. [In 19]56 Hungary rebelled. In 1968 the people [of Cz]echoslovakia (che kuh sloh VAH kee uh) [dema]nded freedom. The Soviet Army quickly [crush]ed these movements.

[How]ever, in the early 1980s, workers in Poland [force]d their government to accept a labor union [that w]as free of communist control. The labor [union] was called **Solidarity.** An electronics tech[nician] named **Lech Walesa** (LEHK vah LEHN sah) [led So]lidarity. Before this time, labor unions in [comm]unist countries had been run by the [gover]nment, rather than by workers.

By 1987 Soviet leader **Mikhail Gorbachev** (mee kah EEL GAWR buh chawf)

▶ In Gdansk, Poland, Solidarity leader Lech Walesa speaks to shipyard workers.

began calling for more freedoms. His call for freedom started a chain reaction throughout Eastern Europe. As a result, Poland held free elections in 1989. In 1990 the Poles elected Lech Walesa as president.

Hungary and Czechoslovakia also broke free of communist rule in 1989. A writer named Vaclav Havel (VAH tslahv HAH vehl) became president of Czechoslovakia. He had been a leading **dissident,** or protester against the government. Later, Czechoslovakia split into two countries, the **Czech Republic** and the **Slovak Republic** (Slovakia). (See the map on page R16.)

The end of communism also led to the breakup of Yugoslavia (yoo goh SLAH vee uh), another country in Eastern Europe. It also helped to form the newly independent nations of **Slovenia,** **Croatia,** **Bosnia and Herzegovina,** and **Macedonia.** In the next chapter, you will read about wars that were caused by the creation of these "breakaway" nations.

REVIEW Why did Eastern Europe change so rapidly after Gorbachev allowed greater freedom?
⟳ Draw Conclusions

▶ During the 1980s, Soviet leader Mikhail Gorbachev became a driving force for political and economic change.

621

Changes in Eastern Europe

🕐 *Quick Summary* Various countries were dismantled and others created as communism came to an end in Eastern Europe.

1 Which of these Eastern European countries was the first to protest communist governments— Czechoslovakia, East Germany, Hungary, or Poland? In what year? East Germany; 1953 Sequence

2 Define Solidarity and describe its goal. Solidarity was led by Polish electronics technician Lech Walesa. It was a labor union that was free from communist control. Main Idea and Details

3 As communism declined, what was one nation that splintered? What new nations were formed? Possible answers: Czechoslovakia split into the Czech Republic and the Slovak Republic; Yugoslavia broke up. Slovenia, Croatia, Bosnia and Herzegovina, and Macedonia were formed. Cause and Effect

4 Which of the people described on this page do you think made the most important contribution to the quality of life in Eastern Europe? Explain. Answers will vary. Students should support their opinions with persuasive facts from the page. Evaluate

---

✓ **REVIEW ANSWER** Many Eastern Europeans had been unhappy with Soviet control. They were ready to take action at the first sign of relaxed control. Gorbachev's call for freedom started a chain reaction throughout Eastern Europe. ⟳ Draw Conclusions

Communism Crumbles

🕐 *Quick Summary* When Mikhail Gorbachev became the Soviet leader, he introduced policies to allow more freedom and to reform the economy. Eventually, the Soviet Union was dismantled.

5 **What effect did the Cold War have on the Soviet economy?** The Soviet Union spent a large amount of money on weapons rather than on other parts of its economy. **Cause and Effect**

Ongoing Assessment

If... students are unable to link cause and effect in discussing the Soviet economy,	**then...** create a cause and effect graphic organizer on the chalkboard. Remind students that an *effect* is something that happened, and a *cause* is the reason that it happened. Ask students to look for clue words that signal cause and effect in the text.

6 **Define *perestroika* and *glasnost*.** *Perestroika* is another word for "restructuring." *Glasnost* means "openness," or freedom of speech. **Main Idea and Details**

7 **How did Boris Yeltsin rise to power in Russia?** When an attempted coup d'état was made to remove Mikhail Gorbachev from office, Yeltsin led demonstrations to stop the coup. As a result, Yeltsin became more popular and powerful than Gorbachev. **Cause and Effect**

🌐 **MAP SKILL**
A New Eastern Europe

Guide students to summarize the changes to Eastern Europe caused by the breakup of the Soviet Union.

8 **Name the members of the Commonwealth of Independent States.** Russia, Belarus, Ukraine, Moldova, Georgia, Armenia, Azerbajjan, Turkmenistan, Tajikistan, Kyrgyzstan, Uzbekistan, Kazakhstan **Interpret Maps**

MAP SKILL Answer Estonia, Latvia, and Lithuania

Communism Crumbles

During the Cold War, the Soviet Union and the United States spent huge sums of money on weapons. As a result, the Soviet Union had little money left over for other parts of the economy. For most people, the communist promise of a "worker's paradise" remained just an unfulfilled promise. Many lost faith in the communist system.

In 1985 Mikhail Gorbachev became the Communist Party leader. During his term, he introduced **perestroika,** or "restructuring," to reform the Soviet economy. Gorbachev also introduced **glasnost,** or "openness," to allow people some freedom of speech. He hoped that these policies would improve the economy, offer political freedom, and democratize the Soviet system.

Glasnost soon made people want greater self-government. In 1990 one of the 15 Soviet republics, Lithuania, declared independence. Other republics then began declaring their independence.

Some Soviet officials were unhappy with these changes. In August 1991, they attempted a coup d'état to overthrow Gorbachev. **Boris Yeltsin** (YEL'T suhn), president of the Russian Republic, successfully led demonstrations to stop the coup.

These events helped strengthen Yeltsin's popularity, and he gained more power than Gorbachev. In December 1991, Yeltsin and other leaders of the republics declared the end of the Soviet Union. Yeltsin then made the **Kremlin,** an old Moscow fort that had been the seat of Soviet government, the center for his government. Rejecting communism, Yeltsin began to change the Russian economy.

🌐 **MAP SKILL** **A New Eastern Europe**

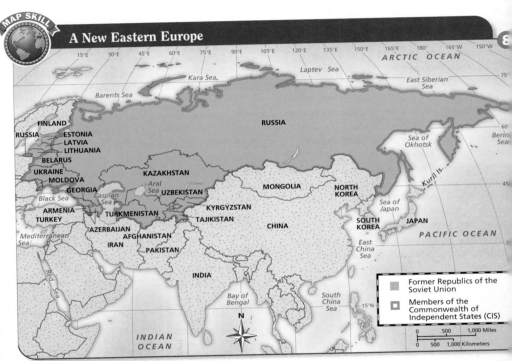

▶ The map of Eastern Europe changed after the fall of communism.

 **MAP SKILL** Use a Map Key *Which former republics of the Soviet Union did not become members of the Commonwealth of Independent States?*

622

Practice and Extend

❄️ **MEETING INDIVIDUAL NEEDS**
Leveled Practice

Write a Series of Journal Entries Students can write journal entries based on the ideas in this lesson.

Easy Students can write a journal entry to explore their own thoughts about what makes a country "free" and why they would want to live in a country that allows freedom of speech. **Reteach**

On-Level Students can write from the point of view of one of the people in this lesson and write ideas about the changes in Eastern Europe. They should explain their goals and how they accomplished them. **Extend**

Challenge Ask students to suppose they could interview the historical figures in this lesson. In their "reporters' journals," students can write questions that they would like to ask various people such as Gorbachev, Yeltsin, Havel, and Walesa. Have students anticipate answers and conduct "live" interviews. **Enrich**

For a Lesson Summary, use Quick Study, pp.146.

ter the failed Soviet coup attempt, crowds
lebrate outside the Kremlin, the center of
e Soviet goverment in Red Square.

e breakup of the Soviet Union in 1991
ed 15 new nations. Look at the map on
622 and locate these nations. Many of the
ns joined a loose association called the
monwealth of Independent States.

Mikhail Gorbachev resigned as president of the
Soviet Union on December 25, 1991. Describing
that day, he wrote:

> "The promise I gave to the
> people . . . was kept: I gave
> them freedom."

REVIEW What was the effect of *glasnost*?
Cause and Effect

Summarize the Lesson

1985 Mikhail Gorbachev became the
Communist Party leader of the Soviet Union.

1989 Communist governments fell in
Eastern Europe, and the gates of the Berlin
Wall opened.

1991 The Soviet Union came to an end.

ESSON 3   REVIEW

heck Facts and Main Ideas

Draw Conclusions Copy the diagram
below on a separate sheet of paper. Then
fill in the conclusion based on the given
facts.

he communist system failed in
Eastern Europe, and many
eople lost faith in communism.

Workers wanted labor unions
free of communist control.

Eastern Europeans protested
against their governments.

→ The
communist
system failed
in Eastern
Europe;
people
became
unhappy with
communism;
and the
communist
system in
Eastern
Europe lost
support from
the people.

What events does "the Revolution of 1989"
describe?

3. Why did Gorbachev start the policy of
perestroika? the policy of *glasnost*?

4. What changes did the end of communism
bring to Eastern Europe?

5. **Critical Thinking:** *Make Generalizations*
How did the Soviet response to protests
in Eastern Europe in the 1950s and 1960s
compare to those of Gorbachev in the
1980s?

Link to  **Writing**

Write an Editorial Suppose you are a member
of Solidarity in Poland in 1980. Write an editorial explaining why your labor union should be
controlled by workers, rather than by the communist government.

623

Workbook, p. 152

Lesson 3: Eastern Europe
Directions: Sequence the events in the order in which they took place by
numbering them from 1 (earliest) to 13 (most recent). You may use your textbook.

____ Mikhail Gorbachev calls for more freedom for Soviet people.

____ The people of Hungary rebel against their communist government.

____ Boris Yeltsin and other leaders of the republics declare the end of the Soviet Union in
December 1991.

____ The destruction of the Berlin Wall is complete.

____ Yeltsin begins to change the Russian economy and 15 new nations are created.

____ People in East Germany protest against their communist government.

____ East Germany and West Germany are reunited into one country.

____ Workers in Poland led by Lech Walesa force their government to accept Solidarity.

____ The people of Czechoslovakia want freedom, but their demands are rejected by the
Soviet Union.

____ After World War II, the Soviet Union forces communist governments on countries in
Eastern Europe.

____ Poland holds free elections in 1989.

____ Russia becomes a communist country.

____ Mikhail Gorbachev resigns as president of the Soviet Union.

**Also on Teacher
Resources CD-ROM.**

Primary Source

Cited in *Memoirs* by Mikhail Gorbachev

9 **Do you think that Gorbachev gave
the Soviet people freedom? Explain.**
Possible answer: Yes, he gave the people
freedom of speech and attempted to
bring openness to the nation.
Analyze Primary Sources

✓ **REVIEW ANSWER** *Glasnost*
encouraged more freedom and self-
government throughout the Soviet Union.
Lithuania declared its independence.
Other republics began to ignore Soviet
laws. **Cause and Effect**

Close and Assess

Summarize the Lesson

Tell students to examine the time line.
Copy it onto the chalkboard and ask
volunteers to place additional events on
the time line to expand it.

✓ **LESSON 3   REVIEW**

1. **Draw Conclusions** For possible
answers, see the reduced pupil page.

2. The fall of communist governments
in Poland, Hungary, Czechoslovakia,
East Germany, and other nations in
Eastern Europe; the opening of the
Berlin Wall

3. He started the policy of *perestroika*
to reform the Soviet economy. He
started the policy of *glasnost* to give
the people some freedom of speech.

4. The end of communism brought many
changes in government and many
new nations. In Eastern Europe it
brought about a new, unified
Germany, the Czech Republic and
Slovakia, Slovenia, Croatia, Bosnia
and Herzegovina, and Macedonia.

5. **Critical Thinking:** *Make
Generalizations* In the 1950s and
1960s, the Soviets sent troops to
crush protests in East Germany,
Hungary, and Czechoslovakia. In the
1980s Gorbachev gave the countries
of Eastern Europe the freedom to
change without fearing Soviet attack.

Link to  **Writing**

Remind students that an editorial
should be persuasive.

Determine Accuracy of Information

Objective

- Evaluate the credibility of print resources.

Resource

- Workbook, p. 153

1 Introduce and Motivate

What does *accuracy of information* mean? Discuss why it is important to use accurate sources. Pose a research scenario for students and ask them why it is important to know whether a source is reliable. Would students, for example, read a newspaper advice column to get facts about a historical event? Do they think that all Internet sites provide equally reliable information? Then have students read the **What?** section of text on p. 624.

Why determine whether information is accurate? Have students read the **Why?** section of text on p. 625. Ask them why some information they find may not be accurate. (Bias, prejudice, censorship)

2 Teach and Discuss

How is this skill used? Examine with students the table on p. 624.

- Point out that the data in the table are from factual sources. These numbers can be proven to be either true or false. Would students call this information accurate? Could this information be biased in any way?

- Ask students how helpful this information would be if they needed information about the year 2001. Emphasize the fact that students need to check copyright dates when they are looking for up-to-date information.

- Have students read the **How?** section of text on p. 625.

Determine Accuracy of Information

What? When you are reading a book, magazine, periodical, or newspaper, how do you know if the source is accurate? You face this issue when you are doing general reading or gathering information for a report. Determining the credibility of a source is an important skill. *Credibility* means "believability." If a source is not credible, then you should not take the information you are reading as fact.

Information is updated from time to time. Updated sources are more likely to be accurate. If you are using a source that is ten or more years old, you may want to double-check the information. This is especially important when you are using statistics or numbers. If you needed to find the population of a country for a research report, the most accurate statistic is from the most recent census. A census is an official national count of the people of a country or state. It is taken by about 90 percent of all countries in the world every ten years. Look at the information below from the U.S. Census Bureau. The population and growth rate of Russia by decade are given for the years 1960–2000.

The information in this table is provided by the U.S. Census Bureau. This bureau is a U.S. government office. A department within the U.S. Census Bureau gathers international population statistics.

Population and Growth Rate of Russia, 1960–2000

Year	Population	Growth Rate
1960	119,632,000	1.6
1970	130,245,000	0.9
1980	139,045,000	0.7
1990	148,082,000	0.6
2000	146,001,000	−0.1

source: U.S. Census Bureau

What conclusion can you draw from this table? The population growth rate, or the rate of population increase, drops after 1970 from 0.9 to 0.7. The rate decreases even more after 1990. From what you have read about the events in the Soviet Union between 1989–1991, make an inference. Does this information seem accurate? For example, people began to leave Russia when communism became weaker in the Soviet Union in the late 1980s. After 1991 Russians who wanted to get out of the former Soviet Union were free to leave.

1

Practice and Extend

 CURRICULUM CONNECTION
Math

Create Line Graphs

- Invite students to create a line graph using the information on the page. For the population growth rate data, for example, students could place the years on the horizontal axis and the population on the vertical axis.

- Remind students to add a title to their graph and the source and date of the data used.

- Students can use their completed graphs to formulate questions that challenge their classmates.

y? Almost anyone can write an article
[b]ook. Sometimes writers have biases or
[opin]ices that affect how they write about a
[…] If you do not check the accuracy of a
[…], you may be reading or using incorrect
[…]ation.

[For] example, under communist rule, the Soviet
[…] had tight rules on releasing information.
[There] was no freedom of the press. The Soviet
[govern]ment often released false information,
[mis]ading its people and other nations.
[Ho]wever, in the mid-1980s, Gorbachev's policy
[gla]snost gave more freedom of the press.
[Ma]nkred Golenpolsky of the Soviet State
[Publis]hing Committee said in 1988, "It's more
[interesti]ng right now to read than to live." Even more
[infor]mation became available to the public and
[w]orld after 1991.

w? Knowing about the author will help you
[deter]mine whether the source is credible.
[Knowi]ng how current the source is, or what the
[public]ation date is, helps you determine the
[accur]acy of information.

Knowing the history of the former Soviet Union
will help you determine the credibility of the
selection below. If you did not know that the
Soviet Union had strict rules on releasing information before 1986, you might think that the
selection is inaccurate.

Think and Apply

Read the selection from *The New Russians* by
Hedrick Smith, who won the Pulitzer Prize for
International Reporting. Then answer the
questions.

> *"Suddenly criticizing the Soviet past,
> the Soviet present, even the Soviet
> leadership, was not only tolerated
> [accepted], it was encouraged—in the
> press, books, theater, films, and on
> television . . . . Other books hidden
> away by Soviet authors came off the
> shelves . . . . Glasnost brought them
> out into the daylight."*

1 What information helps you determine
whether or not the information from
Hedrick Smith's book is accurate or not?

2 What other research might you need to do
before you decide whether or not Smith's
book has provided accurate information?

625

---

1 **Explain the general trend of the
population and its growth rate in
Russia during the last 30 years.** The
population rose between 1970 and
1990, but the growth rate slowed from
decade to decade. Finally in 2000, the
growth rate declined slightly overall.
Analyze Information

2 **If you are evaluating a book for
accuracy of information, what might
you first consider?** The author's
reputation and the context in which it
was written; how recent any data it
contains are (its copyright date).
Sequence

3 Close and Assess

Think and Apply

1. I read in Lesson 3 that the Soviet
Union had strict rules on the reporting
of information before Gorbachev
announced glasnost in 1986, so the
information seems accurate.

2. Research the author, Hedrick Smith.
Students have already been told that
Smith was a Pulitzer Prize winner, so
they have a starting point.

Workbook, p. 153

Determine Accuracy of Information

When gathering information, it is important to use source material that is accurate
and credible. Outdated information can provide old statistics and lead to false
conclusions. An author who projects bias or is not a credible source for a topic can
state opinions as facts, which can mislead the reader.

Directions: Fill in the circle next to the correct answer.

1. Which of the following online sources would be most likely to post unbiased information
   about a recent world crisis?
   Ⓐ government Web site
   Ⓑ online chat room
   Ⓒ family home page
   Ⓓ e-mail from an eyewitness

2. Which of the following print sources would be most likely to provide a firsthand account
   of the fall of the Berlin Wall?
   Ⓐ novel about the reunification of Germany
   Ⓑ article from a recent monthly German teen magazine
   Ⓒ diary entry from an eyewitness to the event
   Ⓓ entry in a world almanac

3. Which of the following print sources would be most likely to provide reliable statistics on
   the population of your state?
   Ⓐ publication of the U.S. Census Bureau
   Ⓑ 1990 almanac
   Ⓒ encyclopedia
   Ⓓ geographic dictionary

4. Which of the following would be most likely an objective source for a report on the
   decolonization of India?
   Ⓐ speech by Mohandas Gandhi
   Ⓑ declaration by the British government
   Ⓒ biography of Jawaharlal Nehru
   Ⓓ encyclopedia entry on the history of India in the twentieth century

Notes for Home: Your child learned how to analyze sources for accuracy of information.
Home Activity: With your child, read two accounts of the same event from different sources. Then
compare the sources for accuracy, correctness, and objectivity.

**Also on Teacher
Resources CD-ROM.**

Resources

- Assessment Book, pp. 109–112
- Workbook, p. 154: Vocabulary Review

Chapter Summary

For possible answers, see the reduced pupil page.

Vocabulary

1. e, **2.** d, **3.** b, **4.** c, **5.** a, **6.** f

People and Terms

Possible answers:

1. Julius Nyerere was elected president of independent Tanzania.

2. Robert Mugabe was the first prime minister of Zimbabwe.

3. Nelson Mandela helped end apartheid and became the first black president of South Africa.

4. Mohandas Gandhi was the leader of the independence movement in India.

5. Arab nationalism is Arab unity.

6. Zionism is the commitment to establishing a Jewish state in Palestine.

7. Kwame Nkrumah was a leader in Ghana who believed that freedom belonged to all people.

8. Solidarity was a labor union in Poland that became independent of communist control.

9. Lech Walesa was the head of Solidarity and a president of post-communist Poland.

10. Mikhail Gorbachev was the Soviet leader whose call for freedoms led to a chain reaction of Eastern European nations seeking freedom.

Facts and Main Ideas

1. Lack of good leadership, internal conflicts

2. Nonviolent civil disobedience is the peaceful refusal to cooperate with unjust laws. Gandhi persuaded millions of Indians to refuse to cooperate with the British, making it impossible for Britain to rule India effectively.

1940   19

1947
India and Pakistan gained independence.

about 1960
Many colonies in sub-Saharan Africa began to gain independence.

1948
State of Israel was created.

Chapter Summary

Draw Conclusions

Target Skill

On a separate piece of paper, fill in a conclusion that the facts support.

Many colonies in sub-Saharan Africa became new nations after World War II.
Most colonies in South and Southeast Asia became new nations after World War II.
New countries and states formed in the middle East after the world wars.
The Soviet Union broke up into 15 new states in the 1990s.

→ Since the end of World War II, many new nations and states have been established.

Vocabulary

Match each word with the correct definition or description.

1 decolonization (p. 607)

2 coup d'état (p. 607)

3 apartheid (p. 609)

4 segregate (p. 609)

5 dissident (p. 621)

6 civil disobedience (p. 611)

a. protester against a harsh government

b. government policy of racial separation

c. to keep people of different races separate

d. overthrow of government by a small group

e. ending of colonial rule

f. refusal to obey unjust laws

People and Terms

Write a sentence explaining why each of the following people or terms was important in decolonization or the creation of new nations. You may use two or more in a single sentence.

1 Julius Nyerere (p. 607)

2 Robert Mugabe (p. 609)

3 Nelson Mandela (p. 609)

4 Mohandas Gandhi (p. 611)

5 Arab nationalism (p. 616)

6 Zionism (p. 61

7 Kwame Nkrum (p. 607)

8 Solidarity (p. 621)

9 Lech Walesa (p. 621)

10 Mikhail Gorbachev (p. 621)

626

Practice and Extend

Assessment Options

✔ **Chapter 21 Assessment**

- Chapter 21 Content Test: Use Assessment Book, pp. 109–110.
- Chapter 21 Skills Test: Use Assessment Book, pp. 111–112.

Standardized Test Prep

- Chapter 21 Tests contain standardized test format.

✔ **Chapter 21 Performance Assessment**

- Students can create a map portfolio to document the changes that occurred in Africa, Asia, and Europe during the second half of the twentieth century.
- Their portfolios should include maps of the various continents annotated with information about "before and after" names
- As you evaluate students' portfolios, assess their understanding of the many changes that took place in the world as new nations were formed.

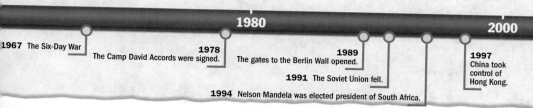

1967 The Six-Day War
1978 The Camp David Accords were signed.
1980
1989 The gates to the Berlin Wall opened.
1991 The Soviet Union fell.
1994 Nelson Mandela was elected president of South Africa.
1997 China took control of Hong Kong.
2000

Facts and Main Ideas

What were two challenges of independence in Africa?

What is nonviolent civil disobedience and how did Gandhi use it to help India gain independence?

Name five nations that have formed in Europe since 1989.

Time Line How many years passed between the opening of the gates to the Berlin Wall and the end of the Soviet Union?

Main Idea How did Africa, South Asia, and Southeast Asia change after World War II?

Main Idea Name two important changes in the Middle East after World War II.

Main Idea How do the structures of the Soviet Union and the Commonwealth of Independent States differ?

Critical Thinking: *Make Inferences* Do you think that Mikhail Gorbachev believed in communism? Explain your answer.

Write About History

Write a poem expressing joy on the independence day of a country.

Write a letter home telling about events in Palestine in 1948 from a journalist's point of view.

Write an editorial about the fall of the Soviet Union.

Apply Skills

Determine Accuracy of Information

Your teacher may ask you to use additional reading materials with your textbook. As you read, you may find different explanations and statistics about an event. How will you decide which source is more accurate?

Read the passages below about the Palestinian population after the 1967 Arab-Israeli war. The first one is taken from your textbook.

"The Gaza Strip and West Bank were home to more than 1 million Palestinians."

"1.3 million Palestinians flee when Israel captures Gaza and West Bank during the Six-Day War."
United Nations Relief and Works Agency (UNRWA)

"Israel . . . acquire[d] the problem of administering more than a million Arabs in Gaza and the West Bank."
Encyclopaedia Britannica

❶ What information do these three sources provide?

❷ Do you think that one source is more accurate than the others? If yes, explain why.

❸ How would you check the accuracy of these sources?

Internet Activity

To get help with vocabulary, people, and terms, select dictionary, encyclopedia, or almanac from *Social Studies Library* at **www.sfsocialstudies.com.**

627

Hands-on Unit Project

Unit 8 Performance Assessment

See p. 678 for information about using the Unit Project as a means of performance assessment. A scoring guide is provided on p. 678.

WEB SITE
Technology

r more information, students can select the ctionary, encyclopedia, or almanac from *Social* udies Library at **www.sfsocialstudies.com.**

Workbook, p. 154

Also on Teacher Resources CD-ROM.

3. Accept any five: Unified Germany, the Czech Republic, the Slovak Republic, Slovenia, Croatia, Bosnia and Herzegovina, Macedonia, Estonia, Latvia, Lithuania, Belarus, Ukraine, Moldova, post-Soviet Russia, Georgia, Armenia, Azerbaijan, Turkmenistan, Krgystan, Tajikistan, Uzbekistan, Kazakhstan

4. Two years

5. Many former colonies in these areas became independent after World War II.

6. Students should cite the creation of Israel. Other possibilities: Arab nationalism became a force in many Arab nations; Israel seized the West Bank, Golan Heights, Sinai Peninsula, and Gaza Strip; Arab states placed an embargo on oil exports to countries that supported Israel.

7. The Soviet Union was a union of republics that had little freedom. The Commonwealth of Independent States is a loose association of independent nations that were once Soviet republics.

8. Possible answer: Yes, Gorbachev introduced policies to try to fix the Soviet Union's problems. He must have believed that if problems were solved and the people given more freedom, they would choose to improve their communist system rather than abandon it.

Write About History

1. Encourage students to use vivid images and figurative language to make their poems more interesting.

2. Encourage students to use correct letter format. Letters should be written from the first-person point of view.

3. Remind students that editorials contain reasoned opinions supported by facts.

Apply Skills

1. The number of Palestinian Arabs living in the Gaza Strip and the West Bank following the Six-Day War

2. Students may say that the UNRWA is more accurate because it gives a more specific number.

3. Check the author; look in additional sources; try to determine how each author gathered statistics.

Chapter Planning Guide

Chapter 22 • Cooperation, Conflict, and Challenges

Locating Time and Place pp. 628–629

Lesson Titles	Pacing	Main Ideas
Lesson 1 **Economic Cooperation** pp. 630–633		• World economies are closely bound together, while people continue to fight for civil rights and freedom
Chart and Graph Skills: Interpret Cartograms pp. 634–635	2 days	• A cartogram, a graph based on a map, represents in an easy-to-use format.
Lesson 2 **Conflicts of Identity** pp. 636–641		• Ethnic, political, and religious differences have led violent conflicts around the world.
Biography: Aung San Suu Kyi p. 642	2 days	• Aung San Suu Kyi won the Nobel Peace Prize for her work to make her country, Myanmar, democratic.
Citizen Heroes: Courage The Struggle for Peace p. 643		• Rigoberta Menchú has worked to create peace and further the cause of human rights in Guatemala.
Lesson 3 **Political Conflicts and Challenges** pp. 644–649		• People around the world continue to stand up against terrorism and work toward peace.
	2 days	

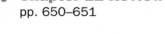
✓ **Chapter 22 Review** pp. 650–651

◀ **Aung San Suu Kyi has devoted her life to bringing democracy to her country.**

✓ = Assessment Options

In 2002, the 15 countries of the European Union replaced their national currencies with the euro.

Vocabulary	Resources	Meeting Individual Needs
oss domestic product (GDP) ading bloc ro de agreement	• Workbook, p. 156 • Transparency 20 • Every Student Learns Guide, pp. 294–297 • Quick Study, pp. 148–149 • Workbook, p. 157	• ESL Support, TE p. 631 • Leveled Practice, TE p. 633
nicity ltiethnic nation nic cleansing ressive	• Workbook, p. 158 • Transparencies 23, 64 • Every Student Learns Guide, pp. 298–301 • Quick Study, pp. 150–151	• Learning Styles, TE p. 635 • ESL Support, TE p. 637 • Leveled Practice, TE p. 639
rorism	• Workbook, p. 159 • Transparency 23 • Every Student Learns Guide, pp. 302–305 • Quick Study, pp. 152–153	• ESL Support, TE p. 646 • Leveled Practice, TE p. 647 • Learning Styles, TE p. 649
	✓ Chapter 22 Content Test, Assessment Book, pp. 113–114 ✓ Chapter 22 Skills Test, Assessment Book, pp. 115–116	✓ Chapter 22 Performance Assessment, TE p. 650

Providing More Depth

Additional Resources
- Vocabulary Cards
- Daily Activity Bank
- Social Studies Plus!
- Big Book Atlas
- Student Atlas
- Outline Maps
- Desk Maps

 Technology

- AudioText
- The test maker
- Teacher Resources CD-ROM
- Map Resources CD-ROM
- **www.sfsocialstudies.com**

 To establish guidelines for your students' safe and responsible use of the Internet, use the Scott Foresman Internet Guide.

Additional Internet Links
To find out more about:
- Myanmar, visit **www.york.cuny.edu**
- Tiananmen Square, visit **www.nmis.org**
- Kosovo, visit **www.care.org**

Key Internet Search Terms
- trading bloc, trade agreement
- Yugoslavia
- Ireland

Workbook Support

Use the following Workbook pages to support content and skills development as you teach Chapter 22. You can also view and print Workbook pages from the Teacher Resources CD-ROM.

Workbook, p. 155

Vocabulary Preview

Use with Chapter 22.

Directions: Match each vocabulary word in the box to its meaning. Write the vocabulary word on the line before the definition. You may use your glossary.

gross domestic product	trade agreement	ethnic cleansing
trading bloc	ethnicity	repressive
euro	multiethnic nation	terrorism

ethnic cleansing   1. policy of driving out or killing people who do not share the same identity

ethnicity   2. sharing the same language, customs, and other aspects of culture

trade agreement   3. understanding that outlines rules about the exchange of goods between countries

trading bloc   4. group of countries that agree to trade under favorable conditions

gross domestic product   5. value of all final goods and services produced in a country in a year

multiethnic nation   6. nation with many different ethnic groups

repressive   7. denies citizens basic civil rights

euro   8. currency issued by the European Union

terrorism   9. use of violence and fear to achieve political goals

 Notes for Home: Your child learned the vocabulary terms for Chapter 22.
Home Activity: With your child, discuss your family's ethnicity and the countries in which family members or ancestors were born. Identify what economic ties, if any, those countries have with the United States.

Use with Pupil Edition, p. 628

Workbook, p. 156

Lesson 1: Economic Cooperation

Use with Pages 630–633.

Directions: Read the following descriptions and decide which regional trading bloc each one describes. Write E for European Union, A for ASEAN, M for Mercosur, and N for NAFTA. You may use your textbook.

M 1. includes Argentina, Brazil, Paraguay, and Uruguay

N 2. includes the United States, Mexico, and Canada

E 3. includes 15 European nations

A 4. includes five Southeast Asian countries

Directions: Answer the following questions on the lines provided.

5. What are three effects of having a global economy?

> Possible answers: What happens in one country soon affects others; products we buy come from all over the world; some people and nations have become very wealthy; it has caused problems for some workers, communities, and economies; some industries have had to shut down because of increased competition.

6. How does a developing country differ from a developed country?

> The industries and economies in a developing country are in the process of developing and generate less wealth than those in developed countries do.

 Notes for Home: Your child learned about global economies and economic cooperation among nations.
Home Activity: With your child, analyze the graph on p. 631. Discuss some of the differences between developing and developed nations. Which countries or regions have the highest and lowest GDP?

Use with Pupil Edition, p. 633

Workbook, p. 157

Interpret Cartograms

Use with Pages 6...

A cartogram is a special kind of graph based on a map. A cartogram stretches and bends a nation's boundaries on a map to represent information.

Directions: Read the table below. Then answer the questions about cartograms.

	Area	Population	Population of Largest City	Gr Dom Pro
Yugoslavia	39,499 sq. mi.	11,206,847	1,168,454	$24.3
Rwanda	10,169 sq. mi.	8,154,933	232,733	$3 b.
Ireland	27,136 sq. mi.	3,632,944	1,056,666	$59.9

1. Which of the countries in the table would be the smallest on a cartogram that was population? Why?

> Ireland; Ireland has the smallest population.

2. For which category would Ireland appear as the largest country on a cartogram? V

> Gross Domestic Product; Ireland has a higher GDP tha Yugoslavia or Rwanda.

3. Which country would appear larger based on the population of its largest city: Yu or Rwanda? Why?

> Yugoslavia; its largest city has a larger population tha Rwanda's largest city.

4. Which country would appear the smallest on a cartogram that was based on area?

> Rwanda; it has the smallest area of the three countrie the table.

Notes for Home: Your child learned how to interpret cartograms.
Home Activity: With your child, review which cities or countries would be the largest and small cartogram based on the amount of rainfall they have received.

Use with Pupil Edition, p. 635

Workbook Support

Workbook, p. 158

Use with Pages 636–641.

on 2: Conflicts of Identity

ns: Read the following descriptions and decide to which region each
rite *Y* for Yugoslavia, *A* for Africa, and *I* for Ireland. Some descriptions
ly to more than one region. Include all regions that fit the description.
wer the questions that follow.

1. Issues over identity or ethnicity lead to violence.

2. Millions of refugees flee or are forced to leave.

3. Conflicts arise over religion.

4. Serbs fight Kosovars.

5. The country is divided geographically.

6. Hutu fight Tutsi.

7. The country begins to break apart when the communists lose power.

8. Catholics fight Protestants.

9. People engage in ethnic cleansing.

10. Outside troops are sent in.

at are two examples of basic human rights?

ossible answers: **Freedom of speech and freedom from**
rrest without just cause or reason

ch basic human rights were women denied under the Taliban's rule?

ossible answers: **The right to work, attend school, practice**
edicine, and make choices in health care

at ways do you think the governments of developed nations such as the United States
nfluence a repressive government?

ossible answers: **Nations might place sanctions on**
untries with repressive governments, cut off economic aid,
send funding to agencies that support basic civil rights.

es for Home: Your child learned how ethnic, political, and religious differences have led to violence
nd the world.
me Activity: With your child, brainstorm ways people can resolve conflicts over identity or ethnicity.

Use with Pupil Edition, p. 641

Workbook, p. 159

Use with Pages 644–649.

Lesson 3: Political Conflicts and Challenges

Directions: Use the terms in the box to complete each sentence with information
from Lesson 3. You may use your textbook.

religion	Oklahoma City	Lockerbie
terrorism	World Trade Center	antiterrorism
Pentagon	Lebanon	Taliban
ethnicity		political beliefs

1. **Terrorism** _____ can take the form of assassinations, bombings, hijackings,
kidnappings, or chemical and germ warfare.

2. People in the military were targeted by terrorists when a car bomb exploded in 1983 at the
U.S. embassy in _____ **Lebanon** _____.

3. In December 1988, an airplane flying over _____ **Lockerbie** _____, Scotland, was
destroyed by a terrorist bomb.

4. In April 1995, a car bomb exploded outside the Murrah Federal Building in
_____ **Oklahoma City** _____, Oklahoma.

5. On the morning of September 11, 2001, hijacked airplanes crashed into the twin towers of
the **World Trade Center** in New York City and the _____ **Pentagon** _____ near
Washington, D.C., killing about 3,000 people.

6. Following the terrorist attacks on September 11, Congress passed tougher
_____ **antiterrorism** _____ laws to support the fight against terrorism.

7. The United States gathered evidence that the _____ **Taliban** _____ government in
Afghanistan was protecting the terrorist group responsible for the attacks on September 11.

8. Acts of terrorism are often caused by differences in _____ **religion** _____,
_____ **ethnicity** _____, or _____ **political beliefs** _____ among people.

Notes for Home: Your child learned about acts of terrorism and the struggle to fight terrorist attacks
around the world.
Home Activity: With your child, brainstorm ways the governments and people around the world can stand
up against terrorism. Discuss how the United States has responded to acts of terrorism in the past.

Use with Pupil Edition, p. 649

Workbook, p. 160

Use with Chapter 22.

Vocabulary Review

Directions: Read each sentence. Then replace the words in italics with the correct vocabulary
term from the box and write it on the line provided. Not all words will be used. You may use
your glossary.

gross domestic product (GDP)	trade agreement	ethnic cleansing
trading bloc	ethnicity	repressive
euro	multiethnic nation	terrorism

1. Sometimes differences in religion and *shared language, customs, and culture* are factors in
war.

   ethnicity

2. Many developed nations have a larger *measure of a nation's wealth* than most developing
countries do.

   gross domestic product (GDP)

3. Yugoslavia is an example of a *nation with many different ethnic groups*.

   multiethnic nation

4. For years, South Africa had a government that was *denying citizens basic civil rights*.

   repressive

5. The *group of countries that agree to trade under favorable conditions* formed by the
United States, Mexico, and Canada signed the NAFTA agreement in 1994.

   trading bloc

6. After Bosnia declared independence, Slobodan Milosevic encouraged Serb soldiers to
carry out a policy of *driving out and sometimes killing the people who do not share the
same identity*.

   ethnic cleansing

7. The partnership between the United States, Canada, and Mexico had its roots in a 1989
understanding that outlines rules about the exchange of goods between countries.

   trade agreement

Notes for Home: Your child learned the vocabulary terms for Chapter 22.
Home Activity: With your child, read a newspaper article about international trade and banking. What
references to trade agreements or trading blocs are made?

Use with Pupil Edition, p. 651

Assessment Support

Use the following Assessment Book pages to assess content and skills in Chapter 22. You can also view and print Assessment Book pages from the Teacher Resources CD-ROM.

Assessment Book, p. 113

Chapter 22 Test

Part 1: Content Test

Directions: Fill in the circle next to the correct answer.

Lesson Objective (1:1, 5)

1. What has been one effect of trading blocs on member nations?
   - Ⓐ Many more blocs have been created.
   - ● Tariffs on goods have been reduced or removed.
   - Ⓒ Fewer products have been offered for sale.
   - Ⓓ The prices of goods around the world have dropped, causing higher profits.

Lesson Objective (1:5)

2. How can a country benefit from belonging to a trading bloc?
   - ● It may enjoy reduced tariffs and increased trade.
   - Ⓑ Higher taxes are placed on traded goods.
   - Ⓒ There is more control over trade.
   - Ⓓ More manufactured goods can be imported.

Lesson Objective (1:2)

3. Which of the following does NOT describe gross domestic product?
   - Ⓐ value of goods and services produced in a country in a year
   - ● a tariff, quota, or embargo that often hinders trade
   - Ⓒ measure of a nation's wealth
   - Ⓓ tool to compare production of developing and developed nations

Lesson Objective (1:3)

4. Which of the following countries is NOT a North American Free Trade Agreement (NAFTA) partner?
   - Ⓐ United States
   - Ⓑ Canada
   - ● Great Britain
   - Ⓓ Mexico

Lesson Objective (1:4)

5. What is the purpose of the World Trade Organization (WTO)?
   - Ⓐ control tariffs
   - Ⓑ set exchange rates
   - ● settle trade disputes
   - Ⓓ allow free trade among all nations

Lesson Objective (2:1, 2)

6. What was one result of the conflicts in Bosnia and Kosovo?
   - Ⓐ The Bosnian and Kosovar fighters surrendered to the Serb soldiers.
   - Ⓑ Serbian president Milosevic was removed from power.
   - Ⓒ The two regions declared independence from Serbia.
   - ● Thousands of refugees were driven from the area.

Lesson Objective (2:3)

7. How were the conflicts in central Africa and Northern Ireland similar?
   - Ⓐ Both involved people with opposing religious beliefs.
   - Ⓑ Both resulted in few casualties.
   - ● Both were caused by hatred related to differences of identity.
   - Ⓓ Both have continued for more than 200 years.

Use with Pupil Edition, p. 650

Assessment Book, p. 114

Lesson Objective (2:1)

8. Which two groups fought for control of Northern Ireland?
   - ● Protestants and Catholics
   - Ⓑ Muslims and Arabs
   - Ⓒ Serbs and Bosnians
   - Ⓓ Hutu and Tutsi

Lesson Objective (2:5)

9. Which of the following is NOT an action taken against women as a result of policies like those of the Taliban?
   - Ⓐ drove women out of the workforce
   - ● forced women to marry at a younger age
   - Ⓒ banned women from getting medical care
   - Ⓓ kept girls from attending school

Lesson Objective (2:4)

10. In which of the following countries do citizens today struggle to receive basic human rights?
    - Ⓐ the Netherlands and Great Britain
    - ● Myanmar (Burma) and Chiapas, Mexico
    - Ⓒ the United States and Japan
    - Ⓓ Canada and France

Lesson Objective (3:2)

11. Which of the following describes terrorism?
    - Ⓐ heroic act in the face of danger
    - Ⓑ fight against chemical warfare
    - ● use of violence and fear to achieve political goals
    - Ⓓ use of violence to perform ethnic cleansing

Lesson Objective (3:2)

12. Which is NOT a method of terrorism?
    - Ⓐ kidnappings
    - Ⓑ hijackings
    - Ⓒ bombings
    - ● robberies

Lesson Objective (3:3)

13. What was the result of the 1914 assassination of Austrian Archduke Francis Ferdinand?
    - Ⓐ An American plane was destroyed.
    - Ⓑ Congress passed tougher antiterrorism laws.
    - ● It started a chain reaction throughout Europe, eventually leading to World War I.
    - Ⓓ The United States began bombing Taliban military targets.

Lesson Objective (3:1, 3)

14. How did Thomas Jefferson respond to the Barbary States' attacks on U.S. and European ships in the eighteenth century?
    - ● He sent a naval squadron to stop the piracy.
    - Ⓑ He declared war against North Africa.
    - Ⓒ He promoted piracy against Barbary States' ships in the Mediterranean.
    - Ⓓ The United States entered World War I.

Lesson Objective (3:3, 5)

15. Which is NOT an action taken by the U.S. government following the attacks on September 11, 2001?
    - ● began bombing military targets in Great Britain
    - Ⓑ passed tougher antiterrorism laws
    - Ⓒ increased security at airports and other public buildings
    - Ⓓ provided the airline industry with funding

Use with Pupil Edition, p. 650

Assessment Support

Assessment Book, p. 115

Part 2: Skills Test

Directions: Use complete sentences to answer questions 1–8. Use a separate sheet of paper if you need more space.

1. Today many countries in Europe, North America, and Asia belong to trading blocs. What do these countries hope to gain from trade agreements? **Main Idea and Details**

   They hope to reduce or eliminate taxes on goods traded to member nations, increase trade, and encourage cooperation among bloc members.

2. How do member nations of the European Union benefit from a single currency? **Summarize**

   Possible answer: By using a single currency, the countries in the European Union do not have to use exchange rates. As a result, EU nations were exporting more manufactured goods than any other single nation.

3. What effect has the North American Free Trade Agreement had on the United States? **Cause and Effect**

   The expanded U.S. trade by removing tariffs on goods made and sold in North America.

4. Why is it important for the nations of the world to support human rights for women? **Express Ideas**

   Possible answer: Basic human rights should extend to both genders. World organizations and nations should support equal rights and freedoms for all citizens.

5. How do the freedoms in the United States compare to those in countries with repressive governments? **Compare and Contrast**

   Possible answer: Americans enjoy greater freedoms than people in many countries do. The basic freedoms and rights given to many Americans are not granted to citizens in other parts of the world.

Use with Pupil Edition, p. 650

Assessment Book, p. 116

6. Why was the student protest at Tiananmen Square in China an important event in world affairs? **Evaluate**

   Possible answer: It brought the world's attention to human rights violations and showed the world that some people must fight for basic freedoms. It also proved to the world that the Chinese communist government denies its citizens certain civil rights.

7. How can adults and children around the world stand up to acts of terrorism? **Express Ideas**

   Possible answer: People can give blood and donate money to organizations set up to help victims and families of terrorism. People can also support their nations by hanging their country's flag and showing pride in their country.

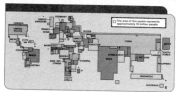

Population of Asia, 2001

8. Use the cartogram to answer the questions. **Interpret Cartograms**
   a. What does the cartogram show?

   the population of Asian countries in 2001

   b. Why are the country shapes not representative of the actual country?

   The cartogram distorts a real map to show population. The larger the population of a country, the greater its area on the cartogram.

   c. Which country has the largest population? **China**

Use with Pupil Edition, p. 650

Cooperation, Conflict, and Challenges

Chapter 22 Outline

Resources

- Workbook, p. 155: Vocabulary Preview
- Vocabulary Cards
- Social Studies Plus!

1991, Maastricht: Lesson 1

This picture shows euros, the currency of the European Union. Ask how euros compare to American bills. (Bills are green and have pictures of presidents on them; the euro shown here is pink and has pictures of buildings on it; both are paper.)

1998, Kosovo: Lesson 2

If necessary, remind students that civil war is a war between different groups of people who live in the same country. Ask students to describe the person in the picture and to explain how this person might be affected by war. (She might not be able to go to school; some of her relatives might leave to fight in the war; her family may have trouble buying food or other supplies.)

2001, The United States: Lesson 3

Tell students that this picture shows firefighters and military personnel hanging a flag from the Pentagon after the September 11, 2001, terrorist attacks. Ask students to describe the size of the flag and discuss why a flag of this size was selected. (Extremely large; to show that the United States was still strong even though it had been attacked)

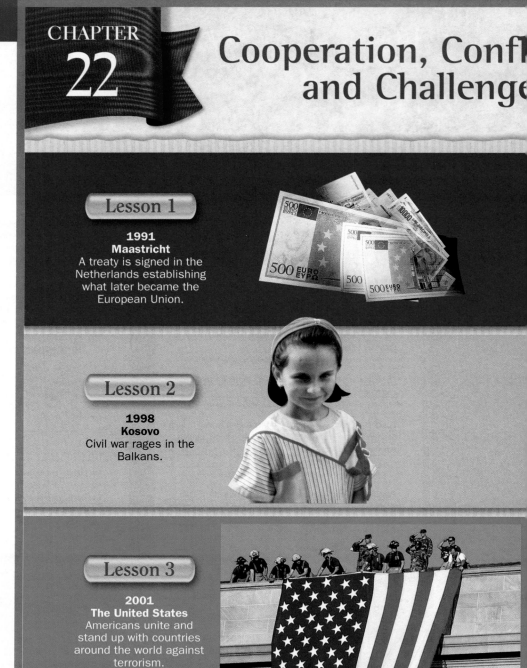

CHAPTER 22 Cooperation, Conf[...] and Challenge[...]

Lesson 1

1991 Maastricht
A treaty is signed in the Netherlands establishing what later became the European Union.

Lesson 2

1998 Kosovo
Civil war rages in the Balkans.

Lesson 3

2001 The United States
Americans unite and stand up with countries around the world against terrorism.

628

Practice and Extend

Vocabulary Preview

- Use Workbook p. 155 to help students preview the vocabulary words in this chapter.
- Use Vocabulary Cards to preview key concept words in this chapter.

Also on Teacher Resources CD-ROM.

Workbook, p. 155

Vocabulary Preview

Directions: Match each vocabulary word in the box to its meaning. Write the vocabulary word on the line before the definition. You may use your glossary.

gross domestic product	trade agreement	ethnic cleansing
trading bloc	ethnicity	repressive
euro	multiethnic nation	terrorism

_____ 1. policy of driving out or killing people who do not share the same identity

_____ 2. sharing the same language, customs, and other aspects of culture

_____ 3. understanding that outlines rules about the exchange of goods between countries

_____ 4. group of countries that agree to trade under favorable conditions

_____ 5. value of all final goods and services produced in a country in a year

_____ 6. nation with many different ethnic groups

_____ 7. denies citizens basic civil rights

_____ 8. currency issued by the European Union

_____ 9. use of violence and fear to achieve political goals

Notes for Home: Your child learned the vocabulary terms for Chapter 22.
Home Activity: With your child, discuss your family's ethnicity and the countries in which family members or ancestors were born. Identify what economic ties, if any, those countries have with the United States.

Locating Time and Place

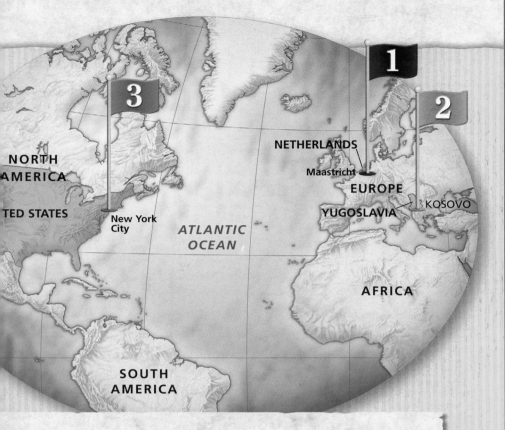

NORTH AMERICA

TED STATES

New York City

ATLANTIC OCEAN

NETHERLANDS

Maastricht

EUROPE

YUGOSLAVIA · KOSOVO

AFRICA

SOUTH AMERICA

Why We Remember

>m your own experience, you know that working and playing together—
her than fighting—makes life richer. After many terrible wars in the
:ntieth century, many people began to cooperate to try to make the
:ld better. They worked together in organizations such as the United
:ions to promote peace. Nations opened up trade to share prosperity
und the world. At the beginning of a new century, we enjoy the results
his cooperation. However, we still have conflicts. Thus, our new
:tury is a time of cooperation, conflicts, and challenges.

629

WEB SITE
Technology

:an learn more about
stricht, Netherlands; Kosovo,
slavia; and New York City, New
by clicking on *Atlas* at
.sfsocialstudies.com.

SOCIAL STUDIES STRAND
Geography

Mental Mapping On an outline map
of the countries of the world, ask
students to label the United States
and major trading partners or regions
of the United States. Discuss how
the world has become a global
economy by having students give
examples of what products their
families use that were made outside
of the United States.

- Have students examine the pictures
  shown on p. 628 for Lessons 1, 2,
  and 3.

- Remind students that each picture
  is coded with both a number and a
  color to link it to a place on the map
  on p. 629.

Why We Remember

Have students read the "Why We
Remember" paragraph on p. 629, and
ask them why events in this chapter
might be important to them. Lead a
discussion of current events, asking
students to describe areas of the world
that are in conflict today. Ask students
if they know what is at the root of any
of these conflicts. Then have students
discuss organizations that try to
promote cooperation rather than
conflict. What can students do to
promote peace in the world? In their
own community?

Economic Cooperation

Objectives

- Explain the causes and effects of trading blocs, trade agreements, and trade disputes.

- Define *gross domestic product*.

- List four trading blocs and their members.

- Explain the role of the World Trade Organization.

- Explain what the benefits are of belonging to a trading bloc.

Vocabulary

gross domestic product, (GDP) p. 631;
trading bloc, p. 632; **euro,** p. 632;
trade agreement, p. 633;

Resources

- Workbook, p. 156
- Transparency 20
- Every Student Learns Guide, pp. 294–297
- Quick Study, pp. 148–149

Quick Teaching Plan

If time is short, have students chart details about the lesson as they read independently.

- Have students create two-column charts with the headings *World Economy* and *Struggle for Equality*.

1 Introduce and Motivate

Preview Write *global economy* on the board and ask students if they can define it. Ask students what items they use that come from other countries. Tell students they will learn more about the global economy as they read Lesson 1.

You Are There Tell students that most economists agree that international trading has benefits. Ask students why this might be true. (People have access to a large, diverse group of goods.)

630 Unit 8 • New Nations and a New Century

NETHERLANDS
Maastricht

1950		1985	
1957 The European Economic Community (EEC) is created.		**1991** Mercosur is organized.	**199** NAF goe effe

Economic Cooperation

PREVIEW

Focus on the Main Idea
World and regional economies have become closely bound together.

PLACES
Maastricht

PEOPLE
Bill Clinton

VOCABULARY
gross domestic product (GDP)
trading bloc
euro
trade agreement

TERMS
European Union (EU)
Association of Southeast Asian Nations (ASEAN)
Mercosur
North American Free Trade Agreement (NAFTA)
World Trade Organization (WTO)

630

You Are There
You're helping Dad fold laundry. pick up a shirt and look at the lab "Made in Turkey. Where is Turkey you ask.

Dad sends you to find the atlas. You look up Turke find that it lies partly in Europe and partly in Asia. Yc pick up other objects around your house to see wher were made.

"How about this picture frame?" asks Dad. "Made i Taiwan." The atlas shows that Taiwan is an island off China's coast.

Now it's your turn. "My baseball cap? Made in the I know where that is."

Dad's face lights up. He grabs the pen in his pocke *"Fabriqué au Canada."*

You're stumped. Then Dad chuckles and says, "That's French for 'Made in Canada'."

▶ **Every day goods from around the world are produced and sold to consumers.**

Cause and Effect As you read, consider how econom cooperation among nations affects the global communit

---

Practice and Extend

READING SKILL
Cause and Effect

In the Lesson Review, students complete a graphic organizer like the one below. You may want to provide students with a copy of Transparency 20 to complete as they read the lesson.

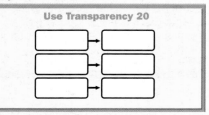

Use Transparency 20

WEB SITE
Technology

- You can look up vocabulary wor by clicking on *Social Studies Lib* and selecting the dictionary at **www.sfsocialstudies.com.**

- Students can learn more about current news by clicking on *Current Events* at **www.sfsocialstudies.com.**

- Explore other events that occurred on this day by clicking on *This Day in History* at **www.sfsocialstudies.com.**

Economies Without Borders

We live in a global economy. That is [why] you have objects that were made [in m]any other countries.

[Li]ving in a global economy also [mea]ns that what happens in one coun[try s]oon affects others. Trade barriers, [th]ings such as tariffs, quotas, or [emb]argos, often hinder trade. As a [resu]lt, many countries remove trade bar[riers] by carrying on free trade with countries [arou]nd the world. This means that they trade [witho]ut tariffs. Removing tariffs can encourage [trade].

[In o]ur global economy, the products we buy [com]e from all over the world. For example, today [auto]mobile makers sell their cars worldwide. [Whe]n your grandparents started driving, however, [most] cars sold in the United States were [Amer]ican-made.

[Th]e global economy has made some people [and n]ations very wealthy. But it has also caused [probl]ems for some workers, communities, and [econo]mies. Industries have had to shut down [beca]use of increased competition. They could no [longe]r compete in the global economy. Increased [comp]etition often leads to lower prices for con[sume]rs. But lower prices can sometimes cause [lower] profits for industries. In the United States, [autom]obile manufacturing is such an industry. [We h]ave far fewer jobs in this industry today than [we di]d 50 years ago.

[Eve]n in a global economy there are still sharp [differ]ences in wealth among countries. Wealthy [area]s include the United States, several [Europ]ean nations, and Japan. These nations are [called] developed nations. Their industries and [econo]mies are well-developed.

[The] global economy also includes developing [nation]s whose industries and economies are in [the pr]ocess of developing. They do not have the

▶ New cars parked at a port in Seattle, Washington, will soon make their way to other ports around the globe.

great wealth that the developed nations have. Many developing nations are in Africa and Asia. Look at the pie graph below which compares gross domestic product of world regions. **Gross domestic product** (GDP) is the value of all final goods and services produced in a country in a year. It is a measure of a nation's wealth.

REVIEW What are some of the positive and negative effects of the global economy on nations? **Cause and Effect**

Gross Domestic Product

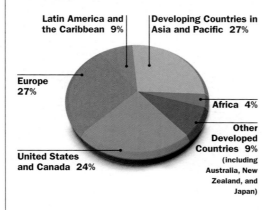

Latin America and the Caribbean 9%

Developing Countries in Asia and Pacific 27%

Europe 27%

Africa 4%

United States and Canada 24%

Other Developed Countries 9% (including Australia, New Zealand, and Japan)

▶ The standard of living of countries and regions can be compared using GDP as an indicator.

GRAPH SKILL Use a Circle Graph *Which countries or regions have the highest GDP?*

Economies Without Borders

🕐 **Quick Summary** In today's global economy people can buy goods from all over the world. Although the global economy has helped some nations prosper, others are still developing.

1 **Explain how removing tariffs encourages trade.** When a tariff is removed, the goods are less expensive, therefore increasing trade by making goods more affordable. **Cause and Effect**

2 **How does the global economy affect developing nations?** It has not made them as wealthy as it has made developed nations. **Draw Conclusions**

3 **What is gross domestic product?** Value of all final goods and services produced in a country in a year. **Main Idea and Details**

✓ **REVIEW ANSWER** Positive: More opportunities to trade, increased wealth for some; Negative: Sharp differences in wealth, increased competition can hurt a nation's economy. **Cause and Effect**

GRAPH SKILL Answer Developing countries in Asia and Pacific

[Dis]cuss Prices and Profits

[U]se manipulatives to help students build on what they already know.

[H]ave one student choose a familiar object, such as a backpack, and attach a [hi]gh price to the object. Tell students that because there is just one of these [ob]jects, people will pay a high price for it.

[A]sk several other students to hold up similar items.

[Di]scuss with students what will happen to the price of the first object now that [m]ore of the objects are available. (It will fall.)

[As]k, *Will the company that sells the first item make more or less money?* (Less) *Will the company have more or fewer jobs?* (Fewer)

[For a]dditional ESL support, use *Every Student Learns Guide*, pp. 294–297.

Developing Nations

- In many developing nations, extreme poverty has caused disease epidemics, starvation, and death.

- In much of Africa, developing nations face harsh environmental conditions, such as deserts. Farmers use up the nutrients in the soil when they farm, so they can no longer grow crops.

- In 1996 two-thirds of the poorest people in the world lived in developing nations in Africa and Latin America. Most of these people lived on less than $1 per day.

Trade and Cooperation

⏰ **Quick Summary** Trading blocs such as the European Union and Association of Southeast Asian Nations encourage favorable trading conditions.

4 **How could trade lead to peaceful relations between countries?** If countries depended on each other for necessary goods, then they might need to cooperate and maintain peace.

💭 Draw Conclusions

Ongoing Assessment

If... students are unable to draw a conclusion about how trading blocs affect economies,

then... ask students to think of someone with whom they might trade games or food. Did students think of a friend?

💲 **SOCIAL STUDIES STRAND**
Economics

Remind students that an exchange rate is the price of one country's currency, or form of money, converted to the price of another country's currency. For example, a pound is a unit of money in England, but not in the United States. A sum of money, in pounds, can be changed into a sum in dollars or yen or lire.

5 **How does the EU benefit from having its own currency?** EU nations using the euro do not have to use exchange rates. They are able to export more manufactured goods.
Main Idea and Details

✓ **REVIEW ANSWER** Members of a trading bloc can trade goods at a reduced tariff rate, which increases trade.
Main Idea and Details

Trading Blocs

6 **Are most of the members of EU in the eastern or western part of Europe?**
Western **Interpret Maps**

MAP SKILL Answer In both images, the countries are all closely grouped. Both maps also show members of a regional trading bloc.

Trade and Cooperation

After World War II, many people believed that free trade between nations would lead to peace and prosperity. As a result, nations signed treaties to open up trade. They reduced or ended **4** the use of tariffs with their trading partners.

Many nations joined regional trading blocs. A **trading bloc** is a group of countries that agree to trade under favorable conditions. Nations in a trading bloc reduce taxes on goods traded by countries within the trading bloc.

The trading bloc with the most nations is the **European Union (EU)**. The origin of the EU began during the Cold War. In 1957 the European Economic Community was created to establish a common market. A common market is an economic union formed to increase trade and encourage cooperation among its members.

In 1991, 12 Western European leaders signed a treaty in **Maastricht** in the Netherlands. Within two years, the treaty had been approved by all members and the organization was

renamed the European Community. The Europe[an] Community later became part of the EU. Three more countries joined, bringing the total to 15. Since the fall of communism in the Soviet Uni[on] many nations in Eastern Europe have been ap[ply]ing for membership in the EU. In 1999 the EU issued its own money, the **euro.** By having its own currency, EU members using the euro do [not] have to use exchange rates. As a result, EU nations began to export more manufactured goods than any other single nation in the worl[d]

Western Europe was not the only place wher[e] trading bloc formed. In 1967 five Southeast As[ian] countries formed the **Association of Southeas[t] Asian Nations (ASEAN).** Like the EU, this orga[ni]zation aimed to reduce tariffs. It also wanted t[o] promote economic cooperation.

REVIEW What are the benefits of belongin[g to] a trading bloc? **Main Idea and Detai[ls]**

▶ **The EU put the euro (pic[tured] here) into circulation in [1999.] International trade requ[ires] a system for exchangin[g] currency between natio[ns.]**

MAP SKILL Trading Blocs

[Map showing EU countries: FINLAND, SWEDEN, North Sea, IRELAND, UNITED KINGDOM, DENMARK, NETHERLANDS, GERMANY, LUXEMBOURG, BELGIUM, FRANCE, AUSTRIA, LIECHTENSTEIN, ITALY, ATLANTIC OCEAN, PORTUGAL, SPAIN, GREECE, Mediterranean Sea; and ASEAN countries: MYANMAR (BURMA), LAOS, THAILAND, VIETNAM, CAMBODIA, South China Sea, PHILIPPINES, BRUNEI, MALAYSIA, SINGAPORE, INDONESIA, INDIAN OCEAN, PACIFIC OCEAN]

▶ The European Union and ASEAN are important trading blocs.
MAP SKILL Compare Maps *What do the countries in these two maps have in common?*

632

Practice and Extend

FAST FACTS

The treaty to create the European Union was signed in Maastricht, the Netherlands, in 1991. Share with students other events from the year 1991:

- The Persian Gulf War ended with a cease-fire on April 3. The United Nations forces were victorious.
- Shortly before apartheid laws were repealed, European nations ended sanctions, or boycotts, against South Africa.
- The population of the world topped 5.4 billion.
- The first user-friendly Internet interface was created. It was named Gopher, aft[er] the mascot of the University of Minnesota, where the technology was created.
- Richard Branson and Per Lindstrand made the first hot air balloon flight acro[ss] the Pacific Ocean.
- The world mourned the death of Theodore Seuss Geisel, or "Dr. Seuss," whose literary works charmed children everywhere.

merican Trading Blocs

g blocs also developed in North and
merica. In 1991 Argentina, Brazil,
y, and Uruguay organized **Mercosur,** the
rn Common Market." Before Mercosur,
ations had mostly traded with Europe and
ed States. Mercosur has expanded and
ened trade among these South American

nited States, Canada, and Mexico
partners in a free trade zone called the
merican Free Trade Agreement (NAFTA),
ent into effect in 1994. The partnership
roots in the 1989 trade agreement
the United States and Canada. A
greement outlines rules about the
e of goods between countries.

.S.–Canada trade agreement was then
d to Mexico. After the leaders of the three
s signed the agreement in 1992, U.S.
nt **Bill Clinton** persuaded Congress to rat-
prove, the full agreement in 1993. Over
AFTA must remove tariffs on most goods

produced and sold in North America. This agreement has greatly expanded trade between the
United States and Mexico.

In addition to specific regions of the world
forming trading blocs, trading nations also set up
several world organizations to promote free
trade. The **World Trade Organization (WTO)** was
created in 1995 to help nations settle trade disputes. The WTO makes sure that member nations
follow their trade agreements.

REVIEW Why do you think President Clinton
persuaded Congress to include Mexico in NAFTA?
Draw Conclusions

Summarize the Lesson

- **1957** The European Economic Community
  (EEC) was created.
- **1991** Mercosur was organized.
- **1994** NAFTA, the trading bloc including
  Canada, the United States, and Mexico,
  became fully operational.

SSON 1 · REVIEW

ck Facts and Main Ideas

use and Effect On a separate piece of
per, copy the diagram below. Write in the
ssing cause and effect.

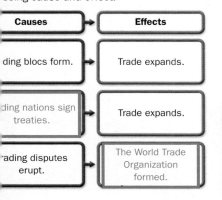

Causes	→	Effects
ding blocs form.	→	Trade expands.
ding nations sign treaties.	→	Trade expands.
rading disputes erupt.	→	The World Trade Organization formed.

2. Define *gross domestic product.*
3. Name four trading blocs and list their members.
4. Explain the role of the World Trade Organization.
5. **Critical Thinking:** *Make Inferences* What might economic conditions be like in coun-tries that belong to no trading blocs? Explain your answer.

Link to 〰 Geography

Use a Map Look at a globe or a map of the world. How do you think physical geography affects how trading blocs form? What pat-terns can you identify?

MEETING INDIVIDUAL NEEDS
Leveled Practice

ain Trading Blocs Students explain and
ss trading blocs.

Ask students to write a short definition of
g *bloc* for a dictionary. **Reteach**

evel As members of a trading bloc, students
rite persuasive letters asking a nation to
me part of the bloc. **Extend**

lenge Have groups of students research one
e trading blocs discussed here and give
ntations about three of the bloc's trade
ments. **Enrich**

Lesson Summary, use Quick Study, p. 148.

Workbook, p. 156

Lesson 1: Economic Cooperation

Directions: Read the following descriptions and decide which regional trading bloc each one describes. Write *E* for European Union, *A* for ASEAN, *M* for Mercosur, and *N* for NAFTA. You may use your textbook.

____ 1. includes Argentina, Brazil, Paraguay, and Uruguay

____ 2. includes the United States, Mexico, and Canada

____ 3. includes 15 European nations

____ 4. includes five Southeast Asian countries

Directions: Answer the following questions on the lines provided.

5. What are three effects of having a global economy?

_____
_____
_____
_____

6. How does a developing country differ from a developed country?

_____
_____
_____
_____

Also on Teacher Resources CD-ROM.

American Trading Blocs

Quick Summary After trading
blocs developed in Europe, they
developed in the Americas.

7 **Compare and contrast Mercosur
with the European Union.** Both are
trading blocs, and both expanded and
strengthened trade among member
nations. The EU has more member
nations, and it has developed its own
common currency. **Compare and Contrast**

✓ **REVIEW ANSWER** To increase trade
and improve economic cooperation
among North American nations
Draw Conclusions

3 Close and Assess

Summarize the Lesson

Give students three minutes to list the
main ideas of the lesson. Check
students' lists for the most important
ideas. Ask probing follow-up questions.

✓ **LESSON 1** **REVIEW**

1. **Cause and Effect** For possible answers, see the reduced pupil page.

2. Measure of a nation's wealth; value of all final goods and services produced in a country in a year.

3. EU—Finland, Sweden, Denmark, Ireland, United Kingdom, the Netherlands, Germany, Belgium, France, Luxembourg, Austria, Liechtenstein, Italy, Greece, Spain, Portugal; ASEAN—Brunei, Cambodia, Indonesia, Laos, Malaysia, Myanmar, the Philippines, Singapore, Thailand, Vietnam; Mercosur—Argentina, Brazil, Paraguay, Uruguay; NAFTA—United States, Canada, Mexico

4. To help nations settle trade disputes

5. **Critical Thinking:** *Make Inferences* Probably poorer because they do not have favorable trade agreements

Link to 〰 Geography

Students should explain that
countries in the same region often
form trading blocs.

Interpret Cartograms

Objective
- Interpret cartograms to find particular information.

Resource
- Workbook, p. 157

1 Introduce and Motivate

What is a cartogram? Discuss with students the different ways that facts can be shown at a glance. Students might mention that maps show information in a visual format and that graphs give concise data. Then have students read the **What?** section of text on p. 634.

Why use a cartogram? Tell students to read the **Why?** section of text on p. 635. Ask students why a cartogram might be easier to use than a written paragraph about the same topic. (Graphic representations of data can be understood at a glance, unlike a written paragraph.)

2 Teach and Discuss

How is this skill used? Examine with students the cartograms on pp. 634–635.

- Point out that the cartograms have descriptive titles to identify the data being represented. Labels make the cartograms easier to use.

- Point out that a cartogram might look distorted. Instruct students to note carefully the labels that accompany graphics so they know what exactly is being represented and do not confuse a cartogram with an actual map.

- Have students read the **How?** section of text on p. 635.

Chart and Graph Skills

Interpret Cartograms

What? A cartogram is a special kind of graph based on a map. It stretches and bends the map outlines to represent data, or information. The cartogram below represents the population of the world by country. It distorts the "real" map to give particular information about these nations.

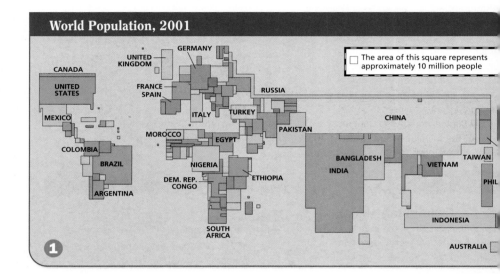

World Population, 2001

The area of this square represents approximately 10 million people

Practice and Extend

CURRICULUM CONNECTION
Math

Create Cartograms

- Invite students to create cartograms to reflect data. Students can gather appropriate information from almanacs or other reference sources. Student could also create cartograms about data in school, such as the number of students in each sixth grade class.

- If students find creating cartograms too challenging, you might have them fi cartograms in science or social studies textbooks. They can write questions about the cartograms or explain what they show.

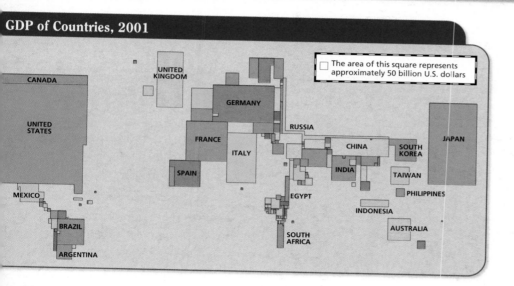

GDP of Countries, 2001

The area of this square represents approximately 50 billion U.S. dollars

CANADA
UNITED KINGDOM
GERMANY
UNITED STATES
FRANCE
ITALY
RUSSIA
CHINA
SOUTH KOREA
JAPAN
SPAIN
INDIA
TAIWAN
MEXICO
EGYPT
PHILIPPINES
INDONESIA
BRAZIL
AUSTRALIA
SOUTH AFRICA
ARGENTINA

1 Which country has the largest population, Japan or Vietnam? Japan
Interpret Graphs

2 How does looking at an actual map help you interpret a cartogram?
Possible answer: You can compare the size of each country on the map with its size on the cartogram. This comparison helps you understand the data in the cartogram. ↺ **Draw Conclusions**

3 How would a map be different from the cartogram on p. 634? The size of each country would be proportional to its area not to data such as GDP or population. Country borders would be curved instead of straight.
↺ **Draw Conclusions**

4 Imagine that you find a 1990 almanac. Would you use it to check the accuracy of these cartograms? Why or why not? No; these cartograms reflect data from 2001. The statistics from 1990 and 2001 would most likely not be the same. **Analyze Information**

y? Graphs help us understand information quick glance. For this reason, they often e a big impact.

w? To use and understand a cartogram, must know what the "real" map looks like. at the map of the world in the atlas in the of your textbook. Now look at the cartogram ge 634. Did you notice that the cartogram es some countries look much larger or much er?
w look at the cartogram above. This car-m represents gross domestic product (GDP) untry. Compare this cartogram with the car-m on page 634. How have the shapes and of some countries changed? To check the nation on the cartograms, look in an ac. You should be able to verify that the ries that look the largest on the cartogram

have the highest GDP in the world. You should also be able to verify that the largest countries on the cartogram have the greatest population in the world. Check to see that the information in the almanac matches the information on the car-tograms. You should be able to confirm your conclusions.

4

Think and Apply

1 Which countries have the largest population?

2 Which countries have the highest GDP?

3 What other data could you use to make a cartogram of the world?

635

Think and Apply

1. China and India

2. The United States, Japan, and Germany

3. Answers will vary. Students may suggest resources, energy use, or life expectancy.

lore Cartograms Students can use their vidual learning styles to explore cartograms.

litory Learning Students can take turns giving listening to oral directions for interpreting or king a cartogram.

ividual Learning Invite students to find mples of cartograms from various books and rnet sites. They can photocopy or download eral cartograms and take notes on what they ned from examining them.

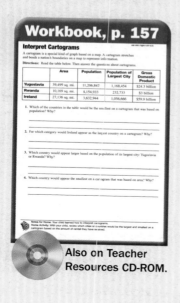

Workbook, p. 157

Interpret Cartograms

A cartogram is a special kind of graph based on a map. A cartogram stretches and bends a nation's boundaries on a map to represent information.

Directions: Read the table below. Then answer the questions about cartograms.

	Area	Population	Population of Largest City	Gross Domestic Product
Yugoslavia	39,499 sq. mi.	11,206,847	1,168,454	$24.3 billion
Rwanda	10,169 sq. mi.	8,154,933	232,733	$3 billion
Ireland	27,136 sq. mi.	3,632,944	1,056,666	$59.9 billion

1. Which of the countries in the table would be the smallest on a cartogram that was based on population? Why?

2. For which category would Ireland appear as the largest country on a cartogram? Why?

3. Which country would appear larger based on the population of its largest city: Yugoslavia or Rwanda? Why?

4. Which country would appear the smallest on a cartogram that was based on area? Why?

Also on Teacher Resources CD-ROM.

Conflicts of Identity

Objectives

- List and describe three major conflicts over identity or ethnicity.

- Explain why thousands of refugees fled Bosnia and Herzegovina in the 1990s.

- Compare and contrast the conflicts in central Africa and Northern Ireland.

- List three places in the world where people have been struggling for freedoms or human rights.

- Explain why some countries do not give equal status to men and women.

Vocabulary

ethnicity, p. 637; **multiethnic nation,** p. 637; **ethnic cleansing,** p. 637; **repressive,** p. 640

Resources

- Workbook, p. 158
- Transparency 23
- Every Student Learns Guide, pp. 298–301
- Quick Study, pp. 150–151

Quick Teaching Plan

If time is short, have students create an outline as they read independently.

- Encourage students to use headings as subtopics or titles in their outlines.

1 Introduce and Motivate

Preview Discuss with students religious or cultural conflicts that they have read about in this book. Tell students they will read about other problems between peoples and nations caused by differences in religion and customs in Lesson 2.

You Are There Marybeth Lorbiecki's first letters, written in 1991, are carefree and happy. Have students discuss how the war affected her life.

LESSON 2

YUGOSLAVIA
SERBIA
KOSOVO
MONTENEGRO

1950	1970	1990

late 1960s Violence in Northern Ireland breaks out.

1989 Protest at Tiananmen Square

1991–1992 Breakup of Yugoslavia

1993–1994 Massacres in Rwanda and Burundi lead to civil war

War breaks o...

PREVIEW

Focus on the Main Idea
Ethnic, political, and religious differences have led to violent conflicts around the world.

PLACES
Yugoslavia
Slovenia
Croatia
Serbia
Montenegro
Bosnia and Herzegovina
Kosovo
Rwanda
Burundi
Northern Ireland
Afghanistan
Myanmar
Chiapas
Tiananmen Square
Beijing

PEOPLE
Slobodan Milosevic
Mairead Corrigan Maguire
Mary Robinson
Aung San Suu Kyi
Rigoberta Menchú

VOCABULARY
ethnicity
multiethnic nation
ethnic cleansing
repressive

636

Conflicts of Identity

 You Are There You pick up Marybeth Lorbiecki's *My Palace of Leaves in Sarajevo.* You've been wondering how the w... that broke out in 1991 in Yugoslavia affected the live... children. You hope that the letters of this 10-year-old... will help give you a better picture of what it was like. You begin to read her book.

We use candles at night. No TV . . . .
Run to cellar many times. Bombs, and more bom...
  Sit hours and hours . . . .
It is difficult to read. Noise is louder than
  thunder, it shakes me inside.
Father and Drini and I make pretend
  plays and stories, songs and dances.
  It is good almost as TV.

▶ This Bosnian girl was among thousands of children affected by the 1991 war.

 Draw Conclusions As you read, identify religious, political, and ethnic conflicts to draw conclusions about conflicts of identity.

Practice and Extend

READING SKILL
Draw Conclusions

In the Lesson Review, students complete a graphic organizer like the one below. You may want to provide students with a copy of Transparency 23 to complete as they read the lesson.

Use Transparency 23

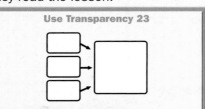

WEB SITE
Technology

- You can look up vocabulary word... by clicking on *Social Studies Libr...* and selecting the dictionary at **www.sfsocialstudies.com.**

- Students can learn more about... current news by clicking on *Current Events* at **www.sfsocialstudies.com.**

- Explore other events that occurred on this day by clicking on *This Day in History* at **www.sfsocialstudies.com.**

Identity and Ethnicity

The war that broke out in Marybeth's country s over identity or ethnicity. When people have e same **ethnicity** that means that they speak e same language, have the same customs, and re other cultural aspects. Many times people go to war for economic and political reasons. metimes ethnic and religious differences are o factors in war.

A nation with many different ethnic groups is ed a **multiethnic nation.** The former country Yugoslavia, in the Balkans in southeastern ope, is one example of a multiethnic nation. en the communists lost power in Yugoslavia, country began to break apart.

ike the Soviet Union, Yugoslavia was a union epublics. In 1991 two of the six republics, venia (sloh VEE nee uh) and **Croatia** (krow AY), declared independence. **Serbia,** the largest ublic in Yugoslavia, and **Montenegro** then ght a bitter war with Croatia. These civil wars e mainly fought over ethnicity. With help from UN, most fighting in Croatia ended in 1998.

VIEW How do differences in ethnicity cause licts? **Cause and Effect**

Kosovo

hen the republic of **Bosnia and Herzegovina** ared independence in 1992, war broke out. president of Serbia, **Slobodan Milosevic** w baw duhn mee LOH shehv ihtch), encouraged s to carry out a policy of ethnic cleansing. **nic cleansing** means to drive out or kill people do not share the same identity. Thousands fugees were forced out of Bosnia. Many tries tried to help end the war. They firmly ved that ethnic cleansing was wrong and ted human rights. With the help of other tries, a 1995 agreement—called the Dayton rds—ended the war in Bosnia.

t wars continued to rage in this region. A dis- of Serbia, called **Kosovo,** became the next

---

trouble spot. Most of the 2 million people there were Muslim Albanians called Kosovars. Kosovars wanted freedom and independence. In 1999 Milosevic sent in a mostly Serbian army. Soldiers burned and looted property and killed thousands of innocent people. They drove about 1 million Kosovars out of Kosovo.

In the end, NATO stepped in to help. NATO fighter jets bombed Belgrade, the capital of Serbia. They forced Milosevic to withdraw his army and provided help for refugees.

REVIEW Why did other countries get involved in the Kosovo conflict? **Draw Conclusions**

MAP SKILL

The Balkans

AUSTRIA   HUNGARY
MOLDOVA
SLOVENIA
CROATIA   Vojvodina
ROMANIA
BOSNIA & HERZEGOVINA
SERBIA   Danube River
YUGOSLAVIA
Black Sea
MONTENEGRO
Kosovo
BULGARIA
MACEDONIA
ALBANIA
TURKEY
GREECE
Aegean Sea
Adriatic Sea
Mediterranean Sea

- Republics of Yugoslavia
- Provinces of Serbia
- Other Balkan countries

N

0   150   300 Miles
0   150   300 Kilometers

▶ The Balkans have been a hot spot for conflicts of identity or ethnicity.

MAP SKILL Use a Locator Map *In what region of Europe are the Balkans located?*

---

lore National Identity Students may have difficulty understanding the cept of *identity*. Relate the concept to personal identity first.

ave each student describe him or herself. Ask simple questions about tudents' likes, dislikes, traditions, and so on. As students describe emselves and answer questions, point out that they are different from each ther. Explain that each person has an identity.

students are able to understand the concept of personal identity, discuss ational identity. Ask students to list what people in other countries might be roud of. Encourage students to say what makes a country special and ifferent from other countries.

additional ESL support, use *Every Student Learns Guide, pp. 298–301.*

Identity and Ethnicity

Quick Summary Many wars, including civil wars in Yugoslavia, have been fought over issues of identity or ethnicity.

1 **How might ethnic diversity be a benefit to a nation?** Possible answer: People share ideas with others. They are exposed to various points of view, and all can be enriched by sharing traditions and ways of thinking. **Evaluate**

✓ **REVIEW ANSWER** People with different languages, religions, and cultures may go to war with one another over these differences. **Cause and Effect**

Kosovo

Quick Summary Slobodan Milosevic, former president of Serbia, encouraged a policy of ethnic cleansing in Bosnia. Later, a Serbian army drove about one million Kosovars out of Kosovo.

2 **What issues fueled conflict in the region that was formerly Yugoslavia?** Slobodan Milosevic promoted ethnic cleansing to rid the region of people of differing ethnicities. In Kosovo, citizens were driven out or killed because they were Muslim Albanians who wanted independence. **Cause and Effect**

✓ **REVIEW ANSWER** They believed that ethnic cleansing was wrong and violated human rights. **Draw Conclusions**

MAP SKILL

The Balkans

3 **What are the republics and provinces in Yugoslavia?** Montenegro and Serbia are republics, and Kosovo and Vojvodina are provinces. **Interpret Maps**

MAP SKILL **Answer** Southeastern Europe

Central Africa

Quick Summary Civil War in Rwanda and Burundi was caused by prejudice between the Hutu and Tutsi ethnic groups.

H **SOCIAL STUDIES STRAND**
History

By the fifteenth century, the Hutu lived in Central Africa. The Tutsi came from the north and conquered the region, forcing the Hutu to live under a repressive government.

4 **Compare and contrast the Hutu and Tutsi.** Same: Bantu-speaking cultures, most have the same religion; Different: distinct ethnic groups with their own traditions **Compare and Contrast**

Literature and Social Studies

Have students read the poem. Ask them how the poem applies to their own lives.

5 **What do you think the poet meant when she wrote "more 'we' and less 'I'"?** Possible answer: People should think about the needs of others more and think about their own needs less. **Express Ideas**

Rwanda and Burundi

6 **Where are these countries in relation to the equator?** South of the equator **Apply Information**

MAP SKILL **Answer** Democratic Republic of the Congo, Uganda, and Tanzania

✓ **REVIEW ANSWER** Ethnic tension between the two groups caused mass killings, which fueled further massacres. **Cause and Effect**

Northern Ireland

Quick Summary Violence has erupted between Protestants and Catholics in Northern Ireland.

Central Africa

In the 1990s, the neighboring central African countries of **Rwanda** and **Burundi** exploded into civil war. The majority of the people in these two countries belong mainly to the Tutsi (TOO tze) and Hutu (HOO too) ethnic groups. Both are Bantu-speaking cultures and practice the same religion. However, they are distinct ethnic groups in that **4** the Tutsi and Hutu have their own traditions. This difference has caused much tension and violence.

The army in Burundi, controlled by the Tutsi, killed thousands of Hutu citizens in 1993. The next year, the Hutu in control of Rwanda tried to wipe out the entire Tutsi population there. No one knows an exact number, but as many as 1 million Tutsi died.

Then the Tutsi took control in Rwanda and drove out the Hutu. More than 1 million Hutu refugees fled, mostly to the neighboring Democratic Republic of the Congo (DRC; Zaire). DRC rebel forces soon attacked the refugee camps and drove the Hutu back to Rwanda.

Literature and Social Studies

5 ## What the World Needs

This poem was written by Elzbieta Jaworska when she was a teenager in Poland. Do you agree with what she thinks the world needs?

A little more kindness, a little less need,
A little more giving, a little less greed,
A little more gladness, a little less care,
A little more faith, a little more prayer,
A little more "we" and a little less "I,"
A little more laughter and a little less sigh,
A little more sunshine and brightening the view,
And a lot more friends, exactly like you.

638

MAP SKILL
Rwanda and Burundi

▶ Civil war also has erupted inside and outside of Rwanda and Burundi over issues of identi

MAP SKILL Understand Borders and Capita
Which countries border Rwanda and Burundi?

The problems the Hutu and Tutsi survivors a returning refugees have faced are enormous. Villages and cities were badly damaged. People could not find jobs, shelter, or food.

REVIEW What caused the fighting between Hutu and Tutsi in Burundi and Rwanda? **Cause and Effect**

▶ The group Doctors Without Borders sends volunteer doctors and other aid to refugees around the world. This German doctor helps a woman care for her child after major flooding h Mozambique in 2000.

Practice and Extend

CURRICULUM CONNECTION
Literature

Write Poems About Peace

- Invite students to write their own poems that give a "formula" for peace. Encourage them to first list their ideas about what is required for peace and then craft their ideas into vivid images and descriptions.
- To inspire student writing about peace, you might share books such as the following:

The Middle East in Search of Peace, by Cathryn J. Long (Millbrook Press, ISBN 0-761-30105-4, 1996) **Easy**

Zlata's Diary: A Child's Life in Sarajevo, by Zlata Filipovic (translated by Christina Pribichevich-Zoric) (Penguin, ISBN 0-140-24205-8, 1995) **On-Level**

The Freedom Writers Diary: How a Teacher and 150 Teens Used Writing to Change Themselves and the World Around Them, by Freedom Writers Staff (Turtleback Books, ISBN 0-606-18104-0, 1999) **Challenge**

Northern Ireland

agreements between ethnic groups are
e only conflicts in the world. Fighting has
d on religious differences between
tants and Catholics in **Northern Ireland.**
nd used to be all one country. But Great
, which held power in Ireland for hundreds
rs, divided Ireland in 1920. Northern
l remained part of the United Kingdom. The
 Ireland became an independent republic.
t Irish are Catholics. However, in the six
es of Northern Ireland, Protestants are the
ty and control much of the economy and
ment.

he 1960s, the Protestant majority controlled
rn Ireland's parliament. As a result, the
ic minority began a movement for civil rights.
 troops were sent in and violence grew.
conflict in Northern Ireland has caused the
of more than 3,000 people. Peace activists
s **Mairead Corrigan Maguire** are calling for
hting to stop. She, like so many others, has
mily members to Catholic-Protestant vio-
 In 1976 she was awarded the Nobel Peace
Prize. Maguire believes that people in the twenty-
first century need to form new ideas of identity:

> *"It is fine to celebrate our diver-
> sity and our roots, but somehow
> we must . . . understand the
> most important identity that we
> have . . . the human family."* ⑨

REVIEW What conclusion can you draw
about the effects of hostility in Northern Ireland?
◉ Draw Conclusions

The Struggle of Women

One struggle in the world involves about half of
the population. This is the struggle of women for
equality and freedom. In many countries, women
have equality with men. In some, they have opportunities for good education and jobs too. But in other
countries, the status of women is very low.

In 1996 a religious political party, called the
Taliban, came to power in **Afghanistan.** The
Taliban drove women out of the workforce and
girls out of schools. Women doctors were not
allowed to practice medicine. Some female
patients were not able to get medical care.

Policies like those of the Taliban caused a
reaction in the global community.
Mary Robinson of Ireland
became the United Nations
High Commissioner for
Human Rights in 1997.
She has encouraged
nations to ratify the
Convention on the
Elimination of Discrimination
Against Women. This document
has been called the "human
rights charter for women." ⑩

▶ **Mary Robinson
served as
president of
Ireland before
heading the UN
Commission for
Human Rights.**

REVIEW Why does the United
Nations support equal rights for
women? ◉ Draw Conclusions

United Kingdom

10°W   0°
60°N

200 Miles

ilometers

RTHERN   SCOTLAND
RELAND

UNITED

KINGDOM

LAND

WALES ENGLAND NETHERLANDS

GERMANY

BELGIUM
FRANCE

thern Ireland is one of four divisions of the
ted Kingdom.
SKILL Use a Map What are the other
ivisions of the United Kingdom?

639

Struggles for Change

 Quick Summary Many nations in the world, such as Myanmar, are struggling for freedom under repressive governments.

⭐ SOCIAL STUDIES STRAND
Citizenship

The U.S. Bill of Rights guarantees basic civil rights to citizens, including freedom of speech and of the press, freedom to choose one's own religion, and the right to peacefully assemble.

11 How is the United States government different from the repressive governments described on this page? The U.S. government has a Constitution and Bill of Rights that guarantee certain rights. Repressive governments deny basic rights to their citizens. **Compare and Contrast**

✓ **REVIEW ANSWER** Aung San Suu Kyi fought to obtain civil rights and political freedom from a repressive government in Myanmar (Burma). Peasants in Chiapas fought for a voice in their government and better living conditions. **Compare and Contrast**

Limited Freedom

Quick Summary The denial of basic civil rights to the citizens of the People's Republic of China led to a mass protest in Tiananmen Square in 1989.

Primary Source

Cited in *Crisis at Tiananmen,* by Yi Mu and Mark V. Thompson

12 What does this quotation reveal about the people involved in the protest? A variety of people were involved (*people, countrymen, classmates*). They died for their beliefs. **Analyze Primary Sources**

✓ **REVIEW ANSWER** These governments both deny civil rights to their citizens. **Compare and Contrast**

Struggles for Change

Many people have fought for human rights and freedom in the world. Even though greater democracy has come to nations such as Taiwan, South Korea, Chile, and others, people still struggle for freedom. Today, some nations have repressive governments. A **repressive** government is one that denies citizens basic human rights. Freedom of speech is one example of a human right. Another is freedom from arrest without just cause or reason.

Aung San Suu Kyi is just one of many people who have fought for human rights and political freedom. She has led the struggle against the repressive government led by military rulers in **Myanmar** (Burma), which has one of the world's worst records on human rights. An army officer named Ne Win took over the government there in a coup d'état in 1962. His ruling group has refused to give up power, even after losing national elections. It has also imprisoned many opponents like Aung San Suu Kyi. Read more about her in the biography on page 642.

People have also fought for political changes in the Americas. In 1994 people living in **Chiapas** (chee AH pahs), Mexico's poorest state, rebelled against the government. They were angry about the living conditions there. Many farm workers and laborers had lost their land to wealthy farmers and landowners. They also wanted more of a voice in the government.

▶ A sign by a tree blocking a road welcomes people to the rebel state of Chiapas.

Some economic and political changes have been made in Chiapas. However, many farmers continue to seek greater rights and better living conditions.

In Guatemala **Rigoberta Menchú** led a group of workers in a strike against plantation owners. Her work earned her world wide recognition. more about Rigoberta Menchú on page 643.

REVIEW What rights did Aung San Suu Kyi peasants in Chiapas fight for? **Compare and Contrast**

Limited Freedom

The People's Republic of China is another nation that has been criticized for its human rights record. The ruling Communist Party that has begun to allow the Chinese people some nomic freedom. For example, they can start own businesses. But the government still deny people human rights, such as freedom of speech. The Chinese Communist Party does not want give up its hold on power.

▶ On May 25, 1989, students seeking more freedom, protested at Tiananmen Square in Beijing.

Practice and Extend

🎨 CURRICULUM CONNECTION
Art

Create a Display

Students can work in small groups to create museum displays or Web site plans for a "Human Rights Hall of Fame."

- Encourage students to find biographical information about a variety of human rights activists.
- They also can draw pictures, download photographs, record speech excerpts, and compile other information to make their projects intriguing and memorable.
- Students could focus on the human rights activists mentioned in this chapter as well as others, such as Mohandas Gandhi or Martin Luther King, Jr. Suggest that they use a search engine and enter *human rights* or *civil rights* as keywords.

...he spring of 1989, students gathered for
...s protest in **Tiananmen** (tyahn ahn mehn)
...re in **Beijing**, China. They demanded more
...m. Chinese leaders sent the army into
...men Square to crush the protests.
...eds were killed. Many students were
...ed and imprisoned. One student leader
...bered it sadly:

> *On a day in June that
> should have belonged to a
> season of fresh flowers,
> my people, my countrymen,
> my classmates . . . fell."*

...n though the mass protest was put down by
...mmunist government, their fight was seen
...ions of people on television. This event
showed people around the world how in some
places others must fight for rights that are often
taken for granted elsewhere.

REVIEW What do the governments of China
and Myanmar have in common? **Compare and
Contrast**

Summarize the Lesson

- **late 1960s** Violence broke out in Northern Ireland.
- **1989** Protest at Tiananmen Square
- **1993–1994** Civil war broke out between Tutsi and Hutu peoples in Rwanda and Burundi.
- **1999** War in Kosovo left millions of refugees.

---

eck Facts and Main Ideas

1. **Draw Conclusions** On a separate piece of paper, copy the diagram below. Write a conclusion based on the given facts.

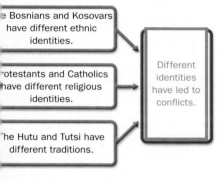

e Bosnians and Kosovars have different ethnic identities.

otestants and Catholics have different religious identities.

he Hutu and Tutsi have different traditions.

Different identities have led to conflicts.

2. What caused thousands of refugees to flee Bosnia and Herzegovina in the 1990s?

3. How are the situations in central Africa and Northern Ireland alike and different?

4. Name three places in the world where people have been struggling for freedom or human rights.

5. **Critical Thinking:** *Detect Bias* Do you think countries that do not give equal status to men and women are showing a bias? Why or why not?

Link to — **Reading**

Vocabulary in Context Read the following statement. Then in your own words, write a definition for the underlined word. Use the surrounding words to help you.

> *In a society where the rights . . .
> of women are <u>constrained</u>, no man
> can be truly free. He may have power,
> but he will not have freedom.*
> —**Mary Robinson**

641

SOCIAL STUDIES
Background

...nanmen Square

•riginally constructed in 1651, Tiananmen Square •as enlarged in 1958 to cover 100 acres.

"The Gate of Heavenly Peace," or Tiananmen, •as once the main gate of the Imperial Palace. ... is located at the north end of the square.

he Great Hall of the People is on the west side •f the square. The annual meetings of the ...ational People's Congress are held there.

t the southern end of the square stands the ...ao Zedong Memorial Hall. The body of Mao lies ...n state inside this hall.

Workbook, p. 158

Lesson 2: Conflicts of Identity

Directions: Read the following descriptions and decide to which region each refers. Write F for Yugoslavia, A for Africa, and I for Ireland. Some descriptions may apply to more than one region. Include all regions that fit the description. Then answer the questions that follow.

_____ 1. Issues over identity or ethnicity lead to violence.
_____ 2. Millions of refugees flee or are forced to leave.
_____ 3. Conflicts arise over religion.
_____ 4. Serbs fight Kosovars.
_____ 5. The country is divided geographically.
_____ 6. Hutu fight Tutsi.
_____ 7. The country begins to break apart when the communists lose power.
_____ 8. Catholics fight Protestants.
_____ 9. People engage in ethnic cleansing.
_____ 10. Outside troops are sent in.

11. What are two examples of basic human rights?

12. Which basic human rights were women denied under the Taliban's rule?

13. In what ways do you think the governments of developed nations such as the United States can influence a repressive government?

Also on Teacher Resources CD-ROM.

Summarize the Lesson

Tell students to examine the vertical time line. Then ask students to compare and contrast the various events on the time line. What has caused the conflicts? How have people been affected by them?

✓ **LESSON 2   REVIEW**

1. **Draw Conclusions** For possible answers, see the reduced pupil page.

2. Serbian policy of ethnic cleansing

3. They are both conflicts of identity. However, Central Africa's conflict is over ethnic groups and Northern Ireland's involves religious differences.

4. Possible answers: Kosovo, Central Africa, Northern Ireland, China, Myanmar

5. **Critical Thinking:** *Detect Bias* Possible answer: Yes. Such countries show bias by denying equal rights to part of the population.

Link to — **Reading**

Students should be able to determine that *constrained* means "inhibited" or "controlled." Encourage students to identify what clues helped them figure out the meaning and to use *constrained* in a sentence about China or Myanmar.

Aung San Suu Kyi

Objective

- Identify the contributions of significant individuals, such as Aung San Suu Kyi.

1 Introduce and Motivate

Preview To activate prior knowledge, ask students to recall information they have already learned about Aung San Suu Kyi in Lesson 1. Tell students that they will learn more about the roots of Suu Kyi's struggle for freedom in Myanmar.

2 Teach and Discuss

1 What role did Aung San play in the history of Burma? He led Burma to its independence from Great Britain.
Main Idea and Details

Primary Source

Cited in *Nobel Prize Winners Supplement 1987–1991*, edited by Paula McGuire

2 What duty was Aung San Suu Kyi speaking about in this quote? Her father had fought for freedom for the nation. She felt that it was her duty to carry on her father's legacy and do the same.
Analyze Primary Sources

3 Why do you think the government freed some pro-democracy leaders, but not Aung San Suu Kyi? Possible answer: Suu Kyi is one of the most popular leaders, especially after winning the Nobel Peace Prize, and the military government might want to keep her away from her supporters. **Draw Conclusions**

3 Close and Assess

Learn from Biographies Answer

Possible answer: She wanted to continue to work in person to get the military government to recognize the results of the election and give up power so that a democratic government could take its place.

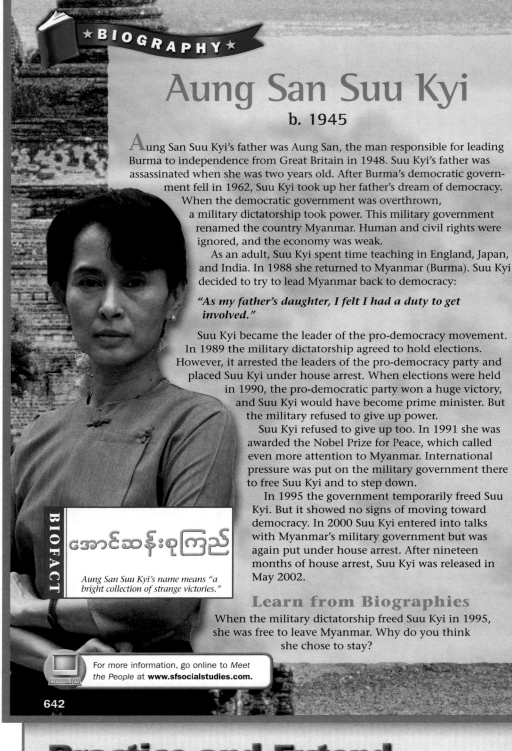

Aung San Suu Kyi
b. 1945

Aung San Suu Kyi's father was Aung San, the man responsible for leading Burma to independence from Great Britain in 1948. Suu Kyi's father was assassinated when she was two years old. After Burma's democratic government fell in 1962, Suu Kyi took up her father's dream of democracy. When the democratic government was overthrown, a military dictatorship took power. This military government renamed the country Myanmar. Human and civil rights were ignored, and the economy was weak.

As an adult, Suu Kyi spent time teaching in England, Japan, and India. In 1988 she returned to Myanmar (Burma). Suu Kyi decided to try to lead Myanmar back to democracy:

"As my father's daughter, I felt I had a duty to get involved."

Suu Kyi became the leader of the pro-democracy movement. In 1989 the military dictatorship agreed to hold elections. However, it arrested the leaders of the pro-democracy party and placed Suu Kyi under house arrest. When elections were held in 1990, the pro-democratic party won a huge victory, and Suu Kyi would have become prime minister. But the military refused to give up power.

Suu Kyi refused to give up too. In 1991 she was awarded the Nobel Prize for Peace, which called even more attention to Myanmar. International pressure was put on the military government there to free Suu Kyi and to step down.

In 1995 the government temporarily freed Suu Kyi. But it showed no signs of moving toward democracy. In 2000 Suu Kyi entered into talks with Myanmar's military government but was again put under house arrest. After nineteen months of house arrest, Suu Kyi was released in May 2002.

BIOFACT

Aung San Suu Kyi's name means "a bright collection of strange victories."

Learn from Biographies

When the military dictatorship freed Suu Kyi in 1995, she was free to leave Myanmar. Why do you think she chose to stay?

For more information, go online to *Meet the People* at **www.sfsocialstudies.com.**

642

Practice and Extend

WEB SITE **Technology**

Students can find out more about Aung San Suu Kyi by clicking on *Meet the People* at **www.sfsocialstudies.com.**

FYI **SOCIAL STUDIES** **Background**

About Aung San Suu Kyi

- *House arrest* means "confineme at home." Someone who is unde house arrest is prohibited from leaving his or her home.

- When Aung San Suu Kyi was under house arrest, she was so cut off from the world that she did not know she had won the Nobel Prize until she heard the news on the radio. Her son delivered her acceptance speec

CITIZEN HEROES

The Struggle
for Peace

e Struggle for Peace

berta Menchú knows poverty and heartbreak first-
. As a Mayan Indian, she was born in 1959 into
rty. Growing up in a small Guatemalan village,
hú watched poor farmers being forced
eir small plots of land by rich landowners.

years Guatemalan soldiers had been killing thousands of poor
s. But Guatemala's military governments had done nothing
this.

e 1970s, many of Guatemala's poor farmers joined
er to stand up for their rights. Rigoberta Menchú's
led one of these organizations but was killed by gov-
nt forces in 1980. Despite the danger involved,
ú took over as leader of her father's organization. She
gar and cotton workers in a massive strike against
tion owners. The government tried to arrest Menchú,
e fled the country. While out of the country, Menchú
about poverty and lack of human rights in Guatemala.
her efforts, Menchú was awarded the 1992 Nobel
r Peace. Upon receiving the award she stated:

1

> *"I consider this prize not as an award to me
> personally, but . . . in the struggle for peace,
> for human rights, and for the rights of
> indigenous [native] people . . . ."* **2**

temala no longer has a military government, but the military
s strong. Poor farmers and political activists still fear
pings and death. Using the $1.2 million she received
e Nobel Peace Prize,
ú has set up a human
foundation and continues
k for peace.

Courage in Action

Link to Current Events What kind of risk did
Menchú take in her fight for peace in Guatemala?
Research a person or a group of people who have
taken risks to make peace.

643

CURRICULUM CONNECTION
Literature

re About Peace and Peacemakers

se books may pique students' interest in the topic of people who work for
ce—or inspire them to work for peace themselves:

ce Crane, by Sheila Hamanaka (William Morrow and Company, ISBN 0-688-
.3815-2, 1995) **Easy**

* of War: True Stories from the Front Lines of the Children's Movement for
Peace in Colombia,* by Sara Cameron (Scholastic Trade, ISBN 0-439-29721-4,
:001) **On-Level**

cemakers: Winners of the Nobel Peace Prize, by Ann T. Keene (Oxford
Iniversity Press, ISBN 0-195-10316-5, 1998) **Challenge**

The Struggle
for Peace

Objective

- Identify a significant individual,
  Rigoberta Menchú, who worked for
  human rights.

1 Introduce and Motivate

Preview To activate prior knowledge,
ask students to discuss the people they
have read about who have fought for the
rights of others. What motivates such
people to take up these causes? Tell
students that this Citizen Heroes page
focuses on Rigoberta Menchú, a woman
who has worked for peace and human
rights in Guatemala.

2 Teach and Discuss

1 **Describe the major problems facing
Guatemalan peasant farmers during
Menchú's early life.** They were forced off
their land by rich landowners. Soldiers
killed thousands of peasants, and the
government did nothing to solve the
problems. **Summarize**

Primary Source

Cited in *Nobel Prize Winners 1992–1996
Supplement* by Clifford Thompson, ed.

2 **Why did Menchú feel the award
belonged to others besides herself?**
Others were struggling for peace as
much as or more than she was. She
considered her award a symbol in the
quest for peace. **Draw Conclusions**

3 Close and Assess

Courage in Action

Link to Current Events

Encourage students to use a variety of
sources as they research. Brainstorm
a list of risk-takers for peace. Write
suggestions on the board and allow
students to choose their subjects.

Political Conflicts and Challenges

Objectives

- Provide examples of how throughout history, people have stood up against terrorism.

- Define *terrorism* and explain how it is used.

- Explain how the United States has responded to acts of terrorism.

- Explain how people around the world have responded to acts of terrorism.

- Explain how governments around the world have stood up against terrorism.

Vocabulary

terrorism, p. 645

Resources

- Workbook, p. 159
- Transparency 23
- Every Student Learns Guide, pp. 302–305
- Quick Study, pp. 152–153

Quick Teaching Plan

If time is short, have students create fact cards.

- Have students prepare several index cards with the categories *Terrorist Event* (International or American), *Who, What, When, Why,* and *Response*.

- Have students add details to each card as they read the lesson independently.

1 Introduce and Motivate

Preview To activate prior knowledge, ask students what they know about the international fight against terrorism. Tell students they will learn more about this fight as they read Lesson 3.

You Are There Share with students that during the tragedy of September 11, 2001, many rescue workers helped save lives, but sadly, some rescue workers lost their own lives. Ask students what makes someone a hero.

LESSON 3

1970   1980   1990

1988
Bomb on airliner explodes over Lockerbie, Scotland.

1995
Truck bomb destroys a federal building in Oklahoma City.

Terrorist attacks occur in New York City and near Washing[ton]

Political Conflict[s] and Challenges

PREVIEW

Focus on the Main Idea
People around the world continue to stand up against terrorism and work toward peace.

PLACES
Barbary States
Lockerbie
Oklahoma City
New York City
Washington, D.C.

PEOPLE
Thomas Jefferson
George W. Bush
Elie Wiesel

VOCABULARY
terrorism

▶ In the United States, there are more than 150,000 emergency medical technicians and paramedics who wear badges such as this one.

You Are There September 11, 2001: You've been watching and listening to news re[ports] with your parents all day long. You[...] stunned by the horrible images on TV.

You're sad but feel safe at home with your family. The TV station shows some live video footage of emer- gency rescue workers.

"Look!" you cry out. "It's Uncle Nat! He's carrying a[...] woman to the ambulance."

A news reporter turns to your uncle and says, "You['re] a hero."

"I'm just doing my job," he replies.

You're so proud of Uncle Nat. Now you know a rea[l] hero!

You wonder if heroes are ever frightened or worried. Do you have to be a rescue worker or soldier to be heroic? You wonder what it takes to be a hero.

Draw Conclusions As you read, put facts together to understand how and why many people have been standing up against terrorism and working toward peace.

644

Practice and Extend

READING SKILL
Draw Conclusions

In the Lesson Review, students complete a graphic organizer like the one below. You may want to provide students with a copy of Transparency 23 to complete as they read the lesson.

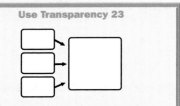

Use Transparency 23

WEB SITE
Technology

- You can look up vocabulary word[s] by clicking on *Social Studies Libr[ary]* and selecting the dictionary at **www.sfsocialstudies.com.**

- Students can learn more about current news by clicking on *Current Events* at **www.sfsocialstudies.com.**

- Explore other events that occurred on this day by clicking on *This Day in History* at **www.sfsocialstudies.com.**

ternational Struggles

ughout world history, many people have
med heroic acts in the face of danger.
eroes have been part of the fight and
e against international terrorism.

sm is the use of violence and fear to
e political goals. Terrorism can take the
f assassinations, bombings, hijackings,
pings, or chemical and germ warfare. It is
sed against civilians, or ordinary citizens.
rism has been a part of world history for
es. In the twentieth century, international
t attacks increased as groups used terror-

ism to carry out their political agendas. For example, in June 1914, a member of the Black Hand
Serbian terrorist organization assassinated
Austrian Archduke Franz Ferdinand. This event
started a chain reaction throughout Europe,
which eventually led to World War I. Beginning in
the late 1950s, a group fighting for Algerian independence from France carried out terrorist
attacks against French colonists.

Look at the map below to locate major international terrorist attacks since 1978. **3**

REVIEW What is terrorism and how is it used?
Main Idea and Details

Major International Terrorist Attacks, 1978–2001

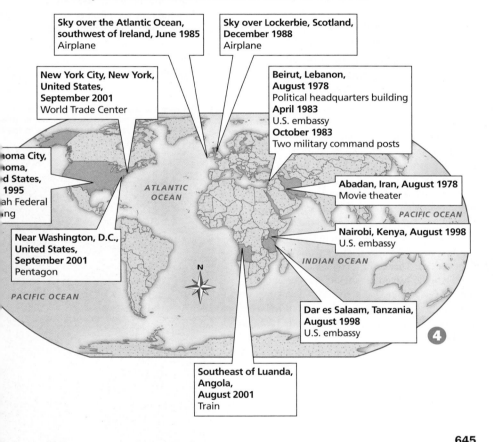

Sky over the Atlantic Ocean,
southwest of Ireland, June 1985
Airplane

Sky over Lockerbie, Scotland,
December 1988
Airplane

New York City, New York,
United States,
September 2001
World Trade Center

Beirut, Lebanon,
August 1978
Political headquarters building
April 1983
U.S. embassy
October 1983
Two military command posts

noma City,
noma,
d States,
1995
ah Federal
ng

ATLANTIC
OCEAN

Abadan, Iran, August 1978
Movie theater

PACIFIC OCEAN

Near Washington, D.C.,
United States,
September 2001
Pentagon

Nairobi, Kenya, August 1998
U.S. embassy

INDIAN OCEAN

N

PACIFIC OCEAN

Dar es Salaam, Tanzania,
August 1998
U.S. embassy **4**

Southeast of Luanda,
Angola,
August 2001
Train

Quick Summary Terrorism has
been carried out in a variety of
forms throughout the world for
centuries and has increased during the
twentieth and twenty-first centuries.

1 What forms can terrorism take?
Assassinations, bombings, hijackings,
kidnappings, and chemical and germ
warfare **Main Idea and Details**

2 What is the goal of most terrorists?
Possible answer: To carry out their
political agendas **Main Idea and Details**

**3 Why did the group fighting for
Algerian independence attack French
colonists?** They wanted independence
from France. **Cause and Effect**

**4 What places and buildings were
targets of major international terrorists
in 1978?** A political headquarters
building in Beirut, Lebanon, and a movie
theater in Abadan, Iran **Interpret Maps**

✓ **REVIEW ANSWER** Terrorism is the use
of violence and fear to achieve political
goals. **Main Idea and Details**

te Historical Fiction

ell students that people in the community can be sources of information.
ave students interview someone in the community about responding to
errorism. Students may choose to interview a neighbor, a local government
fficial, or a family member.

ave small groups of students share what they learned in their interviews.
tudents should use the interview material as they write a short story about
errorism. They may write one group story, or students may write individual
tories.

tudents may be able to use some of the direct quotations from interview
ources as models for dialogue in their stories.

ncourage students to focus their stories on characters' response to
errorism, rather than on the attacks.

Terrorism Against Americans

🕐 **Quick Summary** Terrorism against America has occurred on American soil and in other countries, and the U.S. government has always responded strongly.

Primary Source

Cited in *The Papers of Thomas Jefferson*, by Julian P. Boyd, ed.

5 What does this quotation reveal about America's reputation? What does it suggest is the reason for this reputation? It suggests that other nations thought America was not willing to protect itself. Up to this point America had not responded strongly to the pirate attacks. **Analyze Primary Sources**

6 In what country did terrorists attack a U.S. embassy in 1983? Lebanon **Main Idea and Details**

Test Talk

Locate Key Words in the Text

7 What information suggests that the plane crashes into the World Trade Center were not accidental? Have students locate key words in the text, such as *hijacked* and *crashed,* that will support their answer. The airplanes were hijacked, which means that people other than the pilots and other airline employees were controlling the airplanes. 🔍 **Draw Conclusions**

Terrorism Against Americans

Terrorist attacks on Americans and on American property and interests are not new. In the late eighteenth century, pirates of the **Barbary States** on the coast of North Africa began attacking U.S. and European commercial ships in the Mediterranean Sea. They held the crews for ransom, or in exchange for money.

When **Thomas Jefferson** became President in 1801, he wanted to end piracy overseas to protect American rights. In a letter, Jefferson wrote about the determination of the United States to stand up against piracy:

> *"If we wish our commerce to be free and uninsulted, we must let [other] nations see that we have an energy which at present they disbelieve."*

5

After diplomatic negotiations failed, Jefferson sent a naval squadron to stop piracy in the Mediterranean. As a result, the Barbary States signed a treaty ending the attacks on U.S. commercial ships.

But by the twentieth century, terrorists began to target civilians, as well as military forces. For example, in April 1983, a car bomb exploded at the U.S. embassy in Lebanon. In December 1988, a terrorist bomb destroyed an American airplane over **Lockerbie,** Scotland. In April 1995, a truck bomb exploded outside the Murrah Federal Building in **Oklahoma City,** Oklahoma. In 1998 bombs planted by international terrorists exploded outside two U.S. embassies in Tanzania and Kenya.

6

The United States had been responding to and taking a stand against terrorism for many years. But our country faced a new challenge on September 11, 2001.

646

▶ In this painting, the U.S. Nav[y] shown capturing an Algerian [ship] in the war with the Barbary S[tates]

On that morning, inter[natio]nal terrorists crashed two hijacked airplanes int[o] the 110-story twin towers [of] the World Trade Center in **New York City.** Thousands of pe[ople] working in the twin towers were killed, a[nd] both buildings were completely destroyed. O[n the] same day, international terrorists crashed a [third] hijacked airplane into the Pentagon, the head[–] quarters for the Department of Defense, in Arlington, Virginia, a suburb of **Washington, D[.C.]**

It is believed that passengers on a fourth hijacked airplane performed heroic acts to pr[e]vent the destruction of other possible target[s.] However, the plane crashed in a field in Shanksville, Pennsylvania. About 3,000 peop[le] from some 40 nations were killed in the September 11 terrorist attacks.

▶ The twin towers of the World Trade Center were international symbols of economic powe[r.] They were also important landmarks in the N[ew] York City skyline.

Practice and Extend

History of Terrorist Attacks

Students might be able to access the content of the text more easily if they do the following activities.

- Make a time line indicating dates and locations of terrorist attacks.
- Find locations on a map of several attacks.
- Write sentences about Thomas Jefferson's and George W. Bush's responses to the terrorist attacks.

For additional ESL support, use Every Student Learns Guide, pp. 302–305.

More About September 11, 200[1]

- Following the terrorist attacks o[n] September 11, businesses on Wall Street and in the financial district of New York City were closed for several days.
- The New York Stock Exchange was closed longer than any time since the depression in 1933.
- Police officers and firefighters were among those who rang the opening bell when the stock market reopened on Monday, September 17, 2001.

American people responded to these
st attacks with courage and heroism.
nds of rescue workers, firefighters, police
s, emergency workers, and volunteers
 to the scenes of the attacks. They risked
es to save the lives of others.

ts and children around the country also
ded. Some people donated blood. Others
d money to funds and organizations that
en set up for victims and their families.
ort of the United States, people hung
an flags on houses, businesses, and
ment buildings around the nation and in
es around the world.

U.S. government and military also
ded immediately. President George W.
addressed the nation with these words:

*rrorist attacks can shake
he foundations of our
iggest buildings, but they
annot touch the foundation
f America. These acts shat-
r steel, but they cannot dent
he steel of American resolve
determination]."*

e weeks following the attacks, Congress
tougher antiterrorism laws. Air travel had
d greatly, so funding was made available

▶ After the terrorist attacks of September 11, 2001,
U.S. airports and airlines increased security
measures.

to the airline industry to help with economic
recovery. Airports, skyscrapers, train and bus
stations, and other public buildings increased
security.

The terrorist attacks on the United States on
September 11, 2001, provoked, or caused, a unified response by the United States. By October 7, **9**
the United States, aided by other nations, had
gathered evidence that the Taliban government
in Afghanistan was protecting the terrorist group
responsible for the attacks. On that day, the
United States, with its ally Great Britain, began
bombing Taliban military targets in Afghanistan.

By December Taliban rule over Afghanistan had
been replaced. Efforts to establish a new government had also begun.

REVIEW How did Americans respond to the
terrorist attacks on September 11, 2001?
Summarize

Terrorist Attacks Against Civilians **10**

Location	Target	Attacker
Lockerbie, Scotland	Civilians	International terrorists
Oklahoma City	Civilians	Domestic terrorist
Tanzania and Kenya	Civilians	International terrorists
New York City and near Washington, D.C.	Civilians	International terrorists

orist attacks against Americans have taken different forms.

RT SKILL Use a Chart *How are these terrorist attacks alike and different?*

647

Primary Source
United States President George W. Bush in a speech
to the American people, September 11, 2001

8 **What was the goal of the words
President Bush spoke as he addressed
the nation?** Possible answer: He wanted
to encourage people not to be overcome
by the attacks and to display their pride
and strength as American citizens.
Analyze Primary Sources

SOCIAL STUDIES STRAND
Citizenship

Tell students that in addition to bombing
military targets in Afghanistan, the
United States, Britain, Germany, Norway,
and Russia sent thousands of tons of
food and medicine to help the Afghan
people, who had lived through many
years of internal and external conflict.

9 **What does the response of the
United States to the attacks of
September 11, 2001, suggest about
the United States?** Possible answer:
The United States works hard to protect
its own citizens while continuing to help
people in other countries.
Draw Conclusions

✓ REVIEW ANSWER Americans donated
blood and money and displayed
American flags. The U.S. government
passed tougher antiterrorism laws.
Security was increased in airports and
other public places. U.S. bombing of
Afghanistan began, and Taliban rule over
Afghanistan was replaced. Summarize

10 **How does this chart support the
statement *In the last half of the
twentieth century, terrorists stopped
targeting just military forces*?** All of the
targets on the chart were civilian.
Interpret Charts

✓ Ongoing Assessment

If... students are unable to support the statement,	then... call students' attention to the *Target* column of the chart.

CHART SKILL **Answer** Alike: all the
attacks listed on the chart targeted
civilians; Different: two attacks took
place on American soil, one took place
overseas; two attacks were carried out
by international terrorists, one was
carried out by a domestic terrorist.

MEETING INDIVIDUAL NEEDS
Leveled Practice

cuss Terrorism Using the ideas in this lesson, students explain and discuss
rism.

y Ask students to make a word web for the term *terrorism* and discuss the
ds they used. **Reteach**

Level Have students write a response to one of the attacks described in the
on and suggest an alternative method the terrorists groups might have used
chieve their goals peacefully. **Extend**

llenge Have students research the causes of, responses to, and results of
of the attacks shown on the map on p. 645. Students can present their
ings to the class in an oral report. **Enrich**

a Lesson Summary, use Quick Study, p. 152.

Working Together

🕐 **Quick Summary** Although differences among people can result in acts of terrorism, people around the world are working together for international peace.

Primary Source

Cited in *Parade Magazine*, Oct. 28, 2001

11 What do Elie Wiesel's words mean to you? Possible answer: People should stick together in troubled times and act in an honorable way rather than use revenge and violence to solve problems. **Analyze Primary Sources**

FACT FILE
The World Unites

12 Why do you think the workers in the top photograph hung the large American flag from the roof of the Pentagon after September 11, 2001? Possible answers: To show that they were proud to be Americans and that they were not allowing the terrorists to make them fearful. **Interpret National/Political Symbols**

13 Do you think individuals such as Mairead Corrigan Maguire and Daniel Barenboim can have an effect on peace around the world? Explain. Possible answer: Yes; they demonstrate that people can work together. **Evaluate**

✓ **REVIEW ANSWER** People around the world worked together to promote peace. They have formed peace organizations or have brought people together to perform to help promote peace. Countries have supported the U.S. military response. **Main Idea and Details**

Working Together

The United States was not the only nation to respond to the terrorist attacks on September 11. Countries all over the world have responded and supported the fight against terrorism. As Elie Wiesel, a Holocaust concentration camp survivor and winner of the Nobel Prize for Peace said:

". . . it is incumbent upon [required of] us to choose between escape and solidarity, shame and honor. The terrorists have chosen shame. We choose honor."

FACT FILE
The World Unites

After the terrorist attacks on September 11, Americans and many people around the world vowed to unite in the fight against terrorism. With President George W. Bush, New York City Mayor Rudolph Giuliani, and New York Governor George Pataki, rescue workers, firefighters, police officers, volunteers, and political and religious leaders worldwide also responded. They began working together to help support victims, families of victims, and businesses destroyed and damaged as a result of the attacks.

648

Practice and Extend

🔵 **CURRICULUM CONNECTION**
Art

Create a Peace Display

- Students can work in small groups to create a display showing ways to promote peace.
- Ask students to find information about a variety of peace movements, using reference materials and the Internet.
- Students can also draw pictures and write paragraphs showing what they can do to promote peace around the world.

During a peace vigil in Northern Ireland, people hold up cut-out doves of peace.

Acts of terrorism are often caused by differences—in religion, ethnicity, or political beliefs—among peoples. People around the world have tried to work together to promote peace. For example, disagreements between Protestants and Catholics led to acts of terrorism in Northern Ireland. Mairead Corrigan Maguire founded the Community of the Peace People to help unite Protestants and Catholics.

Disputes between Arabs and Jews in the Middle East have also led to acts of terrorism. In response, some Arabs and Jews have worked together to promote peace and understanding of differences. In the summer of 2001, Chicago Symphony Orchestra conductor Daniel Barenboim led a concert program performed by young Palestinians and Jewish musicians to show that people of different identities can work together. **13**

REVIEW How have people and countries around the world responded to acts of terrorism?
Main Idea and Details

Summarize the Lesson

- **1988** Bomb on airplane exploded over Lockerbie, Scotland.
- **1995** Truck bomb destroyed a federal building in Oklahoma City.
- **2001** Terrorist attacks hit New York City and near Washington, D.C.

LESSON 3   REVIEW

Check Facts and Main Ideas

1. **Draw Conclusions** On a separate piece of paper, copy the diagram below. Fill in the missing facts that support the conclusion.

| President Jefferson sent a naval squadron to stop piracy in the Mediterranean | Some people have formed organizations to bring people together to promote peace. | Airports, skyscrapers, train and bus stations, and other public buildings increased security. |

↓

People throughout history have stood up against terrorism.

2. What is terrorism and when is it used?

3. How has the United States responded to acts of terrorism?

4. How have people around the world responded to acts of terrorism?

5. **Critical Thinking:** *Solve Complex Problems* What can governments around the world do to stand up to terrorists and terrorism?

Link to ⟨⟩ **Writing**

Make of list Write down several objectives for working toward peace. Consider new ways that people can help promote peace together.

649

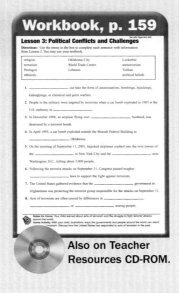

Workbook, p. 159

Lesson 3: Political Conflicts and Challenges

Directions: Use the terms in the box to complete each sentence with information from Lesson 3. You may use your textbook.

religion	Oklahoma City	Lockerbie
terrorism	World Trade Center	
Pentagon	Lebanon	Taliban
ethnicity		political beliefs

1. _____ can take the form of assassinations, bombings, hijackings, kidnappings, or chemical and germ warfare.

2. People in the military were targeted by terrorists when a car bomb exploded in 1983 at the U.S. embassy in _____.

3. In December 1988, an airplane flying over _____, Scotland, was destroyed by a terrorist bomb.

4. In April 1995, a car bomb exploded outside the Murrah Federal Building in _____, Oklahoma.

5. On the morning of September 11, 2001, hijacked airplanes crashed into the twin towers of the _____ in New York City and the _____ near Washington, D.C., killing about 3,000 people.

6. Following the terrorist attacks on September 11, Congress passed tougher _____ laws to support the fight against terrorism.

7. The United States gathered evidence that the _____ government in Afghanistan was protecting the terrorist group responsible for the attacks on September 11.

8. Acts of terrorism are often caused by differences in _____, _____, or _____ among people.

Notes for Home: Your child learned about acts of terrorism and the groups to fight terrorist attacks around the world.
Home Activity: With your child, brainstorm ways the governments and people around the world can stand up to terrorism. Discuss how the United States has responded to acts of terrorism in the past.

Also on Teacher Resources CD-ROM.

Summarize the Lesson

Examine the vertical time line with students. Have them determine whether each attack was international or within the United States and if the attack was by foreign or domestic terrorists. Discuss what conclusion they can draw based on their answers. (Terrorism has no boundaries.)

✓ **LESSON 3   REVIEW**

1. **Draw Conclusions** For possible answers, see the reduced pupil page.

2. Terrorism is the use of violence and fear to achieve political goals.

 **Test Talk**

Write Your Answer to Score High

Tell students to use details from the text to support their written answer

3. The United States has stood up against terrorism. President Jefferson stopped piracy in the Mediterranean by trying to negotiate and then by sending a naval squadron. The United States has increased security and passed stronger antiterrorism laws.

4. They have used military force against terrorist groups, created tougher laws, increased security, and worked together to promote peace and understanding.

5. **Critical Thinking:** *Solve Complex Problems* Answers will vary. Students might suggest that governments could pass more antiterrorism laws, increase security, or work with other governments to track down and stop terrorists.

Link to ⟨⟩ **Writing**

Students should work in groups to brainstorm their lists of objectives and ideas. Have groups share and compare their responses. Consider putting into action ideas students may suggest, such as becoming pen or e-mail pals with other students around the world to share ideas about promoting peace.

Resources

- Assessment Book, pp. 113–116
- Workbook, p. 160: Vocabulary Review

Chapter Summary

For possible answers, see the reduced pupil page.

Vocabulary

1. e, **2.** b, **3.** d, **4.** a, **5.** c

People and Terms

1. The European Union is a European trading bloc that began as the European Economic Community in 1957.

2. Mercosur is a South American trading bloc that includes Brazil, Argentina, Paraguay, and Uruguay.

3. Bill Clinton was the U.S. President who persuaded Congress to approve NAFTA.

4. George W. Bush was the U.S. President at the time of terrorist attacks in New York City and Washington, D.C.

5. Aung San Suu Kyi is a leader in the struggle against Myanmar's repressive government.

6. Rigoberta Menchú of Guatemala fought against repressive government there.

7. Mary Robinson became the United Nations High Commissioner for Human Rights in 1997.

8. Slobodan Milosevic was the president of Serbia who encouraged ethnic cleansing in Bosnia and Kosovo.

9. Mairead Corrigan Maguire is an activist who worked for peace in Northern Ireland and shared the 1976 Nobel Prize for Peace.

10. ASEAN, the Association of Southeast Asian Nations, was set up in 1967 as a trading bloc among five nations.

CHAPTER 22
REVIEW

1950	1960
1957 The European Economic Community was created.	**1962** Military takeover in Burma

Chapter Summary

Draw Conclusions

Target Skill

On a separate piece of paper, fill in three facts that support the given conclusion.

Trading blocs formed to promote economic cooperation.

Differences in identity or ethnicity have caused conflicts.

Terrorism has given way to new challenges.

The world has seen examples of cooperation, conflicts, and challenges.

Vocabulary

Match each word with the correct definition or description.

1. **trading bloc** (p. 632)

2. **ethnicity** (p. 637)

3. **gross domestic product** (p. 631)

4. **repressive** (p. 640)

5. **euro** (p. 632)

a. denying citizens basic civil rights

b. common culture, religion, and customs of a group

c. currency of the EU

d. a measure of a nation's wealth

e. a group of countries that agrees to trade under favorable conditions

People and Terms

Write a sentence explaining why each of the following people or terms was important in wor[ld] events since World War II. You may use two [or] more in a single sentence.

1. European Union (p. 632)

2. Mercosur (p. 633)

3. Bill Clinton (p. 633)

4. George W. Bush (p. 647)

5. Aung San Suu Kyi (p. 640)

6. Rigoberta Menchú (p. 6[ ])

7. Mary Robins[on] (p. 639)

8. Slobodan Milosevic (p. 637)

9. Mairead Cor[rigan] Maguire (p. [ ])

10. ASEAN (p. 6[ ])

650

Practice and Extend

Assessment Options

✓ Chapter 22 Assessment

- Chapter 22 Content Test: Use Assessment Book, pp. 113–114.
- Chapter 22 Skills Test: Use Assessment Book, pp. 115–116.

TEST PREP **Standardized Test Prep**

- Chapter 22 Tests contain standardized test format.

✓ Chapter 22 Performance Assessment

- Have students work in groups to create news magazine shows about an event in Chapter 2[2]
- Remind students that their reports should answer *Who? What? When? Where?* and *Why?* Students should describe events in chronological order and give background information.
- As students present their news shows, listen for facts about the lesson topics. Be tha[t] students show understanding of the global economy and of the roots of conflict between nations and groups of people within nations.

Timeline:

1970   1980   1990   2000

late 1960s Violence broke out in Northern Ireland.

1967 ASEAN was formed.

1989 Tiananmen Square massacre

1991–1992 Breakup of Yugoslavia

1994 NAFTA began.

1996 Taliban takeover in Afghanistan

1999 War in Kosovo

2001 Terrorist attacks hit New York City and near Washington, D.C.

Facts and Main Ideas

What is a trading bloc?

How did Chinese communist leaders react to students protesting in Tiananmen Square in 1989?

Which republics pulled out of Yugoslavia? Which republic used force against them?

Time Line How many years were there between the breakup of Yugoslavia and the war in Kosovo?

Main Idea How has economic cooperation brought about the global economy?

Main Idea Why do differences of identity sometimes lead to conflict?

Main Idea How has the world responded to acts of terrorism?

Critical Thinking: *Fact or Opinion* Acts of terrorism against Americans have been committed for centuries.

Write About History

Write an **advertisement** for a new product your company is trying to market in a foreign nation.

Write an **eyewitness account** of the events in Tiananmen Square in June 1989. Identify your point of view—student, soldier, bystander, or reporter.

Write a **preamble**, or introduction, to a new constitution for a nation that has decided to guarantee full equality for women.

Apply Skills

Interpret Cartograms

Turn to the atlas in the back of your textbook. Look at a map of South America. Then look at the cartogram below representing population and answer the following question.

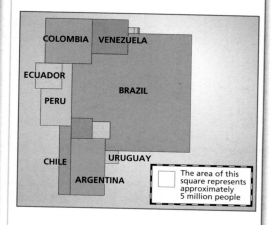

COLOMBIA   VENEZUELA

ECUADOR

PERU

BRAZIL

CHILE

URUGUAY

ARGENTINA

The area of this square represents approximately 5 million people

1 How does the map of South America on page R9 compare to the cartogram?

Internet Activity

To get help with vocabulary, people, and terms, select dictionary, encyclopedia, or almanac from *Social Studies Library* at **www.sfsocialstudies.com**.

651

Hands-on Unit Project

Unit 8 Performance Assessment

See p. 678 for information about using the Unit Project as a means of performance assessment. A scoring guide is provided on p. 678.

WEB SITE
Technology

For more information, students can select the dictionary, encyclopedia, or almanac from *Social Studies Library* at **www.sfsocialstudies.com**.

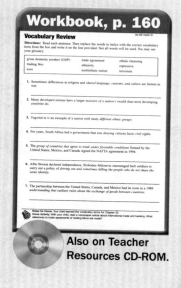

Workbook, p. 160

Vocabulary Review

Also on Teacher Resources CD-ROM.

Facts and Main Ideas

1. A group of nations that agree to trade on favorable terms

2. They sent the army in to stop the demonstration by force, killing many. They also had students arrested and imprisoned.

3. Slovenia, Croatia, and Bosnia and Herzegovina pulled out. Serbia tried to keep them in by force.

4. Seven or eight years

5. Cooperation in trade, such as trading blocs, has tied nations' economies closer together and created the global economy.

6. Differences in identity sometimes cause disagreements and resentments, which can become the spark for conflict.

7. The United States and countries around the world have donated blood, raised money, increased security, passed tougher antiterrorism laws, formed peace organizations, and used their armed forces against terrorists.

8. Fact

Write About History

1. Students' advertisements should be persuasive and take cultural differences into account. What would people in other countries find appealing about the product?

2. Point out that the narrators of their accounts might be biased. For example, a soldier's perspective on the events would differ from a student's. Students should consider these differences as they write. Can classmates figure out which point of view is being used, even if the speaker is not identified?

3. The language they use should be clear and straightforward.

Apply Skills

1. The size of each square or rectangle in the cartogram, which represents each country's population, is about the same as each country's area on the map of South America on page R9.

Chapter Planning Guide

Chapter 23 • Living in the 21st Century

Locating Time and Place pp. 652–653

Lesson Titles	Pacing	Main Ideas
Lesson 1 **Population Growth and Change** pp. 654–657	2 days	• Population growth and movement present challeng in today's world.
Map and Globe Skills: Compare Distribution Maps pp. 658–659		• Distribution maps show the spread of things such population, wildlife, or natural resources.
Lesson 2 **Earth's Environment** pp. 660–663	1 day	• People are working together to repair damage to Earth's environment.
Lesson 3 **Energy** pp. 664–667	1 day	• As energy sources become less plentiful, we look new ways to produce and conserve energy.
Lesson 4 **Technology** pp. 668–671	1 day	• Technology gives us many benefits, but it cannot s every human problem.

✓ **Chapter 23 Review**
pp. 672–673

In 1965 Edward H. White
became the first America
to leave his spacecraft a
"walk" in space.

✓ = Assessment Options

◀ **Pollution from people has reached Antarctica and harmed its environment and wildlife.**

Vocabulary	Resources	Meeting Individual Needs
lennium gacity nographer nigration population growth	• Workbook, p. 162 • Transparency 23 • Every Student Learns Guide, pp. 306–309 • Quick Study, pp. 154–155 • Workbook, p. 163	• ESL Support, TE p. 655 • Leveled Practice, TE p. 656
al warming on dioxide enhouse effect ticide ronmentalist angered species restation ertification ution	• Workbook, p. 164 • Transparency 21 • Every Student Learns Guide, pp. 310–313 • Quick Study, pp. 156–157	• ESL Support, TE p. 661 • Leveled Practice, TE p. 663
ervation l fuel enewable resource wable resource oelectric energy hermal energy	• Workbook, p. 165 • Transparency 23 • Every Student Learns Guide, pp. 314–317 • Quick Study, pp. 158–159	• ESL Support, TE p. 665 • Leveled Practice, TE p. 667
e station lite	• Workbook, p. 166 • Transparency 23 • Every Student Learns Guide, pp. 318–321 • Quick Study, pp. 160–161	• ESL Support, TE p. 669 • Learning Styles, TE p. 670 • Leveled Practice, TE p. 671
	✓ Chapter 23 Content Test, Assessment Book, pp. 117–118 ✓ Chapter 23 Skills Test, Assessment Book, pp. 119–120	✓ Chapter 23 Performance Assessment, TE p. 672

Providing More Depth

Additional Resources

- Vocabulary Cards
- Daily Activity Bank
- Social Studies Plus!
- Big Book Atlas
- Student Atlas
- Outline Maps
- Desk Maps

 Technology

- AudioText
- The test maker
- Teacher Resources CD-ROM
- Map Resources CD-ROM
- **www.sfsocialstudies.com**

 To establish guidelines for your students' safe and responsible use of the Internet, use the Scott Foresman Internet Guide.

Additional Internet Links

To find out more about:

- population in the major cities of the world, visit **www.citypopulation.de**
- the causes and impact of global warming, visit **www.epa.gov**
- space science and relevant activities, visit **ssdoo.gsfc.nasa.gov**

Key Internet Search Terms

- world population
- pollution
- technology

Workbook Support

Use the following Workbook pages to support content and skills development as you teach Chapter 23. You can also view and print Workbook pages from the Teacher Resources CD-ROM.

Workbook, p. 161

Use with Chapter 23.

Vocabulary Preview

Directions: Match each vocabulary word to its meaning. Write the word on the line provided. Not all words will be used. You may use your glossary.

millennium	greenhouse effect	fossil fuel
megacity	pesticide	nonrenewable resource
demographer	environmentalist	renewable resource
immigration	endangered species	hydroelectric energy
zero population growth	deforestation	geothermal energy
global warming	desertification	space station
carbon dioxide	pollution	satellite
	conservation	

__space station__   1. large satellite in space that serves as a scientific base

__renewable resource__   2. natural resource that can be replaced

__millennium__   3. one thousand years

__geothermal energy__   4. energy from super-hot water underground

__immigration__   5. process of people moving to a new country

__satellite__   6. human-made object sent into space

__hydroelectric energy__   7. water power from rapidly flowing rivers or dams

__demographer__   8. scientist who studies population trends

__pesticide__   9. chemical that is used to kill pests

__environmentalist__   10. person who favors taking measures to protect the environment

__endangered species__   11. animals and plants that could die out

__conservation__   12. limiting the use of energy

__megacity__   13. city region with 10 million or more people

 Notes for Home: Your child learned the vocabulary terms for Chapter 23.
Home Activity: Help your child make flash cards for the vocabulary terms for Chapter 23. Make half of them tonight and the other half tomorrow night. Quiz your child on the definition of each word.

Use with Pupil Edition, p. 652

Workbook, p. 162

Use with Pages 654–657.

Lesson 1: Population Growth and Change

Directions: Read the following statements. Then write *T* (True) or *F* (False) on the line before each statement. If the answer is false, rewrite the statement to make it true. You may use your textbook.

1. __F__ Many of the world's people are moving to rural areas.

   Many of the world's people are moving to urban areas.

2. __F__ Calcutta is one of the richest and most populated cities in the world.

   Calcutta is one of the poorest and most populated cities in the world.

3. __T__ The Industrial Revolution in the late 1800s resulted in an increase in migration from rural areas to urban areas.

4. __T__ Unemployment is high in many developing countries and governments cannot provide good housing and clean water.

5. __F__ Developed countries usually have a higher population growth rate than developing countries.

   Developing countries usually have a higher population growth rate than developed countries.

6. __T__ Many demographers believe that there is a connection between the status of women and a country's population growth rate.

Notes for Home: Your child learned about trends in the growth and movement of the world's population.
Home Activity: With your child, discuss the effects of population changes on your community. What advantages or disadvantages has your family experienced?

Use with Pupil Edition, p. 657

Workbook, p. 163

Use with Pages 658–659.

Compare Distribution Maps

Directions: Answer the questions below about distribution maps. You may use your textbook.

1. What is the purpose of distribution maps?

   They show where something is distributed, or spread, across the area shown on the maps.

2. What type of symbols do distribution maps use to show the distribution of something across an area?

   Possible answer: Dots, colors, shading, or other symbols

3. Why might politicians use distribution maps? Why might airlines? Why might city governments?

   Possible answers: To identify possible supporters; to identify routes, frequency of flights along these routes, and locations for hub cities; to predict the type and amount of services needed

4. Look at the two distribution maps on pp. 658–659. Near what kind of physical feature has much of the world's population settled? On which distribution map did you find this information?

   waterways; world population distribution map

5. Look at the world population distribution map on p. 658. According to the map key, what symbol represents population? What does a cluster of these symbols indicate about the population of that area?

   dots; a large population

Notes for Home: Your child learned how to compare distribution maps.
Home Activity: With your child, discuss how changes in the population density of your community affect the people who live and work there. What effects do population shifts have on local governments and our use of natural resources?

Use with Pupil Edition, p. 659

Workbook, p. 164

Use with Pages 660–663.

Lesson 2: Earth's Environment

Directions: Complete the cause-and-effect chart with information from this lesson. You may use your textbook.

Cause	Effect
People burn fuels such as coal and oil.	**Carbon dioxide is released into the atmosphere.**
Rachel Carson writes *Silent Spring*.	**Many people become environmentalists.**
People begin pressing for laws to protect the environment.	**The U.S. Congress sets up the EPA and passes laws to protect endangered species.**
Most nations believe reducing the carbon dioxide they produce will disrupt their economies.	**Most nations have not adopted the Kyoto Protocol.**
Population increases lead people to cut down forests to plant crops on the land.	**Deforestation adds to global warming.**
Farmers overplant and animals overgraze the land.	**Desertification destroys fertile land.**
Humans do not properly dispose of much waste, such as garbage.	**Pollution makes the environment dirty.**

Notes for Home: Your child learned about the causes and effects of damage to Earth's environment.
Home Activity: With your child, set up a recycling system in your home. Create a space to recycle things such as cans, plastic, and newspapers. Decide on a schedule to determine when and how often you will turn in your recyclable products.

Use with Pupil Edition, p. 663

Workbook Support

Workbook, p. 165

Lesson 3: Energy

Use with Pages 664–667.

Directions: Use the information from Lesson 3 to answer the following questions on the lines provided. You may use your textbook.

1. What are two ways we use fossil fuels?

   Possible answers: To run generators in power plants, to power cars, to heat homes and businesses

2. What are two problems related to using fossil fuels to supply energy?

   Possible answers: They take so long to form, are nonrenewable, and give off carbon dioxide when they burn.

3. What were the causes of the oil crisis of the 1970s?

   OPEC members cut petroleum production and raised oil prices.

4. What are the advantages of nuclear power?

   It uses nuclear fuel instead of fossil fuels, does not give off carbon dioxide, and could last for thousands of years.

5. What are some examples of renewable energy sources? What is the advantage of using these to create energy?

   Possible answers: Solar, water, wind, and nuclear energy; they cannot be used up easily.

6. How are hydroelectric energy and geothermal energy different?

   Hydroelectric energy uses rapidly flowing water; geothermal energy comes from super-hot water underground.

7. In what ways are scientists trying to solve the world's energy shortage?

   by creating new ways of producing energy and developing more energy-efficient vehicles and machines

 Notes for Home: Your child learned about the ways we produce and conserve energy.
Home Activity: With your child, read a newspaper article about energy conservation. What new ways of conservation are discussed?

Use with Pupil Edition, p. 667

Workbook, p. 166

Lesson 4: Technology

Use with Pages 668–671.

Directions: Write the events from the box in the chart in the order in which they took place. You may use your textbook.

- Researcher Flossie Wong-Staal helps identify HIV.
- U.S. astronauts Neil Armstrong and Edwin Aldrin walk on the moon.
- UN Secretary-General Kofi Annan urges developed nations to contribute money to help fight AIDS in Africa.
- Desktop computers are introduced for use at home and at work.
- The former Soviet Union launches the *Sputnik I* satellite into space.
- Toolmaking advances from stone to copper.
- Soviet astronaut Yuri Gagarin becomes the first human in space.

1. Toolmaking advances from stone to copper.

2. The former Soviet Union launches the *Sputnik I* satellite into space.

3. Soviet astronaut Yuri Gagarin becomes the first human in space.

4. U.S. astronauts Neil Armstrong and Edwin Aldrin walk on the moon.

5. Desktop computers are introduced for use at home and at work.

6. Researcher Flossie Wong-Staal helps identify HIV.

7. UN Secretary-General Kofi Annan urges developed nations to contribute money to help fight AIDS in Africa.

 Notes for Home: Your child learned about advances in technology and the research scientists continue to conduct.
Home Activity: With your child, make a chart to compare how technology has changed the ways in which people communicate, work, and live from the time you were a child to the present.

Use with Pupil Edition, p. 671

Workbook, p. 167

Vocabulary Review

Use with Chapter 23.

Directions: Complete each sentence with a vocabulary term from Chapter 23. Write the word on the line provided. Not all words will be used.

1. Some farmers spray their crops with a ____pesticide____ to kill insects.

2. Cutting down forests to create areas to plant crops is called ____deforestation____.

3. Petroleum is a ____nonrenewable resource____ because it cannot be easily replaced.

4. Human activities such as burning gasoline in cars produce a gas called ____carbon dioxide____.

5. A gradual increase in the average temperature of Earth's surface is known as ____global warming____.

6. As a solution to ____pollution____, people recycle aluminum, paper, and glass.

7. Coal, petroleum, and natural gas are each a ____fossil fuel____.

8. Tokyo is an example of a ____megacity____ because more than 10 million people live there.

9. The point at which enough babies are born to balance the number of deaths is called ____zero population growth____.

10. Gases trap heat that radiates from Earth's surface in a process called the ____greenhouse effect____.

11. When the topsoil of fertile land becomes loose, dries up, and blows away, the process is called ____desertification____.

12. Limiting our use of energy, or ____conservation____, is one solution to the energy crisis.

13. Water power from rivers or dams provides an alternative source of energy called ____hydroelectric energy____.

 Notes for Home: Your child learned the vocabulary terms for Chapter 23.
Home Activity: Nine vocabulary terms from Chapter 23 were not covered in this exercise. Have your child identify the nine missing terms and use each in an original sentence.

Use with Pupil Edition, p. 673

Workbook, p. 168

8 Project Making Contact

Directions: In a group, design a Web page about the history of communication.

1. Our Web page will feature this communication method or invention:

   _____

2. Description of the method or invention:

   _____

   _____

3. Inventor(s) of this method or invention:

   _____   _____

4. A time line shows the development of the method or invention through history.

   Earliest use in ____ Additions or improvements in ____ Modern form ____
   (year)   (year)   (year)

5. Pictures we will include to represent our method or invention:

   _____   _____
   _____   _____
   _____   _____

You may wish to have students research Web pages on the Internet and discuss features commonly found on Web pages before drawing their own.

☑ **Checklist for Students**

____ We chose a communication method or invention.
____ We wrote important facts and described it.
____ We created a time line and pictures showing how it changed over time.
____ We made a drawing of our Web page.
____ We presented our Web page to the class.

 Notes for Home: Your child learned about the development of communication.
Home Activity: With your child, discuss the different methods of communication used by your family. Which methods have been invented in the last 20 years? What developments in communication do you predict will occur in the next 20 years?

Use with Pupil Edition, p. 678

Assessment Support

Use these Assessment Book pages and the test maker to assess content and skills in Chapter 23 and Unit 8. You can also view and print Assessment Book pages from the Teacher Resources CD-ROM.

Assessment Book, p. 117

Chapter 23 Test
Part 1: Content Test

Directions: Fill in the circle next to the correct answer.

Lesson Objective (1:1, 2)

1. Why do many people move to urban areas?
   - Ⓐ They seek basic necessities.
   - Ⓑ There are fewer economic opportunities in urban areas.
   - Ⓒ Governments can no longer provide basic services.
   - ● They seek more job opportunities.

Lesson Objective (1:4)

2. Which of the following is NOT a result of the increasing population in many cities?
   - Ⓐ housing shortages
   - Ⓑ unclean water
   - ● less pollution
   - Ⓓ crowded conditions

Lesson Objective (1:3)

3. In which part of the world is population growing the fastest?
   - ● in developing countries
   - Ⓑ in countries with many cities
   - Ⓒ in the United States
   - Ⓓ in Europe

Lesson Objective (1:5)

4. What is one way that France has been affected by immigration from North African colonies?
   - Ⓐ More than 600,000 people are now homeless in France.
   - Ⓑ Many of France's people are fleeing to other countries as a result of the immigration.
   - ● More people in France now attend mosques than churches.
   - Ⓓ The population growth in France slowed drastically.

Lesson Objective (2:3)

5. What role does carbon dioxide play in the greenhouse effect?
   - ● It traps heat radiated from Earth's surface.
   - Ⓑ It soaks up oxygen in the air.
   - Ⓒ Earth moves gradually toward the sun.
   - Ⓓ Clouds and carbon dioxide block the sun's heat.

Lesson Objective (2:2)

6. What is the role of an environmentalist?
   - Ⓐ study Earth's natural resources
   - Ⓑ write about plants and nature
   - ● protect Earth's natural environment
   - Ⓓ use natural medicines to cure diseases

Lesson Objective (2:4)

7. What has the U.S. government done to protect the environment?
   - Ⓐ forced farmers to stop using pesticides
   - Ⓑ closed travel on all rivers and lakes
   - Ⓒ outlawed all machines that pollute the air
   - ● passed laws to reduce pollution and protect animals

Lesson Objective (2:1)

8. Which of the following is NOT an example of how humans harm the environment?
   - Ⓐ pollution
   - Ⓑ deforestation
   - Ⓒ desertification
   - ● conservation

Use with Pupil Edition, p. 672

Assessment Book, p. 118

Lesson Objective (2:4)

9. Which is one solution people have found for pollution control?
   - Ⓐ desertification
   - ● recycling
   - Ⓒ global warming
   - Ⓓ pesticides

Lesson Objective (3:2)

10. Which of the following is an example of a fossil fuel?
    - Ⓐ carbon dioxide
    - ● petroleum
    - Ⓒ nuclear power
    - Ⓓ solar energy

Lesson Objective (3:1)

11. Why are fossil fuels considered nonrenewable resources?
    - Ⓐ They can be used over and over.
    - ● They cannot be easily replaced.
    - Ⓒ They will never run out.
    - Ⓓ They burn for a very long time.

Lesson Objective (3:3)

12. What is one effect of using nuclear power?
    - ● radioactive waste
    - Ⓑ carbon dioxide
    - Ⓒ deforestation
    - Ⓓ global warming

Lesson Objective (3:4)

13. What type of resource is used to produce hydroelectricity?
    - ● renewable
    - Ⓑ nonrenewable
    - Ⓒ fossil fuel
    - Ⓓ solar

Lesson Objective (3:5)

14. What would be one characteristic of a perfect energy source?
    - Ⓐ nonrenewable
    - Ⓑ a fossil fuel
    - Ⓒ produces carbon dioxide
    - ● nonpolluting

Lesson Objective (4:1)

15. Which area(s) saw major advances in technology in the twentieth century?
    - Ⓐ space travel
    - Ⓑ communication
    - Ⓒ medicine
    - ● all of the above

Lesson Objective (4:2)

16. Which is NOT a way we use satellites?
    - ● to make more powerful desktop computers
    - Ⓑ to serve as a scientific base
    - Ⓒ as a refueling station for spacecraft
    - Ⓓ as a launching pad for other satellites

Lesson Objective (4:3)

17. What is the main goal of the Human Genome Project?
    - Ⓐ develop faster and smarter computers
    - Ⓑ launch communication satellites into space
    - ● identify the cause of diseases
    - Ⓓ stop global warming

Lesson Objective (4:4)

18. What is one technological accomplishment that has NOT yet been made?
    - Ⓐ space travel
    - ● cure for AIDS
    - Ⓒ information processing
    - Ⓓ genetic research

Use with Pupil Edition, p. 672

Assessment Book, p. 119

Part 2: Skills Test

Directions: Use complete sentences to answer questions 1–7. Use a separate sheet of paper if you need more space.

1. What general trends exist in the world's population, and what are the effects of these trends? **Analyze Information**

   Population is increasing in urban areas and in developing countries. The growing population has led to overcrowding, homelessness, and unhealthy living conditions.

2. Why is the role of demographers important? **Summarize**

   Scientists who study population trends analyze and predict where people live and work to help solve challenges related to housing, services, and use of resources.

3. What causes global warming? **Main Idea and Details**

   Increased levels of gases such as carbon dioxide build up in Earth's atmosphere. These gases trap the heat from the sun and cause the temperature of Earth's surface to increase.

4. Do you believe that humans have done more good or harm to Earth? Provide at least three facts to support your opinion. **Fact and Opinion**

   Possible answers: I believe humans have done more harm to Earth. Deforestation and human activities produce carbon dioxide contributes to global warming. Human activity has caused fertile land to be lost through desertification.

5. Do you think it is important to conserve energy? Explain. **Express Ideas**

   Possible answer: Yes. Some sources of energy, such as oil and coal, may run out someday. By conserving these fuels, we can make them last longer.

Use with Pupil Edition, p. 672

Assessment Book, p. 120

6. In what ways is technology important in improving the quality of life for people? **Express Ideas**

   Possible answers: Technology helps people find cures for diseases, provide new methods of transportation, increase communication, make life easier, and predict trends that can help us make decisions for the future.

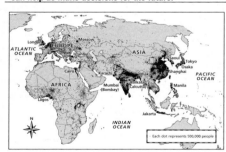

Population of Europe, Africa, and Asia

7. Use the map to answer the questions. **Compare Distribution Maps**
   a. How is population represented on this map?

   by dots, with each dot representing 500,000 people

   b. Where in Asia is the population density the greatest?

   the southern part of the continent

   c. What other types of information could you show on a distribution map?

   Answers will vary. Possible answers: where certain animals live, where certain industries are located, the location of natural resources

Use with Pupil Edition, p. 672

Assessment Support

Assessment Book, p. 121

Unit 8 Test

Part 1: Content Test

Directions: Fill in the circle next to the correct answer.

Lesson Objective (21–1:1)

1. What effect did decolonization have on parts of Africa and Asia after World War II?
   - Ⓐ It strengthened the power of European countries in these areas.
   - ● It resulted in the creation of many new independent countries such as Kenya and Pakistan.
   - Ⓒ It caused conflict between these two areas.
   - Ⓓ It encouraged some European countries to set up new colonies.

Lesson Objective (21–1:2)

2. How did apartheid impact South Africa?
   - Ⓐ It was a law that guaranteed equal rights to all citizens.
   - Ⓑ This movement expanded the power of South Africa.
   - ● This system of segregation resulted in unfair treatment of blacks.
   - Ⓓ It led to a series of protests against communism.

Lesson Objective (21–2:1)

3. What nation was formed as a result of Zionism?
   - ● Israel
   - Ⓑ India
   - Ⓒ Palestine
   - Ⓓ Pakistan

Lesson Objective (21–2:5)

4. What agreement attempted to create a peace process for the Middle East?
   - Ⓐ the Holocaust
   - Ⓑ Balfour Declaration
   - ● Oslo Accords
   - Ⓓ Dayton Accords

Lesson Objective (21–3:1, 2)

5. What significant event occurred in 1989 in Eastern Europe?
   - ● The gates of the Berlin Wall were opened.
   - Ⓑ Students protested at Tiananmen Square.
   - Ⓒ Nelson Mandela was arrested.
   - Ⓓ The Cold War began.

Lesson Objective (21–3:4)

6. How did the fall of communism affect Eastern Europe?
   - Ⓐ Several large countries gained control of smaller nations.
   - Ⓑ The power of the Soviet Union increased in the region.
   - ● Many newly independent nations set up their own governments.
   - Ⓓ War broke out between communist and democratic countries.

Lesson Objective (22–1:3)

7. To which trading bloc does the United States belong?
   - Ⓐ EU
   - ● NAFTA
   - Ⓒ ASEAN
   - Ⓓ Mercosur

Use with Pupil Edition, p. 676

Assessment Book, p. 122

Lesson Objective (22–2:1, 3)

8. What caused conflicts in Northern Ireland?
   - Ⓐ ethnic differences
   - ● opposing religious beliefs
   - Ⓒ different views on government
   - Ⓓ increasing pressure to separate from Great Britain

Lesson Objective (22–2:4)

9. Which country can be described as having a repressive government?
   - ● China
   - Ⓑ United States
   - Ⓒ Great Britain
   - Ⓓ Japan

Lesson Objective (22–3:2)

10. Which is NOT a method of terrorism?
    - Ⓐ assassinations
    - ● mass protests
    - Ⓒ kidnappings
    - Ⓓ chemical and germ warfare

Lesson Objective (23–1:3)

11. Which areas today experience the greatest increase in population?
    - ● urban areas and developing countries
    - Ⓑ rural areas and undeveloped countries
    - Ⓒ megacities in North America
    - Ⓓ countries experiencing strong immigration

Lesson Objective (23–1:4)

12. What is one challenge presented by a growing population?
    - Ⓐ too many available jobs
    - Ⓑ a surplus of farm products
    - ● housing shortages in cities
    - Ⓓ less land in rural areas

Lesson Objective (23–2:3)

13. Which gas produced by gasoline-burning machines is linked to the greenhouse effect?
    - Ⓐ oxygen
    - Ⓑ nitrogen
    - Ⓒ helium
    - ● carbon dioxide

Lesson Objective (23–2:2)

14. Which of the following activities might an environmentalist promote?
    - Ⓐ traveling in an automobile
    - Ⓑ using pesticides
    - ● using solar-powered lights
    - Ⓓ building factories

Lesson Objective (23–3:1, 2)

15. To which category of energy source do coal, petroleum, and natural gas belong?
    - Ⓐ renewable energy
    - Ⓑ alternative energy
    - ● fossil fuels
    - Ⓓ nonpolluting fuels

Lesson Objective (23–3:4)

16. Which of the following is used to produce hydroelectric energy?
    - ● water
    - Ⓑ wind
    - Ⓒ sun
    - Ⓓ steam

Lesson Objective (23–4:4)

17. Which of the following problems had NOT been solved with technology in the late twentieth century?
    - Ⓐ mapping human genes
    - Ⓑ creating satellite communications
    - Ⓒ building a usable space station
    - ● finding an affordable cure for AIDS

Use with Pupil Edition, p. 676

Assessment Book, p. 123

Part 2: Skills Test

Directions: Use complete sentences to answer questions 1–7. Use a separate sheet of paper if you need more space.

1. Which twentieth-century leaders used civil disobedience as a form of protest? What injustice did they protest? **Main Idea and Details**

   Mohandas Gandhi used nonviolent civil disobedience to bring about India's independence from Great Britain. These same methods also were used by Martin Luther King, Jr., to gain equality for black Americans and by black South Africans to fight apartheid in their country.

2. How did conflict between Arabs and Jews in Palestine lead to war in the Middle East? **Point of View**

   Many Jews had migrated to Palestine in the 1930s and wanted to create a separate Jewish nation. The Arabs wanted Palestine to remain a single Arab state. When Palestine was divided in two, war broke out between these two groups for control of the region.

3. What effect on trade should a country experience from joining a regional trading bloc? **Cause and Effect**

   Member countries would trade with one another more freely. Taxes on some goods traded by member countries would be reduced. This savings would encourage one member country to increase trade with other members.

4. What types of differences of identity have led to conflicts in many parts of the world? **Main Idea and Details**

   Ethnic differences have led to wars in Serbia and central Africa. In Northern Ireland, conflicts have erupted because of opposing religious beliefs.

Use with Pupil Edition, p. 676

Assessment Book, p. 124

5. Why is it important for scientists to develop alternative sources of energy? **Make Inferences**

   Many of the energy sources we use today are based on nonrenewable resources. They also add to the world's environmental problems. Scientists are trying to find alternative energy sources that will replace them, will last longer, and will not harm the environment.

6. How has technology improved people's lives? **Draw Conclusions**

   Possible answer: Technology has improved communication and transportation. It has also led scientists to find cures for many diseases and makes daily tasks easier.

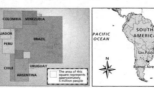

Cartogram: Population of South America

Population Distribution: South America

7. Use the map and graph to answer the questions. **Interpret Cartograms, Compare Distribution Maps**
   a. How do the cartogram and the distribution map differ in the way they show information?

   The cartogram uses different sized boxes to represent the total population in each country. The distribution map uses dots to show population distribution.

   b. Where in South America is the population the densest?   around São Paulo

   c. Which country in South America has the largest population?   Brazil

Use with Pupil Edition, p. 676

Living in the 21st Century

Chapter 23 Outline

- **Lesson 1, *Population Growth and Change,*** pp. 654–657
- **Map and Globe Skills: *Compare Distribution Maps,*** pp. 658–659
- **Lesson 2, *Earth's Environment,*** pp. 660–663
- **Lesson 3, *Energy,*** pp. 664–667
- **Lesson 4, *Technology,*** pp. 668–671

Resources

- Workbook, p. 161: Vocabulary Preview
- Vocabulary Cards
- Social Studies Plus!

2000s, Calcutta: Lesson 1

Have students describe the picture. (Many people are at an outside market shopping for food.) Ask students how the market is similar to and different from the grocery stores in the United States. (Both sell food. In the picture, food is being sold outside, but in the U.S. food is usually sold inside a building.)

2000s, Antarctica: Lesson 2

Ask students what kind of climate is shown in the picture and how they can tell. (A cold climate because penguins live in cold climates and because the ground is covered with snow or ice.)

2000s, Iguaçu Falls: Lesson 3

Have students describe the place in the picture. Can they tell from the picture what the climate is like? Why or why not? (A large waterfall and steep cliff next to a body of water; not really, because the only clue about the temperature is that the water is not frozen.)

2000s, Space: Lesson 4

Ask students to describe the clothing that the person in the picture is wearing. (A thick, reflective suit with an attached helmet and boots.) Point out the tool in the person's hand and have student hypothesize about what it might be for.

CHAPTER 23

Living in the 21st Century

Lesson 1
2000s
Calcutta
Population is growing and changing, especially in megacities.

Lesson 2
2000s
Antarctica
People cause environmental damage and work to repair it.

Lesson 3
2000s
Iguaçu Falls
We seek new energy sources and ways to produce and conserve energy.

Lesson 4
2000s
Space
New technology changes people's lives.

652

Practice and Extend

Vocabulary Preview

- Use Workbook p. 161 to help students preview the vocabulary words in this chapter.
- Use Vocabulary Cards to preview key concept words in this chapter.

 Also on Teacher Resources CD-ROM.

Workbook, p. 161

Vocabulary Preview

Directions: Match each vocabulary word to its meaning. Write the word on the line provided. Not all words will be used. You may use your glossary.

millennium	greenhouse effect	fossil fuel
megacity	pesticide	nonrenewable resource
demographer	environmentalist	renewable resource
immigration	endangered species	hydroelectric energy
zero population growth	deforestation	geothermal energy
global warming	desertification	space station
carbon dioxide	pollution	satellite
	conservation	

_____ 1. large satellite in space that serves as a scientific base

_____ 2. natural resource that can be replaced

_____ 3. one thousand years

_____ 4. energy from super-hot water underground

_____ 5. process of people moving to a new country

_____ 6. human-made object sent into space

_____ 7. water power from rapidly flowing rivers or dams

_____ 8. scientist who studies population trends

_____ 9. chemical that is used to kill pests

_____ 10. person who favors taking measures to protect the environment

_____ 11. animals and plants that could die out

_____ 12. limiting the use of energy

_____ 13. city region with 10 million or more people

Notes for Home: Your child learned the vocabulary terms for Chapter 23.
Home Activity: Help your child make flash cards for the vocabulary terms for Chapter 23. Make half of them tonight and the other half tomorrow night. Quiz your child on the definition of each word.

Locating Time and Place

ATLANTIC OCEAN

Calcutta

INDIA

3

BRAZIL

Iguaçu Falls

2

INDIAN OCEAN

ANTARCTICA

Why We Remember

...ou live your daily life, you are part of history being made. You make ...ices and solve problems that affect other people and places. For example, ... buy products made in a particular country. By doing this, you contribute ... wealth of that country. Decisions you make about how to use ...tricity affect energy supplies and the environment. You use technology, ...ch is constantly being improved. Some day in the future you may look ... social studies textbook. As you thumb through the pages, you may think: ...as there! I was part of history."

653

WEB SITE
Technology

...can learn more about Calcutta,
...; Antarctica; Iguaça Falls, Brazil;
...uter space by clicking on *Atlas*
...ww.sfsocialstudies.com.

SOCIAL STUDIES STRAND
Geography

Mental Mapping On a map of the countries of the world, ask students to label the five countries with the largest populations. Then, have them try to identify the top three by numbering them appropriately. Discuss what special problems overpopulation might bring to developing countries.

- Have students examine the pictures shown on p. 652 for Lessons 1, 2, 3, and 4.

- Remind students that each picture is coded with a number and a color to link it to a place on the map on p. 653.

Why We Remember

Have students read the "Why We Remember" paragraph on p. 653, and ask them why events in this chapter might be important to them. Have students discuss everyday decisions they make that affect the economy, energy supplies, and environment.

Population Growth and Change

Objectives

- Explain why people migrate to urban areas in developed countries.

- Explain why more people migrate to urban than to rural areas.

- Identify the parts of the world where population is growing the fastest.

- List and describe one challenge that population movement presents.

- Explain how immigration affects populations in developed and developing countries.

Vocabulary

millennium, p. 655; **megacity,** p. 655; **demographer,** p. 656; **immigration,** p. 657; **zero population growth,** p. 657

Resources

- Workbook, p. 162
- Transparency 23
- Every Student Learns Guide, pp. 306–309
- Quick Study, pp. 154–155

Quick Teaching Plan

If time is short, have students create a web showing the effects of population growth and movement as they read the lesson independently.

1 Introduce and Motivate

Preview Ask students to share what they know about the population of the town or city in which they live. Tell students they will learn about the effects of population growth and changes around the world as they read Lesson 1.

You Are There Often as the population of a city increases, so does the pollution. Ask students whether they would prefer to live in a big city or in a less densely populated area.

LESSON 1

1850	1900	1950
	about 1900 One out of 10 people live in cities.	**about 1960** More people began moving from developing to developed countries.

Abc th popula

PREVIEW

Focus on the Main Idea
Population growth and movement present challenges in today's world.

PLACES
Mexico City
Calcutta
Madagascar

PEOPLE
Mother Teresa

VOCABULARY
millennium
megacity
demographer
immigration
zero population growth

▶ Mexico City is one of the most populated cities in the world.

Population Growth and Change

You Are There Your family settles into the car Benito Juárez Airport in Mexico You're coming here to live beca your father has been appointed to the U.S. Embass keeps telling you that Mexico City is one of the lar and most interesting cities in the world.

The car moves fast on a busy road. In the distan you see crowded hillsides with thousands of small dwellings. You've read that people are coming to t too fast to get good housing. See all the haze? Tha smog. Dad explains that Mexico City sits in a bowl like Los Angeles, California. Sometimes the pollut settles over the city.

You reach the downtown area and pass by wide bo vards and parks bright with flowers. Everywhere see people—shopping, hurrying, and buying from street vendors. It's not hard to believe Mexico City has nearly 20 million residents begin to look forward to the exciting year a

 Draw Conclusions As you read, pu together to identify how the population growing and changing in many parts of world.

Practice and Extend

READING SKILL
Draw Conclusions

In the Lesson Review, students complete a graphic organizer like the one below. You may want to provide students with a copy of Transparency 23 to complete as they read the lesson.

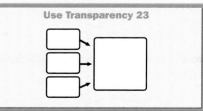

Use Transparency 23

WEB SITE
Technology

- You can look up vocabulary wor by clicking on *Social Studies Lib* and selecting the dictionary at **www.sfsocialstudies.com.**

- Students can learn more about current news by clicking on *Current Events* at **www.sfsocialstudies.com.**

- Explore other events that occurred on this day by clickin on *This Day in History* at **www.sfsocialstudies.com.**

Population Growth

...late twentieth century, **Mexico City** was
...populated city in the world. It was less
...a century ago. However, population
...not unique to Mexico City. It is happen-
...er the world.

...is home to billions of people. A
...**um** is one thousand years. At the begin-
...e second millennium, the world
...on stood at about 6 billion people. When
...ndparents were in school, the world had
...If that many people. The graph below
...ow rapidly population has grown.

...of the world's people are moving to
...city, areas. Cities usually offer more job
...ities than rural, or country, areas. But
...es are growing so fast that they cannot
...ousing for the people who live in them.
...eas cannot always provide basic necessi-
...as clean water and good housing.

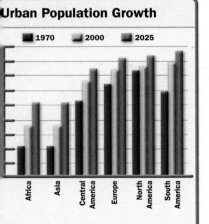

Urban Population Growth

■ 1970 ■ 2000 ■ 2025

Africa, Asia, Central America, Europe, North America, South America

...population growth has increased greatly in
...regions of the world since 1970.

...**SKILL** Use a Bar Graph *Which region is*
...to have the largest urban population by

▶ **Mother Teresa talks to children at an orphanage in Calcutta, India.**

By 2000 there were more than 20 megacities
in the world. A **megacity** is a city region with
10 million or more people. Tokyo, New York City,
and São Paulo are all megacities.

Calcutta, India, is also a megacity, but it is
one of the world's poorest cities. According to
some estimates, 600,000 people are homeless
in Calcutta. They live on the city streets.

You may have heard of **Mother Teresa.** She
was a Roman Catholic nun who wanted to help the
poorest people in Calcutta. She lived and worked
in Calcutta's slums for more than 40 years.

Mother Teresa helped set up soup kitchens,
hospitals, and shelters for homeless people.
She provided hospices, or places for dying people
to be sheltered and cared for.

Like others of the late twentieth century,
Mother Teresa believed in people. She said:

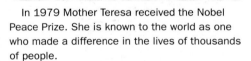

"Do not wait for leaders;
do it alone, person to person." ❷

In 1979 Mother Teresa received the Nobel
Peace Prize. She is known to the world as one
who made a difference in the lives of thousands
of people.

REVIEW How did Mother Teresa help the
people of India? ⟲ Draw Conclusions

655

---

❷ Teach and Discuss
PAGE 655

Population Growth

Quick Summary As population
grows in cities throughout the world,
so do problems of providing necessities
for the people who live there.

**❶ Which two regions will have
doubled their population between
1970 and 2025?** Africa and Asia
Apply Information

GRAPH SKILL Answer South America

✓ Ongoing Assessment

If... students have difficulty using the graph,	then... point out the labels on the horizontal and vertical axes and explain that the third bar is a projected number.

Primary Source

Cited in *Quotable Women of the Twentieth Century,*
edited by Tracy Quinn

**❷ What was Mother Teresa's point of
view about the effect one person can
have?** That each person can make a
difference to others.
Analyze Primary Sources

✓ REVIEW ANSWER She provided food,
shelter, and medical care for the poor.
⟲ Draw Conclusions

ACTIVATE PRIOR KNOWLEDGE
ESL Support

...**e Population Information** Have students share what they know or learn
...family members about population in their home countries.

...**nning** Have students draw an outline map of their country and label the
...st cities. They should draw numerous stick figures to represent the large
...lation of a city and just a few in an area where few people live.

...**mediate** Have students use a web to organize characteristics of a place
...e they or their families have lived, such as population, types of housing, and
...of jobs.

...**nced** Have students take turns giving oral descriptions of their family's
...of origin, such as the approximate population, housing, jobs, water
...es, and so on.

...dditional ESL support, use Every Student Learns Guide, pp. 306–309.

FYI SOCIAL STUDIES Background

Mother Teresa

- Mother Teresa was born in 1910 as Agnes Gonxha Bojaxhiu.
- She entered the Sisters of Loreto in Ireland at age 18.
- She went to India as a teacher.
- She opened the Nirmal Hrdiday (Pure Heart) Home for Dying Destitutes in Calcutta, India, in 1952.

Population Movement

Quick Summary Because of high growth rates in many developing countries, governments have difficulty providing for people's basic needs.

❸ Assume that the population of Madagascar is still increasing at 3 percent a year. Before what year will its population double? Students should add 25 to the current year. **Apply Information**

✓ **REVIEW ANSWER** Governments find it hard to provide clean water and good housing for people. Unemployment is also very high. **Cause and Effect**

Immigration

Quick Summary Immigration changes the population and cultures of the countries to which people move.

C SOCIAL STUDIES STRAND
Culture

❹ How does the status of women affect population growth? Women in developed countries often have good opportunities for education and tend to have fewer children. **Cause and Effect**

✓ **REVIEW ANSWER** It has increased population and changed the culture of countries to which immigrants move. **Main Idea and Details**

Population Movement

You have already learned that people throughout the world are moving to urban areas. The migration of people from rural to urban areas increased during the Industrial Revolution in the late 1800s. By 1900 only about 1 out of 10 people in the world lived in cities. More people moved from the countryside to cities in the first half of the twentieth century for economic opportunities.

By the 1960s, people began moving from developing countries to more developed countries. Today, most of these people on the move continue to seek a better life. Populations in developing countries are rising so fast that many governments can no longer provide good housing and clean water. They also do not have enough jobs for all of the people. Unemployment is high in many developing countries.

The population is growing much faster in many developing nations than in most developed nations. For example, in **Madagascar,** off the coast of East Africa, the population is increasing at more than 3 percent a year. By contrast, the population growth rate in the United States is about 0.9 percent, which means that its population doubles in size in about 77 years. At a 3 **❸** percent growth rate, a country's population doubles in less than 25 years. Population is also growing rapidly in developing nations such as

▶ People crowd a market in Guatemala, a co whose population has nearly doubled since

Guatemala, Ethiopia, and the Philippines.

On the other hand, population is growin or not at all in countries such as Sweden, and Japan. These are all developed nation

REVIEW How are high population grow affecting developing countries? **Cause and**

Immigration

Population changes are important to stu because they affect how people live and w Scientists who study population trends are **demographers** (di MAH gruh furz).

Many demographers believe that the sta of women affects the rate of population gr In developed countries, women often have opportunities for education. Educated won tend to have children later, and fewer of th In developing countries, women sometime fewer job and educational opportunities.

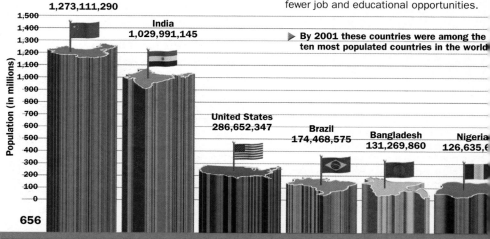

▶ By 2001 these countries were among the ten most populated countries in the world

China 1,273,111,290
India 1,029,991,145
United States 286,652,347
Brazil 174,468,575
Bangladesh 131,269,860
Nigeria 126,635,6

Population (in millions): 1,500 1,400 1,300 1,200 1,100 1,000 900 800 700 600 500 400 300 200 100 0

Practice and Extend

MEETING INDIVIDUAL NEEDS
Leveled Practice

Identify Effects Have students explore population movement.

Easy List the following effects on the chalkboard and ask if each is a commo effect of population movement: *lack of clean water* (yes), *change in geographic features* (no), *spread of new culture* (yes). **Reteach**

On-Level Have students complete a graphic organizer in which the main idea *Immigration has many effects.* **Extend**

Challenge Have students use an atlas or the U.S. Census Web site (**www.census.gov.**) to find current data on the countries of origin of immigrant to the United States. Discuss with students the possible cultural effects that various immigrant groups have on the United States. **Enrich**

For a Lesson Summary, use Quick Study, p. 154.

ration from developing countries is
g the population and cultures of many
ed countries. **Immigration** is the process
e moving to a new country to stay perma-
for a long time. For example, France has
many immigrants from former French
in North Africa. Now one of France's
foods is *couscous,* a hot-cereal dish from
ntries. Some demographers believe that
ople in France now attend mosques than
s. This is because most immigrants from
rica are Muslims.

W   How has immigration changed
s? **Main Idea and Details**

opulation Explosion?

ng ago, demographers spoke of a "popu-
plosion." They compared population to
ng wildly out of control—like the explo-
a bomb. Some of these scientists painted
n pictures of the world's future.

Today, many demographers see evidence of
slowing population growth. In some developed
countries, **zero population growth** has been
reached. This means that just enough babies are
being born to balance population loss.

Some demographers even think that by later
in the twenty-first century, the world's population
might begin to shrink. In the meantime, growing
population remains a challenge in many cities
and developing countries.

REVIEW In your own words, explain the idea
of zero population growth. **Summarize**

Summarize the Lesson

- **c. 1900** One out of 10 people lived in cities.
- **c. 1960** More people began moving from
  developing to developed countries.
- **2000** About half of the population lived in
  urban areas.

SSON 1   REVIEW

ck Facts and Main Ideas

) **Draw Conclusions** On a separate
ece of paper, copy the diagram below.
rite a conclusion based on the facts
the diagram.

More people have
grated to developed
countries.

More people have
ated to urban areas.

More people have
rated to places with
ore opportunities.

More people
have migrated
to urban areas
in developed
countries where
there are more
opportunities.

2. Why are people moving to cities?

3. In which parts of the world is the population
   growing the fastest?

4. Name one challenge that population movement presents.

5. **Critical Thinking:** *Make Generalizations* How
   does immigration affect populations in
   developed and developing countries?

Link to ⬢⬢ Mathematics

Draw a Line Graph Suppose the population of
a megacity was 4 million in 1960, 6 million in
1980, and 12 million in 2000. Sketch a line
graph to show the growth of this megacity, or
describe how the line would look.

657

A Population Explosion?

🕐 ***Quick Summary*** Population
growth seems to be slowing down
during the twenty-first century.

5 **What does *population explosion*
mean?** Population increase that is out of
control. **Analyze Information**

✓ **REVIEW ANSWER** Possible answer:
The population is neither growing nor
shrinking because the number of births
and the number of deaths are in
balance. **Summarize**

3 Close and Assess

Summarize the Lesson

Tell students to examine the vertical time
line. Have them write an explanation for
each of the statistics mentioned.

✓ **LESSON 1   REVIEW**

1. 🔄 **Draw Conclusions** For possible
   answers, see the reduced pupil page.

2. Cities often have better job
   opportunities than do rural areas.

3. Population is growing fastest in
   developing nations.

4. Possible answers: An increased need
   for housing, which may not be
   available; a need for services that
   may be scarce, such as clean water.

5. **Critical Thinking:** *Make
   Generalizations* It may help slow
   the population growth in developing
   countries, and it increases the
   population in developed countries.

Link to ⬢⬢ Mathematics

Help students create an appropriate
scale for their graphs, such as 0, 2
million, 4 million, 6 million, 8 million,
10 million, 12 million.

⬤ CURRICULUM CONNECTION
Math

of Growth

students describe the rate of growth for each
period described in the Link to Mathematics in
esson 1 Review. (Population in the megacity
ased by half between 1960 and 1980, but it
led between 1980 and 2000.)

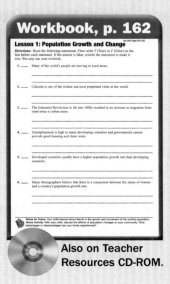

Workbook, p. 162

Lesson 1: Population Growth and Change

Directions: Read the following statements. Then write *T* (True) or *F* (False) on the
line before each statement. If the answer is false, rewrite the statement to make it
true. You may use your textbook.

1. _____ Many of the world's people are moving to rural areas.

2. _____ Calcutta is one of the richest and most populated cities in the world.

3. _____ The Industrial Revolution in the late 1800s resulted in an increase in migration from
   rural areas to urban areas.

4. _____ Unemployment is high in many developing countries and governments cannot
   provide good housing and clean water.

5. _____ Developed countries usually have a higher population growth rate than developing
   countries.

6. _____ Many demographers believe that there is a connection between the status of women
   and a country's population growth rate.

**Also on Teacher
Resources CD-ROM.**

Compare Distribution Maps

Objectives

- Describe and identify the purpose of a distribution map.

- Analyze information from a population density map.

Resource

- Workbook, p. 163

1 Introduce and Motivate

What is a distribution map? Ask students to use their own words to define the term *distribution*. (Possible answer: How and where something is distributed, or spread) Then have students read the **What?** section of text on p. 658.

Why use a distribution map? Have students read the **Why?** section of text on pp. 658–659. Ask them to create questions that could be answered using specific kinds of distribution maps such as population distribution maps or natural resource distribution maps.

2 Teach and Discuss

How is this skill used? Examine with students the distribution maps on pp. 658–659.

- Discuss the different kinds of information shown on each map.

- Point out that the world population map not only shows where people are distributed on the continents, but also which geographical areas tend to become more populated.

- Have students read the **How?** section of text on p. 659.

Compare Distribution Maps

What? Distribution maps are maps that show where something, such as people or natural resources, is distributed, or spread, across the area shown on the map. The world population distribution map below shows where people are distributed around the world.

Distribution maps often use dots to show population density, or where people live. Look at the population distribution map below.

Why? Distribution maps are useful because they are very flexible. You can make distribution maps to show how *anything* is distributed. Do you want to know where certain animals live? Look at a wildlife distribution map. How about where certain kinds of industries are located? Use an economic distribution map.

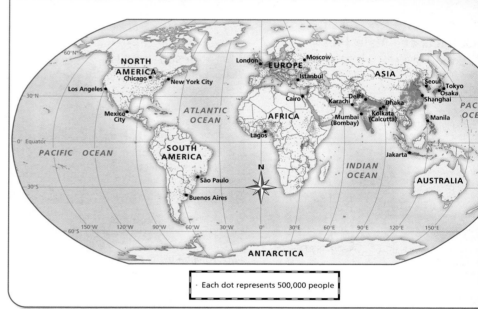

World Population

Each dot represents 500,000 people

658

Practice and Extend

CURRICULUM CONNECTION
Writing

Write a Summary

- Have students summarize in paragraph form the information on the World Population Distribution map.
- Display the following questions to guide students in their summaries:
  Which hemisphere has a higher population?
  In general, do more people live along the coastlines or inland?
  Which continents have the least population? Where are they located?

Major Oil and Gas Fields

ARCTIC OCEAN

NORTH AMERICA

EUROPE

ASIA

PACIFIC OCEAN

ATLANTIC OCEAN

AFRICA

PACIFIC OCEAN

SOUTH AMERICA

INDIAN OCEAN

AUSTRALIA

ANTARCTICA

N

60°N 30°N 30°S 60°S

150°W 120°W 90°W 60°W 30°W 0° 30°E 60°E 90°E 120°E 150°E

☐ Major oil field   ☐ Major natural gas field

eteorologists, or people who study Earth's sphere and weather patterns, use distribu- maps to see where rain has fallen. nmentalists use distribution maps to deter- where pollution is found. Businesses use to show where their offices are located.

w? You can learn a lot by comparing ent types of distribution maps that show the area. For example, by comparing a world ation distribution map to a distribution map ng where oil and gas fields are located, you arn if there are large populations living near tant energy resources. You can also learn important resources are located. compare distribution maps, follow these

ad the title of the maps to learn what each p shows.

dy the map keys on both maps to learn t the symbols and colors on the map an.

3. Note what is alike and different in the distribution of things on both maps.

Think and Apply

Use the World Population map on page 658 and the Major Oil and Gas Fields map on this page to answer the following questions.

1 In what regions of the world is population density the greatest?

2 On which continents are the major oil and gas fields located?

Internet Activity

For more information, go online to the Atlas at **www.sfsocialstudies.com**.

659

1 **Describe the population density of northern Asia and give a possible reason for this distribution.** Possible answer: Few people live in this region; it is far from the equator so the climate is probably cold, and it might be difficult to grow food or make a living there. **Hypothesize**

2 **If the population of the East Coast cities in the United States increases over the next 10 years, how will the population map change?** There will be more dots along the East Coast. **Cause and Effect**

3 **In what part of Africa does a high population density occur in an area with major oil fields?** The area around Lagos in western Africa, just north of the equator. (Some students may also identify the area around Cairo in northeast Africa.) **Interpret Maps**

3 Close and Assess

Think and Apply

1. Europe, South Asia, Southeast Asia, and the Indian subcontinent

2. Every continent except Antarctica has major oil and gas fields.

CURRICULUM CONNECTION
Science

ke a School Population Distribution Map

ave students collect data about the number of eople in three different classrooms and the chool's office.

ave them draw a population distribution map nowing these four locations.

ake sure that students include accurate keys r their maps.

Workbook, p. 163

Compare Distribution Maps

Directions: Answer the questions below about distribution maps. You may use your textbook.

1. What is the purpose of distribution maps?

2. What type of symbols do distribution maps use to show the distribution of something across an area?

3. Why might politicians use distribution maps? Why might airlines? Why might city governments?

4. Look at the two distribution maps on pp. 658–659. Near what kind of physical feature has much of the world's population settled? On which distribution map did you find this information?

5. Look at the world population distribution map on p. 658. According to the map key, what symbol represents population? What does a cluster of these symbols indicate about the population of that area?

Notes for Home: Your child learned how to compare distribution maps.
Home Activity: With your child, discuss how changes in the population density of your community affect the people who live and work there. What affects its population shifts have on local governments and our population?

Also on Teacher Resources CD-ROM.

SOCIAL STUDIES STRAND
Geography

The following map resources are available:

- Big Book Atlas
- Student Atlas
- Outline Maps
- Desk Maps
- Map Resources CD-ROM

Earth's Environment

Objectives

- List and describe how people harm the environment but also provide solutions to help the environment.

- Define *environmentalist*.

- Describe what carbon dioxide is and explain how it has increased in Earth's atmosphere.

- Explain how people have found solutions to help the environment in the last 50 years.

- Express an opinion about whether humans have done more good or harm to Earth.

Vocabulary

global warming, p. 661; **carbon dioxide,** p. 661; **greenhouse effect,** p. 661; **pesticide,** p. 661; **environmentalist,** p. 661 **endangered species,** p. 661; **deforestation,** p. 662; **desertification,** p. 662; **pollution,** p. 663

Resources

- Workbook, p. 164
- Transparency 21
- Every Student Learns Guide, pp. 310–313
- Quick Study, pp. 156–157

Quick Teaching Plan

If time is short, have students create charts with columns labeled *Ways to Help* and *Ways to Harm*. Students should add details as they read independently.

1 Introduce and Motivate

Preview Have students tell how they help keep their community clean. Explain that they will learn more about environmental problems and solutions as they read Lesson 2.

You Are There Controlling litter is one of the environmental challenges of the twenty-first century. Ask students how they can help solve this problem.

660 Unit 8 • New Nations and a New Century

LESSON 2

1960	1970	1980	1990
1962 *Silent Spring* is published.	**1970** The Environmental Protection Agency is established.		**1997** The Kyoto Protocol is written.

PREVIEW

Focus on the Main Idea
People are working together to repair damage to Earth's environment.

PLACES
Antarctica

PEOPLE
Rachel Carson

VOCABULARY
global warming
carbon dioxide
greenhouse effect
pesticide
environmentalist
endangered species
deforestation
desertification
pollution

TERMS
Environmental Protection Agency

▶ People in developed countries generate the most garbage. In response, more people have started recycling programs to reduce waste.

660

Earth's Environment

You Are There Camping in the back country of Yosemite National Park in California one of the best vacations you've ever had. Today, you're hiking to a high lookout with a wide view of the whole valley. It's hard work keeping up with Mom and Dad. But they say this view is really worth the effort.

As you round the last corner, your eyes follow the path out onto the ledge of the lookout. You take a deep breath . . . and then you see it. Just in front of the guardrail is a huge plastic garbage bag. Through a rip, it is spilling out cans, spoiled food, pop bottles, and other junk.

"Tourist trash," says Mom. "Some people have no respect for our planet." Though the view of the valley is awesome, you can't really enjoy it. You're bothered by the way that some people have treated this beautiful place.

Cause and Effect As you read, consider how humans affect Earth's environment and what they are trying to do to take care of it.

Practice and Extend

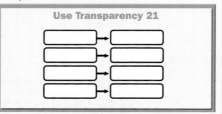

READING SKILL
Cause and Effect

In the Lesson Review, students complete a graphic organizer like the one below. You may want to provide students with a copy of Transparency 21 to complete as they read the lesson.

Use Transparency 21

WEB SITE
Technology

- You can look up vocabulary word by clicking on *Social Studies Libr* and selecting the dictionary at **www.sfsocialstudies.com.**

- Students can learn more about current news by clicking on *Current Events* at **www.sfsocialstudies.com.**

- Explore other events that occurred on this day by clicking on *This Day in History* at **www.sfsocialstudies.com.**

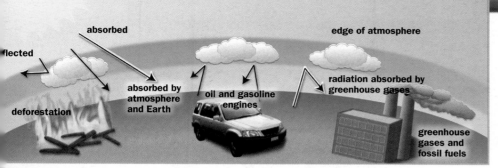

absorbed

edge of atmosphere

flected

absorbed by atmosphere and Earth

oil and gasoline engines

radiation absorbed by greenhouse gases

deforestation

greenhouse gases and fossil fuels

The greenhouse effect is often compared to how air warms inside a greenhouse.

GRAM SKILL Use a Diagram *What conclusion can you draw from the diagram about the greenhouse effect?*

The Environment

lobal warming is a gradual increase in verage temperature of Earth's surface. Many tists agree that Earth's temperature is ris-out they do not agree on why it is rising or the causes and effects might be.

man activities such as burning gasoline in produce a gas called carbon dioxide. on dioxide and other gases trap heat that is ted from the earth. Radiation from the earth warms the atmosphere. This process is d the greenhouse effect.

me scientists estimate that carbon dioxide e atmosphere has increased by about 25 nt since the mid-1800s. Burning fuels such al and oil in factories, houses, and cars has d most of this increase.

he 1960s, many people became more of how human activity ffecting our natural envi-nt. They believed that economic development armful to nature.

962 a scientist named Carson wrote *Silent* . This book described how ides, or chemicals that ed to kill pests such as s, were killing off birds

and other animals. Carson explained how morn-ings were becoming silent:

> *"Early mornings are strangely silent where once they were filled with the beauty of bird song."* ②

Silent Spring convinced some people to become environmentalists. An environmentalist is a person who favors taking measures to protect Earth's natural environment. People began press-ing for laws to protect the environment.

In 1970 the U.S. Congress set up the Environmental Protection Agency. This agency serves as a watchdog for the environment. Later, Congress passed laws to protect endangered species, or animals and plants that could die ③ out. In Europe, "green" political parties formed. Through political action, they worked to pass envi-ronmental laws.

REVIEW How did some people respond to *Silent Spring*? **Cause and Effect**

▶ Rachel Carson holding *Silent Spring,* her book that sparked environmentalism

661

🕐 *Quick Summary* Global warming may result from increased production of carbon dioxide and other gases that trap heat from the Sun in Earth's atmosphere. In the 1960s people in the United States began pressing for laws to protect the environment.

Problem Solving

① **Why has the problem of carbon dioxide in the atmosphere become worse since the mid-1800s?** Burning fuels have increased the amount of carbon dioxide in the atmosphere. **Cause and Effect**

DIAGRAM SKILL **Answer** That they allow some of the Sun's heat to reach Earth but that they do not allow heat radiated from Earth to escape beyond the atmosphere.

Primary Source

Cited in *Silent Spring,* by Rachel Carson

② **Why was Carson concerned about silent mornings?** The birds that used to sing in the morning were being killed off by pesticides. **Analyze Primary Sources**

③ **What does it mean that the Environmental Protection Agency is a watchdog for the environment?** Possible answer: The agency watches for problems affecting the environment and takes steps to fix and protect it; this is similar to how a watchdog protects its owner. **Main Idea and Details**

✓ **REVIEW ANSWER** Some people became environmentalists, pressing for new laws to protect the environment. **Cause and Effect**

EXTEND LANGUAGE
ESL Support

erstand Suffixes Help students focus on the purpose of the suffix *-ist* in *ntist* and *environmentalist,* as well as in other words.

inning Discuss the meanings of *science* and *environment.* Show how the x *-ist* can be used to make a new word with a related meaning. (A scientist e who studies or knows about science; an environmentalist is one who ies or knows about the environment.)

rmediate Help students make a list of simple words with the *-ist* suffix, as *dentist, artist,* and *pianist,* and then conclude that the words with the *-ist* x name people by their work. Have them identify what each person does.

anced Write on the board *science/scientist* and *environment/environmentalist.* students write an original sentence using each of these pairs of words.

dditional ESL support, use Every Student Learns Guide, pp. 310–313.

Problems and Solutions

Quick Summary Human activity affects the environment in positive and negative ways.

Map Adventure Answers

1. First you will see the Andes mountains. As you approach Puerto Francisco de Orellana, you will see a green carpet of rain forest below. **2.** Rain forests cover it; it is closed off from the rest of Ecuador by the high Andes Mountains. **3.** No; paved roads will bring more people to oil fields; air travel is easy and quick. A paved road runs between the Huaorani villages and Puerto Francisco de Orellana.

4 **Why was the Kyoto Protocol created?** The treaty addressed the issue of global warming, urging nations to reduce the carbon dioxide they produce. **Main Idea and Details**

5 **How might the Kyoto Protocol disrupt a nation's economy?** Possible answer: Businesses may have to invest in new equipment and processes to reduce production of carbon dioxide. This could cut into profits. **Hypothesize**

Test Talk

Use Information from the Text

6 **How does deforestation contribute to global warming?** Students should use what they have already learned about global warming and deforestation to formulate their answers. Deforestation has removed the trees that absorb carbon dioxide; this increases the greenhouse effect, which contributes to global warming. **Cause and Effect**

Ongoing Assessment

| If... students cannot describe deforestation's contribution to global warming, | then... have them reread the lesson and list the steps in the process. |

✓ **REVIEW ANSWER** Deforestation and overgrazing of animals **Summarize**

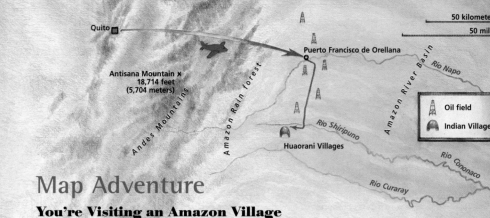

Quito

Antisana Mountain ✗
18,714 feet
(5,704 meters)

Puerto Francisco de Orellana

Andes Mountains

Amazon Rain forest

Amazon River Basin

Rio Napo

Rio Shiripuno

Huaorani Villages

Rio Cononaco

Rio Curaray

50 kilometer
50 mile

Oil field
Indian Village

Map Adventure

You're Visiting an Amazon Village

You begin your visit in Quito, Ecuador (KEE toh, EH kwuh door). You fly over the Andes Mountains to Puerto Francisco de Orellana. Then you ride on a bus to the banks of Rio (river) Shiripuno. From there, you take a boat a few miles up the river. Huaorani (WA or AH nee) villagers will greet you as the boat pulls into the shore.

1. How will the landscape you view through your plane window change as you fly toward Puerto Francisco de Orellana?

2. This part of eastern Ecuador—called "El Oriente"—is part of the Amazon River Basin. From map clues, can you guess why it has been isolated for a long time?

3. Do you think the Huaorani villages will remain isolated much longer? Use clues from the map to explain your answer.

Problems and Solutions

Some environmentalists believe that global warming will continue unless people take steps to slow or stop it. In 1997 officials from more than 160 countries met in Kyoto, Japan, to draw up a treaty on global warming called the Kyoto **4** Protocol. The treaty urged nations to agree to reduce the production of greenhouse gases such as carbon dioxide over time.

But most nations have not adopted the treaty because they believe it will disrupt their **5** economies. The treaty must be ratified by at least 55 countries. For more developed countries, the treaty offers emission credits in return for pollution control efforts.

Another problem in the world is feeding rap growing populations. Farmers have cut down forests to grow crops. This process is called **deforestation.** The deforestation of rain fores in South America, Africa, and Southeast Asia added to global warming. Deforestation has removed the trees, which absorb carbon diox gases. As a solution to deforestation, people have planted trees.

Global warming is not the only example of climate change caused by human activity. Throughout history, fertile land has been lost through a process called **desertification.** In th process, farmers plow fields, and animals ove graze the land. Topsoil becomes loose, dries and blows away. Desertification has been devastating in parts of Africa.

662

Practice and Extend

FYI **SOCIAL STUDIES**
Background

Global Warming

- During the past 100 years, the average temperature of Earth's surface has risen from about 59°F to almost 60°F.
- Scientists estimate that the average temperature may rise another 2.5° F to 10.4° F in the next 100 years.

effect of humans on the environment has
...ched the poles of the earth. For example,
...ica, the fifth largest continent on Earth,
... last continent to be explored. It is also
...est, driest, and coldest continent. Only
...ts live there. However, tourism in
...ca has grown in the past several
...s. Some 15,000 tourists visit there each
...sted cans and plastic wrappers are just
... the ways people have polluted parts of

Antarctica. **Pollution** is the process of making the environment dirty. A visible form of pollution is waste such as garbage. As a solution to pollution, people recycle aluminum, paper, and glass.

REVIEW What agricultural practices have harmed the land? **Summarize**

Summarize the Lesson

— **1970** The U.S. Congress set up the Environmental Protection Agency.
— **1997** The Kyoto Protocol was written.

▶ **Trash left by tourists in Antarctica harms the environment and wildlife.**

...SSON 2 REVIEW

...ck Facts and Main Ideas

...ause and Effect On a separate piece of ...aper, copy the diagram below. Fill in the ...ffects.

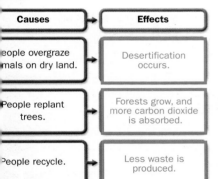

Causes		Effects
...eople overgraze ...mals on dry land.	→	Desertification occurs.
...People replant trees.	→	Forests grow, and more carbon dioxide is absorbed.
...People recycle.	→	Less waste is produced.

2. What is an environmentalist?
3. What has happened to the amount of carbon dioxide in Earth's atmosphere?
4. How have people helped to solve environmental problems in the last 50 years?
5. **Critical Thinking:** *Evaluate Information* Do you think that humans have done more good or harm to Earth? Why or why not?

Link to  **Science**

Research and Report Carbon dioxide is not the only greenhouse gas, although it is the most plentiful. Use an encyclopedia or Internet resource to identify another greenhouse gas. Explain how it is produced.

663

---

3 Close and Assess

Summarize the Lesson

Tell students to read the actions described in the vertical time line. Ask them to identify the problems that caused each action to take place.

✓ **LESSON 2** **REVIEW**

1. **Cause and Effect** For possible answers, see the reduced pupil page.
2. An environmentalist is a person who favors taking action to protect Earth's environment.
3. It has increased by about 25 percent since the mid-1800s.
4. They have worked to pass environmental laws, replanted trees, and recycled.
5. **Critical Thinking:** *Evaluate Information* Answers will vary, but students should include information from the lesson in their answers.

Link to ○○ **Science**

Students might identify methane, which may come from the decomposition of organic wastes in landfills; nitrous oxide, which may come from factories or farms; or hydrofluorocarbons, which may come from factories.

MEETING INDIVIDUAL NEEDS
Leveled Practice

...tify **Problems and Solutions** Have students ...tify and explore environmental problems and ...tions.

...y Have students complete a Problem/Solution ... with problems such as deforestation and ...tions such as planting trees. **Reteach**

...evel Have students create charts showing ...ses of, effects of, and solutions to an ...ronmental problem. **Extend**

...llenge Ask students to identify a local ...ronmental problem and suggest a solution ...t. **Enrich**

...a Lesson Summary, use Quick Study, p. 156.

Workbook, p. 164

Lesson 2: Earth's Environment

Directions: Complete the cause-and-effect chart with information from this lesson. You may use your textbook.

Cause	Effect
People burn fuels such as coal and oil.	
Rachel Carson writes *Silent Spring*.	
People begin pressing for laws to protect the environment.	
Most nations believe reducing the carbon dioxide they produce will disrupt their economies.	
Population increases lead people to cut down forests to plant crops on the land.	
Farmers overplant and animals overgraze the land.	
Humans do not properly dispose of much waste, such as garbage.	

Also on Teacher Resources CD-ROM.

Energy

Objectives

- Explain why fossil fuels are nonrenewable resources that will eventually run out.

- List three fossil fuels, and explain which one will run out first.

- Explain why nuclear energy has advantages and disadvantages as an alternative to energy from fossil fuels.

- List and explain four renewable alternative energy sources.

- Describe the characteristics of a perfect energy source.

Vocabulary

conservation, p. 665; **fossil fuel,** p. 665; **nonrenewable resource,** p. 665; **renewable resource,** p. 666; **hydroelectric energy,** p. 666; **geothermal energy,** p. 667

Resources

- Workbook, p. 165
- Transparency 23
- Every Student Learns Guide, pp. 314–317
- Quick Study, pp. 158–159

Quick *Teaching Plan*

If time is short, have students make a chart showing the advantages and disadvantages of different energy sources.

1 Introduce and Motivate

Preview To activate prior knowledge, ask students to name appliances and tools they use every day that require some form of energy. Tell students that they will learn about a variety of energy sources in Lesson 3.

 You Are There Oil is used as fuel for cars and other machines that people rely on to do work. Ask students whether they have read or heard about new sources of energy that scientists are trying to develop.

LESSON 3

Chernobyl
Iguaçu Falls

1970	1980	1990

1973 First global oil crisis

1986 Chernobyl nuclear accident

George W. Bush begir to help make the U se

Energy

PREVIEW

Focus on the Main Idea
As energy sources become less plentiful, we look for new ways to produce and conserve energy.

PLACES
Chernobyl
Iguaçu Falls
Niagara Falls

PEOPLE
George W. Bush

VOCABULARY
conservation
fossil fuel
nonrenewable resource
renewable resource
hydroelectric energy
geothermal energy

TERMS
Organization of Petroleum Exporting Countries (OPEC)

▶ **An offshore drilling rig in the Gulf of Mexico**

664

You Are There Mom is a petroleum engineer. Wh your friends find out what she do they picture her wearing an oil-s tered outfit and carrying a clipboard.

Actually, Mom does most of her work in an office ing a computer screen. Today, she has let you visit h work!

Mom brings up the 3-D imaging software she uses look at rocks far underground. You see bands of stuff in different colors. It looks like a layered cake. Mom hands you 3-D goggles and says, "Put these on." Wow! Now you feel like you are *inside* the rock layers.

"There!" says Mom. "Look at that pool of liquid. That might be oil."

She tells you that it's important for us to keep looking for more sources of oil so we don't have to rely on oil from other countries. However, she also explains that we should reduce our use of fuels and find alternative sources of energy too.

 Draw Conclusions As you read, identify how energy is produced and where new energy sources might be located.

Practice and Extend

READING SKILL
Draw Conclusions

In the Lesson Review, students complete a graphic organizer like the one below. You may want to provide students with a copy of Transparency 23 to complete as they read the lesson.

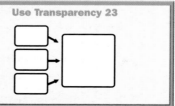
Use Transparency 23

WEB SITE
Technology

- You can look up vocabulary word by clicking on *Social Studies Libr* and selecting the dictionary at **www.sfsocialstudies.com.**

- Students can learn more about current news by clicking on *Current Events* at **www.sfsocialstudies.com.**

- Explore other events that occurred on this day by clicking on *This Day in History* at **www.sfsocialstudies.com.**

Using Energy

nergy keeps our world going. We depend on
ural resources to keep producing the energy
need. As world population has grown rapidly,
and for energy has skyrocketed. A growing
ulation, new industries, and new technologies
and more energy.

eeping up with this demand for energy is one
e biggest challenges we face in the twenty-
century. We need to find new energy sources
new ways to produce energy. We also need to
how to stop wasting energy. **Conservation,**
niting our use of energy, is one solution to
energy crisis.

you ever wonder when you plug in your com-
r or television where the electricity comes
? It is generated in a power plant, which
power lines to get electricity to your home.
power plants burn fuel to produce steam
water. The pressure of the steam then
s a generator.

burn a lot of coal, petroleum (oil), and natu-
as to run generators in power plants. We use
fuels in other ways too. In a huge chemical
called a refinery, gasoline is extracted, or
out, from petroleum. As you know, gasoline
s most of our cars run.

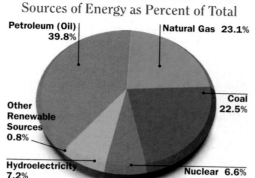
Sources of Energy as Percent of Total

Petroleum (Oil) 39.8%
Natural Gas 23.1%
Coal 22.5%
Nuclear 6.6%
Hydroelectricity 7.2%
Other Renewable Sources 0.8%

GRAPH SKILL Use a Circle Graph **Which source of energy is used more than others?** ②

Coal, petroleum, and natural gas make up more than 80 percent of world energy sources. They are **fossil fuels,** which formed long ago, deep in the earth from rotting plants and animals. Part of the trouble with fossil fuels is that they take so long to form. Fossil fuels are **nonrenewable resources** because they can not be easily replaced. Look at the time line below to see when some scientists believe that fossil fuels will run out. ③

REVIEW What are some causes of the rapidly increasing demand for energy? **Cause and Effect**

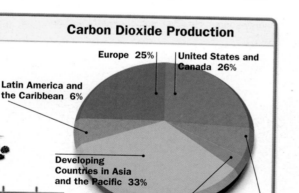
When Might Fossil Fuels Run Out?

| Gas
Coal
Oil

1800 1900 2000 2100 2200 2300 2400
Year

Carbon Dioxide Production

Europe 25%
United States and Canada 26%
Latin America and the Caribbean 6%
Developing Countries in Asia and the Pacific 33%
Africa 3%
Other Developed Countries* 7%

*including Australia, New Zealand, and Japan 665

Quick Summary Keeping up with the world's need for energy will require producing energy in new ways, as well as limiting our energy use.

① What are some important uses of fossil fuels? Run generators to produce electricity, produce gasoline for cars **Main Idea and Details**

② Which of the energy sources specifically named is used least? Nuclear **Interpret Graphs**

GRAPH SKILL **Answer** Petroleum

③ Why will fossil fuels run out? Possible answer: Fossil fuels are used up when they are burned to produce energy, and it takes a long time for new supplies to form. **Draw Conclusions**

✓ **Ongoing Assessment**

| **If...** students do not understand why fossil fuels will run out, | **then...** explain that it takes millions of years for the fuels to form. Ask students how this time period affects our ability to rely on new fossil fuels. |

✓ **REVIEW ANSWER** Rapidly growing populations; new industries; new technologies **Cause and Effect**

Graphic Organizers Students can use assorted graphic organizers to
erstand parts of the lesson.

inning Have students make a two-column chart with the headings *Electricity*
Gas. Help them list in the appropriate column things that use electricity or gas.

ermediate Have students make a web showing various energy sources and
uses to which the energy is put.

anced Have students make Problem-Solution charts. They should identify
problem the text implies (a potential energy shortage) and list possible
tions.

additional ESL support, use Every Student Learns Guide, pp. 314–317.

Petroleum

- In addition to being used as fuel, petroleum is also used to produce medicine, plastic, paint, and cloth.
- Millions of years ago petroleum formed from the decomposition of organisms.
- The time it takes for petroleum to form is between tens of millions of years and one hundred million years.

Meeting Energy Needs

Quick Summary Because of the limited sources of fossil fuels and the pollution they produce, other renewable energy sources must be found.

4 **Why did a global oil crisis occur in 1973?** Many of the world's biggest oil producers cut their production and raised oil prices. **Cause and Effect**

5 **What is one major disadvantage of fossil fuels?** They may cause global warming. **Main Idea and Details**

✓ **REVIEW ANSWER** Advantages: Nuclear power does not produce carbon dioxide and could last thousands of years. Disadvantages: If an accident occurs, harmful radioactive gases can escape into the atmosphere; radioactive waste must be buried.
Main Idea and Details

Alternative Energy

Quick Summary Alternative renewable resources, such as solar energy, water, and wind, can be used as energy sources in addition to fossil fuels and nuclear power.

Meeting Energy Needs

Because most developed countries have relied on fossil fuels for energy, they have faced many challenges. For example, much of the world's oil reserves are located in the Middle East. In 1973 many of the world's biggest oil producers cut their production of petroleum and formed the **Organization of Petroleum Exporting Countries (OPEC).** They also raised oil prices. This caused **4** a global oil crisis. People waited in long lines to fill their cars with gasoline.

Because the United States imports a great deal of the oil it uses, it has relied on OPEC. To avoid a future energy supply crisis, U.S. President **George W. Bush** began a campaign in 2001 toward self-sufficiency.

Another problem with fossil fuels is that they give off carbon dioxide when they burn. You read in Lesson 2 how this gas is collecting in Earth's atmosphere, trapping warmth. Fossil fuels are **5** thought by some to be the main cause of global warming.

One nonrenewable resource that does not give off carbon dioxide is nuclear energy. A nuclear power plant uses steam pressure to drive a generator. But instead of burning a fossil fuel, it uses nuclear fuel. In nuclear fuel, heat is produced by splitting atoms. Though nonrenewable, nuclear fuel could last for thousands of years.

Nuclear power seems to be a good alternative energy source. However, sometimes things can go wrong in a nuclear power plant. In 1986 the **Chernobyl** (chair NOH buhl) nuclear power plant in the Soviet Union (now Ukraine) had a terrible accident. Gases and steam blew off the top of concrete building. Radioactive gases escaped the atmosphere. About 30 people died. However some scientists think an additional 40,000 cancer deaths will occur over time because of the population's exposure to nuclear radiation.

Another problem with nuclear power is the waste it produces. This material, which remain radioactive for thousands of years, must be buried deep underground.

REVIEW What are the advantages and disadvantages of using nuclear power as an alternative energy source? **Main Idea and Detail**

Alternative Energy

Some people think that we should use more **renewable resources** such as solar energy, wa and wind because they cannot be used up ea like nonrenewable resources can. Some powe plants are using giant windmills to drive gene tors. Others use water power from rapidly flow rivers or dams. This type of energy is called **hydroelectric energy.** Waterfalls are a great source of hydroelectricity. **Iguaçu Falls** on the border between Argentina and Brazil is a majo source of hydroelectricity in South America. **Niagara Falls** in Canada provides a portion o the province of Ontario's energy needs.

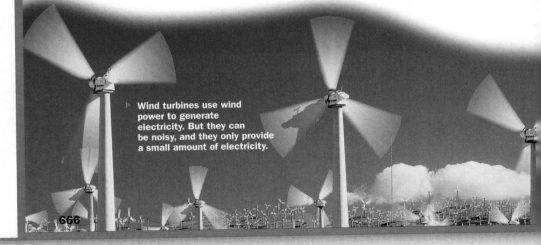
▶ **Wind turbines use wind power to generate electricity. But they can be noisy, and they only provide a small amount of electricity.**

666

Practice and Extend

CURRICULUM CONNECTION
Literature

Books About Energy

Use the following books to extend the content.
Fuels for the Future (Protecting Our Planet), by Edward Parker (Raintree/Steck Vaughn, ISBN 0-817-24937-0, 1998) **Easy**

Energy (Eyewitness), by Jack Challoner, Clive Streeter (Photographer) (DK Publishing, ISBN 0-789-45576-5, 2000) **On-Level**

From Space to Earth : The Story of Solar Electricity, by John Perlin (Aatec Publications, ISBN: 0-937-94814-4, 1999) **Challenge**

FAST FACTS

This page describes various ways to meet energy needs. Here are some other facts about energy.

- **Japan** imports nearly 100% of its total energy needs.
- Demands on the energy supply in **California** ha caused widespread blackouts in recent years.
- Denis Hayes organized the first **Earth Day** in 1970 to help people focus on the need to conserve Earth's resources.

er alternative, or other, energy source
ermal energy. This is energy from
t water underground. Many power
uld tap into this source. But alterna-
gy sources can only make a minor
ion to our energy needs. Some are
in only certain parts of the world.
ists are trying to create entirely new
roducing energy. One area of
is nuclear fusion. *Fusion* means
ogether." In nuclear fusion, atoms are
d instead of split apart. This process
energy and does not produce dangerous
oducts.

kle our energy challenges, we can also
making changes to the fuel-guzzling
s we use. For example, we can try to
tomobiles and trucks more energy effi-
gineers in automobile companies are
g hybrid cars. These cars are smaller
er than traditional cars. They have much
gasoline engines.

▶ Iguaçu Falls consists of some 275 waterfalls.

REVIEW What conclusion can you make about
the alternative energy sources we use?
🔄 Draw Conclusions

Summarize the Lesson

— **1973** The first global oil crisis occurred.

— **1986** The Chernobyl nuclear accident
polluted vast areas of eastern Europe.

— **2001** George W. Bush began an energy
campaign to help make the United States
self-sufficient.

SSON 3   REVIEW

ck Facts and Main Ideas

🔄 Draw Conclusions On a separate piece
paper, copy the diagram below. Write a
nclusion based on the given facts.

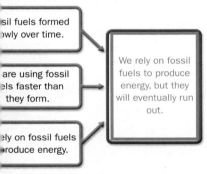

sil fuels formed
wly over time.

are using fossil
els faster than
they form.

ely on fossil fuels
roduce energy.

We rely on fossil
fuels to produce
energy, but they
will eventually run
out.

3. List a benefit and a disadvantage of nuclear
energy.

4. Identify alternative energy sources we use
today.

5. **Critical Thinking:** *Solve Complex Problems*
Make a list of the qualities a good energy
source has.

Link to 🔗 **Science**

Electricity from Lightning In this lesson, you
have read about generating electricity in
power plants. Explain whether or not you
believe lightning could be used to produce
electricity. Explain your conclusion.

hat are fossil fuels and which one will
obably run out first?

667

MEETING INDIVIDUAL NEEDS
Leveled Practice

e **Point of View** Have students express their
s of view about energy problems and solutions.

Have students choose which energy source
think is best and tell why. **Reteach**

evel Have students list all energy sources
the lesson and rank them from most to least
able. **Extend**

lenge Ask students to write and present a
ch explaining which energy source they think
ld receive research funding and why. Have
ents include statistics to support their
ons. **Enrich**

Lesson Summary, use Quick Study, p. 158.

Workbook, p. 165

Lesson 3: Energy

Directions: Use the information from Lesson 3 to answer the following questions
on the lines provided. You may use your textbook.

1. What are two ways we use fossil fuels?

2. What are two problems related to using fossil fuels to supply energy?

3. What were the causes of the oil crisis of the 1970s?

4. What are the advantages of nuclear power?

5. What are some examples of renewable energy sources? What is the advantage of using
these to create energy?

6. How are hydroelectric energy and geothermal energy different?

7. In what ways are scientists trying to solve the world's energy shortage?

Notes for Home: Your child learned about the ways we produce and conserve energy.
Home Activity: With your child, read a newspaper article about energy conservation. What new ways of
conservation are discussed?

**Also on Teacher
Resources CD-ROM.**

❻ **Why would working to develop
energy-efficient cars be a wise plan?**
Possible answer: These cars use less
gasoline; therefore fossil fuels would not
be depleted as quickly. This would give
scientists time to find new energy
sources. 🔄 **Draw Conclusions**

✓ **REVIEW ANSWER** There is no perfect
source; each seems to have one or
more drawbacks. 🔄 **Draw Conclusions**

❸ Close
and Assess

Summarize the Lesson

Tell students to examine the vertical
time line. Ask them to use the events
listed in the time line and others they
read about to write a summary of the
world's energy problems and some
possible solutions.

✓   **LESSON 3**   **REVIEW**

1. 🔄 **Draw Conclusions** For possible
answers, see the reduced pupil page.

2. Fuels formed deep in the earth such
as coal, oil, and natural gas; oil

3. Does not give off carbon dioxide;
produces radioactive waste

4. Nuclear energy, wind power,
hydroelectricity, solar power,
geothermal energy

5. **Critical Thinking:** *Solve Complex
Problems* It would not contribute to
pollution or global warming; it would
pose no danger of radioactive
poisoning to human, plant, or animal
life; it would be renewable; it would
be cheap to produce.

Link to 🔗 **Science**

Possible answer: The power plants
described in this lesson need a
steady source of energy to drive an
electric generator. Though lightning
has lots of energy, that energy is not
a steady source. Another problem is
that we do not know when and where
lightning will strike.

Technology

Objectives

- Explain how we have used technology.
- Explain why and how we have used technology in space.
- Explain what the Human Genome Project is.
- Give an example of a problem that technology can solve and give an example of a problem that technology cannot solve.
- Explain why some forms of technology are more important than others.

Vocabulary

space station, p. 669
satellite, p. 669

Resources

- Workbook, p. 166
- Transparency 23
- Every Student Learns Guide, pp. 318–321
- Quick Study, pp. 160–161

Quick Teaching Plan

If time is short, have students create biographical sketches for the people featured in Lesson 4, including their occupations and contributions to technology.

1 Introduce and Motivate

Preview Have students discuss ways in which technology affects their daily activities. Tell students that they will learn about technological advances in different areas, including health care and space exploration.

You Are There Point out that several years ago the United States was in a race against Russia to make advances in space exploration. Today these two countries are working together on the space station. Have students predict what new forms of technology will be developed during their lifetimes.

668 Unit 8 • New Nations and a New Century

1950	1975

1957 First satellite

1975 First personal computer

199 U.S. *Atlantis* dock with Russia's *Mi*

Human Genome Project identifies thousands of hum

PREVIEW

Focus on the Main Idea
Technology gives us many benefits, but it cannot solve every human problem.

PEOPLE
Yuri Gagarin
Neil Armstrong
Edwin Aldrin
Charles DeLisi
David A. Smith
Flossie Wong-Staal

VOCABULARY
space station
satellite

TERMS
National Aeronautics and Space Administration (NASA)
Human Genome Project

▶ In 1965 Edward H. White II became the first American to leave his spacecraft and "walk" in space.

668

Technology

You Are There
Snug in your spacesuit, you step of the space shuttle and onto a s station. You close your eyes. You dreamed of this day. You remember reading about the space shuttle *Atlantis* docking with the Russian spac tion *Mir* (meer) in 1995. Russian and American crev began working together to do important experimen repair satellites on the space station. Soon, astronau came from many other nations to work on *Mir*.

You're thrilled that you were chosen to work on the International Space Station. You know that you will and sleep here for many days and do important worl wonder if the inside of the space station is like a rail car because other astronauts have described it that You open your eyes and take another step. Now it's y turn to make history.

Draw Conclusions
As you read, put facts together to understand how we solve problems with technology.

Practice and Extend

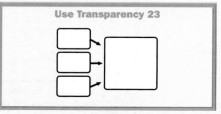

New Technology

...ke the space station *Mir*, technology
...lop quickly. A **space station** is a large
... or human-made object sent into space,
...es as a scientific base. It can also be
... a refueling station for spacecraft or a
...g pad for other satellites.

...ology has helped us learn more about
...erse and change and improve our lives.
... there are problems that come with
...g technology.

...ology includes using knowledge,
...s, and tools to accomplish or improve
...ng. In prehistory, technology was very
...included advancements in toolmaking
...ne to copper. Today, when we make more
...computers to process more information
...at is technology.

In fact, for the past 50 years, computers have played a part in most of our technology. Fast-developing technology has helped space travel skyrocket. The former Soviet Union put the first satellite into orbit in 1957. It was called *Sputnik I*. Today, telephones, cable television, and other communications depend on satellites.

Technology helped astronaut **Yuri Gagarin** of the Soviet Union to become the first human in space in April 1961. The U.S. government space agency, the **National Aeronautics and Space Administration (NASA)**, sent the first humans, **Neil Armstrong** and **Edwin Aldrin**, to walk on the moon in July 1969. All of this was made possible with technology.

REVIEW What are two important new technologies of the twentieth century?
Summarize

Computers

One of the first modern computers was developed by American John Atanasoff. It was completed in 1946 and called an Electronic Numerical Integrator and ...ter, or ENIAC. Weighing some 30 tons and filling the space of a small room, ENIAC ...ly complete one task at a time.

...onal computers (PCs) that fit on your desktop were developed in 1975. PCs could be ...home or work by one person and were much faster than ENIAC. By the mid-1990s, a ...er could be held in someone's hand! With a hand-held computer, you can browse the Internet and download information while you are away from your PC.

▶ The size, speed, and capabilities of computers have improved because of technology.

669

New Possibilities

Quick Summary A new form of technology involves identifying and mapping human genes.

❸ Why is the Human Genome Project important? It is an international effort to map all the human genes. Understanding genes can help researchers explain how genetic diseases develop and may help scientists develop ways to cure these diseases. **Evaluate**

✓ **REVIEW ANSWER** Answers may vary, but students should explain that technology should help researchers identify the genes and learn more about them faster. ❸ **Draw Conclusions**

 **Telecommunication**

❹ When information is communicated by satellite, what steps does it go through? First a signal is transmitted from the ground to the satellite, then the satellite amplifies it and relays it to another location on the ground. **Sequence**

New Possibilities

Another new form of technology that developed in the late twentieth century was the mapping of genes. Genes are the basic blueprint for life. Scientists have learned how to substitute genes from one cell to another. They can even mix genes from different species, or life forms.

The Human Genome Project is an international effort to find all of the more than 30,000 human genes. It was launched in 1990, five years after Charles DeLisi and David A. Smith led the first conference to investigate the possibility of such a project. By 2000 researchers were able to map out thousands of human genes. By understanding genes, researchers can try to ❸ explain how genetic diseases develop and find a cure for such diseases.

Technology has helped researchers and scientists identify human genes. However, there are social and legal issues involved. The information that we learn about genes could be used for other purposes. Even though the cause of disease is the main goal of discovering genes, it may not be the only one.

REVIEW How can technology help researchers learn about human genes? ❸ **Draw Conclusions**

▶ J. Craig Vente[r] leading genor[...] scientist, sta[...] front of a proj[...] from the hum[...] genetic code.

 DORLING KINDERSLEY EYEWITNESS BOOK

Telecommunication

Communication is the sharing of information, ideas, and thoughts. It has been a vital part of human life since prehistory. Over time, methods of communication have improved. Today, we can even rely on telecommunication—messages that can be transmitted by radio, telephones, and satellites—to communicate with people around the world.

Satellite Systems
About 200 communication satellites are in orbit around the Earth. The satellites receive signals from transmitter dishes, amplify them, and then relay them back to a ground station. In this way, the signals are transmitted to other continents, enabling instant worldwide telecommunication.

Geosta[...] satellites a[...] by sola[...]

Ground station receives signals from the satellites

 ❹

Practice and Extend

FYI SOCIAL STUDIES
Background

Human Genome Project
- The idea to study human genomes originated at scientific conferences held between 1985 and 1987.
- The Human Genome project began in the United States in 1990.
- James Watson was one of the first directors of the program in the United States.

MEETING INDIVIDUAL NEEDS
Learning Styles

Report on Future Technology Using their individual learning styles, students predict what technological and scientific advances might occur in their lifetimes.

Verbal Learning Have students discuss a certain topic, such as the future impact of gene mapping, and share their predictions with others.

Linguistic Learning Have students write and present stories that describe life, health, and technology 30 years from now.

Limits

scientists today are doing research on
e called Acquired Immunodeficiency
e, or AIDS. AIDS is a deadly disease that
people's immune systems. Scientists are
chnology to help find a cure.

e **Wong-Staal** has helped lead the way in
search. In the early 1980s, she joined the
the United States that identified human
deficiency virus, or HIV, the AIDS virus.
hers in France made the same discovery
ame time.

illustrates both the power and limits of
gy. Anti-AIDS drugs can now keep
people healthy for years. But these
e very expensive. Only some people
rd them. People in developing countries
usually afford to buy anti-AIDS drugs.
01 UN Secretary-General Kofi Annan
tions to contribute money to help fight

AIDS in Africa. Southern Africa has the largest number of people infected with HIV in the world.

The AIDS crisis in Africa demonstrates that technology cannot solve every problem. Still, technology has been part of our human history from the beginning. It continues to impact how we live.

REVIEW What is the main goal of the technologies discussed in this section?
➲ Draw Conclusions

Summarize the Lesson

- **1957** The Soviet Union launched the world's first artificial satellite, *Sputnik I*.
- **1975** The first personal computer became available to the public.
- **2000** The Human Genome Project identified thousands of genes.

SSON 4 REVIEW

ck Facts and Main Ideas

➲ **Draw Conclusions** On a separate piece paper, copy the diagram below. Write a nclusion based on the given facts.

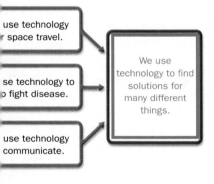

use technology r space travel.

se technology to fight disease.

use technology communicate.

→ We use technology to find solutions for many different things.

plain how we have used technology in ace.

3. What is the Human Genome Project?
4. Give an example of a problem that technology might solve and an example of a problem that it cannot solve.
5. **Critical Thinking:** *Evaluate Information* Of the technologies discussed in this lesson, which do you think is most important? Explain your answer.

Link to ⬡⬡ Technology

Be an Inventor What could you invent that would improve an aspect of human life? Would your invention help solve a problem in your community or school? Describe your invention and then draw a sketch or make a model to present to the class.

671

Workbook, p. 166

Lesson 4: Technology

Directions: Write the events from the box in the chart in the order in which they took place. You may use your textbook.

- Researcher Flossie Wong-Staal helps identify HIV.
- U.S. astronauts Neil Armstrong and Edwin Aldrin walk on the moon.
- UN Secretary-General Kofi Annan urges developed nations to contribute money to help fight AIDS in Africa.
- Desktop computers are introduced for use at home and at work.
- The former Soviet Union launches the *Sputnik I* satellite into outer space.
- Toolmaking advances from stone to copper.
- Soviet astronaut Yuri Gagarin becomes the first human in space.

1.
2.
3.
4.
5.
6.
7.

Also on Teacher Resources CD-ROM.

Limits

⏱ *Quick Summary* Scientists around the world are using technology to help find a cure for AIDS.

5 **Summarize the limits of AIDS drugs.** Although they help infected people live for years, they are very expensive, so some people—particularly those in developing countries—cannot afford them. **Summarize**

✓ **REVIEW ANSWER** To improve human life ➲ **Draw Conclusions**

3 Close and Assess

Summarize the Lesson

Tell students to read the events described in the vertical time line. Ask them to identify one way in which each event helped to improve human life.

1. ➲ **Draw Conclusions** For possible answers, see the reduced pupil page.
2. We have used technology to launch satellites, space stations, and space shuttles into outer space.
3. A project designed to map out the more than 30,000 genes in humans.
4. Possible answer: Technology might find a better treatment or a cure for muscular dystrophy; it might improve a crop to produce more food; it might find a vaccine or a cure for AIDS. On the other hand, technology cannot give money to people who are too poor to pay for the medical care they need.
5. **Critical Thinking:** *Evaluate Information* Students should identify a technology and give reasons to support their answers.

Link to ⬡⬡ Technology

To help students identify an invention, provide a list of fields in which technology is essential (i.e., medicine, space exploration, communication, information, agriculture).

Resources

- Assessment Book, pp. 117–120
- Workbook, p. 167: Vocabulary Review

Chapter Summary

For possible answers, see the reduced pupil page.

Vocabulary

1. d, **2.** b, **3.** c, **4.** a, **5.** e

People and Terms

Possible answers:

1. Mother Teresa was a Roman Catholic nun who spent most of her life helping the very poor of Calcutta, India, one of the world's poorest megacities.

2. Rachel Carson wrote the book *Silent Spring* in 1962; it described environmental damage caused by pesticides and spurred new laws to protect the environment.

3. The Environmental Protection Agency is an environmental watchdog agency in the U.S. government.

4. NASA, (the National Aeronautics and Space Administration) is the U.S. space agency that sent the first humans to the moon.

5. Yuri Gagarin, a Soviet astronaut, became the first human to travel in space in 1961.

6. In 1969 Neil Armstrong and Edwin Aldrin became the first humans to walk on the moon.

7. In 2001 President George W. Bush proposed that the United States pursue a policy of energy self-sufficiency.

8. OPEC (the Organization of Petroleum Exporting Countries) can affect the supply of oil coming from the Middle East and its price.

9. The Human Genome Project was launched in 1990 as an international effort to find all of the more than 30,000 human genes.

10. Flossie Wong-Staal has helped lead the way in AIDS research.

672 Unit 8 • New Nations and a New Century

CHAPTER 23
REVIEW

1950	1960	
1957 First successful satellite	**about 1960** More people began moving from developing to developed countries.	**1962** *Silent* was pu

Chapter Summary

Draw Conclusions

On a separate piece of paper, copy the diagram below. Write a conclusion based on the given facts in the diagram.

Fossil fuels are nonrenewable resources.	→	Our energy decisions have a str effect on the earth's environme
The world's population is increasing.	→	
Technology can improve our lives.	→	

Vocabulary

Match each word with the correct definition or description.

1 demographer (p. 656)

2 environmentalist (p. 661)

3 global warming (p. 661)

4 fossil fuel (p. 665)

5 satellite (p. 669)

a. coal, petroleum, natural gas

b. a person who supports taking measures to protect environment

c. a gradual increase in Earth's average temperature

d. a scientist who studies population trends

e. an object that is sent into space and orbits Earth

People and Terms

Write a sentence explaining why each o lowing people or terms was important i since World War II. You may use two or a single sentence.

1 Mother Teresa (p. 655)

2 Rachel Carson (p. 661)

3 Environmental Protection Agency (p. 661)

4 NASA (p. 669)

5 Yuri Gagarin (p. 669)

6 Neil Arm and Edw (p. 669)

7 George V (p. 666)

8 OPEC (p.

9 Human C Project (p. 670)

10 Flossie V Staal (p.

672

Practice and Extend

Assessment Options

✓ **Chapter 23 Assessment**

- Chapter 23 Content Test: Use Assessment Book, pp. 117–118.
- Chapter 23 Skills Test: Use Assessment Book, pp. 119–120.

Standardized Test Prep

- Chapter 23 Tests contain standardized test format.

✓ **Chapter 23 Performance Assessment**

- Assign small groups one of the scientific fields (the environment, energy, technology) this chapter.
- Have each group work together on a speech telling about the problems and solutions relevant to their scientific field.
- Have one member of each group present th speech to the class.
- Assess students' understanding of problem and solutions in the area addressed.

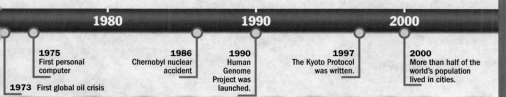

1975 First personal computer

1973 First global oil crisis

1986 Chernobyl nuclear accident

1990 Human Genome Project was launched.

1997 The Kyoto Protocol was written.

2000 More than half of the world's population lived in cities.

ts and Main Ideas

t parts of the world is population g the fastest?

as technology changed since tory?

Line How many years were there en the publication of *Silent Spring* e nuclear accident at Chernobyl?

dea How is the world's population dif- today than it was about 50 years ago?

dea How are we trying to solve nmental problems?

dea How are we trying to solve y problems?

dea Can technology solve every n problem? Explain your answer.

l Thinking: *Evaluate Information* Do ink it is important to use technology a cure for a genetic disease? Why or ot?

ite About History

an energy-saving plan for your family.

a short biography of one of the ing people: Rachel Carson, Mother a of Calcutta, or George W. Bush. Use opedias or the Internet to do your rch.

three personal guidelines for using nmental resources.

Apply Skills

Compare Distribution Maps

Look at the map below. Then answer the questions.

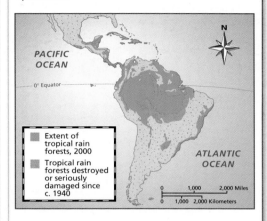

PACIFIC OCEAN

0° Equator

ATLANTIC OCEAN

■ Extent of tropical rain forests, 2000

■ Tropical rain forests destroyed or seriously damaged since c. 1940

0   1,000   2,000 Miles
0   1,000   2,000 Kilometers

1 Look at the map on page 658. What is population density where tropical rain forests are located?

2 What can you conclude from the maps above and on page 658 about rain forests and population density in this region?

Internet Activity

To get help with vocabulary, people, and terms, select dictionary, encyclopedia, or almanac from *Social Studies Library* at **www.sfsocialstudies.com.**

673

Hands-on Unit Project

it 8 Performance Assessment

e p. 678 for information about using the Unit ject as a means of performance assessment. coring guide is provided on p. 678.

WEB SITE Technology

ore information, students can select the nary, encyclopedia, or almanac from *Social es Library* at **www.sfsocialstudies.com.**

Facts and Main Ideas

1. In developing nations

2. It continues to develop more quickly, building on the technology already developed.

3. 24 years

4. The population is much larger now than it was 50 years ago; there are more megacities; there has been an increase in movement of people from developing countries to developed countries.

5. We are looking for more fossil fuels, and also trying to cut back on our use of fossil fuels by using alternative energy resources— nuclear, wind power, solar power, and hydroelectricity. We are trying to conserve energy and use sources that do not cause global warming or pollution.

6. We are using alternative resources such as solar energy, water, and wind. We can also make trucks and automobiles more efficient.

7. No. Accept well-reasoned and supported answers.

8. Accept any well-reasoned and supported answer.

Write About History

1. Students' plans should have specific directions their family could follow to save the energy they use to light, heat, and clean their homes.

2. Students' biographies should include information other than that found in this chapter.

3. Before students write guidelines, have students identify some of the natural resources they will conserve, such as water, oil, forests, and animals.

Apply Skills

1. Rain forests are thinly populated.

2. Rain forests are being destroyed or damaged, but this change does not appear to have affected the population density.

The Garden We Planted Together

Objectives

- Identify figurative language.

- Explain how literature may reflect the times during which it was written.

1 Introduce and Motivate

Preview To activate prior knowledge, ask students to recall what they learned about the United Nations in Chapter 19. Tell students that they will learn more about the goals of this peacekeeping organization in this poem.

Ask students what they think they can learn from a poem about an international organization. (It might provide another viewpoint that they can learn from.)

2 Teach and Discuss

1 **What do the flowers in the poem represent?** The different countries of the world ⮑ Draw Conclusions

2 **What does the poem suggest happens when one member of the United Nations becomes weak or has problems?** Other countries come to its aid by helping to find solutions and sharing their resources. Make Inferences

UNIT
8
End with a Poem

The Garden We Planted Together

by Anuruddha Bose

This poem was written by an 11-year-old boy from India in honor of the fiftieth anniversary of the United Nations. As you have learned, the United Nations was created in 1945 as a world peacekeeping organization. After reading Anuruddha's poem, consider why he chose this subject. What do you think the garden symbolizes?

From all over the world
together they came,
to make a garden
with shovels and spades.

Disagreement crept in—
which flowers to grow?
So they sat in a circle
And agreed row by row.

They wrote down their rules
in a big, mighty book
and promised to keep them
by hook and by crook.

With the book to guide them,
they grew beautiful flowers,
each of them equal,
none higher, none lower. **1**

When some flowers grow weak
or ready to die,
the children get together,
new solutions to try. **2**

They share water and seeds,
all must have enough,
the book just demands it
when the going gets tough.

The garden remains a symbol
to all, its flowers are fifty years
old this fall. The book is known
as a charter of peace—its rules
are still valid, so read if you please. **3** **4**

674

Practice and Extend

FYI **SOCIAL STUDIES**
Background

The United Nations

- On April 25, 1945, fifty nations met for two months and created a United Nations charter.
- The charter listed rules that the nations agreed to follow in order to encour[age] peace around the world.
- The official beginning of the United Nations was on October 24, 1945.
- Each member country has an equal vote, regardless of size.
- By the year 2001, there were 189 member countries in the United Nations.

artwork by Jordan, age 11

675

3 **What does the poet suggest is the main goal of the United Nations?** To keep peace around the world
Analyze Information

4 **What is the author's view of the United Nations?** Possible answer: He feels it is an effective peacekeeping organization that everyone should know about. Point of View

3 Close and Assess

- Have students choose a stanza and paraphrase its meaning in their own words.

- Ask students to write a summary of what they learned about the United Nations from reading this poem.

CURRICULUM CONNECTION
Art

te a Symbolic Garden

vide students with assorted paints, collage materials, or materials that ld be used to create a sculpture.

ve students create a painting, collage, or sculpture of what they visualize en they read this poem.

ve them label or describe their artwork to explain how it is connected to poem.

Resource
- Assessment Book, pp. 121–124

Main Ideas and Vocabulary

1. c, **2.** d, **3.** b, **4.** b

Vocabulary

1. b, **2.** c, **3.** d, **4.** e, **5.** a, **6.** f

Apply Skills

- Provide students with access to reference books, encyclopedias, or the Internet to find the data.

- Encourage students to use the most current data they can find about the country they have chosen.

Test Talk

Use Information from Graphics

Use Apply Skills to model the Test Talk strategy.

Understand the question.

Have students identify places or things in the question. Students should finish the statement "I need to find out ...."

Use information from graphics.

Ask students to skim any graphs or diagrams they find in their research to gather statistics for their cartograms.

Main Ideas and Vocabulary

TEST PREP

Read the passage below and use it to answer the questions that follow.

When World War II ended in 1945, European countries still held many colonies. Most colonies were in Africa and Asia. Soon they began demanding independence.

Mohandas Gandhi used new methods of nonviolent civil disobedience to gain independence for India in 1947.

By the 1960s, many nations in sub-Saharan Africa were becoming independent too. However, black Africans in South Africa had to struggle to gain full civil rights.

The state of Israel was created in 1948, which led to the Arab-Israeli Conflict. Later, the fall of communism in Eastern Europe led to the creation of more new nations.

The world faced many new ideas and challenges in the late twentieth century and early twenty-first century. Cooperation led to free trade and the global economy. Nations drew together and formed trading blocs to help promote regional trade.

Along with cooperation, though, conflict broke out. Many conflicts were based on differences of identity. Ethnic conflict tore apart Yugoslavia and Rwanda. International terrorism posed new challenges.

Scientists developed new areas of research. Industry used the research to create new products. Computers soon changed the way people lived and worked.

Humans blasted into space. Astronauts walked on the moon and set up space stations. Scientists began to research human genes and find cures for diseases.

1 According to the passage, what forces led to creation of so many new nations after 1945?
- **A** communist takeovers
- **B** hatred, greed
- **C** the end of imperialism, the fall of communism
- **D** inflation, unemployment

2 In the passage the term *civil disobedience* means—
- **A** going to prison
- **B** opposing someone by any means necessary
- **C** setting up an new nation
- **D** opposing someone or something by not cooperating

3 In the passage the term *trading blocs* means—
- **A** open-air markets
- **B** groups of countries trading to their advantage
- **C** efforts to stop trade
- **D** tariffs

4 What is the main idea of the passage?
- **A** The world is full of conflict.
- **B** We live in a time of new nations, ideas, and challenges.
- **C** Mohandas K. Gandhi was a great person.
- **D** Science is changing our world.

676

Practice and Extend

Assessment Options

✓ Unit 8 Assessment

- Use Unit 8 Content Test; Use Assessment Book, pp. 121–122.
- Use Unit 8 Skills Test; Use Assessment Book, pp. 123–124.

Standardized Test Prep

- Unit 8 Tests contain standardized test format.

✓ Unit 8 Performance Assessment

- See p. 678 for information about using the Unit Project as a means of Performance Assessment.
- A scoring guide for the Unit Project is provided in the teacher's notes on p. 678.

 Test Talk

- Test Talk Practice Book

WEB SITE
Technology

For more information, students can select the dictionary, encyclopedia, or almanac from *Social Studies Library* at **www.sfsocialstudies.com.**

Vocabulary

vocabulary word to its definition.

illennium
. 655)

eforestation
. 662)

asnost (p. 622)

newable
source (p. 666)

restroika
622)

migration
657)

a. restructuring

b. one thousand
years

c. clearing of trees

d. openness

e. natural resource
that can be
replaced

f. process of people
moving to a new
place to live

Apply Skills

a **Cartogram** using a topic from this
example, compare how much garbage
ced by a country or how much energy is
d by a country or countries. Use encyclo-
books, and the Internet to gather your
s. Use colored paper or markers to
e cartogram.

Energy Consumption

Canada

United States 27%

Write and Share

Present Radio Interviews Choose someone to
be the moderator of a radio talk show. The moderator will interview people that students have
read about in the unit. Let other students volunteer for these guest parts. Have remaining
classmates write questions that the moderator
will ask the guests. Give guests time to write
their answers before showtime.

Read on Your Own

Look for books like these in your library.

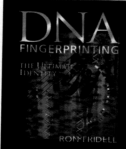

677

Write and Share

- Provide access to encyclopedias,
biographies, and the Internet for
students to use to find answers to
their questions.

- Have students who write the
questions include information they
read about in Unit 8.

- Encourage student guests to portray
their characters the way they believe
they would act, sound, and look.

- Use the following scoring guide.

✓**Assessment Scoring Guide**

Present Radio Interviews	
4	Students' questions reflect insight about and knowledge of the person's accomplishments. Guests answer the questions completely and provide additional, accurate, and related information about the person they are portraying.
3	Students' questions reflect general understanding of the person. Guests answer the questions completely and accurately.
2	Question writers ask general questions. Guests answer some of the questions accurately.
1	Question writers ask irrelevant questions. Guests are unable to answer any relevant questions that were asked.

Read on Your Own

The Storyteller's Beads, by Jane Kurtz
(Gulliver Books, ISBN 0-152-01074-2,
1998) **Easy**

Girl of Kosovo, by Alice Mead (Farrar Straus &
Giroux, ISBN 0-374-32620-7, 2001)
On-Level

DNA Fingerprinting: The Ultimate Identity, by
Ron Fridell, (Franklin Watts, Incorporated,
ISBN 0-531-11858-4, 2001) **Challenge**

visit the Question

ve students look at the lists they
eated about the ways in which they
n be global citizens.

ve students look at the lists of
ys in which citizens around the
rld show their concern for the
bal community and how they
ght struggle to be an active
ce in that community.

- Ask students to compare and
contrast their lists.

- Students should write a persuasive
paragraph explaining how and why
people can and should become
active in the affairs of the global
community.

Making Contact

Objective
- Describe the history of a communications method and create an accompanying Web page.

Resource
- Workbook, p. 168

Materials
paper, pencils, pens, markers, reference materials from the library or Internet, computer with graphics program (optional)

Follow This Procedure
- Tell students that they will design a Web page about the history of a communication method. Brainstorm communication methods.

- Divide students into groups of three or four. Have them research a method and write about its development.

- Have students draw their Web pages, including text, pictures, and other graphics. If possible, have students create their Web pages on a computer.

- Use the following scoring guide.

✓ Assessment Scoring Guide

Making Contact	
4	Creates a web page to describe the history of a communication method using many details and accurate information in a clear visual presentation that includes a variety of elements.
3	Describes the history of a communication method using details and mostly accurate information in a clear visual presentation that includes some variety of elements.
2	Describes the history of a communication method using few details and some inaccurate information in a visual presentation that includes little variety of elements.
1	Describes the history of a communication method using few or no details and inaccurate information in a visual presentation that includes no variety of elements.

UNIT 8 Project

Making Contact

Design a Web page about the history of communication.

1 Form groups and choose a communication method or invention that helped people communicate. Write about the development of the communication method or invention you chose.

2 Use pictures wherever possible. You may choose to include a timeline.

3 Draw your Web page. Include text, pictures, and other graphics that represent your method or invention. If possible, create your Web page on the computer.

4 Present your Web page to the class.

History of Writing
Click on a picture to learn more!

Internet Activity

Explore communication technology. Go to **www.sfsocialstudies.com/activities** and select your grade and unit.

678

Practice and Extend

Hands-on Unit Project

✓ Performance Assessment
- The Unit Project can also be used as a performance assessment activity.
- Use the scoring guide to assess each group's work.

WEB SITE Technology

Students can launch the Internet Activity by clicking on *Grade 6, Unit 8* at **www.sfsocialstudies.com/activities.**

Workbook, p. 1

8 Project Making Contact

Directions: In a group, design a Web page about the history of communication.

1. Our Web page will feature this communication method or invention:

2. Description of the method or invention:

3. Inventor(s) of this method or invention:

4. A timeline shows the development of the method or invention through history.

Earliest use is _____. Additions or improvements in _____. Modern form in _____.
(year) (year) (year)

5. Pictures we will include to represent our method or invention:

✓ Checklist for Students

____ We chose a communication method or invention.
____ We wrote important facts and described it.
____ We created a timeline and pictures showing how it changed over time.
____ We made a drawing of our Web page.
____ We presented our Web page to the class.

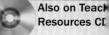

Also on Teach Resources CD

Reference Guide

Table of Contents

R1

Atlas
Satellite Photograph of the Continents

Atlas
The World: Political

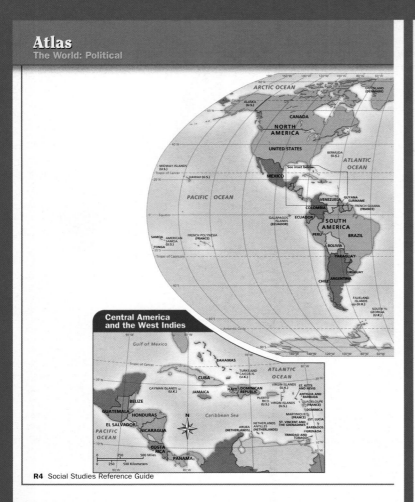

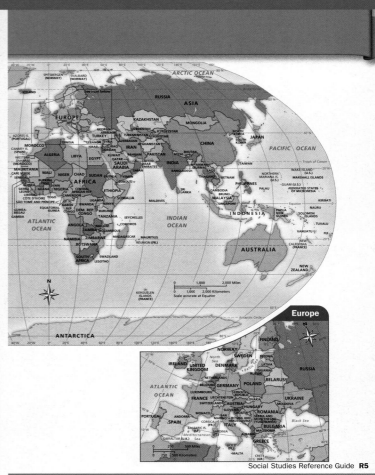

Atlas
The World: Physical

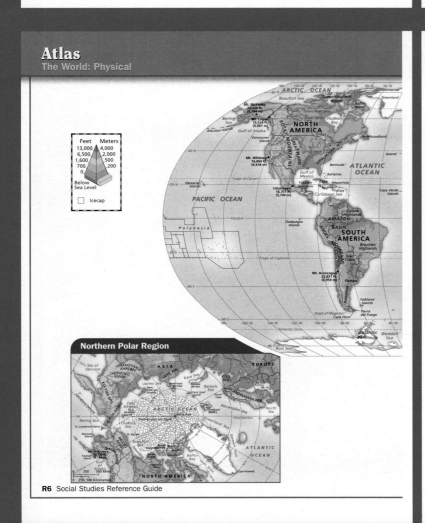

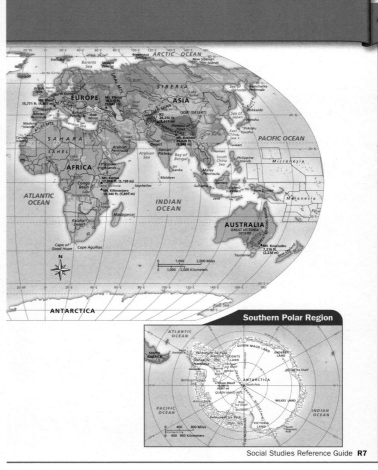

Atlas
The Americas: Political

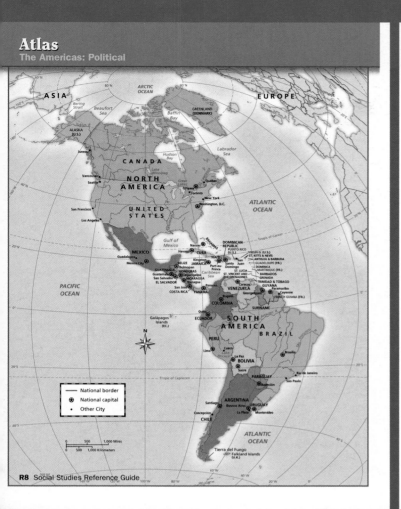

The Americas: Physical

Atlas
Asia and the Pacific Islands: Political

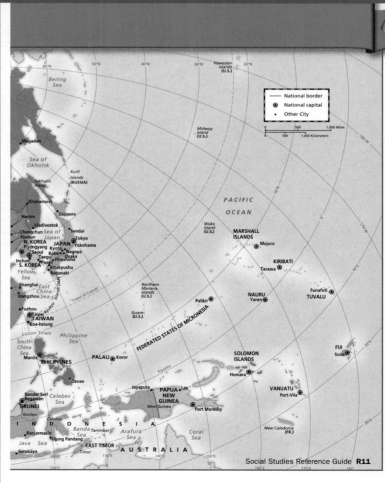

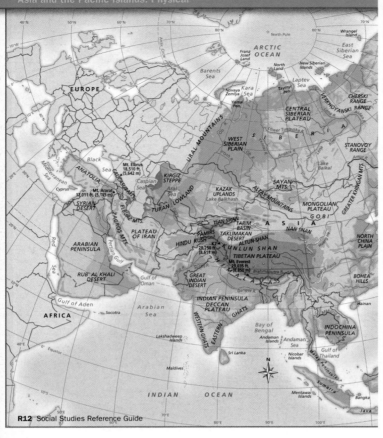

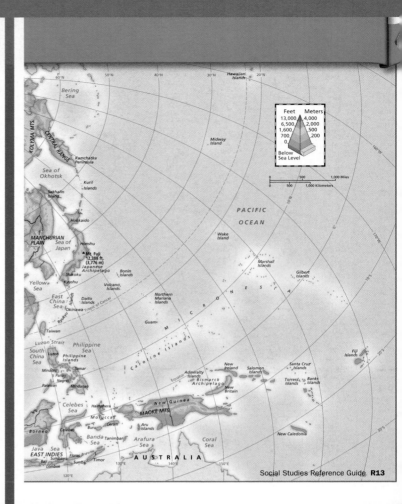

National border
⊛ National capital
• Other City

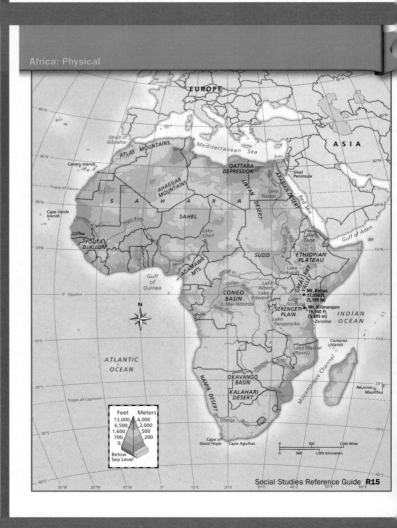

Atlas
Europe: Political

Europe: Physical

Atlas
Australia and New Zealand: Political and Physical

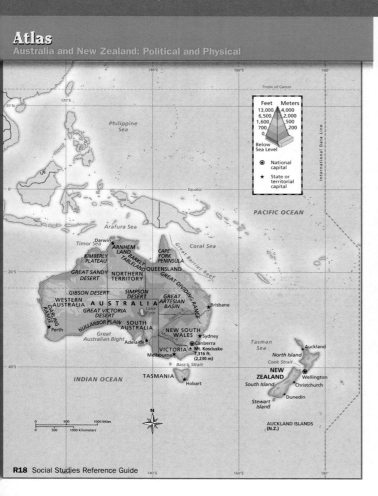

Arctic/Antarctica

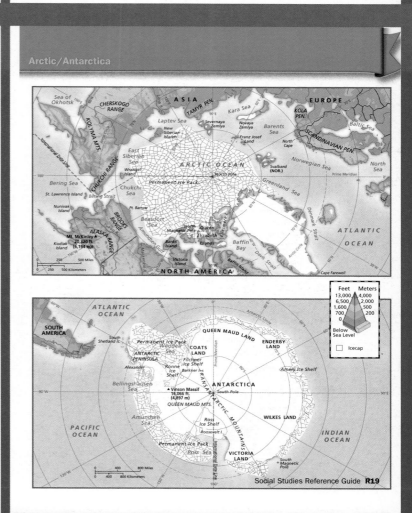

Geography Terms

archipelago group or chain of islands

basin bowl-shaped area of land surrounded by higher land

bay narrower part of an ocean or lake that cuts into land

canal narrow waterway dug across land mainly for ship travel

cataract steep, large waterfall

coast land at the edge of a large body of water such as an ocean

coastal plain area of flat land along an ocean or sea

delta triangle-shaped area of land at the mouth of a river

desert very dry, barren land without trees

dune hill of sand formed by wind

glacier giant sheet of ice that moves very slowly across land

gulf large body of water with land around part of it

island land with water all around it

isthmus narrow strip of land connecting two larger land areas

lake large body of water with land all or nearly all around it

mountain a very high hill

mountain range long row of mountains

mouth place where a river empties into another body of water

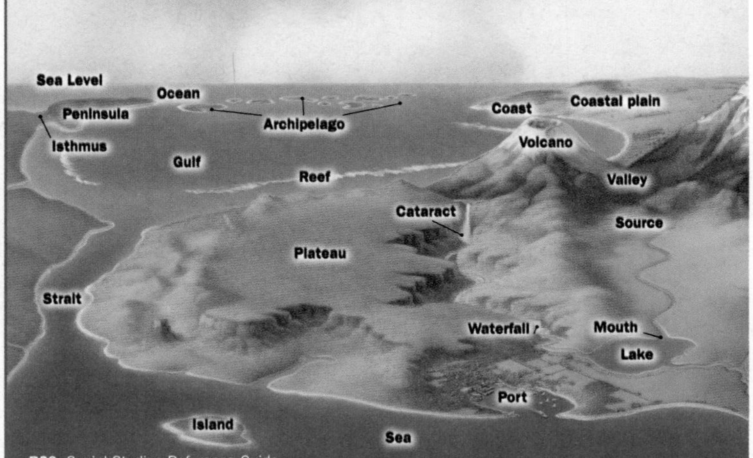

oasis fertile spot in a desert, with water and green vegetation

ocean any of the four largest bodies of water on Earth

peak pointed top of a mountain

peninsula land with water on three sides

plain very large area of flat land

plateau high, wide area of flat land, with steep sides

port place, usually in a harbor, where ships safely load and unload goods and people

reef off-shore ridge, often of limestone, along a coastline, at or near the surface of a sea or ocean

riverbank land at a river's edge

sea large body of water somewhat smaller than an ocean

sea level an ocean's surface, compared to which land can be measured either above or below

source place where a river begins

steppe wide, treeless plain

strait narrow channel of water joining two larger bodies of water

tributary stream or river that runs into a larger river

valley low land between mountains or hills

volcano mountain with an opening at the top formed by violent bursts of steam and hot rock

waterfall steep falling of water from a higher to a lower place

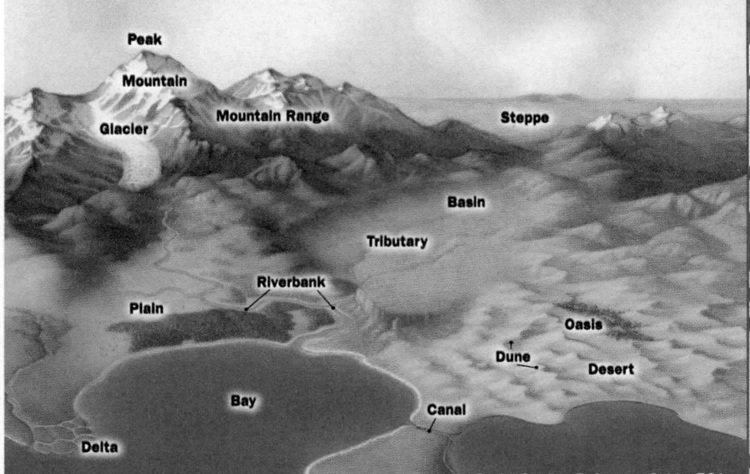

Countries of the World

Afghanistan
Capital: Kabul
Population: 26,813,057
Area: 250,010 sq mi; 647,500 sq km
Leading Exports: fruits and nuts, handwoven carpets, and wool
Location: Asia

Albania
Capital: Tirana
Population: 3,490,435
Area: 11,101 sq mi; 28,750 sq km
Leading Exports: metals and metallic ores, textiles
Location: Europe

Algeria
Capital: Algiers
Population: 31,193,917
Area: 919,626 sq mi; 2,381,740 sq km
Leading Exports: petroleum and natural gas
Location: Africa

Andorra
Capital: Andorra la Vella
Population: 67,627
Area: 181 sq mi; 468 sq km
Leading Exports: tobacco products and furniture
Location: Europe

Angola
Capital: Luanda
Population: 10,366,031
Area: 481,370 sq mi; 1,246,700 sq km
Leading Exports: oil, petroleum products, and diamonds
Location: Africa

Anguilla
Capital: The Valley
Population: 12,132
Area: 35 sq mi; 91 sq km
Leading Exports: lobster and salt
Location: North America (Caribbean Sea)

Antigua and Barbuda
Capital: Saint John's
Population: 66,970
Area: 170 sq mi; 442 sq km
Leading Exports: petroleum products and manufactured goods
Location: North America (Caribbean Sea)

Argentina
Capital: Buenos Aires
Population: 37,384,816
Area: 1,068,339 sq mi; 2,766,890 sq km
Leading Exports: wheat, corn, oilseed, and manufactured goods
Location: South America

Armenia
Capital: Yerevan
Population: 3,336,100
Area: 11,506 sq mi; 29,800 sq km
Leading Exports: diamonds, scrap metal, and copper
Location: Asia

Australia
Capital: Canberra
Population: 19,357,594
Area: 2,968,010 sq mi; 7,686,850 sq km
Leading Exports: coal, gold, wheat, wool, and iron ore
Location: Australia

Austria
Capital: Vienna
Population: 8,150,835
Area: 32,376 sq mi; 83,858 sq km
Leading Exports: machinery and equipment, iron, and steel
Location: Europe

Azerbaijan
Capital: Baku
Population: 7,771,092
Area: 33,438 sq mi; 86,600 sq km
Leading Exports: oil, gas, machinery, and cotton
Location: Asia

The Bahamas
Capital: Nassau
Population: 297, 852
Area: 5,382 sq mi; 13,940 sq km
Leading Exports: pharmaceuticals, rum, and seafood
Location: North America (Caribbean Sea)

Bahrain
Capital: Manama
Population: 645,361
Area: 239 sq mi; 620 sq km
Leading Exports: petroleum and petroleum products
Location: Asia

Bangladesh
Capital: Dhaka
Population: 131,269,860
Area: 55,600 sq mi; 144,000 sq km
Leading Exports: garments, jute and jute goods, and leather
Location: Asia

Barbados
Capital: Bridgetown
Population: 275,330
Area: 166 sq mi; 430 sq km
Leading Exports: sugar, molasses, rum, and clothing
Location: North America (Caribbean Sea)

Belarus
Capital: Minsk
Population: 10,350,194
Area: 79,926 sq mi; 207,600 sq km
Leading Exports: machinery and equipment, chemicals
Location: Europe

Belgium
Capital: Brussels
Population: 10,258,762
Area: 11,780 sq mi; 30,510 sq km
Leading Exports: iron, steel, machinery, and chemicals
Location: Europe

Belize
Capital: Belmopan
Population: 256,052
Area: 8,865 sq mi; 22,960 sq km
Leading Exports: sugar, citrus fruits, bananas, and clothing
Location: North America

Benin
Capital: Porto-Novo
Population: 6,590,782
Area: 43,484 sq mi; 112,620 sq km
Leading Exports: cotton, oil, and palm products
Location: Africa

Bermuda
Capital: Hamilton
Population: 63,503
Area: 23 sq mi; 59 sq km
Leading Exports: re-export of pharmaceuticals
Location: North America (Atlantic Ocean)

Bhutan
Capital: Thimphu
Population: 2,049,412
Area: 18,147 sq mi; 47,000 sq km
Leading Exports: cardamom, gypsum, timber, and handicrafts
Location: Asia

Bolivia
Capital: La Paz and Sucre
Population: 8,300,463
Area: 424,179 sq mi; 1,098,580 sq km
Leading Exports: metals, natural gas, soybeans, gold, and wood
Location: South America

Bosnia and Herzegovina
Capital: Sarajevo
Population: 3,922,205
Area: 19,782 sq mi; 51,233 sq km
Leading Exports: none
Location: Europe

Botswana
Capital: Gaborone
Population: 1,586,119
Area: 231,812 sq mi; 600,370 sq km
Leading Exports: diamonds, copper, and nickel
Location: Africa

Brazil
Capital: Brasilia
Population: 174,486,575
Area: 3,286,600 sq mi; 8,511,965 sq km
Leading Exports: iron ore, soybeans, citrus, and coffee
Location: South America

Brunei
Capital: Bandar Seri Begawan
Population: 336,376
Area: 2,228 sq mi; 5,770 sq km
Leading Exports: oil and natural gas
Location: Asia

Bulgaria
Capital: Sofia
Population: 7,707,495
Area: 42,824 sq mi; 110,910 sq km
Leading Exports: machinery and agricultural products
Location: Europe

Burkina Faso
Capital: Ouagadougou
Population: 12,272,289
Area: 105,873 sq mi; 274,200 sq km
Leading Exports: cotton, gold, and animal products
Location: Africa

Burundi
Capital: Bujumbura
Population: 6,223,897
Area: 10,746 sq mi; 27,830 sq km
Leading Exports: coffee, tea, and cotton
Location: Africa

Cambodia
Capital: Phnom Penh
Population: 12,491,501
Area: 69,902 sq mi; 181,040 sq km
Leading Exports: timber, rubber, and rice
Location: Asia

Cameroon
Capital: Yaounde
Population: 15,803,200
Area: 183,574 sq mi; 475,440 sq km
Leading Exports: petroleum products, coffee, and cotton
Location: Africa

Canada
Capital: Ottawa
Population: 31,592,805
Area: 3,851,940 sq mi; 9,976,140 sq km
Leading Exports: wood pulp, timber, petroleum, and machinery
Location: North America

Cape Verde
Capital: Praia
Population: 405,163
Area: 1,556 sq mi; 4,030 sq km
Leading Exports: fish, bananas, and hides
Location: Africa (Atlantic Ocean)

Central African Republic
Capital: Bangui
Population: 3,576,884
Area: 240,542 sq mi; 622,980 sq km
Leading Exports: diamonds, timber, cotton, coffee, and tobacco
Location: Africa

Chad
Capital: N'Djamena
Population: 8,707,078
Area: 495,772 sq mi; 1,284,000 sq km
Leading Exports: cotton, cattle, textiles, and fish
Location: Africa

Chile
Capital: Santiago
Population: 15,328,467
Area: 292,269 sq mi; 756,950 sq km
Leading Exports: copper, fish, and chemicals
Location: South America

China
Capital: Beijing
Population: 1,273,111,290
Area: 3,705,533 sq mi; 9,596,960 sq km
Leading Exports: textiles, garments, and machinery
Location: Asia

Colombia
Capital: Bogota
Population: 40,349,388
Area: 439,751 sq mi; 1,138,910 sq km
Leading Exports: petroleum, coffee, coal, and bananas
Location: South America

Comoros
Capital: Moroni
Population: 596,202
Area: 838 sq mi; 2,170 sq km
Leading Exports: vanilla, cloves, and perfume oil
Location: Africa (Indian Ocean)

Congo, Democratic Republic of the
Capital: Kinshasa
Population: 53,624,718
Area: 905,599 sq mi; 2,345,410 sq km
Leading Exports: copper, coffee, diamonds, cobalt, and oil
Location: Africa

Congo, Republic of the
Capital: Brazzaville
Population: 2,894,336
Area: 132,051 sq mi; 342,000 sq km
Leading Exports: oil, lumber, sugar, and cocoa
Location: Africa

Costa Rica
Capital: San José
Population: 3,773,057
Area: 19,730 sq mi; 51,100 sq km
Leading Exports: coffee, bananas, textiles, and sugar
Location: North America

Côte d'Ivoire
Capital: Yamoussoukro
Population: 16,393,221
Area: 124,507 sq mi; 322,460 sq km
Leading Exports: cocoa, coffee, wood, and petroleum
Location: Africa

Croatia
Capital: Zagreb
Population: 4,334,142
Area: 21,830 sq mi; 56,538 sq km
Leading Exports: textiles and transportation equipment
Location: Europe

Cuba
Capital: Havana
Population: 11,184,023
Area: 42,805 sq mi; 110,860 sq km
Leading Exports: sugar, tobacco, and nickel
Location: North America (Caribbean Sea)

Cyprus
Capital: Nicosia
Population: 762,887
Area: 3,572 sq mi; 9,250 sq km
Leading Exports: citrus, potatoes, grapes, wine, and clothing
Location: Europe (Mediterranean Sea)

Czech Republic
Capital: Prague
Population: 10,264,212
Area: 30,388 sq mi; 78,703 sq km
Leading Exports: machinery and manufactured goods
Location: Europe

Denmark
Capital: Copenhagen
Population: 5,352,815
Area: 16,630 sq mi; 43,094 sq km
Leading Exports: meat products, dairy products, and furniture
Location: Europe

Djibouti
Capital: Djibouti
Population: 460,700
Area: 8,495 sq mi; 22,000 sq km
Leading Exports: hides and coffee
Location: Africa

Dominica
Capital: Roseau
Population: 70,786
Area: 290 sq mi; 750 sq km
Leading Exports: bananas, soap, bay oil, vegetables, and citrus
Location: Caribbean Sea

Dominican Republic
Capital: Santo Domingo
Population: 8,581,477
Area: 18,815 sq mi; 48,730 sq km
Leading Exports: iron, nickel, sugar, gold, coffee, and cocoa
Location: North America (Caribbean Sea)

Ecuador
Capital: Quito
Population: 13,183,978
Area: 109,487 sq mi; 283,560 sq km
Leading Exports: petroleum, bananas, shrimp, cocoa
Location: South America

Egypt
Capital: Cairo
Population: 69,536,644
Area: 386,675 sq mi; 1,001,450 sq km
Leading Exports: oil and petroleum products, cotton, and textiles
Location: Africa

El Salvador
Capital: San Salvador
Population: 6,237,662
Area: 8,124 sq mi; 21,040 sq km
Leading Exports: coffee, sugar cane, and shrimp
Location: North America

Equatorial Guinea
Capital: Malabo
Population: 486,060
Area: 10,831 sq mi; 28,050 sq km
Leading Exports: coffee, oil, and cocoa
Location: Africa

Eritrea
Capital: Asmara
Population: 4,298,269
Area: 46,844 sq mi; 121,320 sq km
Leading Exports: livestock, sorghum, and textiles
Location: Africa

Estonia
Capital: Tallinn
Population: 1,431,471
Area: 17,414 sq mi; 45,226 sq km
Leading Exports: textiles, food products, and machinery and equipment
Location: Europe

Ethiopia
Capital: Addis Ababa
Population: 65,891,874
Area: 435,201 sq mi; 1,127,127 sq km
Leading Exports: coffee, leather products, and gold
Location: Africa

Countries of the World

Fiji
Capital: Suva
Population: 844,330
Area: 7,054 sq mi; 18,270 sq km
Leading Exports: sugar, gold, processed fish, and lumber
Location: Oceania

Finland
Capital: Helsinki
Population: 5,175,783
Area: 130,132 sq mi; 337,030 sq km
Leading Exports: paper and pulp, machinery, and chemicals
Location: Europe

France
Capital: Paris
Population: 59,551,227
Area: 211,217 sq mi; 547,030 sq km
Leading Exports: machinery and transportation equipment
Location: Europe

Gabon
Capital: Libreville
Population: 1,221,175
Area: 103,351 sq mi; 267,670 sq km
Leading Exports: oil, timber, manganese, and uranium
Location: Africa

The Gambia
Capital: Banjul
Population: 1,411,205
Area: 4,363 sq mi; 11,300 sq km
Leading Exports: peanuts, peanut products, and fish
Location: Africa

Georgia
Capital: T'bilisi
Population: 4,989,285
Area: 26,912 sq mi; 69,700 sq km
Leading Exports: citrus, tea, and wine
Location: Asia

Germany
Capital: Berlin
Population: 83,029,536
Area: 137,808 sq mi; 356,910 sq km
Leading Exports: vehicles, machines, machine tools, and chemicals
Location: Europe

Ghana
Capital: Accra
Population: 19,894,014
Area: 92,104 sq mi; 238,540 sq km
Leading Exports: cocoa, gold, timber, and bauxite
Location: Africa

Greece
Capital: Athens
Population: 10,623,835
Area: 50,944 sq mi; 131,940 sq km
Leading Exports: manufactured goods, foodstuffs, and wine
Location: Europe

Grenada
Capital: Saint George's
Population: 89,227
Area: 131 sq mi; 340 sq km
Leading Exports: bananas, cocoa, nutmeg, fruits, and vegetables
Location: North America (Caribbean Sea)

Guatemala
Capital: Guatemala City
Population: 12,974,361
Area: 42,044 sq mi; 108,890 sq km
Leading Exports: coffee, sugar, bananas, and cardamom
Location: North America

Guinea
Capital: Conakry
Population: 7,613,870
Area: 94,930 sq mi; 245,860 sq km
Leading Exports: bauxite, alumina, diamonds, gold, and coffee
Location: Africa

Guinea Bissau
Capital: Bissau
Population: 1,315,822
Area: 13,946 sq mi; 36,210 sq km
Leading Exports: cashews, peanuts, shrimp, fish, and palm kernels
Location: Africa

Guyana
Capital: Georgetown
Population: 697,181
Area: 83,033 sq mi; 214,970 sq km
Leading Exports: sugar, gold, bauxite, rice, and shrimp
Location: South America

Haiti
Capital: Port-au-Prince
Population: 6,964,549
Area: 10,700 sq mi; 27,712 sq km
Leading Exports: light manufactured products, coffee, and mangoes
Location: Caribbean Sea

Holy See (Vatican City)
Capital: Vatican City
Population: 890
Area: 0.17 sq mi; 0.44 sq km
Leading Exports: none
Location: Europe

Honduras
Capital: Tegucigalpa
Population: 6,406,052
Area: 43,280 sq mi; 112,090 sq km
Leading Exports: bananas, coffee, shrimp, and zinc
Location: North America

Hungary
Capital: Budapest
Population: 10,106,017
Area: 35,920 sq mi; 93,030 sq km
Leading Exports: machinery, equipment, and manufactured goods
Location: Europe

Iceland
Capital: Reykjavik
Population: 277,906
Area: 39,770 sq mi; 103,000 sq km
Leading Exports: fish and fish products
Location: Europe

India
Capital: New Delhi
Population: 1,029,991,145
Area: 1,269,389 sq mi; 3,287,590 sq km
Leading Exports: clothing, chemicals, gems, and jewelry
Location: Asia

Indonesia
Capital: Jakarta
Population: 228,437,870
Area: 636,000 sq mi; 1,919,440 sq km
Leading Exports: oil and gas, textiles, rubber, and plywood
Location: Asia

Iran
Capital: Tehran
Population: 66,128,965
Area: 634,562 sq mi; 1,643,452 sq km
Leading Exports: petroleum, carpets, and fruit and nuts
Location: Asia

Iraq
Capital: Baghdad
Population: 23,331,985
Area: 168,760 sq mi; 437,072 sq km
Leading Exports: oil
Location: Asia

Ireland
Capital: Dublin
Population: 3,840,838
Area: 27,136 sq mi; 70,280 sq km
Leading Exports: machinery, chemicals, and electronics
Location: Europe

Israel
Capital: Jerusalem
Population: 5,938,093
Area: 8,019 sq mi; 20,770 sq km
Leading Exports: machinery, electronics, and cut diamonds
Location: Asia

Italy
Capital: Rome
Population: 57,679,825
Area: 116,310 sq mi; 301,230 sq km
Leading Exports: metals, motor vehicles, textiles, and clothing
Location: Europe

Jamaica
Capital: Kingston
Population: 2,665,636
Area: 4,243 sq mi; 10,990 sq km
Leading Exports: bauxite, sugar, bananas, and rum
Location: Caribbean Sea

Japan
Capital: Tokyo
Population: 126,771,662
Area: 145,888 sq mi; 377,835 sq km
Leading Exports: machinery, motor vehicles, and electronics
Location: Asia

Jordan
Capital: Amman
Population: 5,153,378
Area: 35,637 sq mi; 92,300 sq km
Leading Exports: phosphates, fertilizers, and potash
Location: Asia

Kazakhstan
Capital: Astana
Population: 16,731,303
Area: 1,049,191 sq mi; 2,717,300 sq km
Leading Exports: oil, ferrous and nonferrous metals
Location: Asia

Kenya
Capital: Nairobi
Population: 30,765,916
Area: 224,970 sq mi; 582,650 sq km
Leading Exports: tea, coffee, petroleum products, and cement
Location: Africa

Kiribati
Capital: Tarawa
Population: 91,149
Area: 277 sq mi; 717 sq km
Leading Exports: copra and fish products
Location: Oceania

Korea, North
Capital: P'yongyang
Population: 21,968,228
Area: 46,542 sq mi; 120,540 sq km
Leading Exports: minerals and metallurgical products
Location: Asia

Korea, South
Capital: Seoul
Population: 47,904,370
Area: 38,025 sq mi; 98,480 sq km
Leading Exports: electronics, electrical equipment, and motor vehicles
Location: Asia

Kuwait
Capital: Kuwait
Population: 2,041,961
Area: 6,881 sq mi; 17,820 sq km
Leading Exports: oil
Location: Asia

Kyrgyzstan
Capital: Bishkek
Population: 4,753,003
Area: 76,644 sq mi; 198,500 sq km
Leading Exports: wool, meat, cotton, metal, and shoes
Location: Asia

Laos
Capital: Vientiane
Population: 5,497,459
Area: 91,432 sq mi; 236,800 sq km
Leading Exports: wood products, coffee, and tin
Location: Asia

Latvia
Capital: Riga
Population: 2,385,231
Area: 24,750 sq mi; 64,100 sq km
Leading Exports: timber and ferrous metals
Location: Europe

Lebanon
Capital: Beirut
Population: 3,627,774
Area: 4,016 sq mi; 10,400 sq km
Leading Exports: agricultural products, chemicals, and textiles
Location: Asia

Lesotho
Capital: Maseru
Population: 2,177,062
Area: 11,719 sq mi; 30,350 sq km
Leading Exports: wool, mohair, wheat, cattle, and peas
Location: Africa

Liberia
Capital: Monrovia
Population: 3,225,837
Area: 43,002 sq mi; 111,370 sq km
Leading Exports: iron ore, rubber, coffee, and diamonds
Location: Africa

Libya
Capital: Tripoli
Population: 5,240,599
Area: 679,385 sq mi; 1,759,540 sq km
Leading Exports: oil, refined petroleum products, and food products
Location: Africa

Liechtenstein
Capital: Vaduz
Population: 32,204
Area: 62 sq mi; 160 sq km
Leading Exports: specialty machinery and dental products
Location: Europe

Lithuania
Capital: Vilnius
Population: 3,610,535
Area: 25,175 sq mi; 65,200 sq km
Leading Exports: machinery, mineral products, and foodstuffs
Location: Europe

Luxembourg
Capital: Luxembourg
Population: 442,972
Area: 998 sq mi; 2,586 sq km
Leading Exports: finished steel products and chemicals
Location: Europe

Macedonia
Capital: Skopje
Population: 2,046,209
Area: 9,781 sq mi; 25,333 sq km
Leading Exports: manufactured goods
Location: Europe

Madagascar
Capital: Antananarivo
Population: 15,982,563
Area: 226,665 sq mi; 587,040 sq km
Leading Exports: coffee, vanilla, cloves, shellfish, and sugar
Location: Africa

Malawi
Capital: Lilongwe
Population: 10,548,250
Area: 45,747 sq mi; 118,480 sq km
Leading Exports: tobacco, tea, and sugar
Location: Africa

Malaysia
Capital: Kuala Lumpur
Population: 22,229,040
Area: 127,322 sq mi; 329,750 sq km
Leading Exports: electronic equipment, petroleum, rubber, and palm oil
Location: Asia

Maldives
Capital: Male
Population: 301,475
Area: 116 sq mi; 300 sq km
Leading Exports: fish and clothing
Location: Asia (Indian Ocean)

Mali
Capital: Bamako
Population: 11,008,518
Area: 478,783 sq mi; 1,240,000 sq km
Leading Exports: cotton, livestock, gold, peanuts, and fish
Location: Africa

Malta
Capital: Valletta
Population: 394,583
Area: 122 sq mi; 316 sq km
Leading Exports: machinery and transportation equipment
Location: Europe (Mediterranean Sea)

Marshall Islands
Capital: Majuro
Population: 70,822
Area: 70 sq mi; 181 sq km
Leading Exports: coconut oil, fish, trochus shells
Location: Oceania

Mauritania
Capital: Nouakchott
Population: 2,667,859
Area: 397,969 sq mi; 1,030,700 sq km
Leading Exports: iron ore, fish, fish products, and livestock
Location: Africa

Mauritius
Capital: Port Louis
Population: 1,189,825
Area: 718 sq mi; 1,860 sq km
Leading Exports: textiles, sugar, and clothing
Location: Africa (Indian Ocean)

Mexico
Capital: Mexico City
Population: 101,879,171
Area: 761,632 sq mi; 1,972,550 sq km
Leading Exports: oil, petroleum products, coffee, and silver
Location: North America

Micronesia, Federated States of
Capital: Palikir
Population: 134,597
Area: 271 sq mi; 702 sq km
Leading Exports: fish, bananas, and black pepper
Location: Oceania

Moldova
Capital: Chisinau
Population: 4,430,654
Area: 13,012 sq mi; 33,700 sq km
Leading Exports: foodstuffs, wine, tobacco, fur, and leather
Location: Europe

Monaco
Capital: Monaco
Population: 31,693
Area: 0.77 sq mi; 2 sq km
Leading Exports: none
Location: Europe

Mongolia
Capital: Ulaanbaatar
Population: 2,654,999
Area: 604,270 sq mi; 1,565,000 sq km
Leading Exports: copper, livestock, animal products, and cashmere
Location: Asia

Montenegro
(*See* Serbia and Montenegro)

Countries of the World

Morocco
Capital: Rabat
Population: 30,645,305
Area: 172,420 sq mi; 446,550 sq km
Leading Exports: food, beverages, and phosphates
Location: Africa

Mozambique
Capital: Maputo
Population: 19,371,057
Area: 309,506 sq mi; 801,590 sq km
Leading Exports: shrimp, cashews, cotton, and sugar
Location: Africa

Myanmar (Burma)
Capital: Yangon (Rangoon)
Population: 41,994,678
Area: 261,979 sq mi; 678,500 sq km
Leading Exports: textiles, clothing, teak, rice, and hardwood
Location: Asia

Namibia
Capital: Windhoek
Population: 1,797,677
Area: 318,707 sq mi; 825,418 sq km
Leading Exports: diamonds, copper, gold, zinc, and lead
Location: Africa

Nauru
Capital: no official capital
Population: 11,845
Area: 8 sq mi; 21 sq km
Leading Exports: phosphates
Location: Oceania

Nepal
Capital: Katmandu
Population: 25,284,463
Area: 54,365 sq mi; 140,800 sq km
Leading Exports: carpets, clothing, rice, wheat, and leather goods
Location: Asia

Netherlands
Capital: Amsterdam
Population: 15,981,472
Area: 16,033 sq mi; 41,523 sq km
Leading Exports: machinery and equipment, flowers, and chemicals
Location: Europe

New Zealand
Capital: Wellington
Population: 3,864,129
Area: 103,741 sq mi; 268,680 sq km
Leading Exports: wool, beef, fish, and foodstuffs
Location: Oceania

Nicaragua
Capital: Managua
Population: 4,812,569
Area: 50,000 sq mi; 129,494 sq km
Leading Exports: coffee, cotton, rice, sugar, seafood, and gold
Location: Central America

Niger
Capital: Niamey
Population: 10,355,156
Area: 489,208 sq mi; 1,267,000 sq km
Leading Exports: uranium ore and animal products
Location: Africa

Nigeria
Capital: Abuja
Population: 126,635,626
Area: 356,682 sq mi; 923,770 sq km
Leading Exports: oil, cocoa, timber, and rubber
Location: Africa

Norway
Capital: Oslo
Population: 4,503,440
Area: 125,186 sq mi; 324,220 sq km
Leading Exports: pulp and paper products, petroleum products, and natural gas
Location: Europe

Oman
Capital: Muscat
Population: 2,622,198
Area: 82,034 sq mi; 212,460 sq km
Leading Exports: petroleum and food
Location: Asia

Pakistan
Capital: Islamabad
Population: 144,616,639
Area: 310,414 sq mi; 803,940 sq km
Leading Exports: cotton, textiles, clothing, and rice
Location: Asia

Palau
Capital: Koror
Population: 18,766
Area: 177 sq mi; 458 sq km
Leading Exports: trochus, tuna, copra, and handicrafts
Location: Oceania

Panama
Capital: Panama City
Population: 2,845,647
Area: 30,194 sq mi; 78,200 sq km
Leading Exports: bananas, shrimp, sugar, coffee, and clothing
Location: North America

Papua New Guinea
Capital: Port Moresby
Population: 5,049,055
Area: 178,266 sq mi; 461,690 sq km
Leading Exports: gold, copper ore, oil, and wood products
Location: Oceania

Paraguay
Capital: Asuncion
Population: 5,734,139
Area: 157,052 sq mi; 406,750 sq km
Leading Exports: soybeans, feed, cotton, and beef
Location: South America

Peru
Capital: Lima
Population: 27,483,864
Area: 496,243 sq mi; 1,285,220 sq km
Leading Exports: copper, zinc, and fish products
Location: South America

Philippines
Capital: Manila
Population: 82,841,518
Area: 115,834 sq mi; 300,000 sq km
Leading Exports: electronics, textiles, and food products
Location: Asia

Poland
Capital: Warsaw
Population: 38,633,912
Area: 120,731 sq mi; 312,680 sq km
Leading Exports: machinery, transportation equipment, manufactured goods, and coal
Location: Europe

Portugal
Capital: Lisbon
Population: 10,066,253
Area: 35,553 sq mi; 92,080 sq km
Leading Exports: clothing, machinery, cork, and paper
Location: Europe

Qatar
Capital: Doha
Population: 769,152
Area: 4,416 sq mi; 11,437 sq km
Leading Exports: petroleum products
Location: Asia

Romania
Capital: Bucharest
Population: 22,364,022
Area: 91,702 sq mi; 237,500 sq km
Leading Exports: metals, metal products, and mineral products
Location: Europe

Russia
Capital: Moscow
Population: 145,470,197
Area: 6,592,734 sq mi; 17,075,200 sq km
Leading Exports: petroleum, petroleum products, wood products, and metals
Location: Europe and Asia

Rwanda
Capital: Kigali
Population: 7,312,756
Area: 10,170 sq mi; 26,340 sq km
Leading Exports: coffee, tea, hides, and tin ore
Location: Africa

Saint Kitts and Nevis
Capital: Basseterre
Population: 38,819
Area: 104 sq mi; 261 sq km
Leading Exports: machinery, food, electronics, and beverages
Location: North America (Caribbean Sea)

Saint Lucia
Capital: Castries
Population: 156,260
Area: 239 sq mi; 620 sq km
Leading Exports: bananas, clothing, cocoa, and vegetables
Location: North America (Caribbean Sea)

Saint Vincent and the Grenadines
Capital: Kingstown
Population: 115,461
Area: 150 sq mi; 389 sq km
Leading Exports: bananas and taro
Location: North America (Caribbean Sea)

Samoa
Capital: Apia
Population: 179,466
Area: 1,104 sq mi; 2,860 sq km
Leading Exports: coconut products and fish
Location: Oceania

San Marino
Capital: San Marino
Population: 26,937
Area: 23 sq mi; 60 sq km
Leading Exports: stone, lime, wood, and chestnuts
Location: Europe

São Tomé and Príncipe
Capital: Sao Tome
Population: 165,034
Area: 386 sq mi; 1,001 km
Leading Exports: cocoa, coffee, and palm oil
Location: Africa

Saudi Arabia
Capital: Riyadh
Population: 22,757,092
Area: 757,011 sq mi; 1,960,582 sq km
Leading Exports: petroleum and petroleum products
Location: Asia

Senegal
Capital: Dakar
Population: 10,284,929
Area: 75,752 sq mi; 196,190 sq km
Leading Exports: fish, peanuts, and phosphates
Location: Africa

Serbia and Montenegro (Yugoslavia)
Capital: Belgrade
Population: 11,101,833
Area: 39,436 sq mi; 102,350 sq km
Leading Exports: manufactured goods, food, and raw materials
Location: Europe

Seychelles
Capital: Victoria
Population: 79,326
Area: 176 sq mi; 455 sq km
Leading Exports: fish, cinnamon bark, and copra
Location: Africa (Indian Ocean)

Sierra Leone
Capital: Freetown
Population: 5,426,618
Area: 27,700 sq mi; 71,740 sq km
Leading Exports: diamonds, coffee, and cocoa
Location: Africa

Singapore
Capital: Singapore
Population: 4,300,419
Area: 250 sq mi; 647 sq km
Leading Exports: electronics and refined petroleum products
Location: Asia

Slovakia
Capital: Bratislava
Population: 5,414,937
Area: 18,860 sq mi; 48,845 sq km
Leading Exports: machinery and transportation equipment
Location: Europe

Slovenia
Capital: Ljubljana
Population: 1,930,132
Area: 7,837 sq mi; 20,296 sq km
Leading Exports: metals and transportation equipment
Location: Europe

Solomon Islands
Capital: Honiara
Population: 480,442
Area: 10,985 sq mi; 28,450 sq km
Leading Exports: fish, timber, and cocoa
Location: Oceania

Somalia
Capital: Mogadishu
Population: 7,253,137
Area: 246,210 sq mi; 637,660 sq km
Leading Exports: bananas, animals, fish, and hides
Location: Africa

South Africa
Capital: Pretoria (administrative), Cape Town (legislative), Bloemfontein (judicial)
Population: 43,586,097
Area: 471,027 sq mi; 1,219,912 sq km
Leading Exports: gold, minerals, metals, and diamonds
Location: Africa

Spain
Capital: Madrid
Population: 40,037,995
Area: 194,892 sq mi; 504,750 sq km
Leading Exports: motor vehicles, textiles, olives and olive oil, and manufactured goods
Location: Europe

Sri Lanka
Capital: Colombo
Population: 19,408,635
Area: 25,333 sq mi; 65,610 sq km
Leading Exports: textiles, garments, tea, and diamonds
Location: Asia (Indian Ocean)

Sudan
Capital: Khartoum
Population: 35,080,373
Area: 967,532 sq mi; 2,505,810 sq km
Leading Exports: gum arabic, cotton, and peanuts
Location: Africa

Suriname
Capital: Paramaribo
Population: 433,998
Area: 63,041 sq mi; 163,270 sq km
Leading Exports: aluminum, shrimp, and fish
Location: South America

Swaziland
Capital: Mbabane (administrative) Lobamba (royal and legislative)
Population: 1,104,343
Area: 6,641 sq mi; 17,360 sq km
Leading Exports: beverage concentrates, sugar, and fruit
Location: Africa

Sweden
Capital: Stockholm
Population: 8,873,052
Area: 173,738 sq mi; 449,964 sq km
Leading Exports: machinery, motor vehicles, and paper products
Location: Europe

Switzerland
Capital: Bern
Population: 7,283,274
Area: 15,943 sq mi; 41,290 sq km
Leading Exports: machinery, machine equipment, and food products
Location: Europe

Syria
Capital: Damascus
Population: 16,728,808
Area: 71,501 sq mi; 185,180 sq km
Leading Exports: petroleum, textiles, cotton, and fruit
Location: Asia

Taiwan
Capital: Taipei
Population: 22,370,461
Area: 13,892 sq mi; 35,980 sq km
Leading Exports: electrical machinery, electronics, and textiles
Location: Asia

Tajikistan
Capital: Dushanbe
Population: 6,578,681
Area: 55,253 sq mi; 143,100 sq km
Leading Exports: cotton, aluminum, fruit, and vegetable oil
Location: Asia

Tanzania
Capital: Dodoma (legislative), Dar es Salaam (executive)
Population: 36,232,074
Area: 364,914 sq mi; 945,090 sq km
Leading Exports: coffee, cotton, tobacco, tea, and cloves
Location: Africa

Thailand
Capital: Bangkok
Population: 61,797,751
Area: 198,463 sq mi; 511,770 sq km
Leading Exports: machinery, rice, rubber, and garments
Location: Asia

Togo
Capital: Lome
Population: 5,153,088
Area: 21,927 sq mi; 56,790 sq km
Leading Exports: phosphates, cotton, cocoa, and coffee
Location: Africa

Tonga
Capital: Nuku'alofa
Population: 104,227
Area: 289 sq mi; 748 sq km
Leading Exports: squash, fish, and vanilla
Location: Oceania

Trinidad and Tobago
Capital: Port-of-Spain
Population: 1,169,682
Area: 1,981 sq mi; 5,130 sq km
Leading Exports: petroleum and petroleum products
Location: North America (Caribbean Sea)

Tunisia
Capital: Tunis
Population: 9,705,102
Area: 63,172 sq mi; 163,610 sq km
Leading Exports: phosphates, chemicals, and agricultural products
Location: Africa

Countries of the World

Turkey
Capital: Ankara
Population: 66,493,970
Area: 301,394 sq mi; 780,580 sq km
Leading Exports: manufactured products, cotton, textiles, and foodstuffs
Location: Europe and Asia

Turkmenistan
Capital: Ashgabat
Population: 4,603,244
Area: 188,463 sq mi; 488,100 sq km
Leading Exports: natural gas, cotton, and oil
Location: Asia

Tuvalu
Capital: Funafuti
Population: 10,838
Area: 10 sq mi; 26 sq km
Leading Exports: copra
Location: Oceania

Uganda
Capital: Kampala
Population: 23,985,712
Area: 91,139 sq mi; 236,040 sq km
Leading Exports: coffee, cotton, and tea
Location: Africa

Ukraine
Capital: Kiev
Population: 48,760,474
Area: 233,098 sq mi; 603,700 sq km
Leading Exports: fuel and petroleum products, chemicals, and metals
Location: Europe

United Arab Emirates
Capital: Abu Dhabi
Population: 2,407,460
Area: 32,000 sq mi; 82,877 sq km
Leading Exports: oil, natural gas, and dried fish
Location: Asia

United Kingdom
Capital: London
Population: 59,647,790
Area: 94,529 sq mi; 244,820 sq km
Leading Exports: manufactured goods, machinery, fuels, and chemicals
Location: Europe

United States
Capital: Washington, D.C.
Population: 278,058,881
Area: 3,717,939 sq mi; 9,629,091 sq km
Leading Exports: capital goods, automobiles, and consumer goods
Location: North America

Uruguay
Capital: Montevideo
Population: 3,360,105
Area: 68,041 sq mi; 176,220 sq km
Leading Exports: wool, meat, rice, and leather products
Location: South America

Uzbekistan
Capital: Tashkent
Population: 25,155,064
Area: 172,748 sq mi; 447,400 sq km
Leading Exports: cotton, gold, natural gas, and minerals
Location: Asia

Vanuatu
Capital: Port-Vila
Population: 192,910
Area: 4,710 sq mi; 12,200 sq km
Leading Exports: copra, beef, cocoa, timber, and coffee
Location: Oceania

Venezuela
Capital: Caracas
Population: 23,916,810
Area: 352,156 sq mi; 912,050 sq km
Leading Exports: petroleum, bauxite, aluminum, and steel
Location: South America

Vietnam
Capital: Hanoi
Population: 79,939,014
Area: 127,248 sq mi; 329,560 sq km
Leading Exports: textiles, rice, crude oil, coffee, rubber, and sea products
Location: Asia

Yemen
Capital: Sanaa
Population: 18,078,035
Area: 203,857 sq mi; 527,970 sq km
Leading Exports: oil, cotton, coffee, fish, hides, and fruit
Location: Asia

Yugoslavia
(See Serbia and Montenegro)

Zambia
Capital: Lusaka
Population: 9,770,199
Area: 290,594 sq mi; 752,610 sq km
Leading Exports: copper, zinc, cobalt, and lead
Location: Africa

Zimbabwe
Capital: Harare
Population: 11,365,366
Area: 150,809 sq mi; 390,580 sq km
Leading Exports: agricultural and mineral products and clothing
Location: Africa

World History Time Line
Prehistory

3.5 million | 35,000 B.C. | 30,000 | 25,000 | 20,000 | 15,000 | 10,000 | 5000 | 1000 B.C.

3.5 million years ago
The first humans probably appeared

AFRICA

5500–3500 B.C.
Cave walls painted in Tassili

3000 B.C. or earlier
Farmers in Nile River Valley developed irrigation systems

5000 B.C.
Crops first cultivated in Egypt

THE AMERICAS

9500 or more B.C.
Humans probably crossed the Bering land bridge from Asia into North America

9000 B.C.
Clovis culture established in the Americas

7000 B.C.
"Cave of the Hands" painted

4000 B.C. or earlier
Corn first cultivated in Mexico

ASIA AND PACIFIC

10,000 B.C.
Herding of goats began in Persia (present day = Iran)

8000 B.C.
New Stone Age began in Southwest Asia as agriculture developed

7000 B.C. or earlier
Wheat and barley first cultivated in Southwest Asia

5000 B.C. or earlier
Farmers in Mesopotamia developed irrigation systems

6000 B.C. or earlier
Rice first cultivated in China

EUROPE

30,000 B.C.
Stone-Age people made cave paintings at Chauvet (France)

15,000 B.C.
Cave paintings made at Lascaux (France)

13,000 B.C.
Cave paintings made at Altamira (Spain)

Social Studies Reference Guide **R29**

World History Time Line
Beginning of Recorded History

3500 B.C. | 3250 B.C. | 3000 B.C. | 2750 B.C. | 2500 B.C. | 2250 B.C. | 2000 B.C.

AFRICA

3200 B.C.
Civilization arose in Nubia

3150 B.C.
King Menes united Lower and Upper Egypt

2575 B.C.
Egyptians invaded Nubia

2600 B.C.
Great Pyramid begun at Giza in Egypt

THE AMERICAS

3000 B.C.
Inuit settled in northern Canada

2500 B.C.
Period of drought ended across North America; people returned to the Great Plains and hunted buffalo

ASIA AND PACIFIC

3500 B.C.
People settled in the Indus River Valley

3500 B.C.
City-states of Mesopotamia arose

3200 B.C.
Writing invented in Sumer

2500 B.C.
Height of Harappa and Mohenjo-Daro civilizations

2334 B.C.
Sargon of Akkad united Mesopotamia into world's first empire

2000 B.C.
Xia legendary period began in China

2100 B.C.
City-state of Ur gained control of Mesopotamia

1800 B.C.
Abraham's covenant (agreement) with God marked the beginning of Judaism

EUROPE

3000 B.C.
Minoan culture arose on Crete

1750 B.C. | 1500 B.C. | 1250 B.C. | 1000 B.C. | 750 B.C. | 500 B.C. | 250 B.C. | A.D. 1

AFRICA

1570 B.C.
New Kingdom began in Egypt

814 B.C.
Traditional date of founding of Carthage by seafaring Phoenicians

750 B.C.
Nubian kings began a century of rule as pharaohs of Egypt

600 B.C.
Nubian city-state of Meroë arose as a great trade center

146 B.C.
Rome destroyed Carthage at the end of the Third Punic War

100 B.C.
Bantu people began spreading across Africa

THE AMERICAS

1200 B.C.
Olmec civilization arose in Mexico

900 B.C.
Chavín culture appeared in ancient Peru

700 B.C.
Adena culture appeared in Ohio Valley

300 B.C.
Decline of Olmec civilization

200 B.C.
Chavín culture disappeared from ancient Peru

100 B.C.
Hopewell culture arose in east-central North America

ASIA AND PACIFIC

1760 B.C.
Shang dynasty began rule in China; writing used on oracle bones

before 1750 B.C.
Hammurabi ruled Babylonia, developed first extensive law code

1400 B.C.
Phoenicians developed alphabet

1500 B.C.
Aryans migrated into India

1000 B.C.
King David united the Hebrews

1027 B.C.
Zhou dynasty founded in China

563 B.C.
Siddhartha Gautama, the Buddha, born in India

551 B.C.
Confucius born in Lu Province, China

500 B.C.
Lydians minted the region's first coins

350 B.C.
Mencius began to spread the teachings of Confucius

214 B.C.
Shi Huangdi connected existing walls to form the Great Wall

206 B.C.
During the Han dynasty, civil service exams were set up in China

EUROPE

1600 B.C.
Latins settled along Italy's Tiber River

Minoan culture reached its height

1400 B.C.
Mycenae arose on Greek mainland

1250 B.C.
Troy and Mycenae fought in the Trojan War

900 B.C.
Greek city-state of Sparta began conquering its neighbors

753 B.C.
According to legend, Rome founded

500s B.C.
Democracy appeared in some Greek city-states; Rome set up a republic

336 B.C.
Alexander the Great became king of Macedonia on the death of Philip II

27 B.C.
Augustus became first Roman emperor

Social Studies Reference Guide **R31**

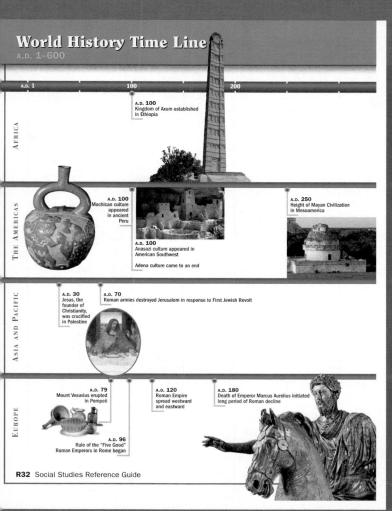

World History Time Line
A.D. 1–600

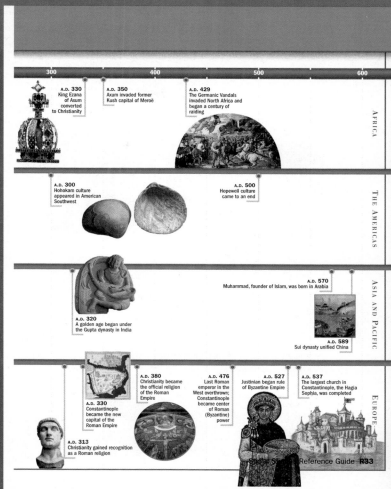

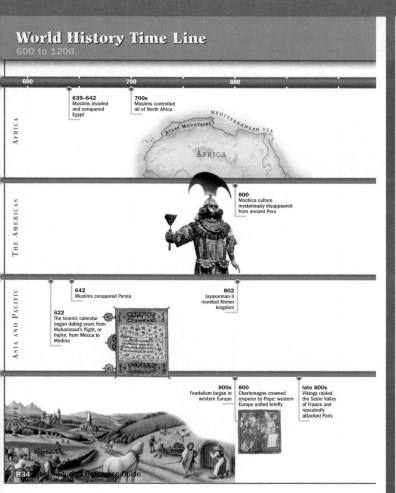

World History Time Line
600 to 1200

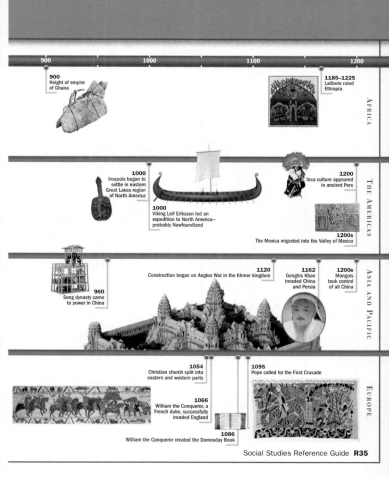

World History Time Line
1200 to 1800

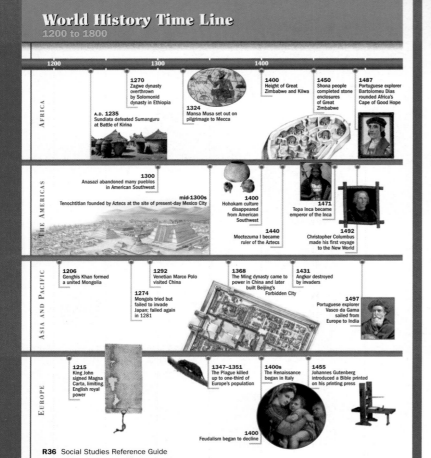
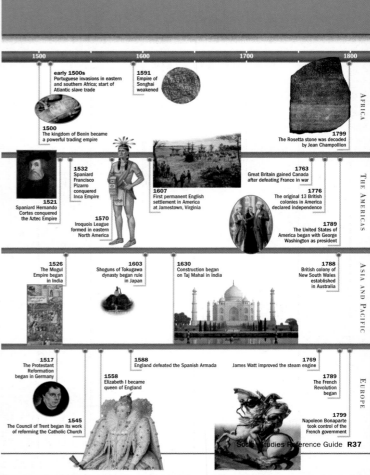

1200 · 1300 · 1400 · 1500 · 1600 · 1700 · 1800

AFRICA

1270 Zagwe dynasty overthrown by Solomonid dynasty in Ethiopia

A.D. 1235 Sundiata defeated Sumanguru at Battle of Kirina

1324 Mansa Musa set out on pilgrimage to Mecca

1400 Height of Great Zimbabwe and Kilwa

1450 Shona people completed stone enclosures of Great Zimbabwe

1487 Portuguese explorer Bartolomeu Dias rounded Africa's Cape of Good Hope

early 1500s Portuguese invasions in eastern and southern Africa; start of Atlantic slave trade

1591 Empire of Songhai weakened

1500 The kingdom of Benin became a powerful trading empire

1799 The Rosetta stone was decoded by Jean Champollion

THE AMERICAS

1300 Anasazi abandoned many pueblos in American Southwest

mid-1300s Tenochtitlan founded by Aztecs at the site of present-day Mexico City

1400 Hohokam culture disappeared from American Southwest

1471 Topa Inca became emperor of the Inca

1440 Moctezuma I became ruler of the Aztecs

1492 Christopher Columbus made his first voyage to the New World

1521 Spaniard Hernando Cortes conquered the Aztec Empire

1532 Spaniard Francisco Pizarro conquered Inca Empire

1570 Iroquois League formed in eastern North America

1607 First permanent English settlement in America at Jamestown, Virginia

1763 Great Britain gained Canada after defeating France in war

1776 The original 13 British colonies in America declared independence

1789 The United States of America began with George Washington as president

ASIA AND PACIFIC

1206 Genghis Khan formed a united Mongolia

1274 Mongols tried but failed to invade Japan; failed again in 1281

1292 Venetian Marco Polo visited China

1368 The Ming dynasty came to power in China and later built Beijing's Forbidden City

1431 Angkor destroyed by invaders

1497 Portuguese explorer Vasco da Gama sailed from Europe to India

1526 The Mogul Empire began in India

1603 Shoguns of Tokugawa dynasty began rule in Japan

1630 Construction began on Taj Mahal in India

1788 British colony of New South Wales established in Australia

EUROPE

1215 King John signed Magna Carta, limiting English royal power

1347–1351 The Plague killed up to one-third of Europe's population

1400s The Renaissance began in Italy

1455 Johannes Gutenberg introduced a Bible printed on his printing press

1400 Feudalism began to decline

1517 The Protestant Reformation began in Germany

1558 Elizabeth I became queen of England

1588 England defeated the Spanish Armada

1545 The Council of Trent began its work of reforming the Catholic Church

1769 James Watt improved the steam engine

1789 The French Revolution began

1799 Napoleon Bonaparte took control of the French government

R36 Social Studies Reference Guide

Social Studies Reference Guide **R37**

World History Time Line
1800 to 1950

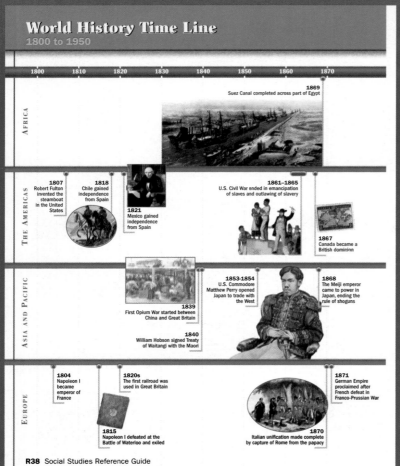
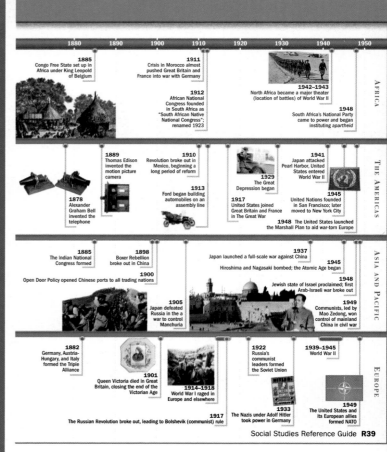

1800 · 1810 · 1820 · 1830 · 1840 · 1850 · 1860 · 1870 · 1880 · 1890 · 1900 · 1910 · 1920 · 1930 · 1940 · 1950

AFRICA

1869 Suez Canal completed across part of Egypt

1885 Congo Free State set up in Africa under King Leopold of Belgium

1911 Crisis in Morocco almost pushed Great Britain and France into war with Germany

1912 African National Congress founded in South Africa as "South African Native National Congress"; renamed 1923

1942–1943 North Africa became a major theater (location of battles) of World War II

1948 South Africa's National Party came to power and began instituting *apartheid*

THE AMERICAS

1807 Robert Fulton invented the steamboat in the United States

1818 Chile gained independence from Spain

1821 Mexico gained independence from Spain

1861–1865 U.S. Civil War ended in emancipation of slaves and outlawing of slavery

1867 Canada became a British dominion

1878 Alexander Graham Bell invented the telephone

1889 Thomas Edison invented the motion picture camera

1910 Revolution broke out in Mexico, beginning a long period of reform

1913 Ford began building automobiles on an assembly line

1917 United States joined Great Britain and France in The Great War

1929 The Great Depression began

1941 Japan attacked Pearl Harbor, United States entered World War II

1945 United Nations founded in San Francisco; later moved to New York City

1948 The United States launched the Marshall Plan to aid war-torn Europe

ASIA AND PACIFIC

1839 First Opium War started between China and Great Britain

1840 William Hobson signed Treaty of Waitangi with the Maori

1853–1854 U.S. Commodore Matthew Perry opened Japan to trade with the West

1868 The Meiji emperor came to power in Japan, ending the rule of shoguns

1885 The Indian National Congress formed

1898 Boxer Rebellion broke out in China

1900 Open Door Policy opened Chinese ports to all trading nations

1905 Japan defeated Russia in the a war to control Manchuria

1937 Japan launched a full-scale war against China

1945 Hiroshima and Nagasaki bombed; the Atomic Age began

1948 Jewish state of Israel proclaimed; first Arab-Israeli war broke out

1949 Communists, led by Mao Zedong, won control of mainland China in civil war

EUROPE

1804 Napoleon I became emperor of France

1820s The first railroad was used in Great Britain

1815 Napoleon I defeated at the Battle of Waterloo and exiled

1871 German Empire proclaimed after French defeat in Franco-Prussian War

1870 Italian unification made complete by capture of Rome from the papacy

1882 Germany, Austria-Hungary, and Italy formed the Triple Alliance

1901 Queen Victoria died in Great Britain, closing the end of the Victorian Age

1914–1918 World War I raged in Europe and elsewhere

1917 The Russian Revolution broke out, leading to Bolshevik (communist) rule

1922 Russia's communist leaders formed the Soviet Union

1933 The Nazis under Adolf Hitler took power in Germany

1939–1945 World War II

1949 The United States and its European allies formed NATO

R38 Social Studies Reference Guide

Social Studies Reference Guide **R39**

World History Time Line

1950 to present-day

1950 | 1960 | 1970 | 1980 | 1990 | 2000 | 2010

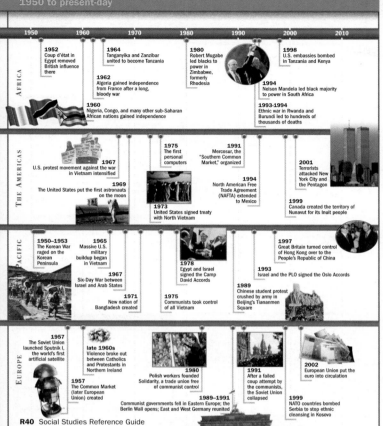

Africa

1952 Coup d'état in Egypt removed British influence there

1960 Nigeria, Congo, and many other sub-Saharan African nations gained independence

1962 Algeria gained independence from France after a long, bloody war

1964 Tanganyika and Zanzibar united to become Tanzania

1980 Robert Mugabe led blacks to power in Zimbabwe, formerly Rhodesia

1993-1994 Ethnic war in Rwanda and Burundi led to hundreds of thousands of deaths

1994 Nelson Mandela led black majority to power in South Africa

1998 U.S. embassies bombed in Tanzania and Kenya

The Americas

1967 U.S. protest movement against the war in Vietnam intensified

1969 The United States put the first astronauts on the moon

1973 United States signed treaty with North Vietnam

1975 The first personal computers

1991 Mercosur, the "Southern Common Market," organized

1994 North American Free Trade Agreement (NAFTA) extended to Mexico

1999 Canada created the territory of Nunavut for its Inuit people

2001 Terrorists attacked New York City and the Pentagon

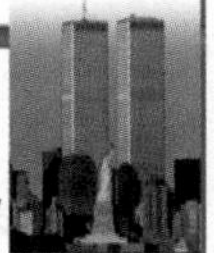

Pacific

1950–1953 The Korean War raged on the Korean Peninsula

1965 Massive U.S. military buildup began in Vietnam

1967 Six-Day War between Israel and Arab States

1971 New nation of Bangladesh created

1975 Communists took control of all Vietnam

1978 Egypt and Israel signed the Camp David Accords

1989 Chinese student protest crushed by army in Beijing's Tiananmen Square

1993 Israel and the PLO signed the Oslo Accords

1997 Great Britain turned control of Hong Kong over to the People's Republic of China

Europe

1957 The Soviet Union launched Sputnik I, the world's first artificial satellite

1957 The Common Market (later European Union) created

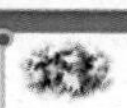

late 1960s Violence broke out between Catholics and Protestants in Northern Ireland

1980 Polish workers founded Solidarity, a trade union free of communist control

1989–1991 Communist governments fell in Eastern Europe; the Berlin Wall opens; East and West Germany reunited

1991 After a failed coup attempt by the communists, the Soviet Union collapsed

1999 NATO countries bombed Serbia to stop ethnic cleansing in Kosovo

2002 European Union put the euro into circulation

Gazetteer

This Gazetteer is a geographic dictionary that will help you locate and pronounce places in this book. Latitude and longitude are given for cities. The page numbers tell you where each place appears on a map (m) or in the text (t).

A

Aegean Sea (i jē′ən sē) the sea that separates Greece from Asia Minor (m. 247, t. 247)

Afghanistan (af gan′ə stan) a country in Southwest Asia (t. 639)

Agra (ä′grə) a city in India; capital of the Mogul Empire and home of the Taj Mahal; 27°N, 78°E (m. 348, t. 347)

Akkad (ak′ad) a city-state in northern Mesopotamia, the ruler of which conquered all the city-states of Mesopotamia and formed the world's first empire (m. 40, t.41)

Albany (ȯl′bə nē) the capital of New York; 42°N, 73°W (t. 475)

Alexandria (al′ig zan′drē ə) an Egyptian seaport city on the Mediterranean, a center of trade and learning in the Hellenistic Age; 31°N, 30°E (m. 267, t. 269)

Altamira (əl tə mē′rə) a site in Spain where prehistoric paintings appear on the ceiling of a cave (t. 28)

Altiplano (äl tə plä′nō) a region of plateaus and plains in the Andes (m. 187, t. 187)

Amazon Rain Forest (am′ə zon rān fôr′ist) the largest rain forest on Earth (m. 187, t. 187)

Amazon River (am′ə zon riv′ər) the world's second longest river, located in the northern half of South America (m. 187, t. 187)

Andes Mountains (an′dēz moun′tənz) the world's longest mountain chain, located in western South America (m. 187, t. 187)

Angkor (ang′kôr) the first royal city of the Khmer Kingdom (m. 356, t. 357)

Angkor Wat (ang′kôr wät) a temple featuring magnificent towers; built in the 1100s by the Khmer people in present-day Cambodia (m. 357, t. 357)

Antarctica (ant′ärk′tə kə) the fifth largest continent on Earth; also the highest, driest, and coldest continent (t. 663)

Anyang (an yāng′) a town in eastern China known for its artifacts of bone (m. 109, t. 107)

Appalachian Mountains (ap′ə lā′chən moun′tənz) a range in eastern North America (m. 210, t. 209)

Arabian Peninsula (ə rā′bē ən pə nin′sə lə) peninsula in Southwest Asia, bounded by the Red Sea, the Persian Gulf, and the Arabian Sea (m. 334, t. 335)

Asia Minor (ā′zhə mī′nər) the western edge of Asia (m. 247, t. 247)

Assyria (ə sir′ē ə) region at the foot of the Zagros Mountains in the Upper Tigris River Valley (t. 52)

Athens (ath′ənz) a city-state that was the best example of ancient Greek democracy; the capital of modern Greece; 38°N, 23°E (m. 247, t. 255)

Atlas Mountains (at′ləs moun′tənz) a mountain range that separates the Sahara from the Mediterranean (m. 371, t. 371)

Australia (ȯ strā′ lyə) an island continent southeast of Asia; became a dominion of Britain (m. 502, t. 502)

Axum (aks′əm) a kingdom in East Africa that began as a trading settlement (m. 380, t. 381)

B

Babylon (bab′ə lon) a city-state in Mesopotamia (m. 49, t. 49)

Babylonia (bab′ə lō′nē ə) an empire that included all of Mesopotamia as well as some neighboring city-states (m. 49, t. 49)

Balkan Peninsula (bȯl′kən pə nin′sə lə) a stretch of land that extends southward into the eastern part of the Mediterranean Sea (m. 247, t. 247)

Pronunciation Key

a	in hat	ō	in open	sh	in she
â	in care	ȯ	in all	th	in thin
ā	in age	ô	in order	ᴛʜ	in then
ä	in far	oi	in oil	zh	in measure
e	in let	ou	in out	ə	= a in about
ē	in equal	u	in cup	ə	= e in taken
ėr	in term	ů	in put	ə	= i in pencil
i	in it	ü	in rule	ə	= o in lemon
ī	in ice	ch	in child	ə	= u in circus
o	in hot	ng	in long		

Beijing (bā′jing′) the capital of China; 40°N, 116°E (m. 101, t. 101)

Benin (be nēn′) a West African kingdom that became an empire by 1500 (m. 380, t. 384)

Beringia (bə rin′jē ə) a prehistoric "land bridge" that once connected Asia and North America (m. 15, t. 14)

Berlin (bər lin′) the capital of Germany and site of the Berlin Conference in 1884; 52°N, 13°E (t. 489)

Berlin Wall (bər lin′ wawl) a wall built in 1961 to divide the German city of Berlin into a communist eastern and a non-communist western half; the wall was finally torn down in 1989 (t. 621)

Black Sea (blak sē) a large sea bordered by Turkey, Bulgaria, Romania, Ukraine, Russia, and Georgia (m. 323, t. 324)

Bodh Gaya (bōd gä′yä) the town in northern India where Siddhartha was enlightened and became Buddha (m. 140, t. 142)

Bosnia and Herzegovina (boz′nē ə and hėr′tsə gə vē′nə) a Balkan country, once part of Yugoslavia (m. 522, t. 521)

Boston (bȯ′stən) the capital of Massachusetts and site of colonial protests against the British; 42°N, 71°W (t. 457)

Brazil (brə zil′) a country in South America; originally a Portuguese colony (m. 446, t. 446)

Burundi (bů rün′dē) a central African nation affected by civil war in the 1990s (t. 638)

Byzantine Empire (biz′n tēn′ em′pīr) an empire of lands that formed the eastern part of the Roman Empire with its center at the city of Constantinople (t. 323)

Byzantium (bi zan′tē əm) an old Greek city, renamed Constantinople, that became the center of the Byzantine Empire; present-day Istanbul (t. 301)

C

Cahokia (ka hō′kē ə) the largest temple mound site in North America (m. 220, t. 221)

Calcutta (kal kut′ə) a megacity in India; 22°N, 88°E (t. 655)

Cambodia (kam bō′ dē ə) a country in Southeast Asia; part of the Khmer civilization (m. 357, t. 357)

Canaan (kā′nən) Eastern Mediterranean land in which Abraham resettled around 1800 B.C. (t. 55)

Canada (kan′ə də) a large nation in the north part of North America (t. 223)

Canadian Shield (kə nā′dē ən shēld) a vast plateau region north of the Interior Plains in North America (m. 210, t. 209)

Canton (kan ton′) a former British treaty port in China; now called Guangzhou (m. 492, t. 494)

Cape of Good Hope (kāp ov gůd hōp) the southern tip of Africa (m. 440, t. 439)

Carthage (kär′thij) an important Phoenician trading post in North Africa (m. 58, t. 58)

Cave of the Hands (kāv ov ᴛʜə handz) a cave in Patagonia, a land in southern South America, where people painted on the walls thousands of years ago (t. 27)

Central Plateau (sen′trəl pla tō′) a high, flat area in the center of the Plateau of Mexico (t. 163)

Central Uplands (sen′trəl up′ləndz) low mountains and high plateaus in the central region of Europe (t. 393)

Chang'an (shəng′än) a capital city in Central Asia on the Silk Road (m. 409, t. 409)

Chauvet (shō vā′) a site in southern France with 32,000-year-old cave paintings and artifacts (m. 26, t. 29)

Chavín (chä vēn′) an ancient city in southern South America; home to the Chavín people (m. 190, t. 191)

Chernobyl (chėr nō′bəl) site in Ukraine of a nuclear power plant accident in 1986 (t. 666)

Chiapas (chē ä′päs) Mexico's poorest state (t. 640)

Chichén Itzá (chē chen′ ēt zä′) an ancient Mayan city located on the Yucatan Peninsula (m. 168, t. 171)

China (chī′nə) a large country in East Asia (m. 350, t. 351)

Clovis (klō′vis) city in New Mexico near where archaeologists found many early human-made objects (m. 15, t. 12)

Coastal Range (kō′stl rānj) a small mountain range in North America, between the Great Basin and the Pacific Ocean (t. 209)

Colosseum (kol′ə sē′əm) a famous Roman arena (m. 288, t. 291)

Congo Free State (kong′gō frē stāt) a Belgian colony in Africa under King Leopold II (t. 489)

Constantinople (kon stan tə nō′pəl) the capital of the Byzantine Empire (m. 322, t. 324)

Crete (krēt) an island in the eastern Mediterranean Sea; the center of Minoan civilization (m. 247, t. 250)

Croatia (krō ā′shə) a Balkan nation, once part of Yugoslavia (t. 621)

Cuba (kyü′bə) Caribbean nation in which the Soviet Union attempted to build missile bases in 1962 (t. 572)

Cuzco (küz′kō) the capital of the Inca empire (m. 198, t. 197)

Czechoslovakia (chək ə slō vä′kē ə) a central European country invaded by Germany in 1939 (t. 545)

Czech Republic (chək ri pub′lik) a nation formed after Czechoslovakia split into two countries in 1993 (t. 621)

D

Danube River (dan′yüb riv′ər) Europe's second longest river (m. 393, t. 394)

Deccan Plateau (dek′ən pla′tō) a dry, high region south of the Indo-Ganges Plain (m. 124, t. 126)

Deir el-Medina (dīr əl mə dē′nə) a village built for workers at the Valley of the Kings in Egypt (t. 88)

Dolores (dō lôr′əs) a village in which the end of colonial rule in Mexico began (t. 459)

Dunhuang (dun hwang′) a Chinese city on the edge of the Taklimakan Desert (m. 406, t. 409)

E

Eastern Ghats (ē′stərn gȯts) rolling mountains east of the Deccan Plateau in southern India (t. 126)

East Germany (ēst jėr′mə nē) a former country created by the Soviet Union after World War II (m. 569, t. 570)

Edo (ē′dō) the Japanese shogun capital, renamed Tokyo; 35°N, 140°E (m. 362, t. 361)

Egypt (ē′jipt) an ancient kingdom and present-day country in northeastern Africa (m. 79, t. 79)

England (ing′glənd) the southernmost and largest part of the island of Great Britain (m. 396, t. 397)

Ethiopia (ē′thē ō′pē ə) a country in East Africa (m. 383, t. 382)

Europe (yür′əp) a continent to the north of Africa, connected to Asia in western Russia (m. 393, t. 393)

F

Fertile Crescent (fėr′tl kres′nt) a curved region with rich soil in the Middle East where one of the first civilizations developed (m. 35, t. 35)

Florence (flôr′əns) an important Italian city-state that became the birthplace of the Renaissance; 44°N, 11°E (t. 431)

Forbidden City, The (fər bid′n sit′ē, ᴛʜə) the palace of the Chinese emperor in Beijing (t. 351)

Formosa (fôr mō′sə) an island colonized by China and later renamed Taiwan (m. 494, t. 495)

G

Ganges River (gan′jēz riv′ər) an important river in India; Hindus believe it represents purity (m. 136, t. 138)

Ganges River Valley (gan′jēz riv′ər val′ē) the land surrounding the Ganges River (m. 124, t. 131)

Gao (gou) a city east of Timbuktu and capital of the Songhai Empire (m. 377, t. 378)

Gaza Strip (gä′zə strip) an area of eastern Mediterranean land seized by Israel in the Six-Day War (m. 617, t. 616)

Genoa (jen′ō ə) a seaport town in Italy (m. 410, t. 410)

Germany (jėr′mə nē) a nation in central Europe (m. 499, t. 499)

Ghana (gä′nə) an ancient kingdom in West Africa (m. 377, t. 375)

Giza (gē′zə) a city in Egypt where the Great Pyramid is located; 30°N, 31°E (m. 84, t. 87)

Golan Heights (gō′län hīts) an area of southwestern Asia seized by Israel in the Six-Day War (m. 617, t. 616)

Pronunciation Key

a	in hat	ō	in open	sh	in she
â	in care	ȯ	in all	th	in thin
ā	in age	ô	in order	ᴛʜ	in then
ä	in far	oi	in oil	zh	in measure
e	in let	ou	in out	ə	= a in about
ē	in equal	u	in cup	ə	= e in taken
ėr	in term	ů	in put	ə	= i in pencil
i	in it	ü	in rule	ə	= o in lemon
ī	in ice	ch	in child	ə	= u in circus
o	in hot	ng	in long		

Gazetteer

Great Basin (grāt bā′sn) an area of basins and ranges west of the Rocky Mountains (m. 210, t. 209)

Great Britain (grāt brit′n) the largest island of Europe; made up of England, Scotland, and Wales (t. 475)

Great European Plain (grāt yůr′ə pē′ən plān) a vast expanse of land in Europe; includes southeastern England (t. 393)

Great Lakes, The (grāt lāks, ᴛʜə) a chain of five freshwater lakes in North America (t. 224)

Great Plains (grāt plānz) a large, grassy region in the western Interior Plains of North America (m. 210, t. 209)

Great Rift Valley (grāt rift val′ē) a valley in East Africa (m. 371, t. 372)

Great Serpent Mound (grāt sėr′pənt mound) a large, snake-shaped mound created by the Adena people (m. 220, t. 219)

Great Zimbabwe (grāt zim bä′bwä) a city in southeastern Africa that reached its height in about 1400; features large stone enclosures (m. 383, t. 384)

Guangxi Zhungzu (gwäng shē zəng jü) a region in southern China that has one of the best climates for farming (m. 101, t. 102)

Guiana Highlands (gē ä′nə hī′ ləndz) a land of vast tropical forests in northern South America (m. 187, t. 188)

Gulf of Mexico (gulf ov mek′sə kō) a part of the Atlantic Ocean east of Mexico (m. 163, t. 164)

Gulf Stream (gulf strēm) a powerful ocean current that brings warm water from the Gulf of Mexico to Europe (t. 394)

H

Hagia Sophia (hä yē′ə sō fē′ə) a great domed cathedral in Constantinople (present-day Istanbul, Turkey) (t. 326)

Haiti (hā′tē) a former French colony in the Caribbean Sea and the first republic led by a person of African descent (m. 460, t. 459)

Hanoi (hä noi′) the former capital of North Vietnam and capital of present-day Vietnam 21°N, 106°E (m. 586, t. 586)

Harappa (hə rä′pə) the site of one of the earliest civilizations in South Asia (m. 122, t. 126)

Himalayas (him′ə lā′əz) a mountain range in southern Asia; includes the highest point on Earth (m. 101, t. 103)

Hippodrome (hip′ə drōm) a huge building in Constantinople and the site of chariot races (t. 324)

Hiroshima (hir′ō shē′mə) Japanese city that was the site of the first atomic bomb dropped in a war, on August 6, 1945; 34°N, 132°E (m. 553, t. 554)

Hong Kong (hong′ kong′) a British colony in China, received after the first Opium War and returned to China in 1997; 22°N, 114°E (m. 494, t. 494)

Huang River (hwäng riv′ər) a river that cuts through the North China Plain (m. 101, t. 102)

Huang River Valley (hwäng riv′ər val′ē) the area surrounding the Huang River (m. 101, t. 102)

Hudson River (hud′sən riv′ər) a river that runs through the state of New York (t. 475)

I

Iguaçu Falls (e′gwä sü fälz) a waterfall on the border between Argentina and Brazil; a major source of hydroelectricity in South America (t. 666)

India (in′dē ə) a large country on the Indian subcontinent (t. 346)

Indian Ocean (in′dē ən ō′shən) an ocean south of Asia, west of Australia, and east of Africa (m. 124, t. 124)

Indochina (in′dō chī′nə) a peninsula in Southeast Asia that includes Vietnam, Cambodia, and Laos (t. 488)

Indo-Ganges Plain (in′dō gan′jēz plān) a region in India through which the Ganges and Brahmaputra Rivers flow (m. 124, t. 125)

Indus River Valley (in′dəs riv′ər val′ē) the land surrounding the Indus River in Pakistan (t. 125)

Interior Plains (in tir′ē ər plānz) large plains between the Rocky Mountains and Appalachian Mountains in North America (m. 210, t. 209)

Ionian Sea (ī ō′nē un sē) the sea that separates western Greece from southeastern Italy (m. 247, t. 248)

Israel (iz′rē əl) Jewish kingdom founded by David around 1000 B.C.; a country in southwestern Asia (m. 54, t. 57)

Italian Peninsula (i tal′yən pə nin′sə lə) an arm of land surrounded by the Mediterranean, Tyrrhenian, and Adriatic seas; location of the country of Italy (m. 277, t. 277)

Italy (it′l ē) a country in southern Europe, on a peninsula in the Mediterranean Sea (m. 501, t. 499)

J

Jamestown (jāmz′ toun′) the first permanent English colony in North America (t. 447)

Japan (jə pan′) a nation that consists of four large islands and many smaller islands in the western Pacific Ocean, east of the Asian mainland (m. 360, t. 361)

Jenne-jenno (je nā′ je nō′) an ancient city in West Africa, located southeast of Timbuktu on the Niger River; the oldest known city in sub-Saharan Africa (m. 377, t. 377)

Jerusalem (jə rü′sə ləm) the capital of the kingdom of Israel; 32°N, 35°E (m. 57, t. 57)

Judah (jü′də) the southern region of Israel that became its own kingdom after the death of Solomon (m. 57, t. 57)

K

Kenya (ken′ yə) an eastern African nation that won its independence in 1963 (t. 607)

Kilwa (kil′wä) a southern African city involved in the gold and ivory trade (m. 383, t. 383)

Kish (kish) an early city-state in Mesopotamia (t. 38)

Kosovo (kō′sə vō) an area in Serbia and site of a violent conflict in 1999 (m. 637, t. 637)

Koumbi (küm′bē) the capital of the kingdom of Ghana (t. 375)

Kush (kůsh) a Nubian kingdom freed from Egypt in 1650 B.C. (m. 93, t. 94)

Kyoto (kyō′tō) a major city in Japan; 35°N, 136°E (m. 362, t. 362)

L

Lagash (lə′gash) an early city-state in Mesopotamia (t. 38)

Lake Texcoco (lāk tā skō′kō) the lake on which the Mexica settled (t. 176)

Lake Titicaca (lāk tit′ə kä′kə) a lake in the Altiplano in South America (m. 187, t. 188)

Laos (lä′ōs) a country in Southeast Asia; once part of the Khmer civilization (m. 357, t. 357)

Lascaux (ləs kou′) a site in southern France with cave art from about 17,000 years ago (t. 28)

London (lun′dən) the capital of Great Britain; 51°N, 0° (t. 549)

Lower Egypt (lō′ər ē′jipt) the region of Egypt that surrounds the Nile Delta (m. 79, t. 79)

Lu Province (lü prä′vins) the birthplace of Confucius (m. 114, t. 115)

M

Maastricht (mäs′trikt) a town in the Netherlands that was the site of the signing of the treaty that created the European Union (m. 630, t. 632)

Macao (mə kou′) a former Portuguese treaty port in China (m. 494, t. 494)

Macedonia (mas′ə dō′nē ə) an ancient country in northern Greece; a nation formed after the breakup of Yugoslavia (m. 263, t. 264)

Machu Picchu (mäch′ü pēk chü) a city built by the Inca people on a mountaintop in the Andes Mountains in present-day Peru (m. 198, t. 197)

Madagascar (mad′ə gas′kər) an island off the coast of East Africa (t. 656)

Mali (mä′lē) an empire in West Africa (m. 377, t. 376)

Manchuria (man chůr′ē ə) the northeastern region of China, seized by Japan in 1931 (m. 494, t. 496)

Marathon (mar′ə thon) a plain northeast of Athens, Greece (t. 261)

Mecca (mek′ə) a city located along the shore of the Red Sea on the Arabian Peninsula; the birthplace of Muhammad; 21°N, 40°E (m. 332, t. 331)

Medina (mə dē′nə) a town on the Arabian Peninsula where Muhammad found people eager to hear his teachings on Islam (m. 332, t. 331)

Pronunciation Key

a	in hat	ō	in open	sh	in she
â	in care	ȯ	in all	th	in thin
ā	in age	ô	in order	ᴛʜ	in then
ä	in far	oi	in oil	zh	in measure
e	in let	ou	in out	ə	= a in about
ē	in equal	u	in cup	ə	= e in taken
ėr	in term	ů	in put	ə	= i in pencil
i	in it	ü	in rule	ə	= o in lemon
ī	in ice	ch	in child	ə	= u in circus
o	in hot	ng	in long		

Gazetteer

Mediterranean Sea (med′ə tə rā′nē ən sē) a large body of water bordered by Europe, Asia, and Africa (m. 247, t. 247)

Memphis (mem′fis) a city on the Nile in Egypt; 25°N, 31°E (m. 82, t. 80)

Menlo Park (mən′lō pärk) a town in New Jersey where Thomas Edison had his laboratory (t. 479)

Meroë (mər′ō ē′) a capital city of Nubia (m. 93, t. 93)

Mesoamerica (mes′ō ə mer′ə kə) a region that extends from southern North America to the central part of Central America (m. 163, t. 163)

Mesopotamia (mes′ə pə ta′me ə) an area of flat land between the Tigris and Euphrates Rivers where one of the first civilizations emerged (m. 35, t. 35)

Mexico City (mek′sə kō sit′ē) capital of Mexico and the most populated city in the world; 19°N, 99°W (t. 655)

Midway Island (mid′wā ī′lənd) site, west of Hawaii, of an important battle in World War II (m. 553, t. 553)

Milan (mi lan′) an important city-state in Italy during the Renaissance; 45°N, 9°E (t. 431)

Mississippi River (mis′ə sip′ē riv′ər) located in North America, the main river of one of the largest river systems in the world (m. 210, t. 209)

Moche Valley (mō′chə val′ē) the home of the Mochica people (m. 190, t. 192)

Mohenjo-Daro (mō hen′jō där′ō) an ancient city in the Indus River Valley in Pakistan (m. 128, t. 129)

Mongolia (mong gō′lē ə) a country in northern Asia (m. 352, t. 352)

Monte Verde (mon′tə vər′dā) site in Chile near where archaeologists found artifacts dating to 12,500 years ago (m. 15, t. 16)

Mount Everest (mount ev′ər ist) the highest peak in the Himalayas and the tallest mountain on Earth (m. 124, t. 123)

Mount Kilimanjaro (mount kil′ə mən jär′ō) the highest mountain in Africa (m. 371, t. 372)

Mount Olympus (mount ō lim′pəs) a mountain in northern Greece thought by the ancient Greeks to be the home of their gods (m. 252, t. 254)

Myanmar (Burma) (mī än′mär) a country in South Asia with a repressive government (t. 640)

Mycenae (mī sē′nē) an early city-state of Greece (m. 247, t. 251)

N

Nagasaki (nä gə sä′kē) a port city in Japan and site of the second atomic bomb dropped in a war, on August 9, 1945; 33°N, 130°E (m. 553, t. 554)

Nanjing (nän′ jing′) the capital of China during the Japanese occupation (m. 546, t. 546)

Napata (nap′ət ə) the capital of the African kingdom of Kush (m. 93, t. 95)

Nazareth (naz′ər əth) a city in ancient Palestine and the home of Jesus (m. 294, t. 295)

New South Wales (nü south wālz) a British colony for convicts in Australia (t. 447)

New York City (nü yôrk sit′ē) the largest city in the United States; 40°N, 74°W (t. 475)

New Zealand (nü zē′lənd) a colony that became a dominion of Britain (m. 502, t. 502)

Niagara Falls (nī ag′rə fälz) waterfalls on the boundary between the United States and Canada; provides a portion of the energy needs of the Canadian province of Ontario (t. 666)

Nile River (nīl riv′ər) the longest river in the world, it flows from East Africa to Egypt (m. 82, t. 79)

Nile River Valley (nīl riv′ər val′ē) the area of land surrounding the Nile River (m. 79, t. 79)

Nineveh (nin′ə və) the capital of the Assyrian Empire and the site of a great library under King Ashurbanipal (m. 49, t. 52)

Nippur (nip ər′) an early city-state in Mesopotamia (t. 38)

Normandy (nôr′mən dē) a region in northern France and the site of the D-Day invasion on June 6, 1944 (m. 552, t. 552)

North China Plain (nôrth chī′nə plān) the region where human settlement and culture began in China (m. 101, t. 101)

Northern Ireland (nôr′ᴛʜərn īr′lənd) a part of the United Kingdom located in the northeastern part of the island of Ireland; the site of fighting between religious groups (m. 639, t. 639)

North European Plain (nôrth yůr′ə pe′ən plān) the northern part of the Great European Plain (m. 393, t. 393)

North Korea (nôrth kô rē′ ə) the communist nation of a divided Korea on the Korean peninsula in eastern Asia (m. 583, t. 583)

North Vietnam (nôrth vē et näm′) the communist nation of Vietnam (m. 586, t. 584)

Northwest Mountains (nôrth′west′ moun′tən) a region in Europe that is poor for farming (m. 393, t. 393)

Nubia (nü′bē ə) a large African kingdom to the south of Egypt (m. 93, t. 93)

Nunavut (nü′nə vüt′) a province in northern Canada and the home of many of the Inuit people (m. 223, t. 223)

O

Oklahoma City (ō′klə hō′mə sit′ē) capital city of the U.S. state of Oklahoma; the sight of a terrorist attack in 1995; 35°N, 97°W (t. 646)

Olympia (ō lim′pē ə) an area of ancient Greece where the Olympic Games were first held (m. 247, t. 254)

Osaka (ō sä′kə) a major city in Japan; 34°N, 135°E (m. 362, t. 362)

P

Pakistan (pak′ə stan) a Muslim nation in southern Asia; created by the division of India in 1947 (m. 610, t. 612)

Palestine (pal′ə stīn) a Roman province on the eastern coast of the Mediterranean Sea (t. 295)

Pampas (pam′pəz) a vast grassland in the southern plains of South America (m. 187, t. 188)

Pantanal (pän tə näl′) the world's largest wetland, located in South America (m. 187, t. 187)

Paris (pär′is) the capital of France; 49°N, 2°E (m. 529, t. 468)

Pearl Harbor (pėrl här′bər) a port in Hawaii attacked by the Japanese on December 7, 1941 (m. 553, t. 550)

Peloponnesus (pel ə pə nē′səs) a part of the Greek peninsula (m. 247, m. 263)

People's Republic of China (pē′pəlz ri pub′lik uv chī′nə) the name given to China after the communist takeover in 1949 (t. 578)

Peru (pə rü′) a dry, rough country in western South America (m. 190, t. 191)

Philippines (fil′ə pēnz′) an island nation in the Pacific Ocean (m. 553, t. 553)

Phoenicia (fə nish′ə) an ancient country on the Mediterranean Sea, south of Asia Minor (t. 267)

Plateau of Mexico (pla tō′ ov mek′sə kō) a high, flat area in central Mexico (t. 163)

Poland (pō′lənd) a country east of Germany (m. 549, t. 549)

Prussia (prush′ə) the largest and most powerful German state before unification (m. 499, t. 500)

Q

Quebec (kwi bek′) the first permanent French settlement in North America (t. 447)

R

Rhineland (rīn′land) the western region of Germany bordering France (t. 536)

Rhine River (rīn riv′ər) the main river of the busiest inland system of waterways in the western part of Europe (m. 393, t. 394)

Rocky Mountains (rok′ē moun′tənz) a mountain range that stretches through western Canada and the United States (m. 210, t. 209)

Rome (rōm) a city near the middle of the western coast of Italy; 42°N, 12°E (m. 277, t. 277)

Russia (rush′ə) a large country in Eastern Europe and north Asia (m. 522, t. 496)

Rwanda (rü än′də) a central African nation affected by civil war in the 1990s (t. 638)

Pronunciation Key

a	in hat	ō	in open	sh	in she
â	in care	ȯ	in all	th	in thin
ā	in age	ô	in order	ᴛʜ	in then
ä	in far	oi	in oil	zh	in measure
e	in let	ou	in out	ə	= a in about
ē	in equal	u	in cup	ə	= e in taken
ėr	in term	ů	in put	ə	= i in pencil
i	in it	ü	in rule	ə	= o in lemon
ī	in ice	ch	in child	ə	= u in circus
o	in hot	ng	in long		

Gazetteer

S

Sahara (sə har′ə) the largest desert in the world (m. 371, t. 371)

Sahiwal (sə ē′wəl) a town in east-central Pakistan; the center of the cotton industry (m. 126, t. 126)

Salamis (sal′ə məs) the site of a mighty sea battle between Greece and Persia (t. 261)

Sandwich Islands (sand′wich ī′ləndz) a group of islands in the Pacific Ocean; now known as the Hawaiian Islands (t. 445)

Sarajevo (sar′ə yä′vō) the capital of Bosnia and Herzegovina; 44°N, 18°E (m. 522, t. 522)

Sardinia (sär din′ē ə) an island near Italy (m. 499, t. 501)

Scandinavia (skan′də nā′vē ə) a northwestern region of Europe; includes the nations of Denmark, Sweden, and Norway (m. 396, t. 397)

Sea of Marmara (sē uv mär′mər ə) a small sea that lies between Europe and Asia Minor (m. 322, t. 324)

Serbia (sėr′bē ə) a country in southeastern Europe (m. 522, t. 521)

Shanghai (shang hī) a former British treaty port in China; 31°N, 121°E (m. 492, t. 494)

Sierra Madre Occidental (sē er′ə mäd′drā ok′sə den′tl) a mountain range to the west of the Plateau of Mexico (m. 163, t. 163)

Sierra Madre Oriental (sē er′ə mäd′drā ôr′ē en′tl) a mountain range to the east of the Plateau of Mexico (m. 163, t. 163)

Sinai Peninsula (sī′nī pə nin′sə lə) an area of land seized by Israel in the Six-Day War (m. 617, t. 616)

Skara Brae (skä′rä brā) a Stone Age village in Northern Scotland discovered by archaeologists in the 1800s (t. 22)

Slovak Republic (slō′vak ri pub′lik) an Eastern European nation formed after Czechoslovakia split into two countries (t. 621)

Slovenia (slō vē′nē ə) a southeastern European nation formed after the breakup of Yugoslavia (t. 621)

Snaketown (snāk toun) the modern name of the Hohokam's largest village (m. 212, t. 213)

Sofala (sō fä′lä) a southern African city involved in the gold and ivory trade (m. 383, t. 383)

Somme, The (səm, ᴛʜə) a river in eastern France (m. 529, t. 529)

Songhai (song gī′) an empire near the Niger River (m. 377, t. 378)

South Africa (south af′rə kə) an African nation that was ruled under a system of apartheid until the early 1990s (m. 608, t. 609)

South Korea (south kô rē′ə) the republic of a divided Korea on the Korean peninsula in eastern Asia (m. 583, t. 583)

South Vietnam (south vē et näm′) the former non-communist part of Vietnam in Southeast Asia (m. 586, t. 584)

Soviet Union (sō′vē et yü nyən) the former country formed by Russia's communist leaders in 1922 (m. 531, t. 531)

Soweto (sō wə′tō) a town in South Africa that was the site of the killing of black children in 1976 (t. 609)

Sparta (spär′tə) an ancient Greek city-state that was under strict military rule (m. 252, t. 255)

Stalingrad (stä′lin grad) a city in the Soviet Union and the site of fierce fighting in World War II; present-day Volgograd (m. 552, t. 551)

Suez Canal (sü ez′ kə nal′) a man-made waterway that connects the Mediterranean Sea with the Indian Ocean (m. 488, t. 488)

Sumer (sü′mər) a powerful city-state in southern Mesopotamia (m. 40, t. 41)

T

Taipei (tī pā′) the capital of Taiwan; 25°N, 121°E (t. 578)

Taiwan (tī wän′) an island nation that became Nationalist China (m. 577, t. 577)

Tanzania (tan′zə nē′ə) an African nation that gained independence in 1961 (m. 608, t. 607)

Tassili (tas ē′le) an area in the North African country of Algeria; the site of ancient cave paintings (m. 13, t. 13)

Tenochtitlan (tā nōch′tē tlan′) the capital city of the Aztecs (m. 175, t. 176)

Thebes (thēbz) a Greek city-state that defeated Sparta (m. 263, t. 264)

Tiananmen Square (tyän′än mən skwâr) an area in Beijing where students gathered for a mass protest in 1989 (t. 641)

Tiber River (tī′bər riv′ər) a river in Italy (m. 277, t. 277)

Tibetan Plateau (ti bət′n pla tō′) a rocky region in the west of China (m. 101, t. 103)

Tikal (tē käl′) a city-state of the Maya that is now an important ruin (m. 170, t. 170)

Timbuktu (tim′buk tü′) a major trading city in Mali (m. 377, t. 377)

Tokyo (tō′kē ō) the capital city of Japan; 35°N, 139°E (t. 554)

Topper site (top′ər sīt) a place in South Carolina where archaeologists found artifacts that were up to 18,000 years old (m. 15, t. 16)

Troy (troi) a city on the western coast of Asia Minor; site of the legendary Trojan War (m. 252, t. 253)

U

Umma (ü′mə) an early city-state in Mesopotamia (t. 38)

Upper Egypt (up′ər ē′jipt) the region south of the Nile Delta (m. 79, t. 79)

Ur (ėr) an early city-state in Mesopotamia (m. 38, t. 38)

Ural Mountains (yür′əl moun′tənz) a mountain range that separates Eastern Europe from Asia (m. 393, t. 393)

Uruk (ėr′ük) a large Sumerian city-state in Mesopotamia (t. 41)

V

Valley of Mexico (val′ē ov mek′sə kō) an area of Mesoamerica (t. 176)

Venice (ven′is) an important city-state during the Renaissance; 45°N, 12°E (t. 431)

Verdun (vər dun′) a city in northeastern France; 49°N, 5°E (m. 529, t. 529)

Volga River (vol′gə riv′ər) the longest river in Europe (m. 393, t. 394)

W

Washington, D.C. (wäsh′ing tən) the capital city of the United States; located between Maryland and Virginia along the Potomac River 38°N, 77°W (t. 646)

West Bank (west bangk) an area of land seized by Israel in the Six-Day War (m. 617, t. 616)

Western Ghats (wə′stərn gôts) rolling mountains west of the Deccan Plateau in southern India (m. 124, t. 126)

West Germany (west jėr′mə nē) a former European country created by the Allies after World War II (m. 569, t. 570)

West Indies (west in′dēz) islands in the Caribbean (m. 438, t. 440)

Y

Yucatán Peninsula (yü kə′tan′ pə nin′sə lə) an arm of land that sticks out into the Gulf of Mexico (m. 163, t. 164)

Yugoslavia (yü′gō slä′vē ə) a former country in southeastern Europe (m. 637, t. 637)

Z

Zimbabwe (zim bä′bwā) a southern African nation, formerly known as Southern Rhodesia (m. 608, t. 609)

Pronunciation Key

a in hat	ō in open	sh in she
ā in care	ȯ in all	th in thin
â in age	ô in order	ᴛʜ in then
ä in far	oi in oil	zh in measure
e in let	ou in out	ə = a in about
ē in equal	u in cup	ə = e in taken
ėr in term	ů in put	ə = i in pencil
i in it	ü in rule	ə = o in lemon
ī in ice	ch in child	ə = u in circus
o in hot	ng in long	

Biographical Dictionary

This Biographical Dictionary tells you about the people in this book and how to pronounce their names. The page numbers tell you where the person first appears in the text.

A

Abraham c. 1800 B.C. A shepherd living in Ur who is considered by Jewish people to be the first Jew. p. 55

Akbar (ak′bär) 1542–1605 Grandson of Babur who became the greatest Mogul emperor. His reign from 1556 to 1605 brought most of the Indian subcontinent under Mogul rule. p. 348

Akhenaten (äk′ə′nät ən) Egyptian ruler who changed his name from Amenhotep IV and called for the worship of one god, Aton. p. 90

Aldrin, Edwin 1930– American astronaut who walked on the moon in 1969. p. 669

Alexander 356 B.C.–323 B.C. Known as "Alexander the Great," the king of Macedonia who conquered a vast empire in Europe, Asia, and Africa. p. 267

Alexius Comnenus (ä leks′ē us kŏm nən′us) 1048–1118 Byzantine emperor who appealed to the pope for Christian knights to fight against the Turks. p. 407

al-Khwarizmi (al kwär′əz mē) c. 780–850 Muslim mathematician who developed algebra. p. 336

Amanirenas first century B.C. Queen of Kush who led military expeditions and built monuments. p. 95

Arafat, Yasir (är′ə fat, yä′sər) 1929– Leader of the PLO who signed a peace pact with Israel in 1993. p. 616

Archimedes (ar kə mē′dēz) c. 287 B.C.–212 B.C. Scientist of the Hellenistic Age who was the first person to explain how levers work. p. 270

Aristotle (ar′ə stot′l) 384 B.C.–322 B.C. Ancient Greek philosopher and student of Plato who wrote more than 170 books. p. 262

Armstrong, Neil 1930– American astronaut who became the first human to walk on the moon in July of 1969. p. 669

Ashoka c. 304 B.C.–237 B.C. Grandson of Chandragupta Maurya. Who used stone columns to mark the territory of his empire and make announcements. p. 133

Ashurbanipal (ash ür bän′ē pal) reign 668 B.C.–627 B.C. King of Assyria from 668 B.C. to 627 B.C. when it was at its largest and most powerful. p. 52

Augustus (ȯ gus′təs) 63 B.C.–A.D. 14 Ancient Roman emperor whose rule began a long period of prosperity and peace called the Pax Romana, or "the Roman Peace." for the Roman Empire. p. 289

B

Babur (bä′bər) 1483–1530 Muslim ruler who conquered parts of northern India and founded the Mogul Empire. p. 348

Ban Zhao (ban jou) c. 100 B.C. Chinese scholar and historian of the Han dynasty who continued the work of Sima Qian. p. 111

Barton, Sir Edmund 1849–1920 Australian leader who drew up his country's first constitution. p. 503

Begin, Menachem (bā′gin, mə nä′kəm) 1913–1992 Israeli prime minister who worked toward peace in the Middle East by signing a peace accord between Egypt and Israel in 1978. p. 619

Ben-Gurion, David 1886–1973 Israeli leader who declared the state of Israel in 1948. p. 615

Bismarck, Otto von 1815–1898 Prussian prime minister who unified Germany in the 1800s. p. 500

Bolívar, Simón (bō lē′vär, sē mōn′) 1783–1830 South American soldier and revolutionary leader who liberated northwestern South America from the Spanish. p. 462

Brittain, Vera 1893–1970 British writer who became a pacifist after serving as a nurse in World War I. p. 533

Bush, George W. 1946– Forty-third president of the United States who began a campaign toward energy self-sufficiency and against terrorism in 2001. p. 647

C

Caligula (kə lig′yə lə) 12–41 Cruel ancient Roman emperor who was assassinated by members of his bodyguard. p. 289

Carson, Rachel 1907–1964 American scientist who wrote *Silent Spring*, warning of the harmful effects of pesticides on the environment. p. 661

Cartier, Jacques (kär tyā′, zhäk) 1491–1557 French explorer who claimed Canada for France. p. 447

Cavour, Camillo di (dē kä vůr′, kä mē′lō) 1810–1861 Prime minister of Sardinia who supported a unified Italy. p. 501

Chamberlain, Neville 1869–1940 British prime minister who pursued a policy of appeasement with Adolf Hitler before World War II. p. 545

Chandragupta Maurya (chən drə gup′tə mou′rē ə) 360 B.C.–298 B.C. Soldier who started the Mauryan Empire, the first Indian empire, and later became a monk. p. 135

Charlemagne (shär′lə mān) 742–814 King of the Franks who was later crowned emperor of the former Roman Empire in western Europe. p. 397

Chiang Kai-shek (chang′ kī′shek) 1887–1975 Leader of the Nationalist Party in China who set up a nationalist government in Taiwan. p. 577

Churchill, Winston 1874–1965 Prime Minister of Great Britain in 1940 who led the country to victory in World War II. p. 549

Ci Xi (tsē shyē′) 1835–1908 Chinese empress who tried to keep out foreigners and prevented further progress in China. p. 495

Claudius (klō′dē əs) 10 B.C.–A.D. 54 Ancient Roman emperor after Caligula who tried to improve conditions in the Empire. p. 289

Clemenceau, Georges (klem′ən sō, jôr′jə) 1841–1929 Leader of France who opposed U.S. President Woodrow Wilson's ideas for a fair peace and cooperation between nations after World War I. p. 536

Clinton, Bill 1946– Forty-second president of the United States who extended free trade throughout North America. p. 633

Columbus, Christopher c. 1451–1506 Italian sailor who sailed to the Americas from Spain in 1492. p. 440

Commodus (kum mō′dəs) 161–192 Ancient Roman emperor who succeeded his father, Marcus Aurelius, and began the decline of the Roman Empire. p. 299

Confucius (kən fyü′shəs) c. 551 B.C.–479 B.C. Chinese teacher of morals that came to embody the core of Confucianism. p. 115

Constantine (kon′stən tēn) c. 275–337 Christian emperor who made Christianity equal to all other religions in Rome and reunited the Roman Empire after Diocletian had divided it into two parts. p. 296

Cook, James 1728–1779 English sea captain who searched for a northern passage to the Pacific. p. 445

Copernicus (kə pėr′nə kəs) 1473–1543 Renaissance scientist who taught that Earth moves around the sun. p. 434

Cortés, Hernando (kôr tez′, hər nan′dō) 1485–1547 Spanish conquistador who defeated the Aztecs in 1521. p. 180

Cyrus II c. 585 B.C.–529 B.C. Persian king who established the Persian Empire. p. 132

D

da Gama, Vasco (də gä′mə, väs′kō) c. 1469–1524 Portuguese explorer who sailed around the Cape of Good Hope to India, establishing the first all-water route from Europe. p. 439

Darius I c. 550 B.C.–486 B.C. Persian king who expanded the Persian Empire to include India. p. 132

David 1030 B.C.–965 B.C. Second king of Israel who unified the kingdom of Israel. p. 57

da Vinci, Leonardo (də vin′chē, lē′ō När′dō) 1452–1519 Renaissance artist who painted the *Mona Lisa* and made contributions to science. p. 432

Deborah c. 1200 B.C. Female Hebrew judge who encouraged a military leader to gather the peoples of Israel to attack the Canaanites. p. 56

de Gouges, Marie-Olympe 1748–1793 French political activist and feminist who wrote the *Declaration of the Rights of Woman and the Female Citizen*, calling for the equality of women. p. 471

Deganawidah (deg än ä wē′də) c. 1550–1600 Native American leader who founded the Iroquois Confederacy. p. 225

de Klerk, F. W. 1936– President of South Africa who ended the policy of apartheid. p. 609

Dias, Bartolomeu (dē′əs, bär tō′lō myü) c. 1450–1500 Portuguese explorer who sailed around the Cape of Good Hope in 1488. p. 439

Dickens, Charles 1812–1870 English writer who often wrote about the London slums. p. 477

Diocletian (dī ō klē′shən) c. 245–316 Ancient Roman emperor who restored order and strengthened the economy of the Roman Empire, dividing it into two parts. p. 300

Pronunciation Key

a in hat	ȯ in all	sh in she
ā in age	ō in open	th in thin
â in care	ô in order	ᴛʜ in then
ä in far	oi in oil	zh in measure
e in let	ou in out	ə = a in about
ē in equal	u in cup	ə = e in taken
ėr in term	ů in put	ə = i in pencil
i in it	ü in rule	ə = o in lemon
ī in ice	ch in child	ə = u in circus
o in hot	ng in long	

Biographical Dictionary

E

Edison, Thomas 1847–1931 American inventor who created many items such as the electric light bulb, the phonograph, and the motion picture. p. 479

Eisenhower, Dwight D. 1890–1969 U.S. general who led the Allied forces on D-Day, history's largest invasion by sea, during World War II. He later became the thirty-fourth president of the United States. p. 552

Elizabeth I 1533–1603 Queen of England who built up the English navy and promoted the arts. p. 442

Enheduanna (en hā′dü wän ä) c. 2330 B.C. Daughter of Sargon and was appointed the high priestess of Ur. p. 45

Euclid (yü′klid) c. 300 B.C. Greek mathematician who developed the system of plane geometry. p. 271

Eudocia (yů′dō shē′ə) c. 400–460 Wife of Eastern Roman Emperor Theodosius II who converted to Christianity and had much influence on her husband's reign. p. 305

Ezana (ā′zä nä) c. 330 King of Axum Ethiopia who converted to Christianity. p. 381

F

Ferdinand, Francis 1863–1914 Archduke of Austria-Hungary whose assassination was a factor that led to World War I. p. 522

Frank, Anne 1929–1945 Young Jewish girl who kept a diary of her experiences during the Holocaust in World War II. p. 561

Fulton, Robert 1765–1815 American inventor who built the first steamboat in 1807. p. 475

G

Gagarin, Yuri 1934–1968 Soviet cosmonaut who became the first human in space in 1961. p. 669

Galileo (gal′ə lē′ō) 1564–1642 Renaissance scientist who studied motion and who was imprisoned by the Church for his belief that Earth moves around the sun. p. 434

Gandhi, Mohandas (gän′dē, mō hän′dəs) 1869–1948 Indian political and religious leader who believed in nonviolent civil disobedience and led India to independence in 1947. p. 611

Gaozu (gou′zü′) 256 B.C.–195 B.C. First ruler of the Han dynasty who lifted the ban on books in China. p. 111

Garibaldi, Giuseppe (gar′ə bòl′dē, jü zep′ā) 1807–1882 Italian patriot and soldier who led a small army called the "Redshirts" to unify southern Italy. p. 501

Genghis Khan (jəng′gis kän) c. 1162–1227 Mongolian leader who united the nomadic tribes of northern Asia to form a unified Mongolia. p. 352

Gilgamesh (gil′gä məsh) c. 2700 B.C. Sumerian king whose adventures were recorded in the *Epic of Gilgamesh.* p. 44

Gorbachev, Mikhail (gôr′bə chóf, mē′kīl′) 1931– Communist Party leader and last president of the Soviet Union who called for and allowed more freedom in Eastern Europe. p. 621

Gutenberg, Johannes (güt′n bėrg, yō′hän) c. 1390–1468 German craftsman who invented the movable-type printing press in the 1440s. p. 435

H

Hammurabi (ham′ů rä′bē) c. 1810 B.C.–1750 B.C. King of Babylon who came to rule all of Mesopotamia and established a written code of laws known as the Code of Hammurabi. p. 51

Hannibal (han′ə bəl) 247 B.C.–183 B.C. Carthaginian general who launched an invasion on the Romans from Spain by crossing the Alps. p. 285

Hatshepsut (hat shəp′süt) reigned c. 1498 B.C.–1483 B.C. Queen of ancient Egypt who proclaimed herself pharaoh and ruled during the New Kingdom. p. 91

Henry the Navigator 1394–1460 Portuguese prince who encouraged expeditions to explore the west coast of Africa. p. 439

Hidalgo, Miguel (ē däl′gō, mē gəl′) 1753–1811 Mexican priest who encouraged a revolt in Mexico. p. 459

Hillary, Edmund 1919–2001 New Zealand mountain climber who was the first person to reach the top of Mount Everest. p. 573

Hippocrates (hi pok′rə tēz) c. 460 B.C.–377 B.C. Ancient Greek doctor who is often called the "father of medicine." p. 270

Hirohito (hir′ō hē′tō) 1901–1989 Emperor of Japan during World War II who surrendered to the United States. p. 546

Hitler, Adolf 1889–1945 German dictator who led Nazi Germany against the Allies in World War II. p. 544

Hobby, Oveta Culp 1905–1995 American commander of the U.S. Women's Army Corps during World War II. p. 552

Hobson, William 1793–1842 British naval officer who signed a treaty making New Zealand a colony. p. 503

Ho Chi Minh (hō′ chē′ min′) 1890–1969 Communist leader of the Viet Cong in Vietnam who was determined to bring communist rule to South Vietnam. p. 584

Homer c. 900 B.C.–800 B.C. Ancient Greek poet who composed two poems, the *Iliad* and the *Odyssey*, about the Trojan War. p. 253

Hussein 1935–1999 King of Jordan who gave up his country's claim to the West Bank in order to foster peace with Israel. p. 618

I

Ibn Battuta (əb′ən ba tü′tä) c. 1304–1368 Great traveler and historian of the Islamic world. p. 336

Inca Viracocha (in kä′ vē rä kō′chä) c. 1435 Incan ruler who fled his empire in 1438 because he thought it would be defeated by the Chancas. p. 198

Isabella 1451–1504 Spanish queen who funded Columbus's expedition to America. p. 440

Iturbide, Agustín de (dā ē tür bē′dā, ò gus tēn′) 1783–1824 Spanish army officer who defeated Spain and proclaimed independence for Mexico. p. 461

J

Jayavarman II (jä yä vär′mən) c. 770–850 God-king of the Khmer who reunited the kingdom in 802. p. 357

Jefferson, Thomas 1743–1826 Third president of the United States who stood up to piracy against Americans off the Barbary coast. p. 646

Jesus c. 4 B.C.–A.D. 29 A young Jewish man who taught in Palestine and founded Christianity. p. 295

Jiang Qing (jyäng chēng) 1914–1991 Wife of Mao Zedong who led the Cultural Revolution in China in the 1960s and 1970s. p. 579

Jinnah, Muhammed Ali 1876–1948 Muslim nationalist and political leader who called for the formation of the separate Muslim state of Pakistan. p. 612

John 1167–1216 English king whose lords forced him to agree to the Magna Carta in 1215, which limited royal power. p. 398

Johnson, Lyndon B. 1908–1973 Thirty-sixth president of the United States who escalated the commitment of U.S. forces in Vietnam in an effort to prevent a communist takeover of South Vietnam. p. 584

Julius, Caesar (jü′lyəs sē′zər) 100 B.C.–44 B.C. Ancient Roman general whose murder led to the end of the Roman Republic. p. 286

Junius Brutus sixth century B.C. Ancient Roman leader who, with his supporters, forced the Etruscans out of Rome. p. 278

Justinian 483–565 Byzantine emperor who brought the Empire to its height under his rule and told his scholars to collect the laws of the ancient Romans and organize them into a code of laws. p. 327

K

Kashta reigned c. 777–750 B.C. King of Kush who conquered Upper Egypt. p. 94

Kennedy, John F. 1917–1963 Thirty-fifth president of the United States who prevented the Soviet Union from building missile bases in Cuba. p. 572

Kenyatta, Jomo (ken yä′tə, jō′mō) 1890–1978 African independence leader in Kenya who became that country's first prime minister and president. p. 607

Khrushchev, Nikita (krüsh′chóf, ni kē′tə) 1894–1971 Leader of the Soviet Communist Party in the 1950s and 1960s who divided Berlin with a wall and tried to build missile bases in Cuba. p. 572

Khufu (kü′fü) c. 2600 B.C. Egyptian pharaoh for whom the Great Pyramid at Giza was built. p. 87

Kublai Khan (kü′blə kän) 1215–1294 Grandson of Genghis Khan and founder of the Mongol (Yuan) dynasty. p. 352

L

Lalibela (lä lē bə′lä) reigned 1185–1225 Zagwe king who built eleven Christian churches in Ethiopia. p. 382

Laozi (lou′dzē′) c. sixth century B.C. First great teacher of Daoism who taught before Confucius. p. 117

Pronunciation Key

a in hat	ò in all	sh in she
ā in age	ō in open	th in thin
â in care	ô in order	TH in then
ä in far	oi in oil	zh in measure
e in let	ou in out	ə = a in about
ē in equal	u in cup	ə = e in taken
ėr in term	ů in put	ə = i in pencil
i in it	ü in rule	ə = o in lemon
ī in ice	ch in child	ə = u in circus
o in hot	ng in long	

Biographical Dictionary

Lenin, Vladimir 1870–1924 Communist leader who took over the government of Russia after the revolution and later formed the Soviet Union. p. 531

Leopold II 1835–1909 Belgian king who cruelly ruled the Congo region of Africa in the late 1800s. p. 489

Louis XVI 1754–1793 French king who was overthrown during the French Revolution. p. 467

Luther, Martin 1483–1546 German priest whose protest to the Roman Catholic Church in 1517, started the Reformation. p. 436

M

MacArthur, Douglas 1880–1964 U.S. general who commanded forces in the Pacific, including the Philippines, during World War II. p. 553

MacDonald, Sir John 1812–1872 Canadian who became the first prime minister of Canada. p. 502

Magellan, Ferdinand c. 1480–1521 Portuguese sailor who led a group of ships, one of which was the first to circumnavigate the world. p. 439

Maguire, Mairead Corrigan 1944– Northern Irish social worker who was awarded the Nobel Prize for Peace in 1976 for her work toward ending the violence in Northern Ireland. p. 639

Manco Capac c. 1200 Founder of the Inca dynasty who led the Inca to settle in Cazco. p. 197

Mandela, Nelson 1918– African National Congress leader who was the first black president of South Africa. p. 609

Manetho c. 300 B.C. Egyptian priest and advisor who began keeping records of the ancient Egyptian kings. p. 85

Mansa Musa (män′sä mü′sä) c. 1324 King of Mali who is best known for his pilgrimage to Mecca. p. 376

Mao Zedong (mou′ zů dùng′) 1893–1976 Chinese communist leader and founder of the People's Republic of China. p. 577

Marco Polo (pō′lō) c. 1254–1324 Venetian merchant, world traveler, and writer who remained in China as a guest for 17 years. p. 409

Marcus Aurelius (mär′kus ò rē′lē əs) 121–180 Ancient Roman philosopher, general, and emperor who was perhaps the greatest of Rome's "Five Good Emperors." p. 293

Marie Antoinette (mə rē′ an′twə net′) 1755–1793 Wife of Louis XVI and Queen of France during the French Revolution. p. 468

Marshall, George 1880–1959 U.S. Secretary of State under President Harry S. Truman who believed the United States should help all countries recover after World War II. p. 560

Marx, Karl 1818–1883 German economist and philosopher who popularized socialist ideals and predicted that a revolution would erase economic classes. p. 481

Mazzini, Giuseppe (mat zē′nē, jü zep′ä) 1805–1872 Italian patriot who fought to create a unified nation. p. 499

McNamara, Robert 1916– U.S. Secretary of Defense under President Lyndon B. Johnson who supported the build-up of U.S. forces in Vietnam but later questioned U.S. involvement in the war. p. 586

Meiji (mā′jē) 1852–1912 Japanese emperor who started Japan on a path of rapid modernization and adoption of Western ways. p. 495

Menchú, Rigoberta (men′chyü, rē gō bər′tä) 1959– Guatemalan woman who was awarded the Nobel Prize for Peace in 1992 for her work toward civil rights for Guatemala's poor farmers. p. 640

Mencius (mən′shē əs) c. 371 B.C.–289 B.C. Disciple of Confucius who is regarded as second only to Confucius as the cofounder of Confucianism. p. 117

Menes (mē′nēz) c. 3150 B.C. Legendary ancient Egyptian king who is credited with uniting Lower and Upper Egypt. p. 85

Michelangelo 1475–1564 Renaissance painter and sculptor who sought realism in his art. p. 432

Milosevic, Slobodan (mē lō′shəv ətch, slò′bò dən) 1941– President of Serbia who encouraged Serb fighters to carry out a policy of ethnic cleansing. p. 637

Minos (mī′nəs) Legendary King of the Minoan civilization in Crete. p. 250

Moctezuma I (mok tə zü′mä) c. 1390–1469 Aztec ruler of the Aztec Empire who increased its size and wealth. p. 178

Moctezuma II (mok tə zü′mä) 1466–1520 Aztec emperor who was the last to reign the Aztec Empire before it fell to Spain. p. 180

Morelos, José María (mō rā′lōs, hō sā′ mä rē′ä) 1765–1815 Mexican farmer and priest who helped lead the fight for Mexican independence. p. 461

Moses c. 1400 B.C.–1200 B.C. Hebrew prophet and teacher who led the Hebrews out of slavery in Egypt and received the Ten Commandments from God. p. 55

Mother Teresa 1910–1997 Roman Catholic nun who helped the poorest people of Calcutta, India, for decades p. 655

Mugabe, Robert (mü gä′bā, rə′bərt) 1924– African nationalist who became the prime minister of Zimbabwe (formerly Rhodesia). p. 609

Muhammad (mu häm′əd) c. 570–632 Founder of Islam. p. 331

Mussolini, Benito (mü′sə lē′nē, bən ē′tō) 1883–1945 Italian dictator who led Italy in World War II against the Allies. p. 544

N

Napoleon Bonaparte (nə pō′lē ən bō′nə pärt) 1769–1821 French general and military genius who named himself emperor of France in 1804. p. 469

Nasser, Gamal Abdel 1918–1970 Modern Egyptian leader who drove the British out of Egypt in 1956. p. 616

Nebuchadnezzar II (nə bə kəd nəz′ər) c. 630 B.C.–562 B.C. Chaldean dynasty king of Babylon who took over much of the former Assyrian Empire and ordered massive building projects. p. 52

Nero (nir′ō) 37–68 Ancient Roman emperor upon whose death civil war broke out. p. 289

Nicholas II 1868–1918 Czar of Russia during World War I who became the last Russian emperor.. p. 522

Nixon, Richard 1913–1994 Thirty-seventh president of the United States who visited China in 1972 and, in 1974, became the only president to resign from office. p. 578

Nkrumah, Kwame (nə krü′mə, kwä′mä) 1909–1972 Ghanaian leader who headed the independence movement and later became Ghana's first prime minister. p. 607

Norgay, Tenzing (nôr′gā, tən′zing) 1914–1986 Sherpa who was one of the first people to reach the top of Mount Everest. p. 573

Nyerere, Julius (nyə rār′ā, jü′lyəs) 1922–1999 Tanganyikan leader who worked for the independence of Tanzania from Great Britain and later became that country's first president. p. 607

O

O'Higgins, Bernardo 1778–1842 South American army leader who helped gain Chile's independence in 1818. p. 462

P

Pachacuti (pä chä kü′tē) c. 1391–1473 Incan emperor and son of Inca Viracocha who defeated the Chancas and extended his empire. p. 203

Paul died c. A.D. 68 Disciple of Jesus who helped spread his teachings throughout the Roman Empire. p. 296

Pericles (per′ə klēz′) c. 490 B.C.–429 B.C. Ancient Athenian leader who strove to make Athens the center of art and literature and who was responsible for building the Parthenon. p. 255

Perry, Matthew 1794–1858 U.S. naval officer who sailed to Japan and opened the country to trade with the West in 1853. p. 495

Peter died c. A.D. 67 Disciple of Jesus who helped spread his teachings throughout the Roman Empire. p. 296

Petrarch, Francesco (pə′trärk, fran səs′kō) 1304–1374 Italian poet and scholar who often encouraged people to speak and write thoughtfully. p. 431

Pizarro, Francisco (pi zär′ō, fran sis′kō) c. 1478–1541 Spanish conquistador who defeated the Incas. p. 201

Plato (plā′tō) c. 428 B.C.–347 B.C. Ancient Greek philosopher and disciple of Socrates who was one of the most famous thinkers of ancient Greece. p. 262

Pythagoras (pə thag′ər əs) c. 580 B.C.–500 B.C. Ancient Greek philosopher and mathematician whose ideas led to the field of geometry. p. 271

R

Rabin, Yitzhak (rä bēn′, yət zäk′) 1922–1995 Israeli prime minister who worked toward peace in the Middle East by signing the Oslo Accords in 1993. p. 618

Raphael 1483–1520 Renaissance painter who is known for his Madonnas. p. 432

Regulus c. 250 B.C. Ancient Roman general who was defeated and captured in a war between Rome and Carthage. p. 283

Pronunciation Key

a in hat	ò in all	sh in she
ā in age	ō in open	th in thin
â in care	ô in order	TH in then
ä in far	oi in oil	zh in measure
e in let	ou in out	ə = a in about
ē in equal	u in cup	ə = e in taken
ėr in term	ů in put	ə = i in pencil
i in it	ü in rule	ə = o in lemon
ī in ice	ch in child	ə = u in circus
o in hot	ng in long	

Biographical Dictionary

Rhodes, Cecil (rōdz, sē′səl) 1853–1902 British imperialist who believed that Europeans were better than non-Europeans in the colonies. p. 487

Robespierre, Maximilien de (də rōbz′pyer, māk′sē mē lyan′) 1758–1794 Radical leader who became a key figure in the French Revolution. p. 469

Robinson, Mary 1944– First female president of the Republic of Ireland who later became the United Nations High Commissioner for Human Rights in 1997. p. 639

Romulus Augustulus (rom′yə las ô gus′tə lus) c. 464–? Last emperor of the Western Roman Empire in A.D. 476 at age twelve and reigned for only eleven months. p. 304

Roosevelt, Eleanor 1884–1962 Wife of U.S. President Franklin D. Roosevelt who became a delegate to the United Nations, a writer, and a public speaker. p. 560

Roosevelt, Franklin D. 1882–1945 Thirty-second president of the United States and the longest serving president who led the country during most of World War II. p. 550

Roosevelt, Theodore 1858–1919 Twenty-sixth president of the United States who was responsible for peace between Japan and Russia in 1905. p. 496

S

el-Sadat, Anwar 1918–1981 Egyptian president who made peace with Israel in 1978. p. 619

San Martín, José de (dā sän mär tēn′, hō sā′) 1778–1850 Argentine soldier who helped defeat the Spanish in Chile. p. 462

Sargon c. 2400 B.C.–2300 B.C. Akkadian king who united all of the city-states of Mesopotamia under his rule, forming the world's first empire. p. 45

Scipio (skip′ē ō) c. 185 B.C.–129 B.C. Ancient Roman general who attacked Carthage and forced Hannibal to retreat from Rome. p. 285

Sese Seko, Mobutu (sə sā′ sā kō, mō bü′tü) 1930–1997 African president of Zaire (Democratic Republic of the Congo) who overthrew the government in 1965 and ruled as dictator until 1997. p. 607

Shah Jahan (shä jə hän′) 1592–1666 Grandson of Akbar and Mogul ruler from 1628 to 1658 who ordered the construction of the Taj Mahal. p. 349

Shi Huangdi (shē′ hwäng dē) c. 259 B.C.–210 B.C. King of Qin who created the first unified Chinese empire and became the first Chinese emperor. p. 110

Shikibu, Murasaki c. 978–1014 Japanese court lady who wrote *The Tale of Genji*, the world's first novel. p. 361

Shulgi c. 2100 B.C. King of the Sumerian dynasty of Ur who was also the son of Ur-Nammu. p. 46

Siddhartha Gautama (sid där′tə gō′tə mə) c. 563 B.C.–483 B.C. Ancient Indian religious leader who came to be known as the Buddha, or the "Enlightened One," and founded Buddhism. p. 141

Sima Qian (sü′mən chə′en) c. 100 B.C. Chinese astronomer who became the first Chinese historian after writing a complete history book on China. p. 111

Socrates (sok′rə tēz′) c. 470 B.C.–399 B.C. Ancient Greek philosopher who developed an approach to teaching based on asking questions. p. 262

Solomon c. 1000 B.C. Son of David and King of Israel. p. 57

Sonni Ali (sün′nē ä lē′) c. 1500 King of Songhai who increased trade and learning in the empire of Songhai. p. 378

Stalin, Joseph 1879–1953 Dictator of the Soviet Union who fought on the side of the Allies during World War II and led the Soviet Union against the United States in the Cold War. p. 546

Stephenson, George 1781–1848 British engineer who invented the locomotive. p. 475

Sumanguru (sü mən gü′rü) c. 1203 King of Ghana who defeated the Soninke king and controlled Koumbi. p. 375

Sundiata (sün′ dē ä′tä) 1210–1255 King of Mali who established a long-lived system of government and made Mali into one of the greatest trading kingdoms in Africa. p. 376

Sun Yat-sen (sün′ yät′sən′) 1866–1925 Chinese leader who led a revolutionary movement in China that began in 1911. p. 577

Suryavarman II (sər yä vär′mən) c. 1150 Khmer king who oversaw the construction of the magnificent towers of Angkor Wat. p. 357

Suu Kyi, Aung San (sü kyē, än sän) 1945– Myanmar opposition leader who was awarded the Nobel Prize for Peace in 1991 for leading a pro-democracy movement in Myanmar (Burma). p. 642

T

Tarquin (tär′kwin) c. 510 B.C. Etruscan leader and the last king of ancient Rome. p. 278

Theodora c. 500–548 Wife of Byzantine Emperor Justinian who was also his most trusted advisor. p. 327

Theodosius (thē ō dō′sē əs) 347–395 Ancient Roman emperor who made Christianity Rome's official religion in 380. p. 296

Thutmose III c. 1400s B.C. New Kingdom pharaoh who conquered Nubia and brought ancient Egypt to the height of its power. p. 94

Tilak 1856–1920 Indian rebel leader who helped guide India to independence. p. 488

Tokugawa Ieyasu (tō kü gä′wä ē yä′sü) 1543–1616 First shogun of the Tokugawa dynasty of Japan who also began a policy of isolation. p. 361

Topa Inca c. 1471 Inca ruler and son of Pachacuti who doubled the size of the empire. p. 198

Toussaint L'Ouverture (tü sän′ lü vər tür′) 1743–1803 Former slave who led a revolt against the French in Haiti. p. 459

Toyotomi Hideyoshi (toi yō tō′mē hi dā yō′shē) 1537–1598 Japanese general who united Japan after civil war in 1590. p. 361

Truman, Harry S. 1884–1972 Thirty-third president of the United States after Franklin Roosevelt died, Truman authorized the use of the atomic bomb on Japan. p. 554

U

Urban II c. 1035–1099 Pope who issued a plea to free the Holy Land Palestine from the Turks, launching the Crusades. p. 407

Ur-Nammu c. 2200 B.C.–2100 B.C. Sumerian king who founded the last and most successful dynasty of Ur. p. 46

V

Victor Emmanuel II 1820–1878 Sardinian king who began to rule a unified Italy in 1860. p. 501

Victoria 1819–1901 Queen of Great Britain who oversaw the expansion of the British Empire and claimed that "the sun never sets" on it. p. 488

Virgil (vėr′jəl) 70 B.C.–19 B.C. Ancient Roman poet who wrote the legend the *Aeneid*. p. 253

W

Walesa, Lech (və wen′sə, lək) 1943– Polish steel worker who led the Solidarity labor union and became president after communists lost control of the Polish government. p. 621

Washington, George 1732–1799 General of the United States in the Revolutionary War who later became the first president of the United States. p. 458

Watt, James 1736–1819 Scottish inventor who improved the steam engine, enabling it to power large machines. p. 475

Wilhelm II 1859–1941 German ruler who insisted on building a big, modern navy to compete with Great Britain. p. 521

William the Conqueror c. 1028–1087 Norman king who conquered England in 1066. p. 397

Wilson, Woodrow 1856–1924 Twenty-eighth president of the United States who, during World War I, negotiated peace based on the Fourteen Points and helped form the League of Nations. p. 530

Wu Di (wü dē) c. 87 B.C. Chinese emperor who increased authority during the Han dynasty. p. 111

Wu Hou (wü jou) 625–705 First Chinese empress who ruled during the Tang dynasty and unified the empire. p. 351

Y

Yeltsin, Boris 1931– First president of the Russian Republic, which formed in 1991 after the breakup of the Soviet Union. p. 622

Z

Zheng He c. 1371–1435 Chinese explorer who led seven voyages westward under the Ming dynasty. p. 355

Pronunciation Key

a in hat	ò in all	sh in she
ā in age	ō in open	th in thin
â in care	ô in order	ᴛʜ in then
ä in far	oi in oil	zh in measure
e in let	ou in out	ə = a in about
ē in equal	u in cup	ə = e in taken
ėr in term	ù in put	ə = i in pencil
i in it	ü in rule	ə = o in lemon
ī in ice	ch in child	ə = u in circus
o in hot	ng in long	

Glossary

The Glossary will help you understand the meanings and pronounce the vocabulary words in this book. The page number tells you where the word or term first appears.

A

absolute power (ab′sə lüt pou′ər) the power to control every part of a society (p. 357)

adobe (ə dō′bē) a brick formed from mud and straw that is dried in the sun (p. 214)

aggression (ə gresh′ən) a policy of launching attacks on the territory of others (p. 545)

agora (ag′ər ə) an outdoor marketplace in ancient Greece (p. 249)

agriculture (ag′rə kul chər) the raising of plants or animals for human use (p. 21)

alliance (ə lī əns) an agreement made between two or more groups or nations (p. 177)

Allied Powers (al′īd pou′ərz) an alliance between Great Britain, France, Russia, and Italy in World War I (p. 527)

Allies (al′īz) an alliance between Great Britain, France, the Soviet Union, China, and the United States in World War II (p. 550)

alpaca (al pak′ə) a domesticated animal from the Andes Mountains (p. 187)

Analects (a nə leks′) a collection of sayings by Confucius (p. 116)

ancestor (an′ses tər) a relative who lived longer ago than a grandparent (p. 111)

annex (ə neks′) to attach or to add (p. 545)

anthropology (an′thrə pol′ə jē) the study of how people have developed and live in cultural groups (p. 27)

apartheid (ə pärt′hāt) a system of laws in South Africa, which kept blacks and whites separate (p. 609)

Apostle (ə pos′əl) one of twelve disciples chosen by Jesus to help him preach and spread the Word of God (p. 295)

appeasement (ə pēz′mənt) to preserve peace by meeting the demands of an aggressor (p. 545)

Appian Way (a′pē′ən wā) a famous ancient Roman road (p. 287)

aqueduct (ak′wə dukt) structures used to carry flowing water from a distance (p. 170)

Arab nationalism (ar′əb nash′ə nə liz′əm) Arab unity, which became a powerful force under Egyptian President Gamal Abdel Nasser (p. 616)

archaeologist (är′kē ol′ə jist) a scientist who uncovers evidence, or proof, from the past (p. 11)

archaeology (är′kē ol′ə jē) the study of past cultures through the things that remain such as buildings, tools, or pottery (p. 11)

archipelago (är′kə pel′ə gō) a close group of islands (p. 188)

arid (ar′id) dry (p. 210)

aristocracy (ar′ə stok′rə sē) a government controlled by a few wealthy people (p. 255)

aristocrat (ə ris′tə krat) a person who is a member of a high social class (p. 361)

Armada (är mä′də) a fleet of warships (p. 442)

armistice (är′mə stis) a cease-fire (p. 530)

artifact (är′tə fakt) an object made by people long ago (p. 11)

artisan (är′tə zən) a craftsperson such as a potter or weaver (p. 38)

Assembly (ə sem′blē) in ancient Greece, an Athenian governing body of all citizens older than eighteen (p. 255)

assembly line (ə sem′blē lin) a way to manufacture items in which each worker contributes one part along a moving belt or line to make a whole product (p. 479)

Association of Southeast Asian Nations, (ASEAN) a trading bloc of Southeast Asian nations (p. 632)

astrolabe (as′trə lāb) and instrument used by navigators to determine latitude (p. 337)

auction (ôk′shən) to sell something to the highest bidder (p. 299)

Axis Powers (ak′sis pou′ərz) alliance between Germany, Italy, and Japan in World War II (p. 550)

B

balsa (bôl′sə) a small reed boat (p. 188)

Bantu (ban′tü) any of a number of languages with word similarities in Africa (p. 373)

barter (bär′tər) to exchange one kind of good or service for another (p. 59)

basin and range (bā′sn and rānj) a low area of land with a small mountain range (p. 209)

Bastille (ba stēl′) a former prison in Paris and site of the beginning of the French Revolution (p. 468)

Big Three (big thrē) the major Allied leaders—Franklin Roosevelt, Joseph Stalin, and Winston Churchill (p. 551)

biome (bī′ōm) a place that has a distinct climate, plants, and animals (p. 188)

Book of Documents (bük ov dok′yə mənts) Zhou dynasty text that Confucius interpreted and revived (p. 115)

Brahman (brä′mən) believed by Hindus to be the universal truth being, which is the source of everything (p. 138)

brahmin (brä′mən) a priest who held the highest position in Aryan society (p. 131)

Bronze Age (bronz āj) a period of history when bronze was mainly used to make items such as tools and weapons (p. 108)

bubonic plague (byü bon′ik plāg) an epidemic spread to humans by fleas from rats (p. 410)

Buddha, the (bü′də) the "Enlightened One," what Siddhartha Gautama came to be known (p. 141)

Buddhism (bü′diz əm) the religion that is based on the teachings of the Buddha (p. 141)

burial mound (ber′ē əl mound) a small hill of dirt built over the grave of a person (p. 219)

Byzantine Empire (biz′n tēn′ em′pīr) an empire of lands formerly part of the Roman Empire with its center at the city of Constantinople (p. 301)

Byzantine Orthodox Church (biz′n tēn′ ôr′thə doks chėrch) the early Christian church in the Eastern Roman Empire of which the emperor was head (p. 302)

C

caesar (sē′zər) an ancient Roman emperor (p. 286)

caliph (kā′lif) a successor to Muhammad (p. 332)

capitalism (kap′ə tə liz′əm) an economic system in which private individuals own most businesses and resources (p. 480)

capitalist (kap′ə tə list) a person who follows capitalism and invests in factories and industries (p. 480)

caravan (kar′ə van) a group of people and animals traveling together (p. 331)

carbon dating (kär′bən dāt′ing) a method of estimating the age of something after it has died (p. 23)

carbon dioxide (kär′bən di ok′sīd) a gas produced by the burning of gasoline (p. 661)

caste (kast) in Hinduism, a lifelong social group into which one is born (p. 139)

casualty (kazh′ü əl tē) a wounded or killed soldier (p. 528)

catacomb (kat′ə kōm) an underground room used as a burial site (p. 295)

cataract (kat′ə rakt′) a waterfall (p. 80)

cathedral (kə thē′drəl) a large, important Christian church (p. 327)

causeway (kôz′wā′) raised bridges made of land (p. 176)

cenote (sä nō′tā) natural wells on the Yucatán Peninsula (p. 171)

Central Powers (sen′trəl pou′ərz) an alliance between Germany, Austria-Hungary, and the Ottoman Empire in World War I (p. 527)

charter (chär′tər) a constitution (p. 560)

chinampa (chən äm′pä) man-made island (p. 176)

chivalry (shiv′əl rē) a knight's code of behavior (p. 401)

Christianity (kris′chē an′ə tē) the monotheistic religion based on the life, teachings, and death of Jesus (p. 295)

circumnavigate (sėr′kəm nav′ə gāt) to travel around the world (p. 439)

city-state (sit′ē stāt) a city that is an individual unit, complete with its own form of government and traditions (p. 38)

civil disobedience (siv′əl dis′ə bē′dē əns) the refusal to obey or cooperate with unjust laws (p. 611)

civilization (siv′ə lə zā′shən) a group of people who have a complex and organized society within a culture (p. 35)

civil service (siv′əl sėr′vis) the practice of using skills and talents to work in the government (p. 111)

climate (klī′mit) the average weather conditions of a place over a long span of time (p. 23)

Pronunciation Key

a in hat	ō in open	sh in she
â in care	ò in all	th in thin
ā in age	ô in order	ᴛʜ in then
ä in far	oi in oil	zh in measure
e in let	ou in out	ə = a in about
ē in equal	u in cup	ə = e in taken
ėr in term	ù in put	ə = i in pencil
i in it	ü in rule	ə = o in lemon
ī in ice	ch in child	ə = u in circus
o in hot	ng in long	

Glossary

Code of Hammurabi (kōd ov ham′ü rä′bē) a set of laws established by Hammurabi (p. 50)

codex (kō′deks) a folding-screen book containing information about predicting the future and religious rituals (p. 172)

Cold War (kōld wôr) the tension between the Soviet Union and the United States after World War II (p. 569)

collective (kə lek′tiv) farms that are grouped together and run by the government (p. 546)

colony (kol′ə nē) a settlement far from the country that governs it (p. 445)

Columbian Exchange (kə lum′bē ən eks chānj′) the transfer of goods and diseases from Europe to America and American items back to Europe (p. 441)

command economy (kə mand′ i kon′ə mē) an economy in which the government or other central authority controls the flow of money (p. 481)

commerce (kom′ərs) the buying and selling of a large quantity of goods (p. 431)

common market (kom′ən mär′kit) an economic union (p. 636)

communism (kom′yə niz′əm) a form of socialism in which all resources are owned by a government led by a dictator (p. 531)

compound (kom′pound) a set-aside area (p. 494)

concentration camp (kon′sən trā′shən kamp) a place that holds imprisoned people of a particular ethnic group or for their political or religious beliefs (p. 559)

concrete (kon′krēt′) a building material made from a mixture of crushed stone, sand, cement, and water (p. 287)

Confucianism (kən fyü′shə niz′əm) a way of thinking and living based on the teachings of Confucius (p. 116)

conquer (kong′kər) to defeat (p. 45)

conquest (kon′kwest) the defeat of another group (p. 52)

conquistador (kon kē′stə dôr) a Spanish conqueror (p. 441)

conservation (kən sər vā′shən) the use of resources carefully and wisely (p. 657)

consul (kon′səl) in ancient Rome, one of two officials who managed the government and the army (p. 283)

containment (kən tān′mənt) a policy of preventing Soviet communism from spreading into new countries or states (p. 570)

convent (kon′vent) a community of nuns (p. 401)

corporation (kôr′pə rā′shən) a business organization (p. 479)

Counter-Reformation (koun′tər-ref′ər mā′shən) response and reforms by the Roman Catholic Church to the Protestant Reformation (p. 437)

coup d'état (kü′dā tä′) the overthrow of a government (p. 607)

covenant (kuv′ə nənt) an agreement (p. 55)

Crusades (krü sādz′) major military expeditions by Christians to win back control of Palestine (Holy Land) and to protect the Byzantine Empire (p. 407)

culture (kul′chər) the way in which individuals and groups react with their environment, including their technology, customs, beliefs, and art (p. 27)

cuneiform (kyü nē′ə fôrm) a form of wedge-shaped writing used in ancient times (p. 43)

D

daimyo (dī myō) a powerful samurai who controlled many other samurai and governed large areas of farmland in Japan (p. 359)

Daoism (dou′izəm) the belief in finding the "way," or the dao, of the universe (p. 117)

D-Day (dē′dā′) June 6, 1944, the date that Allied forces landed in France in World War II in the largest invasion by sea in history (p. 552)

Declaration of Independence (dek lə rā′shən ov in di pen′dəns) the document written in 1776 that said the American colonies were free and independent states and no longer part of Great Britain (p. 458)

Declaration of the Rights of Man and of Citizen a document that established the rights of citizens under a French republic (p. 468)

decolonization (dē kol′ə nə zā′shən) the process of replacing colonial rule with self-rule (p. 607)

deforestation (dē fôr′ist ā′shən) the clearing of land, which causes loss of forests and less fertile land (p. 662)

Delian League (də lē′ən lēg) in ancient Greece, an alliance between Athens and other Greek city-states (p. 263)

delta (del′tə) a triangular-shaped area at the mouth of some rivers (p. 79)

democracy (di mok′rə sē) a government by the people (p. 255)

demographer (di mog′rə fər) a person who studies population trends (p. 656)

depression (di presh′ən) a period of sharp economic decline (p. 543)

descendant (di sen′dənt) a person born later into the same family (p. 55)

desertification (di zėrt′ə fə kā′shən) the drying up of land along a desert (p. 662)

détente (dā tänt′) a relaxation of tensions, especially between nations (p. 587)

deva-raja (dā′və-rä′jə) according to Hindu rites, a god-king (p. 357)

dharma (där′mə) in Hinduism, the order of the universe (p. 138)

dictator (dik′tā tər) a person who has total control over the people (p. 283)

disciple (də sī′pəl) one of a small group of people who followed Jesus (p. 295)

dissident (dis′ə dənt) a protester against a government (p. 621)

diverse (də vėrs′) different (p. 27)

Domesday Book (dümz′dā′ bůk) a book made in 1086 that helped King William keep track of all of the people and property in England (p. 397)

domestic system (də mes′tik sis′təm) a system in which goods were made in the home, rather than in factories (p. 475)

domesticate (də mes′tə kāt) to tame (p. 19)

dominion (də min′yən) a self-governing nation with strong ties to a ruling empire (p. 502)

domino effect (dom′ə nō ə fekt′) a theory that the fall of one item will lead to the fall of all adjoining items like dominoes that are lined up when one is toppled (p. 585)

double cropping (dub′əl krop′ping) a process in which two crops are grown on the same land in the same year (p. 102)

dynasty (dī′nə stē) a ruling family (p. 45)

E

economy (i kon′ə mē) the way people use and manage resources (p. 89)

Eightfold Path (āt′fōld path) the Buddhist way of living that can help Buddhists find relief from their suffering (p. 143)

emperor (em′pər ər) the ruler of an empire (p. 289)

empire (em′pīr) a large territory consisting of many different places under the control of a single ruler (p. 45)

encomienda (en kō mē ən′də) a Spanish system that allowed colonists to demand labor from Native Americans (p. 447)

endangered species (en dān′jərd spē′shēz) an animal or plant that is in danger of dying out completely (p. 661)

enlightenment (en līt′n mənt) in Buddhism, a state of pure goodness, the goal of reincarnation (p. 142)

environmentalist (en vī′rən men′tl ist) a person who tries to solve environmental problems (p. 661)

Environmental Protection Agency a U.S. agency that watches the environment (p. 661)

epidemic (ep′ə dem′ik) a disease that spreads quickly (p. 410)

estate (e stāt′) a class or order in pre-Revolutionary French society (p. 467)

Estates-General (e stātz′jen′ər əl) in pre-Revolutionary France, a representative assembly that advised the king (p. 467)

etching (ech′ing) an imprinted drawing or design (p. 213)

ethnic cleansing (eth′nik klən′zing) to drive out or kill people who do not share the same ethnicity or identity (p. 637)

ethnicity (eth nis′ə tē) a group of people with the same language, customs, and culture (p. 637)

euro (yůr′ō) the money of the European Union (p. 632)

European Union, (EU) (yůr′ə pē′ən yü′nyən) a European trading bloc (p. 632)

excavation site (ek′skə vā′shən sīt) a site where archaeologists uncover artifacts (p. 20)

excommunicate (eks′kə myü′nə kāt) to expel from a church (p. 437)

Pronunciation Key

a in hat	ō in open	sh in she
â in care	ȯ in all	th in thin
ā in age	ô in order	ᴛʜ in then
ä in far	oi in oil	zh in measure
e in let	ou in out	ə = a in about
ē in equal	u in cup	ə = e in taken
ėr in term	ů in put	ə = i in pencil
i in it	ü in rule	ə = o in lemon
ī in ice	ch in child	ə = u in circus
o in hot	ng in long	

F

factory (fak′tər ē) a building that houses many machines (p. 475)

factory system (fak′tər ē sis′təm) the grouping of machines in one place (p. 475)

fascism (fash′iz′əm) a form of government that stresses the nation above individuals (p. 544)

fertile (fėr′tl) rich, as in soil (p. 35)

feudalism (fyü′dl iz′əm) a social, political, and economic system used in the Middle Ages (p. 401)

Five-Year Plan (fīv′yir plan) an economic plan first launched by Soviet Party leader Joseph Stalin in 1928 (p. 546)

fossil fuel (fos′əl fyü′əl) a fuel formed long ago deep in the earth from prehistoric plants and animals (p. 665)

Four Noble Truths (fôr nō′bəl trüᴛʜz) in Buddhism, beliefs about human suffering (p. 143)

Fourteen Points (fôr′tēn′points) U.S. President Woodrow Wilson's blueprint for peace in Europe after World War I (p. 536)

G

geography (jē og′rə fē) the study of the relationship between physical features, climate, and people (p. 27)

geothermal energy (jē ō thėr′məl en′ər jē) energy that is produced from super-hot, underground water (p. 667)

glacier (glā′shər) a huge ice sheet (p. 12)

gladiator (glad′ē ā tər) in ancient Rome, a professional fighter (p. 291)

glasnost (glaz′nost) "openess", a policy introduced by Mikhail Gorbachev in 1985 to allow the Soviet people some freedom of speech (p. 622)

global warming (glō′bəl wôr′ming) a gradual increase in the temperature of Earth's surface (p. 661)

Golden Age (gōl′dən āj) a period of time in ancient Athens when magnificent temples were built; artists created statues and monuments; and philosophers extended human knowledge (p. 262)

Gospels (gos′pəlz) in Christianity, the four books of the Bible known as the New Testament (p. 295)

Great Depression (grāt di presh′ən) a period of economic decline that began in 1929 and lasted until about 1939 (p. 543)

Great Wall (grāt wȯl) a wall in China originally built for protection from northern invaders that over centuries was extended to more than 4,300 miles (p. 110)

Great Zimbabwe (grāt zim bä′bwā) a kingdom in Africa of some 11,000 people that reached its height about 1400 (p. 384)

greenhouse effect (grēn′hous ə′fekt′) the process by which carbon dioxide in Earth's atmosphere traps heat from the sun, raising the temperature of Earth's surface (p. 661)

griot (grēō′) a professional storyteller from Africa (p. 376)

gross domestic product, (GDP) (grōs də mes′tik prod′ekt) a measure of a country's wealth (p. 631)

guerrilla (gə ril′ə) a hit-and-run fighter (p. 584)

guild (gild) a group of craftspeople or merchants who are united by a common interest (p. 404)

H

hajj (haj) a pilgrimage to Mecca (p. 331)

Han dynasty (hän dī′nə stē) a dynasty that lasted from 206 B.C. to A.D. 220 in China (p. 111)

harvest (här′vist) to gather (p. 20)

Hellenistic Age (hel′ə nis′tik āj) a period of time when ancient Greek and Asian cultures mixed (p. 268)

helot (hel′ət) a slave (p. 255)

hieroglyphics (hī′ər ə glif′iks) a form of writing based on pictures (p. 86)

Hinduism (hin′dü iz′əm) the main religion of India that is based on Aryan beliefs (p. 137)

hippodrome (hi′pə′drōm) an ancient Greek stadium used for horse and chariot racing (p. 324)

holocaust (hol′ə kôst) a mass killing (p. 535)

Human Genome Project (hyü′mən je′nōm proj′ekt) an international project launched in 1990, to locate all of the human genes (p. 670)

hydroelectric energy (hī′drō i lek′trik en′ər jē) electricity produced by using the energy of flowing water (p. 666)

I

Ice Age (īs āj) a period of time when glaciers covered great stretches of land (p. 12)

icon (ī′kon) a religious image (p. 328)

immigration (im′ə grā′shən) to leave a home country and go to another country to stay permanently (p. 657)

immortal (i môr′tl) to live forever (p. 254)

imperialism (im pir′ē ə liz′əm) a system of building an empire by conquering lands around the world (p. 487)

imperialist (im pir′ē ə list) a person who promotes imperialism (p. 487)

independent (in′di pen′dənt) free (p. 94)

indulgence (in dul′jəns) in the Roman Catholic Church, a pardon for sin (p. 436)

Industrial Revolution (in dus′trē əl rev′ə lü′shən) a period of time in society when human and animal power changed to machine power (p. 475)

inflation (in flā′shən) a rapid increase in prices (p. 537)

internal combustion engine (in tėr′nl kəm bus′chən en′jən) a machine that uses the power of a controlled burning of fuel (p. 479)

irrigation (ir ə gā′shən) a system of transporting water to crops (p. 36)

Islam (is′lam) the monotheistic religion revealed to and based on the teachings of Muhammad (p. 331)

J

jihad (ji häd′) in Islam, a military or peaceful "struggle" (p. 333)

Judaism (jü′dē iz′əm) the monotheistic religion founded by Abraham (p. 55)

Justinian Code (ju stin′ē ən kōd) laws of the ancient Romans collected by Byzantine scholars and organized into a code of laws for the Byzantine Empire under Emperor Justinian (p. 327)

K

kamikaze (kä′mi kä′zē) World War II Japanese pilots who flew into enemy warships to destroy them (p. 554)

knight (nīt) a feudal warrior trained and prepared to fight on horseback (p. 401)

L

labor union (lā′bər yü′nyən) a group of workers that gathers together to raise wages and improve working conditions (p. 480)

lady (lā′dē) a woman of nobility (p. 405)

laissez faire (les′ā fâr′) "leave it alone," a policy in which the government does not try to control something such as business operations (p. 480)

landform (land′fôrm′) a natural feature of Earth's surface such as a valley, plain, hill, or mountain (p. 27)

Late Stone Age (lāt stōn āj) the end of the New Stone Age (p. 27)

League of Nations (lēg ov nā′shənz) an organization of nations formed after World War I to promote cooperation and peace (p. 536)

legislature (lej′ə slā′chər) a group of elected people who make laws (p. 457)

levee (lev′ē) a dike used to control flooding (p. 102)

llama (lä′mə) a domesticated animal from the Andes Mountains (p. 187)

loess (lō′is) a yellowish brown soil that blows in from a desert (p. 101)

long house (lȯng′ hous′) a large, rectangular building used by the Iroquois that housed many families (p. 224)

M

Magna Carta (mag′nə kär′tə) an English charter (1215) that limited royal power (p. 398)

Mandate of Heaven (man′dāt ov hev′ən) in dynastic China, the divine right to govern for the good of all people (p. 116)

manor system (man′ər sis′təm) in the Middle Ages, a way to manage feudal lands (p. 402)

marathon (mar′ə thon) the longest race in the Olympics, a footrace of about 26 miles (p. 261)

market economy (mär′kit i kon′ə me) an economy in which the people make their own decisions about how to spend money (p. 480)

Marshall Plan (mär′shəl plan) a plan that offered U.S. financial help to Europe after World War II (p. 560)

massacre (mas′ə kər) the killing of many helpless people (p. 457)

Pronunciation Key

a in hat	ō in open	sh in she
â in care	ȯ in all	th in thin
ā in age	ô in order	ᴛʜ in then
ä in far	oi in oil	zh in measure
e in let	ou in out	ə = a in about
ē in equal	u in cup	ə = e in taken
ėr in term	ů in put	ə = i in pencil
i in it	ü in rule	ə = o in lemon
ī in ice	ch in child	ə = u in circus
o in hot	ng in long	

Glossary

meditation (med′ə tā′shən) in Buddhism, a way of clearing the mind (p. 142)

megacity (meg′ə sit′ē) a city region with more than 10 million people (p. 655)

mercantilism (mėr′kən ti liz′əm) a system in which a country uses its colonies to obtain raw materials, makes products from the raw materials, and then sells the goods back to the colonists (p. 445)

mercenary (mėr′sə ner′ē) a hired soldier (p. 264)

Mercosur (mėr kō′sər) a trading bloc of South American countries (p. 633)

Messiah (mə′sī ə) in Judaism, a leader sent by God; in Christianity, the savior, Jesus, God in human form (p. 296)

Middle Ages (mid′l ājs) a period in European history that lasted from about 500 to about 1500 (p. 397)

middleman (mid′l man) a person who goes between buyers and sellers (p. 112)

migrate (mī′grāt) to move from one place to another (p. 12)

millennium (mə len′ē əm) a period of 1,000 years (p. 655)

Ming dynasty (ming dī′nəstē) a dynasty that lasted from 1368 to 1644 in China (p. 353)

Minoan (mi nō′ən) an early Greek civilization that developed on the island of Crete (p. 250)

missionary (mish′ə ner′ē) a person who teaches a religion to people with different beliefs (p. 401)

mobilization (mō′bə lī zā′shən) the preparations nations make before sending their armies into battle (p. 522)

modernization (mod′ər nī zā′shən) the process of bringing ways and standards to those of the present (p. 495)

monarch (mon′ərk) a king or queen who is a supreme leader (p. 401)

monarchy (mon′ər kē) government in which a king, queen, or emperor has supreme power (p. 467)

monastery (mon′ə ster′ē) a community where monks live, study, and pray (p. 401)

Mongol (Yuan) dynasty (mong′gəl dī nə′stē) a dynasty that began with Kublai Khan's conquest of southern China and Burma in 1287 (p. 352)

monk (mungk) a man who devotes his life to religion and lives in a monastery (p. 401)

monotheism (mon′ə thē iz′əm) the worship of only one God (p. 55)

monsoon season (mon sün′) rainy season in monsoon climates in which winds blow from the southwest for six months (p. 125)

mosque (mosk) a Muslim place of worship (p. 332)

movable type (mü′və bəl tīp) small, reusable metal blocks used to print letters and numbers (p. 435)

multiethnic nation (mul′tē eth′nik nā′shən) a nation with different ethnic groups living together (p. 637)

mummy (mum′ē) a preserved dead body (p. 87)

Muslim (muz′ləm) a believer in Islam (p. 331)

myth (mith) a traditional story that may include gods and goddesses and often tries to explain events in nature (p. 253)

N

Napoleonic Code (nə pō′lē on′ik kōd) a system of French laws under Emperor Napoleon I (p. 469)

National Aeronautics and Space Administration, (NASA) the United States space agency (p. 669)

National Assembly (nash′ə nəl ə sem′blē) the revolutionary assembly made up of members of the third estate of France, which served as the French parliament (p. 467)

nationalism (nash′ə nə liz′əm) a strong devotion to one's country (p. 487)

Nationalist Party (nash′ə nə list pär′tē) the party started by Sun Yat-sen after China became a republic in 1911 (p. 577)

navigator (nav′ə gā′tər) a person skilled at guiding ships (p. 337)

Nazis (nä′tsēz) the National Socialists, Germany's former fascist party (p. 544)

neutral (nü′trəl) one that does not take sides (p. 523)

New Stone Age (nü stōn āj) the late period of the Stone Age when humans made great improvements in technology (p. 19)

New Testament (nü tes′tə mənt) the part of the Christian Bible that contains the Gospels (p. 295)

nobility (nō bil′ə tē) a high-ranking social class (p. 115)

nomad (nō′mad) a person who travels from place to place without a permanent home (p. 22)

nonrenewable resource (non ri nü′ə bl ri sôrs′) a resource that cannot be replaced (p. 665)

Normans (nôr′mənz) a group of invaders that settled in northern France (p. 397)

North American Free Trade Agreement, (NAFTA) an agreement that created a free-trade zone between the United States, Canada, and Mexico (p. 633)

North Atlantic Treaty Organization, (NATO) a military alliance set up by the United States and its Western Allies after World War II (p. 571)

nuclear (nü′klē ər) atomic (p. 569)

nun (nun) a woman who devotes her life to religion and lives in a convent (p. 401)

O

oba (ō′bə) a king of Benin (p. 384)

Old Stone Age (ōld stōn āj) the early, longer period of the Stone Age when little progress was made (p. 19)

Olympic Games (ō lim′pik gāmz) athletic contests held by the ancient Greeks about 3,500 years ago and revived in modern times (p. 254)

Open Door Policy (ō′pən dôr pol′ə sē) a policy set up in 1900 by the United States in which any country could trade with China (p. 495)

oracle bone (ôr′ə kəl bōn) a bone commonly used during the Shang dynasty in China to predict the future (p. 108)

oral tradition (ôr′əl trə dish′ən) the passing down of stories from person to person orally (p. 253)

P

papyrus (pə pī′rəs) a plant whose stems are used to make a kind of paper (p. 80)

parliament (pär′lə mənt) an elected legislature (p. 502)

patrician (pə trish′ən) a wealthy, powerful citizen of ancient Rome (p. 283)

patriotism (pā′trē ə tiz′əm) a sense of pride in one's country (p. 285)

Pax Romana (paks′ rō mä′nä) "Roman Peace," a time when ancient Rome was prosperous and peaceful (p. 289)

peninsula (pə nin′sə lə) land that is nearly surrounded by water (p. 164)

perestroika (per′ə stroi′ka) "restructuring"; a reform movement introduced by Mikhail Gorbachev to restructure the Soviet economy (p. 622)

persecute (pėr′sə kyüt) to punish (p. 296)

pesticide (pes′tə sīd) a chemical that is used to kill insects or other pests (p. 661)

pharaoh (fer′ō) in ancient Egypt, a god-king (p. 85)

philosopher (fə los′ə fər) a person who studies truth and knowledge (p. 262)

pictograph (pik′tə graf) a picture that represents a word (p. 107)

pilgrimage (pil′grə mij) a journey to a place of religious importance (p. 331)

pillage (pil′ij) to rob (p. 303)

pit house (pit′ hous) a dwelling used by the Hohokam and made from digging a hole in the ground and covering it with logs (p. 213).

plague (plāg) an epidemic of an often fatal disease (p. 263)

Plague, the (plāg) an attack of bubonic plague that killed about 25–30 percent of Europe's population from 1347 to 1352 (p. 410)

plain (plān) an area of flat land (p. 35)

plateau (pla tō′) an area of high, flat land (p. 36)

plebeian (pli bē′ən) a common citizen of ancient Rome (p. 283)

plunder (plun′dər) valuables taken in war (p. 251)

policy of isolation (pol′ə sē ov ī sə lā′shən) a policy whereby foreigners are forced out of a country and traveling abroad is outlawed (p. 363)

pollution (pə lü′shən) the process of making the environment dirty (p. 663)

polytheism (pol′ē thē′iz əm) the worship of many gods (p. 42)

pope (pōp) the leader of the Roman Catholic Church (p. 302)

prehistory (prē his′tər ē) the long period of time before people developed systems of writing and written language (p. 11)

proletarian (prō′lə târ′ē ən) of, or belonging to, the working class (p. 579)

propaganda (prop′ə gan′də) the planned spread of certain beliefs (p. 545)

Protestantism (prōt′ə stən tiz′əm) the religion of Protestants, or Christians who led a movement against the beliefs and practices of the Roman Catholic Church (p. 437)

Pronunciation Key

a	in hat	ō	in open	sh	in she
â	in care	ȯ	in all	th	in thin
ā	in age	ô	in order	ᴛʜ	in then
ä	in far	oi	in oil	zh	in measure
e	in let	ou	in out	ə	= a in about
ē	in equal	u	in cup	ə	= e in taken
ėr	in term	u̇	in put	ə	= i in pencil
i	in it	ü	in rule	ə	= o in lemon
ī	in ice	ch	in child	ə	= u in circus
o	in hot	ng	in long		

Glossary

pueblo (pweb′lō) a structure of adobe brick (p. 214)

pyramid (pir′ə mid) a large stone building to serve as a house for the dead (p. 87)

Q

Qin dynasty (chin dī′nə stē) the Chinese dynasty founded by the first Chinese emperor, Shi Huangdi in 221 B.C. (p. 110)

quipu (kē′pü) a knotted rope used by the Incas to keep records (p. 199)

Quran (kô rän′) the holy book of Islam (p. 331)

R

Ramadan (räm′ə dän′) the ninth month of the Muslim calendar (p. 332)

reason (rē′zn) logical thinking (p. 262)

Reformation (ref′ər mā′shən) the religious movement in Europe that aimed at reforming the Roman Catholic Church but led to the establishment of Protestantism (p. 437)

reformer (ri fôr′mər) a person who tries to change or improve something (p. 480)

refugee (ref′yə jē′) a person who leaves his or her homeland for a safer place (p. 559)

region (rē′jən) an area on Earth with common physical features (p. 38)

Reign of Terror (ran ov ter′ər) a period of violence during the French Revolution when thousands of citizens were put to death (p. 468)

reincarnation (rē′in kär nā′shən) the Hindu belief that the spirit or soul goes from one life to the next (p. 138)

Renaissance (ren′ə säns′) the intellectual and economic movement that began in the mid-1400s and lasted until the 1600s that saw a revived interest in the art, social, scientific, and political thoughts of ancient Greece and Rome (p. 431)

renewable resource (ri nü′ə bəl ri sôrs′) a natural resource that can be replaced (p. 666)

reparations (rep′ə rā′shənz) a payment for war losses (p. 536)

representative (rep′ri zen′tə tiv) a person elected to represent the people (p. 283)

repressive (ri pres′iv) something that restrains (p. 640)

republic (ri pub′lik) a form of government in which citizens have the right to choose their leaders (p. 283)

Rig Veda (rig vā′də) one of the best-known books of the Vedas, containing more than 1,000 hymns (p. 137)

Roman Catholic Church (rō′mən kath′ə lik chėrch) the early Christian church in the Western Roman Empire of which the Pope was head (p. 302)

Rosetta Stone (rō zet′ə stōn) a stone on which a passage was written in three languages: Greek, Egyptian hieroglyphics, and a form of Egyptian cursive writing (p. 86)

Russian Revolution (rush′ən rev′ə lü′shen) the revolution that overthrew Russian Czar Nicholas I in 1917, later establishing the Bolshevik government under Vladimir Lenin (p. 531)

S

samurai (sam′u̇ rī′) a member of the Japanese warrior class (p. 361)

sanction (sangk′shən) a penalty placed against a country to force it to change its ways or policies (p. 609)

Sanskrit (san′skrit) the main language of the Aryans (p. 130)

satellite (sat′l īt) an object that is sent into space and orbits Earth (p. 669)

savanna (sə van′ə) a short grassy plain (p. 371)

scribe (skrīb) a professional writer (p. 43)

scrub land (skrub land) an area of low-growing vegetation (p. 188)

segregate (seg rə gāt) to separate (p. 609)

Senate (sen′it) a governing body in which ancient Roman representatives served (p. 283)

serf (sėrf) a person who lived on and farmed feudal land (p. 401)

Shang dynasty (shang dī′nə stē) a dynasty that lasted from 1760 B.C. to 1500 B.C. in China (p. 108)

shogun (shō′gun) a high-ranking military commander in Japan (p. 362)

Silk Road (silk rōd) a trading route that connected Europe and lands of the former Roman Empire with China (pp. 112, 409)

silt (silt) a mixture of soil and small rocks (p. 79)

slavery (slā′vər ē) the practice of one person owning another person (p. 55)

snowhouse (snō hous) a house of snow blocks used by the Inuit (p. 223)

social division (sō′shəl də vizh′ən) a group that does a certain type of work (p. 22)

socialism (sō′shə liz′əm) an economic system in which the government owns businesses, land, and natural resources (p. 481)

society (sə sī′ə tē) an organized community with established rules and traditions (p. 42)

Socratic method (sō krat′ik meth′əd) an approach to teaching developed by the Greek philosopher, Socrates, which involves teaching people to think by asking questions (p. 262)

sod house (sod hous) a shelter made from blocks of earth (p. 223)

Solidarity (sol′ə dar′ə tē) a Polish labor union that resisted communist control (p. 621)

Song dynasty (sông dī′nə stē) a dynasty that lasted from 960 to 1279 in China (p. 351)

Soviet (sō′vē et) a Russian workers' council (p. 531)

space station (spās stā′shən) a large, orbiting scientific base used by humans in space (p. 669)

steam engine (stēm en′jən) a machine that uses the power of steam (p. 475)

Stone Age (stōn āj) the period of time when humans relied primarily on stone tools (p. 19)

strike (strīk) the refusal to work until demands are met (p. 480)

subcontinent (sub kon′tə nənt) a large area of land that is separated from other countries by water and land (p. 123)

subsistence farming (səb sis′təns fär′ming) the process of growing food mainly for self-consumption (p. 125)

sudra (sü′dru) a serf in Hindu society (p. 131)

Sui dynasty (swāy dī′nə stē) a dynasty that lasted from 581 to 618 in China (p. 351)

surplus (sėr′pləs) an extra supply (p. 21)

Swahili (swä hē′lē) a culture and language that combines African and Arabic cultures and languages (p. 383)

synagogue (sin′ə gog) a Jewish place of worship (p. 257)

T

Taj Mahal (täj′ mə häl′) a magnificent tomb built by the Indian ruler Shah Jahan in memory of his wife (p. 346)

Tang dynasty (täng dī′nə stē) a dynasty that lasted from 618 to 907 in China (p. 351)

technology (tek nol′ə jē) the way in which humans produce the items they use (p. 19)

temple mound (tem′pəl mound) hill of dirt built for ceremonies (p. 221)

Ten Commandments (ten kə mand′mənts) a set of laws that provides guidance for the worship of God and rules for moral behavior (p. 55)

tenement (ten′ə mənt) an overcrowded slum apartment building (p. 477)

terrace (ter′is) a platform of earth (p. 101)

terrorism (ter′ə riz′əm) the use of violence and fear to achieve political goals (p. 645)

Tet Offensive (tet ə fen′siv) a series of battles launched by the Viet Cong and North Vietnamese across South Vietnam in 1968 (p. 586)

textile (tek′stīl) cloth that is either woven or knitted (p. 475)

theocracy (thē ok′rə sē) a system of government in which the rulers are believed to represent the will of the gods (p. 169)

three-field rotation system (thrē′ fēld′ rō tā′shən sis′təm) in the Middle Ages, a system whereby the planting of crops on manor lands alternates between three fields (p. 403)

Torah (tôr′ə) the first five books of the Hebrew Bible (p. 56)

trade agreement (trād äg rē′mənt) an agreement with rules about the exchange of goods between countries (p. 633)

trading bloc (trā′ding blok) a group of nations that agrees to trade under favorable conditions (p. 632)

Pronunciation Key

a	in hat	ō	in open	sh	in she
â	in care	ȯ	in all	th	in thin
ā	in age	ô	in order	ᴛʜ	in then
ä	in far	oi	in oil	zh	in measure
e	in let	ou	in out	ə	= a in about
ē	in equal	u	in cup	ə	= e in taken
ėr	in term	u̇	in put	ə	= i in pencil
i	in it	ü	in rule	ə	= o in lemon
ī	in ice	ch	in child	ə	= u in circus
o	in hot	ng	in long		

Glossary

treaty port (trē′tē pôrt) Asian port cities that were open to trade with Western countries (p. 494)

Treaty of Tordesillas (trē′tē ov tôr də sē′yə) the 1494 agreement that divided any newly discovered territories between Spain and Portugal (p. 441)

Treaty of Versailles (trē′tē ov vèr sī′) the document signed at the end of World War I between the Allies and Germany (p. 536)

trench warfare (trench wôr′fàr′) the use of deep ditches to shelter troops in battle (p. 528)

triangular trade (tri ang′gyə lər trād) a trade arrangement in which manufactured goods were traded for slaves, slaves were sold for raw materials such as sugar cane, and raw materials were made into manufactured products for sale (p. 449)

tribune (trib′yūn) in ancient Rome, men who were appointed to protect the rights of plebeians (p. 284)

tributary (trib′yə ter′ē) a small stream that flows into a larger stream or river (p. 209)

Triple Alliance (trip′əl ə lī′əns) an alliance formed in 1882 between Germany, Austria-Hungary, and Italy (p. 522)

Triple Entente (trip′əl än tänt′) an alliance formed in 1907 between Russia, France, and Great Britain (p. 522)

Truman Doctrine (trū′mən dok′trən) U.S. President Harry S. Truman's commitment of the U.S. military to help nations resisting communism (p. 570)

tundra (tun′drə) a cold, flat area where trees cannot grow (p. 210)

typhoon (ti fūn′) a tropical storm with heavy winds and rough seas (p. 361)

ulama (ü′lä mə) an ancient Olmec ball game (p. 175)

unify (yü′nə fī) to unite, combine, or bring together (p. 85)

United Nations, (UN) (yü ni′tid nā′shənz) an international peacekeeping organization that was created in 1945 (p. 560)

vandal (van′dl) a person who destroys property (p. 303)

Vedas (vā′dəs) "Books of Knowledge" that contain much of the stories and songs of the Aryans (p. 130)

Viet Cong (vē et′ kông′) Vietnamese communist guerillas (p. 584)

Vietnamization (vē et nä′mə zā′shən) Richard Nixon's plan to reduce the role of the United States in the Vietnam War (p. 586)

Warsaw Pact (wôr′sò pakt) a military alliance of the communist countries of Eastern Europe signed after World War II (p. 570)

wattle (wät′l) a wall material made from branches and vines intertwined with logs (p. 219)

wetland (wet′land′) land that is covered with moist soil (p. 187)

wigwam (wig′wom) a dome-shaped hut made of branches covered with animal skins or woven mats (p. 220)

Women's Army Corps (wim′ənz är′mē kôr) a female division of the U.S. Army in World War II (p. 552)

World Trade Organization, (WTO) (wèrld träd ôr′gə nə zā′shən) an international body created to help nations settle trade disputes (p. 633)

zero population growth (zir′ō pop′yə lā′shən grōth) the balance between new babies born and people lost due to death (p. 657)

Zhou dynasty (jou di′nə stē) the largest of the Chinese dynasties, lasting from 770–221 B.C. (p. 108)

ziggurat (zig′ú rat) a huge, pyramid-shaped structure consisting of a series of stacked, rectangular platforms (p. 41)

Zionism (zī′ə niz′əm) a movement that began in the 1800s to set up a Jewish state in Palestine (p. 615)

Zoroastrianism (zôr′ō as′trē ə niz′əm) a religion founded by the Persian prophet Zoroaster based on the belief of one god as supreme and the enemy of evil (p. 132)

Index

This Index lists the pages on which topics appear in this book. Page numbers after an *m* refer to a map. Page numbers after a *p* refer to a photograph. Page numbers after a *c* refer to a chart, graph, or diagram.

Index

Index

Credits

Text

Dorling Kindersley (DK) is an international publishing company specializing in the creation of high quality reference content for books, CD-ROMs, online and video. The hallmark of DK content it its unique combination of educational value and strong visual style. This combination allows DK to deliver appealing, accessible and engaging educational content that delights children, parents, and teachers around the world. Scott Foresman is delighted to have been able to use selected extracts of DK content within this Social Studies program.

12 from *Eyewitness: North American Indian* by David Murdoch. Copyright ©2000 by Dorling Kindersley Limited.

86 from *Eyewitness: Ancient Egypt* by George Hart. Copyright ©2000 by Dorling Kindersley Limited.

270 from *Eyewitness: Ancient Greece* by Anne Pearson. Copyright ©2000 by Dorling Kindersley Limited.

354 from *Eyewitness: Ancient China* by Arthur Cotterell. Copyright ©2000 by Dorling Kindersley Limited.

670 from *Eyewitness: Media & Communication* by Clive Gifford. Copyright ©2000 by Dorling Kindersley Limited.

"Battling Everest" by Michael Burgan. Reprinted by permission of NGS Image Collection. p. 573

From *The Cambridge Illustrated History of China* by Patricia Buckley Ebrey. © Cambridge University Press 1996. Reprinted with the permission of Cambridge University Press. p. 111

Song "A Boat on the Lake". Reprinted by permission of Pearson Education, Inc. pp. 148-149

Excerpt from *Jataka Tales* edited by Nancy DeRoin. Copyright © 1975 by Nancy DeRoin. Reprinted by permission of Houghton Mifflin. p. 141

"The Garden We Planted Together" by Anuraddha Bose from *A World in Our Hands*. Copyright © 1995 by Peace Child Charitable Trust. With permission of Tricycle Press. p. 674

"What the World Needs" by Elzbieta Jawarska from *A World in Our Hands*. Copyright © 1995 by Peace Child Charitable Trust. Reprinted by permission of Tricycle Press. p. 638

From *My Palace of Leaves in Sarjaveo* by Marybeth Lorbiecki. Copyright © 1997 by Marybeth Lorbiecki. Reprinted by permission of the Selman Literary Agency. p. 636

From *Horizon History of Africa*, pg. 188. Copyright © 1971 by American Heritage Publishing Co., Inc., a subsidiary of McGraw-Hill, Inc. Reprinted by permission of AMERICAN HERITAGE, Inc.

"Over There" by George M. Cohan © 1917 (Renewed) EMI Feist Catalog Inc. All Rights Reserved. Used by permission of Warner Bros. Publications U.S. Inc., Miami, FL 33014 p. 592

From #67 "Hymn of the Nile" from *A Comparative Study of the Literature of Egypt, Palestine and Mesopotamia*, edited by T. Eric Peet, originally published by Oxford University Press. Reprinted by courtesy of The British Academy and The Clarendon Press. p. 80

Excerpt from "The Earth and the People" from *Magic Words* Copyright © 1968, 1967 by Edward Field, reprinted by permission of Harcourt, Inc. p. 232

Cover page from The Parade Magazine, October 28, 2001. Reprinted by permission. p. 648

Fair Use:

Quotes from pgs. 61 & 71 from *Side-By-Side: A Photographic History of America Women in War* by Vickie Lewis. Copyright © 1999 by Vickie Lewis. New York: Stewart, Tabori & Chang, 1999.

From *Mesopotamia: The Mighty Kings*. New York: Time-Life Books, 1995.

From *The Code of Hammurabi*, translated by L.W. King. The Avalon Project at the Yale Law School, 1996. http://www.yale.edu/lawweb/avalon/hamframe.htm.

From *The Sea Traders* by Maitland Edey. New York: Time-Life Books, 1974.

From *The Epic of Gilgamesh*, translated by N.K. Sandars. London: Penguin, 1972.

From *Babylonians* by H.W.G. Saggs. Berkley and Los Angeles, California: University of California Press, 2000.

From *The Sumerians: Their History, Culture and Character* by Samuel Noah Kramer, pages 238 and 341. Chicago & London: The University of Chicago Press, 1963.

From *S.C. dig challenges theory of First Americans* by Henry Eichel. http://www.cgcas.org/topper.htm [central gulf coast archaeology society]

From *Rio Pinturas Cave Paintings The Hands of Time* by Carlos Manuel Conto. http://www.argentime.com/eng/issues/009/02manos.htm.

From "Found Wonders in A Secret Cave" by Nancy Fritz as appeared in *Popular Science*, 6/1/95.

From *The First Cities* by Dora Jane Haroblin. New York: Time-Life Books, 1973.

From *The Life and Death of Adolph Hitler* by Adolph Payne, pg. 131. NewYork: Praeger Publishers, 1973.

From *A Time to Break the Silence* by Martin Luther King, Jr. http://stum.finda.edu/instructor/swensson.king.html.

From *Life and Death in Shanghai* by Nien Cheng, pg. 64 & 65. New York: Grove Press, Inc.

From *Deaths of Man* by Edwin S. Shneidman, pg. 184. New York: Quandrangle/The New York Times Book Co. , 1973.

From *History of the Twentieth Century, Vol. 2* by Martin Gilbert, pg. 659. New York: Wm. Morrow and Company, Inc.

From *Why Lenin? Why Stalin?* by Theodore H. Von Laue, pg. 196. New York: J.B. Lippincott Company.

From *New York Times Great Lives of the Twentieth Century* edited by Galb, Rosenthal and Siegal, pg. 106. New York: Times Books, a division of Random House, Inc., 1988.

From *Twentieth Century Speeches* edited by Biran McArthur, pg. 56. London: The Penguin Group, 1992.

From *British Novelists between the Wars* edited by George M. Johnson, pg. 50. Detroit, Washington, D.C., London: A Bruccoli Clark Layman Book, Gale Research.

Excerpt from *The Clary Marble* by Minfong Ho, pg. 73. New York: Farrar Straus Giroux. Published simultaneously in Canada: HarperCollins Canada, Ltd., 1991.

Excerpt from *The Vietnam Reader*, edited by Walter Capps, pg. 206. New York: Routledge, an imprint of Routledge, Champan and Hall, Inc., 1991.

From *The March of Folly* by Barbara Tuchman, pg. 304. New York: Ballantine Books, a division of Random House, Inc., 1985.

Frank Church quote from http://www.vietnamwarnet/quotations/quotations.htm.

From *The Wit and Wisdom of Winston Churchill*, edited by James C. Humes, pg. 142 & 119-120. New York: HarperPerennial, a division of HarperCollins Publishers, 1994.

Winston Churchill quote from *International Church Society Website*, http://www.winstonchurchill.org/bonmots.htm#owed.

From *Familiar Quotations* by John Bartlett, 15th and 125th anniversary edition, pg. 909. New York: Little, Brown and Company (Inc.), 1980.

From *Oxford Dictionary of Quotations*, pgs. 632 and 488, edited by Elizabeth Knowles. New York: Oxford University Press, 1999.

From *Historic World Leaders*, edited by Anne Commire, pg. 387. Michigan: Gale Research, Inc., 1994.

Quotation from *Premier Chou En-Lai*, pg. 90. New York: Thomas Y. Crowell Company.

Published simultaneously in Canada: Fitzhenry & Whiteside Limited.

From *The First World War* by Martin Gilbert, pg. 133. New York: Henry Holt and Company, 1994.

From *Horizon History of Africa*, pg. 73. Heritage Publishing Company, 1971.

From *The Power of Gold* by Peter L. Bernstein. New York, NY: John Wiley & Sons, Inc. 2000.

From *The Tanner Lectures on Human Values, Volume 18*, edited by Grethe B. Peterson. Salt Lake City, UT: University of Utah Press, 1997.

From *Women Prime Minister and Presidents* by Olga S. Opfell. Jefferson, NC: McFarland & Company, Inc., 1993.

From *Nobel Prize Winners Supplement 1987-1991*, edited by Paula McGuire. New York, NY: The H.W. Wilson Company, 1992.

From *Nobel Prize Winners, 1992-1996 Supplement*, edited by Clifford Thompson. New York, NY: The H.W. Wilson Company, 1997.

From *Crisis in Tiananmen: Reform and Reality in Modern China* by Ti Mu and Mark V. Thompson. San Francisco, CA: China Books & Periodicals, Inc. 1989.

From *Great Lives of the Twentieth Century*, edited by Arthur Gelm, A.M. Rosenthal and Marvin Siegel. New York, NY: Times Books, 1988.

From *Nelson Mandela's life of struggle* found on http://www.bbc.co.uk/leeds/news/042001/26/mandela_biog.shtml.

From *EUROPE: A History* by Norman Davies. New York, NY: Oxford University Press, 1996

From *Encyclopaedia Britannica, Volume 3*. Chicago, IL: The University of Chicago, 1990

From *Simón Boliva: Latin American Liberator* by Frank de Varona. Brookfield, CT: The Millbrook Press, 1993.

From *The History of the Haitian Revolution and the Economic Adjustment to Emancipation: 1791-1804* by Sapna Mehta, Seminar Paper 1999.

From *The Dictionary of Biographical Quotation* edited by Richard Kenin and Justin Wintle. New York, NY: Alfred A. Knopf, 1978.

Quote by Christopher Columbus from *Early European Adventurers and the Opening of Japan* by Richard Pflederer found on http://www.mercatormag.com/103_pfled.html.

Quote by Martin Luther from *Luther at the Imperial Diet of Worms (1521)* found on http://www.luterh.de/e/worms.html.

From *A Global History, From Prehistory to the Present* by L.S. Stavrianos. Englewood Cliffs, NJ: Prentice Hall a division of Simon & Schuster, 1991.

From *Historic World Leaders (4) North & South America A-L*, edited by Anne Commire, Associate editor, Deborah Klezmer. Washington, DC: Gale Research Inc, 1994.

From *Historic World Leaders (2) Europe A-K*, edited by Anne Commire, associate editor, Deborah Klezmer. Washington, DC: Gale Research Inc, 1994.

From *Quotable Women of the Twentieth Century*, edited by Tracy Quinn. New York, NY: William Morrow & Company, Inc., 1999.

From *The New Russians* by Hedrick Smith. New York, NY: Random House, Inc. 1990.

Quote by Mikhail Sergeevich Gorbachev from *Oxford Dictionary of Quotations*. New York, NY: Oxford University Press, 1999.

Quote by Mahatma Gandhi from *Oxford Dictionary of Quotations*. New York, NY: Oxford University Press, 1999.

Quote by Kwame Nkrumah from *Oxford Dictionary of Quotations*. New York, NY: Oxford University Press, 1999.

From *The Nobel Peace Prize for 1978* found on http://www.nobel.se/peace/laureates/1978/press.html.

From *Historic World Leaders, Volume 1, Africa, Middle East, Asia, Pacific* edited by Anne Commire. Washington, DC: Gale Research, 1994.

Quote by Bartolomé de Las Casa from *The Legacy of Bartolomé de Las Casas* by Benjamin Keane found on http://osu.orst.edu/dept/philosophy/ideas/papers/keen.html#11.

From *Simpson's Contemporary Quotations* compiled by James B. Simpson, 1988 found on http://www.bartleby.com/63/82/3082.html.

From *The Dragon Empress* by Marina Warner. New York, NY: The Macmillan Company, 1972.

From *The Clay Marble* by Minfong Ho. New York, NY: A Sunburst Book, Farrar, Straus, Giroux, 1991.

From *Lessons of the Rain Forest* edited by Suzanne Head and Robert Heinzman. San Francisco, CA: Sierra Club Books, 1990.

From *A Concise History of the World* by J.M. Roberts. New York, NY: Oxford University Press, 1995.

Excerpt from Pliny from *The Destruction of Pompeii, 79 AD* found on http://www.ibiscom.com/pompeii.htm.

From *The Horizon Book of Ancient Greece*, edited by William Harlan Hale. New York, NY: American Heritage Publishing Co., Inc., 1965.

From *A Short History of China* by Hilda Hookham. New York, NY: St. Martin's Press, 1970.

From *Theosophy World, November 1998* found on http://www.theosophy.net/tw-text/TW9811.txt.

From *A Traveller's History of India, 2e* by Sinharaja Tammita-Delgoda, edited by Denis Judd. Brooklyn, NY: Interlink Books, 1999.

From http://home.cfl.rr.com/crossland/Ancientcivilizations/Ancient_Egypt/ancient_egypt.html.

From "The Fabled Land Punt" from *Ancient Record of Egypt Historical Documents from the Earliest Times to the Persian Conquest, Vols., II, IV* by James Breasted. Chicago, IL: University of Chicago Press.

From *Historic World Leaders (5): North & South American M-Z*, edited by Anne Commire, associate editor, Deborah Klezmer. Washington DC: Gale Research Inc., 1994.

From *Isaac Asimov's Book of Science and Nature Quotations* by Isaac Asimov. 1988. Found on http://department.stthomas.edu/recycle/forest.htm.

From *What Life Was Like Amid Splendor and Intrigue, Byzantine Empire AD330-1453*. By the editors of Time-Life Books, Alexandria, VA.

From *World Book Encyclopedia "Muhammed" M, Volume 13*. Chicago, IL: World Book, Inc.

From *The Travel of Ibn Battuta: "Ibn Battuta in Mali"* found on http://www.humanitites/ualberta/ca/history111/weeksept29/sept29.tut2.html.

From *Rokugo-no-Watash;, The Rokugo Ferry Crossing* found on http://www.us-japan.org/edomatsu/Rokugo/story.html.

From http://www.visit-mekong/com/cambodia/thigstodo/

From *The Royal Kingdoms of Ghana, Mali, and Songhay* by Patricia & Fredrick McKissack. New York, NY: Henry Holt and Company, 1994.

From *African Empires*...found on http://barney.gonzaga/edu/-sbennet3/mead/lessonplans/africanempires.htm.

From *African Civilization Revisited* by Basil Davidson. African World Press, 1991.

From *World Book Encyclopedia, Volume F*. Chicago, IL: World Book, Inc.

From "Heart of Sky" *The Popul Vuh: The Mayan Book of the Dawn of Life*, translated by Dennis Tedlock.

Maps:

MapQuest.com, Inc.

Illustrations:

8, 11, 14 Yoshi Miyake; 14 Asun Balzola; 16, 19, 24 Higgins Bond; 24, 25, 31, 104, 105, 159, 171, 272, 340, 341, 343, 386, 411, 412, 475, 476, 490, 505, 524, 537, 539, 562, 563, 571, 589, 590, 595, 624, 631, 642, 647, 655, 656, 661, 665 Jeff Grunewald; 32, 41 Randal Birkey; 34, 38, 80, 110, 187, 261, 323, 337, 371, 409, 577 Susan J. Carlson; 37, 85, 94 Ralph Voltz; 43, 55, 292 Dan McGeehan; 44, 47, 51, 176, 213, 219, 353, 368, 384, 616 Robert Lawson; 45, 148, 149, 506 Ilene Robinette; 52, 73, 135, 181, 317, 329, 379 Chris Butler; 64, 148, 308 Eliza Holliday; 64, 65 Carmelo Blandino; 89, 401 Linda Pierce; 100, 101 Neil Slave; 107 Gladys Rosa-Mendoza; 157, 225, 592 Tony Crnkovich; 166, 220, 268, 271, 287, 400 William Graham; 200, 662 Chet Jezierski; 206, 390, 416 Tom Metcalf; 232, 588 Neal Armstrong; 312 Bill & Debbie Farnsworth; 524 Joann Daley; 528, 569, 574 Andy Zito; 674 Jordan Dalton

Photographs:

Every effort has been made to secure permission and provide appropriate credit for photographic material. The publisher deeply regrets any omission and pledges to correct errors called to their attention in subsequent editions. Unless otherwise acknowledged, all photographs are the property of Scott Foresman, a division of Pearson Education.

Cover: (BR) Roy Ooms/Masterfile Corporation, (C) Karen Su/China Span

Endsheets: Left page: (Bkgd) ©The Studio Dog/PhotoDisc, (BL) ©PhotoDisc, (BCL) ©Frans Lemmens/Getty Images, (BC) ©Art Archive, (BR), (TL) ©Dorling Kindersley, Limited, (TR), (LC) ©Corbis, (C) Garry Black/Masterfile; Right page: (BR) ©Anthony Johnson/Getty Images, (TR) ©Jorge Ianiszewski/Art Resource, NY, (TC), (TL) ©Corbis, (CL) ©D. Logan/Robertstock, (C) Karen Su/China Span

Front Matter: III ©Hubert Stadler/Corbis; IV Werner Foreman Archive/Art Resource, NY; V Felipe Davalos/NGS Image Collection; VI Scala/Art Resource, NY; VII Bibliothèque Nationale Paris/The Art Archive; viii Robert Frerck/Odyssey Productions; IX Scala/Art Resource, NY; X U. S. Coast Guard; XI Diana Ong/Superstock; XII Musee du Louvre, Paris/Dagli Orti/Art Archive, Ancient Art & Architecture Collection/Ronald Sheridan Photo Library; H4 (CC) Robin Sachs/PhotoEdit, (CL) Michael Newman/PhotoEdit, (CR) Mary Kate Denny/PhotoEdit, (BL) Rudi Von Briel/PhotoEdit, (BR) ©Comstock, Inc., (BC) Fotopic/Camerique/H. Armstrong Roberts; H5 (CL) Myrleen Ferguson Cate/PhotoEdit, (CR) ©2003 Frank Siteman/Mira Media Image Resource Alliance; H6 (C) Superstock, (BC) ©Antonio M. Rosario/Getty Images, (BR) ©Patrick Ward/Corbis; H7 (BL) Reunion des Musees Nationaux/Art Resource, NY, (BC) ©Yann Arthus-Bertrand/Corbis; H8 Earth Imaging/Getty Images; H16 Jeff Greenberg/Stock Boston; H20 Richard Hutchings/PhotoEdit.

Unit 1:

1 ©Hubert Stadler/Corbis; 2, 3 Kenneth Garrett; 4 (CL) Scala/Art Resource, NY, (L) Archaeological Museum Aleppo/Dagli Orti/Art Archive, (CR) National Gallery Budapest/Dagli Orti/Art Archive, (R) Musée du Louvre Paris/Dagli Orti/Art Archive; 5 (CL), (CR) Corbis-Bettmann, (R) Chris Hellier/The Granger Collection, (L) The Granger Collection; 7 Kenneth Garrett/National Geographic; 8 (C) ©Macduff Everton/Corbis, (B) Archivo Iconografico, S.A/Corbis; 10 British Museum/©Dorling Kindersley; 12 (R), (L) American Museum of Natural History/©Dorling Kindersley; 13 (B), (TR) Erich Lessing/Art Resource, NY; 17 Scala/Art Resource, NY; 18 (B) ©John Garrett/Corbis; 20 (T) ©Doranne Jacobson/International Images, (B) Eileen Tweedy/Art Archive; 21 Butser Ancient Farm/©Dorling Kindersley; 22 (T) Scott Camazine, (B) ©Macduff Everton/Corbis; 23 (CL) Kenneth Garrett; 25 Galleria di Storia ed Arte Udine/Dagli Orti/Art Archive; 26 Reunion des Musées Nationaux/Art Resource, NY; 27 (B) Bettmann/Corbis, (T) Artville; 28 (B) Grant Heilman Photography, (C) Runk/Schoenberger/Grant Heilman Photography, (T) Archivo Iconografico, S.A/Corbis; 29 Kenneth Garrett; 30 Reunion des Musées Nationaux/Art Resource, NY; 32 (B) Scala/Art Resource, NY, (T) British Museum, (BC) ©Art Directors & TRIP Photo Library, (T) Getty Images; 34 (L) Burke/Triolo Productions/FoodPix; 36 Chris Stowers/Panos Pictures; 38 (B) British Museum; 39 (TR) British Museum; 40 National Museum Damascus Syria/Dagli Orti/Art Archive; 42 (TL), (TR) British Museum, (B) Erich Lessing/Art Resource, NY; 43 (B) British Museum; 44 (L) Musée du Louvre Paris/Dagli Orti/Art Archive, (R) Eric Lessing/Art Resource, NY; 46 SEF/Art Resource, NY; 47 (R) Eric Lessing/PhotoEdit, (L) Topham Picturepoint/ Image Works; 48 (BL) Topham Picturepoint/Image Works; 50 ©Gianni Dagli Orti/Corbis; 51 (R), (L) British Museum; 52 The Metropolitan Museum of Art, Gift of John D. Rockefeller, Jr.,1932. (32.143.2) Photograph ©1981 The Metropolitan Museum of Art; 53 ©Art Directors & TRIP Photo Library; 54 Scala/Art Resource, NY; 56 (L) The Jewish Museum, NY/Art Resource, NY, (R) Jewish Museum/©Dorling Kindersley; 57 (TL) ©Chris Hellier/Corbis, (B) Andy Crawford/©Dorling Kindersley; 58 National Geographic; 59 (L), (R) Museum of the American Numismatic Association; 60 (BC) Oriental Institute of the University of Chicago, (R) ©AFP/Corbis; 61 (T) Archaeological Museum Bagdad/Dagli Orti/Art Archive; 63 Topham Picturepoint/Image Works; 66 Getty Images;

Unit 2:

69, 70, 71 Werner Foreman Archive/Art Resource, NY; 72 (CL), (CC) Araldo de Luca/Corbis, (L) Erich Lessing/Art Resource, NY, (R) ©Doranne Jacobson/International Images; 73 (R) Asian Art & Archaeology, Inc./Corbis, (CL) Giraudon/Art Resource, NY, (L) The British Library/Art Archive, (CR) British Museum; 75 (T) Robert Caputo/Stock Boston, (TR) ©Dorling Kindersley; 76 (C) John Woodcock/©Dorling Kindersley, (B) Roger Wood/Corbis, (T) Erich Lessing/Art Resource, NY; 78 Kenneth Garrett; 79 Erich Lessing/Art Resource, NY; 80 North Carolina Museum of Art/Corbis; 81 (TL) Art Directors & TRIP Photo Library, (TR) Dagli Orti/The Art Archive; 83 Robin White/Robin White/FotoLex Associates; 84 Egyptian Museum Cairo/Dagli Orti (A)/Art Archive; 85 (B) Fitzwilliam Museum, University of Cambridge, UK/Bridgeman Art Library International Ltd.; 86 (C),(B) British Museum/©Dorling Kindersley, (TL) Boltin Picture Library, (TR) Art Resource, NY; 87 (T) The Newark Museum/Art Resource, NY, (B) John Woodcock/©Dorling Kindersley; 88 (BR) Dagli Orti (A)/Art Archive, (B) B. Turner/Art Directors & TRIP Photo Library; 89 Erich Lessing/Art Resource, NY; 90 Danita Delimont Stuart Westmorland/Danita Delimont, Agent; 91 (R) H. Rogers/Art Directors & TRIP Photo Library, (Bkgd) ©Wolfgang Kaehler Photography, (L) Boltin Picture Library; 92 ©Roger Wood/Corbis; 93 Kerma beaker, Kerma, Nubia, Sudan, Classic Kerma, about 1700-1550 B.C.; Pottery; Height 11.7cm (4 5/8 in.). Harvard University-Museum of Fine Arts Expedition, 13.4080.; 94 Egyptian Museum Cairo/Dagli Orti (A)/Art Archive; 95 British Museum; 96 Egyptian Museum Cairo/Dagli Orti (A)/Art Archive; 97 Kenneth Garrett; 98 (B) Archivo Iconografico, S.A/Corbis, (TC) Catherine Platt/Panos Pictures, (C) Lowell Georgia/Photo Researchers, Inc.; 100 (BL) WorldSat International/Photo Researchers, Inc., (BR) Catherine Platt/Panos Pictures; 102 (T) Lowell Georgia/Corbis, (B) Picture Press/Corbis; 103 (T) ©Galen Rowell/Corbis; 104 Wolfgang Kaehler; 106 Lowell Georgia/Photo Researchers, Inc.; 107 Genius of China Exhibition/The Art Archive; 108 Art Archive; 109 (T) Court Ladies Preparing Newly Woven Silk, China, Northern Song dynasty, early 12th century; Attributed to Emperor Huizong, Chinese (1082-1135). Handscroll; ink, color and gold on silk; H x W: 14 5/8 x57 3/16 in. (37 x 145.3 cm). Special Chinese and Japenese Fund, 12.886. (BC) British Museum; 110 (T) Asian Art & Archaeology, Inc/Corbis, (B) ©Keren Su/Corbis; 111 (T) Giraudon/Art Resource, NY: 112 Asian Art & Archaeology, Inc/Corbis; 113 (R) The British Library/Art Archive, (Bkgd) ©Mercury Press International, (L) Wolfgang Kaehler; 114 ©Dorling Kindersley; 115 (B) Dennis Cox/ChinaStock, (T) Archivo Iconografico, S.A/Corbis; 116 (B) N. Ray/Art Directors & TRIP Photo Library, (TR) ©Dorling Kindersley; 117 (T) Réunion des Musées Nationaux/Art Resource, NY; 118 WorldSat International/Photo Researchers, Inc.; 119 Asian Art & Archaeology, Inc/Corbis; 120 (B) Neil Cooper/Panos Pictures, (BC) ©Doranne Jacobson/International Images, (TC) Paolo Koch/Photo Researchers, Inc., (T) Mrú tribal village. Chittagong hill tracts. Bangladesh/Panos Pictures; 122 (BL) Frank Schreider/Photo Researchers, Inc., (R) R. Cracknell/Art Directors & TRIP Photo Library; 124 (B) Alan Oddie/PhotoEdit; 125 (T) E.R. Degginger/Color-Pic, Inc., (B) Mrú tribal village. Chittagong hill tracts. Bangladesh/Panos Pictures; 126 (B) Mercury Press International, (T) Art Directors & TRIP Photo Library, (TL) Dinodia/Art Directors & TRIP Photo Library; 127 ©Howard Davies/Corbis; 128 Borromeo/Art Resource, NY; 129 (T) National Museum Karachi/Dagli Orti (A)/Art Archive, (B) Paolo Koch/Photo Researchers, Inc.; 130 Milind A. Ketkar/Dinodia Picture Agency; 131 (T) Victoria & Albert Museum, London/Art Resource, NY, (BR) ©Danny Lehman/Corbis, (BL) Victoria and Albert Museum, London/Art Resource, NY; 132 ©Chris Hellier/Corbis; 133 (T) Giraudon/Art Resource, NY, (B) ©Doranne Jacobson/International Images; 134 British Museum; 135 E.R. Degginger/Color-Pic, Inc.; 136 ©Doranne Jacobson/International Images; 137 (TC) Reunion des Musées Nationaux/Art Resource, NY, (BC) Boltin Picture Library, (B) Musée Guimet Paris/Dagli Orti (A)/Art Archive, (T) M. Amirtham/Dinodia Picture Agency; 139 ©David H. Wells/Corbis; 140 Dinodia Picture Agency; 141 (B) Werner Foreman Archive/Art Resource, NY, (T) Mary Evans Picture Library; 142 (BL) ©Doranne Jacobson/International Images; 143 Neil Cooper/Panos Pictures; 146 (T) Borromeo/Art Resource, NY, (B) Alan Oddie/PhotoEdit

Unit 3:

153, 154, 155 Felipe Davalos/NGS Image Collection; 156 (CR) Archivo Iconografico, S.A./Corbis, (L) North Wind Picture Archives, (CL), (R) Pedro de Osma Museum Lima/Mireille Vautier/Art Archive; 157 (CL) Scala/Art Resource, NY, (L) Réunion des Musées Nationaux photo: Franck Raux/Art Resource, NY, (R) Instituto de Investigaciones Antropoligicas/Alfonso Caso Fund/Instituto de Investigaciones Antropoligicas; 159 (T) Robert Frerck/Odyssey Productions, (R) Werner Forman/Biblioteca Universitaria, Bologna, Italy/Art Resource, NY; 160 (TC) ©Charles & Josette Lenars/Corbis, (C) Robert Frerck/Odyssey Productions; 162 Museum of Mankind London/Eileen Tweedy/Art Archive, (B) ©Charles & Josette Lenars/Corbis; 164 (B) ©Macduff Everton/Corbis, (R) Larry Dunmire/D. Donne Bryant Stock Photography; 165 International Images; 168 ©Gianni Dagli Orti/Corbis; 169 Robert Frerck/Odyssey Productions ; 170 ©Danny Lehman/Corbis; 171 (B) Robert Frerck/Odyssey Productions; 172 (T) ©Charles & Josette Lenars/Corbis, (B) INAH/©Dorling Kindersley; 174 D. Donne Bryant Stock Photography; 175 Werner Forman/Museum fuer Voelkerkunde, Hamburg, Germany/Art Resource, NY; 178 Private Collection/Ancient Art and Architecture Collection Ltd./Bridgeman Art Library International Ltd.; 179 (B), (C) INAH/©Dorling Kindersley; 180 Biblioteca Nacional, Madrid, Spain/Bridgeman Art Library International Ltd.; 181 (L) Museum für Völkerkunde, Wien oder MVK, Wien/Kunsthistorisches Museum, (R) North Wind Picture Archives; 182 ©Danny Lehman/Corbis; 184 (T) Robert Frerck/Woodfin Camp & Associates, (B) Katsuyoshi Tanaka/Woodfin Camp & Associates, (BC) Bruning Museum Lambayeque Peru/Mireille Vautier/The Art Archive, (C) Album/J. Enrique Molina/Art Archive; 186 Robert Frerck/Odyssey Productions; 187 (BL) Robert Frerck/Woodfin Camp & Associates, (TR) Michael & Patricia

Fogden/Corbis, (TL) ©Stephanie Maze/Corbis, (BR) ©Craig Lovell/Corbis; 188 Robert Frerck/Odyssey Productions; 189 ©Doranne Jacobson/International Images; 190 Album/J. Enrique Molina/Art Archive; 191 (B) Archaeological Museum Lima/Dagli Orti/Art Archive, (T) Werner Forman Archive/David Bernstein Fine Art, NY/Art Resource, NY; 192 Robert Frerck/Odyssey Productions ; 193 Robert Frerck/Odyssey Productions; 196 (B) Katsuyoshi Tanaka/Woodfin Camp & Associates; 197 (T) Bruning Museum Lambayeque Peru/Mireille Vautier/The Art Archive; 198 Jorge Ianiszewski/Art Resource, NY; 199 (T) Newberry Library, Chicago, (B) Loren McIntyre/Woodfin Camp & Associates; 200 Robert Frerck/Odyssey Productions; 201 Franck Raux/Réunion des Musées Nationaux/Art Resource, NY; 202 Instituto de Investigaciones Antropoligicas/Alfonso Caso Fund/Instituto de Investigaciones Antropoligicas; 203 (T), (TR) Pedro de Osma Museum Lima/Mireille Vautier/Art Archive, (C) Tom Till Photography, Inc.; 204 (B) Robert Frerck/Odyssey Productions, (T) Jorge Ianiszewski/Art Resource, NY; 206 (T) Bob Clemenz Photography, (BC) Richard A. Cooke/Corbis, (B) Werner Forman/American Museum of Natural History, NY/Art Resource, NY; 208 (L) Bob Clemenz Photography, (BR) R. Hamilton Smith, (C) ©James Randklev/Getty Images; 209 (CL) Willard Clay Photography, (L) ©Layne Kennedy/Corbis, (R) ©Douglas Peebles/Corbis, (CR) ©Danny Lehman/Corbis; 211 ©Doranne Jacobson/International Images; 212 ©Richard A. Cooke/Corbis; 214 Bob & Suzanne Clemenz/Bob Clemenz Photography; 215 Richard A. Cooke/Corbis; 216 (T) The Granger Collection (B) Smithsonian American Art Museum, Washington DC/Art Resource/Art Resource, NY; 218 Cahokia Mounds State Historic Site; 219 ©Richard A. Cooke/Corbis; 221 ©Michael Lewis/Corbis; 222 Werner Forman/American Museum of Natural History, NY/Art Resource, NY; 223 AP/Wide World; 225 With permission of the Royal Ontario Museum ©/Royal Ontario Museum, (CL) ©D. Robert & Lorri Franz/Corbis; 226 Smithsonian Institution; 229 (T) Giraudon/Art Resource, NY, Ben Asen (C) Ben Asen, (B) image courtesy of Pennsylvania State University with permission from Christopher Uhl; 230 ©Doranne Jacobson/International Images

Unit 4:

237, 238 Scala/Art Resource, NY; 240 (L) A.K.G., Berlin/SuperStock, (CL), (CR) ©Araldo de Luca/Corbis, (R) Réunion des Musées Nationaux/Art Resource, NY; 241 (L) Augustus of Primaporta, circa 20 BC/Corbis, (CL) Vanni Archive/Corbis, (CR) SuperStock, (R) Erich Lessing/Art Resource, NY; 243 (B) ©Mimmo Jodice/Corbis, (T) ©Araldo de Luca/Corbis, (TR) ©Gianni Dagli Orti/Corbis; 244 (T) Nimatallah/Art Resource, NY, (TC) North Wind Picture Archives, (BC) Réunion des Musées Nationaux/Art Resource, NY, (B) Archivo Iconografico, S.A./Corbis; 246 ©Wolfgang Kaehler/Corbis; 248 (B) SuperStock, (T) ©Gail Mooney/Corbis; 249 The Granger Collection; 250 (T) Wolfgang Kaehler/Corbis, (B) Werner Forman/Art Resource, NY; 251 Nimatallah/Art Resource, NY; 252 The Granger Collection; 253 Forbes Collection, New York City/Bridgeman Art Library, London/SuperStock; 254 (TC) ©Araldo de Luca/Corbis, (TR) ©Duomo/Corbis, (R) Nimatallah/Art Resource, NY, (BR) ©Andrea Jemolo/Corbis, (BC) The Granger Collection, New York, (BL) Réunion des Musées Nationaux/Art Resource, NY, (L) Scala/Art Resource, NY, (CL) ©Wolfgang Kaehler/Corbis, (CR) The Granger Collection (CC) ©Mimmo Jodice/Corbis; 255 North Wind Picture Archives; 256 British Museum; 257 (R) The Granger Collection, SuperStock, (L) Scala/Art Resource, NY; 260 Fine Art Museum, Budapest, Hungary/Bridgeman Art Library, London/SuperStock; 262 (TR), (BR) SuperStock, (CR) Museo Capitolino, Rome, Italy/ET Archive, London/SuperStock, (B) ©Wolfgang Kaehler/Corbis-Bettmann; 263 Réunion des Musées Nationaux/Art Resource, NY; 264 The Granger Collection; 265 (R) Réunion des Musées Nationaux/Art Resource, NY, (L) Scala/Art Resource, NY, SuperStock; 266 (L) The Granger Collection, (R) Bettmann/Corbis; 267 Archivo Iconografico, S.A./Corbis; 268 R. Sheridan/Ancient Art & Architecture Collection/Ronald Sheridan Photo-Library; 270 (T) Scala/Art Resource, NY, (BR) ©Dorling Kindersley, (TR) British Museum/©Dorling Kindersley; 272 (TR) Fine Art Museum, Budapest, Hungary/Bridgeman Art Library, London/SuperStock; 274 (TL) SEF/Art Resource, NY, (TR) Antonio Calanni/AP/Wide World, (CL) Réunion des Musées Nationaux/Art Resource, NY, (BR) Historical Picture Archive/Corbis, (BL) ©Araldo de Luca/Corbis; 276 ©Mark L Stephenson/Corbis; 278 (T) SEF/Art Resource, NY, (B) Vanni Archives/Corbis; 280 (T) (B) ©Mimmo Jodice/Corbis; 281 (T) University College of Wales, Aberystwyth, Wales/Bridgeman Art Library International Ltd., (B) ©Dorling Kindersley; 282 Hulton/Archive by Getty Images; 283 ©Araldo de Luca/Corbis; 284 (L) Bettmann Archives/Corbis, (C) Bradford City Art Gallery & Museum, England/Bridgeman Art Library, London/SuperStock, (R) British Museum/©Dorling Kindersley; 285 Réunion des Musées Nationaux/Art Resource, NY; 286 (TR) The Granger Collection; 288 ©Araldo de Luca/Corbis; 289 ©Araldo de Luca/Corbis; 290 British Museum/©Dorling Kindersley; 291 (T) British Museum/©Dorling Kindersley, (B) ©Dorling Kindersley; 293 Capitoline Museums, Rome, Italy/Canali PhotoBank, Milan/SuperStock; 294 The Granger Collection; 295 Antonio Calanni/AP/Wide World; 296 Scala/Art Resource, NY; 297 Craig Aurness/Corbis; 298 Art Resource, NY; 299 Art Resource, NY, (T) British Museum/©Dorling Kindersley; 300 Alinari/Art Resource, NY; 301 (T) The Granger Collection, (B) SuperStock, (BR) Historical Picture Archive/Corbis; 302 (B) Jonathan Blair/Corbis, (T) Archivo Iconografico, S.A./Corbis; 303 The Granger Collection; 305 (R) Erich Lessing/Art Resource, NY, Stapleton Collection, UK/Bridgeman Art Library International Ltd., (CL) Guy Clark/www.ancient-art.com/Ancient Coins and Antiquities; 306 British Museum/©Dorling Kindersley

Unit 5:

313, 314, 315 Bibliothèque Nationale Paris/The Art Archive; 316 (L) Musee de Chartres, France/Explorer, Paris/SuperStock, (CL) Ancient Art & Architecture Collection/Ronald Sheridan Photo-Library, (CR) Earl Morse, New York/Werner Forman Archive/Art Resource, NY, (R) Cathedral Treasury Aachen/Dagli Orti (A)/The Art Archive; 317 (L) Ancient Art & Architecture Collection/Ronald Sheridan Photo-Library, (R) Robert Frerck/Odyssey Productions, (CR) Burt Silverman/NGS Image Collection; 319 Robert Frerck/Odyssey Productions; 320 (TC) Archivo Iconografico, S.A./Corbis, (B), (T) Giraudon/Art Resource, NY, (BC) SuperStock; 322 Robert Frerck/Odyssey Productions; 323 ©Paul Almasy/Corbis; 324 Robert Frerck/Odyssey Productions; 325 Giraudon/Art Resource, NY; 326 Archivo Iconografico, S.A./Corbis; 328 Ancient Art & Architecture Collection/Ronald Sheridan Photo-Library; 329 (L) Dagli Orti (A)/The Art Archive, (R), (C) Ancient Art & Architecture Collection/Ronald Sheridan Photo-Library; 330 SuperStock; 331 (B) Christine Osborne Pictures, (T) Ramey/Stock Boston; 332 Paolo Koch/Photo Researchers, Inc.; 333 V. & M. Birley/Tropix Photo Library/www.tropix.co.uk; 335 Werner Foreman Archive/Art Resource, NY; 336 Paolo Koch/Photo Researchers, Inc.; 337 National Maritime Museum, Greenwich/Werner Forman Archive/Art Resource, NY; 338 Giraudon/Art Resource, NY; 339 Burt Silverman/NGS Image Collection; 341 Dortmund, Westfälisches Schulmuseum/AKG London Ltd.; 342 National Maritime Museum, Greenwich/Werner Forman Archive/Art Resource, NY; 344 (T) Wolfgang Kaehler, (BC) ©Christophe Loviny/Corbis, (TC) Private Collection/Bridgeman Art Library International Ltd., (B) SuperStock; 346 Wolfgang Kaehler; 348 Victoria & Albert Museum, London/Art Resource, NY; 349 Roland and Sabrina Michaud/Woodfin Camp & Associates; 350 The Art Archive; 351 (TC) ©British Library/©Dorling Kindersley, (TCC) British Library/©Dorling Kindersley, (BCC) Science Museum/Science & Society Picture Library, (BC) University Museum of Archaeology and Anthropology, Cambridge/© Dorling Kindersley, (B) Victoria & Albert Museum, London, UK/Bridgeman Art Library International Ltd., (T) Bibliothèque Nationale Paris/The Art Archive; 352 (T) Werner Foreman/Art Resource, NY; 354 (CL) ©Dorling Kindersley, (CR), (BR), (BC), (BL) British Library/©Dorling Kindersley, (T) British Museum/©Dorling Kindersley; 355 Yu Zheng/ChinaStock; 356 ©Christophe Loviny/Corbis; 358 (CL) Sean Sprague/Stock Boston, (CR) Michael Yamashita Photography; 359 (L) Musee National de Phnom Penh, Cambodia/Bridgeman Art Library International Ltd., (R) ; ©Leonard de Selva/Corbis; 360 Erich Lessing/Art Resource, NY; 361 (B) SuperStock, (T) ©Dorling Kindersley; 362 Private Collection/Bridgeman Art Library International Ltd.; 363 Werner Forman/Art Resource, NY; 366 Sean Sprague/Stock Boston; 368 (T) John Elk III, (C) Robert Frerck/Odyssey Productions; 370 M. Foster/Christine Osborne Pictures; 371 (CR) John Elk III, (BL) Robin White/Robin White/FotoLex Associates, (BR), (T), (CL) Gerald Cubitt; 372 (L) SuperStock, (R) Daryl Balfour/Gallo Images; 374 Robert Frerck/Odyssey Productions, (B) ©Victor Englebert; 375 (T) ©Victor Englebert; 376 John Elk III; 378 British Museum/©Dorling Kindersley; 379 Werner Forman/Art Resource, NY; 380 Darrel Plowes; 381 (L) ©Victor Englebert, (R) ©Dorling Kindersley; 382 (T) Laura James/Private Collection/Bridgeman Art Library International Ltd., (B) Michelle Burgess/Stock Boston; 384 Gerald Cubitt; 385 Robert Frerck/Odyssey Productions; 387 V. and M. Birley/Tropix Photo Library; 388 John Elk III; 390 (T) Christine Osborne Pictures, (TC) Dept. of the Environment, London, UK/Bridgeman Art Library International Ltd., (B) Bibliotheque Nationale, Paris, France/Bridgeman Art Library International Ltd.; 392 SuperStock; 394 SuperStock; 395 Christine Osborne Pictures; 396 Public Record Office London/The Art Archive; 397 Musee de la Tapisserie, Bayeux, France/Bridgeman Art Library International Ltd.; 398 Dept. of the Environment, London, UK/Bridgeman Art Library International Ltd.; 399 (CL) Bibliotheque Municipale, Castres, France/Giraudon/Bridgeman Art Library International Ltd., Scala/Art Resource, NY, (CR) Hulton Archive/Getty Images; 401 ©Dorling Kindersley; 403 Ancient Art & Architecture Collection/Ronald Sheridan Photo-Library; 404 (BL), (BR) Courtesy of the Provincial Museum of Newfoundland and Labrador, (T) ©Duomo, Orvieto, Umbria, Italy/Roger-Viollet, Paris/Bridgeman Art Library International Ltd.; 405 Art Resource, NY; 406 Kunstindustrimuseet, Oslo, Norway/Bridgeman Art Library International Ltd.; 408 (T) Bibliotheque Nationale, Paris, France/Bridgeman Art Library International Ltd., (B) Robert Frerck/Odyssey Productions; 410 British Museum; 411 ©Dorling Kindersley; 415 Musee de la Tapisserie, Bayeux, France/Bridgeman Art Library International Ltd.

Unit 6:

421, 422, 423 Scala/Art Resource, NY; 424 (L), (R) The Granger Collection, (CL) Private Collection/Index/Bridgeman Art Library International Ltd., (CR) Archivo de Indias, Seville, Spain/Mithra-Index/Bridgeman Art Library International Ltd.; 425 (L) AKG London Ltd., (CL) Mary Evans Picture Library, (CR) Robert Frerck/Odyssey Productions, (R) Bettmann/Corbis; 427 North Wind Picture Archives; 428 (T), Scala/Art Resource, NY, (CC) The Granger Collection (BC) Hulton Archive/Getty Images; 430 Vanni Archive/Corbis; 432 (T) Scala/Art Resource, NY, (B) The Granger Collection; 433 (T) Ian Hessenberg/Hayward Gallery, (BL) Werner Forman/Art Resource, NY, (BR) Fukuhara, Inc/Corbis; 434 (TL) Erich Lessing/Art Resource, NY, (TR) Nimatallah/Art Resource, NY, (BCL), (BCR), (BR) Science Museum/©Dorling Kindersley, (CR) Scala/Art Resource, NY, (BL) Private Collection/Ken Welsh/Bridgeman Art Library International Ltd., (CL) Science & Society Picture Library; 435 (T) Hulton/Archive by Getty Images, (B) Science & Society Picture Library; 436 Jorg Breu the Elder/The Newberry Library, Chicago/Stock Montage Inc.; 437 Mary Evans Picture Library; 438 Stock Montage Inc.; 439 The Granger Collection; 442 Erich Lessing/Art Resource, NY; 443 (R) National Trust/Art Resource, NY, Cornelius de Visscher/Art Resource, NY, (L) Justus Göpel/AKG London Ltd.; 444 Pitt Rivers Museum/©Dorling Kindersley; 445 (T) National Maritime Museum/AKG London Ltd., (B) ©O. Alamany & E. Vicens/Corbis; 447 (T) Werner Forman/Art Resource, NY, (B) HultonArchive/Getty Images, (C) The Granger Collection; 448 The Granger Collection; 450 Peter Jackson, F.S.A.; 451 Courtesy Denver Post; 452 Scala/Art Resource, NY; 454 (T), (TC) The Granger Collection, (BC) North Wind Picture Archives, (BL), (BR) Science Museum/©Dorling Kindersley; 456 Hulton Archive/Getty Images; 457 The Granger Collection; 458 (T), (B) The Granger Collection; 459 (B) Stock Montage Inc., (T) National History Museum Mexico City/Dagli Orti/The Art Archive; 461 (c) 2003 Banco de México Diego Rivera & Frida Kahlo Museums Trust. Av. Cinco de Mayo No. 2, Col. Centro, Del. Cuauhtémoc 06059, México, D.F./ Reproduccion Autorizada por el Instituto Nacional de Bellas Artes y Literatura/(c) Sean Sprague/Mexicolore/SuperStock; 462 The Granger Collection; 463 (R) Bettmann/Corbis, (Bkgd) AKG London Ltd., (L) D. Donne Bryant/DDBryant Stock Photography; 464, 465 The Smithsonian Institution; 466 Hulton Archive/Getty Images; 467 (T) Musée Carnavalet

Paris/Jean-Loup Charmet/The Art Archive, (B) Chateau de Versailles, France/Lauros-Giraudon/Bridgeman Art Library International Ltd.; 468 (T) Ancient Art & Architecture Collection/Ronald Sheridan Photo-Library, (B) The Granger Collection; 469 (L) Hulton Archive/Getty Images, (R) Bibliotheque Nationale, Paris, France/Lauros-Giraudon/Bridgeman Art Library International Ltd.; 470 Réunion des Musées Nationaux/Art Resource, NY; 471 (T) Musee de la Ville de Paris, Musee Carnavalet, Paris, France/Bridgeman Art Library International Ltd., (B) Photographic reproduction by the Bibliothèque Nationale de France; 472 (T), (B) The Granger Collection; 473 The Granger Collection; 474 North Wind Picture Archives; 476 The Art Archive; 477 Museum of London, UK/Bridgeman Art Library International Ltd.; 478 (C), (L) Science Museum/©Dorling Kindersley, (R) ©Dorling Kindersley; 479 (R) Science Museum/©Dorling Kindersley, (L) Beaulieu Motor Museum/©Dorling Kindersley; 480 North Wind Picture Archives; 481 (L) Bettmann/Corbis, (R) Hulton-Deutsch Collection/Corbis; 482 Science Museum/©Dorling Kindersley; 484 (T) Bettmann/Corbis, (BCR) ©Stamps reproduced by kind permission of New Zealand Post Limited from their 1940 Centennial stamp issue ©Australian Postal Corporation, 1813/The Art Archive, (B) ©Canada Post Corporation, 1898. Reproduced with Permission/The Art Archive; 486 Dagli Orti/The Art Archive; 487 (T) Consolidated Goldfields/The Art Archive, (B) Bettmann/Corbis; 488 The Granger Collection; 489 North Wind Picture Archives; 492 Fine Art Photographic Library, London/Art Resource, NY; 493 (T) Private Collection/Dagli Orti/The Art Archive, (B) ©Photograph Courtesy of Peabody Essex Museum E79708/Peabody Essex Museum of Salem; 495 (T) Bettmann/Corbis, (CR) Scala/Art Resource, NY, (B) Bettmann/Corbis; 496 Underwood & Underwood/Corbis; 497 (R) Réunion des Musées Nationaux/Art Resource, NY, (L) "The Blue Sky" -Emperor Meiji. Handwritten by Chiba Taneaki, Painting "Spring Morning" by Kwanzan (1874-1931) Detail. Courtesy of The Board of Chamberlains/Imperial Household Agency, (Bkgd) Ancient Art & Architecture Collection/Ronald Sheridan Photo-Library; 498 ©Dorling Kindersley; 499 Mary Evans Picture Library; 500 (B) Gert Schuetz/AKG London Ltd., (T) Lionel Cironneau/AP/Wide World; 501 Museo del Risorgimento Rome/Dagli Orti/The Art Archive; 502 (C) ©Canada Post Corporation, 1898. Reproduced with Permission/The Art Archive, (L), (R), ©Stamps reproduced by kind permission of New Zealand Post Limited from their 1940 Centennial stamp issue ©Australian Postal Corporation, 1813/The Art Archive; 503 ©Penny Tweedie/Corbis; 504 Museo del Risorgimento Rome/Dagli Orti/The Art Archive

Unit 7:

511, 512 (C) U. S. Coast Guard; 514 (L) National Archives, (CL), (CR) Corbis, (R) Bettmann/Corbis; 515 (L) AP/Wide World, (CL) Bettmann/Corbis, (CR) Mary Evans Picture Library, (R) JAF Collection/©Magnum Photos; 517 Hulton/Archive Photos; 518 (T) Bettmann/Corbis, (C), (B) The Granger Collection; 520 ©Brian Seed 2001; 521 (B) Hulton/Archive Photos, (T) The Granger Collection; 523 Bettmann/Corbis; 526 ©Underwood & Underwood/Corbis; 527 (B) The Granger Collection; 528 The West Point Museum Collections, United States Military Academy. Photographed for Scott Foresman by Joshua Nefsky; 529 The Burns Archive, Ltd; 530 The Granger Collection; 531 Charles Phelps Cushing/H. Armstrong Roberts; 532 Hulton-Deutsch Collection/Corbis; 533 (Bkgd) Library of Congress/Corbis, (R) Hulton/Archive, (L) Christopher Cormack/Corbis; 534 Imperial War Museum/Art Archive; 535 Corbis; 536 (BR), (BL), (T) The Burns Archive, Ltd; 537 The Granger Collection; 538 Imperial War Museum/Art Archive; 540 (C) Bettmann/Corbis, (B) The Granger Collection, (T) Hulton/Archive Photos; 542 Bettmann/Corbis; 543 (B) Bettmann/Corbis, (T) The Granger Collection; 544 (T) Mary Evans Picture Library, (BC) Hulton-Deutsch Collection/Corbis, (BR) ©Michael Jang/Getty Images, (BL) Siede Preis/PhotoDisc, (C) Topham/Image Works; 545 Hulton/Archive Photos; 546 AP/Wide World; 547 Hulton/Archive; 548 Bettmann/Corbis; 550 (B) The Granger Collection, (T) AP/Wide World; 551 (TR) Wings Across America, (TL) ©2001 Owen/Black Star, (B) Hulton-Deutsch Collection/Corbis; 552 National Archives; 555 (Bkgd), (R) Hulton/Archive Photos, (L) Chartwell Manor, Kent, UK/Bridgeman Art Library International Ltd.; 556, 557 Smithsonian Institution; 558 The Granger Collection; 559 (T) Fred Ramage/Keystone/Archive Photos, (B) AP/Wide World; 560 Courtesy of FDR Library, Hyde Park, NY, (B) Ben Shahn, Liberation. (1945)/©The Musem of Modern Art, New York/©Estate of Ben Shahn/Licensed by VAGA, New York, NY; 561 (T) AP/Wide World, (B) The Granger Collection; 564 Wings Across America; 566 (C) Bettmann/Corbis, (B) AP/Wide World, (T) Courtesy of FDR Library, Hyde Park, NY; 568 Bettmann/Corbis; 569 Courtesy of FDR Library, Hyde Park, NY; 570 (B) Bettmann/Corbis, (T) Courtesy North Atlantic Treaty Organization; 571 (T) ©1999 Owen/Black Star, (B) Bettmann/Corbis; 572 ©Magnum Photos; 573 Edmund Hillary/Royal Geographical Society, London; 574 (R) Cecil Stoughton/TimePix, (L) Time Magazine, © Time Inc./TimePix; 575 AP/Wide World; 576 Macduff Everton/Corbis; 578 (T) ©Magnum Photos, (B) ©Dorling Kindersley; 579 Bettmann/Corbis; 580 Hulton/Archive Photos; 581 (R) AP/Wide World, (Bkgd) ©Harry Redl/Black Star (L) David King; 582 ©Steve Raymer/Corbis; 583 AP/Wide World; 584 (B) AP/Wide World, (T) Hulton Archive/Getty Images; 585 (B) Hulton/Archive Photos, (C) ©AFP, (T) Hulton-Deutsch Collection/Corbis; 587 Express Newspaper/Hulton Archive/Getty Images; 589 (T) SuperStock, (C) Douglas Corry/PictureQuest, (B) Bettmann/Corbis; 590 Courtesy North Atlantic Treaty Organisation; 592 ©The Norman Rockwell Museum at Stockbridge/2002 Christie's Images, Inc./Reproduced courtesy of the Norman Rockwell Family Trust; 597, 598 Diana Ong/SuperStock; 600 (L) ©Elliott & Fry/Hulton Archive/Getty Images, (CL) Erich Hartmann/©Magnum Photos, (R) Hulton Archive/Getty Images, (CR) Hulton-Deutsch Collection/Corbis; 601 (L), (CL), (CR) Hulton Archive/Getty Images, (R) Eric Risberg/AP/Wide World; 603 (T) Raghu Rai/©Magnum Photos, (B) Chris Hellier/Corbis; 604 (C) S. Kanno/Photri, Inc., (B) Thomas Kienzle/AP/Wide World; 607 Agence France Press/Archive Photos/Hulton Archive/Getty Images; 609 (T) Reuters/Juda Ngwenya/Hulton Archive/Getty Images, (B) Denis Farrell/AP/Wide World; 610 David Longstreath/AP/Wide World, (T) Stuart Franklin/©Magnum Photos; 611 (B) Vithalbhai Jhaveri/GandhiServe e.K; 613 (R) ©AFP, (Bkgd) Wolfgang Kaehler, (L) Translated by Julius Nyerere/Oxford University Press; 614 S. Kanno/Photri, Inc.; 615 ©Horst Tappe/Hulton Archive/Getty Images; 616 Charles Bonnay/TimePix; 618 Bob Daugherty/AP/Wide World; 619 (BR) Sahm Doherty/TimePix, (T) Corbis, (Bkgd) ©Richard T. Nowitz/Corbis, (BL) Bettmann/Corbis; 620 Thomas Kienzle/AP/Wide World; 621 (T) Bettmann/Corbis, (B) ©David & Peter Turnley/Corbis; 623 ©David & Peter Turnley/Corbis; 625 J. Lee/Tropix Photo Library/www.tropix.co.uk; 628 (B) Reuters/TimePix, (C) ©David & Peter Turnley/Corbis; 630 C Squared Studios/PhotoDisc; 631 ©Bruce Hands/Getty Images; 632 Frank Wing/PhotoDisc; 634 ©Chris Shinn/Getty Images; 636 ©David & Peter Turnley/Corbis; 638 ©Per-Anders Pettersson/Prestige/Getty Images News Services; 639 Paul McErlane/AP/Wide World; 640 (R) Reuters/Arthur Tsang/Hulton Archive/Getty Images, (L) ©AFP; 642 (L) ©Alison Wright/Corbis, (Bkgd) Radhika Chalasani/Sipa Press; 643 Rolando Gonzalez/©AFP; 644 Marc Schauber; 646 (B) ©Joseph Sohm/Visions of America/Corbis, (T) Hulton Archive/Getty Images; 647 Julie Jacobson/AP/Wide World; 648 (T) Reuters/TimePix, (BL) AP/Wide World, (BC) Richard Drew/AP/Wide World, (BR) Antonio Cotrim/©AFP; 649 Peter Mcerlane/AP/Wide World; 650 Frank Wing/PhotoDisc; 652 (T) Fotos & Photos/Index Stock Imagery, (TC) PhotoLink/PhotoDisc, (BC) Paul Schutzer/TimePix; 654 SuperStock; 655 Santosh Basak/AP/Wide World; 656 Fotos & Photos/Index Stock Imagery; 660 Ecoscene/Corbis; 661 AP/Wide World; 663 PhotoLink/PhotoDisc; 664 ©Terry Vine/Getty Images; 666 ©A & L Sinibaldi/Getty Images, (B) ©Mike Agliolo/Science Source/Photo Researchers, Inc.; 667 Paul Schutzer/TimePix; 668 NASA; 669 (L) AP/Wide World, (R) Getty Images; 670 ©Martin Simon/Corbis SABA

Unit 8:

597, 598, 599 Diana Ong/SuperStock; 600 (L) Elliott & Fry/Hulton/Archive by Getty Images, (CL) Erich Hartmann/© Magnum Photos, (R) Hulton/Archive by Getty Images, (CR) Hulton-Deutsch Collection/Corbis; 601 (L), (CL), (CR) Hulton/Archive by Getty Images, (R) Eric Risberg/AP/Wide World; 603 (T) Raghu Rai/© Magnum Photos, (B) © Chris Hellier/Corbis; 604 (C) S. Kanno/Photri, Inc., (B) Thomas Kienzle/AP/Wide World, (T) Dream Maker Software; 606 Dream Maker Software; 607 Agence France Press/Archive Photos/Hulton/Archive by Getty Images; 609 (T) Reuters/Juda Ngwenya/Hulton/Archive/Getty Images, (B) Denis Farrell/AP/Wide World; 610 David Longstreath/AP/Wide World; 611 (T) Stuart Franklin/© Magnum Photos, (B) Vithalbhai Jhaveri/GandhiServe e.K; 613 (R) © AFP, (Bkgd) Wolfgang Kaehler, (L) Translated by Julius Nyerere/Oxford University Press; 614 S. Kanno/Photri, Inc.; 615 Horst Tappe/Hulton/Archive/Getty Images; 616 Charles Bonnay/TimePix; 618 Bob Daugherty/AP/Wide World; 619 (BR) Sahm Doherty/TimePix, (T) Corbis, (Bkgd) © Richard T. Nowitz/Corbis, (BL) Bettmann/Corbis; 620 Thomas Kienzle/AP/Wide World; 621 (T) Bettmann/Corbis, (B) © David & Peter Turnley/Corbis; 623 David & Peter Turnley/Corbis; 625 J. Lee/Tropix Photo Library; 628 (T) © Frank Wing/PhotoDisc, (B) Reuters/TimePix, (C) © David & Peter Turnley/Corbis; 630 C Squared Studios/PhotoDisc; 631 © Bruce Hands/Stone; 632 © Frank Wing/PhotoDisc; 634 © Chris Shinn/Stone; 636 © David & Peter Turnley/Corbis; 638 © Per-Anders Pettersson/Prestige/Getty Images News Services; 639 Paul McErlane/AP/Wide World; 640 (R) Reuters/Arthur Tsang/Hulton/Archive/Getty Images, (L) © AFP; 642 (L) © Alison Wright/Corbis, (Bkgd) Radhika Chalasani/Sipa Press; 643 Rolando Gonzalez/© AFP; 644 Marc Schauber; 646 (B) © Joseph Sohm/Visions of America/Corbis, (T) Hulton/Archive by Getty Images; 647 Julie Jacobson/AP/Wide World; 648 (T) Reuters/TimePix, (BL) AP/Wide World, (BC) Richard Drew/AP/Wide World, (BR) Antonio Cotrim/© AFP; 649 Peter Mcerlane/AP/Wide World; 650 © Frank Wing/PhotoDisc; 652 (T) Fotos & Photos/Index Stock Imagery, (TC) PhotoLink/PhotoDisc, (BC) Paul Schutzer/TimePix, (B) NASA; 654 SuperStock; 655 Santosh Basak/AP/Wide World; 656 Fotos & Photos/Index Stock Imagery; 660 Ecoscene/Corbis; 661 AP/Wide World; 663 PhotoLink/PhotoDisc; 664, 665 © Terry Vine/Getty Images/Stone; 666 © A & L Sinibaldi/Stone; 667 Paul Schutzer/TimePix; 668 NASA; 669 (L) AP/Wide World, (R) The Image Bank

End Matter: R2 Earth Imaging/Stone; R22 (TL) Flag Research Center; R30 (TCR) Detail/Smithsonian American Art Museum, Washington DC/Art Resource, NY/(Detail); R32 (BR) © Arthur Tilley/Getty Images/FPG; R35 (TCL) American Museum of Natural History/© Dorling Kindersley, (TCC) National Maritime Museum/© Dorling Kindersley; R37 (TCR) The Granger Collection, New York; R38 (TCCR) The Granger Collection, New York; R39 (TCR) The Military Picture Library/Corbis, (TCC) Hulton-Deutsch Collection/Corbis, (TCL) Smithsonian Institution; R40 (BL) Hulton/Archive, (TCLB) TimePix, (TL) Flag Research Center; Endsheets: (C) D. Logan/H. Armstrong Roberts; (BC) Frans Lemmens; (TC), (TL), (TR), Corbis; (C) Garry Black/Masterfile Corporation; (BL) Anthony Johnson; (LC) PhotoDisc; INAH/© Dorling Kindersley; Jorge Taniszewski/Art Resource, NY; Museum of Mankind London/Eileen Tweedy/Art Archive; © Canada Post Corporation, 1898. Reproduced with Permission/The Art Archive; © Dorling Kindersley; The Granger Collection, New York; Bob Clemenz Photography; (CC) Robert Frerck/Odyssey Productions; (BC) Christine Osborne Pictures; Gianni Dagli Orti/Corbis; The Studio Dog/PhotoDisc

Notes

Teacher Resources

Graphic Organizers

Vocabulary Words

Family Activities

Scope and Sequence

Unit Bibliographies

Index

Facing Fear: Helping Students Cope with Tragic Events

American Red Cross

Together, we can save a life

As much as we would like to protect our children, we cannot shield them from personal or community tragedies. We can, however, help them to be prepared for unforeseen dangerous events and to learn about facing and moving beyond their fears and related concerns.

Common Responses to Trauma and Disaster

Young people experience many common reactions after a trauma. These include reexperiencing the event (for example, flashbacks), avoidance and numbing of feelings, increased agitation, and changes in functioning. These reactions may be manifested in clingy behaviors, mood changes, increased anxieties, increased startle responses (for example, more jumpy with noises), physical complaints, and aggressive behavior. Increased aggressive behaviors may also be seen. When the trauma or disaster is human-made, such as a terrorist event, young people may react with hurtful talk, behaviors, or play. All of these reactions are normal responses and will, in general, dissipate with time. However, should these persist or increase over time, a referral to a mental health professional might be considered. Similarly, should these reactions result in a danger to self or others, immediate action is warranted.

Issues of Safety, Security, and Trust

In the aftermath of terrorism or other tragic events, students can feel overwhelmed with concerns of safety, security, and trust. Worries about their own safety as well as the safety of those important in their lives are likely heightened. Although they have developed a sense of empathy and are concerned about others, their immediate needs for personal reassurance will take priority. They will need repeated reassurances about their safety and the safety of those around them. They may have concerns about the event reoccurring; this concern may be exacerbated by repeated exposure to media images. At times students may feel as if they are reexperiencing the event. They may have triggers for memories, such as noises, sights, or smells. These "flashbacks" may also occur without an obvious reminder. Reexperiencing can be very frightening for students this age. They may try (without success) to NOT think about the event. Their inability to block the thoughts may produce increased levels of stress. Although students

will continue to process recent events, a return to a classroom routine is one of the best ways to reinforce a sense of security and safety.

Expressing Thoughts and Feelings

Young people seven to twelve years old have the ability to understand the permanence of loss from trauma. They may become preoccupied with details of it and want to talk about it continually. The questions and the details discussed are often disturbing to adults (for example, talk of gore and dismemberment). Such discussions are not meant to be uncaring or insensitive but rather are the way that many students attempt to make sense of a tragedy. Since their thinking is generally more mature than that of students under seven, their understanding of the disaster is more complete. They understand the irreversibility of death but may continue to ask questions about death and dying as they try to understand the repercussions of the event.

Students this age will attempt to create the "story" of the terrorist action or tragic event. Unfortunately, their attempts will contain misinformation as well as misperceptions. Unless addressed directly, the misunderstanding may be perpetuated and lead to increased levels of stress. Students are trying to make the story "fit" into their concept of the world around them. Questions related to the trauma may be equally repetitive. Teachers may answer students' questions only to have the same questions repeated within a few minutes. Having the same answer will increase the students' sense of security and help them process the trauma.

One result of a human-made tragedy may be intense feelings of anger and a sense of revenge. With an inaccurate understanding of events, these feelings may develop into hateful/hurtful talk or play. It may be directed toward classmates or groups of people. This behavior should be immediately addressed. Open discussions with these young students may improve their understanding of the event as well as reduce inappropriate direction of anger toward others.

Identifying Factors to Predict Students at Greatest Risk

Feelings accompanying the event may overwhelm elementary-aged students. In addition to the anger, they may also have feelings of guilt and intense sadness; nervousness is also seen. As they attempt to process these feelings, a change in school performance may be seen. Some students will have a drop in school performance as attention and concentration to their work is diminished. They may not be able to grasp new concepts as easily as before the event and grades may show a decline. Students may become more active in their behaviors as well as more impulsive and reckless. These behaviors often appear similar to attention deficit hyperactivity disorder and/or learning disabilities. Although either may be present, the impact of the event as a reason for the behavior changes should be considered. Students may develop problems in sleep and appetite after a traumatic event or disaster. These changes may contribute to a decrease in school performance.

It is important to note that some students may try to handle feelings of guilt and worry by an intense attention to schoolwork. These students may be worried about disappointing teachers and parents. Through their intense focus on school, they may be attempting to avoid activities and thoughts that are disturbing.

Students' anxiety and fear may be seen in an increased number of physical complaints. These may include headaches, stomachaches, feelings of nausea, or vague aches and pains. Expression of these emotions may also be seen in mood changes. *(continued on the following page)*

TR1

(continued from p. TR1)

Students may become more irritable and quarrelsome. They may become more aggressive at recess. Although some students may act out more, others may become more withdrawn and detached from activities and friends around them. They may be having an equally hard time processing the events, but because of their quietness, they are often overlooked as having any difficulties.

In the face of tragic events, students of this age will be seeking ways to help others. By finding positive avenues for expressing their concerns and need for involvement, initial negative reactions to the event may begin to diminish. Working to guide students in positive directions can be an important aspect of the healing process.

It is important to remember that all of these reactions are normal and, generally, will begin to diminish with time.

Moving Forward in Spite of Life-Affecting Events

Frightening events, such as the terrorist attacks in the United States on September 11, 2001, the Oklahoma City bombing in 1995, earthquakes, tornadoes, and hurricanes here and in other countries, massive transportation accidents, and war or armed conflict or other military action, impact us all. Events that are caused by human beings can be particularly frightening and raise unique concerns.

Terrorist actions and other violent acts are designed to instill fear in individuals and communities, if not countries. Because they happen without warning, there is no time to prepare. This unpredictability leaves us with a heightened sense of vulnerability and anxieties that the event could be repeated again, anywhere. With increased media coverage, even those not directly impacted can be significantly affected by an event. Images make us feel closer to the victims and we may perceive ourselves as victims of the actions as well. The questions that arise from disasters of human design are difficult, if not impossible, to answer. We want answers to "Why?" and "How could they?" and are often left frustrated by the lack of satisfying responses. This frustration also gives rise to intense feelings of anger. The anger toward the perpetrators may be uncomfortable and difficult to express in productive ways. As adults struggle with reactions and feelings in the aftermath of a terrorist action or tragic event, young people are similarly searching for how to best handle their feelings. At all ages, they take cues from adults around them (parents, teachers, and community and national leaders).

Students need to know that their reactions and feelings to such events are normal. They need to recognize that others feel very similarly. Most important, young people need to know that they will begin to feel better with time and that it is acceptable to enjoy friends, family, and activities. They need to know that there are things they can do to help themselves move forward in a positive way.

Activities to Help Students Address Fears

The following activities are designed to help you help your students address their fears and move beyond them.

- **What Happened**—Have students tell what they remember about the trauma/disaster. Validate their experiences, but be sure to correct any misperceptions and misunderstandings.

- **Searching for a Sense of Safety**—Review with students school and family emergency procedures for natural or human-made disasters. Have students list people to contact in an emergency as well as identifying a "buddy family" that will be available to check on their safety.

- **Dealing with Feelings**—Make a chart with *Uncomfortable Feelings* and *What We Can Do About Them* as heads. List feelings students may have following a traumatic event. Then work together to come up with things to do to feel better (examples may include talking to adults, writing letters, helping in the relief effort, relaxation exercises, activities with friends, and watching a funny movie together).

- **Redirecting Thoughts**—Have students make an activity wheel by writing or drawing an activity that they enjoy doing (playing with a pet, singing a song, reading a book, riding a bike, shooting baskets,

kicking soccer balls, stringing beads, watching a favorite show or video). Show them how to put a paper arrow and a pape[r] fastener through the middle of the wheel loosely enough to spin the arrow. Suggest that when an unwanted thought or picture pops in their mind, they can spin to choose an activity to help get rid of the thought or picture.

- **Looking Ahead and Setting Goals**—Hel[p] students identify and write short-range go[als] as well as long-range ones. Discuss setting realistic goals and how they can be achiev[ed.] Also discuss ways of keeping track of the goals and the progress toward meeting the[m,] reminding students of the importance of sharing thoughts and feelings while worki[ng] toward the goals.

Books for Young Readers

Molly's Pilgrim Cohen, Barbara. Illus. by Daniel M. Duffy. Beech Tree Books, 1998[. A] recent Jewish Russian immigrant teaches [her] third-grade class about all kinds of pilgrim[s.]

Number the Stars Lowry, Lois. Laureleaf, 1998. In 1943, Jews in Denmark are hidde[n] and smuggled to safety in Sweden.

Heroes Mochizuki, Ken. Illus. by Dom Lee. Lee and Low Books, 1997. A Japanese American child, treated as an outsider by classmates during the Vietnam War, begs [his] father and uncle to tell how they fought in the U.S. Army during World War II.

The Tenth Good Thing About Barney Viors[t,] Judith. Illus. by Eric Blegvad. Aladdin, 19[.] After the death of a pet cat, a young child tries to think of ten good things about him[.]

Jumping into Nothing Willner-Pardo, Gina. Illus. by Heidi Chang. Houghton Mifflin, 1999. Sophie devises a plan to overcome her fear of jumping off the high dive.

 American Red Cross **Information on American Red Cross** *Facing Fear: Helping Young People Deal with Terrorism and Tragic Events*

The American Red Cross *Facing Fear* curriculum contains lesson plans for teachers and includes hands-on or interactive activities for the classroom that will help students and their families prepare for disastrous situations and equip them with tools to sort out their feelings and fears.

For further information or to obtain copies of the *Facing Fear* curriculum materials, or the curriculum materials that focus on natural disaster preparedness, called *Masters of Disaster*™, contact your local American Red Cross chapter. Visit

http://www.redcross.org to find your nearest Red Cross chapter, and visit **www.redcross.org/disaster/masters** for specific information on the curriculum. American Red Cross products are available exclusively from local Red Cross chapters in the United States.

With permission, parts above were adapted from Healing After Trauma Skills, *Robin H. Gurwitch and Anne K. Messenbaugh, University of Oklahoma Health Sciences Center.*

Cause and Effect

Cause   **Effect**

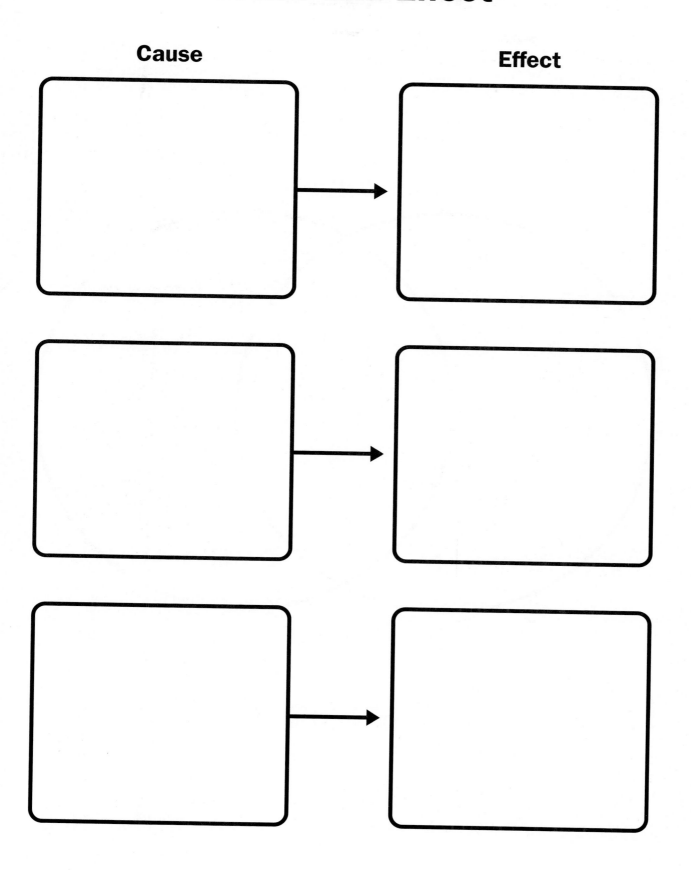

Compare and Contrast

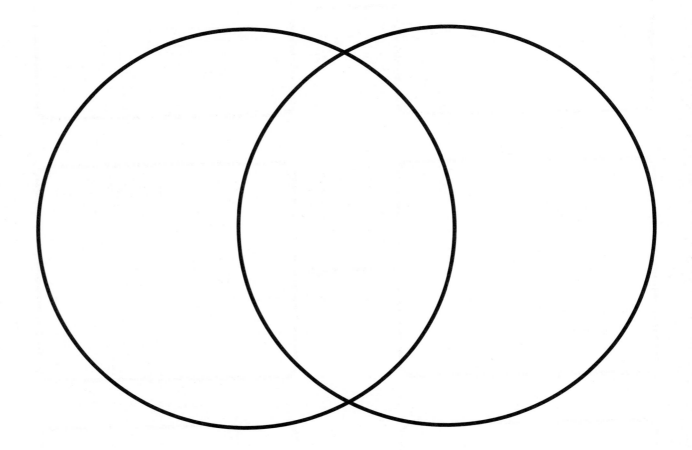

Compare and Contrast

Draw Conclusions

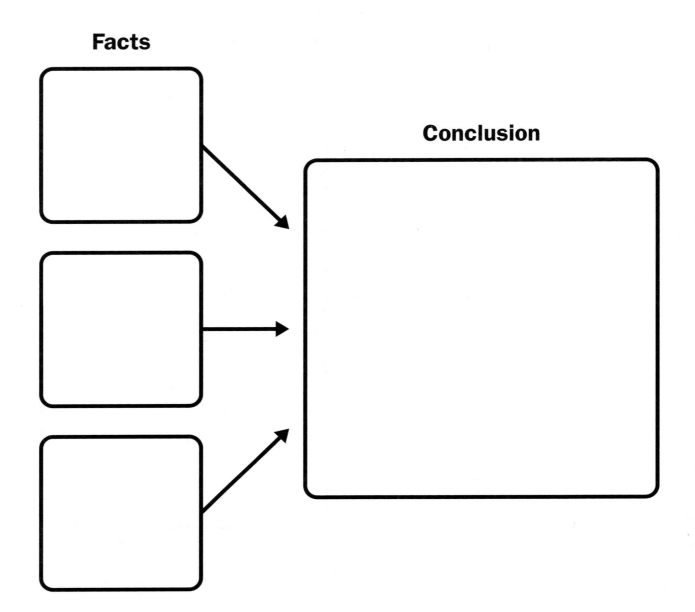

Facts

Conclusion

Main Idea and Details

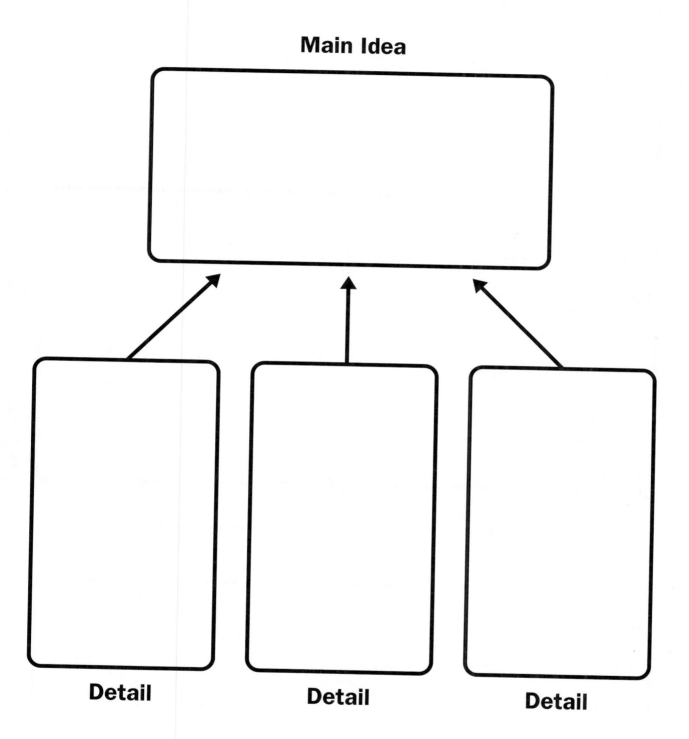

Main Idea

Detail   Detail   Detail

Sequence

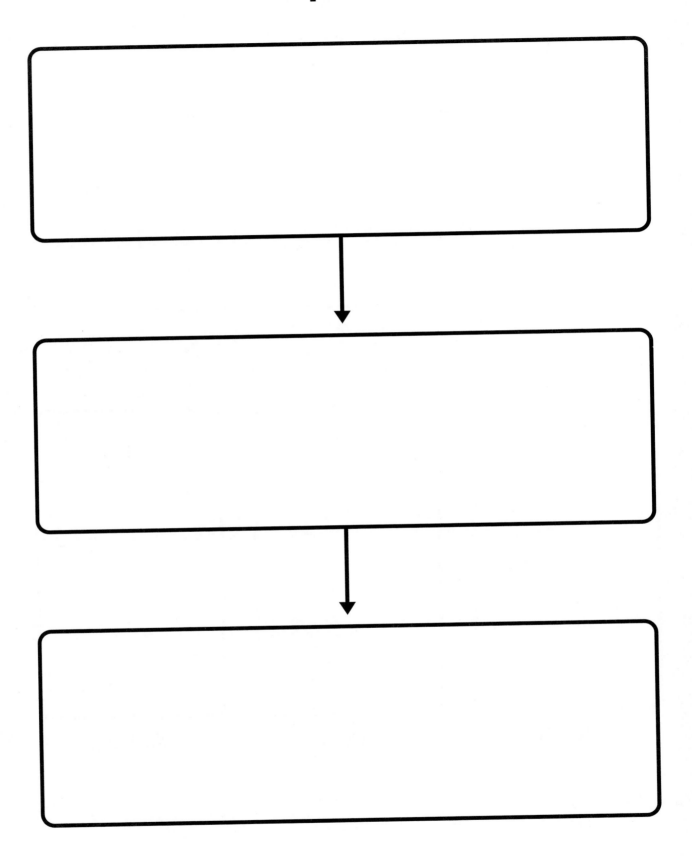

Summarize

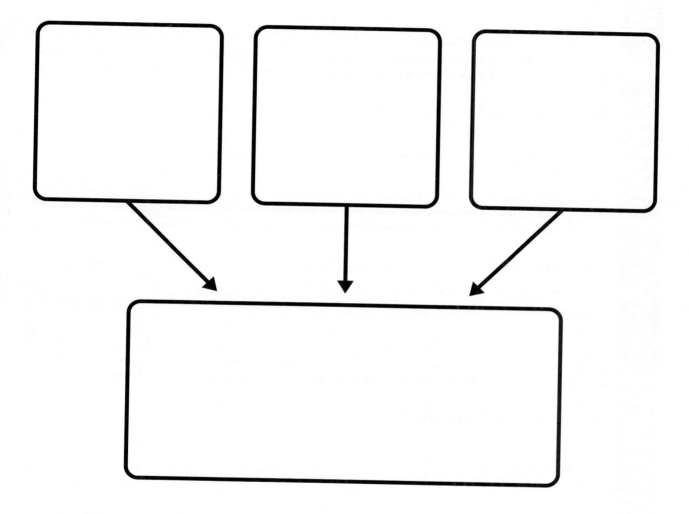

Event Summary

Name of event _____

WHO? Who was part of this event? _____

_____

_____

WHAT? What happened? _____

_____

_____

WHEN? When did this happen? _____

_____

_____

WHERE? Where did this happen? _____

_____

_____

WHY? What caused the event to happen? _____

_____

_____

Use a Decision-Making Process

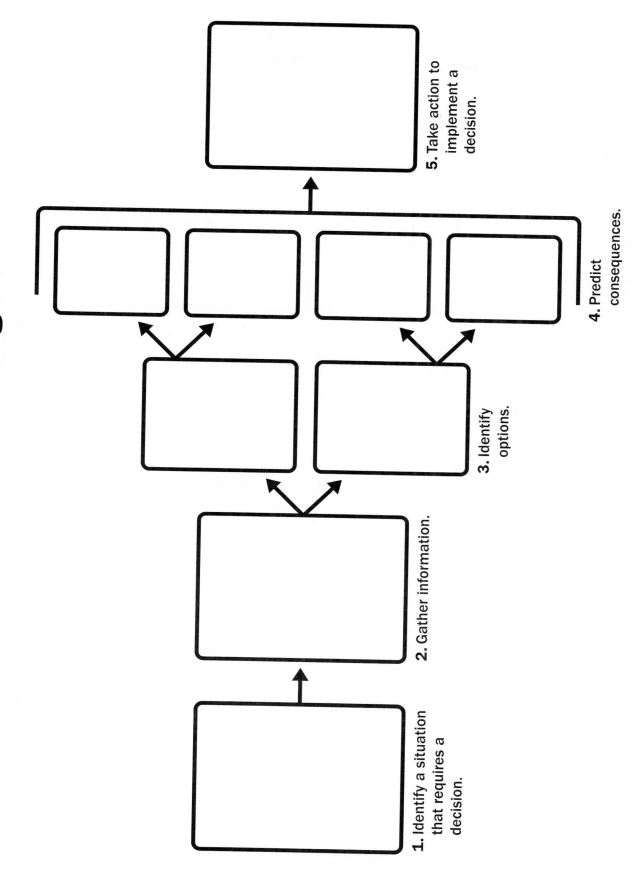

1. Identify a situation that requires a decision.

2. Gather information.

3. Identify options.

4. Predict consequences.

5. Take action to implement a decision.

Use a Problem-Solving Process

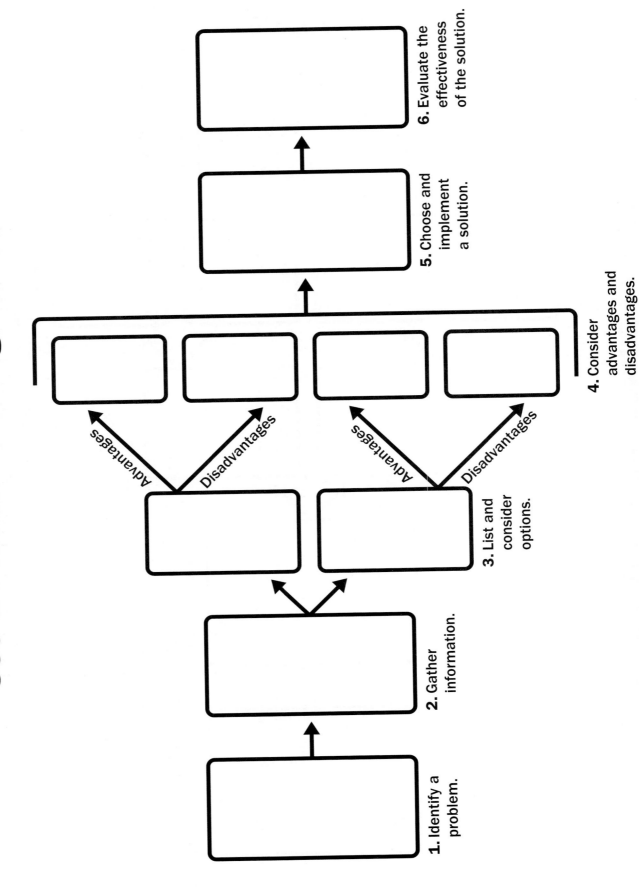

1. Identify a problem.

2. Gather information.

3. List and consider options.

Advantages

Disadvantages

Advantages

Disadvantages

4. Consider advantages and disadvantages.

5. Choose and implement a solution.

6. Evaluate the effectiveness of the solution.

Social Studies Daily Journal

Something important I learned was...

Some new words I learned are...

One way this relates to me is...

I would like to learn more about...

K-W-L Chart

Topic _____

What We **K**now	What We **W**ant to Know	What We **L**earned

Unit 1, Chapter 1

prehistory	archaeology
archaeologist	artifact
migrate	glacier
technology	domesticate
harvest	excavation site
agriculture	surplus
nomad	social division

Vocabulary Words

Unit 1, Chapter 1

climate	carbon dating
culture	anthropology
landform	geography
diverse	

Unit 1, Chapter 2

civilization	fertile
plain	plateau
irrigation	city-state
region	artisan
ziggurat	society
polytheism	scribe
cuneiform	conquer

Unit 1, Chapter 2

empire	dynasty
conquest	covenant
monotheism	slavery
descendant	synagogue
barter	

Unit 2, Chapter 3

delta	silt
papyrus	cataract
unify	pharaoh
hieroglyphics	pyramid
mummy	economy
independent	

Unit 2, Chapter 4

loess	terrace
levee	double cropping
pictograph	oracle bone
province	ancestor
civil service	middleman
nobility	

Unit 2, Chapter 5

subcontinent	monsoon season
subsistence farming	brahmin
sudra	reincarnation
caste	meditation
enlightenment	

Unit 3, Chapter 6

peninsula	cenote
theocracy	aqueduct
codex	mercenary
chinampa	causeway
alliance	

Unit 3, Chapter 7

wetland	biome
scrub land	archipelago
quipu	

basin and range	tributary
tundra	arid
etching	pit house
pueblo	adobe
burial mound	wattle
wigwam	temple mound
snowhouse	sod house

Unit 3, Chapter 8

long house

Unit 4, Chapter 9

✂

agora	plunder
myth	immortal
aristocracy	democracy
marathon	philosopher
reason	plague
mercenary	

Unit 4, Chapter 10

patrician	plebeian
republic	representative
Senate	consul
dictator	tribune
patriotism	caesar
emperor	gladiator
catacomb	synagogue

Unit 4, Chapter 10

disciple	persecute
auction	pope
pillage	vandal

Unit 5, Chapter 11

hippodrome	cathedral
icon	pilgrimage
caravan	mosque
astrolabe	

Unit 5, Chapter 12

aristocrat	samurai
typhoon	daimyo
shogun	

Unit 5, Chapter 13

savanna	griot
Swahili	oba

Vocabulary Words

Unit 5, Chapter 14

✄

monk	nun
monastery	convent
missionary	monarch
serf	knight
chivalry	guild
lady	epidemic

© Scott Foresman 6

Unit 6, Chapter 15

commerce	indulgence
excommunicate	circumnavigate
conquistador	colony
mercantilism	

Unit 6, Chapter 16

legislature	massacre
monarchy	textile
factory	tenement
corporation	reformer
strike	

Unit 6, Chapter 17

nationalism	imperialism
imperialist	treaty port
compound	modernization
dominion	parliament

Unit 7, Chapter 18

mobilization	neutral
casualty	trench warfare
armistice	holocaust
reparations	inflation

Unit 7, Chapter 19

depression	fascism
Nazis	propaganda
aggression	annex
appeasement	collective
refugee	concentration camp
charter	

Unit 7, Chapter 20

✂

nuclear	containment
proletarian	guerrilla
détente	

Unit 8, Chapter 21

decolonization	coup d'état
segregate	apartheid
sanction	civil disobedience
Zionism	dissident
perestroika	*glasnost*

Unit 8, Chapter 22

gross domestic product (GDP)	trading bloc
euro	trade agreement
ethnicity	multiethnic nation
ethnic cleansing	repressive
terrorism	

Unit 8, Chapter 23

millennium	megacity
demographer	immigration
zero population growth	global warming
carbon dioxide	greenhouse effect
pesticide	environmentalist
endangered species	deforestation
desertification	pollution

Unit 8, Chapter 23

conservation	fossil fuel
nonrenewable resource	renewable resource
hydroelectric energy	geothermal energy
space station	satellite

SCOTT FORESMAN
SOCIAL STUDIES
UNIT 1 FAMILY ACTIVITY

Dear Family:

Here is what we're learning in Social Studies!

Unit 1 Main Ideas

★ We use archaeology to learn about early peoples.

★ Communities began to develop during the Stone Age.

★ We use archaeology to learn about early cultures.

★ One of the first civilizations developed in the Fertile Crescent.

★ The Mesopotamian civilizations of Sumer and Akkad flourished from about 3500 B.C. to 2000 B.C.

★ New empires in the Fertile Crescent advanced by adopting earlier Mesopotamian culture.

★ Judaism was one of the first religions in the world to worship only one God.

Talk Together

Discuss with your child what people might learn about your way of life by studying the objects in your home. What might small kitchen tools tell about your family? Relate the discussion to the work of archaeologists who study ancient objects to draw conclusions about how earlier peoples lived.

★ Activity ★

Help your child learn more about early civilizations.

✔ Provide your child with index cards.

✔ Have your child use the cards to write facts about the different early civilizations he or she is learning about in Unit 1.

✔ Ask your child to sort the cards so that he or she can compare and contrast the civilizations.

Fast Facts

In the 1980s, a Clovis-like spear point was found in Siberia. Scientists are looking for more such points in Siberia. If they find them, scientists may have to change their ideas about where and when Clovis points were first used.

Thank you for supporting your child's Social Studies education!

Estimada familia:

¡Esto es lo que estamos aprendiendo en estudios sociales!

Unidad 1 Ideas principales

★ Hacemos uso de la arqueología para aprender cosas sobre los pueblos antiquos.

★ Durante la Edad de Piedra se empezaron a desarrollar comunidades.

★ Con la arqueología aprendemos la forma en que se desarrollaron las primeras culturas.

★ Una de las primeras civilizaciones se desarrolló en la Fértil Medialuna.

★ Las civilizaciones mesopotámicas de Sumeria y Acadia florecieron de 3500 a.C. a 2000 a.C.

★ Los nuevos imperios de la Fértil Medialuna progresaron adoptando culturas mesopotámicas anteriores.

★ El judaísmo se convirtió en una de las primeras religiones del mundo en que se adoraba a un solo Dios.

Para conversar

Hable con su niño o niña acerca de lo que la gente podría aprender sobre su forma de vida estudiando los objetos de su hogar. ¿Qué podría indicar sobre su familia la presencia de pequeños utensilios de cocina? Relacione esta conversación con el trabajo de los arqueólogos que estudian objetos antiguos para sacar conclusiones sobre la forma de vida de pueblos antiguos.

★ Actividad ★

Ayude a su niño o niña a aprender más cosas sobre las primeras civilizaciones.

✔ Proporcione fichas a su niño o niña.

✔ Pídale que las use para escribir datos sobre las distintas civilizaciones antiguas que está estudiando en la Unidad 1.

✔ Pida a su niño o niña que clasifique las fichas de modo que pueda comparar y contrastar las civilizaciones.

Datos curiosos

En la década de 1980, se encontró una punta de lanza de tipo Clovis en Siberia. Los científicos están buscando más puntas de este tipo en Siberia. Si las encuentran, tal vez los científicos tengan que cambiar sus ideas sobre dónde y cuándo se usaron puntas Clovis por primera vez.

¡Gracias por ayudar a su niño o niña con su educación de estudios sociales!

Dear Family:

Here is what we're learning in Social Studies!

Unit 2 Main Ideas

★ The Egyptians have depended on the Nile River to survive for thousands of years.

★ The first civilizations in ancient Egypt were great and complex.

★ The Egyptians and Nubians interacted with each other and with other peoples.

★ A tour of China reveals great diversity in the land, water, and ways of life.

★ China's history, organized by dynasties, includes many inventions and ideas.

★ Confucianism is a way of thought that became a way of life in China.

★ South Asia is home to different peoples making homes across magnificent landscapes, from mountains to islands.

★ Indian civilization developed with influences from the Aryans and Persians.

★ Hinduism combines spiritual beliefs, gods, and practices.

★ Finding peace and happiness is at the heart of Buddhism.

Talk Together

Talk with your child about the exchange of ideas and technology in the early civilizations. What kinds of ideas did people share? How did the people come in contact with one another? Discuss how people today learn about other people's ideas and technologies.

★ Activity ★

Help your child learn about early African and Asian civilizations.

✔ Together, use index cards to make question-and-answer cards for the early African and Asian civilizations discussed in the text.

✔ Write a question on one card and the answer to the question on another card. Focus questions and answers on the geography, ways of life, ideas, leadership, and technologies of the civilizations.

✔ Play a matching game with your child. Spread out the cards, facedown. Take turns matching questions and answers.

Fast Facts

Buddhism and Hinduism still thrive today, mostly in Asia. About 350 million people are Buddhists and almost 800 million are Hindus.

Thank you for supporting your child's Social Studies education!

Estimada familia:

¡Esto es lo que estamos aprendiendo en estudios sociales!

Unidad 2 Ideas principales

★ Los egipcios han dependido del río Nilo para sobrevivir durante miles de años.

★ Las primeras civilizaciones del antiguo Egipto fueron grandes y complejas.

★ Los egipcios y los nubios establecieron relaciones entre sí y con otros pueblos.

★ Un viaje por China permite observar una gran diversidad de tierras, extensiones de agua y formas de vida.

★ La historia de China, organizada en dinastías, incluye muchos inventos e ideas.

★ El confucianismo es una manera de pensar que se convirtió en una forma de vida en China.

★ En el sur de Asia viven diferentes pueblos en unos paisajes magníficos, que van desde montañas hasta islas.

★ La civilización india se desarrolló con la influencia de los arios y persas.

★ El hinduismo combina creencias espirituales, dioses y prácticas.

★ El hallazgo de la paz y la felicidad es la base del budismo.

Para conversar

Hable con su niño o niña sobre el intercambio de ideas y tecnología en las primeras civilizaciones. ¿Qué clases de ideas las personas? ¿Cómo se pusieron en contacto unos pueblos con otros? Hable de la forma en que hoy en día las personas aprenden las ideas y tecnologías de otras personas.

★ Actividad ★

Ayude a su niño o niña a aprender cosas sobre las primeras civilizaciones africanas y asiáticas.

✔ Usen fichas para escribir preguntas y respuestas sobre las primeras civilizaciones africanas y asiáticas tratadas en el texto.

✔ Escriban una pregunta en una ficha y la respuesta en otra. Concentren las preguntas y respuestas en la geografía, formas de vida, ideas, liderazgo y tecnologías de las civilizaciones.

✔ Juegue a un juego de correspondencia con su niño o niña. Esparza las fichas boca abajo. Túrnense para hacer corresponder las preguntas y las respuestas.

Datos curiosos

El budismo y el hinduismo siguen prosperando hoy en día, en su mayor parte en Asia. Hay alrededor de 350 millones de budistas y casi 800 millones de hindúes.

¡Gracias por ayudar a su niño o niña con su educación de estudios sociales!

Dear Family:

Here is what we're learning in Social Studies!

Unit 3 Main Ideas

★ Early civilizations in Mesoamerica used the rich natural resources of the region.

★ The Olmec and the Maya developed complex civilizations in Mesoamerica.

★ The Aztecs built a great empire in Mesoamerica.

★ South America is a large continent of many landscapes.

★ The Chavín and Mochica developed civilizations in ancient Peru.

★ The Inca ruled a vast empire in the Andes Mountains.

★ North America is a diverse continent that has been home to many different cultures.

★ The Hohokam and Anasazi cultures thrived in the Southwest.

★ Native American peoples built burial and ceremonial mounds throughout eastern North America.

★ Early Canadians survived by using what their environment provided them.

Talk Together

Ask your child to tell you about the different kinds of housing and occupations early North Americans had. Encourage your child to note how climate and geography affected housing and occupation. Why didn't the Anasazi build their pueblos with wood? Why did Inuit who were traveling build snowhouses?

★ Activity ★

Help your child learn more about the Aztec and Inca.

✔ On a sheet of paper, write the names *Aztec* and *Inca*.

✔ With your child, review information about the Aztec and Inca civilizations. Write the information on the paper.

✔ Have your child use the information to identify ways in which the two civilizations were alike and different. Underline or highlight similarities.

Fast Facts

The name for the Hopewell culture came from Captain Mordecai Hopewell, whose farm near Chillicothe, Ohio, was the site of more than 20 Native American burial and ceremonial mounds.

Thank you for supporting your child's Social Studies education!

Estimada familia:

¡Esto es lo que estamos aprendiendo en estudios sociales!

Unidad 3 Ideas principales

★ Las primeras civilizaciones de Mesoamérica hacían uso de la riqueza de recursos naturales de la región.

★ Los olmecas y los mayas desarrollaron civilizaciones complejas en Mesoamérica.

★ Los aztecas formaron un gran imperio en Mesoamérica.

★ América del Sur es un continente grande de paisajes variados.

★ Los chavín y los mochica desarrollaron civilizaciones en el antiguo Perú.

★ Los incas gobernaron un gran imperio en los Andes.

★ América del Norte es un continente diverso que ha sido cuna de muchas culturas diferentes.

★ Las culturas de los hohokams y anasazis prosperaron en el Suroeste.

★ Los pueblos indígenas norteamericanos construyeron montículos funerarios y ceremoniales en toda la región este de América del Norte.

★ Los primeros canadienses sobrevivieron haciendo uso de lo que les proporcionaba su medio ambiente.

Para conversar

Hable con su niño o niña acerca de los distintos tipos de vivienda y ocupaciones que tenían los primeros pobladores de América del Norte. Anímele a observar cómo afectó el clima y la geografía a sus viviendas y ocupaciones. ¿Por qué los anasazis no construyeron sus pueblos de madera? ¿Por qué construían casas de nieve los inuits que viajaban?

★ Actividad ★

Ayude a su niño o niña a aprender más cosas sobre los aztecas e incas.

✔ En una hoja de papel, escriba los nombres *aztecas* e *incas*.

✔ Junto con su niño o niña, repase la información sobre las civilizaciones de los aztecas y los incas. Escriba la información en el papel.

✔ Pida a su niño o niña que use la información para identificar maneras en que las dos civilizaciones se parecían y se diferenciaban. Subraye o resalte las similitudes.

Datos curiosos

El nombre de la cultura hopewell proviene del capitán Mordecai Hopewell, en cuya granja ubicada cerca de Chillicothe, Ohio, había al menos más de 20 montículos funerarios y ceremoniales de indígenas norteamericanos.

¡Gracias por ayudar a su niño o niña con su educación de estudios sociales!

Dear Family:

Here is what we're learning in Social Studies!

Unit 4 Main Ideas

★ Surrounded by mountains and water, the ancient Greeks developed communities and traveled on the sea to trade with other peoples.

★ Two very different cultures grew in the city-states of Athens and Sparta.

★ During the Golden Age of Athens, Athenians excelled in the arts, philosophy, and government.

★ The conquests of Alexander the Great built a new culture that mixed Greek and Asian ways.

★ Rome's location helped it to grow from a village into a powerful city.

★ Rome's republic became very powerful, but its conquests created major problems.

★ The Roman Empire was one of the world's most powerful empires.

★ Christianity grew to become the official religion of the Roman Empire.

★ Rome fell to invaders, but the Roman Empire continued in the East.

Talk Together

Ask your child to explain the meaning of the word *democracy* as applied to ancient Greek civilization and the word *republic* as applied to ancient Roman civilization. Then discuss how these words are used in reference to the United States today.

★ Activity ★

Help your child compare the gods and goddesses of Greek myth with their Roman counterparts.

✔ List the names and roles of the gods and goddesses of Greek myth. See the Fact File on page 254 of your child's social studies text.

✔ Look up the Greek name in a dictionary or an encyclopedia. There you should find the name of the equivalent god or goddess from Roman myth. Write the Roman name on your list.

✔ Point out to your child that the Romans adopted some gods and goddesses from Greek mythology. Others, however, came from their own myths, which were similar to those of the Greeks.

Fast Facts

Many of the planets in our solar system are named for gods and goddesses of Roman myths. Many constellations also bear the names of figures from Greek mythology.

Thank you for supporting your child's Social Studies education!

Estimada familia:

¡Esto es lo que estamos aprendiendo en estudios sociales!

Unidad 4 Ideas principales

★ Los antiguos griegos, rodeados de montañas y extensiones de agua, desarrollaron comunidades y viajaban por mar para comerciar con otros pueblos.

★ Se desarrollaron dos culturas muy diferentes en las ciudades-estado de Atenas y Esparta.

★ Durante la Edad de Oro de Atenas, sus habitantes se destacaron en las artes, la filosofía y el gobierno.

★ Las conquistas de Alejandro Magno crearon una cultura nueva que mezclaba formas griegas y asiáticas.

★ La ubicación de Roma contribuyó a que pasara de ser un pueblo a una ciudad poderosa.

★ La república de Roma se hizo muy poderosa, pero sus conquistas crearon problemas importantes.

★ El Imperio Romano fue uno de los imperios más poderosos del mundo.

★ El cristianismo se convirtió en la religión oficial del Imperio Romano.

★ Roma cayó derrotada por invasores, pero el Imperio Romano continuó en el Este.

Para conversar

Pida a su niño o niña que explique el significado del término democracia según se aplica a la antigua civilización griega y república según se aplica a la antigua civilización romana. Hable luego de cómo se usan estas palabras con referencia a los Estados Unidos en la actualidad.

★ Actividad ★

Ayude a su niño o niña a comparar los dioses y diosas de la mitología griega con los de la romana.

✔ Hagan una lista de los nombres de los dioses y diosas de la mitología griega. Vea el Banco de datos de la página 254 del libro de texto de estudios sociales.

✔ Consulten el nombre griego en un diccionario o enciclopedia. Debería aparecer el nombre del dios o la diosa equivalente de la mitología romana. Escriban el nombre romano en la lista.

✔ Señale a su niño o niña que los romanos adoptaron algunos dioses y diosas de la mitología griega. Otros, sin embargo, procedieron de sus propios mitos, que eran similares a los de los griegos.

Datos curiosos

Muchos de los planetas de nuestro sistema solar tienen nombres de dioses y diosas de mitos romanos. Muchas constelaciones llevan también los nombres de figuras de la mitología griega.

¡Gracias por ayudar a su niño o niña con su educación de estudios sociales!

Dear Family:

Here is what we're learning in Social Studies!

Unit 5 Main Ideas

★ Physical features, climate, and Roman and Greek culture influenced how people lived in the Byzantine Empire.

★ Under the rule of Justinian, the Byzantine Empire became great.

★ Islam brought changes to lands in Southwest Asia.

★ Trade and conquest helped spread religion and language throughout the Islamic world.

★ Asia has a variety of climates and landforms that influenced several different cultures.

★ Medieval Chinese dynasties made several significant contributions to trade and technology.

★ For hundreds of years, the Khmer culture dominated the peninsula of Southeast Asia.

★ Japan became isolated, or separated, from most of the world but still carried on some trade.

★ People throughout Africa have adapted to a variety of environments.

★ Many kingdoms developed in the savanna and forested areas of West Africa.

★ Trading empires developed in eastern, central, and southern Africa that interacted with Arabia, India, and China.

★ The landforms and climate of Europe affect the way Europeans live.

★ After a series of rulers and invaders, medieval government in Europe experienced a change.

★ The Church, feudalism, and manor life formed the foundation of European medieval life.

★ Routes promoted trade, travel, and communication, as well as the Plague, between Europe, Africa, and Asia.

Talk Together

Ask your child to tell you about where medieval empires were established. Talk about how trade helped empires grow.

★ Activity ★

Help your child understand the importance of trade to the exchange of ideas.

✔ Ask your child to list goods that Muslim traders traded with other groups. From the list, choose goods to trade.

✔ Role-play trading situations in which you and your child negotiate a trade. Think about how the exchange could lead to sharing ideas. For example, you might point out some of the uses and benefits of a particular good.

✔ Explore how you exchange ideas as you trade goods.

Fast Facts

The longest structure ever built is the Great Wall of China, which stretches more than 4,000 miles. Built to keep out invaders, the wall is now a major tourist attraction.

Thank you for supporting your child's Social Studies education!

Estimada familia:

¡Esto es lo que estamos aprendiendo en estudios sociales!

Unidad 5 Ideas principales

★ Las características físicas, el clima y las culturas romana y griega influyeron en la forma de vivir de los habitantes del Imperio Bizantino.

★ Bajo el reinado de Justiniano, el Imperio Bizantino creció.

★ El Islam introdujo cambios en las tierras del suroeste asiático.

★ El comercio y las conquistas ayudaron a propagar la religión y el idioma a través del mundo islámico.

★ Asia tiene una variedad de climas y accidentes geográficos que influyeron en varias culturas diferentes.

★ Las dinastías medievales chinas hicieron varias contribuciones importantes al comercio y a la tecnología.

★ Durante cientos de años, la cultura jemer dominó la península del sureste asiático.

★ Japón se aisló, o se separó, de la mayoría del mundo, pero seguía efectuando algunas operaciones comerciales.

★ Los habitantes de toda África se han adaptado a una variedad de ambientes.

★ Muchos reinos se desarrollaron en la sabana y las áreas boscosas de África occidental.

★ Se desarrollaron imperios comerciales en las regiones del este, centro y sur de África, que tenían relaciones con Arabia, India y China.

★ Los accidentes geográficos y el clima de Europa afectan la manera en que viven los europeos.

★ Después de una serie de gobernantes e invasores, el gobierno medieval europeo experimentó un cambio.

★ La Iglesia, el feudalismo y la vida en los feudos formaban los cimientos de la vida medieval europea.

★ Las rutas promovieron el comercio, los viajes y las comunicaciones, así como la peste, entre Europa, África y Asia.

Para conversar

Pida a su niño o niña que le cuente dónde se establecieron los imperios medievales. Hable de cómo contribuyó el comercio al crecimiento de los imperios.

★ Actividad ★

Ayude a su niño o niña a entender la importancia del comercio para el intercambio de ideas.

✔ Pida a su niño o niña que haga una lista de los bienes que intercambiaban los comerciantes musulmanes con otros grupos. Escojan de la lista los bienes con los que vayan a comerciar ustedes.

✔ Simulen situaciones comerciales en las que usted y su niño o niña intercambian bienes. Piensen en la forma en que el intercambio de bienes puede hacer que compartan ideas. Por ejemplo, puede señalar algunos de los usos y ventajas de cierto producto.

✔ Hablen de cómo se intercambian ideas a medida que se comercia con bienes.

Datos curiosos

La estructura más larga jamás construida es la Gran Muralla China, que se extiende más de 4,000 millas. La muralla, construida para resistir a los invasores, es ahora una atracción turística importante.

¡Gracias por ayudar a su niño o niña con su educación de estudios sociales!

SCOTT FORESMAN
SOCIAL STUDIES
UNIT 6 FAMILY ACTIVITY

Dear Family:

Here is what we're learning in Social Studies!

Unit 6 Main Ideas

★ From the mid-1400s to the 1600s, Europeans had a renewed interest in art, literature, education, and the cultures of ancient Greece and Rome.

★ European traders wanted additional trade routes and rulers wanted to increase their empires.

★ As Europeans came across new lands, they spread their culture through settlement and colonization.

★ New nations in the Americas broke free of European rule.

★ The path of revolution turned violent in France.

★ The Industrial Revolution began in Great Britain and soon spread to other nations.

★ While business owners gained more freedom from government controls, workers struggled to improve their working conditions.

★ By the 1800s, many European nations were building empires by conquering and colonizing other countries and territories.

★ China and Japan experienced Western imperialism in different ways.

★ Nationalism led to new nations in Europe and the British colonies.

Talk Together

Talk with your child about how political points of view may change over time.

★ Activity ★

Help your child learn more about political cartoons.

✔ Review with your child the lesson about political cartoons, found on pages 450–451 in the textbook. If possible, show your child political cartoons in a current newspaper or a magazine.

✔ Ask your child to draw and label a political cartoon. The political cartoon should be based in some way on the subject matter in Unit 6.

✔ Ask your child to decribe the point of view that he or she is portraying in the political cartoon.

Fast Facts

Today, Canada is a bilingual nation in which English and French are the official languages, reflecting the French and English history of the nation.

Thank you for supporting your child's Social Studies education!

Estimada familia:

¡Esto es lo que estamos aprendiendo en estudios sociales!

Unidad 6 Ideas principales

★ Desde mediados del siglo XV hasta el siglo XVII, los europeos mostraron un interés renovado en el arte, la literatura, la educación y las culturas de Grecia y Roma antiguas.

★ Los comerciantes europeos querían rutas de comercio adicionales y los gobernantes querían aumentar sus imperios.

★ A medida que los europeos llegaron a nuevas tierras, propagaron su cultura por medio de asentamientos y colonización.

★ Se formaron nuevas naciones en las Américas que se hicieron independientes de los gobiernos europeos.

★ El camino de la revolución se hizo violento en Francia.

★ La Revolución Industrial empezó en Gran Bretaña y se propagó en poco tiempo a otras naciones.

★ Mientras que los propietarios de negocios se liberaron más de los controles del gobierno, los trabajadores tuvieron que luchar para mejorar sus condiciones laborales.

★ Hacia el siglo XIX, muchas naciones europeas formaron imperios conquistando y colonizando otros países y territorios.

★ China y Japón experimentaron el imperialismo del Occidente de distintas maneras.

★ El nacionalismo condujo a la aparición de nuevas naciones en Europa y en las colonias británicas.

Para conversar

Hable con su niño o niña acerca de cómo cambian los puntos de vista políticos con el tiempo.

★ Actividad ★

Ayude a su niño o niña a aprender más cosas sobre las caricaturas políticas.

✔ Repase con su niño o niña la lección sobre caricaturas políticas de las páginas 450 y 451 del libro del estudiante. Si es posible, muéstrele las caricaturas políticas de un periódico o revista actual.

✔ Pida a su niño o niña que dibuje y titule una caricatura política. La caricatura política debe basarse de alguna manera en el tema de la Unidad 6.

✔ Pida a su niño o niña que describa el punto de vista que está representando en la caricatura política.

Datos curiosos

Hoy en día, Canadá es una nación bilingüe donde el inglés y el francés son los idiomas oficiales, lo cual refleja el pasado francés e inglés de la nación.

¡Gracias por ayudar a su niño o niña con su educación de estudios sociales!

Dear Family:

Here is what we're learning in Social Studies!

Unit 7 Main Ideas

★ Competition among nations pushed Europe toward war.

★ The Great War caused much destruction.

★ The Allies tried to make a peace treaty that would solve all of Europe's problems.

★ Hard times set the stage for another world war.

★ World War II caused millions of deaths and great destruction.

★ The Allies formed the United Nations and helped shattered nations rebuild.

★ After 1945 the Soviet Union and the Allies broke off relations.

★ In a century of revolution, communists took control of China.

★ The Cold War became a "hot" war in Korea and Vietnam.

Talk Together

Discuss with your child the international roles that nations play. How did the nations help one another during wartime? How does the United Nations try to encourage peaceful solutions to international problems?

★ Activity ★

Help your child learn about the time frame of American involvement in international events during the twentieth century.

✔ Have your child identify the wars and international conflicts in which the United States was involved during the twentieth century.

✔ Write the names of the international conflicts on index cards and have your child place the events on a time line.

✔ Discuss the role the United States played in each war or conflict.

Fast Facts

About 70 million people served in the Allied and Axis militaries during World War II.

Thank you for supporting your child's Social Studies education!

Estimada familia:

¡Esto es lo que estamos aprendiendo en estudios sociales!

Unidad 7 Ideas principales

★ La competencia entre las naciones causó el estallido de una guerra en Europa.

★ La Gran Guerra causó mucha destrucción.

★ Los Aliados trataron de redactar un tratado de paz para resolver todos los problemas de Europa.

★ Los tiempos difíciles sentaron las bases para otra guerra mundial.

★ La Segunda Guerra Mundial causó millones de muertes y una gran destrucción.

★ Los Aliados formaron las Naciones Unidas y ayudaron a reconstruir los países destruidos.

★ Después de 1945, la Unión Soviética y los Aliados suspendieron sus relaciones.

★ En un siglo de revolución, los comunistas se hicieron con el control de China.

★ La Guerra Fría se convirtió en una guerra "caliente" en Corea y Vietnam.

Para conversar

Hable con su niño o niña acerca de las funciones internacionales que desempeñan las naciones. ¿Cómo se ayudaron las naciones entre sí en tiempos de guerra? ¿Cómo intentan las Naciones Unidas llegar a soluciones pacíficas para los problemas internacionales?

★ Actividad ★

Ayude a su niño o niña a aprender acerca de los períodos de participación de los Estados Unidos en los acontecimientos internacionales del siglo XX.

✔ Pídale que identifique las guerras y los conflictos internacionales en los que se vieron involucrados los Estados Unidos durante el siglo XX.

✔ Escriba los nombres de los conflictos internacionales en fichas y pida a su niño o niña que ordene los acontecimientos en una línea cronológica.

✔ Hable de la función que desempeñaron los Estados Unidos en cada guerra o conflicto.

Datos curiosos

Unos 70 millones de personas sirvieron en los ejércitos aliados y del Eje durante la Segunda Guerra Mundial.

¡Gracias por ayudar a su niño o niña con su educación de estudios sociales!

Dear Family:

Here is what we're learning in Social Studies!

Unit 8 Main Ideas

★ The end of colonialism brought an end to imperialism and European rule in Africa and Asia.

★ The end of European control and the creation of Israel changed the Middle East.

★ Calls for greater freedom brought an end to communism in Eastern Europe.

★ World and regional economies have become closely bound together.

★ Ethnic, political, and religious differences have led to violent conflicts around the world.

★ People around the world continue to stand up against terrorism and work toward peace.

★ Population growth and movement present challenges in today's world.

★ People are working together to repair damage to Earth's environment.

★ As energy sources become less plentiful, we look for new ways to produce and conserve energy.

★ Technology gives us many benefits, but it cannot solve every human problem.

Talk Together

Ask your child to tell you about different aspects of each of the following issues in the present-day world: civil rights, energy, technology, and the environment.

★ Activity ★

Help your child learn about environmental concerns.

✔ Together, skim newspapers or news magazines for a story related to the environment.

✔ Identify the issues addressed in the article. Does the article identify problems? Does it propose solutions?

✔ Discuss why environmental issues are important. Have your child think of ways your family can help the environment. Make a list of your child's suggestions.

Fast Facts

The United States is the leading producer and consumer of energy in the world. It uses about 25 percent of the energy produced every year.

Thank you for supporting your child's Social Studies education!

Estimada familia:

¡Esto es lo que estamos aprendiendo en estudios sociales!

Unidad 8 Ideas principales

★ El fin del colonialismo dio por terminado el imperialismo y el dominio europeo en África y Asia.

★ El fin del control europeo y la creación de Israel cambió el Oriente Medio.

★ Las demandas de mayor libertad terminaron con el comunismo en Europa del Este.

★ Las economías mundiales y regionales han pasado a depender estrechamente entre sí.

★ Las diferencias étnicas, políticas y religiosas han conducido a conflictos violentos en el mundo.

★ Los habitantes de todo el mundo siguen enfrentándose al terrorismo y trabajando por la paz.

★ El crecimiento y el movimiento de la población son desafíos del mundo actual.

★ Las personas trabajan juntas para reparar los daños causados en el medio ambiente.

★ A medida que las fuentes de energía se hacen más escasas, buscamos nuevas formas de producir y conservar energía.

★ La tecnología nos da muchos beneficios, pero no puede resolver todos los problemas humanos.

Para conversar

Pida a su niño o niña que le hable sobre diversos aspectos de cada uno de los siguientes asuntos del mundo actual: derechos civiles, energía, tecnología y ecología.

★ Actividad ★

Ayude a su niño o niña a aprender cosas sobre asuntos del medio ambiente.

✔ Juntos, hojeen periódicos o revistas de noticias para encontrar una historia relacionada con la ecología.

✔ Identifiquen los asuntos tratados en el artículo. ¿Identifica problemas el artículo? ¿Propone soluciones?

✔ Hablen de por qué son importantes los asuntos de ecología. Pida a su niño o niña que piense en formas en que su familia puede ayudar al medio ambiente. Prepare una lista de las sugerencias de su niño o niña.

Datos curiosos

Los Estados Unidos son el productor y consumidor principal de energía del mundo. Utilizan alrededor del 25 por ciento de la energía producida cada año.

¡Gracias por ayudar a su niño o niña con su educación de estudios sociales!

Scope and Sequence

ESSENTIAL KNOWLEDGE	K	1	2	3	4	5	6
History							
Understand human influence in shaping communities, states, and nations	★	★	★	★	★	★	★
Contributions of ordinary people	★	★	★	★	★	★	★
Historic figures and their lives		★	★	★	★	★	★
Understand the origins and significance of customs, holidays, celebrations, and landmarks in the community, state, nation, and world	★	★	★	★	★	★	★
Understand the concepts of time and chronology	★	★	★	★	★	★	★
Order of events	★	★	★	★	★	★	★
Past, present, future	★	★	★	★	★	★	★
Political, economic, and social change	★	★	★	★	★	★	★
Cause and effect		★	★	★	★	★	★
Understand how various sources provide information			★	★	★	★	★
Primary sources			★	★	★	★	★
Secondary sources			★	★	★	★	★
Understand how human needs, ideas, issues, and events influence past and present	★	★	★	★	★	★	★
Exploration, colonization, and settlement	★	★	★	★	★	★	★
Conflict and revolution	★	★	★	★	★	★	★
Immigration			★	★	★	★	★
Growth and expansion			★	★	★	★	★
Understand that the past influences the present	★	★	★	★	★	★	★
Connecting past and present	★	★	★	★	★	★	★
Comparing past and present	★	★	★	★	★	★	★
Geography							
Understand concept of location	★	★	★	★	★	★	★
Relative and exact	★	★	★	★	★	★	★
Factors influencing location		★	★	★	★	★	★
Understand concept of place	★	★	★	★	★	★	★
Landforms, bodies of water, vegetation, animal life	★	★	★	★	★	★	★
Climate, weather, and seasonal patterns	★	★	★	★	★	★	★
Understand human-environment interactions	★	★	★	★	★	★	★
Natural resources and land use	★	★	★	★	★	★	★
Human features (housing, roads)	★	★	★	★	★	★	★
Human adaptations to and modifications of their environments		★	★	★	★	★	★
Understand the concept of movement	★	★	★	★	★	★	★
Movement of ideas through cultural sharing	★	★	★	★	★	★	★
Colonization, immigration, settlement patterns (people)		★	★	★	★	★	★
Physical characteristics affect trade (products)			★	★	★	★	★
Physical characteristics affect human activities (culture)			★	★	★	★	★
Understand concept of region		★	★	★	★	★	★
Physical characteristics		★	★	★	★	★	★
Political characteristics			★	★	★	★	★

Scope and Sequence

ESSENTIAL KNOWLEDGE	K	1	2	3	4	5	6
Population characteristics			★	★	★	★	★
Economic characteristics			★	★	★	★	★
Time zones					★	★	★
Understand and use geographic tools to collect, analyze, and interpret information	★	★	★	★	★	★	★
Maps and globes	★	★	★	★	★	★	★
Comparison of world regions and countries		★	★	★	★	★	★
Read, interpret, and construct charts, maps, and diagrams		★	★	★	★	★	★

Economics

ESSENTIAL KNOWLEDGE	K	1	2	3	4	5	6
Understand how scarcity of resources leads to economic choice	★	★	★	★	★	★	★
Basic human needs and wants	★	★	★	★	★	★	★
Goods and services	★	★	★	★	★	★	★
Production, distribution, and consumption	★	★	★	★	★	★	★
Work and income	★	★	★	★	★	★	★
Saving and spending	★	★	★	★	★	★	★
Opportunity cost	★	★	★	★	★	★	★
Understand markets and price	★	★	★	★	★	★	★
Exchange of goods and services	★	★	★	★	★	★	★
Impact of mass production and specialization			★	★	★	★	★
Supply and demand				★	★	★	★
Competition				★	★	★	★
Economic interdependence				★	★	★	★
Imports, exports, and trade				★	★	★	★
Understand economic patterns and systems	★	★	★	★	★	★	★
Effects of transportation and communication	★	★	★	★	★	★	★
Free enterprise			★	★	★	★	★
Entrepreneurship			★	★	★	★	★

Government

ESSENTIAL KNOWLEDGE	K	1	2	3	4	5	6
Understand the purposes of government	★	★	★	★	★	★	★
Promotion of the common good	★	★	★	★	★	★	★
Order and security			★	★	★	★	★
Distribution of services			★	★	★	★	★
Protection of individual rights and freedoms			★	★	★	★	★
Understand the structure of government	★	★	★	★	★	★	★
Purpose of rules and laws	★	★	★	★	★	★	★
Roles and responsibilities of authority figures and public officials	★	★	★	★	★	★	★
Levels of government (local, state, and national)		★	★	★	★	★	★
Government services		★	★	★	★	★	★
Branches of government			★	★	★	★	★
Government documents			★	★	★	★	★
Political parties						★	★
Understand the functions of government	★	★	★	★	★	★	★

ESSENTIAL KNOWLEDGE	K	1	2	3	4	5	6
Making, amending, and removing laws	★	★	★	★	★	★	★
Enforcing laws		★	★	★	★	★	★
Financing of services			★	★	★	★	★
Understand types of governments		★	★	★	★	★	★

Citizenship

ESSENTIAL KNOWLEDGE	K	1	2	3	4	5	6
Understand good citizenship	★	★	★	★	★	★	★
Historic figures and ordinary people	★	★	★	★	★	★	★
Citizenship traits (caring, respect, responsibility, fairness, honesty, courage)	★	★	★	★	★	★	★
Working for the common good	★	★	★	★	★	★	★
Believing in truth and justice	★	★	★	★	★	★	★
Treating all people equally	★	★	★	★	★	★	★
Solving problems	★	★	★	★	★	★	★
Making decisions	★	★	★	★	★	★	★
Understand state and national identities	★	★	★	★	★	★	★
Flags, symbols, anthems, pledges	★	★	★	★	★	★	★
Customs and celebrations	★	★	★	★	★	★	★
Mottoes		★	★	★	★	★	★
Understand the freedoms, rights, and responsibilities of citizens		★	★	★	★	★	★
Individual freedoms (choosing your associates, choosing where you live)		★	★	★	★	★	★
Economic freedoms (choosing your own work, owning property)		★	★	★	★	★	★
Political freedoms (joining a political party, running for office, purpose of and need for free elections)		★	★	★	★	★	★
Rights (free speech, voting rights, freedom of religion, equal protection and opportunity under the law)		★	★	★	★	★	★
Responsibilities/ participating, voting		★	★	★	★	★	★
Responsibilities/ keeping informed			★	★	★	★	★
Understand democratic principles		★	★	★	★	★	★
Due process and equal protection under the law				★	★	★	★
Majority rule with minority respect				★	★	★	★
Government by law				★	★	★	★

Culture

ESSENTIAL KNOWLEDGE	K	1	2	3	4	5	6
Understand social groups and institutions	★	★	★	★	★	★	★
Family and community	★	★	★	★	★	★	★
Education	★	★	★	★	★	★	★
Religion		★	★	★	★	★	★
Politics			★	★	★	★	★
Understand similarities and differences among people	★	★	★	★	★	★	★
Culture and culture region	★	★	★	★	★	★	★
Language	★	★	★	★	★	★	★
Customs, holidays, and traditions	★	★	★	★	★	★	★
Similarities among diverse groups	★	★	★	★	★	★	★
Contributions of diverse groups	★	★	★	★	★	★	★

Scope and Sequence

ESSENTIAL KNOWLEDGE	K	1	2	3	4	5	6
Understand how the arts express cultural heritage	★	★	★	★	★	★	★
Literature	★	★	★	★	★	★	★
Music, drama, dance	★	★	★	★	★	★	★
Role of writers and artists		★	★	★	★	★	★
Art			★	★	★	★	★
Architecture			★	★	★	★	★

Science, Technology, and Society

	K	1	2	3	4	5	6
Understand how technology has affected life	★	★	★	★	★	★	★
Tools and appliances	★	★	★	★	★	★	★
Communication	★	★	★	★	★	★	★
Transportation	★	★	★	★	★	★	★
Recreation	★	★	★	★	★	★	★
Work, education, and learning	★	★	★	★	★	★	★
Medicine				★	★	★	★
Understand the significance of the inventions or creations of people in technology	★	★	★	★	★	★	★
Understand the changes brought about by scientific discoveries and technological inventions	★	★	★	★	★	★	★
Predict how future discoveries and innovations could affect life in the United States	★	★	★	★	★	★	★

ESSENTIAL SKILLS	K	1	2	3	4	5	6

Map and Globe Skills

	K	1	2	3	4	5	6
Understand directions		★	★	★	★	★	★
Cardinal directions		★	★	★	★	★	★
Intermediate directions			★	★	★	★	★
Understand globes	★	★	★	★	★	★	★
Purpose of globe	★	★	★	★	★	★	★
Equator			★	★	★	★	★
Hemispheres				★	★	★	★
Poles				★	★	★	★
Prime meridian/International Date Line				★	★	★	★
Arctic and Antarctic Circles				★	★	★	★
Latitude and longitude				★	★	★	★
Understand, use, and create maps	★	★	★	★	★	★	★
Location of cities, states, countries, continents, oceans	★	★	★	★	★	★	★
Comparison of map with photograph	★	★	★	★	★	★	★
Comparison of map with globe	★	★	★	★	★	★	★
Locator map		★	★	★	★	★	★
Routes and mental mapping		★	★	★	★	★	★
Grids			★	★	★	★	★
Inset maps				★	★	★	★

ESSENTIAL SKILLS	K	1	2	3	4	5	6
Map projections						★	★
Understand and use map symbols	★	★	★	★	★	★	★
Landforms and bodies of water	★	★	★	★	★	★	★
Symbols	★	★	★	★	★	★	★
Key and legend		★	★	★	★	★	★
Direction symbols and compass rose		★	★	★	★	★	★
Borders			★	★	★	★	★
Scale and distance				★	★	★	★
Lines of latitude and longitude						★	★	★
Elevation tints					★	★	★
Understand and use special purpose maps		★	★	★	★	★	★
Historical map		★	★	★	★	★	★
Political map		★	★	★	★	★	★
Physical map			★	★	★	★	★
Climate map				★	★	★	★
Product and resource map				★	★	★	★
Transportation map					★	★	★
Distribution map					★	★	★
Precipitation map					★	★	★
Elevation map					★	★	★
Population map					★	★	★
Population density map					★	★	★
Understand time zones					★	★	★
Understand cartograms							★

Chart and Graph Skills

	K	1	2	3	4	5	6
Understand charts and graphs	★	★	★	★	★	★	★
Charts	★	★	★	★	★	★	★
Diagrams	★	★	★	★	★	★	★
Calendars and time lines	★	★	★	★	★	★	★
Bar graphs	★	★	★	★	★	★	★
Pie (circle) graphs				★	★	★	★
Line graphs				★	★	★	★
Climographs						★	★

Critical Thinking Skills

	K	1	2	3	4	5	6
Problem solving	★	★	★	★	★	★	★
Identify a problem	★	★	★	★	★	★	★
Gather information	★	★	★	★	★	★	★
List and consider options	★	★	★	★	★	★	★
Consider advantages and disadvantages	★	★	★	★	★	★	★
Choose and implement a solution	★	★	★	★	★	★	★
Evaluate the effectiveness of a solution	★	★	★	★	★	★	★

Scope and Sequence

ESSENTIAL SKILLS	K	1	2	3	4	5	6
Decision making	★	★	★	★	★	★	★
Identify a situation that requires a decision	★	★	★	★	★	★	★
Gather information	★	★	★	★	★	★	★
Consider the options	★	★	★	★	★	★	★
Predict the consequences	★	★	★	★	★	★	★
Take action	★	★	★	★	★	★	★
Analysis of information	★	★	★	★	★	★	★
Sequence	★	★	★	★	★	★	★
Categorize and classify	★	★	★	★	★	★	★
Compare and contrast	★	★	★	★	★	★	★
Identify main ideas and details	★	★	★	★	★	★	★
Predict		★	★	★	★	★	★
Identify cause-and-effect relationships			★	★	★	★	★
Summarize				★	★	★	★
Generalize				★	★	★	★
Make inferences and draw conclusions				★	★	★	★
Identify different points of view and frames of reference (detection of bias)				★	★	★	★
Fact and opinion				★	★	★	★
Evaluation of arguments and sources				★	★	★	★

Research Skills

	K	1	2	3	4	5	6
Tables and charts	★	★	★	★	★	★	★
Time lines	★	★	★	★	★	★	★
Bar graphs	★	★	★	★	★	★	★
Diagrams	★	★	★	★	★	★	★
Pie (circle) graphs				★	★	★	★
Line graphs				★	★	★	★
Flowcharts						★	★
Primary and secondary sources	★	★	★	★	★	★	★
Audio and video recordings	★	★	★	★	★	★	★
Art	★	★	★	★	★	★	★
Photographs	★	★	★	★	★	★	★
Biographies, autobiographies, and oral histories	★	★	★	★	★	★	★
Internet	★	★	★	★	★	★	★
Computer software	★	★	★	★	★	★	★
Artifacts and historical records		★	★	★	★	★	★
Atlases and gazetteers		★	★	★	★	★	★
News sources and current events		★	★	★	★	★	★
Speeches				★	★	★	★
Encyclopedias				★	★	★	★
Dictionaries and thesauruses				★	★	★	★
Almanacs				★	★	★	★

ESSENTIAL SKILLS	K	1	2	3	4	5	6
Political cartoons						★	★
Use appropriate math skills to interpret maps and graphs		★	★	★	★	★	★

Reading Skills

	K	1	2	3	4	5	6
Vocabulary	★	★	★	★	★	★	★
Context clues (synonym, antonym, definition)	★	★	★	★	★	★	★
Abbreviations and acronyms		★	★	★	★	★	★
Classification and categorization of words		★	★	★	★	★	★
Multiple meanings		★	★	★	★	★	★
Dictionary and glossary			★	★	★	★	★
Gazetteer				★	★	★	★
Comprehension	★	★	★	★	★	★	★
Order	★	★	★	★	★	★	★
Picture clues	★	★	★	★	★	★	★
Sequence	★	★	★	★	★	★	★
Compare and contrast	★	★	★	★	★	★	★
Use of visuals (pictures, maps, time lines, graphs, charts, models, graphic organizers)	★	★	★	★	★	★	★
Recall and retell	★	★	★	★	★	★	★
Main idea and details	★	★	★	★	★	★	★
Picture analysis		★	★	★	★	★	★
Prediction		★	★	★	★	★	★
Understand and use graphic and typographical features (boldface, headings, captions, phonetic respellings)		★	★	★	★	★	★
Summarize a chapter or section		★	★	★	★	★	★
Context clues			★	★	★	★	★
Understand and use book parts (table of contents, glossary, atlas, gazetteer, index, bibliography, appendices)			★	★	★	★	★
Scan for specific facts or ideas				★	★	★	★
Understand and use textbook study features (prereading questions, preview and focus statements, summary statements, postreading questions)				★	★	★	★
Make outlines				★	★	★	★
Cause and effect			★	★	★	★	★
Drawing conclusions				★	★	★	★
Summarize				★	★	★	★
Understand characteristics of text types (autobiography, biography, essay, expository, historical fiction, informational, journal/diary, legend, letter, narrative, poetry, speech)					★	★	★	★
Generalize					★	★	★
Take notes						★	★	★

Speaking and Listening

	K	1	2	3	4	5	6
Understand and use speaking and listening skills	★	★	★	★	★	★	★
Dramatization	★	★	★	★	★	★	★
Song	★	★	★	★	★	★	★
Poems	★	★	★	★	★	★	★

Scope and Sequence

Scope and Sequence

ESSENTIAL SKILLS	K	1	2	3	4	5	6
Stories	★	★	★	★	★	★	★
Oral directions	★	★	★	★	★	★	★
Interviews		★	★	★	★	★	★
Debates				★	★	★	★
Use standard grammar and sentence structure				★	★	★	★
Oral reports						★	★

Writing Skills

	K	1	2	3	4	5	6
Understand forms of writing	★	★	★	★	★	★	★
Descriptive	★	★	★	★	★	★	★
Narrative	★	★	★	★	★	★	★
Expository		★	★	★	★	★	★
Persuasive				★	★	★	★
Understand and use writing skills and processes	★	★	★	★	★	★	★
Lists	★	★	★	★	★	★	★
Captions and labels	★	★	★	★	★	★	★
Use standard grammar, spelling, sentence structure, and punctuation	★	★	★	★	★	★	★
Report		★	★	★	★	★	★
Letter		★	★	★	★	★	★
Collect, organize, and record information		★	★	★	★	★	★
Identify and use reliable sources		★	★	★	★	★	★
Use multimedia tools		★	★	★	★	★	★
Journal/diary			★	★	★	★	★
Essay				★	★	★	★
Research paper				★	★	★	★
Summary				★	★	★	★
News report and feature story				★	★	★	★
Editorials and opinion articles				★	★	★	★
Biography and autobiography						★	★
Speech						★	★
Bibliography						★	★
Historical fiction						★	★
Legend						★	★

Unit 1 Bibliography

Archaeologists Dig for Clues, by Kate Duke (HarperTrophy, ISBN 0-06-445175-5, 1997) **Easy**

Assyria and Mesopotamia, by Lorna Oakes (Anness Publishing, Inc., ISBN 0-754-80656-1, 2001) **Easy**

Beowulf the Warrior, edited by Ian Serraillier (Ignatius Press, ISBN 1-883937-03-5, 1997) **Easy**

Exploring the Ice Age, by Margaret Cooper (Atheneum Books for Young Readers, ISBN 0-689-82556-0, 2001) **Easy**

Step Into . . . The Stone Age, by Charlotte Hurdman (Anness Publishing, Ltd., ISBN 1-85967-684-7, 1998) **Easy**

The Stone Age News, by Fiona MacDonald (Candlewick, ISBN 0-7636-0451-8, 1998) **Easy Parent's Choice Silver Honor**

The Sumerians, by Pamela Odijk (Silver Burdett, ISBN 0-382-09892-7, 1990) **Easy**

The Assyrians, by Elaine Landau (Millbrook Press, ISBN 0-7613-0217-4, 1997) **On-Level**

The Atlas of the Bible Lands: History, Daily Life and Traditions, by Andrea Dué (Peter Bedrick Books, ISBN 0-87226-559-5, 1998) **On-Level**

Exploring the Ice Age, by Margaret Cooper (Simon & Schuster Children's, ISBN 0-689-82556-0, 2001) **On-Level**

Eyewitness: Prehistoric Life, by William Lindsay (Dorling Kindersley, ISBN 0-7894-5868-3, 2000) **On-Level**

Mesopotamia, by Pamela F. Service (Marshall Cavendish Corp., ISBN 0-7614-0301-9, 1998) **On-Level**

The Mystery of the Mammoth Bones and How It Was Solved, by James Cross Giblin (HarperCollins, ISBN 0-06-027493-X, 1999) **On-Level NCSS Notable Book, 2000**

The Seven Wise Princesses: A Medieval Persian Epic, by Wafa Tarnowska and Nilesh Mistry (Barefoot Books, ISBN 1-84148-022-3, 2000) **On-Level**

The Seven Wonders of the Ancient World, by Reg Cox and Neil Morris (Chelsea House, ISBN 0-7910-6046-2, 2000) **On-Level**

The Dead Sea Scrolls, by Ilene Cooper (Morrow Junior, ISBN 0-688-14300-8, 1997) **Challenge NCSS Notable Book, 1998**

Gilgamesh: A New Rendering in English Verse, by David Ferry (Farrar, Straus & Giroux, ISBN 0-374-52383-5, 1992) **Challenge**

Gilgamesh the King, by Ludmila Zeman (Tundra Books, ISBN 0-88776-437-1, 1998) **Challenge**

Great Wonders of the World, by Russell Ash (Dorling Kindersley, ISBN 0-7894-6505-1, 2000) **Challenge Parent's Choice Silver Honor**

The Israelites, by Pamela Odijk (Silver Burdett, ISBN 0-382-09888-9, 1990) **Challenge**

Mesopotamia and the Fertile Crescent, by John Malam and Mavis Pilbeam (Raintree-Steck-Vaughn, ISBN 0-817-25434-X, 1999) **Challenge**

The Odyssey, by Homer, translated by Robert Fitzgerald (Knopf, ISBN 0-679-41047-3, 1992) **Challenge**

The Story of Mankind, by Hendrik Willem van Loon, ed. John Merriman (W. W. Norton, ISBN 0-87140-175-4, 1999) **Challenge Newbery Award Winner**

Dawn of Art: The Chauvet Cave: The Oldest Known Paintings in the World, by Jean-Marie Chauvet et al. (Abrams, ISBN 0-810-93232-6, 1996) **Teacher reference**

Discovery Channel School Videos

Discover Magazine: The Earliest Immigrants A skeleton sheds light on human migration to North America. (Item # 745133, 17 minutes)

Discovery Atlantis Follow scientists to Bolivia as they search for this legendary lost city. (Item # 7167027, 51 minutes)

 Look for this symbol throughout the Teacher's Edition to find **Award-Winning Selections**.

Unit 2 Bibliography

The Complete Book of Map and Geography Skills (American Educational Publishing, ISBN 1-56189-503-2, 1998) **Easy**

Confucius: Philosopher and Teacher, by Josh Wilker (Franklin Watts, ISBN 0-531-11436-8, 1999) **Easy**

Cut from the Same Cloth: American Women of Myth, Legend, and Tall Tale, by Robert D. San Souci (Puffin, ISBN 0-698-11811-1, 2000) **Easy**

The Great Wall, by Elizabeth Mann (Mikaya Press, ISBN 0-9650493-2-9, 1997) **Easy**

Growing Up in Ancient Egypt, by Rosalie David, Angus McBride (illustrator) (Troll Associates, ISBN 0-8167-2718-X, 1997) **Easy**

Hatshepsut, His Majesty, Herself, by Catherine M. Andronik (Atheneum, ISBN 0-689-82562-5, 2001) **Easy**

A Place in the Sun, by Jill Rubalcaba (Houghton Mifflin, ISBN 0-395-82645-4, 1997) **Easy**

 The Riddle of the Rosetta Stone: Key to Ancient Egypt, by James Cross Giblin (HarperTrophy, ISBN 0-06-446137-8, 1993) **Easy ALA Notable Children's Book, 1991**

Weather, by Seymour Simon (HarperCollins, ISBN 0-688-17521-X, 2000) **Easy**

The Great Wall of China, by Leonard Everett Fisher (Aladdin Paperbacks, ISBN 0-689-80178-5, 1995) **On-Level**

Hatshepsut and Ancient Egypt, by Miriam Greenblatt (Benchmark Books, ISBN 0-7614-0911-4, 1999) **On-Level**

How to Draw Maps and Charts, by Pam Beasant and Alastair Smith (E. D. C. Publications, ISBN 0-7460-1002-8, 1993) **On-Level**

How Would You Survive as an Ancient Egyptian? by Jacqueline Morley (Franklin Watts, ISBN 0-531-15303-7, 1996) **On-Level**

One World, Many Religions: The Ways We Worship, by Mary Pope Osborne (Knopf, ISBN 0-679-83930-5, 1996) **On-Level Orbis Pictus Honor**

Pyramid, by David Macaulay (Houghton Mifflin, ISBN 0-395-21407-6, 1975) **On-Level ALA Notable Book**

Shower of Gold: Girls and Women in the Stories of India, by Uma Krishnaswami (Linnet Books, ISBN 0-208-02484-0, 1999) **On-Level**

Weather and Climate, by Alvin Silverstein, Virginia Silverstein, and Laura Silverstein Nunn (Twenty-First Century Books, ISBN 0-7613-3223-5, 1998) **On-Level**

Wisdom Tales from Around the World, by Heather Forest (August House Publishing, ISBN 0-87483-479-1, 1996) **On-Level**

Ancient Chinese Dynasties, by Eleanor J. Hall (Lucent Books, ISBN 1-56006-624-5, 2000) **Challenge**

Child of the Morning, by Pauline Gedge (Sophia Books, ISBN 0-937-14985-0, 1993) **Challenge**

The Emerald Lizard: Fifteen Latin American Tales to Tell in English and Spanish, by Pleasant DeSpain (August House Publishing, ISBN 0-87483-552-6, 1999) **Challenge**

The Great Wall of China: From History to Myth, by Arthur Waldron (Cambridge University Press, ISBN 0-521-42707-X, 1992) **Challenge**

King Asoka and Buddhism, by Anuradha Seneviratna (Vipassana Research Publications, ISBN 9-552-40065-1, 1995) **Challenge**

Mapping the Unknown, by Peter Chrisp (Raintree-Steck-Vaughn, ISBN 0-8172-4535-9, 1996) **Challenge**

Science Explorer: Weather and Climate, by Prentice Hall (Prentice Hall School Group, ISBN 0-13-434494-4, 2000) **Challenge**

Stories from the Silk Road, by Cherry Gilchrist (Barefoot Books, ISBN 1-902283-25-2, 1999) **Challenge**

The Story of Mankind, by Hendrik Willem van Loon (W. W. Norton and Company, ISBN 0-87140-175-4, 1999) **Challenge Newbery Award Winner**

Tales Mummies Tell, by Patricia Lauber (HarperCollins, ISBN 0-690-04389-9, 1985) **Challenge**

Ancient Egyptians and Their Neighbors: An Activity Guide, by Marian Broida (Chicago Review Press, ISBN 1-55652-360-2, 1999) **Teacher reference**

The Egyptians, by Gillian Chapman (Beech Tree Books, ISBN 0-688-17746-8, 2000) **Teacher reference**

The Oxford History of Ancient Egypt, by Ian Shaw (Oxford University Press, ISBN 0-19-815034-2, 1999) **Teacher reference**

Discovery Channel School Videos

Ancient Egypt A three-segment video highlights ancient Egyptian culture, hieroglyphics, and pyramids. (Item # 717363, 22 minutes)

Great Egyptians A three-segment video features Hatshepsut, Tutankhamen, and Cleopatra. (Item # 745273, 22 minutes)

Great Egyptians 5-Pack A ten-segment, five-video set includes Akhenaten, Cleopatra, Hatshepsut, Sneferu, and Ramses the Great. (Item # 718262, 260 minutes)

The Great Wall of China This video explores the 2,000-year-old Great Wall and its influence on China and Europe. (Item # 745091, 54 minutes)

Mummies A three-segment video unwraps mummies in ancient Egypt and South America. (Item # 764738, 26 minutes)

Seven Wonders of the World: Simply the Best This video includes animation and video footage of each wonder. (Item # 716779, 26 minutes)

Look for this symbol throughout the Teacher's Edition to find **Award-Winning Selections**.

Unit 3 Bibliography

Aztec, Inca & Maya, by Elizabeth Baquedano (Dorling Kindersley, ISBN 0-7894-6115-3, 2000) **Easy**

Aztec Times, by Antony Mason (Simon & Schuster, ISBN 0-689-81199-3, 1997) **Easy**

The Aztecs, by Philip Ardagh (Peter Bedrick, ISBN 0-87226-632-X, 2000) **Easy**

Aztecs: The Fall of an Empire, by Richard Platt, Peter Dennis (illustrator) (Dorling Kindersley, ISBN 0-7894-3957-3, 1998) **Easy**

Inca Town, by Fiona MacDonald (Franklin Watts, ISBN 0-531-15361-4, 1999) **Easy**

The Iroquois, by Virginia Driving Hawk Sneve (Holiday House, ISBN 0-8234-1163-X, 1995) **Easy**

Montezuma and the Fall of the Aztecs, by Eric A. Kimmel, Daniel San Souci (illustrator) (Holiday House, ISBN 0-8234-1452-3, 2000) **Easy**

The Polar Bear Son: An Inuit Tale, by Lydia Dabcovich (Clarion Books, ISBN 0-395-72766-9, 1999) **Easy**

The Trail of Tears, by Joseph Bruchac (Random Library, ISBN 0-679-99052-6, 1999) **Easy**

The Corn Grows Ripe, by Dorothy Rhoads (Puffin, ISBN 0-14-036313-0, 1993) **On-Level** *Newbery Honor Book*

The Encyclopedia of the Ancient Americas: Step into the World of the Inuit, Native American, Aztec, Maya, and Inca Peoples, by Jen Green et. al. (South Water Publishing, ISBN 1-842-15186-X, 2000) **On-Level**

Hernando Cortés and the Conquest of Mexico, by Gina De Angelis (Chelsea House, ISBN 0-7910-5516-7, 1999) **On-Level**

Hiawatha: Founder of the Iroquois Confederacy, by Nancy Bonvillain (Chelsea House Publishing, ISBN 0-7910-1707-9, 1994) **On-Level**

Scholastic Encyclopedia of the North American Indian, by James Ciment and Ronald LaFrance, edited by C. Jackson (Scholastic Trade, ISBN 0-590-22790-4, 1996) **On-Level**

Secret of the Andes, by Ann Nolan Clark (Viking Press, ISBN 0-14-030926-8, 1976) **On-Level** *Newbery Award Winner*

Step Into the . . . Inca World, by Philip Steele (Lorenz Books, ISBN 0-7548-0476-3, 2000) **On-Level**

Wounded Knee: The Death of a Dream, by Laurie O'Neill (Millbrook, ISBN 1-56294-253-0, 1993) **On-Level**

The Earliest Americans, by Helen Roney Sattler (Clarion Books, ISBN 0-395-54996-5, 1993) **Challenge**

The Girl Who Dreamed Only Geese and Other Tales of the Far North, by Howard Norman (Harcourt Brace, ISBN 0-15-230979-9, 1997) **Challenge**

The Inca Empire (World History Series), by Dennis Nishi (Lucent Books, ISBN 1-560-06538-9, 2000) **Challenge**

The Iroquois, by Barbara Graymont (Chelsea House Publishing, ISBN 0-7910-0361-2, 1989) **Challenge**

The Life and Death of Crazy Horse, by Russell Freedman (Holiday House, ISBN 0-8234-1219-9, 1996) **Challenge**

Lost Treasure of the Inca, by Peter Lourie (Boyds Mills, ISBN 1-56397-743-5, 1999) **Challenge**

Pizarro and the Conquest of the Incan Empire in World History, by Richard Worth (Enslow Publishers, Inc., ISBN 0-7660-1396-0, 2000) **Challenge**

Sweat of the Sun, Tears of the Moon: A Chronicle of an Incan Treasure, by Peter Lourie (University of Nebraska Press, ISBN 0-8032-7980-9, 1998) **Challenge**

Along the Inca Road: A Woman's Journey into an Ancient Empire, by Karin Muller (National Geographic Society, ISBN 0-7922-7685-X, 2000) **Teacher reference**

The Art of Mesoamerica: From Olmec to Aztec, by Mary Ellen Miller (Thames & Hudson, ISBN 0-500-20345-8, 2001) **Teacher reference**

Conquest: Montezuma, Cortés, and the Fall of Old Mexico, by Hugh Thomas (Simon & Schuster, ISBN 0-671-51104-1, 1995) **Teacher reference**

History of the Inca Empire: An Account of the Indians' Customs and Their Origin Together with a Treatise on Inca Legends, History, and Social Institutions, by Bernabe Cobo (University of Texas Press, ISBN 0-292-73025-X, 1983) **Teacher reference**

Discovery Channel School Videos

Discover Magazine: Ancient Sky Watchers Learn about the cliff-dwelling ancestors of the Pueblo who created an amazingly accurate calendar. (Item # 715938, 26 minutes)

In Search of the Maya See how these hieroglyphics begin to tell the story of a culture that disappeared without explanation. (Item # 745125, 27 minutes)

 Look for this symbol throughout the Teacher's Edition to find **Award-Winning Selections**.

Unit 4 Bibliography

Alexander the Great: The Legend of a Warrior King, by Peter Chrisp (DK Publishing, ISBN 0-7894-6166-8, 2000) **Easy**

Ancient Greece, by Anne Pearson, Nick Nicholls (photographer) (DK Publishing, ISBN 0-7894-5750-4, 2000) **Easy**

Ancient Rome, by Peter Chrisp and Kate Hayden (World Book, Inc., ISBN 0-716-69400-X, 1998) **Easy**

Athens, by R. Conrad Stein (Children's Press, ISBN 0-516-26142-8, 1997) **Easy**

Emperors and Gladiators, by Anita Ganeri (NTC/Contemporary Publishing, ISBN 0-87226-661-3, 2001) **Easy**

First Facts About the Ancient Romans, by Fiona MacDonald and David Salariya (Peter Bedrick Books, ISBN 0-87226-496-3, 1996) **Easy**

 The Librarian Who Measured the Earth, by Kathryn Lasky (Little Brown & Co., ISBN 0-316-51526-4, 1994) **Easy Children's Choice Award**

Maps and Mapmaking, by Fran Sammis (Marshall Cavendish, Inc., ISBN 0-7614-0367-1, 1999) **Easy**

The World of the Roman Emperor, by Peter Chrisp (Peter Bedrick Books, ISBN 0-87226-296-0, 1999) **Easy**

Ancient Greece, by Peter Connolly (Oxford University Press Children's Books, ISBN 0-19-910810-2, 2001) **On-Level**

The Ancient Olympic Games, by Judith Swaddling (University of Texas Press, ISBN 0-292-77751-5, 2000) **On-Level**

Ancient Rome, by Mike Corbishley (Checkmark Books, ISBN 0-8160-1970-3, 1989) **On-Level**

Arachne Speaks, by Kate Hovey (Margaret McElderry, ISBN 0-689-82901-9, 2001) **On-Level**

Daily Life in Ancient and Modern Athens, by Dawn Kotapish (Lerner Publications, ISBN 0-8225-3216-6, 2000) **On-Level**

Famous Men of Rome, by John Haaren and A. B. Poland (Greenleaf Press, ISBN 1-882514-04-1, 1989) **On-Level**

Gladiator, by Richard Ross Watkins (Houghton Mifflin, ISBN 0-395-82656-X, 1997) **On-Level**

Herodotus and the Explorers of the Classical Age, by Ann Graham Gaines (Chelsea House Publishing, ISBN 0-7910-1293-X, 1993) **On-Level**

The Trial of Socrates, by Don Nardo (Lucent Books, ISBN 1-56006-267-3, 1996) **On-Level**

The Ancient City: Life in Classical Athens and Rome, by Peter Connolly and Hazel Dodge (Oxford University Press, ISBN 0-19-521582-6, 2000) **Challenge**

Augustus and Imperial Rome, by Miriam Greenblatt (Benchmark Books, ISBN 0-7614-0912-2, 1999) **Challenge**

 Black Ships Before Troy: The Story of the Iliad, by Rosemary Sutcliff (Delacorte Press, ISBN 0-385-31069-2, 1993) **Challenge ALA Best Book**

City: A Story of Roman Planning and Construction, by David Macaulay (Houghton Mifflin, ISBN 0-395-34922-2, 1983) **Challenge**

Encyclopedia of Ancient Greece, by Lisa Miles (Usborne Publishers, ISBN 0-7460-3403-2, 2000) **Challenge**

Knossos: Searching for the Legendary Palace of King Minos, by Alexandre Farnoux and David J. Baker, trans. (Harry N. Abrams, ISBN 0-810-92819-1, 1996) **Challenge**

Outcast, by Rosemary Sutcliff (Sunburst, ISBN 0-374-45673-9, 1995) **Challenge**

The Trojan War and the Adventures of Odysseus, by Pedraic Colum (William Morrow and Company, ISBN 0-688-14588-4, 1997) **Challenge**

The Young Oxford Companion to Maps and Mapmaking, by Rebecca Stefoff (Oxford University Press, ISBN 0-19-508042-4, 1995) **Challenge**

Barrington Atlas of the Greek and Roman World, by Richard J. A. Talbert (Princeton University Press, ISBN 0-691-03169-X, 2000) **Teacher reference**

Gods, Heroes and Men of Ancient Greece, by W. H. D. Rouse (New American Library Trade, ISBN 0-451-52790-9, 2001) **Teacher reference**

Discovery Channel School Videos

Ancient Greece The three segments of this video feature Alexander the Great, great philosophers, and Greek mythology. (Item # 764704, 26 minutes)

Life in Ancient Rome This five-video series explores the history of Rome. *Rise to Power* is about the birth of the Roman Republic. *Struggle for Power* centers on Julius Caesar. *Expansion and Conquest* details the building of the Roman Empire. *Fall of an Empire* follows the invasion of Rome by Germanic tribes. *Prosperity and Decline* includes the Pax Romana and the eventual decay of the empire. (Item # 730150, 53 minutes per video)

 Look for this symbol throughout the Teacher's Edition to find **Award-Winning Selections**.

Unit 5 Bibliography

Amazon: A Young Reader's Look at the Last Frontier, by Peter Lourie (Boyds Mills Press, ISBN 1-56397-712-5, 1998) **Easy**

Cambodia, by Dayaneetha De Silva (Gareth Stevens, ISBN 0-8368-2322-2, 2000) **Easy**

Cathedral: The Story of Its Construction, by David Macaulay (Houghton Mifflin Co., ISBN 0-395-17513-5, 1973) **Easy** *Caldecott Honor Book,* **New York Times Best Illustrator**

Empress of China Wu Ze Tian, by Cheng-An Jiang (Victory Press, ISBN 1-878217-32-1, 1998) **Easy**

Fa Mulan: The Story of a Woman Warrior, by Robert D. San Souci (Hyperion Press, ISBN 0-7868-2287-2, 1998) **Easy**

The Kitchen Knight: A Tale of King Arthur, by Margaret Hodges (Holiday House, ISBN 0-8234-0787-X, 1990) **Easy**

Maples in the Mist: Children's Poems from the Tang Dynasty, edited by Minfong Ho (Lothrop, Lee, & Shephard, ISBN 0-688-12044-X, 1996) **Easy** *ALA Notable Book*

Marguerite Makes a Book, by Bruce Robertson (Getty Publications, ISBN 0-89236-372-X, 1999) **Easy**

Sebgugugu the Glutton: A Bantu Tale from Rwanda, by Verna Aardema and Nancy Clouse (Africa World Press, Inc., ISBN 0-86543-377-1, 1993) **Easy**

The Silk Route: 7,000 Miles of History, by John S. Major (HarperTrophy, ISBN 0-06-443468-0, 1996) **Easy**

If You Lived in the Days of the Knights, by Ann McGovern (Scholastic Trade, ISBN 0-439-10565-X, 2001) **On-Level**

Indonesia, Cambodia, and Thailand: Stencils, edited by Mira Bartok-Baratta (Good Year Publishing Company, ISBN 0-673-36313-9, 1996) **On-Level**

Justinian, by John Moorhead (Longman Publishing Group, ISBN 0-582-06303-5, 1994) **On-Level**

King Arthur, by Rosalind Kerven (DK Publishing, ISBN 0-7894-2887-3, 1998) **On-Level**

Muhammad of Mecca: Prophet of Islam, by Elsa Marston (Franklin Watts, Inc., ISBN 0-531-15554-4, 2001) **On-Level**

One World, Many Religions: The Ways We Worship, by Mary Pope Osborne (Knopf, ISBN 0-679-83930-5, 1996) **On-Level** *Orbis Pictus Honor*

Son of Charlemagne, by Barbara Willard (Bethlehem Books, ISBN 1-883937-30-2, 1998) **On-Level**

Sundiata: Lion King of Mali, by David Wisniewski (Clarion Books, ISBN 0-395-76481-5, 1999) **On-Level**

Tokoloshi: African Folktales Retold, by Diana Pitcher (Tricyle Press, ISBN 1-883672-03-1, 1993) **On-Level**

Voices of the River: Adventures on the Delaware, by Jan Cheripko (Boyds Mills Press, ISBN 1-56397-622-6, 2001) **On-Level**

Catherine, Called Birdy, by Karen Cushman (Houghton Mifflin, ISBN 0-395-68186-3, 1994) **Challenge** *Newbery Honor Book*

Chantrea Conway's Story: A Voyage from Cambodia in 1975, by Clare Pastore (Berkley Publishing Group, ISBN 0-425-17889-7, 2001) **Challenge**

Charlemagne, by Roger Collins (University of Toronto Press, ISBN 0-8020-8218-1, 1998) **Challenge**

The Cow-Tail Switch and Other West African Stories, by Harold Courlander and George Herzog (Henry Holt & Company, Inc., ISBN 0-8050-0298-7, 1987) **Challenge**

Genghis Khan, by R. P. Lister (Cooper Square Press, ISBN 0-8154-1052-2, 2000) **Challenge**

In the Land of the Taj Mahal: The World of the Fabulous Mughals, by Ed Rothfarb (Henry Holt and Co., Inc., ISBN 0-8050-5299-2, 1998) **Challenge**

The Midwife's Apprentice, by Karen Cushman (HarperTrophy, ISBN 0-06-440630-X, 1996) **Challenge** *Newbery Award Winner*

Stories of Young Pioneers in Their Own Words, by Violet T. Kimball (Mountain Press Publishing Company, ISBN 0-87842-423-7, 2000) **Challenge**

The Story of King Arthur and His Knights, by Howard Pyle (Dover Publications, ISBN 0-486-21445-1, 1996) **Challenge**

The Story of Mankind, by Hendrik Willem van Loon (W. W. Norton and Company, ISBN 0-87140-175-4, 1999) **Challenge** *Newbery Award Winner*

A Companion to Justinian's Institutes, edited by Ernest Metzger (Cornell University Press, ISBN 0-8014-8584-3, 1999) **Teacher reference**

Discovery Channel School Video

Times Medieval This four-segment video features medieval feudal life, castles, knights' armor, and the legend of King Arthur. (Item # 717470, 26 minutes)

 Look for this symbol throughout the Teacher's Edition to find **Award-Winning Selections**.

Unit Bibliographies

Unit 6 Bibliography

Bound for America: The Forced Migration of Africans to the New World, by James Haskins, et al. (Lothrop Lee & Shepard, ISBN 0-688-10258-1, 1999) **Easy**

 Good Queen Bess: The Story of Elizabeth I of England, by Peter Vennema (HarperCollins, ISBN 0-688-17961-4, 2001) **Easy** *ALA Notable Book, Boston Globe Horn Book Honors*

Jamestown Colony, by Gail Sakurai (Children's Press, ISBN 0-516-26138-X, 1997) **Easy**

Leonardo da Vinci, by Diane Stanley (HarperTrophy, ISBN 0-688-16155-3, 2000) **Easy** *ALA Notable Book, Boston Globe Horn Book Honors, Orbis Pictus Award*

The Lightbulb, by Joseph Wallace (Atheneum, ISBN 0-689-82816-0, 1999) **Easy**

A Long and Uncertain Journey: The 27,000 Mile Voyage of Vasco da Gama, by Joan Elizabeth Goodman (Mikaya Press, ISBN 0-9650493-7-X, 2001) **Easy**

Simón Bolívar: Latin American Liberator, by Frank De Varona (Millbrook Press, ISBN 1-56294-812-1, 1993) **Easy**

The Dream Keeper and Other Poems, by Langston Hughes (Knopf, ISBN 0-679-94421-4, 1994) **On-Level**

Elizabeth I, by Catherine Bush (Chelsea House, ISBN 0-87754-579-0, 1987) **On-Level**

Let It Shine: Stories of Black Women Freedom Fighters, by Andrea Davis Pinkney (Harcourt, ISBN 0-15-201005-X, 2000) **On-Level**

The Lyons Throne, by M. L. Stainer (Chicken Soup Press, ISBN 1-893337-02-2, 1999) **On-Level**

Morning Girl, by Michael Dorris (Hyperion Books, ISBN 0-7868-1358-X, 1999) **On-Level** *Scott O'Dell Award*

Renaissance, by Andrew Langley (Knopf, ISBN 0-375-80136-7, 1999) **On-Level**

Sarny: A Life Remembered, by Gary Paulsen (Random House Inc., ISBN 0-440-21973-6, 1999) **On-Level**

Simón Bolívar: South American Liberator, by David Goodnough (Enslow Publishers, ISBN 0-7660-1044-9, 1998) **On-Level**

The Spanish Armada, by John Tincey (Osprey Publishing, ISBN 1-84176-028-5, 2000) **On-Level**

They Came in Chains: The Story of the Slave Ships, by Milton Meltzer (Benchmark Books, ISBN 0-7614-0967-X, 2000) **On-Level**

Beware, Princess Elizabeth, by Carolyn Meyer (Harcourt, ISBN 0-15-202659-2, 2001) **Challenge**

Bolívar: Liberator of a Continent, by Bill Boyd (Capital Books, ISBN 1-892123-16-9, 2000) **Challenge**

Dream Freedom, by Sonia Levitin (Silver Whistle, ISBN 0-15-202404-2, 2000) **Challenge**

Elizabeth I: Red Rose of the House of Tudor, by Kathryn Lasky (Scholastic, ISBN 0-590-68484-1, 1999) **Challenge**

Escape from the Slave Traders, by Dave Jackson and Neta Jackson (Bethany House, ISBN 1-55661-263-X, 1992) **Challenge**

Leonardo Da Vinci for Kids: His Life and Times, by Janis Herbert (Chicago Review Press, ISBN 1-55652-298-3, 1998) **Challenge**

Midnight Magic, by Avi (Scholastic, Inc., ISBN 0-590-36035-3, 1999) **Challenge**

The Voyage of the Armada: The Spanish Story, by David Howarth (Lyons Press, ISBN 1-585-74424-7, 2001) **Challenge**

What Life Was Like Among Samurai and Shoguns: Japan, A.D. 1000–1700, by Time-Life Books, ed. (Time-Life Inc., ISBN 0-7835-5462-1, 1999) **Challenge**

Famous Men of the Renaissance and Reformation, by Robert G. Shearer (Greenleaf Press, ISBN 1-882514-10-6, 1996) **Teacher reference**

A Short History of the French Revolution, by Jeremy D. Popkin (Prentice Hall, ISBN 0-13-060032-6, 2001) **Teacher reference**

Discovery Channel School Videos

Conquerors: Napoleon This video explores the accomplishments of a man who seized control by virtue of his brilliant military strategy and excellent timing. (Item # 722769, 27 minutes)

Conquerors: Peter the Great Discover how this Russian monarch's passion and perseverance spawned military victories, modern cities, and a renewed national pride. (Item # 715912E, 26 minutes)

Conquerors: Suleyman the Magnificent Explore how this sultan transformed Constantinople into Istanbul, allowed conquered subjects to have autonomy, and defended his Ottoman Empire. (Item # 722744E, 27 minutes)

The Revolutionary War This video provides a concise and compelling look at America's birth. (Item # 716746, 53 minutes)

 Look for this symbol throughout the Teacher's Edition to find **Award-Winning Selections**.

Unit 7 Bibliography

Churchill and the British, by John Bradley (Gloucester Press, ISBN 0-531-17227-9, 1990) **Easy**

The Glorious Flight: Across the Channel with Louis Blériot, by Alice Provensen and Martin Provensen (Viking Press, ISBN 0-14-050729-9, 1987) **Easy Caldecott Medal Winner**

Lost in the War, by Nancy Antle (Puffin, ISBN 0-14-130836-2, 2000) **Easy**

Meet A. A. Milne, by S. Ward (PowerKids Press, ISBN 0-8239-5708-X, 2001) **Easy**

Passage to Freedom: The Sugihara Story, by Ken Mochizuki (Lee & Low Books, ISBN 1-880000-49-0, 1999) **Easy American Bookseller Pick of the Lists**

Sweet Dried Apples: A Vietnamese Wartime Childhood, by Rosemary Breckler, Deborah Kogan Ray (illustrator) (Houghton Mifflin, ISBN 0-395-73570-X, 1996) **Easy**

The Top of the World: Climbing Mount Everest, by Steve Jenkins (Houghton Mifflin, ISBN 0-395-94218-7, 1999) **Easy**

Vietnam Veterans Memorial, by Jason Cooper (Rourke Book Company, ISBN 0-86593-549-1, 1999) **Easy**

The Wit and Wisdom of Winston Churchill: A Treasury of More than 1,000 Quotations and Anecdotes, by James C. Humes (HarperPerennial, ISBN 0-06-092577-9, 1995) **Easy**

Air Raid—Pearl Harbor! by Theodore Taylor (Harcourt, ISBN 0-15-216421-9, 2001) **On-Level**

Bud, Not Buddy, by Christopher Paul Curtis (Delacorte Press, ISBN 0-385-32306-9, 1999) **On-Level Newbery Award Winner**

Frances Hodgson Burnett: Beyond the Secret Garden, by Angelica Shirley Carpenter and Jean Shirley (First Avenue Editions, ISBN 0-8225-9610-5, 1992) **On-Level**

Out of the Dust, by Karen Hesse (Scholastic Paperbacks, 0-590-37125-8, 1999) **On-Level Newbery Award Winner**

Sing for Your Father, Su Phan, by Stella Pevsner and Fay Tang (Clarion Books, ISBN 0-395-82267-X, 1997) **On-Level**

Triumph on Everest: A Photobiography of Sir Edmund Hillary, by Broughton Coburn (National Geographic Society, ISBN 0-7922-7114-9, 2000) **On-Level**

The Valiant Women of the Vietnam War, by Karen Zeinert (Millbrook Press, ISBN 0-7613-1268-4, 2000) **On-Level**

When the Soldiers Were Gone, by Vera W. Propp (Puffin, ISBN 0-698-11881-2, 2001) **On-Level**

Winston Churchill: Soldier, Statesman, Artist, by John Severance (Clarion, ISBN 0-395-69853-7, 1996) **On-Level**

Woodrow Wilson, by Sallie Randolph (Walker & Co., ISBN 0-8027-8143-8, 1992) **On-Level**

At Home with Beatrix Potter: The Creator of Peter Rabbit, by Susan Denyer (Harry N. Abrams, ISBN 0-8109-4112-0, 2000) **Challenge**

Eleanor Roosevelt: A Life of Discovery, by Russell Freedman (Houghton Mifflin Corp., ISBN 0-395-84520-3, 1997) **Challenge Newbery Honor Book, ALA Notable Book**

Flags of Our Fathers, by James Bradley and Ron Powers (adapted for young readers) (Delacorte Press, ISBN 0-385-72932-4, 2001) **Challenge**

The Good Fight: How World War II Was Won, by Stephen E. Ambrose (Atheneum, ISBN 0-689-84361-5, 2001) **Challenge**

Good Night, Maman, by Norma Fox Mazer (Harcourt, Brace, ISBN 0-15-201468-3, 1999) **Challenge**

The Nazi Olympics, by Susan D. Bachrach (Little, Brown, ISBN 0-316-07087-4, 2000) **Challenge**

Never Give In: The Extraordinary Character of Winston Churchill, by Stephen Mansfield (Cumberland House, ISBN 1-888952-19-9, 1997) **Challenge**

Touching My Father's Soul: A Sherpa's Journey to the Top of Everest, by Jamling Tenzing Norgay and Broughton Coburn (Harper, ISBN 0-06-251687-6, 2001) **Challenge**

The Vietnam War: "What Are We Fighting For?" by Deborah Kent (Enslow Publishers, ISBN 0-7660-1731-1, 2000) **Challenge**

Atlas of World History, by John Haywood (Metro Books, ISBN 1-58663-099-7, 2000) **Teacher reference**

The Timetables of History: A Horizontal Linkage of People and Events, by Bernard Grun (Simon & Schuster, ISBN 0-671-74271-X, 1991) **Teacher reference**

Discovery Channel School Videos

Jerusalem: City of Heaven Visit this city, which is holy to Jews, Christians, and Muslims and which continues to attract conflict and controversy. (Item # 716266D, 51 minutes)

Normandy: The Great Crusade Watch footage of the actual landing at Omaha Beach on D-Day, hear personal accounts of soldiers, and learn about the evolution of D-Day. (Item # 718361D, 53 minutes)

 Look for this symbol throughout the Teacher's Edition to find **Award-Winning Selections**.

Unit Bibliographies

Unit 8 Bibliography

Fuels for the Future, by Edward Parker (Raintree-Steck-Vaughn, ISBN 0-8172-4937-0, 1998) **Easy**

Gandhi, by Demi (Margaret McElderry, ISBN 0-689-84149-3, 2001) **Easy**

The Middle East in Search of Peace, by Cathryn J. Long (Millbrook Press, ISBN 0-7613-0105-4, 1996) **Easy**

Peace Crane, by Sheila Hamanaka (William Morrow and Company, ISBN 0-688-13815-2, 1995) **Easy**

Rachel Carson: Pioneer of Ecology (Women of Our Time), by Kathleen V. Kudlinski (Penguin Putnam, ISBN 0-14-032242-6, 1989) **Easy**

Sitti's Secrets, by Naomi Shihab Nye (Aladdin Paperbacks, ISBN 0-689-81706-1, 1997) **Easy** *Jane Addams Book Award*

The Storyteller's Beads, by Jane Kurtz (Gulliver Books, ISBN 0-15-201074-2, 1998) **Easy**

World Population, by Nance Fyson (Franklin Watts, Inc., ISBN 0-531-14479-8, 1998) **Easy**

The Arab-Israeli Conflict, by Tony McAleavy (Cambridge University Press, ISBN 0-521-62953-5, 1998) **On-Level**

Aung San Suu Kyi: Fearless Voice of Burma, by Whitney Stewart (Lerner Publications, ISBN 0-8225-4931-X, 1997) **On-Level**

Biodiversity, by Dorothy Hinshaw Patent (Clarion Books, ISBN 0-395-68704-7, 1996) **On-Level**

Causes and Consequences of the Arab-Israeli Conflict, by Stewart Ross (Raintree-Steck-Vaughn, ISBN 0-8172-4051-9, 1995) **On-Level**

Energy, by Jack Challoner, Clive Streeter (photographer)(DK Publishing, ISBN 0-7894-5576-5, 2000) **On-Level**

The Environmental Movement: From Its Roots to the Challenges of a New Century, by Laurence Pringle (Morrow/Avon, ISBN 0-688-15626-6, 2000) **On-Level**

Girl of Kosovo, by Alice Mead (Farrar Straus & Giroux, ISBN 0-374-32620-7, 2001) **On-Level**

No More Strangers Now: Young Voices from a New South Africa, by Tim McKee, Anne Blackshaw (photographer) (DK Publishing, ISBN 0-7894-2663-3, 2000) **On-Level** *ALA Notable Book for Children*

Out of War: True Stories from the Front Lines of the Children's Movement for Peace in Colombia, by Sara Cameron (Scholastic Trade, ISBN 0-439-29721-4, 2001) **On-Level**

Zlata's Diary: A Child's Life in Sarajevo, by Zlata Filipovic (translated by Christina Pribichevich-Zoric) (Penguin, ISBN 0-14-024205-8, 1995) **On-Level**

The Chain Reaction: Pioneers of Nuclear Science, by Karen Fox (Franklin Watts, ISBN 0-531-11425-2, 1998) **Challenge**

DNA Fingerprinting: The Ultimate Identity, by Ron Fridell (Franklin Watts, Inc., ISBN 0-531-11858-4, 2001) **Challenge**

The Freedom Writers Diary: How a Teacher and 150 Teens Used Writing to Change Themselves and the World Around Them, by Freedom Writers Staff (Turtleback Books, ISBN 0-606-18104-0, 1999) **Challenge**

From Space to Earth: The Story of Solar Electricity, by John Perlin (aatec publications, ISBN 0-937948-14-4, 1999) **Challenge**

Gandhi: Great Soul, by John B. Severance (Houghton Mifflin Co., ISBN 0-395-77179-X, 1997) **Challenge**

Habibi, by Naomi Shihab Nye (Aladdin Paperbacks, ISBN 0-689-82523-4, 1999) **Challenge** *ALA Notable Book for Children*

Israel: An Illustrated History, by Daniel J. Schroeter (Oxford University Press, ISBN 0-19-510885-X, 1999) **Challenge**

Peacemakers: Winners of the Nobel Peace Prize, by Ann T. Keene (Oxford University Press, ISBN 0-19-510316-5, 1998) **Challenge**

Samir and Yonatan, by Daniella Carmi (Arthur A. Levine, ISBN 0-439-13504-4, 2000) **Challenge** *Mildred L. Batcheldor Award*

Mandela's Children: Growing Up in Post-Apartheid South Africa, by Oscar A. Barbarin and Linda M. Richter (Routledge, ISBN 0-415-92469-3, 2001) **Teacher reference**

Silent Spring, by Rachel Carson (Houghton Mifflin, ISBN 0-395-68329-7, 1994) **Teacher reference**

Discovery Channel School Videos

Technology at Work 2-Pack One of the seven segments in this video follows an electronic signal from the Daytona 500 to a television in a viewer's living room. (Item # 765628, 60 minutes)

Understanding: Television This video explores the impact of television on life in America, beginning with the introduction of television at the 1939 World's Fair. (Item # 717686A, 51 minutes)

 Look for this symbol throughout the Teacher's Edition to find **Award-Winning Selections**.

Index

Index

Index

266, 276, 282, 288, 294, 298, 322, 326,
330, 334, 346, 350, 356, 360, 370, 374,
380, 392, 396, 400, 406, 430, 438, 444,
456, 466, 474, 478, 486, 492, 498, 520,
526, 534, 542, 548, 558, 568, 576, 582,
606, 614, 620, 630, 636, 644, 654, 660,
664, 668

Read Aloud, 1h, 69h, 153h, 237h, 313h,
421h, 511h, 597h

Reading

Curriculum Connection, 1f, 69f, 153f,
237f, 313f, 421f, 511f, 597f
Link to Reading, 53, 256, 287, 292,
363, 523, 537, 547, 641

Reading Skills

Analyze Information, H12, 3, 5, 15, 36,
42, 47, 71, 73, 133, 138, 143, 155,
157, 167, 169, 171, 172, 180, 239,
241, 255, 261, 267, 315, 347, 357,
371, 372, 377, 397, 402, 404, 409,
410, 413, 417, 434, 451, 494, 513,
515, 521, 527, 528, 530, 531, 535,
578, 599, 601, 616, 625, 635, 657,
675
Analyze Pictures, H4, H16, 137, 233,
465, 500
Analyze Primary Sources, 14, 37, 43,
52, 65, 91, 111, 116, 137, 181, 229,
253, 270, 284, 286, 289, 291, 293,
295, 305, 308, 328, 329, 331, 335,
339, 352, 353, 358, 363, 379, 383,
399, 401, 407, 409, 410, 431, 437,
440, 443, 457, 458, 459, 463, 471,
477, 487, 495, 499, 500, 501, 523,
530, 533, 536, 547, 549, 550, 552,
559, 561, 569, 570, 577, 586, 589,
607, 609, 611, 623, 640, 642, 646,
647, 648, 655, 661
Apply Information, H4, H12, 15, 20,
25, 49, 83, 93, 102, 105, 111, 129,
178, 215, 241, 259, 268, 270, 281,
290, 303, 308, 384, 387, 403, 431,
457, 493, 523, 544, 563, 615, 638,
655, 656
Categorize, 20, 27
Cause and Effect, H15, 21, 27, 34,
41, 64, 79, 86, 89, 94, 95, 101, 110,
115, 117, 123, 132, 133, 139, 142,
164, 165, 169, 177, 180, 181, 188,
193, 197, 198, 199, 201, 215, 217,
224, 225, 228, 248, 249, 263, 264,
266, 269, 271, 284, 285, 286, 296,
298, 299, 301, 323, 331, 334, 335,
336, 339, 347, 349, 353, 356, 357,
360, 361, 362, 363, 371, 373, 379,
382, 383, 385, 392, 393, 394, 395,
402, 404, 406, 407, 408, 409, 410,

411, 416, 431, 435, 439, 440, 443,
447, 457, 461, 468, 469, 471, 473,
475, 477, 479, 487, 488, 492, 495,
499, 500, 503, 516–517, 520, 521,
523, 526, 528, 529, 530, 531, 534,
536, 542, 543, 544, 545, 546, 548,
550, 551, 552, 554, 558, 559, 568,
570, 571, 572, 573, 575, 576, 577,
578, 579, 580, 582, 583, 585, 589,
593, 615, 617, 621, 622, 623, 630,
631, 637, 638, 645, 656, 659, 660,
661, 662, 665, 666
Compare and Contrast, H6, H7, H19,
5, 25, 27, 35, 41, 49, 55, 59, 73, 83,
86, 89, 90, 93, 102, 107, 109, 111,
116, 117, 139, 141, 142, 157,
158–159, 162, 163, 164, 165, 168,
169, 172, 175, 178, 186, 187, 188,
189, 192, 195, 198, 208, 209, 210,
212, 213, 218, 220, 221, 222, 223,
227, 229, 241, 252, 254, 262, 277,
281, 283, 284, 289, 295, 296, 299,
302, 317, 323, 329, 333, 341, 348,
352, 358, 361, 371, 378, 382, 385,
425, 440, 441, 442, 447, 456, 459,
465, 474, 479, 481, 491, 497, 502,
522, 527, 528, 529, 546, 551, 560,
563, 570, 583, 585, 601, 615, 633,
638, 640, 669
Draw Conclusions, H4, H7, H11, H14,
11, 12, 13, 14, 17, 19, 20, 22, 23, 29,
37, 43, 49, 50, 53, 56, 58, 59, 80, 81,
83, 85, 87, 89, 90, 94, 107, 110, 115,
125, 127, 131, 132, 133, 135, 137,
138, 141, 142, 145, 148, 155, 163,
164, 169, 170, 171, 172, 177, 200,
201, 203, 214, 219, 220, 224, 226,
239, 247, 248, 249, 250, 253, 254,
256, 257, 267, 269, 270, 283, 284,
285, 287, 288, 289, 291, 292, 295,
296, 299, 303, 304, 305, 308, 315,
317, 327, 351, 354, 359, 361, 365,
379, 383, 401, 403, 404, 408, 417,
432, 433, 443, 445, 458, 461, 463,
468, 473, 475, 480, 488, 489, 493,
494, 496, 503, 507, 529, 531, 543,
547, 549, 553, 554, 557, 561, 569,
571, 574, 578, 587, 599, 602–603,
607, 609, 610, 611, 612, 614, 617,
620, 621, 631, 632, 633, 635, 636,
637, 639, 642, 643, 644, 646, 647,
654, 655, 664, 665, 667, 668, 669,
670, 671, 674
Evaluate, H17, 50, 52, 85, 88, 103,
108, 132, 145, 167, 172, 203, 225,
257, 267, 269, 278, 281, 290, 305,
348, 351, 365, 461, 493, 502, 530,
535, 573, 575, 579, 587, 588, 609,
611, 621, 637, 648, 670
Express Ideas, 51, 79, 124, 149, 382,
577, 579, 584, 638, 639

Fact and Opinion, 113, 200, 213, 217,
268, 324, 337
Generalize, 17, 105, 141, 290, 460,
491, 507
Hypothesize, 65, 85, 93, 113, 187,
219, 223, 224, 233, 331, 381, 476,
529, 581, 586, 659, 662
Interpret Charts, 351, 536, 544, 647
Interpret Graphs, 340–341, 491, 563,
571, 635, 665
Interpret Maps, H8, H11, H14, H15,
15, 21, 57, 58, 79, 101, 109, 124,
130, 132, 142, 163, 170, 175, 198,
210, 214, 220, 259, 263, 267, 277,
286, 300, 327, 332, 347, 348, 352,
362, 373, 377, 383, 393, 397, 407,
409, 413, 436, 441, 446, 448, 460,
469, 488, 494, 499, 501, 502, 522,
531, 546, 549, 552, 569, 583, 586,
608, 610, 611, 617, 622, 632, 637,
639, 645, 659
Interpret National/Political Symbols,
648
Interpret Time Lines, 3, 25, 71, 73,
155, 157, 239, 241, 315, 317, 423,
425, 525, 571, 601
Main Idea and Details, H10, H14, H17,
H19, 5, 12, 14, 17, 19, 20, 21, 22, 23,
26, 27, 28, 35, 36, 37, 38, 40, 41, 42,
43, 44, 45, 46, 47, 49, 51, 53, 54, 55,
56, 57, 61, 64, 85, 86, 87, 91, 93, 95,
101, 107, 108, 110, 111, 112, 113,
116, 124, 129, 130, 131, 133, 134,
137, 138, 143, 170, 171, 172, 173,
174, 176, 178, 179, 187, 188, 190,
191, 192, 195, 196, 197, 198, 199,
209, 210, 213, 214, 223, 227, 232,
242–243, 246, 247, 248, 249, 251,
253, 255, 260, 261, 262, 263, 265,
268, 269, 276, 277, 278, 279, 282,
283, 284, 286, 289, 290, 292, 293,
294, 295, 296, 297, 299, 300, 302,
304, 324, 327, 330, 331, 332, 333,
336, 338, 347, 349, 350, 351, 354,
359, 362, 365, 372, 373, 375, 376,
377, 378, 381, 382, 384, 393, 394,
395, 397, 398, 399, 400, 401, 402,
403, 405, 407, 408, 409, 416, 435,
442, 446, 448, 451, 461, 462, 467,
469, 473, 475, 476, 478, 481, 488,
493, 496, 499, 502, 506, 507, 521,
525, 527, 529, 530, 532, 535, 536,
544, 547, 549, 550, 551, 552, 553,
560, 579, 585, 586, 588, 608, 610,
612, 613, 615, 616, 618, 619, 621,
622, 631, 632, 642, 645, 646, 648,
656, 661, 662, 665, 666
Make Decisions, H5, H14, 125, 176,
263, 265, 300, 480, 527, 545
Make Inferences, H4, H10, H20, 13, 22,
41, 49, 60, 79, 109, 125, 135, 179,
189, 192, 214, 220, 223, 226, 228,

Index

Index

Credits

Photographs

Every effort has been made to secure permission and provide appropriate credit for photographic material. The publisher deeply regrets any omission and pledges to correct errors called to its attention in subsequent editions.

Unless otherwise acknowledged, all photographs are the property of Scott Foresman, a division of Pearson Education.

Cover:

(C) Karen Su/China Span

Front Matter:

SF1 (C) Karen Su/China Span; SF4 (CL) Smithsonian Institution; SF6 (BL) Lexington Historical Society; SF12 (B) © Mark L Stephenson/Corbis

Unit 1: 1A (C) © Hubert Stadler/Corbis; 1B (B) National Museum Damascus Syria/Dagli Orti/Art Archive; 1B-C (T) Kenneth Garrett; 1D (B) © Gianni Dagli Orti/Corbis; 1D-E (T) Kenneth Garrett; 1F-G (T) Kenneth Garrett; 1H (T) Kenneth Garrett; 8A (B) Réunion des Musées Nationaux/Art Resource, NY; 8B (T) Erich Lessing/Art Resource, NY; 32A (B) American Numismatic Association; 32B (T) British Museum; **Unit 2:** 69A (C) Werner Foreman Archive/Art Resource, NY; 69B (B) Archivo Iconografico, S.A/Corbis; 69B-C (Bkgd) Werner Foreman Archive/Art Resource, NY; 69C (TL) Art Resource, NY; 69D-E (Bkgd) Werner Foreman Archive/Art Resource, NY; 69F-G (Bkgd) Werner Foreman Archive/Art Resource, NY; 69H (Bkgd) Werner Foreman Archive/Art Resource, NY, (TC) Sagli Orti/The Art Archive; 76A (B) © Araldo de Luca/Corbis; 76B (T) Kenneth Garrett; 98A (B) Art Archive; 98B (T) Réunion des Musées Nationaux/Art Resource, NY; 120A (B) Werner Foreman Archive/Art Resource, NY; 120B (T) Borromeo/Art Resource, NY; **Unit 3:** 153A (C) Felipe Davalos/NGS Image Collection; 153B-C (T) Felipe Davalos/NGS Image Collection; 153C (T) Robert Frerck/Odyssey Productions; 153D (B) © Richard A. Cooke/Corbis; 153D-E (T) Felipe Davalos/NGS Image Collection; 153F-G (T) Felipe Davalos/NGS Image Collection; 153H (T) Felipe Davalos/NGS Image Collection, (CT) Werner Foreman/Biblioteca Universitaria, Bologna, Italy/Art Resource, NY; 160A (B) INAH/© Dorling Kindersley; 160B (T) © Danny Lehman/Corbis; 184A (B) Jorge Ianiszewski/Art Resource, NY; 184B (T) Album/J. Enrique Molina/Art Archive; 206A (B) Werner Foreman/American Museum of Natural History, New York, N.Y., U.S.A./Art Resource, NY; 206B (T) © Richard A. Cooke/Corbis; **Unit 4:** 237A (C) Scala/Art Resource, NY; 237B (B) The Granger Collection, New York; 237C (B) Scala/Art Resource, NY; 237C (B) © Araldo de Luca/Corbis; 237D (B) © Dorling Kindersley; 237D-E (T) Scala/Art Resource, NY; 237F-G (T) Scala/Art Resource, NY; 237H (T) Scala/Art Resource, NY, (TC) Réunion des Musées Nationaux/Art Resource, NY; 244A (B) Scala/Art Resource, NY; 244B (T) British Museum; 274A (B) British Museum/© Dorling Kindersley; 274B (T) British Museum/© Dorling Kindersley; **Unit 5:** 313A (C) Bibliothèque Nationale Paris /The Art Archive; 313B-C (T) Bibliothèque Nationale Paris /The Art Archive; 313D-E (T) Bibliothèque Nationale Paris /The Art Archive; 313F-G (T) Bibliothèque Nationale Paris /The Art Archive; 313H (T) Bibliothèque Nationale Paris /The Art Archive, (TL) Robert Frerck/Odyssey Productions; 320A (B) SuperStock; 320B (T) Giraudon/Art Resource, NY; 344A (B) Musée National de Phnom Penh, Cambodia/Bridgeman Art Library International Ltd.; 344B (T) Science Museum/Science & Society Picture Library; 368A (B) Darrel Plowes; 368B (B) ©Victor Englebert; 390A (B) Bibliothèque Nationale, Paris, France/Bridgeman Art Library International Ltd.; 390B (T) Public Record Office, London/The Art Archive; **Unit 6:** 421A (C) Scala/Art Resource, NY; 421B-C (T) Scala/Art Resource, NY; 421C (T) Science Museum/© Dorling Kindersley; 421D-E (T) Scala/Art Resource, NY; 421F-G (T) Scala/Art Resource, NY; 421H (T) Scala/Art Resource, NY; 421H (T) Ian Hessenberg/Hayward Gallery; 428A (B) The Granger Collection, New York; 428B (T) Science & Society Picture Library; 454A (B) Science Museum/© Dorling Kindersley; 454B (T) Bridgeman Giraudon/Lauros/Bridgeman Art Library International Ltd.; 484A (B) Private Collection/Dagli Orti/The Art Archive; 484B (T) Réunion des Musées Nationaux/Art Resource, NY; **Unit 7:** 511A (CC) U.S. Coast Guard; 511B (B) © Magnum Photos; 511B-C (Bkgd) U.S. Coast Guard; 511C (TL) Hulton/Archive Photos; 511D-E (Bkgd) U.S. Coast Guard; 511F-G (Bkgd) U.S. Coast Guard; 511H (Bkgd) U.S. Coast Guard; 518A (B) Hulton-Deutsch Collection/Corbis; 518B (T) The West Point Museum Collections, United States Military Academy. Photographed for Scott Foresman by Joshua Nefsky; 540A (B) Courtesy of FDR Library, Hyde Park, NY; 540B (T) Wings Across America; 566A (B) Hulton-Deutsch Collection/Corbis; 566B (T) David King; **Unit 8:** 597A (C) Diana Ong/SuperStock; 597B-C (T) Diana Ong/SuperStock; 597C (T) Thomas Kienzle/AP/Wide World; 597D-E (T) Diana Ong/SuperStock; 597F-G (T) Diana Ong/SuperStock; 597H (T) Diana Ong/SuperStock, (TL) Vithalbhai Jhaveri/GandhiServe e.K; 604A (B) Corbis; 604B (T) Translated by Julius Nyerere/Oxford University Press; 628A (B) © Alison Wright/Corbis; 628B (T) © Frank Wing/PhotoDisc; 652A (B) NASA; 652B (T) PhotoLink/PhotoDisc; **End Matter:** TR67 (B) National Geographic; TR69 (B) Werner Foreman Archive/David Bernstein Fine Art, NY/Art Resource, NY; TR70 (B) © Araldo de Luca/Corbis; TR71 (B) © Dorling Kindersley; TR72 (B) Werner Foreman/Art Resource, NY; TR73 (B) © Steve Raymer/Corbis; TR74 (B) © Mike Agliolo/Science Source/Photo Researchers, Inc.

Notes

Notes